Social Psychology

Social Psychology

FOURTH EDITION

SHARON S. BREHM

Ohio University

SAUL M. KASSIN

Williams College

STEVEN FEIN

Williams College

HOUGHTON MIFFLIN COMPANY   Boston   New York

Editor-in-Chief: Kathi Prancan
Senior Associate Editor: Jane Knetzger
Developmental Editor: Joanne M. Tinsley
Senior Project Editor: Rosemary R. Jaffe
Senior Production/Design Coordinator: Jennifer Waddell
Senior Manufacturing Coordinator: Priscilla J. Abreu
Marketing Manager: Pamela Laskey

Cover design: Deborah Azerrad Savona
Cover image: Alberto Incrocci/The Image Bank

Credits are found following the References at the end of the book.

Printed in the U.S.A.

Library of Congress Catalog Card Number: 98-72001

ISBN: 0-395-90922-8

1 2 3 4 5 6 7 8 9-DW-02 01 00 99 98

We dedicate this book to our families, friends, and colleagues.

Brief Contents

Contents

The Social Self   54

Perceiving Persons   90

Perceiving Groups   126

Group Processes   246

PART THREE Social Relations

Attraction and Close Relationships   292

Helping Others   336

Aggression   382

PART FOUR Applying Social Psychology

12

Law   428

Business 466

Health 498

Preface

We authors used to think of social psychology as a discipline that is stable and slow to change. As in other sciences, we thought, knowledge accumulates in small increments, one step at a time. There are, after all, no "critical" experiments, and no single study can literally "prove" a theory or hypothesis. While all this remains true, and while future social psychologists of the next millennium will stand firmly on the shoulders of their twentieth-century predecessors, for us the process of revising this textbook has put a spotlight on just how dynamic and responsive our field can be. As the world around us rapidly changes—socially, politically, and technologically—so too does social psychology.

We had two main goals for this revision. First, we wanted to accurately, impartially, and comprehensively represent the most important recent advances in the field, both basic and applied. We have no theoretical or political axes to grind. As such, we sought a balanced presentation of perspectives within the field as a whole—biological as well as sociocultural, and affective as well as cognitive. Second, we wanted this textbook to serve as a good teacher outside the classroom. To us, this means speaking the student's language while introducing a new one; making connections to current events in politics, sports, business, entertainment, and other life domains; and encouraging students to rethink their commonsense assumptions and seek out new knowledge. Good teachers are dynamic, interactive, and challenging—and so, we think, is this textbook. We wanted the Fourth Edition of *Social Psychology* to be a better teacher than it has been before. We hope that our readers will find that we've succeeded.

WHAT'S NEW IN THIS EDITION

We are pleased to welcome a new coauthor to the book, Steven Fein, of Williams College. Steve brings to this edition not only his expertise in stereotyping, prejudice, and the sociocultural and motivational influences on social cognition, but also his experience as a dynamic instructor.

In preparing this revision, we carefully—and with helpful feedback from many users—examined every aspect of the book. The results of this process can be seen in the content, organization, and presentation of this new edition, as well as in the supplemental materials that accompany it.

The Content

Comprehensive, Up-to-Date Scholarship   The bedrock of teaching is knowledge. Like its predecessors, the Fourth Edition offers a broad, balanced, mainstream look at social psychology. Thus, there are detailed descriptions of classic studies from the historical warehouse as well as the latest research findings, some hot off the presses, from over 800 new references. In particular, we draw your attention to the following topics, which are either new to this edition or have received expanded coverage:

- Social psychology and common sense (Chapter 1)
- Using the internet for research purposes (Chapter 2)
- Using meta-analysis as a research tool (Chapter 2)
- Interpersonal drawbacks of positive illusions (Chapter 3)
- Ironic effects of mental self-control (Chapter 3)
- Counterfactual thinking and regret (Chapter 4)

- The need for closure (Chapter 4)
- Ironic effects of stereotype suppression (Chapter 5)
- Stereotype threat and academic achievement of women and minorities (Chapter 5)
- Individual, situational, and cultural differences in prejudice (Chapter 5)
- Bivariate view of attitudes (Chapter 6)
- Positive emotions and persuasion (Chapter 6)
- The automaticity of social behavior (Chapter 7)
- Social impact in cyberspace communications (Chapter 7)
- Cultural differences in responses to social dilemmas (Chapter 8)
- Computer-based brainstorming (Chapter 8)
- The need for affiliation (Chapter 9)
- The evolution of desire, mate selection, and jealousy (Chapter 9)
- Cultural influences on conceptions of love (Chapter 9)
- Overhelping (Chapter 10)
- The altruistic personality (Chapter 10)
- Evolutionary and cultural origins of helping (Chapter 10)
- Cultures of honor (Chapter 11)
- Gender differences in aggression (Chapter 11)
- Police interrogations and confessions (Chapter 12)
- Overt and covert integrity testing in the workplace (Chapter 13)
- Affirmative action (Chapter 13)
- Escalation effects in economic decision-making (Chapter 13)
- Effects of stress on the immune system (Chapter 14)
- Proactive coping (Chapter 14)
- The health effects of opening up versus keeping secrets (Chapter 14)

Connections with Current Events   To cover the world of social psychology is one thing. To use the principles to explain events in the real world is quite another. We are convinced that making this connection is the single best way to heighten student interest and involvement, so we do both. Over the years, teachers and students alike have told us how much they value this "newsy" feature of our book.

The Fourth Edition continues in our commitment to making social psychology relevant to real world events. Indeed, we invite you to flip the book open to any page and start reading. Very soon, you'll come across a passage, a figure, a table, a photo, or a cartoon that refers to people, places, events, and issues that are prominent in contemporary culture. Some of what you'll see includes stories about President Clinton; peacemaking efforts in Israel and Northern Ireland; the deaths of Princess Diana and Mother Theresa; Good Samaritan laws; the trials of Marv Albert, Timothy McVeigh and British au pair Louise Woodward; the race discrimination suit against Texaco; the Chicago zoo gorilla that rescued a young child; the recent contagion of shootings in American schools; road rage; the marine blood-pinning scandal; the "V" chip; entertainment figures Cindy Crawford, Oprah Winfrey, Bruce Springsteen, and Bill Cosby; the mass suicide of the Heaven's Gate cult; *Titanic;* the natural disasters spawned by El Niño; fluctuations in the stock market; Microsoft CEO Bill Gates; sports figures Michael Jordan, Mike Tyson, Tara Lipinski, and Tiger Woods; the cast of *Seinfeld.*

New to this edition, you will also find—within the margins—various quotations, song lyrics, public opinion poll results, "factoids," and relevant website addresses. These high-interest items are designed to further illustrate the connectedness of social psychology to a world that extends beyond the borders of a college campus.

The Evolutionary Perspective   In recent years, psychology in general has been influenced heavily by brain research, drug studies, behavioral genetics, and other biological perspectives on the human experience. In this regard, social psychology is no exception. At the heart of this perspective is the notion that we humans, like other species, have an evolutionary past that predisposes us to behave in ways that are adapted to promote survival and reproduction. Increasingly, evolutionary psychologists have sought to explain a wide range of social behaviors such as prejudice, helping, aggression, physical beauty, mate selection, love, and romantic jealousy. We realize that this theoretical perspective is often provocative and controversial. And we realize that while many of our colleagues embrace it, others are skeptical, if not cynical of, this approach. Like it or not, the pages of our most respected journals are filled with both studies and critiques of evolutionary psychology. This edition of our textbook discusses this trend, particularly in Part Three on Social Relations.

Sociocultural Perspectives   Social psychologists have long been fascinated by similarities and differences—among cultural groups, racial and ethnic groups within cultures, men and women, gays and straights. Our coverage of cross-cultural research, and of studies involving race and ethnicity, gender, and sexual orientation, are fully incorporated in the main body of the text. And this coverage is extensive. On virtually all topics—from the social self and perception of persons and groups, to attitudes, conformity and obedience, interpersonal behavior, interpersonal attraction, and group influences—sociocultural perspectives are embedded throughout. We believe that the study of human diversity can help students become more informed about interpersonal relations as well as about ethics and values.

Social Psychology and Common Sense   This edition introduces a new feature that we are excited about. Building upon a discussion in Chapter 1 about the links between social psychology and common sense, each substantive chapter opens with *Putting Common Sense to the Test*, a set of true-false questions designed to assess the student's intuitive beliefs about material later contained in that chapter. Some examples: "Sometimes the harder you try to control a thought, feeling, or behavior, the less likely you are to succeed," "People often come to like what they suffer for," "Opposites attract," and "Groups are less likely than individuals to invest more in a project that is failing." The answers to these questions are revealed in a marginal box after the topic is presented in the text. These answers are then more fully explained at the end of each chapter. We think that students will find this exercise engaging. It will also enable them, as they read, to check their intuitive beliefs against the findings of social psychology—and notice the discrepancies that exist.

The Organization

Of all the challenges faced by teachers and textbooks, perhaps the greatest is to put information together in a way that is accurate and understandable. A strong organizational framework helps in meeting this challenge. There is nothing worse for a student than having to wade through a "laundry list" of endless studies whose connection with each other remains a profound mystery. A strong structure thus facilitates the development of conceptual understanding.

But the tail should not wag the dog. Since organizational structure is a means to an end, not an end in itself, we believe that it should be kept simple and relatively unobtrusive. In this edition, as in the previous ones, we present social psychology within four major Parts, a heuristic structure that teachers and students have found sensible and easy to follow. We realize, of course, that some instructors prefer to reshuffle the deck to develop a chapter order that better fits their own approach. There is no problem in doing this. Each chapter stands on its own and does not require that others be read first. In response to user comments, however, we have re-ordered the Parts from previous editions to make the structure more compatible with common practice.

As before, we start with an internal focus on *Social Perception* (Part One) and conclude with *Applying Social Psychology* (Part Four). In contrast to previous editions, however, the section on *Social Influence* (Part Two) now precedes rather than follows the material on *Social Relations* (Part Three). This shift enables us to move forward our basic coverage of attitudes—a change that just about everyone we talked to finds desirable.

In addition to re-ordering the Parts of this book, we made two organizational changes to suit the way many instructors like to teach the course. First, we added a chapter on research methods, thus separating it from the introduction and definition of social psychology, its history, and main perspectives, all presented in Chapter 1. Research methods help us to teach students to think like social psychologists, which is why some instructors dedicate one or even two full class days to the topic. Thus, we felt it was important to present research as an ongoing process—from the germ of an idea to the publication of a body of studies suitable for meta-analysis—and to set that material aside in its own chapter.

The second major change was to bring together the study of attraction and close relationships in a single chapter. Wanting to tell a conceptually coherent story self-contained within a single chapter, we have now combined these topics. Opening with the notion that the need to belong is a fundamental human motive, and moving on to the initial attraction process, mate selection, love, sex, and the formation, development, and breakup of close relationships, this chapter presents a comprehensive and up-to-date look at this growing, active, and important area of research.

The Presentation

Even when the content of a textbook is accurate and up-to-date, and even when its organization is sound, there is still the matter of presentation. As the teacher outside the classroom, a good textbook should facilitate learning. Thus, each and every chapter comes complete with the following pedagogical features:

- A narrative preview, chapter outline, and commonsense quiz.
- Key terms highlighted in the text, defined in the margin, listed at the end of the chapter, and reprinted in an alphabetized glossary at the end of the book. Both the list and the glossary provide page numbers for easy location of the term.
- Numerous bar graphs, line graphs, tables, sketches, photographs, flow charts, and cartoons that not only illustrate material in the text but extend, enhance, and enliven that material. Some of these depict classic images and studies from social psychology's past; others, new to the Fourth Edition, are contemporary, often "newsy."
- A comprehensive bulleted review summarizing the major sections and points at the end of each chapter.

Supplemental Materials

All students who purchase this textbook in North America will receive a reader, *Readings in Social Psychology: The Art and Science of Research*. This item comes shrink-wrapped free with the textbook and contains sixteen original articles—each with a brief introduction and questions to stimulate critical thinking about "doing" social psychology. These articles represent some of the most creative and accessible research in the field, both classic and contemporary, of topical interest to students.

Two other supplemental readers are available to students. *Perspectives: Social Psychology*, by Michele Acker, Otterbein College, reprints recent relevant articles from a variety of newspapers, magazines, and other sources. *Stand! Social Psychology*, by Brad Caskey, University of Wisconsin–River Falls, features articles and essays presenting conflicting opinions on the most fundamental controversies in the field, with learning aids that help students develop critical thinking skills and formulate reasoned opinions on issues. These two readers, published by **coursewise publishing,** are available through Houghton Mifflin representatives. Also available with our book is a subscription to courselinks™, a coursewise website guiding students to sites recommended by an editorial board of social psychology instructors, with worksheets for the links, self-quizzes, discussion opportunities, and other resources. Visit www.coursewise.com for more information.

The *Study Guide*, *Test Bank*, and *Instructor's Resource Manual* have been completely revised and considerably expanded. As in the Third Edition, these materials are absolutely first-rate, and we believe they will receive an enthusiastic response from both teachers and students.

Each chapter of the *Study Guide* facilitates student learning through the use of a chapter outline, learning objectives, a review of key terms and concepts, multiple-choice questions with explanations for why the correct answer is the best choice, and a new set of practice essay questions with sample answers.

The *Test Bank* features an extensive and half-new set of multiple-choice questions and essay questions with sample answers. Three types of objective questions are provided: factual, conceptual, and applied. All items are keyed to learning objectives and text pages. The computerized test bank for IBM or Macintosh computers contains all of the questions in the test bank in an easy-to-use, menu-driven format that allows for customization to each instructor's needs.

The *Instructor's Resource Manual* contains many learning objectives, lecture outlines, discussion topics, classroom exercises, handouts, and audiovisual resource suggestions. The classroom exercises, which were completely revised in the Third Edition and augmented again for the Fourth, feature a "What if This Bombs?" section that offers tips for making the most of every activity—even if it does not work.

An extensive set of *overhead transparencies* includes images from within and outside the text's illustration program. *Electronic slides* are now also available with the book for lecture presentation purposes.

Created especially for the Fourth Edition, *Social Psychology Lecture Starter Videoclips* offers instructors who use this text an hour of footage containing brief clips perfectly suited for classroom use. A wide variety of full-length *videos and films* is also available through your Houghton Mifflin sales representative.

Also new to the Fourth Edition is *Psychabilities*, a website featuring additional teaching and learning resources that support the social psychology course. Visit the Psychology page of the Houghton Mifflin College Division site located at http://www.hmco.com/hmco/college/College.html for entry to this site.

ACKNOWLEDGMENTS

Textbooks are the product of a team effort. As always, we are grateful to Houghton Mifflin Company for its commitment to quality as the first priority. First, we want to thank Kathi Prancan, our guardian angel whose commitment and oversight in the early stages of this edition helped bring it to fruition. This book would not have been possible without her. We also want to express our deep appreciation to all those whose considerable talents and countless hours of hard work can be seen on every page of this book: Jane Knetzger, Senior Associate Editor; Joanne M. Tinsley, Developmental Editor; Rosemary R. Jaffe, Senior Project Editor; Jennifer Waddell, Senior Production/Design Coordinator; Catherine Hawkes, Designer; Jessyca Broekman, Art Editor; and Naomi Kornhauser and Linda Sykes, Photo Editors.

Then there are our colleagues who guided us through their feedback on the Third Edition. Each and every one of these teachers and scholars has helped to make this a better book. For their invaluable insights, comments, and suggestions, we thank:

Scott Allison, *University of Richmond*
Craig A. Anderson, *University of Missouri*
Robin A. Anderson, *St. Ambrose University*
C. Daniel Batson, *University of Kansas*
Beth Benoit, *University of Massachusetts, Lowell & Middlesex Community College*
Brad J. Bushman, *Iowa State University*
Melissa A. Cahoon, *University of Dayton*
Nathaniel Carter, *Lane College*
Keith E. Davis, *University of South Carolina*
Joseph R. Ferrari, *DePaul University*
J.H. Forthman, *San Antonio College*
Traci Giuliano, *Southwestern University*
Karen L. Harris, *Western Illinois University*
Robert D. Johnson, *Arkansas State University*
William M. Klein, *Colby College*

LaRue Kobrin, *College of the Redwoods*
Doug Krull, *Northern Kentucky University*
Margaret A. Lloyd, *Georgia Southern University*
David C. Lundgren, *University of Cincinnati*
Roque V. Mendez, *Southwest Texas State University*
Cynthia R. Nordstrom, *Illinois State University*
Randall E. Osborne, *Indiana University East*
Patricia A. Oswald, *Iona College*
Carol K. Oyster, *University of Wisconsin–La Crosse*
Margaret M. Pulsifer, *Johns Hopkins University School of Medicine*
Todd K. Shackelford, *Florida Atlantic University*
Laura S. Sidorowicz, *Nassau Community College*
Anthony Stahelski, *Central Washington University*
William von Hipple, *Ohio State University*
Kipling D. Williams, *University of New South Wales*

Finally, we are very grateful to Steven Spencer for helping put together a top-of-the-line *Study Guide, Instructor's Resource Manual,* and *Reader*. We are also deeply indebted to William Klein and Lisa Klein, authors of the excellent new *Test Bank*. These works have added a whole new dimension to this text.

Sharon S. Brehm

Saul M. Kassin

Steven Fein

About the Authors

Sharon S. Brehm is Provost at Ohio University, where she is also Professor of Psychology and of Interpersonal Communication. Born and raised in Roanoke, Virginia, she received both her B.A. and Ph.D. from Duke University. She completed an internship in clinical psychology at the University of Washington Medical Center in Seattle. From 1975 to 1990, she was on the faculty of the University of Kansas, and from 1990 to 1996 she was Dean of Harpur College of Arts and Sciences at the State University of New York at Binghamton. Brehm has held visiting appointments in France, Germany, and Italy. Her books include *The Application of Social Psychology to Clinical Practice*, a recognized classic in the field, and *Intimate Relationships*, a popular textbook. Representing Division 8, Personality and Social Psychology, she is currently serving her second term on the Council of Representatives of the American Psychological Association.

Saul M. Kassin is Professor of Psychology at Williams College in Williamstown, Massachusetts. Born and raised in New York City, he graduated with a B.S. from Brooklyn College. After receiving his Ph.D. in personality and social psychology from the University of Connecticut, he spent one year at the University of Kansas and two years at Purdue University. In 1984, he was awarded a prestigious U.S. Supreme Court Judicial Fellowship, and in 1985 he worked as a postdoctoral fellow in the Psychology and Law Program at Stanford University. Kassin is author of the textbook *Psychology* (second edition) and has coauthored or edited six scholarly books, including *Developmental Social Psychology*, *The Psychology of Evidence and Trial Procedure*, and *The American Jury on Trial: Psychological Perspectives*. His research interests are in social perception and its applications to legal evidence, trial procedure, and jury decision-making.

Steven Fein is Associate Professor of Psychology at Williams College, Williamstown, Massachusetts. Born and raised in Bayonne, New Jersey, he received his A.B. from Princeton University and his Ph.D. in social psychology from the University of Michigan. He has been teaching at Williams College since 1991, with time spent teaching at Stanford University in 1999. His edited books include *Emotion: Interdisciplinary Perspectives*, and *Readings in Social Psychology: The Art and Science of Research*. He is on the executive committee of the Society of Personality and Social Psychology. His research interests concern stereotyping and prejudice, suspicion, and sociocultural and motivational influences on person perception.

Social Psychology

1 | Introduction

PREVIEW

This chapter introduces you to the study of social psychology. We begin by defining social psychology and identifying how it is distinct from but related to some other areas of study, both outside and within psychology. Next, we review the history of the field. We conclude by looking forward, with a discussion of the important themes and perspectives that are propelling social psychology into a new century.

A few years from now, you may receive a letter in the mail, inviting you to a high-school or college reunion. You'll probably feel a bit nostalgic, and you'll begin to think about those old school days. What thoughts will come to mind first? Will you remember the poetry you finally began to appreciate in your junior year? Will you think about the excitement you felt when you completed your first chemistry lab? Will a tear form in your eye as you remember how inspiring your social psychology class was?

Perhaps. But what will probably dominate your thoughts are the people you knew in school and the interactions you had with them—the long and intense discussions about everything imaginable; the loves you had, lost, or wanted so desperately to experience; the time you made a fool of yourself at a party; the effort of trying to be accepted by a fraternity, sorority, or clique of popular people; the day you sat in the pouring rain with your friends while watching a football game.

We focus on these social situations because we are social beings. We forge our individual identities not alone but in the context of other people. We work, play, and live together. We hurt and help each other. We define happiness and success for each other. And we don't fall passively into social interactions; we actively seek them. People go home for the holidays, play the dating game, make friends, give parties, build networks, pledge an enduring commitment, decide to have children. We watch others, speculate about them, and predict who will wind up with whom.

"Man is a social animal."
—Benedict Spinoza, *Ethics*

You've probably seen the movie *It's a Wonderful Life*. When the hero, George Bailey, was about to kill himself, the would-be angel Clarence didn't save him by showing him how much personal happiness he'd miss if he ended his life. Instead, he showed George how much his life had touched the lives of others and how many people would be hurt if he were not a part of their world. It was these social relationships that saved George's life, just as they define our own.

Precisely because we need and care so much about social interactions and relationships, the social contexts in which we find ourselves can influence us profoundly. In an episode of the television series *Seinfeld*, for example, Kramer redecorates his apartment so that it resembles a talk-show set. When his friends Jerry, George, and Elaine stop by, they inadvertently behave like guests on a talk show; the social setting has shaped their behaviors. You can find many examples of this kind of influence in your own life. Have you ever laughed at a joke you didn't get just because those around you were laughing? Do you present yourself in one way with one group of people and in quite a different way with another group? The power of the situation can also be much more subtle, and yet powerful, than in these examples, as when another's unspoken expectations about you literally seem to cause you to become a different person.

For those of us fascinated by our own social behavior and that of others, social psychology is a dream come true. Just look at Table 1.1 and consider a small sample of the questions you'll explore in this textbook. As you can see, the social nature of the human animal is what social psychology is all about. Learning about social psychology is learning about ourselves and our social worlds. And because social psychology is scientific rather than anecdotal, systematic rather than haphazard, it provides insight that would be impossible to gain through intuition or experience alone.

The value of social psychology's perspective on human behavior is widely recognized. Courses in social psychology are often required for undergraduate majors in business, education, and journalism as well as in psychology and sociology. Although most advanced graduates with a Ph.D. in social psychology hold faculty appointments in colleges or universities, they also work in medical centers, law firms, business organizations, and government agencies. Constantly expanding their horizons, social psychologists seek new knowledge and new opportunities to apply what they have learned.

The purpose of this chapter is to provide you with a broad overview of the field. By the time you finish it, you should be ready and (we hope) eager for what lies ahead.

T A B L E 1.1   **Examples of Social Psychological Questions**

Social Perception: What Affects How We Perceive Ourselves and Others?

- Why do people sometimes sabotage their own performance, making it more likely that they will fail? (Chapter 3)

- Why do first impressions often stick like glue regardless of what happens afterward? (Chapter 4)

- Where do stereotypes come from, and why are they so resistant to change? (Chapter 5)

Social Influence: How Do We Influence Each Other?

- Why do we often come to like what we suffer for? (Chapter 6)

- Why would people inflict intense pain on another human being simply because they are told to? (Chapter 7)

- Why are mobs typically more violent than the individuals who are in them? (Chapter 8)

Social Interaction: What Causes Us to Like, Love, Help, and Hurt Others?

- How similar or different are the sexes in what they look for in a mate? (Chapter 9)

- When is a bystander more or less likely to help you in an emergency? (Chapter 10)

- Does exposure to TV violence, or watching pornography, trigger aggressive behavior? (Chapter 11)

Applying Social Psychology: How Does Social Psychology Help Us Understand Questions About Law, Business, and Health?

- How can the wording of an attorney's question alter an eyewitness's memory? (Chapter 12)

- How can a business leader most effectively motivate his or her employees? (Chapter 13)

- How does stress affect one's health, and what are the most effective ways of coping with stressful experiences? (Chapter 14)

Our social relationships and interactions are extremely important to us. Most people seek out and are profoundly affected by other people. This social nature of the human animal is what social psychology is all about.

What Is Social Psychology?

We begin by defining the new territory you're about to enter. Then we map out the relationship of social psychology to sociology and some other disciplines within the field of psychology.

Defining Social Psychology

Social psychology is the scientific study of how individuals think, feel, and behave in regard to other people and how individuals' thoughts, feelings, and behaviors are affected by other people. Let's look at each part of this definition.

Scientific Study   There are many approaches to understanding how people think, feel, and behave. We can learn about human behavior from novels, films, history, and philosophy—to name just a few possibilities. What makes social psychology different from these artistic and humanistic endeavors is that social psychology is a science. It applies the *scientific method* of systematic observation, description, and measurement to the study of the human condition. How, and why, social psychologists do this is explained in Chapter 2.

How Individuals Think, Feel, and Behave   In addition to social psychology, many other disciplines employ scientific techniques to study human behavior. Examples include anthropology, communication studies, economics, political science, and sociology. All of these disciplines, including social psychology, are called *social sciences*.

The social sciences differ in what aspects of behavior they examine. Some concentrate on relatively limited, specific content areas. Economists, for instance, conduct research on economic issues, and political scientists on political ones. Social psychology opts for a broader view, studying many different behaviors that occur in many different settings. Research on attitudes (see Chapter 6) offers a

> **social psychology** The scientific study of how individuals think, feel, and behave in regard to other people and how individuals' thoughts, feelings, and behaviors are affected by other people.

A well-like celebrity like Oprah Winfrey can influence the attitudes and behaviors of millions of people. When Oprah recommends a book, for example, sales of the book are likely to skyrocket.

good illustration. By investigating a variety of specific attitudes (including, but not limited to, those about economics and politics), social psychologists attempt to establish general principles of attitude formation and change that apply in a variety of situations. This search for general principles is characteristic of social psychology's approach to a diverse array of human behaviors.

The level of analysis also sets social psychology apart from some other social sciences. Sociology, for instance, classifies people in terms of their nationality, race, socioeconomic class, and other *group factors*. In contrast, social psychology typically focuses on the psychology of the *individual*. Even when social psychologists study groups of people, they usually emphasize the behavior of the individual in the group context.

Research methods provide another distinction. Far more than other social sciences, social psychology uses experiments to investigate human behavior. Later in this chapter, we describe the basic features of an experiment. In sum, social psychology is characterized by a broad perspective, a focus on the individual, and the frequent use of an experimental methodology.

Other People—The Social Element   The last part of the definition, "in regard to other people, and how individuals' thoughts, feelings, and behaviors are affected by other people," is where the "social" in social psychology comes into play and how social psychology is distinguished from other branches of psychology. As a whole, the discipline of psychology is an immense, sprawling enterprise, the 800-pound gorilla of the social sciences, concerned with everything from neurotransmitters in the brain to why there was a backlash against the Spice Girls within a year of their rise to fame. Nevertheless, much of psychology emphasizes the scientific method, takes a broad perspective with a focus on the individual, and employs experimental techniques. What makes social psychology unique is its emphasis on the social nature of individuals.

However, the "socialness" of social psychology varies. Attempting to establish general principles of human behavior, social psychologists sometimes examine nonsocial factors that affect people's thoughts, emotions, motives, and actions. For example, they may study whether heat causes people to behave more aggressively (Anderson & Anderson, 1998). What is social about this is the behavior: people hurting each other. In addition, social psychologists sometimes study people's thoughts or feelings about nonsocial things, such as people's attitudes toward Nike versus New Balance basketball shoes. How can attitudes toward basketball shoes be of interest to social psychologists? One way is if these attitudes are influenced by something social, such as whether Michael Jordan's endorsement of Nike makes people like Nike. Both examples, determining whether heat causes an increase in aggression or whether Michael Jordan causes an increase in sales of Nike shoes, are social psychological pursuits because the thoughts, feelings, or behaviors either (a) concerned other people or (b) were influenced by other people.

The "other people" referred to in the definition of *social psychology* do not have to be real or present. Even the implied or imagined presence of others can have important effects on individuals (Allport, 1985). For example, if people imagine receiving positive or negative reactions from others, their self-esteem can be affected significantly (Leary, Haupt, et al., 1998).

The Power of the Situation: An Example of a Social Psychology Experiment

Two of the authors of this text recently conducted an experiment that can serve as an example of how social psychologists study the influence of the imagined or implied presence of others on individuals (Fein et al., 1998). We had college students watch a tape of a 1984 debate between Ronald Reagan and Walter Mondale, two candidates for the presidency of the United States. During that debate, Reagan fired off a pair of one-liners that elicited a great deal of laughter from the audience. Political analysts have wondered whether those one-liners may have won the debate, and possibly the election, for Reagan. The one-liners comprised only seconds of a ninety-minute debate concerning the most important issues of the day. Could their effect have been so great?

To study this issue, we had students watch the debate under one of three conditions. One-third of the students saw the debate as it was, without any editing. One-third of the students saw the debate with the one-liners and the ensuing audience reaction edited out. By comparing these two conditions, we could see whether the presence versus absence of this pair of jokes could make a large difference in people's impressions of Reagan and Mondale from the debate. However, there was also a third condition. One-third of the students saw the debate with the one-liners intact but with the audience reaction edited out. That is, Reagan told his jokes, but there appeared to be no audience response, and the debate continued uninterrupted.

After watching the debate, the students judged the performance of the candidates on a scale ranging from 0 *(terrible)* to 100 *(excellent)*. As you can see from the first two bars in Figure 1.1, the students who saw the entire unedited tape did not rate Reagan much more positively than did the students who saw the debate without the one-liners. This suggests that the jokes did not have much impact on these viewers' perceptions of the candidates. But look at the third bar in the figure. As it indicates, the students who saw

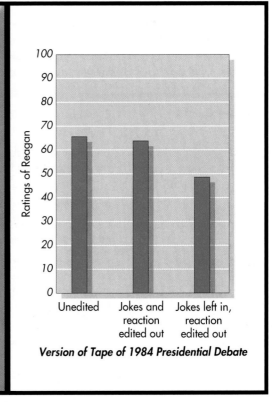

FIGURE 1.1 Influence of Others' Reactions

This graph shows the results of research in which participants saw different versions of a tape of a 1984 presidential debate between Ronald Reagan and Walter Mondale. During the debate, Reagan had delivered a pair of witty one-liners that elicited a positive audience reaction. Participants who saw an unedited version of the tape and participants who saw a version with the jokes and the audience reaction edited out judged Reagan's performance similarly. Participants who saw a version with the jokes left in but the audience reaction edited out (suggesting that the audience didn't find the jokes funny) rated Reagan much more negatively. *(Adapted from Fein et al., 1998.)*

Version of Tape of 1984 Presidential Debate

the version of the debate with the one-liners kept in but the audience reaction edited out rated Reagan much less positively than did either of the other groups. What could explain their negativity toward Reagan's debate performance? Perhaps when Reagan's jokes appeared to elicit no reaction, the students unknowingly used the lack of reaction as an indication that Reagan's attempts at wit were inept, causing them to see Reagan in a much less positive light.

What is interesting about these results from a social psychological standpoint was that the students' judgments were influenced more by other people's *reactions* to what Reagan said (that is, whether or not the audience appeared to laugh) than by the *content* of what he said (that is, whether or not the one-liners were edited out of the tape). And it is important to note that these "other people" were not in the room with the students; they were simply sounds on a videotape recorded more than a decade earlier.

The power of the immediate situation is an important theme in social psychological research, but it is not the only one. Other themes focus on the roles of individuals' cultural backgrounds; the biases in the way that people make judgments; and the motivations that people have to be liked, to belong to respected social groups, and to achieve material and social rewards. In later chapters we will examine the influences of each of these factors on people's thoughts, feelings, and behaviors.

Social Psychology and Related Fields: Distinctions and Intersections

Social psychology is sometimes confused with certain other fields of study. Before we go on, it is important to clarify how social psychology is distinct from these other fields. At the same time, it is important to illustrate some of the ways in which interesting and significant questions can be addressed through interactions between social psychology and these other fields (see Table 1.2).

Social Psychology and Sociology Sociologists and social psychologists share an interest in many issues, such as violence, prejudice, cultural differences, and marriage. Sociology, however, tends to focus on the group level, whereas social psychology tends to focus on the individual level. For example, sociologists might track the political attitudes of the middle class in the United States, whereas social psychologists might examine some of the specific factors that make individuals like one political candidate better than another.

In addition, sociologists most often study the relation

TABLE 1.2   Distinctions Between Social Psychology and Related Fields: The Case of Research on Prejudice

To see the differences between social psychology and related fields, consider an example of how researchers in each field might conduct a study of prejudice.

Field of Study	Example of How a Researcher in the Field Might Study Prejudice
Sociology	Track how Americans' prejudice toward Japanese has changed since World War II
Clinical psychology	Test various therapies for people with antisocial personalities who exhibit great degrees of prejudice
Personality psychology	Develop a questionnaire to identify men who are very high or low in degree of prejudice toward women
Cognitive psychology	Manipulate exposure to a member of some category of people and measure the thoughts and concepts that are automatically activated *(A study of prejudice in this field would, by definition, be at the intersection of cognitive and social psychology.)*
Social psychology	Manipulate various kinds of contact between individuals of different groups and examine the effect of these manipulations on the degree of prejudice exhibited

between people's behaviors and *societal* variables, such as social class. In contrast, social psychologists are more likely to study the relation between people's behaviors and more specific, immediate variables, such as manipulations of mood and exposure to particular models of behavior. Finally, although there are many exceptions, social psychologists are more likely than sociologists to use experiments in which they manipulate some variable and determine the effects of this manipulation using precise, quantifiable measures.

Despite these differences, sociology and social psychology are clearly related. When these two fields intersect, the result can be a more complete understanding of important issues. For example, inter-disciplinary research on gender differences in math proficiency has examined how both societal and immediate factors can affect these differences, as will be examined in Chapter 5 (Benbow et al., 1997; Spencer et al., 1998).

Do provocative, sexualized images in advertising, such as on the billboard seen here (near the sign about "student body cards"), make people more sexist or prone to sexual aggression? This is one of the questions that social psychology addresses.

Social Psychology and Clinical Psychology Tell people not very familiar with psychology that you are taking a social psychology class, and they are likely to say things like, "Oh, great, now you're going to start psychoanalyzing me," or, "Finally, maybe you can tell me why everyone in my family is so messed up." The assumption underlying these reactions, of course, is that you are studying clinical, or abnormal, psychology. Clinical psychologists seek to understand and treat people with psychological difficulties or disorders. Social psychologists do not focus on disorders; rather, they focus on the more typical ways in which individuals think, feel, behave, and influence each other.

There are, however, many fascinating ways in which clinical and social psychology intersect. Both, for example, may address how people cope with anxiety or pressure in social situations; how depressed and nondepressed individuals differ in the way they process social information, explain the causes of behavior, and seek out interactions; and how people who are labeled as having various psychological disorders can be helped or hurt by others' expectations concerning these disorders (e.g., Giesler & Swann, 1998; Haupt & Leary, 1997; Markman & Weary, 1996).

Social Psychology and Personality Psychology Both personality psychology and social psychology are concerned with individuals and their thoughts, feelings, and behaviors. However, personality psychology seeks to understand differences between individuals that remain relatively stable across a variety of situations, whereas social psychology seeks to understand how social factors affect most individuals, *despite* their different personalities.

In other words, personality psychologists are interested in cross-situational consistency. They may ask, "Is this person outgoing and friendly almost all the time, in just about any setting?" Social psychologists are interested in how different situations cause different behaviors. They may ask, "Are people in general more likely to seek out companionship when they are made anxious by a situation than when they are made to feel relaxed?"

These examples show the contrast between the fields; but in fact, personality psychology and social psychology are very closely linked. The American Psychological Association has more than fifty different divisions, and yet personality psychologists and social psychologists share the same division. Many of these scholars belong to an organization called the Society of Personality and Social Psychology, and two important journals that publish research in these fields are the *Journal of Personality and Social Psychology* and *Personality and Social Psychology Bulletin*. So personality and social psychologists see a lot of each other.

The reason for the high degree of connection between social psychology and personality psychology is that the two areas complement each other so well. For example, some social psychologists examine how receiving negative feedback (a situational factor) can have different effects on people as a function of whether their self-esteem is high or low (an individual difference factor) (Baumeister et al., 1996). Other questions at the intersection of personality psychology and social psychology include the following: "Do people tend to be attracted to others whose personalities are the opposite of their own?" "Does watching a lot of TV cause more antisocial behavior in some types of children than in others?" "When is it better for a group or business to have a leader who has a very controlling, domineering personality, and when is it better to have a leader who is more cooperative and warm?"

Social Psychology and Cognitive Psychology   Cognitive psychologists study mental processes such as thinking, learning, remembering, and reasoning. Social psychologists are often interested in these same processes. More specifically, though, social psychologists are interested in how people think, learn, remember, and reason with respect to social information and in how these processes are relevant to social behavior.

The last two decades have seen an explosion of interest in the intersection of cognitive and social psychology. The study of *social cognition* is discussed in more detail later in this chapter, and it is a focus throughout this text, especially in Part I on Social Perception.

Social Psychology and Common Sense

After reading about a theory or finding of social psychology, you may sometimes think, "Of course. I knew that all along. Anyone could have told me that." This "knew-it-all-along" phenomenon often causes people to question how social psychology is different from common sense, or traditional folk wisdom. After all, why would any of the following social psychological findings be surprising?

- Physically attractive individuals tend to be seen as less intellectually competent than physically unattractive individuals.
- To change people's behavior for more than a brief period of time, it is necessary to change their attitudes first.
- People tend to underestimate the extent to which others share their opinions, attributes, and behavior.
- Most people are less likely to commit an act of physical aggression against someone if they have had the chance to release their tensions by playing a violent sport.

We will have more to say about these statements below.

Common sense may seem to explain many social psychological findings after the fact. The problem is distinguishing common-sense fact from common-sense myth. After all, for most common-sense notions, there is an equally sensible-sounding notion that says the opposite. Is it "Birds of a feather flock together" or "Opposites attract"? Is it "Two heads are better than one" or "Too many cooks spoil the broth"?

Social psychology, unlike common sense, uses the scientific method to put its theories to the test. How it does so will be discussed in greater detail in the next chapter. But before we leave this section, one word of caution: Those four "findings" listed on page 10? *They are all false.* Although there may be sensible reasons to believe each of the statements to be true, research indicates otherwise. Therein lies the problem with relying on common sense.

To emphasize this point, and to encourage you to think critically about social psychological issues *before* as well as after learning about them, this textbook contains a feature called "Putting Common Sense to the Test." Beginning with Chapter 3, each chapter opens with a few statements about social psychological issues that will be covered in that chapter. Some of the statements are true, and some are false. As you read each statement, make a prediction about whether it is true or false, and think about *why* this is your prediction. Marginal notes throughout the chapter will tell you

whether the statements are true or false. In reading the chapter, check not only whether your prediction was correct but also whether your reasons for the prediction were appropriate. If your intuition wasn't quite on the mark, think about what the right answer is and how the evidence supports that answer. There are few better ways of learning and remembering than through this kind of critical thinking.

Unlike the research in Duh *magazine, most social psychology research goes far beyond—and often contradicts—common-sense notions and intuitions.* Roz Chast © 1996 from The New Yorker Collection. All Rights Reserved.

From Past to Present: A Brief History of Social Psychology

People have probably been asking social psychological questions for as long as humans could think about each other. Certainly, early philosophers such as Plato offered keen insights into many social psychological issues. But no systematic and scientific study of social psychological issues developed until the end of the nineteenth century. The field of social psychology is therefore a very young one. As a testament to this youth, the social psychologist Dorwin Cartwright said in 1979 that 90 percent of social psychologists who had ever lived were still alive at that time. Recent years have marked a tremendous interest in social psychology and an injection of many new scholars into the field. As social psychology begins its second century, it is instructive to look back to see how the field today has been shaped by the people and events of its first century.

"Psychology has a long past, but only a short history."

—Herman Ebbinghaus, *Summary of Psychology*

The Birth and Infancy of Social Psychology: 1880s–1920s

Would these runners race faster or slower if they were running individually against the clock rather than running simultaneously with their competitors? More generally, will the performance of individuals improve or decline when in the presence of others? The two founders of social psychology, American psychologist Norman Triplett and French agricultural engineer Max Ringelmann, sought answers to questions such as these. Chapter 8 on Group Processes brings you up-to-date on the latest research in this area.

Like most such honors, the title "founder of social psychology" has many potential recipients, and not everyone agrees on who should prevail. Most point to the American psychologist Norman Triplett, who is credited with having published the first research article in social psychology at the end of the nineteenth century (1897–1898). Triplett's work was noteworthy because, after observing that bicyclists tended to race faster when racing in the presence of others than when simply racing against a clock, he designed an experiment to study this phenomenon in a carefully controlled, precise way. This scientific approach to studying the effects of the social context on individuals' behavior can be seen as marking the birth of social psychology.

A case can also be made for the French agricultural engineer Max Ringelmann. Ringelmann's research was conducted in the 1880s but wasn't published until 1913. In an interesting twist of fate, Ringelmann also studied the effects of the presence of others on the performance of individuals. In contrast to Triplett, however, Ringelmann noted that individuals often performed worse on simple tasks such as pulling rope when they performed the tasks with other people. The issues addressed by these two early researchers continue to be of vital interest, as will be seen later in Chapter 8 on Group Processes.

Despite their place in the history of social psychology, neither Triplett nor Ringelmann actually established social psychology as a distinct field of study. Credit for this creation goes to the writers of the first three textbooks in social psychology: the English psychologist William McDougall (1908) and two Americans, Edward Ross (1908) and Floyd Allport (1924). Allport's book in particular, with its focus on the interaction of individuals and their social context and its emphasis on the use of experimentation and the scientific method, helped establish social psychology as the discipline it is today. These authors announced the arrival of a new approach to the social aspects of human behavior. Social psychology was born.

A Call to Action: 1930s–1950s

What one person would you guess has had the strongest influence on the field of social psychology? Various social psychologists, as well as psychologists of other areas, might be mentioned in response to this question. But someone who was not a psychologist at all may have had the most dramatic impact on the field: Adolf Hitler.

Hitler's rise to power and the ensuing turmoil caused people around the world to become desperate for answers to social psychological questions about what

causes violence, prejudice and genocide, conformity and obedience, and a host of other social problems and behaviors. In addition, many social psychologists living in Europe in the 1930s fled to the United States and helped establish a critical mass of social psychologists who would give shape to the rapidly maturing field. The years just before, during, and soon after World War II marked an explosion of interest in social psychology.

In 1936, Gordon Allport (younger brother of Floyd, author of the 1924 textbook) and a number of other social psychologists formed the Society for the Psychological Study of Social Issues. The name of the society illustrates these psychologists' concern for making important, practical contributions to society. Also in 1936, a social psychologist named Muzafer Sherif published a groundbreaking study of social influence. As a youth in Turkey, Sherif had witnessed groups of Greek soldiers brutally killing his friends. After emigrating to the United States, Sherif drew on this experience and began to conduct research on the powerful influences groups can exert on their individual members. As described in more detail in Chapter 7 on Conformity, participants in Sherif's 1936 research observed a visual illusion—a dot of light that was actually stationary but appeared to move. Watching alone, participants differed considerably in their individual estimates of the light's movement. When they watched together in groups, however, their estimates of the light's movement converged. The light itself never budged, but opinions moved toward a common perception.

Sherif's research was crucial for the development of social psychology because it demonstrated that it is possible to study complex social processes such as conformity and social influence in a rigorous, scientific manner. This innovation laid the foundation for what was to become one of the major topics in social psychology. Research and theory on social influence are discussed throughout this text, particularly in Part II on Social Influence.

Another great contributor to social psychology, Kurt Lewin, fled the Nazi onslaught in Germany and emigrated to the United States in the early 1930s. Lewin was a bold and creative theorist whose concepts have had lasting effects on the field. Among the fundamental principles of social psychology that Lewin (1935, 1947) helped establish were the following:

What we do depends to a large extent on how we perceive and interpret the world around us. Different people can see the same situation differently, and their

Built on the legacy of Kurt Lewin, one of the leading figures in the development of the field, applied social psychology contributes to the solution of social problems. Throughout this text, we describe the application of social psychological principles to societal concerns such as classroom interaction (see Chapter 5 on Perceiving Groups) and environmental conservation (see Chapter 8 on Group Processes).

behavior will vary accordingly. This theme continues to be important in social psychology. You will encounter it throughout this textbook, especially in Part I, on Social Perception.

Behavior is a function of the interaction between the person and the environment. Lewin's conviction that both internal and external factors affect behavior helped create a unified view that was distinct from the other major psychological paradigms during his lifetime: psychoanalysis, with its emphasis on internal motives and fantasies; and behaviorism, with its focus on external rewards and punishments. Lewin's position was an early version of what today is known as the **interactionist perspective** (Blass, 1984). This approach combines personality psychology (stressing internal, psychological differences among individuals) with social psychology (stressing differences among external situations). Throughout this book, we examine the impact of both individual and situational differences, alone and together.

Social psychological theories should be applied to important, practical issues. Lewin researched a number of practical issues, such as how to persuade Americans at home during the war to conserve materials to help the war effort; how to promote more economical and nutritious eating habits; and what kinds of leaders elicit the best work from group members. Through these studies, Lewin showed how social psychology could enlarge our understanding of social problems and contribute to their solution. Built on Lewin's legacy, applied social psychology flourishes today in areas such as advertising, business, education, environmental protection, health, law, politics, public policy, religion, and sports. Throughout this text, we draw on the findings of applied social psychology to illustrate the implications of social psychological principles for our daily lives. In Part IV, three prominent areas of applied social psychology are discussed in detail: law, business, and health. One of Lewin's statements can be seen as a call to action for the entire field: "No research without action, no action without research."

During World War II, many social psychologists answered Lewin's call as they worked for the U.S. government to investigate how to protect soldiers from the propaganda of the enemy, how to persuade citizens to support the war effort, how to select officers for various positions, and other practical issues. During and after the war, social psychologists sought to understand the prejudice, aggression, and conformity the war had brought to light. The 1950s saw many major contributions to the field of social psychology; Table 1.3 lists some of these contributions. With this remarkable burst of activity and impact, social psychology was clearly, and irrevocably, on the map.

This World War II poster featuring "Rosie the Riveter" was part of the United States government's campaign to encourage American women to take jobs in traditionally male-dominated occupations, such as in welding. When the war was over and the men who had served in the military returned to the workforce, new advertisements were designed to encourage women to leave these jobs and concentrate on raising families.

Confidence and Crisis: 1960s–Mid-1970s

In spectacular fashion, Stanley Milgram's research in the early and middle 1960s linked the post–World War II era with the coming era of social revolution. Milgram's research was inspired by the destructive obedience demonstrated by Nazi officers and ordinary citizens in World War II, but it also looked ahead to the civil disobedience that was beginning to challenge institutions in many parts of the world. Milgram's experiments, which demonstrated individuals' vulnerability to the destructive commands of authority, became the most famous research in the history

interactionist perspective
An emphasis on how both an individual's personality and environmental characteristics influence behavior.

of social psychology. This research is discussed in detail in Chapter 7.

With its foundation firmly in place, social psychology entered a period of expansion and enthusiasm. The sheer range of its investigations was staggering. Social psychologists considered how people thought and felt about themselves (Bem, 1967) and others (Jones & Davis, 1965; Kelley, 1967). They studied interactions in groups (Moscovici & Zavalloni, 1969) and social problems such as why people fail to help others in distress (Latané & Darley, 1970). They also examined aggression (Bandura, 1973), physical attractiveness (Berscheid & Walster, 1974b), and stress (Glass & Singer, 1972). All of these topics are discussed in this text. For the field as a whole, it was a time of great productivity.

Ironically, it was also a time of crisis and heated debate. Many of the strong disagreements during this period can be understood as a reaction to the dominant research method of the day: the laboratory experiment. Those social psychologists who questioned this type of research maintained that certain practices were unethical (Kelman, 1967), that experimenters' expectations influ-

TABLE 1.3	Some Major Contributions to Social Psychology During the 1950s	
Contributor	**Contribution**	**Discussed in This Text**
Theodor Adorno and colleagues	Published *The Authoritarian Personality*, an influential book on prejudice	Perceiving Groups (Chapter 5)
Gordon Allport	Published *The Nature of Prejudice*, which continues to inspire research on stereotyping and prejudice	Perceiving Groups (Chapter 5)
Solomon Asch	Demonstrated individuals' tendency to conform to an obviously wrong majority; studied how individuals form impressions of others	Conformity (Chapter 7); Perceiving Persons (Chapter 4)
Leon Festinger	Introduced theory of social comparison, concerning how people look to others to learn about themselves; introduced theory of cognitive dissonance, concerning people's desire to maintain consistency in their thoughts and behaviors	The Social Self (Chapter 3), Perceiving Groups (Chapter 5); Attitudes (Chapter 6)
Fritz Heider	Introduced attribution theory, concerning how people judge others and the causes of their behavior; introduced balance theory, concerning people's desire for consistency in their thoughts, feelings, and relationships	Perceiving Persons (Chapter 4); Attraction and Close Relationships (Chapter 9)
Carl Hovland and colleagues	Conducted experiments on attitudes and persuasion, which was influential not only to social psychology but to the rapidly growing advertising industry	Attitudes (Chapter 6)
John Thibaut and Harold Kelley	Studied how people consider costs and rewards in their relationships	Attraction and Close Relationships (Chapter 9)

enced their participants' behavior (Orne, 1962; Rosenthal, 1966), and that the theories being tested in the laboratory were historically and culturally limited (Gergen, 1973). Those who favored laboratory experimentation, on the other hand, contended that their procedures were ethical, their results valid, and their theoretical principles widely applicable (McGuire, 1967). For a while, social psychology seemed split in two.

An Era of Pluralism: Mid-1970s–1990s

Fortunately, both sides won. As we will see in the next chapter, more rigorous ethical standards for research were instituted, more stringent procedures to guard against bias were adopted, and more attention was paid to possible cross-cultural differences in behavior. But the baby was not thrown out with the bath water. Laboratory experiments continued. They did, however, get some company, as a single-minded attachment to one research method evolved into a broader acceptance of many methods. The logic behind a pluralistic approach is compelling (Houts et al., 1986):

- Because different topics require different kinds of investigations, a range of research techniques is needed.
- Because no research method is perfect, a *multimethod* investigation of a topic increases our confidence that the results obtained do not simply reflect the peculiar characteristics of any one approach.

The various research methods used by today's social psychologists are described in the next chapter.

"Hot" versus "Cold" Perspectives   Pluralism in social psychology extends far beyond its methods. There are also important variations in what aspects of human behavior are emphasized. People think, feel, desire, and act. But how do you slice the pie? One approach, which we might call "hot," focuses on *emotion* and *motivation* as determinants of our thoughts and actions (Zajonc, 1984). Another, which we could call "cold," places the emphasis on *cognition*, holding that people's thoughts affect how they feel, what they want, and what they do (Lazarus, 1984). Of course, some social psychologists prefer to put both slices on their plate or to divide up the behavioral whole into entirely different pieces. Nevertheless, the contrast between the "hot" and "cold" perspectives reflects some very real differences in how to conceptualize human behavior.

In this text, we describe both points of view. For instance, the theory of cognitive dissonance (Festinger, 1957), discussed in Chapter 6 on Attitudes, is one of the most influential theories ever developed in social psychology. Dissonance theory is, in our terms, very "hot." When what we do conflicts with what we believe, we feel uncomfortable, and we are motivated to reduce this discomfort, often by changing our attitudes and opinions.

Even though dissonance is a classic example of a "hot" drive-reduction model (when hungry, eat; when dissonant, strive for consistency), it is—as the name indicates—strongly cognitive as well. Dissonance and consonance exist in the mind of the individual. In this sense, dissonance theory served as at least one parent to what became known as **social cognition,** the study of how we perceive, remember, and interpret information about ourselves and others.

Social Cognition   Social cognition is social psychology's contribution to the "cognitive revolution" of the 1980s (Friman et al., 1993). Suddenly, or so it seemed, researchers from a wide array of disciplines—including psychology, philosophy, computer science, and the burgeoning interdisciplinary field of neuroscience—discovered a common interest in cognitive processes and the effects of cognition on behavior. Today, social cognition remains a creative and exciting area in social psychology. Theory and research in social cognition are discussed throughout this text, particularly in Part I on Social Perception.

International and Cultural Perspectives   Another source of pluralism in contemporary social psychology is found in the increasing effort to develop an international and multicultural perspective. Although, as we have seen, individuals from many countries helped establish the field, social psychology achieved its greatest professional recognition in the United States and Canada. It is estimated that today some 75 to 90 percent of social psychologists live in North America (Smith & Bond, 1993; Triandis, 1994). Indeed, some have called social psychology "culture-bound" (Berry et al., 1992) and "largely monocultural" (Moghaddam et al., 1993).

social cognition   The study of how people perceive, remember, and interpret information about themselves and others.

Social psychologists are becoming increasingly interested in cross-cultural research, which helps us break out of our culture-bound perspective. Many of our behaviors differ across cultures. In some cultures, for example, people are expected to negotiate about the price of the products they buy, as in this market in Tunisia. In other cultures, such bargaining would be highly unusual and cause confusion and distress.

This aspect of social psychology is rapidly changing, with profound consequences for our view of human behavior.

- The greater emphasis by European social psychologists on the meaning and impact of group membership has vastly increased the "socialness" of social psychology (Moreland et al., 1994). Major contributions described later in this book include social identity theory (Tajfel, 1982; Turner, 1987) and minority influence (Moscovici, 1980; Mugny, 1982).
- Cross-cultural research has revealed important distinctions between collectivist cultures (more typical in Africa, Asia, and Latin America) and individualistic ones (more typical in North America and Europe). Those distinctions are discussed in many chapters in the book and are introduced in more detail in Chapter 3 on the Social Self.

These are but two examples of the cross-cultural interactions and comparisons that are taking place today. In this text, we describe research conducted in dozens of countries, representing every continent on earth. As our knowledge expands, we should be able to see much more clearly both the behavioral differences among cultures and the similarities we all share.

Social Psychology in a New Century

As we begin the twenty-first century, social psychology begins its second hundred years. The field today continues to grow in numbers and diversity of researchers and research topics, areas of the world in which research is conducted, and industries that hire social psychologists and apply their work.

Throughout this text, we emphasize the most current, cutting-edge research in the field, along with the classic findings of the past. In the remainder of the chapter we focus on a few of the exciting themes and perspectives emerging from current research—research that is helping to shape the social psychology of the new century.

Integration of Emotion, Motivation, and Cognition

If any one perspective dominated the final quarter of social psychology's first century, it may have been social cognition. Social psychologists demonstrated that how individuals perceive, integrate, interpret, and remember information about themselves and others is critically important to virtually every area in the field. Social-cognitive explanations were so powerful that the roles of more "hot" influences, such as emotions and motivations, often took a back seat. Social cognition continues to flourish, but one of the more exciting developments in the field is the re-emergence of interest in how individuals' emotions and motivations influence their thoughts and actions. Especially exciting is the fact that the social-cognitive approach is not necessarily seen as being at odds with approaches that emphasize motivations and emotions. Instead, there is a new push to integrate these perspectives, such as in investigating how people's motivations influence nonconscious cognitive processes, and vice versa.

One issue illustrating the integration of "hot" and "cold" variables concerns the conflict between wanting to be right and wanting to feel good about oneself. Most of us hold two very different motivations simultaneously: On the one hand, we want to be accurate in our judgments about ourselves and others. On the

"On the one hand, eliminating the middleman would result in lower costs, increased sales, and greater consumer satisfaction; on the other hand, we're the middleman."

Our desire to be accurate in our judgments can sometimes interfere with our desire to feel good about ourselves. Robert Mankoff © 1997 from The New Yorker Collection. All Rights Reserved.

other hand, we *don't* want to be accurate if it means we will learn something bad about ourselves or those closest to us. These goals try to steer our cognitive processes in different directions—sometimes slightly different and sometimes drastically different. How we perform the required mental gymnastics is an ongoing concern for social psychologists.

Biological and Evolutionary Perspectives

As the technology available to researchers evolves, biological perspectives are increasingly being integrated into all branches of psychology, and this integration should continue to grow in social psychology. We are, of course, biological organisms, and it is clear that our brains and bodies influence, and are influenced by, our social experiences.

Social psychologists have been concerned with physiological influences and responses for many years. Examples of this interest can be found throughout the textbook, such as in discussions of self-perception, attribution, attitude change, attraction, and aggression. Recent advances in **behavioral genetics**—a subfield of psychology that examines the effects of genes on behavior—has triggered new research to investigate such matters as the extent to which aggression is an inherited trait and the roles genes play in individuals' sexual orientation or identity.

Evolutionary psychology, which uses the principles of evolution to understand human behavior, is another growing area that is sparking new research in social psychology. According to this perspective, to understand a social psychological issue such as jealousy, we should ask how the psychological mechanisms under-

behavioral genetics A subfield of psychology that examines the role of genetic factors on behavior.

evolutionary psychology A subfield of psychology that uses the principles of evolution to understand human social behavior.

lying jealousy today may have evolved from the natural selection pressures our ancestors faced. Evolutionary psychological theories can then be used to explain and predict gender differences in jealousy, what situational factors are most likely to trigger jealousy, and the like. This perspective is discussed in many places in the textbook, especially in Part III on Social Relations.

Sociocultural Perspectives

Because of such developments as satellite communications, the Internet, and the globalization of the world's economies, it is faster, easier, and more necessary than ever before for people from vastly different cultures to interact with one another. Thus, our need and desire to understand how we are similar to and different from one another is greater than ever as well. Earlier work by social scientists has given us an understanding and appreciation of the role of culture in all aspects of social psychology, but our appetites have only been whetted; we also have an understanding and appreciation of how much more we need to know about cultural influences and differences.

Increasing numbers of social psychologists are evaluating the universal generality or cultural specificity of their theories and findings by conducting **cross-cultural research,** in which they examine the similarities and differences across a variety of cultures. More and more social psychologists are also conducting **multicultural research,** in which they examine racial and ethnic groups within cultures.

Sociocultural factors clearly contribute to differences between men and women on a number of dimensions; and for years, social psychologists have studied gender differences in a variety of domains, such as conformity, leadership style, and aggression. Recent research is not only extending this tradition; it is sometimes turning it on its ear by illustrating that many research programs were flawed as a result of taking a male-dominated approach. New research on aggression, for example, illustrates that most of the older research focused almost exclusively on the forms of aggression typical of boys, thereby failing to recognize important issues relevant to aggression among girls.

Some social psychology textbooks devote a separate chapter to culture or to culture and gender. We chose not to do so. Because we believe that sociocultural influences are inherent in all aspects of social psychology, we chose instead to integrate discussions of the role of culture and gender throughout the textbook.

New Technologies

"Awesome" is an overused word, but it surely is appropriate to describe the revolution that is taking place in how we access information and communicate with each other. In writing this new edition of *Social Psychology*, we have been amazed to discover how much more information is available through our computers today than just a few years ago. We would be presumptuous, and probably naive, to try to predict how new communication and computer technologies will influence the ways in which people interact in the coming years; but it probably is safe to predict that their influence will be great. As more and more people fall in love on line, or fall into social isolation, or react with anxiety or violence to the loss of individual privacy, social psychology will explore these issues. We expect that some of the students reading this textbook today will be among those explorers in the coming years.

cross-cultural research
Research designed to compare and contrast people of different cultures.

multicultural research
Research designed to examine racial and ethnic groups within cultures.

Review

What Is Social Psychology?

Defining Social Psychology

- Social psychology is the scientific study of how individuals think, feel, and behave in regard to other people and how individuals' thoughts, feelings, and behaviors are affected by other people.
- Like other sciences, social psychology relies on the systematic approach of the scientific method.
- Distinctive characteristics of social psychology include a broad perspective on a variety of social contexts and behaviors, a focus on the individual, and the frequent use of experiments.
- The "socialness" of social psychology varies, as social psychologists sometimes examine how nonsocial factors affect social thoughts, feelings, and behaviors and sometimes study how social factors influence nonsocial thoughts, feelings, and behaviors.

The Power of the Situation: An Example of a Social Psychology Experiment

- In one experiment, participants' judgments of a political candidate's performance in a debate were influenced more by the reactions of other people to some remarks made by the candidate than by the remarks themselves.

Social Psychology and Related Fields: Distinctions and Intersections

- Social psychology is related to a number of different areas of study, including sociology, clinical psychology, personality psychology, and cognitive psychology. Important work is being done at the intersection of social psychology and each of these fields.
- Social psychology tends to focus on individuals, whereas sociology tends to focus on groups. In addition, social psychology is less likely than sociology to study the relation between broad societal variables and people's behaviors and is more likely to use experimentation.
- In contrast to clinical psychology, social psychology does not focus on disorders but rather on the more typical ways in which individuals think, feel, behave, and interact.
- Personality psychology focuses on differences between individuals that remain relatively stable across a variety of situations; social psychology focuses on how social factors affect most individuals, despite their different personalities.
- Cognitive and social psychologists share an interest in mental processes such as thinking, learning, remembering, and reasoning; but social psychologists focus on the relevance of these processes to social behavior.

Social Psychology and Common Sense

- Many social psychological theories and findings may seem like common sense. The problem with common sense, however, is that it may offer conflicting explanations and provides no way to test which is correct.

From Past to Present: A Brief History of Social Psychology

The Birth and Infancy of Social Psychology: 1880s–1920s

- Early research by Triplett and Ringelmann established an enduring topic in social psychology: how the presence of others affects an individual's performance.
- The first social psychology textbooks in 1908 and 1924 began to give the emerging field of social psychology its shape.

A Call to Action: 1930s–1950s

- Trying to explain, and offer solutions to, a world at war, social psychology began to flourish.
- Sherif's work laid the foundation for later studies of social influence, and the legacy of Kurt Lewin is still evident throughout much of social psychology.
- The 1940s and 1950s saw a burst of activity in social psychology that firmly established it as a major social science.

Confidence and Crisis: 1960s–Mid-1970s

- Stanley Milgram's experiments demonstrated individuals' vulnerability to the destructive commands of authority.
- While social psychology was expanding in many new directions, there was also intense debate about the ethics of research procedures, the validity of research results, and the generalizability of conclusions drawn from the research.

An Era of Pluralism: Mid-1970s–1990s

- During the 1970s, social psychology began to take a pluralistic approach that continues today in its research methods, views on human behavior, and development of international and multicultural perspectives.

Social Psychology in a New Century

- Several exciting themes and perspectives are helping to shape the beginning of social psychology's second century.

Integration of Emotion, Motivation, and Cognition

■ Researchers are becoming more interested in how emotion, motivation, and cognition can operate together in influencing individuals' thoughts, feelings, and behaviors.

Biological and Evolutionary Perspectives

■ Biological perspectives, including perspectives based on genetics and evolutionary principles, are being applied to the study of social psychological issues such as gender differences, relationships, and aggression.

Sociocultural Perspectives

■ Increasing numbers of social psychologists are evaluating the universal generality or cultural specificity of their theories and findings by examining similarities and differences across cultures as well as between racial and ethnic groups within cultures.

New Technologies

■ As rapidly advancing technologies change how individuals access information and communicate, changes in how individuals interact are likely to follow. The social psychology of the next era will explore these issues.

Key Terms

behavioral genetics *18*
cross-cultural research *19*
evolutionary psychology *18*
interactionist perspective *14*
multicultural research *19*
social cognition *16*
social psychology *5*

2 Doing Social Psychology Research

PREVIEW

This chapter examines how social psychologists do their research. We begin by asking, "Why should you learn about research methods?" We answer this question by discussing how learning about research methods can benefit you both in this course and beyond. Then we consider how researchers come up with and develop ideas and begin the research process. Next, we provide an overview of the research designs that social psychologists use to test their ideas. Finally, we turn to important questions about ethics and values in social psychology.

(Continued on next page)

1 t's a familiar situation. You're starting a new semester or quarter at school, and you're just beginning to settle in to a new schedule and routine. You're looking forward to your new courses. In general, it's an exciting time. But there's one major catch: As you spend more and more time with your new classmates and new responsibilities, you're leaving someone behind. It could be a boyfriend or girlfriend, a spouse, or a close friend—someone who is not involved in what you are now doing. You may now live far apart from each other, or you may still be in the same location but your new commitments in school are keeping you apart from each other much more than you'd like. The romantic in you says, "Together forever." Or at least, "No problem." But the realist in you worries a bit. Will your love or friendship be the same? Can it survive the long distance, or the new demands on your time, or the new people in your respective environments? Your friends or family may have advice to offer in this situation. Some might smile and reassure you, "Don't worry. Remember what they say, 'Absence makes the heart grow fonder.' This will only strengthen your relationship." Others might call you aside and whisper, "Don't listen to them. Everybody knows, 'Out of sight, out of mind.' You'd better be careful."

Taking your mind off this problem, you begin to work on a class project. You have the option of working alone or as part of a group. Which should you do? You consult the wisdom of common sense. Maybe you should work in a group. After all, everyone knows that "two heads are better than one." As some members of your group begin to miss meetings and shirk responsibilities, though, you remember that "too many cooks spoil the broth." Will you regret having been so quick to decide to join this group? After all, haven't you been taught to "look before you leap"? Then again, if you had waited and missed the chance to join the group, you might have regretted your inaction, recalling that "he who hesitates is lost."

Questions about the course of relationships, the efficiency of working in groups, and the regret of action versus inaction are social psychological questions. And because we all are interested in predicting and explaining people's behaviors and their thoughts and feelings about each other, we all have our own opinions and intuitions about social psychological matters. If the discipline of social psychology were built on the personal experiences, observations, and intuitions of everyone who is interested in social psychological questions, it would be chock-full of interesting theories and ideas; but it would also be a morass of contradictions, ambiguities, and relativism. Instead, social psychology is built on the scientific method.

Scientific? It's easy to see how chemistry is scientific. When you mix two specific compounds in the lab, you can predict exactly what will happen. The compounds will act the same way every time you mix them if the general conditions in the lab are the same. But what happens when you mix together two chemists, or any two people, in a social context? Sometimes you get great chemistry between them; other times you get apathy or even repulsion. How, then, can social behavior, which seems so variable, be studied scientifically?

To many of us in the field, that's the great excitement and challenge of social psychology—the fact that it is so dynamic and diverse. Furthermore, in spite of these characteristics, social psychology can, and should, be studied according to scientific principles. Social psychologists develop specific, quantifiable hypotheses that can be tested empirically. If these hypotheses are wrong, they can be proven wrong. In addition, social scientists report the details of how they conduct their tests so that others can try to replicate their findings. They integrate evidence from across time and place. And slowly but steadily, they build a consistent and ever more precise understanding of human nature. How social psychologists investigate social psychological questions scientifically is the focus of this chapter. Before we explain the methodology they use, we first explain a bit about why it's important and interesting for you to learn about these matters.

Based on the results of a study of undergraduate students, VanderStoep and Shaughnessy (1997) concluded that studying research methods in psychology can give students "some general skills that they can use while watching the evening news, shopping for automobiles, voting, or deciding whether to adopt a new weight-loss technique they saw advertised."

Why Should You Learn About Research Methods?

One very practical reason for learning about research methods is that it will help you better understand and learn the material in this book, which will in turn help you on tests and in subsequent courses. Let's look more closely at why this is so. Because social psychology is so relevant to our everyday lives, and because there are so many common-sense notions about social psychological questions, separating myths from truths can be difficult. Most of us don't have an intuition about particular questions concerning quantum mechanics, but we do have intuitions about, say, whether people work better alone or in groups. If you simply read a list of social psychological findings about issues such as this, without knowing and understanding the evidence that social psychologists have produced to support the findings, you may discover later that the task of remembering the findings and distinguishing them from your original intuitions about the issues is a difficult one. This task is sometimes especially difficult in multiple-choice exams. The right answer might seem very plausible; but then again, so might some of the wrong answers, just as there are good reasons to believe both that "two heads are better than one" and that "too many cooks spoil the broth."

But the benefits of learning about research methods go far beyond the academic. Training in research methods in psychology can improve your reasoning about real-life events (Lehman et al., 1988; VanderStoep & Shaughnessy, 1997). It can make you a better, more sophisticated consumer of information in general. We are constantly bombarded with "facts" from the media, from sales pitches, and from other people. Much of this information turns out to be wrong or, at best, oversimplified and misleading. We are told about the health benefits of eating certain kinds of food, the college entrance exam score benefits of certain preparation

courses, or the social-status benefits of driving a certain kind of car or wearing a certain kind of shoes. To each of these pronouncements, we should say, "Prove it." What is the evidence? What alternative explanations might there be? For example, a commercial tells us that most doctors prefer a particular (and rather expensive) brand of aspirin. So should we buy the expensive brand of aspirin? Think about what that brand was compared with. Perhaps the doctors didn't prefer that brand of aspirin over other (and cheaper) brands of aspirin; perhaps they simply preferred that brand of aspirin over non-aspirin products for a particular problem. Thinking like a scientist while reading this text will foster a healthy sense of doubt about claims like these. You will be in a better position to critically evaluate the information to which you're exposed and separate fact from fiction.

We are bombarded with information in our everyday lives, such as in the countless advertisements designed to persuade us to buy particular products or adopt particular opinions or attitudes. Learning the methods used in social psychology research can help students become more sophisticated consumers of this information.

Developing Ideas: Beginning the Research Process

The research process involves coming up with ideas, refining them, testing them, and interpreting the meaning of the results obtained. This section describes the first stage of research, coming up with ideas. It also discusses the role of hypotheses and theories and of basic and applied research.

Asking Questions

Every social psychology study begins with a question. And the questions come from everywhere. As discussed in Chapter 1, the first social psychology experiment published was triggered by the question, "Why do bicyclists race faster in the presence of other bicyclists?" (Triplett, 1897–1898). Inspiration can come from a vari-

In March 1998, an injured student in Jonesboro, Arkansas, is rushed to an ambulance after two boys, ages eleven and thirteen, opened fire on their schoolmates, killing four girls and a teacher. Over the years, tragic incidents like this one have inspired social psychologists to conduct research on violence and a wide range of other important social problems.

ety of sources, from the distressing, such as a gruesome murder and the inaction of witnesses to that murder (Latané & Darley, 1970), to the amusing, such as the lyrics of a country song that suggests that people in bars look more attractive to other patrons as closing time approaches (Pennebaker et al., 1979).

Questions also come from reading about research that has already been done. Solomon Asch (1946), for example, read about Muzafer Sherif's (1936) demonstration of how individuals in a group conform to others in the group when making judgments about a very ambiguous stimulus (described in Chapter 1 and in Chapter 7 on Conformity). Asch questioned whether people would conform to the opinions of others in a group even when it was quite clear that the group was wrong. He tested this question, and the results surprised him and the rest of the field: People did conform to a very high degree. Thus, one of the most famous experiments in the field inspired an even more famous experiment.

Searching the Literature

Once the researcher has an idea, whether it came from personal observation, folk wisdom, an event in the news, or previous findings, it is important to see what research has already been done on this topic and related topics. Textbooks such as this one offer a starting point. Another good resource is the journal *Psychological Abstracts*, which lists summaries of articles published in psychology journals. One of the best ways to search for published materials on topics of interest is by using an electronic database. Electronic databases can store tremendous amounts of information on computers, and the information can be accessed very quickly and easily. Some of these databases, such as PsycLIT and PsycINFO, are specific to the psychology literature, and others are more general. When you use an electronic database, you can search hundreds of thousands of published articles and books in seconds. You can type in names of authors, key words or phrases, years, or the like and instantly receive summaries of articles that fit your search criteria. In addition to searching databases specific to the psychology literature, you can also learn about other research by searching more generally, such as on the World Wide Web, or in databases containing references to newspaper and magazine articles.

"The currency of science is not truth, but doubt."

— Dennis Overbye

Once you have found some relevant articles, there is a good chance that those articles will refer to other articles that are relevant. Going from article to article, sometimes called *treeing*, can prove very valuable in tracking down information about the research question.

More often than not, the researcher's original question is changed in one way or another during the course of searching the literature. The question should become more precise, more specific to particular sets of conditions that are likely to have different effects, and more readily testable.

Hypotheses and Theories

An initial idea for research may be so vague that it amounts to little more than a hunch or an educated guess. Some ideas vanish with the break of day. But others can be shaped into a **hypothesis**—an explicit, testable prediction about the conditions under which an event will occur. Formulating a hypothesis is a critical step toward planning and conducting research. It allows us to move from the realm of common sense to the rigors of the scientific method.

As hypotheses proliferate and data are collected to test the hypotheses, a more advanced step in the research process may take place: the proposal of a **theory**—an organized set of principles used to explain observed phenomena. Theories are usually evaluated in terms of three criteria: simplicity, comprehensiveness, and generativity. All else being equal, the best theories are elegant and precise; encompass all of the relevant information; and lead to new hypotheses, further research, and better understanding.

In social psychology, there are many theories. Social psychologists do not attempt the all-encompassing grand theory, such as those of Freud or Piaget, which you may have studied in introductory psychology. Instead, they rely on more precise "mini-theories" that address limited and specific aspects of the way people behave, make explicit predictions about behavior, and allow meaningful empirical investigation. Most social psychological theories are highly generative. They stimulate systematic programs of research by their advocates. They may also provoke sharp criticism from their opponents. Beginning students of social psychology are often surprised by the lack of consensus in the field. In part, such disagreement reflects the fact that social psychology is a very young science. At this stage in its development, premature closure is a worse sin than contradiction or even confusion. But debate is an essential feature of even the most mature science. It is the fate of all scientific theories to be criticized and, eventually, surpassed.

Basic and Applied Research

Is testing a theory the purpose of research in social psychology? For some researchers, yes. **Basic research** seeks to increase our understanding of human behavior and is often designed to test a specific hypothesis from a specific theory. **Applied research** has a different purpose: to make use of social psychology's theories or methods to enlarge our understanding of naturally occurring events and to contribute to the solution of social problems.

Despite their differences, basic and applied research are closely connected in social psychology. Some researchers switch back and forth between the two—today basic, tomorrow applied. Some studies test a theory and examine a real-world phenomenon simultaneously. As a pioneer in both approaches, Kurt Lewin (1951) set the tone when he encouraged basic researchers to be concerned with complex social problems and urged applied researchers to recognize how important and practical good theories are.

"[Close cooperation between theoretical and applied psychology] can be accomplished ... if the theorist does not look toward applied problems with highbrow aversion or with a fear of social problems, and if the applied psychologist realizes that there is nothing so practical as a good theory."

—Kurt Lewin

hypothesis A testable prediction about the conditions under which an event will occur.

theory An organized set of principles used to explain observed phenomena.

basic research Research whose goal is to increase the understanding of human behavior, often by testing hypotheses based on a theory.

applied research Research whose goals are to enlarge the understanding of naturally occurring events and to find solutions to practical problems.

Refining Ideas: Defining and Measuring Social Psychological Variables

No matter what method researchers plan to use to test their hypotheses, they always must decide how they will define and measure the variables in which they are interested. This sometimes can be a straightforward process. For example, if you are interested in comparing how quickly people run a 100-yard dash when alone and when racing against another person, you can rely on well-established ways to define and measure the variables in question. Many other times, however, the process is less straightforward. If you are interested in studying the effects of self-esteem on altruistic behavior, you must first define self-esteem and altruistic behavior. There may be countless ways to do this. Which ones should you pick?

Conceptual Variables and Operational Definitions: From the Abstract to the Specific

When a researcher first develops a hypothesis, the variables typically are in an abstract, general form. These are *conceptual variables*. Examples of conceptual variables include prejudice, conformity, attraction, love, violence, group pressure, and social anxiety. In order to test specific hypotheses, we must then transform these conceptual variables into variables that can be manipulated or measured in a study. The specific way in which a conceptual variable is manipulated or measured is called the *operational definition* of the variable. For example, a researcher might operationally define "conformity" in a particular study as the number of times a participant indicated agreement with the obviously wrong judgments made by a group of confederates. Part of the challenge and fun of designing research in social psychology is taking an abstract conceptual variable such as love or group pressure and deciding how to operationally define it so as to manipulate or measure it.

Often, there is no single best way to transform a variable from the abstract (conceptual) to the specific (operational). A great deal of trial and error may be involved. However, sometimes there are systematic, statistical ways of checking how valid various manipulations and measures are, and researchers spend a great deal of time fine-tuning their operational definitions so that these definitions best capture the conceptual variables in which they are interested.

Researchers evaluate the manipulation and measurement of variables in terms of their **construct validity.** Construct validity refers to the extent to which the manipulations in an experiment really manipulate the conceptual variables they were designed to manipulate and the measures used in a

From this picture, we can guess that the boy sitting by himself on the playground is lonely, but how do researchers precisely define and measure conceptual variables like loneliness? Researchers may use any of a number of approaches, such as asking people how they feel or observing their behavior.

study (experimental or otherwise) really measure the conceptual variables they were designed to measure. Later in this chapter, for example, we discuss a study (Leonard, 1989) in which one of the conceptual variables was whether participants were intoxicated. There are several ways of measuring this variable, most of which are relatively straightforward: assessing participants' blood alcohol concentration after some number of drinks, measuring their ability to perform simple motor tasks, or asking them how drunk they feel, for example. Thus, one researcher might operationally define intoxication as when a participant has a blood alcohol level of .10, whereas another might define it as when a participant says that he or she feels drunk. Another conceptual variable in this study was aggression. Measuring aggression in experiments is particularly difficult because of ethical and practical issues—researchers can't let participants in their studies attack each other. Researchers interested in measuring aggression are thus often forced to measure relatively unusual behaviors, such as administering shocks to another person as part of a specific task. Does this really measure aggression? It's hard to tell. Some researchers say that such measures often are valid; others say they often aren't (Anderson & Bushman, 1997; Tedeschi, 1997).

Measuring Variables: Self-Reports and Observations

Social psychologists measure variables in many ways, but most can be placed into one of two categories: self-reports and observations.

Self-Reports: Going Straight to the Source Collecting *self-reports*—in which participants disclose their thoughts, feelings, desires, and actions—is a widely used measurement technique in social psychology. Self-reports can consist of individual questions or sets of questions that together measure a single conceptual variable. One popular self-report measure, the Rosenberg Self-Esteem Scale, consists of a set of questions that together measure individuals' overall self-esteem. This scale is presented in Table 2.1. Do the items on this scale seem to you to measure what you think of as self-esteem? This scale is used in a wide variety of settings, and many researchers consider it to have good construct validity (e.g., Bagley et al., 1997).

Self-reports give the researcher access to an individual's beliefs and perceptions. But self-reports are not always accurate and can be misleading. For example, the desire to look good to ourselves and others can influence how we respond. As Shakespeare put it in the play *Measure for Measure*, "It oft falls out, to have what we would have, we speak not what we mean." Research using a procedure called the "bogus pipeline" indicates that participants who are led to believe that their responses will be verified by an infallible lie-detector report facts about themselves more accurately and endorse socially *un*acceptable opinions more frequently than those not told about such a device. The bogus pipeline is, in fact, bogus; no such infallible device exists. But belief in its powers enhances truth-telling (Aguinis et al., 1993; Roese & Jamieson, 1993; Tourangeau et al., 1997).

Self-reports are also affected by the way in which questions are asked. Consider some of the effects of wording and context in the following instances:

TABLE 2.1 The Rosenberg Self-Esteem Scale

Self-reports are a widely used measurement technique in social psychology. The Rosenberg Self-Esteem Scale measures an individual's perception of his or her self-worth. *(Rosenberg, 1965)*

Indicate whether you *strongly agree, agree, disagree,* or *strongly disagree* with each of these statements.

1. I feel that I'm a person of worth, at least on an equal plane with others.
2. On the whole, I am satisfied with myself.
3. I wish I could have more respect for myself.
4. I certainly feel useless at times.
5. At times I think I am no good at all.
6. I feel that I have a number of good qualities.
7. All in all, I am inclined to feel that I am a failure.
8. I am able to do things as well as most other people.
9. I feel that I do not have much to be proud of.
10. I take a positive attitude toward myself.

To score responses on this scale, score items 1, 2, 6, 8, and 10 in a positive direction (*strongly agree* = 4, etc.) and items 3, 4, 5, 7, and 9 in a reversed direction (*strongly agree* = 1, etc.). The highest possible score is 40; the lowest possible is 10. Higher scores indicate higher self-esteem.

construct validity The extent to which the measures used in a study measure the variables they were designed to measure and the manipulations in an experiment manipulate the variables they were designed to manipulate.

This person would probably score low on Rosenberg's Self-Esteem Scale. Dean Vietor © 1997 from The New Yorker Collection. All Rights Reserved.

"Clemson here. How may I disappoint you?"

■ When asked on a survey, "How much special consideration should black students receive in college admissions?" more than 70 percent of the UCLA freshmen in the sample said that at least some special consideration should be given. However, when asked, "Should affirmative action be abolished?" 50 percent said yes (Shea, 1996).

■ Asked about government spending "on assistance to the poor," only 23 percent of respondents in a 1994 *Time* magazine survey said that too much was being spent. Asked about "welfare," however, 53 percent said that too much was being spent.

■ Should people have the freedom to express their opinions publicly? Participants in a survey were more likely to answer yes to that question if the previous question was about the Catholic church than if it was about Nazis (Ottati et al., 1989).

■ When German adults were asked how many hours a day they watched TV, only 16.2 percent said they watched more than 2.5 hours per day when "more than 2.5 hours" was the maximum possible response. But when "up to 2.5

TABLE 2.2   How Many Hours of TV Did They Watch?

Depending on which scale was presented to them, only a small number (16.2 percent) or a much larger number (37.5 percent) of the German adults in this survey said they watched more than 2.5 hours of TV each day. Changing the response alternatives given to respondents can change their self-reports. *(Adapted from Schwarz et al., 1985.)*

Maximum = "More than 2.5 hours"	Percentage	Minimum = "Up to 2.5 hours"	Percentage
Up to 0.5 hour	7.4	Up to 2.5 hours	62.5
0.5 to 1 hour	17.7	2.5 hours to 3 hours	23.4
1 hour to 1.5 hours	26.5	3 hours to 3.5 hours	7.8
1.5 hours to 2 hours	14.7	3.5 hours to 4 hours	4.7
2 hours to 2.5 hours	17.7	4 hours to 4.5 hours	1.6
More than 2.5 hours	16.2	More than 4.5 hours	0

(The 2.5 hours to 3 hours through More than 4.5 hours rows are bracketed together as 37.5)

hours" was the minimum response alternative, 37.5 percent reported they watched TV for more than 2.5 hours per day (Schwarz et al., 1985). These results are displayed in Table 2.2.

■ In one study, 88 percent of participants indicated that they thought condoms were effective in stopping AIDS when condoms were said to have a "95 percent success rate." However, when condoms were said to have a "5 percent failure rate," only 42 percent indicated that they thought condoms were effective (Linville et al., 1992).

Another reason self-reports can be inaccurate is that they often ask participants to report on thoughts or behaviors from the past, and their memory for these thoughts or behaviors may be suspect. To reduce this problem, psychologists have developed ways to reduce the time that elapses between an actual experience and the person's report of it (Wheeler & Reis, 1991). For example, some use *interval-contingent* self-reports, in which respondents report their experiences at regular intervals, usually once a day. They may report events since the last report, or how they feel at the moment, or both. Researchers may also collect *signal-contingent* self-reports. Here, respondents report their experiences as soon as possible after being signaled to do so, usually by means of a beeper. Finally, some researchers collect *event-contingent* self-reports, in which respondents report on a designated set of events as soon as possible after such events have occurred. For example, the Rochester Interaction Record (RIR) is an event-contingent self-report questionnaire used by respondents to record every social interaction lasting ten minutes or more that occurs during the course of the study, usually a week or two (Nezlek et al., 1994).

Whatever their differences, most self-report methods require participants to provide specific answers to specific questions. In contrast, *narrative studies* collect lengthy responses on a general topic. Narrative materials can be generated by participants at the researcher's request or taken from other sources (such as diaries, letters, speeches, press conferences, and books). These accounts are then analyzed in terms of a coding scheme developed by the researcher. For example, the researcher might code participants' diaries for particular goals they mention (Lavallee & Campbell, 1995), or they might code sports articles in newspapers for examples of athletes' explanations for winning or losing (Roesch & Amirkhan, 1997).

Observational methods provide a useful alternative to self-reports. For example, studies of young children, whose verbal skills are limited, often rely on observations.

Observations: Looking On　　Self-reports are not the only available window on human behavior. Researchers can also observe people's actions. Sometimes these observations are very simple, as when a researcher notes which of two items a person selects. At other times, however, the observations are more elaborate and (like the coding of narrative accounts) require that interrater reliability be established. **Interrater reliability** refers to the level of agreement among multiple observers of

interrater reliability　The degree to which different observers agree on their observations.

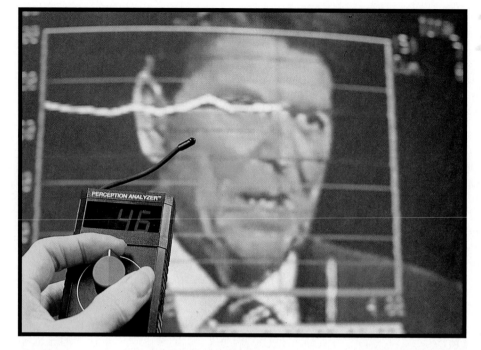

Computerized video technology, such as this Perception Analyzer™, allows researchers to track participants' moment-by-moment reactions to events on the screen (in this case a presidential debate). It can also simultaneously display the average ratings of groups of participants in a graph superimposed over the video. This technology can help researchers study the dynamics of social influence.

the same behavior. Only when different observers agree can the data be trusted. For example, in the Dyadic Interaction Paradigm developed by William Ickes and his colleagues (1990), the interaction between two strangers meeting for the first time is videotaped. Two independent observers then work from the videotapes to assess such behaviors as interpersonal distance, body posture, looking at each other, and smiling. The extent to which the two observers agree on each behavior determines the degree of interrater reliability.

Machines, too, can do the watching. Various kinds of equipment are used to measure physiological responses such as changes in heart rate, levels of particular hormones, and sexual arousal. Social psychologists use computers to record the speed with which participants respond to stimuli, such as how quickly they respond to positive or negative words after exposure to a black male versus a white male face (Dovidio, Kawakami, et al., 1997). Indeed, throughout social psychology, much of what used to be done by human voice or hand—instructions given, materials presented, measures taken—is now computerized.

The advantage of observational methods is that they avoid our sometimes faulty recollections and distorted interpretations of our own behavior. Actions can speak louder than words. But if individuals know they are being observed, some observational methods are as vulnerable as self-reports to people's desire to present themselves in a favorable light.

Testing Ideas: Research Designs

Social psychologists use several different methods to test their research hypotheses and theories. Although methods vary, in general, the field emphasizes objective, systematic, and quantifiable approaches. Social psychologists do not simply seek out evidence that supports their ideas; rather, they test their ideas in ways that could very clearly prove them wrong.

The most popular and preferred research method in social psychology is experimentation, in which researchers can test cause-and-effect relationships, such as whether exposure to a violent television program causes viewers to behave more aggressively. We emphasize the experimental approach in this book. In addition, we report the results of many studies that use another popular approach: correlational research, which looks for associations between two variables without establishing cause and effect. We also report the results of studies that use a relatively new technique called meta-analysis, which integrates the research findings of many different studies. Before describing these approaches, though, we turn to an approach with which we all are very familiar: descriptive research. This is the approach used in opinion polls, ratings of the popularity of TV shows, box scores in the sports section, and the like.

Descriptive Research: Discovering Trends and Tendencies

One obvious way of testing ideas about people is simply to record how frequently or how typically people think, feel, or behave in particular ways. The goal of *descriptive* research in social psychology is, as the term implies, to describe people and their thoughts, feelings, and behaviors. This method can test questions such as: Do most people support capital punishment? What percentage of people who encounter a person lying on the sidewalk would offer to help that person? What do men and women say are the things most likely to make them jealous of their partner? Particular methods of doing descriptive research include observing people, studying records of past events and behaviors, and surveying people. We discuss each of these methods in this section.

Observational Studies   We can learn about other people simply by observing them, of course, and some social psychological questions can be addressed through observational studies. For example, Debra Pepler and Wendy Craig (1995) wanted to know how common bullying is among schoolchildren in Canada. Is it an infrequent occurrence at most schools, centered around a handful of bullies, or is it a widespread problem? To investigate this question, these researchers used hidden video cameras and microphones to record the incidents of bullying in a number of schoolyards in Canada (with the permission of the schools). This peek into the schoolyard enabled Pepler and Craig to discover that the problem of bullying is much more pervasive than many people believe, and they were able to report the frequency with which various forms of aggression occurred.

TV news magazine shows like *Prime Time Live* and *Dateline NBC* also often use hidden cameras to record the behaviors of various individuals. The ethics of this can be troublesome; we return to the issue of ethics in research later in the chapter. In addition to the ethical issues, though, issues of accuracy may arise in connection with these news programs. TV reporters and journalists are often more interested in telling a good story than being scientifically sound, so we should be careful when drawing general conclusions from their presentations. A news program may show footage that is consistent with the point of view of their overall story—for example, footage showing that certain kinds of people are treated worse by car salespeople or auto mechanics than others—but may not show footage that is inconsistent with this point of view. Social psychologists are trained to be systematic and unbiased in their observations and to report all of the data that are relevant to the research question, not just the data that support a particular hypothesis.

"For crying out loud, gentlemen! That's us! Someone's installed the one-way mirror in backward!"

Archival Studies   Archival research involves examining existing records of past events and behaviors, such as newspaper articles, medical records, diaries, sports statistics, personal ads, legal documents, crime statistics, suicide notes, or hits on a World Wide Web page. A major advantage of archival measures is that, because the researchers are observing behavior secondhand, they can be sure that they did

Many social psychological questions are addressed using surveys, which can be conducted over the phone, by mail, via the Internet, or face-to-face in field settings such as this street fair.

not influence the behavior by their presence. A limitation of this approach is that available records are not always complete or detailed enough, and they may have been collected in a non-systematic manner.

Archival measures are particularly valuable for examining cultural and historical trends. In Chapter 11 on Aggression, for example, we report a number of trends concerning the rate of violent crime in the United States and how it has changed in recent years, and we report differences in homicide rates in countries around the world. These data come from archival records, such as the records of police stations, the Federal Bureau of Investigations (FBI), and the United Nations. Other examples of archival research include a study that tracked the proportion of *New Yorker* cartoons over the years that featured black men and women in various roles (Thibodeau, 1989) and a study that examined the waist-to-hip ratio of Miss America winners and *Playboy* playmates over the past several decades (Singh, 1993).

Surveys   It is said that nobody in politics these days sneezes without first conducting an opinion poll. Surveys have become increasingly popular in recent years, and surveys have been conducted on everything from politics, to attitudes about social issues, to the percentages of women and men who squeeze the toothpaste tube from the bottom (O.K., we'll tell you: 37 percent of women and 18 percent of men; Weiss, 1991). Conducting surveys involves asking people questions about their attitudes, beliefs, and behaviors. Surveys can be conducted in person, over the phone, by mail, or via the Internet. Many social psychological questions can only be addressed with surveys because they involve variables that are impossible or unethical to observe directly or manipulate, such as people's sexual behaviors or their optimism about the future.

Although anyone can conduct a survey (and sometimes it seems that everyone does), there is a science to designing, conducting, and interpreting the results of surveys. Like other self-report measures, surveys can be affected strongly by subtle aspects of the wording and context of questions, and survey researchers are trained to consider these issues and to test various kinds of wording and question ordering before conducting their surveys.

One of the most important issues that survey researchers face is how to select the people who will take part in the survey. The researchers first must identify the *population* in which they are interested. Is this survey supposed to tell us about the attitudes of North Americans in general, shoppers at Wal-Mart, or students in Introduction to Social Psychology at University X, for example? From this general population, the researchers select a subset, or *sample*, of individuals. For a survey to be accurate, the sample must be similar to, or representative of, the population on important characteristics such as age, sex, race, income, education, and cultural background. The best way to achieve this representativeness is to use **random sampling**, a method of selection in which everyone in a population has

random sampling A method of selecting participants for a study so that everyone in a population has an equal chance of being in the study.

an equal chance of being selected for the sample. Survey researchers use randomizing procedures, such as tables of randomly distributed numbers generated by computers, to decide how to select individuals for their samples.

To see the importance of random sampling, consider a pair of U.S. presidential elections (Rosnow & Rosenthal, 1993). Just before the 1936 election, a magazine called the *Literary Digest* predicted that Alfred Landon, the Republican governor of Kansas, would win by 14 percentage points over Franklin Roosevelt. The *Digest* based its prediction on a survey of more than 2 million Ameri-

cans. In fact, though, Landon *lost* the election by 24 percentage points. The magazine, which had been in financial trouble before the election, declared bankruptcy soon after.

Twenty years later, the Gallup survey's prediction of Dwight Eisenhower's victory was off by less than 2 percent. The size of its sample? Only about 8,000. How could the results of the 1936 survey, with its much larger sample, be so far off and the results of the 1956 survey so accurate? The answer is that the 1936 sample was not randomly selected. The *Digest* got the names of the people it contacted from sources such as phone books and club membership lists. In 1936, a great many people could not afford to have telephones or belong to clubs. The people in the sample, therefore, tended to be wealthier than the population, and wealthier people preferred Landon. In contrast, in 1956, Gallup pollsters randomly selected election districts throughout the country and then randomly selected households within those districts. Today, because of improved sampling procedures, surveys

A representative sample includes individuals who possess the characteristics of the population that is being studied. Suppose we're interested in the people who attended this baseball game. A representative sample drawn from this population would be much smaller in number (making it possible for us to interview them), but have a similar composition in terms of basic demographic factors such as gender, race, ethnicity, age, and occupation.

In the 1948 U.S. presidential election, pollsters nationwide predicted that Thomas Dewey would defeat Harry Truman by a wide margin. As Truman basked in his victory, pollsters realized that their predictions were based on nonrandom samples of voters. Random sampling would have led to much more accurate predictions.

conducted on little more than 1,000 Americans can be used to make accurate predictions about the entire U.S. population.

Correlational Research: Looking for Associations

Although there is much to learn from descriptive research, social psychologists typically want to know more. Most research hypotheses in social psychology concern the relationship between variables. For example, is there a relationship between people's gender and their tendency to conform to others in certain situations or between how physically attractive people are and how much money they make?

One way to test such hypotheses is with correlational research. **Correlational research** can be conducted using observational, archival, or survey methods. Unlike descriptive research, however, correlational approaches are designed to measure how different variables relate to each other. Determining how variables relate to each other, or correlate, can suggest to researchers how similar or different two psychological measures are (for example, whether there is any similarity between people's self-esteem and their popularity) and how well one variable can be used to predict another (for example, how well we can predict academic success in college from high school GPA or college entrance exam scores). It is important to note that researchers doing correlational research typically do not manipulate the variables they study; they simply measure them.

Being in a relationship is correlated with having similar levels of physical attractiveness. But a correlation cannot identify the cause of this association. Chapter 9 on Attraction and Close Relationships discusses both correlational and experimental research on the role of similarity in the attraction process.

Correlation Coefficient   When researchers examine the relationship between variables that vary in quantity (such as temperature or degree of self-esteem), they can measure the strength and direction of the relationship between the variables and calculate a statistic called a **correlation coefficient.** Correlation coefficients can range from +1.0 to –1.0. The absolute value of the number (the number itself, without the positive or negative sign) indicates how strongly the two variables are associated. The larger the absolute value of the number, the stronger the association between the two variables, and thus the better either of the variables is as a predictor of the other. Whether the coefficient is positive or negative indicates the direction of the relationship. A positive correlation coefficient indicates that as one variable increases, so does the other. For example, college entrance exam scores correlate positively with grades. The positive direction of this relationship indicates that higher entrance exam scores are associated with higher grades and lower entrance exam scores are associated with lower grades. This correlation is not perfect; some people with high entrance exam scores have poor grades, and vice versa. Therefore, the correlation is less than +1.0; but it is greater than 0, because there is some association between the two. A negative coefficient indicates that the two variables go in opposite directions: As one

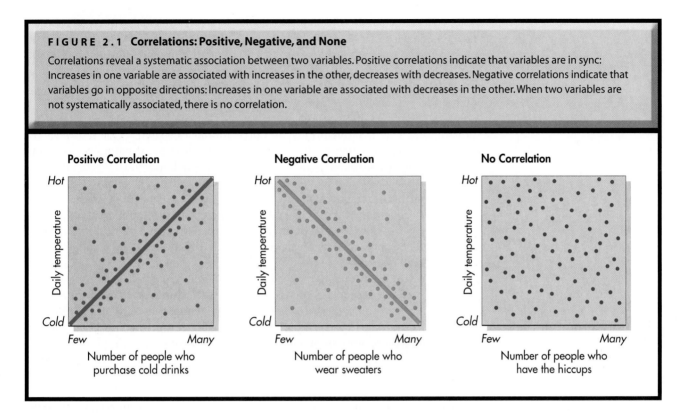

FIGURE 2.1 Correlations: Positive, Negative, and None
Correlations reveal a systematic association between two variables. Positive correlations indicate that variables are in sync: Increases in one variable are associated with increases in the other, decreases with decreases. Negative correlations indicate that variables go in opposite directions: Increases in one variable are associated with decreases in the other. When two variables are not systematically associated, there is no correlation.

goes up, the other tends to go down. For example, number of classes missed and GPA are likely to be negatively correlated. And a correlation close to 0 indicates that there is no consistent relationship at all. These three types of patterns are illustrated in Figure 2.1. Because few variables are perfectly related to each other, most correlation coefficients do not approach +1.0 or –1.0 but have more moderate values, such as –.39 or +.57.

Correlations obtained at a single point in time across a number of individuals are called *concurrent*. For example, you might be interested in testing the hypothesis that physically attractive people tend to make more money than physically unattractive people. You could measure the physical attractiveness of many different people somehow (such as by taking their pictures and asking a dozen other people to rate their physical appearance) and also ask them how much money they make. Correlations can also be obtained at different times from the same individuals. These correlations are called *prospective*. Prospective studies are especially useful in determining whether certain behaviors at a particular age are associated with other behaviors at a later age. For example, you might want to see whether people's degree of optimism at the age of twenty is correlated with how happy they feel at the age of forty. You would record the level of optimism of a number of twenty-year-olds by using a questionnaire designed to measure optimism; and twenty years later, you'd ask these same individuals to complete a questionnaire designed to measure how happy they are. Chapter 11 on Aggression discusses prospective studies examining correlations between children's early viewing of TV violence and later aggressive behavior.

Some correlational studies involve a variable that does not vary in quantity, such as race, gender, political affiliation, or preference for Italian, Mexican, or Thai food. In this case, researchers cannot compute a typical correlation coefficient. Nevertheless, such studies can reveal relationships between variables. For example, some research indicates that students who study Latin and take the Latin Achievement Tests do more than 100 points better on verbal and math SATs than other

correlational research
Research designed to measure the association between variables that are not manipulated by the researcher.

correlation coefficient A statistical measure of the strength and direction of the association between two variables.

students (Costa, 1982). This research indicates a relationship between whether or not a student studies Latin (which is an either/or variable that does not vary in quantity—a student either does or does not study Latin) and students' success on the SAT (which is a variable that does vary in quantity from zero points to a perfect score). (Does this correlation mean that studying Latin causes students to do better on the SAT? Think about it; we'll return to this question later.)

Advantages and Disadvantages of Correlational Research   Correlational research has many advantages. It can study the associations of naturally occurring variables that cannot be manipulated or induced—such as gender, race, ethnicity, and age. It can examine phenomena that would be difficult or unethical to create for research purposes, such as love, hate, and abuse. Correlational research also offers researchers a great deal of freedom in where variables are measured. Participants can be brought into a laboratory specially constructed for research purposes, or they can be approached in a real-world setting (often called "the field") such as a shopping mall or airport.

Despite these advantages, however, correlational research has one very serious disadvantage. And here it is in bold letters: **Correlation is not causation.**

In other words, a correlation cannot demonstrate a cause-and-effect relationship. Instead of revealing a specific causal pathway from one variable (A) to another variable (B), a correlation between variables A and B contains within it three possible causal effects: A could cause B; B could cause A; or a third variable, C, could cause both A and B. For example, imagine learning that the number of hours per night one sleeps is negatively correlated with the number of colds one gets. This means that as the amount of sleep increases, colds decrease in frequency; conversely, as sleep decreases, colds become more frequent. One reasonable explanation for this relationship is that lack of sleep (variable A) causes people to become more vulnerable to colds (variable B). Another reasonable explanation, however, is that people who have colds can't sleep well, and so colds (variable B) cause lack of sleep (variable A). A third reasonable explanation is that some other variable (C) causes both lack of sleep and greater frequency of colds. This third variable could be stress. Indeed, stress has many effects on people, as will be discussed in Chapter 14 on Health. Figure 2.2 describes another correlation that can be explained in many ways—the correlation between TV watching and aggression, which will be discussed in Chapter 11 on Aggression.

As sure as death and taxes, there will be many, many times in your life when you will encounter reports in the media that suggest cause-and-effect relationships

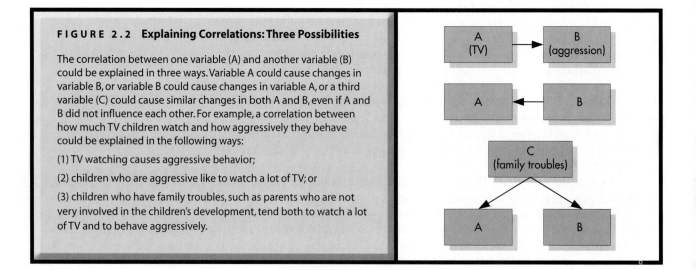

FIGURE 2.2   Explaining Correlations: Three Possibilities

The correlation between one variable (A) and another variable (B) could be explained in three ways. Variable A could cause changes in variable B, or variable B could cause changes in variable A, or a third variable (C) could cause similar changes in both A and B, even if A and B did not influence each other. For example, a correlation between how much TV children watch and how aggressively they behave could be explained in the following ways:

(1) TV watching causes aggressive behavior;

(2) children who are aggressive like to watch a lot of TV; or

(3) children who have family troubles, such as parents who are not very involved in the children's development, tend both to watch a lot of TV and to behave aggressively.

based on correlational research. One of the great benefits of learning and gaining experience with the material in this chapter is that you can see the flaws in media reports like these and not be taken in by them. Correlation is not causation.

To illustrate how even such respected representatives of the media as the *New York Times* make this mistake, let's return to the Latin and SAT correlation discussed above. This relationship was reported in an Op-Ed piece in the *Times* entitled "Latin and Greek Are Good for You" (Costa, 1982). The author cited the SAT figures indicating that students who took the Latin Achievement Test did much better on their SATs than other students and concluded that "Latin is good for you." So why is this conclusion wrong? It *is* possible that studying Latin caused an improvement on SAT scores, but other causal explanations are possible as well. In terms of Figure 2.2, A (Latin) might have caused B (elevated SAT scores). Although B could not have caused A, because the students took the SATs only after they had been studying Latin, it is very possible that some other variable (C) caused both A and B. For example, high school students who decide to study Latin may in general be more intelligent than students who show no interest in the subject, and schools that offer study in languages such as Latin and Greek may in general be better academically than schools that do not. So, it is possible that studying Latin had no effect on the students' SAT scores, despite the correlation between these two variables (Lehman et al., 1988).

Do we learn nothing, then, from correlations? To say that would be to take caution too far. Correlations tell us about the strength and direction of relationships between variables. This helps researchers understand these variables better and allows them to use one variable to predict the other. Correlations can be extremely useful in developing new hypotheses to guide future research. And by gathering large sets of correlations and using complicated statistical techniques to crunch the data, we can develop highly accurate predictions of future events. But still, correlation is not causation.

Experiments: Looking for Cause and Effect

Social psychologists often do want to examine cause-and-effect relationships. Although it is informative to know, for example, that watching a lot of TV is correlated with violent behavior in real life, the inevitable next question is whether watching a lot of TV *causes* an increase in violent behavior. If we want to examine cause-and-effect relationships, we need to conduct an **experiment.** Experiments in social psychology range from the very simple to the almost incredibly elaborate. All of them, however, share two essential characteristics.

1. The researcher has *control* over the experimental procedures, manipulating the variables of interest while ensuring uniformity elsewhere. All participants in the research are treated in exactly the same manner—except for the specific differences the experimenter wants to create. By exercising control, the researcher attempts to ensure that differences obtained after the experimental manipulation are produced only by that manipulation and are not affected by other events in the experiment.

2. Participants in the study are *randomly* assigned to the different manipulations (called "conditions") included in the experiment. If there are two conditions, who goes where may be determined by simply flipping a coin. If there are many conditions, a computer program may be used. However it's done, **random assignment** means that participants are not assigned to a condition on the basis of their personal or behavioral characteristics. By randomly assigning participants to experimental conditions, the experimenter attempts to ensure a level playing field. On the average, the participants assigned to one condition

experiment A form of research that can demonstrate causal relationships because (1) the experimenter has control over the events that occur and (2) participants are randomly assigned to conditions.

random assignment A method of assigning participants to the various conditions of an experiment so that each participant in the experiment has an equal chance of being in any of the conditions.

TABLE 2.3 Correlations Versus Experiments

	Correlational Research	Experimental Research
What does it involve?	Measuring variables and the degree of association between them	Random assignment to conditions and control over the events that occur; determining the effects of manipulations of the independent variable(s) on changes in the dependent variable(s)
What is the biggest advantage of using this method?	Enables researchers to study naturally occurring variables, including variables that would be too difficult or unethical to manipulate	Enables researchers to determine cause-and-effect relationships—that is, whether the independent variable can cause a change in an experiment in the dependent variable

TABLE 2.4 Random Sampling Versus Random Assignment

	Random Sampling	Random Assignment
What does it involve?	Selecting participants to be in the study so that everyone from a population has an equal chance of being a participant in the study	Assigning participants (who are already in the study) to the various conditions of the experiment so that each participant has an equal chance of being in any of the conditions
What is the biggest advantage of using this procedure?	Enables researchers to collect data from samples that are representative of the broader population; important for being able to generalize the results to the broader population	Equalizes the conditions of the experiment so that it is very unlikely that the conditions differ in terms of pre-existing differences among the participants; essential to determine that the independent variable(s) caused an effect on the dependent variable(s)

are no different from those assigned to another condition. Differences that appear between conditions after an experimental manipulation can therefore be attributed to the impact of that manipulation and not to any pre-existing differences between participants.

Because of experimenter control and random assignment of participants, an experiment is a powerful technique for examining cause and effect. Both characteristics serve the same goal: to eliminate the influence on participants' behavior of any factors other than the experimental manipulation. By ruling out alternative explanations for research results, we become more confident that we understand just what has, in fact, caused a certain behavior to occur. Table 2.3 summarizes the distinctions between correlational and experimental research.

Random Sampling Versus Random Assignment
You may recall that we mentioned random sampling earlier, in connection with surveys. It's important to remember the differences between random *sampling* and random *assignment*. Table 2.4 summarizes these differences. Random sampling concerns how individuals are selected to be in a study; it is important for generalizing the results obtained from a sample to a broader population, and it is therefore very important for survey research. Random assignment concerns not who is selected to be in the study but rather how participants in the study are assigned to different conditions, as explained above. Random assignment is essential to experiments because it is essential to establishing cause-and-effect relationships; without it, it is always possible that any differences found between the conditions in a study were caused by pre-existing differences among participants. Random sampling, in contrast, is not necessary for establishing causality. For that reason, and because random sampling is difficult and expensive, very few experiments use random sampling. We consider the implications of this fact later in the chapter.

Laboratory and Field Experiments Most experiments in social psychology are conducted in a *laboratory* setting, usually located in a university, so that the environment can be controlled and the participants carefully studied. Social psychology labs do not necessarily look like stereotypical laboratories with liquid bubbling in beakers or expensive equipment everywhere (although many social psychology labs are indeed very "high-tech"). They can resemble ordinary living rooms or even game rooms. The key point is that the laboratory setting enables researchers to have control over the setting, measure participants' behaviors precisely, and keep conditions identical for participants.

Field research is conducted in real-world settings outside of the laboratory. Researchers interested in studying helping behavior, for example, might conduct an experiment in a public park. The advantage of field experiments is that people are more likely to act naturally in a natural setting than in a laboratory in which they know they are being studied. The disadvantage of field settings is that the experimenter often has less control and cannot ensure that the participants in the various conditions of the experiment will be exposed to the same things.

Independent and Dependent Variables In an experiment, researchers manipulate one or more **independent variables** and examine the effect of these manipulations on one or more **dependent variables.** For example, in Chapter 1, we described an experiment in which participants watched one of three versions of a presidential debate between Ronald Reagan and Walter Mondale (Fein et al., 1998). Some participants saw an unedited version of the debate; others saw a version in which funny remarks made by Reagan, and the audience's positive reaction to those remarks, were edited out; and others saw a version in which the remarks were left in but the positive audience reaction was edited out. The version of the debate shown to the participants was the independent variable—that is, we manipulated this variable to determine its effect on another variable, the dependent variable. In this study, the dependent variable was the participants' ratings of Reagan on a 100-point scale, ranging from "terrible" to "excellent." The ratings were the dependent variable because we were interested in seeing if they would *depend* on (that is, be influenced by) the manipulation of the independent variable. As discussed in Chapter 1, the manipulation did have a significant effect on the dependent variable; the participants who saw the version of the debate in which Reagan's remarks were left in but the audience reaction was edited out rated Reagan much more negatively than did the participants in the other two conditions.

In field research, people are observed in real-world settings. Field researchers may observe children in a schoolyard, for example, to study any of a variety of social psychological issues, such as friendship patterns, group dynamics, conformity, helping, aggression, and cultural differences.

Main Effects and Interactions Some experiments include multiple independent variables. In such cases, researchers can examine the separate effects of each independent variable on the dependent variable or variables and can also study how the different independent variables combine to create interactive effects. For example, consider an experiment by Kenneth Leonard (1989) on the effects of alcohol on aggression. The participants were male undergraduates who had agreed to take part in a study on "the influence of alcohol on perceptual-motor skills." Only participants who indicated that they drank alcohol were included. When each participant arrived at the research laboratory, he was randomly assigned to receive either no drink of any kind or a combination of vodka and ginger ale designed to produce the level of blood alcohol concentration legally defined as intoxication. Thus, one independent variable was whether or not the participants were given alcohol.

Each participant was then informed that he would be competing against another participant on an experimental task and that the loser on each trial would receive an electric shock administered by the winner. Actually, there was no other

independent variables In an experiment, the factors experimenters manipulate to see if they affect the dependent variables.

dependent variables In an experiment, the factors experimenters measure to see if they are affected by the independent variables.

participant; tape-recorded messages and programmed responses during the task were used to simulate the opponent's behavior. At the beginning of the first trial, half of the participants (randomly assigned within the alcohol and no-alcohol conditions) were led to believe that their opponent intended to administer the most severe shock available; the other half were led to believe that the opponent intended to use only the mildest possible shock. This was the second independent variable. After the first trial was over, however, all participants were told that their opponent had set the minimum shock level. They then prepared for the second trial.

The outcome being studied—the dependent variable—was the level of shock that a participant selected before each trial to be administered to the opponent in the event that the participant was the winner on that trial. Thus, the questions addressed in this experiment were what effects (1) intoxication and (2) original beliefs about the opponent's aggressive intentions would have on how much shock a participant was prepared to give to the opponent before each trial. Table 2.5 summarizes the design of the experiment.

Figure 2.3a depicts the results for the first trial. In general, participants who believed that the opponent had aggressive intentions selected higher levels of shock than did participants who believed that the opponent had nonaggressive intentions. This result, in which the levels of a single independent variable produce differences in the dependent variable, is called a *main effect*. There is another possible main effect in this experiment—the effect of intoxication on the dependent variable. This effect turned out not to be significant in the first trial. As you can see in Figure 2.3a, intoxicated participants selected about the same level of shock as sober participants.

Figure 2.3b depicts the results for the second trial. Remember, before setting their shock levels for this second trial, all the participants had been told that their opponents had not acted aggressively in the first trial. On the second trial, both independent variables affected the dependent variable. Let's look first at the effects of the independent variables separately. What was the main effect for the manipulation of alcohol? To examine this main effect, ignore the effect of participants' original belief about the opponent's intent. As you can see from Figure 2.3b, intoxicated participants set higher shock levels, on average, than sober participants. Now, what is the main effect for the participants' original beliefs about the opponent? To examine this main effect, ignore the effect of alcohol. In general, participants who had originally believed that their opponents had aggressive intentions set their shock levels higher than did the participants who had not had this belief.

When we look at the *interaction* of the two independent variables, the results become even more interesting. To look for an interaction, ask yourself, "Does the effect of one independent variable change as a function of the other independent variable?" To the extent that it does, there is an interaction between the two variables. So, did the effect of the manipulation of participants' original beliefs change as a function of whether or not they were intoxicated? Yes. Although *in general* intoxicated participants responded more aggressively than sober participants, this effect was much stronger among the

TABLE 2.5 Alcohol and Aggression: The Conditions

Participants in Leonard's experiment on alcohol and aggression either drank alcohol until intoxicated or did not drink alcohol. Then they were led to expect their opponent to have either aggressive or nonaggressive intentions toward them. Combining these two independent variables creates the four conditions displayed here. *(Based on Leonard, 1989.)*

	Intoxicated	Sober
Expected opponent to be aggressive	Condition 1: Intoxicated / Expected aggressive intent	Condition 2: Sober / Expected aggressive intent
Expected opponent to be nonaggressive	Condition 3: Intoxicated / Expected nonaggressive intent	Condition 4: Sober / Expected nonaggressive intent

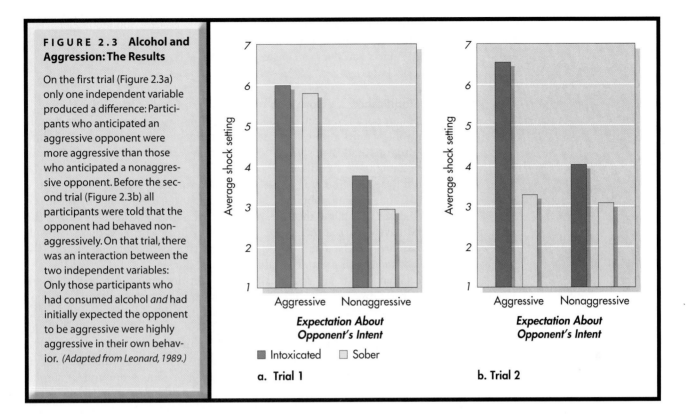

FIGURE 2.3 Alcohol and Aggression: The Results

On the first trial (Figure 2.3a) only one independent variable produced a difference: Participants who anticipated an aggressive opponent were more aggressive than those who anticipated a nonaggressive opponent. Before the second trial (Figure 2.3b) all participants were told that the opponent had behaved nonaggressively. On that trial, there was an interaction between the two independent variables: Only those participants who had consumed alcohol *and* had initially expected the opponent to be aggressive were highly aggressive in their own behavior. *(Adapted from Leonard, 1989.)*

participants who had been led to believe that their opponent had aggressive intentions. Similarly, although *in general* participants set higher shock levels if they had been led to believe that their opponent would be aggressive, this effect was much stronger among the intoxicated participants than among the sober ones. Thus, neither alcohol by itself nor beliefs about the opponent's aggressive intent by itself caused the most aggressive responses. Rather, those who were both intoxicated *and* had expected the opponent to be aggressive were most likely to set particularly high shock levels.

What explains this interaction? One possibility is that when sober, participants who had originally believed that their opponent would be aggressive were able to adjust their feelings about him when they were told that he in fact had not behaved aggressively. When drunk, however, they were less able or less motivated to adjust their initial negative expectations about the opponent; thus, they remained aggressive toward him.

Subject Variables   Some experiments include variables that are neither dependent nor truly independent. In Leonard's experiment, all of the participants were male. But suppose that Leonard had been interested in potential gender differences in his study and that he had included both male and female participants. The sex of the participants cannot be manipulated and randomly assigned, so it is not a true independent variable; and it is not influenced by the independent variables, so it is not a dependent variable. Variables such as these are called **subject variables,** because they characterize pre-existing differences among the subjects, or participants, in the experiment. If a study includes subject variables but no true, randomly assigned independent variable, it is not an experiment. But experiments often include subject variables along with independent variables so that researchers can test whether the independent variables have the same or different effects on different kinds of participants. Would intoxicated women have behaved in the same way as

subject variables Variables that characterize pre-existing differences among the participants in a study.

intoxicated men in Leonard's experiment? Would gun control opponents behave in the same way as gun control proponents? Looking for interactions between independent and subject variables can answer questions such as these.

Statistical Significance A close look at the results in Figures 2.3a and 2.3b reveals that the average shock levels set in the four conditions in Leonard's experiment differed by only a few units on the shock setting. Are such differences large enough to be meaningful, or could they simply be due to chance? After all, if you flip a coin ten times, you might get six tails and four heads. Is the difference between 6 and 4 a meaningful difference? Surely it isn't—one could expect differences like this from random luck alone. Results obtained in an experiment are examined by means of statistical analyses that allow the researcher to determine how likely it is that the results could have occurred by chance. The standard convention is that if a result could have occurred by chance 5 or fewer times in 100 possible outcomes, then the result is *statistically significant* and should be taken seriously.

The fact that results are statistically significant does not mean that they are absolutely certain. In essence, statistical significance is an attractive betting proposition. The odds are quite good (at least 95 out of 100) that the effects obtained in the study were due to the experimental manipulation of the independent variable. But there is still the possibility (as high as 5 out of 100) that the findings occurred by chance. This is one reason why it is important to try to *replicate* the results of an experiment—repeat the experiment and see if similar results are found. If similar results are found, the probability that these results could have occurred by chance both times is five percent times five percent, or one-quarter of one percent (which equals 1 time in 400 possible outcomes).

Let's look again at Leonard's experiment. In the first trial, the main effect for the manipulation of participants' beliefs about the opponent was statistically significant. This means that there is a probability of less than 5 percent that the difference in average shock levels found between the participants who expected the opponent to be aggressive and those who expected him to be nonaggressive was due to chance. In the second trial, each of the two main effects, as well as the interaction between the two independent variables, was statistically significant.

internal validity The degree to which there can be reasonable certainty that the independent variables in an experiment caused the effects obtained on the dependent variables.

experimenter expectancy effects The effects produced when an experimenter's expectations about the results of an experiment affect his or her behavior toward a participant and thereby influence the participant's responses.

external validity The degree to which there can be reasonable confidence that the results of a study would be obtained for other people and in other situations.

Internal Validity: Did the Independent Variable Cause the Effect? When an experiment is properly conducted, its results are said to have **internal validity:** There is reasonable certainty that the independent variable did, in fact, cause the effects obtained on the dependent variable (Cook & Campbell, 1979). As noted earlier, both experimenter control and random assignment seek to rule out alternative explanations of the research results, thereby strengthening the internal validity of the research.

Experiments also include *control groups* for this purpose. Typically, a control group consists of participants who experience all of the experimental procedures except the experimental manipulations. In Leonard's study on alcohol and aggression, participants who didn't drink alcohol and didn't hear their supposed opponent express aggressive intentions served as a control group. As a sort of "dry run," the control group provides a baseline against which to compare what happens when the independent variables are activated.

Outside the laboratory, creating control groups in natural settings that examine real-life events raises many practical and ethical problems. For example, research on new medical treatments for deadly diseases, such as AIDS, faces a terrible dilemma. Individuals randomly assigned to the control group receive the standard treatment, but they are excluded for the duration of the study from what could turn out to be a life-saving new intervention. Yet without such a comparison, it is extremely difficult to determine which new treatments are effective and which are useless. Although AIDS activists used to oppose including control groups in treatment research, they have recently become more supportive of this approach (Gorman, 1994).

In assessing internal validity, researchers need to consider their own role as well. Unwittingly, they can sometimes sabotage their own research. Here's how:

- Before they conduct a study, experimenters usually make an explicit prediction, or at least have a strong expectation, about the effect of an independent variable.
- If they know what conditions participants have been assigned to, they may, without realizing it, treat participants in different conditions differently.
- Because the experimenters' behavior can affect the participants' behavior, the results could then be produced by the experimenters' actions rather than by the independent variable.

The best way to protect an experiment from the influence of experimenters' expectations—called **experimenter expectancy effects** (Rosenthal, 1976)—is to keep them uninformed about assignments to conditions. If experimenters do not know the condition to which a participant has been assigned, they cannot treat participants differently as a function of their condition. Leonard's study of alcohol and aggression was conducted by a single experimenter who was aware of participants' experimental assignments. Since the experimenter did sometimes interact directly with the participant, experimenter expectancy effects, though unlikely, could have affected the results. In an effort to reduce the opportunity for such effects to occur, Leonard minimized the interaction between the experimenter and each participant by the use of tape-recorded instructions at various points in the experiment.

External Validity: Do the Results Generalize?   In addition to guarding internal validity, researchers are concerned about **external validity,** the extent to which the results obtained under one set of circumstances would also occur in a different set of circumstances (Berkowitz & Donnerstein, 1982). When an experiment has external validity, its findings can be assumed to generalize to other people and to other situations. As we will see, both the participants in the experiment and the setting in which it takes place affect external validity.

Because social psychologists often seek to establish universal principles of human behavior, their ideal sample of participants should be representative of all human beings all over the world. Such an all-inclusive representative sample has never been seen and probably never will be. Representative samples of more limited populations do exist and can be achieved by random sampling of a population, which was discussed earlier in the chapter. But, as also men-

As this participant in an experiment on the effects of television violence watches scenes of violence, his pulse and blood pressure are measured. Even if this experiment had strong internal validity, its external validity would be weak if the results could not be generalized beyond the circumstances of the experiment, such as to more natural settings and with different types of people.

tioned earlier, social psychologists rarely study representative samples. Usually, they rely on convenience samples drawn from populations that are readily available to them, which accounts for why so much of social psychological research is conducted on college students. The common practice of using convenience samples in social psychological research poses a crucial question: Is it possible to establish universal principles of human behavior with research on nonrepresentative samples?

Those who favor the use of convenience samples point to some very real practical issues. Representative samples are fine for surveys requiring short answers to a short list of questions. But what about complex, time-consuming experiments like Leonard's? The expense of bringing participants from diverse geographic areas into the lab would be staggering. And various extraneous variables (travel fatigue, disruptions in regular routines) could distort the results. Advocates of convenience samples also contend that there is no contradiction between universal principles and particular participants. Indeed, the more basic the principle, the less it matters who participates in the research. For example, various people or cultures might differ in the form of aggression they typically exhibit when angry; but the situational factors that cause people to be more likely to aggress, however that aggression is expressed, may be similar for most individuals no matter where they are from or what experiences they have had.

In spite of these arguments, the drawbacks to convenience samples are clear. Strictly speaking, the results of Leonard's research can be generalized only to young adult males who currently drink alcohol, attend a specific university, and are willing to participate in a psychology experiment in order to earn some money. Presumably, Leonard wants to generalize his results much more broadly, but our confidence in the external validity of any study that uses a convenience sample is necessarily reduced. Reacting against the prevalence of convenience samples in social psychology, David Sears (1986) offered a spirited argument for the many advantages of including participants from a variety of backgrounds and life experiences.

Have social psychologists taken Sears' advice to heart? Partly. As noted in Chapter 1, social psychological research is now conducted in many countries, ensuring the participation of participants from different societies.

But what about research on racial and ethnic minorities living in the United States? Here, the record is much less encouraging. To determine the percentage of research articles on African Americans that appeared in six leading journals published by the American Psychological Association from 1970 to 1989, Sandra Graham (1992) selected articles that met two criteria: (1) African Americans were included as participants, and (2) African Americans were the population of interest or the results were analyzed by race. In all the journals surveyed, the percentage of articles on African Americans declined from the earliest time period (1970–1974) to the most recent one covered by Graham's study (1985–1989). The *Journal of Personality and Social Psychology*, the only social psychology journal in the study, consistently had the lowest percentage (1.6 percent) among the six journals. Graham's research provides only a partial view of the bigger picture: Other minority groups were not studied, nor were other psychology journals, and the data do not address the 1990s. Even so, these data establish an important goal for all of psychology and especially for social psychology—a branch of psychology that has a strong tradition of research on such topics as stereotypes, prejudice, social norms, and intergroup conflict. To become a better science, social psychology must become more inclusive.

External validity is also affected by the place where research is conducted. Because field research occurs in real-life natural settings rather than in the artificial arrangements of a laboratory, aren't its results more generalizable to actual behavior? The answer depends on where you stand on the issue of mundane versus experimental realism (Aronson & Carlsmith, 1968).

Mundane realism refers to the extent to which the research setting resembles the real-world setting of interest. In order to study interpersonal attraction, Theodore Newcomb (1961) set up an entire college dormitory—a striking example of mundane realism. Advocates of mundane realism contend that if research procedures are more realistic, research findings are more likely to reveal what really goes on.

In contrast, **experimental realism** refers to the degree to which the experimental setting and procedures are real and involving to the participant, regardless of whether they resemble real life or not. The setting of Leonard's research on alcohol and aggression was a far cry from the bars and sporting events where this volatile mixture is often found. But extensive research conducted with similar procedures indicates that this experimental scenario is highly involving for participants. According to those who favor experimental realism, if participants' experiences are real to them, their behavior in the lab—even if the lab is in the basement of the psychology building—will be as natural and spontaneous as their behavior in the real world would be. The majority of social psychologists who conduct experiments emphasize experimental realism.

Like many researchers who strive to create a highly involving experience for participants, Leonard had to rely on **deception,** providing participants with false information about experimental procedures. In Leonard's study, the supposed opponent didn't actually exist. Sometimes, however, social psychologists employ **confederates,** who act as though they are participants in the experiment but are really working for the experimenter. Deception not only strengthens experimental realism but also confers other benefits: It allows the experimenter to manufacture situations in the laboratory that would be difficult to observe in a natural setting; to study potentially harmful behaviors, such as aggression, in a regulated, safe manner; and to assess people's spontaneous reactions rather than socially acceptable presentations. Studies have shown that participants are rarely bothered by deception and often particularly enjoy studies that use it (Smith & Richardson, 1983). Nevertheless, the use of deception creates some serious ethical concerns, which we examine later in this chapter.

Meta-Analysis: Combining Results Across Studies

We have seen that social psychologists conduct original descriptive, correlational, and experimental studies to test their hypotheses. Another way to test hypotheses in social psychology is to use a set of statistical procedures to examine in a new way relevant research that has already been conducted and reported. This technique is called **meta-analysis.** By "meta-analyzing" the results of a number of studies that have been conducted in different places and by different researchers, a social psychologist can measure precisely how strong and reliable particular effects are. For example, studies published concerning alcohol and aggression, such as Leonard's, may sometimes contradict each other. Sometimes alcohol increases aggression; sometimes it doesn't. By combining the data from all the studies that are relevant to this hypothesis and conducting a meta-analysis, a researcher can determine what effect alcohol typically has, how strong that effect typically is, and perhaps under what specific conditions that effect is most likely to occur. This technique, which was developed relatively recently, is being used with increasing frequency in social psychology today (Rosenthal, 1991; Schmidt, 1992). We report the results of many meta-analyses in this textbook. Meta-analyses concerning alcohol and aggression, for example, are described in Chapter 11 on Aggression.

mundane realism The degree to which the experimental situation resembles places and events in the real world.

experimental realism The degree to which experimental procedures are involving to participants and lead them to behave naturally and spontaneously.

deception In the context of research, a method that provides false information to participants.

confederate Accomplice of an experimenter who, in dealing with the real participants in an experiment, acts as if he or she is also a participant.

meta-analysis A set of statistical procedures used to review a body of evidence by combining the results of individual studies to measure the overall reliability and strength of particular effects.

Ethics and Values in Social Psychology

Regardless of where research is conducted and what method is used, ethical issues must always be considered. Researchers in all fields have a moral and legal responsibility to abide by ethical principles. In social psychology, the use of deception has caused particular concern (Ortmann & Hertwig, 1997), and several studies have provoked fierce debate about whether they went beyond the bounds of ethical acceptability. For example, Stanley Milgram (1963) designed a series of experiments to address the question, "Would people obey orders to harm an innocent person?" To test this question, he put volunteers into a situation in which an experimenter commanded them to administer painful electric shocks to someone who they thought was another volunteer participant (in fact, the other person was a confederate who was not actually receiving any shocks). The experiment had extremely high experimental realism—many of the participants experienced a great deal of anxiety and stress as they debated whether they should disobey the experimenter or continue to inflict pain on another person. The details and results of this experiment will be discussed in Chapter 7 on Conformity, but suffice it to say that the results of the study made people realize how prevalent and powerful obedience can be.

Milgram's research was inspired by the obedience displayed by Nazi officers in World War II. No one disputes the importance of his research question. What has been debated, however, is whether the significance of the research topic justified exposing participants to possibly harmful psychological consequences. Under today's provisions for the protection of human participants, Milgram's classic experiments probably could not be conducted in their original form.

Milgram's research was by no means the only social psychological research to trigger debates about ethics. Several studies in the history of social psychology have sparked a great deal of controversy. And it is not only the controversial studies that receive scrutiny. Today, virtually every social psychology study conducted is evaluated for its ethics by other people before the study can be conducted. In the following sections, we describe current policies and procedures as well as continuing concerns about ethics and values in social psychological research.

Institutional Review Boards: The Ethical Watchdogs

informed consent An individual's deliberate, voluntary decision to participate in research, based on the researcher's description of what will be required during such participation.

debriefing A disclosure, made to participants after research procedures are completed, in which the researcher explains the purpose of the research, attempts to resolve any negative feelings, and emphasizes the scientific contribution made by the participants' involvement.

In 1974, the agency then called the United States Department of Health, Education, and Welfare established regulations for the protection of human participants in research. These regulations created institutional review boards (IRBs) at all institutions seeking federal funding for research involving human participants. Charged with the responsibility for reviewing research proposals to ensure that the welfare of participants was adequately protected, IRBs were to be the "watchdogs" of research.

Although researchers have become accustomed to submitting their proposals to IRBs, questions persist about the appropriate role of these boards. For example, should IRBs act as censors? Few, if any, researchers or board members would endorse such a practice. But an experiment by Stephen Ceci and his colleagues (1985) found that university IRBs were more likely to approve politically neutral proposals than socially sensitive ones having implications for societal groups or policies. Socially sensitive topics often raise serious ethical questions that require careful scrutiny by investigators and IRBs (Sieber & Stanley, 1988). Properly conducted, however, socially sensitive research can offer vital information needed to address major societal issues.

Informed Consent: Do You (Really) Want to Participate?

Besides submitting their research to government-mandated IRBs, researchers must also abide by their profession's code of ethics. The statement of ethics of the American Psychological Association (APA), called *Ethical Principles of Psychologists* (1992), considers a wide range of ethical issues, including those related to research procedures and practices. The APA code stipulates that researchers are obligated to guard the rights and welfare of all those who participate in their studies.

One such obligation is to obtain **informed consent.** Individuals must be asked whether they wish to participate in the research project and must be given enough information to make an informed decision. Deceiving research participants about "significant aspects that would affect their willingness to participate, such as physical risks, discomfort, or unpleasant emotional experiences" is explicitly prohibited, although withholding less vital information is presumably allowed. The APA code also recognizes that research "involving only anonymous questionnaires, naturalistic observations, or certain kinds of archival research" may not require informed consent.

In principle, informed consent is absolutely essential for the protection of human participants. Only if you know what you would be getting into can you decide whether you want to get involved. In practice, however, it can be difficult to ensure that consent is, in fact, informed. Often, the information given to participants is vague because the researchers do not want to tell the participants so much that their responses during the study will be affected. Other times, the information can be so detailed and complex that many participants don't fully understand it (Mann, 1994). To make the practice of obtaining informed consent as effective as the principle says it should be, we will need more research on how best to communicate this information.

Social psychology experiments don't reach this level of deception, nor are participants likely to be so startled by the debriefing! But whenever participants are deceived about research procedures or purposes, it is especially important to provide a full and thorough debriefing. The Far Side

Debriefing: Telling All

Have you ever participated in psychological research? If so, what was your reaction to this experience? Have you ever been deceived about the hypothesis or procedures of a study in which you were a participant? If so, how did you feel about it? Most research on participants' reactions indicates that they have positive attitudes about their participation, even when they were deceived about some aspects of a study (Christensen, 1988). Indeed, deceived participants sometimes have expressed more favorable opinions than those who have not been deceived, presumably because studies involving deception are often interesting and creative (Smith & Richardson, 1983).

These findings are reassuring, but they do not remove the obligation of researchers to use deception only when nondeceptive alternatives are not feasible. In addition, whenever deception has been used, there is a special urgency to the requirement that, once the data have been collected, researchers fully inform their participants about the nature of the research in which they have participated. This process of disclosure is called **debriefing.** During a debriefing, the researcher goes over all procedures, explaining exactly what happened and why. Deceptions are revealed, the purpose of the research is discussed, and the researcher makes every effort to help the participant feel good about having participated. A skillful debriefing takes time and requires close attention to the individual participant (Aronson et al., 1985).

Values and Science: Points of View

Ethical principles are based on moral values. These values set standards for and impose limits on the conduct of research, just as they influence individuals' personal behavior. When the potential benefits of research for humankind are high and the potential costs are ethically acceptable, there is a moral imperative to try to carry out the research. But when the human costs are too high in terms of the suffering of participants, the moral imperative is to refrain.

Ethical issues are an appropriate focus for moral values in science, but do values affect science in other ways as well? Consider this statement by Senator Orrin Hatch: "We in Congress look to social science to provide us unbiased and objective information" (1982, p. 1036). Is it possible for social psychology or any other social science to do this? Is it desirable? If what the senator has in mind is a *totally* unbiased, value-free science, the odds for meeting this goal are not good. For example, in his presidential address to the National Council on Family Relations, Brent Miller (1993) cited his own increasing awareness of the role of values: "In the early 1980s I considered adolescent pregnancy as an area of research that I could approach as an objective social scientist. Since then I have come to realize how naive I was and that even the definitions of the problems, let alone their potential solutions, are absolutely riddled with values—those deeply held beliefs about right and wrong" (p. 12). And, after describing how investigators have emphasized individual rather than societal factors in substance abuse, Keith Humphreys and Julian Rappaport (1993) commented that, "Researchers are just doing what they often unwittingly do—perpetuating the status quo by being uncritical about the problems that are handed to them by powerful others" (p. 897).

Infatuated by important topics, wrestling with beliefs about right and wrong, under the thumb of those who control funding for research—this all seems a long way from "unbiased and objective." It's such a long way that perhaps the search for objectivity is only a self-serving illusion. Perhaps the more forthright approach is to adopt a psychology of political advocacy: "championing causes that one believes good for the culture; . . . condemning movements or policies that seem inimical to human welfare" (Gergen, 1994, p. 415).

> *"[Objectivity in science] is the willingness (even the eagerness in truly honorable practitioners) to abandon a favored notion when testable evidence disconfirms key expectations."*
>
> —Stephen Jay Gould

But there is another view. From this perspective, science can never be completely unbiased and objective because it is a human enterprise. Scientists choose what to study and how to study it; their choices are affected by personal values as well as by professional rewards. To acknowledge these influences, however, is not to embrace them. Quite the contrary. Such influences are precisely why the scientific method is so important.

As Stanley Parkinson (1994) puts it, "Scientists are not necessarily more objective than other people; rather, they use methods that have been developed to minimize self-deception" (p. 137). By scrutinizing their own behavior and adopting the rigors of the scientific method, scientists attempt to free themselves of their preconceptions and, thereby, to see reality more clearly, even if never perfectly.

You've read what others have said about values and science. But what do you think about all this? How *do* values influence science? How *should* values affect scientific inquiry?

Your introduction to the field of social psychology is now complete. In these first two chapters, you have gone step by step through a definition of social psychology, a review of its history and discussion of its future, an overview of its research methods, and a consideration of ethics and values. As you study the material presented in the coming chapters, the three of us who wrote this book invite you to share our enthusiasm. You can look forward to information that overturns common-sense assumptions, to lively debate and heated controversy, and to a better understanding of yourself and other people. Welcome to the world according to social psychology. We hope you enjoy it!

Review

Why Should You Learn About Research Methods?

- Because common sense and intuitive ideas about social psychological issues can be misleading and contradictory, it is important to understand the scientific evidence on which social psychological theories and findings are based.
- Studying research methods in psychology improves people's reasoning about real-life events and information presented by the media and other sources.

Developing Ideas: Beginning the Research Process

Asking Questions

- Ideas for research in social psychology come from everywhere—personal experiences and observations, events in the news, and other research.

Searching the Literature

- Before pursuing a research idea, it is important to see what research has already been done on this and related topics.
- Electronic databases provide access to a wealth of information, both in the psychology literature and in more general sources.

Hypotheses and Theories

- Formulating a hypothesis is a critical step toward planning and conducting research.
- Theories in social psychology are specific rather than comprehensive and generate research that can support or disconfirm them.

Basic and Applied Research

- The goal of basic research is to increase understanding of human behavior.
- The goal of applied research is to increase understanding of real-world events and contribute to the solution of social problems.

Refining Ideas: Defining and Measuring Social Psychological Variables

Conceptual Variables and Operational Definitions: From the Abstract to the Specific

- Researchers often must transform abstract, conceptual variables into specific operational definitions that indicate exactly how the variables are to be manipulated or measured.
- Construct validity is the extent to which the operational definitions successfully manipulate or measure the conceptual variables to which they correspond.

Measuring Variables: Self-Reports and Observations

- In self-reports, participants indicate their thoughts, feelings, desires, and actions.
- Self-reports can be distorted by efforts to make a good impression, as well as by the effects of the wording and context of questions.
- To increase the accuracy of self-reports, some approaches emphasize the need to collect self-reports as soon as possible after participants experience the relevant thoughts, feelings, or behaviors.
- Narrative studies analyze the content of lengthy responses on a general topic.
- Observations can be made by human observers or by machines.

Testing Ideas: Research Designs

- Most social psychologists test their ideas by using objective, systematic, and quantifiable methods.

Descriptive Research: Discovering Trends and Tendencies

- In descriptive research, social psychologists record how frequently or typically people think, feel, or behave in particular ways.
- One form of descriptive research is observational research, in which researchers observe individuals systematically, often in natural settings.

- In archival research, researchers examine existing records and documents such as newspaper articles, diaries, and published crime statistics.
- Surveys involve asking people questions about their attitudes, beliefs, and behaviors.
- Survey researchers identify the population to which they want the results of the survey to generalize, and they select a sample of people from that population to take the survey.
- To best ensure a sample that is representative of the broader population, researchers should randomly select people from the population to be in the survey.

Correlational Research: Looking for Associations

- Correlational research examines the association between variables.
- A correlation coefficient is a measure of the strength and direction of the association between two variables.
- Positive correlations indicate that as scores on one variable increase, scores on the other variable increase; and that as scores on one variable decrease, scores on the other decrease.
- Negative correlations indicate that as scores on one variable increase, scores on the other decrease.
- Correlation does not indicate causation; the fact that two variables are correlated does not necessarily mean that one causes the other.
- Correlations can be used for prediction and for generating hypotheses.

Experiments: Looking for Cause and Effect

- Experiments require (1) control by the experimenter over events in the study and (2) random assignment of participants to conditions.
- Random sampling concerns how people are selected to be in a study, whereas random assignment concerns how people who are in the study are assigned to the different conditions of the study.
- Experiments are often conducted in a laboratory so that the researchers can have control over the context and can measure variables precisely.
- Field experiments are conducted in real-world settings outside the laboratory.
- Experiments examine the effects of one or more independent variables on one or more dependent variables.
- In a main effect, the levels of a single independent variable produce differences in the dependent variable; this effect is independent of (not related to) the effects of any other independent variables.

- In an interaction, the effect of one independent variable on the dependent variable changes as a function of another independent variable; thus, the independent variables jointly affect the dependent variable.
- Subject variables are variables that characterize pre-existing differences among the participants.
- Results that are statistically significant could have occurred by chance 5 or fewer times in 100 possible outcomes.
- Experimental findings have internal validity to the extent that changes in the dependent variable can be attributed to the independent variables.
- Control groups strengthen internal validity; experimental expectancy effects weaken it.
- Research results have external validity to the extent that they can be generalized to other people and other situations.
- A representative sample strengthens external validity; a convenience sample weakens it.
- Mundane realism is the extent to which the research setting seems similar to real-world situations.
- Experimental realism is the extent to which the participants experience the experimental setting and procedures as real and involving.
- Deception is sometimes used to increase experimental realism.
- Confederates act as though they are participants in an experiment but actually work for the experimenter.

Meta-Analysis: Combining Results Across Studies

- Meta-analysis uses statistical techniques to integrate the quantitative results of different studies.

Ethics and Values in Social Psychology

- Ethical issues are particularly important in social psychology because of the use of deception in some research.

Institutional Review Boards: The Ethical Watchdogs

- Established by the federal government, IRBs are responsible for reviewing research proposals to ensure that the welfare of participants is adequately protected.

Informed Consent: Do You (Really) Want to Participate?

- The American Psychological Association's code of ethics requires psychologists to secure informed consent from research participants.

Debriefing: Telling All

■ Most participants have positive attitudes about their participation in research, even if they were deceived about some aspects of the study.

■ Whenever deception has been used in a study, a full debriefing is essential; the researchers must disclose the facts about the study and make sure that the participant does not experience any distress.

Values and Science: Points of View

■ Moral values set standards for and impose limits on the conduct of research.

■ There are various views on the relation between values and science. Few believe that there can be a completely value-free science, but some advocate trying to minimize the influence of values on science, whereas others argue that values should be recognized and encouraged as an important factor in science.

Key Terms

applied research *27*

basic research *27*

confederates *47*

construct validity *28*

correlation coefficient *36*

correlational research *36*

debriefing *49*

deception *47*

dependent variables *41*

experiment *39*

experimental realism *47*

experimenter expectancy
    effects *45*

external validity *45*

hypothesis *27*

independent variables *41*

informed consent *49*

internal validity *44*

interrater reliability *31*

meta-analysis *47*

mundane realism *47*

random assignment *39*

random sampling *34*

subject variables *43*

theory *27*

3 | The Social Self

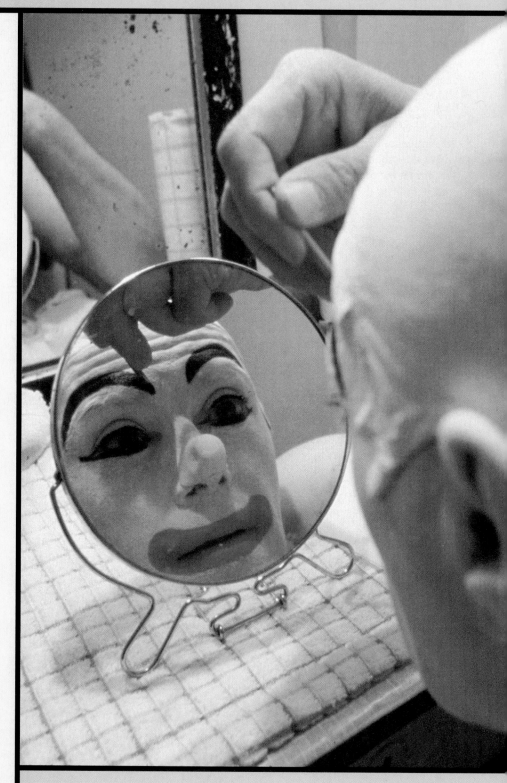

PREVIEW

This chapter examines three interrelated aspects of the "social self." First, it considers the *self-concept* and the question of how people come to understand their own actions, emotions, and motivations. Second, it considers *self-esteem,* the affective component, and the question of how people evaluate themselves and defend against threats to their self-esteem. Third, it considers *self-presentation,* a behavioral manifestation of the self, and the question of how people present themselves to others. As we will see, the self is complex and multifaceted.

Can you imagine living a meaningful or coherent life without a clear sense of who you are? In *The Man Who Mistook His Wife for a Hat*, neurologist Oliver Sacks (1985) described such a person—a patient named William Thompson. According to Sacks, Thompson suffered from an organic brain disorder that impairs a person's memory of recent events. Unable to recall anything for more than a few seconds, Thompson was always disoriented and lacked a sense of inner continuity. The effect on his behavior was startling. Trying to grasp a constantly vanishing identity, Thompson would construct one tale after another to account for who he was, where he was, and what he was doing. From one moment to the next, he would improvise new identities—a grocery store clerk, minister, or medical patient, to name just a few. In social settings, Thompson's behavior was especially intriguing. As Sacks (1985) observed,

> *The presence of others, other people, excite and rattle him, force him into an endless, frenzied, social chatter, a veritable delirium of identity-making and -seeking; the presence of plants, a quiet garden, the nonhuman order, making no social demands upon him, allow this identity-delirium to relax, to subside. (p. 110)*

Thompson's plight is unusual, but it highlights two important points—one about the private "inner" self, the other about the "outer" self we show to others. First, the capacity for self-reflection is necessary for people to feel as if they understand their own motives and emotions and the causes of their behavior. Unable to ponder his own actions, Thompson appeared vacant and without feeling—"de-souled," as Sacks put it. Second, the self is heavily influenced by social factors. Thompson himself seemed compelled to put on a face for others and to improvise characters for the company he kept. We all do, to some extent. We may not create a kaleidoscope of multiple identities as Thompson did, but the way we manage ourselves is influenced by the people around us.

PUTTING COMMON SENSE TO THE TEST

T / F

_____ Humans are the only animals who recognize themselves in the mirror.

_____ Smiling can make you feel happier.

_____ Sometimes the harder you try to control a thought, feeling, or behavior, the less likely you are to succeed.

_____ People tend to be overly optimistic about their future.

_____ People often sabotage their own performance in order to protect their self-esteem.

_____ It's more adaptive to alter one's behavior than to stay consistent from one social situation to the next.

This chapter examines the ABCs of the self: *affect, behavior,* and *cognition.* First, we ask a cognitive question: How do people come to know themselves, develop a self-concept, and maintain a stable sense of identity? Second, we explore an affective, or emotional, question: How do people evaluate themselves, enhance their self-images, and defend against threats to their self-esteem? Third, we confront a behavioral question: How do people present themselves to others and regulate their actions according to interpersonal demands? As we'll see, the self is a topic that in recent years has attracted unprecedented interest among social psychologists (Baumeister, 1998).

The Self-Concept

Have you ever been at a noisy gathering and yet managed to hear someone at the other end of the room mention your name? If so, then you have experienced the "cocktail party effect"—the ability to pick a personally relevant stimulus out of a complex environment (Moray, 1959; Wood & Cowan, 1995). To the cognitive psychologist, this phenomenon shows that people are selective in their attention. To the social psychologist, it also shows that the self is an important object of our own attention.

Beginnings of the Self-Concept

When you stand in front of a mirror, what do you see? If you were a dog, a cat, or some other animal, you would not realize that the image you see is you, your own reflection. Except for human beings, only great apes—chimpanzees, gorillas, and orangutans—seem capable of self-recognition. How can we possibly know what nonhumans think about mirrors? In a series of studies, Gordon Gallup (1977) placed different species of animals in a room with a large mirror. At first, they greeted their own images by vocalizing, gesturing, and making other social responses. After several days, the great apes—but not the other animals—began to use the mirror to pick food out of their teeth, groom themselves, blow bubbles, and make faces for their own entertainment. From all appearances, they recognized themselves.

In other studies, Gallup anesthetized the animals, then painted an odorless red dye on their brows, and returned them to the mirror. Upon seeing the red spot, only the apes reached for their brows—proof that they perceived the image as their own. By using a similar red dye test (but without anesthetizing the infants), developmental psychologists have found that most human infants begin to recognize themselves

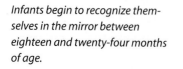

Infants begin to recognize themselves in the mirror between eighteen and twenty-four months of age.

in the mirror between the ages of eighteen and twenty-four months (Lewis & Brooks-Gunn, 1979). Today, many researchers believe that self-recognition among great apes and human infants is the first clear expression of the concept "me" (Asendorpf et al., 1996; Povinelli et al., 1994).

The ability to see yourself as a distinct entity is a necessary first step in the evolution and development of a **self-concept,** the sum total of beliefs you have and can communicate about yourself (Sedikides & Skowronski, 1997). The second step involves social factors.

"Look, babe. At this point, you've reinvented yourself so many times you're back to who you were at the start."

In some ways, our sense of self is malleable and subject to change.
Robert Mankoff © 1998 from The New Yorker Collection. All Rights Reserved.

Sociologist Charles Horton Cooley (1902) introduced the term *looking-glass self* to suggest that other people serve as a mirror in which we see ourselves. Expanding on this idea, George Herbert Mead (1934) added that we often come to know ourselves by imagining what significant others think of us and then incorporating these perceptions into our self-concepts. It is interesting that when Gallup tested his apes, those that had been raised in isolation—without exposure to peers—did not recognize themselves in the mirror. Only after such exposure did they begin to show signs of self-recognition. Among human beings, our self-concepts match our *perceptions* of what others think of us, as Cooley and Mead would have predicted. But there's a hitch: What we think of ourselves often does not match what specific others *actually* think of us (Felson, 1989; Kenny & DePaulo, 1993; Shrauger & Schoeneman, 1979).

In recent years, social psychologists have broken new ground in the effort to understand the social self. People are not born thinking of themselves as reckless, likable, shy, or outgoing. So where do their self-concepts come from? In the coming pages, five sources are considered: introspection, perceptions of our own behavior, the influences of other people, autobiographical memories, and culture. Then we look at self-schemas, the actual components of the self-concept.

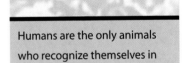

Humans are the only animals who recognize themselves in the mirror. **False.**

Introspection

Let's start at the beginning: How do people achieve insight into their own beliefs, attitudes, emotions, and motivations? Common sense makes this question seem ludicrous. After all, don't you know what you think because *you* think it? And don't you know how you feel because *you* feel it? Look through popular books on how to achieve self-insight, and you'll find the answers to these questions to be yes. Whether the prescribed technique is meditation, psychotherapy, religion, dream analysis, or hypnosis, the advice is basically the same: Self-knowledge is derived from introspection, a looking inward at one's own thoughts and feelings.

If these how-to books are correct, it stands to reason that no one can know you as well as you know yourself. Indeed, for others to know you at all, they would need information about your inner states, not just about your behavior. Do you agree? Susan Andersen and Lee Ross (1984) interviewed college students and asked them to discuss their social relationships, career goals, important life decisions, conflicts, and other personal topics. Before the interview, participants were instructed to

self-concept The sum total of an individual's beliefs about his or her own personal attributes.

focus on their thoughts and feelings, their overt behavior, or a mixture of both. Afterward, participants who had described their thoughts and feelings rated the interviews as more informative about themselves than did those who had focused only on behavior. Independent observers (who were strangers to the participants themselves) felt the same way. In another study, people were asked to write down the most important ways they have of knowing themselves, and the processes of self-reflection topped the list (Sedikides & Skowronski, 1995).

People assume that to truly know someone you must have access to private, subjective experiences. But is this really the case? Some social psychologists are not sure that this faith in introspection is justified. Several years ago, Richard Nisbett and Timothy Wilson (1977) found that research participants often cannot accurately explain the causes or correlates of their own behavior. This observation has forced researchers to confront a thorny question: Does introspection improve the *accuracy* of self-knowledge?

Wilson (1985) says no, that introspection can sometimes impair self-knowledge. In a series of studies, he found that the attitudes people reported having about different objects corresponded closely to their behavior toward those objects. The more participants said they enjoyed a task, the more time they spent on it; the more attractive they found a scenic landscape, the more pleasure they revealed in their facial expressions; the happier they said they were with a current dating partner, the longer the relationship ultimately lasted. Ironically, after participants had been told to analyze the reasons for how they felt, reported attitudes no longer correspond to behavior.

Too much introspection can also impair certain types of judgments. In one study, Wilson and Jonathan Schooler (1991) had people taste and rate five brands of strawberry jam. Those who were asked to list the reasons for their taste preferences agreed less with *Consumer Reports* experts than did those who made their ratings without analysis. In another study, Wilson and Suzanne LaFleur (1995) had college students make predictions about their relationship with a fellow student in the upcoming semester—predictions that were later verified. Students who were told to write down the reasons before making the predictions were ultimately less accurate than those who made predictions without explicit analysis. Apparently, it is possible to think too much, only to get confused.

Is introspection futile? Not necessarily. As Murray Millar and Abraham Tesser (1989) point out, people can reflect on their own behavior by listing either *reasons* or *feelings*. Whether this reflection provides valuable self-insight depends on whether the behavior in question is caused more by cognitive or affective factors, thoughts or feelings. For behaviors that are cognitively driven, such as making business investment decisions, a listing of reasons may well increase the accuracy of self-knowledge. But for behaviors that are affectively determined, such as romantic relationships, it may not. To determine why you like a certain puzzle, enjoy a work of art, or love another person, focusing on your feelings is more helpful than making a list of reasons.

The usefulness of introspection may also depend on the amount of time people have and the cognitive resources available for self-reflection. Gregory Hixon and William Swann (1993) asked people to rate themselves on various attributes (intelligence, athletic ability, physical attractiveness, social skills, and musical and artistic talent). Some participants were asked to think simultaneously about another task, while others were free to concentrate only on the self-ratings. Each participant's responses were later compared with a friend's ratings of that participant on the same attributes. The result: The self-friend ratings were more highly correlated when participants could focus on the task than when they could not. According to Hixon and Swann, introspection can increase self-insight—provided that we have enough time and cognitive resources.

Perceptions of Our Own Behavior

Regardless of what we can learn from introspection, Daryl Bem (1972) believes that people can learn about themselves the same way outside observers do—by watching their own behavior. Bem's **self-perception theory** is simple yet profound. To the extent that internal states are weak or difficult to interpret, people infer what they think or how they feel by observing their own behavior and the situation in which it takes place. Think about it. Have you ever listened to yourself argue with someone, only to realize with amazement how angry you were? Have you ever devoured a sandwich in record time, only then to conclude that you must have been incredibly hungry? In each case, you made an inference about yourself by watching your own actions.

There are limits to self-perception, of course. According to Bem, people do not infer their own internal states from behavior that occurred in the presence of compelling situational pressures such as reward or punishment. If you argued vehemently or wolfed down a sandwich because you were paid to do so, you probably would not assume that you were angry or hungry. In other words, people learn about themselves through self-perception only when the situation alone seems insufficient to have caused their behavior.

A good deal of research supports self-perception theory. When people are gently coaxed into doing something, and when they are not otherwise certain about how they feel, they come to view themselves in ways that are consistent with the behavior (Chaiken & Baldwin, 1981; Fazio, 1987; Schlenker & Trudeau, 1990). Thus, research participants induced to describe themselves in flattering terms scored higher on a later test of self-esteem than did those who were led to describe themselves more modestly (Jones et al., 1981; Rhodewalt & Agustsdottir, 1986). Similarly, those who were maneuvered by leading questions into describing themselves as introverted or extroverted— whether or not they really were— came to define themselves as such later on, unless they were certain of this aspect of their personality (Fazio et al., 1981; Swann & Ely, 1984). British author E. M. Forster anticipated the theory well when he asked, "How can I tell what I think 'til I see what I say?"

"I don't sing because I am happy. I am happy because I sing."

Self-Perceptions of Emotion   Draw the corners of your mouth back and up and tense your eye muscles. Okay, relax. Now raise your eyebrows, open your eyes wide, and let your mouth drop open slightly. Relax. Now pull your brows down and together and clench your teeth. Relax. If you followed these directions, you would have appeared to others to be feeling first happy, then fearful, and finally angry. The question is, How would you have appeared to yourself?

Social psychologists who study emotion have asked precisely that question. Viewed within the framework of self-perception theory, the **facial feedback hypothesis** states that changes in facial expression can trigger corresponding changes in the subjective experience of emotion. In the first test of this hypothesis, James Laird (1974) told participants that they were taking part in an experiment on activity of the facial muscles. After attaching electrodes to their faces, he showed them a series of cartoons. Before each one, the participants were instructed to contract certain facial muscles in ways that created either a smile or a frown. As Laird predicted, participants rated what they saw as funnier, and reported feeling

self-perception theory The theory that when internal cues are difficult to interpret, people gain self-insight by observing their own behavior.

facial feedback hypothesis The hypothesis that changes in facial expression can lead to corresponding changes in emotion.

happier, when they were smiling than when they were frowning. In follow-up research, people were similarly induced through posed expressions to experience fear, anger, sadness, and disgust (Duclos et al., 1989). Apparently, facial expressions—though not *necessary* for the experience of emotion—can evoke and magnify certain of our emotional states (McIntosh, 1996)

But why? With eighty muscles in the human face, which can create over 7,000 expressions, can we actually vary our own emotions by contracting certain muscles and wearing different expressions? Research suggests that we can, though it is not clear what the results mean. Laird argues that facial expressions affect emotion through a process of self-perception: "If I'm smiling, I must be happy." Consistent with this hypothesis, Chris Kleinke and his colleagues (1998) asked people to emulate either the happy or angry facial expressions that were depicted in a series of photographs. Half the participants saw themselves in a mirror during the task; the others did not. Did these manipulations affect mood states? Yes. Compared to participants in a no-expression control group, those who put on happy faces felt better—and those who put on angry faces felt worse. As predicted by self-perception theory, these differences were particularly pronounced among participants who saw themselves in a mirror.

Other researchers maintain that facial movements spark emotion by producing physiological changes in the brain (Izard, 1990). For example, Robert Zajonc (1993) argues that smiling causes facial muscles to increase the flow of air-cooled blood to the brain, a process that produces a pleasant state by lowering brain temperature. Conversely, frowning decreases blood flow, producing an unpleasant state by raising temperature. To demonstrate, Zajonc and his colleagues (1989) conducted a study in which they asked participants to repeat certain vowels twenty times each, including the sounds *ah*, *e*, *u*, and the German vowel *ü*. In the meantime, temperature changes in the forehead were measured and participants reported on how they felt. As it turned out, *ah* and *e* (sounds that cause people to mimic smiling) lowered forehead temperature and elevated mood, whereas *u* and *ü* (sounds that cause us to mimic frowning) increased temperature and dampened mood. In short, people need not infer how they feel. Rather, facial expressions evoke physiological changes that produce an emotional experience.

Other expressive behaviors, such as body posture, can also provide us with sensory feedback and influence the way we feel. When people feel proud, they stand erect with their shoulders raised, chest expanded, and head held high *(expansion)*. When dejected, however, people slump over with their shoulders drooping and head bowed *(contraction)*. Clearly, your emotional state is revealed in the way you carry yourself. But is it also possible that the way you carry yourself affects your emotional state? Can people lift their spirits by expansion or lower their spirits by contraction? Yes. Sabine Stepper and Fritz Strack (1993) arranged for people to sit in either a slumped or an upright position by varying the height of the table they had to write on. Those forced to sit upright reported feeling more pride after succeeding at a task than did those who were placed in a slumped position. In another study, participants who were instructed to lean forward with their fists clenched during the experiment reported feeling anger, while those who sat slumped with their heads down said they felt sadness (Duclos et al., 1989).

Emotional states can even be evoked by vocal cues. Research shows that people tend to speak quickly and raise their voices when fearful or anxious but to slow down and lower their voices when sad or depressed. Can the way you speak influence the way you feel? Aron Siegman and Stephen Boyle (1993) had research participants talk about experiences that had made them anxious or sad. For some events, they spoke at a normal rate; for others, they were instructed to speak either fast and loud or slow and soft. As predicted, speech style amplified the experience. Speaking fast and loud made participants more anxious when they talked about anxiety-related events, whereas speaking slow and soft made them feel sadder when they talked about sad events. Thus, our emotions can be influenced by sensory feedback from the voice as well as from the face and body.

Self-Perceptions of Motivation Without quite realizing it, Mark Twain was a self-perception theorist. In *The Adventures of Tom Sawyer*, written in the late 1800s, he quipped, "There are wealthy gentlemen in England who drive four-horse passenger coaches twenty or thirty miles on a daily line, in the summer, because the privilege costs them considerable money; but if they were offered wages for the service that would turn it into work then they would resign."

Twain's hypothesis—that reward for an enjoyable activity undermines interest in that activity—seems to contradict our intuition and a good deal of psychological research. After all, aren't we all motivated by reward, as declared by B. F. Skinner and other behaviorists? The answer depends on how *motivation* is defined.

As a keen observer of human behavior, Twain anticipated a key distinction between intrinsic and extrinsic motivation. *Intrinsic motivation* originates in factors within a person. People are said to be intrinsically motivated when they engage in an activity for the sake of their own interest, the challenge, or sheer enjoyment. Eating a fine meal, listening to music, spending time with friends, and having a hobby are among the activities that you might find intrinsically motivating. In contrast, *extrinsic motivation* originates in factors outside the person. People are said to be extrinsically motivated when they engage in an activity as a means to an end, for tangible benefits. It might be for money, grades, or recognition; to fulfill obligations; or to avoid punishment. As the behaviorists have always said, people do strive for reward. The question is, What happens to the intrinsic motivation once that reward is no longer available?

Posing in front of her paintings, ten-year-old Alexandra Nechita is a prodigy artist. At four, she spent hours at a time coloring with crayons. Now, with the help of an agent, her paintings are selling in galleries for thousands of dollars apiece. Looking ahead, one wonders: Will the pressure to paint for money diminish Alexandra's intrinsic love of art?

From the standpoint of self-perception theory, Twain's hypothesis makes sense. When someone is rewarded for listening to music, playing games, or eating tasty food, his or her behavior becomes *over*justified, or *over*rewarded, and can be attributed to extrinsic as well as intrinsic motives. This **overjustification effect** can be dangerous: Observing that their own efforts have paid off, people begin to wonder if the activity was ever worth pursuing in its own right.

Research shows that when people start getting "paid" for a task they already enjoy, they sometimes lose interest in it. In an early demonstration of this effect, Mark Lepper and others (1973) gave preschool children an opportunity to play with colorful felt-tipped markers—an opportunity most could not resist. By observing how much time the children spent on the activity, the researchers were able to measure their intrinsic motivation. Two weeks later, the children were divided into three groups, all about equal in terms of initial levels of intrinsic motivation. In one, the children were simply asked to draw some pictures with the markers. In the second, they were told that if they used the markers they would receive a "Good Player Award," a certificate with a gold star and a red ribbon. In a

overjustification effect
The tendency for intrinsic motivation to diminish for activities that have become associated with reward or other extrinsic factors.

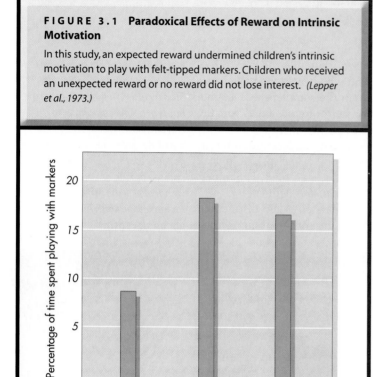

FIGURE 3.1 Paradoxical Effects of Reward on Intrinsic Motivation

In this study, an expected reward undermined children's intrinsic motivation to play with felt-tipped markers. Children who received an unexpected reward or no reward did not lose interest. *(Lepper et al., 1973.)*

third group, the children were not offered a reward for drawing pictures, but—like those in the second group—they received a reward when they were done.

About a week later, the teachers placed the markers and paper on a table in the classroom while the experimenters observed through a one-way mirror. Since no rewards were offered on this occasion, the amount of free time the children spent playing with the markers reflected their intrinsic motivation. As predicted, those children who had expected and received a reward for their efforts were no longer as interested in the markers as they had been. Children who had not received a reward were not adversely affected, nor were those who had unexpectedly received the reward. Having played with the markers without the promise of reward, these children remained intrinsically motivated (see Figure 3.1).

The paradox that reward can undermine rather than enhance intrinsic motivation has been observed in many settings and with both children and adults (Deci & Ryan, 1985; Enzle & Anderson, 1993; Pittman & Heller, 1987; Tang & Hall, 1995). Accept money for a leisure activity, and before you know it, what used to be "play" may come to feel more like "work." In the long run, this can have negative effects on the quality of performance. In a series of studies, Teresa Amabile (1996) and others had participants write poems, draw or paint pictures, make paper collages, and generate creative solutions to business dilemmas. Consistently, they found that people are more creative when they feel interested and challenged by the work itself than when they feel pressured to make money, fulfill obligations, meet deadlines, win competitions, or impress others. In one study, Amabile had art experts rate the works of professional artists and found that the artists' commissioned work (art they were contracted for) was judged as lower in quality than their noncommissioned work. People are likely to be more creative when they are intrinsically motivated in relation to the task, not compelled by outside forces.

But wait. If extrinsic benefits serve to undermine intrinsic motivation, should teachers and parents *not* offer rewards to their children? And are the employee incentive programs so often used in business doomed to fail, as some have suggested (Kohn, 1993)? It all depends on how the reward is perceived—and by whom. If a reward is presented in the form of verbal praise or as a special "bonus" for superior performance, then it can actually *enhance* intrinsic motivation by providing positive feedback about competence—as when people win competitions, earn scholarships, and receive other forms of recognition (Cameron & Pierce, 1994; Eisenberger & Cameron, 1996; Reeve & Deci, 1996).

Individual differences in motivational orientation toward work must also be considered. For intrinsically oriented people who say that "What matters most to me is enjoying what I do" and that "I seldom think about salary and promotions," reward may be unnecessary—and may even be detrimental (Amabile et al., 1994). Yet for those who tend to be focused on the achievement of specific goals, such extrinsic inducements as reward, game scores, and competition can have a positive effect on intrinsic motivation (Elliot & Harackiewicz, 1994; Harackiewicz & Elliot, 1993).

Influences of Other People

As we noted earlier, Cooley's (1902) theory of the looking-glass self emphasized that other people help us define ourselves. In this section, we will see the importance of this proposition to our self-concepts.

Social Comparison Theory   Suppose a stranger were to ask, "Who are you?" If you had only five minutes to answer, would you mention your ethnic or religious background? What about your hometown? Would you describe your talents and your interests or your likes and dislikes? When asked this question, people tend to describe themselves in ways that set them apart from others in their immediate environment (McGuire & McGuire, 1988). Among children, boys are more likely to cite their gender when they grow up in families that are predominantly female, and girls do the same when they live in families that are predominantly male (McGuire et al., 1979). On the college campus, "nontraditional" older students are more likely to mention their age than are traditional younger students (Kite, 1992). Regardless of whether the unique attribute is gender, age, height, or eye color, this pattern is basically the same. The implication is intriguing: Change someone's social surroundings, and you can change that person's spontaneous self-description.

This reliance on distinguishing features in self-description indicates that the self is a social construct and that we define ourselves in part by using others as a benchmark. Indeed, that is what Leon Festinger (1954) proposed in his **social comparison theory.** Festinger argued that when people are uncertain of their abilities or opinions—that is, when objective information is not readily available—they evaluate themselves through comparisons with similar others. The theory seems reasonable, but is it valid? Over the years, social psychologists have put social comparison theory to the test, focusing on two key questions: (1) *When* do we turn to others for comparative information? (2) Of all the people who inhabit the earth, *with whom* do we choose to compare ourselves? (Suls & Wills, 1991; Wood, 1989).

As Festinger proposed, the answer to the "when" question appears to be that people engage in social comparison in states of uncertainty, when more objective means of self-evaluation are not available. In fact, recent studies suggest that Festinger may have understated the role of social comparison processes—that people may judge themselves in relation to others even when more objective standards are available. For example, William Klein (1997) asked college students to make a series of judgments of artwork. Giving false feedback, he then told the students that 60 percent or 40 percent of their answers were correct—and that this was 20 percent higher or lower than the average among students. When they later rated their own skill at the task, participants were influenced not by their absolute scores, but by where they stood in relation to their peers. For them, it was better to have had a 40 percent score that was above average than a 60 percent score that was below average.

The "with whom" question has also been the subject of many studies. The answer seems to be that when we evaluate our own taste in music, value on the job market, or athletic ability, we look to others who are similar to us in relevant ways (Goethals & Darley, 1977; C. T. Miller, 1984; Wheeler et al., 1982)—a choice that we make automatically, without necessarily being aware of it (Gilbert et al., 1995). If you are curious about your flair for writing, for example, you're more likely to compare yourself with other college students than with high schoolers or best-selling authors. There are exceptions to this rule, of course. Later in the chapter, we will see that people often cope with personal inadequacies by focusing on others who are *less* able or *less* fortunate than themselves.

Two-Factor Theory of Emotion   People seek social comparison information to evaluate their abilities and opinions. Do we also turn to others to determine some-

social comparison theory
The theory that people evaluate their own abilities and opinions by comparing themselves to others.

thing as personal and subjective as our own emotions? In experiments on affiliation, Stanley Schachter (1959) found that when people were frightened into thinking they would receive painful electric shocks, most sought the company of others
who were in the same predicament. Nervous and uncertain about how they should
be feeling, participants wanted to affiliate with similar others, presumably for the
purpose of comparison. Yet when they were not fearful, and expected only mild
shocks, or when the "others" were not taking part in the same experiment, participants preferred to be alone. As Schachter put it, "Misery doesn't just love any kind
of company; it loves only miserable company" (p. 24).

Intrigued by the possibilities, Schachter and his research team took the next
step. Could it be, they wondered, that when people are uncertain of how they feel,
their emotional state is actually determined by the reactions of others around
them? In answer to this question, the researchers proposed that two factors are
necessary to feel a specific emotion. First, the person must experience physiological arousal—a racing heart, perspiration, rapid breathing, a tightening of the stomach. Second, the person must make a *cognitive interpretation* that explains the source
of the arousal. And that is where the people around us come in: Their reactions
help us interpret our own arousal.

To test this provocative **two-factor theory of emotion**, Schachter and Jerome
Singer (1962) injected male participants with epinephrine, a drug that produces
physiological arousal. Although one group was forewarned about the drug's effects,
a second group was not. Members of a third group were injected with a harmless
placebo. Before the drug (which was described as a vitamin supplement) actually
took effect, participants were left alone with a male confederate introduced as
another participant who had received the same injection. In some sessions, the
confederate behaved in a euphoric manner. For twenty minutes, he bounced
around happily, doodling on scratch paper, sinking jump shots into the wastebasket, flying paper airplanes across the room, and playing with a hula-hoop. In other
sessions, the confederate displayed anger, ridiculing a questionnaire they were filling out and, in a fit of rage, ripping it up and hurling it into the wastebasket.

Think for a moment about these various situations. As the drug takes effect,
participants in the *drug-informed* group begin to feel their hearts pound, their
hands shake, and their faces flush. Having been told to expect these symptoms,
however, they need not search for an explanation. Participants in the *placebo* group
do not become aroused in the first place, so they have no symptoms to explain. But
now consider the plight of those in the *drug-uninformed* group, who suddenly
become aroused without knowing why. Trying to identify the sensations, these participants, according to the theory, should take their cues from someone else in the
same predicament—namely, the confederate.

In general, the experimental results supported Schachter and Singer's line of
reasoning. Drug-uninformed participants reported feeling relatively happy or
angry depending on the confederate's performance. In many instances, they even
exhibited similar kinds of behavior. One participant, for example, "threw open the
window and, laughing, hurled paper basketballs at passersby." In the drug-
informed and placebo groups, however, participants were, as expected, less influenced by these social cues.

Schachter and Singer's two-factor theory has attracted a good deal of controversy, as some experiments have corroborated their findings but others have not.
Overall, however, one limited but important conclusion can safely be drawn: When
people are unclear about their own emotional states, they sometimes interpret how
they feel by watching others (Reisenzein, 1983). The "sometimes" part of the conclusion is important. For others to influence your emotion, your level of physiological arousal cannot be too intense, or else it will be experienced as
aversive—regardless of the situation (Maslach, 1979; Zimbardo et al., 1993). Also,
research shows that other people must be present as a possible explanation for

two-factor theory of emotion
The theory that the experience
of emotion is based on two
factors: physiological arousal
and a cognitive interpretation
of that arousal.

arousal *before* its onset. Once people are aroused, they turn for an explanation to events that preceded the change in their physiological state (Schachter & Singer, 1979; Sinclair et al., 1994).

In subsequent chapters, we will see that the two-factor theory of emotion has far-reaching implications for passionate love, anger and aggression, and other affective experiences.

Autobiographical Memories

Philosopher James Mill once said, "The phenomenon of the Self and that of Memory are merely two sides of the same fact." If the story of patient William Thompson at the start of this chapter is any indication, Mill was right. Without autobiographical memories—recollections of the sequences of events that have touched your life (Rubin, 1996)—you would have no coherent self-concept. Think about it. Who would you be if you could not remember your parents or childhood playmates, your successes and failures, the places you lived, the schools you attended, the books you read, and the teams you played for? Clearly, memories shape the self-concept. In this section, we'll see that the self-concept shapes our memories as well (Ross, 1989).

When people are prompted to recall their own experiences, they typically report more events from the recent than from the distant past. There are, however, two consistent exceptions to this recency rule. The first is that older adults retrieve a large number of personal memories from their adolescence and early adult years—a "reminiscence peak" that may occur because these years are busy and formative in one's life (Fitzgerald, 1988; Jansari & Parkin, 1996). A second exception is that people tend to remember transitional "firsts." Reflect for a moment on your college career. What events pop to mind—and when did they occur? Did you come up with the day you arrived on campus or the first time you met your closest friend? What about notable classes, parties, or sports events? When David Pillemer and others (1996) asked juniors and seniors to recount the most memorable experiences of their first year, 32 percent of all recollections were from the transitional month of September. When college graduates were given the same task, they too cited a disproportionate number of events from the opening two

Although adults recall more experiences from the recent than distance past, we retain many memories from late adolescence and early adulthood. These formative years are best captured by high-school yearbook photos—such as those of actors Sharon Stone and Tom Hanks.

months of their first year—followed, interestingly, by the next major transitional period, the last month of their senior year.

Obviously, not all experiences leave the same impression. Ask people old enough to remember November 22, 1963, and they probably can tell you exactly where they were, whom they were with, and what was happening the moment they heard the news that John F. Kennedy had been shot. Roger Brown and James Kulik (1977) coined the term *flashbulb memories* to describe these enduring, detailed, high-resolution recollections and speculated that humans are biologically equipped for survival purposes to "print" these dramatic events in memory. These flashbulb memories are not necessarily accurate, but they "feel" special and serve as prominent landmarks in the biographies we write about ourselves (Conway, 1995).

By linking the present to the past and providing us with a sense of inner continuity, autobiographical memory is a vital part of our identity. There are two ways in which memory is shaped by the self. First, people are motivated to distort the past in ways that are self-inflated, a tendency known as the **egocentric bias.** According to Anthony Greenwald (1980), "The past is remembered as if it were a drama in which the self was the leading player" (p. 604). To illustrate this bias at its best (or worst), let's turn the clock back to a momentous event in American history: the Senate Watergate hearings of 1973. The witness was John Dean, former counsel to President Richard Nixon. Dean had submitted a 245-page statement in which he recounted word for word the details of many conversations. Dean's memory seemed so impressive that he was called "the human tape recorder." But then, in an ironic twist of fate, investigators discovered that Nixon had taped the meetings that Dean recalled. Was Dean accurate? A comparison of his testimony with the actual tapes revealed that although he correctly remembered the gist of his White House meetings, he consistently exaggerated his own role and his own importance in the events. Ulric Neisser (1981), who analyzed Dean's testimony, wondered, "Are we all like this? Is everyone's memory constructed, staged, self-centered?" The answer is yes—there is a bit of John Dean in all of us. Thus, when college basketball players from opposing teams were asked to cite turning points in the games they played against each other, 80 percent of them referred to plays initiated by their own teams (Ross & Sicoly, 1979).

A second way in which autobiographical memory is shaped by the self is the **hindsight bias,** our tendency to think after an event that we knew beforehand what would happen. Historians are sometimes criticized for making the past seem inevitable in hindsight. Apparently, we all do. After learning a new fact or the outcome of some event—whether it's a drop in the stock market, the outcome of a trial, an earthquake, or the winner of the Super Bowl—people are quick to say, "I knew it all along" (Fischhoff, 1975; Hawkins & Hastie, 1990; Wood, 1978).

When it comes to autobiographical memory, 20/20 hindsight can lead people to revise their fading personal histories in ways that reflect favorably on the self. For example, George Goethals and Richard Reckman (1973) found that people whose attitudes about school busing were changed by a persuasive speaker later assumed that they had held their new attitude all along. Similarly, Michael Ross (1989) found that after people were persuaded by an expert who said that frequent tooth brushing was desirable, they reported in the context of a subsequent experiment having brushed more often in the previous two weeks. Illustrating that memory can be biased rather than objective, these participants "updated" the past in light of their new attitude. More recently, Bahrick and others (1996) had ninety-nine college students recall all of their high-school grades and then checked the accuracy of these reports against the actual transcripts. Overall, most grades were recalled correctly. But most of the errors in memory were grade *inflations*—and most of these were made when the actual grades were *low* (see Figure 3.2).

Contemplating the social ramifications of such findings, Ross (1989) suggested that our revisionist tendencies could account for why successive generations of parents bemoan how today's children are not as responsible as those who grew up in

FIGURE 3.2   Distortions in Memory of High School Grades

Students were asked to recall their high school grades, which were then checked against their actual transcripts. These comparisons revealed that most errors in memory were grade inflations. Lower grades were recalled with the least accuracy (and the most inflation). It appears that people sometimes revise their own past to suit their current self-image. *(Bahrick et al., 1996.)*

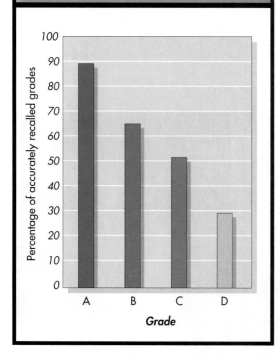

egocentric bias Bias toward perceiving and recalling oneself as a central actor in past events.

hindsight bias The tendency, once an event has occurred, to overestimate one's ability to have foreseen the outcome.

the good old days. According to Ross, adults do not compare the younger generation with what they themselves were like at a comparable age. Instead, adults for-
getfully assume that they used to be as they are in the present. By comparison, the
next generation is sure to appear deficient. From his studies of adult development,
psychiatrist George Vaillant (1977) drew a similar conclusion: "It is all too common for caterpillars to become butterflies and then to maintain that in their youth
they had been little butterflies. Maturation makes liars of us all" (p. 197).

Reflecting an interdependent *view of the self, children in Japan are taught to fit in to the community. Reflecting a more* independent *view of the self, children in the United States are encouraged to express their individuality.*

Cultural Perspectives

The self-concept is also influenced by cultural factors. In America, it is said that
"the squeaky wheel gets the grease." In Japan, it is said that "the nail that stands out
gets pounded down." In America, parents tell their children to be independent,
self-reliant, and assertive, a "cut above the rest." In Japan, children are raised to fit
into the community.

   These differences illustrate two cultural orientations. One values *individualism*
and the virtues of independence, autonomy, and self-reliance. The other values *collectivism* and the virtues of interdependence, cooperation, and social harmony.
Under the banner of individualism, personal goals take priority over group allegiances. In collectivist cultures, however, the person is, first and foremost, a loyal
member of a family, team, company, church, and state (Triandis, 1994). In what
countries are these contrasting orientations the most extreme? In a worldwide
study of 116,000 employees of IBM, Geert Hofstede (1980) found that the most
fiercely individualistic people were from the United States, Australia, Great
Britain, Canada, and the Netherlands, in that order. The most collectivist people
were from Venezuela, Colombia, Pakistan, Peru, Taiwan, and China.

   Individualism and collectivism are so deeply ingrained in a culture that they
mold our very self-conceptions and identities. According to Hazel Markus and Shi-
nobu Kitayama (1991), most North Americans and Europeans have an *independent*
view of the self. In this view, the self is an entity that is distinct, autonomous, self-
contained, and endowed with unique dispositions. Yet in much of Asia, Africa, and
Latin America, people hold an *interdependent* view of the self. Here, the self is part
of a larger social network that includes one's family, co-workers, and others with
whom one is socially connected. People with an independent view say that "the
only person you can count on is yourself" and "I enjoy being unique and different
from others." In contrast, those with an interdependent view are more likely to
agree that "I'm partly to blame if one of my family members or co-workers fails"
and "my happiness depends on the happiness of those around me" (Rhee et al.,

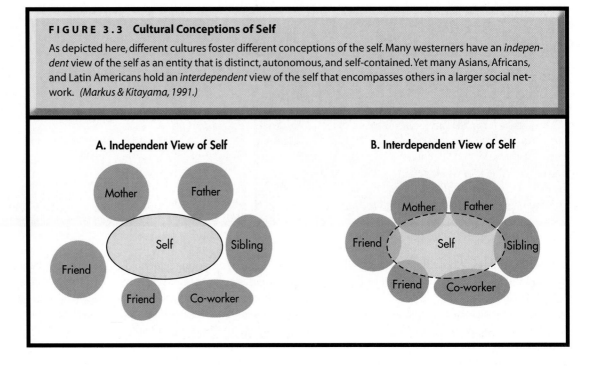

FIGURE 3.3   Cultural Conceptions of Self

As depicted here, different cultures foster different conceptions of the self. Many westerners have an *independent* view of the self as an entity that is distinct, autonomous, and self-contained. Yet many Asians, Africans, and Latin Americans hold an *interdependent* view of the self that encompasses others in a larger social network. *(Markus & Kitayama, 1991.)*

1995; Singelis, 1994; Triandis, 1995). These contrasting orientations are depicted in Figure 3.3.

Research confirms that there is a close link between cultural orientation and conceptions of the self. David Trafimow and his colleagues (1991) had North American and Chinese college students complete twenty sentences beginning with "I am. . . ." The Americans were more likely to fill in the blank with trait descriptions ("I am shy"), whereas the Chinese were more likely to identify themselves by group affiliations ("I am a college student"). It's no wonder that in China, one's family name comes *before* one's personal name. Similar differences are found between Australians and Malaysians (Bochner, 1994).

How do these cultural orientations influence the way we perceive, evaluate, and present ourselves in relation to others? Markus and Kitayama (1991) report on three interesting differences. First, American college students see themselves as less similar to others than do Asian Indian students, reinforcing the idea that people with independent conceptions of the self believe that they are unique. Second, Americans are more likely to express jealousy, pride, and other "ego-focused" emotions that affirm the self as an autonomous entity, whereas non-westerners experience more "other-focused" emotions that foster social harmony. In Japan, for example, people often report feelings of *oime* (indebtedness to someone), *fureai* (connection with someone), and *shitashimi* (familiarity to someone). Third, people in individualistic cultures strive for personal achievement, while those living in collectivist cultures derive more satisfaction from the status of a valued group. Thus, North Americans overestimate their own contributions to a team effort, take credit for success, and blame others for failure, whereas people from collectivist cultures tend to underestimate their own role and present themselves in more modest, self-effacing terms (Kitayama et al., 1997). In a study that illustrates this point, Steven Heine and Darrin Lehman (1995) had students from Canada and Japan estimate the odds that certain positive and negative events would happen to them and to their peers. The result: Canadian students saw themselves, relative to their peers, as more likely to undergo the positive events and less likely to experience the negatives. But Japanese students rated themselves and peers as equally likely to experience the two types of events.

So, are people from disparate cultures locked into thinking about the self in either personal or collective terms? Or are both aspects of the self present in everyone, to be expressed according to the situation? Consider again the study noted above, where American students described themselves more in terms of personal traits and Chinese students cited more group affiliations. In a fascinating follow-up, Trafimow and his colleagues (1997) tested students from Hong Kong, all of whom spoke English as a second language. One half of the students were given the "Who am I?" test in Chinese, and the other half took the test in English. Did this variation influence the results? Look at Figure 3.4, and you'll see that among these students those who took the test in English focused more on personal traits, while those who took the test in Chinese focused more on group affiliations. Perhaps all of us have both personal and collective aspects of the self to draw on, and the part that comes to mind depends on the situation we are in.

If there are cultural influences on conceptions of the self, it stands to reason that there are also individual variations within a culture. For example, research conducted in North America indicates that men are more likely to derive a positive self-image from fulfilling the goals of independence and autonomy, while women define themselves somewhat more by their social connections (Cross & Madson, 1997; Josephs et al., 1992). As we'll see in subsequent chapters, these differing representations of the self can help explain the differences often observed between men and women in various aspects of our social lives.

Self-Schemas

Thus far, we have seen that people learn about themselves through introspection, by observing their own behavior, by comparing themselves with others, and by organizing their autobiographical memories. We have also seen that culture influences the way people see themselves in relation to others. But what, specifically, does the self-concept consist of, and how does it affect our views of the world?

According to Hazel Markus (1977), the self-concept is made up of cognitive molecules called **self-schemas:** beliefs about oneself that guide the processing of self-relevant information. Self-schemas are to an individual's total self-concept what hypotheses are to a theory, or what books are to a library. You can think of yourself as masculine or feminine, as independent or dependent, as liberal or conservative, as introverted or extroverted. Indeed, any specific attribute may have relevance to the self-concept for some people but not for others. The self-schema for body weight is a good example. People who regard themselves as extremely overweight or underweight, or for whom body image is a conspicuous aspect of the self-concept, are considered *schematic* with respect to weight. In contrast, those who do not regard their own weight as extreme or as an important part of their lives are *aschematic* on that attribute (Markus et al., 1987).

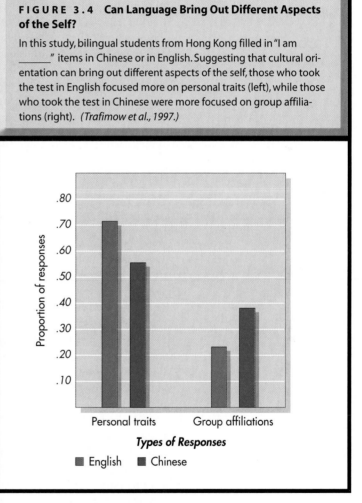

FIGURE 3.4 Can Language Bring Out Different Aspects of the Self?

In this study, bilingual students from Hong Kong filled in "I am _____" items in Chinese or in English. Suggesting that cultural orientation can bring out different aspects of the self, those who took the test in English focused more on personal traits (left), while those who took the test in Chinese were more focused on group affiliations (right). *(Trafimow et al., 1997.)*

self-schemas Beliefs people hold about themselves that guide the processing of self-relevant information.

Self-schemas are important because they lead us to interpret and recall our life experiences according to personally relevant themes. For body-weight schematics, a wide range of otherwise mundane events—a trip to the supermarket, new clothing, dinner at a restaurant, a day at the beach, or a friend's eating habits—may trigger self-relevant thoughts. When processing information, people (1) make rapid judgments about themselves on matters relevant to self-schemas, (2) are quick to notice, recall, or reconstruct past events that fit their own self-schemas, and (3) reject information that is inconsistent with their self-schemas (Kihlstrom & Cantor, 1984). People often view others through the lens of their self-schemas as well. Body-weight schematics, for example, always seem to notice whenever someone else eats too much or gains another pound.

Consisting of many self-schemas, the self is multifaceted. In fact, people tend to think not only about their current selves but also about *possible selves*—what they might become, would like to become, and are afraid of becoming in the future. Thus, when college students were asked to rate themselves on a list of attributes, there were marked differences between current views of the self and possible selves. Most imagined possibilities were in a positive direction, as students could see themselves becoming good parents, happy, physically fit, well-respected, secure, and successful (Markus & Nurius, 1986). Conceptions of possible selves provide us with an imaginary blueprint for future goals and plans (Ruvolo & Markus, 1992).

Self-Esteem

How do you feel about yourself? Are you generally satisfied with your appearance, personality, abilities, and friendships? Are you optimistic about your future? When it comes to the self, people are hardly cool, objective, dispassionate observers. Rather, we are judgmental, emotional, and highly protective of our **self-esteem**—an affectively charged component of the self.

The word *esteem* comes from the Latin *aestimare*, which means "to estimate or appraise." Self-esteem thus refers to our positive and negative evaluations of ourselves (Coopersmith, 1967). Some individuals have higher self-esteem than others do—and this attribute can have a profound impact on the way they think and feel about themselves. It is important to keep in mind, however, that although some people have higher self-esteem than others, a feeling of self-worth is not a single trait etched permanently in stone. Rather, it is a state of mind that varies in response to success, failure, changes in fortune, social interactions, and other life experiences (Heatherton & Polivy, 1991). People who have an unstable, fluctuating self-esteem react more strongly to positive and negative events than do people whose sense of self-worth is stable and secure (Kernis & Wascholl, 1995). Also, because the self-concept is made up of many self-schemas, individuals typically view parts of the self differently: Some parts they judge more favorably, or see more clearly or as more important, than other parts (Fleming & Courtney, 1984; Pelham, 1995; Pelham & Swann, 1989).

The Need for Self-Esteem

self-esteem An affective component of the self, consisting of a person's positive and negative self-evaluations.

You and just about everyone else on the planet has a need for self-esteem, as you want to see yourself in a positive light. This observation about human motivation is beyond dispute. But let's step back for a moment and ask, Why? Why do we have this need for self-esteem?

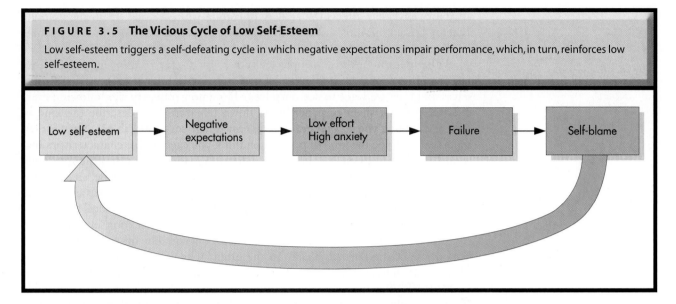

FIGURE 3.5 The Vicious Cycle of Low Self-Esteem
Low self-esteem triggers a self-defeating cycle in which negative expectations impair performance, which, in turn, reinforces low self-esteem.

At present, there are two social psychological answers to this question. One theory, proposed by Mark Leary and his colleagues (1995), is that people are inherently social animals and that the need for self-esteem is driven by this more primitive need to connect with others and gain their approval. Our self-esteem thus serves as an indicator of how we are doing in the eyes of others. A second theory, proposed by Jeff Greenberg, Sheldon Solomon, and Tom Pyszczynski (1997), is that people are motivated to see themselves as valuable members of society as a way of coping with a deeply rooted fear of death that privately haunts us all. In a series of experiments, these investigators found that after participants were given positive feedback that boosted their self-esteem, they reacted to graphic scenes of death, or to the thought of their own death, with less defensiveness and anxiety.

In many ways, satisfying the need for self-esteem is critical to our entire outlook on life. People with positive self-images tend to be happy, healthy, productive, and successful. They tend to persist longer at difficult tasks, sleep better at night, and have fewer ulcers. They are also more accepting of others and less likely to conform to peer pressure. In contrast, people with negative self-images are more anxious, depressed, pessimistic about the future, and prone to failure (Brown, 1991).

People high in self-esteem are confident and bring to new challenges a winning and motivating attitude. In contrast, people low in self-esteem lack confidence and bring to new tasks a losing attitude that traps them in a vicious, self-defeating cycle (see Figure 3.5). Expecting to fail, and fearing the worst, they become anxious, exert less effort, and "tune out" on important challenges. Then, when they do fail, people with low self-esteem often blame themselves, which makes them feel even less competent (Brockner, 1983; Brown & Dutton, 1995). Low self-esteem may even be bad for one's health. Some research suggests that becoming aware of one's own negative

attributes adversely affects the activity of certain white blood cells in the immune system, thus compromising the body's capacity to ward off disease (Strauman et al., 1993).

What determines how people feel about themselves? According to E. Tory Higgins (1989), our self-esteem is defined by the match between how we see ourselves and how we want to see ourselves. To demonstrate, try the following exercise. On a blank sheet of paper, write down ten traits that describe the kind of person you think you *actually* are (smart? easygoing? sexy? excitable?). Next, list ten traits that describe the kind of person you think you *ought* to be, characteristics that would enable you to meet your sense of duty, obligation, and responsibility. Then make a list of traits that describe an *ideal* of what you would like to be, an ideal that embodies your hopes, wishes, and dreams. If you follow these instructions, you should have three lists—your actual self, your ought self, and your ideal self.

Research has shown that these lists can be used to predict your self-esteem and emotional well-being. The first list is your self-concept. The others represent your personal standards, or *self-guides*. To the extent that you fall short of these standards, you will have a lowered self-esteem, negative emotion, and in extreme cases a serious affective disorder. The specific consequence depends on which self-guide you fail to achieve. If there's a discrepancy between your actual and ought selves, you will feel guilty, ashamed, and resentful. You might even suffer from excessive fears and anxiety-related disorders. If the mismatch is between your actual and ideal selves, you'll feel disappointed, frustrated, sad, and unfulfilled. In extreme cases, you might even become depressed (Scott & O'Hara, 1993; Strauman, 1992).

It's clear that every one of us must cope with some degree of self-discrepancy. Nobody is perfect. Yet we do not all suffer from the emotional consequences. The reason, according to Higgins, is that self-esteem depends on two factors. The first is simply the amount of discrepancy. The more of it there is, the worse we feel. The second factor is the extent to which we focus on these self-discrepancies. The more focused we are, the greater the harm. This second factor raises an important question: What makes us more or less focused on our personal shortcomings? For an answer, we turn to self-awareness theory.

The Self-Awareness "Trap"

If you carefully review your daily routine—classes, work, chores at home, leisure activities, social interactions, and meals—you will probably be surprised at how little time you actually spend thinking about yourself. In a study that illustrates this point, more than a hundred people, ranging in age from nineteen to sixty-three, were equipped for a week with electronic beepers that sounded every two hours or so between 7:30 A.M. and 10:30 P.M. Each time the beepers went off, participants interrupted whatever they were doing, wrote down what they were thinking at that moment, and filled out a brief questionnaire. Out of 4,700 observations, only 8 percent of all recorded thoughts were about the self. For the most part, attention was focused on work and other activities. In fact, when participants were thinking about themselves, they reported feeling relatively unhappy and wished they were doing something else (Csikszentmihalyi & Figurski, 1982).

Self-Focusing Situations   The finding that people may be unhappy when they are thinking about themselves is interesting, but what does it mean? Does self-reflection bring out our personal shortcomings the way staring into a mirror draws our gaze to every blemish on the face? Is self-awareness an unpleasant mental state from which we need to retreat?

Robert Wicklund and others believe that the answer is yes (Duval & Wicklund, 1972; Wicklund, 1975; Wicklund & Frey, 1980). According to their

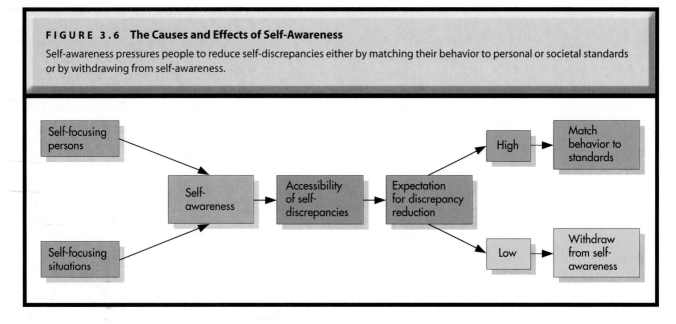

FIGURE 3.6 The Causes and Effects of Self-Awareness
Self-awareness pressures people to reduce self-discrepancies either by matching their behavior to personal or societal standards or by withdrawing from self-awareness.

self-awareness theory, people are not usually self-focused, but certain situations predictably force us to turn inward and become the objects of our own attention. When we talk about ourselves, glance in a mirror, stand before an audience or camera, watch ourselves on videotape, or behave in a conspicuous manner, we enter a state of heightened self-awareness that leads us naturally to compare our behavior to some standard. This comparison often results in a negative discrepancy and a temporary reduction in self-esteem as we discover that we fall short. Thus, people often experience a negative mood state when placed in front of a mirror (Hass & Eisenstadt, 1990). In fact, the more self-absorbed people are in general, the more likely they are to suffer from alcoholism, depression, anxiety, and other clinical disorders (Ingram, 1990).

Is there a solution? Self-awareness theory suggests that there are essentially two ways to cope with such discomfort: (1) "shape up" by behaving in ways that reduce our self-discrepancies or (2) "ship out" by withdrawing from self-awareness. According to Charles Carver and Michael Scheier (1981), the solution chosen depends on whether people think they can reduce their self-discrepancy—and whether they're pleased with the progress they make once they try (Duval et al., 1992). If so, they tend to match their behavior to personal or societal standards; if not, they tune out, look for distractions, and turn attention away from the self. This process is depicted in Figure 3.6.

In general, research supports the prediction that when people are self-focused, they tend to behave in ways that are consistent either with their own personal values or with socially accepted ideals (Gibbons, 1990). In an interesting field study, for example, Halloween trick-or-treaters—children wearing masks, costumes, and painted faces—were greeted at a researcher's door and left alone to help themselves from a bowl of candy. Although the children were asked to take only one piece, 34 percent violated the request. When a full-length mirror was placed behind the candy bowl, however, the number of violators dropped to 12 percent. Apparently, the mirror forced the children to become self-focused, leading them to behave in a way that was consistent with public standards of desirable conduct (Beaman et al., 1979). In another study that illustrates this positive effect of self-awareness, C. Neil Macrae and his colleagues (1998) found that participants were less likely than normal to use stereotypes in describing others—a social taboo known to us all—when they were seated in front of a mirror, when they could see themselves on a TV monitor, or when their names were flashed briefly on a screen.

"I have the true feeling of myself only when I am unbearably unhappy."

—Franz Kafka

self-awareness theory
The theory that self-focused attention leads people to notice self-discrepancies, thereby motivating either an escape from self-awareness or a change in behavior.

Self-awareness theory states that if a successful reduction of self-discrepancy seems unlikely, individuals will take a second route: escape from self-awareness. Roy Baumeister (1991) speculates that drug abuse, sexual masochism, spiritual ecstasy, binge eating, and even suicide all serve this escapist function. One disturbing health implication thus concerns the use of alcohol. According to Jay Hull, people often drown their sorrows in a bottle as a way to escape the negative implications of self-awareness. To test this hypothesis, Hull and Richard Young (1983) administered what was supposed to be an IQ test to male participants and gave false feedback suggesting that they had either succeeded or failed. Supposedly as part of a separate study, those participants were then asked to taste and rate different wines. As they did so, experimenters kept track of how much they drank during a fifteen-minute tasting period. As predicted, participants who were prone to self-awareness drank more wine after failure than after success, presumably to dodge the blow to their self-esteem. Among participants not prone to self-awareness, there was no difference in alcohol consumption. Similar results were obtained in a study of men hospitalized for alcoholism and released. After three months, those who were both self-conscious and under stress were the most likely to relapse into heavy drinking (Hull et al., 1986). These results come as no surprise. Indeed, many of us expect alcohol to grant this form of relief (Leigh & Stacy, 1993) and help us manage our emotional highs and lows (Cooper et al., 1995).

Claude Steele and Robert Josephs (1990) believe that alcoholic intoxication provides more than just a means of tuning out on the self. By causing people to lose touch with reality and shed their inhibitions, it also evokes a state of "drunken self-inflation." In one study, for example, participants rated their actual and ideal selves on various traits—some important to self-esteem, others not important. After drinking either an 80-proof vodka cocktail or a harmless placebo, they re-rated themselves on the same traits. As measured by the perceived discrepancy between actual and ideal selves, participants who were drinking expressed inflated views of themselves on traits they considered important (Banaji & Steele, 1989).

Self-Focusing Persons Just as *situations* evoke a state of self-awareness, certain *individuals* are characteristically more self-focused than others. Research has revealed an important distinction between **private self-consciousness**—the tendency to introspect about our inner thoughts and feelings—and **public self-consciousness**—the tendency to focus on our outer public image (Buss, 1980; Fenigstein et al., 1975). Table 3.1 presents a sample of items used to measure these traits.

Private and public self-consciousness are distinct traits. People who score high on a test of private self-consciousness tend to fill in incomplete sentences with first-person pronouns, are quick to make self-descriptive statements, and are acutely aware of changes in their internal bodily states (Mueller, 1982; Scheier et al., 1979). In contrast, those who score high on a measure of public self-consciousness are sensitive to the way they are viewed from an outsider's perspective. Thus, when people were asked to draw a capital letter E on their foreheads, 43 percent of those with high levels of public self-consciousness, compared with only 6 percent of those with low levels, oriented the E so that it was backward from their own standpoint but correct for an outside observer (Hass, 1984). People who are high in public self-consciousness are also particularly sensitive to the extent to which others share their opinions (Fenigstein & Abrams, 1993).

T A B L E   3 . 1   How Self-Conscious Are You?

These sample items appear in the Self-Consciousness Scale. How would you describe yourself on the public and the private aspects of self-consciousness? *(Fenigstein et al., 1975.)*

Items That Measure Private Self-Consciousness

- I'm always trying to figure myself out.
- I'm constantly examining my motives.
- I'm often the subject of my fantasies.
- I'm alert to changes in my mood.
- I'm aware of the way my mind works when I work on a problem.

Items That Measure Public Self-Consciousness

- I'm concerned about what other people think of me.
- I'm self-conscious about the way I look.
- I'm concerned about the way I present myself.
- I usually worry about making a good impression.
- One of the last things I do before leaving my house is look in the mirror.

---

private self-consciousness
A personality characteristic of individuals who are introspective, often attending to their own inner states.

public self-consciousness
A personality characteristic of individuals who focus on themselves as social objects, as seen by others.

The distinction between private and public self-awareness has implications for the ways in which we reduce self-discrepancies. According to Higgins (1989), people are motivated to meet either their own standards or the standards held for them by significant others. If you're privately self-conscious, you listen to an inner voice and try to reduce discrepancies relative to your own standards; if you're publicly self-conscious, however, you try to match your behavior to socially accepted norms. As illustrated in Figure 3.7 there may be "two sides of the self: one for you and one for me" (Scheier & Carver, 1983, p. 123).

Ironic Effects of Self-Control   Up to this point, we have seen that self-focused attention can motivate people to control their behavior and strive toward personal or social ideals. But there's a possible downside to self-awareness that is often seen in sports, when athletes become so self-focused under pressure that they stiffen up and "choke." Indeed, controlled studies have shown that being self-conscious—say, by thinking about one's limbs, bodily position, or breathing—can disrupt the smooth and natural flow of athletic performance (Baumeister, 1984; Lewis & Linder, 1997).

The paradoxical effects of attempted self-control are evident in other situations, too. Studying what he calls *ironic processes*, Daniel Wegner (1994) has found that, at times, the harder you try to inhibit a thought, feeling, or behavior, the less likely you are to succeed. Try not to think about a white bear for the next thirty seconds, he finds, and that very image intrudes upon consciousness with remarkable frequency. Instruct a jury to disregard an item of evidence, and the censored material is sure to pop to mind as they deliberate. Try not to worry about how long it's taking to fall asleep, and you'll stay awake. Try not to laugh in class, think about the chocolate cake in the fridge, or scratch the itch on your nose—well, you get the idea.

According to Wegner, every conscious effort at maintaining control is met by a concern about failing to do so. This concern automatically triggers an "ironic operating process" as the person, trying hard *not* to fail, searches his or her mind for the unwanted thought. The ironic process will not necessarily prevail, says Wegner. Sometimes we can put the imaginary white bear out of mind. But if the person is cognitively busy, distracted, tired, hurried, or under stress, then the ironic process, because it "just happens," will prevail over the intentional process—which requires conscious attention and effort. Thus, Wegner (1997) notes that "any attempt at mental control contains the seeds of its own undoing" (p. 148).

FIGURE 3.7 Revolving Images of Self
According to self-awareness theory, people try to meet either their own standards or standards held for them by others—depending, perhaps, on whether they are in a state of private or public self-consciousness. As Scheier and Carver (1983, p. 123) put it, there are "two sides of the self: one for you and one for me." *(Snyder et al., 1983.)*

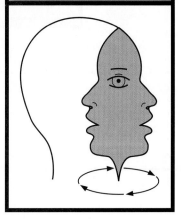

"The highest possible stage in moral culture is when we recognize that we ought to control our thoughts."

—Charles Darwin

At age twenty-one, Tiger Woods became the youngest golfer to win the coveted Masters Tournament—and broke the course record. Woods was called the greatest golfer ever. Yet soon he was struggling like never before. Why? Could it be that being under the spotlight of high expectations caused Woods to become self-conscious—and choke under the pressure?

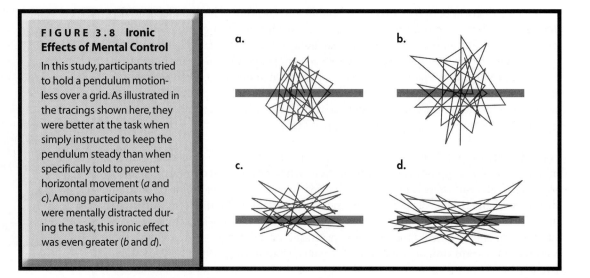

FIGURE 3.8 Ironic Effects of Mental Control

In this study, participants tried to hold a pendulum motionless over a grid. As illustrated in the tracings shown here, they were better at the task when simply instructed to keep the pendulum steady than when specifically told to prevent horizontal movement (*a* and *c*). Among participants who were mentally distracted during the task, this ironic effect was even greater (*b* and *d*).

Sometimes the harder you try to control a thought, feeling, or behavior, the less likely you are to succeed. **True.**

"We don't see things as they are, we see them as we are."

—Anaïs Nin

Ironic processes have now been observed in a wide range of behaviors. In an intriguing study of this effect on the control of motor behavior, Wegner and his colleagues (1998) had participants hold a pendulum (a crystalline pendant suspended from a nylon fishing line) over the center of two intersecting axes on a glass grid, which formed a +. Some participants were instructed simply to keep the pendulum steady, while others were more specifically told not to allow it to swing back and forth along the horizontal axis. Try this yourself, and you'll see that it's not easy to prevent all movement. In this experiment, however, the pendulum was more likely to swing horizontally when this direction was specifically forbidden. To further examine the role of mental distraction, the researchers instructed some participants to count backward from a thousand by sevens while controlling the pendulum. In this situation, the ironic effect was even greater. Among those who specifically tried to prevent horizontal movement but could not concentrate fully on the task, the pendulum swayed freely back and forth—in the forbidden direction (see Figure 3.8). Using a similar method, these researchers found that people were most likely to overshoot a golf putt when they specifically tried *not* to overshoot but were distracted while putting. It may seem both comic and tragic, but at times our efforts at self-control backfire, thwarting even the best of intentions.

Mechanisms of Self-Enhancement

We have seen that self-awareness can create discomfort and lower self-esteem by focusing attention on discrepancies. People often avoid focusing on themselves and turn away from unpleasant truths, but such avoidance is not always possible. How, then, does the average person cope with his or her faults, inadequacies, and uncertain future?

Let's begin with a stark fact about human behavior. Most people, most of the time, think highly of themselves. Consistently, research has shown that participants see positive traits as more self-descriptive than negative ones, rate themselves more highly than they rate others, rate themselves more highly than they are rated *by* others, overestimate their contribution to team efforts, exaggerate their control over life events, and predict that they have a bright future (Taylor, 1989). People also evaluate their own personality traits as being more desirable than traits that are not self-descriptive (Dunning et al., 1991). Illustrating the "mere ownership effect," people even rate the letters in their name more favorably than the other letters of the alphabet (Hoorens & Nuttin, 1993) and judge various consumer products that they own as better than comparable products they do not own (Beggan, 1992).

It's not that we consciously or openly flatter ourselves. The response is more like a reflex. Indeed, when research people are busy or distracted as they make self-ratings, their judgments are quicker and even more favorable (Hixon & Swann, 1993; Paulhus et al., 1989). We can't all be perfect, nor can we all be better than average. So what supports this common illusion? In this section, we examine four methods that people use to rationalize or otherwise enhance their self-esteem: self-serving cognitions, self-handicapping, basking in the glory of others, and downward social comparisons.

Self-Serving Cognitions How well did you do on the Scholastic Assessment Test (SAT)? James Shepperd (1993b) asked college students about their performance on this infamous test and uncovered two interesting patterns. First, the students over-estimated their actual scores by an average of 17 points. This inflationary distortion was most pronounced among those with relatively low scores, and it persisted somewhat even when students knew that the experimenter would check their academic files. Second, a majority of students whose SAT scores were low described their scores as inaccurate and the test in general as invalid. In fact, the SATs for the group as a whole were predictive of their grade point averages.

When students receive exam grades, those who do well take credit for their success; those who do poorly complain about the instructor and the test questions. When researchers have articles accepted for publication, they credit the quality of their work; when articles are rejected, they blame the editor and reviewers. When gamblers win a bet, they see themselves as skillful; when they lose, they moan and groan about fluke events that transformed near victory into defeat. Whether people are high or low in self-esteem, explain their outcomes publicly or in private, and try to be honest or to make a good impression, there is bias: People tend to take credit for success and distance themselves from failure (Schlenker et al., 1990).

People are also unrealistically optimistic. Students who were asked to predict their own future compared with that of the average person believed that they would graduate higher in their class, get a better job, have a happier marriage, and bear a gifted child. They also believed they were less likely to get fired or divorced, have a car accident, become depressed, or suffer from a heart attack (Weinstein, 1980). There are many other examples as well. Polls taken between 1952 and 1980 revealed that, by a 4-to-1 ratio, American voters—regardless of whether they supported the ultimate winner or loser—expected their candidate to prevail (Granberg & Brent, 1983). Similarly, sports fans often let their team preferences interfere with the bets they place, even when they are trying to be "objective" (Babad & Katz, 1991).

Obviously, the future is not always bright, so what supports this unwavering optimism? Ziva Kunda (1987) finds that people bolster their rosy outlook with elaborate theories that link their personal attributes to desirable outcomes. In one study, for example, people who had been involved in a serious high school relationship said they believed that such an experience promotes a stable marriage. Yet those who had

In casinos, racetracks, and lotteries, people lose billions of dollars a year in gambling. This self-defeating behavior persists in part because people exaggerate their control over random events and then make excuses for their losses.

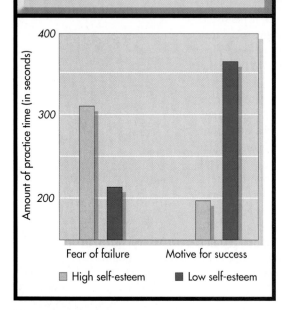

FIGURE 3.9   Self-Handicapping: To Protect or Enhance Self-Esteem?

Participants worked on a task that supposedly measured intelligence. When participants were focused on succeeding, those with high self-esteem practiced less. When participants were led to become fearful of failure, those with low self-esteem practiced less. This pattern suggests that self-handicapping is a face-saving defense against failure for people low in self-esteem and an opportunity for enhancement through success for those high in self-esteem. *(Tice, 1991.)*

People tend to be overly optimistic about their future.

True.

self-handicapping Behaviors designed to sabotage one's own performance in order to provide a subsequent excuse for failure.

not been romantically involved said they believed that a *lack* of experience promotes a happy-ever-after ending. It is no wonder that the participants in Kunda's study predicted that there was only a 20 percent chance that their own future marriages would end in divorce—despite knowing that the population divorce rate is 50 percent.

Self-Handicapping   "My dog ate my homework." "I had a flat tire." "My alarm didn't go off." "My computer crashed." "I had a bad headache." On occasion, people make excuses for past performance. Sometimes we come up with excuses in anticipation of future performance as well. Particularly when people are afraid that they might fail in an important situation, they use illness, shyness, anxiety, pain, trauma, and other complaints as excuses (Kowalski, 1996; Snyder & Higgins, 1988). Why? By admitting to a limited physical or mental weakness, we can shield ourselves from what could be the most shattering implication of failure—a lack of ability.

Making verbal excuses is one way to cope with the threatening implications of failure. Under certain conditions, this strategy is taken one step further: People actually sabotage their own performance. It seems like the ultimate paradox, but there are times when people purposely set themselves up for failure in order to preserve their self-esteem (Higgins et al., 1990).

First described by Stephen Berglas and Edward Jones (1978), **self-handicapping** refers to actions people take to handicap their own performance in order to build an excuse for anticipated failure. To demonstrate, Berglas and Jones recruited college students for an experiment supposedly involving the effects of drugs on intellectual performance. All participants worked on a twenty-item test of analogies and were told that they had done well, after which they expected to work on a second, similar test. For one group, the problems in the first test were relatively easy, leading participants to expect more success in the second test; for a second group, the problems were insoluble, leaving participants confused about their initial success and worried about possible failure. Before seeing or taking the second test, participants were given a choice of two drugs: Actavil, which was supposed to improve performance, and Pandocrin, which was supposed to impair it.

Although no drugs were actually administered, most participants who were confident about the upcoming test selected the Actavil. In contrast, males—but not females—who feared the outcome of the second test chose the Pandocrin. By handicapping themselves, these men set up a convenient excuse for failure—an excuse, we should add, that may have been intended more for the experimenter's benefit than for the benefit of the participants themselves. Indeed, a follow-up study showed that although self-handicapping occurs when the experimenter witnesses the participants' drug choice, it is reduced when the experimenter is not present while that choice is being made (Kolditz & Arkin, 1982).

Some people use self-handicapping as a defense more than others do (Rhodewalt, 1990)—and there are different ways to use it. For example, men often handicap themselves by taking drugs (Higgins & Harris, 1988), neglecting to practice (Hirt et al., 1991), and giving a performance enhancer to their rival (Shepperd & Arkin, 1991). Women instead tend to report stress and physical symptoms (Hirt et al., 1991; Smith et al., 1983). People also differ in their reasons for self-handicapping. Dianne Tice (1991) found that people who are low in self-esteem use self-handicapping to set up a defensive, face-saving excuse in case they fail, while those who are high in self-esteem use it as an opportunity to claim extra credit if they succeed (see Figure 3.9). Other researchers have also found this difference in orientation (Rhodewalt et al., 1991; J. V. Wood et al., 1994).

Whatever the goal, self-handicapping seems like an ingenious strategy: With the odds stacked against us, the self is insulated from failure and enhanced by success. By easing the pressure to succeed, it might even enable us to enjoy what we're doing without worrying so much about performance (Deppe & Harackiewicz, 1996). Of course, this strategy is not without cost. Sabotaging ourselves—by not practicing, or by drinking too much, using drugs, or faking illness—objectively increases the risk of failure. What's worse, it may not endear us to others. For example, Frederick Rhodewalt and his colleagues (1995) found that participants did not like their partners in an experiment when they thought that these partners had self-handicapped by claiming they did not care, were anxious, or were medically impaired.

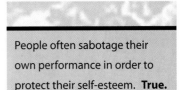

People often sabotage their own performance in order to protect their self-esteem. **True.**

Basking in the Glory of Others   To some extent, your self-esteem is influenced by individuals and groups with whom you identify. According to Robert Cialdini and his colleagues (1976), people often **bask in reflected glory (BIRG)** by showing off their connections to successful others. Cialdini's team first observed BIRGing on the university campuses of Arizona State, Louisiana State, Notre Dame, Michigan, Pittsburgh, Ohio State, and Southern California. On the Monday mornings after football games, they counted the number of school sweatshirts worn on campus and found that more of them were worn if the team had won its game on the previous Saturday. In fact, the larger the margin of victory, the more school shirts were counted.

When Vietnam veterans returned in defeat more than twenty-five years ago, they were neglected, even scorned by the American public. It seems that the tendency to bask in reflected glory is matched by an equally powerful need to cut off reflected failure.

To evaluate the effects of self-esteem on BIRGing, Cialdini gave students a general-knowledge test and rigged the results so half would succeed and half would fail. The students were then asked to describe in their own words the outcome of a recent football game. In these descriptions, students who thought they had just failed a test were more likely than those who thought they had succeeded to share in their team's victory by exclaiming that "*we* won" and to distance themselves from defeat by lamenting how "*they* lost." In another study, participants coming off a recent failure were quick to point out that they had the same birth date as someone known to be successful—thus BIRGing by a merely coincidental association (Cialdini & De Nicholas, 1989).

If self-esteem is influenced by our links to others, how do we cope with friends, family members, teammates, and co-workers of low status? Again, consider sports fans, an interesting breed. As loudly as they cheer in victory, they often turn and jeer their teams in defeat. This behavior seems fickle, but it is consistent with the notion that people derive part of their self-esteem from associations with others. In one study, participants took part in a problem-solving team that either succeeded, failed, or received no feedback about its performance. Participants were later offered a chance to take home a team badge. In the success and no-feedback groups, 68 and 50 percent, respectively, took badges; in the failure group, only 9 percent did (Snyder et al., 1986). It seems that the tendency to bask in reflected glory is matched by an equally powerful tendency to CORF—that is, to "cut off reflected failure." In fact, Edward Hirt and his colleagues (1992) have found that avid sports fans temporarily lose faith in their own mental and social abilities after their favorite team suffers defeat.

bask in reflected glory (BIRG) Increasing self-esteem by associating with others who are successful.

"Your mother and I have seen your report card, and we've decided to distance ourselves from you."

To preserve their own self-esteem, people dissociate from others who fail. Leo Cullum © 1992 from The New Yorker Collection. All Rights Reserved.

downward social comparisons Defensive tendencies to compare ourselves with others who are worse off than we are.

Downward Social Comparisons Earlier, we discussed Festinger's (1954) theory that people evaluate themselves by social comparison with similar others. But let's contemplate the implications. If the people around us achieve more than we do, what does that do to our self-esteem? Perhaps adults who shy away from class reunions in order to avoid having to compare themselves with former classmates are acting out an answer to that question.

Festinger fully realized that people don't always seek out objective information and that social comparisons are sometimes made in self-defense. When a person's self-esteem is at stake, he or she often benefits from making **downward social comparisons**—comparisons with others who are inferior, less successful, less happy, or less fortunate (Hakmiller, 1966; Wills, 1981; Wood, 1989). When people who are low in self-esteem suffer a setback, downward comparisons have an uplifting effect on their mood and on their outlook for the future (Aspinwall & Taylor, 1993; Gibbons & McCoy, 1991).

This benefit can be seen in the classroom. Educators used to be puzzled by the finding that disadvantaged elementary school children often score higher on measures of academic self-esteem than do children from affluent, academically minded schools. The reason: Students feel better about themselves when surrounded by classmates who are lower rather than higher in their levels of achievement. Apparently, it's better to be a big fish in a small pond than a small fish in a big pond (Marsh & Parker, 1984).

There are also striking implications for health-related issues. When victimized by tragic life events (perhaps a crime, an accident, a disease, or the death of a loved one) people like to *affiliate* with others in the same predicament who are adjusting well, role models who offer hope and guidance. But they tend to *compare* themselves with others who are worse off, a form of downward social comparison (Taylor & Lobel, 1989).

Clearly, it helps to know that life could be worse, which is why most cancer patients compare themselves with others who are not adjusting well (J. V. Wood et al., 1985) and believe they are in better shape than their peers (Taylor et al., 1986). Interviews of women with breast cancer tell the story. One woman who had only a lump removed wondered "how awful it must be for women who have had a full mastectomy." An older woman who had a mastectomy said: "The people I really feel sorry for are these young gals. To lose a breast when you're so young must be awful." Yet a young mastectomy patient derived comfort from the fact that "if I hadn't been married, this thing would have really gotten to me" (Taylor, 1989, p. 171). As these quotes poignantly illustrate, there's always someone else with whom we can favorably compare—and this downward comparison makes us feel better (VanderZee et al., 1996). In the words of a terminally ill patient who appeared on a CBS documentary *A Time to Die*, "It's not the worst thing that could happen."

Unfortunately, it's not always possible to defend the self via downward comparison. Think about it. When a sibling, spouse, or close friend has more success than you do, what happens to your self-esteem? Abraham Tesser (1988) predicts two possible reactions. On the one hand, you might feel proud of your association with this successful other, as in the process of basking in reflected glory. If you've ever bragged about the achievements of a loved one as if they were your own, you know how "reflection" can bolster self-esteem. On the other hand, you may feel overshadowed by the success of this other person and experience social comparison jealousy—a mixture of emotions that include envy, resentment, and a drop in self-esteem.

According to Tesser, the key to whether one feels the pleasure of reflection or the pain of jealousy is whether the other person's success is self-relevant. When close friends surpass us in ways that are vital to our self-concepts, we become jealous and distance ourselves from them in order to keep up our own self-esteem. When intimate others surpass us in ways that are not important, however, we take pride in their triumphs through a process of reflection (Tesser & Collins, 1988; Tesser et al., 1989). Applying this model to family dynamics, Tesser (1980) found that college students were most likely to report friction with their brothers or sisters when the two were close in age and when there was a disparity in their levels of ability.

How do we cope when forced to make upward social comparisons in an important, self-relevant domain? When we are outperformed by someone else—whether it's in class, at work, or on the athletic field—it is not realistic to deny the implication that this other person is superior. Yet research suggests that people can escape this situation with their self-esteem relatively intact (Collins, 1996). How is this possible? In a series of studies, Mark Alicke and his colleagues (1997) had pairs of participants and confederates take a "perceptual intelligence test" and rigged it so that the confederates would always score higher. Afterward, participants rated their own and the confederates' level of perceptual intelligence. Compared with neutral observers who secretly watched the sessions through a one-way mirror and then made the same ratings, participants consistently *over*rated the confederate's ability. Why? "If the person who beats me is a genius, then I'm not so bad after all."

At their 25th reunion, these Wellesley College graduates, Class of '69, stand alongside a lifesize figure of Hillary Clinton, their most famous classmate. For these women, the association is a source of pride.

Are Positive Illusions Adaptive?

Psychologists used to maintain that an accurate perception of reality is vital to mental health. In recent years, however, this view has been challenged by research on the mechanisms of self-defense. Consistently, as we have seen, people preserve their self-esteem by deluding themselves and others with biased cognitions, self-handicapping, BIRGing, and making downward comparisons. Are these strategies a sign of health and well-being, or are they symptoms of disorder?

When Shelley Taylor and Jonathon Brown (1988) reviewed the relevant research, they found that individuals who are depressed or low in self-esteem actually have more realistic views of themselves than do most others who are better adjusted. Their self-appraisals are more likely to match appraisals of them made by neutral observers; they make fewer self-serving attributions to account for success and failure; they are less likely to exaggerate their control over uncontrollable events; and they make more balanced predictions about their future. They are also more likely to compare themselves with similar others rather than make downward comparisons (Swallow & Kuiper, 1993; Wheeler & Miyake, 1992). Based on these results, Taylor and Brown (1988) reached the provocative conclusion that positive illusions promote happiness, the desire to care for others, and the ability to engage in productive work—hallmark attributes of mental health: "These illusions help make each individual's world a warmer and more active and beneficent place in which to live" (p. 205).

Not everyone agrees with the notion that it is most adaptive to wear rose-colored lenses. Randall Colvin and Jack Block (1994) argued that even if positive illusions temporarily elevate one's mood and self-esteem, the long-term effects are unclear. Baumeister and Scher (1988) warned that such illusions give rise to chronic patterns of self-defeating behavior—as when people escape from self-awareness through the use of alcohol and other drugs, self-handicap themselves into failure and underachievement, deny health-related problems until it's too late for treatment, and rely on the illusion of control to protect them from the tender mercies of the gambling casino.

From an interpersonal standpoint, C. Randall Colvin and his colleagues (1995) found that people who have inflated rather than realistic views of themselves were rated less favorably on certain dimensions by their own friends. In their studies, self-enhancing men were seen as assertive and ambitious—which are okay—but also as boastful, condescending, hostile, and less considerate of others. Self-enhancing women were seen as more hostile, more defensive and sensitive to criticism, more likely to overreact to minor setbacks, and less well-liked. In fact, Baumeister and his colleagues (1996) suggested that people endowed with high self-esteem are more likely to lash out angrily and violently in response to negative feedback, rejection, and other bruises to the ego. Citing this research, *U.S. News & World Report* commentator John Leo (1996) offers this advice: "Let's lower our self-esteem."

Realism or illusion, which orientation is more adaptive? As social psychologists debate the short-term and long-term effects of positive illusions, it's clear that there is no simple answer (Colvin & Block, 1994; Taylor & Brown, 1994). For now, the picture that has emerged is this: People who harbor positive illusions of themselves are likely to enjoy the benefits and achievements of high self-esteem. But these same individuals may pay a price in other ways—as in their relations with others. So what are we to conclude? Do positive illusions motivate personal achievement but alienate us socially from others? Is it adaptive to see oneself in slightly inflated terms, but maladaptive to take a view that is too much biased? It will be interesting to see how this thorny debate is resolved in the years to come.

Self-Presentation

The human quest for self-knowledge and self-esteem tells us about the inner self. The portrait is not complete, however, until we paint in the outermost layer, the behavioral expression of the social self. Most people are acutely concerned about the image they present to others. The fashion industry, diet centers, cosmetic surgeries designed to reshape everything from eyelids to breasts, and the endless search for miracle drugs that grow hair, remove hair, whiten teeth, freshen breath, and smooth out wrinkles, all exploit our preoccupation with physical appearance. Similarly, people are concerned about the impressions they convey through their public behavior. What, as they say, will the neighbors think?

In *As You Like It*, William Shakespeare wrote, "All the world's a stage, and all the men and women merely players." This insight was first put into social science terms by sociologist Erving Goffman (1959), who argued that life is like a theater and that each of us acts out certain *lines,* as if from a script. Most important, said Goffman, is that each of us assumes a certain *face,* or social identity, that others politely help us to maintain. Inspired by Goffman's theory, social psychologists study **self-presentation:** the process by which we try to shape what others think of us and what we think of ourselves (Schlenker & Weigold, 1992; Tedeschi, 1981).

self-presentation Strategies people use to shape what others think of them.

In his 1997 tour of the United States, Chinese President Jiang Zemin opens trading on the New York Stock Exchange—an ironic image for a communist leader. Seeking improved economic ties with the United States, Jiang engaged in strategic self-presentation.

An act of self-presentation may take many different forms. It may be conscious or unconscious, accurate or misleading, intended for an external audience or for ourselves. In this section, we look at the various goals of self-presentation and the ways in which people try to achieve these goals.

The Two Faces of Self-Presentation

There are basically two types of self-presentation, each serving a different motive. *Strategic self-presentation* consists of our efforts to shape others' impressions in specific ways in order to gain influence, power, sympathy, or approval. Prominent examples of strategic self-presentation are everywhere: in personal ads, in political campaign promises, in defendants' appeals to the jury. The specific goals include the desire to be seen as likable, competent, moral, dangerous, or helpless. Whatever the goal, people try to control their self-presentations in part through the use of nonverbal behaviors (DePaulo, 1992). For example, women often eat less in front of men in order to appear appropriately feminine (Mori et al., 1987; Pliner & Chaiken, 1990).

The specific identities that people try to present vary from one person and situation to another (Leary & Kowalski, 1990). There are, however, two strategic self-presentation goals that are very common. The first is ingratiation, a term used to describe acts that are motivated by the desire to "get along" and be liked. The second goal is self-promotion, a term used to describe acts that are motivated by a desire to "get ahead" and be respected for one's competence (Arkin, 1981; Jones & Pittman, 1982). These goals are so basic to social behavior that they develop at an early age. When driven by a desire to be selected as a partner for a competitive game, even second-grade children talk themselves up (Aloise-Young, 1993).

On the surface, it seems easy to achieve these goals. When people want to be liked, they put their best foot forward, smile a lot, nod their heads, express agreement, and, if necessary, use favors, compliments, and apple-polishing flattery. When people want to be admired for their competence, they try to impress others by talking about themselves and immodestly showing off their status, knowledge, and exploits. In both cases, there are tradeoffs. As the term "brown-nosing" all too graphically suggests, ingratiation tactics need to be subtle or else they will backfire (Jones, 1964). Similarly, people who constantly trumpet their own achievements are seen as self-absorbed and boastful—and are disliked as a result (Godfrey et al., 1986).

"Great-looking tie!"

Ingratiation is a strategy often used to curry favor. Mischa Richter © 1992 from The New Yorker Collection. All Rights Reserved.

Self-presentation may give rise to other problems as well. In a provocative article entitled "Self-Presentation Can Be Hazardous to Your Health," Mark Leary and his colleagues (1994) reviewed evidence suggesting that the need to project a favorable public image can lure us into unsafe patterns of behavior. For example, self-presentation concerns can increase the risk of AIDS (when men are too embarrassed to buy condoms and talk openly with their sex partners), skin cancer (when people bake under the sun to get an attractive tan), eating disorders (when women overdiet or use amphetamines, laxatives, and forced vomiting to stay thin), drug abuse (when teenagers smoke, drink, and use drugs to impress their peers), and accidental injury (when young men drive recklessly to appear brave and fearless to others).

The second self-presentation motive is *self-verification*: the desire to have others perceive us as we truly perceive ourselves. According to William Swann (1987), people are highly motivated to verify their existing self-concept in the eyes of others. Swann and his colleagues have gathered a great deal of evidence for this hypothesis—and have found, for example, that people selectively elicit, recall, and accept personality feedback that confirms their self-conceptions. In fact, people sometimes bend over backward to correct others whose impressions are positive but mistaken. In one study, participants interacted with a confederate who later said that they seemed dominant or submissive. When the comment was consistent with the participant's self-concept, it was accepted at face value. Yet when it was inconsistent, participants went out of their way to prove the confederate wrong: Those who perceived themselves as dominant but were labeled submissive later behaved more assertively than usual; those who viewed themselves as submissive but were labeled dominant subsequently became even more docile (Swann & Hill, 1982).

Self-verification seems desirable, but wait—Do people who have a negative self-concept want others to share that impression? Nobody is perfect, and everyone has some faults. But do we really want to verify these faults in the eyes of others? Do those of us who feel painfully shy, socially awkward, or insecure about an ability want others to see these weaknesses? Or would we prefer to present ourselves as bold, graceful, or competent? What happens when the desire for self-verification clashes with the need for self-enhancement?

Seeking to answer this question, Swann, Stein-Seroussi, and Giesler (1992) asked each participant to fill out a self-concept questionnaire and then choose an interaction partner from two other participants—one who supposedly had evaluated the participant favorably; the other, unfavorably. The result? Although participants with a positive self-concept chose partners who viewed them in a positive light, a majority of those with a negative self-concept preferred partners who confirmed their admitted shortcomings (see Figure 3.10). In a more recent study, 64 percent of participants with low self-esteem, compared with only 25 percent of those with high self-esteem, sought clinical feedback about their weaknesses rather than their strengths when given a choice (Giesler et al., 1996).

If people seek self-verification from laboratory partners, it stands to reason that they would want the same from their close relationships. In a study of married couples, husbands and wives separately answered questions about their self-concepts, spouses, and commitment to the marriage. As predicted, people who had a positive self-concept expressed more commitment to partners who appraised them favorably, while those with a negative self-concept felt more committed to partners who appraised them *un*favorably (Swann, Hixon, & De La Ronde, 1992).

Regarding important aspects of the self-concept, research shows that people would rather reflect on and learn more about their own positive qualities than their negative ones (Sedikides, 1993). Still, it appears that the desire for self-verification is powerful—and can even, at times, overwhelm the need for self-enhancement. We all want to make a good impression, but we also want others in our lives to have an accurate impression, one that is compatible with our own self-concept (Swann, 1997).

Individual Differences in Self-Monitoring

Although self-presentation is a way of life for all of us, it differs considerably among individuals. Some people are generally more conscious of their public image than others. Also, some people are more likely to engage in strategic self-presentation, while others seem to prefer self-verification. According to Mark Snyder (1987), these differences are related to a personality trait he called **self-monitoring:** the tendency to regulate one's own behavior to meet the demands of social situations.

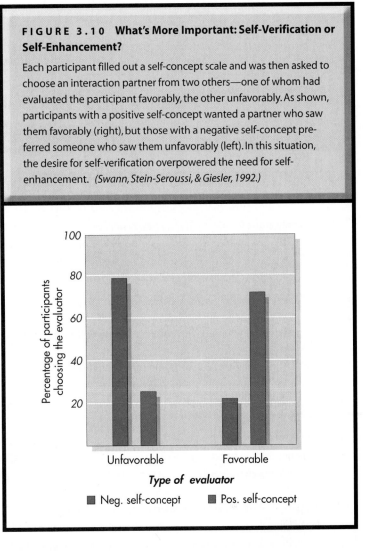

FIGURE 3.10 **What's More Important: Self-Verification or Self-Enhancement?**

Each participant filled out a self-concept scale and was then asked to choose an interaction partner from two others—one of whom had evaluated the participant favorably, the other unfavorably. As shown, participants with a positive self-concept wanted a partner who saw them favorably (right), but those with a negative self-concept preferred someone who saw them unfavorably (left). In this situation, the desire for self-verification overpowered the need for self-enhancement. *(Swann, Stein-Seroussi, & Giesler, 1992.)*

Individuals who are high in self-monitoring appear to have a repertoire of selves from which to draw. Sensitive to strategic self-presentation concerns, they are poised, ready, and able to modify their behavior as they move from one situation to another. As measured by the Self-Monitoring Scale (Snyder, 1974; Snyder & Gangestad, 1986), they are likely to agree with such statements as "I would probably make a good actor" and "In different situations and with different peo-ple, I often act like very different persons." In contrast, low self-monitors are self-verifiers by nature, appearing less concerned about the propriety of their behavior. Like character actors always cast in the same role, they express themselves in a consistent manner from one situation to the next, exhibiting what they regard as their true and honest self. On the Self-Monitoring Scale, low self-monitors say that "I can only argue for ideas which I already believe" and "I have never been good at games like charades or improvisational acting" (see Table 3.2 on page 86).

Social psychologists disagree on whether the Self-Monitoring Scale measures one global trait or a combination of two or more specific traits (Briggs & Cheek, 1988; John et al., 1996) and on whether high and low self-monitors represent two discrete types of people or just points along a continuum (Gangestad & Snyder, 1991; Miller & Thayer, 1989). Either way, the test scores do appear to predict important social behaviors. Concerned with public image, high self-monitors go out of their way to learn about others with whom they might interact and about the

self-monitoring The tendency to change behavior in response to the self-presentation concerns of the situation.

TABLE 3.2 Self-Monitoring Scale

Are you a high or low self-monitor? For each statement, answer *True* or *False*. When you are done, give yourself one point if you answered *T* to items 4, 5, 6, 8, 10, 12, 17, and 18. Then give yourself one point if you answered *F* to items 1, 2, 3, 7, 9, 11, 13, 14, 15, and 16. Count your total number of points. This total represents your Self-Monitoring Score. Among North American college students, the average score is about 10 or 11. *(Snyder & Gangestad, 1986.)*

1. I find it hard to imitate the behavior of other people.

2. At parties and social gatherings, I do not attempt to do or say things that others will like.

3. I can only argue for ideas which I already believe.

4. I can make impromptu speeches even on topics about which I have almost no information.

5. I guess I put on a show to impress or entertain others.

6. I would probably make a good actor.

7. In a group of people I am rarely the center of attention.

8. In different situations and with different people, I often act like very different persons.

9. I am not particularly good at making other people like me.

10. I'm not always the person I appear to be.

11. I would not change my opinions (or the way I do things) in order to please someone or win their favor.

12. I have considered being an entertainer.

13. I have never been good at games like charades or improvisational acting.

14. I have trouble changing my behavior to suit different people and different situations.

15. At a party I let others keep the jokes and stories going.

16. I feel a bit awkward in company and do not show up quite as well as I should.

17. I can look anyone in the eye and tell a lie with a straight face (if for a right end).

18. I may deceive people by being friendly when I really dislike them.

It's more adaptive to alter one's behavior than to stay consistent from one social situation to the next. **False.**

rules for appropriate conduct. Then, once they have the situation sized up, they modify their behavior (Danheiser & Graziano, 1982; Shaffer et al., 1982). If a situation calls for conformity, high self-monitors conform; if the same situation calls for autonomy, they refuse to conform. In contrast, low self-monitors maintain a relatively consistent posture across situations (Snyder & Monson, 1975).

In the coming chapters, we will see that because so much of our behavior is influenced by social norms, self-monitoring is relevant to many aspects of social psychology. This fact may also have interesting developmental implications. A survey of eighteen- to seventy-three-year-olds revealed that self-monitoring scores tend to drop with age—presumably because people become more settled and secure about their personal identities as they get older (Reifman et al., 1989). For now, however, ponder this question: Is it better to be a high or low self-monitor? Is one orientation inherently more adaptive than the other?

The existing research does not enable us to make this kind of value judgment. Consider high self-monitors. Quite accurately, they regard themselves as *pragmatic*, flexible, and adaptive and as able to cope with the diversity of life's roles. But wait—they could also be described as fickle or phony opportunists, more concerned with appearances than with reality and willing to change colors like a chameleon just to fit in. Now think about low self-monitors. They describe themselves as *principled* and forthright; they are without pretense, always speaking their minds so others know where they stand. Of course, they could also be viewed as stubborn, insensitive to their surroundings, and unwilling to compromise in order to get along. Concerning the relative value of these two orientations, then, it is safe to conclude that neither high nor low self-monitoring is necessarily undesirable—unless carried to the extreme. Goffman (1955) made the same point many years ago, when he wrote:

> *Too little perceptiveness, too little* savoir faire, *too little pride and considerateness, and the person ceases to be someone who can be trusted to take a hint about himself or give a hint that will save others embarrassment. . . . Too much* savoir faire *or too much considerateness and he becomes someone who is too socialized, who leaves others with the feeling that they do not know how they really stand with him, nor what they should do to make an effective long-term adjustment. (p. 227)*

Epilogue: The Multifaceted Self

Throughout human history, writers, poets, philosophers, and personality theorists have portrayed the self as an enduring aspect of personality, as an invisible "inner core" that is stable over time and slow to change. The struggle to "find yourself" and "be true to yourself" is based on this portrait. Indeed, when people over eighty-five years old were asked to reflect on their lives, almost all said that despite having changed in certain ways, they had remained essentially the same person (Troll & Skaff, 1997). In recent years, however, social psychologists have focused on change. In doing so, they have discovered that at least part of the self is malleable—molded by life experiences and varying from one situation to the next. From this perspective, the self has many different faces.

When you look into the mirror, what do you see, one self or many? Do you see a person whose self-concept is enduring or one whose identity seems to change from time to time? Do you see a person whose strengths and weaknesses are evaluated with an objective eye or one who is insulated from unpleasant truths by mechanisms of self-defense? Do you see a person who has an inner, hidden self that is different from the face shown to others?

Based on the material presented in this chapter, the answer to such questions seems always to be the same: The self has all these characteristics. More than a hundred years ago, William James (1890) said that the self is not simple but complex and multifaceted. Based on current theories and research, we can now appreciate just how right James was. Sure, there's an aspect of the self-concept that we come to know only through introspection and that is stable over time. But there's also an aspect that changes with the company we keep and the information we get from others. When it comes to self-esteem, there are times when we are self-focused enough to become acutely aware of our shortcomings. Yet there are also times when we guard ourselves through self-serving cognitions, self-handicapping, BIRGing, and downward social comparisons. Then there is the matter of self-presentation. It's clear that each of us has a private self consisting of our inner thoughts, feelings, and memories. But it is equally clear that we also have an outer self, portrayed by the roles we play and the masks we wear in public. As you read through the pages of this text, you will see that the cognitive, affective, and behavioral components of the self are not separate and distinct but interrelated. They are also of great significance for the rest of social psychology.

Review

The Self-Concept

- The self-concept is the sum total of a person's beliefs about his or her own attributes. It is the cognitive component of the self.

Beginnings of the Self-Concept

- Recognizing oneself as a distinct entity is the first step in the development of a self-concept.
- Human beings and apes are the only animals to recognize their mirror-image reflections as their own.

- Cooley's "looking-glass self" suggests that social factors are a necessary second step.

Introspection

- People believe that introspection is a key to knowing the true self.
- But research shows that introspection sometimes diminishes the accuracy of self-reports.

Perceptions of Our Own Behavior

- Bem's self-perception theory holds that when internal states are difficult to interpret, we infer our inner states by observing our own behavior and the surrounding situation.
- Based on self-perception theory, the facial feedback hypothesis states that facial expressions can produce, not just reflect, an emotion state (smiling can cause us to feel happy).
- But it's unclear if the emotion occurs via self-perception or because facial expressions trigger physiological changes that produce the emotional response.
- Also derived from self-perception theory, studies of the overjustification effect show that people sometimes lose interest in activities for which they are rewarded.
- But if a reward is seen as a "bonus" for superior performance, then it can enhance intrinsic motivation by providing positive feedback.

Influences of Other People

- According to social comparison theory, people often evaluate their own opinions and abilities by comparing themselves to similar others.
- Schachter and Singer proposed that the experience of emotion is based on two factors: physiological arousal and a cognitive label for that arousal.
- Under certain conditions, people interpret their own arousal by watching others in the same situation.

Autobiographical Memories

- Memory of one's life events is critical to the self-concept.
- When people recall life experiences, they typically report more events from the recent past than from the distant past, though some types of memories are generally more vivid and lasting than others.
- There are two ways in which the self guides memory.
- First, autobiographical memories are shaped by an egocentric bias, as people overemphasize their own roles in past events.
- Second, the hindsight bias leads people to revise their personal histories in light of new information about themselves.

Cultural Perspectives

- Cultures foster different conceptions of self.
- Many Europeans and North Americans hold an independent view of the self that emphasizes autonomy.
- People in certain Asian, African, and Latin American cultures hold an interdependent view of the self that encompasses social connections.
- These cultural differences influence the way we perceive, feel about, and present ourselves in relation to others.

Self-Schemas

- A self-schema is a specific belief about oneself that guides the processing of information.
- On matters relevant to self-schemas, people make rapid judgments about themselves and are quick to recall past actions or predict future actions.

Self-Esteem

- Self-esteem refers to a person's positive and negative evaluations of the self.

The Need for Self-Esteem

- People have a need for high self-esteem and want to see themselves in a positive light.
- People with low self-esteem often find themselves caught in a vicious cycle of self-defeating behavior.
- Self-esteem can be defined by the match between how we see ourselves and how we want to see ourselves. Large self-discrepancies are associated with negative emotional states.
- Discrepancies between the actual and ideal selves are related to feelings of disappointment and depression.
- Discrepancies between the actual and the ought selves are related to shame, guilt, and anxiety.
- These emotional effects depend on the amount of discrepancy and whether we are consciously focused on it.

The Self-Awareness "Trap"

- In general, people spend little time actually thinking about themselves.
- But certain situations (mirrors, cameras, audiences) increase self-awareness, and certain people are generally more self-conscious than others.
- Self-awareness forces us to notice self-discrepancies and can produce a temporary reduction in self-esteem.
- To cope, we either adjust our behavior to meet our standards or withdraw from the self-focusing situation.
- Heavy drinking can be viewed as a means of escaping from self-awareness.
- Due to the operation of ironic processes, our efforts at self-control sometimes backfire, causing us to think, feel, and act in ways that are opposite to our intentions.

Mechanisms of Self-Enhancement

- Most people think highly of themselves and protect their self-esteem. There are four ways of achieving this.
- The first is through self-serving cognitions, such as taking credit for success but denying the blame for failure.
- Second, people make excuses and even self-handicap (through drug use or reduced effort) in order to excuse anticipated failure.
- Third, people often bask in reflected glory, boosting self-esteem through their associations with successful others.
- Fourth, people often compare themselves with others who are less happy, less successful, or less fortunate.

- When others surpass us in ways that are important to us, we become jealous and distance ourselves from them. When surpassed in ways that are not self-relevant, we feel pride and seek closeness.

Are Positive Illusions Adaptive?

- Recent research suggests that certain positive illusions may foster high self-esteem and mental health.
- An alternative view is that such illusions promote self-defeating behavior patterns and that people with inflated views of themselves are liked less by others.

Self-Presentation

- Self-presentation is the process by which we try to shape what others think of us and even what we think of ourselves.

The Two Faces of Self-Presentation

- There are basically two motives for self-presentation.
- The first is strategic, when we try to shape others' impressions in order to be liked or seen as competent.
- The second is self-verification, by which we try to get others to perceive us as we perceive ourselves.

Individual Differences in Self-Monitoring

- Individuals differ in the tendency to regulate their behavior to meet the demands of social situations.
- High self-monitors modify their behavior, as appropriate, from one situation to the next.
- Low self-monitors express themselves in a more consistent manner, exhibiting at all times what they see as their true self.

Epilogue: The Multifaceted Self

- As this chapter has shown, the self is not simple but complex and multifaceted.

Key Terms

bask in reflected glory (BIRG) *79*

downward social comparisons *80*

egocentric bias *66*

facial feedback hypothesis *59*

hindsight bias *66*

overjustification effect *61*

private self-consciousness *74*

public self-consciousness *74*

self-awareness theory *73*

self-concept *57*

self-esteem *70*

self-handicapping *78*

self-monitoring *85*

self-perception theory *59*

self-presentation *82*

self-schemas *69*

social comparison theory *63*

two-factor theory of emotion *64*

PUTTING COMMON SENSE TO THE TEST

Humans are the only animals who recognize themselves in the mirror.

False. *Studies have shown that the great apes (chimpanzees, gorillas, and orangutans) are also capable of self-recognition.*

Smiling can make you feel happier.

True. *Consistent with the facial feedback hypothesis, facial expressions can trigger or amplify the subjective experience of emotion.*

Sometimes the harder you try to control a thought, feeling, or behavior, the less likely you are to succeed.

True. *Research on ironic processes in mental control have revealed that trying to inhibit a thought, feeling, or behavior often backfires.*

People tend to be overly optimistic about their future.

True. *In general, people see themselves as more likely than average to have positive outcomes and less likely to have negative ones.*

People often sabotage their own performance in order to protect their self-esteem.

True. *Studies have shown that people often handicap their own performance in order to build an excuse for anticipated failure.*

It's more adaptive to alter one's behavior than to stay consistent from one social situation to the next.

False. *High and low self-monitors differ in the extent to which they alter their behavior to suit the situation they are in, but neither style is inherently more adaptive.*

4 Perceiving Persons

PREVIEW

This chapter examines how people come to know, or think that they know, other persons. First, we introduce the elements of social perception—those aspects of persons, situations, and behavior that guide initial observations. Next, we examine how people make explanations, or attributions, for the behavior of others and how they form integrated impressions based on initial perceptions and attributions. We then consider confirmation biases, the subtle ways in which initial impressions lead people to distort later information, setting in motion a self-fulfilling prophecy.

_____ The impressions we form of others are influenced by superficial aspects of their appearance.

_____ Adaptively, people are skilled at knowing when someone is lying rather than telling the truth.

_____ Like social psychologists, people are sensitive to situational causes when explaining the behavior of others.

_____ People are slow to change their first impressions on the basis of new information.

_____ The notion that we can create a "self-fulfilling prophecy" by getting others to behave in ways we expect is a myth.

_____ People are more accurate at judging the personality of friends and acquaintances than of strangers.

After Princess Diana was killed in a high-speed car accident in Paris, investigators and grief-stricken observers throughout the world wanted to know what had happened: Was her limousine driver drunk? Was another car involved? Was the tragedy caused by photographers gawking and chasing for pictures? When boxer Mike Tyson bit off a chunk of Evander Holyfield's ear in a heavyweight championship bout, stunned sports fans wondered: Was his barbaric act premeditated, or had Tyson simply snapped under the pressure of the moment? When President Bill Clinton and Vice President Al Gore were mired in various campaign financing scandals, voters were suspicious: Had they broken the law, or were the allegations motivated by partisan politics? After Louise Woodward, a nineteen year-old British au pair, was convicted in Massachusetts for the murder of eight month-old Matthew Eappen, everyone tried to predict whether the judge would affirm or reduce the jury's verdict and life sentence. And when couples divorce after years of marriage, friends and relatives often ask, Whose fault was it?

Whatever the topic—world news, sports, politics, crime and punishment, or personal events closer to home—we are all active and interested participants in **social perception,** the processes by which people come to understand one another. This chapter is divided into four sections. First we look at the "raw data" of social perception—persons, situations, and behavior. Second, we examine how people explain and analyze behavior. Third, we consider how people integrate their observations into a coherent impression of other persons. Fourth, we discuss some of the subtle ways in which our impressions create a distorted picture of reality,

social perception A general term for the processes by which people come to understand one another.

Soon after Princess Diana was pulled from the wreckage of a high-speed car accident, people all over the world wanted to know what happened—and why. In all aspects of life, human beings are active and interested social perceivers.

often setting in motion a self-fulfilling prophecy. As you read this chapter, you will notice that the various processes are considered from a perceiver's vantage point. Keep in mind, however, that in the events of life, you are both a *perceiver* and a *target* of others' perceptions.

Observation: The Elements of Social Perception

As our opening examples suggest, understanding others may be difficult, but it's a vital part of everyday life. How do we do it? What kinds of evidence do we use? One cannot actually "see" someone's mental or emotional state, motives, or intentions, any more than a detective can see a crime that has already been committed. So, like a detective who tries to reconstruct events by turning up witnesses, fingerprints, blood samples, and other evidence, the social perceiver comes to know others by relying on indirect clues—the elements of social perception. These clues arise from three sources: persons, situations, and behavior.

Persons: Judging a Book by Its Cover

Have you ever met someone for the first time and immediately formed an impression based only on a quick "snapshot" of information? As children, we were told not to judge a book by its cover, that things are not always what they seem, that appearances are deceptive, and that all that glitters is not gold. As adults, however, we can't seem to help ourselves.

In 500 B.C.E., the mathematician Pythagoras looked into the eyes of prospective students to determine if they were gifted. At about the same time, Hippocrates—the founder of modern medicine—used facial features to make diagnoses of life and death. In the nineteenth century, Viennese physician Franz Gall introduced a carnival-like science called phrenology and claimed that he could assess people's character by the shape of their skulls. And in 1954, psychologist

William Sheldon mistakenly concluded from flawed studies of adult men that there is a strong link between physique and personality.

People may not measure each other by bumps on the head, as phrenologists used to do, but first impressions are influenced in subtle ways by a person's height, weight, skin color, hair color, eyeglasses, and other aspects of appearance (Alley, 1988; Bull & Rumsey, 1988; Herman et al., 1986). As social perceivers, we are influenced by the color of a person's clothing. Indeed, Aldert Vrij (1997) found that crime suspects are seen as more aggressive when dressed in black—a color that is associated with evil and death in many cultures—than when they wear lighter clothing. We are even influenced by a person's name. For example, Robert Young and his colleagues (1993) found that fictional characters with "old generation" names such as Harry, Walter, Dorothy, and Edith are judged less popular and intelligent than those with "young generation" names such as Kevin, Michael, Lisa, and Michelle.

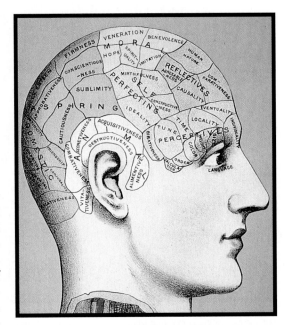

The human face in particular attracts more than its share of attention. For example, Diane Berry and Leslie Zebrowitz-McArthur (1986) have found that adults who have baby-faced features—large, round eyes, high eyebrows, round cheeks, a large forehead, smooth skin, and a rounded chin—tend to be seen as warm, kind, naive, weak, honest, and submissive. In contrast, adults who have mature features—small eyes, low brows and a small forehead, wrinkled skin, and an angular chin—are seen as stronger, more dominant, and more competent. Thus, in small claims court, judges are more likely to favor baby-faced defendants accused of intentional wrongdoing, but they tend to rule against baby-faced defendants accused of negligence (Zebrowitz-McArthur & McDonald, 1991). And in the work setting, baby-faced job applicants are more likely to be recommended for employment as day-care teachers, whereas mature-faced adults are considered to be better suited for work as bankers (Zebrowitz-McArthur et al., 1991). Results like these have been found in a variety of studies (Zebrowitz-McArthur, 1996).

In the nineteenth century, Franz Gall introduced phrenology, the pseudo-scientific theory that personality traits and abilities could be "seen" in the bumps on the skull.

What accounts for these findings? And why, in general, are people so quick to judge others by appearances? There are three possible explanations. One is that human beings are genetically programmed to respond gently to infantile features so that real babies are treated with tender loving care. Another possibility is that we simply learn to associate infantile features with helplessness and then generalize this expectation to baby-faced adults. Third, maybe there is an actual link between appearance and behavior—a possibility suggested by the fact that research participants exposed only to photos or brief videotapes of strangers formed impressions that correlated with the self-descriptions of these same strangers (Berry & Finch Wero, 1993; Kenny et al., 1992). Whatever the explanation, the perceived link between appearance and behavior may account for the shock that we often experience when our expectations are disconfirmed (see photo on page 94).

The impressions we form of others are influenced by superficial aspects of their appearance. **True.**

Situations: The Scripts of Life

In addition to the beliefs we hold about persons, each of us has preset notions about certain types of situations—"scripts" that enable us to anticipate the goals, behaviors, and outcomes likely to occur in a particular setting (Abelson, 1981; Read, 1987). Based on past experience, people can easily imagine the sequences of events likely to unfold in a typical greeting or at the shopping mall or dinner table. The more experience you have in a given situation, the more detail your scripts will contain. As described in Roger Axtell's (1993) best-seller, *Do's and Taboos Around the World*, many scripts are culture-specific. As a dinner guest in Bolivia,

If you're interested in perceptions of the human face, you can visit FACIAL ANALYSIS, a fascinating site in which studies of the face are presented through links to research labs all over the world. (mambo.ucsc.edu/psl.fanl /html)

When "Son of Sam" David Berkowitz was arrested in 1977, New Yorkers anxiously waited for a glimpse of him. What would the monster who murdered six innocent people look like? When this babyfaced image first appeared in the news (center), people were shocked.

you should clean your plate to prove that you enjoyed the meal. Eat in an Indian home, however, and you'll see that many native guests leave some food on the plate to show the host that they had enough to eat.

In a study of the American "first date" script, John Pryor and Thomas Merluzzi (1985) asked college students to list the sequence of events that take place in this situation. From these lists, a picture of a typical first date emerged. Sixteen steps were identified, including: (1) male arrives; (2) female greets male at door; (3) female introduces date to parents or roommate; (4) male and female discuss plans and make small talk; (5) they go to a movie; (6) they get something to eat or drink; (7) male takes female home; (8) if interested, he remarks about a future date; (9) they kiss; (10) they say good night. Sound familiar? Additional research shows that dating is a clearly scripted event about which men and women show high levels of agreement (Rose & Frieze, 1993). Pryor and Merluzzi then randomized their list of events and asked participants to arrange them into the appropriate order. They found that those with extensive dating experience were able to organize the statements more quickly than those who had less dating experience. For people who are familiar with a script, the events fall into place like the pieces of a puzzle.

A knowledge of social settings provides an important context for understanding other people's verbal and nonverbal behavior. For example, this knowledge leads us to expect someone to be polite during a job interview, playful at a picnic, and rowdy at a keg party. Scripts influence social perceptions in two ways. First, we sometimes see what we expect to see in a particular situation. In one study, participants looked at photographs of human faces that had ambiguous expressions. When told that the person in the photo was being threatened by a vicious dog, they saw the expression as fearful; when told that the individual had just won money, participants interpreted the *same* expression as a sign of happiness (Trope, 1986). Second, people use what they know about social situations to explain the causes of human behavior. As described later in this chapter, an action seems to offer more information about a person when it departs from the norm than when it is common. In other words, you would learn more about someone who is rowdy during a job interview or polite at a keg party than if it were the other way around.

Behavioral Evidence

An essential first step in social perception is to recognize what someone is doing at a given moment. Identifying actions from movement is surprisingly easy. Even when actors dressed in black move about in a dark room with point lights attached only to the joints of their bodies, people easily recognize such complex acts as walking, running, jumping, exercising, and falling (Johansson et al., 1980).

More interesting, perhaps, is that people derive *meaning* from their observations by dividing the continuous stream of human behavior into discrete units. By having participants observe someone on videotape and press a button whenever they detect a meaningful action, Darren Newtson and his colleagues (1987) have found that some perceivers break the behavior stream into a large number of fine units, whereas others break it into a small number of gross units. While watching a baseball game, for example, you might press the button after each pitch, after each batter, after every inning, or only after runs are scored.

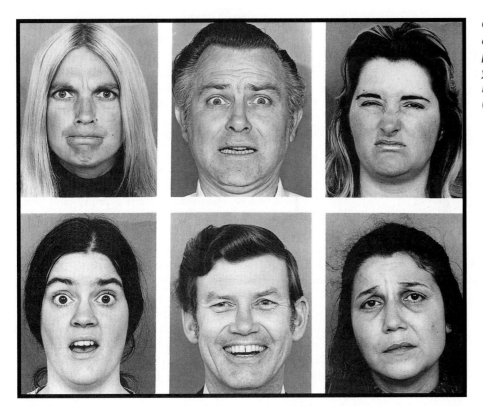

Can you tell how these individuals are feeling? If you are like most people, regardless of your culture, you will have little trouble recognizing the emotions portrayed. (Copyright by Paul Ekman 1975.)

The manner in which people divide a stream of behavior can influence perceptions in important ways. Research participants who are told to break an event into fine units rather than gross units attend more closely, detect more meaningful actions, and remember more details about the actor's behavior than do gross-unit participants (Lassiter et al., 1988). Fine-unit participants become more familiar with the actor they've observed, so they also come to view that actor in more positive terms (Lassiter, 1988). As we will see in Chapter 9, familiarity often heightens attraction.

The Silent Language of Nonverbal Behavior   Behavioral cues are used not only to identify someone's actions but also to determine his or her inner states. Knowing how another person is feeling can be tricky because people often try to hide their true emotions. Think about it. Have you ever had to suppress your rage at someone, mask your disappointment after failure, feign surprise, make excuses, or pretend to like something just to be polite? Sometimes people come right out and tell us how they feel. At other times, however, they do not tell us, they are themselves not sure, or they actively try to conceal their true feelings. For these reasons, we often tune in to the silent language of **nonverbal behavior.**

What kinds of nonverbal cues do people use in judging how someone else is feeling? In *The Expression of the Emotions in Man and Animals,* Charles Darwin (1872) proposed that the face expresses emotion in ways that are innate and understood by people all over the world. Contemporary research supports this notion. Numerous studies have shown that when presented with photographs similar to those above, people can reliably identify at least six "primary" emotions: happiness, fear, sadness, anger, surprise, and disgust. In one study, participants from ten different countries—Estonia, Germany, Greece, Hong Kong, Italy, Japan, Scotland, Sumatra, Turkey, and the United States—exhibited high levels of agreement in their recognition of these emotions (Ekman et al., 1987). Not everyone agrees that the results are strong enough to support the claim that emotions are "universally" recognized in the face (Russell, 1994). Indeed, sometimes we infer how others are feeling not from the expressions on their faces but from the situations they're in

nonverbal behavior Behavior that reveals a person's feelings without words—through facial expressions, body language, and vocal cues.

"You find that surprising, or is it just your pierced eyebrow?"

People are quick to "see" emotional states in others on the basis of facial expressions. Danny Shanahan © 1995 from The New Yorker Collection. All Rights Reserved.

(Carroll & Russell, 1996). It is clear, however, that from one end of the world to the other, a smile is a smile and a frown is a frown, and just about everyone knows what they mean—even when the expressions are "put on" by actors and not genuinely felt (Gosselin et al., 1995).

Darwin believed that the ability to recognize emotion in others has survival value for all members of a species. This hypothesis suggests that some emotions are more important to identify than others. Thus, it may be more adaptive to know when someone else is angry (and hence prone to lash out in violence) than to know when someone is happy, a nonthreatening emotion. So, are people more sensitive to signs of anger than to signs of happiness? In a series of experiments, Christine and Ranald Hansen (1988) asked participants to find discrepant facial expressions in photographs of crowds consisting of happy, neutral, or angry faces. In some pictures, all individuals wore the same expression; in others, there was a single discrepant expression. As Darwin would have predicted, participants were quicker to spot discrepant angry faces than they were to locate discrepant faces that were happy or neutral. Other studies have shown that angry faces are arousing to people even when presented subliminally—that is, without their awareness (Dimberg & Ohman, 1996). Joel Aronoff and others (1992) believe that anger is universally associated with certain fixed geometric patterns in the face. As shown in Figure 4.1, anger can be "seen" in triangular eyes that point toward the nose and other hard, downward lines in the forehead, cheeks, mouth, and chin. Such patterns are common in the threatening ceremonial masks worn in many cultures.

It's interesting to note that the social value of the face has become evident to those who communicate online. When e-mail first became popular, the written word was often misinterpreted—especially when the writer was trying to be funny—because it lacked the nonverbal cues that normally animate and clarify live interactions. To fill in this gap, e-mailers created smiley faces and other "emoticons" (emotion icons) from standard keyboard characters. Some routinely used emoticons, meant to be viewed with

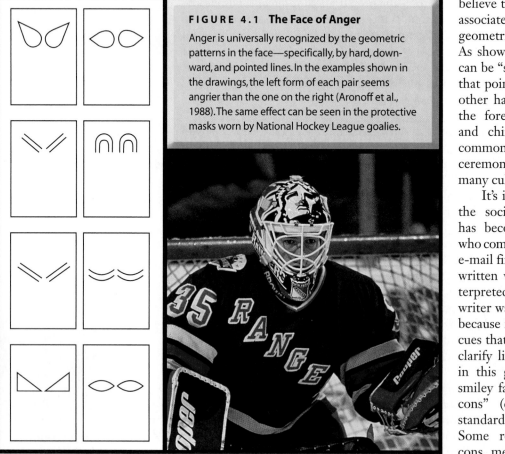

FIGURE 4.1 The Face of Anger

Anger is universally recognized by the geometric patterns in the face—specifically, by hard, downward, and pointed lines. In the examples shown in the drawings, the left form of each pair seems angrier than the one on the right (Aronoff et al., 1988). The same effect can be seen in the protective masks worn by National Hockey League goalies.

one's head tilted 90 degrees to the left, are shown in Figure 4.2 (Sanderson, 1993).

Other nonverbal cues can also influence social perception, enabling us to make quick and often accurate judgments of others (Ambady & Rosenthal, 1993). For example, social perceivers are often fluent readers of *body language*—the ways in which people stand, sit, walk, and express themselves with various gestures. In communicating with others, people use conversational hand gestures such as the raised fist, the bye-bye wave, the thumbs up, and the extended middle finger, sometimes referred to as "flipping the bird" (Krauss et al., 1996). People even form impressions of others based on how they walk. For example, research shows that men and women who have a youthful walking style—who sway their hips, bend their knees, lift their feet, and swing their arms—are seen as happier and more powerful than those who walk slowly, take shorter steps, and stiffly drag their feet (Montepare & McArthur, 1988).

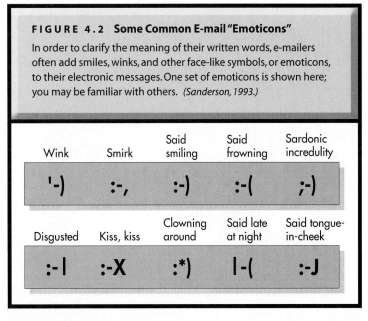

FIGURE 4.2 Some Common E-mail "Emoticons"
In order to clarify the meaning of their written words, e-mailers often add smiles, winks, and other face-like symbols, or emoticons, to their electronic messages. One set of emoticons is shown here; you may be familiar with others. *(Sanderson, 1993.)*

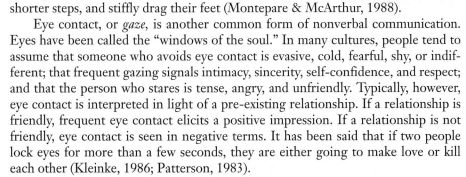

Wink	Smirk	Said smiling	Said frowning	Sardonic incredulity
'-)	:-,	:-)	:-(	;-)

Disgusted	Kiss, kiss	Clowning around	Said late at night	Said tongue-in-cheek
:-|	:-X	:*)	|-(	:-J

Eye contact, or *gaze*, is another common form of nonverbal communication. Eyes have been called the "windows of the soul." In many cultures, people tend to assume that someone who avoids eye contact is evasive, cold, fearful, shy, or indifferent; that frequent gazing signals intimacy, sincerity, self-confidence, and respect; and that the person who stares is tense, angry, and unfriendly. Typically, however, eye contact is interpreted in light of a pre-existing relationship. If a relationship is friendly, frequent eye contact elicits a positive impression. If a relationship is not friendly, eye contact is seen in negative terms. It has been said that if two people lock eyes for more than a few seconds, they are either going to make love or kill each other (Kleinke, 1986; Patterson, 1983).

Another powerful, primitive form of nonverbal behavior is *touch*—the congratulatory high-five, the sympathetic pat on the back, the joking elbow in the ribs, and

"Our faces, together with our language, are social tools that help us navigate the social encounters that define our 'selves' and fashion our lives."

—Alan J. Fridlund

Why were Israeli Prime Minister Netanyahu and Palestinian leader Arafat shaking hands? Did they feel warmly toward each other, or was the greeting compelled by the situation? Look at the cool distance that separates these rival leaders and you'll "see" that this 1996 meeting was filled with tension. In the past, Netanyahu had said that he would never shake Arafat's hand.

People often communicate nonverbally through various hand gestures. In the United States, the "thumbs up" is used to signal that all is well. In Australia, this same gesture is considered rude.

Many animals communicate nonverbally. For example, ants send chemical signals to indicate food, and vervet monkeys give off loud alarm calls that differ depending on whether the predator they see is a snake, eagle, or leopard.

the loving embrace being just a few familiar examples. Physical touching has long been regarded as an expression of friendship, nurturance, and sexual interest. However, it may also serve other functions. Several years ago, Nancy Henley (1977) observed that men, older persons, and those of high socioeconomic status were more likely to touch women, younger persons, and individuals of lower status than the other way around. Henley's interpretation: that touching may be an expression not only of intimacy but of dominance and control.

As described by Axtell (1993), nonverbal communication norms vary from one culture to the next. So watch out. In Bulgaria, nodding your head means "no" and shaking your head sideways means "yes." In Germany and Brazil, the American "okay" sign (forming a circle with your thumb and forefinger) is an obscene gesture. Personal space habits also vary across cultures. Japanese people like to keep a comfortable distance while interacting. But in Puerto Rico and much of Latin America, people stand very close—and backing off is considered an insult. Also beware of what you do with your eyes. In Latin America, locking eyes is a must; yet in Japan, too much eye contact shows a lack of respect. If you're in the habit of stroking your cheek, you should know that in Italy, Greece, and Spain it means that you find the person you're talking to attractive. And whatever you do, don't ever touch someone's head in Buddhist countries, especially Thailand. The head is sacred.

Different cultures also have vastly different rules for greeting someone. In Finland, you should give a firm handshake; in France, you should loosen the grip; in Zambia, you should use your left hand to support the right; and in Bolivia, you should extend your arm if your hand is dirty. In Japan, people bow; in Thailand, they put both hands together in a praying position on the chest; and in Fiji, they smile and raise their eyebrows. In certain parts of Latin America, it is common for people to hug, embrace, and kiss upon meeting. And in most Arab countries, men greet one another by saying *salaam alaykum*, then shaking hands, saying *kaif halak*, and kissing each other on the cheek.

Distinguishing Truth from Deception   It was September 1997 when the drama unfolded in a Virginia courtroom. Sportscaster Marv Albert was the defendant, accused of sexually assaulting Vanessa Perhach, a longtime sexual companion. Perhach testified that Albert had pinned her to his hotel bed, bit her on the back, and forced himself upon her. Albert denied the charges, said the interaction was consensual, and claimed that Perhach was lying because he was engaged to be married and wanted to terminate their relationship. The trial ended abruptly when Albert pleaded guilty in exchange for a reduction in charges and later a suspended sentence. He never apologized, however; and to this day, he maintains his innocence. This was a classic "he said, she said" trial. But who should be believed, Albert or Perhach, and why?

Social perception is tricky because people sometimes try to hide or stretch the truth about themselves. Poker players bluff to win money, witnesses lie to protect themselves, and public officials make campaign promises they don't intend to keep. On occasion, everyone tells something less than "the truth, the whole truth, and nothing but the truth." Can social perceivers tell the difference? Can you tell when someone is lying?

Sigmund Freud, the founder of psychoanalysis, once said that "no mortal can keep a secret. If his lips are silent, he chatters with his fingertips; betrayal oozes out of him at every pore" (1905, p. 94). Paul Ekman and Wallace Friesen (1974) revised Freud's observation by pointing out that some pores "ooze" more than others. Specifically, Ekman and Friesen proposed that some channels of communication are difficult for deceivers to control, while others are relatively easy. To test this hypothesis, they showed a series of films—some pleasant, others disgusting—to a group of female nurses. While watching, participants were instructed either to report their honest impressions of these films or to conceal their true feelings. Through the use of hidden cameras, the participants were videotaped. Others acting as observers then viewed the tapes and judged whether the participants had been truthful or deceptive. The results showed that the level of judgment accuracy was influenced by which types of nonverbal cues the observers were exposed to. Observers who watched tapes that focused on the body were better at detecting deception than were those who saw tapes focused on the face. The face can communicate emotion, but it is relatively easy for deceivers to control—unlike nervous movements of the hands and feet.

This study was the first of many. In other studies as well, one group of participants made truthful or deceptive statements while another group read the transcripts, listened to audiotapes or watched videotapes, and then tried to evaluate the statements. This research showed that people frequently make mistakes in their judgments of truth and deception and too often accept what others say at face value. Even more sobering, people don't have a good sense of their own lie-detection skills. Specifically, it seems that people are confident in these judgments regardless of whether they are correct or incorrect (DePaulo et al., 1997). As you might expect, some people are better than others at this task (Frank & Ekman, 1997). Surprisingly, however, professionals who regularly make these kinds of judgments for a living—police detectives, trial judges, psychiatrists, and those who

In 1997, Vanessa Perhach accused Marv Albert of sexual assault. She vividly described a hotel room incident that he vehemently denied. So who was telling the truth? Public opinion was split over this case— illustrating how difficult it is to make accurate judgments of truth and deception.

TABLE 4.1 Can the "Experts" Catch a Liar?

Lie-detection experts with experience at making judgments of truth and deception were shown brief videotapes of ten women telling the truth or lying about their feelings. Considering that there was a fifty-fifty chance of guessing correctly, the accuracy rates were remarkably low. Only a sample of U.S. Secret Service agents posted a better-than-chance performance. *(Ekman & O'Sullivan, 1991.)*

Observer Groups	Accuracy Rates
College Students	52.82
CIA, FBI, and military	55.67
Police investigators	55.79
Trial judges	56.73
Psychiatrists	57.61
U.S. Secret Service agents	64.12

Adaptively, people are skilled at knowing when someone is lying rather than telling the truth. **False.**

administer lie-detector tests for the CIA, FBI, and military—are, like the rest of us, highly prone to error (Ekman & O'Sullivan, 1991; see Table 4.1).

What seems to be the problem? After reviewing over thirty studies, Miron Zuckerman and his colleagues (1981) concluded that there is a *mismatch* between the behaviors that actually signal deception and those used by perceivers to detect deception. To be specific, four channels of communication provide relevant information: words, the face, the body, and the voice. When people have a reason to lie, *words* alone cannot be trusted. The *face* is also controllable. We tend to think that people do not smile when they lie, but it is common for deceivers to mask their real feelings with false smiles that do not stretch up to the eye muscles (Ekman et al., 1990). Indeed, psychophysiological research confirms that there are two types of smiles—one more genuine than the other (Ekman & Davidson, 1993; Frank et al., 1993). The *body* is somewhat more revealing than the face, as deception is often accompanied by fidgety movements of the hands and feet and by restless shifts in posture. Finally, the *voice* is the leakiest, most revealing cue. When people lie, especially when they are highly motivated to do so, their voices rise in pitch, and the number of speech hesitations increases.

In light of these findings, it appears that perceivers tune in to the wrong channels of communication. Too easily seduced by the silver tongue and the smiling face, we often fail to notice the restless body and quivering voice. Ironically, research participants become more accurate in their judgments of truth and deception when they are too busy to attend closely to what a speaker says (Gilbert & Krull, 1988), when they're instructed to pay more attention to the telltale cues of the body or voice than to the face (DePaulo et al., 1982), and when they are not themselves anxious about social interaction (DePaulo & Tang, 1994).

Attribution: From Elements to Dispositions

To interact effectively with others, we need to know how they feel and when they can be trusted. But to understand people well enough to predict their future behavior, we must also identify their *dispositions:* stable characteristics such as personality traits, attitudes, and abilities. Since we cannot actually see dispositions, we infer them indirectly from what a person says and does. In this section, we look at the processes that lead us to make these inferences.

Attribution Theories

Do you ever think about the influence you have on other people? What about the roles of heredity, childhood experiences, and social forces? Do you wonder why some people succeed while others fail? Individuals differ in the extent to which they feel a need to explain the uncertain events of human behavior (Weary & Edwards, 1994). Among college students, for example, psychology majors are more curious about such matters than are natural-science majors (Fletcher et al., 1986). Although there are vast differences among us, people in general tend to ask "why?"

when they confront important events that are negative or unexpected (Hastie, 1984; Weiner, 1985)—and when understanding these events has personal relevance (Malle & Knobe, 1997).

To make sense of our social world, we try to understand the causes of other people's behavior. But what kinds of explanations do we make, and how do we go about making them? In a classic book entitled *The Psychology of Interpersonal Relations*, Fritz Heider (1958) took the first step toward answering these questions. To Heider, we are all scientists of a sort. Motivated to understand others well enough to manage our social lives, we observe, analyze, and explain their behavior. The explanations we come up with are called *attributions*, and the theory that describes the process is called **attribution theory.** The questions posed at the beginning of the chapter—questions regarding the accidental death of Princess Diana, the Tyson-Holyfield fight, the campaign financing charges against President Clinton, the judge's decision on the British au pair, and couples that divorce—are questions of attribution.

"It's not you, Frank, it's me—I don't like you."

People make attributions all the time in an effort to make sense of their social world. But what kind of attribution is being made here?

Robert Mankoff © 1997 from The New Yorker Collection. All Rights Reserved.

Although people come up with different kinds of explanations for the events of human behavior, Heider found it useful to group these explanations into two categories: personal and situational. Consider the following example. In December 1997, basketball star Latrell Sprewell of the Golden State Warriors physically assaulted P. J. Carlesimo, his coach. The team then terminated Sprewell's contract, the NBA suspended him for one year, and everyone tried to explain his actions. Some observers said the incident occurred because Sprewell is young, brash, and hot-tempered (a **personal attribution**), while others speculated that his actions were provoked by the in-your-face style of his coach and by the circumstances of their encounter (a **situational attribution**). The task for the attribution theorist is to determine not the *true* causes of such an event but our *perceptions* of the causes. For now, two major attribution theories are described.

Jones's Correspondent Inference Theory   According to Edward Jones and Keith Davis (1965), each of us tries to understand others by observing and analyzing their behavior. Jones and Davis's **correspondent inference theory** predicts that people try to infer from an action whether the act itself corresponds to an enduring personal characteristic of the actor. Is the person who commits an act of aggression a beast? Is the person who donates money to charity an altruist? To answer these kinds of questions, people make inferences on the basis of three factors.

The first factor is a person's degree of *choice*. Behavior that is freely chosen is more informative about a person than behavior that is coerced. In one study, participants read a speech, presumably written by a college student, that either favored or opposed Fidel Castro, the communist leader of Cuba. Some participants were told that the student had freely chosen this position, and others were told that the student had been assigned the position by a professor. When asked to determine the student's true attitude, participants were more likely to assume a correspondence between his or her essay (behavior) and attitude (disposition) when the student had had a choice than when he or she had been assigned to the role (Jones & Harris, 1967; see Figure 4.3). Keep this study in mind. It supports correspondent inference theory; but as we will see later, it also demonstrates one of the most tenacious biases of social perception.

The second factor that leads people to make dispositional inferences is the *expectedness* of behavior. As previously noted, an action tells us more about a person

attribution theory A group of theories that describe how people explain the causes of behavior.

personal attribution
Attribution to internal characteristics of an actor, such as ability, personality, mood, or effort.

situational attribution
Attribution to factors external to an actor, such as the task, other people, or luck.

correspondent inference theory A theory holding that we make inferences about a person when his or her actions are freely chosen, are unexpected, and result in a small number of desirable effects.

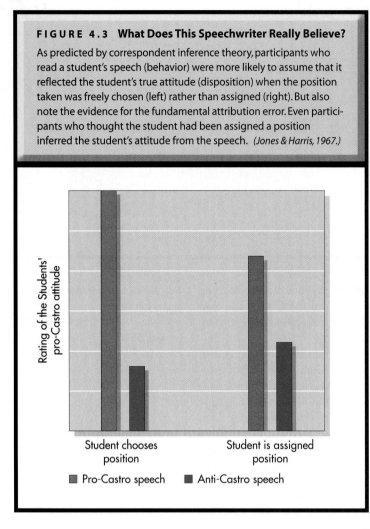

Rating of the Students' pro-Castro attitude

Student chooses position   Student is assigned position

■ Pro-Castro speech   ■ Anti-Castro speech

when it departs from the norm than when it is typical, part of a social role, or otherwise expected under the circumstances (Jones et al., 1961). Thus, people think they know more about a student who wears three-piece suits to class or a citizen who openly refuses to pay taxes than about a student who wears blue jeans to class or a citizen who files tax returns on April 15.

Third, people consider the intended *effects* or consequences of someone's behavior. Acts that produce many desirable outcomes do not reveal a person's specific motives as clearly as acts that produce only a single desirable outcome (Newtson, 1974). For example, you are likely to be uncertain about exactly why a person stays on a job that is enjoyable, high paying, and in an attractive location—three desirable outcomes, each sufficient to explain the behavior. In contrast, you may feel more certain about why a person stays on a job that is tedious and low paying but is in an attractive location—only one desirable outcome.

Kelley's Covariation Theory Correspondent inference theory seeks to describe how perceivers try to discern an individual's personal characteristics from a slice of behavioral evidence. However, behavior can be attributed not only to personal factors but to situational factors as well. How is this distinction made? In the opening chapter, we noted that the causes of human behavior can be derived only through *experiments*. That is, one has to make more than a single observation and compare behavior in two or more settings in which everything stays the same except for the independent variables. Like Heider, Harold Kelley (1967) believes that people are much like scientists in this regard. They may not observe others in a laboratory, but they too make comparisons and think in terms of "experiments." According to Kelley, people make attributions by using the **covariation principle:** In order for something to be the cause of a behavior, it must be present when the behavior occurs and absent when it does not. Three kinds of covariation information are particularly useful: consensus, distinctiveness, and consistency.

To illustrate these concepts, imagine you are standing on a street corner one hot, steamy evening minding your own business, when all of a sudden a stranger comes out of an air-conditioned movie theater and blurts out, "Great flick!" Looking up, you don't recognize the movie title, so you wonder what to make of this "recommendation." Was the behavior (the rave review) caused by something about the person (the stranger), the stimulus (the film), or the circumstances (say, the air-conditioned theater)? Possibly interested in spending a night at the movies, how would you proceed to explain what happened? What kinds of information would you want to obtain?

Thinking like a scientist, you might seek out *consensus information* to see how different persons react to the same stimulus. In other words, how do other moviegoers feel about this film? If others also rave about it, the stranger's behavior is

covariation principle A principle of attribution theory holding that people attribute behavior to factors that are present when a behavior occurs and absent when it does not.

high in consensus and is attributed to the stimulus. If others are critical of the same film, the behavior is low in consensus and is attributed to the person.

Still thinking like a scientist, you might also want to have *distinctiveness information* to see how the same person reacts to different stimuli. In other words, how does this moviegoer react to other films? If the stranger is critical of other films, the target behavior is high in distinctiveness and is attributed to the stimulus. If the stranger raves about everything, however, then the behavior is low in distinctiveness and is attributed to the person.

Finally, you might seek *consistency information* to see what happens to the behavior at another time when the person and the stimulus both remain the same. How does this moviegoer feel about this film on other occasions? If the stranger raves about the film on video as well as in the theater, the behavior is high in consistency. If the stranger does not always enjoy the film, the behavior is low in consistency. According to Kelley, behavior that is consistent is attributed to the stimulus when consensus and distinctiveness are also high and to the person when they are low. In contrast, behavior that is low in consistency is attributed to transient circumstances, such as the temperature of the movie theater.

Kelley's theory and the predictions it makes are represented in Figure 4.4. Does this model describe the kinds of information *you* seek when you try to determine what causes people to behave as they do? Yes, research shows that research participants who are instructed to make attributions for various events do, in general, follow the logic of covariation (Cheng & Novick, 1990; Fosterling, 1992; McArthur, 1972).

Attribution Biases

When the theories of attribution were first proposed, they were represented by such complicated flow charts, formulas, and diagrams that many social psychologists began to wonder: Do people really analyze behavior in the way that one might

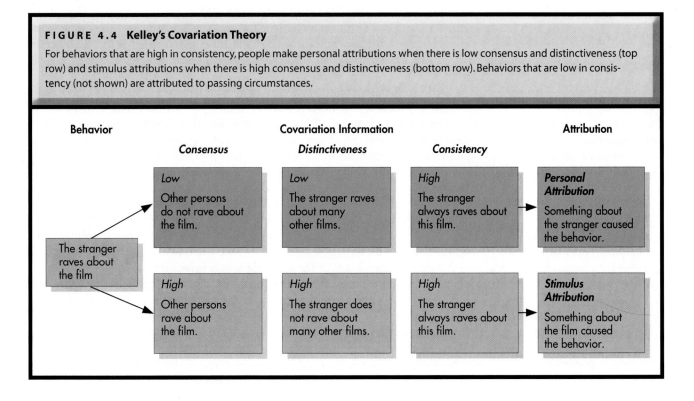

FIGURE 4.4 Kelley's Covariation Theory

For behaviors that are high in consistency, people make personal attributions when there is low consensus and distinctiveness (top row) and stimulus attributions when there is high consensus and distinctiveness (bottom row). Behaviors that are low in consistency (not shown) are attributed to passing circumstances.

expect of computers? Do people have the time, the motivation, or the cognitive capacity for such elaborate and mindful processes? The answer is sometimes yes, sometimes no. As social perceivers, we are limited in our ability to process all relevant information, or we may lack the kinds of training needed to employ fully the principles of attribution theory. More important, we often don't make an effort to think carefully about our attributions. With so much to explain and not enough time in a day, people take mental shortcuts, cross their fingers, hope for the best, and get on with life. The problem is that with speed comes bias and perhaps even a loss of accuracy. In this section, we examine some of these shortcuts—and their consequences.

Cognitive Heuristics   According to Daniel Kahneman, Amos Tversky, and others, we often make attributions and other types of social judgments by using cognitive heuristics—information-processing rules of thumb that enable us to think in ways that are quick and easy but that frequently lead to error (Gilovich, 1991; Kahneman et al., 1982; Nisbett & Ross, 1980).

One rule of thumb that has particularly troublesome effects on attribution is the **availability heuristic,** a tendency to estimate the odds that an event will occur by how easily instances of it pop to mind. To demonstrate this phenomenon, Tversky and Kahneman (1973) asked research participants: Which is more common, words that start with the letter *r* or words that contain *r* as the third letter? In actuality, the English language has many more words with *r* as the third letter than as the first. Yet most people guessed that more words begin with *r*. The reason? It's easier to bring to mind words in which *r* appears first. Apparently, our estimates of likelihood are heavily influenced by events that are readily available in memory (MacLeod & Campbell, 1992).

The availability heuristic can lead us astray in two ways. First, it gives rise to the **false-consensus effect,** a tendency for people to overestimate the extent to which others share their opinions, attributes, and behaviors (Ross, Greene, & House, 1977). This bias is pervasive. Regardless of whether people are asked to predict how others feel about military spending, abortion, gun control, Campbell's soup, certain types of music, or norms for appropriate behavior, they exaggerate the percentage of others who behave similarly or share their views. This occurs most strongly when the actual percentage of others who agree is low (Gross & Miller, 1997).

To illustrate the effect, Joachim Krueger and Russell Clement (1994) asked participants in a study to indicate whether they agreed or disagreed with a series of statements taken from a well-known personality test. Later, they were asked to estimate the percentage of people in general who would agree with these same statements. As shown in Table 4.2, participants' beliefs about other people were biased by their own responses. In part, the false-consensus bias is a by-product of the availability heuristic. We tend to associate with others who are like us in important ways, so we are more likely to notice and recall instances of similar rather than dissimilar behavior (Deutsch, 1989). Interestingly, people do *not* exhibit this bias when asked to predict the behavior of people from groups other than their own (Mullen et al., 1992).

A second consequence of the availability heuristic is that social perceptions are influenced more by one vivid life story than by hard statistical facts. Have you ever wondered why so many people buy lottery tickets despite the astonishingly low odds or why so many travelers are afraid to fly even though they are more likely to perish in a car accident? These behaviors are symptomatic of the **base-rate fallacy**—the fact that people are relatively insensitive to numerical base rates, or probabilities, and are influenced instead by graphic, dramatic events such as the sight of a multimillion-dollar lottery winner celebrating on TV or a photograph of

availability heuristic The tendency to estimate the likelihood that an event will occur by how easily instances of it come to mind.

false-consensus effect The tendency for people to overestimate the extent to which others share their opinions, attributes, and behaviors.

base-rate fallacy The finding that people are relatively insensitive to consensus information presented in the form of numerical base rates.

bodies being pulled from the wreckage of a plane crash. The base-rate fallacy can thus lead to various misperceptions of risk. Indeed, people overestimate the number of those who die in shootings, fires, floods, and terrorist bombings and underestimate the death toll caused by heart attacks, strokes, diabetes, and other mundane events (Slovic et al., 1982).

Every day, we are besieged by both types of information: We read the unemployment rate, and we watch personal interviews with frustrated job seekers; we read the casualty figures of war, and we witness the agony of a parent who has lost a child in combat. Logically, statistics that summarize the experiences of many people are more informative than a single and perhaps atypical case, but perceivers march to a different drummer. As long as a personal anecdote is seen as relevant (Schwarz, Strack, Hilton, & Naderer, 1991) and the source as credible (Hinsz et al., 1988), it seems that one good image is worth a thousand numbers.

People can also be influenced by how easy it is to imagine events that did *not* occur. As thoughtful and curious beings, we often are not content to accept what happens to us or to others without wondering, at least in private, "What if…?" According to Daniel Kahneman and Dale Miller (1986), people's emotional reactions to events are often colored by **counterfactual thinking,** the tendency to imagine alternative outcomes that might have occurred but did not. If the imagined result is better than the actual result, we are likely to experience disappointment, regret, and frustration. If the imagined result is worse, then we react with emotions that range from relief and satisfaction to elation. In interesting ways, the psychological impact of positive and negative events depends on the way we think about "what might have been" (Roese, 1997; Roese & Olson, 1995).

People don't immerse themselves in counterfactual thought after every experience, obviously. But according to Victoria Medvec and Kenneth Savitsky (1997), certain situations—such as being on the *verge* of a better or worse outcome, just above or below some cutoff point—make it easy to conjure up images of what might have happened. The implications are intriguing. Imagine, for example, that you are an Olympic athlete and have just won a silver medal—a remarkable feat. Now imagine that you have just won the bronze medal. Which situation would make you feel better? Rationally speaking, you should feel more pride and satisfaction with the silver medal. But what if your achievement had prompted you to engage in counterfactual thinking? What alternative would preoccupy your mind if you had finished in second place? Where would your focus be if you had placed third? Is it possible that the athlete who is better off objectively will feel worse?

To examine this question, Medvec and her colleagues (1995) videotaped forty-one athletes in the 1992 summer Olympic Games at the moment they realized that they had won a silver or a bronze medal and again, later, during the medal ceremony. Then they showed these tapes, without sound, to people who did not know the order of finish. These participants were asked to observe the medalists and rate their emotional states on a scale ranging from "agony" to "ecstasy." The intriguing result, as you might expect, was that the bronze medalists, on average, seemed happier than the silver medalists. Was there any more direct evidence of counterfactual thinking? In a second study, participants who watched interviews with many of these same athletes rated the silver medalists as more negatively focused on finishing second rather than first and the bronze medalists as more positively focused on

TABLE 4.2 The False-Consensus Effect

In this study, participants who agreed or disagreed with forty statements estimated the percentage of other people who would agree with the same statements. As shown in this sample of items, participants' estimates of population consensus were biased by their own views. *(Krueger & Clement, 1994.)*

Statements	Agree %	Disagree %
I sweat very easily on cool days.	44.54	29.26
I enjoy reading love stories.	53.49	47.12
I would like to be a singer.	56.50	39.71
I think most people would lie to get ahead.	66.12	48.36
I am a very sociable person.	65.16	59.17

"A single death is a tragedy; a million is a statistic."

—Joseph Stalin

counterfactual thinking
A tendency to imagine alternative events or outcomes that might have occurred but did not.

Kramer, George, Jerry, and Elaine played distinctive roles on the TV show, Seinfeld. But what are these individuals really like? Illustrating the fundamental attribution error, viewers often assume that actors in real life are like the characters they play on TV.

finishing third rather than fourth. For these great athletes, feelings of satisfaction were based more on their thoughts of what might have been than on the reality of what was.

The Fundamental Attribution Error   By the time you finish reading this textbook, you will know the cardinal lesson of social psychology: People are profoundly influenced by the *situational* context of behavior. This point is not as obvious as it may seem. For instance, parents are often surprised to hear that their mischievous child, the family monster, is a perfect angel in the classroom. And students are often surprised to observe that their favorite professor, so eloquent in the lecture hall, may stumble over words in less formal gatherings. These reactions are symptomatic of a well-documented aspect of social perception. When people explain the behavior of others, they tend to overestimate the role of personal factors and overlook the impact of situations. Because this bias is so pervasive, and sometimes so misleading, it has been called the **fundamental attribution error** (Ross, 1977).

Evidence of the fundamental attribution error was first reported in the Jones and Harris (1967) study described earlier, in which participants read an essay presumably written by a student. In that study, participants were more likely to infer the student's true attitude when the position taken had been freely chosen than when they thought that the student had been assigned to it. But look again at Figure 4.3, and you'll notice that even when participants thought that the student had no choice but to assert a position, they still used the speech to infer his or her attitude. This finding has been repeated many times. Whether the essay topic is nuclear power, abortion, drug laws, or the death penalty, the results are essentially the same (Jones, 1990).

People fall prey to the fundamental attribution error even when they are fully aware of the situation's impact on behavior. In one experiment, the participants themselves were assigned to take a position, whereupon they swapped essays and rated each other. Remarkably, they still jumped to conclusions about each other's attitudes (Miller et al., 1981). In another experiment, participants inferred attitudes from a speech even when they were the ones who had assigned the position to be taken (Gilbert & Jones, 1986).

A fascinating study by Ross, Amabile, and Steinmetz (1977) demonstrates the fundamental attribution error in a more familiar setting, the TV quiz show. By a flip of the coin, participants in this study were randomly assigned to play the role of either the questioner or the contestant in a quiz game while spectators looked on. In front of the contestant and spectators, the experimenter instructed the questioner to write ten challenging questions from his or her own store of general knowledge. If you are a trivia buff, you can imagine how esoteric such questions can be: Who was the first governor of Idaho? What team won the NHL Stanley Cup in 1968? It is no wonder that contestants correctly answered only about 40 percent of the questions asked. When the game was over, all participants rated the

fundamental attribution error The tendency to focus on the role of personal causes and underestimate the impact of situations on other people's behavior.

questioner's and contestant's general knowledge on a scale of 0 to 100.

Picture the events that transpired. The questioners appeared more knowledgeable than the contestants. After all, they knew all the answers. But a moment's reflection should remind us that the situation put the questioner at a distinct advantage (there were no differences between the two groups on an objective test of general knowledge). Did participants take the questioner's advantage into account, or did they assume that the questioners actually had greater knowledge? The results were startling. Spectators rated the questioners as above average in their general knowledge and the contestants as below average. The contestants even rated themselves as inferior to their partners. Like the spectators, they too were fooled by the loaded situation (see Figure 4.5).

What's going on here? Why do social perceivers consistently make assumptions about persons and fail to appreciate the impact of situations? According to Daniel Gilbert and Patrick Malone (1995), the problem stems in part from *how* we make attributions. Attribution theorists used to assume that people survey all the evidence and then decide on either a personal or a situational attribution. Instead, it now appears that social perception is a two-step process: First we identify the behavior and make a quick personal attribution; then we correct or adjust that inference to account for situational influences. The first step is simple and automatic, like a reflex; the second requires attention, thought, and effort (see Figure 4.6).

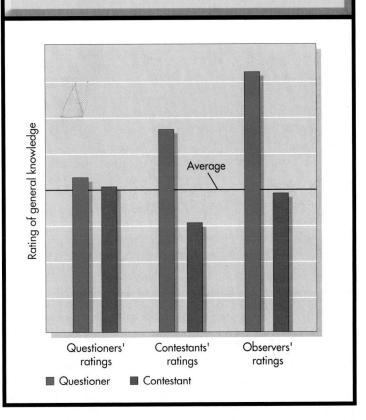

FIGURE 4.5 Fundamental Attribution Error and the TV Quiz Show

Even though the simulated quiz show situation placed questioners in an obvious position of advantage over contestants, observers rated the questioners as more knowledgeable (right). Questioners did not overrate their general knowledge (left); but contestants rated themselves as inferior (middle) and observers rated them as inferior as well. These results illustrate the fundamental attribution error. *(Ross, Amabile, and Steinmetz, 1977.)*

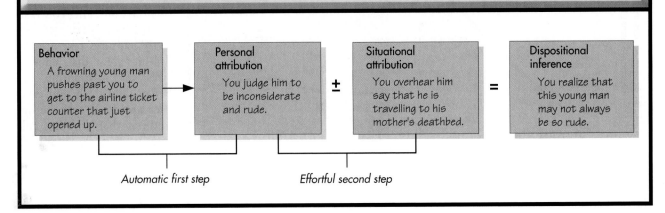

FIGURE 4.6 Two-Step Model of the Attribution Process

Traditional attribution theories assumed that we analyze behavior by searching for a personal or situational cause. The two-step model suggests that people make personal attributions *automatically* and then must consciously adjust that inference in order to account for situational factors.

Several research findings support this hypothesis. First, without realizing it, people often form quick impressions of others based on a brief sample of behavior (Lupfer et al., 1990; Moskowitz, 1993; Newman & Uleman, 1989). Second, perceivers are *more* likely to commit the fundamental attribution error when they are cognitively busy, or distracted, as they observe the target person than when they pay full attention (Gilbert et al., 1992; Trope & Alfieri, 1997). Third, people are *less* likely to commit the fundamental attribution error when they take time before making their judgments (Burger, 1991), when they are highly motivated to be careful and accurate (Webster, 1993), and when they are suspicious that the target has ulterior motives for his or her behavior (Fein, 1996).

Since the two-step model predicts that personal attributions are automatic but that later adjustment for situational factors requires conscious thought, it makes sense to suggest that when attention is divided, when the attribution is made hastily, or when perceivers lack motivation, the second step suffers more than the first. As Gilbert and his colleagues (1988) put it, "The first step is a snap, but the second one's a doozy" (p. 738). Why is the first step such a snap, and why does it seem so natural for people to assume a link between acts and personal dispositions? There are two possible explanations. The first is based on Heider's (1958) insight that people see dispositions in behavior because of a perceptual bias, something like an optical illusion. When you listen to a speech or watch a quiz show, the actor is the conspicuous *figure* of your attention; the situation fades into the *background* ("out of sight, out of mind," as they say). According to Heider, people attribute events to factors that are perceptually conspicuous, or *salient*. To test this hypothesis, Shelley Taylor and Susan Fiske (1975) varied the seating arrangements of research participants who watched as two actors had a carefully staged conversation. In each session, the participants were seated so that they faced actor A, actor B, or both actors. When later questioned about their observations, they rated the actor they faced as the more dominant member of the pair, the one who set the tone and direction.

A second explanation is that perhaps culture teaches us to commit the fundamental attribution error. As we saw in Chapter 1, westerners tend to believe that persons are autonomous, motivated by internal forces, and responsible for their own actions. In contrast, many nonwestern "collectivist" cultures take a more holistic view that emphasizes the relationship between individuals and their social roles. To test the hypothesis that differing cultural worldviews are related to attributions, Joan Miller (1984) asked Americans and Asian Indians of varying ages to describe the causes

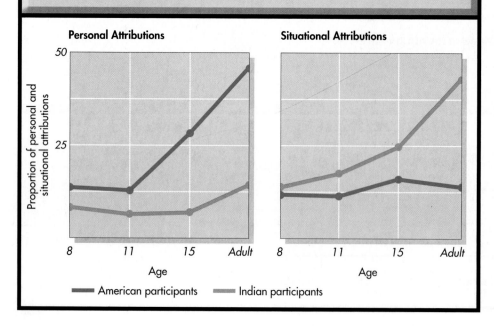

FIGURE 4.7   Fundamental Attribution Error: A Western Bias?

American and Asian Indian participants of varying ages described the causes of negative actions they had observed. Among young children, there were no cultural differences. With increasing age, however, Americans made more personal attributions, and Indian participants made more situational attributions. Explanations for positive behaviors followed a similar pattern. This finding suggests that the fundamental attribution error is a western phenomenon. *(J. G. Miller, 1984.)*

of positive and negative behaviors they had observed in their lives. Among young children, there were no cultural differences. With increasing age, however, the Americans made more personal attributions, while the Indians made more situational attributions (see Figure 4.7). In another study, Michael Morris and Kaiping Peng (1994) compared students from the United States and China. They found no cultural differences in the perception of *physical* events; but for social behaviors, the American students made attributions that were more personal and less situational. It is important to recognize that individuals within a culture also differ in their individualist versus collectivist orientations. These differences are related to the attributions they make and the inferences they draw from behavior (Duff & Newman, 1997; Newman, 1993).

The Actor-Observer Effect   People may commit the fundamental attribution error when they explain the behavior of others, but do we exhibit the same bias in explaining our own behavior? Think about it. Are you shy or outgoing, or does your behavior depend on the situation? Are you calm or intense, quiet or talkative, lenient or firm? Or, again, does your behavior in these regards depend primarily on the situation? Now pick a friend, and answer the same questions about his or her behavior. Do you notice a difference? Chances are, you do. Research shows that people are more likely to say "It depends on the situation" to describe themselves than to describe others. When Lewis Goldberg (1978) administered 2,800 English trait words to fourteen groups, each containing 100 people, he found that 85 percent checked off more traits for others than for themselves.

The tendency to make personal attributions for the behavior of others and situational attributions for ourselves is called the **actor-observer effect** and has been widely demonstrated (Jones & Nisbett, 1972; Watson, 1982). In one study, sixty prison inmates and their counselors were asked to explain why the inmates had committed their offenses. The counselors cited enduring personal characteristics; the prisoners referred to transient situational factors (Saulnier & Perlman, 1981). In a second study, an analysis of "Dear Abby" letters appearing in a newspaper revealed that people seeking advice explained the behavior of others in terms more dispositional than the terms they used to explain their own actions (Schoeneman & Rubanowitz, 1985). In a third study, college roommates rated themselves or each other in terms of how consistently they exhibited various traits—such as inquisitiveness, happiness, patience, and impulsiveness. Compared with the way students saw themselves, the roommates rated others as more consistent in their behavior (Krueger, 1998).

There are two bases for the difference between actors and observers. First, people have more privileged *information* about themselves than about others—enough to know that their behavior changes from one situation to the next (Prentice, 1990; White & Younger, 1988). Second, observers focus *attention* on the actor whose behavior they are trying to explain, but actors must attend to the situation that guides their behavior. Absorbed in a conversation, you gaze at your partner; playing tennis, you keep your eye on the ball; taking an exam, you concentrate on the questions. The result is that actors see as causal key aspects of the situation they are in, while observers see as causal the persons they are watching (Robins et al., 1996). Thus, when an actor and an observer later review the actor's behavior on videotape from each other's visual perspective, the usual effect is reversed (Storms, 1973).

Motivational Biases   As we saw in Chapter 1, people tend to make more favorable, self-serving, and one-sided attributions for their own behavior. Research conducted with students, teachers, parents, workers, athletes, and others shows that we take more credit for success than for failure. Similarly, people seek more information about their strengths than about their weaknesses, overestimate their contribution to group efforts, exaggerate their control, and predict a rosy future. The

Like social psychologists, people are sensitive to situational causes when explaining the behavior of others. **False.**

actor-observer effect   The tendency to attribute our own behavior to situational causes and the behavior of others to personal factors.

false-consensus effect described earlier also has a self-serving side to it. Research suggests that we overestimate the extent to which others think, feel, and behave as we do, in part to reassure ourselves that our own ways are correct, normal, and socially appropriate (Alicke & Largo, 1995; Sherman et al., 1984).

Additional motives can influence our attributions for the behavior of others. For example, William Klein and Ziva Kunda (1992) showed research participants the performance on a practice quiz of another participant—a male target who was later expected to become either their partner or their opponent in a competition. In all cases, the target had answered the practice questions correctly. The reason for his success? Hoping he was not too competent, participants who thought that the target was to be their opponent perceived him as less able than those who thought he was their prospective partner. To justify their wishful thinking, these participants reasoned that the task was easy and that luck was a contributing factor.

At times, personal defensive motives lead us to blame others for their misfortunes. Consider the following classic experiment. Participants thought they were taking part in an emotion-perception study. One person, actually a confederate, was selected randomly to take a memory test while the others looked on. Each time the confederate made a mistake, she was jolted by a painful electric shock (actually, there was no shock; what participants saw was a staged videotape). Since participants knew that only the luck of the draw had kept them off the "hot seat," you might think they would react with sympathy and compassion. Not so. In fact, they belittled the hapless confederate (Lerner & Simmons, 1966).

Melvin Lerner (1980) argues that the tendency to be critical of victims stems from our deep-seated **belief in a just world.** According to Lerner, people need to view the world as a just place in which we "get what we deserve" and "deserve what we get"—a world where hard work and clean living always pay off and where laziness and a sinful lifestyle are punished. To believe otherwise is to concede that we, too, are vulnerable to the cruel twists and turns of fate. So how do people defend themselves from this realization? If people cannot help or compensate the victims of misfortune, they turn on them. Thus, it is often assumed that poor people are lazy, that crime victims are careless, that battered wives provoke their violent and abusive husbands, and that gay men with AIDS lack moral integrity. As you might expect, cross-national comparisons reveal that people in poorer countries are less likely than those in more affluent countries to believe in a just world (Furnham, 1993).

The tendency to disparage victims may seem like just another symptom of the fundamental attribution error: too much focus on the person and not enough on the situation. But the conditions that trigger this tendency suggest there is more to it. Studies have shown that accident victims are held more responsible for their fate when the consequences of the accident are severe rather than mild (Walster, 1966), when the victim's situation is similar to the perceiver's (Shaver, 1970), and when the perceiver is emotionally aroused by the event (Thornton et al., 1986) or generally anxious about threats to the self (Thornton, 1992). The more threatened we feel by an apparent injustice, the greater is the need to protect ourselves from the implication that it could happen to us. One way to defend against this implication is to psychologically distance ourselves from victims by disparaging them. Fortunately, people do not resort to derogation when they can restore justice by helping the victim (Lerner & Simmons, 1966) or when they are prompted to take the victim's perspective (Aderman et al., 1974).

Some people openly disparage gay men with AIDS and blame them for their fate. This reaction may stem from the need to believe that the world is just, and that tragedy strikes only those who are sinful or careless—not us.

belief in a just world The belief that individuals get what they deserve in life, an orientation that leads people to disparage victims.

"And see that you place the blame where it will do the most good."

Integration: From Dispositions to Impressions

When behavior is attributed to situational factors, we do not generally make inferences about the actor. However, personal attributions often lead us to infer that the actor has a certain trait, or disposition—that the leader of a failing business is incompetent or that a former enemy who extends the olive branch is peaceful. Human beings are not one-dimensional, however, and one trait does not a person make. To have a complete picture of someone, social perceivers must assemble the various bits and pieces into a unified impression.

Information Integration: The Arithmetic

Once personal attributions are made, how are they combined into a single coherent picture of a person? How do we approach the process of **impression formation?** Do we simply add up all of a person's traits and calculate a mental average, or do we combine the information in more complicated ways? Anyone who has written or received letters of recommendation will surely appreciate the practical implications. Suppose you're told that an applicant is friendly and intelligent, two highly favorable qualities. Would you be more or less impressed if you then learned that this applicant was also prudent and even-tempered, two moderately favorable qualities? If you are more impressed, then you are intuitively following a *summation* model of impression formation: The more positive traits there are, the better. If you are less impressed, then you are using an *averaging* model: The higher the average value of all the various traits, the better.

To quantify the formation of impressions, Norman Anderson (1968) had research participants rate the desirability of 555 traits on a 7-point scale. By calculating the average ratings, he obtained a *scale value* for each trait (*sincere* had the highest scale value; *liar* had the lowest). In an earlier study, Anderson (1965) used similar values and compared the summation and averaging models. Specifically, he asked a group of participants to rate how much they liked a person described by

---

impression formation
The process of integrating information about a person to form a coherent impression.

two traits with extremely high scale values *(H, H)*. A second group received a list of four traits, including two that were high and two that were moderately high in their scale values *(H, H, M+, M+)*. In a third group, participants received two extremely low, negative traits *(L, L)*. In a fourth group, they received four traits, including two that were low and two that were moderately low *(L, L, M-, M-)*. What effect did the moderate traits have on impressions? As predicted by an averaging model, the moderate traits diluted from rather than added to the impact of the highly positive and negative traits. The practical implication for those who write letters of recommendation is clear. Applicants are better off if their letters include only the most glowing comments and omit favorable remarks that are somewhat more guarded in nature.

After extensive amounts of research, it now appears that although people tend to combine traits by averaging, the process is somewhat more complicated. Consistent with Anderson's (1981) **information integration theory,** impressions formed of others are based on a combination, or integration, of (1) personal dispositions of the perceiver and (2) a *weighted* average, not a simple average, of the target person's characteristics (Kashima & Kerekes, 1994). Let's look more closely at these two sets of factors.

Deviations from the Arithmetic

Like other aspects of our social perceptions, impression formation does not follow the rules of cold logic. Weighted averaging may describe the way most people combine different traits, but the whole process begins with a warm-blooded human perceiver, not a computer. Thus, certain deviations from the "arithmetic" are inevitable.

Perceiver Characteristics   To begin with, perceivers differ in the kinds of impressions they form of others. Some people seem to measure everyone with an intellectual yardstick; others look for physical beauty, a warm smile, a good sense of humor, or a firm handshake. Whatever the attribute, each of us is more likely to notice and recall certain traits than others (Higgins et al., 1982; Bargh et al., 1988). Thus, when people are asked to describe a group of target individuals, there's typically more overlap between the various descriptions provided *by* the same *perceiver* than there is between those provided *for* the same *target* (Dornbusch et al., 1965; Park, 1986). Part of the reason for the differences among perceivers is that we tend to use ourselves as a standard, or frame of reference, when evaluating others. Compared with the inert couch potato, for example, the serious jock is more likely to see others as less active and athletic (Dunning & Hayes, 1996).

A perceiver's current, temporary *mood* can also influence the impressions formed of others (Forgas, 1995). For example, Joseph Forgas and Gordon Bower (1987) told research participants that they had performed very well or poorly on a test of social adjustment. As expected, this feedback altered their moods; it also affected their outlook on others. When presented with behavioral information about various characters, participants spent more time attending to positive facts and formed more favorable impressions when they were happy than when they were sad. Follow-up research shows that the biasing influence of mood is most pronounced when we are forming impressions of others who are atypical and who require more thought and effort in order to be understood (Forgas, 1992). In short, the combined effects of perceiver differences and fluctuating mood point to an important conclusion: that to some extent, impression formation is in the eyes of the beholder.

Priming Effects   The characteristics we tend to notice in other people also change from time to time, depending on recent experiences. Have you ever noticed that

information integration theory The theory that impressions are based on (1) perceiver dispositions and (2) a weighted average of a target person's traits.

once a novel word slips into a conversation, it is repeated over and over again? If so, you have observed **priming,** the tendency for frequently or recently used concepts to come to mind easily and influence the way we interpret new information.

The effect of priming on impressions was first demonstrated by E. Tory Higgins and others (1977). Research participants were presented with a list of trait words, ostensibly as part of an experiment on memory. In fact, the task was designed as a priming device to plant certain ideas in their minds. Some participants read words that evoked a positive image: *brave, independent, adventurous.* Others read words that evoked a more negative image: *reckless, foolish, careless.* Later, in what they thought to be an unrelated experiment, participants read about a man who climbed mountains, drove in a demolition derby, and tried to cross the Atlantic Ocean in a sailboat. As predicted, their impressions were shaped by the trait words they had earlier memorized. Those exposed to positive words later formed more favorable impressions of the character than those exposed to negative words. All participants read exactly the same description, yet they formed different impressions depending on what was already on their minds. In fact, priming seems to work best when the prime words are presented so rapidly that people are not even aware of the exposure (Bargh & Pietromonaco, 1982).

In a provocative series of experiments, John Bargh and his colleagues (Bargh, Chen, & Burrows, 1996) found that our social behavior—not just our judgments of others—may also be subject to the effects of priming without awareness. In one study, for example, research participants were given thirty sets of words presented in scrambled order ("he it hides finds instantly") and told to use some of the words in each set to form grammatical sentences. After explaining the test, which would take about five minutes, the experimenter told participants to locate him down the hall when they were finished so he could administer a second task. So far so good. But when participants found the experimenter, he was in the hallway engaged in a conversation—and he stayed in that conversation for ten full minutes without even acknowledging their presence. What's a person to do, wait patiently or interrupt? The participants didn't know it, but some had worked on a scrambled word test that contained many "politeness" words *(yield, respect, considerate, courteous)*, while others had been exposed to many words related to rudeness *(disturb, intrude, bold, bluntly)*. Would these test words secretly prime participants, a few minutes later, to behave in one way or the other? Yes. Compared with those given neutral words to unscramble, participants primed for rudeness were more likely—and those primed for politeness were less likely—to break in and interrupt the experimenter (see Figure 4.8).

Target Characteristics Just as not all social perceivers are created equal, neither are all traits created equal. In recent years, personality researchers have discovered, across cultures, that individuals can reliably be distinguished from one another along five broad traits, or factors: extroversion, emotional stability, openness to experience, agreeableness, and conscientiousness (Goldberg, 1993; McCrae & Costa, 1997; Wiggins, 1996). Are some of these factors easier to judge than others? Yes. Based on their review of thirty-two studies, David Kenny and his colleagues (1994) found that social perceivers are most likely to agree in their judgments of a target's extroversion—that is, in the extent to which he or she is sociable, friendly, fun-loving, outgoing, and

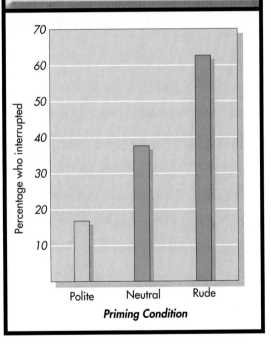

FIGURE 4.8 The Priming of Social Behavior Without Awareness
Would waiting participants interrupt the busy experimenter? Compared with those who had previously been given neutral words to unscramble (center), participants given politeness words were less likely to cut in (left) and those given rudeness words were more likely to cut in (right). These results show that priming can influence not only our social judgments but our behavior as well. *(Bargh, Chen, & Burrows, 1996.)*

priming The tendency for recently used words or ideas to come to mind easily and influence the interpretation of new information.

adventurous. It seems that this characteristic is easy to spot—and different perceivers often agree on it even when rating a target person whom they are seeing for the first time.

The valence of a trait—whether it is considered socially desirable or undesirable—also determines its impact on our final impressions. Specifically, research shows that people exhibit a *trait negativity bias*, the tendency for negative information to weigh more heavily than positive information (Coovert & Reeder, 1990; Skowronski & Carlston, 1989). This means that we are likely to form more extreme impressions of a person who is said to be untrustworthy than of one who is said to be honest. We tend to view others favorably, so we are quick to take notice and pay careful attention when this expectation is violated (Pratto & John, 1991). One bad trait may be enough to destroy a person's reputation—regardless of other qualities. Research on American political campaigns confirms the point: Public opinion is shaped more by a candidate's "negatives" than by positive information (Klein, 1991; Lau, 1985).

The impact of trait information on our impressions of others depends not only on characteristics of the perceiver and target but on context as well. Two contextual factors are particularly important in this regard: (1) implicit theories of personality and (2) the order in which we receive information about one trait relative to other traits.

Implicit Personality Theories   When O. J. Simpson was charged with brutally murdering his ex-wife Nicole and her friend Ron Goldman, everyone was shocked. Simpson was a national hero—athletic, attractive, charming, intelligent, and successful. Once the premier running back in the National Football League, Simpson went on to become a sports broadcaster, Hollywood actor, and father of four children.

It is easy to understand why people reacted to the charges with such disbelief. Simpson just didn't seem like *the kind of person* who would commit a cold-blooded murder. That reaction was based on an **implicit personality theory**—a network of assumptions that we hold about relationships among various types of people, traits, and behaviors. Knowing that someone has one trait thus leads us to infer that they have other traits as well (Bruner & Tagiuri, 1954; Schneider, 1973; Sedikides & Anderson, 1994). For example, you might assume that a person who is unpredictable is also dangerous or that someone who speaks slowly is also slow-witted. You might also assume that certain traits are linked to certain behaviors (Reeder, 1993; Reeder & Brewer, 1979)—that a beloved sports hero like O. J. Simpson, for example, could not possibly stab two people to death.

Solomon Asch (1946) was the first to discover that the presence of one trait often implies the presence of others. Asch told one group of research participants that an individual was "intelligent, skillful, industrious, warm, determined, practical and cautious." Another group read an identical list of traits, except that the word *warm* was replaced by *cold*. Only the one term was changed, but the two groups formed very different impressions. Participants inferred that the warm person was also happier and more generous, good-natured, and humorous than the cold person. When two other words were varied (*polite* and *blunt*), however, the differences were less pronounced. Why? Asch concluded that *warm* and *cold* are **central traits,** meaning that they imply the presence of certain other traits and exert a powerful influence on final impressions. The impact of central traits is not limited to studies using trait lists, either. When college students in different classes were led to believe that a guest lecturer was a warm or a cold person, their impressions after the lecture were consistent with these beliefs—even though he gave the same lecture to everyone (Kelley, 1950; Widmeyer & Loy, 1988).

The Primacy Effect   The order in which a trait is discovered can also influence its impact. It is often said that first impressions are critical, and social psychologists

implicit personality theory A network of assumptions people make about the relationships among traits and behaviors.

central traits Traits that exert a powerful influence on overall impressions.

primacy effect The tendency for information presented early in a sequence to have more impact on impressions than information presented later.

are quick to agree. Studies show that information often has greater impact when presented early in a sequence rather than late—a phenomenon known as the **primacy effect.**

In another of Asch's (1946) classic experiments, one group of participants learned that a person was "intelligent, industrious, impulsive, critical, stubborn, and envious." A second group received exactly the same list but in reverse order. Rationally speaking, the two groups should have felt the same way about the person. But instead, participants who heard the first list—in which the more positive traits came first—formed more favorable impressions than did those who heard the second list. Similar findings were obtained among participants who watched a videotape of a woman taking an SAT-like test. In all cases, she correctly answered fifteen out of thirty multiple-choice questions. But participants who observed a pattern of initial success followed by failure perceived the woman as more intelligent than did those who observed the opposite pattern of failure followed by success (Jones et al., 1968). There are exceptions, but as a general rule, people tend to be more heavily influenced by the "early returns."

What accounts for this primacy effect? There are two basic explanations. The first is that once perceivers think they have formed an accurate impression of someone, they tend to pay less attention to subsequent information. Thus, when research participants read a series of statements about a person, the amount of time they spent reading the items declined steadily with each succeeding statement (Belmore, 1987). Does this mean we are doomed to a life of primacy? No, not at all. If unstimulated or tired, our attention may wane. But if perceivers are sufficiently motivated to avoid tuning out and are not pressured to form a quick first impression, primacy effects are diminished (Anderson & Hubert, 1963; Kruglanski & Freund, 1983). Thus, in one study, college students "leaped to conclusions" about a target person on the basis of preliminary information when they were mentally fatigued from having just taken a two-hour exam—but not when they were fresh, alert, and motivated to pay attention (Webster et al., 1996). In addition, Arie Kruglanski and Donna Webster (1996) have found that some people are more likely than others to "seize" upon and "freeze" their first impressions. According to these researchers, individuals differ in their **need for closure,** the desire to reduce ambiguity. People who are low in this regard are open-minded, deliberate, and perhaps even reluctant to draw firm conclusions about others. In contrast, those who are high in the need for closure tend to be impulsive and impatient and form quick and lasting judgments of others.

More unsettling is the second reason for primacy, known as the *change-of-meaning hypothesis.* Once people have formed an impression, they interpret inconsistent information in light of that impression. Asch's research shows just how malleable the meaning of a trait can be. When people are told that a kind person is *calm,* they assume that he or she is gentle, peaceful, and serene. When a cruel person is said to be *calm,* however, the same word is interpreted to mean cool, shrewd, and calculating. There are many examples to illustrate the point. Based on your first impression, the word *proud* can mean self-respecting or conceited, *critical* can mean astute or picky, and *impulsive* can mean spontaneous or reckless.

It is remarkable just how creative we are in our efforts to transform a bundle of contradictions into a coherent, integrated impression. For example, the person who is said to be "good" but also "a thief" can be viewed as a Robin Hood type of character (Burnstein & Schul, 1982). Or, that person can be seen to have changed over time (Silka, 1989). Asch and Henri Zukier (1984) presented people with inconsistent trait pairs and found that they used different strategies to reconcile the conflicts. For example, a brilliant-foolish person may be seen as "very bright on abstract matters, but silly about day-to-day practical tasks," a sociable-lonely person has "many superficial ties but is unable to form deep relations," and a cheerful-gloomy person may simply be someone who is "moody."

People are slow to change their first impressions on the basis of new information. **True.**

need for closure A desire to reduce cognitive uncertainty, which heightens the importance of first impressions.

Confirmation Biases: From Impressions to Reality

"Please, your majesty," said the knave, "I didn't write it and they can't prove I did; there's no name signed at the end." "If you didn't sign it," said the King, "that only makes the matter worse. You must have meant some mischief, or else you'd have signed your name like an honest man."

This exchange, taken from Lewis Carroll's *Alice's Adventures in Wonderland*, illustrates the power of existing impressions. It is striking but often true: Once people make up their minds about something—even if they have incomplete information—they become more and more unlikely to change their minds when confronted with new evidence. Political leaders thus refuse to withdraw their support for government programs that don't work, and scientists stubbornly defend their theories in the face of conflicting research data. These instances are easy to explain. Politicians and scientists have personal investments in their opinions, for pride, funding, and reputation may be at stake. But what about people who more innocently fail to revise their opinions, often to their own detriment? What about the baseball manager who clings to old strategies that are ineffective or the trial lawyer who always selects juries according to false stereotypes? Why are they often so slow to face the facts? As we will see, people are subject to various **confirmation biases**—tendencies to *interpret*, *seek*, and *create* information in ways that verify existing beliefs.

"It is a capital mistake to theorize before you have all the evidence. It biases the judgment."

—Arthur Conan Doyle

Perseverance of Beliefs

Imagine you are looking at a slide that is completely out of focus. Gradually, it becomes focused enough so that the image is less blurry. At this point, the experimenter wants to know if you can recognize the picture. The response you're likely to make is interesting. Participants in experiments of this type have more trouble making an identification if they watch the gradual focusing procedure than if they simply view the final, blurry image. In the mechanics of the perceptual process, people apparently form early impressions that interfere with their subsequent ability to "see straight" once presented with improved evidence (Bruner & Potter, 1964). As we will see in this section, social perception is subject to the same kind of interference—which is another reason why first impressions often stick like glue even after we are forced to confront information that discredits them.

Consider what happens when you're led to expect something that does not materialize. In one study, John Darley and Paget Gross (1983) asked participants to evaluate the academic potential of a nine-year-old girl named Hannah. One group was led to believe that Hannah came from an affluent community in which both parents were well-educated professionals (high expectations). A second group thought that she was from a run-down urban neighborhood and that both parents were uneducated blue-collar workers (low expectations). As shown in Figure 4.9, participants in the first group were slightly more optimistic in their ratings of Hannah's potential than were those in the second group. In each of these groups, however, half the participants then watched a videotape of Hannah taking an achievement test. Her performance on the tape seemed average. She correctly answered some difficult questions but missed others that were relatively easy. Look again at Figure 4.9 and you'll see that even though all participants saw the same tape, Hannah now received much lower ratings of ability from those who thought

confirmation bias The tendency to seek, interpret, and create information that verifies existing beliefs.

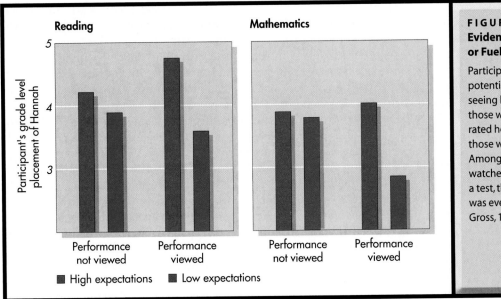

FIGURE 4.9 Mixed Evidence: Does it Extinguish or Fuel First Impressions?

Participants evaluated the potential of a schoolgirl. Without seeing her test performance, those with high expectations rated her slightly higher than did those with low expectations. Among participants who watched a tape of the girl taking a test, the expectations effect was even greater. (Darley & Gross, 1983.)

she was poor and higher ratings from those who thought she was affluent. Apparently, presenting an identical body of mixed evidence did not extinguish the biasing effects of beliefs—it *fueled* these effects.

Events that are ambiguous enough to support contrasting interpretations are like inkblots: We see in them what we want or expect to see. So what about information that plainly disconfirms our beliefs? What then happens to our first impressions? Craig Anderson and his colleagues (1980) addressed this question by supplying participants with false information. After they had time to think about the information, they were told that it was untrue. In one experiment, half the participants read case studies suggesting that people who take risks make better firefighters than do those who are cautious. The others read cases suggesting the opposite conclusion. Next, participants were asked to come up with a theory for the suggested correlation. The possibilities are easy to imagine: "He who hesitates is lost" supports risk-taking, whereas "You have to look before you leap" supports caution. Finally, participants were led to believe that the session was over and were told that the information they had received was false, manufactured for the sake of the experiment. Participants, however, did not abandon their firefighter theories. Instead they exhibited **belief perseverance,** sticking to initial beliefs even after they had been discredited. Apparently, it's easier to get people to build a theory than to convince them to tear it down. Even social psychologists are slow to change their pet theories in light of inconsistent research data (Greenwald et al., 1986).

Why do beliefs often outlive the evidence on which they are supposed to be based? The reason is that when people conjure up explanations that make sense, those explanations take on a life of their own. In fact, once people form an opinion, that opinion is strengthened by merely *thinking* about the topic—even without articulating the reasons for it (Tesser, 1978). And therein lies the solution. By asking people to consider why an *alternative* theory might be true, belief perseverance effects can be reduced or eliminated (Anderson & Sechler, 1986).

Confirmatory Hypothesis Testing

Social perceivers are not passive recipients of information. Like detectives, we ask questions and actively search for clues. But do we seek information objectively, or

belief perseverance The tendency to maintain beliefs even after they have been discredited.

are we inclined to confirm the suspicions we already hold? Mark Snyder and William Swann (1978) addressed this question by having pairs of participants who were strangers to one another take part in a getting acquainted interview. In each pair, one participant was to interview the other. But first, that participant was falsely led to believe that his or her partner was either introverted or extroverted (actually, the participants were assigned on a random basis to these conditions) and was then told to select questions from a prepared list. Those who thought they were talking to an introvert chose mostly introvert-oriented questions ("Have you ever felt left out of some social group?"), while those who thought they were talking to an extrovert asked extrovert-oriented questions ("How do you liven up a party?"). Expecting a certain kind of person, participants unwittingly sought evidence that confirmed their expectations. By asking loaded questions, in fact, the interviewers actually gathered support for their beliefs. Thus, neutral observers who later listened to the tapes were also left with the mistaken impression that the interviewees really were as introverted or extroverted as the interviewers had assumed.

This last part of the study is powerful but, in hindsight, not all that surprising. Imagine yourself on the receiving end of an interview. Asked about what you do to liven up parties, you would probably talk about organizing group games, playing dance music, and telling jokes. On the other hand, if you were asked about difficult social situations, you might talk about being nervous before oral presentations or about what it feels like to be the new kid on the block. In other words, simply by going along with the questions that are asked, you supply evidence confirming the interviewer's beliefs. Thus, perceivers set in motion a vicious cycle: Thinking someone has a certain trait, they engage in a one-sided search for information; and in doing so, they create a reality that ultimately supports their beliefs (Zuckerman et al., 1995).

Are people so blinded by their existing beliefs that they cannot manage an objective search for evidence? It depends. In the task devised by Snyder and Swann, people conduct a biased, confirmatory search for information. Even professional counselors trained in psychotherapy select questions designed to confirm their own hypotheses (Haverkamp, 1993). Thankfully, different circumstances produce less biasing results. When people are not certain of their beliefs and are concerned about the accuracy of their impressions (Kruglanski & Mayseless, 1988), when they are allowed to prepare their own interviews (Trope et al., 1984), or when the available nonconfirmatory questions are better than the confirmatory questions (Skov & Sherman, 1986), then they pursue a more balanced search for information.

The Self-fulfilling Prophecy

In 1948, sociologist Robert Merton told a story about Cartwright Millingville, president of the Last National Bank during the Depression. Although the bank was solvent, a rumor began to spread that it was floundering. Within hours, hundreds of depositors were lined up to withdraw their savings before no money was left to withdraw. The rumor was false, but the bank eventually failed. Using stories such as this, Merton proposed what seemed like an outrageous hypothesis: that a perceiver's expectation can actually lead to its own fulfillment, a **self-fulfilling prophecy**.

Merton's hypothesis lay dormant within psychology until Robert Rosenthal and Lenore Jacobson (1968) published the results of a study entitled *Pygmalion in the Classroom*. Noticing that teachers had higher expectations for better students, they wondered if teacher expectations *influenced* student performance rather than

self-fulfilling prophecy
The process by which one's expectations about a person eventually lead that person to behave in ways that confirm those expectations.

the other way around. To address the question, they told teachers in a San Francisco elementary school that certain pupils were on the verge of an intellectual growth spurt. The results of an IQ test were cited but, in fact, the pupils had been randomly selected. Then eight months later, when real tests were administered, the "late bloomers" exhibited an increase in their IQ scores compared with children assigned to a control group. They were also evaluated more favorably by their classroom teachers.

When the Pygmalion study was first published, it was greeted with chagrin. If positive teacher expectations can boost student performance, can negative expectations have the opposite effect? And what about the social implications? Could it be that affluent children are destined for success and disadvantaged children are doomed to failure because educators hold different expectations for them? Many researchers were critical of the study itself and skeptical about the generality of the results. Unfortunately, though, these findings cannot be swept under the proverbial rug. In a review of additional studies, Rosenthal (1985) found that teacher expectations significantly predicted student performance 36 percent of the time.

How might teacher expectations be transformed into reality? There are two points of view. According to Rosenthal, the teacher forms an initial impression of students early in the school year—based, perhaps, on their background or reputation, physical appearance, initial classroom performance, and standardized-test scores. The teacher then alters his or her behavior in ways that are consistent with that impression. If initial expectations are high rather than low, the teacher gives the student more praise, attention, and challenging homework. In turn, the student adjusts his or her own behavior. If the signals are positive, the student may become energized, work hard, and succeed. If negative, there may be a loss of interest and self-confidence. The cycle is thus complete and the expectations confirmed.

While recognizing that this effect can occur, Lee Jussim and his colleagues (1996) question whether teachers in real life are so prone in the first place to form erroneous impressions of their students. It's true, in many naturalistic studies, that the expectations teachers have at the start of a school year are later confirmed by their students—a result that is consistent with the notion that the teachers had a hand in producing that outcome. But wait. That same result is also consistent with a more innocent possibility: that perhaps the expectations teachers form of their students are *accurate*. There are times, Jussim admits, when teachers may stereotype a student and, without realizing it, behave in ways that create a self-fulfilling prophecy. But there may also be times when teachers predict how their students will perform without necessarily influencing that performance.

Either way, it's clear that self-fulfilling prophecies are at work in many settings—not only schools but also business organizations and the military. For example, in a study of a thousand men assigned to twenty-nine platoons in the Israeli Defense Forces, Dov Eden (1990) led some platoon leaders but not others to expect that the groups of trainees they were about to receive had great potential (in fact, these groups were of average ability). After ten weeks, the trainees assigned to the high-expectation platoons scored higher than the others on written exams and on the ability to operate a weapon. Both inside and outside the classroom, the self-fulfilling prophecy is a powerful phenomenon (Cooper & Good, 1983; Darley & Fazio, 1980; Harris et al., 1994; Harris & Rosenthal, 1985).

When our expectations lead us to alter the behavior of others, the prophecy we fulfill is called a self-fulfilling prophecy. But how does it work? How do social perceivers transform their own expectations of others into reality? Research indicates that the phenomenon occurs as a three-step process. First, a perceiver forms an impression of a target person—an impression that may be based on interactions with the target or on other information. Second, the perceiver behaves in a man-

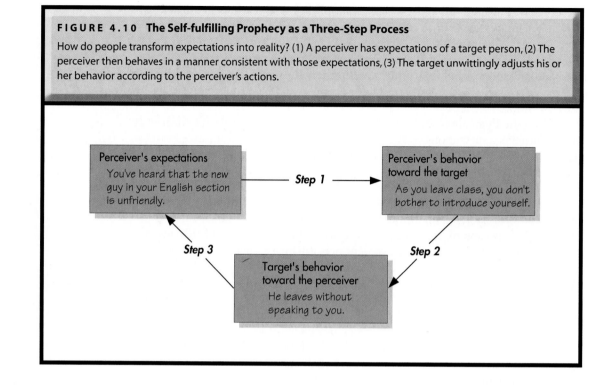

FIGURE 4.10 The Self-fulfilling Prophecy as a Three-Step Process

How do people transform expectations into reality? (1) A perceiver has expectations of a target person, (2) The perceiver then behaves in a manner consistent with those expectations, (3) The target unwittingly adjusts his or her behavior according to the perceiver's actions.

ner that is consistent with that first impression. Third, the target person unwittingly adjusts his or her behavior to the perceiver's actions. The net result: behavioral confirmation of the first impression (see Figure 4.10).

But now let's straighten out this picture. It would be a sad commentary on human nature if each of us were so easily molded by others' perceptions into appearing brilliant or stupid, introverted or extroverted, competitive or cooperative, warm or cold. The effects are well established, but there are limits. By viewing the self-fulfilling prophecy as a three-step process, social psychologists can identify the links in the chain that can be broken to prevent the vicious cycle.

Consider the first step, the link between one's expectations and one's behavior toward the target person. In the typical study, perceivers try to get to know the target on only a casual basis and are not necessarily driven to form an accurate impression. But when perceivers are highly motivated to seek the truth (as when they are considering the target as a possible teammate or opponent), they become more objective—and often do not confirm prior expectations (Harris & Perkins, 1995; Hilton & Darley, 1991).

The link between expectations and behavior depends in other ways as well on a perceiver's goals and motivations in the interaction (Snyder, 1993). In one study, John Copeland (1994) put either the perceiver or the target into a position of relative power. In all cases, the perceiver interacted with a target who was said to be introverted or extroverted. In half the pairs, the perceiver was given the power to accept or reject the target as a teammate for a money-winning game. In the other half, it was the target who was empowered to choose a teammate. The two participants interacted, the interaction was recorded, and neutral observers listened to the tapes and rated the target person. So, did perceivers cause the targets to behave as introverted or extroverted, depending on initial expectations? Yes and no. Illustrating what Copeland called "prophecies of power," Figure 4.11 shows that high-power perceivers triggered the self-fulfilling prophecy, as in past research, but that low-power perceivers did not. In the low-power situation, the

The notion that we can create a "self-fulfilling prophecy" by getting others to behave in ways we expect is a myth.

False.

perceivers spent less time getting to know the target person and more time trying to be liked. Other researchers have similarly found that perceivers do not confirm expectations when they're primarily motivated to self-present and get along (Neuberg et al., 1993; Snyder & Haugen, 1994).

Now consider the second step, the link between a perceiver's behavior and the target's response. In much of the past research, as in much of life, target persons are not aware of others' false impressions. Thus, it is unlikely that Rosenthal and Jacobson's (1968) "late bloomers" knew of their teachers' high expectations or that Snyder and Swann's (1978) "introverts" and "extroverts" knew of their interviewers' misconceptions. But what if they had known? How would *you* react if you found yourself being cast in a particular light? When it happened to participants in one experiment, they managed to overcome the effect by behaving in ways that forced the perceivers to abandon their expectations (Hilton & Darley, 1985).

As you may recall from the discussion of self-verification in Chapter 3, this result is most likely to occur when perceiver expectations clash with a target person's self-concept. When targets who viewed themselves as extroverted were interviewed by perceivers who believed they were introverted (and vice versa), what changed as a result of the interaction were the perceivers' beliefs—not the targets' behavior (Swann & Ely, 1984). Social perception is a two-way street. It's important to recognize that the persons we judge have their own prophecies to fulfill.

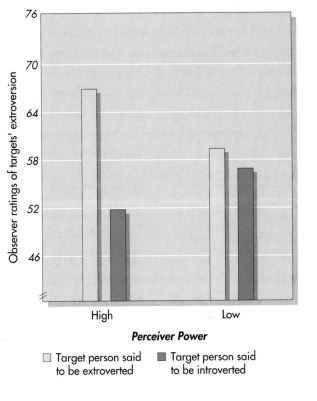

FIGURE 4.11 Prophecies of Power

In this study, perceivers interacted with a target person said to be introverted or extroverted. In half the pairs, the perceiver was in a position of power; in the other half, the target had power. Did perceivers cause targets to behave according to expectations? As shown, only high-power perceivers produced the self-fulfilling prophecy. In contrast, apparently, low-power perceivers spent less time trying to know the target person and more time trying to be liked. *(Copeland, 1994.)*

Social Perception: The Bottom Line

Trying to understand people—whether they are world leaders, professional athletes, politicians, trial judges, or loved ones closer to home—is no easy task. As you reflect on the material in this chapter, you will notice that there are two radically different views of social perception. One suggests that the process is quick and relatively automatic. Without much thought, effort, or awareness, people make rapid-fire snap judgments about others based on physical appearance, preconceptions, or just a hint of behavioral evidence. According to a second view, however, the process is relatively mindful. People observe others carefully and reserve judgment until their analysis of the target person, behavior, and situation is complete. As suggested by theories of attribution and information integration, the process is eminently logical.

FIGURE 4.12   The Processes of Social Perception

Summarizing Chapter 4, this diagram depicts the processes of social perception. As shown, it begins with the observation of persons, situations, and behavior. Sometimes, we make snap judgments from these cues. At other times, we form impressions only after making attributions and integrating these attributions. Either way, our impressions are subject to confirmation biases and the risk of a self-fulfilling prophecy.

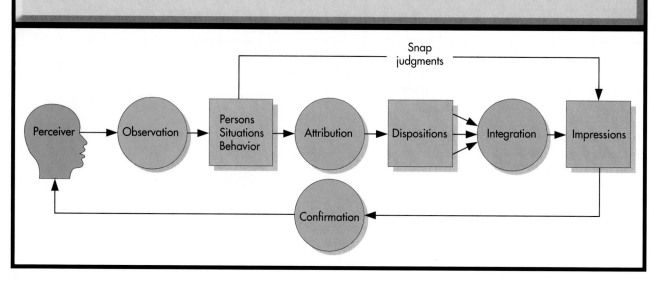

In light of recent research, it is now safe to conclude that both accounts of social perception are correct. Sometimes, our judgments are made instantly; at other times, they are based on a more painstaking analysis of behavior (Brewer, 1988; Fiske & Neuberg, 1990). Either way, we often steer our interactions with others along a path that is narrowed by first impressions, a process that can set in motion a self-fulfilling prophecy. The various aspects of social perception, as described in this chapter, are summarized in Figure 4.12.

At this point, we must confront an important question: How *accurate* are people's impressions of each other? For years, this question has proved provocative but hard to answer (Cronbach, 1955; Kenny, 1994). Granted, people often depart from the ideals of logic and exhibit bias in their social perceptions. In this chapter alone, we have seen that perceivers tend to use cognitive heuristics without regard for numerical base rates; overlook situational influences on behavior; disparage victims whose misfortunes threaten their sense of justice; form premature first impressions; and interpret, seek, and create evidence in ways that support these impressions.

To make matters worse, we often have little awareness of our limitations, leading us to feel *overconfident* in our judgments. In a series of studies, David Dunning and his colleagues (1990) asked college students to predict how a target person would react in various situations. Some made predictions about a fellow student whom they had just met and interviewed, and others made predictions about their roommates. In both cases, participants reported their confidence in each prediction, and accuracy was determined by the responses of the target persons themselves. The results were clear: Regardless of whether they judged a stranger or a roommate, the students consistently overestimated the accuracy of their predictions. People even overestimate their ability to predict their own behavior. When ninety-eight first-year students made 3,800 self-predictions about the upcoming academic year—predictions that were later verified ("Will you decide on a major?" "Will you call your parents more than twice a month?" "Will you have a steady boyfriend/girlfriend?")—they estimated that they would be accurate 82 percent of the time. As it turned out, their accuracy rate was only 68 percent (Vallone et al., 1990).

Standing back from the material presented in this chapter, you may find the list of shortcomings, punctuated by the problem of overconfidence, to be long and depressing. So, how can this list be reconciled with the triumphs of civilization? Or to put it another way, "If we're so dumb, how come we made it to the moon?" (Nisbett & Ross, 1980, p. 249). Part of the answer stems from the realization that *bias*—that is, a deviation from the rules of logic—does not necessarily result in *error*—defined as real-life judgments that are incorrect (Funder, 1987). The fundamental attribution "error" is a good example: We may make personal attributions to the neglect of situations, but sometimes behavior really *is* caused by personal factors (Funder, 1982; Harvey et al., 1981).

It is true that people fall prey to the biases identified by social psychologists and probably even to some biases that have not yet been noticed. It is also true that we often get fooled by con artists, misjudge our partners in marriage, and hire the wrong job applicants. As Thomas Gilovich (1991) points out, more Americans believe in ESP than in evolution, and there are twenty times more astrologers than astronomers. The problem is, these biases can have harmful consequences—giving rise, as we'll see in Chapter 5, to stereotypes, prejudice, and discrimination. Yet despite our imperfections, there are four reasons to be guardedly optimistic about our competence as social perceivers:

1. The more experience people have with each other, the more accurate they are. For example, although people have a limited ability to assess the personality of strangers they meet in the laboratory, they are generally better at judging their own friends and acquaintances (Levesque, 1997; Malloy & Albright, 1990; Paunonen, 1989).

2. Although people are not good at making global judgments of others (that is, at knowing what people are like across a range of settings), we are able to make more circumscribed predictions of how others will behave in our own presence. You may misjudge the personality of a roommate or co-worker, but to the extent that you can predict your roommate's actions at home or your co-worker's actions on the job, the mistakes may not matter (Swann, 1984).

> People are more accurate at judging the personality of friends and acquaintances than of strangers. **True.**

3. Social perception skills can be enhanced in people who are taught the rules of probability and logic (Nisbett et al., 1987). For example, graduate students in psychology—because they take courses in statistics—tend to improve in their ability to reason about everyday social events (Lehman et al., 1988).

4. People can form more accurate impressions of others when motivated by a concern for accuracy and open-mindedness than when motivated by a need for immediacy, confirmation, and closure (Kruglanski & Webster, 1996). Thus, many studies described in this chapter have shown that people exhibit less bias when there is an incentive for accuracy within the experiment (Kunda, 1990; Neuberg, 1989) or when they make judgments that have adaptive significance (Baron, 1988).

To summarize, research on the accuracy of social perceptions offers a valuable lesson: To the extent that we observe others with whom we have had time to interact, make judgments that are reasonably specific, have some knowledge of the rules of logic, and are sufficiently motivated to form an accurate impression, the problems can be minimized. Indeed, being aware of the biases described in this chapter may well be a necessary first step toward a better understanding of others.

Review

Observation: The Elements of Social Perception

- To understand others, social perceivers rely on indirect clues—the elements of social perception.

Persons: Judging a Book by Its Cover

- People often make snap judgments of others based on physical appearances (for example, adults with baby-faced features are seen as having childlike qualities).

Situations: The Scripts of Life

- People have preconceptions, or "scripts," about certain types of situations. These scripts guide our interpretations of behavior.

Behavioral Evidence

- People derive meaning from behavior by dividing it into discrete, meaningful units.
- Nonverbal behaviors are often used to determine how others are feeling.
- From facial expressions, people all over the world can identify the emotions of happiness, fear, sadness, surprise, anger, and disgust.
- Body language, gaze, and touch are also important forms of nonverbal communication.
- People use nonverbal cues to detect deception but are often not accurate in making these judgments because they pay too much attention to the face and neglect cues that are more revealing.

Attribution: From Elements to Dispositions

- Attribution is the process by which we explain people's behavior.

Attribution Theories

- People begin to understand others by making personal or situational attributions for their behavior.
- Correspondent inference theory states that people learn about others from behavior when it is freely chosen, unexpected, and results in a small number of desirable outcomes.
- From multiple behaviors, we base our attributions on three kinds of covariation information: consensus, distinctiveness, and consistency.

Attribution Biases

- People depart from the logic of attribution theory in several ways.

- First, we use cognitive heuristics—rules of thumb that enable us to make judgments that are quick but often in error.
- Second, we tend to commit the fundamental attribution error, overestimating the role of personal factors and underestimating the impact of situations.
- Third, the actor-observer effect reveals that although people tend to make personal attributions for others, they attribute their own behavior to situational factors.
- Fourth, we often make biased attributions for the behavior of others. Needing to believe in a just world, for example, people often criticize victims and hold them responsible for their fate.

Integration: From Dispositions to Impressions

Information Integration: The Arithmetic

- The impressions we form are based on an averaging of a person's traits, not on a summation.
- According to information integration theory, impressions are based on perceiver predispositions and a weighted average of individual traits.

Deviations from the Arithmetic

- Perceivers differ in their sensitivity to certain traits and in the impressions they form.
- Differences stem from stable perceiver characteristics, recent experiences, implicit personality theories, and the primacy effect.

Confirmation Biases: From Impressions to Reality

- Once an impression is formed, people become less likely to change their minds when confronted with nonsupportive evidence.
- People tend to interpret, seek, and create information in ways that confirm existing beliefs.

Perseverance of Beliefs

- First impressions may survive in the face of inconsistent information.
- Ambiguous evidence is interpreted in ways that bolster first impressions.
- The effect of evidence that is later discredited perseveres because people formulate theories to support their initial beliefs.

Confirmatory Hypothesis Testing

- Once perceivers have beliefs about someone, they seek further information in ways that confirm those beliefs.

The Self-fulfilling Prophecy

- As shown by the effects of teacher expectancies on student achievement, first impressions set in motion a self-fulfilling prophecy.
- This is the product of a three-step process: (1) a perceiver forms an expectation of a target person, (2) the perceiver behaves accordingly, and (3) the target adjusts to the perceiver's actions.
- This self-fulfilling prophecy effect is powerful but limited in important ways.

Social Perception: The Bottom Line

- Sometimes, people make snap judgments; at other times, they evaluate others by carefully analyzing their behavior.
- Research suggests that our judgments are often biased and that we are overconfident.
- Still, there are conditions under which we are more competent as social perceivers.

Key Terms

actor-observer effect *109*

attribution theory *101*

availability heuristic *104*

base-rate fallacy *104*

belief in a just world *110*

belief perseverance *117*

central traits *114*

confirmation bias *116*

correspondent inference theory *101*

counterfactual thinking *105*

covariation principle *102*

false-consensus effect *104*

fundamental attribution error *106*

implicit personality theory *114*

impression formation *111*

information integration theory *112*

need for closure *115*

nonverbal behavior *95*

personal attribution *101*

primacy effect *115*

priming *113*

self-fulfilling prophecy *118*

situational attribution *101*

social perception *91*

PUTTING COMMON SENSE TO THE TEST

The impressions we form of others are influenced by superficial aspects of their appearance.

True. *Research shows that first impressions are influenced by height, weight, clothing, facial characteristics, and other aspects of appearance.*

Adaptively, people are skilled at knowing when someone is lying rather than telling the truth.

False. *People frequently make mistakes in their judgments of truth and deception, too often accepting what others say at face value.*

Like social psychologists, people are sensitive to situational causes when explaining the behavior of others.

False. *In explaining the behavior of others, people overestimate the importance of personal factors and overlook the impact of situations—a bias known as the "fundamental attribution error."*

People are slow to change their first impressions on the basis of new information.

True. *Studies have shown that once people form an impression of someone, they become resistant to change even when faced with contradictory new evidence.*

The notion that we can create a "self-fulfilling prophecy" by getting others to behave in ways we expect is a myth.

False. *In the laboratory and in the classroom, a perceiver's expectation can actually lead to its own fulfillment.*

People are more accurate at judging the personality of friends and acquaintances than of strangers.

True. *People often form erroneous impressions of strangers but tend to be more accurate in their judgments of friends and acquaintances.*

5 | Perceiving Groups

PREVIEW

This chapter considers how people think, feel, and behave toward members of social groups. We begin by examining *stereotypes,* beliefs about groups that influence our judgments of individuals. Next, we examine *prejudice,* negative feelings toward others based on their group membership. To illustrate these problems, we then focus on *sexism* and *racism,* forms of discrimination based on a person's gender and racial background. After considering some of the effects of being the *targets* of stereotypes and prejudice, we discuss some ways to reduce discrimination.

(Continued on next page)

"I'm kind of a deep thinker and I walked through town that night after work. You know I'd had my gun in my waist as I was walking around and I'd seen the black guy there at the bus stop and I kind of just thought to myself you know, that he really didn't belong where he was at. And I just thought how easy it would be for me to kind of just take him out right there. It really didn't seem like much to me." To nineteen-year-old Nathan John Thill, it didn't seem like much to murder a man he saw on the street simply because of the color of the man's skin.

In November 1997, Thill and another man encountered Oumar Dia, a thirty-eight-year-old immigrant from the West African nation of Mauritania and father of three children, at a downtown bus stop in Denver. According to police reports and interviews, the two white men made racist remarks to Dia and grabbed his hat and threw it on the sidewalk. A white woman, Jeannie Van Velkinburg, thirty-six, witnessed what was going on and picked up the hat and gave it back to Dia. Then Thill allegedly shot Dia, killing him instantly, and shot Van Velkinburg, severing her spine. Van Velkinburg, a nurse's aide and mother of two, was paralyzed from the waist down. "There was really no emotion involved when I did it," Thill, a self-proclaimed white supremacist, said a few days later, "so it's really hard to know what emotion to feel now" (Vaughan, 1997, p. 5).

T / F

_____ Stereotypes allow people to save time and effort when processing information about others, freeing them to pay attention to other tasks or information.

_____ Members of low-status, stereotyped groups have lower self-esteem than members of high-status groups.

_____ Even brief exposure to sexist television commercials can significantly influence the behaviors of men and women.

_____ Groups with a history of prejudice toward each other tend to become much less prejudiced soon after they are made to interact with each other in a desegregated setting.

_____ The tendency for minority students to underperform relative to white students on a particular academic test is not likely to be affected by slight changes in the test setting but instead requires gradual, long-term societal changes.

A Threat in the Air: Effects on Stigmatized Targets
  Perceiving Discrimination
  Stereotype Threat and Academic Achievement of Women and Minorities

Problems and Prospects

Review

Key Terms

That same month, several other racist acts of violence occurred in the Denver area, including one that resulted in the killing of a police officer. The people of Denver, a city with a reputation for tolerance, were stunned. But the incidents did not receive a great deal of national attention, in part because instances of violence based on racism are all too common. Just a few weeks after the killings in Denver, for example, two white supremacists in Little Rock, Arkansas, were charged with murder and conspiracy to overthrow the U.S. government and replace it with a whites-only Aryan People's Republic. On that same day in Philadelphia, a thirty-nine-year-old man was arraigned on charges of planting eight pipe bombs at local businesses and painting swastikas on politicians' offices (Kaplan et al., 1997).

Violence due to racism is by no means limited to the United States; the plague seems universal. Open a newspaper, and you might read stories about genocide in Sudan, "ethnic cleansing" in Bosnia, and neo-Nazi violence in Germany and France. And for every bit of violence, there are countless other, more subtle ways in which we hurt each other through racism.

Race, of course, is but one way in which we divide the world into different groups. Another is gender; and here, too, we find disturbing occurrences. Consider the case of Ann Hopkins. She was hoping to become a partner in one of the largest accounting firms in the country. Her record was impeccable. In just a few years, Hopkins had single-handedly brought in more than $25 million in contracts, tops among her peers. Yet she was denied a partnership even though several less productive men were promoted. According to Hopkins, it was because she was a woman. As in most disputes, however, there are two sides to the story. The firm claimed that Hopkins was abrasive, overbearing, and hard to work with. Some partners complained that she used profanity and was insensitive to co-workers. One member of the firm was even said to have quit because he could not tolerate working with her.

Was Ann Hopkins rejected because of her personality, her gender, or a combination of the two? Hopkins took the case to court and claimed she was described by partners as a "macho" woman who needed to take a course at "charm school." One partner advised her to "wear make-up, have my hair styled, and wear jewelry." What do these comments prove? To address this question, Hopkins sought expert testimony from social psychologist Susan Fiske. Citing the research presented in this chapter, Fiske concluded that Hopkins was a likely victim of sex discrimina-

(Left) At an anti-hate rally in Denver, friends mourn the death of Oumar Dia, an immigrant from the African country of Mauritania who was murdered on the streets of downtown Denver. (Right) Nathan Thill, who described himself as a white supremacist and a "warrior" in a race war, confessed to shooting Dia and a woman who had tried to help him.

Ann Hopkins and Hunter Tylo are two women who sued their employers, charging discrimination. Despite an exceptional record of productivity, Hopkins (left) was denied partnership in a large accounting firm. Tylo (right) was fired from the cast of Melrose Place *soon after becoming pregnant. Were these women victims of sexist double standards about how women should look and behave? Both won their respective lawsuits.*

tion. The trial judge agreed, and by a 6 to 3 vote so did the U.S. Supreme Court (Fiske et al., 1991, 1997).

More recently, actress Hunter Tylo sued the producers of the television series *Melrose Place*, arguing that the producers had discriminated against her by firing her because of her pregnancy. The producers claimed that Tylo had been hired to play a sexy character and could no longer do so because she had gained so much weight. Supporters of Tylo argued that men on television who gain weight are not fired and that a double standard therefore exists. Others argued that Tylo knew that she had to look a certain way in order to play the part that she had agreed to play. Was her firing an act of discrimination? A Los Angeles jury thought so and awarded her almost $5 million—almost twice as much as she had asked for.

Discrimination of this sort raises important questions about social perception and interaction, and examining these questions has been a fundamental part of social psychology for more than half a century.

The term **discrimination** is used to describe *behaviors* directed against persons because of their membership in a particular group. What do we mean by group? Actually, there are many kinds of groups—such as families, political parties, nations, states, religions, and ethnic subcultures. For the purposes of this chapter, a **group** is defined as two or more people perceived as having at least one of the following characteristics: (1) direct interactions with each other over a period of time; (2) joint membership in a social category based on sex, race, or other attributes; (3) a shared, common fate, identity, or set of goals. We see people in fundamentally different ways if we consider them to comprise a group rather than simply an aggregate of individuals. How does this happen, and why? How are people's thoughts, feelings, and behaviors affected? Examining these questions is the focus of this chapter.

The chapter is divided into five parts. First, we consider the causes and effects of *stereotypes*—beliefs that people have about individuals based on their membership in a social group. Second, we examine *prejudice*, which consists of negative feelings about others because of their connection to a social group. To put these

discrimination Any behavior directed against persons because of their membership in a particular group.

group Two or more persons perceived as related because of their interactions with each other over time, membership in the same social category, or common fate.

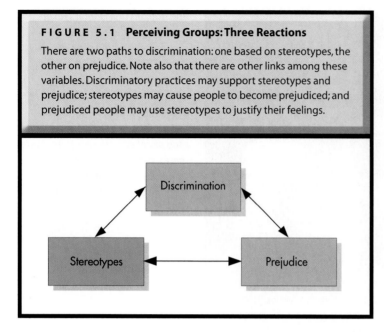

FIGURE 5.1   Perceiving Groups: Three Reactions

There are two paths to discrimination: one based on stereotypes, the other on prejudice. Note also that there are other links among these variables. Discriminatory practices may support stereotypes and prejudice; stereotypes may cause people to become prejudiced; and prejudiced people may use stereotypes to justify their feelings.

problems in concrete terms, we then focus on sexism and racism, two historically common forms of discrimination. Next, we shift the focus from the perceivers to the perceived: What are some of the ways in which people are affected by being the targets of stereotypes, prejudice, and discrimination? The chapter concludes with a discussion of some ways in which discrimination can be reduced. For the most part, the chapter discusses stereotypes and prejudice separately. Note, however, that our beliefs and feelings influence each other, that both give rise to discrimination, and that discriminatory behavior, in turn, fuels stereotypes and prejudices (see Figure 5.1).

Stereotypes

A stereotype is a belief that associates a whole group of people with certain traits. When you stop to think about it, the list of well-known stereotypes seems endless. Consider some examples: The Japanese are sneaky, athletes are brainless, librarians are quiet, Italians are emotional, accountants are dull, Californians are laid back, white men can't jump, and used-car salesmen can't be trusted as far as you can throw them. In this section, we raise four questions: (1) How do stereotypes form? (2) How do they influence our perceptions of individuals? (3) What keeps them alive when so often they prove to be wrong? (4) What aspects of stereotyping can we control, and what aspects are automatic and outside of our conscious awareness?

How Stereotypes Form

The origins of stereotypes can be traced to a number of sources (Allport, 1954). From a historical perspective, stereotypes spring from past events. Thus, it can be argued that slavery in America gave rise to the portrayal of Blacks as inferior, just as the sneak attack on Pearl Harbor in World War II fostered a belief that the Japanese cannot be trusted. From a political perspective, stereotypes are viewed as a means by which groups in power come to rationalize war, religious intolerance, and economic oppression. And from a sociocultural perspective, it has been argued that real differences between social groups contribute to perceived differences. Each of these perspectives has something unique to offer. Social psychologists, however, also pose an additional question: Regardless of how stereotypes are born within a culture, how do they grow and operate in the minds of individuals?

The formation of stereotypes involves two related processes. The first is *categorization*, in which we sort people into groups. The second is a process by which we perceive groups to which we belong *(ingroups)* as being different from groups to which we do not belong *(outgroups)*. These two processes reflect not only basic cognitive operations but also sociocultural and motivational factors.

Social Categorization   As perceivers, we routinely sort single objects into groups rather than think of each as unique. Biologists classify animals into families; archaeologists divide time into eras; geographers split the earth into regions. Like-

stereotype A belief that associates a group of people with certain traits.

wise, people sort each other into groups on the basis of gender, race, and other common attributes in a process called **social categorization.** In some ways, social categorization is natural and adaptive. By grouping people the way we group foods, animals, and other objects, we form impressions quickly and use past experience to guide new interactions. With so many things to pay attention to in our social worlds, we can save time and effort by using people's group memberships to make inferences about them. For example, Neil Macrae and his colleagues tested the hypothesis that by simplifying the way we form impressions of others, stereotypes free up cognitive resources that can be used in other activities (Macrae, Milne, & Bodenhausen, 1994). In their study, participants simultaneously worked on two tasks: They made judgments of target persons based on trait lists printed on a computer screen, and at the same time they tried to monitor a tape-recorded passage on an unfamiliar topic (the economy and geography of Indonesia). In the judgment task, some participants but not others received stereotype labels along with the trait lists (for example, a person described as creative, sensitive, and temperamental was also said to be an "artist").

How well did participants perform at the two tasks? There were three key results. First, participants given the stereotype labels later recalled more of the stereotypic traits on the lists (for example, participants were more likely to recall that the person was creative, temperamental, and sensitive if they had been exposed to the "artist" label). Second, participants given the stereotype labels were able to do the other, simultaneous task better: They monitored the tape-recorded passage more effectively. This result suggests that stereotypes function as "energy-saving devices." To the extent that perceivers judge others they meet by falling back on old preconceptions, they have more cognitive resources available for other activities. Third, the stereotype labels had these effects even if the participants were not consciously aware that they had been exposed to these labels. That is, the stereotype labels were given to some participants through a **subliminal presentation,** in which information is presented so faintly or rapidly that people do not have any conscious awareness of having been exposed to it. Despite not realizing that they had seen the stereotype labels, these participants showed similar "energy-saving" effects. This illustrates how subtle, and yet powerful, the effects of social categorizations can be.

There is, however, a serious drawback to the time and energy saved through social categorization. Like lumping apples and oranges together because both are fruit, categorizing people leads us to overestimate the differences between groups and to underestimate the differences within groups (Stangor & Lange, 1994; Wilder, 1986). Aware of the social categories to which individuals belong, we can fail even to perceive information about these individuals that does not conform to our stereotypes about their groups (von Hippel et al., 1995).

Ingroups Versus Outgroups   The second process that promotes stereotyping follows directly from the first. Although grouping humans is much like grouping objects, there is a key difference. When it comes to social categorization, perceivers themselves are members or nonmembers of the categories they use. Groups that you identify with—your country, your religion, your political party, even your hometown sports team—are called *ingroups,* whereas groups other than your own are called *outgroups.* This strong tendency to carve the world into "us" and "them" has important consequences.

One consequence is a phenomenon known as the **outgroup homogeneity effect,** a pervasive tendency for social perceivers to assume that a greater similarity exists among members of outgroups than among members of ingroups. In other words, there may be fine and subtle differences among "us," but "they" are all alike (Linville & Jones, 1980). There are three types of evidence for this bias. First, when people are asked to estimate how many group members share a certain

Stereotypes allow people to save time and effort when processing information about others, freeing them to pay attention to other tasks or information. **True.**

social categorization The classification of persons into groups on the basis of common attributes.

subliminal presentation A method of presenting stimuli so faintly or rapidly that people do not have any conscious awareness of having been exposed to them.

outgroup homogeneity effect The tendency to assume that there is greater similarity among members of outgroups than among members of ingroups.

stereotyped characteristic, percentage estimates are higher in ratings of outgroups than in ratings of ingroups. Second, when people are asked to estimate the range of differences within a population, that range is seen as narrower when the population being considered is an outgroup than when it is an ingroup. Third, when people are asked to rate a group of individuals in terms of how alike they are, outgroup members are seen as being more similar to each other than are ingroup members. Linville et al. (1996) recently identified another form of this bias, the *outgroup covariation effect,* which is the tendency for people to perceive outgroup members as more likely to have clusters of traits that go together. For example, younger people are more likely than older people to believe that an older person who is unsociable is also unhappy, aimless, and lazy.

Research shows that outgroup homogeneity effects are common (Linville, 1998; Ostrom & Sedikides, 1992; Vonk & van Knippenberg, 1995). Indeed, there are many real-life examples. Americans who arrive from China, Korea, Taiwan, and Vietnam see themselves as different, but to the western eye they are all Asian. Business majors like to talk about engineering types; engineers talk about business types; liberals lump together all conservatives; teenagers lump together all old people; and as the natives of New York City proclaim their cultural and ethnic diversity, outsiders talk of the typical New Yorker. To people outside the group, outgroup members can even seem to look alike—people are less accurate in distinguishing and recognizing faces of members of racial groups other than their own, especially to the extent that they are unfamiliar with these other groups (Bothwell et al., 1989; Teitelbaum & Geiselman, 1997). As a result of the outgroup homogeneity effect, people are quick to generalize from a single individual to a whole group (Quattrone & Jones, 1980). Also, the more that people believe an outgroup is homogeneous, the more confident they are in their judgments of any individual from the outgroup (Ryan et al., 1996).

There are two reasons for the tendency to perceive outgroups as homogeneous. First, we often do not notice subtle differences among outgroups because we have little personal contact with them. Think about your family or your favorite sports team, and specific individuals come to mind. Think about an unfamiliar outgroup, however, and you are likely to think in abstract terms about the group as a whole. Indeed, research shows that the more familiar people are with an outgroup, the less likely they are to perceive it as homogeneous (Linville et al., 1989). A second problem is that people often do not encounter a representative sample of outgroup members. A student from one school who only encounters students from a rival school when they cruise into town for a Saturday football game, screaming at the top of their lungs, sees only the most avid rival fans—hardly a diverse lot (Quattrone, 1986).

People often have a great deal of detailed, diverse information about their own groups, and much less information about other groups. This can contribute to the outgroup homogeneity effect, in which people assume that "they" are all alike.

Sociocultural and Motivational Factors   Social categorization and ingroup-outgroup distinctions reflect basic cognitive processes; they are, in part, by-products of how humans think and process information about their world. They are, however, also influenced by situational factors, such as the cultural context in which people live and the motivations that people have in particular settings. For example, there are countless ways in which people can divide others into social categories. Why are some categorizations—such as race, gender, and sexual preference—more likely to dominate our perceptions than others? Why, and when, are people quicker to categorize a black male firefighter as black than as a man or as a firefighter? Cognitive factors can determine this; if perceivers have recently been primed to think about one of the categories, that category becomes more likely to dominate perceptions, making alternative categories especially unlikely to come to mind (Dijksterhuis & van Knippenberg, 1996; Macrae et al., 1995). But sociocultural and motivational factors can also play important roles. The sociocultural factors include how different groups are portrayed by the media and how parents, peers, and schools promote particular ways of dividing people. If, for example, the media tend to portray people very differently as a function of race, or if parents warn their children about playing with boys and girls of other races, then race becomes a critically important way to divide up the world (Bar-Tal, 1996; Schaller, 1998). In addition, cultures differ in what categorizations they emphasize and how they make ingroup-outgroup distinctions (Han & Park, 1995; Lee & Ottati, 1995).

Motivational factors also affect how people categorize others. People in relatively powerful positions in society may be motivated to categorize others in ways that help them maintain the status quo and justify their feelings of superiority (Jost & Banaji, 1994; Operario & Fiske, 1998; Pratto et al., 1997). More situationally specific motivations also are important: If your house is on fire, you are much more likely to categorize a black male firefighter as a firefighter than as black or male (Bodenhausen & Macrae, 1998; Zárate & Sandoval, 1995). Motivational factors also influence perceptions of ingroups and outgroups (Brewer & Brown, 1998). People who are motivated to protect their group or their group identity, perhaps because they perceive that the ingroup is being threatened by an outgroup, may see their *ingroup* as relatively homogeneous (Thompson et al., 1997).

How Stereotypes Distort Perceptions of Individuals

Social categorization and the outgroup homogeneity effect help to explain how beliefs about groups develop. Now, let's consider how these beliefs influence the perception of individuals. Imagine learning that a mother yelled at a fourteen-year-old girl, that a lawyer behaved aggressively, and that a Boy Scout grabbed the arm of an elderly woman crossing the street. Now imagine that a construction worker yelled at a fourteen-year-old girl, that an ex-con behaved aggressively, and that a skinhead grabbed the arm of an elderly woman crossing the street. Do very different images of these actions come to mind? This is a fundamental effect of stereotyping: Stereotypes of groups distort people's perceptions and interpretations of the behaviors of group members. Perceivers are likely to see members of stereotyped groups as more similar to the stereotype than they actually are. This is especially likely when a target of a stereotype behaves in an ambiguous way; perceivers reduce the ambiguity by interpreting the behavior as consistent with the stereotype (Dunning & Sherman, 1997; Kunda et al., 1997). For example, in one study, black and white sixth-grade boys saw pictures and descriptions of ambiguously aggressive behaviors (such as one child bumping into another). Both the black and the white boys judged the behaviors as more mean and threatening if the behaviors were performed by black boys than white boys (Sagar and Schofield, 1980).

Not only do stereotypes affect how we perceive and interpret others' behaviors, they also often cause us to remember stereotype-consistent information about others better than stereotype-inconsistent information (Hense et al., 1995; Dijksterhuis & van Knippenberg, 1996). In a classic demonstration, Gordon Allport and Leo Postman (1947) showed participants a picture of a subway train filled with passengers. In the picture were a black man dressed in a suit and a white man holding a razor (see Figure 5.2). One participant viewed the scene briefly and then described it to a second participant who had not seen it. The second participant communicated the description to a third participant and so on, through six rounds of communication. The result: In more than half the sessions, the final participant's report indicated that the black man, not the white man, held the razor. Some participants even reported that he had waved it in a threatening manner. As Allport and Postman explained, "The distortion may occur even in participants who have no anti-Negro bias. It is an unthinking cultural stereotype that the Negro is hot tempered and addicted to the use of razors and weapons" (p. 63).

Not all behaviors are distorted to seem more consistent with stereotypes. Sometimes the opposite effect occurs. As a general rule, judgments of a stimulus are influenced by the discrepancy between that stimulus and one's expectations. When a stimulus differs only slightly from expectations, the difference is barely noticed, if at all. When a stimulus varies considerably from expectations, however, the perceived difference is magnified as the result of a **contrast effect.** To illustrate, imagine that you've been presented with three buckets of water—one cold, one hot, and the third at room temperature. After placing your right hand into the cold water and your left hand into the hot water, you place both hands simultaneously into the third bucket. You can probably predict the odd result: Even though both hands are in the same water, your right hand now feels warm, and your left hand feels cool. The temperature you feel depends on the sensation that preceded it.

Just as contrast effects can influence physical sensations, they can also affect social perceptions (Biernat et al., 1998; Manis et al., 1988; Stapel & Koomen, 1998). For example, based on negative stereotypes about the intelligence of African Americans, perceivers may see an African American who behaves in a very intelligent way as more intelligent than a European American who behaves in the same way (Jussim et al., 1987). Was Ann Hopkins, the productive but abrasive accountant described earlier, denied a partnership because of a contrast effect? In her court case, Hopkins claimed that her aggressive manner proved offensive only because it clashed with traditional conceptions of women. Was her claim justified? Is the same tough-mindedness more acceptable in a man? The research on the contrast effect supports Ann Hopkins's analysis of the workplace. As we'll see, gender stereotypes lead people to expect warm, gentle women and assertive, forceful men. Since those who break the mold are subject to contrast effects, it is conceivable that Ann Hopkins seemed tougher and more abrasive than a man would under

FIGURE 5.2   How Racial Stereotypes Distort Social Perceptions

After briefly viewing this picture, one participant described it to a second participant, who described it to a third, and so on. After six rounds of communication, the final report often placed the razor held by the white man into the black man's hand. This study illustrates how racial stereotypes can distort social perception. *(Adapted from Allport & Postman, 1947.)*

contrast effect A tendency to perceive stimuli that differ from expectations as being even more different than they really are.

the same circumstances. Similarly, a gentle man would seem more passive and weak than a woman would in the same situation.

There are some limits to the contrast effect (Hilton & von Hippel, 1996). In each of the following conditions, perceivers are more likely to fall back on their stereotypes and see others' behaviors as more rather than less consistent with the stereotypes: (1) when their ability to process information is impaired, such as when they are in anxiety-provoking situations (Wilder, 1993); (2) when they have a particularly high need to perceive consistency and structure in their environments (Neuberg & Newsom, 1993); and (3) when they are making judgments about members of relatively small and homogeneous groups for which they have very strong expectations of consistency (Hilton & von Hippel, 1990).

How Stereotypes Survive: Self-Perpetuating Mechanisms

Stereotypes offer us quick and convenient summaries of social groups. In general, it is difficult to determine the accuracy of a stereotype (Ryan et al., 1996). It is clear, however, that they often cause us to overlook the diversity within categories and to form mistaken impressions of specific individuals. Given their shortcomings, why do stereotypes endure? Researchers have identified several mechanisms that help answer this question; they include illusory correlations, attributions, subtyping, and confirmation biases.

Illusory Correlations   One answer can be found in the **illusory correlation,** a tendency for people to overestimate the link between variables that are only slightly or not at all correlated (Chapman, 1967). Illusory correlations result from two different processes. First, when two variables are occasionally associated with each other, people are likely to overestimate their association if the variables are *distinctive*—that is, if they capture attention simply because they are novel or deviant. To illustrate this, imagine observing 100 behaviors performed by people from group X and 20 behaviors performed by people from group Y (see Table 5.1). For each group, three-quarters of the behaviors are positive and sociable, and one-quarter are negative and anti-social. In this situation, people from group Y are more distinctive than people from group X, because they are in the minority; and negative behaviors are more distinctive than positive behaviors, because they are in the minority. Despite the fact that negative behaviors are no more associated with group Y than with group X (25 percent of the behaviors in each group are negative), people who observe these behaviors tend to overestimate the association between the minority group and minority behaviors. Therefore, they perceive group Y people as more negative and antisocial than group X people (Hamilton & Gifford, 1976). The implications for stereotyping are important: Unless otherwise motivated, people overestimate the joint occurrence of distinctive variables such as minority groups and deviant acts (Schaller, 1991).

Second, when two variables are occasionally associated with each other, people are likely to overestimate their association if the variables are already meaningfully

TABLE 5.1   The Illusory Correlation

Perceivers often overestimate the frequency with which distinctive variables co-occur, such as when minority group members (group Y) behave in a relatively rare, negative way. Although the proportion of group X members who behave negatively is the same as the proportion of group Y members who do, perceivers see group Y members as disproportionately likely to behave negatively.

Reality	Perception
100 Group X People	**100 Group X People**
75 positive behaviors (75%)	75 positive behaviors (75%)
25 negative behaviors (25%)	25 negative behaviors (25%)
20 Group Y People	**20 Group Y People**
15 positive behaviors (75%)	10 positive behaviors (50%)
5 negative behaviors (25%)	10 negative behaviors (50%)

illusory correlation   An overestimate of the association between variables that are only slightly or not at all correlated.

associated in their own minds. For example, in one study, participants were presented with lists of paired words, such as *lion-tiger*, *lion-eggs*, *bacon-tiger*, and *bacon-eggs*, and then were asked to estimate how particular word pairs were presented. The participants tended to overestimate the frequency of pairings that had meaningful, expected associations *(lion-tiger, bacon-eggs)*, even if such pairings actually occurred no more frequently than less expected pairings *(lion-eggs, bacon-tiger)* (Chapman, 1967). David Hamilton and Terrence Rose (1980) found that stereotypes can lead people to expect social groups and traits to fit together like bacon and eggs and to overestimate the frequency with which they actually observed these associations. The implications for stereotyping are important here as well: People overestimate the joint occurrence of variables they expect to be associated with each other, such as stereotyped groups and their corresponding stereotypic behaviors.

Research on illusory correlations helps to explain the formation and stubborn persistence of stereotypes. First, members of minority groups—precisely because they are distinctive in the population—are under the spotlight, so everything they do is blown out of numerical proportion. Second, pre-existing stereotypes may be sustained by false support. The person who thinks politicians are dishonest will overestimate the number of corruption scandals that occur in government compared to other settings. Likewise, someone who believes that the mentally ill are dangerous will overestimate the number of murders committed by deranged psychiatric patients compared to those by other violent criminals. Once a stereotype is in place, we are quick to notice the supporting evidence.

Attributions   Illusory correlations are one way in which people develop and maintain stereotypes. People also maintain their stereotypes through the attributions that they make about other people and their behaviors. Chapter 4 on Perceiving Persons discusses how perceivers attribute other people's behaviors to personal factors, such as their personalities and attitudes, and to situational factors, such as the circumstances in which the behaviors occurred. One important attributional bias discussed in Chapter 4 is the fundamental attribution error, the tendency to focus on the role of personal causes and underestimate the impact of situations on other people's behaviors. This bias can help perpetuate stereotypes. Because perceivers often fail to take into account situational factors that affect others' behavior, they are likely to fail to recognize how stereotypes and discrimination can affect the behaviors of a stereotyped group. Even when the perceivers' own behaviors toward the target of a stereotype interfere with the target's performance, perceivers are likely to attribute the poor performance to the individual and not account for the negative influence that they played (Gilbert & Jones, 1986). For example, a teacher who has very low expectations about a particular student because of a negative stereotype may behave toward the student in ways that reveal his or her low expectations, causing the student to lose confidence and underperform. The teacher is likely to attribute the student's poor performance to the student's lack of ability or motivation rather than to his or her own influence on the student.

The fundamental attribution error represents a way in which perceivers fail to take into account situational influences when making attributions. However, when a perceiver's expectations about others are violated, the perceiver becomes much more likely to think about situational factors in order to explain the surprising behavior. Stereotypes create expectations about group members, and perceivers try to explain the potential causes of a group member's behavior if it is inconsistent with the group stereotype. Rather than accept a stereotype-disconfirming behavior at face value, perceivers imagine the situational factors that might explain away this apparent exception to the rule, such as random luck, ulterior motives, or other special circumstances (Hastie, 1984; Hilton et al., 1993; Wilder et al., 1996).

The role of attribution can also be seen in the subtleties of the language we use (Ruscher, 1998). Anne Maass and her colleagues (1995) have found that people are more likely to use personal, trait-like terms to describe behavior when it is consistent with a stereotype than when it is inconsistent. For example, imagine learning that a student got a B+ on a test. People who expect members of an outgroup to be unintelligent relative to members of their ingroup may describe this student as "smart" if she is a member of their ingroup, whereas they may describe her as "someone who got a B+ on a test" if she is a member of the outgroup. By failing to use a positive trait when describing the outgroup member, perceivers can more easily maintain their negative stereotype of this group. This linguistic bias helps perceivers maintain their stereotypes and expectancies (Karpinski & von Hippel, 1996). It is especially likely to be used by perceivers who feel that their ingroup is threatened and are thus motivated to perceive the outgroup in less positive ways (Maass, Ceccarelli, & Rudin, 1996), or by perceivers who are motivated to maintain their impressions of the outgroup (Webster et al., 1997).

Subtyping Have you ever noticed that people often manage to hold negative views about a social group even when they like individual members of that group? One of the unnerving paradoxes of social perception is that stereotypes stubbornly survive one disconfirmation after the next. The question is, Why? Gordon Allport (1954) recognized this phenomenon almost half a century ago. He wrote, "There is a common mental device that permits people to hold prejudgments even in the face of much contradictory evidence. It is the device of admitting exceptions.... By excluding a few favored cases, the negative rubric is kept intact for all other cases" (p. 23). Confronted with Ann Hopkins, or with any woman who does not seem particularly warm and nurturant, people can either develop a more diversified image of females or toss the mismatch into a special subtype—say, *"career women."* To the extent that people create this subtype, their existing image of women-in-general will remain relatively intact. Similarly, to the extent that white Americans dismiss their amiable black neighbors as atypical "middle-class Blacks," unflattering images of Blacks-in-general may also resist change. This problem was depicted in the 1989 movie *Do the Right Thing*, in which a white bigot was asked to reconcile his racist views with the fact that Magic Johnson was his favorite basketball player and Eddie Murphy his favorite actor. "Let me explain myself," he replied. "They're black, but they're not really black.... It's different."

Women who play rough contact sports—such as these members of the United States women's hockey team, which won the first Olympic gold medal awarded in women's ice hockey—defy gender stereotypes. But rather than change their gender stereotypes, many perceivers subtype these women and dismiss them as exceptions.

When does disconfirming evidence about individual members lead people to revise their beliefs, and when are these members dismissed as subtypes that do not reflect the group? The research on this question suggests the following conclusions:

■ Target persons who disconfirm a stereotype can force a revision of that stereotype if they are otherwise viewed as representative members of the group. A lawyer who deviates from the stereotype of lawyers by being interpersonally warm and generous will have more effect on the overall stereotype of lawyers if he or she fits the usual image in other ways (such as by being well-dressed and wealthy) than if he or she seems atypical in these other ways (Desforges et al., 1997; Hewstone & Lord, 1998; Weber & Crocker, 1983; Wilder et al., 1996).

■ If the exceptions to the stereotype are dispersed across many individuals rather than concentrated in a few notable individuals, the overall stereotype is more likely to change (Hewstone et al., 1994).

■ People who deviate dramatically from the stereotype on some dimension are *less* likely to change the stereotype than are people who deviate more moderately. Indeed, extreme exceptions may make the stereotype even *stronger*. This "boomerang" effect may result from perceivers' being so surprised by the exceptional person that they react by bringing to mind thoughts of people who confirm the stereotype (Kunda & Oleson, 1997).

Thus, to change negative stereotypes about the intelligence of African Americans or the athleticism of European Americans, it is better to expose people to many examples of African Americans who are intelligent or European Americans who are athletic than it is to expose people to a few African American geniuses or a few European American athletic superstars.

Confirmation Biases and Self-fulfilling Prophecies

In Chapter 4 on Perceiving Persons, we saw that first impressions are often slow to change because people process information in ways that tend to verify their existing beliefs. Similar biases are at work in the stubborn maintenance of stereotypes. One problem is that people given an opportunity to learn more about a person or a stereotyped group seek information that is likely to confirm the stereotype (Johnston & Macrae, 1994). This can lead to a second problem: Our expectations about others can lead us to act in ways that cause them to behave consistently with our expectations. Chapter 4 discussed the self-fulfilling prophecy, the process by which a perceiver's expectation can actually lead to its own fulfillment. Stereotypes of groups can lead to self-fulfilling prophecies just as expectations about individuals can. Stereotypes shape the information we seek—and find—about others.

These processes can be extremely subtle, as is illustrated in an experiment by Mark Chen and John Bargh (1997) in which white participants were shown black male or white male faces subliminally. As will be discussed later in this chapter, these subliminal presentations can trigger thoughts of stereotypes without the perceiver's awareness. After this exposure, each participant was teamed up to play a verbal game

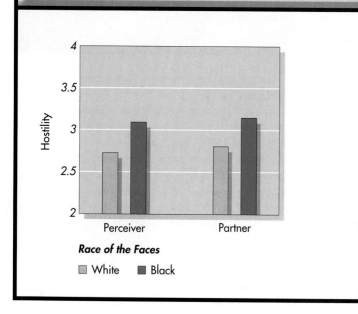

FIGURE 5.3   Eliciting Stereotype-Consistent Behavior

White participants (perceivers) were shown black male or white male faces for fractions of a second, without their awareness. Next, each perceiver interacted with another white participant (partner) who had not been exposed to the faces. The perceivers who had been shown black faces were rated by judges as acting more hostile than the participants who had been shown white faces (left). In addition, partners who interacted with perceivers who had been shown black faces were judged to be more hostile than partners who interacted with perceivers who had been shown white faces (right). Presumably, perceivers exposed to the black male faces activated negative stereotypes about black men, triggering behavior consistent with their stereotypes for both themselves and their partners. *(Adapted from Chen & Bargh, 1997.)*

Hostility

Race of the Faces
■ White   ■ Black

with another white participant who had not been exposed to the faces. Their inter-actions were audiotaped. Judges listened to each participant's verbal behavior inde-pendently of the partner's and rated the hostility exhibited by each participant. Chen and Bargh found that participants who had been exposed to the black faces behaved in a more hostile way in their subsequent interactions with their partners, presumably because the exposure to the black faces had triggered stereotypes about Blacks, including the trait of hostility. Because these participants acted in a hostile way toward their partners, their partners in turn behaved with greater hostility (see Figure 5.3). Thus, even though these participants had no conscious awareness of seeing any black men at any point in the study, the subliminal exposure to black male faces triggered behavior that led to hostility for both the perceivers and the people with whom they interacted.

> *"Not everybody's life is what they make it. Some people's life is what other people make it."*
>
> —Alice Walker

Is Stereotyping Inevitable? Automatic Versus Intentional Processes

Stereotypes are born of the human tendency to categorize others, and they can have very powerful effects on how we think, feel, and behave toward group mem-bers. Part of the power of stereotypes is that they often are activated without our awareness, and they operate at an unconscious, or "implicit," level (Greenwald & Banaji, 1995). But is stereotyping inevitable? When we encounter people from other groups, do our stereotypes of these groups always become activated in our minds? Can we do anything to prevent this from happening? Most people believe that they can resist stereotyping others, but recent research paints a far more com-plex picture.

Stereotypes as (Sometimes) Automatic   Patricia Devine (1989) distinguished between automatic and controlled processes in stereotyping. She argued that peo-ple have become highly aware of the contents of many stereotypes through socio-cultural mechanisms such as lessons learned from parents and images in the media. Because of this high awareness, people automatically activate stereotypes whenever they are exposed to members of groups for which popular stereotypes exist. Thus, just as many of us are automatically primed to think "eggs" after hearing "bacon," we are also primed to think of concepts relevant to a stereotype when we think of a stereotyped group. To be sure, we can try to prevent this activated stereotype from influencing our judgments or behaviors. However, we are often unaware that a par-ticular stereotype has been activated or how it can influence our perceptions and behaviors (Bargh, 1997; Greenwald & Banaji, 1995; Monteith et al., 1998). Thus, the stereotype can affect us in spite of our good intentions. Devine's theory sparked an explosion of interest in these issues. Recent research suggests some qualifica-tions to the notion that stereotype activation is inevitable. Several conclusions can be drawn at this point:

1. *When perceivers are primed to think even briefly of particular aspects of a popular stereotype, they are very likely to automatically activate the general stereotype in their minds.* This stereotype activation can influence their subsequent thoughts, feelings, and behaviors. In addition, this process occurs even if perceivers are unaware of their exposure to the stereotype and even if they are relatively low in prejudice. Lorella Lepore and Rupert Brown (1997), for example, exposed some white British students to subliminal presentations on a computer moni-tor of words relevant to negative stereotypes about Blacks, such as *crime* and *unemployed*, as well as category labels, such as *Blacks* and *West Indians*. Other students were exposed to neutral, stereotype-irrelevant words. The words

were presented so quickly that the students didn't even realize that they had seen them. Soon after, in what appeared to be an unrelated task, the students read about a series of behaviors describing a person whose race was unspecified (for example, "He plays football regularly"). The students who had been primed with the stereotype-relevant words rated this person more negatively on traits relevant to the stereotype, such as *careless* and *aggressive*, than did the students who had been primed with neutral words. These results indicate that thinking about *some* of the content of a stereotype can automatically trigger thoughts of the stereotype *in general*, which can in turn influence subsequent judgments and behaviors. These results were found regardless of the students' individual levels of prejudice against Blacks. In another study, American undergraduates were subtly primed to think about either aggression, a stereotypically masculine trait, or dependence, a stereotypically feminine trait. Soon after, they read about a male or female target person. Participants who had been primed to think about aggression rated the male target more stereotypically, and those who had been primed to think about dependence rated the female target more stereotypically (Banaji et al., 1993). This kind of automatic gender stereotyping does not appear to depend on the perceivers' degree of sexism (Banaji & Hardin, 1996).

2. *When perceivers are exposed to information or cues about a stereotyped group, as opposed to the content of the stereotype itself, stereotype activation is not inevitable.* Whether the stereotype is activated can depend on how prejudiced the perceiver is. Lepore and Brown conducted an additional study in which they presented some participants with category labels, such as *Blacks* and *West Indians*, but no stereotypic content. The participants then made judgments about another person. Participants tended to exhibit activation of the negative stereotype of Blacks only if they were relatively high in prejudice against Blacks. The judgments made by those who were relatively low in prejudice were unaffected by the category labels. Bernd Wittenbrink and his colleagues (1997) also found that white Americans relatively high in prejudice toward Blacks were more likely than those lower in prejudice to exhibit stereotype activation when exposed subliminally to the category label *Black*.

3. *When perceivers are exposed to a member of a stereotyped group, stereotype activation can depend on whether they pay attention to the group member.* Participants in a study by Daniel Gilbert and Gregory Hixon (1991) watched a videotape of a woman holding cards containing word fragments, such as *ri_e* and *s_ort*, and were instructed to complete the word fragments. When the woman holding the cards was Asian, participants who were not otherwise distracted created words that are stereotypic of Asians, words such as *rice* and *short*. However, participants who were kept very busy with a cognitively demanding task while watching the tape showed no evidence of stereotype activation. Similarly, participants in another study (Pendry & Macrae, 1996) were less likely to show stereotype activation if they watched a woman on videotape while involved in a situation that compelled them to pay less attention to her. In contrast, if perceivers already have activated a stereotype, then being busy or distracted should make them *more* likely to use this stereotype. Because stereotypes are easy to use and can save perceivers time and effort in making inferences about others, busy perceivers are more prone to use stereotypes than non-busy perceivers if the stereotype has been activated. In other words, being busy or distracted can interfere with the stereotype coming to mind at all, but once the stereotype has been activated, then being busy or distracted increases the likelihood that the activated stereotype will be applied to subsequent judgments (Gilbert & Hixon, 1991).

4. *Perceivers' goals can make stereotype activation more likely.* When people's self-esteem has been threatened, such as by failure on an important task, they may

become motivated to negatively stereotype others so that they will feel better about themselves (Crocker & Luhtanen, 1990; Fein & Spencer, 1997). Steven Spencer and his colleagues (1998) proposed that in these situations, perceivers become more likely to activate stereotypes when exposed to members of stereotyped groups. One of their experiments used the same procedure as the study by Gilbert and Hixon described above: Participants saw a tape of a woman holding cards with word fragments, and they made words from these fragments. In the study by Spencer and colleagues, however, some participants received negative feedback about their performance on an intelligence test before watching the videotape—feedback that represented a threat to their self-esteem. Other participants did not receive any self-esteem threat. In addition, while watching the videotape, *all* of the participants were kept busy with a distracting task. According to Gilbert and Hixon's results, this distracting task should have made stereotype activation unlikely. Consistent with Gilbert and Hixon's results, those who had not received the self-esteem threat showed no evidence of stereotype activation. However, those who had received a self-esteem threat *did* show stereotype activation. Presumably, their motivation to stereotype facilitated stereotype activation despite the demands of the other task.

Stereotypes as Explicit and Controlled   The evidence just discussed indicates that stereotype activation is automatic under some conditions and not others (Bargh, 1997). Once activated, stereotypes can influence our perceptions and reactions in important ways. But regardless of stereotype activation, none of us needs to be trapped into evaluating specific persons only in terms of social categories. Research shows that three factors enable us to overcome stereotypes and judge others on a more individual basis (Brewer, 1988; Fiske & Neuberg, 1990).

The first factor is the amount of *personal information* we have about someone. Once such information is available, stereotypes and other preconceptions lose relevance and impact. Thus, when participants in one study read about a man or woman who consistently reacted to difficult situations by behaving assertively or passively, their impressions of that person were influenced more by his or her actions than by gender (Locksley et al., 1980). In fact, people will often set aside their stereotypes even when the personal information they have is not clearly relevant to the judgment they have to make (Hilton & Fein, 1989; Lord et al., 1994).

The second factor is a perceiver's cognitive *ability* to focus on an individual member of a stereotyped group. People are most likely to form an impression that is based on a stereotype that already has been activated if they're busy (Gilbert & Hixon, 1991) or pressed for time (Pratto & Bargh, 1991) and unable to think carefully about the unique attributes of a single person. In an intriguing test of this ability hypothesis, Galen Bodenhausen (1990) classified participants by their circadian arousal patterns, or biological rhythms, into two types: "morning people" (who describe themselves as most alert early in the morning) and "night people" (who say they peak much later, in the evening). By random assignment, participants took part in an experiment in human judgment that was scheduled at either 9 A.M. or 8 P.M. The result? Morning people were more likely to use stereotypes when tested at night; night owls were more likely to do so early in the morning. Other research shows that people are also more likely to use stereotypes when they are under the influence of alcohol than when they are sober (von Hippel et al., 1995) and when positive or negative moods interfere with their processing of information (Bless et al., 1996; Lambert et al., 1997).When we are tired, drunk, rushed, distracted, or lack the mental energy to individualize our judgments, we fall back on simple-minded rules of thumb.

The third factor is *motivation*. When social perceivers are highly motivated to form an accurate impression of someone (say, if they're in an interdependent relationship with the person or if they need to compete against the person), they often manage to set aside their pre-existing beliefs (Hilton & Darley, 1991; Snyder, 1992). In one study, participants expected to interact with a former mental patient who had supposedly been treated for schizophrenia. Ordinarily, people would pre-judge this individual according to their beliefs about mental illness. But when participants were told that they would be working with the person to earn money based on their joint performance, they paid more attention to the patient's personal characteristics (Neuberg & Fiske, 1987). Sufficiently motivated, people can make individualized judgments of others—provided they are not otherwise distracted (Pendry & Macrae, 1994). Motivation can work in the opposite direction, too. Do you know some people who tend to think a lot about every decision and others who always seem motivated to make quick decisions and never look back? People in the latter category—who have a high need for closure—are particularly unlikely to pay attention to individuating information about group members (Kruglanski & Webster, 1996).

Ironic Effects of Trying to Suppress Stereotypes   To summarize, research shows that we can stop ourselves from making hasty, stereotypic judgments when we have personalized information and are able and willing to use that information. But you might wonder about a strategy that seems even more direct: What if you simply try really hard to resist thinking about the stereotype? Research in other contexts suggests that sometimes the harder you try to suppress an unwanted thought, the less likely you are to succeed. Try not to think about a white bear for the next thirty seconds, and that image will come to mind with remarkable frequency. Try not to worry about how long it's taking you to fall asleep, and you'll stay awake. Try not to think about an itch, or the chocolate cheesecake in the fridge, or a particular sexist thought …well, you get the idea (Wegner, 1997).

> "The highest possible stage in moral culture is when we recognize that we ought to control our thoughts."
>
> —Charles Darwin

Knowing how difficult it is to suppress unwanted thoughts, Neil Macrae and his colleagues have conducted a series of experiments to examine when stereotype inhibition works and when it does not work. They have found that trying to suppress stereotypes not only is ineffective under some conditions but also can make stereotypes exert even *more* influence. In one study participants saw a photograph of a male skinhead and wrote a paragraph describing the person. Half the participants were warned that social perceptions are often biased by stereotypes and that they should try to avoid this bias. After completing the task, all participants were given a second skinhead photograph to evaluate, this time without special instructions. So, was the warning effective? Consistent with the notion that people can control the use of stereotypes, analyses of the descriptions revealed that the warning did reduce stereotyping in the first task. The effect, however, was short-lived. In fact, the same participants who managed to control themselves in the first task later used more stereotypes in the second task than did the participants who had not tried to suppress their stereotypes earlier (see Figure 5.4). This post-suppression "rebound" suggests that it may be hard for us to keep from using stereotypes on a consistent, long-term basis. And the rebound can be seen in behaviors as well as judgments. In another study, participants who had been instructed to suppress their stereotypes of skinheads later sat further away from another person who appeared to be a skinhead than did participants who hadn't suppressed their stereotypes earlier (Macrae, Bodenhausen, Milne, & Jetten, 1994).

In these studies, the participants were instructed by the experimenter to suppress their stereotypes. But what if people want to suppress stereotypes because of their *own* motivation to be fair and unbiased? Will they be more successful than people who try to suppress stereotypes simply because an experimenter tells them to? To address this question, Macrae and his colleagues (1998) conducted another series of experiments in which they used a subtle manipulation of self-focus to cause some participants to be motivated not to stereotype. As mentioned in Chapter 3 on The Social Self, when people focus on themselves, they become more likely to behave consistently with their internalized standards and norms. Macrae and colleagues put some participants in situations that increased their self-focus (such as seeing their images on a TV monitor or being exposed subliminally to their own sur-names). This situation caused participants to suppress unwanted stereotypic thoughts when describing a member of a stereotyped group—unless the participants actually condoned the stereotype, in which case the self-focus increased their stereotyping of the individual. For those who did suppress the stereotype while in the self-focus situation, however, a rebound effect emerged. That is, later—once they had been removed from the self-focus context—these participants stereotyped a different member of the stereo-typed group more than did participants who had not been in a self-focus situation.

So, are attempts to suppress stereotypes doomed to failure? First of all, it is important to note that people often can success-fully suppress stereotypes in the short run if they are motivated to do so and have the necessary attentional resources and energy (Wegner, 1997). But will the stereotypic thoughts soon pop back up with renewed force like a volleyball that's been held under water, as the results just described would suggest? Margo Mon-teith and her colleagues (1998) are more optimistic. They note that the stereotypes used in the suppression studies described above typically involve groups that most perceivers don't feel that bad about stereotyping, such as skinheads and yuppies. Although fair-minded people might prefer to treat everyone as an individual rather than stereotype them, they probably are not highly moti-vated to suppress stereotypes of this kind. However, many people are highly motivated to suppress stereotypes based on race, gen-der, and sexual orientation. Research by Monteith and her col-leagues suggests that rebound effects are less likely to occur after suppression of stereotypes that people are highly motivated to reject. Low-prejudice people in particular may be able to consider individuating information about members of stereotyped groups and thus have an easier time keeping stereotyped thoughts out of mind. This may indeed be the best strategy for avoiding the influences of stereo-types: Rather than try to suppress thoughts about a stereotyped group, try instead to activate thoughts about the individual who happens to be a member of that group.

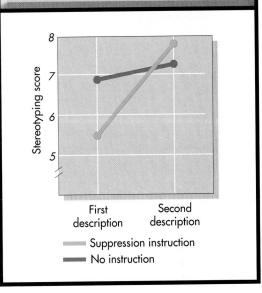

FIGURE 5.4 Stereotypes on the Rebound

Participants were shown a picture of a skinhead and asked to write a description. Some were instructed to avoid the use of stereotypes; others were not. Later, all participants evaluated a second skinhead, this time without instruction. As shown, instructed participants suppressed the use of stereotypes in the first task, thus demonstrating an ability to control themselves (left). But the same participants were later more likely to use stereo-types in the second task—evidence of a post-sup-pression "rebound" effect (right). This result suggests that it's hard to inhibit the use of stereo-types on a long-term basis. *(Data from Macrae, Bodenhausen, Milne, & Jetten, 1994.)*

Prejudice

S tereotypes may form and endure as a result of the way we categorize people and distinguish between ingroups and outgroups. This cognitive perspec-tive—in which stereotypes are considered a by-product of the way human beings think—suggests that if people could be prevented from viewing each other in categorical terms, or were enlightened by accurate information, discrimination throughout the world would be eliminated. But would it, really? Is the way we *think* about groups all that matters? If you look back at Figure 5.1, you'll see that there is another potent factor to consider: how people *feel* about the social groups they encounter. In this section, we trace a second path to discrimination, one based on **prejudice**—a term used to describe our negative feelings toward persons based on their membership in a group.

prejudice Negative feelings toward persons based on their membership in certain groups.

Robbers Cave: Setting the Stage

Clearly, some people are more prejudiced than others. The problem is so widespread, however, that it seems nobody is immune. Social psychologists have thus sought to identify the situational factors that give rise to prejudice. This section describes a classic study of intergroup conflict, a study that sets the stage for theories focusing on the role of social situations.

We begin our analysis in an unlikely place: Robbers Cave State Park, Oklahoma. In the summer of 1954, a small group of eleven-year-old boys—all white, healthy, middle-class youngsters, all strangers to one another—arrived at a 200-acre camp located in a densely wooded area of the park. The boys spent the first week or so hiking, swimming, boating, and camping out. After a while, they gave themselves a group name and printed it on their caps and T-shirts. At first, the boys thought they were the only ones at the camp. Soon, however, they discovered that there was a second group and that tournaments had been arranged between the two groups.

What these boys didn't know was that they were participants in an elaborate study conducted by Muzafer Sherif and his colleagues (1961). Parents had given permission for their sons to take part in an experiment for a study of competitiveness and cooperation. The two groups were brought in separately, and only after each had formed its own culture was the other's presence revealed. Now, the "Rattlers" and the "Eagles" were ready to meet. They did so under tense circumstances, competing against each other in football, a treasure hunt, a tug-of-war, and other events. For each event, the winning team was awarded points; and the tournament winner was promised a trophy, medals, and other prizes. Almost overnight, the groups turned into hostile antagonists; and their rivalry escalated into a full-scale war. Group flags were burned, cabins were ransacked, and a food fight that resembled a riot exploded in the mess hall. Keep in mind that the participants in this study were well-adjusted boys, not street-gang members. Yet as Sherif (1966) noted, a naive observer would have thought the boys were "wicked, disturbed, and vicious" (p. 85).

Creating a monster through competition was easy. Restoring the peace, however, was not. First the experimenters tried saying nice things to the Rattlers about the Eagles and vice versa, but the propaganda campaign did not work. Then the two groups were brought together under noncompetitive circumstances, but that didn't help either. What did eventually work was the introduction of **superordinate goals,** mutual goals that could be achieved only through cooperation between the groups. For example, the experimenters arranged for the camp truck to break down, and both groups were needed to pull it up a steep hill. This strategy worked like a charm. By the end of camp, the two groups were so friendly that they insisted on traveling home on the same bus. In just three weeks, the Rattlers and Eagles experienced the kinds of changes that often take generations to unfold: They formed close-knit groups, went to war, and made peace.

Realistic Conflict Theory

The events of Robbers Cave mimicked the kinds of conflict that plague people all over the world. The simplest explanation for this conflict is competition. Assign strangers to groups, throw the groups into contention, stir the pot, and soon there's conflict. This recipe is not limited to boys at summer camp, either. Intense animosity was also aroused, for example, among a thousand corporate executives who were placed in competing groups as part of a management training program (Blake & Mouton, 1984).

superordinate goals Shared goals that can be achieved only through cooperation among individuals or groups.

The view that direct competition for valuable but limited resources breeds hostility between groups is called **realistic conflict theory** (Levine & Campbell, 1972). As a simple matter of economics, one group may fare better in the struggle for land, jobs, or power than another group. The loser becomes frustrated and resentful, the winner feels threatened and protective—and before long, conflict heats to a rapid boil. Chances are, a good deal of prejudice in the world is driven by the realities of competition (Olzak & Nagel, 1986; Taylor & Moghaddam, 1994).

But there is much more to prejudice than real competition. First, the "realistic" competition for resources may in fact be imagined—a perception in the mind of an individual who is not engaged in any real conflict. The opening of this chapter described how a young white man named Nathan Thill shot and killed Oumar Dia simply because he was black. In Thill's mind, his group, "the white race," was threatened by an ongoing race war; and Thill considered himself a "warrior" in that war (Vaughan, 1997). Second, people may become resentful of other groups not because they believe their own security or resources are threatened by these groups but because of their sense of **relative deprivation**—the belief that they fare poorly compared with others (Crosby, 1976; Olson et al., 1986). What matters to the proverbial Smiths is not the size of their house per se but whether it is larger than the Jones's house next door. There are two sources of discontent: *egoistic* deprivation, a concern for one's own self-interest, and *fraternal* deprivation, a concern for the interest of one's group (Runciman, 1966; Tyler & Smith, 1998). This distinction is crucial to the theory that competition breeds prejudice. In the United States, anti-Black feelings are related not to personal gains or losses but to the fear that Whites as a group are falling behind (Bobo, 1988). The same result—resentment against those who threaten the ingroup—can account for the negative feel-

Increased global economic competition triggers hostilities between countries.

ings of black Americans for white Americans (Abeles, 1976), French Canadians for their English-speaking neighbors (Guimond & Dubé-Simard, 1983), and Muslims for the Hindus in India (Tripathi & Srivastava, 1981).

Social Identity Theory

Why are people so sensitive about the status and integrity of their ingroups relative to rival outgroups, even when personal interests are not at stake? Could it be that personal interests really *are* at stake, that our protectiveness of ingroups is nourished by a concern for the self? If so, could that explain why people all over the world believe that their own nation, culture, language, and religion are better and more deserving than others?

These questions were first raised in a study of high school boys in Bristol, England, conducted by Henri Tajfel and his colleagues (1971). The boys were

realistic conflict theory The theory that hostility between groups is caused by direct competition for limited resources.

relative deprivation Feelings of discontent aroused by the belief that one fares poorly compared with others.

shown a series of dotted slides, and their task was to estimate the number of dots on each. The slides were presented in rapid-fire succession, so the dots could not be counted. Later, the experimenter told the participants that some people are chronic "overestimators" and that others are "underestimators." As part of a second, entirely separate task, participants were supposedly divided for the sake of convenience into groups of overestimators and underestimators (in fact, they were divided randomly). Knowing who was in their group, participants were told to allocate points to each other, points that could be cashed in for money.

This procedure was designed to create *minimal groups*—persons categorized on the basis of trivial, minimally important similarities. Tajfel's overestimators and underestimators were not long-term rivals, did not have a history of antagonism, were not frustrated, did not compete for a limited resource, and were not even acquainted with each other. Still, participants consistently allocated more points to members of their own group than to members of the other group. This pattern of discrimination, called **ingroup favoritism,** has been found in studies performed in many countries. Even in groups that are constructed by the flip of a coin, participants favor others with whom they are aligned (Messick & Mackie, 1989).

At the World Cup Soccer games of 1994, patriotic sports fans basked in the glory of their team's success. The American fans shown here enjoyed the first World Cup victory by a U.S. team in forty-four years.

They also make more favorable attributions for the successes and failures of fellow ingroup members than for the successes and failures of members of other groups (Weber, 1994). The preference for ingroups is so powerful that its effects can be measured by the language we use. Charles Perdue and his colleagues (1990) found evidence using a subtle priming procedure that "ingroup" pronouns such as *we, us,* and *ours* trigger positive emotions, while "outgroup" pronouns such as *they, them,* and *theirs* elicit negative emotions.

To explain ingroup favoritism, Tajfel (1982) and John Turner (1987) proposed **social identity theory.** According to this theory, each of us strives to enhance our self-esteem, which has two components: a *personal* identity and various collective or *social* identities that are based on the groups to which we belong. In other words, people can boost their self-esteem through their own personal achievements or through affiliation with successful groups. What's nice about the need for social identity is that it leads us to derive pride from our connections with others, even if we don't receive any direct benefits from these others (Gagnon & Bourhis, 1996). What's sad, however, is that we often feel the need to belittle "them" in order to feel secure about "us." Religious fervor, racial and ethnic conceit, and patriotism may all fulfill this more negative side of our social identity. The theory is summarized in Figure 5.5.

ingroup favoritism The tendency to discriminate in favor of ingroups over outgroups.

social identity theory The theory that people favor ingroups over outgroups in order to enhance their self-esteem.

Basic Predictions   Social identity theory makes two basic predictions: (1) threats to one's self-esteem heighten the need for ingroup favoritism and (2) expressions of ingroup favoritism enhance one's self-esteem. Research generally supports these predictions (Brewer & Brown, 1998; Hogg & Abrams, 1990; Rubin & Hewstone,

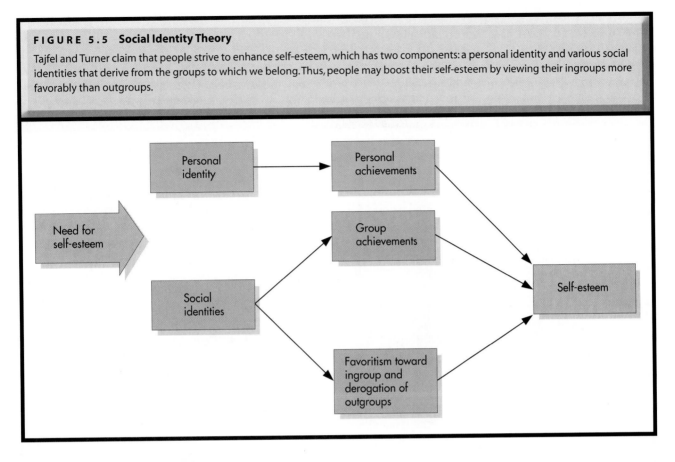

FIGURE 5.5 Social Identity Theory

Tajfel and Turner claim that people strive to enhance self-esteem, which has two components: a personal identity and various social identities that derive from the groups to which we belong. Thus, people may boost their self-esteem by viewing their ingroups more favorably than outgroups.

1998; Turner et al., 1994). In one study, Steven Fein and Steven Spencer (1997) gave participants positive or negative feedback about their performance on a test of social and verbal skills—feedback that temporarily raised or lowered their self-esteem. These participants then took part in what was supposed to be a second experiment in which they evaluated a job applicant. All participants received a photograph of a young woman, her resumé, and a videotape of a job interview. In half the cases, the woman was called Maria D'Agostino and depicted as Italian; in the other half, she was called Julie Goldberg and depicted as Jewish (on the campus where the study was held, a negative stereotype of the "Jewish American Princess" was evoked by upper-middle-class Jewish women from New York).

As predicted by social identity theory, there were two important results (see Figure 5.6 page 148). First, among participants whose self-esteem had been lowered by negative feedback, Julie Goldberg was rated more negatively than Maria D'Agostino—even though their pictures and their credentials were the same. Second, negative-feedback participants given a chance to belittle the Jewish woman later exhibited a post-experiment increase in self-esteem. A blow to one's self-image evokes prejudice—and the expression of prejudice helps to restore that image.

Other researchers have also found support for this theory. For example, Nyla Branscombe and Daniel Wann (1994) found that ingroup members derogated outgroups in response to a threat to the esteem of their ingroup and that this derogation was particularly likely among people who identified strongly with their ingroup. And when people's self-esteem is threatened more generally by concerns brought on by thoughts of their own mortality, they exhibit greater prejudice against outgroups. In one study, Christian participants rated Christian targets more positively and Jewish targets more negatively when they were made to think about their own mortality (Greenberg et al., 1990).

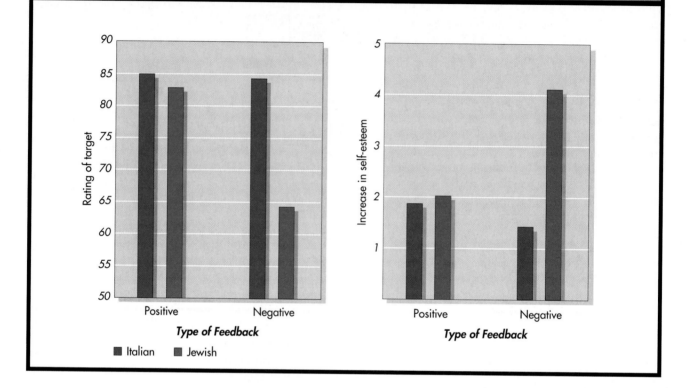

FIGURE 5.6   Self-Esteem and Social Identity

Participants received positive or negative feedback and then evaluated a female job applicant believed to be Italian or Jewish. There were two key results: (1) participants whose self-esteem had been lowered by negative feedback evaluated the woman more negatively when she was Jewish than when she was Italian (left); and (2) negative-feedback participants given the opportunity to belittle the Jewish woman showed a post-experiment increase in self-esteem (right).   *(Fein & Spencer, 1997.)*

Situational, Individual, and Cultural Differences   What precise conditions arouse social identity motives? According to Marilynn Brewer (1991), one important consideration is the relative size of one's ingroup. Noting that people want to belong to groups that are small enough for them to feel unique, Brewer points out that ingroup loyalty—and outgroup prejudice—are more intense for groups that are in the minority than for members of large and inclusive majorities. Indeed, when Brewer (1993) told participants they were in the majority or minority in their dot-estimation performance, she found greater ingroup favoritism among those believing that their group was in the minority.

A second important factor is a person's status relative to others in the ingroup. Jeffrey Noel and his colleagues (1995) found that people are most motivated to derogate outsiders when their ingroup status is marginal—such as pledge (under initiation) rather than active (fully initiated) members of fraternities and sororities—and when they are in the presence of fellow ingroup members. Wanting to prove themselves worthy members of the group, they publicly derogate outsiders in part to win the favor of fellow ingroup members.

In addition, individuals differ in the extent to which their total self-esteem is influenced by ingroups. People whose self-esteem is very invested in their groups are more likely to view others in ways that are consistent with social identity theory (Crocker & Luhtanen, 1990; Kowalski & Wolfe, 1994). Highly prejudiced individuals are particularly motivated to maintain the distinction between their own group and outgroups when they perceive or judge others (Blascovich et al., 1997; Yzerbyt et al., 1995).

Finally, cultural differences can also influence social identity processes. Steven Heine and Darrin Lehman (1997) propose that people from collectivist cultures such as those in Asia are less likely than people from individualist cultures such as those in North America to show biases favoring their ingroups in order to boost their self-esteem. In one study, for example, Japanese students exhibited less ingroup-enhancing biases than did Japanese-Canadian students, who, in turn, exhibited less of these biases than did European-Canadian students. However, although collectivists may be less likely to exaggerate the strengths of their ingroups, some research indicates that they draw sharper distinctions between ingroup and outgroup members than individualists (Gudykunst & Bond, 1997). Among a sample of sixth graders in Korea, for example, children who were more collectivistic exhibited greater discrimination between ingroup and outgroup members than did more individualistic children (Han & Park, 1995).

"It's not enough that we succeed. Cats must also fail."

Reactions to Low Status   Social identity theory poses another interesting question: If self-esteem is influenced by the status of our ingroups relative to outgroups, how do people cope with ingroups of low status or with weak ingroup members? How do *you* cope with associations you find embarrassing? The theory predicts two possible reactions: risk a loss of self-esteem or distance yourself from those in question. So which is it? To examine the question, José Marques (1990) and his colleagues conducted studies in which participants had to evaluate ingroup and outgroup members who behaved in positive or negative ways. In one study, participants listened to two taped speeches, one of high quality and one of low quality. One was made by a fellow law student, the other by a philosophy student. The researchers varied which of the two made the better speech. As it turned out, participants overrated the ingroup speaker who performed well but underrated the ingroup speaker who performed poorly. To preserve the integrity of the ingroup, people may be excessively harsh in their treatment of less able fellow members—at least when the ingroup is important to their social identities (Branscombe et al., 1993).

Even if people don't or can't distance themselves from weak ingroup members, their self-esteem may not be deflated by being members of low-status ingroups: People who are members of low-status, stereotyped groups do not tend to have lower overall self-esteem than people in high-status groups (Crocker et al., 1998). Self-esteem is a flexible quality. If an ingroup is relatively low in status in a particular domain (such as academics), ingroup members may de-emphasize the importance of this domain and instead invest their self-esteem in domains for which their ingroups have higher status (such as popularity) (Steele, 1997). In addition, Heather Smith and Tom Tyler (1997) propose that although pride in the status of one's ingroup is important for one's self-esteem, so too is the respect that one feels within the ingroup. Thus, even if the ingroup is low in status, individuals who are high in status *within* the ingroup can derive positive self-esteem from it.

So far, we have seen that stereotypes are enduring images of social groups that lead people to overlook diversity within outgroups and rush to judgment about specific individuals. We have also seen that prejudice can stem from competition

Derogating outgroups can make ingroup members feel better about themselves. Leo Cullum © 1997 from The New Yorker Collection. All Rights Reserved.

Members of low-status, stereotyped groups have lower self-esteem than members of high-status groups. **False.**

for resources or the need to favor ingroups in the service of self-esteem. We now put these problems into concrete terms by focusing on sexism and racism. Although there are many other forms of prejudice and discrimination, these have received the most attention in social psychological research.

Sexism

When a baby is born, the first words uttered ring loud and clear: "It's a boy!" or "It's a girl!" In many hospitals, the newborn boy immediately is given a blue hat and the newborn girl a pink hat. The infant receives a gender-appropriate name and is showered with gender-appropriate gifts. Over the next few years, the typical boy is supplied with toy trucks, baseballs, hammers, guns, and chemistry sets; the typical girl is furnished with dolls, stuffed animals, toy make-up kits, sewing machines, and tea sets. As they enter school, many expect the boy to earn money by delivering newspapers and to enjoy math and computers, while they expect the girl to babysit and to enjoy crafts, music, and social activities. These distinctions persist in college, as more male students major in economics and the sciences and more female students in the arts, languages, and humanities. In the work force, more men become doctors, construction workers, auto mechanics, airplane pilots, investment bankers, and engineers. In contrast, more women become secretaries, schoolteachers, nurses, flight attendants, bank tellers, and housewives. Back on the home front, the life cycle begins again when a man and woman have their first baby and discover that "It's a girl!" or "It's a boy!"

The traditional pinks and blues are not as distinct today as they used to be. Many gender barriers of the past have broken down, and the colors have somewhat blended together. Nevertheless, **sexism**—prejudice and discrimination based on a person's gender—still exists. Indeed, it begins with the fact that sex is the most conspicuous social category we use to identify ourselves and others (Stangor et al., 1992).

"I don't think you can distance yourself from the White House on this one. After all, you are the President."

When their self-esteem is threatened because of their association with a particular group, group members may try to distance themselves from their group. Arnie Levin © 1997 from The New Yorker Collection. All Rights Reserved.

Gender Stereotypes: Blue for Boys, Pink for Girls

What do people say when asked to describe the typical man and woman? Males are said to be more adventurous, assertive, aggressive, independent, and task-oriented; females are thought to be more sensitive, gentle, dependent, emotional, and people-oriented. These images are so universal that they were reported by 2,800 college students from thirty different countries of North and South America, Europe, Africa, Asia, and Australia (Williams & Best, 1982). The images are also salient to young children—who identify themselves and others as boys or girls by three years of age, form gender-stereotypic beliefs about toys and other objects soon after that, and then use their simplified stereotypes in judging others and favoring their own

sexism Prejudice and discrimination based on a person's gender.

gender over the other in intergroup situations (C. L. Martin et al., 1990; Powlishta, 1995). Preschool-age boys and girls like a new toy less if they are told that it is a toy that opposite-sex children like (Martin et al., 1995). Even infants can tell the difference. In one study, nine-month-olds who were shown pictures of all-male or all-female faces spent less and less time looking—until a face of the opposite sex appeared. This result tells us what the infants themselves could not: that they distinguish between men and women (Leinbach & Fagot, 1993). Another study using a similar procedure found that ten-month-olds can learn associations between gender and social information (Levy & Haaf, 1994).

Take this pink ribbon off my eyes
I'm exposed
And it's no big surprise
Don't you think I know
Exactly where I stand
This world is forcing me
To hold your hand

'Cause I'm just a girl, little ol' me
Don't let me out of your sight
I'm just a girl, all pretty and petite
So don't let me have any rights
Oh…I've had it up to here!

Girls and women are frequently confronted with gender stereotypes and sexist attitudes that devalue their abilities and roles in society. The frustration of having to so frequently encounter and challenge them is illustrated in these lyrics from No Doubt's song "Just a Girl."

Beliefs about males and females are so deeply ingrained that they influence the behavior of adults literally the moment a baby is born. In a fascinating study, the first-time parents of fifteen girls and fifteen boys were interviewed within twenty-four hours of the babies' births. There were no differences between the male and female newborns in height, weight, or other aspects of physical appearance. Yet the parents of girls rated their babies as softer, smaller, and more finely featured. The fathers of boys saw their sons as stronger, larger, more alert, and better coordinated (Rubin et al., 1974). Could it be there really were differences that only the parents were able to discern? Doubtful. In another study, men and women were shown a videotape of a nine-month-old baby. Half were told they were watching a boy; the other half, a girl. All participants saw the same tape, yet their perceptions were biased by gender beliefs. At one point, for example, the baby burst into tears over a jack-in-the-box. How did the participants interpret this reaction? *He* was angry, and *she* was frightened (Condry & Condry, 1976).

People all over the world make sharp distinctions between boys and girls, men and women. The issue is not whether these stereotypes exist but (1) when they influence our social perceptions, (2) whether they are accurate, and, if not, (3) why they endure. Let's begin with the first question: When do gender stereotypes bias our perceptions of men and women? In other words, what activates gender stereotypes?

What Activates Gender Stereotypes?

According to Kay Deaux and Brenda Major (1987), three types of factors determine whether gender stereotypes will be activated: the perceiver, the target, and the situation. To begin with, some *perceivers* are more gender-focused than others. Sandra Bem (1981) refers to people who have masculine or feminine gender-role orientations as "gender schematics" and claims that they tend to divide the world into masculine and feminine terms. In contrast, people who are balanced in their orientations are "gender aschematic" perceivers for whom sex is not a dominant social category. In general, gender schematics are

Gayle Murray is a welder in Massachusetts. A male co-worker once told her, "You're a nice girl, but I can't help but feel you are taking a job from a man with a family. She answered, "I took the test, and I passed, and this is my job." (Parade, January 25, 1998, p. 5)

more likely to pay attention to the sex of others, such as a job applicant, and to form negative impressions of those who violate cultural norms for acceptable male and female behavior (Frable, 1989).

Characteristics of the *target* person can also activate gender stereotypes. People who are highly masculine or feminine in their physical appearance elicit the perception that they are masculine or feminine in other ways as well (Deaux & Lewis, 1984). Even a simple title can activate the stereotype, as when a woman chooses to use *Ms.* rather than *Miss* or *Mrs.* (Dion & Cota, 1991). Certain kinds of clothing also bring our attention to gender. Consider the case of Brenda Taylor, a Florida attorney, who was fired because she dressed for work in designer blouses, tight-fitting skirts, and ornate jewelry. Her supervisor complained that her appearance in court "created the impression that she was a bimbo interested only in meeting men" (Associated Press, 1988). Did Taylor's attire undermine her credibility? Studies show that clothing can have this effect. When business administrators viewed videotaped interviews of female applicants for a management position, they gave the women more positive recommendations when they were dressed in a "masculine" navy suit than when they wore a softer, more "feminine" light-colored dress (Forsythe, 1990). However, recall the case of Ann Hopkins. When she was denied a promotion in her accounting firm, she was told that she should try to appear more feminine. Sexism can make impossible, contradictory demands on women.

Finally, certain *situations* are more likely than others to make gender salient. Especially important is a person's prominence relative to others in the situation. Picture a man in an all-female group or a woman in an all-male group. These individuals draw an abundance of attention, which makes them self-conscious and impairs their performance on cognitive tasks (Saenz, 1994). Tokens are also likely to be viewed in gender-stereotypic terms: The token male is seen as more masculine ("father figure, leader, or macho type"), and the token female as more feminine ("motherly type, a bitch, or the group secretary"), than when the same individuals are judged in balanced, mixed-sex groups (Fiske et al., 1991). Again, we're reminded of Ann Hopkins and others who have minority status in an organization. In the spotlight, whatever they do is noticed and scrutinized—and blown out of proportion.

Are Gender Stereotypes Accurate?

Gender stereotypes are so widespread that one wonders if they are accurate. Of course, what is meant by "accurate" can be debated. Accurate in this context could mean that gender stereotypes reflect universal, stable, possibly genetic differences; or it could mean that gender stereotypes reflect differences that exist under particular sets of societal and historic conditions, with no presumption that the differences will persist if these conditions change. Most social psychologists focus on the latter meaning.

Based on years of research, two conclusions can be drawn. First, people's beliefs about the differences between men and women contain a kernel of truth (Eagly & Wood, 1991; Feingold, 1994; Maccoby & Jacklin, 1974; Swim, 1994). Second, at least some of these beliefs may oversimplify and exaggerate that truth (Spence et al., 1985; Tavris, 1992). Yes, most men are somewhat more aggressive, competitive, assertive, and task-focused than most women. And yes, most women are more sensitive, cooperative, nurturant, and people-focused than most men. But our stereotypes about men and women may be stronger and more numerous than the differences themselves (Allen, 1995; Martin, 1987). Like the cartoonist who draws caricatures, we tend to stretch, expand, and enlarge the ways in which men and women differ.

According to Gallup polls conducted almost 50 years apart, men in 1997 are more involved with household duties than men were in 1949. Of the married people surveyed in 1949, 62% said that the husband helped with the housework, 40% said he helped with the cooking, and 31% said he helped with the dishes. In 1997, these numbers rose to 85%, 73%, and 47%, respectively.

—Press release from Gallup Poll (www.gallup.com/poll/news/970320.html)

Why Do Gender Stereotypes Endure?

If men and women are more similar than people think, why do exaggerated perceptions of difference endure? Earlier in this chapter, we described several reasons why a stereotype, like the proverbial cat, can have many lives. The same mechanisms apply to perceptions of gender. Expecting male-female differences, people tend (1) to perceive illusory correlations, overestimating the percentage of masculine men and feminine women, (2) to make attributions about men's and women's behaviors in ways that support the stereotypes, such as attributing stereotype-inconsistent behaviors to unusual circumstances, (3) to dismiss individuals who don't match the gender stereotype as unrepresentative subtypes, and (4) to seek out evidence that supports the stereotype, sometimes causing the targets of the stereotype to behave in ways that confirm it. Additional explanations have also been proposed to explain why gender stereotypes in particular are so stubborn. These include explanations that focus on media images and popular culture and on social role theory.

Media Images and Popular Culture   Sociocultural factors, such as societal institutions and popular culture, foster male-female distinctions in many ways. Gone are the days when the media almost exclusively portrayed women in stereotypical, powerless roles. Still, research indicates that some gender stereotyping persists— for example, in TV commercials and programs in countries around the world (Furnham & Skae, 1997; Lovdal, 1989; Mwangi, 1996), children's books (Turner-Bowker, 1996), magazine advertisements (Kang, 1997), and music videos presented on MTV (Gan et al., 1997; Signorielli et al., 1994).

More to the point is the fact that media depictions can influence viewers, often without their realizing it. Think about TV commercials for beer or men's cologne. There's a good chance that the commercials that come to mind include images of women as sex objects whose primary purpose in the ads is to serve as "the implied 'reward' for product consumption" (Rudman & Borgida, 1995, p. 495). Can these commercials affect not only men's attitudes toward women but their immediate behavior as well? Laurie Rudman and Eugene Borgida (1995) conducted an experiment to find out. They recruited male undergraduate students for a "market research project." Participants watched a videotape containing either sexist commercials (taped from network and cable TV) or commercials for similar products that contained no sexual imagery. The participants' task was to rate the ads on dimensions such as "likable—not likable" and "attention getting—not attention getting." After performing this task and spending a few minutes performing a different task on a computer, the participants were told that the study was over. But they were then asked to do a favor for the experimenter and interview a woman for a job as a confederate in a different research project. All but one of the participants agreed to do this.

Each participant who agreed to conduct the interview was taken to a room to meet and interview the woman, who actually *was* a confederate of the experimenter. The participant was given some interview questions to use and was left alone in the room with the woman while the experimenter secretly videotaped the interaction through a one-way mirror. Later, female judges watched these videotaped interactions and evaluated the participants' behavior toward the female confederate on dimensions including *proximity* (How close to the confederate did the participant sit?), *dominance* (How interpersonally dominating did he appear to be? How much did he interrupt her?), and *sexualized behavior* (How much did he look at her body? How sexually motivated did he appear to be?). The men who had seen the sexist TV commercials were rated significantly higher on each of these dimensions than were the men who had seen the control commercials (see

TABLE 5.2   TV Commercials and Men's Behavior

Male undergraduate students were exposed either to sexist television commercials or to control commercials for similar products. Later, these male students interviewed a female student who appeared to be applying for a research job. The interaction between each male participant and the female job candidate was secretly videotaped, and judges watched the videotaped interactions. The judges used a 7-point scale to evaluate the men's behavior in terms of proximity, dominance, and sexualized behavior. Compared with the men who had seen the control commercials (right), those who had seen the sexist commercials (left) were rated significantly higher on each of these dimensions. *(Rudman & Borgida, 1995.)*

	Type of Commercials Seen	
	Sexist	Control
Proximity		
■ How close did he sit to the confederate?	4.12	2.66
Dominance		
■ How much did he control the interaction, interrupt her, etc.?	4.42	3.13
Sexualized Behavior		
■ How frequently did he look at the confederate's body, appear to be sexually motivated, appear to be sexist, etc.?	4.27	3.13

Even brief exposure to sexist television commercials can significantly influence the behaviors of men and women. **True.**

social role theory The theory that small gender differences are magnified in perception by the contrasting social roles occupied by men and women.

Table 5.2). Having been primed with images of women as sex objects on TV, the men treated a woman in objectifying ways.

TV commercials influence women as well. In a series of studies, Florence Geis and her colleagues created two sets of TV commercials (Geis et al., 1984; Jennings et al., 1980). In one set, male and female characters were portrayed in stereotypic fashion: A woman served her working man his dinner or behaved in a coy, alluring manner. In the other, the roles were reversed, with the man playing the domestic, seductive role. Female college students watched one of the two sets. Those who saw the stereotypical ads later expressed lower self-confidence, less independence, and fewer career aspirations in experimental tasks than did those who viewed counter-stereotypical ads. Whether or not consumers purchase the products explicitly advertised on television, they do seem to buy the implicit messages about gender—messages that may set in motion a self-fulfilling prophecy.

Media images of men and women also differ in other, more subtle ways. When Dane Archer and his colleagues (1983) inspected 1,750 photographs from *Time*, *Newsweek*, and other magazines, they found what they called "face-ism"—a bias toward greater facial prominence in pictures of men than in pictures of women. This phenomenon is so prevalent that it appeared in analyses of 3,500 photographs from different countries, classic portraits painted in the seventeenth century, and the amateur drawings of college students. Although there are multiple explanations for this bias (Schwarz & Kurz, 1989), one popular interpretation is that facial prominence signals power and dominance. Consistent with this hypothesis, Miron Zuckerman and Suzanne Kieffer (1994) examined magazine photos, portraits, and postage stamps and uncovered a bias toward greater facial prominence in pictures of Whites than in pictures of Blacks. They also found that people pictured with high facial prominence were seen as more dominant—regardless of their race. Whatever the explanation, it's clear that stereotypes can be perpetuated by the subtleties of the human portrait.

Social Role Theory   The media and popular culture are not the only sociocultural factors that contribute to the durability of gender stereotypes. Imagine a secretary typing a letter for a corporate president. Did you visualize a *female* secretary working for a *male* president? Alice Eagly's (1987) **social role theory** states that although the perception of sex differences may be based on actual differences, it is magnified by the unequal social roles occupied by men and women. The process involves three steps. First, through a combination of biological and social factors, a division of labor between the sexes has emerged over time—at home and in the work setting. Men are more likely to work in construction or business; women are more likely to care for children and take lower-status jobs. Second, since people behave in ways that fit the roles they play, men are more likely than women to wield physical, social, and economic power. Third, these behavioral differences

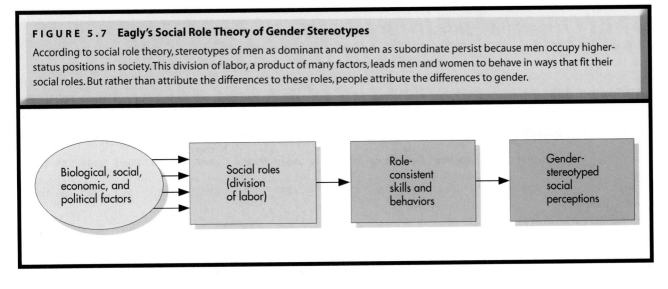

FIGURE 5.7 Eagly's Social Role Theory of Gender Stereotypes
According to social role theory, stereotypes of men as dominant and women as subordinate persist because men occupy higher-status positions in society. This division of labor, a product of many factors, leads men and women to behave in ways that fit their social roles. But rather than attribute the differences to these roles, people attribute the differences to gender.

provide a continuing basis for social perception, leading us to perceive men as dominant "by nature" and women as domestic "by nature," when in fact the differences reflect the roles they play. In short, sex stereotypes are shaped by—and often confused with—the unequal distribution of men and women into different social roles (see Figure 5.7). According to this theory, perceived differences between men and women are based on real behavioral differences that are mistakenly assumed to arise from gender rather than from social roles. When the roles are reversed, the gender stereotypes disappear (Eagly & Wood, 1982).

Sex Discrimination: A Double Standard?

It could be argued that variety is the spice of life and that there's nothing inherently wrong with gender stereotypes as long as men and women are portrayed as different but equal. But are masculine and feminine attributes equally valued? Are men and women judged by the same standard, or is there—as Ann Hopkins maintained—a "double standard"?

Many years ago, Philip Goldberg (1968) asked students at a small women's college to evaluate the content and writing style of some articles. When the material was supposedly written by John McKay rather than Joan McKay, it received higher ratings, a result that led Goldberg to wonder if even women were prejudiced against women. Certain other studies showed that people often devalue the performance of women who take on tasks usually reserved for men (Lott, 1985) and attribute their achievements to luck rather than ability (Deaux & Emswiller, 1974; Nieva & Gutek, 1981). It now appears, however, that the devaluation of women is not common. More than a hundred studies modeled after Goldberg's indicate that people are not generally biased by gender in the evaluation of performance (Swim et al., 1989, 1996; Top, 1991).

TABLE 5.3 Gender Differences in Specific Occupations in the United States

Recent labor statistics reveal that men and women occupy very different positions in the U.S. work force. *(Data from U.S. Bureau of the Census, 1994.)*

Occupation	% Men	% Women
Airline Pilot	96	4
Auto Mechanic	99	1
Bartender	47	53
Child-care worker	3	97
Computer programmer	66	34
Dentist	90	10
Dental assistant	1	99
Lawyer, judge	77	23
Physician	78	22
Registered nurse	6	94
Real estate sales	49	51
Secretary	1	99
Teacher, elementary	14	86
Teacher, college	57	43
Telephone operator	13	87
Telephone repairer	88	12

TABLE 5.4   Women in Work Settings Around the World

Recent international labor statistics indicate that in most of the countries represented, women are especially likely to work in clerical, sales, and service occupations, and especially unlikely to work in production/transport occupations. *(Data from International Labor Office, 1996.)*

Percent of Workers Who Are Women

	Australia	Brazil	Canada	Costa Rica	Egypt	Israel	Italy	Japan	Mexico	Nether-lands	New Zealand	Niger	Spain	USA	UK
Total	42%	39%	45%	30%	20%	42%	35%	40%	32%	41%	44%	8%	34%	46%	45%
Professional/technical (scientists, teachers, engineers, doctors, lawyers, writers, artists)	25	63	56	45	30	54	15	43	45	45	50	8	48	53	44
Administrative/managerial (legislative officials, managers)	43	39	42	33	12	19	54	9	20	17	24	8	12	43	33
Clerical (clerical workers, bookkeepers, postal workers)	47	41	80	49	35	71	34	60	55	59	77	30	51	79	76
Sales (salespeople, insurance, real estate, and securities workers)	10	86	45	37	14	38	50	38	51	47	48	—	45	50	64
Service (bookkeepers, cooks, hairdressers and barbers, building caretakers)	78	35	57	58	6	59	46	55	39	65	65	—	58	60	66
Production/transport (metal workers, woodworkers, tailors and dressmakers, plumbers, miners)	29	25	14	19	4	13	22	28	19	10	16	2	12	18	15

In other ways, however, sex discrimination still exists. Look at Table 5.3 (page 155) and Table 5.4 (above), and you'll notice some striking sex differences in occupational choice. How many female airline pilots have you met lately? What about male secretaries? Sex discrimination during the early school years paves the way for diverging career paths in adulthood. Then, when equally qualified men and women compete for a job, gender considerations enter in once again, as some research indicates that business professionals favor men for so-called masculine jobs (such as a manager for a machinery company) and women for so-called feminine jobs (such as a receptionist) (Glick et al., 1988).

Racism

Nathan Thill's cold-blooded murder of Oumar Dia clearly was an act of **racism**—prejudice and discrimination based on a person's racial background. Such blatant racism remains far too common throughout the world today. But racism can also be much more subtle, lurking beneath surfaces and behind corners. We may see its shadow and not be sure whether it is real or an apparition. Subtle, undercover forms of racism can be just as hurtful as more blatant forms, in part because their subtlety allows them to slip through people's defenses. People who truly want to be fair-minded don't realize the extent to which their reactions and behaviors are influenced by racial stereotypes and prejudices. And often, it seems impossible to know whether and to what extent racism exists in a particular situation. What role did racism play in the arrest, trial, and contradictory verdicts in the two trials of O. J. Simpson? Few events in recent memory triggered more debates about racism than the Simpson case, and people continue to have different opinions about it. In this section of the chapter, we consider some of the blatant and subtle forms and consequences of racism.

More than Just Black and White

Our earlier discussion of prejudice emphasized how people favor their ingroups and discriminate against outgroups. So it should come as no surprise that in much of the world, people discriminate against each other on the basis of race. None of us is completely immune from perpetrating, or being the targets of, some form of racism. But it is important to consider that there are multiple levels of racism. At an *individual* level, any of us can be racist toward anyone else. However, there are also *institutional* and *cultural* factors that unfairly give privilege to some people in society while causing discrimination against others. Children who grow up surrounded by these institutions and cultures quickly learn to read the signs pointing to how society seems to value its citizens unequally.

Just as there are multiple levels of racism, there are also multiple targets. Social psychological research concerning racism has focused primarily on racism by Whites toward Blacks, but many social psychologists also study prejudice and discrimination concerning other races and ethnicities, such as against Asians, Jews, and Latinos. Indeed, it is likely that social psychological research will become more broadly focused as a growing number of people identify themselves in multiple racial and ethnic categories. The U.S. Bureau of the Census reports that the number of multiracial children has quadrupled since 1970 to more than 2 million. According to Jack White (1997), "The color line once drawn between blacks and whites—or more precisely between whites and nonwhites—is breaking into a polygon of dueling erthnicities, each fighting for its place in the sun" (p.33).

Despite the multiple racial or ethnic backgrounds of such individuals, many perceivers categorize these individuals in oversimplified ways. For example, the media have labeled Tiger Woods as one of the best black golfers in history, and a hero and role model for African American children. But Tiger Woods doesn't consider himself "black" or "African American"—not because he denies this part of his identity, but because he also embraces other parts of it as well. His heritage is a quarter Thai, a quarter Chinese, a quarter white, an eighth American Indian and an eighth black. When asked who is he, Woods says, "I'm just who I am, whoever you see in front of you." As a boy, he made up the term "Cablinasian" to describe himself, combining Caucasian, Black, Indian, and Asian (White, 1997, p. 34). What Woods frequently experiences, however, is that many others like to use more

racism Prejudice and discrimination based on a person's racial background.

simple, familiar labels—and these labels make it easier for perceivers to rely on familiar stereotypes and prejudices.

Going Under Cover: Modern Racism

In spite of Tiger Woods's prominence, some other golfers and numerous fans have made racist remarks to him. Clearly, we are a long way from a racism-free society. More generally, however, a close examination of legislation, opinion polls, sociological data, and social psychological research indicates that racial prejudice and discrimination have been lessening over the last several decades (Dovidio & Gaertner, 1997). After all, not so long ago, Tiger Woods would not even have been allowed to play professional golf.

In a classic study of ethnic stereotypes published in 1933, Daniel Katz and Kenneth Braly found that white college students viewed the average white American as smart, industrious, and ambitious. Yet they saw the average African American as superstitious, ignorant, lazy, and happy-go-lucky. In multiple follow-up surveys with demographically similar samples of white students conducted from 1951 through 1993, these negative images of Blacks largely faded (Dovidio et al., 1996). Table 5.5 reports some of the changes in racial prejudice illustrated by these and other studies. According to public opinion polls, racial prejudice in the United States has dropped sharply since World War II. These are all reasons to cheer, but a question remains: Can these results be trusted, or has racism simply gone underground?

People tend to associate anti-Black prejudice with images of blatant racism characterized by slavery, lynch mobs, the Ku Klux Klan, the segregation of public facilities, the claim that African Americans are inferior, and the kinds of violence described in the opening of this chapter. Although blatant racism continues to exist, some call this kind of racism "old-fashioned" to contrast it with more subtle, covert forms of racism that have emerged in more recent years. That is, although overt bigotry has declined, it has been replaced in part by **modern racism**—a subtle form of prejudice that surfaces in less direct ways whenever it is safe, socially acceptable, or easy to rationalize. In short, the overt symptoms of racism may have changed, but the underlying disease remains (Dovidio & Gaertner, 1997; Katz et al., 1986; McConahay, 1986).

According to theories of modern racism, many people are racially ambivalent. They want to see themselves as fair, but they still harbor feelings of anxiety and discomfort in the presence of other racial groups (Hass et al., 1992). There is a good deal of evidence for this ambivalence. For example, many white Americans pay lip

TABLE 5.5 Changes in Overt Racism

The results of many studies and surveys like these demonstrate that overt, negative stereotyping and racism have declined dramatically over the years. Although these results are encouraging, research on more subtle, modern racism reveals that the picture is much more complex than these self-reports suggest. *(Dovidio et al., 1996; Peterson, 1997.)*

Percentage of White Participants Selecting a Trait to Describe Black Americans

Trait	1933	1967	1993
Superstitious	84%	13%	1%
Lazy	75	26	5
Happy-go-lucky	38	27	2
Ignorant	38	11	5
Musical	26	47	12
Very religious	24	8	17
Stupid	22	4	0

Percentage of White Participants Who Report Being Willing to Admit Blacks into Various Relationships with Them

	1949	1968	1992
Willing to Admit Blacks to:			
Employment in my occupation	78%	98%	99%
My club as personal friends	51	97	96
My street as neighbors	41	95	95
Close kinship by marriage	0	66	74

Percentage of Adult Participants Who Agree with the Statement, "It's All Right for Blacks and Whites to Date Each Other."

	1987	1997
	48%	69%

modern racism A form of prejudice that surfaces in subtle ways when it is safe, socially acceptable, and easy to rationalize.

service to the *principles* of racial equality; but in *practice*, they oppose mixed marriages, black political candidates, and racially symbolic policies (Sears & Allen, 1984). There are several specific theories of modern racism, but they all emphasize contradictions and tensions that lead to subtle, often unconscious forms of prejudice and discrimination.

Detecting Modern Racism   If people who are prejudiced will not admit it and may not even be aware of it, how do we know that this form of racism exists? Several methods have been used to identify modern racism. One is the *bogus pipeline*, a phony lie-detector test in which participants are attached with electrodes to a machine that supposedly records their true feelings. Since people don't want to get caught lying, this method elicits more honest answers to sensitive questions. For example, white college students rated Blacks in more negative terms when the bogus pipeline was used than when it was not (Sigall & Page, 1971).

But because modern racism is so subtle, people can't detect the extent to which their attitudes and behaviors reflect such racism, even if they are highly motivated to do so. Therefore, rather than ask direct questions, social psychologists develop other ways of measuring subtle forms of racism. Samuel Gaertner, John Dovidio, and others have found that *reaction time*—the time it takes to answer a question— can be used to uncover hidden prejudices. In one study, white participants read word pairs and pressed a button whenever they thought the words fit together. In each case, the word *Blacks* or *Whites* was paired with either a

The burning cross stands as a terrifying symbol of the Ku Klux Klan and its old-fashioned racism.

positive term *(clean, smart)* or a negative term trait *(stupid, lazy)*. The results were revealing. Participants did not openly associate Blacks with negative terms or Whites with positive terms, and they were equally quick to reject the negative terms in both cases. However, participants were *quicker* to respond to positive terms when paired with *Whites* than with *Blacks*. Since it takes less time to react to stimuli that fit existing attitudes, this finding suggests that participants were unconsciously more predisposed to associate positive traits with Whites than with Blacks. What is also revealing is that covert biased reactions of this kind typically cannot be predicted by participants' explicit, self-reported prejudice levels. In contrast, people's reactions in more explicit, consciously controlled tasks—such as making a decision about a white or black defendant's guilt in a mock trial—*are* predicted by people's self-reported degree of prejudice (Dovidio et al., 1986; Dovidio, Kawakami, et al., 1997).

In modern racism, prejudice against minorities surfaces primarily under circumstances when the expression of prejudice is safe, socially acceptable, and easy to rationalize because of its ambiguity. For example, in a study of helping behavior, white female participants worked in groups in which either a black or a white confederate needed assistance to complete the task. When participants were led to believe that the confederate had tried hard, or when the request was made by a third party, most were willing to help. But when participants were led to believe that the confederate had not worked hard and there was no third-party request, they refused to help the black confederate more often than they refused to help the white one. When circumstances allowed participants to excuse a negative response, they discriminated on the basis of race (Frey & Gaertner, 1986).

These results may seem subtle, but they suggest that racial prejudice is so deeply ingrained in our culture that negative stereotypes are as difficult to break as a bad habit (Devine, 1989). In fact, many Whites who consider themselves nonprejudiced admit that they sometimes do not react toward Blacks, or to other groups such as gay men, as they should—an insight that causes them to feel embarrassed, guilty, and ashamed of themselves (Monteith et al., 1993). Indeed, when they have reason to suspect that racism could bias their judgments, low-prejudice Whites may show an opposite bias on explicit, consciously controlled tasks, responding more favorably to Blacks than to Whites (Dovidio, Kawakami, et al., 1997; Fein et al, 1997).

A troubling aspect of modern racism, however, is that it can be invisible to its perpetrators. Carl Word and his colleagues (1974), for example, conducted an experiment concerning job interviews and found that racial stereotypes can hurt the performance of black job candidates. Without realizing it, white participants sat farther away, made more speech errors, and held shorter interviews when interviewing a black applicant than a white applicant. This colder interpersonal style caused the interviewees to behave in a more nervous and awkward manner. For black men and women in the job market, the implications are sobering. Once past the interview and hiring, the predicament is not eliminated; Thomas Pettigrew and Joanne Martin (1987) note that when minorities enter the workplace, they confront three biases: (1) Negative racial stereotypes lead employers and co-workers to hold low expectations that are hard to overcome; (2) in organizations with few minorities, those who are hired draw more than their share of attention, leading perceivers to exaggerate both the positive and the negative; and (3) it is often believed that minorities are hired as "tokens," a belief that raises even more doubts about their competence. Together, these biases subject minority employees to what Pettigrew and Martin call "triple jeopardy."

Measuring Modern Racism and Other Subtle Prejudices   Just as with any other form of prejudice, individuals differ in the degree to which they exhibit modern racist tendencies. But because of the covert nature of modern racism, measuring these differences is difficult. John McConahay (1986) developed the Modern Racism Scale, which asks people to respond to symbolic questions that reflect modern racism. McConahay tried to design the questions so that respondents would not realize that the questions measured racism as opposed to more abstract, ambiguous attitudes. This scale has been used successfully in numerous studies, such as in predicting individuals' likelihood of activating negative stereotypes about African Americans (Wittenbrink et al., 1997) and in predicting racial discrimination in evaluation of job candidates (McConahay, 1983). Based in part on the popularity of this scale, social psychologists subsequently developed a number of scales to measure other subtle forms of prejudice, including the Modern Sexism Scale (Swim et al., 1995) and the Neo-Sexism Scale (Tougas et al., 1995), and to measure blatant versus subtle racism in western Europe (Pettigrew & Meertens, 1995). Some research, however, suggests that scales such as the Modern Racism Scale are not nearly as able to detect prejudice today as they were originally designed to be (Dovidio, Kawakami, et al., 1997; Fazio et al., 1995). People who are highly motivated to control their expressions of prejudice may score low on the Modern Racism Scale and yet still exhibit a great deal of modern racism (Dunton & Fazio, 1997).

How, then, can we measure individual differences in modern racism? The answer seems to be to use covert measures that do not require individuals to answer questions about their attitudes. Just as researchers have measured people's reaction time to detect the presence of modern racism, they are now using these kinds of procedures to measure individual differences in modern racism. Russell Fazio and his colleagues (1995) developed a procedure they call a *bona fide pipeline* to measure people's racial prejudice. In this procedure, participants perform a series of memory and judgment tasks in what seems to be a study of information processing. While watching a presentation of photographs of students of various races, participants respond as quickly as they can to adjectives by pressing a button to indicate whether they think each adjective is good or bad. What the participants do not realize is that the race of the person they see in the photo presented just before the presentation of an adjective can influence how quickly they make a positive or negative judgment about the adjective. In one study, for example, white participants were slower to rate a positive adjective as good if the adjective was presented immediately after an image of a black student than if it was presented after an image of a white student. Black participants were faster to rate a negative adjective as bad if the adjective was presented immediately after an image of a white student. Individuals' degree of prejudice is measured by the degree to which their responses are influenced by the race of the people seen in the pictures. Even more recently, Anthony Greenwald and his colleagues (1998) developed what they call the Implicit Association Test, which measures the extent to which two concepts (such as *black-good/white-bad* versus *black-bad/white-good*) are associated.

An important advantage of tasks like these is that they require participants to make quick judgments that are influenced by their racial attitudes without their being consciously aware of this influence or able to control it. Therefore, the tasks reveal prejudices that cannot be detected through self-report measures. And although differences revealed on these tasks are measured in fractions of seconds, they predict real, meaningful judgments and behaviors. For example, Fazio and his colleagues found that their bona fide pipeline measure predicted white participants' nonverbal behaviors toward Blacks in an interaction much better than did these participants' scores on the Modern Racism Scale.

Intergroup Contact: A Cure?

Modern racism is difficult to overcome because it lurks like a wolf in sheep's clothing and manifests itself in indirect ways. Is there a solution? Can stereotypes and prejudice be wiped out by a mass media blitz designed to inform people that their expectations and fears are unfounded? Social psychologists used to think that such efforts at persuasive communication would work, but their effectiveness is very limited. There is, however, reason for hope.

School Desegregation: The Great Experiment   In the historic 1954 case of *Brown v. Board of Education of Topeka*, the U.S. Supreme Court ruled that racially separate schools were inherently unequal, in violation of the Constitution. In part, the decision was informed by empirical evidence supplied by thirty-two eminent social scientists on the harmful effects of segregation on the self-esteem and academic achievement of black students as well as on race relations (Allport et al., 1953). The Supreme Court's decision propelled the nation into a large-scale social experiment. What would be the effect?

At the time, the *Brown* decision was controversial. Many Americans opposed school desegregation, arguing that morality cannot be legislated and that forcing interracial contact would only escalate the conflict. Meanwhile, others advanced the **contact hypothesis,** which states that under certain conditions, direct contact between members of rival groups will reduce stereotyping, prejudice, and discrimination (Allport, 1954; Amir, 1969; Stephan, 1985).

contact hypothesis The theory that direct contact between hostile groups will reduce prejudice under certain conditions.

Despite the Court's ruling, desegregation proceeded slowly. There were stalling tactics, lawsuits, and vocal opposition to busing. Many schools remained untouched until the early 1970s. Then, as the dust began to settle, research brought the grave realization that little had changed—that contact between black and white schoolchildren was not having the intended effect. Walter Stephan (1986) reviewed studies conducted during and after desegregation and found that although 13 percent reported a decrease in prejudice among Whites, 34 percent reported no change, and 53 percent reported an *increase*. These findings forced social psychologists to challenge the wisdom of their testimony to the Supreme Court and to re-examine the contact hypothesis that had guided that advice in the first place (Cook, 1984; Miller & Brewer, 1984).

Students at Central High School in Little Rock, Arkansas, in September, 1957, shout insults at Elizabeth Eckford, 16, as she walks toward the school entrance. National Guardsmen blocked the entrance and would not let her enter.

"See that man over there?"

"Yes."

"Well, I hate him."

"But you don't know him."

"That's why I hate him."

—Gordon Allport

The Contact Hypothesis: A Re-examination Is the original contact hypothesis wrong? No. Although desegregation did not immediately produce the desired changes, the conditions necessary for successful intergroup contact did not exist in the public schools. Nobody ever said that deeply rooted prejudices can be erased just by throwing groups together. According to the contact hypothesis, four conditions must exist for contact to succeed.

First, the two groups should be of *equal status*, at least in the contact situation. Blacks and Whites had interacted long before 1954, but too often in situations where Blacks worked at a clear disadvantage in lower-status jobs or in outright servitude. If anything, such unequal-status contacts only perpetuated existing negative stereotypes. You may recall Eagly's (1987) theory that gender stereotypes are sustained by the different social roles played by men and women. The same logic applies to the perception of Blacks and Whites. Desegregation situations that have promoted equal-status contact—as in the army and public housing projects—have been successful (Pettigrew, 1969). When the public schools were desegregated, however, white children were coming from more affluent families, were better prepared, and were academically more advanced than their black peers (Cohen, 1984).

Second, successful contact requires *personal interactions* between individuals. When people are divided into social categories, as we have seen, ingroups tend to assume that outgroup members are all alike. Through intimate, one-on-one interactions, these categories should break down, and outgroup members should be perceived in more individualized terms (Brewer & Miller, 1984; Wilder, 1986). In schools, however, interracial contact among individual children is uncommon. The school is not a melting pot. After the bus arrives, students gravitate toward members of their own race on the playground, in the cafeteria, and in the classroom. What's more, the problem is compounded when students are "tracked" based on grades, a policy that further separates advantaged white students from disadvantaged black students. In short, *desegregation* does not ensure *integration* (Epstein, 1985; Schofield, 1982).

The third condition for successful contact is that the opposing groups engage in *cooperative activities* to achieve superordinate goals. In the Robbers Cave study described earlier, this strategy transformed bitter enemies into allies. Cooperation and shared goals break down the psychological barrier between groups, leading members to re-categorize the two groups into one and reducing ingroup favoritism: "They" become part of "us" (Bettencourt et al., 1992; Gaertner et al., 1990). Yet the typical classroom is filled with competition, the wrong ingredient. Picture the scene. The teacher stands in front of the class and asks a question. Many children wave their hands, each straining to catch the teacher's eye. Then, as soon as one student is called on, the others groan in frustration. In the competition for the teacher's approval, they are losers—hardly a scenario suited to positive intergroup contact (Aronson, 1988).

Finally, intergroup contact can work only if it is supported by *social norms*. When it comes to racial attitudes and behavior, people are profoundly influenced by what others say and do. Like their hairstyles and their taste for music, individuals' racial prejudices are affected dramatically by those of their peers, family, and immediate culture (Pettigrew, 1991). Even overhearing a racial slur by a stranger can increase people's expressions of prejudice (Greenberg & Pyszczynski, 1985). Norms have a powerful impact on us. Yet in the case of school desegregation, the social climate was not supportive. Many principals, teachers, and local officials objected; and many parents boycotted busing. The four necessary conditions of the contact hypothesis are summarized in Table 5.6.

Although many problems have plagued school desegregation efforts, research shows that prejudice can be reduced in situations that satisfy the chief requirements of the contact hypothesis (Cook, 1985). One of the most successful demonstrations of this point took place on the baseball diamond. On April 15, 1947, Jackie Robinson played first base for the Brooklyn Dodgers—and became the first black man to break the color barrier in American sports. Robinson's opportunity came through Dodgers owner Branch Rickey, who felt that integrating baseball was both moral and good for the game (Pratkanis & Turner, 1994). Rickey knew all about the contact hypothesis and was assured by a social scientist friend that a team could furnish the conditions needed for it to work: equal status among teammates, personal interactions, dedication to a common goal, and a positive climate from the owner, managers, and coaches. The rest is history. Rickey signed Robinson and tried to create the situation necessary for

TABLE 5.6 The Contact Hypothesis: Necessary Conditions

Four conditions are deemed necessary for intergroup contact to serve as a treatment for racism. However, many desegregated schools have failed to create a setting that meets these conditions.

1. ***Equal Status*** The contact should occur in circumstances that place the two groups in an equal status.

2. ***Personal interaction*** The contact should involve one-on-one interactions among individual members of the two groups.

3. ***Cooperative activities*** Members of the two groups should join together in an effort to achieve superordinate goals.

4. ***Social norms*** The social norms, defined in part by relevant authorities, should favor intergroup contact.

Groups with a history of prejudice toward each other tend to become much less prejudiced soon after they are made to interact with each other in a desegregated setting. **False.**

Jackie Robinson and Branch Rickey discuss Robinson's contract with the Brooklyn Dodgers. The deal had great historical significance. The two men also went on to become good friends.

success. Although Robinson did face a great deal of racism, he endured, and base-ball was integrated. At the end of his first year, Jackie Robinson was named rookie of the year; and in 1962, he was elected to the Baseball Hall of Fame. At his induc-tion ceremony, Robinson asked three people to stand beside him: his mother, his wife, and his friend Branch Rickey.

The Jigsaw Classroom   Work- ing in the classroom, Elliot Aronson and his col-leagues (1978) developed a cooperative learning method called the **jigsaw class-room.** In newly desegregated public schools in Texas and California, they assigned fifth-graders to small racially and academically mixed groups. The material to be learned within each group was divided into subtopics, much the way a jigsaw puz-zle is broken into pieces. Each student was responsible for learning one piece of the puzzle, after which all members took turns teaching their material to one another. In this system, everyone—regardless of race, ability, or self-confidence—needs everyone else if the group as a whole is to succeed.

The method produced impressive results. Compared with children in tradi-tional classes, those in jigsaw classrooms grew to like each other more, liked school more, were less prejudiced, and had higher self-esteem. What's more, academic test scores improved for minority students and remained the same for white stu-dents. Much like an interracial sports team, the jigsaw classroom offers a promising way to create a truly integrated educational experience. It also provides a model of how to use interpersonal contact to promote greater tolerance of diversity.

A Threat in the Air: Effects on Stigmatized Targets

We are all the targets of other people's stereotypes and prejudices. We are stereotyped and treated differently based on how we look, how we talk, and where we come from. People infer numerous things about us by whether we are "morning people" or "night owls," what sports teams we root for, and whether we think Sean Connery or Pierce Brosnan makes a better James Bond. None of us is immune from having our work evaluated in a biased way, our motives questioned, or our attempts at making new friends rejected because of stereotypes and prejudices.

But for the targets of some stereotypes and prejudices, these concerns are relentless and profound. To targets of these stereotypes, there seem to be few safe havens. Social psychologists often refer to these targets as *stigmatized*—"individuals who, by virtue of their membership in a particular social group, or by possession of particular characteristics, are targets of negative stereotypes, are vulnerable to being labeled as deviant, and are devalued in society" (Major & Crocker, 1993, p. 345). What are some of the effects of being stigmatized by stereotypes and prejudice? In this section we first examine some of the effects that perceiving discrimination can have on individuals, and then we focus on the impact that the perceived threat of being stereotyped can have on the academic achievement of women and minorities.

Perceiving Discrimination

Members of different groups disagree dramatically about the prevalence and mag-nitude of discrimination that is directed at their groups. Surveys show that most white Americans believe that racial discrimination is on the decline in housing,

jigsaw classroom   A cooperative learning method used to reduce racial prejudice through interaction in group efforts.

education, and employment, but most black Americans maintain that the problem still exists (Sigelman & Welch, 1991). The more covert, subtle forms of racism characterized as modern racism may often be barely visible to perceivers, but their effects can be humiliating to their targets. In *Color-Blind*, writer Ellis Cose (1997), who is African American, tells a story about how he was treated in a job interview twenty years ago. He was an award-winning newspaper reporter at the time and was hoping to land a job

with a national magazine. The editor he met with was pleasant and gracious, but he said that the magazine didn't have many black readers. "All the editor saw was a young black guy, and since *Esquire* was not in need of a young black guy, they were not in need of me…he had been so busy focusing on my race that he was incapable of seeing *me* or my work" (p. 150). Then a few years later, and in light of affirmative action, Cose was asked if he was interested in a position in a firm as corporate direc-tor of equal opportunity. "I was stunned, for the question made no sense. I was an expert neither on personnel nor on equal employment law; I was, however, black, which seemed to be the most important qualification" (p. 156).

The targets of stigmatizing stereotypes wonder frequently whether and to what extent others' impressions of them are distorted through the warped lens of social categorization. Over time, such suspicions can be deeply frus-trating. In particular situations, however, they can have both positive and negative conse-quences. In a study by Jennifer Crocker and her colleagues (1991), black participants described themselves on a questionnaire, supposedly to be evaluated by an unknown white student who sat in an adjacent room. Participants were told that they were either liked or disliked by this student on the basis of the questionnaire; then they took a self-esteem test. If the participants thought that the white student could not see them and did not know their race, their self-esteem scores predictably rose after positive feedback and declined after negative feedback (see Figure 5.8). But when participants thought the evaluating student had seen them through a one-way mir-ror, negative feedback did *not* lower their self-esteem. In this situation, participants blamed the unfavorable evaluations on prejudice. However, there was a drawback: One-way mirror partici-pants who received positive feedback showed a *decrease* in self-esteem. The reason? Instead of

FIGURE 5.8 Attributions to Prejudice: Benefits and Drawbacks

Black participants received a positive or negative evaluation from a white student in a nearby room. They thought the white student had or had not seen them through a one-way mirror. In the unseen condition, self-esteem increased after positive feedback and decreased after neg-ative feedback. For participants who thought the evaluator had seen them, negative feedback did not lower self-esteem (the benefit), but positive feedback did (the drawback). Thinking the evaluator knew they were black, participants attributed the feedback to racial factors; thus, they denied themselves both the blame for failure and the credit for success. *(Data from Crocker et al., 1991.)*

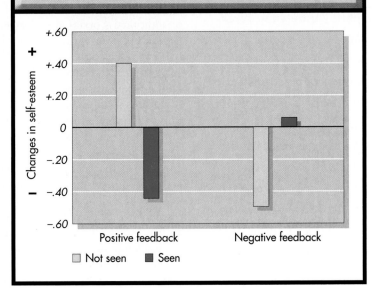

internalizing the credit for success, these participants attributed the praise to patronizing, reverse discrimination.

Attributing negative feedback to discrimination can have its costs as well. First, such an attribution can sometimes be inaccurate, and the recipient of the feedback might miss an opportunity to learn information relevant for self-improvement. Second, although attributing negative feedback to discrimination can protect one's overall self-esteem, it can also make people feel as if they have less personal control over their lives (Ruggiero & Taylor, 1997). Possibly because they do not want to sacrifice their sense of personal control, people in relatively low status groups are sometimes particularly unlikely to perceive discrimination targeted toward them *personally*, even though they perceive discrimination targeted toward their *group* (Crosby, 1984; Kobrynowicz & Branscombe, 1997; Ruggiero & Major, 1998).

Stereotype Threat and Academic Achievement of Women and Minorities

Claude Steele (1997) proposes that in situations in which a negative stereotype can apply to certain groups, "members of these groups can fear being reduced to that stereotype" (p. 614). Steele calls this predicament *stereotype threat*, for it hangs like "a threat in the air" while the individual is in the stereotype-relevant situation. The predicament can be particularly threatening for individuals whose identity and self-esteem are invested in domains for which the stereotype is relevant. Steele argues that stereotype threat plays a crucial role in influencing the intellectual performance and identity of stereotyped group members.

Steele cites disturbing statistics pointing to the underperformance of African Americans in school and of women in domains requiring advanced math skills. According to his theory, stereotype threat can hamper achievement in academic domains in two ways. First, the cognitive and emotional reactions to the activation of stereotype threats in an academic setting can directly interfere with performance. Second, if this stereotype threat is chronic in the academic domain, it can cause individuals to *disidentify* from that domain—to dismiss the domain as no longer relevant to their self-esteem and identity. To illustrate, imagine a black student and a white student who enter high school equally qualified in academic performance. Imagine that while taking a particularly difficult test at the beginning of the school year, each student struggles on the first few problems. The white student may begin to worry about failing, but the black student may have a whole set of additional worries about appearing to confirm a negative stereotype of African Americans. Even if the black student doesn't believe the stereotype at all, the threat of being reduced to a stereotype in the eyes of those around her can trigger anxiety and distraction, impairing her performance. And if she experiences this threat in school frequently—perhaps because she stands out as one of only a few African Americans in the school or because of the way she is treated by others—the situation may become too threatening to her self-esteem. To buffer herself against the threat, she may disidentify with school; if so, her academic performance will become less relevant to her identity and self-esteem. In its place, some other domain of life, such as social success or a particular non-academic talent, will become a more important source of identity and pride.

Steele and his colleagues conducted a series of experiments in which they manipulated factors likely to increase or decrease stereotype threat as students took academic tests. The good news is that when stereotype threat is reduced, so too is the academic underperformance of the threatened group members. For example, Steele and Joshua Aronson (1995) had black and white students from a highly selective university take a very difficult standardized verbal test. To some partici-

Sports Illustrated surveyed almost 2,000 students in U.S. middle schools and high schools and asked them to choose from a list of careers the ones they thought they could successfully pursue. Of all the careers listed, professional sports was the only one selected more often by black students than by white or Hispanic students.

—S. L. Price

pants, it was introduced as a test of intellectual ability; to others, as a laboratory problem-solving task unrelated to ability. Steele and Aronson reasoned that because of the difficulty of the test, *all* the students would struggle with it. If the test was said to be related to intellectual ability, however, the black students would also feel the threat of a negative stereotype. In contrast, if the test was simply a laboratory task and not a real test of intelligence, then negative stereotypes would be less applicable, and the stereotype threat would be reduced. In that case, black students would be less impaired while taking the test. The results supported these predictions. Even though each student's score on the test was adjusted according to his or her past verbal SAT score in order to equalize initial differences in ability, black students did significantly worse on the test if it had been introduced as a test of intellectual ability. In contrast, if the test had been introduced as unrelated to ability, then black students' scores were much higher, showing no difference from the scores of the white students (see Figure 5.9).

Thus, a seemingly minor change in the setting—a few words about the meaning of a test—had a powerful effect on the black students' performance. In a second study, the researchers used an even more slight manipulation of stereotype threat: whether or not the students were asked to report their race just before taking the test (which was described as unrelated to ability). Making them think about race for a few seconds just before taking the test impaired the performance of black students but had no effect on white students.

Steele's theory predicts that because negative stereotypes concerning women's advanced math skills are prevalent, women may often experience stereotype threat in settings relevant to these skills. Reducing stereotype threat in these settings, therefore, should reduce the underperformance that women tend to exhibit in these areas. To test this idea, Steven Spencer and his colleagues (1999) recruited male and female students who were good at math and felt that math was important to their identities. The researchers gave these students a very difficult standardized math test, one on which all of them would perform poorly. Before taking the test, some students were told that the test generally showed no gender differences—thereby implying that the negative stereotype of women's ability in these areas was *not* relevant to this particular test. Other students were told that the test *did* generally show gender differences. As Steele's theory predicted, women performed worse than men when they were told that the test typically produced gender differences, but they performed the same as men when they were told that the test typically did not produce gender differences. A subsequent experiment found that women experienced more anxiety when they were told that the test produced gender differences, and this anxiety was related to their underperformance.

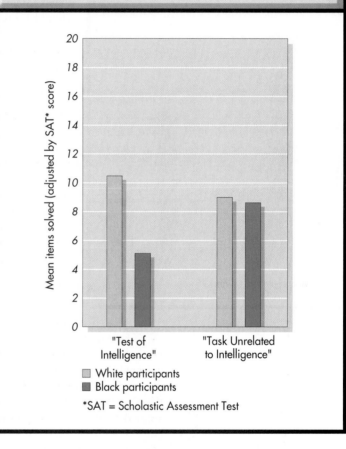

FIGURE 5.9 Stereotype Threat and Academic Performance
Black and white students took a very difficult standardized verbal test. Before taking the test, some students were told that it was a test of their intellectual ability, but others were told that it was simply a laboratory task unrelated to intellectual ability. All students' scores on this test were adjusted based on their scores from standardized college entrance verbal examinations. Despite this adjustment, black students did significantly worse than white students on the test if it had been introduced as a test of intellectual ability (left). In contrast, among the students who had been told that the test was unrelated to ability, black students and white students performed equally well (right). *(Steele & Aronson, 1952.)*

The tendency for minority students to underperform relative to white students on a particular academic test is not likely to be affected by slight changes in the test setting but instead requires gradual, long-term societal changes. **False.**

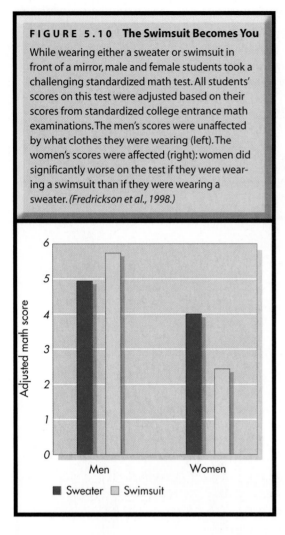

FIGURE 5.10   The Swimsuit Becomes You

While wearing either a sweater or swimsuit in front of a mirror, male and female students took a challenging standardized math test. All students' scores on this test were adjusted based on their scores from standardized college entrance math examinations. The men's scores were unaffected by what clothes they were wearing (left). The women's scores were affected (right): women did significantly worse on the test if they were wearing a swimsuit than if they were wearing a sweater. *(Fredrickson et al., 1998.)*

An interesting experiment by Barbara Fredrickson and her colleagues (1998) also examined how anxiety triggered by the context in which women take a math test can impair their performance. Male and female participants in their study were asked to sample and evaluate some consumer products, including an item of clothing that they tried on and wore for some amount of time. For some participants, the clothing was a one-piece swimsuit; for others, it was a crewneck sweater. While wearing the clothing alone in a room in front of a mirror, each participant took a math test. Fredrickson and her colleagues proposed that because women in our society are made to feel more shame and anxiety about their bodies than are men, they should feel more anxious when taking the test while wearing the swimsuit, whereas men should be relatively unaffected by the manipulation of clothing. As can be seen in Figure 5.10, the results supported their predictions. After adjusting the participants' test scores based on their past performance on standardized math tests, these researchers found that women did significantly worse when wearing a swimsuit than a sweater, whereas men's performance was unaffected by the clothing manipulation.

Stereotype threat can affect any group for which strong, well-known, negative stereotypes are relevant in particular settings. For example, many white athletes feel stereotype threat whenever they step onto a court or playing field where they comprise the minority. Will the white athlete feel the added weight of this threat while struggling against other athletes in a game? Former professional basketball star Isiah Thomas, an African American, thinks so: "I'd think blacks would always want to keep the stereotype that we're better than whites; it's an advantage. When two guys walk on the court to play basketball, and the white athlete's dealing with the guy's blackness and the black guy's dealing with the business of basketball, the black guy beats him" (Price, 1997, p. 44).

The experiments conducted by Steele and his colleagues give us reason for hope that stereotype threat can be overcome, however. Through changes in the situational factors that give rise to stereotype threat, the tremendous weight of negative stereotypes can be reduced, allowing the targets of stereotypes to perform to their potential. In fact, outside of the laboratory, Steele and his colleagues have applied their theory in a university setting. By creating what Steele calls a "wise" environment that fosters interracial contact and cooperation and reduces factors that contribute to stereotype threat, these researchers found that the black students in their program showed almost no underperformance in their grades and were very unlikely to drop out of school (Steele, 1997).

Problems and Prospects

The description of the racism-fueled murder in Denver that opens the chapter, and the exciting research of Claude Steele and his colleagues that helps close it, illustrate the problems and prospects concerning stereotypes, prejudice, and discrimination today. Let's review what we know and can expect from the future.

Stereotypes are beliefs that ultimately lead us to overlook the diversity within groups and jump to conclusions about specific persons. Once formed, stereotypes are hard to erase. Indeed, even if individual perceivers are not biased, stereotypes are often preserved by the forces of culture and can be slow to change. The problems stemming from prejudice and intergroup conflict are equally daunting. Negative feelings toward outgroups arise from competition for limited resources and from the need to favor ingroups over outgroups in order to boost self-esteem. Modern racism is a particularly acute problem, one that is poised and ready to strike at the first provocation.

Sexism and racism are similar in some respects but different in others. Both women and racial minorities often occupy low-status social roles, and both are known victims of discrimination. But sexism rests heavily on caricatures of men and women, whereas racism is further inflamed by negative emotions toward racial outgroups. In addition, research shows that people believe sex differences are more likely than race differences to be biologically rooted (Martin & Parker, 1995).

It is interesting that despite the differences, there may be a single solution to both problems: change behavior, and hearts and minds should follow. Hire men for "feminine" jobs and women for "masculine" jobs, and gender stereotypes may well begin to fade. Likewise, bring Whites, Blacks, and other minorities together as close, cooperative equals, and racial prejudice may also diminish. It's not reasonable to expect these changes overnight, and we may even have to conclude that at least some degree of discrimination is inevitable among human beings. But there is much room, and much hope, for improvement.

According to a 1997 USA Today *survey of U.S. teenagers, 82% of Whites, 81% of Blacks, and 89% of Hispanics say that at least a few of their friends are from a different racial or ethnic group.*

—Karen S. Peterson

Review

- Discrimination is influenced by both beliefs and feelings about social groups.

Stereotypes

- Stereotypes are beliefs that associate groups of people with certain types of characteristics.

How Stereotypes Form

- The formation of stereotypes begins with the tendency for people to group themselves and others into social categories.
- Social categories can be energy-saving devices, allowing perceivers to make quick inferences about group members, but this can lead to inaccurate judgments.
- Social categorization spawns the outgroup homogeneity effect, a tendency to assume that there is more similarity among members of outgroups than ingroups.
- This bias leads us to generalize from individuals to whole groups and vice versa.
- Sociocultural and motivational factors can influence social categorization and outgroup homogeneity effects.

How Stereotypes Distort Perceptions of Individuals

- Stereotypes cause perceivers to see members of stereotyped groups as more similar to the stereotype than they actually are.
- Behaviors that differ markedly from stereotypic expectations, however, are judged to be even more discrepant than they really are as the result of a contrast effect.

How Stereotypes Survive: Self-Perpetuating Mechanisms

- People perceive illusory correlations between groups and traits when the traits are distinctive or when the correlations fit prior notions.
- People tend to make attributions about the causes of group members' behaviors in ways that help maintain their stereotypes.
- Group members who do not fit the mold are often subtyped, leaving the overall stereotype intact. They force a revision of beliefs only when they are otherwise typical members of the group.
- People tend to seek and interpret events in ways that confirm existing stereotypes, sometimes causing the stereotyped targets to behave consistently with the stereotypes.

Is Stereotyping Inevitable? Automatic Versus Intentional Processes

- Stereotypes are often activated without our awareness and operate at an unconscious, or "implicit," level.
- Stereotype activation occurs automatically under some conditions but can also be influenced by how prejudiced the perceivers are, how cognitively busy or distracted they are, and how motivated they are to stereotype others.
- Perceivers can ignore stereotypes and form more individualized impressions of others when they have personal information and the ability and motivation to use that information.
- But research also suggests that it may be hard for people to suppress the use of stereotypes on a consistent, long-term basis.

Prejudice

- Prejudice refers to negative feelings toward persons based on their membership in certain groups.

Robbers Cave: Setting the Stage

- In the Robbers Cave study, boys divided into rival groups quickly showed intergroup prejudice, which was reduced when they were brought together through tasks that required intergroup cooperation.

Realistic Conflict Theory

- Realistic conflict theory maintains that direct competition for resources gives rise to prejudice.
- Prejudice is aroused by perceived threats to an important ingroup.

Social Identity Theory

- Participants categorized into arbitrary minimal groups discriminate in favor of the ingroup.
- Social identity theory proposes that self-esteem is influenced by the fate of social groups with which we identify.
- Research shows that threats to the self cause derogation of outgroups, which in turn increases self-esteem.
- Ingroup favoritism is more intense among people in small minority groups and people who need to elevate their ingroup status.
- People's tendency to exhibit ingroup favoritism may vary across cultures.
- People sometimes distance themselves from ingroups, or from individual members, that fail. Even so, people can derive positive self-esteem from low-status groups.

Sexism

- Sexism is a form of prejudice and discrimination based on a person's gender.

Gender Stereotypes: Blue for Boys, Pink for Girls

- Across the world, men are described as assertive, independent, and task-oriented; women as sensitive, dependent, and people-oriented.
- Gender stereotypes are so deeply ingrained that they bias perceptions of males and females from the moment they are born.

What Activates Gender Stereotypes?

- Gender stereotypes bias the social judgments of some perceivers more than others. They also influence perceptions of target persons who are highly masculine or feminine in appearance or who are viewed in situations that heighten the salience of gender.

Are Gender Stereotypes Accurate?

- Although there are differences between men and women, stereotypes are often stronger than the actual differences.

Why Do Gender Stereotypes Endure?

- Cultural institutions foster gender distinctions in portrayals of males and females.
- Perceived differences between men and women are magnified by the contrasting social roles they occupy.

Sex Discrimination: A Double Standard?

- There are some striking sex differences in occupational choices.
- Men and women are judged more favorably when they apply for jobs that are consistent with gender stereotypes.

Racism

- Racism is a form of prejudice and discrimination based on a person's racial background.

More than Just Black and White

- Institutional and cultural factors fuel racism.

Going Under Cover: Modern Racism

- Over the years, surveys have recorded a decline in negative views of black Americans.
- However, more subtle, modern racism surfaces in less direct ways when people can rationalize racist behavior.
- Researchers use covert measures to detect and measure modern racism and other subtle forms of prejudice and discrimination.

Intergroup Contact: A Cure?

- In its 1954 ruling in *Brown* v. *Board of Education*, the U.S. Supreme Court ordered public schools to desegregate.
- According to the contact hypothesis, desegregation should reduce prejudice.

- Desegregation did not cure the problem; but the key conditions of intergroup contact—equal status, personal interactions, the need to achieve a common goal, and social norms—did not exist.
- As in the jigsaw classroom, positive changes can occur when the conditions necessary for intergroup contact do exist.

A Threat in the Air: Effects on Stigmatized Targets

- Stigmatized groups are negatively stereotyped and devalued in society.

Perceiving Discrimination

- When members of stigmatized groups perceive others' reactions to them as discrimination, they experience both benefits and drawbacks for their self-esteem.

Stereotype Threat and Academic Achievement of Women and Minorities

- Situations that activate stereotype threat cause individuals to worry that others will see them in negative, stereotypic ways.
- Stereotype threat can impair the intellectual performance and identity of stereotyped group members.
- Reducing stereotype threat through slight changes in a setting can dramatically improve the performance of stereotyped group members.

Problems and Prospects

- Despite the differences between sexism and racism, one solution may serve both problems: Change behavior, and hearts and minds will follow.

Key Terms

PUTTING COMMON SENSE TO THE TEST

Stereotypes allow people to save time and effort when processing information about others, freeing them to pay attention to other tasks or information.

True. *People who use stereotypes, even if they don't realize they are using them, save time and effort by using people's group memberships to make inferences about them.*

Members of low-status, stereotyped groups have lower self-esteem than members of high-status groups.

False. *Because people are adaptive in what they take pride in and emphasize, being in a low-status, stereotyped group often does not cause an individual to develop low self-esteem.*

Even brief exposure to sexist television commercials can significantly influence the behaviors of men and women.

True. *Exposure to sexist commercials can make men behave in more sexist ways toward women and can make women engage in more stereotypical behaviors.*

Groups with a history of prejudice toward each other tend to become much less prejudiced soon after they are made to interact with each other in a desegregated setting.

False. *When the contact between groups involves unequal status between them, lacks personal interaction between individual group members, and does not involve cooperation to achieve shared goals, contact is* not *likely to reduce prejudice.*

The tendency for minority students to underperform relative to white students on a particular academic test is not likely to be affected by slight changes in the test setting but instead requires gradual, long-term societal changes.

False. *Although gradual, long-term societal changes may be essential for more long-term effects, slight changes in the setting of an academic test, such as how a test is introduced to students, can result in dramatic effects on the performance of minority students who are targets of negative stereotypes.*

6 | Attitudes

PREVIEW

This chapter examines social influences on attitudes. We define *attitudes* and then discuss how they are measured and when they are related to behavior. Then we consider two methods of changing attitudes. First, we look at source, message, and audience factors that win persuasion through the media of *communication*. Second, we consider theories and research showing that people often change their attitudes as a consequence of their own *actions*.

OUTLINE

T / F

_____ Researchers can tell if someone has a positive or negative attitude by measuring physiological arousal.

_____ In reacting to persuasive communications, people are influenced more by superficial images than by logical arguments.

_____ People are most easily persuaded by commercial messages that are presented without their awareness.

_____ The more money you pay people to tell a lie, the more they will come to believe it.

_____ People often come to like what they suffer for.

A bortion. Affirmative action. The death penalty. Family values. Gay and lesbian marriages. Gun control. School prayer. Multiculturalism. Bill Gates. The SATs. Anyone who has followed recent events in the United States—or anywhere else, for that matter—knows how passionately people feel about the issues of the day. Attitudes and the mechanisms of attitude change, or persuasion, are a vital part of human social life. This chapter addresses three sets of questions: (1) What is an attitude, how can it be measured, and what is its link to behavior? (2) What kinds of persuasive communications lead people to change their attitudes? (3) Why do we often change our attitudes as a result of our own actions?

The Study of Attitudes

D o you favor or oppose a ban on assault weapons? Should smoking be prohibited in public places? Would you rather listen to rock music or jazz, drink Coke or Pepsi, work on a PC or a Mac? As these questions suggest, each of us has positive and negative reactions to various persons, objects, and ideas. These reactions are called **attitudes.** Skim the chapters in this book, and you'll see just how pervasive attitudes are. For example, self-esteem is an attitude that each of us holds about himself or herself, attraction is a positive attitude toward another person, and prejudice is a negative attitude often directed against certain groups.

There are two schools of thought on how the term *attitude* should be defined (Eagly & Chaiken, 1998; Petty et al., 1997). One view holds that an attitude is a combination of affective, behavioral, and cognitive reactions to an object (Breckler, 1984; Rajecki, 1982). According to this *tricomponent* approach, an attitude is (1) a positive, negative, or mixed *affective* reaction consisting of our emotions, moods, and feelings about an object; (2) a *behavioral* disposition, or tendency to act in a certain manner toward an object; and (3) a *cognitive* reaction, as our evaluation of the object is based on relevant beliefs, images, and memories.

attitude A positive, negative, or mixed reaction to a person, object, or idea.

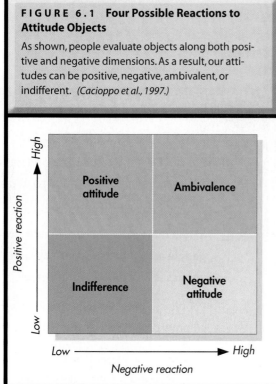

FIGURE 6.1 Four Possible Reactions to Attitude Objects

As shown, people evaluate objects along both positive and negative dimensions. As a result, our attitudes can be positive, negative, ambivalent, or indifferent. *(Cacioppo et al., 1997.)*

Thoughts and feelings are not always related to each other, nor do they necessarily guide our behavior. Because of this lack of consistency, many social psychologists prefer to keep the three components separate and use the word *attitude* in primarily affective terms (Petty & Cacioppo, 1986; Zanna & Rempel, 1988). In this *single-component* definition, an attitude is a positive, negative, or mixed evaluation of an object, expressed at some level of intensity—nothing more, nothing less. *Like, dislike, love, hate, admire,* and *detest* are the kinds of words that people use to describe their attitudes.

It's important to realize that attitudes cannot simply be represented along a single continuum ranging from wholly positive to wholly negative—as you might expect if our attitudes were like the balance knob on a stereo that directs sound to the left or right speaker or like the lever on a thermostat that raises or lowers temperature. Rather, as depicted in Figure 6.1, our attitudes can vary in strength along both positive and negative dimensions. In other words, we can react to something with positive affect, with negative affect, with ambivalence (strong but mixed emotions), or with apathy and indifference (Cacioppo et al., 1997).

At times, everyone forms positive and negative evaluations of the people, objects, and ideas they encounter. In fact, this process appears to be automatic, like a reflex action (Bargh, Chaiken, Raymond, & Hymes, 1996). It's important to realize, however, that individuals differ in the extent to which they react to stimuli in strong positive and negative terms. What about you—do you form opinions easily? Do you have strong likes and dislikes? Or, do you tend to react in more objective, non-evaluative ways? People who describe themselves as high rather than low in the **need for evaluation** are more likely to view their daily experiences in judgmental terms. They are also more opinionated on a whole range of social, moral, and political issues (Jarvis & Petty, 1996).

How Attitudes Are Measured

To experience attitude measurement firsthand by taking part in a nationwide survey, you can visit the Gallup Organization online (www.gallup.com/poll).

In 1928, Louis Thurstone published an article entitled "Attitudes Can Be Measured." What Thurstone failed to anticipate, however, is that measurement is a tricky business. Several years ago, one review of the research uncovered more than five hundred different methods of determining an individual's attitudes (Fishbein & Ajzen, 1972).

Self-Report Measures   The easiest way to assess a person's attitude about something is to ask. The method of *self-report* is direct and straightforward. But attitudes are sometimes too complex to be measured by a single question. As you may recall from Chapter 2, one problem recognized by public opinion pollsters is that responses to attitude questions can be influenced by their wording, the context in which they are asked, and other extraneous factors (Schwarz & Sudman, 1996; Tourangeau et al., 1991). In one survey, for example, six hundred Americans were asked if the government spent too much money on "assistance to the poor," and only 23 percent agreed. Yet when the very same question was asked about "welfare," the agreement rate rose to 53 percent (*Time*, 1994). In another survey, respondents were asked if "People should have the freedom to express their opinions publicly" and were more likely to say yes if the preceding question was about the Catholic Church than if it was about the American Nazi Party (Ottati et al., 1989).

need for evaluation A tendency to form positive and negative attitudes toward the people, objects, and issues we encounter.

Recognizing the problems with single-question measures, researchers often use multiple-item questionnaires known as **attitude scales** (Robinson et al., 1991; Schwarz et al., 1998). Attitude scales come in different forms, perhaps the most popular being the *Likert Scale*, named after its inventor, Rensis Likert (1932). In this technique, respondents are presented with a list of statements about an atti-

As seen in this confrontation between pro-choice and anti-abortion forces, people are often very passionate about their attitudes.

tude object and are asked to indicate on a multiple-point scale how strongly they agree or disagree with each statement. Each respondent's total attitude score is derived by summing his or her responses to all the items. However, regardless of whether attitudes are measured by one question or by a full-blown scale, the results should be taken with caution. All self-report measures assume that people express their true opinions. Sometimes this assumption is reasonable and correct, but often it is not. Wanting to make a good impression on others, people are generally reluctant to admit to their failures, vices, weaknesses, unpopular opinions, and prejudices.

One approach to this problem is to increase the accuracy of self-report measures. To get respondents to answer attitude questions more truthfully, researchers sometimes use the **bogus pipeline**, an elaborate mechanical device that supposedly records our true feelings—like a lie-detector test. Not wanting to get caught in a lie, respondents tend to answer attitude questions with less social desirability bias when they think that deception would be detected by the bogus pipeline (Jones & Sigall, 1971; Roese & Jamieson, 1993). For example, Roger Tourangeau and his colleagues (1997) found that people were more likely to admit to drinking too much, using cocaine, having frequent oral sex, and not exercising enough when the bogus pipeline was used than when it was not.

Covert Measures   A second approach to the self-report problem is to collect indirect, covert measures of attitudes. One possibility in this regard is to use observable behavior—such as facial expressions, tone of voice, and body language. In one study, Gary Wells and Richard Petty (1980) secretly videotaped college students as they listened to a speech and noticed that when the speaker took a position that the students agreed with (that tuition costs should be lowered), most made vertical head movements. But when the speaker took a contrary position (that tuition costs should be raised), head movements were in a horizontal direction. Without realizing it, the students had signaled their attitudes by nodding and shaking their heads.

Although behavior provides clues, it is far from perfect as a measure of attitudes. Sometimes, we nod our heads because we agree; at other times, we nod to be polite. The problem is that people monitor their overt behavior just as they monitor self-reports. But what about internal, physiological reactions that are difficult, if not impossible, to control? Does the body betray how we feel? In the past, researchers tried to divine attitudes from involuntary physical reactions such as perspiration, heart rate, and pupil dilation. The result, however, was always the

attitude scale A multiple-item questionnaire designed to measure a person's attitude toward some object.

bogus pipeline A phony lie-detector device that is sometimes used to get respondents to give truthful answers to sensitive questions.

FIGURE 6.2 The Facial EMG: A Covert Measure of Attitudes?

The facial EMG makes it possible to detect differences between positive and negative attitudes. Notice the major facial muscles and recording sites for electrodes. When people hear a message with which they agree rather than disagree, there is a relative increase in EMG activity in the depressor and zygomatic muscles but a relative decrease in the corrugator and frontalis muscles. These changes cannot be seen with the naked eye. *(Cacioppo & Petty, 1981.)*

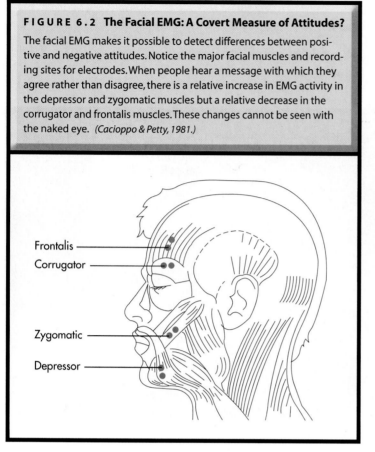

Researchers can tell if someone has a positive or negative attitude by measuring physiological arousal. **False.**

same: Measures of arousal reveal the intensity of one's attitude toward an object but not whether that attitude is positive or negative. On the physiological record, love and hate look very much the same (Petty & Cacioppo, 1983).

Although physiological arousal measures cannot distinguish between positive and negative attitudes, some exciting alternatives have been discovered. One is the **facial electromyograph (EMG).** As shown in Figure 6.2, certain muscles in the face contract when we are happy, and different facial muscles contract when we are sad. Some of the muscular changes cannot be seen with the naked eye, however, so the facial EMG is used. To determine whether the EMG can be used to measure the affect associated with attitudes, John Cacioppo and Richard Petty (1981) recorded facial muscle activity of participants as they listened to a message with which they agreed or disagreed. The agreeable message increased activity in the cheek muscles—the facial pattern characteristic of happiness. The disagreeable message sparked activity in the forehead and brow area—the facial patterns associated with sadness and distress. Outside observers who later watched the participants were unable to see these subtle changes. The muscles in the human face reveal smiles, frowns, and other reactions to attitude objects that otherwise are hidden from view (Cacioppo et al., 1986; Tassinary & Cacioppo, 1992).

Electrical activity in the brain may also assist in the measure of attitudes. In 1929, Hans Burger invented a machine that could detect, amplify, and record "waves" of electrical activity in the brain through electrodes pasted to the surface of the scalp. The instrument is called an *electroencephalograph*, or EEG, and the information it provides takes the form of line tracings called *brain waves*. Based on an earlier discovery—that certain patterns of electrical brain activity are triggered by exposure to stimuli that are novel or inconsistent—Cacioppo and his colleagues (Cacioppo, Crites, Bernston, & Coles, 1993) had participants list ten items they liked and ten they did not like within various object categories (fruits, sports, movies, universities, etc.). Later, these participants were brought into the laboratory, wired to an EEG, and presented with a list of category words that depicted the objects they liked and disliked. The result: The brain-wave pattern normally triggered by inconsistency increased more when a disliked stimulus appeared after a string of positive items, or when a liked stimulus was shown after a string of negative items, than when either stimulus evoked the same attitude as the items that preceded it. Although more research is needed, this discovery suggests that attitudes may be measurable by electrical activity in the brain.

facial electromyograph (EMG)
An electronic instrument that records facial muscle activity associated with emotions and attitudes.

The Link Between Attitudes and Behavior

People take for granted the notion that attitudes influence behavior. We assume that voters' opinions of opposing candidates predict the decisions they make on election day, that consumers' attitudes toward competing products influence the purchases they make, and that feelings of prejudice trigger negative acts of discrimination. Yet as sensible as these assumptions seem, the link between attitudes and behavior is far from perfect.

Sociologist Richard LaPiere (1934) was the first to notice that attitudes and behavior don't always go hand in hand. In the 1930s, LaPiere took a young Chinese-American couple on a three-month, 10,000-mile automobile trip, visiting 250 restaurants, hotels, and campgrounds throughout the United States. Although prejudice against Asians was widespread at the time, the couple was refused service only once. Yet when LaPiere wrote back to the places they had visited and asked if they would accept Chinese patrons, more than 90 percent of those who returned an answer said they would not. Self-reported attitudes did not correspond with behavior.

This study was provocative but seriously flawed. LaPiere measured attitudes several months after his trip, and during that time the attitudes may have changed. He also did not know whether those who responded to his letter were the same people who had greeted the couple in person. It was even possible that the Chinese couple were served wherever they went only because they were accompanied by LaPiere himself.

Despite these problems, LaPiere's study was the first of many to reveal a lack of correspondence between attitudes and behavior. In 1969, Allan Wicker reviewed the applicable research and concluded that attitudes and behavior are correlated only weakly, if at all. Sobered by this conclusion, researchers were puzzled: Could it be that the votes we cast do *not* follow from our political opinions, that consumer purchases are *not* based on attitudes toward a product, or that discrimination is *not* related to underlying prejudice? Is the study of attitudes useless to those interested in human social behavior? No, not at all. During the next few years, researchers went on to identify some of the conditions under which attitudes and behavior are correlated. Stephen Kraus (1995) recently analyzed all of this research and concluded that "attitudes significantly and substantially predict future behavior" (p. 58). In fact, Kraus calculated that there would have to be 60,983 new studies reporting a zero correlation before this conclusion would have to be revised!

Attitudes in Context   One important factor is the level of *correspondence*, or similarity, between attitude measures and behavior. Perhaps the reason that LaPiere (1934) did not find a correlation between self-reported prejudice and discrimination was that he had asked proprietors about Asians in general but then observed their actions toward only one couple. To predict a single act of discrimination, he should have measured people's more specific attitudes toward a young, well-dressed, attractive Chinese couple accompanied by an American professor.

Analyzing more than a hundred studies, Icek Ajzen and Martin Fishbein (1977) found that attitudes correlate with behavior only when attitude measures closely match the behavior in question. Illustrating the point, Andrew Davidson and James Jaccard (1979) tried to use attitudes to predict whether women would use birth control pills within the next two years. Attitudes were measured in a series of questions ranging from very general ("How do you feel about birth control?") to very specific ("How do you feel about using birth control pills during the next two years?"). The more specific the initial attitude question was, the better it predicted the behavior. Other researchers as well have replicated this finding (Kraus, 1995).

The link between our feelings and our actions should also be placed within a broader context. Attitudes are one determinant of social behavior, but there are other determinants as well. This limitation formed the basis for Fishbein's (1980) theory of reasoned action, which Ajzen (1991) then expanded into his **theory of planned behavior.** According to these theories, our attitudes influence our

theory of planned behavior
The theory that attitudes toward a specific behavior combine with subjective norms and perceived control to influence a person's actions.

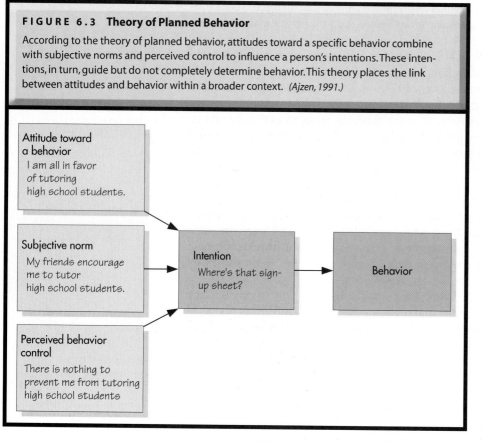

FIGURE 6.3   Theory of Planned Behavior
According to the theory of planned behavior, attitudes toward a specific behavior combine with subjective norms and perceived control to influence a person's intentions. These intentions, in turn, guide but do not completely determine behavior. This theory places the link between attitudes and behavior within a broader context. *(Ajzen, 1991.)*

Attitude toward a behavior
I am all in favor of tutoring high school students.

Subjective norm
My friends encourage me to tutor high school students.

Perceived behavior control
There is nothing to prevent me from tutoring high school students

Intention
Where's that sign-up sheet?

Behavior

behavior through a process of deliberate decision making—and their impact is limited in four respects (see Figure 6.3).

First, as just described, behavior is influenced less by general attitudes than by attitudes toward a specific behavior. Second, behavior is influenced not only by attitudes but by *subjective norms*—our beliefs about what others think we should do. As we'll see in Chapter 7, social pressures to conform often lead us to behave in ways that are at odds with our inner convictions. Third, according to Ajzen, attitudes give rise to behavior only when we perceive the behavior to be within our *control*. To the extent that people lack confidence in their ability to engage in some behavior, they are unlikely to form an intention to do so. Fourth, although attitudes (along with subjective norms and perceived control) contribute to an *intention* to behave in a particular manner, people often do not or cannot follow through on their intentions.

A good deal of research supports the theories of reasoned action and planned behavior (Ajzen & Madden, 1986; Fishbein & Stasson, 1990; Madden et al., 1992). Indeed, this general approach—which places the link between attitudes and behavior in a broader context—has successfully been used to predict a wide range of behaviors, such as losing weight, using condoms, donating blood, exercising, smoking cigarettes, voting, attending church, shoplifting, choosing an occupation, and making moral and ethical decisions (Kurland, 1995; Sheppard et al., 1988).

Strength of the Attitude   According to the theories of reasoned action and planned behavior, specific attitudes combine with social factors to produce behavior. Sometimes attitudes have more influence on behavior than do other factors; sometimes they have less. In large part, it depends on the importance, or *strength*, of the attitude. Each of us has some views that are nearer and dearer to the heart than others. Computer jocks often become attached to IBM PCs, Macs, or other competing brands, while political activists have fiery passions for one political party over others. In each case, the attitude is held with great confidence and is difficult to change (Petty & Krosnick, 1995).

Why are some attitudes stronger than others? One provocative hypothesis, as advanced by Abraham Tesser (1993), is that strong attitudes are rooted in our genetic make-up. Research shows that on some issues, the attitudes of identical twins are more similar than those of fraternal twins; and twins raised apart are as similar to each other as are those raised in the same home. This pattern of evidence suggests that people may be predisposed by nature to hold certain attitudes. Indeed, Tesser found that when asked about attitudes for which there seems to be a genetic link (such as attitudes toward sexual promiscuity, religion, and the death penalty), research participants were quicker to respond and less likely to alter their views in the direction of social norms. Tesser speculates that as a result of inborn physical, sensory, and cognitive abilities, temperament, and personality traits, individuals are biologically predisposed to hold certain strong attitudes.

Whether or not there is a genetic link, David Boninger and his colleagues (1995) have identified three psychological factors that consistently distinguish between our strongest and weakest attitudes. These investigators asked people to reflect on their views toward defense spending, gun control, the legalization of marijuana, abortion rights, and other issues. They found that those attitudes that people held the most passionately concerned issues that (1) directly affected their own outcomes and self-interests; (2) related to deeply held philosophical, political, and religious values; and (3) were of concern to their close friends, family, and social ingroups.

Several factors indicate the strength of an attitude and its link to behavior. One is that people tend to behave in ways that are consistent with their attitudes when they are well informed. For example, college students were asked which of two candidates they preferred in an upcoming local election for mayor. Those who knew the campaign issues were later the most likely to actually vote for their favored candidate (Davidson et al., 1985). In another study, students were questioned about their views on various environmental issues and later were asked to take action—to sign petitions, participate in a recycling project, and so on. Again, the more informed students were, the more consistent their environmental attitudes were with their behavior (Kallgren & Wood, 1986).

Second, the strength of an attitude is indicated not only by the amount of information on which it is based but also by how that information was acquired in the first place. Research shows that attitudes are more stable and more predictive of behavior when they are formed through direct personal experience than when they are based on indirect, secondhand information. In a series of experiments, for example, Russell Fazio and Mark Zanna (1981) introduced two groups of participants to a set of puzzles. One group actually worked on sample puzzles; the other group merely watched someone else work on them. Participants were then asked to rate their interest in the puzzles (attitude) and were given an opportunity to spend time on them (behavior). As it turned out, attitudes and behaviors were more consistent

among participants who had previously sampled the puzzles. Other researchers, too, have found that people feel more strongly about an object when their attitudes toward it were born of direct experience (Millar & Millar, 1996).

A third key factor is that strong attitudes are highly *accessible* to awareness, which means they are quickly and easily brought to mind (Fazio, 1990). To return to our earlier examples, computer jocks think often about their computer preferences, and political activists think often about their party allegiances. It turns out

Chances are, these identical twins have more in common than being firefighters. Research suggests that people may be genetically predisposed to hold certain attitudes.

that many attitudes—not just those we feel strongly about—are easily brought to mind by the mere sight or even just the mention of an attitude object (Bargh et al., 1992). Of course, situational factors can also bring an attitude into awareness. Attitudes thus correlate with behavior more when people become self-focused by staring into a mirror (Gibbons, 1978), when they overhear others discussing the issue (Borgida & Campbell, 1982), or when they are questioned repeatedly (Powell & Fazio, 1984). Interestingly, people are quick to assume a connection between attitude strength and accessibility. When researchers activated a particular attitude by having participants express it over and over again, the participants later came to perceive that attitude as personally more important (Roese & Olson, 1994).

To summarize, research on the link between attitudes and behavior leads to an important conclusion. Our feelings toward an object do not always determine our actions because other factors must be taken into account. However, when attitudes are strong and specific to a behavior, the effects are beyond dispute. Under these conditions, voting *is* influenced by political opinions, consumer purchasing *is* affected by product attitudes, and racial discrimination *is* rooted in feelings of prejudice. Attitudes are important determinants of behavior. The question now is, How can attitudes be changed?

Persuasion by Communication

Television provides a major outlet for commercial persuasion. The average American watches 30 hours of TV per week—and views roughly 37,822 commercials per year.

On a day-to-day basis, we are all involved in the process of changing attitudes. Advertisers flood consumers with ad campaigns designed to sell new cars, soft drinks, sneakers, and laundry detergents. Likewise, politicians make speeches, pass out bumper stickers, and kiss babies to win votes. Attitude change is sought whenever parents socialize their children, scientists advance theories, religious groups seek converts, or trial lawyers argue cases to a jury. Some appeals work; others do not. Some are soft and subtle; others are hard and blatant. Some serve the public interest, while others serve personal interests. The point is, there is nothing inherently evil or virtuous about changing attitudes, a process known as **persuasion.** We do it all the time.

If you wanted to change someone's attitude on an issue, you would probably try by making a persuasive *communication*. Appeals made in person and through the mass media rely on the spoken word, the written word, and the image that is worth a thousand words. What determines whether an appeal succeeds or fails? To understand why certain approaches are effective while others are not, we need to know *how* and *why* persuasive communications work. For that, we need a road map of the persuasion process.

If you're generally interested in advertising history, news, or employment prospects, you can visit the web site for Advertising Age, a great resource on the subject (www.adage.com).

Two Routes to Persuasion

It's a familiar scene in American politics: Every four years, presidential candidates launch extensive campaigns for office. In a way, if you've seen one election, you've seen them all. The names and dates may change; but over and over again, opposing candidates accuse each other of ducking the issues and turning the election into a flag-waving popularity contest. True or not, these accusations show that politicians are keenly aware that they can win votes through two completely different methods. They can stick to the issues, or they can base their appeals on other grounds.

To account for these alternative approaches, Richard Petty and John Cacioppo (1986) proposed a dual-process model of persuasion. This model assumes that we

persuasion The process by which attitudes are changed.

"And I'd like to ask my mud-slinging opponent if he's been faithful to that moose he married."

Persuasive communication is big business. During the 1998 Super Bowl, advertisers spent an average of $2.6 million per ad minute.

do not always process communications the same way. When people think critically about the contents of a message, they are said to take a **central route to persuasion** and are influenced by the strength and quality of the arguments. When people do not think critically about the contents of a message but focus instead on other cues, they take a **peripheral route to persuasion.** As we'll see, the route taken depends on whether one is willing and able to scrutinize the information contained in the message itself. Over the years, this model has provided an important framework for understanding the factors that elicit persuasion (Petty & Wegener, 1998; Petty et al., 1997).

According to Advertising Age, *the ten companies that spent the most money on advertising in 1997 were, in order: Chevrolet, McDonald's, Ford, Sears, Dodge, AT&T, MCI, Burger King, Toyota, and Kelloggs.*

The Central Route   In the first systematic attempt to study persuasion, Carl Hovland and his colleagues (1949, 1953) started the Yale Communication and Attitude Change Program. They proposed that for a persuasive message to have influence, the recipients of that message must learn its contents and be motivated to accept it. According to this view, people can be persuaded only by an argument they attend to, comprehend, and retain in memory for later use. Regardless of whether the message takes the form of a personal appeal, a newspaper editorial, a Sunday sermon, a TV commercial, or an advertising banner on a Web site, these basic requirements remain the same.

Several years later, William McGuire (1969) reiterated the information-processing steps necessary for persuasion and, like the Yale group before him, distinguished between the learning, or *reception*, of a message—a necessary first step—and its later *acceptance*. In fact, McGuire (1968) used this distinction to explain the surprising finding that a recipient's self-esteem and intelligence are unrelated to persuasion. In McGuire's scheme, these characteristics have opposite effects on reception and acceptance. People who are smart or high in self-esteem are better able to learn a message but are less likely to accept its call for a change in attitude. People who are less smart or low in self-esteem are more willing to accept the message but may have trouble learning its contents. Overall, then, neither group is generally more vulnerable to persuasion than the other—a prediction that is supported by a good deal of research (Rhodes & Wood, 1992).

central route to persuasion
The process by which a person thinks carefully about a communication and is influenced by the strength of its arguments.

peripheral route to persuasion   The process by which a person does not think carefully about a communication and is influenced instead by superficial cues.

In presidential politics, candidates try to win votes by addressing the issues, as in a press conference (the central route), or through the use of banners, music, and other theatrics, as in a convention (the peripheral route).

Getting the audience's attention is not a first step to persuasion that can be taken for granted. In a recent Harris poll, 7 out of 10 Americans said they often lower the volume or switch channels to avoid TV commercials.

elaboration The process of thinking about and scrutinizing the arguments contained in a persuasive communication.

Anthony Greenwald (1968) and others then argued that persuasion requires a third, intermediate step: **elaboration.** To illustrate, imagine you are offered a job and your prospective employer tries to convince you over lunch to accept. You listen closely, learn the terms of the offer, and understand what it means. But if it's an important interview, your head will spin with questions as you weigh the pros and cons and contemplate the implications: Would I have to move? Is there room for growth? Am I better off staying where I am? When confronted with personally significant messages, we don't just listen for the sake of collecting information—we think about that information. The message is then effective to the extent that it leads us to focus on favorable rather than unfavorable thoughts.

These theories of attitude change all share the assumption that the recipients of persuasive appeals are attentive, active, critical, and thoughtful. This assumption is correct—some of the time. When it is, and when people consider a message carefully, their reaction to it depends on the strength of its contents. In these instances, messages have greater impact when they are easily learned rather than difficult, when they are memorable rather than forgettable, and when they stimulate favorable rather than unfavorable elaboration. Ultimately, strong arguments are persuasive, and weak arguments are not. On the central route to persuasion, the process is eminently thoughtful.

The Peripheral Route "The receptive ability of the masses is very limited, their understanding small; on the other hand, they have a great power of forgetting." The author of this statement was Adolf Hitler (1933, p. 77). Believing that people are incompetent processors of information, Hitler relied heavily in his propaganda on the use of slogans, uniforms, marching bands, flags, and other symbols. For Hitler, "Meetings were not just occasions to make speeches, they were carefully planned theatrical productions in which settings, lighting, background music, and the timing of entrances were devised to maximize the emotional fervor of an audience" (Qualter, 1962, p. 112). Do these ploys work? Can the masses be so handily manipulated into persuasion? Audiences are not always thoughtful. Sometimes people do not follow the central route to persuasion but instead take a short cut through the peripheral route. Rather than try to learn the message and think through the issues, they respond with little effort on the basis of superficial, peripheral cues.

On the peripheral route to persuasion, people often evaluate a communication by using simple-minded heuristics, or rules of thumb (Chaiken, 1987; Chaiken et al., 1989). If a communicator has a good reputation, speaks fluently, or writes well, we tend to assume that his or her message must be correct. And when a speaker has a reputation for being honest, people think in less critical terms about the contents of his or her communication (Priester & Petty, 1995). Likewise, we assume that a message must be correct if it contains a long litany of arguments, numerous statistics, or an impressive list of supporting experts; if it elicits cheers from an audience; or if the speaker seems to be arguing against his or her own interests. In some cases, simply knowing that an argument has majority support can get people to change their attitudes (Giner-Sorolla & Chaiken, 1997).

On the mindless peripheral route, people are also influenced by a host of attitude-irrelevant factors—such as cues from their own body movements. In one study, participants were induced to nod their heads up and down (as if saying "yes") or shake them from side to side (as if saying "no") while listening via headphones to an editorial—presumably to test whether the headphones could endure the physical activity. Those coaxed into nodding later agreed with the arguments more (Wells & Petty, 1980). In other studies, participants viewed and rated graphic symbols or wordlike stimuli (*surtel, primet*) while using an exercise bar to either stretch their arms out (which mimics what we do to push something away) or flex their arms in (which we do to bring something closer). These stimuli were later judged to be more pleasant when associated with the flexing of the arm than with the stretching-out motion (Cacioppo, Priester, and Bernston, 1993; Priester et al., 1996).

Route Selection   Thanks to Petty and Cacioppo's (1986) two-track distinction between central and peripheral routes, we can better understand why the persuasion process seems so logical on some occasions yet so illogical on others—why voters may select candidates according to issues or images, why juries may base their verdicts on evidence or a defendant's appearance, and why consumers may base their purchases on marketing reports or product images. The process that is engaged depends on whether the recipients of a persuasive message have the *ability* and the *motivation* to take the central route or whether they rely on peripheral cues instead.

To understand the conditions that lead people to take one route or the other, it's helpful to view persuasive communication as the outcome of three factors: a *source* (who), a *message* (says what and in what context), and an *audience* (to whom). Each of these factors influences a recipient's approach to a persuasive communication. If a source speaks clearly, if the message is important, if there is a bright and captive audience that cares deeply about the issue and has time to absorb the information, then audience members will be willing and able to take the effortful central route. But if the source speaks at a rate too fast to comprehend, if the message is trivial, or if audience members are distracted, pressed for time, or uninterested, then the less strenuous peripheral route is taken.

A key determinant in the selection of a route is one's level of personal involvement—that is, the extent to which a message has relevance for one's values and goals (Johnson & Eagly, 1989; Petty & Cacioppo, 1990). Certain techniques can be employed to heighten a recipient's level of involvement. For example, the use of rhetorical questions—a technique used in roughly 30 percent of all radio commercials (Howard, 1990b)—motivates people to think about a message and process it more carefully (Burnkrant & Howard, 1984; Petty, Cacioppo, & Heesacker, 1981).

FIGURE 6.4 Two Routes to Persuasion

Based on characteristics of the source, message, and audience, recipients of a communication take either a central or a peripheral route to persuasion. On the central route, people are influenced by strong arguments and evidence. On the peripheral route, persuasion is based more on heuristics and other superficial cues. This two-process model helps explain how persuasion can seem logical on some occasions and illogical on others.

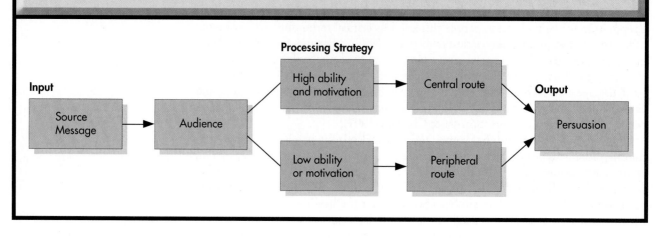

Figure 6.4 presents a road map of persuasive communication. In the next three sections, we will follow this map from the input factors, through the central or peripheral route, to the final destination: persuasion.

The Source

Basketball star Michael Jordan is a living legend, one of the most gifted athletes of our time. He is also being paid more millions of dollars per year than anyone else—to endorse Nike, Oakley, Gatorade, Wheaties, and other products. Why is Jordan considered such an effective spokesman? Indeed, what makes some communicators, in general, more effective than others? As we'll see, there are two key attributes: credibility and likability.

Credibility   Imagine you are waiting in line in a supermarket, and you catch a glimpse of a swollen headline: "Doctors Report Cure for AIDS!" As your eye wanders across the front page, you discover that you are reading the *National Enquirer.* What would you think? Now imagine that you are reading through scientific periodicals in a university library, and you come across a similar article—but this time it appears in the *New England Journal of Medicine.* Now what would you think?

Chances are, you would react with more excitement to the medical journal than to the supermarket tabloid—even though both sources report the same news item. In a study conducted during the cold war era of the 1950s, participants read a speech advocating the development of nuclear submarines. The speech elicited more agreement when it was attributed to an eminent American physicist than when the source was said to be the Soviet newspaper *Pravda* (Hovland & Weiss, 1951). Likewise, when participants read a speech favoring more lenient treatment of juvenile offenders, they changed their attitudes more when they thought the speaker was a judge rather than a convicted drug dealer (Kelman & Hovland, 1953).

Why are some sources more believable than others? Why were the medical journal, the physicist, and the judge more credible than the tabloid, *Pravda,* and the drug dealer? For communicators to be seen as credible, they must have two characteristics: (1) competence, or expertise, and (2) trustworthiness. *Competence* refers to a speaker's ability. People who are knowledgeable, smart, or well spoken or who

In reacting to persuasive communications, people are influenced more by superficial images than by logical arguments. **False.**

have impressive credentials are persuasive by virtue of their expertise (Hass, 1981). Experts can have a disarming effect on us. We assume they know what they're talking about. So when they speak, we listen. And when they take a position, even one that is extreme, we yield. Unless an expert contradicts us on issues that are personally important, we tend to accept what he or she says without much scrutiny (Maddux & Rogers, 1980)—even when the message itself is ambiguous (Chaiken & Maheswaran, 1994).

Still, we are confronted by plenty of experts in the world whose opinions do not sway us. The reason is that expertise is not enough. To have credibility, communicators must also be *trustworthy*—that is, they must be seen as willing to report what they know truthfully and without compromise. What determines whether we trust a communicator? To some extent, we make these judgments on the basis of stereotypes. In 1997, for example, the Gallup Organization asked about a thousand Americans to rate how honest people were in various occupational categories. As shown in Table 6.1, pharmacists topped the list as the most trustworthy occupational group. Car salesmen were the least trusted.

In 1997, Michael Jordan was paid $31 million to play basketball. Forbes *magazine estimates that he earned an extra $47 million in product endorsements.*

In judging the credibility of a source, common sense arms us with a simple rule of caution: Beware of those who have something to gain from successful persuasion. Thus, if a speaker has been bought off, has an ax to grind, or is simply telling us what we want to hear, we suspect that speaker of bias. This rule sheds light on a classic problem in advertising concerning the value of celebrity spokespersons: The more products a celebrity endorses, the less trustworthy he or she appears to consumers (Tripp et al., 1994). The same rule also explains why speakers are seen as more credible when they present a balanced, two-sided message in which they acknowledge and refute opposing arguments than when their message is purely one-sided (Crowley & Hoyer, 1994).

The self-interest rule has other interesting implications. One is that people are impressed by others who take unpopular stands or argue against their own interests. When research participants read a political speech accusing a large corporation of polluting a local river, those who thought that the speechmaker was a pro-environment candidate addressing an environmentalist group perceived him to be biased, while those who thought he was a pro-business candidate talking to company supporters assumed he was sincere (Eagly et al., 1978). Trust is also established by speakers who are not purposely trying to change our views. For this reason, people are influenced more when they think that they are accidentally overhearing a persuasive communication than when they receive a sales pitch intended for their ears (Walster & Festinger, 1962). That's why advertisers often use the "overheard communicator" trick, in which the source tells a buddy about a new product that really works. Feeling as if they are eavesdropping on a personal conversation, viewers assume that what one friend says to another can be trusted.

Likability   More than anything else, Michael Jordan's celebrity power is based on his athletic talent, his popularity, his charm, and

TABLE 6.1   Who Do You Trust?

In 1997, a Gallup poll was conducted to determine the level of honesty attributed to people from various occupational groups. Indicated below are the percentages of respondents who rated each group as "high" or "very high" in honesty.

Occupation	Honest?
Pharmacists	69%
Clergy	59%
Medical doctors	56%
College teachers	55%
Policemen	49%
Bankers	34%
Journalists	23%
Business executives	20%
Building contractors	20%
Stockbrokers	18%
Real estate agents	16%
Lawyers	15%
Advertisers	12%
Insurance salesmen	12%
Car salesmen	8%

his winning smile. But do these qualities enhance someone's impact as a communicator? Yes. As Dale Carnegie (1936) implied in the title of his classic best seller, *How to Win Friends and Influence People*, being liked and being persuasive go hand in hand. The question is, what makes a communicator likable? As we'll see in Chapter 9, two factors that enhance attraction are *similarity* and *physical attractiveness*.

A study by Diane Mackie and others (1990) illustrates the importance of similarity. Students enrolled at the University of California at Santa Barbara read a strong or a weak speech that argued against continued use of the SATs in college admissions. Half the participants were led to believe that the speech was written by a fellow UCSB student; the other half thought the author was a student from the University of New Hampshire. Very few participants were persuaded by the weak arguments. In contrast, many of those who read the strong message did change their attitudes—but only when they believed it was given by a fellow UCSB student.

The effect of source similarity on persuasion has obvious implications for those who wish to exert influence. Think about it. We're all similar to one another in some respects. We might agree in politics, share a common friend, have similar tastes in food, or enjoy spending summers on the same beach. Aware of the social benefits of similarity, the astute communicator can thus use common bonds to enhance his or her impact on an audience. This approach is particularly effective when the similarities seem relevant to the content of the communication (Berscheid, 1966).

When it comes to physical attractiveness, advertising practices presuppose that beauty is also persuasive. After all, billboards, magazine ads, and TV commercials are filled with young and glamorous "supermodels" who are tall and slender (for women) or muscular (for men) and who have glowing complexions and radiant smiles. Sure, these models can turn heads, you may think, but can they change attitudes and behaviors?

In a study that addressed this question, Shelly Chaiken (1979) had male and female college students approach others on campus. They introduced themselves as members of an organization that was trying to get the university to stop serving meat during breakfast and lunch. In each case, these student assistants gave reasons for the position and then asked re-spondents to sign a petition. The result: Attractive communicators were able to get 41 percent of the respondents to sign the petition, whereas those who were less attractive succeeded only 32 percent of the time. Sometimes, a speaker's physical appearance matters more than the quality of the arguments and presentation (Kahle & Homer, 1985; Pallak, 1983). In advertising, beauty is particularly persuasive when the physical "image" is important to the product being sold (Shavitt et al., 1994).

Advertisers are so convinced that beauty sells products that they pay millions of dollars for supermodels like Cindy Crawford to appear in their ads. This award-winning TV commercial for Pepsi was considered a huge success.

When What You Say Is More Important Than Who You Are   To this point, it must seem as if the source of a persuasive message is more important than the message itself. Is this true? Advertisers have long debated the value of high-priced celebrity endorsements. David Ogilvy (1985), a giant in advertising, used to say that celebrities are not effective because viewers know they've been bought and paid for. Ogilvy was not alone in his skepticism. Still, many advertisers scramble furiously to sign high-priced models, entertainers, and athletes. From Michael Jordan to Cindy Crawford, Bill Cosby, Tiger Woods, and Jerry Seinfeld, TV commercials regularly feature a parade of stars. The bigger the star, supposedly the more valuable the endorsement.

Compared with the contents of a message, does the source really make the difference that advertisers pay for? Are we so impressed by the expert, and so drawn to the charming face, that we embrace whatever they have to say? And are we so scornful of nonexperts and unattractive people that their presentations fall on deaf ears? In light of what is known about the central and peripheral routes to persuasion, the answer to these questions is, it depends.

First, a recipient's level of involvement plays an important role. When a message has personal relevance to your life, you pay attention to it and think critically about its arguments and implications. When a message does not have relevance, however, you may take the source at face value and spend little time scrutinizing the information. For example, Richard Petty and his colleagues had students listen to a speaker who proposed that seniors should be required to take comprehensive exams in order to graduate (Petty, Cacioppo, & Goldman, 1981). Three aspects of the communication situation were varied. First, participants were led to believe that the speaker was either an education professor at Princeton University or a high school student. Second, participants heard either well-reasoned arguments and hard evidence or a weak message based only on anecdotes and personal opinion. And third, participants were told either that the proposed exams might be used the following year (Uh oh, that means me!) or that they would not take effect for another ten years (Who cares, I'll be long gone by then!).

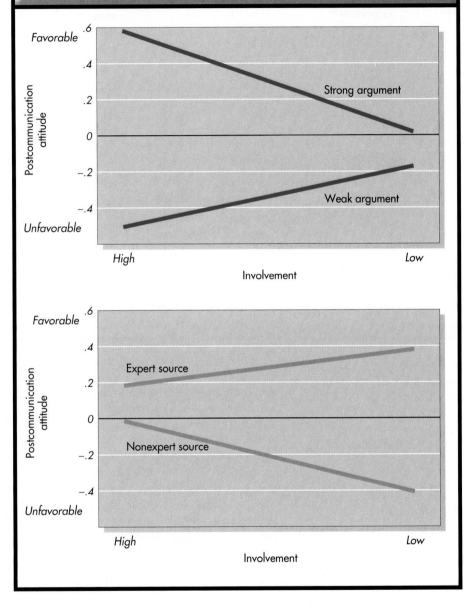

FIGURE 6.5 Source Versus Message: The Role of Audience Involvement
People who were high or low in their personal involvement heard a strong or weak message from an expert or nonexpert. For high-involvement participants (left), persuasion was based on the strength of arguments, not on source expertise. For low-involvement participants (right), persuasion was based more on the source than on the arguments. Source characteristics have more impact on those who don't care enough to take the central route to persuasion. *(Petty, Cacioppo, & Goldman, 1981.)*

As predicted, personal involvement determined the relative impact of source expertise and speech quality. Among participants who would not be affected by the proposed change, attitudes were based largely on the speaker's credibility: The professor was persuasive, the high school student was not. Among participants who thought that the proposed change would affect them directly, attitudes were based on the quality of the speaker's proposal: Strong arguments were persuasive, weak arguments were not. As depicted in Figure 6.5, people followed the source rather

FIGURE 6.6   The Sleeper Effect

In Experiment 1, participants changed their immediate attitudes more in response to a message from a high-credibility source than in response to a message from a low-credibility source. When attitudes were remeasured after three weeks, the high-credibility source lost impact, and the low-credibility source gained impact—the sleeper effect. In Experiment 2, the sleeper effect disappeared when participants were reminded of the source.   *(Kelman & Hovland, 1953.)*

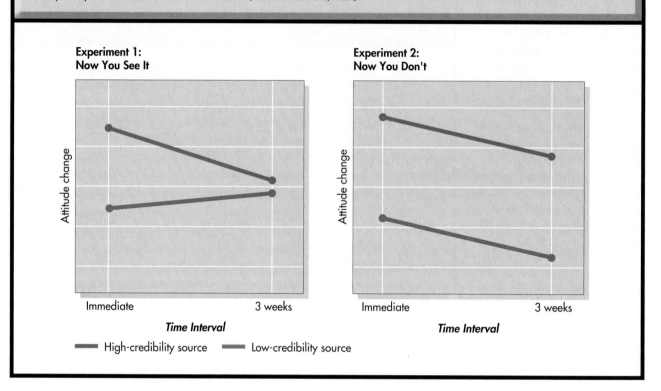

than the message under low levels of involvement, illustrating the peripheral route to persuasion. But message factors outweighed the source under high levels of involvement, when participants cared enough to take the central route to persuasion. Likewise, research has shown that the tilt toward likable and attractive communicators is reduced when recipients take the central route (Chaiken, 1980).

There is a second limit to source effects. It is often said that time heals all wounds. Well, it may also heal the effects of a bad reputation. Hovland and Weiss (1951) varied communicator credibility (for example, the physicist versus *Pravda*) and found that the change had a large and immediate effect on persuasion. But when they remeasured attitudes four weeks later, the effect had vanished. Over time, the attitude change produced by the credible source decreased, and the change caused by the noncredible source increased. This latter finding—the delayed persuasive impact of a noncredible communicator—is called the **sleeper effect.**

To explain this unforeseen result, the Hovland research group proposed the *discounting cue hypothesis.* According to this hypothesis, people immediately discount the arguments made by noncredible communicators; but over time, they dissociate what was said from who said it. In other words, people tend to remember the message but forget the source (Pratkanis et al., 1988). To examine the role of memory in this process, Herbert Kelman and Carl Hovland (1953) reminded a group of participants of the source's identity before their attitudes were reassessed. If the sleeper effect was due to forgetting, they reasoned, then it could be eliminated through reinstatement of the link between the source and the message. As shown in Figure 6.6, they were right. When participants' attitudes were measured after three weeks, those who were not reminded of the source showed the usual

sleeper effect A delayed increase in the persuasive impact of a noncredible source.

sleeper effect. Those who were reminded of the source did not. For these latter participants, the effects of high and low credibility endured.

The sleeper effect generated a good deal of controversy. There was never a doubt that credible communicators lose some impact over time. But researchers had a harder time finding evidence for delayed persuasion by noncredible sources. Exasperated by their own failures to obtain this result, Paulette Gillig and Anthony Greenwald (1974) thus wondered, "Is it time to lay the sleeper effect to rest?" The answer, as it turned out, was no.

More recent research shows that the sleeper effect is reliable—provided that participants do not learn who the source is until *after* they have received the original message (Greenwald et al., 1986; Gruder et al., 1978; Pratkanis et al., 1988). To appreciate the importance of timing, imagine that you're flipping through a magazine and you come across what appears to be a review of a new CD. Before you begin reading, however, you notice in the fine print that this so-called review is really an advertisement. Aware that you can't trust what you read, you skim the ad and reject it. Now imagine the same situation, except that you read the entire ad before realizing what it is. Again, you reject it. But notice the difference. This time, you have read the message with an open mind. You may then have rejected it; but after a few weeks, the information sinks in and influences your evaluation of the CD. This experience illustrates the sleeper effect.

"It is a superb vision of America, all right, but I can't remember which candidate projected it."

Research on the sleeper effect shows that people often remember the message but forget the source. Ed Fisher © 1996 from The New Yorker Collection. All Rights Reserved.

The Message

Obviously, not all sources are created equal, as some are more credible or likable than others. On the peripheral route to persuasion, audiences are influenced heavily, maybe too heavily, by these and other source characteristics. But when people care about an issue, the strength of a message determines its success. On the central route to persuasion, what matters most is whether a scientist's theory is supported by the data, whether a company has a sound product. Keep in mind, however, that the target of a persuasive appeal comes to know a message only through the medium of communication: *what* a person has to say and *how* that person says it.

Informational Strategies Communicators often struggle over how to present an argument to maximize its impact. Should a message be long and crammed with facts or short and to the point? Is it better to present a highly partisan, one-sided message or to take a more balanced, two-sided approach? And how should the various arguments be ordered—from strongest to weakest or the other way around? These are the kinds of questions often studied by persuasion researchers (Petty & Wegener, 1998; Petty et al., 1997).

Often, the most effective strategy to use depends on whether members of the audience process the message on the central or the peripheral route. Consider message length. When people process a message lazily, with their eyes and ears half-closed, they often fall back on a simple heuristic: The longer a message, the more valid it must be. In this case, word length gives the superficial appearance of factual support—regardless of the quality of the arguments (Petty & Cacioppo, 1984; Wood et al., 1985). Thus, as David Ogilvy (1985) concluded from his many years of advertising experience, "The more facts you tell, the more you sell" (p. 88).

"The truth is always the strongest argument."

—Sophocles

TABLE 6.2   Effects of Presentation Order and Timing on Persuasion

A study by Miller and Campbell (1959) demonstrated the effect of presentation order and the timing of opposing arguments on persuasion. As applied to our example, the Democratic and Republican conventions resemble the fourth row of this table. From these results, it seems that the scheduling of such events is fair, promoting neither primacy nor recency.

	Conditions					Results
1.	**Message 1**	**Message 2**	One week	Decision		**Primacy**
2.	**Message 1**	One week	**Message 2**	Decision		**Recency**
3.	**Message 1**	**Message 2**	Decision			None
4.	**Message 1**	One week	**Message 2**	One week	Decision	None

When people process a communication carefully, however, length is a two-edged sword. If a message is long because it contains lots of supporting information, then longer does mean better. The more supportive arguments you can offer, or the more sources you can find to speak on your behalf, the more persuasive will be your appeal (Harkins & Petty, 1981). But if the added arguments are weak, or if the new sources are redundant, then an alert audience will not be fooled by length alone. When adding to the length of a message dilutes its quality, an appeal might well *lose* impact (Friedrich et al., 1996; Harkins & Petty, 1987).

When opposing sides try to persuade an audience, the order of presentation becomes a relevant factor as well. In the summer of 1996, before the November presidential election, the Republicans held their national convention about a month before the incumbent Democrats held theirs. These events were watched on television by millions of voters. Do you think the order in which they were scheduled put one party at an advantage? If you believe that information presented first has more impact, you'd be predicting a *primacy effect* (advantage to the Republicans). If you believe that information presented last has the edge, you'd be predicting a *recency effect* (advantage to the Democrats).

There are good reasons for both predictions. On the one hand, first impressions are important. On the other hand, memory fades over time, and people often recall only the last argument they hear before making a decision. In light of these contrasting predictions, Norman Miller and Donald Campbell (1959) searched for the "missing link" that would determine the relative effects of primacy and recency. They discovered that the missing link is *time*. In a jury simulation study, they had people (1) read a summary of the plaintiff's case, (2) read a summary of the defendant's case, and (3) make a decision. The researchers varied how much time separated the two messages and then how much time elapsed between the second message and the decisions. When participants read the second message right after the first and then waited a whole week before reporting their opinion, a primacy effect prevailed, and the side that came first was favored. Both messages faded equally from memory, so only the greater impact of first impressions was left. Yet when participants made a decision immediately after the second message but a full week after the first, there was a recency effect. The second argument was fresher in memory, thus favoring the side that went last. Using these results as a guideline, let's return to our original question: What is the impact on election day of how the national conventions are scheduled? Think for a moment about the placement and timing of these events. The answer appears in Table 6.2.

Message Discrepancy   Persuasion is a process of changing attitudes. But just how much change should be sought? Before addressing an audience, all speakers confront what is perhaps the most critical strategic question: How extreme a position should they take? How *discrepant* should a message be from the audience's position in order to have the greatest impact? Common sense suggests two opposite answers. One approach is to take an extreme position in the hope that the more change you advocate, the more you get. Another approach is to exercise caution and not push for too much change so that the audience will not reject the message outright. Which approach seems more effective? Imagine trying to convert your politically conservative friends into liberals, or the other way around. Would you stake out a radical position in order to move them toward the center, or would you preach moderation so as not to be cast aside?

Research shows that communicators should adopt the second, more cautious approach. To be sure, some discrepancy is needed to produce a change in attitude. But the relationship to persuasion can be pictured as an upside-down U—with the most change being produced at moderate amounts of discrepancy (Bochner & Insko, 1966). A recent study by Kari Edwards and Edward Smith (1996) helps to explain why taking a more extreme counter-attitudinal position is counterproductive. These investigators first measured people's attitudes on a number of hot social issues—for example, whether gay and lesbian couples should adopt children, whether employers should give preference in hiring to minorities, and whether the death penalty should be abolished. Several weeks later, they asked these same people to read, think about, and rate arguments that were either consistent or inconsistent with their own prior attitudes. The result: When given arguments to read that preached attitudes that were discrepant from their own, the participants spent more time scrutinizing the material and judged the arguments to be weak (see Figure 6.7). Apparently, people are quick to refute and reject persuasive messages they don't agree with. In fact, the more personally important the issue is to us, the more stubborn and resistant to change we become (Zuwerink & Devine, 1996).

Fear Appeals Many trial lawyers say that to win cases, they have to appeal to jurors through the heart rather than through the mind. The evidence is important, they admit; but what really matters is whether the jury reacts to their client with anger, disgust, sympathy, or sadness. Of course, very few messages are entirely based on rational argument or on emotion. And it's possible that the best approach to take depends on whether the attitude is rooted more in a person's beliefs or in his or her feelings about the object in question (Edwards, 1990; Millar & Millar, 1990).

The use of fear appeals, or scare tactics, is particularly common. In political campaigns, candidates often use negative advertising to frighten voters about their opponents. Certain religious cults also use scare tactics to indoctrinate new members. So do public health organizations that graphically portray the victims of

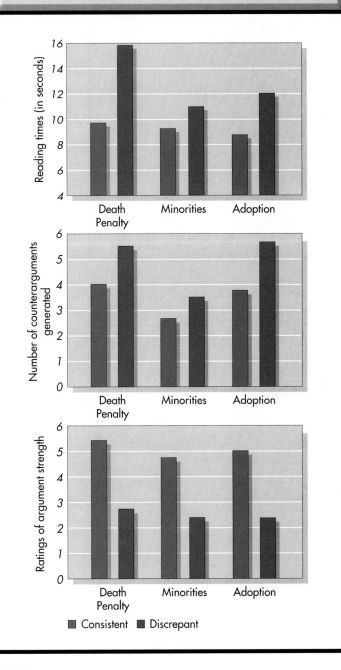

FIGURE 6.7 Reactions to Attitude-Discrepant Messages: Why Too Much Discrepancy Does Not Persuade

Participants read arguments on various social issues. In response to those that were attitude-discrepant rather than attitude-consistent, they spent more time reading (top), generated more counterarguments (center), and judged the arguments as weaker (bottom). *(Edwards & Smith, 1996.)*

What pickled this frog,   Could pickle your lungs.

The same formaldehyde that preserves
dead frogs is found in cigarettes.

Public health organizations often use fear, or scare tactics, to change attitudes and behavior.

Since the Ad Council initiated its "Friends don't let friends drive drunk" campaign, 79% of Americans say that they have personally stopped someone who had been drinking from taking the wheel of a car.

cigarette smoking, drugs, and unsafe sex. That is why magazine ads for condoms often use fear appeals—the most extreme being "I enjoy sex but I don't want to die for it" (Struckman-Johnson et al., 1990). Even commercial advertisers try to frighten consumers into buying their products. After all, who would want to get caught with dandruff, bad breath, or body odor?

Is fear effective? If so, is it better to arouse just a little nervousness or trigger a full-blown anxiety attack? To answer these questions, social psychologists have compared the effects of communications that vary in their fearfulness. In the first such study, Irving Janis and Seymour Feshbach (1953) found that high levels of fear arousal did not generate increased agreement with a communication. Since then, however, research has shown that high fear often does motivate change—in part, by increasing our incentive to think carefully about the persuasive arguments contained in the message (Baron et al., 1994).

Fear arousal increases the incentive to change, but its ultimate impact depends on the strength of the arguments—and on whether the message also contains reassuring advice on how to avoid the threatened danger (Leventhal, 1970; Rogers, 1983; Witte, 1992). This last point is important. Without specific instructions on how to cope, people may feel helpless, panic, and tune out. In one study, for example, participants with a chronic fear of cancer were less likely than others to detect the logical errors in a message that called for regular cancer checkups (Jepson & Chaiken, 1990). When clear instructions are included, however, high dosages of fear are effective. Anti-smoking films that tell smokers how to quit thus elicit more negative attitudes about cigarettes when they show gory lung-cancer operations than charts filled with dry statistics (Leventhal et al., 1967). And driving-safety films are more effective when they show broken bones and bloody accident victims than controlled collisions involving plastic crash dummies (Rogers & Mewborn, 1976).

Positive Emotions   It's interesting that just as fear helps to induce a change in attitude, so do positive emotions. In one study, people were more likely to agree with a series of controversial arguments when they snacked on peanuts and soda than when they did not eat (Janis et al., 1965). In another study, participants liked a TV commercial more when it was embedded in a program that was upbeat rather than sad (Mathur & Chattopadhyay, 1991). Research shows that people are "soft touches" when they are in a good mood. Depending on the situation, food, drinks, a soft reclining chair, tender memories, a success experience, breathtaking scenery, and pleasant music can lull us into a positive emotional state—ripe for persuasion (Schwarz, Bless, & Bohner, 1991).

According to Alice Isen (1984), people see the world through rose-colored glasses when they are feeling good. Filled with high spirits, we become more sociable, more generous, and generally more positive in our outlook. We also make decisions more quickly and with relatively little thought. The result: Positive feelings activate the peripheral route to persuasion, facilitating change, and allowing superficial cues to take on added importance (Petty et al., 1993; Worth & Mackie, 1987).

What is it about feeling good that leads us to take short cuts rather than the more effortful central route to persuasion? There are three possible explanations. One is that a positive emotional state is cognitively distracting, causing the mind to wander and impairing our ability to think critically about the persuasive arguments (Mackie & Worth, 1989; Mackie et al., 1992). A second explanation is that when people are in a good mood, they assume that all is well, let down their guard, and become lazy processors of information (Schwarz, 1990). A third explanation is that when people are happy, they become motivated to savor the moment and maintain their happy mood—not spoil it by thinking critically about new information (Wegener & Petty, 1994).

This last notion raises an interesting question: What if happy people were presented with a positive, uplifting persuasive message? Would they still appear cognitively distracted, or lazy, or would they pay close attention in order to prolong the rosy glow? To test this hypothesis, Duane Wegener and his colleagues (1995) showed some college students a funny segment from the TV show *Late Night with David Letterman*. Others, less fortunate, watched a somber scene from an HBO movie, *You Don't Have to Die*. All students were then asked to read and evaluate either an uplifting, pro-attitudinal article about a new plan to cut tuition or a distressing, counter-attitudinal article about a new plan to raise tuition. In half the cases, the article they read contained strong arguments; in the others, the arguments were weak. Did the students read the material carefully enough to distinguish between the strong and weak arguments? Those in the somber condition clearly did. Among those in the happy condition, however, the response depended on whether they expected the message to be one they wanted to hear. When the happy students read about a tuition increase, they tuned out and were equally persuaded by the strong and weak arguments. When they read about the proposal to cut tuition, however, they were persuaded more when the arguments were strong than when they were weak. Being in a good mood, and receiving a pro-attitudinal message that would not spoil it, these happy students took the effortful central route to persuasion.

Subliminal Messages   In 1957, Vance Packard published *The Hidden Persuaders*, an exposé of Madison Avenue. As the book climbed the best-seller list, it awakened in the public a fear of being manipulated by forces that could not be seen or heard. What had Packard uncovered? In the 1950s, amid growing fears of communism and the birth of rock 'n' roll, a number of advertisers were said to be using *subliminal advertising*, the presentation of commercial messages outside of conscious awareness. It all started in a drive-in movie theater in New Jersey, where the words "Drink Coke" and "Eat popcorn" were secretly flashed on the screen during intermissions for a third of a millisecond. Although the audience never noticed the message, Coke sales were said to have increased 18 percent and popcorn sales 58 percent over a six-week period (Brean, 1958).

This incident was followed by many others. A Seattle radio station presented subaudible anti-TV messages during its programs ("TV is a bore"), and department stores played music tapes over public address systems that contained subaudible anti-theft warnings ("If you steal, you'll get caught"). Later, in books entitled *Subliminal Seduction* (1973) and *The Age of Manipulation* (1989), William Bryan Key charged that advertisers routinely sneak faint sexual images in visual ads to heighten the appeal of their products. Recently, concerns have been raised about subliminal messages in rock music. In one case, the families of two young men who committed suicide blamed the British rock group Judas Priest for subliminal lyrics that promoted satanism and suicide (National Law Journal, 1990). It's clear that many people believe in the power of hidden persuaders.

At the time of the New Jersey theater scandal, research on the topic was so sketchy, and the public so outraged by the sinister implications, that the matter was quickly dropped. But today there is renewed interest in subliminal influences, as well as new research developments. In what has become a multimillion dollar industry, companies sell self-help tapes that play new age music or nature sounds and also contain fleeting messages that promise to help you relax, lose weight, stop smoking, make friends, raise self-esteem, and even improve your sex life. Can

If you're interested in public service advertising, visit the Ad Council (www.adcouncil.org), an organization that created such highly effective public service characters as Smokey the Bear ("Only you can prevent forest fires") and the Crash Test Dummies ("Don't be a dummy—buckle up").

subliminal messages really induce us, without our awareness, to drink Coke, eat popcorn, purchase a particular product, or commit a violent act? In 1982, Timothy Moore reviewed the existing research and concluded that "what you see is what you get"—nothing, "complete scams." Moore was right. In fact, the original Coke-and-popcorn incident was later exposed as a publicity stunt, a hoax (Pratkanis, 1992).

But what about the subliminal self-help tapes for which consumers pay $29.95? Is there any evidence to support the claims of covert therapeutic influence? No. In a controlled experiment, Anthony Greenwald and his colleagues (1991) had people listen every day for five weeks to a music tape that contained hidden messages designed either to improve memory ("My ability to recall is increasing daily") or raise self-esteem ("I have high self-worth"). For half the participants, the tapes were correctly labeled; for others, the labels were reversed. Participants were tested both before and after the five-week period. They were also questioned afterward about their beliefs concerning the tapes.

Did participants believe they were helped by the tapes? More important, did they actually improve? There were two key results. First, test scores on *objective* measures of memory and self-esteem were no higher after exposure to the tapes than before. Second, however, participants *perceived* an improvement in their memory or self-esteem—depending on which label was on the tape, not on which message the tape actually contained. In short, participants believed in the power of the hidden message, but the tapes themselves had no real effect. Other researchers have found that subliminal weight-loss tapes are similarly ineffective (Merikle & Skanes, 1992). Apparently, "What you expect is what you believe, but not necessarily what you get" (Pratkanis et al., 1994, p. 251).

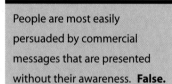

People are most easily persuaded by commercial messages that are presented without their awareness. **False.**

The Audience

Although source and message factors are important, the astute communicator must also take his or her audience into account. Presentation strategies that succeed with some people fail with others. Audiences on the central route to persuasion, for example, bear little resemblance to those found strolling along the peripheral route. In this section, we'll see that the impact of a message is influenced by two additional factors: the recipient's personality and his or her expectations.

Individual Differences: What Turns You On?   Right from the start, social psychologists tried to identify types of people who were more or less vulnerable to persuasion. But it turned out that few individuals are *consistently* easy or difficult to persuade. As a result of this insight, the search for individual differences is now guided by an interactionist perspective. Assuming that each of us can be persuaded more in some settings than in others, researchers look for an appropriate "match" between characteristics of the message and the audience. Thus we ask, What kinds of messages turn *you* on?

Earlier, we saw that people tend to process information more carefully when they are highly involved. Involvement can be determined by the importance and self-relevance of a message. According to Cacioppo and Petty (1982), however, there are also individual differences in the extent to which people become involved and take the central route to persuasion. Specifically, they have found that individuals differ in the extent to which they enjoy and participate in effortful cognitive activities, or, as they call it, the **need for cognition (NC).** People who are high rather than low in their need for cognition like to work on hard problems, search for clues, make fine distinctions, and analyze situations. These differences can be identified by the items contained in the Need for Cognition Scale, some of which appear in Table 6.3.

need for cognition (NC)
A personality variable that distinguishes people on the basis of how much they enjoy effortful cognitive activities.

The need for cognition has interesting implications for changing attitudes. If people are prone to approach or avoid effortful cognitive activities, then the prepared communicator could design messages unique to a particular audience. In theory, the high-NC audience should receive information-oriented appeals, and the low-NC audience should be treated to appeals that rely on the use of peripheral cues. The theory is fine, but does it work? Can a message be customized to fit the information-processing style of its recipients? In one test of this hypothesis, participants read an editorial that consisted of either a strong or a weak set of arguments. As predicted, the higher their NC scores were, the more the participants thought about the material, the better they recalled it, and the more persuaded they were by the strength of its arguments (Cacioppo et al., 1983). In contrast, people who are low in the

TABLE 6.3 Need for Cognition Scale: Sample Items

Are you high or low in the need for cognition? These statements are taken from the NC Scale. If you agree with items 1, 3, and 5 and disagree with items 2, 4, and 6, you would probably be regarded as high in NC. *(Cacioppo & Petty, 1982.)*

1. I really enjoy a task that involves coming up with new solutions to problems.
2. Thinking is not my idea of fun.
3. The notion of thinking abstractly is appealing to me.
4. I like tasks that require little thought once I've learned them.
5. I usually end up deliberating about issues even when they do not affect me personally.
6. It's enough for me that something gets the job done; I don't care how or why it works.

need for cognition are persuaded by cues found along the peripheral route—such as a speaker's reputation and physical appearance, the reactions of others in the audience, and a positive mood state (Cacioppo et al., 1996).

Just as people high in the need for cognition seem to crave information, other personality traits are associated with an attraction to other kinds of messages. Consider the trait of *self-monitoring*. As described in Chapter 3, high self-monitors regulate their behavior from one situation to another out of concern for public self-presentation. Low self-monitors are less image conscious and behave instead according to their own beliefs and preferences. In the context of persuasion, high self-monitors may be particularly responsive to messages that promise desirable social images. Whether the product is beer, soda, blue jeans, or a car, this technique is common in advertising, where often the image is the message.

To test the self-monitoring hypothesis, Mark Snyder and Kenneth DeBono (1985) showed image- or information-oriented print ads to high and low self-monitors. In an ad for Irish Mocha Mint coffee, for example, a man and woman

In a recent series of star-studded ads, Apple Computer showed clips of Muhammad Ali, Albert Einstein, Pablo Picasso, Ted Turner, and other creative geniuses who dared to "think different." A USA Today *poll revealed that this image-oriented message had its greatest appeal among young adults (Enrico, 1998.)*

The Marlboro man stands as a classic symbol of the lone, rugged, individualistic image that tends to attract American consumers.

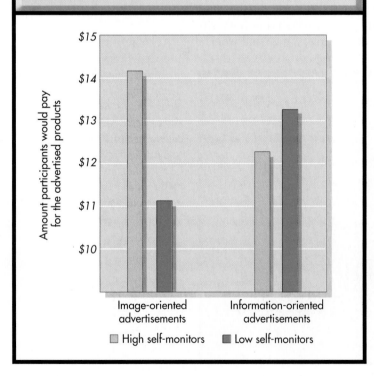

FIGURE 6.8   Informational and Image-Oriented Ads: The Role of Self-Monitoring

High and low self-monitors estimated how much they would pay for products presented in image-oriented or informational magazine ads. As shown, high image-oriented self-monitors preferred products depicted in image-oriented ads (left), while low self-monitors preferred those depicted in informational ads (right). *(Adapted from Snyder & DeBono, 1985.)*

---

were depicted as relaxing in a candlelit room over a cup of coffee. The image-oriented version promised to "Make a chilly night become a cozy evening," while the informational version offered "A delicious blend of three great flavors—coffee, chocolate, and mint." As predicted, high self-monitors were willing to pay more for products after reading imagery ads, while low self-monitors were influenced more by the information-oriented appeals (see Figure 6.8). This study—and others that followed—suggest that a message is persuasive to the extent that it meets the psychological needs of its audience (DeBono, 1987; Lavine & Snyder, 1996).

In this regard, cultural factors also play an important role. In Chapter 3, we saw that cultures differ in the extent to which they are oriented toward individualism versus collectivism. In light of these differences, Sang-Pil Han and Sharon Shavitt (1994) compared the contents of magazine advertisements in the United States, an individualistic country, and Korea, a country with a collectivistic orientation. They found that while American ads were focused more on personal benefits, individuality, competition, and self-improvement, Korean ads appealed more to the integrity, achievement, and well-being of one's family and other ingroups. Clearly, there are different ways to appeal to the members of these two cultures (see Table 6.4). In a second study, Han and Shavitt created two sets of ads for various products. One set portrayed individuals ("Treat yourself to a breath-freshening experience"), and the other set featured groups ("Share this breath-freshening experience"). Both sets were presented to American and Korean participants. The result: Americans were persuaded more by individualistic ads, and Koreans preferred collectivistic ads. To be persuasive, a message should appeal to the culturally shared values of its audience.

Forewarning: Ready or Not, Here I Come!   Probably the toughest audience to persuade is the one that knows you're coming. When people are aware that someone is trying to change their attitude, they become motivated to resist. All they need is some time to collect their thoughts and come up with a good defense. Jonathan Freedman and David Sears (1965) first discovered this when they told high school seniors to expect a speech on why teenagers should not be allowed to drive (an unpopular position, as you can imagine). The students were warned either two or ten minutes before the talk began or not at all. Those who were the victims of a sneak attack were the most likely to succumb to the speaker's position. Those who had a full ten minutes' warning were the least likely to agree. To be forewarned is to be forearmed. But why?

At least two processes are at work here. To understand them, let's take a closer look at what forewarning does. Participants in the Freedman and Sears (1965) study were put on notice in two ways: (1) They were informed of the position the speaker would take, and (2) they were told that the speaker intended to change their attitudes. Psychologically, these two aspects of forewarning have different effects.

The first effect is purely cognitive. Knowing in advance what position a speaker will take enables us to come up with counterarguments and, as a result, to become more resistant to change. To explain this effect, William McGuire (1964) drew an analogy: Protecting a person's attitudes from persuasion, he said, is like inoculating the human body against disease. In medicine, injecting a small dose of infection into a patient stimulates the body to build up a resistance to it. According to this **inoculation hypothesis,** an attitude can be immunized the same way. As with flu shots and other vaccines, our defenses can be reinforced by exposure to weak doses of the opposing position before we actually encounter the full presentation. Studies of negative political ads show that inoculation can be used to combat the kinds of attack messages that sometimes win elections (Pfau et al., 1990). It has even been suggested that parents can protect children from advertising propaganda by exposing them to small doses of TV commercials and then critically discussing the claims that are made (Pratkanis & Aronson, 1992).

Simply knowing that someone is trying to persuade us also elicits a motivational reaction, as we brace ourselves to resist the attempt—regardless of what position is taken. As a TV viewer, you have no doubt heard the phrase "And now, we pause for a message from our sponsor." What does this warning tell us? Not knowing yet who the sponsor is, even the grouchiest among us is in no position to object. Yet imagine how you would feel if an experimenter said to you, "In just a few minutes, you will hear a message prepared according to well-established principles of persuasion and designed to induce you to change your attitudes." If you are like the participants who actually heard this forewarning, you might be tempted to reply, "Oh yeah? Try me!" Indeed, subjects rejected that message without counterargument and without much advance notice (Hass & Grady, 1975).

TABLE 6.4 Cultural Values in Advertising
The statements listed here were taken from American and Korean ads. Note the differences between those classified as individualistic and those classified as collectivistic. *(Han and Shavitt, 1994, pp. 346–347.)*

Some Individualistic Ads

"She's got a style all her own"

"You, only better"

"How to protect the most personal part of the environment: Your skin"

"A leader among leaders"

"Make your way through the crowd"

Some Collectivistic Ads

"A more exhilarating way to provide for your family"

"We have a way of bringing people closer together"

"Celebrating a half-century of partnership"

"Our family agrees with this selection of home furnishings"

"Your business success: Harmonizing with Sunkyong"

---

inoculation hypothesis The idea that exposure to weak versions of a persuasive argument increases later resistance to that argument.

Psychological reactance often triggers attitude change in a direction opposite to the one advocated—even when the speaker's position is consistent with one's own.
Mort Gerberg © 1994 from The New Yorker Collection. All Rights Reserved.

"And just who the hell are you to tell me I'm entitled to my opinion?"

"To do just the opposite is also a form of imitation."

—Lichtenberg

When people think that someone is trying to change their attitude or otherwise manipulate them, a red flag goes up. That red flag is called **psychological reactance.** According to Jack Brehm's theory of psychological reactance, all of us want the freedom to think, feel, and act as we (not others) choose. When we sense that a cherished freedom is being threatened, we become motivated to maintain it. And when we sense that a freedom is slipping away, we try to restore it (Brehm & Brehm, 1981). One possible result is that when a communicator comes on too strong, we may react with *negative attitude change*, by moving in the direction opposite the one advocated—even, ironically, when the speaker's position agrees with our own (Heller et al., 1973). Sometimes, the motive to protect our freedom to think as we choose can supersede our desire to hold a specific opinion.

Persuasion by Our Own Actions

Anyone who has ever acted on stage knows how easy it is to become so absorbed in a role that the experience seems real. Feigned laughter can make an actor feel happy, and crocodile tears can turn into sadness. Even in real life, the effect can be dramatic. In 1974, Patty Hearst—a sheltered college student from a wealthy family—was kidnapped. By the time she was arrested months later, she was a gun-toting revolutionary who called herself Tania. How could someone be so totally converted? In Hearst's own words, "I had thought I was humoring [my captors] by parroting their clichés and buzzwords without believing in them. . . . In trying to convince them I convinced myself."

Role Playing: All the World's a Stage

The Patty Hearst case illustrates the powerful effects of *role playing*. Of course, you don't have to be kidnapped or terrorized to know how it feels to be coaxed into behavior that is at odds with your inner convictions. People frequently engage in attitude-discrepant behavior as part of a job, for example, or to please others. As commonplace as this seems, it raises a profound question. When we play along, saying and doing things that are privately discrepant with our own attitudes, do we begin to change those attitudes as a result? How we feel can determine the way we act. Is it also possible that the way we act can determine how we feel?

psychological reactance
The theory that people react against threats to their freedom by asserting themselves and perceiving the threatened freedom as more attractive.

According to Irving Janis (1968), attitude change persists more when it is inspired by our own behavior than when it stems from passive exposure to a persuasive communication. Janis conducted a study in which one group of participants listened to a speech that challenged their positions on a topic and others were handed an outline and asked to give the speech themselves. As predicted, participants changed their attitudes more after giving the speech than after listening to it (Janis & King, 1954). According to Janis, role playing works because it forces people to learn the message. That is why people remember arguments they come up with on their own better than they remember arguments provided by others (Slamecka & Graff, 1978). In fact, attitude change is more enduring even when people who read a persuasive message merely *expect* that they will later have to communicate it to others (Boninger et al., 1990).

But there's more to role playing than improved memory. The effects of enacting a role can be staggering—in part because it is so easy to confuse what we do, or what we say, with how we really feel. Think about the times you've dished out compliments you didn't mean, or smiled at someone you didn't like, or nodded your head in response to a statement you disagreed with. We often shade what we say just to please a particular listener. What's fascinating is not that we make adjustments to suit others but that this role playing has such powerful effects on our own private attitudes. For example, participants in one study read about a man and then described him to someone else, who supposedly liked or disliked him. As you might expect, participants described the man in more positive terms when their listener was favorably disposed. In the process, however, they also convinced themselves. At least to some extent, "saying is believing" (Higgins & Rholes, 1978).

Consider the implications. We know that attitudes influence behavior—as when people help those whom they like and hurt those whom they dislike. But research on role playing emphasizes the flip side of the coin—that behavior can determine attitudes. Perhaps we come to like people because we have helped them and blame people whom we have hurt. To change people's inner feelings, then, maybe we should begin by focusing on their behavior. Why do people experience changes of attitude in response to changes in their own behavior? One answer to this question is provided by the theory of cognitive dissonance.

Posing as a revolutionary named Tania, Patty Hearst was converted by the role her captors forced her to play. "In trying to convince them I convinced myself," she said.

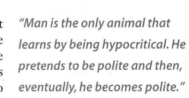

"Man is the only animal that learns by being hypocritical. He pretends to be polite and then, eventually, he becomes polite."

—Jean Kerr

Cognitive Dissonance Theory: The Classic Version

Many social psychologists believe that people are motivated by a desire for cognitive consistency—a state of mind in which one's beliefs, attitudes, and behaviors are all compatible with each other (Abelson et al., 1968). Cognitive consistency theories seem to presuppose that people are generally logical. However, Leon Festinger (1957) turned this assumption on its head. Struck by the irrationalities of human behavior, Festinger proposed **cognitive dissonance theory,** which states that a powerful motive to maintain cognitive consistency can give rise to irrational and sometimes maladaptive behavior.

According to Festinger, all of us hold many cognitions about ourselves and the world around us. These cognitions include everything we know about our own

cognitive dissonance theory
The theory that holding inconsistent cognitions arouses psychological tension that people become motivated to reduce.

TABLE 6.5 Ways to Reduce Dissonance

"I need to be on a diet, yet I just dived head first into a chocolate mousse." If this were you, how would you reduce dissonance aroused by the discrepancy between your attitude and your behavior?

Techniques	Examples
Change your attitude.	"I don't really need to be on a diet."
Change your perception of the behavior.	"I hardly ate any chocolate mousse."
Add consonant cognitions.	"Chocolate mousse is very nutritious."
Minimize the importance of the conflict.	"I don't care if I'm overweight— life is short!"
Reduce perceived choice.	"I had no choice; the mousse was prepared for this special occasion."

beliefs, attitudes, and behavior. Although generally our cognitions coexist peacefully, at times they clash. Consider some examples. You say you're on a diet, yet you just dived head first into a chocolate mousse. Or you waited in line for hours to get into a rock concert, and then the band was disappointing. Or you baked for hours under the hot summer sun, even though you knew of the health risks. Each of these scenarios harbors inconsistency and conflict. You have already committed yourself to one course of action, yet you realize that what you did is inconsistent with your attitude.

Under certain specific conditions, discrepancies such as these can evoke an unpleasant state of tension known as cognitive dissonance. But discrepancy doesn't always produce dissonance. If you broke a diet for a Thanksgiving dinner with the family, your indiscretion would not lead you to experience dissonance. Or if you mistakenly thought the mousse you ate was low in calories, only later to find out the truth, then, again, you would not experience much dissonance. As we'll see, what really hurts is knowing that you committed yourself to an attitude-discrepant behavior freely and with some knowledge of the consequences. When that happens, dissonance is aroused, and you become motivated to reduce it. There are many possible ways to do so, as shown in Table 6.5. Often, the easiest is to change your attitude to bring it in line with your behavior.

Right from the start, cognitive dissonance theory captured the imagination. Festinger's basic proposition is simple, yet its implications are far-reaching. In this section, we examine three research areas that demonstrate the breadth of what dissonance theory has to say about attitude change.

One way to reduce dissonance is to minimize the importance of the conflict. From the Wall Street Journal. Permission, Cartoon Features Syndicate.

"It's a crazy idea, but it just might work."

Justifying Attitude-Discrepant Behavior: When Doing Is Believing   Imagine for a moment that you are a participant in a classic study by Leon Festinger and J. Merrill Carlsmith (1959). As soon as you arrive, you are greeted by an experimenter who says that he is interested in various measures of performance. Wondering what that means, you all too quickly find out. The experimenter hands you a wooden board containing forty-eight square pegs in square holes and asks you to turn each peg a quarter turn to the left, then a quarter turn back to the right, then back to the left, then back again to the right. The routine seems endless. After thirty minutes, the experimenter comes to your rescue. Or does he? Just when you think things are looking up, he hands you another board, another assignment. For the next half-hour, you are to take twelve spools of thread off the board, put them back, take them off, and put them back again. By now, you're just about ready to tear your hair out. As you think back over better times, even the first task begins to look good.

Finally, you're done. After one of the longest hours of your life, the experimenter lets you in on a secret: There's more to this experiment than meets the eye. You were in the control group. To test the effects of motivation on performance, other participants are being told that the experiment will be fun and exciting. You don't realize it, but you are now being set up for the critical part of the study. Would you be willing to tell the next participant that the experiment is enjoyable? As you hem and haw, the experimenter offers to pay for your services. Some participants are offered one dollar; others are offered twenty dollars. In either case, you agree to help out. Before you know it, you find yourself in the waiting room trying to dupe an unsuspecting fellow student (who is really a confederate).

By means of this elaborate, staged presentation, participants were goaded into an attitude-discrepant behavior, an action that was inconsistent with their private attitudes. They knew how dull the experiment really was, yet they raved about it. Did this conflict arouse cognitive dissonance? It depends on how much the participants were paid. Suppose you were one of the lucky ones offered twenty dollars for your assistance. By today's standards, that payment would be worth eighty dollars—surely a sufficient justification for telling a little white lie, right? Feeling well compensated, these participants experienced little if any dissonance. But wait a minute. Suppose you were paid only one dollar. Surely your integrity is worth more than that, don't you think? In this instance, you have **insufficient justification** for going along—so you need a way to cope. According to Festinger (1957), unless you can deny your actions (which is not usually possible), you will feel pressured to change your attitude about the task. If you can convince yourself that the experiment wasn't all bad, then saying it was interesting is all right.

The results were just as Festinger and Carlsmith had predicted. When the experiment was presumably over, participants were asked how they felt about the peg-board tasks. Those in the control group who did not mislead a confederate openly admitted that the tasks were boring. So did those in the twenty-dollar condition, who had ample justification for what they did. However, participants who were paid only one dollar rated the experiment as somewhat enjoyable. Having engaged in an attitude-discrepant act without sufficient justification, these participants reduced cognitive dissonance by changing their attitude. The results can be seen in Figure 6.9.

Two aspects of this study are noteworthy. First, it showed the phenomenon of self-persuasion: When people behave in ways that are discrepant with their attitudes, they sometimes go on to change those attitudes—without exposure to a persuasive communication. To appreciate the powerful implications of this phenomenon, consider that in a recent study, Michael Leippe and Donna Eisenstadt (1994) found that white college students who were coaxed into writing essays in favor of new scholarship funds only for black students later reported more favorable attitudes in general toward African Americans. The second major contribution of Festinger and Carlsmith's results is that they contradicted the time-honored belief that big rewards produce greater change. In fact, the more participants were

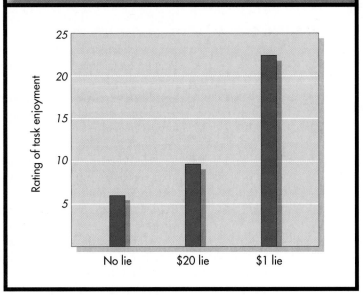

FIGURE 6.9   The Dissonance Classic

Participants in a boring experiment (attitude) were asked to say that it was enjoyable (behavior) to a fellow student. Those in one group were paid a dollar to lie; those in a second group were offered twenty dollars. Members of a third group, who did not have to lie, admitted that the task was boring. So did the participants paid twenty dollars—ample justification for what they did. Participants paid only one dollar, however, rated the task as more enjoyable. Behaving in an attitude-discrepant manner without justification, the one-dollar participants reduced dissonance by changing their attitude. *(Festinger & Carlsmith, 1959.)*

insufficient justification A condition in which people freely perform an attitude-discrepant behavior without receiving a large reward.

The more money you pay people to tell a lie, the more they will come to believe it. **False.**

offered for their inconsistent behavior, the more justified they felt and the *less* likely they were to change their attitudes.

Just as a small reward provides insufficient justification for attitude-discrepant behavior, mild punishment is **insufficient deterrence** for attitude-discrepant *non*behavior. Think about it. What happens when people refrain from doing something they really want to do? Do they devalue the activity and convince themselves that they never really wanted to do it in the first place? In one study, children were prohibited from playing with an attractive toy by being threatened with a mild or a severe punishment. All participants refrained. As cognitive dissonance theory predicts, however, only those faced with the mild punishment—an insufficient deterrent—later showed disdain for the forbidden toy. Those who confronted the threat of severe punishment did not (Aronson & Carlsmith, 1963). Once again, cognitive dissonance theory turned common sense on its head: The less severe the threatened punishment, the greater the attitude change produced.

Justifying Effort: Coming to Like What We Suffer For   Have you ever spent tons of money or tried really hard to achieve something, only to discover later that it wasn't worth all the effort? This kind of inconsistency between effort and outcome can arouse cognitive dissonance and motivate a change of heart toward the unsatisfying outcome. The hypothesis is simple but profound: We alter our attitudes to justify our suffering.

In a classic test of this hypothesis, Eliot Aronson and Judson Mills (1959) invited female students to take part in a series of group discussions about sex. But there was a hitch. Because sex is a sensitive topic, participants were told that they would have to pass an "embarrassment test" before joining the group. The test consisted of reading sexual material aloud in front of a male experimenter. One group of participants experienced what amounted to a *severe* initiation in which they had to recite obscene words and lurid passages taken from paperback novels. A second group underwent a *mild* initiation in which they read a list of more ordinary words pertaining to sex. A third group was admitted to the discussions without an initiation test.

Moments later, all participants were given headphones and permitted to eavesdrop on the group they would soon be joining. Actually, what they heard was a tape-recorded discussion about "secondary sex behavior in the lower animals." It was dreadfully boring. When it was over, participants were asked to rate how much they liked the group members and their discussion. Keep in mind what dissonance theory predicts: The more time or money or effort you choose to invest in something, the more anxious you will feel if the outcome proves disappointing. One way to cope with this inconsistency is to alter your attitudes. That's exactly what happened. Participants who had endured a severe initiation rated the discussion group more favorably than did those who had endured little or no initiation.

It's important to note that embarrassment is not the only kind of "effort" we feel the need to justify to ourselves. As a general rule, the more you pay for something—whether you pay in physical exertion, pain, time, or money—the more you will come to like it. This principle has provocative implications. For example, research suggests that the harder psychotherapy patients have to work at their own treatment, the more likely they are to feel better when that treatment is over (Axsom, 1989; Axsom & Cooper, 1985). Effort justification may also help to explain why college fraternities and sororities foster lifelong loyalties and why 58 percent of Vietnam veterans, compared with only 29 percent of other Americans, say that "The U.S. was right to get involved in the Vietnam war" (Witteman, 1990). Perhaps even today, those who risked their lives need to justify the nightmare they experienced.

Justifying Difficult Decisions: When Good Choices Get Even Better   Whenever we make difficult decisions—whether to marry, what school to attend, or what job

insufficient deterrence A condition in which people refrain from engaging in a desirable activity, even when only mild punishment is threatened.

to accept—we feel dissonance. By definition, a decision is difficult when the alternative courses of action are about equally desirable. Marriage offers comfort and stability; staying single enables us to seek out exciting new relationships. One job might pay more money; the other might involve more interesting work. Once people make tough decisions like these, they are at risk, as negative aspects of the chosen alternatives and positive aspects of the unchosen alternatives are at odds with their decisions. According to dissonance theory, people try to rationalize whatever they decide by exaggerating the positive features of the chosen alternative and the negative features of the unchosen alternative.

People often come to like what they suffer for. **True.**

In an early test of this hypothesis, Jack Brehm (1956) recruited female participants to evaluate various consumer products, presumably as part of a marketing research project. After rating a toaster, a coffee pot, a radio, a stopwatch, and other products, participants were told that they could take one home as a gift. In the high-dissonance condition, they were offered a difficult choice between two items they found equally attractive. In the low-dissonance group, they were offered an easier choice between a desirable and an undesirable item. After receiving the gift, participants read a few research reports, then re-evaluated all the products. The results provided strong support for dissonance theory. In the low-dissonance group, participants' post-decision ratings were about the same as their pre-decision ratings. But in the high-dissonance condition, ratings increased for the chosen item and decreased for the nonchosen item. Participants torn between two equivalent alternatives coped by reassuring themselves that they had made the right choice.

This phenomenon appears in a wide range of settings. For example, Robert Knox and James Inskter (1968) took dissonance theory to the racetrack and found that bettors who had already placed two-dollar bets on a horse were more optimistic about winning than were those still standing in line. Similarly, Dennis Regan and Martin Kilduff (1988) visited several polling stations on election day and found that voters were more likely to think that their candidates would win when interviewed after submitting their ballots than before. Since bets and votes cannot be taken back, people who had committed themselves to a decision were motivated to reduce post-decision dissonance. So they convinced themselves that the decision they made was right.

Cognitive Dissonance Theory: A New Look

Following in Festinger's bold footsteps, generations of social psychologists have studied and refined the basic theory. Nobody disputes the fact that when people are gently coaxed into performing an attitude-discrepant behavior, they often go on to change their attitudes. In fact, individuals who have a high need for consistency are the most likely to show the effect (Cialdini et al., 1995). Through systematic research, however, it became evident early on that Festinger's (1957) original theory was not to be the last word. People do change their attitudes to justify attitude-discrepant behavior, effort, and difficult decisions. But for dissonance to be aroused, certain conditions must be present. As summarized by Joel Cooper and Russell Fazio's (1984) "new look" at dissonance theory, we now have a pretty good idea of what those conditions are, and why.

According to Cooper and Fazio, four steps are necessary for the arousal and reduction of dissonance. First, one's attitude-discrepant behavior must produce unwanted *negative consequences*. Recall Festinger and Carlsmith's (1959) initial study. Not only did participants say something they knew to be false, they also deceived a fellow student into taking part in a painfully boring experiment. Had these participants lied without causing hardship, they would *not* have changed their attitudes to justify the action (Cooper et al., 1974). To borrow an expression from schoolyard basketball, "no harm, no foul." In fact, it appears that negative consequences arouse dissonance even when people's actions are consistent with their attitudes—as when college students who wrote against fee hikes were led to believe that their essays had backfired, leading a university committee to favor an increase (Scher & Cooper, 1989).

The second necessary step in the process is a feeling of *personal responsibility* for the unpleasant outcomes of behavior. Personal responsibility consists of two factors. The first is the freedom of *choice*. When people believe they had no choice but to act as they did, there is no dissonance and no attitude change (Linder et al., 1967). Had Festinger and Carlsmith coerced participants into raving about the boring experiment, the participants would not have felt the need to further justify what they did by changing their attitudes. But the experimental situation led participants to think that their actions were voluntary and that the choice was theirs. Pressured without realizing it, participants believed that they did not have to comply with the experimenter's request.

For people to feel personally responsible, they must also believe that the potential negative consequences of their actions were *foreseeable* at the time (Goethals et al., 1979). When the outcome could not really have been anticipated, then there's no dissonance and no attitude change. Had Festinger and Carlsmith's participants lied in private, only later to find out that their statements had been tape-recorded for subsequent use, then, again, they would not have felt the need to further justify their behavior.

The third necessary step in the process is physiological *arousal*. Right from the start, Festinger viewed cognitive dissonance as a state of discomfort and tension that people seek to reduce—much like hunger, thirst, and other basic drives. Research has shown that this emphasis was well placed. In a study by Robert Croyle and Joel Cooper (1983), participants wrote essays that supported or contradicted their own attitudes. Some were ordered to do so, but others were led to believe that the choice was theirs. During the session, electrodes were attached to each participant's fingertips to record physiological arousal. As predicted by cognitive dissonance theory, those who freely wrote attitude-discrepant essays were the most aroused—an observation made by other researchers as well (Elkin & Leippe, 1986). In fact, participants who write attitude-discrepant essays in a "free-choice" situation report feeling high levels of discomfort—which subside once they change their attitudes (Elliot & Devine, 1994).

The fourth step in the dissonance process is closely related to the third. It isn't enough to feel generally aroused. The person must also make an *attribution* for that arousal to his or her own behavior. Suppose you just lied to a friend, or studied for an exam that was canceled, or made a tough decision that you might soon regret. Suppose further that although you are upset, you believe that your discomfort is caused by some external factor, not by your dissonance-producing behavior. Under these

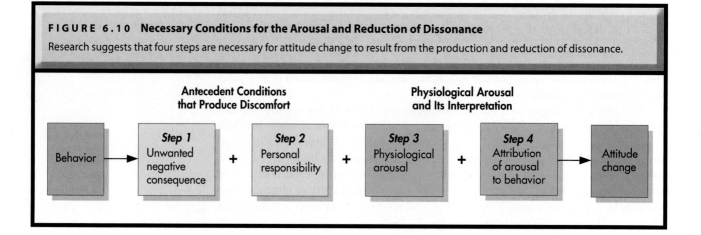

FIGURE 6.10   Necessary Conditions for the Arousal and Reduction of Dissonance
Research suggests that four steps are necessary for attitude change to result from the production and reduction of dissonance.

circumstances, will you exhibit attitude change as a symptom of cognitive dissonance? No, probably not. When participants were led to attribute their dissonance-related arousal to a drug they had supposedly taken (Zanna & Cooper, 1974), to the anticipation of painful electric shocks (Pittman, 1975), or to a pair of prism goggles that they had to wear (Losch & Cacioppo, 1990), attitude change did not occur. Figure 6.10 summarizes the four steps in the production and reduction of dissonance.

To this day, social psychologists continue to debate the "classic" versus "new look" theories of cognitive dissonance. On the one hand, research has shown that attitude-discrepant actions do not always produce dissonance—in part because not everyone cares about being cognitively consistent (Cialdini et al., 1995) and in part because a change in attitude often seems to require the production of negative consequences (R. W. Johnson et al., 1995). On the other hand, some researchers have found that inconsistency alone can trigger cognitive dissonance—even without the negative consequences. For example, Eddie Harmon-Jones and others (1996) had people drink a Kool-Aid beverage that was mixed with sugar or vinegar. The researchers either told participants (no choice) or asked them (high choice) to state in writing that they liked the beverage and then toss these notes, which were not really needed, into the wastebasket. Afterward, they rated how much they really liked the drink. You may have noticed that this experiment parallels the classic Festinger and Carlsmith study, with one key exception: For participants in the high-choice situation who consumed vinegar and said they liked it, the lie—although it contradicted their true attitudes—did not cause harm to anyone. Did they experience dissonance that they would have to reduce by overrating the vinegar Kool-Aid? Look at Figure 6.11, and you'll see that they did. Compared with participants who lied about the vinegar in the no-choice situation, those in the high-choice situation rated its taste as more pleasant. The lie was harmless, but the feeling of inconsistency still forced a change in attitude.

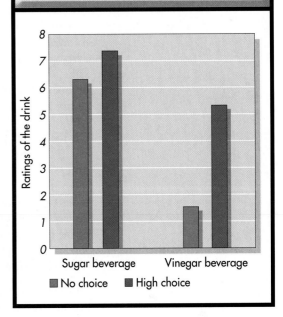

FIGURE 6.11 Cognitive Dissonance: When Behavior Is Inconsistent but Without Harmful Consequence

Participants drank a beverage containing sugar or vinegar and then were told (no choice) or asked (high choice) to write down that they liked it. Compared with those in the vinegar–no choice situation, subjects in the vinegar–high choice situation rated the taste as more pleasant. Their lie did not harm anyone, but the inconsistency forced a change in attitude. *(Harmon Jones et al., 1996.)*

Alternative Routes to Self-Persuasion

It is important to distinguish between the empirical facts as uncovered by dissonance researchers and the theory that is used to explain them. The facts themselves are clear: Under certain conditions, people who behave in attitude-discrepant ways go on to change their attitudes. Whether this phenomenon reflects a human need to reduce dissonance, however, is a matter of some controversy. Over the years, three other explanations have been proposed.

Self-Perception Theory Daryl Bem's (1965) *self-perception theory*, as described in Chapter 3, posed the first serious challenge to dissonance theory. Noting that people don't always have firsthand knowledge of their own attitudes, Bem proposed that we infer how we feel by observing ourselves and the circumstances of our own behavior. This sort of self-persuasion is not fueled by the need to reduce tension or justify our actions. Instead, it is a cool, calm, and rational process in which people interpret ambiguous feelings by observing their own behavior. But can Bem's theory replace dissonance theory as an explanation of self-persuasion?

Bem confronted this question head-on. What if neutral observers who are not motivated by the need to reduce dissonance were to read a step-by-step description of a dissonance study and predict the results? This approach to the problem was ingenious. Bem reasoned that observers can have the same behavioral information as the participants themselves but not experience the same personal conflict. If observers generate the same results as real participants, it shows that dissonance arousal is not necessary for the resulting changes in attitudes.

To test his hypothesis, Bem (1967) described the Festinger and Carlsmith study to observers and had them guess participants' attitudes. Some were told about the one-dollar condition, some were told about the twenty-dollar condition, and others read about the control group procedure. The results closely paralleled the original study. As observers saw it, participants who said the task was interesting for twenty dollars didn't mean it—they just went along for the money. But those who made the claim for only one dollar must have been sincere. Why else would they have gone along? As far as Bem was concerned, participants themselves reason the same way. No conflict, no arousal—just inference by observation.

So should we conclude that self-perception, not dissonance, is what's necessary to bring about attitude change? That's a tough question. It's not easy to come up with a critical experiment to distinguish between these theories. Both predict the same results, but for different reasons. And both offer unique support for their own points of view. On the one hand, Bem's observer studies show that dissonance-like results *can* be obtained without arousal. On the other hand, the subjects of dissonance manipulations *do* experience arousal, which seems necessary for attitude change to take place. Can we say that one theory is right and the other wrong?

Fazio and his colleagues (1977) concluded that both theories are right but in different situations. When people behave in ways that are strikingly at odds with their attitudes, they feel the unnerving effects of dissonance and change their attitudes to rationalize their actions. When people behave in ways that are not terribly discrepant with how they feel, however, they experience relatively little tension and form their attitudes as a matter of inference. In short, highly discrepant behavior produces attitude change through dissonance, whereas slightly discrepant behavior produces change through self-perception.

Impression-Management Theory   Another alternative to a dissonance view of self-persuasion is based on *impression-management theory*, which says that what matters is not a motive to *be* consistent but a motive to *appear* consistent. Nobody wants to be called fickle or be seen by others as a hypocrite. So we calibrate our attitudes and behaviors only publicly—just to present ourselves to others in a particular light (Baumeister, 1982; Tedeschi et al., 1971). Or perhaps we are motivated not by a desire to appear consistent but by a desire to avoid being held responsible for the unpleasant consequences of our actions (Schlenker, 1982). Either way, this theory places the emphasis on our concern for self-presentation. According to this view, participants in the Festinger and Carlsmith study simply did not want the experimenter to think they had sold out for a paltry sum of money.

If the impression-management approach is correct, then cognitive dissonance does not produce attitude change at all—only reported change. In other words, if research participants were to state their attitudes anonymously, or if they were to think that the experimenter could determine their true feelings through covert measures, then dissonance-like effects should vanish. Sometimes, the effects do vanish; but other times, they do not. In general, studies have shown that although self-persuasion can be motivated by impression management, it can also occur in situations that do not clearly arouse self-presentation concerns (Baumeister & Tice, 1984).

Self-Affirmation Theory   A third competing explanation relates self-persuasion to the self. According to Elliot Aronson, acts that arouse dissonance do so because they threaten the self-concept, making the person feel guilty, dishonest, or hypocritical— and motivating a change in attitude or future behavior (Aronson, 1969; Stone et al., 1997; Thibodeau & Aronson, 1992). This being the case, perhaps Festinger and Carlsmith's participants wanted to change their attitudes toward the boring task in order to repair damage to the self, not to resolve cognitive inconsistency.

Claude Steele (1988) takes the notion two steps further. First, a dissonance-producing situation—engaging in attitude-discrepant behavior, exerting wasted effort, or making a difficult decision—sets in motion a process of *self-affirmation* that is designed to revalidate the integrity of the self-concept. Second, this revalidation can be achieved in many ways, not just by resolving dissonance. Self-affirmation theory makes a unique prediction: If the active ingredient in dissonance situations is a threat to the self, then people who have an opportunity to affirm the self in other ways will not suffer from the effects of dissonance. Give Festinger and Carlsmith's one-dollar participants a chance to donate money, help a victim in distress, or solve a problem, and their self-concepts should bounce back without further need to justify their actions.

Research provides support for this hypothesis. For example, Steele and his colleagues (1993) gave people positive or negative feedback about a personality test they had taken. Next, they asked them to rate ten popular music albums and then offered them a choice of keeping either their fifth- or sixth-ranked album. Soon after making the decision, participants were asked to re-rate the albums. As predicted by dissonance theory, most inflated their ratings of the chosen album relative to the unchosen album. The key word, however, is *most*. Among positive-feedback participants, ratings did not change. Why not? According to Steele, these participants had just enjoyed a self-affirming experience—enough to overcome the need to reduce dissonance. This result suggests that there are many possible ways to repair the dissonance-damaged self.

To summarize, dissonance theory maintains that people change their attitudes to justify their attitude-discrepant behaviors, efforts, and decisions. Self-perception theory argues that the change occurs because people infer how they feel by observing their own behavior. Impression-management theory claims that the attitude change is spurred by self-presentation concerns. And self-affirmation theory says that the change is motivated by threats to the self (see Figure 6.12).

Attitudes and attitude change are an important part of social life. In this chapter, we have seen that persuasion can be achieved in different ways. The most common approach is through communication from *others*. Faced with newspaper editorials, junk mail, books, TV commercials, and other messages, we take one of two routes to persuasion. On the central route, attitude change is based on the

---

FIGURE 6.12 Theories of Self-Persuasion: Critical Comparisons

Here we compare the major theories of self-persuasion. Each alternative challenges a different aspect of dissonance theory. Self-perception theory assumes that attitude change is a matter of inference, not motivation. Impression-management theory maintains that the change is more apparent than real, reported for the sake of public self-presentation. Self-affirmation theory contends that the motivating force is a concern for the self and that attitude change will not occur when the self-concept is affirmed in other ways.

Theories

	Cognitive Dissonance	Self-Perception	Impression Management	Self-Affirmation
Is the attitude change motivated by a desire to reduce discomfort?	Yes	No	Yes	Yes
Does a person's private attitude really change?	Yes	Yes	No	Yes
Must the change be directly related to the attitude-discrepant behavior?	Yes	Yes	Yes	No

merits of the communication. On the peripheral route, it is based on superficial cues. A second, less obvious means of persuasion originates within *ourselves*. When people behave in ways that run afoul of their true convictions, they often go on to change their attitudes. Once again, there is not one route to change, but many. In this regard, dissonance, self-perception, impression management, and self-affirmation are among the possible avenues.

Review

The Study of Attitudes

■ An attitude is a combination of affective, behavioral, and cognitive reactions toward an object.

How Attitudes Are Measured

■ The most common way to measure attitudes is through self-reports, such as attitude scales.
■ To get respondents to answer questions honestly, the bogus pipeline may be used.
■ Covert measures may also be used. Such measures include nonverbal behavior, the facial electromyograph (EMG), and brain-wave patterns.

The Link Between Attitudes and Behavior

■ Attitudes do not necessarily correlate with behavior; but under certain conditions, there is a high correlation.
■ Attitudes predict behavior best when they're specific rather than general and strong rather than weak.
■ Attitudes compete with other influences on behavior.

Persuasion by Communication

■ The most common approach to changing attitudes is through a persuasive communication.

Two Routes to Persuasion

■ When people think critically about a message, they take the central route to persuasion and are influenced by the strength of the arguments.
■ When people do not think carefully about a message, they take the peripheral route to persuasion and are often influenced by peripheral cues.
■ The route taken depends on whether people have the ability and the motivation to fully process the communication.

The Source

■ Attitude change is greater for messages delivered by a source that is credible (competent and trustworthy).
■ Attitude change is also greater when the source is likable (similar and attractive).

■ When an audience has a high level of personal involvement, source factors are less important than message quality.
■ The sleeper effect shows that people often forget the source but not the message, so the effects of source credibility tend to dissipate over time.

The Message

■ On the peripheral route, lengthy messages are persuasive. On the central route, length works only if the added information does not dilute the message.
■ Whether it is best to present an argument first or second depends on how much time elapses—between the two arguments and between the second argument and the final decision.
■ Messages that are moderately discrepant from an audience's attitudes will inspire change, but highly discrepant messages will be scrutinized and rejected.
■ High-fear messages motivate attitude change when they contain strong arguments and instructions on how to avoid the threatened danger.
■ Positive emotion also facilitates attitude change because people are easier to persuade when they're in a good mood.
■ Research shows that subliminal messages do not produce meaningful or lasting changes in attitudes.

The Audience

■ People are not consistently difficult or easy to persuade. Rather, different kinds of messages influence different kinds of people.
■ People who are high in the need for cognition are persuaded more by the strength of the arguments.
■ People who are high in self-monitoring are influenced more by appeals to social images.
■ To be persuasive, a message should also appeal to the cultural values of its audience.
■ Forewarning increases resistance to persuasive influence. It inoculates the audience by providing the opportunity to generate counterarguments, and it arouses psychological reactance.

Persuasion by Our Own Actions

Role Playing: All the World's a Stage

■ The way people act can influence how they feel, as behavior can determine attitudes.

Cognitive Dissonance Theory: The Classic Version

■ Under certain conditions, inconsistency between attitudes and behavior produces an unpleasant psychological state called cognitive dissonance.

■ Motivated to reduce the tension, people often change their attitudes to justify (1) attitude-discrepant behavior, (2) wasted effort, and (3) difficult decisions.

Cognitive Dissonance Theory: A New Look

■ According to the "new look" version of cognitive dissonance theory, four conditions must be met for dissonance to be aroused: (1) an act with unwanted consequences, (2) a feeling of personal responsibility, (3) arousal or discomfort, and (4) attribution of the arousal to the attitude-discrepant act.

■ Social psychologists continue to debate whether dissonance can be aroused by cognitive inconsistency when no unwanted consequences are produced.

Alternative Routes to Self-Persuasion

■ Alternative explanations of dissonance-related attitude change have been proposed.

■ Self-perception theory states that people logically infer their attitudes by observing their own behavior.

■ Impression-management theory says that people are motivated only to appear consistent to others.

■ Self-affirmation theory states that dissonance is triggered by threats to the self and can be reduced indirectly, without a change in attitude, through self-affirming experiences.

Key Terms

PUTTING COMMON SENSE TO THE TEST

Researchers can tell if someone has a positive or negative attitude by measuring physiological arousal.

False. *Measures of arousal can reveal how intensely someone feels, but not whether the person's attitude is positive or negative.*

In reacting to persuasive communications, people are influenced more by superficial images than by logical arguments.

False. *As indicated by the dual-process model of persuasion, people can be influenced by images or arguments—depending on their ability and motivation to think critically about the information.*

People are most easily persuaded by commercial messages that are presented without their awareness.

False. *There is no research evidence to support the presumed effects of subliminal ads.*

The more money you pay people to tell a lie, the more they will come to believe it.

False. *Cognitive dissonance studies show that people believe the lies they are under paid to tell as a way to justify their own actions.*

People often come to like what they suffer for.

True. *Studies show that the more people work or suffer for something, the more they come to like it as a way to justify their effort.*

7 | Conformity

PREVIEW

This chapter examines three ways in which our behavior is influenced by others. First, we consider the reasons why people exhibit *conformity* to group norms. Second, we describe the kinds of strategies used to elicit *compliance* with direct requests. Third, we analyze the causes and effects of *obedience* to the commands of authority. The chapter concludes with a discussion of the *continuum of social influence*.

1t was April 1997 when a bizarre news story broke out of southern California: Marshall Applewhite and thirty-eight followers of the Heaven's Gate cult had committed the largest mass suicide in U.S. history. Members of the group were found lying in bed on their backs—identically dressed in black pants, flowing black shirts, and brand new Nike sneakers, with purple shrouds over their faces. The death scene was calm and orderly, not chaotic. Believing that they would be taken to the Kingdom of Heaven in a spacecraft that trailed the Hale-Bopp comet, all the members packed suitcases, prepared identification papers and farewell videotapes, and took their lives by drinking vodka and phenobarbital and then placing plastic bags over their heads. Why would twenty-one women and eighteen men, ranging in age from twenty-six to seventy-two, follow Applewhite to their deaths? What social influences could have operated to produce such self-destructive behavior? One member explained, "All of us at this time are finding ourselves aligning with others of common mind." In contrast, a cult expert who studied Heaven's Gate argued that Applewhite had controlled their minds: "These people were pawns in his personal fantasy" (Gleick, 1997).

The mass suicide of the Heaven's Gate cult reveals the

T / F

_____ When all members of a group give an incorrect response to an easy question, most people most of the time conform with that response.

_____ An effective way to get someone to do you a favor is to make a first request that is so large the person is sure to reject it.

_____ In experiments on obedience, most people who were ordered to administer severe shocks to an innocent person refused to do so.

_____ As the number of people in a group increases, so does their impact on an individual.

_____ Conformity rates vary across different cultures and from one generation to the next.

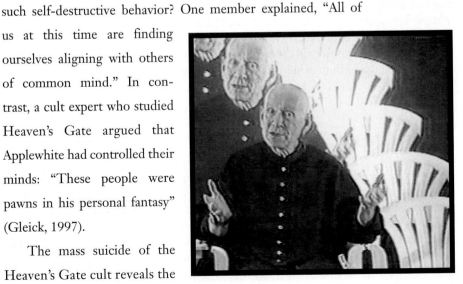

Addressing his followers on videotape, Marshall Applewhite, leader of the Heaven's Gate cult, convinced thirty-eight people to commit mass suicide.

211

In sports stadiums, restaurants, and other settings, people often imitate each other automatically and without conflict.

"We are discreet sheep; we wait to see how the drove is going and then go with the drove."

—Mark Twain

awesome and potentially deadly power of social influence. But the effects that people have on each other can also be seen in the most mundane of human events. Sports fans spread the "wave" around a stadium or chant "defense" in a spectacular show of unison. TV producers insert canned laughter into sitcoms as a way of increasing viewer responsiveness. Political candidates trumpet the inflated results of their own public opinion polls to attract new voters to the winning side. And bartenders, waiters, and waitresses stuff dollar bills into their own tip jars as a way to get customers to follow suit.

These examples illustrate that people sometimes imitate one another automatically and without conflict. Of course, you don't need to be a social psychologist to know that we have an impact on each other's behavior. But how, and with what effect? The term *social influence* refers to the ways in which people are affected by real and imagined pressures from others (Kiesler & Kiesler, 1969; Cialdini & Trost, 1998). The kinds of influences brought to bear on an individual come in different shapes and sizes. In this chapter, we consider three that vary in the degree of pressure exerted on a person—*conformity, compliance,* and *obedience.*

As depicted in Figure 7.1, conformity, compliance, and obedience are not distinct, qualitatively different "types" of influence. In all three cases, the influence may emanate from a person, a group, or an institution. And in all instances, the behavior in question may be constructive (helping oneself or others), or destructive (hurting oneself or others), or neutral. It is useful to note, however, that social influence varies, as points along a continuum, according to the degree of pressure exerted on the individual. It is also useful to note that we do not always succumb under pressure. People may conform or maintain their independence from others; they may comply with direct requests or react with assertiveness; they may obey the commands of authority or oppose powerful others in an act of defiance. In this chapter, we consider the factors that lead human beings to yield to or resist social influence.

Conformity

t is hard to find behaviors that are *not* in some way affected by exposure to the actions of others. As social animals, we are vulnerable to a host of subtle, almost reflex-like influences. We often yawn when we see others yawning and laugh when we hear others laughing. To demonstrate the point, research confederates stopped on a busy street in New York City, looked up, and gawked at the sixth-floor window of a nearby building. Films shot from behind the window indicated that about 80 percent of passers-by stopped and gazed up when they saw the confederates (Milgram et al., 1969).

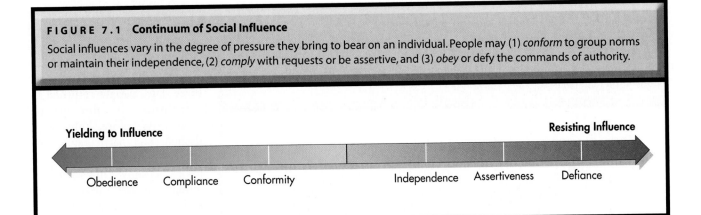

FIGURE 7.1 Continuum of Social Influence

Social influences vary in the degree of pressure they bring to bear on an individual. People may (1) *conform* to group norms or maintain their independence, (2) *comply* with requests or be assertive, and (3) *obey* or defy the commands of authority.

When social psychologists talk of **conformity,** they refer to the tendency for people to *change* their perceptions, opinions, and behavior in ways that are consistent with group norms. With this definition in mind, would you call yourself a conformist or a nonconformist? Do you ever feel pressured to follow what others are doing? At first, you may deny the tendency to conform and, instead, declare your individuality. But think about it. When was the last time you appeared at a formal wedding dressed in blue jeans or remained seated during the national anthem at a sports event? People find it remarkably difficult to breach social norms. In an interesting demonstration of this point, social psychology research assistants were supposed to ask subway passengers to give up their seats—a conspicuous violation of the norm of acceptable conduct. As it turned out, however, many of the assistants could not carry out their assignment. In fact, some of those who tried it became so anxious that they pretended to be ill just to make their request appear justified (Milgram & Sabini, 1978).

With conformity being so widespread, it is interesting and ironic that research participants (at least in North America) who are coaxed into conforming to a group norm will often not admit it. Instead, they try to reinterpret the task and rationalize their own behavior as a way to see themselves as independent (Buehler & Griffin, 1994). People understandably have mixed feelings about conformity. After all, some degree of conformity is essential if individuals are to coexist peacefully, as when people assume their rightful place in a waiting line. Yet at other times, conformity can have harmful consequences, as when people drink too heavily at parties or tell offensive ethnic jokes because others are doing the same. For the social psychologist, the goal is to understand the conditions that promote conformity and the reasons for that behavior.

The Early Classics

In 1936, Muzafer Sherif published a classic laboratory study of how norms develop in small groups. His method was ingenious. Male students, who believed they were participating in a visual perception experiment, sat in a totally darkened room. Fifteen feet in front of them, a small dot of light appeared for two seconds, after which participants were asked to estimate how far it had moved. This procedure was repeated several times. Although participants didn't realize it, the dot of light always remained motionless. The movement they thought they saw was merely an optical illusion known as the *autokinetic effect:* In darkness, a stationary point of light appears to move, sometimes erratically, in various directions.

At first, participants sat alone and reported their judgments to the experimenter. After several trials, Sherif found that they settled in on their own stable

conformity The tendency to change our perceptions, opinions, or behavior in ways that are consistent with group norms.

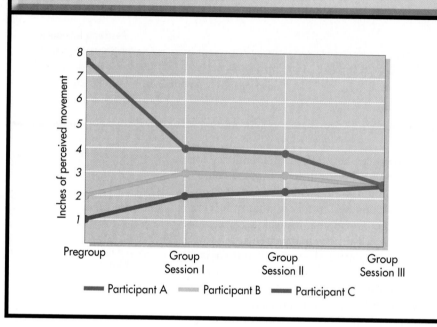

FIGURE 7.2   A Classic Case of Suggestibility

This graph, taken from Sherif's study, shows how three participants' estimates of the apparent movement of light gradually converged. Before they came together, their perceptions varied considerably. Once in groups, however, participants conformed to the norm that had developed. *(Sherif, 1936.)*

perceptions of movement, with most estimates ranging from one to ten inches (although one participant gave an estimate of eighty feet!). During the next three days, people returned to participate in three-person groups. As before, lights were flashed, and participants, one by one, announced their estimates. As shown in Figure 7.2, initial estimates varied considerably, but participants later converged on a common perception. Eventually, each group established its own set of norms.

Some fifteen years after Sherif's demonstration, Solomon Asch (1951) constructed a very different task for testing how people's beliefs affect the beliefs of others. To appreciate what Asch did, imagine yourself in the following situation. You sign up for a psychology experiment; and when you arrive, you find six other students waiting around a table. Soon after you take an empty seat, the experimenter explains that he is interested in the ability to make visual discriminations. As an example, he asks you and the others to indicate which of three comparison lines is identical in length to a standard line.

That seems easy enough. The experimenter then says that after each set of lines is shown, you and the others should take turns announcing your judgments out loud in the order of your seating position. Beginning on his left, the experimenter asks the first person for his judgment. Seeing that you are in the next-to-last position, you patiently await your turn. The opening moments pass uneventfully. The discriminations are clear, and everyone agrees on the answers. On the third set of lines, however, the first participant selects what is quite clearly the wrong line. Huh? What happened? Did he suddenly lose his mind, his eyesight, or both? Before you have the chance to figure this one out, the next four participants choose the same wrong line. Now what? Feeling as if you have entered the Twilight Zone, you wonder if you misunderstood the task. And you wonder what the others will think if you have the nerve to disagree. It's your turn now. You rub your eyes and take another look. What do you see? Better yet, what do you do?

Figure 7.3 gives an idea of the bind in which Asch's participants found themselves—caught between the need to be right and a desire to be liked (Insko et al., 1982; Ross et al., 1976). As you may suspect by now, the other "participants" were actually confederates—and had been trained to make incorrect judgments on twelve out of eighteen presentations. There seems little doubt that the real participants knew the correct answers. In a control group, where they made judgments in isolation, they made almost no errors. Yet Asch's participants went along with the incorrect majority about 37 percent of the time—far more often than most of us would ever predict. Not everyone conformed, of course. About 25 percent refused to agree on any of the incorrect judgments. Yet 50 percent went along on at least half of the critical presentations, with the remaining participants

When all members of a group give an incorrect response to an easy question, most people most of the time conform with that response . **False.**

conforming on an occasional basis. Similarly high levels of conformity were observed when Asch's study was repeated thirty years later and in recent studies involving other cognitive tasks (Larsen, 1990; Schneider & Watkins, 1996).

Looking at Sherif's and Asch's research, let's compare these classic studies of social influence. Obviously, both demonstrate that our perceptions can be heavily influenced by others. But how similar are they, really? Did Sherif's and Asch's participants exhibit the same kind of conformity, and for the same reasons, or was the resemblance in their behavior more apparent than real?

From the start, it was clear that these studies differed in some important ways. In Sherif's research, participants were quite literally "in the dark," so they naturally turned to others for guidance. When physical reality is ambiguous and we are uncertain of our own judgments, as in the autokinetic situation, others can serve as a valuable source of information (Festinger, 1954). Asch's participants found themselves in a much more awkward position. Their task was relatively simple, and they could see with their own eyes what answers were correct. Still, they often followed the incorrect majority. In interviews, many of Asch's participants reported afterward that they went along with the group even though they were not convinced. Many of those who did not conform said they felt "conspicuous" and "crazy," like a "misfit" (Asch, 1956, p. 31).

It's important to realize that these group influences are not limited to the judgments people make in simple laboratory tasks. In a series of experiments, researchers tested the hypothesis that voters are influenced by others in their perceptions of the candidates in presidential debates. In one study, large groups of college students watched a 1992 debate between George Bush, Bill Clinton, and Ross

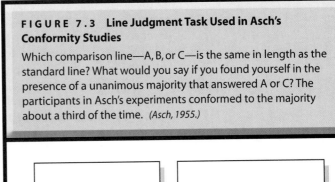

FIGURE 7.3   Line Judgment Task Used in Asch's Conformity Studies

Which comparison line—A, B, or C—is the same in length as the standard line? What would you say if you found yourself in the presence of a unanimous majority that answered A or C? The participants in Asch's experiments conformed to the majority about a third of the time. *(Asch, 1955.)*

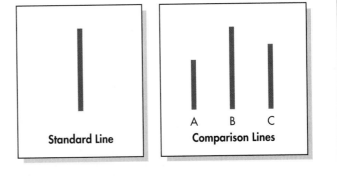

Standard Line   Comparison Lines

After two uneventful rounds in Asch's study, the participant (seated second from the right) faces a dilemma. The answer he had to give in the third test of visual discrimination differs from that of the first five confederates, who are all in agreement. Should he give his own answer, or conform to theirs?

Perot (a videotape of the debate was shown thirty minutes after it ended). In one room, the participants were accompanied by confederates who were programmed to cheer for Bush. In a second room, the confederates cheered for Clinton. In a third room, there were no confederates. Would this manipulation actually influence the way participants perceived the debate? Yes. On a 100-point scale, there was a 45-point shift in the relative evaluations of Bush and Clinton. The reactions of others in the audience altered the way participants saw the debate—even during a heated presidential campaign, and even though many had strong preferences for one candidate or the other (Fein, Goethals, & Kassin, 1998).

Why Do People Conform?

The Sherif and Asch studies demonstrate that people conform for two very different reasons: one informational, the other normative (Crutchfield, 1955; Deutsch & Gerard, 1955). Through **informational influence,** people conform because they want to be correct in their judgments and they assume that when others agree on something, they must be right. In Sherif's autokinetic task, as in other difficult or ambiguous tasks, it's natural to assume that four eyes are better than two. **Normative influence,** however, leads people to conform because they fear the consequences of appearing deviant. Wanting to be accepted and liked, we often avoid behaving in ways that make us stick out like a sore thumb. To be sure, people like to think of themselves as unique. But disagreement can be stressful. It's easy to see why. Research shows that individuals who stray from a group norm are often disliked, rejected, ridiculed, and laughed at (Levine, 1989; Schachter, 1951)—especially when the group needs to reach a consensus (Kruglanski & Webster, 1991).

Usually, informational and normative influences operate jointly (Insko et al., 1983). Even some of Asch's participants admitted that they came to agree with their group's erroneous judgments. Still, the distinction between the two types of influence is important not just for understanding why people conform but because the two types of influence produce different types of conformity: private and public (Allen, 1965; Kelman, 1961). Like beauty, conformity may be skin deep, or it may penetrate beneath the surface. **Private conformity,** also called true acceptance or conversion, describes instances in which others cause us to change not only our overt behavior but our minds as well. To conform at this level is to be truly persuaded that others are correct. In contrast, **public conformity** (sometimes called compliance, a term that is used later in this chapter to describe a different form of influence) refers to a superficial change in behavior. People often respond to normative pressures by pretending to agree even when privately they do not. This often happens when we want to curry favor with others. The politician who tells constituents whatever they want to hear is a case in point.

How, you might be wondering, can social psychologists ever tell the difference between the private and public conformist? After all, both exhibit the same change in their observable behavior. The difference is that compared with someone who merely acquiesces in public, the individual who is truly persuaded maintains that change long after the others are out of the picture. When this distinction is applied to Sherif's and Asch's research, the results come out as expected. At the end of his study, Sherif (1936) retested participants alone and found that their estimates continued to reflect the norm previously established in their group—even among those who were retested a full year after the experiment (Rohrer et al., 1954). In contrast, when Asch (1956) had participants write their answers privately, their level of conformity dropped sharply (Deutsch & Gerard, 1955; Mouton et al., 1956).

In a study that demonstrates both processes, Robert S. Baron and his colleagues (Baron, Vandello, & Brunsman, 1996) had people, in groups of three (the

informational influence Influence that produces conformity when a person believes others are correct in their judgments.

normative influence Influence that produces conformity when a person fears the negative social consequences of appearing deviant.

private conformity The change of beliefs that occurs when a person privately accepts the position taken by others.

public conformity A superficial change in overt behavior, without a corresponding change of opinion, produced by real or imagined group pressure.

other two were confederates), act as eyewitnesses: First they would see a picture of a person, then they would try to pick that person out of a line-up. In some groups, the task was difficult, like Sherif's, as participants saw each picture only once, for half a second. For other groups, the task was easier, like Asch's, in that they saw each picture twice for a total of ten seconds. How often did participants conform when the confederates made the wrong identification? It depended on how motivated they were. When the experimenter downplayed the task as only a "pilot study," the conformity rates

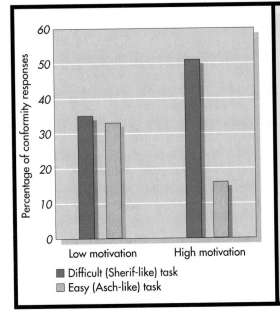

FIGURE 7.4
Distinguishing Types of Conformity

People made judgments under conditions in which they had a high or a low level of motivation. Regardless of whether the judgment task was difficult or easy, there were moderate levels of conformity when participants had low motivation (left). But when they were highly motivated (right), participants conformed more when the task was difficult— as in Sherif's study—and less when it was easy—as in Asch's study. *(Baron et al., 1996.)*

were 35 percent when the task was difficult and 33 percent when it was easy. But when participants were offered a financial incentive to do well, conformity went up to 51 percent when the task was difficult—and down to 16 percent when it was easy (see Figure 7.4). With pride and money on the line, the Sherif-like participants conformed more, and the Asch-like participants conformed less.

Table 7.1 summarizes the comparison of Sherif's and Asch's studies and the depths of social influence that they demonstrate. Looking at this table, you can see that the difficulty of the task is crucial. When reality cannot easily be validated by physical evidence, as in the autokinetic situation, people turn to others for information and conform because they are truly persuaded by that information. When reality is clear, however, the cost of dissent becomes the major issue. As Asch found, it can be difficult to depart too much from others even when you know that they—not you—are wrong. So you play along. Privately, you don't change your mind. But you nod your head in agreement anyway.

Majority Influence

Realizing that people often succumb to peer pressure is only the first step in understanding the process of social influence. The next step is to identify the situational and personal factors that make us more or less likely to conform. We know that people tend to conform when the social pressure is intense and they are insecure about how to behave (Campbell & Fairey, 1989; Santee & Maslach, 1982). But what creates these feelings of pressure and insecurity? Here, we look at four factors: the size of the group, awareness

TABLE 7.1 Two Types of Conformity

A comparison of Sherif's and Asch's studies suggests different kinds of conformity for different reasons. Sherif used an ambiguous task, so others provided a source of information and influenced the participants' true opinions. Asch used a task that required simple judgments of a clear stimulus, so most participants exhibited occasional public conformity in response to normative pressure but privately did not accept the group's judgments.

Experimental Task	Primary Effect of Group	Depth of Conformity Produced
Sherif's ambiguous autokinetic effect	Informational influence	Private acceptance
Asch's simple line judgments	Normative influence	Public conformity

of the norms, the presence of an ally, and the personal characteristics of the individual.

Group Size: The Power in Numbers Common sense would suggest that as the number of people in a majority increases, so should their impact. Actually, it is not that simple. Asch (1956) varied the size of groups, using one, two, three, four, eight, or fifteen confederates, and he found that conformity increased with group size—but only up to a point. Once there were three or four confederates, the amount of *additional* influence exerted by the rest was negligible. Other researchers have obtained similar results (Gerard et al., 1968).

Beyond the presence of three or four others, additions to a group are subject to the law of "diminishing returns" (Knowles, 1983; Mullen, 1983; Tanford & Penrod, 1984). As we will see later, Bibb Latané (1981) likens the influence of people on an individual to the way light bulbs illuminate a surface. When a second bulb is added to a room, the effect is dramatic. When the tenth bulb is added, however, its impact is barely felt, if at all. Economists say the same about the perception of money. An additional dollar seems greater to the person who has only three dollars than to the person who has three hundred.

Another possible explanation is that as more and more people express the same opinion, an individual is likely to suspect that they are acting either in "collusion" or as "spineless sheep." According to David Wilder (1977), what matters is not the actual number of others but one's perception of how many distinct others, thinking independently, there are. Indeed, Wilder found that people were more influenced by two groups of two than by one four-person group and by two groups of three than by one six-person group. Conformity increased even further when people were exposed to three two-person groups. When faced with a majority opinion, we do more than just count the number of warm bodies—we try to assess the number of independent minds.

Awareness of the Norms The size of a majority may influence the amount of pressure that is felt, but social norms give rise to conformity only when we know and focus on those norms. This may sound like an obvious point, yet we often misperceive what is normative—particularly when others are too afraid or embarrassed to publicly present their true thoughts, feelings, and behaviors. One common example of this "pluralistic ignorance" concerns perceptions of alcohol usage. In a number of college-wide surveys, Deborah Prentice and Dale Miller (1996) found that most students overestimated how comfortable their peers were with the level of drinking on campus. Those who most overestimated how others felt about drinking at the start of the school year eventually conformed to this misperception in their own attitudes and behavior. What's more, students who participated in discussion sessions about alcohol that were designed to correct these misperceptions—compared with those who took part in sessions that focused on personal responsibility—were actually drinking less alcohol six months later. Clearly, we are influenced not by social norms per se but by our *perceptions* of the norms.

Knowing how others are behaving in a situation is necessary for conformity, but these norms are likely to influence us only when they are brought to our awareness, or "activated." This point is demonstrated in a series of studies on littering. In the first study, researchers had confederates pass out handbills to amusement park visitors and varied the amount of litter that appeared in one section of the park (an indication of how others behave in that setting). The result: The more litter there was, the more likely visitors were to toss their handbills to the ground (Cialdini et al., 1990).

A second study showed that passers-by were most influenced by the prior behavior of others when their attention was drawn to the existing norm. In this instance, people were observed in a parking garage that was either clean or cluttered with cigarette butts, candy wrappers, paper cups, and trash. In half of the cases, the norm that was already in place—clean or cluttered—was brought to their attention by a confederate who threw paper to the ground as he walked by. In the other half, the confederate passed by without incident. As participants reached their cars, they found a "Please Drive Safely" handbill tucked under the windshield wiper. So, did they toss the paper to the ground or take it with them? The results showed that people were most likely to conform (by littering more when the garage was cluttered than when it was clean) when the confederate had littered—an act that drew attention to the existing norm. In short, social norms had to be "activated," or brought to mind, to influence behavior (Cialdini et al., 1991).

In a third study, which was set in a clean or cluttered outdoor parking lot, some participants watched a confederate toss a fast-food restaurant bag to the ground, while others saw him bend over and pick a bag up—also an act that led participants to take notice of the existing norm. So, did they litter? As it turned out, the second confederate had the greater influence. In this situation, littering was inhibited not only when the parking lot was clean but even when it was cluttered. Apparently, the two situations activated different types of social norms. When the confederate littered, participants were made aware of *descriptive norms* that simply informed them of how most others *do* behave. When the confederate went out of his way to pick up someone else's trash, however, participants were exposed to *injunctive norms* that specify how people in general *should* behave. By linking behavior to signs of social approval and disapproval, injunctive norms have a powerful influence on us (Reno et al., 1993).

An Ally in Dissent: Getting By with a Little Help   In Asch's initial experiment, participants found themselves pitted against unanimous majorities. But what if they had an ally, a partner in dissent? Investigating this issue, Asch found that the presence of a single confederate who agreed with the participant reduced conformity by almost 80 percent. This finding, however, does not tell us why the presence of an ally was so effective. Was it because he or she *agreed* with the participant or because he or she *disagreed* with the majority? In other words, were the views of the participants strengthened because a dissenting confederate offered validating *information* or because dissent per se reduced *normative* pressures?

A series of experiments explored these two possibilities. In one, Vernon Allen and John Levine (1969) led participants to believe they were working together with four confederates. Three of these others consistently agreed on the wrong judgment. The fourth either followed the majority, agreed with the participant, or made a third judgment, which was also incorrect. This last variation was the most interesting: Even when the confederate did not validate their own judgment, participants conformed less often to the majority. In another study, Allen and Levine (1971) varied the competence of the ally. Some participants received support from an average person. In contrast, others found themselves supported by someone who wore very thick glasses and complained that he could not see the visual displays. Not a very reassuring ally, right? Wrong. Even though participants derived less comfort from this supporter than from one who seemed more competent at the task, his presence still reduced their level of conformity.

Two important conclusions follow from this research. First, it is substantially more difficult for people to stand alone for their convictions than to be part of even a tiny minority. Second, *any* dissent—whether it validates an individual's opinion or not—can break the spell cast by a unanimous majority and reduce the normative pressures to conform.

Age and Sex Differences   We all know some people who conform more than others. Asch found individual differences in his research. Attempts to identify

"The young always have the same problem—how to rebel and conform at the same time. They have now solved this by defying their parents and copying one another."

—Quentin Crisp

personality traits that breed conformity, however, have met with little success. Conformist traits may exist, but the effects on behavior vary from one situation to another. Consistent with the interactionist perspective described in the introductory chapter, someone who conforms in one setting may behave autonomously in another setting (Marlowe & Gergen, 1969; Moscovici, 1985).

Although personality factors are hard to pin down, there are age differences in conformity. Many parents know, for example, that their adolescent sons and daughters are all too quick to turn to peers for guidance on how to dress, what music to listen to, and how to behave in ways that are "cool." Are students in junior and senior high school more vulnerable to peer pressure than younger children or adults? The answer is yes, at least during the early stages of adolescence. Thomas Berndt (1979) asked students in grades 3, 6, 9, and 12 how they would react if friends tried to get them to see a movie, help a new kid on the block, cheat on a test, soap windows on Halloween, or participate in other activities. As shown in Figure 7.5, conformity rose steadily, peaked in the ninth grade, and then declined. The tendency to conform is weaker for actions that are immoral or illegal, but young adolescents are particularly at risk, wanting desperately to "fit in" (Brown et al., 1986; Gavin & Furman, 1989).

Are there also gender differences in conformity? Based on Asch's initial studies, social psychologists used to think that women, once considered the "weaker" sex, conform more than men. In light of more recent research, however, it appears that two additional factors have to be considered. First, sex differences depend on how comfortable people are with the experimental task. Frank Sistrunk and John McDavid (1971) had male and female participants answer questions on stereotypically masculine, feminine, and gender-neutral topics. Along with each question, participants were told the percentage of others who agreed or disagreed. Although females conformed to the contrived majority more on the masculine items, males conformed more on the feminine items (there were no sex differences on the neutral questions). This finding suggests that one's familiarity with the issue at hand, not gender, is what affects conformity. Ask about football or video war games, and most women acquiesce more than most men. Ask about family planning and fashion design, and the pattern is reversed (Eagly & Carli, 1981).

A second factor is the type of social pressure people face. As a general rule, sex differences are weak and unreliable. But there is an important exception: In face-to-face encounters, where people must openly disagree with each other, small differences do emerge. In fact, when participants think they are being observed, women conform more and men conform less than they do in a more private situation (Eagly & Chravala, 1986; Eagly et al., 1981). Why does being "in public" create such a divergence in behavior? Alice Eagly (1987) argues that in front of others, people worry about how they come across and feel pressured to behave in ways that are viewed as acceptable within traditional gender-role constraints. At least in public, men make it a point to behave with fierce independence and autonomy, while women play a gentler, more docile role.

Cultural Influences   Cultures vary in their implicit rules of conduct, or social norms. In *Do's and Taboos Around the World*, Axtell (1993) warns world travelers about some of these differences. Dine in an Indian home, he notes, and you should leave food on the plate to show the host that the portions were generous and that

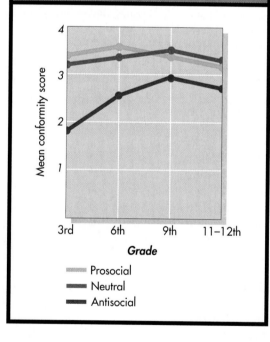

FIGURE 7.5   Conformity in Childhood and Adolescence

Students in grades 3, 6, 9, and 12 reported on how they would react if pressured by peers to participate in certain activities. As shown, conformity rose steadily, peaked in the ninth grade, and then declined. Particularly for young adolescents, who want desperately to fit in—in the way they act, dress, and wear their hair—it's difficult to "just say no." *(Berndt, 1979.)*

you had enough to eat. Yet as a dinner guest in Bolivia, you would show your appreciation by cleaning your plate. Shop in an outdoor market in Iraq, and you should expect to negotiate the price of everything you buy. Plan an appointment in Brazil, and the person you're scheduled to meet is likely to be late. Nothing personal. Even the way we space ourselves from each other is culturally determined. Americans, Canadians, British, and Northern Europeans keep a polite distance between themselves and others—and feel "crowded" by the touchier, nose-to-nose style of the French, Greeks, Arabs, Mexicans, and people of South America.

Just as cultures differ in their social norms, so too do they differ in the extent to which people adhere to those norms. As we saw in Chapter 3, there are two different cultural orientations toward persons and their relationships to groups. Some cultures value **individualism**—and the virtues of independence, autonomy, and self-reliance, while others value **collectivism**—and the virtues of interdependence, cooperation, and social harmony. Under the banner of individualism, personal goals take priority over group allegiances. Yet in collectivistic cultures, the person is, first and foremost, a loyal member of a family, team, company, church, and state.

What determines whether a culture becomes individualistic or collectivistic? Speculating on the origins of these orientations, Harry Triandis (1995) suggests that there are three key factors. The first is the *complexity* of a society. As people come to live in more complex industrialized societies (compared, for example, with a life of food gathering among desert nomads), there are more groups to identify with, which means less loyalty to any one group and a greater focus on personal rather than collective goals. Second is the *affluence* of a society. As people begin to prosper, they gain financial independence from each other, a condition that promotes social independence as well as mobility and a focus on personal rather than collective goals. The third factor is *heterogeneity*. Societies that are homogeneous or "tight" (where members share the same language, religion, and social customs) tend to be rigid and intolerant of those who veer from the norm. Societies that are culturally diverse or "loose" (where two or more cultures coexist) are more permissive of dissent—thus allowing for more individual expression.

Research shows that autonomy and independence are most highly valued in the United States, Australia, Great Britain, Canada, and the Netherlands, in that order. In contrast, many cultures of Asia, Africa, and South America value social harmony and "fitting in" for the sake of the community (Hofstede, 1980). Among the Bantu of Zimbabwe, an African people in which deviance is scorned, 51 percent of the participants placed in an Asch-like study conformed—more than the number typically obtained in the United States (Whittaker & Meade, 1967). In

These photographs were taken of "average-income" families posing in front of their homes and material possessions. Representing the individualistic orientation common among affluent societies is the Skeen family of Pearland, Texas (left). Representing the collectivist orientation found in more impoverished societies is the Natoma family of Kouakourou, Mali (right).

individualism A cultural orientation in which independence, autonomy, and self-reliance take priority over group allegiances.

collectivism A cultural orientation in which interdependence, cooperation, and social harmony take priority over personal goals.

fact, John Berry (1979) compared participants from seventeen cultures and found that conformity rates ranged from a low of 18 percent among Inuit hunters of Baffin Island to a high of 60 percent among village-living Temne farmers of West Africa. More recent analyses have shown that conformity rates are generally higher in cultures that are collectivistic rather than individualistic in their orientation (Bond & Smith, 1996).

Minority Influence

There's a funny episode of the TV show *Seinfeld* in which Elaine publicly admits that she did not like the award-winning film *The English Patient*. As if she had just confessed to a heinous crime, she lost her friend, her boyfriend, and then her job.

It's not easy for individuals to express unpopular views or enlist support from others. Philosopher Bertrand Russell once said that "Conventional people are roused to frenzy by departure from convention, largely because they regard such departure as criticism of themselves." He may have been right. Although people who stand up for their beliefs against the majority are generally seen as competent and honest, they are also disliked and often rejected (Bassili & Provencal, 1988; Levine, 1989).

Resisting the pressure to conform and maintaining one's independence may be socially difficult, but it is not impossible. History's famous heroes, villains, and creative minds are the living proof: Joan of Arc, Muhammad, Charles Darwin, and Gandhi, to name just a few, were dissenters of their time who continue to capture the imagination. So are some of the people of everyday life who make waves and rock boats. In his book *The Dissenters*, anthropologist Langston Gwaltney (1986) interviewed "ordinary" nonconformists such as an Irish man who befriended African Americans in a racist community, a New England grandmother who risked arrest to protest nuclear weapons, and a group of nuns who sued their church. Then there's human behavior in the laboratory. Social psychologists were so intrigued by Asch's initial finding that participants conformed 37 percent of the time that textbooks such as this one routinely refer to "Asch's conformity study." Yet the overlooked flip side of the coin is that Asch's participants refused to acquiesce 63 percent of the time—thus also indicating the power of independence (Friend et al., 1990).

In Twelve Angry Men, *actor Henry Fonda single-handedly convinces eleven fellow jurors to return a not-guilty verdict. Illustrating Moscovici's theory of minority influence, Fonda was persuasive by arguing a consistent position—without wavering.*

Twelve Angry Men, a classic film starring Henry Fonda, provides a good illustration of how a lone dissenter can resist the pressure to conform—and convince others to follow. Almost as soon as the jury room door closes, the jury in this film takes a show-of-hands vote. The result is an eleven-to-one majority in favor of conviction, with Fonda the lone holdout. Through ninety minutes of heated deliberation, Fonda works relentlessly to plant a seed of doubt in the minds of his trigger-happy peers. In the end, the jury reaches a unanimous verdict: *not* guilty.

Sometimes art imitates life; sometimes it does not. In this instance, Henry Fonda's heroics are highly atypical. When it comes to jury decision making, we'll see in Chapter 12 that the majority usually wins. Yet in juries, as in other small groups, there are occasional exceptions. Thanks to Serge Moscovici, Edwin Hollander, and others, we now know quite a bit about **minority influence** and about the strategies that effective nonconformists use to act as agents of social change (Hollander, 1985; Maass & Clark, 1984; Moscovici, 1980; Mugny & Perez, 1991).

The Power of Style   According to Moscovici, majorities are powerful by virtue of their sheer *numbers* and inherent power, while nonconformists derive power from the *style* of their behavior. It is not just what they say that matters, but how they say it. To exert influence, says Moscovici, those in the minority must be forceful, persistent, and unwavering in support of their position. Yet at the same time, they must appear flexible and open-minded. Confronted with a consistent but evenhanded dissenter, members of the majority will sit up, take notice, and rethink their own positions.

Why should a consistent behavioral style prove effective? One possible reason is that unwavering repetition draws attention from those in the mainstream, which is a necessary first step to social influence. Another possibility is that consistency signals that the dissenter is unlikely to yield, which leads those in the majority to feel pressured to seek compromise. A third possible reason is that when confronted with someone who has the self-confidence and dedication to take an unpopular stand without backing down, people assume that he or she must have a point. Unless a dissenter is perceived in negative terms—as biased, obstinate, or just plain crazy—this situation stimulates others to re-examine their own views (Moskowitz, 1996). Of course, it helps to be seen as part of "us" rather than "them." Research shows that dissenters have more influence when people identify with them—and perceive them to be similar in ways that are positive and relevant (Turner, 1991; Wood et al., 1996).

Based on a meta-analysis of ninety-seven experiments investigating minority influence, Wendy Wood and her colleagues (1994) concluded that there is strong support for the consistency hypothesis. In one classic study, for example, Moscovici and others (1969) turned Asch's procedure on its head by confronting people with a *minority* of confederates who made incorrect judgments. In groups of six, participants took part in what was supposed to be a study of color perception. They viewed a series of slides—all blue, but varying in intensity. For each slide, the participants took turns naming the color. The task was simple, but two confederates announced that the slides were green. When the confederates were *consistent*—that is, when both made incorrect green judgments for all slides—they had a surprising degree of influence. About a third of all participants incorrectly reported seeing at least one green slide, and 8 percent of all responses were incorrect. Subsequent research confirmed that the perception of consistency is a key factor.

Based on the fact that dissent often breeds hostility, Edwin Hollander (1958) recommends a different approach. Hollander warns that people who seek positions of leadership or challenge a group without first becoming accepted full-fledged members of that group run the risk that their opinions will fall on deaf ears. As an alternative to Moscovici's consistency strategy, Hollander says that to influence a majority, people should first conform in order to establish their credentials as competent insiders. By becoming members of the mainstream, they accumulate **idiosyncrasy credits,** or "brownie points." Then, as soon as they have collected enough good will within the group, a certain amount of their deviance will be tolerated. Several studies have shown that this "first conform, then dissent" strategy, like the "consistent dissent" approach, can be effective (Bray et al., 1982; Lortie-Lussier, 1987).

A Chip off the Old Block?   Regardless of which strategy is used, minority influence is a force to be reckoned with. But does it work just like the process of confor-

minority influence The process by which dissenters produce change within a group.

idiosyncrasy credits Interpersonal "credits" that a person earns by following group norms.

mity, or is there something different about the way that minorities and majorities effect change? There are two opposing viewpoints. Some theorists believe that a *single process* accounts for both directions of social influence—that minority influence is just like a "chip off the old block" (Latané & Wolf, 1981; Tanford & Penrod, 1984). Others have taken a *dual-process* approach (Moscovici, 1980; Nemeth, 1986). In this second view, majorities and minorities both exert influence, but in very different ways. Majorities, because they have power and control, elicit public conformity by bringing stressful normative pressures to bear on the individual. But minorities, because they are seen as seriously committed to their views, produce a deeper and more lasting form of private conformity, or *conversion*, by leading others to rethink their original positions.

To evaluate these competing single- and dual-process theories, researchers have compared the effects of majority and minority viewpoints on participants who are otherwise neutral on an issue in dispute. On the basis of this research, two conclusions can be drawn. First, the relative impact of majorities and minorities depends on whether the judgment that is being made is objective or subjective, a matter of fact or opinion. In a study conducted in Italy, Ann Maass and her colleagues (Maass, Volpato, & Mucchi-Faina, 1996) found that majorities have greater influence on factual questions, for which only one answer is correct ("What percentage of its raw oil does Italy import from Venezuela?"), but that minorities exert equal impact on opinion questions, for which there is a range of acceptable responses ("What percentage of its raw oil *should* Italy import from Venezuela?"). People feel freer to stray from the mainstream on matters of opinion—when there is no right or wrong answer.

The second conclusion is that the relative effects of majority and minority viewpoints depend on how conformity is measured. To be sure, majorities have a decisive upper hand on direct or public measures of conformity. After all, people are reluctant to stray conspicuously from the group norm. But on more indirect or private measures of conformity—when participants can respond without a fear of appearing deviant—minorities exert a strong impact (Clark & Maass, 1990; Moscovici & Personnaz, 1991; Wood et al., 1996). As Moscovici so cogently argued, each of us is changed in a meaningful but subtle way by minority opinion. Because of social pressures, we may be too intimidated to admit it; but the change is unmistakable (Wood et al., 1994).

According to Charlan Nemeth (1986), dissenters serve a highly valuable purpose. Sometimes, their views are correct; at other times, they are not. But simply by their willingness to stay independent, minorities can force other group members to think more carefully, more openly, and more creatively about a problem, thus enhancing the quality of a group's decision making. In one study, participants exposed to a minority viewpoint on how to solve anagram problems later found more novel solutions themselves (Nemeth & Kwan, 1987). In a second study, those exposed to a consistent minority view on how to recall information later recalled more words from a list they were trying to memorize (Nemeth et al., 1990). And in a third study, interacting groups that contained one dissenting confederate produced more original analyses of complex business problems (Van Dyne & Saavedra, 1996).

Compliance

compliance Changes in
behavior that are elicited
by direct requests.

I n conformity situations, people follow implicit group norms. But another common form of social influence occurs when others make direct *explicit* requests of us in the hope that we will comply. Situations calling for **compliance** take many forms. These include a friend's request for help, sheepishly prefaced by the question "Can you do me a favor?" They also include a salesperson's pitch for business, prefaced by the dangerous words "Have I got a deal for you!" Sometimes, the request itself is up front and direct; what you see is what you get. At other times, it is part of a subtle and more elaborate manipulation.

How do people get others to comply with self-serving requests? How do police interrogators get crime suspects to confess? How do TV evangelists draw millions of dollars in contributions for their ministries? How do *you* exert influence over others? Do you use threats, promises, deceit, politeness, or reason? Do you hint, coax, sulk, negotiate, throw tantrums, or pull rank whenever you can? The compliance strategies we use depend on how well we know a person, on our status within a relationship, and on our personality, our culture, and the nature of the request (Bisanz & Rule, 1989; Buss et al., 1987; Holtgraves & Yang, 1992).

By observing the masters of influence—advertisers, fund raisers, politicians, and business leaders—social psychologists have learned a great deal about the subtle but effective strategies that are commonly used. What we see is that people often get others to comply with their requests by setting traps. Once caught in one of these traps, the unwary victim often finds it difficult to escape.

The Discourse of Making Requests

In a memorable scene in the film *Beverly Hills Cop II*, comedian Eddie Murphy, speaking at a rate far too fast for anyone to comprehend, manages to convince a team of builders to abandon work on a house that he wants to use for the weekend. This scene illustrates the rapid-fire sales pitch at its best. The other guys never had a chance. Murphy capitalized on the fact that fast talkers are assumed to be intelligent and well informed (Apple et al., 1979). He also benefited from the element of surprise. Caught off guard, people tend to capitulate quickly. For example, when New York City subway passengers were forewarned that someone might ask for their seats, only 28 percent said yes when later approached. When the request caught the passengers by surprise, however, the compliance rate doubled to 56 percent (Milgram & Sabini, 1978).

People can also be disarmed by the phrasing of a request. As illustrated by Eddie Murphy's masterful use of doubletalk, *how* you ask for something can be more important than *what* you ask for. Consider, for example, requests that sound reasonable but offer no real reason for compliance. Ellen Langer and her colleagues (1978) found that words alone can sometimes trick us into submission. In their research, an experimenter approached people who were using a library copying machine and asked to cut in. Three different versions of the same request were used. In one, participants were simply asked, "Excuse me. I have five pages. May I use the Xerox machine?" In a second version, the request was justified by the added phrase "because I'm in a rush." As you would expect, more participants stepped aside when the request was justified (94 percent) than when it was not (60 percent). A third version of the request, however, suggests that the reason offered had little to do with the increase in compliance. In this case, participants heard the following: "Excuse me. I have five pages. May I use the Xerox machine because I have to make some copies?" If you read this request closely, you'll see that it really offered no reason at all. Yet 93 percent in this condition complied! It was as if the appearance of a reason, triggered by the word *because*, was all that was necessary. Indeed, Langer (1989) finds that the mind is often on "automatic pilot," as we respond

Con artists prosper from the tendency for people to respond mindlessly to requests that sound reasonable but offer no real basis for compliance.

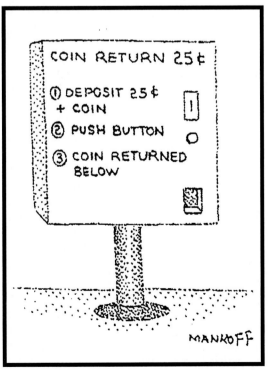

mindlessly to words without fully processing the information they are supposed to convey. At least for requests that are small, "sweet little nothings" may be enough to win compliance.

It is interesting that although the state of mindlessness can make us vulnerable to compliance, it can also have the opposite effect. For example, many city dwellers automatically, as in a reflex action, walk past panhandlers on the street looking for a handout. According to Michael Santos and his colleagues (1994), the way to increase compliance in such situations is to disrupt this mindless refusal response by making a request that is so unusual that it piques the target person's interest. To test the effect of this technique, they hired a confederate to approach people on the street and make a request that was either typical ("Can you spare a quarter?") or atypical ("Can you spare 37 cents?"). The result: Atypical pleas elicited more comments and questions from those who were targeted—and produced a 60 percent increase in the number of people who gave money.

The Norm of Reciprocity

A simple, unstated, but powerful rule of social behavior known as the *norm of reciprocity* dictates that we treat others as they have treated us (Gouldner, 1960). On the negative side, this norm can be used to sanction retaliation against those who cause us harm: "An eye for an eye." On the positive side, it leads us to feel obligated to repay others for acts of kindness. Thus, when we receive gifts, invitations, and free samples, we usually go out of our way to return the favor.

The norm of reciprocity contributes to the predictability and fairness of social interaction. However, it can also be used to exploit us. Dennis Regan (1971) examined this possibility in the following study. Individuals were brought together with a confederate—who was trained to act in a likable or unlikable manner—for an experiment on "aesthetics." In one condition, the confederate did the participant an unsolicited favor. He left during a break and returned with two bottles of Coca-Cola, one for himself and the other for the participant. In a second condition, he returned from the break empty-handed. In a third condition, participants were treated to a Coke—but by the experimenter, not the confederate. The confederate then told participants in all conditions that he was selling raffle tickets at twenty-five cents apiece and asked if they would be willing to buy any. On the average, participants bought more raffle tickets when the confederate had earlier brought them a soft drink than when he had not. The norm of reciprocity was so strong that they returned the favor even when the confederate was not otherwise a likable character. In fact, participants in this condition spent an average of forty-three cents on raffle tickets. At a time when soft drinks cost less than a quarter, the confederate made a handsome quick profit on his investment!

Clearly, the norm of reciprocity can be used to trap us into compliance. But does receiving a favor make us feel indebted for an indefinite period, or is there a time limit to this social rule of thumb? In an experiment designed to answer this question, Jerry Burger and others (1997) used Regan's soft drink favor and had the confederate try to "cash in" with a request either immediately or one week later. The result: Compliance levels increased in the immediate condition but not after a full week had passed. People may feel compelled to reciprocate, but that feeling—at least for small acts of kindness—is relatively short-lived.

Some people are more likely than others to exploit the norm of reciprocity. According to Martin Greenberg and David Westcott (1983), individuals who use reciprocity to elicit compliance are called "creditors" because they always try to keep others in their debt so they can cash in when necessary. On a questionnaire that measures *reciprocation ideology*, people are identified as creditors if they agree with such statements as "If someone does you a favor, it's good to repay that person with a greater favor." On the receiving end, some people more than others try not to accept favors that might later set them up to be exploited. On a scale that measures *reciprocation wariness*, people are said to be wary if they express the suspicion, for example, that "Asking for another's help gives them power over your life" (Eisenberger et al., 1987).

Setting Traps: Sequential Request Strategies

People who raise money or sell for a living know that it often takes more than a single plea to win over a potential donor or customer. Social psychologists share this knowledge and have studied several compliance techniques that are based on making two or more related requests. *Click!* The first request sets the trap. *Snap!* The second captures the prey. In a fascinating book entitled *Influence*, Robert Cialdini (1993) describes a number of sequential request tactics in vivid detail. These methods are presented in the following pages.

The Foot in the Door   Folk wisdom has it that one way to get a person to comply with a sizable request is to start small. First devised by traveling salespeople peddling vacuum cleaners, hair brushes, cosmetics, magazine subscriptions, and encyclopedias, the trick is to somehow get your "foot in the door." The expression need not be taken literally, of course. The point of the **foot-in-the-door technique** is to break the ice with a small initial request that the customer can't easily refuse. Once that first commitment is elicited, the chances are increased that another, larger request will succeed.

Jonathan Freedman and Scott Fraser (1966) tested the impact of this technique in a series of field experiments. In one, an experimenter pretending to be employed by a consumer organization telephoned a group of female homemakers in Palo Alto, California, and asked if they would be willing to answer some questions about household products. Those who consented were then asked a few innocuous questions and thanked for their assistance. Three days later, the experimenter called back and made a considerable, almost outrageous, request. He asked the women if they would allow a handful of men into their homes for two hours to rummage through their drawers and cupboards so they could take an inventory of household products.

The foot-in-the-door technique proved to be very effective. When participants were confronted with only the very intrusive request, 22 percent consented. Yet among those surveyed earlier, the rate of agreement more than doubled, to 53 percent. This basic result has now been repeated over and over again. People are more likely to donate time, money, blood, the use of their home, and other resources once they have been induced to go along with a small initial request. Although the effect is seldom as dramatic as that obtained by Freedman and Fraser, it does appear in a variety of circumstances (Beaman et al., 1983; Dillard, 1991).

The practical implications of the foot-in-the-door technique are obvious. But *why* does it work? Several explanations have been suggested. One that seems plausible is based on self-perception theory—that people infer their attitudes by observing their own behavior. This explanation suggests that a two-step process is at work (DeJong, 1979). First, by observing your own behavior in the initial situation, you come to see yourself as the kind of person who is generally cooperative when approached with that kind of request. Second, when confronted with the more burdensome request, you seek to respond in ways that maintain this new self-image. By this logic, the foot-in-the-door technique should succeed only when you attribute an initial act of compliance to your own personal characteristics.

Research evidence generally supports this explanation. If the first request is too trivial or if participants are paid for the first act of compliance, they won't come

foot-in-the-door technique A two-step compliance technique in which an influencer sets the stage for the real request by first getting a person to comply with a much smaller request.

to view themselves as inherently cooperative. Under these conditions, the technique does *not* work (Seligman et al., 1976; Zuckerman et al., 1979). Likewise, the effect occurs only when people are motivated to be consistent with their self-images. If participants are unhappy with what the initial behavior implies about them, if they are too young to appreciate the implications, or if they don't care about behaving in ways that are personally consistent, then again the technique does not work (Eisenberg et al., 1987; Kraut, 1973). These results suggest that the foot may open the door by altering *self*-perceptions. It's also possible, however, that the technique works by getting people to define the *situation* they're in as one that calls for helpfulness (Gorassini & Olson, 1995).

Knowing that a foot in the door increases compliance is both exciting and troubling—exciting for the owner of the foot, but troubling for the owner of the door. As Cialdini (1993) put it, "You can use small commitments to manipulate a person's self-image; you can use them to turn citizens into 'public servants,' prospects into 'customers,' prisoners into 'collaborators.' And once you've got a person's self-image where you want it, he or she should comply *naturally* with a whole range of requests that are consistent with this new self-view" (p. 64).

Low-Balling   Another two-step trap, perhaps the most unscrupulous of all compliance techniques, is also based on the "start small" idea. Imagine yourself in the following situation. You're at a local automobile dealership. After some negotiation, the salesperson offers a great price on the car of your choice. You cast aside other considerations and shake hands on the deal; and as the salesperson goes off to "write it up," you begin to feel the thrill of owning the car of your dreams. Absorbed in fantasy, you are interrupted by the sudden return of the salesperson. "I'm sorry," he says. "The manager would not approve the sale. We have to raise the price by another $450. I'm afraid that's the best we can do." As the victim of an all-too-common trick known as **low-balling,** you are now faced with a difficult decision. On the one hand, you are wild about the car. You've already enjoyed the pleasure of thinking it's yours; and the more you think about it, the better it looks. On the other hand, you don't want to pay more than you bargained for, and you have an uneasy feeling in the pit of your stomach that you're being duped. What do you do?

Salespeople who use this tactic are betting that you'll go ahead with the purchase despite the added cost. If the behavior of research participants is any indication, they are often right. In one study, experimenters phoned introductory psychology students and asked if they would be willing to participate in a study for extra credit. Some were told up front that the session would begin at the uncivilized hour of 7 A.M. Knowing that, only 31 percent volunteered. But other participants were low-balled. Only *after* they agreed to participate did the experimenter inform them of the 7 A.M. starting time. Would that be okay? Whether or not it was, the procedure achieved its objective—the sign-up rate rose to 56 percent (Cialdini et al., 1978).

Low-balling is an interesting technique. Surely, once the low ball has been thrown, many recipients suspect that they were misled. Yet they go along. Why? The reason appears to be based on the psychology of commitment (Kiesler, 1971). Once people make a particular decision, they justify it to themselves by thinking of all its positive aspects. As they become increasingly committed to a course of action, they grow more resistant to changing their mind, even if the initial reasons for the action have been changed or withdrawn entirely. In the automobile dealership scenario, you might very well have decided to purchase the car because of the price. But then you would have thought about its sleek appearance, the leather interior, the moon roof, and the CD player. By the time you learned that the price would be more than you'd bargained for, it was too late—you were already hooked.

Low-balling also produces another form of commitment. When people do not suspect duplicity, they feel a nagging sense of unfulfilled obligation to the person with whom they negotiated. Thus, even though the salesperson was unable to

low-balling A two-step compliance technique in which the influencer secures agreement with a request but then increases the size of that request by revealing hidden costs.

complete the original deal, you might feel obligated to buy anyway, having already agreed to make the purchase. This commitment to the other person may account for why low-balling works better when the second request is made by the same person than by someone else (Burger & Petty, 1981).

For consumer advice on how to buy a car without falling into the compliance traps often set by dealers, visit the Edmunds Automobile Buyer's Guide (www.edmunds.com)

The Door in the Face   Although shifting from an initial small request to a larger one can be effective, as in the foot-in-the-door and low-ball techniques, oddly enough the opposite is also true. In *Influence*, Cialdini (1993) describes the time he was approached by a Boy Scout and asked to buy two five-dollar tickets to an upcoming circus. Having better things to do with his time and money, he declined. Then the boy asked if he would be interested in buying chocolate bars at a dollar apiece. Even though he doesn't like chocolate, Cialdini—an expert on social influence—bought two of them! After a moment's reflection, he realized what had happened. Whether the Boy Scout planned it that way or not, Cialdini had fallen for what is known as the **door-in-the-face technique.**

The technique is as simple as it sounds. An individual makes an initial request that is so large it is sure to be rejected and then comes back with a second, more reasonable request. Will the second request fare better after the first one has been declined? Plagued by the sight of uneaten chocolate bars, Cialdini and his colleagues (1975) evaluated the effectiveness of the door-in-the-face technique. They stopped college students on campus and asked if they would volunteer to work without pay at a counseling center for juvenile delinquents. The commitment of time would be forbidding: roughly two hours a week for the next two years! Not surprisingly, everyone who was approached politely slammed the proverbial door in the experimenter's face. But then the experimenter followed up with a more modest proposal, asking the students if they would be willing to take a group of delinquents on a two-hour trip to the zoo. The strategy worked like a charm. Only 17 percent of the students confronted with *only* the second request agreed. But of those who initially declined the first request, 50 percent said yes to the zoo trip. You should note that the door-in-the-face technique does not elicit only empty promises. Most research participants who comply subsequently do what they've agreed to do (Cialdini & Ascani, 1976).

Why is the door-in-the-face technique such an effective trap? One possibility involves the principle of *perceptual contrast:* To the person exposed to a very large initial request, the second request "looks smaller." Two dollars' worth of candy bars is not bad compared with ten dollars for circus tickets. Likewise, taking a group of kids to the zoo seems trivial compared with two years of volunteer work. As intuitively sensible as this explanation seems, Cialdini and his colleagues (1975) concluded that perceptual contrast is only partly responsible for the effect. When participants heard the large request without actually having to reject it, their rate of compliance with the second request (25 percent) was only slightly larger than the 17 percent rate of compliance exhibited by those who heard only the small request.

A second, more compelling explanation for the effect involves *reciprocal concessions.* A close cousin of the reciprocity norm, this refers to the pressure to respond to changes in a bargaining position. When an individual backs down from a large request to a smaller one, we view that move as a concession that we should match by our own compliance. Thus, the door-in-the-face technique does not work if the second request is made by a different person (Cialdini et al., 1975). Nor does it work if the first request is so extreme that it comes across as an insincere "first offer" (Schwarzwald et al., 1979). On an emotional level, refusing to help on one request may trigger feelings of guilt—which we can reduce by complying with the second, smaller request (O'Keefe & Figge, 1997).

That's Not All, Folks!   If the notion of reciprocal concessions is correct, then a person shouldn't actually have to refuse the initial offer in order for the shift to a smaller request to work. Indeed, another familiar sales strategy manages to use

An effective way to get someone to do you a favor is to make a first request that is so large the person is sure to reject it. **True.**

door-in-the-face technique A two-step compliance technique in which an influencer prefaces the real request with one that is so large that it is rejected.

concession without first eliciting refusal. In this strategy, a product is offered at a particular price; but then, before the buyer has a chance to respond, the seller adds, "And that's not all!" At that point, either the original price is reduced, or a bonus is offered to sweeten the pot. The seller, of course, intends all along to make the so-called concession.

This ploy, known as the **that's-not-all technique,** seems awfully transparent, right? Surely, no one falls for it, right? Jerry Burger (1986) was not so sure. He predicted that people are more likely to make a purchase when a deal seems to have improved than when the same deal is offered right from the start. To test this hypothesis, Burger set up a booth at a campus fair and sold cupcakes. Some customers who approached the table were told that the cupcakes cost 75 cents each. Others were told that they cost a dollar; but then, before they could respond, the price was reduced to 75 cents. Rationally speaking, Burger's manipulation did not affect the ultimate price, so it should not have affected sales. But it did. When customers were led to believe that the final price represented a reduction, sales increased from 44 to 73 percent.

At this point, let's step back and look at the various compliance techniques described in this section. All of them are based on a two-step process that involves a shift from a request of one size to another. What differs is whether the small or large request comes first and how the transition between steps is made (see Table 7.2). Moreover, all these strategies work in subtle ways by manipulating the target person's self-image, commitment to the product, feelings of obligation to the seller, or perceptions of the real request. It is even possible to increase compliance by making a chain of requests that use a combination of techniques (Goldman, 1986) or by prefacing the request with "How are you feeling?"—a question that tends to elicit a favorable first response from strangers (Howard, 1990a). When you consider these various traps, you have to wonder whether it's ever possible to escape.

that's-not-all technique A two-step compliance technique in which the influencer begins with an inflated request, then decreases its apparent size by offering a discount or bonus.

TABLE 7.2   Sequential Request Strategies

Various compliance techniques are based on a sequence of two related requests. *Click!* The first request sets the trap. *Snap!* The second captures the prey. Research has shown that the four sequential request strategies summarized in this table are all effective.

Request Shifts	Technique	Description
From small to large	Foot in the door	Begin with a very small request; secure agreement; then make a separate, larger request.
	Low-balling	Secure agreement with a request, and then increase the size of that request by revealing hidden costs.
From large to small	Door in the face	Begin with a very large request that will be rejected; then follow that up with a more modest request.
	That's not all	Begin with a somewhat inflated request; than immediately decrease the apparent size of that request by offering a discount or bonus.

Assertiveness: When People Say No

Robert Cialdini (1993) opened his book with a confession: "I can admit it freely now. All my life I've been a patsy." As a past victim of compliance traps, Cialdini is not alone. Many people find it difficult to be assertive in interpersonal situations. Faced with an unreasonable request from a friend, spouse, or stranger, they become anxious at the mere thought of putting a foot down and refusing to comply. Indeed, there are times when it is uncomfortable for anyone to say no. However, just as we can maintain our autonomy in the face of conformity pressures, we can also refuse direct requests—even clever ones. The trap may be set, but you don't have to get caught.

According to Cialdini, the ability to resist the pressures of compliance rests, first and foremost, on being vigilant. If a stranger hands you a gift and then launches into a sales pitch, you should recognize the tactic for what it is and not feel indebted by the norm of reciprocity. And if you strike a deal with a salesperson who later reneges on the terms, you should be aware that you're being thrown a low ball. Indeed, that is exactly what happened to one of the authors of this book. After a full Saturday afternoon of careful negotiation at a local car dealer, Mr. and Mrs. Kassin finally came to terms on a price. Minutes later, however, the salesman returned with the news that the manager would not approve the deal. The cost of an air conditioner, which was to be included, would now have to be added on. Familiar with the research, Saul turned to his wife and exclaimed, "Carol, it's a trick; they're low-balling us!" Realizing what had happened, Carol was furious. She went straight to the manager and made such a scene in front of other customers that he backed down and honored the original deal.

What happened in this instance? Why did recognizing the attempted manipulation produce such anger and resistance? As this story illustrates, compliance techniques work smoothly only if they are hidden from view. The problem is not only that they are attempts to influence us but that they are based on deception. Flattery, gifts, and other ploys often elicit compliance—but not if they are perceived as insincere (Jones, 1964) and not if the target has a high level of reciprocity wariness (Eisenberger et al., 1987). Likewise, the sequential request traps are powerful to the extent that they are subtle and cannot be seen for what they are (Schwarzwald et al., 1979). People don't like to be hustled. Indeed, feeling manipulated leads us to react with anger, psychological reactance, and stubborn noncompliance…unless the request is a command and the requester is a figure of authority.

"Knowledge is power, and if you know when a clever technique is being used on you, then it becomes easier to ignore it."

—Burke Leon

"Bernie's problem is his technique draws attention to itself."

Compliance techniques are powerful only if they are not transparent.
Robert Weber © 1987 from The New Yorker Collection. All Rights Reserved.

Obedience

Allen Funt, the creator and producer of the original TV program *Candid Camera*, spent as much time observing human behavior in the real world as most psychologists do. When asked what he learned from his people-watching, he replied, "The worst thing, and I see it over and over, is how easily people can be led by any kind of authority figure, or even the most minimal signs

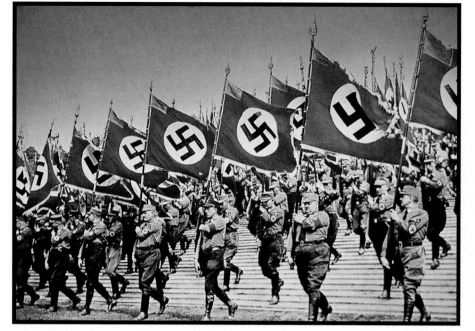

Taken to the extreme, blind obedience can have devastating results. In World War II, Nazi officials killed millions, many said, "because I was just following orders."

"Far more, and far more hideous, crimes have been committed in the name of obedience than have ever been committed in the name of rebellion."

—C. P. Snow

obedience Behavior change produced by the commands of authority.

of authority." He went on to cite the time he put up a road sign that read "Delaware Closed Today." The reaction? "Motorists didn't question it. Instead they asked, 'Is Jersey open?'" (Zimbardo, 1985, p. 47).

Funt is right about the way we react to authority. Taught from birth that it's important to respect legitimate forms of leadership, people think twice before defying parents, teachers, employers, coaches, and government officials. In fact, children seem to understand at a young age that certain authority figures have power in some domains but not others (Laupa & Turiel, 1993). The problem is, mere symbols of authority—titles, uniforms, badges, or the trappings of success, even without the necessary credentials—can sometimes turn ordinary people into docile servants. Leonard Bickman (1974) demonstrated this phenomenon in a series of studies in which a male research assistant stopped passers-by on the streets of Brooklyn and ordered them to do something unusual. Sometimes, he pointed to a paper bag on the ground and said, "Pick up this bag for me!" At other times, he pointed to an individual standing beside a parked car and said, "This fellow is over-parked at the meter but doesn't have any change. Give him a dime!" Would anyone really take this guy seriously? When he was dressed in street clothes, only a third of the people stopped followed his orders. But when he wore a security guard's uniform, nearly nine out of every ten people obeyed! Even when the uniformed assistant turned the corner and walked away after issuing his command, the vast majority of passers-by followed his orders. Clearly, uniforms signify the power of authority (Bushman, 1984, 1988).

Blind **obedience** may seem funny; but if people are willing to take orders from a total stranger, how far will they go when it really matters? As the pages of history attest, the implications are sobering. In World War II, Nazi officials participated in the deaths of millions of Jews, as well as Poles, Russians, Gypsies, and homosexuals. Yet when tried for these crimes, their defense was always the same: "I was just following orders."

Surely, you may be thinking, the Holocaust was a historical anomaly that says more about the Nazis as prejudiced, frustrated, and sick individuals than about the situations that lead people in general to commit acts of destructive obedience. In *Hitler's Willing Executioners*, historian Daniel Goldhagen (1996) argues on the basis of past records that many Germans were willing anti-Semitic participants in the Holocaust—not ordinary people forced to follow orders. But two lines of evidence suggest that blaming the German people is far too simple as an explanation for what happened. First, interviews with Nazi war criminals such as the notorious Adolf Eichmann and doctors who worked in concentration camps have suggested the provocative and disturbing conclusion that these people were "utterly ordinary" (Arendt, 1963; Lifton, 1986; Von Lang & Sibyll, 1983). Second, the monstrous events of World War II do not stand alone in modern history. Even today, crimes of obedience are being committed in ruthless totalitarian regimes throughout the world (Kelman & Hamilton, 1989). On one extraordinary occasion, such obedience was carried to its limit. In 1978, nine hundred members of the People's Temple cult obeyed an order from the Reverend Jim Jones to kill themselves.

Milgram's Research: Forces of Destructive Obedience

During the time that Adolph Eichmann was being tried for his Nazi war crimes, Stanley Milgram (1963) began a dramatic series of experiments that culminated in his 1974 book *Obedience to Authority*. For many years, the ethics of this research has been the focus of much debate. Those who say it was not ethical point to the potential psychological harm to which the participants were exposed. In contrast, those who believe that Milgram's research met appropriate ethical standards emphasize the contribution it makes to our understanding of an important social problem. They conclude that, on balance, the extreme danger that destructive obedience poses for all humankind justified Milgram's unorthodox methods. Consider both sides of the debate, which were summarized in Chapter 2, and make your own judgment. Now, however, take a more personal look. Imagine yourself as one of the approximately one thousand participants who found themselves in the following situation.

The experience begins when you arrive at a Yale University laboratory and meet two men. One is the experimenter, a stern young man dressed in a gray lab coat and carrying a clipboard. The other is a middle-aged gentleman named Mr. Wallace, an accountant who is slightly overweight and average in appearance. You exchange introductions, and then the experimenter explains that you and your co-participant will take part in a study on the effects of punishment on learning. After lots have been drawn, it is determined that you will serve as the teacher and that Mr. Wallace will be the learner. So far so good.

Soon, however, the situation takes on a more ominous tone. You find out that your job is to test the learner's memory and administer electric shocks of increasing intensity whenever he makes a mistake. You are then escorted into another room, where the experimenter straps Mr. Wallace into a chair, rolls up his sleeves, attaches electrodes to his arms, and applies "electrode paste" to prevent blisters and burns. As if that isn't bad enough, you overhear Mr. Wallace telling the experimenter that he has a heart problem. The experimenter responds by conceding that the shocks will be painful but reassures Mr. Wallace that they will not cause

The shock generator used in Milgram's research is similar to the machine used in the studies of aggression described in Chapter 11. The subjects in Milgram's study were instructed to administer shocks of increasing intensity to Mr. Wallace, the confederate being strapped into his chair.

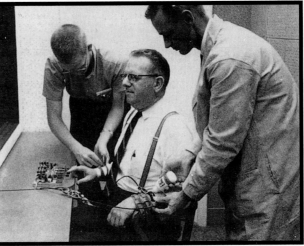

TABLE 7.3   The Learner's Protests in the Milgram Experiment

As participants administered progressively more intense shocks, they heard the learner moan, groan, protest, and complain. All participants heard the same programmed set of responses. Eventually, the learner fell silent and ceased to respond. *(Milgram, 1974.)*

75 volts	Ugh!
90 volts	Ugh!
105 volts	Ugh! *(louder)*
120 volts	Ugh! Hey this really hurts.
135 volts	Ugh!!
150 volts	Ugh!!! Experimenter! That's all. Get me out of here. I told you I had heart trouble. My heart's starting to bother me now. Get me out of here, please. My heart's starting to bother me. I refuse to go on. Let me out.
165 volts	Ugh! Let me out! *(shouting)*
180 volts	Ugh! I can't stand the pain. Let me out of here! *(shouting)*
195 volts	Ugh! Let me out of here. Let me out of here. My heart's bothering me. Let me out of here! You have no right to keep me here! Let me out! Let me out of here! Let me out! Let me out of here! My heart's bothering me. Let me out! Let me out!
210 volts	Ugh!! Experimenter! Get me out of here. I've had enough. I won't be in the experiment any more.
225 volts	Ugh!
240 volts	Ugh!
255 volts	Ugh! Get me out of here.
270 volts	*(Agonized scream.)* Let me out of here. Let me out of here. Let me out of here. Let me out. Do you hear? Let me out of here.
285 volts	*(Agonized scream.)*
300 volts	*(Agonized scream.)* I absolutely refuse to answer any more. Get me out of here. You can't hold me here. Get me out. Get me out of here.
315 volts	*(Intensely agonized scream.)* I told you I refuse to answer. I'm no longer part of this experiment.
330 volts	*(Intense and prolonged agonized scream.)* Let me out of here. Let me out of here. My heart's bothering me. Let me out, I tell you. *(Hysterically)* Let me out of here. Let me out of here. You have no right to hold me here. Let me out! Let me out! Let me out! Let me out of here! Let me out! Let me out!

"permanent tissue damage." In the meantime, you can personally vouch for the painfulness of the shocks because the experimenter stings you with one that is supposed to be mild. From there, the experimenter takes you back to the main room, where you are seated in front of a "shock generator," a machine with thirty switches that range from 15 volts, labeled "slight shock," to 450 volts, labeled "XXX."

Your role in this experiment is straightforward. First you read a list of word pairs to Mr. Wallace through a microphone. Then you test his memory with a series of multiple-choice questions. The learner answers each question by pressing one of four switches that light up signals on the shock generator. If his answer is correct, you move on to the next question. If it is incorrect, you announce the correct answer and shock him. When you press the appropriate shock switch, a red light flashes above it, relay switches click inside the machine, and you hear a loud buzzing sound go off in the learner's room. After each wrong answer, you are told, the intensity of the shock should be increased by 15 volts.

You aren't aware, of course, that the experiment is rigged and that Mr. Wallace—who is actually a confederate—is never really shocked. As far as you know, he gets zapped each time you press one of the switches. As the session proceeds, the learner makes more and more errors, leading you to work your way up the shock scale. As you reach 75, 90, and 105 volts, you hear the learner grunt in pain. At 120 volts, he begins to shout. If you're still in it at 150 volts, you hear the learner cry out, "Experimenter! That's all. Get me out of here. My heart's starting to bother me now. I refuse to go on!" Screams of agony and protest continue. At 300 volts, he says he absolutely refuses to continue. By the time you surpass 330 volts, the learner falls silent and fails to respond—not to be heard from again. Table 7.3 lists his responses in grim detail.

Somewhere along the line, you turn to the experimenter for guidance. What should I do? Don't you think I should stop? Shouldn't we at least check on him? You might even confront the experimenter head-on and refuse to continue. Yet in answer to your inquiries, the experimenter—firm in his tone and seemingly unaffected by the learner's distress—prods you along as follows:

- Please continue (or please go on).
- The experiment requires that you continue.
- It is absolutely essential that you continue.
- You have no other choice; you must go on.

What do you do? In a situation that begins to feel more and more like a bad dream, do you follow your own conscience or obey the experimenter?

Milgram described this procedure to psychiatrists, college students, and middle-class adults, and he asked them to predict how they would behave. On average, these groups estimated that they would call it quits at the 135-volt level. Not a single person thought he or she would go all the way to 450 volts. When asked to predict the percentage of *other* people who would deliver the maximum shock, those interviewed gave similar estimates. The psychiatrists estimated that only one out of a thousand people would exhibit that kind of extreme obedience. They were wrong. In Milgram's initial study, involving forty men from the surrounding New Haven community, participants exhibited an alarming degree of obedience, administering an average of twenty-seven out of thirty possible shocks. In fact, twenty-six of the forty participants—*65 percent*—delivered the ultimate punishment of 450 volts. The complete results are shown in Table 7.4.

> In experiments on obedience, most people who were ordered to administer severe shocks to an innocent person refused to do so. **False.**

The Obedient Participant   At first glance, it is easy to view these results as a lesson in the psychology of cruelty and conclude that Milgram's participants were seriously disturbed (Bierbrauer, 1979; Safer, 1980). But research does not support such a simple explanation. To begin with, those in a control group who were not prodded along by an experimenter refused to continue early in the shock sequence. Moreover, Milgram found that virtually all participants, including those who administered severe shocks, were tormented by the experience. Many of them pleaded with the experimenter to let them stop. When he refused, they went on. But in the process, they trembled, stuttered, groaned, perspired, bit their lips, and dug their fingernails into their flesh. Some participants burst into fits of nervous laughter. On one occasion, said Milgram, "we observed a [subject's] seizure so violently convulsive that it was necessary to call a halt to the experiment" (1963, p. 375).

Was Milgram's 65 percent baseline level of obedience attributable to his unique sample of male participants? Not at all. Forty women who participated in a later study exhibited precisely the same level of obedience: 65 percent threw the 450-volt switch. Before you jump to the conclusion that something was amiss in New Haven, consider the fact that Milgram's basic finding has been obtained in several different countries and with children as well as college students and older adults (Shanab & Yahya, 1977, 1978). Obedience in the Milgram situation is so universal that it led one author to ask, "Are we all Nazis?" (Askenasy, 1978).

The answer, of course, is no. An individual's character can make a difference; and some people, depending on the situation, are far more obedient than others (Blass, 1991). In the aftermath of World War II, a group of social scientists, searching for the root causes of prejudice,

TABLE 7.4 Milgram's Baseline Results

In Milgram's original experiment, participants exhibited a troubling inclination to obey blindly. This table shows the number and percentage of male participants who delivered shocks of varying maximum intensity in response to the experimenter's commands. *(Milgram, 1974.)*

	Participants Who Stopped at This Level	
Shock Level (Volts)	Number	Percent
300	5	12.5
315	4	10.0
330	2	5.0
345	1	2.5
360	1	2.5
375	1	2.5
450	26	65.0

FIGURE 7.6　Factors That Influence Obedience

Milgram varied many factors in his research program. Without commands from an experimenter, fewer than 3 percent of the participants exhibited full obedience. Yet in the standard baseline condition, 65 percent of male and female participants followed the orders. To identify factors that might reduce this level, Milgram varied the location of the experiment, the status of the authority, the participant's proximity to the victim, and the presence of confederates who rebel. The effects of these variations are illustrated here. *(Milgram, 1974.)*

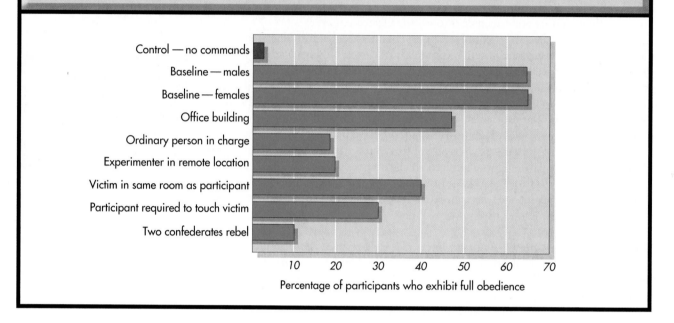

Percentage of participants who exhibit full obedience

sought to identify individuals with an *authoritarian personality* and developed a questionnaire known as the F-Scale to measure it (Adorno et al., 1950; Stone et al., 1993). What they found is that people who get high scores on the F-Scale (F stands for "Fascist") are rigid, dogmatic, sexually repressed, ethnocentric, intolerant of dissent, and punitive. They are submissive toward figures of authority but aggressive toward subordinates. Indeed, people with high F scores are also more willing than low scorers to administer high-intensity shocks in Milgram's obedience situation (Elms & Milgram, 1966).

Although personality characteristics may make someone vulnerable or resistant to destructive obedience, what seems to matter most is the situation in which people find themselves. By carefully varying particular aspects of his basic scenario, as shown in Figure 7.6, Milgram was able to identify factors that increase and decrease the 65 percent baseline rate of obedience. Three factors in particular are important: the authority figure, the proximity of the victim, and the experimental procedure (Blass, 1992; Miller, 1986).

The Authority　What is most remarkable about Milgram's findings is that a lab-coated experimenter is *not* a powerful figure of authority. Unlike a military superior, employer, or teacher, the psychology experimenter in Milgram's research could not ultimately enforce his commands. Still, his physical presence and his apparent legitimacy played major roles in drawing obedience. When Milgram diminished the experimenter's status by moving his lab from the distinguished surroundings of Yale University to a rundown urban office building in nearby Bridgeport, Connecticut, the rate of total obedience dropped to 48 percent. When the experimenter was replaced by an ordinary person—supposedly another participant—there was a dramatic reduction to 20 percent. Similarly, Milgram found that when the experimenter was in charge but issued his commands by telephone, only

21 percent fully obeyed. (In fact, when the experimenter was not watching, many participants in this condition feigned obedience by pressing the 15-volt switch.) One conclusion, then, is clear. At least in the Milgram setting, destructive obedience requires the physical presence of a prestigious authority figure.

If an experimenter can exert such control over research participants, imagine the control wielded by truly powerful authority figures— present or not. An intriguing field study examined the extent to which hospital nurses would obey unreasonable orders from a doctor (Hofling et al., 1966). Using a fictitious name, a male physician called several female nurses on the phone and told them to administer a drug to a specific patient. His order violated hospital regulations: The drug was uncommon, the dosage was too large, and the effects could have been harmful. Yet out of the twenty-two nurses contacted, twenty-one of them had to be stopped as they prepared to obey the doctor's orders.

"Nice touch, Jenkins. I like a man who salutes."

The Victim Situational characteristics of the victim are also important in destructive obedience. Milgram noted that Nazi war criminal Adolf Eichmann felt sick when he toured concentration camps but only had to shuffle papers from behind a desk to play his part in the Holocaust. Similarly, the B-29 pilot who dropped the atom bomb on Hiroshima in World War II said of his mission, "I had no thoughts, except what I'm supposed to do" (Miller, 1986, p. 228). These events suggest that because Milgram's participants were physically separated from the learner, they were able to distance themselves emotionally from the consequences of their actions.

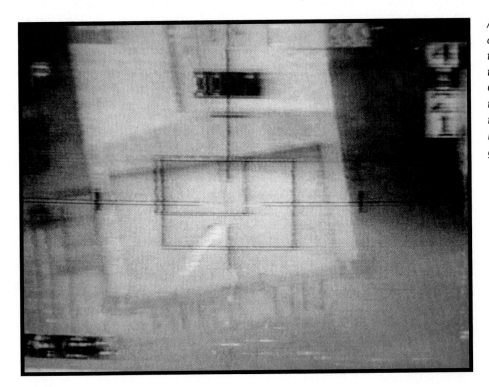

As seen through the missile guidance scope of a French bomber, this Iraqi ammunition site is about to be destroyed during the Persian Gulf War. Notice how the pilot's view from the cockpit is so far removed from the targets below that the mission feels almost like a video-game.

To examine the effects of a victim's proximity on destructive obedience, Milgram seated the learner in one of his studies in the same room as the participant. Under these conditions, only 40 percent fully obeyed. When participants were required to physically grasp the victim's hand and force it onto a metal shock plate, full obedience dropped to 30 percent. These findings represent significant reductions from the 65 percent baseline. Still, three out of ten participants were willing to use brute force in the name of obedience.

The Procedure   Finally, there is the situation created by Milgram. A close look at the dilemma his participants faced reveals two particularly important aspects of the experimental procedure. First, participants were led to feel relieved of any personal sense of *responsibility* for the victim's welfare. The experimenter said up front that he was accountable. When participants are led to believe that *they* are responsible, their level of obedience drops considerably (Tilker, 1970). The ramifications of this finding are immense. In military and other organizations, individuals often occupy positions in the middle of a hierarchical chain of command. Eichmann was a middle-level bureaucrat who received orders from Hitler and transmitted them to others for implementation. Caught between individuals who make policy and those who carry it out, how personally responsible do those in the middle feel? Wesley Kilham and Leon Mann (1974) examined this issue in an obedience study that cast participants in one of two roles: the transmitter (who took orders from the experimenter and passed them on) and the executant (who actually delivered the shocks). As predicted, transmitters were more obedient (54 percent) than executants (28 percent).

The second feature of Milgram's scenario that promoted obedience is gradual escalation. Participants began the session by delivering mild shocks and then, only gradually, escalated to voltage levels of high intensity. After all, what's another 15 volts compared with the current level? By the time participants realized the frightening implications of what they were doing, it had become more difficult for them to escape (Gilbert, 1981). This sequence is much like the foot-in-the-door technique. In Milgram's words, people become "integrated into a situation that carries its own momentum. The subject's problem…is how to become disengaged from a situation which is moving in an altogether ugly direction" (1974, p. 73). We should point out that obedience by momentum is not unique to Milgram's research paradigm. As reported by Amnesty International, many countries today torture political dissidents—and those who are recruited for the dirty work are trained, in part, through an escalating series of commitments (Haritos-Fatouros, 1988).

Obedience to authority is a social issue of such critical importance that social psychologists all over the world continue to ponder and debate its ramifications—in print and in Internet newsgroups. One question often asked is whether Milgram's results would be repeated today in a different but analogous situation. The answer seems to be yes. In a series of experiments, Dutch social psychologists Wim Meeus and Quinten Raaijmakers (1995) constructed a moral dilemma much like Milgram's. Rather than commanding participants to inflict physical pain, however, they engaged participants in behavior intended to cause psychological harm. When participants arrived at a university laboratory, they met a man—actually a confederate—who was there to take a test as part of a job interview. If the applicant passed the test, he would get the job; if he failed, he would not. Supposedly without the applicant's knowledge, the experimenter told participants that he was interested in the ability to work under stress. The participant's task was to read various test questions to the applicant over a microphone from a nearby room and to harass the applicant by making an escalating series of negative remarks. As the applicant worked on the test, then, participants made statements such as "If you continue like this, you will fail the test" and "This job is much too difficult for you. You are more suited for lower functions."

As the events proceeded, the applicant protested. He pleaded with the participant to stop, then angrily refused to tolerate the abuse, eventually falling into a state of despair. Exhibiting visible signs of tension, the applicant faltered in his test performance and failed to get the job. As in Milgram's research, the obedience question was straightforward: How many participants would obey the experimenter's orders through the entire set of fifteen stress remarks, despite the apparent harm caused to a real-life job applicant? In a control group that lacked a prodding experimenter, not a single participant persisted. But when the experimenter ordered participants to go on, 92 percent of them, male and female, exhibited complete obedience—even though they saw the task as unfair and distasteful. This result led the investigators to conclude that obedience is a compelling social phenomenon brought about by the docile manner in which people relate to figures of authority—even today.

Defiance: When People Rebel

It is easy to despair in light of the impressive array of forces that compel people toward blind obedience. But there's also good news. Just as social influence processes can breed subservience to authority, they can also breed rebellion and defiance. Few people realize it, but this phenomenon too was seen during World War II. In *Resistance of the Heart*, historian Nathan Stoltzfus (1996) describes a civil protest in Berlin in which the non-Jewish wives of two thousand newly captured Jews congregated outside the prison. The women were there, initially, seeking information about their husbands. Soon they were filling the streets chanting and refusing to leave. After eight straight days of protest, the defiant women prevailed. Fearing the negative impact on public opinion, the Nazis backed down and released the men.

"A little rebellion now and then is a good thing."

—Thomas Jefferson

Are the actions of a group harder to control than the behavior of a single individual? Consider the following study. Pretending to be part of a marketing research firm, William Gamson and his colleagues (1982) recruited people to participate in a supposed discussion of "community standards." Scheduled in groups of nine, participants were told that their discussions would be videotaped for a large oil company that was suing the manager of a local service station who had spoken out against higher gas prices. After receiving a summary of the case, most participants sided with the station manager. But there was a hitch. The oil company wanted evidence to win its case, said the experimenter—posing as the discussion coordinator. He told each of the group members to get in front of the camera and express the company's viewpoint. Then he told them to sign an affidavit giving the company permission to edit the tapes for use in court.

In light of what is known about blind obedience, people might benefit from a simple reminder—to "question authority."

You can see how the obedience script was supposed to unfold. Actually, only one of thirty-three groups even came close to following the script. In all others, people became incensed by the coordinator's behavior and refused to continue. Some groups were so outraged that they planned to take action. One group even threatened to blow the whistle on the firm by calling the local newspapers. Faced with one emotionally charged mutiny after another, the researchers had to discontinue the experiment.

Why did this study produce such active, often passionate revolt when Milgram's revealed such utterly passive obedience? Could it reflect a difference between the 1960s, when Milgram's studies were run, and the 1980s? Although many college students believe that people would conform less today than in the past, there is no relationship between the year in which a study was conducted and the level of obedience that it produced (Blass & Krackow, 1991). So what accounts for the contrasting results? One key difference is that people in Milgram's studies participated alone and those in Gamson's participated in groups. As Michael Walzer notes, "Disobedience, when it is not criminally but morally, religiously, or politically motivated, is always a *collective* act" (cited in R. Brown, 1986, p. 17).

Our earlier discussion of conformity indicated that the mere presence of one ally in an otherwise unanimous majority gives individuals the courage to dissent. Perhaps the same holds true for obedience. Notably, Milgram never had more than one participant present in the same session. But in one experiment, he did use two confederates who posed as co-teachers along with the real participant. In these sessions, one confederate refused to continue at 150 volts, and the second refused at 210 volts. These models of disobedience had a profound influence on participants' willingness to defy the experimenter: In their presence, only 10 percent delivered the maximum level of shock (see Figure 7.6).

We should add that groups are not a perfect safeguard against destructive obedience. Groups can trigger aggression, as we'll see in Chapter 11. For example, the followers of Jim Jones were together when they collectively followed his command to die. And lynch mobs are just that—groups, not individuals. Clearly, there is power in sheer numbers. That power can be destructive, or it can be used for constructive purposes. Indeed, the presence and support of others often provides the extra ounce of courage that people need to resist orders they find offensive.

The Continuum of Social Influence

As we have seen, social influence on behavior ranges from the implicit pressure of group norms, to the traps set by direct requests, to the powerful commands of authority. In each case, people choose whether to react with conformity or independence, compliance or assertiveness, obedience or defiance. At this point, let's step back and consider two important questions. First, although different kinds of pressure influence us for different reasons, is it possible to predict all the effects with a single, overarching principle? Second, what does the theory and research on social influence say about human nature?

Social Impact Theory

social impact theory The theory that social influence depends on the strength, immediacy, and number of source persons relative to target persons.

In 1981, Bibb Latané proposed that a common bond among the different processes leads people toward or away from social influence. Specifically, Latané proposed **social impact theory,** which states that social influence of any kind—the total impact of others on a target person—is a function of the others' strength, immediacy, and number. According to Latané, social forces act on individuals in

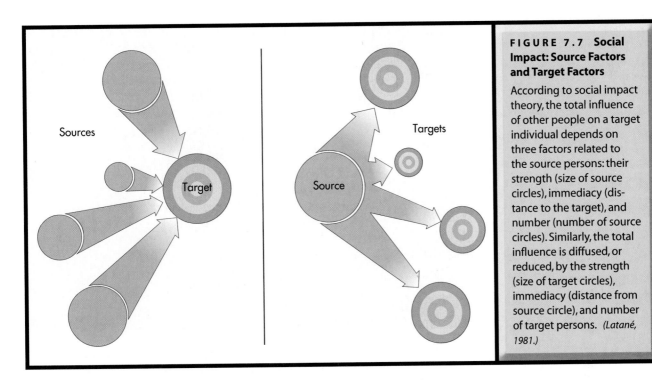

FIGURE 7.7 Social Impact: Source Factors and Target Factors

According to social impact theory, the total influence of other people on a target individual depends on three factors related to the source persons: their strength (size of source circles), immediacy (distance to the target), and number (number of source circles). Similarly, the total influence is diffused, or reduced, by the strength (size of target circles), immediacy (distance from source circle), and number of target persons. *(Latané, 1981.)*

the same way that physical forces act on objects. Consider, for example, how overhead lights illuminate a surface. The total amount of light cast on a surface depends on the strength of the bulbs, their distance from the surface, and their number. As illustrated in the left portion of Figure 7.7, the same factors apply to social impact.

The *strength* of a source is determined by his or her status, ability, or relationship to a target. The stronger the source, the greater the influence. When people view the other members of a group as competent, they are more likely to conform in their judgments. When it comes to compliance, sources enhance their strength by making targets feel obligated to reciprocate a small favor. And to elicit obedience, authority figures gain strength by wearing uniforms or flaunting their prestigious affiliations.

Immediacy refers to a source's proximity in time and space to the target. The closer the source, the greater its impact. Milgram's research offers the best example. Levels of obedience were higher when the experimenter issued commands in person rather than from a remote location. When the victim suffered in close proximity to the participant, he acted as a contrary source of influence, and obedience levels dropped. Consistent with this hypothesis, Latané and his colleagues (1995) asked individuals to name up to seven people in their lives and to indicate how far away those people lived and how many memorable interactions they'd had with those people. In three studies, the correlation was the same: The closer others are, geographically, the more impact they have on us.

Finally, the theory predicts that as the *number* of sources increases, so does their influence—at least up to a point. You may recall that when Asch (1956) increased the number of live confederates from one to four, conformity levels rose. Further increases, however, had only a negligible additional effect.

Social impact theory also predicts that people sometimes resist social pressure. According to Latané, this resistance is most likely to occur when social impact is *divided* among many strong and distant *targets*, as seen in the right part of Figure 7.7. There should be less impact on a target who is strong and far from the source than on one who is weak and close to the source; and there should be less impact on a target person who is accompanied by other targets than on one who stands

As the number of people in a group increases, so does their impact on an individual. **False.**

According to social impact theory, an army officer will exert influence to the extent that he is strong (in a position of power), immediate (physically close), and numerous (backed by others in the institution) relative to his trainees.

alone. Thus, we have seen that conformity is reduced by the presence of an ally and that levels of obedience drop when people are in the presence of rebellious peers.

Over the years, social impact theory has been challenged, defended, and refined on various grounds (Jackson, 1986; Mullen, 1985; Sedikides & Jackson, 1990). On the one hand, critics say that it does not enable us to *explain* the processes that give rise to social influence or answer *why* questions. On the other hand, the theory enables us to *predict* the emergence of social influence and determine *when* it will occur. Whether the topic is conformity, compliance, or obedience, this theory has set the stage for interesting new research in the years to come.

Most recently, Latané and L'Herrou (1996) have refined the theory by conceiving of social impact as a dynamic, ever-changing process. By having large groups of participants interact through e-mail, for example, and by controlling their lines of communication, they found that the individuals within the network formed "clusters." Over time, neighbors (participants who were in direct contact) became more similar to each other than did those who were more distant (not in direct contact) within the network. Referring to the geometry of social space, Latané and L'Herrou note that in the real world, immediacy cannot be defined strictly in terms of physical distance. "Walls between houses, rivers through towns, open spaces between cities, these and other spatial discontinuities all tend to prevent the equal flow of influence among all members of a population" (p. 1229). Speculating on the role of computer technology, they also note that social impact theory may have to account for the fact that, increasingly, we interact in cyberspace—perhaps making physical proximity a less relevant factor.

Perspectives on Human Nature

From the material presented in this chapter, what general conclusions might you draw about human nature? Granted, social influence is more likely to occur in some situations than in others. But are people generally malleable or unyielding? Is there a tilt toward accepting influence or toward putting up resistance? Did those in the Heaven's Gate cult who committed suicide act of their own free will, or were they victims of programmatic group influence?

There is no single, universal answer to these questions. As we saw earlier, some cultures value autonomy and independence, while others emphasize conformity to one's group. Even within a given culture, values may change over time. To demonstrate the point, ask yourself: If you were a parent, what traits would you like your child to have? When this question was put to American mothers in 1924, they chose "obedience" and "loyalty," key characteristics of conformity. Yet when mothers were asked the same question in 1978, they cited "independence" and "tolerance of others," key characteristics of autonomy. Similar trends were found in surveys conducted in West Germany, Italy, England, and Japan (Remley, 1988)—and in laboratory experiments, where conformity rates are somewhat lower today than in the past (Bond & Smith, 1996).

Is it possible that today's children—tomorrow's adults—will exhibit greater resistance to the various forms of social influence? If so, what effects will this trend have on society as a whole? Cast in a positive light, conformity, compliance, and obedience are good and necessary human responses. They promote group solidarity and agreement—qualities that keep groups from being torn apart by dissension. Cast in a negative light, a lack of independence, assertiveness, and defiance are undesirable behaviors that lend themselves to narrow-mindedness, cowardice, and destructive obedience—often with terrible costs. For each of us, and for society as a whole, the trick is to strike a balance.

Conformity rates vary across different cultures and from one generation to the next. **True.**

Review

- Conformity, compliance, and obedience are three kinds of social influence, varying in the degree of pressure brought to bear on an individual.

Conformity

- Conformity is the tendency for people to change their behavior to be consistent with group norms.

The Early Classics

- Two classic experiments illustrate contrasting types of conformity.
- Sherif presented groups of participants with an ambiguous task and found that their judgments gradually converged.
- Using a simpler line-judgment task, Asch had confederates make incorrect responses and found that participants went along about a third of the time.

Why Do People Conform?

- Sherif found that people exhibit private conformity, using others for information in an ambiguous situation.
- Asch's studies indicated that people conform in their public behavior to avoid appearing deviant.

Majority Influence

- As the size of an incorrect unanimous majority increases, so does conformity—up to a point.

- People conform to perceived social norms when these norms are brought to mind—particularly when they are injunctive rather than descriptive.

- The presence of one dissenter reduces conformity, even when he or she disagrees with the participant and lacks competence at the task.
- Young adolescents are particularly vulnerable to peer pressure.
- Women conform more than men on "masculine" tasks and in face-to-face settings, but not on "feminine" or gender-neutral tasks or in private settings.
- Conformity rates are higher in cultures that value collectivism than in those that value individualism.

Minority Influence

- Sometimes minorities resist pressures to conform and are able to influence majorities.
- In general, minority influence is greater when the source is an ingroup member.
- According to Moscovici, minorities exert influence by taking a consistent and unwavering position.
- Hollander claims that to exert influence, a person should first conform, then dissent.
- Majority influence is greater on direct and public measures of conformity, but minorities show their impact in indirect or private measures of conformity.
- By forcing other group members to think more openly about a problem, minorities enhance the quality of a group's decision making.

- People gain courage to resist conformity pressures after watching others do the same.

Compliance

- A common form of social influence occurs when we respond to direct requests.

The Discourse of Making Requests

- People are more likely to comply when they are taken by surprise and when the request *sounds* reasonable.

The Norm of Reciprocity

- We often comply when we feel indebted to a requester who has done us a favor.
- People differ in the extent to which they use reciprocity for personal gain and are wary of falling prey to this strategy.

Setting Traps: Sequential Request Strategies

- Four compliance techniques are based on a two-step request: the first step sets a trap, and the second elicits compliance.
- Using the foot-in-the-door technique, a person sets the stage for the "real" request by first getting someone to comply with a smaller request.
- In low-balling, one person gets another to agree to a request but then increases the size of it by revealing hidden costs. Despite the increase, people often follow through on their agreement.
- With the door-in-the-face technique, the real request is preceded by a large one that is rejected. People then comply with the second request because they see it as a concession to be reciprocated.
- The that's-not-all technique begins with a large request. Then the apparent size of the request is reduced by the offer of a discount or bonus.

Assertiveness: When People Say No

- Many people find it hard to be assertive. Doing so requires that we be vigilant and recognize the traps.

Obedience

- When the request is a command, and the requester is a figure of authority, the resulting influence is called obedience.

Milgram's Research: Forces of Destructive Obedience

- In a series of experiments, participants were ordered by an experimenter to administer increasingly painful shocks to a confederate.
- Sixty-five percent obeyed completely but felt tormented by the experience.

- Obedience levels are influenced by various situational factors, including a participant's physical proximity to both the authority figure and the victim.
- Two aspects of Milgram's procedure also contributed to the high levels of obedience: (1) participants did not feel personally responsible, and (2) the orders escalated gradually.
- In more recent studies, people exhibited high rates of obedience when told to inflict psychological harm on another person.

Defiance: When People Rebel

- Just as processes of social influence breed obedience, they can also support acts of defiance, as groups are more difficult to control than individuals.

The Continuum of Social Influence

Social Impact Theory

- Social impact theory predicts that social influence depends on the strength, immediacy, and number of sources who exert pressure relative to target persons who absorb that pressure.

Perspectives on Human Nature

- There is no single answer to the question of whether people are conformists or nonconformists.
- There are cross-cultural differences in social influence, and values change over time even within specific cultures.

Key Terms

collectivism *221*

compliance *224*

conformity *213*

door-in-the-face technique *229*

foot-in-the-door technique *227*

idiosyncrasy credits *223*

individualism *221*

informational influence *216*

low-balling *228*

minority influence *223*

normative influence *216*

obedience *232*

private conformity *216*

public conformity *216*

social impact theory *240*

that's-not-all technique *230*

PUTTING COMMON SENSE TO THE TEST

When all members of a group give an incorrect response to an easy question, most people most of the time conform with that response.

False. In Asch's classic conformity experiments, respondents conformed only about a third of the time.

An effective way to get someone to do you a favor is to make a first request that is so large the person is sure to reject it.

True. This approach, known as the door-in-the-face technique, increases compliance by making the person feel bound to make a concession.

In experiments on obedience, most participants who were ordered to administer severe shocks to an innocent person refused to do so.

False. In Milgram's classic research, 65 percent of all participants obeyed the experimenter and administered the maximum possible shock.

As the number of people in a group increases, so does their impact on an individual.

False. Increasing group size boosts the impact on an individual only up to a point, beyond which further increases have very little added effect.

Conformity rates vary across different cultures and from one generation to the next.

True. Research shows that conformity rates are higher in cultures that are collectivistic rather than individualistic in orientation, and values change over time even within specific cultures.

8 Group Processes

T / F

_____ People will cheer louder when they cheer as part of a group than when they cheer alone.

_____ Group members' attitudes about a course of action usually become more moderate after group discussion.

_____ People brainstorming as a group come up with a greater number of better ideas than the same number of people working individually.

_____ Groups are less likely than individuals to invest more and more resources in a project that is failing.

_____ Large groups are more likely than small groups to exploit a scarce resource that the members collectively depend on.

People are often at their best—and their worst—in groups. It is through groups that individuals form communities, pool resources, and share successes. But it is also through groups that stereotypes turn into oppression, frustrations turn into mob violence, and conflicts turn into wars.

The most far-reaching decisions that humans make are typically made by groups. Governments, businesses, and other organizations make decisions and implement actions that we can hardly imagine being left to any one person. Individuals rely on groups for everything from the practical, such as raising a barn or a building; to the political, such as raising awareness for a cause by marching or protesting together; to the personal, such as raising one's status by becoming accepted by the right crowd.

Clearly, it is important that we understand how groups work and how individuals influence, and are influenced by, groups. The research reported in this chapter reveals a fascinating fact: Groups are quite different from the sum of their parts.

Working together in a group, people can create magnificent spectacles, such as this scene from the Broadway musical Rent. *Working against each other, groups can produce death and destruction, as is evident in this photo of a war-torn section of the Bosnian city of Mostar.*

Consider, for example, one of the greatest blunders the U.S. government has ever made: the decision to invade Cuba in 1961. When John F. Kennedy became president of the United States in 1961, he assembled one of the most impressive groups of advisors in the history of American government. These individuals—highly intelligent, educated at the best universities, led by a new president brimming with ambition, charisma, and optimism—were called "the best and the brightest" that America had to offer (Halberstam, 1972). The Kennedy administration had inherited a plan from the previous administration of President Dwight Eisenhower to support an invasion of Cuba at the Bay of Pigs. In the invasion, 1,400 Cuban refugees trained and given supplies by the U.S. Central Intelligence Agency (CIA) would land in Cuba and lead a people's revolt to overthrow Fidel Castro's government. Kennedy and his advisors, after much deliberation, eventually approved an invasion plan that, in hindsight, was hopelessly flawed in many ways. For example, once the invaders landed at the Bay of Pigs, they were to be supported by anti-Castro guerrillas camped in the mountains nearby. But had Kennedy and his advisors consulted a map, they might have noticed that the invaders were to land eighty miles away from these mountains, separated from them by a huge swamp. Ultimately, the invasion was carried out and failed miserably. The invaders were quickly killed or captured, the world was outraged at the United States, and Cuba allied itself more closely with the Soviet Union—exactly the opposite of what Kennedy had intended. The United States was humiliated. After the fiasco, Kennedy himself wondered, "How could we have been so stupid?" (Janis, 1982).

This "stupidity" was especially shocking given the intelligence of the individual advisers. It was the dynamics of the *group*, rather than the individuals within the group, that led to the catastrophe (Janis, 1982). How could this be? The research discussed in this chapter will help answer this question, illustrating in many ways how groups are indeed different from the sums of their parts. To understand group processes, we need to examine groups on several different levels: At the individual level, we explore how individuals are influenced by groups; at the group level, we explore how groups perform; and at the inter-group level, we explore how groups interact with each other in cooperation and competition.

Collective Processes: The Presence of Others

In one of her most memorable lines, the American writer Gertrude Stein insisted that a "rose is a rose is a rose." No such claim of uniformity has ever been made for groups. Groups vary tremendously in size, organization, and purpose. Indeed, even defining *group* is not straightforward—dozens of definitions have been used (Levine & Moreland, 1998).

In Chapter 5, we focused on how individuals perceive groups. In that context, we characterized a group as a set of individuals having at least one of the following characteristics: (1) direct interactions with each other over a period of time; (2) joint membership in a social category based on sex, race, or other attributes; (3) a shared, common fate, identity, or set of goals. The current chapter focuses on groups themselves rather than others' perceptions of groups and group members. In this context, we emphasize the first and third criteria: direct interactions among group members over a period of time and a shared, common fate, identity, or set of goals.

Based on these criteria, people attending a concert or working out near each other in a gym are not real groups. Such assemblages are sometimes called **collectives**—people engaging in a common activity but having little direct interaction with each other (Milgram & Toch, 1969). Although some important social psychological processes are unique to real groups, some processes that affect groups also affect collectives. We begin our discussion by examining these *collective processes*, which influence individuals when they are in the presence of others, whether in real groups or collectives.

Social Facilitation: When Others Arouse Us

Social psychologists have long been fascinated by how the presence of others affects behavior. In Chapter 1, we reported that one of the founders of social psychology was Norman Triplett, whose article "The Dynamogenic Factors in Pacemaking and Competition" (1897–1898) is often cited as the earliest publication in the field. Triplett began his research by studying the official bicycle records from the Racing Board of the League of American Wheelmen for the 1897 season. He noticed that cyclists who competed against others performed better than those who cycled alone against the clock. After dismissing various theories of the day (our favorite is "brain worry"), he proposed his own hypothesis: The presence of another rider releases the competitive instinct, which increases nervous energy and enhances performance. To test this proposition, Triplett got forty children to wind up fishing reels, alternating between performing alone and working in parallel. On the average, winding time was faster when the children worked side by side rather than when they worked alone.

Later research following Triplett's studies proved disappointing. Sometimes the presence of others (side by side or with an audience out front) enhanced performance; at other times, performance declined. It seemed that Triplett's promising lead had turned into a blind alley, and social psychologists had largely abandoned this research by World War II. But years later, Robert Zajonc (1965, 1980) saw a way to reconcile the contradictory results by integrating research from experimental psychology with social psychological research. Zajonc offered an elegant solution: The presence of others increases arousal, which can affect performance in different ways, depending on the task at hand. Let's see how this works.

The Zajonc Solution   According to Zajonc, the road from presence to performance requires three steps.

1. The presence of others creates general physiological *arousal*, which energizes behavior. Based on experimental psychology research and principles of evolution, Zajonc argued that all animals, including humans, tend to become aroused when in the presence of *conspecifics*—that is, members of their own species.
2. Increased arousal enhances an individual's tendency to perform the *dominant response*. The dominant response is the reaction elicited most quickly and easily by a given stimulus. Here again, Zajonc drew from experimental psychology research, particularly research concerning learning.

collective People engaged in common activities but having minimal direct interaction.

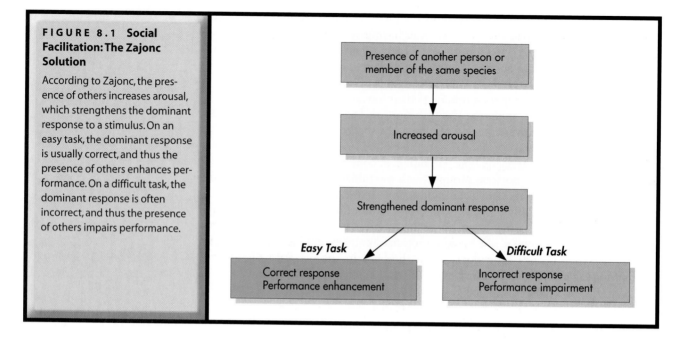

FIGURE 8.1 Social Facilitation: The Zajonc Solution

According to Zajonc, the presence of others increases arousal, which strengthens the dominant response to a stimulus. On an easy task, the dominant response is usually correct, and thus the presence of others enhances performance. On a difficult task, the dominant response is often incorrect, and thus the presence of others impairs performance.

Under the spotlight, the best performers rise to the occasion, as figure skater Tara Lipinski did here, winning the United States Nationals championship in 1997. Through social facilitation, athletes like Lipinski benefit from the presence of an audience when performing well-learned routines.

3. The quality of an individual's performance varies according to the type of *task*. On an easy task (one that is simple or well learned), the dominant response is usually correct or successful. But on a difficult task (one that is complex or unfamiliar), the dominant response is often incorrect or unsuccessful.

Putting these three steps together (see Figure 8.1) yields the following scenarios. Suppose you are playing the violin. If you're an excellent player and are performing a well-learned, familiar arrangement, having other people around should enhance your performance—the presence of others will increase your arousal, which will enhance your dominant response. Because this arrangement is so well learned, your dominant response will be to perform it well. However, if you are just learning to play the violin and you are unfamiliar with this arrangement, the presence of others is the last thing you'll want. The increase in arousal should enhance the dominant response, which in this case would be *unsuccessful* violin playing.

When you think about it, this makes intuitive sense. If you are just learning how to perform some complicated task, such as play the violin or ride a bike, it helps if you are not aroused. In contrast, if you are already good at the task, you may need the extra "juice" that comes from performing in front of others to help you rise to new heights and perform even better than you would if performing alone. Sports fans may be able to think of many instances in which the best athletes, such as basketball player Michael Jordan and figure skater Tara Lipinski, seem to rise to the occasion when the pressure is on, while lesser athletes "choke" under the same kind of pressure. And physical performances are not the only ones influenced; the effects also hold for cognitive tasks, such as trying to memorize a list of words.

Taken as a package, these two effects of the presence of others—helping performance on easy tasks but hurting performance on difficult tasks—are known as **social facilitation.** Unfortunately, this term has been a prime source of confusion for countless students. The trick is to remember that the presence of others facilitates the dominant response, not necessarily the task itself. This facilitation of the dominant response does, in effect, facilitate easy tasks, but it makes difficult tasks even more difficult.

Zajonc says that social facilitation is universal—occurring not only in human activities but also among other animals, even insects. Consider, for instance, cockroaches. How fast will they run? In a study by Zajonc and his colleagues (1969), participating insects were placed in a brightly lit start box connected to a darkened goal box. When the track was a simple one, with a straight runway between the start box and the goal box, cockroaches running in pairs ran more quickly toward the goal box than did those running alone. But in a more complex maze, with a right turn required to reach the goal box, solitary cockroaches outraced pairs. In a particularly creative follow-up experiment, Zajonc and his colleagues found that cockroaches completed the easy maze faster, and the difficult maze slower, if they raced in front of a crowd of spectator cockroaches than if they raced with no audience. You may wonder, How did the researchers get cockroaches to participate as spectators? The researchers placed cockroaches in plexiglass "audience boxes" along either side of the maze, and this "audience" produced social facilitation.

Zajonc's formulation revived interest in the issues raised by Triplett's early research, and suddenly the inconsistent findings that had been reported began to make sense. However, not all of Zajonc's theory has received universal support. Zajonc proposed that the **mere presence** of others is sufficient to produce social facilitation. Indeed, one recent experiment suggests that even a computer can serve as the "other" and can cause social facilitation if the computer interface is designed to look like another person (Sproull et al., 1996). Some have argued, however, that the presence of others will produce social facilitation only when the others have certain characteristics or have certain effects on the individual who is performing. These issues have produced various alternative explanations of social facilitation, and we turn now to two of the major variations on Zajonc's theme.

Evaluation Apprehension   The first and most thoroughly researched alternative, **evaluation apprehension theory,** proposes that performance will be enhanced or impaired only in the presence of others who are in a position to evaluate that performance (Cottrell, 1968; Henchy & Glass, 1968). In other words, it's not simply because others are around that I'm so aroused and therefore inept as I try to learn to snowboard on a crowded mountain. Rather, it's because I worry that the others are watching and probably laughing at me. I imagine them telling stories about me at dinner, or perhaps sending a videotape of my performance to one of those "funniest videos" shows. These concerns increase my dominant response, which is falling.

Usually, presence and potential evaluation go hand in hand. To pry them apart, researchers have come up with some rather unusual procedures. In one study, for example, participants worked on a task alone, in the presence of two other supposed participants (actually confederates), or in the presence of two blindfolded confederates supposedly preparing for a perception study. Compared with participants working alone, those working in the presence of seeing confederates were more likely to come up with dominant responses. In the presence of the blindfolded confederates, however, dominant responses were no more frequent than among participants working alone (Cottrell et al., 1968).

Distraction   Another approach to social facilitation, **distraction-conflict theory,** points out that being distracted while we're working on a task creates attentional conflict (Baron, 1986; Sanders, 1981). We're torn between focusing on the task and inspecting the distracting stimulus. Conflicted about where to pay attention, our arousal increases. Distraction-conflict theory maintains that there's nothing uniquely social about "social" facilitation. People, of course, can be distracting, but

social facilitation A process whereby the presence of others enhances performance on easy tasks but impairs performance on difficult tasks.

mere presence theory A theory holding that the mere presence of others is sufficient to produce social facilitation effects.

evaluation apprehension theory A theory holding that the presence of others will produce social facilitation effects only when those others are seen as potential evaluators.

distraction-conflict theory A theory holding that the presence of others will produce social facilitation effects only when those others distract from the task and create attentional conflict.

TABLE 8.1   Social Facilitation: Questions and Answers

For theories of social facilitation, the major issues in dispute are whether it is produced only by social stimuli and whether the mere presence of others is sufficient to produce it. As you can see, the three theories described in the text provide different answers to these questions.

Questions	Answers		
	Mere Presence	Evaluation Apprehension	Distraction-Conflict
Is it uniquely social?	Yes	Yes	No
Is mere presence sufficient?	Yes	No	No

so can crashing objects, blaring music, and glittering lights. The effect of mere presence is also called into question. People are not always distracting; a familiar presence we take for granted should leave our performance untouched.

Table 8.1 compares the three theories of social facilitation we have described. Is one of them right and the others wrong? Probably not. For example, the mere presence account can explain social facilitation among cockroaches better than the evaluation apprehension account can, but evaluation apprehension is better than mere presence at explaining why blindfolded others have less impact than others who are not blindfolded. Comprehensive reviews of the research evidence have drawn different conclusions about which theory has the best track record (Bond & Titus, 1983; Guerin, 1986). It seems likely that all three of the basic elements described by these theories (mere presence, evaluation, and attention) contribute to the impact others have on our own performance. And there's more to come.

Social Loafing: When Others Relax Us

The tasks employed in research on social facilitation produce individually identifiable results. That is, behavior can be identified and evaluated. But on some tasks, efforts are pooled so that the specific performance of any one individual cannot be determined. That other founder of social psychology, French agricultural engineer Max Ringelmann, investigated group performance on these kinds of collective endeavors. In research conducted during the 1880s, Ringelmann discovered that, compared with what people produced when they worked on their own, individual output declined when they worked together on simple tasks like pulling a rope or pushing a cart (Kravitz & Martin, 1986; Ringelmann, 1913).

Why did individual output decline? One explanation is that the individuals exerted less effort when they acted collectively, but another explanation is that the individuals simply demonstrated poor coordination when working together—some pulled while others relaxed and vice versa. How can you distinguish lack of effort from poor coordination in a task like this? Nearly a hundred years after Ringelmann's research, Alan Ingham and his colleagues (1974) answered this question by using a rope-pulling machine and blindfolding participants. In one condition, participants were led to *think* that they were pulling with a bunch of other participants; and in another condition, the participants were informed that they were pulling alone (which, in fact, they were). The researchers told the participants to pull as hard as they could. Ingham and colleagues were able to measure exactly how hard each individual participant pulled, and they observed that the participants pulled almost 20 percent harder when they thought they were pulling alone than when they thought they were pulling with others.

Bibb Latané and his colleagues (1979) found that group-produced reductions in individual output, which they called **social loafing,** are common in other types of tasks as well. For example, imagine being asked as part of a psychology experiment to cheer or clap as loudly as you can. Common sense might lead you to think that you would cheer and clap louder when doing this together with others in a group

social loafing A group-produced reduction in individual output on easy tasks where contributions are pooled.

than when performing alone because you would be less embarrassed and inhibited if others were doing the same thing as you. But Latané and his colleagues found that when performing collectively, individual students loafed—they exerted less effort. The sound pressure generated by each individual decreased as the size of the group increased (see Figure 8.2). This social loafing occurred even among cheerleaders, who are supposed to be experts at cheering and clapping with others! And social loafing is not restricted to simple motor tasks. Sharing responsibility with others reduces the amount of effort that people put into more complex motor tasks, such as swimming in a relay race (Miles & Greenberg, 1993; Williams et al., 1989); cognitive tasks, such as evaluating a poem, editorial, or job (Petty et al., 1977; Weldon & Gargano, 1988) or generating uses for objects (Harkins & Petty, 1982); and important, enduring real-world behaviors, such as working on collective farms (Latané et al., 1979). When others are there to pick up the slack, people slack off.

Steven Karau and Kipling Williams (1993) conducted a meta-analysis of seventy-eight studies and found social loafing to be a reliable phenomenon, displayed across numerous tasks and in countries around the world. But they also found that social loafing is not inevitable; a number of factors can reduce it (Karau &

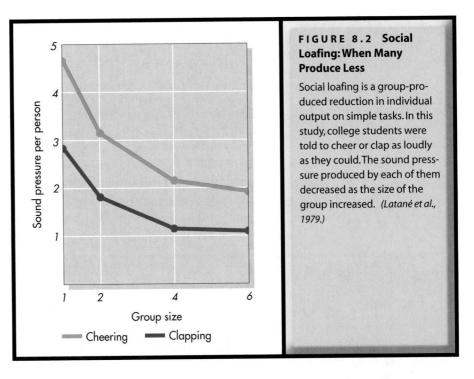

FIGURE 8.2 Social Loafing: When Many Produce Less

Social loafing is a group-produced reduction in individual output on simple tasks. In this study, college students were told to cheer or clap as loudly as they could. The sound pressure produced by each of them decreased as the size of the group increased. *(Latané et al., 1979.)*

People will cheer louder when they cheer as part of a group than when they cheer alone.
False.

"We just haven't been flapping them hard enough."

Individuals often don't try as hard in groups as they do alone. If they can be convinced that their efforts will pay off, however, their output can soar. Sam Gross © 1995 from The New Yorker Collection. All Rights Reserved.

Williams, 1993, 1997; Sheppard, 1993a). Social loafing is less likely to occur when one of the following conditions is present:

- People believe that their own performance can be identified and thus evaluated, by themselves or others.
- The task is important or meaningful to those performing it.
- People believe that their own efforts are necessary for a successful outcome.
- The group expects to be punished for poor performance.
- The group is small.
- The group is cohesive—that is, membership in the group is valuable and important to the members, and the individuals like each other.

In addition, although men and women in a wide variety of populations and cultures exhibit social loafing, it is less prevalent among women than men and less prevalent among people from eastern, collectivist cultures (such as China, Japan, and Taiwan) than among people from western, individualist cultures (such as Canada and the United States).

To explain findings about when social loafing is more or less likely to occur, Karau and Williams (1993, 1997) proposed the **collective effort model.** This model asserts that individuals try hard on a collective task when they think their efforts will help them achieve outcomes that they personally value. If the outcome is not personally important to the individual, or if the individual believes that his or her contribution won't affect the outcome very much, then the individual is likely to socially loaf. The next time you work on a group project, such as a paper that you and several other students are supposed to write together, consider the factors that increase and decrease social loafing. You might want to try to change aspects of the situation so that all group members are motivated to do their share of the work.

Here, Chinese farmers cooperate on a task in which individual contributions cannot be identified. Social loafing on such tasks occurs less often in eastern cultures than in western ones.

Facilitation and Loafing: Unifying the Paradigms

Social facilitation and social loafing represent two separate research traditions, but the connection between them—the fact that both arise in the presence of others—has prompted some investigators to attempt a unified approach that highlights the arousal associated with possible performance evaluation (Harkins & Szymanski, 1987; Sanna, 1992).

- When individual contributions can be identified (social facilitation), the presence of others *increases* arousal and the possibility of being evaluated: The individual is in the spotlight.
- When individual contributions are pooled (social loafing), the presence of others *decreases* arousal and the possibility of being evaluated: Each person's performance is swallowed up in the group product, and the individual can relax and be lost in the crowd.

collective effort model
The theory that individuals will exert effort on a collective task to the degree that they think their individual efforts will be important, relevant, and meaningful for achieving outcomes that they value.

Now, how do arousal and possible evaluation affect performance? It depends on the difficulty of the task to be performed. Four predictions can be made.

■ When the presence of others increases the possibility of evaluation of an individual's work: (1) Performance on easy tasks is enhanced because the individual is more motivated. That's social facilitation, part one. (2) Performance on difficult tasks is impaired because the pressure gets to the individual. That's social facilitation, part two.

■ When the presence of others decreases the possibility of evaluation of an individual's work: (3) Performance on easy tasks is impaired because the individual is uninspired. That's social loafing. (4) Performance on difficult tasks is enhanced because being lost in the crowd frees the individual from anxiety. There's no official name for this effect, but we're inclined to call it "social security."

These predictions have been confirmed in several studies using different methods and measures (Jackson & Williams, 1985; Sanna, 1992). The typical pattern of results is diagrammed in Figure 8.3. A unified view of social facilitation and social loafing has important practical implications for maximizing performance when individuals are working together. In team sports, for example, coaches would be well advised to evaluate each player's performance against a weak opponent but to stress team spirit and overall group effort during a tough game. Unification is

FIGURE 8.3 Unifying the Paradigms: Presence and Evaluation

The relationship between the presence of others and the potential for evaluation is the key to a unified paradigm of social facilitation and social loafing. When individual performance can be evaluated, the presence of others enhances performance on easy tasks but impairs performance on difficult endeavors. When contributions are pooled across individuals, the pattern reverses, as performance declines on easy tasks but improves on difficult ones. *(Adapted from Jackson & Williams, 1985; Sanna, 1992.)*

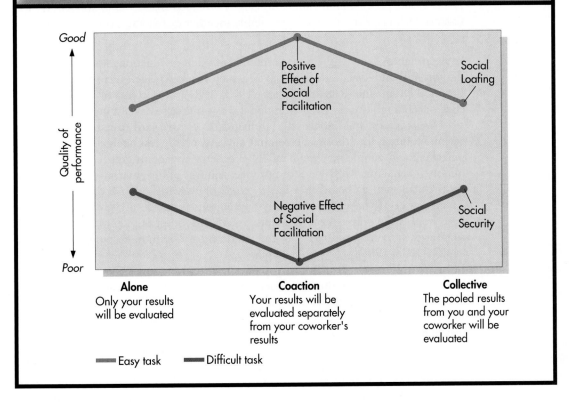

Death in Rwanda, where no sanctuary was sufficient to protect the Tutsi people from the violence of their Hutu neighbors.

also historically satisfying: the two founders of social psychology, Triplett and Ringelmann, together at last.

Deindividuation: When People Lose Control

Some pioneers in social psychology regarded the presence of others as considerably more profound and more troubling. Based on their research in France, Gabriel Tarde (1890) and Gustave Le Bon (1895) thought of collective influence as virtually mesmerizing. They maintained that, under the sway of the crowd, people turn into copycat automatons or, worse still, uncontrollable mobs.

The destructive capacity of collectives has left a bloody trail through human history: pogroms against Jews in Eastern Europe and Russia; lynchings of African Americans in the United States; the indiscriminate murder and rape of the civilian population when the Japanese Army entered undefended Nanking, China, in 1937; neo-Nazi attacks against immigrant workers from Asia and Africa living in today's unified Germany; the slaughter of an estimated 500,000 Tutsi by the Hutu in Rwanda.

What turns an unruly crowd into a violent mob? No doubt many of the factors described in Chapter 11 on Aggression contribute to violence by groups as well as by individuals. These include imitation of aggressive models, intense frustration, high temperatures, alcohol consumption, and the presence of weapons that trigger aggressive thoughts and actions. But there's also **deindividuation,** the loss of a person's sense of individuality and the reduction of normal constraints against deviant behavior. Most investigators believe that deindividuation is a collective phenomenon that occurs only in the presence of others (Diener et al., 1976; Festinger et al., 1952). Philip Zimbardo (1969) observed that arousal, anonymity, and reduced feelings of individual responsibility together contribute to deindividuation.

Environmental Cues In order to understand deindividuation, we must examine the physical and social environment in which it takes place. According to Steven Prentice-Dunn and Ronald Rogers (1982, 1983), two types of environmental cues—accountability cues and attentional cues—increase deviant behavior.

Accountability cues affect the individual's cost-reward calculations. When accountability is low, those who commit deviant acts are less likely to be caught and punished, and people may deliberately choose to engage in gratifying but usually inhibited behaviors. Consider, for instance, features of the environment that create anonymity (such as being in a large crowd or wearing a mask or hood). What would *you* do if you could be totally anonymous—indeed, invisible—for twenty-four hours? Among college students asked this question, their most frequent responses involved criminal acts; the single most common response was "rob a bank" (Dodd, 1985).

Research on actual behavior provides even more compelling evidence of the effects of anonymity. In the laboratory, anonymity is created by various devices: not mentioning participants' names; telling them they will remain unidentified; and sometimes, having them dress up in enveloping clothing, complete with hoods masking their faces from view. In contrast, control participants are addressed by name, wear large name tags, and retain their regular clothing. Compared with controls, those who are anonymous are more aggressive (Zimbardo, 1970), especially when all participants have been physiologically aroused without their awareness (Taylor et al., 1991). Gender differences may also be reduced. In one study, men

deindividuation The loss of a person's sense of individuality and the reduction of normal constraints against deviant behavior.

were more aggressive than women when individuals were identifiable. But protected by anonymity, women behaved as aggressively as men did (Lightdale & Prentice, 1994).

Attentional cues, the second type of environmental characteristic that increases deviant behavior, focus a person's attention away from the self. When a person's self-awareness declines, a change in consciousness takes place. In this "deindividuated state," the individual attends less to internal standards of conduct, reacts more to the immediate situation, and is less sensitive to long-term consequences of behavior (Diener, 1980). Behavior slips out from the bonds of cognitive control, and people act on impulse.

Have you ever been at a party with flashing strobe lights and music so loud that you could feel the room vibrate? If so, did it seem that you were somehow merging with the pulsating crowd and that your individual identity was slipping away? Intense stimulation from the environment is probably the most common attentional

cue reducing self-awareness. In laboratory research, groups of participants placed in a highly stimulating environment (loud rock music, colorful video games) were more uninhibited, extreme, and aggressive in their actions (Diener, 1979; Prentice-Dunn & Rogers, 1980; Spivey & Prentice-Dunn, 1990).

One particularly creative set of field experiments by Edward Diener and Arthur Beaman and their colleagues (Beaman et al., 1979; Diener et al., 1976) demonstrated how accountability cues and attentional cues can affect behavior on a night when many otherwise well-behaved individuals act in antisocial ways: Halloween. When you think about

After the Denver Broncos' victory in the Super Bowl in January, 1998, about 20,000 fans celebrated on the streets of downtown Denver. In the ensuing mayhem, fires were started, cars overturned, and stores looted. In the midst of a crowd like this, people may feel deindividuated, which can lead to deviant behavior.

it, Halloween can be a perfect time to study deindividuation; children often wear costumes with masks, travel in large groups at night, and are highly aroused. In one study, the researchers unobtrusively observed more than 1,300 children who came trick-or-treating to twenty-seven homes spread around Seattle. At each of these homes, a researcher met and greeted the children, who were either alone or in groups. In one condition, the researcher asked the children their names and where they lived; in another condition, the researcher did not ask them any questions about their identities. When asked to identify themselves, the children should have become more self-aware and more accountable for their actions. Children who were not asked to reveal their identities should have felt relatively deindividuated, safe and anonymous in their costumes.

The children were then invited to take *one* item from a bowl full of candy and were left alone with the bowl. Hidden observers watched to see how many pieces of candy each child took. What did the observers see? The children took the most candy when they were the most deindividuated: when they were in a group and had not been asked to identify themselves. In another experiment, the researchers placed a mirror behind the candy bowl in some conditions. As noted in Chapter 3, the presence of a mirror tends to increase people's self-awareness. Children who had been asked their names, especially older children, were much less likely to steal candy if there was a mirror present than if there wasn't. Older children are

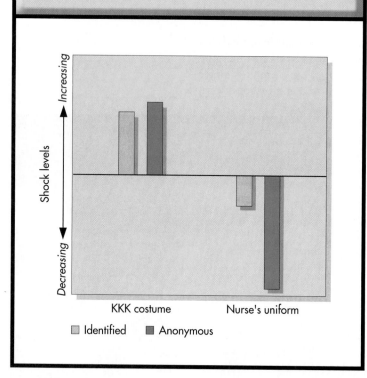

FIGURE 8.4   Anonymous Goodness

Regardless of whether they were individually identified or anonymous, female participants wearing KKK robes increased the intensity of shocks they administered to an experimental confederate. Among those wearing nurses' uniforms, however, anonymous participants *decreased* shock intensity much more than did individually identified participants. *(Data from Johnson & Downing, 1979.)*

more likely to have internal standards against stealing, and making these children self-aware made them more likely to act according to those standards.

Crowds and Identity   In terms of personal responsibility, there is a vast difference between the effects of accountability cues and the effects of attentional cues. To engage in a forbidden action because you think you won't get caught is a deliberate decision. But to lose the ability to exercise self-control is a case of diminished capacity. Although the theoretical distinction is clear, the application to real life is more complicated. Being in a large crowd, for instance, can increase anonymity and decrease self-awareness. Perhaps because of this double impact, larger groups are associated with greater violence. Research by Brian Mullen (1986) on newspaper accounts of sixty lynchings of African Americans that occurred between 1899 and 1946 found that as the size of the mob increased relative to the number of victims, the brutality of the lynching intensified. Leon Mann (1981) found that when a crowd gathers to watch someone who is threatening to commit suicide by jumping from a building or other tall structure, those in the crowd are more likely to jeer and taunt the person if the crowd is large rather than small, especially at night, when the people in the crowd can feel more anonymous.

Despite the association between crowds and violence, the loss of personal identity does not always produce antisocial behavior. In a study conducted by Robert Johnson and Leslie Downing (1979), female undergraduates donned garments resembling either robes worn by Ku Klux Klan members or nurses' uniforms. Half of the participants were individually identified throughout the study; the others were not. All of the participants were then given the opportunity to increase or decrease the intensity of electric shocks delivered to a supposed other participant (actually, an experimental confederate) who had previously behaved in an obnoxious manner. Participants wearing Ku Klux Klan costumes increased shock levels in both the identified and anonymous conditions. However, among those in nurse's apparel, anonymous participants *decreased* shock intensity four times more frequently than did identified participants!

These findings (displayed in Figure 8.4) make a telling point: Sometimes becoming less accountable, or less self-aware, allows us to be more responsive to the needs of others. Whether deindividuation affects people for better or for worse seems to reflect the characteristics of the group (Postmes & Spears, 1998; Reicher & Levine, 1994). As personal identity and internal controls are submerged, social identity and social standards emerge. If a group defines itself ("us") in terms of prejudice and hatred against another group ("them"), deindividuation can ignite an explosion of violence. But if a group defines itself in terms of concern for the welfare of others, deindividuation can spark an expansion of goodness. The consequences of losing your personal identity depend on what you lose it to.

Group Processes: Interacting with Others

Influential as they can be, collectives are only minimally social. People are in the same place at the same time working on a common task or reacting to the same event, but they don't engage in extensive interaction with each other. In this section, we examine social influence and other processes in groups, where interaction among members is more direct and meaningful.

Joining a Group

Groups come in all shapes and sizes: large and small, highly organized and quite informal, short term and long lasting. Sometimes group membership is involuntary. You didn't choose your family. But membership in most groups is voluntary. You decide to join an existing group or get together with others to create a brand-new one. Why do people join groups? How do groups develop over time? We address these questions next.

Why Join a Group?   There are several reasons for joining groups. At a fundamental level, people may have an innate need to belong to groups, stemming from evolutionary pressures that increased people's chances of survival and reproduction when in groups than in isolation (Baumeister & Leary, 1995). Further, people join specific groups in order to accomplish things that they cannot accomplish as individuals. Neither symphonies nor football games can be played by one person alone, and many types of work require team effort. People also join groups because of the social status and identity that they offer (Brewer, 1991; Hogg et al., 1993; Prentice et al., 1994). According to social identity theory, which was discussed in Chapter 5 on Perceiving Groups, an important part of people's feelings of self-worth comes from their identification with particular groups (Crocker & Luhtanen, 1990; Tajfel, 1982). Even a relatively low-status group can be a source of pride for individu-

als who are held in high esteem within the group (Gagnon & Bourhis, 1996); being big fish in small ponds can make people feel good about themselves, particularly people from individualist cultures (McFarland & Buehler, 1995). People may also join groups simply because they like the members and want to have the opportunity to interact with them. Whatever their reasons for joining a particular group, individuals preparing to do so are usually optimistic about the group and believe that they will benefit by belonging (Brinthaupt et al., 1991). In contrast, being rejected by a group is one of life's most painful experiences (Leary, Springer, et al., 1998; Williams, 1998).

People join a group for any of several reasons, such as to affiliate with others, to obtain social status, and to interact with individual group members.

Group Development   Once an individual has joined a group, a process of adjustment takes place. The individual assimilates into the group, making whatever changes are necessary to fit in. At the same time, the group accommodates to the newcomer, making whatever changes are necessary to include that individual. Not surprisingly, groups are likely to accommodate newcomers to the extent that they need more members (Cini et al., 1993).

Socialization of a new member into a group often relies heavily on the relationship between newcomers and established members (Levine et al., 1998). Newcomers model their behavior on what the old-timers do; old-timers may hold explicit training sessions for newcomers. Acting as mentors, old-timers may also develop close personal relationships with newcomers to help them be successful in the group. Having a mentor is useful to anyone joining a new group but may be especially helpful to those, such as women and people of color, who are joining groups from which they were previously excluded (Irons & Moore, 1985).

The socialization of group members is one way in which groups develop and maintain themselves. Group development may proceed through several stages. Group members first evaluate each other and the group as a whole. To the extent that the members accept each other and the group at large, their commitment to the group increases. Eventually, however, individuals may begin to diverge from the group, and the group may try to resocialize them. If the resocialization is unsuccessful, these individuals may exit the group, or the group may dissolve (Levine & Moreland, 1994, 1998).

Bruce Tuckman (1965; Tuckman & Jensen, 1977) proposed a particularly memorable set of stages through which groups develop: forming, storming, norming, performing, and adjourning. These stages are described in Table 8.2. According to this model, groups gradually progress from a period of initial orientation through stages of conflict, compromise, and action, followed by a period of withdrawal if the group no longer satisfies members' needs. Although many groups do seem to pass through these stages, not all groups do (Seeger, 1983).

For example, Connie Gersick (1988, 1994) observes that groups often do not proceed gradually through a uniform series of stages but instead operate in starts and stops, going through periods of relative inactivity until triggered by awareness of time and deadlines. According to Gersick, many groups adopt a problem-solving strategy very quickly—much quicker than Tuckman's theory suggests—but then they procrastinate until they have wasted about half the time they have allotted for the task, after which point they spring into action. Think about the work groups that *you've* been a part of—do the stages described in Table 8.2 seem to apply, or do the groups described by Gersick seem more familiar to you?

TABLE 8.2 Stages of Group Development

- **Forming:** Members try to orient themselves to the group. They often act in polite, exploratory ways with each other.

- **Storming:** Members try to influence the group so that it best fits their own needs. They become more assertive about the group's direction and what roles they would like to play in the group. A great deal of conflict and hostility may arise, along with feelings of excitement about what might be achieved.

- **Norming:** Members try to reconcile the conflicts that emerged during storming and develop a common sense of purpose and perspective. They establish norms and roles and begin to feel more commitment to the group.

- **Performing:** Members try to perform their tasks and maximize the group's performance. They operate within their roles in the group and try to solve problems to allow them to achieve their shared goals.

- **Adjourning:** Members disengage from the group, distancing themselves from the other members and reducing their activities within the group. This may occur if members believe that the benefits of staying in the group no longer outweigh the costs.

(Based on Tuckman, 1965; Tuckman & Jensen, 1977.)

Roles, Norms, and Cohesiveness

Despite their variation in specific characteristics, all groups can be described in terms of three essential components: roles, norms, and cohesiveness (Forsyth, 1990; Levine & Moreland, 1990). People's *roles* in a group, their set of expected behaviors, can be formal or informal. Formal roles are designated by titles: teacher or student in a class, vice president or account executive in a corporation. Informal roles are less obvious but still powerful. For example, Robert Bales (1958) proposed that regardless of people's titles, enduring groups give rise to two fundamental types of roles: an *instrumental* role to help the group achieve its tasks and an *expressive* role to provide emotional support and maintain morale. The same person can fill both roles, but often they are assumed by different individuals.

Bales's view of group roles is patterned after the division of labor in the traditional family between the "breadwinner" father and the "caretaking" mother. Does this pattern still hold? Are males more likely to take an instrumental, task-oriented role and females an expressive, socially oriented role? Under some circumstances, yes. In mixed-sex groups working on tasks that allowed for both kinds of roles, males often engage in more task-oriented activity and females in more positive social behavior (Wood, 1987; Wood, Polek, & Aiken, 1985). But under other circumstances, no. When participants in a mixed-sex group in one experiment were given feedback indicating either high or low competence, those who believed they were highly competent were more task oriented, while those who perceived themselves as lacking competence engaged more often in positive

"I've had to be both hunter and gatherer."

When roles in a group are not distributed properly, group performance suffers. Tom Cheney © 1997 from The New Yorker Collection. All Rights Reserved.

social behaviors (Wood & Karten, 1986). The same pattern of results was obtained for both men and women. Thus, among men and women who feel equally competent about task performance, the roles they adopt and the manner in which they behave are often quite similar (Dovidio et al., 1988).

Having a set of clear roles can be beneficial to a group (Barley & Bechky, 1994). However, when a person's role in the group is ambiguous, when it conflicts with other roles the person plays in the group (as when a group member needs to be demanding while at the same time providing emotional support to others), or when it must change after a period of time, stress and loss of productivity are likely to result (Abramis, 1994; Antonioni, 1996; Jackson & Schuler, 1985).

Groups also establish *norms*, rules of conduct for members. Like roles, norms may be either formal or informal. Fraternities and sororities, for example, usually have written rules for the behavior expected from their members. Informal norms are more subtle. What do I wear? Is it OK for me to call him? Who double-dates with whom? Who pays for this or that? Figuring out the unwritten rules of the group can be a time-consuming and, sometimes, anxiety-provoking endeavor.

The third characteristic of groups, *cohesiveness*, refers to the forces exerted on a group that push its members closer together (Cartwright & Zander, 1960; Festinger, 1950). Such forces can be positive (rewards obtained within the group) or negative (costs involved in leaving the group). Various factors contribute to cohesiveness, including commitment to the group task, attraction to group members,

group pride, and number and intensity of interactions (Cota et al., 1995; Fershtman, 1997; Zaccaro & McCoy, 1988). Outside forces, too, affect cohesiveness—groups in dangerous or unusual environments and groups threatened by other groups often become more cohesive—if the groups' members think that they can cope with these forces effectively as a group (Dion, 1979; Harrison & Connors, 1984; Lanzetta, 1955).

Cohesiveness and group performance are causally related, but the relationship is not a simple one.

First, the causal direction can run both ways: Cohesiveness can influence group performance, and group performance can influence cohesiveness. In their meta-analysis of the research on cohesiveness and group performance, Brian Mullen and Carolyn Copper (1994) found more evidence for an effect of performance on cohesiveness than for an effect of cohesiveness on performance.

Second, Mullen and Copper's meta-analysis also revealed that the positive relationship between cohesiveness and group performance is stronger in small groups than in large groups.

Third, a separate meta-analysis conducted by Stanley Gully and his colleagues (1995) indicates that the positive relationship between cohesiveness and performance is much stronger for tasks that require interdependence among group members than for tasks that do not require interdependence. Interdependent tasks are those in which group members must interact, communicate, cooperate, and observe each other (such as a military operation or a game of football).

Fourth, because cohesiveness increases conformity, cohesiveness should help group performance in situations in which deviance and lack of coordination can endanger a group (again, such as in a military operation); but it can hurt performance in situations in which creative, innovative ideas and behaviors are needed (such as in designing a new advertising campaign for a product that is not selling well).

Finally, the effect of cohesiveness on group performance depends on the norms that have been established in the group. If the norms are positive and consistent with an organization's goals, then high cohesiveness should improve group performance. If, however, a group has established negative, counterproductive norms, then high cohesiveness should lead to *poor* group performance. For example, a group of workers might establish a relatively low work standard as a norm. If this group is cohesive, its members may threaten or socially reject any group member who deviates from the others by working harder than the norm; so cohesiveness promotes poor performance. In contrast, other groups set very ambitious goals for each other and establish positive norms; the more cohesive these groups are, the more likely they are to push each other to succeed (Greene, 1989; Prapavessis & Carron, 1997; Stogdill, 1972; Widmeyer & Ducharme, 1997).

Although blowing the whistle on wrongdoing within a group can be very difficult, Bari-Ellen Roberts, a senior financial analyst at Texaco, went public with accusations of racial discrimination at Texaco and revealed tape recordings of company officials making racially offensive remarks. She and a co-worker filed a class action lawsuit, and Texaco settled in 1996 by agreeing to pay 176.1 million dollars.

Sometimes, breaking a norm in a cohesive group can be very difficult and even traumatic for a group member. Co-workers are especially reluctant to report the unethical behavior of others on their work teams, fearing the social consequences of reporting on a member of the group. Consultants involved in employee relations frequently observe the dilemma that workers in cohesive teams face when they witness unethical conduct. As one consultant noted, "[Team workers] have a fear they'll be seen as divisive. We're social animals, and we so very much want to belong" (Armour, 1998, p. 6B).

Group Polarization: Gaining Conviction

Once a group has formed—with roles, norms, and some degree of cohesiveness—it begins to make decisions and take actions. The issues faced by groups range from the trivial ("Where do we party?") to the profound ("Should we make war—or peace?"). Whatever the issue, the attitudes of group members affect what they do. How does being in a group influence people's opinions?

The key to answering this question is to realize that most groups consist of individuals who hold roughly similar views. People are attracted to groups that share their attitudes, and those who disagree with the group usually leave by their own choice or are ejected by the others. But similar does not mean identical. Although the range of opinion is relatively restricted, there are still differences.

What do you think should be the result of a group discussion of these differing points of view? For example, imagine that a group is discussing whether someone should behave in a risky or a cautious manner, such as whether an entrepreneur should risk trying to expand his or her business or whether an employee in a stable but boring job should quit and take a more creative job in a new but unproven company. Are groups more likely to advocate risky or cautious decisions about issues like these?

Common sense suggests two alternative predictions. Perhaps the most reasonable prediction is that after the group members discuss their differing points of view, the group decision will represent an overall compromise as everyone moves toward the group average. But common sense also suggests another prediction. Many people familiar with committees agree that forming a committee is a good way *not* to get something done. The idea is that individuals are willing to take risks and implement new ideas, whereas groups tend to be cautious and slow moving. Wary of leading the group toward a risky decision, people become more cautious in their views as they discuss them with the other group members.

So, which prediction is the correct one—movement toward the average attitude or movement toward caution? James Stoner (1961) tested this question by comparing decisions made by individuals with decisions made by groups, and he found that *neither* prediction was correct: Group decisions tended to be *riskier* than individuals' decisions. Was this a fluke? Several subsequent studies found similar results, and the tendency for groups to become riskier than the average of the individuals became known as the *risky shift* (Cartwright, 1971).

But the story doesn't end there. Later studies seemed to contradict the idea of the risky shift, finding that for some choices, groups tended to become more *cautious* (Knox & Safford, 1976). How can we make sense of these contradictory findings?

Researchers concluded that group discussion tends to enhance or exaggerate the initial leanings of the group. Thus, if most group members initially lean toward a risky position on a particular issue, the group's position becomes even riskier after the discussion; but if group members in general initially lean toward a cautious position, the group discussion leads to greater caution. This effect is called **group polarization**—the exaggeration through group discussion of initial tendencies in the thinking of group members (Moscovici & Zavalloni, 1969; Myers & Lamm, 1976).

"A committee is a cul-de-sac down which ideas are lured and then quietly strangled."

—Barnett Cocks

group polarization The exaggeration through group discussion of initial tendencies in the thinking of group members.

Group members' attitudes about a course of action usually become more moderate after group discussion. **False.**

Group polarization is not restricted to decisions involving risk versus caution. Any group decision can be influenced by group polarization, even a sorority's decision about what theme to use at its next party (Chandrashekaran et al., 1996). Group polarization is more likely to occur when important, rather than unimportant, issues are being discussed, however (Kerr, 1992b). Consider, for example, racial prejudice. In one study, high school students responded to an initial questionnaire and were classified as high, medium, or low on racial prejudice. Groups of like-minded students then met for a discussion of racial issues, with their individual attitudes on these issues assessed before and after their interaction. Group polarization was dramatic. Students low in prejudice to begin with were even less prejudiced after the group discussion; students moderate or high in prejudice became even more prejudiced (Myers & Bishop, 1970).

What creates group polarization? Three processes are usually emphasized:

1. According to *persuasive arguments theory*, the greater the number and persuasiveness of the arguments to which group members are exposed, the more extreme their attitudes become (Vinokur & Burnstein, 1974). Some arguments provide new information to group members hearing them for the first time. If most group members favor a cautious decision, for example, most of the arguments discussed will favor caution, giving the members more and more reason to want to be cautious. In addition, realizing that others favor caution, members may focus on pro-caution arguments when talking to each other and fail to bring up pro-risk arguments that may also be important to consider (Pavitt, 1994). Simply hearing others repeat our arguments (without offering any new ones) can validate our own reasoning, giving us more confidence in what may originally have been only a slight leaning. Group polarization thus intensifies when a participant makes an argument and then hears it repeated by others in the group (Baron, Hoppe, et al., 1996; Brauer et al., 1995).

2. Group polarization is also created as group members simply discover other people's opinions, even if no arguments are presented (Brown, 1965; Sanders & Baron, 1977). Here, *social comparison* is at work. As described in Chapter 3, individuals develop their view of social reality by comparing themselves with others (Festinger, 1954). The construction of social reality in like-minded groups is a two-step process. First, people discover more support for their own opinion than they had originally anticipated. Second, this discovery sets up a new, more extreme norm and motivates group members to go beyond that norm. If believing X is good, then believing double X is even better. By adopting a more extreme attitudinal position, people can distinguish themselves in the group in a manner approved by the group (Lamm & Myers, 1978).

3. In addition, group polarization is influenced by a concept you may recall from Chapter 5: *social categorization*, the tendency for people to categorize themselves and others in terms of social groups (Turner & Oakes, 1989). The social categorization approach compares how individuals react to information from ingroups (to which they belong or want to belong) and outgroups (to which they don't belong and don't want to). Ingroup members may want to distinguish their group from other groups, and so they overestimate the extremity of their group's position and distance themselves from the position of an outgroup (Hogg et al., 1990; Mackie & Cooper, 1984; McGarty et al., 1992).

" 'It is always best on these occasions to do what the mob do.' 'But suppose there are two mobs?' suggested Mr. Snodgrass. 'Shout with the largest,' replied Mr. Pickwick."

—Charles Dickens

Groupthink: Losing Perspective

The processes involved in group polarization may set the stage for an even greater, and perhaps more dangerous, bias in group decision making. Recall the discussion at the opening of this chapter about the Bay of Pigs invasion in 1961. This was not the only case in which high-level groups associated with the U.S. government made decisions that in hindsight seem remarkably ill-conceived. Take, for instance, these decisions:

- Toward the end of 1941, American military commanders received word that Japan planned to launch an aerial attack on the United States somewhere in the Pacific. Just before the attack on Pearl Harbor, American military intelligence reported losing track of Japanese aircraft carriers that had begun moving toward Pearl Harbor. Rather than take precautions, U.S. military leaders discounted the warning signs and decided to do nothing, leaving the important base completely unprepared and vulnerable. The attack proved disastrous for the United States, costing almost four thousand lives and a significant portion of the nation's arsenal of ships and planes.

- Three burglars associated with a committee to re-elect President Richard Nixon were caught breaking into the Democratic Party's national headquarters at the Watergate complex in Washington, D.C., during Nixon's re-election campaign in 1972. Nixon and his advisers met to discuss how to respond to the incident. The group decided to pay the burglars to keep quiet about their association with the administration; and they planned an elaborate cover-up, which they continued to execute despite increasing evidence that it could not work. When the cover-up was eventually revealed, Nixon was forced to resign in disgrace.

- In the mid-1980s, President Ronald Reagan and his advisers deliberated about selling arms to Iran in return for Iran's promise to help secure the release of U.S. and other hostages being held by terrorists in the Middle East—even though the United States had earlier banned arms sales to Iran. Several members of the administration had serious reservations about this risky plan, but they often failed to voice their concerns. Not only were the arms sales made, but profits from the sales were secretly—and illegally—used to support the *contras*, rebel forces attempting to overthrow the government of Nicaragua. News leaked of the affair, and an investigation was launched that lasted more than a year, culminating in a long list of charges of criminal dealings at the White House, including conspiracy, fraud, theft, and cover-up.

- On January 28, 1986, the U.S. National Aeronautics and Space Administration (NASA) decided to proceed with a risky launch of the space shuttle *Challenger*. Several engineers at the Morton Thiokol Corporation, which had made the shuttle's solid rocket boosters, had warned that launching in cold temperatures could cause the O-ring seals in the rocket boosters to fail, which would cause a catastrophic explosion. Some wanted to ban a liftoff if the temperature was below about 50 degrees. On the morning of January 28, the temperature at the launch pad was below freezing. But high-level officials at Morton Thiokol and NASA were motivated not to delay the launch. The mission had been heavily

On January 20, 1986, the space shuttle Challenger *exploded shortly after liftoff, killing all seven crew members. The mechanical cause of the disaster was soon identified. But human error was also involved, as the decision-making process leading up to the launch was flawed by inadequate communication, political pressure, and factors that promote groupthink.*

promoted by NASA because it marked the first time that "an ordinary citizen," a New Hampshire high school teacher named Christa McAuliffe, would travel into space along with the astronauts. The decision was made to launch; and seventy-three seconds after liftoff, the *Challenger* exploded, killing all seven people on board. Apparently, the O-ring seals had indeed failed.

As we now know, these decisions were seriously flawed and resulted in disastrous consequences. We also know that most of the people in the groups that made the decisions were intelligent individuals. What went wrong? According to Irving Janis (1982), a culprit in fiascoes such as these is **groupthink,** an excessive tendency to seek concurrence among group members. Groupthink emerges when the need for agreement takes priority over the motivation to obtain accurate information and make appropriate decisions. Janis believed that three characteristics contribute to the development of groupthink:

1. Since *highly cohesive groups* are more likely to reject members with deviant opinions, Janis thought they would be more susceptible to groupthink.
2. *Group structure* is also important. Groups that are composed of people from similar backgrounds, isolated from other people, directed by a strong leader, and lacking in systematic procedures for making and reviewing decisions should be particularly likely to fall prey to groupthink.
3. Finally, Janis emphasized that *stressful situations* can provoke groupthink. Under stress, urgency can overrule accuracy, and the reassuring support of other group members becomes highly desirable.

Behavioral Symptoms   In Janis's formulation, groupthink is a kind of social disease, and infected groups display behavioral symptoms such as the following:

■ *Overestimation of the group:* Members maintain an illusion of invulnerability and an exaggerated belief in the morality of the group's positions. Kennedy and his advisers may not have sufficiently questioned the wisdom of the invasion plan they had inherited from the Eisenhower administration. And they may have thought that, as the "best and brightest," they could surely pull off a little invasion. Similarly, American military leaders in 1941 may have discounted warnings about a Japanese attack because they didn't consider Japan a serious threat.

■ *Closed-mindedness:* Members rationalize the correctness of the group's actions and believe stereotypes about the characteristics of the targets of these actions. Did Nixon and his advisers ever think seriously about what was appropriate for political activities in a democracy? Or were they convinced that anything goes against "the enemy"?

■ *Increased pressures toward uniformity:* The pressures to sustain group cohesiveness grow increasingly strong. Group members censor their own thoughts and act as "mindguards" to discourage deviant thoughts by other group members. People who refuse to conform are expelled from the group. An illusion of unanimity can result—it can seem that all members agree with the group consensus, even though many of them may actually have serious reservations that they do not voice. For example, during the planning of the Bay of Pigs invasion, the president's brother, Robert Kennedy, served as a "mindguard" and warned dissenting members to keep quiet. During the Iran-Contra affair, former national security advisor Robert McFarlane had reservations about the plans but, as he would later admit, didn't have "the guts to stand up and tell the president" about them, fearing that if he did, others in the group would say that he "was some sort of commie" (Martz, 1987, p. 19). A high-level engineer at Morton Thiokol testified that his superiors pressured him to drop his resistance against launching *Challenger.* Although he initially opposed the launch, he changed his position "after being told to take off his engineering hat and put on one representing management" (Kruglanski, 1986, p. 48).

groupthink A group decision-making style characterized by an excessive tendency among group members to seek concurrence.

By preventing an open consideration of alternatives, the behavioral symptoms of groupthink can result in the defective decision making outlined in Figure 8.5. In turn, a defective decision-making process increases the likelihood that a group will make bad decisions.

Research on Groupthink Much of the research on groupthink has involved case studies and historical analyses, frequently focusing on the deliberations and actions of government and military officials (McCauley, 1989; Tetlock et al., 1992). But the potential range of groupthink is much broader. Groupthink tendencies have been identified in groups as diverse as university boards of trustees (Hensley & Griffin, 1986) and autonomous work groups in a battery assembly plant (Manz & Sims, 1982).

If Janis's model is to be adequately tested, however, more rigorous experimental or correlational studies are essential. Some researchers disagree with Janis about the specific conditions that make decision-making groups vulnerable to groupthink (Mohamed & Wiebe, 1996; Neck & Moorhead, 1995; Street, 1997; Tetlock, 1998; t'Hart et al., 1995). The role of cohesiveness is especially controversial. Some evidence favors Janis's view that cohesiveness can damage information processing by a group. For instance, Tatsuya Kameda and Shinkichi Sugimori (1993) found that strong pressures toward cohesiveness produced poor decision making: Requiring unanimity rather than majority rule for a new decision decreased group members' use of information that conflicted with their initial decision. The combination of high cohesiveness and the threat of public knowledge of a bad decision has also been shown to reduce the quality of group decision making (Turner et al., 1992). But some other research suggests that cohesiveness may have little, if any, direct impact on groupthink (Leana, 1985; Tetlock et al., 1992). It is even possible that cohesiveness sometimes *reduces* groupthink (Longley & Pruitt, 1980; McCauley, 1989). Deviant opinions may be easier to express and more likely to be taken seriously in a well-established group whose members have strong personal relationships with each other.

What conclusion can we draw about whether cohesiveness makes groups more susceptible to groupthink? Recall our earlier discussion about the role of cohesiveness in group performance: We said that whether or not cohesiveness is associated with better performance depends on other factors, such as group norms. The same applies to groupthink—whether or not cohesiveness promotes groupthink may depend on the presence or absence of other factors. This is exactly what a recent meta-analysis of the groupthink literature suggests: High cohesiveness impairs a group's decisions when other conditions leading to groupthink are present, but not when these other antecedent conditions are absent (Mullen et al., 1994).

As you can see in Figure 8.5, antecedent conditions that contribute to groupthink include

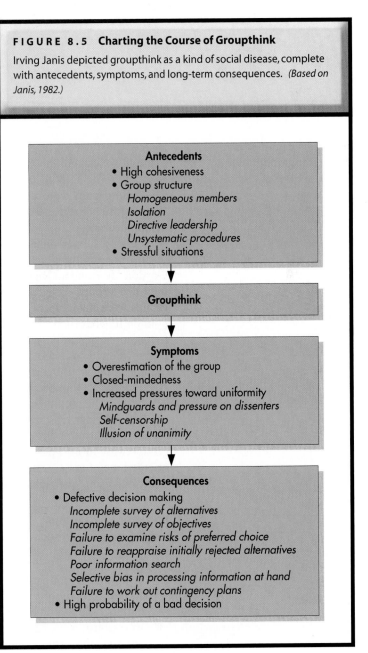

FIGURE 8.5 Charting the Course of Groupthink

Irving Janis depicted groupthink as a kind of social disease, complete with antecedents, symptoms, and long-term consequences. *(Based on Janis, 1982.)*

Antecedents
- High cohesiveness
- Group structure
  Homogeneous members
  Isolation
  Directive leadership
  Unsystematic procedures
- Stressful situations

Groupthink

Symptoms
- Overestimation of the group
- Closed-mindedness
- Increased pressures toward uniformity
  Mindguards and pressure on dissenters
  Self-censorship
  Illusion of unanimity

Consequences
- Defective decision making
  Incomplete survey of alternatives
  Incomplete survey of objectives
  Failure to examine risks of preferred choice
  Failure to reappraise initially rejected alternatives
  Poor information search
  Selective bias in processing information at hand
  Failure to work out contingency plans
- High probability of a bad decision

"On second thought, don't correct me if I'm wrong."

A controlling leader who discourages disagreement can promote group-think, leading to bad decisions.

certain structural aspects of the group. Some structural factors may be particularly important in setting the stage for groupthink. Groups perceived by their members as isolated from others perform more poorly than do groups perceived as more open to outsiders (Moorhead & Montanari, 1986). In addition, groups led by highly directive leaders who voice their preference for a specific course of action are more susceptible to groupthink (Chen et al., 1996; Hodson & Sorrentino, 1997). However, Ramon Aldag and Sally Fuller (1993) caution against the oversimplified notion that directive leadership always impairs group performance. As described in Chapter 13 on Business, a vigorous, inspiring leader is often highly effective.

Under stressful conditions, individuals differ in their resistance to groupthink (Callaway et al., 1985). But there appears to be a general tendency for groups to close ranks and reject deviant opinions when coping with stressful events such as an impending deadline (Kruglanski & Webster, 1991). Again, like cohesiveness, stressors may be sufficient to create groupthink only in combination with other antecedents (Tetlock et al., 1992). High stress together with high cohesiveness, for example, may promote groupthink. In one laboratory experiment, Marlene Turner and colleagues (1992) assembled small problem-solving groups and found that when the groups were made to be cohesive and when they were under pressure (fearing the consequences of faulty decision making), they came up with lower-quality decisions.

Finally, the personalities of the members of the group may interact with some of the antecedents of groupthink to affect the group's decision-making processes. Gordon Hodson and Richard Sorrentino (1997) conducted an experiment in which they had groups of participants make decisions about a legal case. Some of the groups were made up of *certainty-oriented* participants—individuals who prefer to hold on to what they already know and avoid learning new information that might reduce their certainty. Other groups were made up of *uncertainty-oriented* participants—individuals who tend to be motivated and energized in situations that require them to try to resolve uncertainty. The researchers also manipulated the types of leaders the groups had. Some groups were led by strong, directive leaders who stated their opinions at the outset and did not appear to welcome debate, whereas other groups were led by less directive, more open leaders. The results revealed that groups with directive, closed leaders made more biased decisions than groups with more open leaders, especially if the groups consisted of certainty-oriented members. Certainty-oriented groups may not want to risk creating uncertainty by raising questions about the position established by a directive leader.

Preventing Groupthink   To guard against groupthink, Janis urged groups to make an active effort to process information more carefully and accurately. He recommended that decision-making groups use the following strategies:

- To avoid isolation, groups should consult widely with outsiders.
- To reduce conformity pressures, leaders should explicitly encourage criticism and not take a strong stand early in the group discussion.
- To establish a strong norm of critical review, subgroups should separately discuss the same issue, a member should be assigned to play devil's advocate and

question all decisions and ideas, and a "second chance" meeting should be held to reconsider the group decision before taking action.

Indeed, President Kennedy himself appeared to arrive at similar conclusions after the Bay of Pigs disaster. In the following year, 1962, the United States and the Soviet Union appeared to be at the brink of war after U.S. military intelligence discovered that Soviet missiles in Cuba were aimed at the United States. During this crisis, Kennedy stayed away from initial meetings about how to respond to the situation; he consulted with experts outside his inner circle of advisers; and he told his brother Robert to play the devil's advocate and challenge all ideas—in sharp contrast to Robert's role of mindguard during the Bay of Pigs planning. Unlike the Bay of Pigs invasion, the Cuban missile crisis ended exactly as Kennedy had hoped: The Soviet Union withdrew its missiles from Cuba, and a war was avoided.

Recent research suggests some additional strategies for avoiding groupthink. If individual group members anticipate that they will be held personally accountable for their decisions, they will be more likely to voice their true opinions and risk challenging the group (Kroon et al., 1991). Inserting someone into the group to play the role of a "reminder" who is responsible for informing the group about the dangers of biased decision-making processes can also be beneficial (Schultz et al., 1995). The more group members focus on consensus in decision making, the more likely the group is to make biased decisions influenced by groupthink-like tendencies (Kim, 1997; Sundstrom et al., 1997); therefore, leaders or others in groups should try to discourage group members from being concerned with consensus and agreement rather than with independent

---

TABLE 8.3 How Computerized Group Support Systems Help Groups Avoid Groupthink

1. Allow group members to raise their concerns anonymously through the computer interface, enabling them to risk challenging group consensus without fear of direct attacks

2. Reduce the directive role of the leader

3. Enable group members to provide input simultaneously, so they don't have to wait for a chance to raise their ideas

4. Allow the least assertive group members to state their ideas as easily as the most dominating

5. Provide a systematic agenda of information gathering and decision making

6. Keep the focus in the group meetings on the ideas themselves rather than on the people and relationships within the group

(Based on Miranda, 1994.)

---

thought and information seeking. And computer-based technology can be used during meetings to help avoid groupthink (Miranda, 1994). Table 8.3 lists some of the ways in which computerized "group support systems," in which groups use specialized programs to guide their meetings, can enhance group decision making.

Group Performance: Are More Heads Better than One?

Group polarization and groupthink are examples of how groups can go wrong, ending up with attitudes that are too extreme and decisions that are seriously flawed. But aren't two, or more, heads generally better than one? How does the performance of a group compare with the performance of the same number of people working individually? According to Ivan Steiner (1972), it depends on the type of task.

On an *additive* task, the group product is the *sum* of all the members' contributions. Donating to a charity is an additive task, and so is making noise at a pep rally. As we have seen, people often indulge in social loafing during additive tasks. Even

"You think because you understand 'one,' you must understand 'two,' because one and one make two. But you must also understand 'and.'"

—Ancient Sufi saying

Just as the strength of a chain depends on its weakest link, the group product on a conjunctive task is determined by the individual with the poorest performance. In mountain climbing, for example, if one person slips or falls, the whole team is endangered.

On the Internet, you can find dozens of sites containing information about work teams, case studies of organizations and businesses, tips for meetings and leadership, and so forth. To get started, try the following sites: users.ids.net/~brim/ sdwth.html and www. teambuildersplus.com/ links.html

so, groups usually outperform a single individual. Each member's contribution may be less than it would be if that person worked alone, but the group total is still greater than what could be provided by one person.

On a *conjunctive* task, the group product is determined by the individual with the *poorest* performance. Mountain-climbing teams are engaged in such a task; the "weakest link" will determine their success or failure. Because of this vulnerability to the poor performance of a single group member, group performance on conjunctive tasks tends to be worse than the performance of a single, average individual.

On a *disjunctive* task, the group product is (or can be) determined by the performance of the individual with the *best* performance. Trying to solve a problem or develop a strategy is a disjunctive task: What the group needs is a single successful idea, regardless of the number of failures. In principle, groups have an edge on individuals in the performance of disjunctive tasks: The more people involved, the more likely it is that someone will make a breakthrough. In practice, however, group processes can interfere with coming up with ideas and getting them accepted—a phenomenon that Steiner called *process loss.*

Process loss is not restricted to disjunctive tasks. It can result from lack of motivation, as in social loafing on additive tasks. Lack of coordination can also cause process loss, as when the group is slowed down by weaker members on conjunctive tasks. On disjunctive tasks, groups may not realize which group members have the best ideas or are most expert. Unless the best solution for a particular problem is easily identifiable once it has been suggested, the group may fail to implement it; as a result, the group performs worse than its best members (Gigone & Hastie, 1997; Laughlin & Ellis, 1986; Stasser et al., 1995; Stasson & Bradshaw, 1995). Have you ever had the experience of *knowing* you had the right idea but being unable to convince others in your group until it was too late? If so, then you have experienced first-hand the problem of process loss on a disjunctive task. Fortunately, when groups are encouraged to try to determine the most appropriate group members for a task, their performance improves (Henry, 1995). As groups gain experience with each other, they can become better able to recognize and utilize the expertise of their members (Littlepage et al., 1997).

Groups may also underperform on any kind of task simply because they do not set their goals high enough. Verlin Hinsz (1995) found that groups selected goals that were less difficult than the goals individuals selected. Groups may set less ambitious goals so that group members are more likely to appear successful. Some groups may be more likely to set low goals than others. Groups that are high in *efficacy*—the belief that they can be effective at a task—set higher goals, and achieve higher performance, than other groups (Silver & Bufiano, 1996). Even though the goals they set may be less ambitious than those established by individuals, groups that set goals typically perform much better than groups that do not (O'Leary-Kelly et al., 1994).

Other problems in coordination and communication can also reduce the effectiveness of group performance. Next, we take a closer look at some of these problems, as well as some strategies to improve the performance of groups and help them reap the potential benefits of people working together.

Brainstorming: Coming Up with Ideas   During the 1950s, advertising executive Alex Osborn developed a technique called **brainstorming,** designed to enhance the productivity of problem-solving groups. The ground rules for brainstorming call for a free-wheeling, creative approach:

- Express *all* ideas that come to mind, even if they sound crazy.
- The more ideas, the better.
- Don't worry whether the ideas are good or bad, and don't criticize anyone's ideas; they can be evaluated later.
- All ideas belong to the group, so members should feel free to build on each other's work.

Osborn (1953) claimed that by using these procedures, groups could generate more and better ideas than could individuals working alone. The gimmick caught on. Brainstorming was soon a popular exercise in business, government, and education; and it remains so today. But when the research caught up with the hype, it turned out that Osborn's faith in the group process was unfounded. In fact, "nominal groups" (several individuals working alone) produce a greater number of better ideas than do real groups in which members interact with each other. Brainstorming can indeed be effective, but people brainstorming individually produce more and higher-quality ideas than the same number of people brainstorming together. One meta-analysis concluded that brainstorming groups are only about half as productive as an equal number of individuals working alone (Mullen et al., 1991). Rather than being inspired by each other and building on each other's ideas,

"*Nor is the people's judgment always true: The most may err as grossly as the few.*"

—John Dryden

TABLE 8.4   Brainstorming in Groups: Problems and Solutions

Factors That Reduce the Effectiveness of Group Brainstorming

- **Production blocking:** When people have to wait for their turn to speak, they may forget their ideas, may be too busy trying to remember their ideas to listen to others or to generate new ones, or may simply lose interest.

- **Free riding:** As others contribute ideas, individuals may feel less motivated to work hard themselves. They see their own contributions as less necessary or less likely to have much impact.

- **Evaluation apprehension:** In the presence of others, people may be hesitant to suggest wild, off-the-wall ideas for fear of looking foolish and being criticized. Even if they are willing to suggest such ideas, they may spend time preparing to justify them—time that they otherwise could have spent coming up with more ideas.

- **Performance matching:** Group members work only as hard as they see others work. Once the other three factors have reduced the performance of a brainstorming group, performance matching can help maintain this relatively inferior performance.

Why Electronic Brainstorming Is Effective

- Production blocking is reduced because members can type in ideas whenever they come to mind.

- Free riding can be reduced by having the computer keep track of each member's input.

- Evaluation apprehension is reduced because group members contribute their ideas anonymously.

- Performance matching is reduced because group members spend less time focusing on the performance of others as they type in their own ideas. In addition, performance matching is less of a problem because the initial performance of groups brainstorming electronically is likely to be high.

- Group members can benefit by seeing the ideas of others, which can inspire new ideas that they might not otherwise have considered.

---

people brainstorming in a group underperform (Brown & Paulus, 1996; Paulus & Paulus, 1997).

A number of possible explanations have been proposed for why brainstorming is ineffective (see the top of Table 8.4). One prime candidate is *production blocking* (Stroebe & Diehl, 1994). Alone, people produce at their own pace without any distractions. In a group, they have to listen to what others are saying while they wait their turn to speak up. Distracted by listening to others, people forget some of their ideas. Another factor is *free riding* (Kerr & Bruun, 1983), which is a form of

brainstorming A technique that attempts to increase the production of creative ideas by encouraging group members to speak freely without criticizing their own or others' contributions.

People brainstorming as a group come up with a greater number of better ideas than the same number of people working individually. **False.**

"A committee should consist of three men, two of whom are absent."

—Hebert Beerbohm Tree

Although people often feel productive when brainstorming in a group, that feeling can be an illusion.

Richard Cline © 1995 from The New Yorker Collection. All Rights Reserved.

social loafing. Group members sit back and let others do most of the work, feeling that their own efforts are not that important. A third factor that inhibits group brainstorming is *evaluation apprehension* (Camacho & Paulus, 1995). Despite the fact that they're encouraged to express all ideas, no matter how crazy, people may fear being negatively evaluated by other group members; so they become less creative and more inhibited. A fourth factor is *performance matching* (Paulus & Dzindolet, 1993). Alone, people set their own standards. In a group, each person's standard can be influenced by the performance of other participants; and an initially poor performance by group members can perpetuate itself as each individual matches the low standard that prevails. Because of the other three factors—production blocking, free riding, and evaluation apprehension—group brainstorming is likely to begin relatively poorly; and performance matching then contributes to maintaining that poor performance.

It's particularly ironic, then, that people who engage in group brainstorming typically think that it works wonderfully. Despite the research evidence, brainstorming is still a popular device in many organizations. People who participate in interactive brainstorming groups evaluate their own performance more favorably than do individuals in nominal groups. They also enjoy themselves more. And those who have not participated in an interactive brainstorming group believe that such groups are highly productive. Both the experienced and the inexperienced cling to the illusion that group brainstorming is much better than individual brainstorming (Paulus et al., 1993; Stroebe et al., 1992).

Group brainstorming may indeed benefit the group in indirect ways—for example, it can be a fun experience that promotes goodwill and cohesion—but as we have seen, its effect on idea generation is much poorer than most group members realize. One strategy to improve productivity while also promoting the enjoyment that group brainstorming can produce is to alternate brainstorming sessions, having members brainstorm together and then individually (Paulus & Paulus, 1997). Another strategy is to use a facilitator trained to understand the factors that impair group brainstorming. The facilitator can cut people off who stray from the task, discourage evaluation, call on individuals to prevent them from free riding, and keep motivating them to do more ("Come on, a few more ideas and we break fifty!") (Offner et al., 1996; Oxley et al., 1996).

Computers offer a new and promising way to improve group brainstorming. Electronic brainstorming combines the freedom of working alone at a computer with the stimulation of receiving the ideas of others on a screen. The bottom of Table 8.4 presents some of the factors that make this type of brainstorming effective. The research on electronic brainstorming is encouraging, suggesting that interactive groups often perform about as well as nominal groups, and—in some situations, such as when the group is relatively large—may even perform better than nominal groups. Brainstorming may have found its true home on the information superhighway (Gallupe et al., 1991; Paulus et al., 1996; Roy et al., 1996; Valacich et al., 1994).

"Are we thinking here, or is this just so much pointing and clicking?"

Biased Sampling and Communication: Getting Ideas on the Table   Brainstorming stresses the need for creativity. On some tasks, however, simply sharing information is crucial for good performance. Unfortunately, as Garold Stasser (1992) points out, not all the information available to individual members will necessarily be brought before the group. Rather, information that is known to many group members is more likely to enter the group discussion than information known to only one or a few group members. Stasser calls this process *biased sampling*. Because of biased sampling, a group may fail to consider important information that is not common knowledge in the group. Inadequately informed, the group may make a bad decision (Stasser & Titus, 1985).

Recent research has discovered several conditions in which biased sampling is less likely to occur. For example, if individuals who have unique information are made aware that others do not, or may not, have this information, they are more likely to share their information with the group. Imagine, for example, that your group is discussing which of several candidates should be supported for an election. You read some potentially damaging personal information about one of the candidates, and you assume that the others are also aware of it. On the one hand, if you observe during group discussion that nobody else mentions this information, you may assume that the others don't think the information is relevant or credible; so you may not mention it yourself. On the other hand, if you suspect that you are the only one with the information, you may be more likely to introduce the information into the group discussion (Henry, 1995; Schittekatte & van Hiel, 1996). Similarly, if group members are assigned expert roles and are told who in the group has unique information, the group is more likely to share all of the relevant information and make correct decisions (Stasser et al., 1995). In addition, when two group members know the uncommon information rather than just one member, it is more likely to be discussed and used by the rest of the group, possibly because the other person can validate the information if it is brought up (Schittekatte & van Hiel, 1996). It is important, however, that group members who introduce new information are trusted and taken seriously. In one study, for example, Kathleen Propp (1995) found that when the unique information was presented by a woman, it was less likely to be used by the group to make decisions than if it was presented by a man. Another problem is that as groups gain experience both with each other and with a task, they may focus even more on common information and be even less likely to use information that is unique to particular group members (Kim, 1997).

Sometimes, biased sampling can have tragic consequences. The commission formed to investigate the explosion of the space shuttle *Challenger* concluded that inadequate sharing of information contributed to the disaster. Some engineers had information indicating that it would be unsafe to launch the shuttle that morning because of the low temperature, but this information was not shared with everyone. The people who ultimately made the decision to launch therefore were not aware of all the information that was relevant for their decision. The commission concluded, "If the decision-makers had known all the facts, it is highly unlikely that they would have decided to launch" (*Report of the Presidential Commission*, 1986, p. 82).

Part of the problem in the *Challenger* situation was that the *communication network*, which defines who can speak with whom based on a group's structure, made it difficult for information to be distributed to all of the decision makers. In many organizations, information is passed up a chain of command, through layers of middle management, and only some of this information makes it all the way up to the executives who make the final decisions. This may have been the case at NASA. The engineers who were most familiar with the details of the O-rings did not communicate directly with the NASA officials at the top of the chain of command.

Those who occupied positions in the middle of the chain felt pressure from both sides—they were pressured by some engineers below them to delay the launch, but they were pressured by administrators above them not to delay. The high-level engineer who was told to "take off his engineering hat and put on one representing management" illustrates this position. Because warnings were suppressed as the flow of information moved up the chain of command, the people at the top did not know about the concerns of those lower in the chain.

We should note that not everyone agrees that failure to get the facts on the table was the major cause of the accident. As we noted earlier in the chapter, groupthink seems to have been a factor. In addition, Barbara Romzek and Melvin Dubnick (1987) cite the political pressures put on NASA to complete the launch of the space shuttle, as well as the transfer of decision-making authority within NASA from expert professionals to administrators. These developments changed the grounds on which the launch decision was made and increased the likelihood that safety would not come first. Under some circumstances, group discussion has little impact on later decisions, serving primarily as a justification for individuals to act according to their prior judgments (Gigone & Hastie, 1993).

Information Processing   Once a group has all the available information, group members must process that information and use it to make judgments or perform tasks. How well do groups process information, compared with individuals? In general, groups are susceptible to the same information-processing biases as individuals—only more so. For example, as explained in Chapter 4, when individuals process information and make judgments, they often rely on *cognitive heuristics*—information-processing rules of thumb that enable them to think in ways that are quick and easy but that frequently lead to error. These heuristics bias the judgments made by groups even more extremely than they bias the judgments made by individuals. For example, individuals tend to overuse representativeness—that is, they tend to judge the likelihood of an event occurring by how typical it seems (Argote et al., 1990). Groups tend to overuse this heuristic even more. Groups also exaggerate the individual tendency to commit the base-rate fallacy—that is, to underutilize numerical base rates, or probabilities, when making judgments and rely instead on more vivid but less predictive information (Nagao et al., 1985). In reviewing the research on group information processing, Verlin Hinsz and his colleagues (1997) conclude, "If some bias, error, or tendency predisposes individuals to process information in a particular way, then groups exaggerate this tendency. However, if this bias, error, or tendency is unlikely among individuals processing the information (e.g., less than half the sample), then groups are even less likely to process information in this fashion" (pp. 49–50).

An information-processing bias that can be particularly costly to organizations and businesses is **entrapment** (Brockner & Rubin, 1985). Entrapment occurs when commitment to a failing course of action is increased to justify investments already made. In numerous instances, groups, businesses, and governments have incurred huge costs because they kept throwing more money, time, and other resources into a project that should have been terminated long before. One example is British Columbia's escalation of its commitment to host a world's fair in 1986 despite rapidly growing budget deficits (from a projection of $6 million in 1978 to a projection of over $300 million in 1985) (Ross & Staw, 1986). Another is the U.S. government's escalation of the war in Vietnam in the mid-1960s despite mounting evidence that its strategy would not succeed (Janis, 1982). Laboratory experiments show that groups are more likely to escalate commitment to a failing project, and are likely to do so in more extreme ways, than are individuals (Dietz-Uhler, 1996; Whyte, 1993).

Another problem for people working in groups is that they often recall information more poorly than the same number of individuals working alone (Basden et

Groups are less likely than individuals to invest more and more resources in a project that is failing. **False.**

entrapment   The condition in which commitments to a failing course of action are increased to justify investments already made.

al., 1997; Weldon & Bellinger, 1997). However, the information-processing story is not all bad for groups. For example, education programs that have students work in cooperative teams can be very effective in helping students learn (Aronson et al., 1978; Hertz-Lazarowitz & Miller, 1992; Lloyd et al., 1996). In addition, just as individuals can learn and improve their skills over time, so can groups. As groups gain experience in production, for example, their productivity typically improves significantly, particularly if group membership is stable (Argote et al., 1995).

Diversity   As we begin the twenty-first century, groups around the world, whether in schools, organizations, businesses, sports, arts, or governments, are becoming increasingly diverse, most obviously in terms of sex, race, ethnicity, and cultural background. How does diversity affect group performance? How can a group best use diversity to its advantage? The answers to such questions—and even the meaning of *diversity*—are likely to change as society changes in terms of its demographics and attitudes. Thus, the issues surrounding diversity are particularly challenging. In the meantime, though, a great deal of new research is addressing these issues (Brewer, 1995; Chemers et al., 1995; Jackson et al., 1995; Milliken & Martins, 1996; Northcraft et al., 1995), and some tentative conclusions can be offered.

Stunned by the escalation of the Vietnam War and paralyzed by the feeling of entrapment in the conflict, President Lyndon Johnson decided not to seek re-election in 1968. Here, he listens to a tape-recorded message from his son-in-law, who was serving in the U.S. military in Vietnam.

Much of the empirical research has demonstrated that diverse groups often perform less well than homogeneous groups and that diversity is associated with negative group dynamics (Levine & Moreland, 1998; Maznevski, 1994). Miscommunications and misunderstandings are more likely to arise among heterogeneous group members, causing frustration and resentment and damaging group performance by weakening coordination, morale, and commitment to the group. Cliques often form in diverse groups, causing some group members to feel alienated (Jackson et al., 1995; Maznevski, 1994). And even if diversity doesn't appear to hurt a group in any objective way, group members may *think* that it does. For example, S. Gayle Baugh and George Graen (1997) compared how diverse and homogeneous project teams rated their own effectiveness. Project teams that were diverse in terms of gender and race rated themselves as less effective—even though external evaluators judged the diverse teams to be no less effective than the homogeneous teams.

Research has also demonstrated positive effects of diversity. Diversity can give a group flexibility, creativity, and the ability to succeed on tasks that require innovative approaches (Levine & Moreland, 1998). As more and more organizations try to attract customers and investors from diverse cultures, diversity in personnel should offer more and more advantages. In one study, for example, ethnically diverse groups and all-white groups brainstormed to come up with ideas to get more tourists to visit the United States, a topic that the researchers chose for its relevance to diversity. The ideas produced by the ethnically diverse groups were judged to be more effective and feasible than the ideas produced by the all-white groups (McLeod et al., 1996).

In reviewing the literature on diversity and group performance, Martha Maznevski (1994) concluded that diversity can enhance a group's performance if the group is integrated. Heterogeneity is not as likely to help a group if there are many cliques, if there is little communication or equal-status interaction among the diverse group members, and if there is a lack of shared identity. Maznevski proposes that strategies to improve communication can promote true integration of diverse group members, which should help groups reap the benefits that diversity can offer.

Cooperation, Competition, and Conflict: Responding to Differences

The importance of group performance is crystal clear for some of the crucial issues confronting our world today. What determines whether people will act responsibly to protect the environment? What factors contribute to the escalation of conflict? Are there ways to reduce conflict once it has started? For answers to these questions, both individual characteristics and group processes must be considered. In Chapter 13, we examine the effectiveness of specific kinds of leadership in specific organizational circumstances. Here, we describe individual and group influences on cooperation, competition, and conflict. When there are differences between us, how do we respond?

Mixed Motives and Social Dilemmas

Imagine that you have to make a choice between cooperating with others in your group and pursuing your own self-interests, which can hurt the others. Examples of these mixed-motive situations are everywhere. An actor in a play may be motivated to try to "steal" a scene, a basketball player may be inclined to hog the ball, an executive may want to keep more of the company's profits, a family member may want to eat more than her fair share of the leftover birthday cake, and a citizen of the earth may want to use more than his fair share of finite, valuable resources. In each case, the individual can gain something by pursuing his or her self-interests; but if everyone in the group pursues self-interests, all of the group members will ultimately be worse off than if they had cooperated with each other. Each option, therefore, has possible benefits along with potential costs. When you are in a situation like this, you may feel torn between wanting to cooperate and wanting to compete, and these mixed motives create a difficult dilemma. What do you do?

The notion that the pursuit of self-interest can sometimes be self-destructive forms the basis for what is called a **social dilemma.** In a social dilemma, what is good for one is bad for all. If everyone makes the most self-rewarding choice, everyone suffers the greatest loss. This section examines how people resolve the tension between their cooperative and competitive inclinations in social dilemmas.

The Prisoner's Dilemma   We begin with a detective story. Two partners in crime are picked up by the police for questioning. Although the police believe they have committed a major offense, there is only enough evidence to convict them on a minor charge. In order to sustain a conviction for the more serious crime, the police will have to convince one of them to testify against the other. Separated during questioning, the criminals weigh their alternatives (see Figure 8.6). If neither confesses, they will both get light sentences on the minor charge. If both confess and plead guilty, they will both receive moderate sentences. But if one confesses and the other stays silent, the confessing criminal will secure immunity from prosecution while the silent criminal will pay the maximum penalty.

This story forms the basis for the research paradigm known as the *prisoner's dilemma.* In the two-person prisoner's dilemma, participants are given a series of choices in which they have the option of cooperating or competing. If both individuals make the cooperative choice, both obtain a moderate reward. If both make the competitive choice, both suffer a moderate loss. But if one cooperates while the other competes, the competitor obtains a large reward, and the cooperator suffers a large loss. Consider an example: Imagine that you're Prisoner A in Figure 8.6. It appears that no matter what Prisoner B does, you're better off if you compete with B and confess. If B doesn't confess to the police (in other words, if he cooperates

An extensive Web site containing essays, books, and other information about social dilemmas is the following: www.magnolia.net/~leonf/sd/sd.html

social dilemma A situation in which a self-interested choice by everyone creates the worst outcome for everyone.

with you), you get a lighter sentence if you do confess (in other words, if you compete with him by not staying quiet) than if you don't confess—if you confess, you get no jail; if you don't confess, you get one year. If B does confess, you still get a lighter sentence if you confess than if you don't—five versus ten years. So, clearly, you should confess, right? But here's the dilemma: If you *both* confess, each of you gets five years. If *neither* of you confesses, each of you gets only one year. It's really a perplexing situation. What do you think *you* would do?

This kind of social dilemma is not limited to situations involving only two individuals at a time. Imagine, for example, being in a burning building or a sinking ship, as

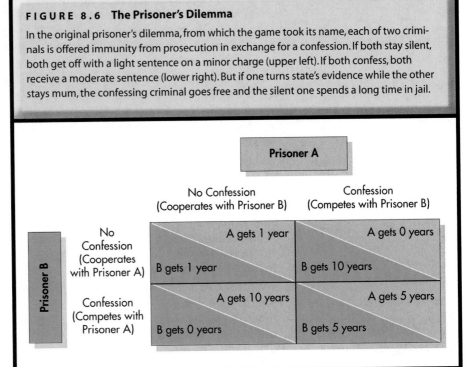

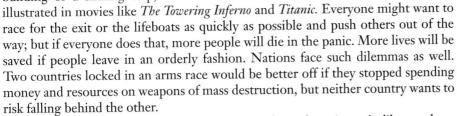

FIGURE 8.6 The Prisoner's Dilemma
In the original prisoner's dilemma, from which the game took its name, each of two criminals is offered immunity from prosecution in exchange for a confession. If both stay silent, both get off with a light sentence on a minor charge (upper left). If both confess, both receive a moderate sentence (lower right). But if one turns state's evidence while the other stays mum, the confessing criminal goes free and the silent one spends a long time in jail.

illustrated in movies like *The Towering Inferno* and *Titanic*. Everyone might want to race for the exit or the lifeboats as quickly as possible and push others out of the way; but if everyone does that, more people will die in the panic. More lives will be saved if people leave in an orderly fashion. Nations face such dilemmas as well. Two countries locked in an arms race would be better off if they stopped spending money and resources on weapons of mass destruction, but neither country wants to risk falling behind the other.

By now, thousands of participants in research on the prisoner's dilemma have confronted various versions of this mixed-motive problem. One strategy that many people eventually adopt over the course of multiple trials is known as *tit-for-tat*—a reciprocal strategy in which cooperation by one elicits cooperation by the other, while competition by one provokes competition by the other (Enzle et al., 1975). This strategy tends to result in relatively positive joint outcomes for the people involved in the dilemma, eliciting much higher levels of cooperation than most other strategies (Axelrod, 1984; Pruitt, 1998). But cooperation and competitiveness are not equally powerful. Competitiveness is a very strong determinant of reciprocity. Once one party makes a competitive move, the other party is highly likely to follow suit (Kelley & Stahelski, 1970). In contrast, a cooperative move, may not elicit cooperation: People who are consistently and unconditionally cooperative can be exploited and taken advantage of (Komorita et al., 1993). When British Prime Minister Neville Chamberlain tried to prevent war in the 1930s by cooperating with Hitler, it gave Hitler the opportunity to become more aggressive.

An alternative to simple reciprocity that is often successful is *win-stay, lose-shift*—a strategy consistent with basic learning principles and conditioning. Using this strategy, individuals continue to compete or cooperate as long as the payoff they receive is high, but they shift to the opposite action whenever the payoff is low (Kraines & Kraines, 1995; Nowak & Sigmund, 1993).

Resource Dilemmas   The prisoner's dilemma sets up a trap for those who play it: Attempts to gain an advantage will backfire if the other party also makes the competitive choice. This conflict of motives also forms the basis for another category

Would you like to try participating in a prisoner's dilemma game online? Some Web sites offer a chance for you to do this. For example, check out the following: ucsub.Colorado.EDU/~danielsm/PD/PD.html

of social dilemmas: *resource dilemmas*, which concern how two or more people share a limited resource. Resource dilemmas come in two basic types: (1) commons dilemmas and (2) public goods dilemmas.

The *commons dilemma* is a situation in which, if people take as much as they want of a limited resource that does not replenish itself, nothing will be left for anyone. Garrett Hardin (1968) called this process the "tragedy of the commons." In former times, people would let their animals graze on the town's lush, grassy commons. But if all the animals grazed to their hearts' content, and to their own-ers' benefit, the commons would be stripped, the animals' food supply diminished, and the owners' welfare threatened. Today, the tragedy of the commons is a clear and present danger on a global scale. Deforestation, air pollution, ocean dumping, massive irrigation, overfishing, commercial development of wilderness areas, a rapidly increasing population in some developing countries, and an overconsuming population in the richest nations—all pit individual self-interest against the common good. Selfish responses to commons dilemmas are social sins of commission; people take too much.

In contrast, selfish responses to *public goods dilemmas* are social sins of omission. In public goods dilemmas, all of the individuals are supposed to contribute resources to a common pool. Examples of these public goods include the blood supply, public broadcasting, schools, libraries, roads, and parks. If no one gives, the service can't continue (Olson, 1965). If club members don't pay their dues or contribute their time, the club will fail. Again, private gain conflicts with the public good.

Solving Social Dilemmas   When does individual desire prevail in social dilem-mas? When, in contrast, do people see beyond their own immediate potential for gain and consider the long-term benefits of cooperation? Social dilemmas pose a serious threat to the quality of life and even to life itself. How do people try to solve them? Although there are many factors that influence people's attempts to solve these dilemmas (Bazerman et al., 1997; Komorita & Parks, 1994; McCusker & Carnevale, 1995), in this section we focus on two general categories. One emphasizes psychological factors, and the other highlights structural arrangements (see Table 8.5).

The psychological factors that influence people's behavior in a social dilemma include a variety of personal characteristics. One way in which individuals differ from each other is in how concerned they are for their own outcomes relative to others' outcomes (Van Lange, 1992). People with a *cooperative orientation* seek to maximize joint gains. Those with an *individualist orientation* seek to maximize their own gain, and those with a *competitive orientation* seek to maximize their own gain relative to that of others. People with a cooperative orientation are less likely to behave in a competitive, resource-consuming fashion than are people with

"If a free society cannot help the many who are poor, it cannot save the few who are rich."

—John F. Kennedy

A social dilemma is created by a con-flict between private benefit and the public good. When individuals dump trash at their convenience, they spoil the environment for everyone.

individualistic or competitive orientations (Parks, 1994). For example, researchers in the Netherlands found that commuters with a cooperative orientation are more likely than commuters with individualist or competitive orientations to use public transportation instead of their cars (Van Vugt et al., 1996). Another individual difference concerns how trusting people are. Individuals low in trust continue to compete against another in a prisoner's dilemma even when this other person announces an intention to cooperate (Parks et al., 1996).

There are also cultural differences in how people behave in social dilemmas. People from individualist cultures tend to cooperate less and compete more than people from collectivist cultures. For example, Craig Parks and Anh Vu (1994) found that participants from the United States, an individualist culture, were less likely to cooperate in the prisoner's dilemma, commons dilemma, and public goods dilemma than were people from South Viet-

TABLE 8.5 Solving Social Dilemmas
Behavior in a social dilemma is influenced by both psychological factors and structural arrangements. The characteristics listed here contribute to the solution of a social dilemma through direct effects on individuals or through deliberate modifications of social structures.

Psychological Factors

- Individual and cultural differences

    Having a cooperative personal orientation

    Trusting others

    Having a collectivist cultural orientation

- Situational factors

    Being in a good mood

    Having had successful experience managing resources and working cooperatively

    Seeing unselfish models

    Having reason to expect others to cooperate

- Group dynamics

    Acting as an individual rather than in a group

    Being in a small group

Structural Arrangements

- Creating a payoff structure that rewards cooperative behavior and/or punishes selfish behavior

- Removing resources from the public domain and handing them over to private ownership

- Establishing an authority to control the resources

nam, a collectivist culture. Taylor Cox and his colleagues (1991) demonstrated that even within the United States, different cultural orientations are associated with different kinds of responses. In their research, groups composed of participants from more collectivist cultural traditions (African, Asian, and Hispanic Americans) displayed more cooperation in a prisoner's dilemma than did groups composed of participants from individualist cultural traditions (European Americans).

To be sure, collectivist cultures are not immune from competitive behavior in social dilemmas. Kaori Sato (1987) had groups of students in Japan manage twenty trees in a simulated forest. The group members could harvest the trees and receive money. If all the group members waited to harvest the trees until they had grown to maximum height, the students would receive more money. But if a group member waited while others harvested the trees first, he or she would be left out of the profits. American students in this kind of commons dilemma often fail to show patience and trust; instead, they gobble up the common resource right away, before the resource can grow to its potential (Edney, 1979). What about the collectivist Japanese students? They too tended to take from their shared resource too early, harvesting the trees before they had a chance to grow fully and provide the group with maximum profit.

Situational factors also influence competitiveness and cooperation. Mood, for instance, affects behavior concerning scarce resources. People experiencing negative moods, such as anger and sadness, have difficulty delaying gratification and tend to take what they want without sufficient regard for the long-term consequences (Knapp & Clark, 1991). In a highly competitive environment, a good mood increases efforts to preserve the common good (Hertel & Fiedler, 1994). Prior experience also has an impact. Individuals given a chance to manage their own, privately controlled resource are more socially responsible in using a collectively controlled resource than are those without this preliminary opportunity (Allison & Messick, 1985). And people who have had a successful experience in working cooperatively are more likely to contribute to a public good (Allison & Kerr, 1994).

Information about what others are doing, or are likely to do, is another important determinant of responses to a social dilemma. Imagine that you live in an area suffering from a water shortage, and you learn that others are making a serious effort to conserve. What's your reaction? The socially responsible behavior of others may encourage you to cooperate as well (Orbell et al., 1988). Even people with a competitive orientation are willing to cooperate if they are confident that others will cooperate (Van Lange & Liebrand, 1991). Expectations about whether others will cooperate often derive from group stereotypes. In one set of studies involving students in the Netherlands, Carsten De Dreu and colleagues (1995) placed participants in a prisoner's dilemma situation with a stranger who they were told was either a business major or a religion major. The students expected more competitiveness if they thought the other person was a business major, and so they behaved more competitively themselves. If the students learned other information about the person that weakened this stereotype, however, the effect of the other person's major was reduced.

Groups as well as individuals can participate in a prisoner's dilemma or can take action together in a resource dilemma. Typically, groups are less cooperative and more competitive than individuals. According to John Schopler, Chester Insko, and their colleagues (1993; Insko & Schopler, 1998; Insko et al., 1994), the competitiveness of groups has its roots in fear and greed—the fear that the other group will exploit one's own group and the greedy desire to maximize the outcomes achieved by one's own group at the other group's expense. Individuals, too, can be driven by fear and greed, but competition between groups intensifies such motives. Another reason why groups are more competitive than individuals is that group members feel less identifiable by members of the other group. The greater anonymity that a group offers frees individual group members to act in a self-interested, aggressive manner (Schopler et al., 1995).

The size of the group also affects responses to social dilemmas. Large groups are more likely to exploit scarce resources than are small ones (Allison et al., 1992). There are three major reasons for the influence of group size. First, it's harder to identify with the welfare of others when the group is large; and people are more socially responsible when they share a meaningful group membership with the other people affected by the dilemma (Kramer & Brewer, 1984). Second, people believe that their actions have more of an impact in a small group; and the more they think that their contribution matters, the more likely they are to contribute to a public good (Kerr, 1992a; Shepperd, 1993a). Third, people are likely to have more face-to-face interactions and greater communication with the others in a small group, making group members more likely to establish and enforce commitments and norms to cooperate, recognize common interests, and engage in long-range thinking (Bouas & Komorita, 1996; Kerr & Kaufman-Gilliland, 1994; Pruitt, 1998).

But many social dilemmas involve very large groups—a city, a state, a nation, the whole world. In these circumstances, the psychological factors we have described may be less effective. Various structural arrangements, such as those listed in Table 8.5, offer an alternative. The most commonly employed structural solution to social dilemmas is to set up a controlling authority (Messick et al., 1983;

Sato, 1987). The Environmental Protection Agency (EPA) was established by the U.S. government to protect the quality of the environment. But maintaining a regulating authority such as the EPA is not cost-free. If regulatory agencies fail to work effectively, the society suffers a double loss—of the endangered resource and of the funds used to support the agency. To solve a social dilemma, people often have to decide where to place their trust: in their fellow citizens or in government authorities.

Large groups are more likely than small groups to exploit a scarce resource that the members collectively depend on. **True.**

Conflict Escalation

Social dilemmas can create important conflicts between groups, and how groups resolve these dilemmas can make the difference between war and peace. There are, of course, many other sources of conflict between groups. The very fact that groups differ from each other on any of a number of dimensions—religious, ethnic, racial, cultural, political—can spark conflict. Again and again, throughout human history, differences between groups explode in hatred and bloodshed. What fans the flames of an escalating conflict? No doubt, many factors are involved (Rubin et al., 1994). *Conflict spirals* are frequent, as one party annoys the other party, who retaliates, prompting a more extreme reaction from the first party, and so on (Holmes & Murray, 1996; Rubin et al., 1994; Youngs, 1986). Earlier in this chapter, we discussed entrapment, in which groups escalate commitments to a failing plan to justify the commitment they have already made. Entrapment contributes to conflict escalation by motivating those on the losing side of a conflict

Group conflict is hard to stop. After Israel and the Palestinian Liberation Organization signed initial peace accords, groups opposed to the peace process increased their violent attacks. In one of the worst incidents, two Palestinian suicide bombers killed twenty-one people at an Israeli army bus stop.

to keep trying to come out on top or by motivating both sides in an enduring conflict that shows no signs of progress to keep fighting. In this section, we concentrate on two other factors that can intensify conflict: threat capacity and biased perceptions of others.

Threat Capacity   It seems obvious that the ability to punish someone who engages in a prohibited behavior can act as a deterrent to conflict escalation. You're less likely to mess with someone who can mess right back with you. If both parties hold their fire, a balance of terror can work. But having the capacity to attack can present an irresistible temptation to do so.

A classic study conducted by Morton Deutsch and Robert Krauss (1960) makes the point. These investigators had pairs of female participants engage in a simulated work environment in which each was in charge of a trucking company carrying merchandise over a road to a specific destination. Because they had to share parts of the road, they had to coordinate their efforts. However, in one condition of the study, one of the women in each pair had the capacity to take control of the road and block the other's progress, which would increase her own profit and reduce the other participant's profit. In another condition, both participants in each pair had this capacity. What was the result?

In general, when a participant had the ability to block the other, she did—and both participants suffered. Overall, participants earned more money if neither could block the other than if one of them could, and when *both* members of the pair could block the other, the participants earned least of all. These results suggest that once coercive means are available, people tend to use them, even when doing so damages their own outcomes.

Perceptions of the Other   Stereotypes and prejudice also play a major role in conflict escalation between groups. During conflict, the opposing group and its members are often perceived as "the other"—strange, foreign, alien. They are characterized in simplistic, exaggerated ways (Tetlock, 1988). Held at a psychological distance, the other becomes a screen on which it is possible to project one's worst fears. Here's what people see:

First, there's a *mirror image:* What we see in our enemies is what our enemies see in us. As Urie Bronfenbrenner (1961) discovered when he visited the Soviet Union during the Cold War, the Soviets saw Americans as aggressive, exploitative, and untrustworthy—just like the Americans saw them.

Second, there's a *double standard:* Whatever we do is good; whatever our enemies do is bad. When Stuart Oskamp (1965) asked American college students to evaluate identical actions taken by the United States and the Soviet Union, he found that U.S. actions were evaluated more favorably than those taken by the Soviets. This double standard persisted through the 1980s among American students and, to a lesser extent, among French-Canadian students (Tobin & Eagles, 1992).

Third, there are *conflict-maintaining attributions:* The most negative explanation is always preferred. Like the partners in an unhappy intimate relationship, opponents are inclined to believe the worst about each other and to discount more positive indications. For example, John Foster Dulles, U.S. secretary of state during the 1950s, attributed declines in Soviet hostility to economic weakness, ulterior motives, policy failures, and internal problems (Holsti, 1962). The possibility of more peaceful intentions seems never to have been considered.

Taken to extremes, negative views of the other can result in *dehumanization,* the perception that people lack human qualities or are "subhuman." Based on malicious stereotypes about outgroups, dehumanization is both a consequence of hostility between groups and an incitement to intergroup conflict (Bandura, 1990; Struch & Schwartz, 1989). Indeed, fueled by dehumanization, the sporadic violence of rampaging mobs can escalate into systematic state-sanctioned genocide: Aggression against the outgroup is justified by dehumanization, which is used to excuse more aggression, which requires more dehumanization to justify, and so on (Bar-Tal, 1990). As the Nazis began the Holocaust, they released propaganda that characterized Jews as less than human—as rats that spread disease and needed to be exterminated. During World War II, the United States portrayed the Japanese people as cold, identical robots. At the same time, the Japanese media portrayed Americans as bloodthirsty animals, as in cartoons depicting eagles flying off with bloodied Japanese citizens in their talons.

Dehumanization is the ultimate version of "us" versus "them," removing all religious and ethical constraints against the taking of human life. As George Orwell (1942) discovered during the Spanish Civil War, the cure for dehumanization is to restore the human connection. Sighting an enemy soldier holding up his trousers with both hands while running beside a nearby trench, Orwell was unable to take the easy shot: "I had come here to shoot at 'Fascists'; but a man who is holding up his trousers isn't a 'Fascist,' he is visibly a fellow creature, similar to yourself, and you don't feel like shooting at him" (p. 254).

Reducing Conflict

With all the forces pressing it forward (see Table 8.6 for a summary), conflict escalation is hardly surprising. But the desire for peace is still strong and pervasive. In this section, we examine the kind of sustained effort that peacemaking requires.

True GRIT Every once in a while, individual leaders try to break the gridlock of intergroup conflict by taking a unilateral step toward peace. U.S. President John Kennedy banned atmospheric nuclear tests without a pledge from the Soviets to do likewise; Egyptian President Anwar Sadat flew to Jerusalem uncertain of the reception he would receive; Soviet General Secretary Mikhail Gorbachev withdrew Soviet forces from Afghanistan before meeting with U.S. President Ronald Reagan in Moscow. The notion that unilateral concessions can reverse an escalating conflict is central to a peacemaking strategy developed by Charles Osgood (1962): **graduated and reciprocated initiatives in tension-reduction (GRIT).**

To see how GRIT works, imagine yourself using its four basic components (Lindskold et al., 1986).

1. You issue a general statement of your intention to reduce conflict. You also clearly announce your peaceful intentions each time you take a tension-reducing initiative. Throughout, you invite the other party to reciprocate. By taking these steps, you hope to enlist public support and put pressure on the other party to respond cooperatively.

> **TABLE 8.6** **Factors That Promote and Sustain the Escalation of Between-Group Conflict**
>
> - The group polarization process, which increases the extremity of group members' attitudes and opinions
> - Pressures for conformity, such as group cohesiveness and groupthink, which make it difficult for individuals to oppose the group's increasingly aggressive position
> - Entrapment, which seeks to justify past investments through the commitment of additional resources
> - Premature use of threat capacity, which triggers aggressive retaliation
> - Negative perceptions of "the other," which promote acceptance of aggressive behavior and enhance cohesiveness of the ingroup "us" against the outgroup "them"

Nelson Mandela and F. W. DeKlerk in a televised debate during their campaigns for the South African presidency. The cordial and dignified behavior of both candidates helped reduce tensions during the election. Mandela's historic victory marked the end of apartheid.

graduated and reciprocated initiatives in tension-reduction (GRIT) A strategy for unilateral, persistent efforts to establish trust and cooperation between opposing parties.

2. You carry out your tension-reducing initiatives as announced, even if there is no immediate reciprocation. These acts serve to establish your credibility. You enhance your credibility further by employing tension-reducing initiatives that can be verified by the other party or by neutral outside observers.

3. Once the other party makes a cooperative move, you quickly reciprocate. Your cooperative response risks at least as much as—and, if possible, more than—the other party's cooperative behavior.

4. You maintain a retaliatory capability in order to deter exploitation by the other party. If the other party attacks, you retaliate at precisely the same level. Once you have retaliated, you resume your unilateral tension-reducing efforts.

Reciprocal, tit-for-tat strategies like GRIT are maximally responsive: Cooperation is met with cooperation, attack with attack. Because the other party is given a greater sense of control over the interaction, the perceived risk of being cooperative is reduced (Friedland, 1990). GRIT also prevents exploitation by allowing for retaliation if it is necessary and avoids conflict escalation by keeping retaliatory actions within the level established by the other party. But GRIT is not simply reactive. It patiently, persistently, and proactively seeks peace. Research on GRIT is encouraging; even people with a competitive orientation tend to respond cooperatively to this strategy, and the positive effects of GRIT can be enduring (Lindskold & Han, 1988; Stone et al., 1996). These findings also suggest that it is not necessary to like an opponent to cooperate on various ventures. Instead, the essential elements are establishing at least a minimal level of trust and recognizing that one's own interests will benefit.

Negotiating with car dealers is a form of negotiation in which many of us engage from time to time. Want some tips? Try Edmund's Web site at: www.edmunds.com/edweb/usedinfo/ngtation.html

Negotiating   Unilateral concessions are useful for beginning the peace process, but extended negotiations are usually required to reach a final agreement. Negotiations on complex issues such as nuclear arms control and international environmental protection, as well as efforts to make peace in volatile regions such as the Middle East, often go on for years or even decades.

But negotiations are not restricted to the international scene. Unions and management engage in collective bargaining to establish employee contracts. Divorcing couples negotiate the terms of their divorce, by themselves or through their lawyers. Dating couples negotiate about which movie to attend. Families negotiate about who does which annoying household chores. Indeed, negotiations occur whenever there is a conflict that the parties wish to resolve without getting into an open fight or relying on an imposed legal settlement. There is an immense amount of research on negotiation and bargaining (Levine & Thompson, 1996; Pruitt & Carnevale, 1993). Here, we focus on those findings most relevant to conflict reduction.

Flexibility is one of the most important factors in successful negotiations. The most effective strategy combines flexibility and strength. For example, compromising late in a bargaining session is often a more successful approach than compromising early or not at all. A weak negotiator who compromises early invites exploitation; a rigid one who refuses to compromise at all sets the stage for the breakdown of negotiations (McGillicuddy et al., 1984; Nemeth & Brilmayer, 1987).

Flexible behavior at the negotiating table requires complex information processing that allows negotiators to consider various perspectives and strategies (Tetlock, 1988). Unfortunately, escalating conflict often interferes with complex information processing. A study of the statements of fourteen Middle Eastern leaders during the Persian Gulf crisis in the early 1990s found that the statements of some leaders supposedly involved in negotiations became less complex and more simplistic as the conflict progressed (Suedfeld et al., 1993).

The other key elements in negotiating successfully are communicating and trying to understand the point of view of the other person. It is always difficult for participants in a dispute to listen carefully to each other and to reach some reasonable understanding of each other's perspective. Communication difficulties are especially

TABLE 8.7 Cultural Assumptions About Negotiating

People from different cultures make different assumptions about the negotiation process. This table summarizes some assumptions commonly made by U.S. and other western negotiators. It also presents some alternative assumptions that may be held by negotiators from other cultures. As you can see, such different assumptions could make it very difficult to reach a successful agreement. *(Based on Kimmel, 1994.)*

Assumptions Made by Negotiators from the U.S. and other Western Countries	Alternatives
Negotiation is a business, not a social activity.	The first step in negotiating is to develop a trusting relationship between the individual negotiators.
Substantive issues are more important than social and emotional issues.	If you don't feel strongly about an issue, then it isn't important to you.
Communication is direct and verbal.	Some of the most important communications are nonverbal.
Written contracts are binding; oral commitments are not.	Written contracts are less meaningful than oral communications because the nonverbal context clarifies people's intentions.
Current information and ideas are more valid than historical or traditional opinions and information.	History and tradition are more valid than current information and ideas.
The representatives at the table have a great deal of latitude in reaching acceptable agreements for their sponsors.	Representatives have very little latitude.
Time is very important; punctuality is expected; deadlines should be set and adhered to.	Building a relationship takes time and is more important than punctuality; setting deadlines is an effort to humiliate the other party.

likely during negotiations between individuals and groups from different cultures (Berry et al., 1992; Fiske et al., 1998). Table 8.7 lists some common assumptions made by negotiators from the United States and other western countries that are not always shared by representatives from other cultures (Kimmel, 1994). If negotiators are not aware of these kinds of cross-cultural differences, the inevitable misunderstandings may prevent them from achieving a successful outcome.

But what constitutes success in negotiations? Perhaps the most common successful outcome is a 50-50 compromise, or what Jeffrey Rubin (1994) calls "concession-convergence." Here, the negotiators start at extreme positions and gradually work toward a mutually acceptable midpoint. Rubin emphasizes that under some circumstances, this is an entirely appropriate approach and a perfectly acceptable result.

Some negotiators, however, achieve a higher level of success. Most negotiations are not simply fixed-sum situations in which each side must give up something until a middle point is reached. Instead, there often exist ways in which both sides can benefit (Bazerman & Neale, 1992). When an **integrative agreement** is reached, both parties obtain outcomes that are superior to a 50-50 split. Take, for instance, the tale of the orange and the two sisters (Follett, 1942). One sister wanted the juice to drink; the other wanted the peel for a cake. So they sliced the orange in half and each one took her portion. These sisters suffered from an advanced case of the *"fixed pie" syndrome*. They assumed that whatever one of them won, the other lost. In fact, however, each of them could have had the whole thing: all of the juice for one, all of the peel for the other. An integrative agreement was well within their grasp, but they failed to see it. Unfortunately, research indicates that this happens all too often. Leigh Thompson and Dennis Hrebec (1996) conducted a meta-analysis of thirty-two experiments and found that in over 20 percent of negotiations that could have resulted in integrative agreements, the participants agreed to settlements that were worse for both sides. The ability to achieve integrative agreements is an acquired skill: Experienced negotiators obtain them more often than do inexperienced ones (Thompson, 1990).

Communication in which both sides disclose their goals and needs is critically important in allowing each side to see opportunities for joint benefits. This may seem obvious, and yet people in negotiations very often fail to communicate their goals and needs. In conflict negotiations, each party is likely to distrust and fear the other. Neither wants to reveal too much for fear of losing power at the bargaining table. Again, this is part of the fixed-pie syndrome. These fixed-pie perceptions often emerge very early, even before the negotiations have begun, and they can linger after negotiations are over. For example, negotiators in one set of studies (Thompson et al., 1995) felt better about the negotiation if they were told that the other party was disappointed with the outcome.

integrative agreement A negotiated resolution to a conflict in which all parties obtain outcomes that are superior to what they would have obtained from an equal division of the contested resources.

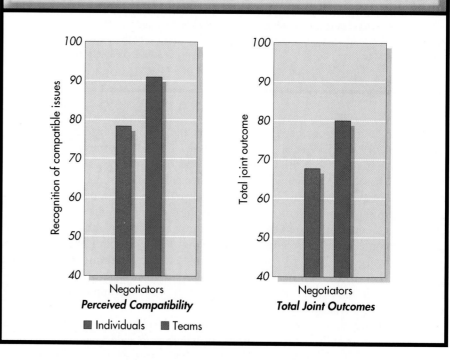

FIGURE 8.7   Negotiating by Individuals and Teams
Participants engaged in negotiations either in teams or as individuals. The two sides in the negotiations had some compatible issues—issues that lent themselves to mutually beneficial outcomes. Teams of negotiators were more likely than individual negotiators to perceive compatible issues, and they reached settlements that resulted in better joint outcomes. *(Adapted from Thompson et al., 1996)*

Although fixed-pie perceptions can prevent the two sides from disclosing information about themselves, if one party does disclose information, the disclosure can have dramatic effects. If one side discloses, the other party becomes much more likely to do so, enhancing the likelihood of integrative agreement (Thompson, 1991). The information disclosed should be honest and accurate, however. Sometimes people pretend to have opposing goals during negotiations so that they can appear to be compromising when in fact they are not. For example, in a divorce negotiation, one spouse may want custody of the children, and the other spouse may feign the same desire so that he or she can use this as a bargaining chip (O'Connor & Carnevale, 1997).

In addition to honest disclosure of information, several other factors can improve negotiations and increase the chances that both sides will benefit. These factors include training negotiators in conflict-resolution techniques (Dudley et al., 1996), using computerized negotiation support systems (Foroughi et al., 1995), and using GRIT (Lindskold & Han, 1988). One other factor that can improve negotiations might surprise you, given earlier discussions in this chapter about how groups often underperform compared to individuals: A team of negotiators is more likely to elicit integrative agreement than an individual negotiator. Figure 8.7 illustrates the results of one study that demonstrates this effect (Thompson et al., 1996). Why are teams more successful than individuals in producing integrative agreements? Teams need to coordinate their efforts and reduce ambiguity more than individuals. Teams therefore may be more likely than individuals to seek out as much information as they can, leading to more communication and a greater likelihood of discovering opportunities for integrative agreements (Polzer, 1996; Thompson et al., 1996).

During particularly difficult or significant negotiations, outside assistance may be sought. The more intense the conflict, the more likely it is to require forceful intervention (Fisher & Keashly, 1990). Some negotiations rely on an *arbitrator*, who has the power to impose a settlement. But it is more common for conflicting parties to request the participation of a *mediator*, who works with them to try to reach a voluntary agreement. Traditionally, mediators have been employed in labor-management negotiations and international conflicts (Carnevale, 1985). But increasingly, mediators help resolve a wide range of other disputes, such as those involving tenants and landlords, divorcing couples, and feuding neighbors (Pruitt & Kressel, 1985). Trained in negotiation and conflict management, mediators can often increase the likelihood of reaching a cooperative solution (Cahn, 1992).

Finding Common Ground   Every conflict is unique, as is every attempt at conflict resolution. Still, all efforts to find a constructive solution to conflict require some common ground to build upon. Recognition of a **superordinate identity** is one way to establish common ground between groups in conflict. When group members perceive that they have a shared identity—a sense of belonging to something larger than and encompassing their own groups—the attractiveness of outgroup members increases, and interactions between the groups often become more peaceful (Coombs, 1987; Dovidio, Kawakami, et al., 1997; Gaertner et al., 1989).

But how can groups engaged in violent conflict, bashing each other both verbally and physically, identify with each other? As described in Chapter 5, Muzafer Sherif and his colleagues (1961) faced this problem when the fierce intergroup competition and rivalry they had created between two groups of boys at summer camp resisted all initial efforts to restore the peace. Propaganda about how nice the other group was didn't work, nor did having the boys get together under pleasant circumstances. Only when the Rattlers and the Eagles had to cooperate to get what both groups wanted did negative perceptions and aggressive behaviors cease. *Superordinate goals* elicit cooperation by appealing to people's self-interest. Because everyone stands to benefit, no one has to be altruistic or compassionate to cooper-

superordinate identity The perception by members of different groups that they all belong to a larger whole.

Germans demonstrate against neo-Nazi groups and anti-Semitism. The sign, "I am a foreigner worldwide," proclaims that since we are all foreigners somewhere, there is no "them," only a superordinate human identity as "us."

ate in the pursuit of a mutual goal. During World War II, for example, the United States and the Soviet Union temporarily de-escalated their conflict when they shared the goal of defeating Nazi Germany.

Superordinate goals have another valuable characteristic: They can produce a superordinate identity. The experience of intergroup cooperation increases the sense of belonging to a single superordinate group (Gaertner et al., 1990). Even the mere expectation of a cooperative interaction increases empathy (Lanzetta & Englis, 1989), which plays a constructive role in human affairs—enhancing helpfulness and reducing aggression. Empathy can be narrowly focused, eliciting concern for only one individual instead of the group as a whole (Batson, Batson, et al., 1995). But extensive empathic connections between various members of each group could lay the foundation for an inclusive, rather than exclusive, social identity.

On the road to peace, both kinds of common ground are needed. Cooperation to meet shared goals makes similarities more visible, and a sense of a shared identity makes cooperation more likely. Those who would make peace, not war, realize that it is in their own self-interest to do so and understand that the cloak of humanity is large enough to cover a multitude of lesser differences.

Review

Collective Processes: The Presence of Others

■ In collectives, people engage in common activities but have minimal direct interaction.

Social Facilitation: When Others Arouse Us

■ In an early experiment, Triplett found that children performed faster when they worked side by side rather than alone.

■ Social facilitation refers to two effects that occur when individual contributions are identifiable: The presence of others enhances performance on easy tasks but impairs performance on difficult tasks.

- The theories of mere presence, evaluation apprehension, and distraction-conflict give different answers to questions concerning (1) whether social facilitation is necessarily social and (2) whether the mere presence of others is sufficient to affect performance.

Social Loafing: When Others Relax Us

- In early research on easy tasks involving pooled contributions, Ringelmann found that individual output declined when people worked with others.
- But social loafing is reduced or eliminated when people think their individual efforts will be important, relevant, and meaningful.

Facilitation and Loafing: Unifying the Paradigms

- A unified paradigm integrates social facilitation, social loafing, and what we've called "social security": when the presence of others enhances performance on difficult tasks involving pooled contributions.

Deindividuation: When People Lose Control

- Deindividuation diminishes a person's sense of individuality and reduces constraints against deviant behavior.
- Two types of environmental cues can increase deviant behavior: (1) Accountability cues, such as anonymity, signal that individuals will not be held responsible for their actions; and (2) attentional cues, such as intense environmental stimulation, produce a deindividuated state in which the individual acts impulsively.
- Large crowds can both increase anonymity and decrease self-awareness, which together can increase violent or other deviant behavior.
- The effects of deindividuation depend on the characteristics of the group. In the context of an antagonistic social identity, antisocial behavior increases; in the context of a benevolent social identity, prosocial behavior increases.

Group Processes: Interacting with Others

Joining a Group

- People join a group for a variety of reasons, including to perform tasks that can't be accomplished alone, to enhance self-esteem and social identity, and to interact with group members.
- The socialization of newcomers into a group relies on the relationships they form with old-timers, who act as models, trainers, and mentors.
- Groups often proceed through several stages of development, from initial orientation through periods of conflict, compromise, and action.

- Some groups pass through periods of inactivity followed by sudden action in response to time pressures.

Roles, Norms, and Cohesiveness

- Interacting groups have three major features: an expected set of behaviors for members (roles), rules of conduct for members (norms), and forces that push members together (cohesiveness).
- When men and women feel equally competent about task performance, they adopt similar roles.
- Establishing clear roles can help a group; but when members' roles are ambiguous, conflict with other roles, or change, stress and poor performance can result.
- The relationship between cohesiveness and group performance is complex, depending on factors such as the size of the group, the kind of task that the group is performing, and the kinds of norms that have been established.
- The pressures toward conformity in a cohesive group make it hard to blow the whistle on misconduct.

Group Polarization: Gaining Conviction

- When individuals who have similar, although not identical, opinions participate in a group discussion, their opinions become more extreme.
- Explanations for group polarization emphasize the number and persuasiveness of arguments heard, social comparison with a perceived group norm, and the influence of one's own ingroup.

Groupthink: Losing Perspective

- Groupthink refers to an excessive tendency to seek concurrence among group members.
- The symptoms of groupthink produce defective decision making, which can lead to a bad decision.
- A highly cohesive group is more likely to experience groupthink if other contributors to groupthink are present, such as a controlling leader and a stressful situation.
- Strategies that have been successful in helping groups avoid groupthink include consulting with outsiders, having the leader play a less controlling role, encouraging criticism and thorough information search, and having a group member play the devil's advocate and challenge the consensus.
- Computer-based technology can help groups avoid groupthink by guiding them to follow systematic agendas and focus on ideas.

Group Performance: Are More Heads Better than One?

- Group performance is influenced by the type of task (additive, conjunctive, or disjunctive).

- Because of process loss, a group may perform worse than it would if every individual performed up to his or her potential.
- Among the factors that create process loss are social loafing, poor coordination, failure to recognize the expertise of particular group members, and goals set too low.
- Contrary to illusions about the effectiveness of interactive brainstorming, groups in which members interact face-to-face produce fewer creative ideas than the same number of people working alone.
- Computer-based technology can improve group brainstorming.
- Biased sampling refers to the tendency for groups to pay more attention to shared information than to unshared information.
- Information may not be communicated adequately in a group because of problems in the group's communication network, such as suppression of relevant information at some point in the decision-making chain.
- Groups are susceptible to the same information-processing biases as individuals—only more so.
- The effects of diversity on group performance depend on the nature of the task and how well integrated the group is.

Cooperation, Competition, and Conflict: Responding to Differences

Mixed Motives and Social Dilemmas

- In mixed-motive situations, such as the prisoner's dilemma, there are incentives for both competition and cooperation.
- In a social dilemma, personal benefit conflicts with the overall good.
- Resource dilemmas involve sharing limited resources. In the commons dilemma, a group of people can take resources from a common pool; whereas in the public goods dilemma, the maintenance of a common resource requires the contributions of a group of people.
- Behavior in a social dilemma is influenced by psychological factors—including individual and cultural differences, situational factors, and group dynamics—as well as structural arrangements.

Conflict Escalation

- Conflicts can escalate for many reasons, including conflict spirals and entrapment.
- The premature use of the capacity to punish can elicit retaliation and escalate conflict.

- Perceptions of the other that contribute to conflict escalation include unfavorable mirror images, a double standard, conflict-maintaining attributions, and dehumanization.

Reducing Conflict

- GRIT—an explicit strategy for the unilateral, persistent pursuit of trust and cooperation between opposing parties—is a useful strategy for beginning the peace process.
- Flexibility and understanding of the other party's perspective are two key ingredients of successful negotiation.
- Many negotiations have the potential to result in integrative agreements, in which outcomes exceed a 50–50 split, but negotiators often fail to achieve such outcomes.
- Communication in which both sides disclose their goals can help the negotiating parties obtain mutual benefits.
- Teams are more likely than individuals to reach integrative agreements.
- Mediators can often be helpful in achieving success in negotiations.
- Superordinate goals and a superordinate identity increase the likelihood of a peaceful resolution of differences.

Key Terms

brainstorming *271*

collective *249*

collective effort model *254*

deindividuation *256*

distraction-conflict theory *251*

entrapment *274*

evaluation apprehension theory *251*

graduated and reciprocated initiatives in tension-reduction (GRIT) *283*

group polarization *263*

groupthink *266*

integrative agreement *286*

mere presence theory *251*

social dilemma *276*

social facilitation *250*

social loafing *252*

superordinate identity *287*

PUTTING COMMON SENSE TO THE TEST

People will cheer louder when they cheer as part of a group than when they cheer alone.

False. *People tend to put less effort into collective tasks, such as group cheering, than into tasks when their individual performance can be identified and evaluated.*

Group members' attitudes about a course of action usually become more moderate after group discussion.

False. *Group discussion often causes attitudes to become more extreme as the initial tendencies of the group are exaggerated.*

People brainstorming as a group come up with a greater number of better ideas than the same number of people working individually.

False. *Groups in which members interact face-to-face produce fewer creative ideas when brainstorming than the same number of people brainstorming alone.*

Groups are less likely than individuals to invest more and more resources in a project that is failing.

False. *Although individuals often feel entrapped by previous commitments and make things worse by throwing good money (and other resources) after bad, groups are even more prone to have this problem.*

Large groups are more likely than small groups to exploit a scarce resource that the members collectively depend on.

True. *Large groups are more likely to behave selfishly when faced with resource dilemmas, in part because people in large groups are less committed to one another, feel that their actions have less impact, and are less likely to establish norms of cooperation.*

9 Attraction and Close Relationships

PREVIEW

This chapter examines how people form relationships with each other. First, we describe the fundamental human need for *being with others,* why people affiliate, and the problem of loneliness. Then we consider various personal and situational factors that influence our *initial attraction* to specific others. Third, we examine different types of *close relationships*—what makes them rewarding, how they differ, the types of love they arouse, and the factors that often break them apart.

No one had expected that audiences would rave about a long disaster film that told the story of the 1912 sinking of a cruise ship, which resulted in the death of 1,500 passengers. But early in 1998, *Titanic* was a monster box office hit, the biggest ever, and on its way to winning several Academy Awards. People loved it—not because it cost a staggering $200 million to produce, not because of the Hollywood special effects, and not because of the starring cast, but because the film was at its core a simple love story.

A few years earlier, also to everyone's surprise, Robert Waller's *The Bridges of Madison County* had become a runaway best-seller. The story was too short; its author, a former professor of management, too obscure; its plot, too trite. And yet this novel about a four-day romance between Robert Kincaid, a world-traveling photographer, and Francesca Johnson, a midwestern housewife, quickly rose to the top of the charts. People snatched it from the racks in city bookstores, suburban malls, airports, supermarkets, and college campuses. The book had struck a deep, responsive chord in millions of readers. The reason? At its heart, it too celebrated a most human phenomenon: attraction and the development of a close relationship. People were just plain fascinated by the possibility that such an unlikely and intense bond might be just around the corner.

T / F

_____ People seek out the company of others, even strangers, in times of stress.

_____ Infants do not discriminate between faces considered attractive and unattractive in their culture.

_____ People who are physically attractive are happier and have higher self-esteem than those who are unattractive.

_____ When it comes to romantic relationships, opposites attract.

_____ Men are more likely than women to interpret friendly gestures by the opposite sex in sexual terms.

_____ After the honeymoon period, there is a consistent decline in levels of marital satisfaction.

Starring in the box office smash Titanic, Leonardo DiCaprio and Kate Winslett played a young couple very much in love.

All of us, at one time or another, have been startled by our reaction to someone we've met. Why, in general, are human beings drawn to each other? Why are we attracted to some people and yet indifferent to, or even repelled by, others? What determines how our intimate relationships evolve? What does it mean to love someone, and what problems are likely to arise along the way? As these questions reveal, attraction among people—from the first spark through the flames of an intimate connection—often seem like a kind of wild card in the deck of human behavior. This chapter unravels some of the mysteries.

Being with Others: A Fundamental Human Motive

Although born helpless, human infants are equipped with reflexes that orient them toward people. They are uniquely responsive to human faces, they turn their head toward voices, and they are able to mimic certain facial gestures on cue. Then, a few weeks later, there is the baby's first smile, surely the warmest sign of all. Much to the delight of parents all over the world, the newborn seems an inherently social animal. But wait. If you reflect on the amount of time you spend talking to, being with, flirting with, pining for, confiding in, or worrying about other people, you'll realize that we are all social animals. It seems that people need people.

According to Roy Baumeister and Mark Leary (1995), the need to belong is a basic human motive, "a pervasive drive to form and maintain at least a minimum quantity of lasting, positive, and significant interpersonal relationships" (p. 497). This general proposition is supported by everyday observation and a great deal of research. All over the world, people feel joy when they form new social attachments and react with anxiety, loneliness, and grief when these bonds are broken—as when separated from a loved one by distance, divorce, or death.

We care deeply about what others think of us, which is why we spend so much time and money to make ourselves presentable and attractive. In fact, some people are so worried about how they come across to others that they experience *social anxiety*, intense feelings of discomfort in situations that invite public scrutiny (Leary & Kowalski, 1995). One very familiar example is public-speaking anxiety, or "stage fright"—a performer's worst nightmare. If you've ever had to make a public presentation, only to feel weak in the knees and hear your voice quiver, you will have endured a hint of this disorder. When sufferers are asked what there is to fear, the most common responses are: shaking and showing other signs of anxiety, going blank,

When babies only weeks old crinkle up their eyes and smile, adults respond with warmth and nurturing. Because humans are social creatures, the smile helps to lubricate the parent-infant relationship.

saying something foolish, and being unable to continue (Stein et al., 1996). For people with high levels of social anxiety, the problem is also evoked by other social situations, such as eating at a public lunch counter, signing a check in front of a store clerk, and, for males, urinating in a crowded men's room. In extreme cases, the reaction can become so debilitating that the person just stays at home (Turner & Beidel, 1989).

Our need to belong runs deep. We'll see in Chapter 14 that people who have a network of close social ties—in the form of lovers, friends, co-workers, and relatives—tend to be happier and more satisfied with life than those who are more isolated (Myers & Diener, 1995). In fact, people who are socially connected are also physically healthier and less likely to die a premature death (House et al., 1988; Uchino et al., 1996).

The Thrill of Affiliation

As social beings, humans are drawn to each other. We work together, play together, live together, and often make lifetime commitments to grow old together. This social motivation begins with the **need for affiliation,** defined as a desire to establish social contact with others (McAdams, 1989). Individuals differ in the strength of their need for affiliation, but it seems that people are motivated to establish and maintain an *optimum* balance of social contact—sometimes craving the company of others, sometimes wanting to be alone—the way the body maintains a certain level of caloric intake. In an interesting study, Bibb Latané and Carol Werner (1978) found that laboratory rats were more likely to approach others of their species after a period of isolation and were less likely to approach others after prolonged contact. These researchers suggested that rats, like many other animals, have a built-in "sociostat" (social thermostat) to regulate their affiliative tendencies.

People are motivated to establish and maintain an optimum level of social contact. Robert Mankoff © 1996 from The New Yorker Collection. All rights reserved.

"At this point, my privacy needs are interfering with my intimacy goals."

Is there evidence of a similar mechanism in humans? Shawn O'Connor and Lorne Rosenblood (1996) recently recruited college students to carry portable beepers for four days. Whenever the beepers went off (on average, every hour), the students wrote down whether, at the time, they were *actually* alone or in the company of other people and whether, at the time, they *wanted* to be alone or with others. The results showed that the students were in the state they desired two-thirds of the time—and that the situation they wished to be in on one occasion predicted their actual situation the next time they were signaled. Whether it was solitude or social contact that the students sought, they successfully managed to regulate their own personal needs for affiliation.

People may well differ in the strength of their affiliative needs, but there are times when we all want to be with other people. Picture the scene at Yankee Stadium, in October 1996, the night the New York Yankees won the World Series. There were more than 60,000 fans at the game, and when it ended, nobody wanted to go home. Nobody rushed to the parking lot or raced to the subway. For nearly half an hour, people did not even leave their seats. In the streets, jubilant

need for affiliation The desire to establish and maintain many rewarding interpersonal relationships.

When the New York Yankees won the World Series in 1996, jubilant fans stayed in their seats to celebrate. Even in this large and sometimes impersonal city, people sought to affiliate with one another rather than be alone.

pedestrians exchanged high-fives, slaps on the back, hugs, and kisses. In this city of strangers—as in Chicago, Dallas, Atlanta, Miami, Denver, and other recent championship sports cities—it is clear that people want to celebrate together rather than alone. Affiliating can satisfy us for other reasons as well. From others, we get energy, attention, stimulation, information, and emotional support (Hill, 1987).

One condition that strongly arouses our need for affiliation is stress. Have you ever noticed the way neighbors who never stop to say hello come together in snowstorms, hurricanes, power failures, and other major crises? Many years ago, Stanley Schachter (1959) theorized that external threat triggers fear and motivates us to affiliate—particularly with others who are facing a similar threat. In a laboratory experiment that demonstrated the point, Schachter found that people who were expecting to receive painful electric shocks chose to wait with other nervous participants rather than alone. So far so good. But when Irving Sarnoff and Philip Zimbardo (1961) led participants to expect that they would be engaging in a highly embarrassing behavior—sucking on large nipples and pacifiers—their desire to be with others fell off. It seemed puzzling. Why do people in fearful misery love company, while those in embarrassed misery seek solitude?

Yacov Rofé (1984) proposed a simple answer: utility. Rofé argued that stress increases the desire to affiliate only when being with others is seen as useful in reducing the negative impact of the stressful situation. Schachter's participants had good reason to believe that affiliation would be useful. They would have the opportunity to compare their emotional reactions with those of others to determine whether they really needed to be fearful. For participants in the Sarnoff and Zimbardo study, however, affiliation had little to offer. Facing embarrassment, being with others is more likely to increase the stress than reduce it.

Turning to Schachter's initial study, what specific benefit do people get from being in the presence of others in times of stress? Recent research suggests that people facing an imminent threat seek each other out in order to gain *cognitive clarity* about the danger they are in. In one study, James Kulik and Heike Mahler (1989) found that hospital patients awaiting open-heart surgery preferred to have as roommates other patients who were post-operative rather than pre-operative, presumably because they were in a position to provide information about the experience. Patients in a second study who had been assigned post-operative rather than pre-operative roommates became less anxious about the experience and were later quicker to recover from the surgery (Kulik et al., 1996).

Even in a laboratory setting, Kulik and others (1994) found that people anticipating the painful task of soaking a hand in ice-cold water (compared with those

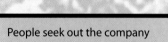

People seek out the company of others, even strangers, in times of stress. **True.**

told that the task would not be painful) preferred to wait with someone who had already completed the task than with someone who had not. They also asked more questions of these experienced peers. Under stress, we adaptively become motivated to affiliate with others who can help us cope with an impending threat. Summarizing his own work, Schachter (1959) had noted that misery loves only miserable company. Based on their more recent research, Gump and Kulik (1997) further amended this assertion: "Misery loves the company of those in the same miserable situation" (p. 317).

The Agony of Loneliness

People need other people—to celebrate, to share news with, to commiserate with, to talk to and learn from. But some people are painfully shy, socially awkward, inhibited, and reluctant to approach others (Bruch et al., 1989). Shyness is a pervasive problem. Roughly 40 percent of all Americans describe themselves as shy, as do 31 percent in Israel, 40 percent in Germany, 55 percent in Taiwan, and 60 percent in Japan (Zimbardo, 1977).

"Loneliness and the feeling of being unwanted is the most terrible poverty."

—Mother Teresa

People who are shy find it difficult to approach strangers, make small talk, telephone someone for a date, participate in small groups, or mingle at parties. What's worse, they often reject others—perhaps because they fear being rejected themselves. The sad result is a pattern of risk avoidance that sets them up for unpleasant and unrewarding interactions (De-Paulo et al., 1990; Meleshko & Alden, 1993; Nezlek & Pilkington, 1994).

Shyness can arise from different sources. In some cases, it may be an inborn personality characteristic. Jerome Kagan (1994) and others have found that some infants are highly sensitive to stimulation, inhibited, and cautious shortly after birth. In other cases, shyness may develop as a learned reaction to failed interactions with others. Thus, interpersonal problems of the past can ignite social anxieties about the future (Leary & Kowalski, 1995). Whatever the source,

---

TABLE 9.1   The Loneliness Scale   *(Russell et al., 1978.)*

Directions: Indicate how often each of the statements below is descriptive of you.

    O indicates "I *often* feel this way"

    S indicates "I *sometimes* feel this way"

    R indicates "I *rarely* feel this way"

    N indicates "I *never* feel this way"

1. How often do you feel unhappy doing so many things alone?   O   S   R   N
2. How often do you feel you have nobody to talk to?   O   S   R   N
3. How often do you feel you cannot tolerate being so alone?   O   S   R   N
4. How often do you feel as if nobody really understands you?   O   S   R   N
5. How often do you find yourself waiting for people to call or write?   O   S   R   N
6. How often do you feel completely alone?   O   S   R   N
7. How often do you feel you are unable to reach out and communicate with those around you?   O   S   R   N
8. How often do you feel starved for company?   O   S   R   N
9. How often do you feel it is difficult for you to make friends?   O   S   R   N
10. How often do you feel shut out and excluded by others?   O   S   R   N

Scoring: For each question, give yourself 1 point if you responded "never" (N), 2 points if you responded "rarely" (R), 3 points if you responded "sometimes" (S), and 4 points if you responded "often" (O). Your total loneliness score is computed by adding your score on each of the ten questions together. Using this scale, the average score among college students is 20.

---

the problem is a real one—and has painful consequences. Studies show that shy people evaluate themselves negatively, expect to fail in their social encounters, blame themselves when they do, and conform out of a fear of rejection. Worst of all, many shy people go into self-imposed isolation, which makes them feel lonely (Cheek & Melchior, 1990).

Loneliness is a sad and heart-wrenching emotion (see Table 9.1). To be lonely is to feel deprived about the nature of one's existing social relations. Some

loneliness A feeling of deprivation about existing social relations.

researchers have maintained that loneliness is triggered by a discrepancy between the level of social contact that a person has and the level he or she wants (Peplau & Perlman, 1982). Others find, more simply, that the less social contact people have, the more lonely they feel (Archibald et al., 1995). Who is lonely, and when? Loneliness is most likely to occur during times of transition or disruption—as in the first year at college, after a romantic breakup, or when a loved one moves far away. Surveys show that people who are unattached are lonelier than those who have romantic partners—but that those who are widowed, divorced, and separated are lonelier than people who have never been married (Peplau & Perlman, 1982). And contrary to the stereotypic image of the lonely old man passing time on a park bench, the loneliest groups in American society are adolescents and young adults eighteen to thirty years old. In fact, loneliness seems to decline over the course of adulthood—at least until health problems in old age limit social activities (Peplau & Perlman, 1982; Rubenstein & Shaver, 1982; Schultz & Moore, 1984).

How do people cope with this distressing state? When college students were asked about the behavioral strategies they use to combat loneliness, 96 percent said they sometimes or often tried harder to be friendly to other people, 94 percent took their mind off the problem by reading or watching TV, and 93 percent tried extra hard to succeed at another aspect of life. Others said that they distracted themselves by running, shopping, washing the car, or staying busy at other activities. Still others sought new ways to meet people, tried to improve their physical appearance, or talked to a friend, relative, or therapist about the problem. Though fewer in number, some are so desperate that they use alcohol or drugs to wash away feelings of loneliness (Rook & Peplau, 1982).

The Initial Attraction

Affiliation is a necessary first step in the formation of a social relationship. But each of us is drawn to some people more than to others. If you've ever had a crush on someone, felt the tingly excitement of a first encounter, or enjoyed the first few moments of a new friendship, then you know the meaning of the term *attraction*. When you meet someone for the first time, what do *you* look for? Does familiarity breed fondness or contempt? Do birds of a feather flock together, or do opposites attract? Is beauty the object of your desire, or do you believe that outward appearances are deceiving? And what is it about a situation, or the circumstances of an initial meeting, that draws you in for more?

According to one perspective, people are attracted to others with whom a relationship is rewarding (Byrne & Clore, 1970; Lott & Lott, 1974). The rewards may be direct—as when people provide us with attention, support, money, status, information, and other valuable commodities. Or the rewards may be indirect—as when it feels good to be with someone who is beautiful, smart, or funny, or who happens to be in our presence when times are good. A new perspective on attraction has also emerged in recent years—that of evolutionary psychology, a subdiscipline that uses principles of evolution to understand human social behavior. According to this view, human beings all over the world exhibit patterns of attraction and mate selection that favor the conception, birth, and survival of their offspring. This approach has a great deal to say about the differences in this regard between men and women (Buss, 1994; Simpson & Kenrick, 1997).

Recognizing the role of rewards and the call of our evolutionary past provides broad perspectives for understanding human attraction. But there's more to the story. Much more. Over the years, social psychologists have identified many determinants of attraction and the development of relationships (Berscheid & Reis,

1998). It's important to note that most of the research has focused on heterosexuals, so we often do not know how well specific findings apply to the homosexual population. At the same time, we'll see that certain basic processes described in this chapter influence the lives of many individuals and couples—regardless of their sexual orientation (Kurdek, 1992).

Familiarity: Being There

It seems so obvious that people tend to overlook it: We are most likely to become attracted to someone whom we have seen and become familiar with. So let's begin with two basic and necessary factors in the attraction process: proximity and exposure.

The Proximity Effect   The single best predictor of whether two people will get together is physical proximity, or nearness. Sure, we interact at remote distances with the help of telephones, online chat rooms, and electronic bulletin boards. But most social interaction still occurs among people who are in the same place at the same time (Latané et al., 1995).

To begin with, where we live influences the friends we make. Many years ago, Leon Festinger and his colleagues (1950) studied friendship patterns in married-student college housing and found that people were more likely to become friends with residents of nearby apartments than with those who lived farther away. More recent research has also shown that college students—who live in off-campus apartments, dormitories, or fraternity and sorority houses—tend to date those who live either nearby (Hays, 1985) or in the same type of housing as they do (Whitbeck & Hoyt, 1994).

The Mere Exposure Effect   Proximity does not necessarily spark attraction, but to the extent that it increases frequency of contact, it's a good first step. Folk wisdom often suggests a dim view of familiarity, which is said to "breed contempt." Not so. In a series of experiments, Robert Zajonc (1968) found that the more often people saw a novel stimulus—whether it was a foreign word, a geometric form, or a human face—the more they came to like it. This phenomenon, which Zajonc called the **mere exposure effect,** has since been observed in more than two hundred experiments (Bornstein, 1989).

People do not even have to be aware of their prior exposures for this effect to occur. In a typical study, participants are shown pictures of several stimuli, each for one to five milliseconds, which is too quick to register in awareness—and too quick for anyone to realize that some stimuli are presented more often than others. After the presentation, participants are shown each of the stimuli and asked two questions: Do you like it, and have you ever seen it before? Perhaps you can predict the result. The more frequently the stimulus is presented, the more people like it. Yet when asked if they've ever seen the liked stimulus before, they say no. These results demonstrate that the mere exposure effect can influence us without our awareness (Kuntz-Wilson & Zajonc, 1980). In fact, the effect is stronger under these conditions (Bornstein & D'Agostino, 1992).

To appreciate the implications in a naturalistic situation, imagine yourself in a psychology class that is held in a large lecture hall. Three times a week, you trudge over to class, shake the cobwebs out of your head, and try your best to be alert. The room holds several hundred students. You come in and look down the tiered seats to the front where your instructor stands. During the semester, you're vaguely aware of another student who sits up front, but you never talk to her, and you probably would not recognize her if you saw her somewhere else. Then, at the end of

mere exposure effect
The phenomenon whereby the more often people are exposed to a stimulus, the more positively they evaluate that stimulus.

the semester, you attend a special session where you are shown photographs of four women and asked some questions about them. Only then do you learn that you have participated in a study of the mere exposure effect.

Now view these same events from the perspective of Richard Moreland and Scott Beach (1992). These researchers selected four women who looked like typical students to be confederates in this study. One had a very easy job: She had her picture taken. But the other three also attended the class—either five, ten, or fifteen times. Did the frequency of exposure spark attraction among the real students in this situation? Yes. In questionnaires they completed after viewing pictures of all four women, students rated each woman on various traits (such as popularity, honesty, intelligence, and physical attractiveness) and recorded their beliefs about how much they would like her, enjoy spending time with her, and want to work with her on a mutual project. The results lined up like ducks in a row: The more classes a woman attended, the more attracted the students were to her.

Familiarity can even influence our self-evaluations. Imagine that you had a portrait photograph of yourself developed into two pictures—one that depicted your actual appearance and the other a mirror-image copy. Which image would you prefer? Which would a friend prefer? Theodore Mita and his colleagues (1977) tried this interesting experiment with female college students and found that most preferred their own mirror images, while their friends liked the actual photos. In both cases, the preference was for the view of the face that was most familiar.

Powerful as it is, the mere exposure effect is limited in two respects. The first is that if you initially dislike someone or something, repeated exposure may actually make the situation worse, breeding contempt instead of attraction (Perlman & Oskamp, 1971). The second limitation is based on the sheer frequency of exposure. Have you ever listened over and over to a new song you liked, or eaten the same food again and again, only to become sick of it after a while? This reaction is common. Experiments have shown that a stimulus that is frequently presented loses impact if it becomes "overexposed"—especially if it is repeatedly presented to people who are easily bored (Bornstein, 1989).

Physical Attractiveness: Getting Drawn In

What do you look for most in a friend or romantic partner? Intelligence? Kindness? A sense of humor? How important, really, is a person's looks? As children, we were told that "beauty is only skin deep." Yet as adults, we react more favorably to others who are physically attractive than to those who are unattractive. In the affairs of our social world, beauty is a force to be reckoned with (Bull & Rumsey, 1988; Hatfield & Sprecher, 1986).

"Beauty is a greater recommendation than any letter of introduction."

—Aristotle

The bias for beauty is pervasive. In one study, fifth grade teachers were given background information about a boy or girl, accompanied by a photograph. All teachers received identical information, yet those who saw an attractive child saw that child as being smarter and more likely to do well in school (Clifford & Walster, 1973). In a second study, male and female experimenters approached students on a college campus and tried to get them to sign a petition. The more attractive the experimenters were, the more signatures they were able to get (Chaiken, 1979). In a third study, Texas judges set lower bail and imposed smaller fines on suspects who were rated as attractive rather than unattractive on the basis of photographs (Downs & Lyons, 1991). In a fourth study, mothers of highly attractive babies were observed to be more attentive, affectionate, and playful in their interactions than were mothers of less attractive infants (Langlois et al., 1995). And in interviews conducted in the United States and Canada, economists discovered that across occupational groups, physically attractive men and women earn more money than others who are comparable except for being less attractive in their appearance (Hamermesh & Biddle, 1994).

It all seems so shallow, so superficial. But before we go on to accept the notion that people prefer others who are physically attractive, let's stop for a moment and consider a fundamental question: What constitutes physical beauty? Is it an objective and measurable human characteristic like height, weight, or hair color; or is beauty a subjective quality, existing more in the eye of the beholder? There are advocates on both sides.

What Is Beauty? Some researchers believe that certain faces are inherently more attractive than others. There are three sources of evidence for this proposition. First, when people are asked to rate faces on a 10-point scale, there is typically a high level of agreement—even across cultural groups. For example, Michael Cunningham and his colleagues (1995) asked Asian and Latino students, along with black and white American students, to rate the appearance of women from all these groups. Overall, the ratings were highly consistent, leading these investigators to argue that people everywhere share a sense of what is beautiful. People also tend to agree about what constitutes an attractive body. For example, men are drawn to the "hourglass" figure seen in women of average weight whose waists are a third narrower than their hips—a shape said to be associated with reproductive fertility (Singh, 1993). In contrast, women like men of average weight with a waist-to-hip ratio that forms a tapering V-shaped physique (Singh, 1995).

Second, some researchers have identified physical features of the human face that are reliably associated with judgments of attractiveness. For example, women who are seen as attractive tend to have large eyes, prominent cheekbones, a small nose, and a wide smile (Cunningham, 1986), while men are seen as attractive if they have a broad jaw (Cunningham, Barbee, & Pike, 1990). Even more intriguing, perhaps, are studies showing that people like faces in which the eyes, noses, lips, and other features are not too different from the average. Judith Langlois and Lori Roggman (1990) showed college students actual yearbook photos as well as computerized facial composites that "averaged" the features of four, eight, sixteen, or thirty-two of the photos. Consistently, the students preferred the averaged composites to the individual faces. In fact, the more faces used to form the composite, the more highly it was rated. Other studies have since confirmed this result (Langlois et al., 1994; Perrett et al., 1994; Rhodes & Tremewan, 1996).

"To tell people to not take pleasure in beauty is like telling them to stop enjoying food or sex or love."

—Nancy Etcoff

Facial attractiveness appears to be relatively consistent across different cultures. Those who are regarded as good-looking in one culture are also judged to be attractive by people from other cultures. The individuals pictured here are from Venezuela, Kenya, and Japan.

Which image do you find more attractive—the actual photo of Lyle Lovett (left) or the re-shaped, symmetrical photo that combines his two left sides (right)? Research shows that people prefer symmetrical faces.

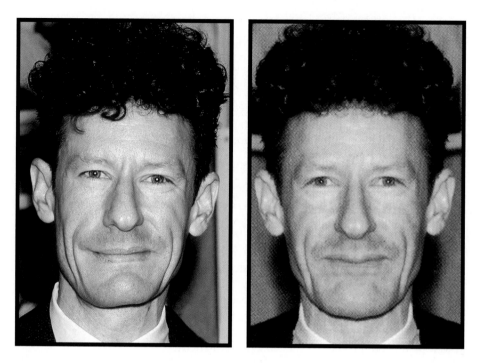

It seems odd that "averaged" faces are judged attractive when, after all, the faces we find most attractive are anything but average. What accounts for these findings? Langlois and her colleagues (1994) believe that people like averaged faces because they are more prototypically facelike and, as such, seem more familiar to us. Others point out that the computerized averaging technique produces faces that are also symmetrical—and that symmetry is what we find attractive (Grammer & Thornhill, 1994). Why would people prefer symmetrical faces in which the paired features on the right and left sides "line up"? Evolutionary psychologists have speculated that facial symmetry is associated with health, fitness, and fertility—qualities that are highly desirable in a mate. At this point, however, support for this hypothesis is mixed (Kalick et al., 1998; Shackelford & Larsen, 1997).

A third source of evidence for the view that beauty is an objective quality is that babies who are far too young to have learned their culture's standards of beauty exhibit a nonverbal preference for faces considered attractive by adults. Indeed, judging from their eye movements, two-month-old infants spend more time gazing at attractive than unattractive faces (Langlois et al., 1991). "These kids don't read *Vogue* or watch TV," notes Langlois, "yet they make the same judgments as adults" (Cowley, 1996, p. 66).

In contrast to this objective perspective, other researchers argue that physical attractiveness is subjective, and they point to the influences of culture, time, and the circumstances of our perception. One source of support for this view is that people from different cultures enhance their beauty in very different ways—through face painting; makeup; plastic surgery; scarring; hairstyling; the molding of bones; the filing of teeth; braces; and the piercing of ears, noses, and other body parts. Indeed, what people find attractive in one part of the world is often seen as repulsive elsewhere (Landau, 1989). Even when it comes to bodies, ideals vary. Looking at preferences on female body size in fifty-four cultures, Judith Anderson and her colleagues (1992) found that heavy women are considered more attractive than slender women in places where food is frequently in short supply. Perhaps body weight is desirable when it signals an ability to survive.

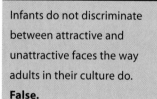

Infants do not discriminate between attractive and unattractive faces the way adults in their culture do.
False.

Standards of beauty also change over time, from one generation to the next. When Brett Silverstein and others examined the measurements of female models appearing in women's magazines from 1901 to 1981, they found that "curvaceousness" (as measured by the bust-to-waist ratio) varied over time, with a boyish, slender look becoming particularly desirable in recent years (Silverstein, Perdue, Peterson, & Kelly, 1986). Apparently, the ideal body for women has changed a great deal from the ample proportions preferred in the past to the slender, athletic form currently in vogue (Lamb et al., 1993).

Conceptions of an attractive face are also subject to change over time. Would the face that launched a thousand ships toward the Trojan War get more than a passing glance today? Look at the pictures below. As constructed by video artist Nancy Burson, the face on the left combines the features of Bette Davis, Audrey Hepburn, Grace Kelly, Sophia Loren, and Marilyn Monroe—beautiful actresses of the 1950s. The portrait on the right combines the faces of Jane Fonda, Meryl Streep, Brooke Shields, Jacqueline Bisset, and Diane Keaton—admired women of the 1980s. Compare these images, and you'll probably prefer the more recent composite, suggesting that our tastes have changed. And once that happens, the rest of us must hurry to catch up. Or, as writer Harold Brodkey (1993) suggests, perhaps it goes the other way around: "We have come to resemble one another, and our celebrated figures have moved along with us in the trend" (p. 31).

Still other evidence for the subjective nature of beauty comes from many research laboratories. Time and again, social psychologists have found that our judgments of someone's beauty can be inflated or deflated by various circumstances. Research shows, for example, that people often see others as more physically attractive after they have grown to like them (Gross & Crofton, 1977). In fact, the more in love people are, the less attracted they are to other members of the opposite sex (Johnson & Rusbult, 1989; Simpson et al., 1990). On the other hand, men who viewed ravishing nude models in *Playboy* and *Penthouse* magazines later gave lower attractiveness ratings to average-looking women, including their own wives—the unfortunate result of a contrast effect (Kenrick et al., 1989). Even our self-evaluations are malleable in this regard. There may be exceptions (Brown et al., 1992), but people feel less attractive after viewing supermodel-like members of the same sex than homelier persons (Thornton & Moore, 1993). And they aren't happy about it. Douglas Kenrick and others found that although exposure to attractive members of the opposite sex put people into a good mood, exposure to

"Love looks not with the eyes, but with the mind; And therefore is wing'd Cupid painted blind."

—William Shakespeare, *A Midsummer Night's Dream*

The computer-generated composite on the left combines the beautiful faces of the 1950s: Bette Davis, Audrey Hepburn, Grace Kelly, Sophia Loren, and Marilyn Monroe. The one on the right combines the beauties of the 1980s: Jane Fonda, Jacqueline Bisset, Diane Keaton, Brooke Shields, and Meryl Streep. Which one do you find more attractive? (Burson et al., 1986.)

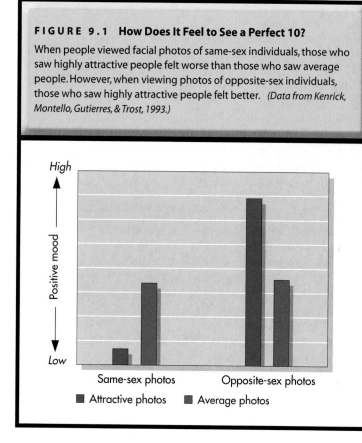

FIGURE 9.1   How Does It Feel to See a Perfect 10?
When people viewed facial photos of same-sex individuals, those who saw highly attractive people felt worse than those who saw average people. However, when viewing photos of opposite-sex individuals, those who saw highly attractive people felt better.   *(Data from Kenrick, Montello, Gutierres, & Trost, 1993.)*

attractive members of the same sex had the opposite effect (Kenrick, Montello, Gutierres, & Trost, 1993) (see Figure 9.1).

Why Are We Blinded by Beauty?   Regardless of how beauty is defined, it's clear that people seen as physically attractive are at a social advantage. Perhaps that's why more than a million Americans a year undergo cosmetic surgery to remove varicose veins; plump up sunken skin; peel and scrape wrinkles from the face; vacuum out fat deposits; restore and transplant hair; lift faces, eyelids, and foreheads; reshape noses; enlarge breasts; and tuck in tummies (*U.S. News & World Report*, 1996).

What creates the bias for beauty, and why are we drawn like magnets to people who are physically attractive? One possibility is that it's inherently rewarding to be in the company of people who are aesthetically appealing—that we derive pleasure from beautiful men and women the same way that we enjoy a breathtaking landscape or magnificent work of art. Or perhaps the rewards are more extrinsic. Perhaps, for example, we expect the glitter of another's beauty to rub off on us. When average-looking men and women are seen together with someone else of the same sex, they are rated as more attractive when this other person is good-looking and as less attractive when he or she is plain-looking (Geiselman et al., 1984).

A second possible reason for the bias for beauty is that people associate physical attractiveness with other desirable qualities—an assumption known as the **what-is-beautiful-is-good stereotype** (Dion et al., 1972). In children's fairy tales, Snow White and Cinderella are portrayed as beautiful *and* kind, while the witch and stepsisters are said to be both ugly *and* cruel. Similarly, studies have shown that good-looking people are judged to be intelligent, successful, happy, well-adjusted, socially skilled, confident, and assertive—though also vain (Eagly et al., 1991). This stereotype seems to operate with amazing speed. Asked to judge various applicants for a job, college students viewed head-and-shoulders slides for just 100 milliseconds. As the pictures whizzed by, they rated the more attractive individuals as better suited for the job and more likely to be cooperative at work (Locher et al., 1993).

Is the physical attractiveness stereotype accurate? Only to a limited extent. Research shows that good-looking people do have more friends, better social skills, and a more active sex life. But beauty is *not* related to objective measures of intelligence, personality, adjustment, or self-esteem. In these ways, it seems that popular perceptions exaggerate the reality (Feingold, 1992b). It also seems that the specific nature of the stereotype depends on cultural conceptions of what is "good." Ladd Wheeler and Youngmee Kim (1997) asked people in Korea to rate photos of various men and women and found that people seen as physically attractive were also assumed to have "integrity" and "a concern for others"—traits that are highly valued in this collectivist culture. In contrast to what is considered desirable in more individualistic cultures, attractive people in Korea were not assumed to be dominant or assertive. What is beautiful is good; but what is good is, in part, culturally defined.

Why does the physical attractiveness stereotype endure? One possibility is that each of us creates support for the bias via the *self-fulfilling prophecy* model described

what-is-beautiful-is-good stereotype The belief that physically attractive individuals also possess desirable personality characteristics.

in Chapter 4. In a classic study of interpersonal attraction, Mark Snyder and his colleagues (1977) brought together unacquainted pairs of male and female college students. All the students were given biographical sketches of their partners. Each man also received a photograph of a physically attractive or unattractive woman, supposedly his partner. At that point, the students rated each other on several dimensions and had a phone-like conversation over headphones. The results were provocative. Men who thought they were interacting with a woman who was attractive rather than unattractive: (1) formed more positive impressions of her personality and (2) were friendlier in their conversational behavior. And now, for the clincher: (3) The female students whose partners had seen the attractive picture were rated by listeners to the conversation as warmer, more confident, and more animated. Fulfilling their own prophecies, men who expected an attractive partner actually created one. These findings call to mind the Greek myth of Pygmalion, who fell in love with a statue he had carved—and brought it to life.

The Benefits and Costs of Beauty　No doubt about it, good-looking people have a significant social edge. As a result, they are more popular, more sexually experienced, and more socially skilled. Thus, it's interesting that physical attractiveness is not a sure ticket to health, happiness, or high self-esteem (Diener et al., 1995; Feingold, 1992b). The life and death of Marilyn Monroe is a case in point. Monroe was considered one of the most ravishing women of her time and one of the hottest actresses in Hollywood. Yet she was terribly vulnerable and insecure. Why?

One problem is that highly attractive people can't tell if all the attention and praise they receive from others is due to their talent or just their good looks. An experiment by Brenda Major and her colleagues illustrates the point (Major, Carrington, & Carnevale, 1984). Male and female participants who saw themselves as physically attractive or unattractive wrote essays that were later positively evaluated by an unknown member of the opposite sex. Half the participants were told that their evaluator would be watching them through a one-way mirror as they wrote the essay; the other half were led to believe that they could not be seen. In actuality, there was no evaluator, and all participants received identical, very positive evaluations of their work. Participants were then asked why their essay had been so favorably reviewed. The result: those who saw themselves as unattractive

Individuals who are judged by others as extremely attractive, but who do not see themselves this way, are unlikely to benefit psychologically from being beautiful.

"I remember when the first boy liked me, I couldn't believe it."
　　　　　　—Michelle Pfeiffer, movie star

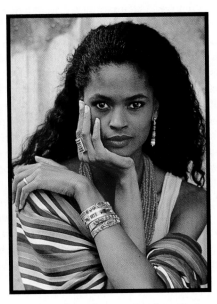

"I grew up the ugliest, scariest, beastliest creature you ever saw."
　　　　　　—Karen Alexander, model

"That I'm found attractive is bizarre to me."
　　　　　　—Uma Thurman, movie star

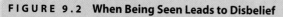

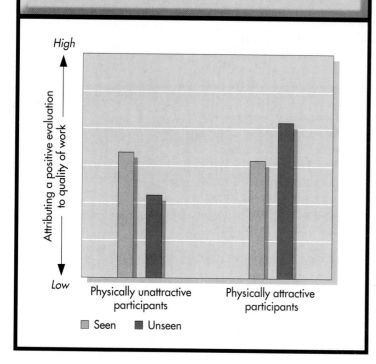

FIGURE 9.2   When Being Seen Leads to Disbelief

People who believed they were physically unattractive were more likely to cite the quality of their work as the reason for receiving a positive evaluation when they thought they were seen by the evaluator. However, people who believed they were attractive were less likely to credit the quality of their work when they thought they were seen.

(Data from Major, Carrington, & Carnevale, 1984.)

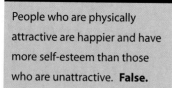

People who are physically attractive are happier and have more self-esteem than those who are unattractive. **False.**

felt better about the quality of their work after getting a glowing evaluation from someone who had seen them. Yet those who viewed themselves as attractive and thought that they had been seen attributed the glowing feedback to their looks—not to the quality of their work. For people who are highly attractive, positive feedback from others can be hard to interpret (see Figure 9.2).

Another cost of having physical attractiveness as a social asset is the pressure to maintain one's appearance. In contemporary American society, such pressures are particularly strong when it comes to the body. This focus on the human form can produce a healthy emphasis on nutrition and exercise. But it can also have distinctly unhealthy consequences—as when men pop steroids to build muscles or when women over-diet to lose weight. Particularly among young women, an obsession with thinness can give rise to serious eating disorders such as *bulimia* (food binges followed by purging) and *anorexia nervosa* (self-imposed starvation, which can be fatal). Although estimates vary, recent studies indicate that fewer than 1 percent of women suffer from anorexia, that 2 to 3 percent have bulimia, and that these rates are higher among female college students than among nonstudents (Brownell & Fairburn, 1995).

Women are more likely than men to suffer from what Janet Polivy and others (1986) call the "modern mania for slenderness." This slender ideal is projected in the mass media. Studies have shown that young women who see magazine ads or TV commercials that feature ultra-thin models become more unhappy, ashamed, and dissatisfied with their own bodies than those who view more neutral materials (Heinberg & Thompson, 1995; Stice & Shaw, 1994). Trying to measure up to multi-million-dollar supermodels can only prove frustrating to most. What's worse, the cultural ideal for thinness may be set early in childhood. Kevin Norton and his colleagues (1996) recently projected the life-size dimensions of the world popular Ken and Barbie dolls and found that both were unnaturally thin compared with the average young adult. In fact, the estimated odds of a young woman having Barbie's shape is approximately 1 in 100,000.

In sum, being beautiful may be a mixed blessing. There are some real benefits that cannot be denied, but there may be some costs as well. This tradeoff makes you wonder about the long-term effects. Some years ago, Ellen Berscheid and others (1972) compared the physical attractiveness levels of college students (based on yearbook pictures) to their adjustment when they reached middle age. There was little relationship between their appearance in youth and their later happiness. Those who were especially good-looking in college were more likely to have married, but they were not more satisfied with marriage or more content with life. Beauty may confer advantage, but it is not destiny.

First Encounters: Getting Acquainted

Proximity increases the odds that we will meet someone, familiarity puts us at ease, and beauty draws us in like magnets to a first encounter. But what determines whether sparks fly in the early getting-acquainted stages of a relationship? In this section, we consider three characteristics of others that can influence our attraction: similarity, liking, and being hard to get.

Liking Others Who Are Similar

The problem with proverbial wisdom is that it very often contradicts itself. Common sense tells us that "birds of a feather flock together." Yet we also hear that "opposites attract." So which is it? Before answering this question, imagine sitting at a computer, meeting someone in an online chat room, and striking up a conversation about politics, sports, restaurants, where you live, or your favorite band—only to

Barbie—the most popular, best-selling doll in the world—is almost impossibly thin compared to the average woman. Just recently, the Mattell toy company introduced Barbie dolls with more realistic figures.

realize that the two of you have a lot in common. Now imagine the opposite experience, of chatting with someone who is very different from you in his or her background, interests, values, and outlook on life. Which of the two strangers would you want to meet, the one who is similar or the one who is different?

Over the years, research has consistently shown that people tend to associate with others who are similar to themselves. On a whole range of demographic variables—including age, education, race, religion, height, level of intelligence, and socioeconomic status—people who go together as friends, dates, or partners in marriage resemble each other more than randomly paired couples (Warren, 1966). These correlations cannot be used to prove that similarity causes attraction. A more compelling case could be made, however, by first measuring people's demographic characteristics and then determining whether these people, when they met others, liked those who were similar to them more than those who were dissimilar. This is what Theodore Newcomb (1961) did. In an elaborate study, Newcomb set up an experimental college dormitory and found that students who were similar in their backgrounds grew to like each other more than did those who were dissimilar. Is demographic similarity still a factor, even today? Yes. In our increasingly multicultural society, people of different religious, racial, and ethnic backgrounds are marrying more than ever before (Smolowe, 1993). Yet sociologists continue to note that even in this age of diversity and choice, "Cupid's arrow is aimed by society more than we like to think" (Macionis, 1997).

People can also be similar to us in other ways that we find attractive—as when we share certain opinions, interests, and values. Again, Newcomb's (1961) experimental dormitory provided a unique setting for tracking attraction over time. During the course of the school year, he found that students who liked each other right from the start also perceived each other to

"The minute you walked into the room, I said to myself, 'Now, he looks interesting.'"

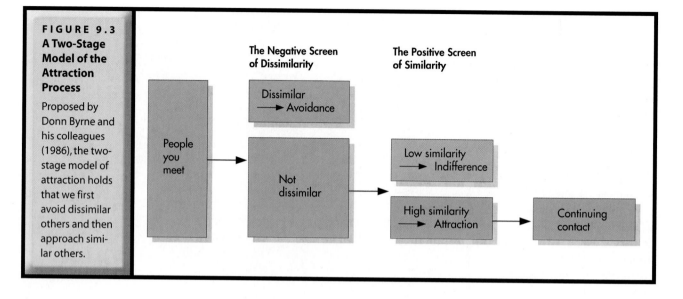

FIGURE 9.3
A Two-Stage Model of the Attraction Process

Proposed by Donn Byrne and his colleagues (1986), the two-stage model of attraction holds that we first avoid dissimilar others and then approach similar others.

be similar in attitudes. Since this link was established before the students knew each other, attraction was the active ingredient. When we like someone, we assume that he or she shares our views (Marks & Miller, 1982).

But what about the effects of actual attitude similarity on attraction? Here, the time course is slower, because people have to get to know each other first. In Newcomb's study, the link between actual similarity and liking increased gradually during the school year. Many laboratory experiments have confirmed the point. For example, Donn Byrne (1971) had people give their opinions on a whole range of issues and then presented them with an attitude survey supposedly filled out by another person (the responses were actually rigged). In study after study, he found that participants liked this other person better when they perceived his or her attitudes as being more similar to theirs. Even in marriage, the more similar two people are—in the roles they like to play and in how they like to spend their leisure time—the more compatible they are (Houts et al., 1996). It appears that birds of a feather not only flock together but stay together (Byrne, 1997).

According to Milton Rosenbaum (1986), attraction researchers have overplayed the role of attitudinal similarity. Similarity does not spark attraction, he says; rather, *dis*similarity triggers repulsion—the desire to avoid someone. Rosenbaum maintains that people expect most others to be similar, which is why others who are different grab our attention. Taking this hypothesis one step further, David Lykken and Auke Tellegen (1993) argue that in mate selection, *all* forms of interpersonal similarity are irrelevant. After a person discards the 50 percent of the population who are least similar, they claim, a random selection process takes over.

So which is it: Are we turned on by others who are similar in their attitudes, or are we turned off by those who are different? As depicted in Figure 9.3, Donn Byrne and his colleagues proposed a two-step model that takes both reactions into account. First, they claim, we avoid associating with others who are dissimilar; then, among those who remain, we are drawn to those who are most similar (Byrne et al., 1986; Smeaton et al., 1989).

In addition to demographics and attitudes, there is a third source of similarity and difference that is also at work, at least in romantic relationships. Have you ever noticed the way people react to couples in which one partner is gorgeous and the other plain? Typically, we are startled by such "mismatches," as if expecting people to pair off with others who are similarly attractive—not more, not less. This reaction has a basis in reality. Early on, laboratory studies showed that both men and women yearn for partners who are highly attractive. Thus, when incoming first-year students at the University of Minnesota were randomly coupled for a dance, their desire for a second date was influenced more by their partner's physical attractiveness than by any other variable (Walster et al., 1966). In real-life situations, however, where one can be accepted or rejected by a prospective partner, people shy away from romantic encounters with others who are "out of their league" (Berscheid et al., 1971). Correlational studies of couples who are dating, engaged, living together, or married thus support a **matching hypothesis**—the idea that people tend to become romantically involved with others who are equivalent in their physical attractiveness (Feingold, 1988).

Matching is also predictive of progress in a relationship. When paired with others who are similar rather than dissimilar in physical attractiveness, clients of a professional dating service were more likely to begin and continue dating (Folkes, 1982)—and couples were more likely to grow closer and more in love (Murstein, 1972). In the economics of the social marketplace, physical matching seems to occur automatically, as people seek the very best but settle for what they can get (Kalick & Hamilton, 1986).

Before concluding that similarity is the key to attraction, though, what about the common-sense notion that opposites attract? Many years ago, sociologists proposed the *complementarity* hypothesis, which holds that people seek others whose needs "oppose" their own—that people who need to dominate, for example, are drawn to those who need to be submissive (Winch et al., 1954). Is there any support for this view? Surprisingly, the answer is no. Sure, most human beings are romantically attracted to others of the opposite sex. But when it comes to fitting mutual needs and personality traits the way keys fit locks, research shows that complementarity does not influence attraction (O'Leary & Smith, 1991).

Liking Others Who Like Us Many years ago, Fritz Heider (1958) theorized that people prefer relationships that are psychologically "balanced" and that a state of imbalance causes distress. In groups of three or more individuals, a balanced social constellation exists when we like someone whose relationships with others parallel our own. Thus, we want to like the friends of our friends and the enemies of our enemies (Aronson & Cope, 1968). If you've ever had a good friend who dated someone you detested, then you know just how awkward and unpleasant an *un*balanced relationship can be. The fact is, we don't expect our friends and enemies to get along (Chapdelaine et al., 1994).

Between two people, a state of balance exists when the relationship is characterized by **reciprocity**—a mutual exchange between what we give and what we receive. Liking is mutual, which is why we tend to like others who indicate that they like us. In one experiment, Rebecca Curtis and Kim Miller (1986) brought pairs of students into the laboratory, arranged for them to talk, and then "revealed" to one member in each pair that he or she was liked by the partner or disliked. When the students were later reunited for conversation, those who thought that they were liked were, in turn, warmer, more agreeable, and more self-disclosing. Feeling liked is important. When groups of men and women were asked to reflect on how they fell in love or developed friendships with specific people, many spontaneously said they had been turned on initially by the realization that they were liked (Aron et al., 1989).

But wait. Does reciprocity mean, simply, that the more people like us, the more we will like them back? Elliot Aronson and Darwyn Linder (1965) conducted an interesting study in which female college students met in pairs several times to discuss various topics. In each pair, one student was a research participant, and her partner was a confederate. After each meeting, the participant overheard a follow-up conversation between the experimenter and the confederate in which she was discussed and evaluated. Over time, the confederate's evaluation of the participant either was consistently positive or negative or underwent a change—either from

When it comes to romantic relationships, opposites attract. **False.**

matching hypothesis The proposition that people are attracted to and form relationships with those who are similar to them in particular characteristics, such as physical attractiveness.

reciprocity A mutual exchange between what we give and receive—for example, liking those who like us.

negative to positive (gain) or from positive to negative (loss). Put yourself in the participant's shoes. All else being equal, in which condition would you like your partner most? In this study, participants liked the partner more when her evaluation changed from negative to positive than when it was positive all along. As long as the "conversion" is gradual and believable, people like others more when their affection took time to earn than when it came easily.

Pursuing Those Who Are Hard to Get The Aronson and Linder (1965) finding suggests that we like others who are socially selective. This seems to support an old popular notion that you can spark romantic interest in someone by playing hard to get. Recently, Ellen Fein and Sherri Schneider (1996) wrote a paperback book for women seductively titled *The Rules: Time-Tested Secrets for Capturing the Heart of Mr. Right.* And what are the rules? Here's one: "Don't call him and rarely return his calls." Here's another: "Let him take the lead." In all cases, the theme is that men are charmed by women who are hard to get. It's an interesting hypothesis. Yet researchers have found that the **hard-to-get effect** is harder to get than they had originally anticipated (Walster et al., 1973). One problem, say Rex Wright and Richard Contrada (1986), is that we are turned *off* by people who reject us because they are committed to someone else or have little interest in us. Second, we prefer people who are moderately selective compared with those who are nonselective (they have no taste) or too selective (they are arrogant).

But now suppose that someone you are interested in is hard to get for external reasons. What if a desired relationship is opposed or forbidden by parents, as in the story of Romeo and Juliet? What about a relationship threatened by catastrophe, as in the love story portrayed in *Titanic*? What about distance, a lack of time, or renewed interest from a partner's old flame? As you may recall from Chapter 6, the theory of psychological reactance states that people are highly motivated to protect their freedom to choose and behave as they please. When a valued freedom is threatened, people reassert themselves, often by seeing the endangered behavior as even more desirable—like the proverbial forbidden fruit (Brehm & Brehm, 1981).

Consider what happens when you think that your chance to get a date for the evening is slipping away. Is it true, to quote the lyrics of country-and-western musician Mickey Gilley, that "the girls all get prettier at closing time"? To find out, researchers entered some bars in Texas and asked patrons three times during the night to rate the physical attractiveness of other patrons of the same and opposite sex. As Gilley had suggested, people of the opposite sex were seen as more attractive as the night wore on (Pennebaker et al., 1979). The study is cute, but the correlation between time and attraction can be interpreted in other ways (perhaps attractiveness ratings rise with blood-alcohol levels!). In a recent study, however, Scott Madey and his colleagues (1996) also had patrons in a bar make attractiveness ratings throughout the night. They found that these ratings increased as the night wore on only among patrons who were not committed to a relationship. As reactance theory would predict, closing time posed a threat—which sparked desire—only to those on the lookout for a late-night date (see Figure 9.4).

Another possible instance of passion fueled by reactance can be seen in "the allure of secret relationships." In a fascinating experiment, Daniel Wegner and others (1994) paired up male and female college students to play bridge. Within each foursome, one couple was instructed in writing to play footsie under the

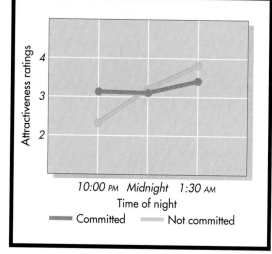

FIGURE 9.4 Perceptions of Attraction as the Night Wears On: The Role of Commitment

In this study, bar patrons made attractiveness ratings throughout the night. As shown, ratings increased over time—but only among men and women not committed to a relationship. It appears that closing time poses a threat—and sparks desire—only among those on the lookout for a late-night date. *(Data from Madey et al., 1996.)*

hard-to-get effect The tendency to prefer people who are highly selective in their social choices over those who are more readily available.

Consistent with reactance theory, studies conducted in bars like this one have shown that men and women who are not in committed relationships see each other as more attractive as the night wears on.

table—either secretly or in the open. Got the picture? After a few minutes, the game was stopped, and the players were asked to indicate privately how attracted they were to their own partner and to the opposite-sex member of the other team. The result: Students who played footsie in secret were more attracted to each other than those who played in the open or not at all. This finding is certainly consistent with reactance theory. But there may be more to it. As we'll see later, the thrill of engaging in a forbidden act, or the sheer excitement of having to keep a secret, may help fan the flames of attraction.

Finally, it's important to realize that there are situations in which reactance may reduce interpersonal attraction. Think about it. Have you ever tried to play the matchmaker by insisting that two of your unattached, single friends get together? Be forewarned: Setting people up can backfire. Determined to preserve the freedom to make their own romantic choices, your friends may become *less* attracted to each other than they would have been without your encouragement (Wright et al., 1992).

"Love ceases to be a pleasure when it ceases to be a secret."

—Aphra Behn

Mate Selection: The Evolution of Desire?

Before moving on to the topic of close relationships, let's stop for a moment and ponder this question: Among heterosexuals, are men and women similarly motivated? For years, sex researchers have found that men and women differ in certain aspects of their sexuality. When respondents were asked to pick ten private wishes from a list, for example, most men and women similarly wanted love, health, peace on earth, unlimited ability, and wealth. But more men than women wanted "to have sex with anyone I choose" (Ehrlichman & Eichenstein, 1992). This finding is common. In surveys, men report being sexually more promiscuous than women. They are more likely to enjoy sex without emotional commitment (Laumann et al., 1994), they are more permissive when it comes to casual sex (Oliver & Hyde, 1993), and they are more likely to fantasize about sex with multiple partners at once (Leitenberg & Henning, 1995).

The Evolutionary Perspective Why do these differences exist and what do they mean? In *The Evolution of Desire*, David Buss (1994) argues that the answer can be derived from evolutionary psychology. According to this perspective, men and women by nature must differ in their optimal mating behaviors (Buss & Schmitt, 1993; Trivers, 1972). A woman must be highly selective because she is biologically limited in the number of children she can bear and raise in a lifetime. A woman must, therefore, search for a mate who possesses (or has the potential to possess) economic resources and who is willing to commit those resources to support her offspring. The result is that women should be attracted to men who are older and financially secure or who have intelligence, ambition, stability, and other traits predictive of future success.

In contrast, men can father an unlimited number of children and ensure their reproductive success by inseminating many women. Men are restricted, however, by their ability to attract fertile partners and by their lack of certainty as to whether the babies born are actually their own. With these motives springing from their evolutionary past, men seek out women who are young and physically attractive (having smooth skin, full lips, lustrous hair, good muscle tone, and other youthful features)—attributes that signal health and reproductive fertility. To minimize their paternal uncertainty, men should also seek women who are likely to be sexually faithful rather than promiscuous.

"Men seek to propagate widely, whereas women seek to propagate wisely."

—Robert Hinde

To test this theory, Buss (1989) and a team of researchers surveyed 10,047 men and women in thirty-seven cultures in North and South America, Asia, Africa, Eastern and Western Europe, and the Pacific. All respondents were asked to rank-order and rate the importance of various attributes in choosing a mate. The results were consistent with predictions. Both men and women gave equally high ratings to certain attributes, such as "having a pleasant disposition." But in the vast majority of countries, "good looks" and "no previous experience in sexual intercourse" were valued more by men, whereas "good financial prospect" and "ambitious and industrious" were more important to women. Analyses of personal ads appearing in magazines and newspapers have also revealed that in the dating marketplace the "deal" is that women offer beauty, while men offer wealth (Feingold, 1992a; Rajecki et al., 1991; Sprecher et al., 1994). In the words of one investigator, the search for a heterosexual mate seems to feature "men as success objects and women as sex objects" (Davis, 1990).

Also consistent with the evolutionary perspective is a universal tendency for men to seek younger women (who are most likely to be fertile) and for women to desire older men (who are most likely to have financial resources). Buss (1989) found this age-preference discrepancy in all the cultures he studied, with men on average wanting to marry women who were 2.7 years younger and women wanting men who were 3.4 years older. Based on their analysis of personal ads, Douglas Kenrick and Richard Keefe (1992) found that men in their twenties are equally interested in younger women and slightly older women still of fertile age. But men in their thirties seek out women who are five years younger, while men in their fifties prefer women ten to twenty years younger. In contrast, girls and women of all ages are attracted to men who are older than themselves. These patterns can also be seen in marriage statistics collected from different cultures and generations. There is one interesting exception: Teenage boys say they are most attracted to women who are slightly *older* than they are, women in their fertile twenties (Kenrick et al., 1996).

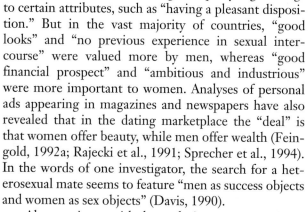

"I'm rich, you're thin. Together, we're perfect."

Another line of research concerns *sexual jealousy*, a negative emotional state that arises from a perceived threat to one's sexual relationship (Salovey, 1991; White & Mullen, 1989). Although jealousy is a common and normal human reaction, men and women are aroused by different triggering events. According to evolutionary theory, a man should be particularly upset by *sexual* infidelity because a wife's extramarital affair increases the risk that the children he supports are not his own. In contrast, a woman should feel threatened more by *emotional* infidelity because a husband who falls in love with another woman might leave and withdraw his financial support.

Two studies support this hypothesis. In one study, male and female college students were asked whether they would be more upset if their romantic partner had formed a deep emotional attachment or had had sexual intercourse with another person. Think for a moment about this awful choice. Which situation would *you* find more distressing? The results revealed a striking sex difference: 60 percent of the men said they would be more upset by a partner's sexual infidelity, but 83 percent of the women felt that emotional infidelity was worse (Buss et al., 1992). This difference has been found not only in the United States but also in Germany and the Netherlands (Buunk et al., 1996). In a second study, newly married husbands and wives were interviewed about how they would react if they suspected their partner of cheating. Interestingly, the men were most likely to say they would use various "mate-retention" tactics (concealing or threatening the wife or taking violent action against the male rival) if their wives were young and relatively attractive. In contrast, women were more likely to say they would use mate-retention tactics (being more watchful or enhancing their appearance) if their husbands were status-driven and had higher incomes (Buss & Shackelford, 1997).

"And do you, Rebecca, promise to make love only to Richard, month after month, year after year, and decade after decade, until one of you is dead?"

Sociocultural Perspectives Although the differences between the sexes are intriguing, critics of the evolutionary approach are quick to argue that some of the results can be interpreted in terms that are more "psychological" than "evolutionary." One common argument is that women trade youth and beauty for money not for reproductive purposes but, rather, because they often lack *direct* access to economic power. With this hypothesis in mind, Steven Gangestad (1993) examined women's access to wealth in each of the countries in Buss's cross-cultural study. He found that the more economic power women had, the more important male physical attractiveness was to them. This result suggests that it may be the generally low social and economic status of women relative to men that leads them to care less about the physical attributes of a potential mate. It's interesting, however, that increased economic power among women does *not*, at the same time, reduce their desire for men with good financial prospects (Wiederman & Allgeier, 1992).

Another argument concerns the finding that men are more fearful of a mate's sexual infidelity (which threatens paternal certainty), while women worry more about emotional infidelity (which threatens future support). This difference is consistent. But what does it mean? In contrast to the explanations provided by evolutionary theory, some researchers have found that men become most upset over sexual infidelity not because of uncertain paternity but because they reasonably assume that a married woman who has a sexual affair is also likely to have intimate feelings for her extramarital partner. In other words, the man's concern, like the woman's, may be over the threat to the relationship—not fatherhood issues (DeSteno & Salovey, 1996; Harris & Christenfeld, 1996).

A third argument is that the differences typically found between the sexes are small compared with the similarities. This is an important point. In Buss's cross-cultural study, both men and women gave their highest ratings to such characteristics as kindness, dependability, a good sense of humor, and a pleasant disposition (physical attractiveness and financial prospects did not top the lists). Moreover, research shows that women desire physical attractiveness as much as men do—when asked about what they want in a short-term casual sex partner (Regan & Berscheid, 1997).

The evolutionary approach offers social psychologists a fascinating but controversial new perspective on mate selection. Untangling the influences of culture from those of evolution is challenging—and will ensure that these dueling perspectives on human attraction will continue to provoke debate in the years to come.

Close Relationships

Being attracted to people can be exhilarating or frustrating—depending on how the initial encounters develop. How important is a good relationship to you? Researchers asked three hundred students to weigh the importance of having a satisfying romantic relationship against the importance of other life goals (like getting a good education, having a successful career, contributing to a better society) and found that 73 percent said they would sacrifice most other goals before giving up a good relationship (Hammersla & Frease-McMahan, 1990).

People have many significant relationships in their lives, but social psychologists have concentrated on adult friends, dating partners, lovers, and married couples (Brehm, 1992; Fehr, 1996; Harvey, 1995; Hatfield & Rapson, 1993; Hendrick & Hendrick, 1992). These **intimate relationships** often involve three basic components: (1) feelings of attachment, affection, and love; (2) fulfillment of psychological needs; and (3) interdependence between partners, each of whom has a meaningful influence on the other (Berscheid & Peplau, 1983).

Not all intimate relationships contain all these ingredients. A summer romance is emotionally intense; but in the fall, people resume their separate lives. An "empty shell" marriage revolves around coordinated daily activities; but emotional attachment is weak, and psychological needs go unmet. Clearly, relationships come in different shapes and sizes. Some are sexual; others are not. Some involve partners of the same sex; others, partners of the opposite sex. Some partners commit to a future together; others drop by for a brief stay. Feelings run the gamut from joyful to painful and from loving to hateful—with emotional intensity ranging all the way from mild to megawatt.

How do two people advance from their first encounters to the intimate relationships that warm our lives? Do we proceed in stages, step by step, or by leaps and bounds? According to one perspective, relationships progress in order through a specific set of stages. For example, Murstein's (1986) *stimulus-value-role (SVR) theory* says there are three: (1) the stimulus stage, in which attraction is sparked by external attributes such as physical appearance; (2) the value stage, in which attachment is based on similarity of values and beliefs; and (3) the role stage, in which commitment is based on the performance of such roles as husband and wife. All three factors are important throughout a relationship, but each one is said to be first and foremost during only one stage (see Figure 9.5).

In evaluating any stage theory, the critical issue is *sequence*. Does the value stage always precede the role stage, or might a couple work out roles before

intimate relationship A close relationship between two adults involving at least one of the following: emotional attachment, fulfillment of psychological needs, and interdependence.

exploring whether their values are compatible? Most investigators do not believe that intimate relationships progress through a fixed sequence of stages. In a series of studies, for example, newlywed couples asked to recall how their relationships had developed reported a number of different paths in the road to marriage. Significant shifts did not occur in the same order for every couple, nor did every couple go through the same shifts. One size did not fit all (Surra & Huston, 1987).

If intimate relationships don't all follow the same script, what does account for how they change? Every relationship has a developmental history with ups, downs, stalls, and accelerations. What pushes a relationship up, pulls it down, or keeps it steady? One common answer is, rewards. Love, like attraction, depends on the experience of positive emotions in the presence of a partner. Step by step, as rewards pile up, love develops. Or, as rewards diminish, love erodes. In reward theories of love, quantity counts. But some would disagree, and it's easy to see why. Think about your own relationships. Are your feelings toward someone you love simply a more intense version of your feelings toward someone you like? Is the love of a close

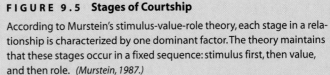

FIGURE 9.5 Stages of Courtship

According to Murstein's stimulus-value-role theory, each stage in a relationship is characterized by one dominant factor. The theory maintains that these stages occur in a fixed sequence: stimulus first, then value, and then role. *(Murstein, 1987.)*

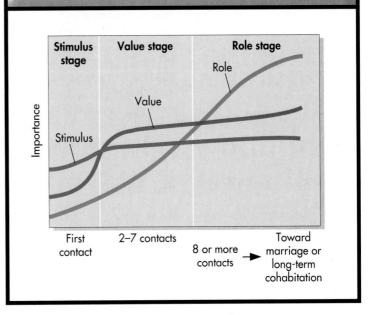

friend the same as the love of a romantic partner? If not, then you can appreciate the argument that there are important qualitative differences among relationships. In this perspective, a great leap is required to take us from liking to loving—and love itself comes in different forms. Both of these views have something to offer. Progress on the road from attraction to love depends on the quantity of fuel in the tank *and* on the kind of engine providing the power. The next section examines the reward-based approach to building a relationship. Then we consider differences among the various types of relationships.

The Intimate Marketplace: Tracking the Gains and Losses

Earlier, we saw that people are initially attracted to others who provide them with direct or indirect rewards. But is "What's in it for me?" still important in a relationship that has blossomed and grown? Can an economic approach be used to predict the future of a close relationship?

Social Exchange Theory **Social exchange theory** is an economic model of behavior according to which people are motivated by a desire to maximize profit and minimize loss in their social relationships just as they are in business (Homans, 1961; Thibaut & Kelley, 1959). The basic premise of social exchange theory is simple: Relationships that provide more rewards and fewer costs will be more satisfying and endure longer. Between intimates, the rewards include love, companionship, consolation in times of distress, and sexual gratification if the relationship is of this nature. The costs include the work it takes to maintain the relationship, conflict, compromise, and the sacrifice of opportunities elsewhere.

social exchange theory A perspective that views people as motivated to maximize benefits and minimize costs in their relationships with others.

The development of an intimate relationship is very clearly associated with the overall level of rewards. Research has shown that dating couples who have many rewarding interactions early on are less likely to break up later than those who start out with relatively few rewards (Lloyd et al., 1984). Dating couples who experience greater increases in rewards as their relationship continues are also more likely to stay together than are those who experience only small increases or declines (Berg & McQuinn, 1986). During the "honeymoon" period of a relationship, costs may not be too important (Hays, 1985). Honeymoons can't last forever, though. In a study of dating couples, Caryl Rusbult (1983) found that costs first entered into the equation at about three months. After that point, both rewards and costs contributed to levels of satisfaction—both in married couples (Margolin & Wampold, 1981) and in gay and lesbian couples living together (Kurdek, 1991a).

Rewards and costs do not arise in a psychological vacuum. People bring to their relationships certain expectations about the balance sheet to which they are entitled. John Thibaut and Harold Kelley (1959) coined the term *comparison level (CL)* to refer to this average, expected outcome in relationships. A person with a high CL expects to have rewarding relationships; someone with a low CL does not. Situations that meet or exceed a person's expectations are more satisfying than those that fall short (Michaels et al., 1984). Even a bad relationship can look pretty good to someone who has a low CL.

According to Thibaut and Kelley (1959), a second kind of expectation is also important. They coined the term *comparison level for alternatives (CLalt)* to refer to people's expectations about what they would receive in an alternative situation. If the rewards available elsewhere are believed to be high, a person will be less committed to staying in the present relationship (Drigotas & Rusbult, 1992). If people perceive few acceptable alternatives (a low CLalt), they will tend to remain—even in an unsatisfying relationship that fails to meet expectations (CL). Of course, just as alternatives can influence our commitment, commitment can influence alternatives as well. To someone who is in love, other prospective partners are seen as less appealing (Johnson & Rusbult, 1989; Simpson et al., 1990).

A third element in the social exchange is investment. An *investment* is something a person puts into a relationship that he or she cannot recover if the relationship ends (Kelley, 1983). If you don't like the way a relationship is working out, you can pack your clothes, grab your CD player, and drive away. But what about the time you put into trying to make it last? What about all the romantic and career opportunities you gave up along the way? As you might expect, investments increase commitment. Because of those things we can't take with us, we're more likely to stay (Rusbult & Buunk, 1993).

Over the years, research has shown that the social exchange framework can be used to predict the commitment of partners to their relationship. This is important because commitment—which is greater for engaged or married couples than for those who are only dating (Stanley & Markman, 1992)—predicts how long premarital relationships will last (Cate & Lloyd, 1992) and whether someone will return to an abusive situation (Rusbult & Martz, 1995). The social exchange framework is diagrammed in Figure 9.6.

Equity Theory   **Equity theory** is a specific version of how social exchange operates in interpersonal interactions (Messick & Cook, 1983; Walster, Walster, & Berscheid, 1978). According to this theory, people are most content with a relationship when the ratio between what they get out of it (benefits) and what they put into it (contributions) is similar for both partners. Thus, the basic equity formula is:

$$\frac{\text{Your Benefits}}{\text{Your Contributions}} = \frac{\text{Your Partner's Benefits}}{\text{Your Partner's Contributions}}$$

equity theory The theory that people are most satisfied with a relationship when the ratio between benefits and contributions is similar for both partners.

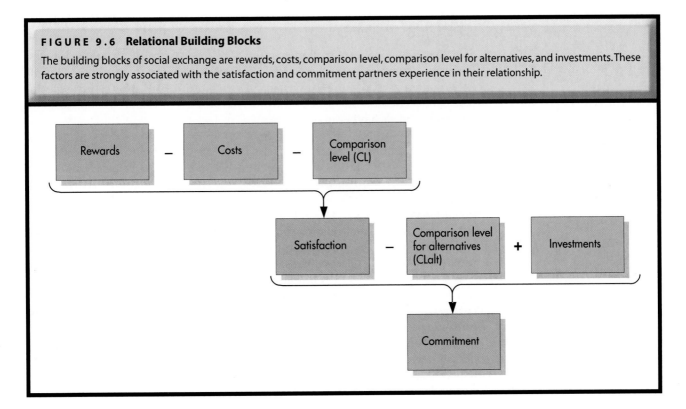

FIGURE 9.6 Relational Building Blocks

The building blocks of social exchange are rewards, costs, comparison level, comparison level for alternatives, and investments. These factors are strongly associated with the satisfaction and commitment partners experience in their relationship.

Equity is different from equality. According to equity theory, the balance is what counts. So if one partner benefits more from the relationship but also makes a greater contribution, then the situation is still equitable. In an *in*equitable relationship, the balance is disturbed: One partner (called the *overbenefited*) receives more benefits than he or she deserves on the basis of contributions made, while the other partner (called the *underbenefited*) receives fewer benefits than deserved.

Both overbenefit and underbenefit are often unhappy states. Underbenefited partners feel angry and resentful because they are giving more than their partner for the benefits they receive. At the same time, overbenefited partners feel guilty because they are profiting unfairly. Both kinds of inequity are associated with negative emotions in dating couples (Walster, Walster, & Berscheid, 1978), married couples (Schafer & Keith, 1980), and the friendships of elderly widows (Rook, 1987). When it comes to satisfaction with a relationship, however, it is usually more unpleasant to feel underbenefited than overbenefited (Hatfield et al., 1982). In a national survey of married women with children, those who saw their relationship as inequitable as opposed to equitable saw divorce as a more likely outcome (Katzev et al., 1994). But among the women in the inequitable group, those who saw themselves as underbenefited ("unfair to me") saw divorce as more likely than those who saw themselves as overbenefited ("unfair to him"). Apparently, people prefer to receive too much in life rather than too little—even if they feel bad about it.

It may strike you that although equity is important, determining whether or not a given relationship is equitable can be difficult. You have to tally up your own benefits, tally up your contributions, compute your partner's benefits and contributions, and compare the two. Rodney Cate and Sally Lloyd (1988) wonder whether people really go to all this trouble when much simpler calculations might suffice. In a series of studies, they found that the absolute level of rewarding outcomes was actually a better predictor of relationship satisfaction and endurance than was either equality of rewards or equity. Simply put, the more good things people said they received from a relationship, the better they felt about it.

Types of Relationships

Social exchange models focus on quantity: The more (rewards, equity), the better (satisfaction, endurance). But is reward always necessary? And what about the qualitative differences in our relationships? Does more reward turn casual acquaintances into friends, and friends into lovers, or are these types of relationships different from each other in other ways?

Exchange and Communal Relationships　According to Margaret Clark and others, people operate on the reward-based model when they are in **exchange relationships,** which are characterized by an immediate tit-for-tat repayment of benefits. In these situations, people want costs to be quickly offset by compensation, leaving the balance at zero. But not all relationships fit this mold. Clark maintains that in **communal relationships,** partners respond to each other's needs and well-being over time, without regard for whether they have given or received a benefit (Clark, 1984; Clark & Mills, 1979; Williamson & Clark, 1989).

Exchange relationships most often exist between strangers and casual acquaintances and in certain long-term arrangements—such as business partnerships. In contrast, strong communal relationships are usually limited to close friends, romantic partners, and family members (Clark & Mills, 1993). Based on fieldwork in West Africa, Alan Fiske (1992) is convinced that this distinction applies to human interactions all over the world. But the cynics among us wonder: Are communal relationships truly free of social exchange considerations? Can people really give without any desire to receive, or do partners in a communal relationship rely on a more subtle version of social exchange, assuming that benefits will balance out in the long run? Clark and Judson Mills (1993) argue that true communal relationships do exist—that once a communal norm has been adopted in a relationship, regardless of how it started, the motivation to respond to the other's needs becomes automatic.

Secure and Insecure Attachment Styles　Another interesting approach to understanding relationships is provided by Phillip Shaver, Cindy Hazan, and their colleagues, who have theorized that just as infants display different kinds of attachment toward their parents, so do adults exhibit specific **attachment styles** in their romantic relationships (Shaver et al., 1998).

For many years, child development psychologists have noticed that infants form intense, exclusive bonds with their primary caretakers. This first relationship is highly charged with emotion, and it emerges with consistency from one culture to the next. By observing the way babies react to both separations from and reunions with the primary caretaker, usually the mother, researchers also noticed that babies have very different attachment styles. Those with *secure* attachments cry in distress when the mother leaves and beam with sheer delight when she returns. Those with insecure attachments show one of two patterns. Some, described as *anxious,* cling and cry when the mother leaves but then greet her with anger or apathy upon her return. Others are generally more detached and *avoidant,* not reacting much on either occasion (Ainsworth et al., 1978).

How important is this first attachment? Does a secure and trusting bond in the first year of life lay a foundation for close relationships later in life? Some have suggested that there is a link. Research shows that infants classified as securely attached are later more positive in their outlook toward others (Cassidy et al., 1996). And looking back, adults with a secure attachment style described having positive family relationships, while avoidant and anxious adults recalled having difficulties with one or both parents (Feeney & Noller, 1990; Hazan & Shaver, 1987).

Whether or not adult attachment styles are rooted in the first year of life, the distinction among adults has proved to be useful. Read the descriptions of three

exchange relationship
A relationship in which the participants expect and desire strict reciprocity in their interactions.

communal relationship
A relationship in which the participants expect and desire mutual responsiveness to each other's needs.

attachment style　The way a person typically interacts with significant others.

attachment types in Table 9.2. Which one fits you best? Hazan and Shaver (1987) presented this task initially in a "love quiz" that appeared in a Denver newspaper and then in a study of college students. As shown in Table 9.2, the distribution of responses was similar in both samples, and it proved similar again in a recent nation-wide sample of eight thousand adults (Mickelson et al., 1997). In addition, the researchers found that people who have a secure attachment style report having satisfying relationships that are happy, friendly, based on mutual trust, and enduring. Cognitively, they see people as good-hearted; and they believe in romantic love. In contrast, avoidant lovers fear intimacy and believe that romantic love is doomed to fade; and anxious lovers report a love life full of emotional highs and lows, obsessive preoccupation, a greater willingness than others to make long-term commitments, and extreme sexual attraction and jealousy.

To some extent, our attachment styles can be seen in our everyday behavior. For example, Jeffrey Simpson and others (1996) videotaped dating couples as they tried to resolve various conflicts and then showed the tapes to outside observers. They found that men who had an insecure-avoidant attachment style were the least warm and supportive and that women with an insecure-anxious style were the most upset and negative in their behavior. In another study, Marie Tidwell and others (1996) asked participants to keep a one-week diary. Analyses of the diary entries revealed that in opposite-sex interactions, avoidant attachment types derived the least enjoyment, while anxious types experienced the widest range of emotions, from high and low.

What about the future: Does the attachment style you endorse today foretell relational outcomes tomorrow? On this question, the evidence is mixed. People who are secure do tend to have more lasting relationships. But the prognosis for those classified as insecure is harder to predict, with the results less consistent. What's important to realize is that although styles of attachment are somewhat stable over time—perhaps as holdovers from infancy and childhood—they are not fixed, or completely set in stone. For instance, Lee Kirkpatrick and Cindy Hazan (1994) tracked down participants from an earlier study and found, four years later, that 30 percent had apparently changed their attachment styles. In keeping with social psychology's theme that people are profoundly shaped by the situations they are in, research suggests that people may continuously revise their attachment styles in response to their own relationship experiences (Baldwin & Fehr, 1995; Keelan et al., 1994; Scharfe & Bartholomew, 1994).

TABLE 9.2 Attachment Style *(Hazan & Shaver, 1987.)*

Question: Which of the following best describes your feelings?

Answers and Percentages	Newspaper Sample	University Sample
Secure I find it relatively easy to get close to others and am comfortable depending on them and having them depend on me. I don't often worry about being abandoned or about someone getting too close to me.	56%	56%
Avoidant I am somewhat uncomfortable being close to others; I find it difficult to trust them completely, difficult to allow myself to depend on them. I am nervous when anyone gets too close, and often, love partners want me to be more intimate than I feel comfortable being.	25%	23%
Anxious I find that others are reluctant to get as close as I would like. I often worry that my partner doesn't really love me or won't want to stay with me. I want to merge completely with another person, and this desire sometimes scares people away.	19%	21%

How Do I Love Thee? Counting the Ways

The poet Elizabeth Barrett Browning asked, "How do I love thee?" and then went on to "count the ways"—of which there are many. When college students were asked to list all the kinds of love that came to mind, they produced 216 items—such as friendship, parental, brotherly, sisterly, romantic, sexual, spiritual, obsessive, possessive, and puppy love (Fehr & Russell, 1991).

Over the years, various schemes for classifying different types of love have been proposed (Sternberg & Barnes, 1998). On the basis of ancient writings, sociologist John Alan Lee (1988) identified three primary love styles—*eros* (erotic love), *ludus* (game-playing, uncommitted love), and *storge* (friendship love). As with primary colors, Lee theorized, these three styles can be blended together to form new secondary types of love, such as *mania* (demanding and possessive love), *pragma* (pragmatic love), and *agape* (other-oriented, altruistic love). On a scale designed to measure these "colors of love," men tend to score higher than women on *ludus*, while women score higher on *storge*, *mania*, and *pragma* (Hendrick & Hendrick, 1995).

Another popular taxonomy is derived from Robert Sternberg's (1986) **triangular theory of love.** According to Sternberg, there are eight basic subtypes of love (seven different forms of love and an eighth combination that results in non-love)—and all can be derived from the presence or absence of three components. The combination can thus be viewed as the vertices of a triangle (see Figure 9.7). These three components—and sample items used to measure each one—are described below:

Intimacy. The emotional component, which involves liking and feelings of closeness. ("I have a comfortable relationship with ___.")

Passion. The motivational component, which contains drives that trigger attraction, romance, and sexual desire. ("Just seeing ___ is exciting for me.")

Commitment. The cognitive component, which reflects the decision to make a long-term commitment to a loved partner. ("I will always feel a strong responsibility for___.")

Research provides strong support for Sternberg's tri-component model. In one study, Arthur Aron and Lori Westbay (1996) asked people to rate sixty-eight prototypical features of love and found that all the various features fell into three categories: passion (*gazing at the other, euphoria, butterflies in the stomach*), intimacy (*feeling free to talk about anything, supportive, understanding*), and commitment (*devotion, putting the other first, long-lasting*). In a second study, Sternberg (1997) asked people to indicate what they see as important in different kinds of relationships and found that the results were consistent with the theory. For example, "ideal lover" scored high on all three components, "friend" scored high on intimacy and commitment but low on passion, and "sibling" scored high on commitment but low on intimacy and passion.

In light of infant attachments, colors, triangles, and other classification schemes that have been proposed over the years, one wonders: How many types of love are there, really? It's hard to tell. But there are two basic types of love that are built into all models. Look at the questions listed in Table 9.3, and on a scale from 1 (not at all) to 10 (totally), answer them based on your feelings toward a *friend*. Next, answer the same questions based on your feelings toward a current or past *romantic partner*. Then follow the scoring procedure described at the bottom of the table. When Zick Rubin (1973) had college students respond to items like these, he found that they gave high ratings to friends on the odd-numbered items and high ratings to romantic partners on the even-numbered items. From these responses, Rubin developed a Liking Scale and a Loving Scale to measure the two types of relationships.

triangular theory of love
A theory proposing that love has three basic components—intimacy, passion, and commitment—which can be combined to produce eight subtypes.

Rubin's approach treated liking and loving as two distinct reactions to an intimate relationship. There is some question, however, about how sharp the difference is. Kenneth and Karen Dion (1976) gave Rubin's two scales to casual daters, exclusive daters, engaged couples, and married couples. Although casual daters reported more liking than loving, liking and loving did not differ among those in the more committed relationships. One possible reason for the overlap between the two scales is that Rubin's version of love is pretty tame. More pointed is the two-pronged distinction made by Elaine Hatfield (1988) and others between passionate and companionate love. According to Hatfield, **passionate love** is an emotionally intense *and often erotic* state of absorption in another person, whereas **companionate love** is a secure, trusting, and stable partnership, similar to what Rubin called liking.

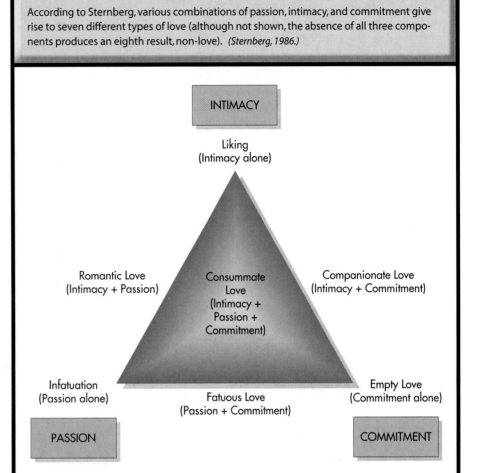

FIGURE 9.7 **Sternberg's Triangular Theory of Love**
According to Sternberg, various combinations of passion, intimacy, and commitment give rise to seven different types of love (although not shown, the absence of all three components produces an eighth result, non-love). *(Sternberg, 1986.)*

INTIMACY

Liking
(Intimacy alone)

Romantic Love
(Intimacy + Passion)

Consummate
Love
(Intimacy +
Passion +
Commitment)

Companionate Love
(Intimacy + Commitment)

Infatuation
(Passion alone)

Fatuous Love
(Passion + Commitment)

Empty Love
(Commitment alone)

PASSION

COMMITMENT

TABLE 9.3 **Liking and Loving**
Some items from the two scales used by Rubin to distinguish between liking and loving. *(Based on Rubin, 1973.)*

Answer each of the following questions on a scale from 1 = *not at all* to 10 = *totally*. Answer them first with a good friend in mind and then while thinking of a romantic partner.

	Friend	Partner
1. This person is one of the most likable people I know.	___	___
2. I feel I can confide in this person about virtually anything.	___	___
3. This person is the sort of person I would like to be.	___	___
4. I would forgive this person for practically anything.	___	___
5. I have great confidence in this person's good judgment.	___	___
6. I would do almost anything for this person.	___	___

A. Sum of your responses to questions 1 + 3 + 5 =
B. Sum of your responses to questions 2 + 4 + 6 =
Which is greater: A or B?

"As soon as you cannot keep anything from a woman, you love her."

—Paul Geraldy

passionate love Romantic love characterized by high arousal, intense attraction, and fear of rejection.

companionate love A secure, trusting, stable partnership.

TABLE 9.4   The Passionate Love Scale

This questionnaire asks you to describe how you feel when you are passionately in love. Think of the person whom you love most passionately *right now*. If you are not in love right now, think of someone you loved before. Enter that person's name in the blank line in each question, and respond according to how you felt at the time your feelings were most intense. Higher scores on this scale indicate greater passionate love. *(Based on Hatfield & Rapson, 1987.)*

Answer each of the following items according to this scale:

1	2	3	4	5	6	7	8	9
Not at all true				Moderately true				Definitely true

1. I would feel deep despair if _____ left me.
2. Sometimes I feel I can't control my thoughts; they are obsessively on _____.
3. I feel happy when I am doing something to make _____ happy.
4. I would rather be with _____ than anyone else.
5. I'd get jealous if I thought _____ were falling in love with someone else.
6. I yearn to know all about _____.
7. I want _____—physically, emotionally, mentally.
8. I have an endless appetite for affection from _____.
9. For me, _____ is the perfect romantic partner.
10. I sense my body responding when _____ touches me.
11. _____ always seems to be on my mind.
12. I want _____ to know me—my thoughts, my fears, and my hopes.
13. I eagerly look for signs indicating _____'s desire for me.
14. I possess a powerful attraction for _____.
15. I get extremely depressed when things don't go right in my relationship with _____.

Passionate Love: The Thrill of It

Passionate love is an intense emotional state of absorption in another person (see Table 9.4). From the ecstatic highs to the agonizing lows, passionate love is the bittersweet stuff of romance paperbacks, popular music, poems, and soap operas. What is it, and where does it come from? According to Ellen Berscheid and Elaine Walster (later Hatfield) (1974a), the key to understanding passionate love is to recognize that it is an emotion—and can be analyzed like any other emotion. Drawing on Schachter's (1964) two-factor theory of emotion (see Chapter 3), they theorized that passionate love requires two key ingredients: (1) a heightened state of physiological *arousal* and (2) the *belief* that this arousal was triggered by the beloved person.

Sometimes, the arousal-love connection is obvious—as when a person feels a surge of sexual desire at the sight of a romantic partner. At other times, however, the symptoms of arousal—such as a pounding heart, sweaty palms, and weak knees—can be hard to interpret. In the company of an attractive person, these symptoms may be attributed or "misattributed" to passionate love. Dolf Zillmann (1984) calls the process **excitation transfer.** According to Zillmann, the arousal triggered by one stimulus can be transferred or added to the arousal from a second stimulus. The combined arousal is then perceived as having been caused only by the second stimulus.

Donald Dutton and Arthur Aron (1974) tested this provocative hypothesis in a field study that took place on two bridges above British Columbia's Capilano River. One was a narrow, wobbly suspension bridge (450 feet long and 5 feet wide, with a low handrail) that sways 230 feet above rocky rapids—a nightmare for anyone the least bit afraid of heights. The other bridge was wide, sturdy, and only 10 feet from the ground. Whenever an unaccompanied young man walked across one of these bridges, he was met by an attractive young woman who introduced herself as a research assistant, asked him to fill out a brief questionnaire, and gave her phone number in case he wanted more information about the project. As predicted, men who crossed the scary bridge were later more likely to call her than those who crossed the stable bridge (interestingly, men on the scary bridge who were interviewed by a male assistant rarely called). Perhaps terror can fan the hot flames of romance.

Or maybe not. Maybe it's just a relief to be with someone when we're in distress. To rule out the possibility that it's relief rather than arousal that fuels attraction, Gre-

excitation transfer The process whereby arousal caused by one stimulus is added to arousal from a second stimulus and the combined arousal is attributed to the second stimulus.

gory White and his colleagues (1981) had to create arousal without distress. How? A little exercise can do it. Male participants ran in place for either two minutes or fifteen seconds and then saw a videotape of a woman they expected to meet. The woman had been made up to look physically attractive or unattractive. After watching the video, participants rated her appearance. The result: Those who exercised for two minutes as opposed to only fifteen seconds saw the physically attractive woman as even more attractive and the unattractive woman as less attractive. This study, and others like it (Allen et al., 1989), showed that arousal—even without distress—intensifies emotional reactions, positive or negative.

The implication of this research—that our passions are at the mercy of bridges, exercise, and anything else that causes the heart to race—is intriguing. It is certainly consistent with the common observation that people are vulnerable to falling in love when their lives are turbulent. But does the effect occur, as theorized, because people *mis*attribute their arousal to a person they have just met? Yes and no. Based on their review of thirty-three experiments, Craig Foster and his colleagues (1998) confirmed that the arousal-attraction effect does exist. They also found, however, that the effect occurs even when people know the actual source of their arousal—in other words, even without a misattribution. According to these investigators, just being aroused—even if we know why—facilitates whatever is the most natural response. If the person we meet is good looking and of the right sex, we become more attracted. If the person is not good looking or of the wrong sex, we become less attracted. No thought is required. The response is automatic.

Whatever its moment-by-moment determinants, passionate love is a widespread, perhaps even universal, human phenomenon. Looking at anthropological research on 166 cultures, William Jankowiak and Edward Fischer (1992) detected at least some indications of passionate love in 147 of them. In light of the highly sexual nature of passionate love, this should come as no surprise. In a book entitled *Lust: What We Know About Human Sexual Desire*, Pamela Regan and Ellen Berscheid (1999) present compelling evidence for the proposition that intense sexual desire and excitement are a vital part of the experience. In this regard, they are quick to note that "love" is different from "being in love." To illustrate, Berscheid and Meyers (1996) asked college men and women to make three lists: people they loved, people they were in love with, and people they were sexually attracted to. As it turned out, only 2 percent of those in the "love" category also appeared in the sex list. Yet among those in the "in love" category, the overlap with sex was 85 percent. And when Regan and her colleagues (1998) asked people to list the characteristics of romantic love, two-thirds cited sexual desire—more than the number who put happiness, loyalty, communication, sharing, or commitment on the list.

Although most people in the world agree that sexual desire is what injects the passion into passionate love, not everyone sees it as necessary for marriage. Think about this question: If a man or woman had all other qualities you desired, would you marry this person if you were *not* in love? When American students were surveyed in 1967, 35 percent of men and 76 percent of women said yes. Twenty years

"I'm looking for a good man who won't get in the way."

"To an American in love, his/her emotions tend to overshadow everything else . . . to a Chinese in love, his/her love occupies a place among other considerations."

—Hsu

later, only 14 percent of men and 20 percent of women said they would marry someone with whom they were not in love (Simpson et al., 1986). The shift among women may reflect the pragmatic point that marrying for love is an economic luxury that few women of the past could afford.

The willingness to marry without love is also subject to cultural variation. Today, that number ranges from 4 percent in the United States, 5 percent in Australia, and 8 percent in England up to 49 percent in India and 51 percent in Pakistan (Levine, 1993). The influence of culture on love is interesting. On the one hand, it could be argued that the rugged individualism found in western cultures would inhibit the tendency to become intimate and interdependent with others. On the other hand, this same individualistic orientation leads people to give priority in making marital decisions to their own feelings—rather than to family concerns, social obligations, religious constraints, income, and the like (Dion & Dion, 1996).

In a wedding ceremony that took place in Bombay, Tushar Agarwal and his bride Richa are married. Fulfilling a tradition that seems strange to most Americans, for whom being in love is necessary for marriage, this Indian marriage was arranged.

In an illustration of this point, Fred Rothbaum and Bill Yuk-Piu Tsang (1998) compared popular love songs in the United States and China. They found that the American lyrics focused more on the two lovers as isolated entities, independent of social context ("There is nobody here, it's just you and me, the way I want it to be").

Even in the United States, home of a strong and consistent romantic ideology, people have doubts about the staying power of passionate love. Does the fire within a relationship burn hot and bright over time, or is it just a passing fancy? Comparisons of couples at different stages of their relationships (Acker & Davis, 1992) and longitudinal studies that measure changes in the same couples over time (Tucker & Aron, 1993) suggest that passionate love does diminish somewhat over time. In fact, researchers interested in the "chemistry of love" believe that the passionate high that new lovers feel is produced by natural stimulants in the body—which inevitably lose some of their intensity over time (Liebowitz, 1983).

"True love never grows old."

—proverb

Companionate Love: The Self-Disclosure in It   In contrast to the intense, emotional, and erotic nature of passionate love, companionate love is a form of affection that can exist between close friends as well as lovers. Companionate relationships rest more on a foundation of mutual trust, caring, respect, friendship, and long-term commitment—characteristics that John Harvey and Julie Omarzu (1997) call "minding" of the close relationship.

Compared with the passionate form of love, companionate love is less intense but in some respects deeper and more enduring. Susan Sprecher and Pamela Regan (1998) administered passionate and companionate love scales to heterosexual couples who had been together for varying amounts of time and found that passionate love scores of both men and women initially rose over time but then peaked and declined somewhat during marriage. Companionate love scores, however, did not similarly decline. Like the sturdy, steady tortoise in Aesop's fable, companion-

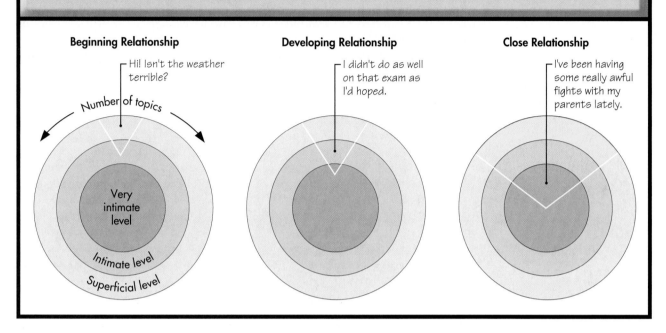

FIGURE 9.8 From a Sliver to a Wedge

According to the theory of social penetration, as a relationship becomes closer, partners increase the breadth of their exchanges (covering a wider range of topics) and also the depth (revealing more intimate information).

ate love may seem outpaced by the flashier start of passionate love, but it can still manage to cross the finish line well ahead.

Companionate love is characterized by high levels of **self-disclosure,** a willingness to open up and share intimate facts and feelings. In a way, self-disclosure is to companionate love what arousal is to passionate love. Think for a moment about your most embarrassing experience, your most cherished ambitions, or your sex life. Would you bare your soul on these private matters to a complete stranger? To an acquaintance? To a friend or a lover? This willingness to disclose intimate facts and feelings lies at the heart of our closest and most intimate relationships (Derlega et al., 1993). Indeed, research shows that the more emotionally involved people are in a dating relationship (Rubin et al., 1980) and the more satisfied they are in marriage (Hansen & Schuldt, 1984), the more they self-disclose to each other. Why? Nancy Collins and Lynn Miller (1994) note three possible reasons for this correlation: (1) We disclose to those we like, (2) we like those who disclose to us, and (3) we like those to whom we have disclosed.

Over the years, researchers have made three observations about self-disclosure patterns in relationships. One is that partners reveal more to each other as their relationship grows over time. According to Irving Altman and Dalmas Taylor (1973), self-disclosure is a basic form of social exchange that unfolds as relationships develop. Their *social penetration theory* holds that relationships progress from superficial exchanges to more intimate ones. At first, people give relatively little of themselves to another person and receive little in return. If initial encounters prove rewarding, however, the exchanges become both *broader* (covering more areas of their lives) and *deeper* (involving more sensitive areas). As shown in Figure 9.8, social interaction grows from a narrow, shallow sliver to a wider, more penetrating wedge.

This increase in self-disclosure can be seen in the fact that the more intimate people are in a relationship, the less likely they are to lie to each other. In an interesting naturalistic study of this point, Bella DePaulo and Deborah Kashy (1998) asked participants to keep a one-week diary of all social interactions and record

self-disclosure Revelations about the self that a person makes to others.

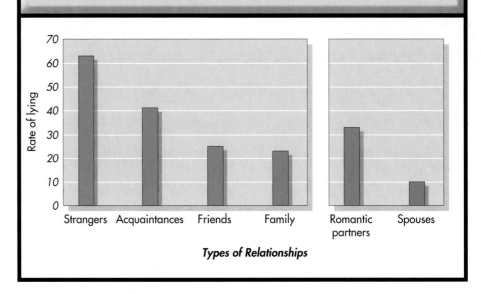

FIGURE 9.9   To Whom Do People Lie?

For one week, people recorded every instance in which they tried to mislead someone. As you can see, they lied most to strangers, followed by acquaintances, family members and friends (left). Also shown is that people lied more often to their unmarried romantic partners than to their spouses (right). These results suggest that the closer two people are, the less likely they are to lie to each other.   *(Data from Depaulo & Kashy, 1998.)*

every instance in which they tried to mislead someone—regardless of how self-serving or well-meaning the intent (some lies are told to advance the liar's self-interest, and others are told for the other person's benefit). As it turned out, the rate of lying among participants decreased according to the closeness of their relationships. On average, they lied most to strangers, followed by casual acquaintances, then family members and friends. Also consistent with the presumed patterns of self-disclosure is that unmarried participants lied three times more often to their romantic partners than married participants did to their spouses. These results are presented in Figure 9.9.

A second observation is that patterns of self-disclosure tend to change according to the state of a relationship. During a first encounter, and in the budding stages of a new relationship, people tend to reciprocate another's self-disclosure with their own—at a comparable level of intimacy. If a new acquaintance opens up, it is polite to match that self-disclosure by revealing more of ourselves. Once a relationship is well established, strict reciprocity occurs less frequently (Altman, 1973; Derlega et al., 1976). Among couples in distress, two different self-disclosure patterns have been observed. For some, both breadth and depth decrease as partners withdraw from each other and cease to communicate (Baxter, 1987). For others, the breadth of self-disclosure declines, but depth increases as the partners hurl cruel and angry statements at each other (Tolstedt & Stokes, 1984). In this case, the social *de*penetration process resembles neither the sliver of a superficial affiliation nor the wedge of a close, intimate relationship—but, rather, a long, thin dagger of discontent.

A third common observation is that individuals differ in the tendency to share private, intimate thoughts with others. For example, Kathryn Dindia and Mike Allen (1992) conducted a meta-analysis of 205 studies involving 23,702 white North Americans and found, on average, that women are more open than men—and that people in general are more self-disclosing to women than to men. This being the case, it comes as no surprise that women rate their same-sex friendships more highly than men rate theirs (Aukett et al., 1988; Wheeler et al., 1989; Wright & Keple, 1981). At least in North America, male friends seem to bond more by taking part in common activities, while female friends engage more in a sharing of feelings (Duck & Wright, 1993). As Paul Wright (1982) put it, women tend to interact "face-to-face"; men go "side-by-side."

It's important to realize that these gender differences in self-disclosure are not universal. In one study, Ladd Wheeler and his colleagues (1989) compared the everyday social interactions of American students with those of Chinese students in Hong Kong and found that whereas American women self-disclosed more to each other than American men did, there were no same-sex interaction differences between the Chinese women and men. In another study, Peter Nardi and Drury Sherrod (1994) examined same-sex friendships among homosexuals and found that gay men and lesbians did *not* differ in their self-disclosures, tendency to engage in common activities, or satisfaction with the friendship. Clearly, more research is needed to understand individual differences in self-disclosure.

Relationship Issues: The Male-Female "Connection"

Browse the shelves of any bookstore, and you'll see one paperback title after another on the general topic of gender. There are books for men and books for women, books that preach the masculine ideal and books that tell us how to be more feminine, books that portray men and women as similar and books that focus on differences, the so-called gender gap. Is it true, to borrow John Gray's (1997) provocative book title, that "Men are from Mars, women are from Venus"? And if so, what are the implications when it comes to male-female relationships?

Sexuality   One hundred years ago, Sigmund Freud shocked the scientific community by proposing psychoanalytic theory, which placed great emphasis on sex as a driving force in human behavior. At the time, Freud's closest colleagues rejected this focus on sexual motivation. But was he wrong? Sexual images and themes appear, literally, in our dreams, in the jokes we tell, in the TV shows we watch, in the novels we read, in the music we hear, and in the sex scandals that swirl around public figures in the news. It's no wonder that advertisers use sex to sell everything from jeans to mouthwash, perfumes, and soft drinks.

Because sex is the most private aspect of human relations, it is difficult to study. During the 1940s, biologist Alfred Kinsey and his colleagues (1948, 1953) conducted the first large-scale survey of sexual practices in the United States. Based on confidential interviews of more than 17,000 men and women, these investigators sought to describe what nobody would openly talk about: patterns of sexual activity. Some of Kinsey's results were shocking, as he revealed that sexual activity was more frequent and more varied than expected. His books became best sellers. His methods were flawed (for example, most respondents were young, white, urban, and middle class), but his findings are still often used as a basis for comparison. Today, using more sophisticated methods, the Kinsey Institute continues to study sexual behavior (Bancroft, 1997).

Since Kinsey's groundbreaking study, numerous sex surveys and studies have been conducted. Although one can never know for sure how accurate the self-report results are, certain findings do emerge with some consistency. First, although there is much variability *within* the sexes, men report being sexually more permissive and active than women do (Simpson & Gangestad, 1992). In heterosexual interactions, men and women also differ in the sexual roles they play—a division of sexual labor that has been summarized in the description of men as

Men are more likely than women to interpret friendly gestures by the opposite sex in sexual terms. **True.**

"go-getters" and of women as "gate-keepers" (Zillmann & Weaver, 1989, p. 95). Of the two roles, the gate-keeper is the more influential because in any *joint* activity, the more restrictive partner calls the shots.

Research also shows that men and women see sex differently in everyday interactions. Compared with women, men view the world in more "sexualized" terms. In one study, Antonia Abbey (1982) arranged for pairs of male and female college students to talk for five minutes, while other students observed these sessions. When she later questioned the actors and observers, Abbey found that the males were more sexually attracted to the females than vice versa. The males also rated the female actors as being more seductive and flirtatious than the women had rated themselves as being. In another study, male participants who read stories of various heterosexual dating scenarios were more likely than female participants to assume that the women in these stories wanted to have sex (Muehlenhard, 1988). Among men more than women, eye contact, a compliment, a friendly remark, a brush against the arm, and an innocent smile are often seen as sexual come-ons (Kowalski, 1993). These differing perceptions occur not only in the laboratory but also between strangers, acquaintances, and casual friends who meet at parties, at school, at work, and in other settings (Abbey, 1987; Saal et al., 1989).

Jealousy Jealousy has a long, tragic history. The Song of Solomon says it's "cruel as the grave." Shakespeare called it "the green-eyed monster." And in the highly publicized 1995 trial of O. J. Simpson, prosecutor Christopher Darden charged that Simpson had killed his ex-wife "for a reason almost as old as mankind itself. He killed her because he couldn't have her."

Jealousy is an emotion that is triggered by the perception of a threat to a valued relationship. The threat doesn't have to actually exist. Neither does the relationship itself; all celebrities know the danger of becoming the target of a stalker's obsessive fantasies. According to Gregory White and Paul Mullen (1989), jealousy begins with an appraisal of the possible threat. Some people have a shorter fuse than others in this regard. Those who feel insecure and inequitably treated by their partner are the most volatile (White, 1981)—particularly when the relationship is new (Melamed, 1991) and the person is highly dependent on it (Buunk, 1991).

The strongest and most destructive feelings of jealousy seem to arise specifically from threats of a sexual nature (Mathes, 1992). We saw earlier that among heterosexual couples, the threat of sexual infidelity is more disturbing to men than to women (Buss et al., 1992), especially in traditional societies (Betzig, 1989; Buss & Schmitt, 1993). Bram Buunk and Ralph Hupka (1987) have also observed cross-cultural differences in the sorts of behaviors that elicit jealousy. Relative to other national groups, kissing elicited high levels of sexual jealousy from Hungarians; dancing and sexual relations, from those in the former Soviet Union; flirting, from those in what used to be Yugoslavia; and sexual fantasies, from the Dutch. In Ireland, Mexico, and the United States, people reported lower levels of sexual jealousy in response to these behaviors.

People also differ in the way they react once jealousy has been aroused. Generally speaking, jealousy is a negative emotion and is accompanied by the distrust, anxiety, and anger that people often feel when they fear the loss of something they already have (Parrott & Smith, 1993). But coping with the threat can take different forms, some more constructive than others. For example, people who are prone to depression tend to blame themselves (Radecki-Bush et al., 1993). Don Sharpsteen and Lee Kirkpatrick (1997) measured people's attachment orientations and then asked them to reflect on how they had coped with past jealousy experiences. They found that people with secure attachment styles had been the most angry and the

jealousy The reaction to a perceived threat to a relationship.

most likely to lash out at their partners. In contrast, those with insecure-anxious or insecure-avoidant styles had tended to feel sad and inadequate, rather than to confront their partners openly, or redirect their anger toward the intruder. Finally, Jeff Bryson (1991) asked college students from different countries to describe how they reacted when jealous and discovered several cross-cultural differences in the way people cope. With tongue in cheek, Bryson summarized his results as follows: "When jealous, the French get mad, the Dutch get sad, the Germans would rather not fight about it, the Italians don't want to talk about it, and the Americans are concerned about what their friends think!" (p. 191).

Communication and Conflict Disagreements about sex and other matters can stir conflict in close relationships (Kurdek, 1994). Whatever the cause, all couples experience some degree of friction. The issue is not whether it occurs but how the couple responds to it. One source of conflict is the difficulty people have talking about their disagreements. When relationships break up, communication problems are among the most common causes cited by heterosexual and homosexual couples alike (Kurdek, 1991b; Sprecher, 1994). But what constitutes "bad communication"? Comparisons between happy and distressed couples have revealed two communication patterns that often occur in troubled relationships.

The first pattern is called *negative affect reciprocity*—a tit-for-tat exchange of expressions of negative feelings (Gottman & Levenson, 1988; Noller & Fitzpatrick, 1990). In all couples, expressions of negative affect elicit more in-kind responses than expressions of positive affect. But negative affect reciprocity, especially in nonverbal behavior, is greater in couples that are distressed—and locked into a duel. Smiles pass by unnoticed, but every glare, every disgusted look, provokes a sharp response. An inability to terminate unpleasant interactions has been observed among distressed couples in Germany and Australia as well as in the United States (Halford et al., 1990).

Men and women react differently to conflict. Women usually report more intense emotions and are more expressive (Grossman & Wood, 1993). She tells him to "warm up," while he urges her to "calm down." Unhappy marriages also tend to be characterized by a *demand/withdraw interaction pattern*, in which the wives demand to discuss relationship problems, only to become frustrated when their husbands withdraw from such discussions (Christensen & Heavey, 1993). In any event, couples caught in this bind often find themselves echoing the title of Deborah Tannen's (1990) popular book on gender differences in communication, *You Just Don't Understand*. According to John Gottman (1994), there is nothing wrong with either approach to dealing with conflict. The problem, he says, lies in the discrepancy. Gottman maintains that healthy relationships are most likely when both partners have similar styles of dealing with conflict.

Whatever one's style, there are two approaches to reducing the negative effects of conflict. The first is so obvious that it is often overlooked: Increase rewarding behavior in other aspects of the relationship. According to Gottman and Levenson (1992), marital stability rests on a "fairly high balance of positive to negative behaviors" (p. 230). If there's conflict over one issue, partners can and should search for other ways to be rewarding to each other. As the balance of positives to negatives improves, so should overall satisfaction, which can reduce conflict (Huston & Vangelisti, 1991; Noller et al., 1994). The second approach is to try to understand the other's point of view. Being sensitive to what the partner thinks and how he or she feels enhances the quality of the relationship (Honeycutt et al., 1993; Long & Andrews, 1990). What motivates individuals in the heat of battle to make that effort to understand? Presumably, it helps if they believe that there is, in fact, a communication problem.

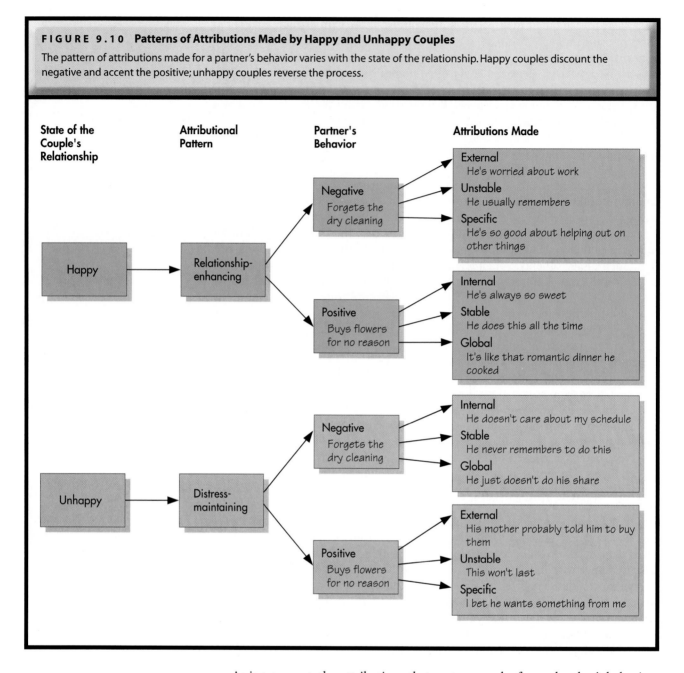

FIGURE 9.10   Patterns of Attributions Made by Happy and Unhappy Couples

The pattern of attributions made for a partner's behavior varies with the state of the relationship. Happy couples discount the negative and accent the positive; unhappy couples reverse the process.

As it turns out, the attributions that partners make for each other's behaviors are correlated with the quality of their relationship (Bradbury & Fincham, 1990; Holtzworth-Munroe & Jacobson, 1987). Happy couples tend to make *relationship-enhancing attributions:* They see the partner's undesirable behaviors as caused by factors that are situational ("a bad day"), temporary ("It'll pass"), and limited in scope ("That's just a sore spot"). Conversely, they see desirable behaviors as caused by factors that are inherent in the partner, permanent, and generalizable to other aspects of the relationship. As illustrated in Figure 9.10, unhappy couples flip the attributional coin on its tail by making the opposite attributions, called *distress-maintaining attributions.* Thus, while happy couples minimize the bad and maximize the good, distressed couples don't give an inch. In light of these very different attributional patterns, it would seem, over time, that happy couples would get happier and miserable couples more miserable. Do they? Yes. Frank Fincham and Thomas Bradbury (1993) found that people who made more distress-maintaining causal attributions at one point in time reported less marital satisfaction one year later. The link between attributions and satisfaction may be reciprocal, with each influencing the other.

Breaking Up Because we are social beings, having close relationships is important to us all—for our happiness and emotional well-being and even for our physical health and longevity. As noted at the start of this chapter, 73 percent of American college students surveyed said they would sacrifice most other life goals rather than give up a satisfying relationship (Hammersla & Frease-McMahan, 1990). Yet sadly, these students live in a society in which 50 to 60 percent of first marriages are likely to end in divorce (Spanier, 1992). With at least one previously divorced partner, the

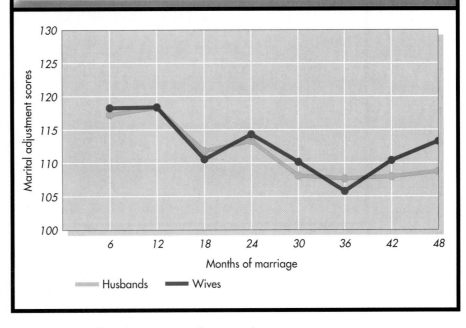

FIGURE 9.11
The Average Course of Marital Satisfaction

Married couples were asked to rate their satisfaction every six months for the first four years of marriage. As shown, the initial honeymoon period was followed by an average decline in satisfaction which, for both husbands and wives, stabilized by the fourth year. *(Data from Karney & Bradbury, 1997.)*

odds of divorce are even greater (Cherlin, 1992). This discrepancy—between the endurance most people want and the disruption they may have to confront—is dramatic. Couples break up, separate, and divorce. How do marriages evolve over time, and why do some last while others dissolve?

Ellen Berscheid and Harry Reis (1998) note that among social psychologists who study intimate relationships, this is the most frequently asked and vexing question. Over the years, researchers have found that newlyweds tend to idealize each other, producing an initial state of marital bliss (Murray et al., 1996). Then, after the honeymoon period, among both husbands and wives, there is typically a steep drop in satisfaction, which stabilizes by the fourth year (Bradbury, 1998). Part of the decline results from the stress of being new parents, which is common, but a similar trajectory is also found among nonparents. To some extent, it appears that our close relationships, like our bodies, age over time (Heaton, 1991). This pattern can be seen in Figure 9.11, which plots satisfaction ratings given every six months over the first four years of marriage. As for factors that predict future outcomes, Benjamin Karney and Thomas Bradbury (1995) reviewed 115 longitudinal studies involving 45,000 married couples and found only that certain positively valued variables (education, employment, constructive behaviors, similarity in attitudes) were somewhat predictive of positive outcomes. They did find, however, that the steeper the initial decline in satisfaction was, the more likely couples were to break up later (Karney & Bradbury, 1997).

When an intimate relationship ends, the experience can be traumatic (Kitson & Morgan, 1990). How do people cope? The answer is, it depends on the nature of the loss. One important factor is the closeness of a relationship, or the extent to which the line between self and other becomes so blurred that *mine* and *yours* are one and the same. Indeed, Arthur Aron and others (1992) found that the longevity of a romantic relationship can be predicted simply by which diagram in

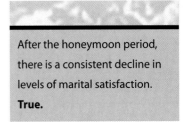

After the honeymoon period, there is a consistent decline in levels of marital satisfaction.
True.

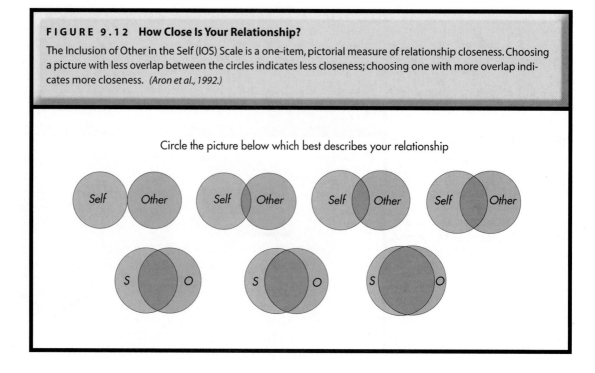

FIGURE 9.12   How Close Is Your Relationship?

The Inclusion of Other in the Self (IOS) Scale is a one-item, pictorial measure of relationship closeness. Choosing a picture with less overlap between the circles indicates less closeness; choosing one with more overlap indicates more closeness. *(Aron et al., 1992.)*

Figure 9.12 people choose to describe their relationship. The more one incorporates a partner into the self, the more lasting the relationship is likely to be—but the more distress one anticipates if there is a breakup.

Another important factor in this regard is interdependence—the social glue that bonds us together. Research shows that the more interdependent couples are (as measured by the amount of time spent together, the variety of shared activities, and the degree of influence each partner has on the other), and the more invested they are in the relationship, the longer it is likely to last (Berscheid et al., 1989; Rusbult & Buunk, 1993)—and the more devastated they become when it ends (Fine & Sacher, 1997; Simpson, 1987). People also differ in the extent to which their associations with others are important to their identity. Among students who had recently experienced a romantic breakup, those for whom relationships play a more central role in identity were more upset (Smith & Cohen, 1993).

An ironic theme runs through much of the research on coping. We are, to put it mildly, darned if we do and darned if we don't. Those factors that contribute to the endurance of a relationship (closeness, interdependence, and the importance of the relationship to one's own identity) turn out to be the same factors that intensify distress and make coping more difficult after a relationship ends. So, how do you balance making the psychological investment necessary for a lasting relationship against holding back enough for self-protection?

In the United States and other Western countries, various demographic markers indicate how problematic traditional forms of commitment have become: a high divorce rate, more single-parent families, more couples living together, and more never-married individuals. But the desire for enduring intimate relationships has never wavered or disappeared. Quite the contrary. Gays and lesbians seek legal recognition of same-sex marriages, the vast majority of divorced individuals remarry, and stepfamilies forge a new sense of what it means to be a "family." It seems that we are in the midst of a great and compelling search, as millions of men and women try to find ways to affiliate with, attract, get closer to, love, and commit themselves with permanence to others.

Review

Being with Others: A Fundamental Human Motive

- The need to belong is a basic human motive, a pervasive drive to form and maintain lasting relationships.

The Thrill of Affiliation

- This social motivation begins with the need for affiliation, a desire to establish social contact with others.
- People differ in the strength of their affiliative needs.
- Stressful situations in particular motivate us to affiliate with others who face a similar threat.

The Agony of Loneliness

- Shyness is a pervasive problem that sets people up to have unrewarding interactions with others.
- People who are painfully shy are at risk for loneliness, a feeling of isolation and social deprivation.

The Initial Attraction

- According to one perspective, people are attracted to others with whom the relationship is rewarding; rewards can be direct, indirect, or by association.
- Evolutionary psychologists argue that human beings exhibit patterns of attraction and mate selection that favor the passing on of their own genes.

Familiarity: Being There

- Proximity sets the stage for social interaction, which is why friendships are most likely to form between people who live near each other.
- Supporting the mere exposure effect, studies show that the more often people see a stimulus, the more they come to like it.
- We do not have to be aware of our prior exposures for the increase in liking to occur.
- Mere exposure might not occur, however, if the target person is initially disliked or becomes "overexposed."

Physical Attractiveness: Getting Drawn In

- In a wide range of social settings, people respond more favorably to men and women who are physically attractive.
- Some researchers believe that certain faces are inherently attractive—across cultures and to infants as well as adults.
- Others argue that beauty is in the eye of the beholder and point to the influences of culture, time, and context.

- One reason for the bias for beauty is that it's rewarding to be in the company of others who are attractive.
- A second reason is that people associate beauty with other positive qualities, an assumption known as the what-is-beautiful-is-good stereotype.
- People seen as physically attractive are more popular, more sexually experienced, and more socially skilled—but they are not happier or higher in self-esteem.
- One reason for the latter is that people who see themselves as attractive often discount the praise they get for nonsocial endeavors.
- Another problem with having beauty as a social asset is that people, notably women, feel pressured to keep up their appearance and are often dissatisfied with how they look.

First Encounters: Getting Acquainted

- People tend to associate with, befriend, and marry others who are similar in their demographic backgrounds, attitudes, and interests.
- People first avoid others who are dissimilar and then are drawn to those remaining who are most similar.
- Supporting the matching hypothesis, people tend to become romantically involved with others who are equivalent in physical attractiveness.
- Contrary to popular belief, complementarity in needs or personality does not affect attraction.
- Indicating the effects of reciprocity, we tend to like others who indicate that they like us.
- But indiscriminate likers can be taken for granted and not liked as much in return.
- Research on the hard-to-get-effect shows that people like others best who are moderately selective in their social choices.

Mate Selection: The Evolution of Desire?

- Evolutionary psychologists say that women seek men with financial security or traits predictive of future success in order to ensure the survival of their offspring.
- In contrast, men seek women who are young and attractive (physical attributes that signal health and fertility)—and not promiscuous (an attribute that diminishes certainty of paternity).
- Cross-cultural studies tend to support these predicted sex differences, but critics note that many of the results can be viewed in terms that are more psychological than evolutionary.

Close Relationships

- Intimate relationships include at least one of three components: feelings of attachment, fulfillment of psychological needs, and interdependence.

- Stage theories propose that close relationships go through specific stages, but evidence for a fixed sequence is weak.
- Two other views emphasize either a gradual accumulation of rewards or a sharp distinction between types of relationships.

The Intimate Marketplace: Tracking the Gains and Losses

- According to social-exchange theory, people seek to maximize gains and minimize costs in their relationships.
- Higher rewards, lower costs, and an outcome that meets or exceeds a partner's comparison level (CL) predict high levels of satisfaction.
- Lower expectations about alternatives (CLalt) and more investment in the relationship are associated with higher levels of commitment.
- Equity theory holds that satisfaction is greatest when the ratio between benefits and contributions is similar for both partners.
- Both overbenefit and underbenefit elicit negative emotions, but the underbenefited are usually less satisfied.

Types of Relationships

- In exchange relationships, people are oriented toward reward and immediate reciprocity; in communal relationships, partners are responsive to each other's needs.
- People with secure attachment styles have more satisfying romantic relationships than do those with insecure (anxious or avoidant) styles.

How Do I Love Thee? Counting the Ways

- According to the triangular theory of love, there are eight subtypes of love produced by different combinations of intimacy, passion, and commitment.
- Inherent in all classifications of love are two types: passionate and companionate.
- Passionate love is an intense, emotional, often erotic state of positive absorption in another person.
- In one theory, passionate love is sparked by physiological arousal and the belief that the arousal was caused by the loved person.
- Consistent with excitation transfer, research shows that arousal can increase or decrease attraction, depending on the initial attractiveness of the person whom one is with.
- Compared with passionate love, companionate love is less intense but in some respects deeper and more enduring.
- Companionate love rests on mutual trust, caring, friendship, commitment, and willingness to share intimate facts and feelings.

- Self-disclosure between partners often becomes broader and deeper over time, though self-disclosure levels vary with the state of the relationship.

Relationship Issues: The Male-Female "Connection"

- On average, men report being sexually more active than women and see opposite-sex interactions in more sexualized terms.
- Jealousy is an emotion that arises from the perception of a threat to the relationship.
- People differ by gender, culture, and other factors in terms of the situations that trigger jealousy and the ways they cope with it.
- When relationships break up, communication problems are among the most common causes.
- Unhappy couples engage often in negative affect reciprocity and exhibit a demand/withdraw interaction pattern.
- During conflict, women are more likely to be demanding; men are more likely to withdraw.
- Partners can reduce conflict by behaving in rewarding ways in other areas and by trying to understand each other's point of view.
- Happy couples make relationship-enhancing attributions, while unhappy couples make distress-maintaining attributions.
- On average, marital satisfaction starts high, then declines steeply for four years before stabilizing.
- Partners who are close and interdependent and for whom relationships are important to the self-concept (characteristics that normally promote stability) suffer more after breaking up.

Key Terms

attachment style *318*

communal relationship *318*

companionate love *321*

equity theory *316*

exchange relationship *318*

excitation transfer *322*

hard-to-get effect *310*

intimate relationship *314*

jealousy *328*

loneliness *297*

matching hypothesis *309*

mere exposure effect *299*

need for affiliation *295*

passionate love *321*

reciprocity *309*

self-disclosure *325*

social exchange theory *315*

triangular theory of love *320*

what-is-beautiful-is-good stereotype *304*

PUTTING **COMMON SENSE** TO THE TEST

People seek out the company of others, even strangers, in times of stress.

True. *Research has shown that external threat causes stress and leads people to affiliate with others who are facing or have faced a similar threat.*

Infants do not discriminate between faces considered attractive and unattractive in their culture.

False. *Two-month-old infants spend more time gazing at attractive than unattractive faces, indicating that they do make the distinction.*

People who are physically attractive are happier and have higher self-esteem than those who are unattractive.

False. *Attractive people are at an advantage in their social lives, but they are not happier, better adjusted, or higher in self-esteem.*

When it comes to romantic relationships, opposites attract.

False. *Consistently, people are attracted to others who are similar—not opposite or complementary—on a whole range of dimensions.*

Men are more likely than women to interpret friendly gestures by the opposite sex in sexual terms.

True. *Experiments have shown that men are more likely than women to interpret friendly opposite-sex interactions as sexual come-ons.*

After the honeymoon period, there is a consistent decline in levels of marital satisfaction.

True. *High marital satisfaction levels among newlyweds are often followed by a steep drop, which stabilizes by the fourth year—a pattern found among parents and nonparents alike.*

10 | Helping Others

Once you've read the book or seen the movie, it's hard to forget *Schindler's List*. At first glance, Oskar Schindler was the classic shady operator: selling pots and pans on the black market; bribing officers in the German Army to award contracts to his company; cheating on his wife; partying with Amon Goeth, the sadistic killer in charge of the local forced-labor camp. Schindler didn't seem the type to look after anyone other than himself. And yet from 1939 to 1945, against incredible odds, in constant danger of being found out, this most unlikely hero rescued over four thousand Jewish men, women, and children from Hitler's "final solution."

Schindler's List is a story of heroism on a grand scale. But it also raises some troubling questions. If Oskar was such an ordinary human being, flawed in so many ways, why weren't there more like him? Why was his heroic helping such an exception to the general rule of active complicity or passive compliance with a murderous regime? In other words, why did Oskar help when so many others didn't?

T / F

_____ People are more likely to help someone in an emergency if the potential rewards seem high and the potential costs seem low.

_____ In an emergency, a person who needs help has a much better chance of getting it if three other people are present than if only one other person is present.

_____ People are much more likely to help someone when they're in a good mood.

_____ People are much less likely to help someone when they're in a bad mood.

_____ Attractive people have a better chance than unattractive people of getting help when they need it.

_____ In any situation, people are more likely to help a friend succeed than a stranger.

_____ Women seek help more often than men do.

Oskar Schindler (second from left) loved to party. His drinking buddies in the German military and the Nazi Party would never have guessed that Schindler was using his contacts with them to help Jews survive.

Dortha Word, second from left, and friends pray on the bridge from which Dortha's daughter, Deletha, jumped to her death three days earlier, trying to escape a man who had been attacking her. About forty people witnessed the attack but did not intervene. Their failure to help her daughter stunned Dortha: "I can't believe all those people stood around and watched."

We don't have to look back in history to find stories that raise questions like these. Consider, for example, the views from two bridges, the Belle Isle Bridge in Detroit and the Tappan Zee Bridge near New York City:

■ Shortly after 2 A.M. on a Saturday night in 1995, Deletha Word, thirty-three, was involved in a traffic accident with Martell Welch, Jr., nineteen, on a traffic-clogged bridge over the Detroit River. Welch, who was over six feet tall and weighed about 270 pounds, got out of his car and ran toward Word, who was under five feet tall and weighed about 115 pounds. He dragged her out of her car, ripped off some of her clothes, and hit her repeatedly while yelling threats at her. Reportedly, this outburst lasted from ten to twenty-five minutes. The attack itself was shocking; but perhaps even more shocking was the fact that about forty people witnessed it, and not one of them attempted to come to the woman's aid. Finally, as Welch approached Word, allegedly holding his car jack, she climbed over the bridge rail and jumped into the river. Orlando Brown, twenty-two, and Lawrence Walker, twenty-one, arrived late to the scene and saw the crowd looking over the railing. When the two men saw Word struggling in the water below, they jumped in to try to save her, risking their own lives. Possibly fearing that these men were trying to harm rather than help her, she pushed away from them. Within moments, she disappeared into the water, and her body was found hours later. Ultimately, Martell Welch was convicted of second-degree murder (*Detroit News*, 1997).

■ Daniel Santos, a twenty-one-year-old mechanic, was driving home from work one evening in 1996 when he saw Maria Capozza, twenty-four, slam her car into the side rail of the Tappan Zee Bridge in a suicide attempt. She then got out of the car and jumped off the bridge into the Hudson River below—a drop of about 150 feet. Santos parked his pickup truck, handed his wallet to an onlooker for safekeeping, and jumped after her, hitting the water at about sixty-three miles per hour. Santos was almost knocked unconscious from the dive, but he recovered and swam toward the young woman. He reached her just as a man from a nearby marina got there in a boat. Although Santos and Capozza had numerous injuries, both survived (Olmeda & Gentile, 1996).

Like *Schindler's List*, these more recent incidents illustrate both the positive and negative sides of social interaction. Why did Orlando Brown, Lawrence Walker, and Daniel Santos risk their lives to save total strangers? And why did approximately forty witnesses to the beating of Deletha Word stand by and do nothing?

There is no simple answer to the question of why some help and others don't or why some situations lead to quick assistance and others to shocking displays of inaction. The determinants of helping behavior are complex and multifaceted (Schroeder et al., 1995). But social psychologists have learned a great deal about these determinants over the last three decades; and as you will see in the pages to come, some of their findings are quite surprising.

In this chapter, we examine several questions about helping: *Why* do people help? *When* do they help? *Who* is likely to help? *Whom* do they help? We then explore the other side of helping: how people react to the help they receive. The concluding section concentrates on a major, recurring theme—social connection—that underlies much of the theory and research on helping.

Motivational Factors: Why Do People Help?

Although few individuals reach the heights of heroic helping, virtually everyone helps somebody sometime. People give their friends a ride on a bad car day; donate money, food, and clothing for disaster relief; baby-sit for a relative; work as a volunteer for charitable activities; pick up the mail for a neighbor who's out of town. The list of everyday acts of kindness is endless. But *why* do people help? Several motivational factors have an impact.

Evolutionary Factors in Helping

We begin with evolution. Evolutionary psychologists and biologists use principles of evolution to understand human social behavior. Can evolutionary principles help explain why people help? At first glance, some may think it unlikely. From an evolutionary perspective, what possible function can there be in helping others, especially at the risk of one's own life? Doesn't risking one's own life for others fly in the face of evolutionary principles like "survival of the fittest"?

The "Selfish Gene"   In fact, evolutionary perspectives emphasize not the survival of the fittest individuals but the survival of the individuals' genes. From the perspective of evolution, then, human social behavior should be analyzed in terms of its contribution to reproductive success: the conception, birth, and survival of offspring. If a specific social behavior enhances reproductive success, the genetic underpinnings of that behavior are more likely to be passed on to subsequent generations and could eventually become part of the common inheritance of the species.

Of course, in order to reproduce, the individual must survive long enough to do so. Being helped *by* others should increase the chances of survival. But what about being helpful *to* others? Since helping others can be costly in terms of time and effort, and is sometimes dangerous to the helper, being helpful would seem to decrease one's chances of survival. Shouldn't any genetically based propensities for helping have dropped out of the gene pool long ago?

Maybe not. There is an alternative to individual survival. You can also preserve your genes by promoting the survival of those who share your genetic make-up, even if you perish in the effort to help them. By means of this indirect route to genetic survival, the tendency to help genetic relatives, called **kinship selection,** could become an innate characteristic—that is, a characteristic that is not contingent on learning for its development, although it can be influenced by learning,

kinship selection Preferential helping of genetic relatives, so that genes held in common will survive.

FIGURE 10.1   The Evolution of Helping: The Role of Kinship

American and Japanese students indicated how they would respond in a variety of situations in which someone needed help. Consistent with an evolutionary perspective, their willingness to offer help increased according to how closely related they were to the person in need. This kinship effect was particularly pronounced in life-or-death situations. *(Adapted from Burnstein et al., 1994.)*

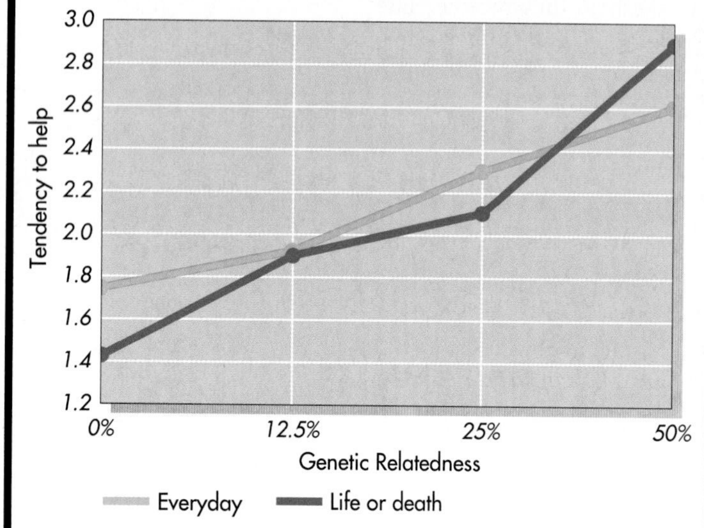

Everyday — *Life or death*

culture, and other factors. Kinship selection is evident in the behavior of many organisms, from bees that allow only related bees into their nests (Greenberg, 1979) to humans that risk their lives trying to save close relatives (Sime, 1983). From the outside, helping a relative may look self-sacrificing. On the inside, however, the "selfish gene" plots its immortality (Dawkins, 1989; Hamilton, 1964).

Because kinship selection serves the function of genetic survival, preferential helping of genetic relatives should be strongest when the biological stakes are particularly high. This appears to be the case. Eugene Burnstein and his colleagues (1994) conducted a series of studies testing several predictions based on evolutionary theory. These researchers asked students in the United States and Japan to report how they would respond to a variety of situations in which someone needed help. As can be seen in Figure 10.1, participants indicated they were more likely to help a person who was closely related (for example, a sibling or parent) than a person who was more distantly related (for example, an uncle or grandmother); the closer the relationship, the greater the genetic similarity. Furthermore, this preference for helping close relatives was stronger for life-and-death situations than for more everyday situations. Finally, intentions to help kin in life-threatening situations were influenced by reproductive-related factors. For example, participants reported they would help youthful relatives more than older adults, and healthy relatives more than those in poor health. The importance of kin selection can also be seen in the helping intentions indicated by early adolescents. Marie Tisak and John Tisak (1996) found that children in fourth, sixth, and eighth grades reported greater likelihood of helping a sibling in a threatening situation than a friend.

Reciprocal Altruism   At best, however, kinship selection provides only a partial explanation for helping. Relatives are not always helpful to each other. And even though relatives may get preferential treatment, most people help out non-kin as well. What's the reproductive advantage of helping someone who isn't related to you? The most common answer is reciprocity. Through *reciprocal altruism*, helping someone else can be in your best interests because it increases the likelihood that this other person will help you when you need it (Krebs, 1987; Trivers, 1985). If Chris helps Sandy and Sandy helps Chris, both Chris and Sandy increase their chances of survival and reproductive success.

Robert Trivers (1971) cites several examples of reciprocal altruism in animals. Many animals groom each other; for example, monkeys groom other monkeys and cats groom other cats. Large fish (such as groupers) allow small fish (such as wrasses) to swim in their mouths without eating them; the small fish get food for themselves and at the same time remove parasites from the larger fish. Chimps who share with other chimps at one feeding are repaid by the other chimps at another feeding; those who are selfish are rebuffed, sometimes violently, at a later feeding (de Waal, 1996). In some human environments, reciprocal altruism is essential for survival even today. Burnstein and his colleagues (1994) cite the !Kung

"Scratch my back and I'll scratch yours."

—Proverb

of Africa as an example. The !Kung have been pushed by other groups into barren lands where food and water are scarce. As a result, the !Kung share all resources within the band. An individual who gets food will share with the others and will expect the same in return. "The idea of eating alone is shocking to the !Kung. It makes them shriek with an uneasy laughter. Lions could do that, they say, not men" (Marshall, 1979, p. 357).

The Cooperative Group Kinship selection and reciprocal altruism emphasize helping specific others based on genetic relatedness or the probability of being helped in return. But much helping goes beyond these limits. For example, injured or sick animals are often aided by others in their group, even if they are unrelated and there is little chance that the recipients will return the favor (de Waal, 1996). Can altruism operate at a broader level than specific genes or specific reciprocal relationships between individuals? Some evolutionary theorists believe that natural selection operates across the full biological hierarchy, from genes, to organisms, to groups, to species (Gould, 1992).

> *Among the Amish, cooperation within the group is an essential feature of their way of life. Some evolutionary theorists believe that helping other members of one's social group is an innate tendency among all human beings.*

According to David Wilson and Elliott Sober (1994), group selection may play a role in accounting for the evolution of human psychology: Human beings can sometimes increase their reproductive success by protecting their own self-interest in relation to other individuals *and* by protecting their group's interest in relation to other groups. Kinship selection is a form of group selection that occurs only in groups of genetic relatives. But the kind of group selection proposed by Wilson and Sober can also operate in groups of unrelated individuals, producing helping behavior based on a social connection rather than a genetic relationship. Thus, say Wilson and Sober, cooperation and helpfulness among members of a social group (especially when the group faces an external threat) could be an innate, universal tendency. There is considerable evidence that people cooperate with and help others much more if they consider these others to be part of their ingroup (Cadenhead & Richman, 1996; Dovidio, Gaertner, et al., 1997). Franz de Waal (1996) reports remarkable instances of within-group helping among animals—for example, a Japanese monkey born without hands and feet who was fully accepted and helped by the other monkeys in its group and a retarded rhesus monkey given special care by the other monkeys in its group.

Rewards of Helping: Helping Others to Help Oneself

Whether or not it can be traced to evolutionary factors, one important reason why people help others is because it often is rewarding. We all like the idea of being the

People are more likely to help someone in an emergency if the potential rewards seem high and the potential costs seem low. **True.**

A Peace Corps worker teaches English in Honduras. Volunteering one's time, energy, and skills to help others can make one feel good about oneself. Even if not financial, the rewards can be tremendous.

hero, lifted onto the shoulders of our peers for coming to the rescue of someone in distress. Helping helps the helper.

The empirical evidence on this point is clear: People are much more likely to help when the potential rewards of helping seem high relative to the potential costs (Dovidio, 1984; Piliavin et al., 1975; Shotland & Stebbins, 1983). This effect does not appear to be limited to the very individualistic cultures of the United States, Canada, and Western Europe; evidence has been found also in Sudan and in Japan, for example (Hedge & Yousif, 1992; Imai, 1991). The research of Jane Piliavin, John Dovidio, and their colleagues suggests that potential helpers conduct a cost-benefit analysis not only when making deliberate decisions to behave prosocially, such as in donating blood, but also in more impulsive, sudden decisions to intervene in an emergency (Dovidio et al., 1991; Piliavin et al., 1981). The process is not necessarily conscious, although it can be. For example, participants in one study rated the relative importance of a number of considerations in deciding whether to help someone else. Two of the three considerations that the participants rated as most important concerned the rewards ("It would make me feel good about myself") and costs ("I might get hurt") of helping. The other consideration was, "It's the right thing to do" (Smitherman, 1992).

Children learn that helping others can be rewarding (Grusec, 1991). Younger children focus on the rewards they get from parents and others. As children develop into adolescence, they begin to reward themselves for helping, taking pride in their actions. Their helpful behavior can then be internally motivated, leading them to help even without the promise of immediate material or social rewards (Cialdini et al., 1981; Piliavin & Callero, 1991).

Helping often simply *feels* good (Smith et al., 1989; Williamson & Clark, 1992). People whose high self-esteem has been threatened by failure become particularly helpful, presumably because they feel the need to reclaim their positive feelings about themselves and they realize that they can achieve this by helping others (Brown & Smart, 1991). Even when helping doesn't feel good immediately, it can pay off in the long run. When parents reluctantly sacrifice watching *Ally McBeal* at the end of a hard day to help their child finish some homework, they might not feel immediate joy from giving help; but in the long run, they will reap the benefits of their behavior (Salovey et al., 1991).

Clearly, helping has its rewards; but clearly, it has its costs as well. Many people who helped Jews during the Holocaust, as Oskar Schindler did, were killed or punished. Daniel Santos suffered painful injuries after his jump from the Tappan Zee Bridge; and he lost his job during his recovery, in part because of the media attention he received. Rudy Tomjanovich, currently coach of the Houston Rockets basketball team, had his professional playing career cut short when he intervened to break up a fight on the court and was punched so hard that bones in his face shattered.

For most people, when the potential costs of helping outweigh the probable benefits, helping is inhibited. Many of the witnesses to the beating of Deletha Word in Detroit said that they hadn't intervened because they had feared that her attacker and his friends would injure them. As one witness said, "She could have been my daughter, my sister, anyone. Why didn't I do anything? I should have just let her in the car, but I would have gotten beat up. Still, I wish I would have done something" (Fields-Meyer et al., 1995, p. 99). It may be that some people intervene in particularly dangerous emergencies only because they simply do not think about the costs involved. After surviving his jump from the Tappan Zee Bridge, Daniel Santos explained, "I just prayed and closed my eyes and I didn't even think about the bad things that could happen to me.... It was crazy, but if you see somebody in the water like that, afraid they're going to drown, you're going to do something to help" (Olmeda & Gentile, 1996, p. 4). For situations in which the potential costs are so high, however, Santos's assumption about how most people would react is wrong.

To shift the balance between the costs and benefits of helping more toward the benefits, some legislatures have created "Good Samaritan" laws that require people to provide or summon aid in an emergency. Such laws are not uncommon in Europe. In fact, several photographers were initially accused by French authorities of breaking France's Good Samaritan laws after the automobile crash that killed Princess Diana, her companion, and their driver in Paris in 1997 (*Daily Telegraph*, 1997). Reportedly, these photographers arrived early at the crash scene and took pictures rather than attempting to help the victims. Good Samaritan laws are relatively rare in the United States (although such a law played an important role in the final episode of the popular TV series, *Seinfeld*, as the four main characters were arrested and sentenced to a year in prison for callously failing to help someone in need). Rather than raise the cost of not helping by adopting Good Samaritan laws, a few states have attempted to lower the cost of helping by enacting laws that protect Good Samaritans against lawsuits. These states encourage bystanders to intervene in emergencies by offering them legal protection, particularly doctors who volunteer medical care when they happen upon emergencies (*Nando Times*, 1997).

Overhelping: Being Cruel by Being Kind

When a child feels threatened by the attention given to a younger sibling, that child may be seen intentionally "helping" the toddler right off his or her feet and onto the floor with a crash. "Oops," says the older child. "I was only trying to help." Adults can be more subtle in their approach, but they may have a similar motivation: to appear to help another only to hurt him or her. According to Daniel Gilbert and David Silvera (1996), people sometimes offer help to another who doesn't really need it, or they offer more help than the recipient needs, in order to raise suspicions about the recipient's successful performance. Imagine the following: Ryan knows that Christina doesn't need any help on a project she's completing, but he makes a public display of assistance, hoping that she'll get less of the credit than she deserves. He hopes others will say, "Sure, Christina did a great job on the project, but I wonder if she could have done it without Ryan."

In one experiment, Gilbert and Silvera motivated some participants to help a job candidate get a job and motivated other participants to hinder his chances. The participants were informed that the candidate would be evaluated on the basis of his performance on a job aptitude test. The participants were led to believe either that the candidate had the skills to ace the test ("Mr. Brilliant"), or that he might struggle with the test ("Mr. Normal"). The participants were given the chance to provide hints to the candidate on the test; they were also informed that the

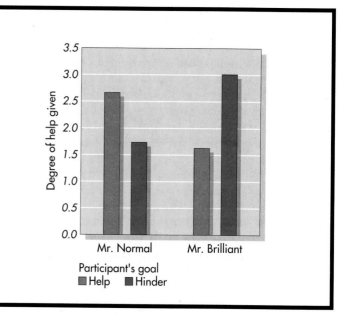

FIGURE 10.2 Overhelping

Participants were given the opportunity to offer hints to a job candidate taking a test. Some participants thought that the candidate ("Mr. Normal") could use some help. Others thought that he ("Mr. Brilliant") would do well without assistance, and that any help given would only make his performance seem less impressive. In addition, some participants were motivated to help the candidate get the job, and others were motivated to hinder his chances. As shown, participants gave more help to Mr. Normal if they were motivated to help rather than hinder him. Yet they gave more "help" to Mr. Brilliant if they wanted to hinder him rather than help him. (Data from Gilbert & Silvera, 1996.)

employer would see these hints along with the results of the test. How many hints would the participants give? Because Mr. Normal needed the assistance, participants should have given him more hints if they wanted to help him than if they wanted to hurt him. In contrast, because Mr. Brilliant didn't need any help, participants should have given him more hints if they wanted to hurt him than help him; after all, in his case, any hints would simply steal his thunder by seeming to make the test easier. As can be seen in Figure 10.2, the participants' help-giving behavior conformed to these predictions: They gave more help to Mr. Normal if they wanted him to succeed than if they wanted him to fail, and they did the opposite for Mr. Brilliant.

Altruism or Egoism: The Great Debate

Binti Jua, a gorilla in the Brookfield Zoo, near Chicago, gently rocks a three-year-old boy who had fallen eighteen feet into the primate exhibit. The gorilla was acclaimed a hero for her role in saving the boy. Did Binti Jua act out of kindness and empathy? Or did she simply do what she was taught—fetch objects that fall into her cage? This episode brings the altruism debate to life—even in the animal world.

At the end of 1996, *People* magazine honored Binti Jua as one of the twenty-five "most intriguing people" of the year; and *Newsweek* named her "hero of the year." On August 16, while caring for her own seventeen-month-old daughter, Binti had come across a three-year-old boy who had fallen about twenty feet onto a cement floor and been knocked unconscious. She had picked up the boy and gently held him, rocking him softly, and then turned him over to paramedics. The "intriguing" thing about Binti was that she is a gorilla.

When the boy climbed over a fence and fell into the primate exhibit at the Brookfield Zoo, near Chicago, witnesses feared the worst. One paramedic said, "I didn't know if she was going to treat him like a doll or a toy." With her own daughter clinging to her back the entire time, Binti "protected the toddler as if he were her own," keeping other gorillas at bay and eventually placing him gently at the entrance where zoo keepers and paramedics could get to him. "I

could not believe how gentle she was," observed a zoo director (O'Neill et al., 1996, p. 72).

It was, of course, a terrific story; and it soon sparked national debate about whether or not Binti's act was a heartwarming example of altruism, motivated by kindness and compassion. At the Democratic National Convention, held in Chicago a few weeks after the incident, Hillary Rodham Clinton referred to the gorilla as "a typical Chicagoan. Tough on the outside but with a heart of gold underneath" (Rubenstein, 1996, p. A17). Others countered that Binti had been trained to pick up and fetch things that fell into her cage and had simply acted as she had been trained to act—with no kindness or compassion involved.

The same debate exists about human behavior. Are humans ever truly **altruistic**—motivated by the desire to increase another's welfare? Or are our helpful behaviors always **egoistic**—motivated by selfish concerns or simple conformity to socialized norms? Although most psychological theories assume an egoistic, self-interested bottom line, not everyone is content with this account of the motives of human behavior. Consider, for example, the many college students who participate in volunteer activities: tutoring refugees and disadvantaged youngsters, serving meals at food kitchens, signing up potential bone-marrow donors, working in community service agencies—the list goes on and on (Sanoff & Leight, 1994). Are they all just looking out for number one?

Daniel Batson (1991) thinks not. He believes that some helpful actions are truly altruistic. Batson defines *altruistic* as we defined it above: motivated by the desire to increase another's welfare. This definition is narrower than some, which characterize any helpful action in the absence of a clear external reward as altruistic. At the same time, it is broader than others, which restrict altruism to helpful actions requiring personal sacrifice by the helper. For Batson, it's the nature of the helper's motive that counts. Regardless of whether you win the gold or lose your shirt, so long as your primary motive is to help the other person, your behavior is altruistic.

According to the empathy-altruism hypothesis, taking the perspective of someone in need is the first step toward altruism. When Sarah DeCristoforo returned to school after receiving chemotherapy for leukemia, her teacher and two friends actually put themselves in her place in one highly visible respect— they shaved their heads. Here, Sarah, wearing a scarf, is surrounded by her supporters.

The Empathy-Altruism Hypothesis Batson's model of altruism is based on his view of the consequences of empathy, which has long been viewed as a basic factor in promoting positive behavior toward others. Although the definition of *empathy* has been much debated, most researchers regard empathy as a multidimensional phenomenon with both cognitive and emotional components (Davis, 1994; Eisenberg et al., 1996). The major cognitive component of empathy is *perspective taking*: using the power of imagination to try to see the world through someone else's eyes. There are two basic emotional components. One is *personal distress*: self-oriented reactions to a person in need, such as feeling alarmed, troubled, or upset. In contrast, *empathic concern* involves other-oriented feelings, such as sympathy, compassion, and tenderness.

According to Batson, perspective taking is the first step toward altruism. If you perceive someone in need and imagine how *that person* feels, you are likely to experience other-oriented feelings of empathic concern, which in turn produce the altruistic motive to reduce the other person's distress. However, if you perceive

altruistic Motivated by the desire to increase another's welfare.

egoistic Motivated by the desire to increase one's own welfare.

FIGURE 10.3   The Empathy-Altruism Hypothesis

According to the empathy-altruism hypothesis, taking the perspective of a person in need creates feelings of empathic concern, which produce the altruistic motive to reduce the other person's distress. When people do *not* take the other's perspective, they experience feelings of personal distress, which produce the egoistic motive to reduce their own discomfort. *(Based on Batson, 1991.)*

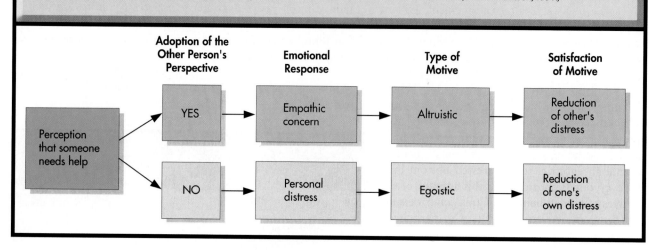

someone in need and focus on your *own* feelings or on how *you* would feel in that person's situation, you are not adopting the perspective of the needy person; rather, you should experience self-oriented feelings of personal distress, which elicit the egoistic motive to reduce your distress (Batson, Early, & Salvarini, 1997; Stotland, 1969). The basic features of Batson's **empathy-altruism hypothesis** are outlined in Figure 10.3.

Now comes the hard part. As outside observers, how can we tell the difference between egoistic and altruistic motives? In both cases, people help someone else, but the helpers' reasons are different. Confronted with this puzzle, Batson came up with an elegant solution. It depends, he says, on how easy it is to escape from a helping situation. When empathic concern is low, people can satisfy their motive to reduce their own distress through helping the person in need *or* through escaping from the scene of the victim's suffering. Out of sight, out of mind—so long, *personal* distress. But when empathic concern is high, people have no such choice. Only by helping the victim can the motive to reduce the *victim's* distress be satisfied. This logic lets us separate the sheep from the goats. When a person's motive is egoistic, helping should decline if it's easy for the individual to escape from the situation. When a person's motive is altruistic, however, help will be given regardless of the ease of escape.

To see how this works, put yourself in the position of a participant in an experiment conducted by Batson and his colleagues (1981). Arriving at the research laboratory, you're told that although another participant, Elaine, is a few minutes late, you should go ahead and read an information sheet. The material you're given informs you that the upcoming study will investigate task performance under unpleasant conditions. One of the participants will perform a task while receiving random electric shocks; the other will observe. Drawing lots to determine assignments, you're relieved at your good fortune: You'll be the observer while Elaine performs the task.

You are then escorted to the observation room. Over closed-circuit TV, you see that Elaine has arrived and is hooked up to some scary-looking equipment. After receiving a number of shocks, she appears quite uncomfortable. Asking for a glass of water, she tells the experimenter about a frightening childhood experience when she was thrown from a horse against an electric fence. For Elaine, the shocks

empathy-altruism hypothesis
The proposition that empathic concern for a person in need produces an altruistic motive for helping.

she is now receiving are very unpleasant, but she says she wants to go on. The experimenter hesitates; perhaps Elaine should stop at this point. And then the experimenter has a bright idea. Would *you* be willing to trade places?

Actually, Elaine was a trained confederate and never got shocked. But the experimental procedures created a compelling dilemma for participants. Would they suffer for someone else? The answer rests on the combinations of *empathic concern* and *difficulty of escape* manipulated in the experiment:

- Because similarity increases empathic thoughts and feelings, half of the participants were told that Elaine's personal values and interests were very similar to their own. The other half were told they were quite different.
- To create an easy-escape condition, half the participants were informed that they could leave after witnessing two of the ten trials during which Elaine would receive random shocks. Those in the difficult-escape condition were required to witness all ten trials. The experimenter's invitation to trade places came at the end of two trials, letting easy-escape participants off the hook but keeping difficult-escape participants still dangling.

So, who agreed to trade places with Elaine? As you can see in Figure 10.4, the vast majority of high-empathic-concern participants helped out, regardless of the ease or difficulty of escape. For the low-empathic-concern participants, in contrast, the ease or difficulty of escape did make a difference: Most of them helped if they thought they would have to continue to watch Elaine suffer unless they took her place, but most did not come to Elaine's rescue if they believed they could leave right away. Just as the empathy-altruism hypothesis predicted, when the escape hatch was wide open, participants with little empathic concern took the easy way out. Those with high empathic concern stayed to help.

In subsequent research, Batson and his colleagues have manipulated empathic concern in other ways, such as by having the experimenter or the person in need of help appeal to the participants either to remain objective and "not get caught up" in what the person in need is experiencing (low empathy) or to try to imagine what the person in need is feeling (high empathy). In more than two dozen experiments, these researchers have demonstrated that empathy promotes altruistic motivation (Batson, Sager, et al., 1997; Batson & Weeks, 1996).

Egoistic Alternatives   Can we conclude, then, that altruism really does exist? Batson and his colleagues believe so. Others are not so sure and offer egoistic alternatives. The debate between these different perspectives has been as intense as a championship tennis match at Wimbledon.

One serve fired by the egoistic side of the debate is that empathy encourages helping not because of concern for the other but because of concern about the costs to the *self* of not helping. People may learn that they will feel guilty after experiencing empathy for others in need but failing to help them. Having learned to anticipate such guilt, these people may help others simply to avoid it. This explanation, however, does not seem to hold. Guilt cannot account for the helpful inclinations associated with empathic concern (Batson et al., 1988; Batson & Weeks, 1996).

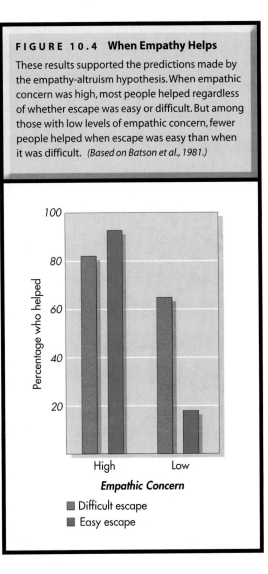

FIGURE 10.4   When Empathy Helps
These results supported the predictions made by the empathy-altruism hypothesis. When empathic concern was high, most people helped regardless of whether escape was easy or difficult. But among those with low levels of empathic concern, fewer people helped when escape was easy than when it was difficult. *(Based on Batson et al., 1981.)*

A second alternative is that empathy highlights the potential *rewards* for helping others. As we noted earlier in this chapter, helping makes people feel good. In their **negative state relief model,** Robert Cialdini and his colleagues (1987) propose that because of this positive effect of helping, people who are feeling bad may be inclined to help others in order to improve their mood. Thus, perhaps empathy promotes helping in the following way: Empathic concern for a person in need increases feelings of sadness, which in turn increase the need for mood enhancement, which in turn brings about helping behavior. During a flurry of volleys back and forth across the net, some evidence was secured in favor of this explanation (Schaller & Cialdini, 1988), but other evidence argued against it (Batson et al., 1989; Schroeder et al., 1988).

Another egoistic alternative involving empathy-specific rewards emphasizes positive well-being rather than negative relief. Kyle Smith and his colleagues (1989) maintain that empathic concern enhances the helper's sensitivity to the good feelings experienced by the person receiving help, causing the helper to experience *empathic joy*. Thus, we help those with whom we empathize because helping them makes us feel especially good. Here again, some evidence has supported the egoism side of the debate (Smith et al., 1989); other evidence, the empathy-altruism side (Batson, 1998; Batson et al., 1991).

Is Altruism Limited?   Despite the egoistic alternatives that continue to be proposed, the evidence for the empathy-altruism hypothesis is quite strong. Nevertheless, it has its limits. First of all, Batson has never claimed that *all* helping is altruistically motivated. No doubt, there are multiple motives for helping, and many helpful acts are best explained in terms of the processes we consider elsewhere in this chapter. And any single helpful action can be the result of a mixture of egoistic and altruistic motives. Mark Snyder (1993) suggests, for example, that the most effective way to increase helping is to encourage people to recognize and feel comfortable with the convergence of self-oriented and other-oriented concerns.

Another limit is created by the fact that motives do not guarantee behavior. Empathy leads to altruistic motivations, but not necessarily to helpful behaviors. For example, someone with empathic concern for another might not help this person if he or she fears that the potential cost of offering the help is very high (Batson et al., 1983). In Batson's view, such findings indicate that altruism does not exist in a cost-free psychological universe. When egoistic costs are greater than the altruistic motive can bear, the other-oriented impulse cannot prevail. Perhaps in order to avoid such internal conflicts, people who anticipate being asked for high-cost assistance often avoid empathy-inducing experiences (Shaw et al., 1994).

A possible third limitation cuts even closer to the fundamental nature of altruism. Distinguishing between egoistic and altruistic motives requires the assumption that there is a clear divide between the self and the other. What if there isn't? What if, as Daniel Wegner (1980, p. 133) suggests, empathy reflects "a basic confusion between ourselves and others"? What if, as Arthur Aron and his colleagues (1991, 1992) propose, those in close relationships incorporate the other into the self? When one and one equals "oneness" or "we-ness," helping this close other person may be seen as helping oneself, or at least helping an important part of oneself (Cialdini et al., 1997; Piliavin et al., 1981). Cialdini and his colleagues believe that in such situations, helping is caused by the recognition of the self in the other, not by empathic concern for the other (Cialdini et al., 1997; Neuberg et al., 1997); Batson and his colleagues counter that empathy triggers altruism regardless of feelings of oneness (Batson, 1997; Batson, Sager, et al., 1997). But perhaps there is a different way to think about the debate on oneness: Perhaps the egoistic account and the altruistic account actually merge on this point. If you feel someone else's

negative state relief model
The proposition that people help others in order to counteract their own feelings of sadness.

needs as deeply as you feel your own, then perhaps there is no true difference between an egoistic motive and an altruistic one.

Is there a level of love, compassion, and caring that lies beyond altruism? This debate—and the more general debate about whether, and when, true altruism exists—will no doubt rage on. As each side continues to score points with impressive shots of evidence, we all win by gaining new and more specific insights into the motivations underlying helping behavior.

Distinguishing Among the Motivations to Help: Why Does It Matter?

On the surface, the debate between altruistic and egoistic accounts of helping may seem to be irrelevant quibbling about semantics or philosophy. After all, if someone pulls you out of a burning car, you don't care if your rescuer did it to increase the chances that your similar genes will be passed down to future generations, to be lauded as a hero as the action news team approaches with its cameras, or simply because he or she was concerned for your safety. You just are thankful that the person helped, no matter what the motivation. So why does it matter whether we attribute the motivation of the helper to altruism or egoism?

We will consider three reasons why these distinctions can be important. First, distinguishing between egoistic and altruistic motives is important for determining whether and what kind of help may be offered in a particular situation. Second, how perceivers interpret the motives of a helper can have significant effects on the feelings and future responses of the helper. Third, how helpers interpret their *own* motives for helping can affect the likelihood that they will behave similarly in the future.

Determining Behavior and Emotional Responses Perhaps the most important reason to consider people's motivations is that they help us determine whether or not the helping will occur in the first place. According to Batson's research, if a witness to your accident doesn't feel true empathy for you, the witness might fail to help you if there is an easy way for him or her to escape the situation and not experience personal distress.

People's motivation for helping can also determine whether or not they will "overhelp." As was discussed earlier in this chapter, individuals sometimes provide help that the recipient doesn't need in order to cast doubt on the recipient's abilities. In other situations, people may provide too much help in order to keep the recipient dependent on them, or because they are unaware of the negative long-term effects of their assistance. If people's motivation stems from empathic concern, however, such overhelping is less likely to occur (Sibicky et al., 1995).

In addition to determining whether and how much someone is likely to help in a particular situation, motivational factors also influence how the helper feels after giving help. Helpers motivated by rewards and costs should feel good or bad as a function of the rewards and costs they receive, whether or not the person in need actually benefitted much from the help. Helpers motivated by empathy should feel good or bad simply as a function of the other person's fate.

Attributions for Helping Whatever the actual motivations that caused someone to help, the helper's and observers' *perceptions* of these motivations can have important effects. In one study illustrating the divergence of these perceptions, Kevin Doherty and colleagues (1990) had undergraduates perform helpful acts. These

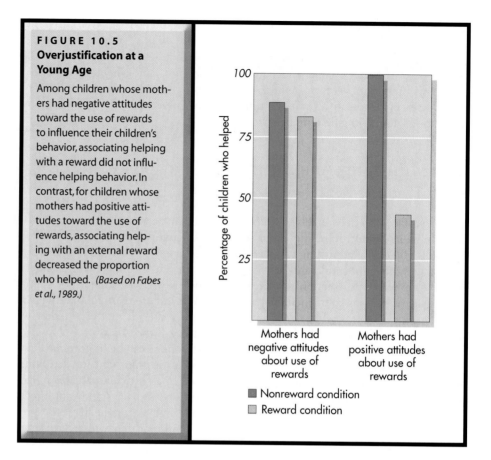

FIGURE 10.5
Overjustification at a Young Age

Among children whose mothers had negative attitudes toward the use of rewards to influence their children's behavior, associating helping with a reward did not influence helping behavior. In contrast, for children whose mothers had positive attitudes toward the use of rewards, associating helping with an external reward decreased the proportion who helped. *(Based on Fabes et al., 1989.)*

students attributed their helpfulness primarily to positive motives (e.g., to aid the other) rather than nonpositive motives (e.g., to create a good impression). Other students who observed these acts attributed positive and nonpositive motives equally for the helpers' behaviors. The students who had performed the helpful acts were offended by the suggestion that their motives were less than altruistic, denouncing the validity of the more egoistic explanations.

According to a poll conducted by the American Association of Retired Persons and published in 1998 in USA Today, *adults say they volunteer for the following reasons: to help people (87%), to make the community a better place (72%), to be with people they enjoy (56%), to be with people with the same ideals (51%), to learn about the issue/problem (41%), and to fulfill a civic duty (39%).*

The Role of Rewards   The effects of rewards for helping can be both positive and negative. If the anticipated rewards do not outweigh the anticipated costs, helping is much less likely to occur. But receiving external rewards for helping can reduce self-perceptions of being a helpful person (Batson, Coke, et al., 1978), which suggests that helping might be vulnerable to the overjustification effect. As indicated in Chapter 3, people rewarded for engaging in an intrinsically enjoyable activity subsequently engage less in that activity if rewards are no longer provided. Research by Richard Fabes and his colleagues (1989) confirms that helping, too, can be overjustified. In this study, elementary school children who had previously been rewarded for helping "poor, sick children in the hospital" were less likely to continue to help in the absence of rewards for doing so. Even children who had simply seen another child rewarded for helping were less helpful in the later, free-choice situation. (Note, however, that this decline in helping occurred only among children whose mothers reported a favorable attitude toward using rewards to influence their children's behavior, as shown in Figure 10.5. Perhaps the extensive use of rewards in child-rearing weakens children's sense of their own internal motivation, making them more susceptible to overjustification.)

Now let's take the next step. If *external* rewards can decrease subsequent helping, will self-perceived *internal* rewards also reduce helpful inclinations? Maybe yes; maybe no. On the one hand, volunteers at a crisis center who emphasized altruistic reasons for helping were more likely to complete their nine-month term of service than were those who placed more importance on egoistic reasons for helping (Clary & Orenstein, 1991). On the other hand, consider the five categories of motives, which are listed in Table 10.1, that Allen Omoto and Mark Snyder found compelled people to volunteer to help persons with AIDS. AIDS volunteers who had initially endorsed self-oriented motives, such as gaining understanding and developing personal skills, remained active volunteers longer than did those who had initially emphasized other-oriented motives, such as humanitarian values and community concern (Omoto & Snyder, 1995).

The difference between the findings of these two studies may lie in the costs of helping. Working at a crisis center requires hard work and dedication, to be sure; but the stresses and strains of helping persons with AIDS can be enormous. It has been said that "the good, and perhaps romanticized, intentions related to humanitarian concern simply may not be strong enough to sustain volunteers faced with the tough realities and personal costs of working with [persons with AIDS]" (Snyder, 1993, p. 258). When helping demands more of us, does self-interest keep us going?

Self-interest in this context is not necessarily a bad thing. Indeed, the fact that many people find helping others to be so personally rewarding is a positive aspect of human nature. One's feelings of empathic concern for others are usually limited to a few other people at a time and perhaps to relatively brief periods. Those people who derive a great deal of personal satisfaction from helping others, however, may be motivated much more frequently and consistently to engage in helping behaviors.

TABLE 10.1 Motivations to Volunteer to Help People with AIDS

Allen Omoto and Mark Snyder identified five categories of motivations underlying people's initial decisions to become volunteers to help people with AIDS. Within each category, three examples of specific statements representative of the general motive are presented. *(Omoto & Snyder, 1995.)*

Values

Because of my humanitarian obligation to help others
Because I enjoy helping other people
Because I consider myself a loving and caring person

Understanding

To learn more about how to prevent AIDS
To learn how to help people with AIDS
To deal with my personal fears and anxiety about AIDS

Personal Development

To get to know people who are similar to myself
To meet new people and make new friends
To gain experience dealing with emotionally difficult topics

Community Concern

Because of my sense of obligation to the gay community
Because I consider myself an advocate for gay-related issues
Because of my concern and worry about the gay community

Esteem Enhancement

To feel better about myself
To escape other pressures and stress in my life
To feel less lonely

"When you give to someone else, you get so much more."

—Retired General Colin Powell

Situational Influences: When Do People Help?

Thus far, we have focused on *why* people help others. We now turn to the question of *when* people help. We begin by discussing a remarkably creative and provocative set of research findings that make a surprising point: If you need help in an emergency, you may be better off if there is only one witness to your plight than if there are several. We then focus on a wide range of other situational factors on helping, including where we live, whether we are experiencing time pressure, what kind of mood we're in, and whether we've been exposed to particular role models or social norms.

The murder of Kitty Genovese, pictured here, shocked the nation in 1964. How could thirty-eight witnesses stand by and do nothing? Research conducted in the aftermath of this tragedy suggests that if there had been only one witness rather than almost forty, Kitty Genovese might have had a better chance of receiving help, and she might be alive today.

In an emergency, a person who needs help has a much better chance of getting it if three other people are present than if only one other person is present. **False.**

bystander effect The effect whereby the presence of others inhibits helping.

The Unhelpful Crowd

At about 3:20 on the morning of March 13, 1964, twenty-eight-year-old Kitty Genovese was returning home from her job as a bar manager. Suddenly, a man attacked her with a knife. She was stalked, stabbed, and sexually assaulted just thirty-five yards from her own apartment building in the New York City borough of Queens. Lights went on and windows went up as she screamed, "Oh my God! He stabbed me! Please help me!" She broke free from her attacker twice, but only briefly. Thirty-eight of her neighbors witnessed her ordeal, but not one intervened. Finally, after nearly forty-five minutes of terror, one man called the police; but by then, Genovese was dead.

The murder of Kitty Genovese shocked the nation. Were her neighbors to blame? It seemed unlikely that all thirty-eight of them could have been moral monsters. Most of the media attention focused on the decline of morals and values in contemporary society and the anonymity and apathy seen in large American cities such as New York. A few days after the incident, Bibb Latané and John Darley discussed over dinner the events and the explanations being offered for it. They were not convinced that these explanations were sufficient to account for why Kitty Genovese didn't get the help she needed; and they wondered if other, social psychological processes might have been at work. They speculated that because each witness to the attack could see that many other witnesses had turned on their lights and were looking out their windows, each witness may have assumed that others would, or should, take responsibility and call the police. To test their ideas, Latané and Darley (1970) set out to see if they could produce unresponsive bystanders under laboratory conditions. Let's take a look at one of their studies.

When a participant arrived, he or she was taken to one of a series of small rooms located along a corridor. Speaking over an intercom, the experimenter explained that he wanted participants to discuss personal problems often faced by college students. Participants were told that, to protect confidentiality, the group discussion would take place over the intercom system, and the experimenter would not be listening. They were required to speak one at a time, taking turns. Some participants were assigned to talk with one other person; others joined larger groups of three or six people.

Although one participant did mention in passing that he suffered from a seizure disorder that was sometimes triggered by study pressures, the opening moments of the conversation were uneventful. But soon, an unexpected problem developed. When the time came for this person to speak again, he stuttered badly, had a hard time speaking clearly, and sounded as if he were in very serious trouble:

> *I could really-er-use some help so if somebody would-er-give me a little h-help-uh-er-er-er-er c-could somebody-er-er-help-er-uh-uh-uh [choking sounds].... I'm gonna die-er-er-I'm...gonna die-er-help-er-er-seizure-er [chokes, then quiet].*

Confronted with this situation, what would *you* do? Would you interrupt the experiment, dash out of your cubicle, and try to find the experimenter? Or would you sit there—concerned, but unsure how to react?

As it turns out, participants' responses to this emergency were strongly influenced by the size of their group. Actually, all participants were participating alone, but tape-recorded material led them to believe that others were present. All the participants who thought that only they knew about the emergency left the room quickly to try to get help. In the larger groups, however, participants were less likely and slower to intervene. Indeed, 38 percent of the participants in the six-person groups never left the room at all! This research led Latané and Darley to a chilling conclusion: The more bystanders, the *less* likely the victim will be helped. This is the **bystander effect,** whereby the presence of others inhibits helping.

Before the pioneering work of Latané and Darley, most people would have assumed just the opposite. Isn't there safety in numbers? Don't we feel more secure rushing in to help when others are around to lend their support? Latané and Darley overturned this common-sense assumption and provided a careful, step-by-step analysis of the decision-making process involved in emergency interventions. In the following sections, we examine each of five steps in this process: noticing something unusual, interpreting it as an emergency, taking responsibility for getting help, deciding how to help, and providing assistance. We also consider the reasons why people sometimes fail to take one of these steps and, therefore, do not help. These steps, and the obstacles along the way, are summarized in Figure 10.6.

Noticing The first step toward being a helpful bystander is to notice that someone needs help or, at least, that something out of the ordinary is happening.

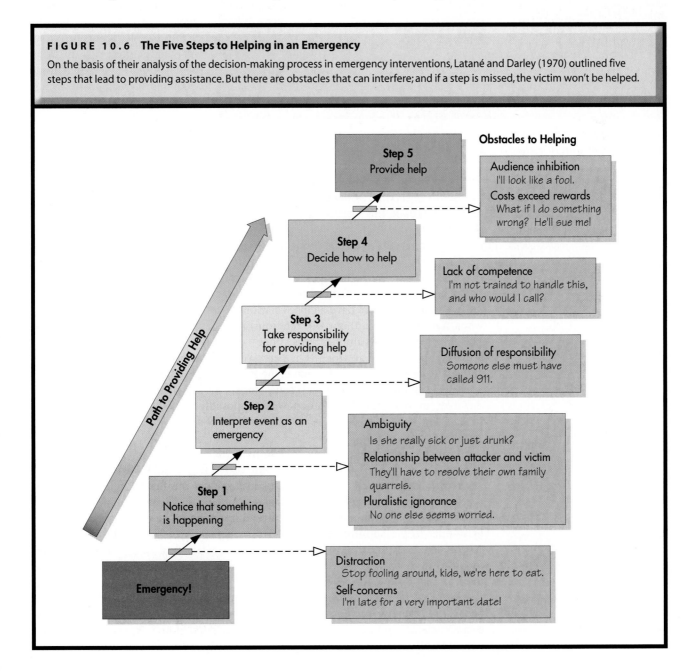

FIGURE 10.6 The Five Steps to Helping in an Emergency
On the basis of their analysis of the decision-making process in emergency interventions, Latané and Darley (1970) outlined five steps that lead to providing assistance. But there are obstacles that can interfere; and if a step is missed, the victim won't be helped.

Participants in the seizure study could not help but notice the emergency. In many situations, however, the problem isn't always perceived. The presence of others can be distracting and can divert attention away from indications of a victim's plight. In addition, people may fail to notice that someone needs help because they are caught up in their own self-concerns. People who live in big cities and noisy environments may become so used to seeing people lying on sidewalks or hearing screams that they begin to tune them out, becoming victims of what Stanley Milgram (1970) called *stimulus overload.*

The first step toward providing help is to notice that someone needs assistance. Distracted by their own concerns or by the overwhelming stimuli of a big, bustling city, these people walking in midtown Manhattan may not even notice the homeless couple begging for spare change.

Interpreting   Noticing the victim is a necessary first step toward helping, but it is not enough. People must interpret the meaning of what they notice. Cries of pain can be mistaken for shrieks of laughter; heart-attack victims can appear to be drunk. So observers wonder: Does that person really need help? In general, the more ambiguous the situation, the less likely it is that bystanders will intervene (Clark & Word, 1972).

Interpretations of the relationship between a victim and an attacker also affect whether help will be provided. Consider, for example, how people react when they see a woman attacked by a man. Research by Lance Shotland and Margaret Straw (1976) indicates that many observers of such an incident believe that the attacker and the victim have a close relationship as dates, lovers, or spouses—even when no information about the relationship is actually available. This inference can have very serious implications, since—as Shotland and Straw documented—intervening in domestic violence is perceived to be more dangerous to the helper and less desired by the victim than is intervening in an attack by a stranger. Given such beliefs, the response to a scene staged by Shotland and Straw was predictable: In the scene, a woman was supposedly being assaulted either by a stranger or by her husband. More than three times as many observers tried to stop the assault by the stranger.

It's not only women who are in danger if they are perceived as having a close relationship with their attacker: Children also suffer. The 1993 murder of two-year-old James Bulger by two ten-year-old boys was the British equivalent of the Kitty Genovese slaying. James was dragged, kicking and screaming, for two and a half miles from a shopping mall to a railroad track, where he was battered to death. Sixty-one people admitted that they had seen the boys. Most did nothing. One asked a few questions but didn't intervene. The reason? As one witness put it, he thought the boys were "older brothers taking a little one home." When people think "family," they think "It's OK, it's safe." But sometimes it isn't.

Perhaps the most powerful information available during an emergency is the behavior of other people. Startled by a sudden, unexpected, possibly dangerous event, each person looks quickly to see what others are doing. As everyone looks at everyone else for clues about how to behave, the entire group is paralyzed by indecision. When this happens, the person needing help is a victim of **pluralistic ignorance.** In this state of ignorance, each individual believes that his or her own thoughts and feelings are different from those of other people, even though everyone's behavior is the same. Each bystander thinks that other people aren't acting because somehow they know there isn't an emergency. Actually, everyone is confused and hesitant; but, imputing wisdom to others, each observer concludes that help is not required.

Latané and Darley (1968) put this phenomenon to the test in an experiment in which participants completed a questionnaire in a room in which they were either alone or with two other participants. A few minutes after participants had started to fill out the questionnaire, smoke began to seep into the room through a vent. Was this an emergency? How do you think *you* would respond? Within four minutes, half of the participants who were working alone took some action, such as leaving the room to report the smoke to someone. Within six minutes—the maximum time allotted before the researchers terminated the experiment—three-quarters of these participants took action. Clearly, they interpreted the smoke as a potential emergency. But what about the participants working in groups of three? Common sense suggests that the chances that somebody will take action should be greater when more people are present. But only one of the twenty-four participants in this condition took action within four minutes, and only three did so before the end of the study—even though at that point, the smoke was so thick they had to fan it away from their faces to see the questionnaire. If these participants had interpreted the smoke as a potential emergency, they would have acted, because their own lives would have been at stake. But instead, they quickly, cooly looked at the reactions of the others in the room, saw that nobody else seemed too concerned, and so became convinced that nothing could be wrong.

Pluralistic ignorance is not restricted to emergency situations (Miller & McFarland, 1987; Prentice & Miller, 1993). Have you ever sat through a class feeling totally lost? You want to ask a question, but you're too embarrassed. No one else is saying anything, so you assume they all find the material a snap. Finally, you dare to ask a question. And suddenly, hands shoot up in the air all over the classroom. No one understood the material, yet everyone assumed that everyone else was breezing along. Pluralistic ignorance in the classroom interferes with learning. In an emergency situation, it can lead to disaster—unless someone breaks out of the pack and dares to help. Then others are likely to follow.

Taking Responsibility Noticing a victim and recognizing an emergency are crucial steps; but by themselves, they don't ensure that a bystander will come to the rescue. The issue of responsibility remains. When help is needed, who is responsible for providing it? If a person knows that others are around, it's all too easy to place the responsibility on *them*. People often fail to help because of the **diffusion of responsibility**—the belief that others will or should intervene. Presumably, each of those thirty-eight people who watched and listened to Kitty Genovese's murder thought someone else would do something to stop the attack. But remember those helpful participants in the seizure study who thought that they alone heard the other person's cry for help? Diffusion of responsibility cannot occur if an individual believes that only he or she is aware of the victim's need.

Diffusion of responsibility usually takes place under conditions of anonymity. Bystanders who do not know the victim personally are more likely to see others as responsible for providing help. Accordingly, if the psychological distance between a bystander and the victim is reduced, there will be less diffusion of responsibility and more help. In one study, the mere anticipation of meeting someone, who then needed help before the meeting actually took place, was sufficient to eliminate diffusion of responsibility (Gottlieb & Carver, 1980). Reducing the psychological

pluralistic ignorance The state in which people mistakenly believe that their own thoughts and feelings are different from those of others, even though everyone's behavior is the same.

diffusion of responsibility The belief that others will or should take the responsibility for providing assistance to a person in need.

Soon after the 1995 Oklahoma City bombing, a police officer found one-year-old Baylee Almon in the rubble and handed her over to a firefighter. As trained professionals with specific assignments, emergency workers were not hindered by the diffusion of reponsibility and knew exactly what kind of direct intervention they could provide. They saved many lives, but not Baylee's, who died minutes after this picture was taken.

distance among bystanders can also counteract the diffusion of responsibility. Established groups in which the members know each other are usually more helpful than groups of strangers (Rutkowski et al., 1983).

In addition, the diffusion of responsibility can be defeated by a person's role. A group leader, even if only recently assigned to that position, is more likely than other group members to act in an emergency (Baumeister et al., 1988). And some occupational roles increase the likelihood of intervention. Registered nurses, for example, do not diffuse responsibility when confronted by a possible physical injury (Cramer et al., 1988). Even when there's no direct relationship between one's occupation and the type of assistance that's needed, job requirements can still influence helping behavior. In 1994, Jack Santos, a YMCA security guard, ran across two highways, passed a dozen passive observers, and put out the fire from the burning clothes of Jack Ordner, who had been thrown from his gasoline tanker when it overturned and burst into flames. Santos was neither a professional firefighter nor a medical specialist, but he was used to taking charge during an emergency. Daniel Santos (no relation to Jack, as far as we know), who jumped off the Tappan Zee Bridge to save the woman who had attempted suicide, *was* a volunteer firefighter; and he, too, immediately took action in the presence of several stunned witnesses.

Deciding How to Help   Having assumed the responsibility to help, the person must now decide how to help. Bystanders are more likely to offer direct help when they feel competent to perform the actions required. For instance, individuals who have received Red Cross training in first-aid techniques are more likely to provide direct assistance to a bleeding victim than are those without training (Shotland & Heinold, 1985).

But people who do not possess the skills that would make them feel competent to intervene directly often do have an option available. They can decide to help indirectly by calling for assistance from others. In many situations, indirect helping is by far the wiser course of action. Physical injuries are best treated by medical personnel; dangerous situations such as domestic violence are best handled by police officers; and that friendly looking individual standing by the side of a stalled car on a lonely road is best picked up by the highway patrol. Even people trained in CPR are now advised to call 911 before starting CPR on an adult victim. Calling others in to help is safe, simple, and effective. A prompt phone call can be a lifeline. Such a call might have saved Kitty Genovese's life.

Providing Help   The final step in the intervention process is to take action. Here, too, the presence of others can have an impact. Latané and Darley point out that people sometimes feel too socially awkward and embarrassed to act helpfully in a public setting. When observers do not act in an emergency because they fear making a bad impression on other observers, they are under the influence of **audience inhibition.** Worrying about how others will view us does not, however, always reduce helping. When people think they will be scorned by others for failing to help, the presence of an audience *increases* their helpful actions (Schwartz & Gottlieb, 1980).

Letting concerns about social approval affect emergency helping may seem inappropriate. It makes a potential helper sound like a cold, calculating sort of person. But according to Jane Piliavin and her colleagues (1981), potential helpers do take rewards and costs into account when deciding whether to respond to an emergency. The **arousal: cost-reward model** of helping stipulates that both emotional and cognitive factors determine whether bystanders to an emergency will intervene. Emotionally, bystanders experience the shock and alarm of personal distress; this unpleasant state of arousal motivates them to do something to reduce it. What they do, however, depends on the "bystander calculus," their computation of the costs and rewards associated with helping. When potential rewards (to self and victim) outweigh potential costs (to self and victim), bystanders will help (Dovidio et al., 1991). But raise those costs and lower those rewards, and victims stand a good chance of having to do without.

Getting Help in a Crowd   As you can see in Figure 10.6, providing help in an emergency is a challenging process. At each step along the way, barriers and diversions can prevent a potential helper from becoming an actual one. Most of these obstacles are social in nature, demonstrating Latané and Darley's point that an individual is less likely to intervene in an emergency when others are present than when he or she is alone with the victim.

But what if you need help in the presence of many people? Is there anything you can do to enhance the chances that someone will come to your aid? Try to counteract the ambiguity of the situation by making it very clear that you do need help, and try to reduce diffusion of responsibility by singling out particular individuals for help, such as with eye contact, pointing, or direct requests (Moriarty, 1975; Shotland & Stebbins, 1980).

The Place We Live

If the presence of others often inhibits helping, do individuals have a worse chance of being helped in an emergency in a big city than in a small town? In the midst of the hectic pace and large crowds of a big city, are pleas for help more likely to go unanswered?

Although place of residence does not seem to affect how much those in close relationships help each other (Franck, 1980; Korte, 1980), a large city does have a number of characteristics that might reduce help to strangers. For example, as we discussed earlier, in the context of "noticing" an emergency, Stanley Milgram (1970) proposed that cities produce stimulus overload among their inhabitants. Bombarded by sights and sounds, city residents may wear a coat of unresponsive armor to protect themselves from being overwhelmed by stimulation. Claude Fischer (1976) noted that the residents of large urban areas are a heterogeneous group—composed of diverse nationalities, races, and ethnic backgrounds. Such diversity could diminish the sense of similarity with others, reduce empathic concern, and result in less helping. Also, people may feel more anonymous and less accountable for their actions in large cities than in smaller communities in which people are more likely to know their neighbors.

audience inhibition Reluctance to help for fear of making a bad impression on observers.

arousal: cost-reward model The proposition that people react to emergency situations by acting in the most cost-effective way to reduce the arousal of shock and alarm.

TABLE 10.2   Helping in the U.S.A.

Six types of helping (returning a pen dropped by a researcher who was walking past; helping a researcher with a leg brace pick up dropped magazines; checking for change when asked for change by a researcher; helping a researcher, who was in dark glasses and carrying a white cane, cross the street; mailing a stamped, addressed letter apparently dropped by someone; and average per capita contributions to the United Way in 1990) were studied in 36 U.S. cities. The top ten and bottom ten cities are listed in this table. Although there was a great deal of variability from one helping measure to the next, some overall patterns emerged, including the findings that higher density (population per square mile) and higher cost of living were strongly associated with less helping. *(Based on data from Levine et al., 1994.)*

Top Ten Cities for Helping		Bottom Ten Cities for Helping	
Overall Rank	Region	Overall Rank	Region
1. Rochester, NY	Northeast	27. Salt Lake City, UT	West
2. Houston, TX	South	28. Boston, MA	Northeast
3. Nashville, TN	South	29. Providence, RI	Northeast
4. Memphis, TN	South	30. Chicago, IL	North Central
5. Knoxville, TN	South	31. Shreveport, LA	South
6. Louisville, KY	South	32. Philadelphia, PA	Northeast
7. St. Louis, MO	North Central	33. Fresno, CA	West
8. Detroit, MI	North Central	34. Los Angeles, CA	West
9. E. Lansing, MI	North Central	35. New York, NY	Northeast
10. Chattanooga, TN	South	36. Patterson, NJ	Northeast

Whatever the exact causes, people are less likely to help in urban areas than in rural ones. This relationship has been found in several countries, including Canada, Israel, Great Britain, and the Sudan (Hedge & Yousif, 1992; Steblay, 1987). For example, Paul Amato (1983) studied fifty-five Australian communities, ranging in population from 999 to over 3 million; and he found that spontaneous, informal help to strangers was greater where the population was smaller. Robert Levine and his colleagues (1994) examined six kinds of helping in thirty-six U.S. cities with populations ranging from 350,000 to over 2 million. As you can see in Table 10.2, Rochester, New York, wins the title of "Most Helpful City." Although greater population was associated with less helping, density (population per square mile) was a more powerful predictor. High-density conditions are often quite stressful (Paulus, 1988). Helping in these U.S. cities was also associated with the cost of living: The higher the costs, the less help was provided, suggesting that feeling strapped can interfere with being helpful.

Time Pressure

The presence of others can create obstacles at each step on the way toward helping in an emergency. Other factors, too, can affect multiple steps in this process. Our good intentions to help those in need can sometimes conflict with other motivations. One such source of conflict is time pressure. When we are in a hurry or have a lot on our minds, we may be so preoccupied that we fail to notice others who need help, we may become less likely to accept responsibility for helping someone, or we may decide that the costs of helping are too high because of the precious time that will be lost. When we have other demands on us that seem very important, getting involved in someone else's problems may seem like a luxury we can't afford (Batson, Cochran, et al., 1978). John Darley and Daniel Batson (1973) examined the role of time pressure in an experiment that produced what may be the most ironic finding in the history of social psychology.

Their study was based on the parable of the Good Samaritan, from the Gospel of Luke. This parable tells the story of three different people—a priest, a Levite, and a Samaritan—each traveling on the road from Jerusalem to Jericho. Each passes a man lying half-dead by the roadside. The priest and the Levite—both considered busy, important, and relatively holy people—pass by the man without stopping. The only one who helps is the Samaritan, a social and religious outcast of that time. The moral of the tale is that people with low status are sometimes more virtuous than those enjoying high status and prestige. Why? Perhaps in part because high-status individuals tend to be busy people, preoccupied with their own concerns and rushing around to important engagements. Such characteristics may prevent them from noticing or deciding to help a victim in need of assistance.

Darley and Batson brought this ancient story to life. They asked seminary students to think about what they wanted to say in an upcoming talk. Half of them were told that the talk was to be based on the parable of the Good Samaritan; the other half expected to discuss the jobs that seminary students like best. All participants were then instructed to walk over to a nearby building where the speech would be recorded. At this point, participants were told that they were running ahead of schedule, that they were right on time, or that they were already a few minutes behind schedule. On the way to the other building, all participants passed a research confederate slumped in a doorway, coughing and groaning. Which of these future ministers stopped to lend a helping hand?

Perhaps surprisingly, the topic of the upcoming speech had little effect on helping. The pressure of time, however, made a real difference. Of those who thought they were ahead of schedule, 63 percent offered help—compared with 45 percent of those who believed they were on time and only 10 percent of those who had been told they were late. In describing the events that took place in their study, Darley and Batson noted that "on several occasions a seminary student going to give his talk on the parable of the Good Samaritan literally stepped over the victim as he hurried on his way!" These seminary students unwittingly demonstrated the very point that the parable they would be discussing warns against.

Emotional Factors in Helping

When you're under time pressure and have a lot on your mind, you may be in a bad mood. After you've finished your project and met the deadline, you may feel much happier. Does how we feel affect how we respond to a person in need? Are we more likely to help when we're feeling good? Are we less likely to help when we're feeling bad? What's your prediction?

Good Mood: A Spirit of Generosity   Sunshine in Minneapolis and pleasant odors in Albany give us some clues about the relationship between good mood and helping. Over the course of a year, pedestrians in Minneapolis were stopped and asked to participate in a survey of social opinions. When Michael Cunningham (1979) tabulated their responses according to the weather conditions, he discovered that people answered more questions on sunny days than on cloudy ones. Moving his investigation indoors, Cunningham found that sunshine is truly golden: The more the sun was shining, the more generous were the tips left by restaurant customers. Sunshine and helping seem to go together, but what's the connection? Probably it's the mood we're in, as a sunny day cheers us up and a cloudy day damps us down.

When the sun is not shining, many people head for the mall. One of the more powerful sensations you can count on experiencing while strolling through the mall comes when you pass a bakery or coffee shop, the pleasant aroma of freshly baked chocolate chip cookies or freshly brewed French roast stopping you in your tracks. Robert Baron (1997) believed that these pleasant scents put people in a good mood, and he wondered if this good mood would make them more likely to help someone in need. He tested this with passers-by in a large shopping mall in Albany, New York. Each selected passer-by was approached by a member of the research team and asked for change for a dollar. This interaction took place in a

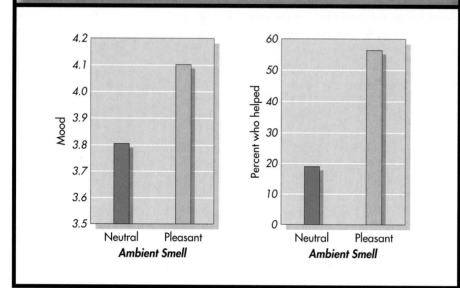

FIGURE 10.7   Scents and Sensibilities
People walking in a mall were approached by someone who asked them for change. This encounter took place in areas of the mall with either pleasant ambient odors or no clear odors. The stranger also gave the individuals a questionnaire that measured their mood on a 5-point scale, ranging from 1 (very bad) to 5 (very good). As shown on the left, the people approached in a pleasant-smelling area were in a better mood than those approached in neutral-smelling locations. In addition (right), people were more likely to help the stranger by giving him change if they were in a pleasant-smelling area than if they were in a neutral-smelling area.   *(Data from Baron, 1997.)*

People are much more likely to help someone when they're in a good mood. **True.**

location containing either strong, pleasant odors (such as near a bakery or a coffee-roasting cafe) or no discernible odor (such as near a clothing store). As can be seen in Figure 10.7, people approached in a pleasant-smelling location were much more likely to help than people approached in a neutral-smelling location. Baron also found that people were in a better mood when they were in the pleasant-smelling environments. This effect on their mood appears to have caused their greater tendency to help.

Of course, sunshine and sweet scents are not the only enhancers of mood and helping. In fact, helping is increased by all kinds of pleasant, mood-lifting experiences, such as being successful on a task (Isen, 1970), reading pleasant positive statements (Aderman, 1972), being offered a cookie (Isen & Levin, 1972), imagining a Hawaiian vacation (Rosenhan et al., 1981), and listening to a comedy routine by Steve Martin (Wilson, 1981). On the job, being in a good mood seems to be the major determinant of a wide range of behaviors (such as helping co-workers, making constructive suggestions, and spreading good will) that improve workplace quality and increase organizational effectiveness (George & Brief, 1992). When we're happy, we're helpful—a state of affairs known as the **good mood effect.**

Despite strong evidence of the effect itself, it's not clear how it occurs (Carlson et al., 1988). One possibility, called the *mood maintenance hypothesis,* is that happy people are motivated to keep their good mood going. For example, individuals in a happy mood have a strong preference for viewing videotapes they expect to make them happy rather than those they expect to be agreeable or interesting (Wegener & Petty, 1994). So do people expect that helping others will make them happy? Among readers of *Better Homes and Gardens,* the answer is a resounding yes. Those who responded to a questionnaire in the magazine extolled the self-benefits of helping, saying it gave them a "helper's high" (Luks, 1988). And it does. Helping others, particularly those with whom we desire a closer relationship, makes us feel good (Williamson & Clark, 1992).

Alternatively, people in a good mood may be more helpful because they have more happy thoughts. Various kinds of positive thoughts can influence helping. When we feel good, we are more aware of the rewards of helping and expect helping to be a more pleasant experience (Isen et al., 1978). A good mood also increases positive thoughts about other people (Forgas & Bower, 1987); and the more we like someone, the more we should be willing to help that person. Or perhaps good moods increase helping by means of positive thoughts about the rewarding nature of social activities (Cunningham, Shaffer, et al., 1990). There is ample evidence

good mood effect   The effect whereby a good mood increases helping behavior.

that individuals who are usually in a good mood engage in more social activities (Watson et al., 1992). Positive thoughts about interacting with others in social activities might, in turn, promote interacting with others in prosocial ways, including helping. Table 10.3 summarizes some of the reasons why feeling good often leads to doing good, and it also describes some of the forks in this road that can lead away from helping.

Whatever its exact cause, the good mood effect has two striking features. First, it doesn't last very long. Typically, the increase in helping produced by a good mood is of short duration (Isen et al., 1976). Second, it kicks in quite early in life. The good mood effect occurs among people of all ages, and even young children help more when they feel happy and cheerful (Moore et al., 1973).

Negative Emotions: Do They Help? Since a good mood increases helping, does a bad mood decrease it? Not necessarily. Under many circumstances, negative feelings can elicit positive behavior toward others (Carlson & Miller, 1987). One such circumstance is when people feel **guilt.** We feel guilty when we believe that we have violated our own personal standards or fear that others may perceive such a violation. Have you ever felt guilty about getting too worked up during a trivial disagreement with a friend? Did you gratefully seize the next available opportunity to help that individual? In such cases, being helpful restores an existing relationship that we value. But the impact of guilt on helping can be much more widespread.

Imagine yourself in the following situation. A stranger approaches you on the street and asks you to use his camera to take his picture for a school project. You get ready, aim, and…nothing. The camera

---

TABLE 10.3 Good Moods Lead to Helping: Reasons and Limitations

Research shows that people in positive moods are more likely to help someone in need than are people in neutral moods. There are several explanations for this effect, as well as some limiting conditions that can weaken or reverse the help-promoting effects of good moods.

Why Feeling Good Leads to Doing Good

- *Desire to maintain one's good mood.* When we are in a good mood, we are motivated to maintain that mood. Helping others makes us feel good, and so it can help maintain a positive mood.

- *Positive expectations about helping.* If we have more positive expectations about the rewards of helping, we are more likely to help.

- *Positive thoughts.* Positive moods trigger positive thoughts, and if we have positive thoughts about others, we should like them more, which makes us more likely to help them.

- *Positive thoughts and expectations about social activities.* Positive moods trigger positive thoughts and expectations about interacting with others and engaging in social activities. These positive thoughts and expectations can promote interacting with others in prosocial ways, including helping them.

When Feeling Good Might *Not* Lead to Doing Good

- *Costs of helping are high.* If the anticipated costs of helping in a particular situation seem high, helping would put our good mood at risk. In this case, if we can avoid getting involved and thus maintain our good mood (for example if we can justify our failure to help), we are less likely to help.

- *Positive thoughts about other social activities that conflict with helping.* If our good mood makes us want to go out and party with our friends, our motivation to engage in this social activity may prevent us from taking the time to notice or take responsibility for helping someone in need.

---

doesn't work. Looking concerned, the stranger says the camera is rather delicate, asks you if you touched any of the dials, and informs you that it will have to be fixed. You continue on your way down the street. As you pass a young woman, she drops a file folder containing some papers. Now, here's the question: Are you more likely to help the woman pick up her papers because you think you broke the other person's camera?

Probably. In an experiment that used this setup, 80 percent of participants who had been led to believe that they had broken the man's camera helped the woman pick up her papers; only 40 percent of participants who had had no broken-camera

guilt Feelings of discomfort or distress produced by people's belief that they have violated their own personal standards or their fear that others will perceive such violations.

TABLE 10.4   Bad Moods and Helping: When Does Feeling Bad Lead to Doing Good, and When Doesn't It?

Research shows that people in negative moods are often more likely to help someone in need than are people in neutral moods. However, there are several limitations to this effect. This table summarizes some of the factors that make it more or less likely for people to do good when they feel bad.

When Negative Moods Make Us More Likely to Help Others

- If we take responsibility for what caused our bad mood ("I feel guilty for what I did")
- If we focus on other people ("Wow, those people have suffered so much")
- If we are made to think about our personal values that promote helping ("I really shouldn't act like such a jerk next time; I have to be nicer")

When Negative Moods Make Us Less Likely to Help Others

- If we blame others for our bad mood ("I feel so angry at that jerk who put me in this situation")
- If we become very self-focused ("I am so depressed")
- If we are made to think about our personal values that do not promote helping ("I have to wise up and start thinking about my own needs more")

People are much less likely to help someone when they're in a bad mood. **False.**

experience stopped to help (Cunningham et al., 1980). Thus, participants who unintentionally harmed one individual were more helpful to the next person. According to Roy Baumeister and his colleagues (1994), such spillover effects provide an especially vivid demonstration of the interpersonal nature of guilt and its function of enhancing, maintaining, and repairing relationships. Feeling guilty, they contend, motivates us to strengthen whatever social relations are at hand.

More generally, negative moods often promote helping. Why might this be? As noted earlier, people know that helping makes them feel good. Recall that in our discussion of the motivations that promote helping, we described the negative state relief model, which holds that people who are feeling bad are motivated to repair their mood and they realize that one way to do it is by helping others (Cialdini et al., 1987). This model seems reasonable, but the evidence is mixed—leading to a vigorous debate on the pros (Cialdini & Fultz, 1990) and cons (Miller & Carlson, 1990) of the negative state relief model. Subsequent research offers an even split, with some results supporting and other results refuting the key assumption that sadness elicits a desire for positive experiences. In one study, for example, greater expectations of feeling sad were correlated with a stronger preference for listening to a pleasant radio broadcast (Fultz & Nielsen, 1993). In another, however, participants in a sad mood did not differ from those in a neutral mood in their preference for watching a happy videotape and were less likely than those in a happy mood to prefer the happy video (Wegener & Petty, 1994). At this point, more research is needed to test the negative state relief model.

An interesting aspect of the negative state relief model involves children. Although young children are more helpful when they are happy, they do not help more when they are sad. Robert Cialdini and his colleagues (1981) propose that helping is not as rewarding to young children as it is to older children and adults. As they develop, children become not only more empathic but also more aware of the potential benefits of helping, which may in turn give them more experience with using helping others to make themselves feel better.

In sum, the relationship between good moods and helping is a strong and consistent one. The relationship between negative moods and helping is more complex. Although feeling bad often leads to helping behavior, there are several limits to this effect (see Table 10.4). One important variable is whether people accept responsibility for their bad feelings (Rogers et al., 1982). Negative moods are less likely to promote helping if we blame others for them (such as when we're angry at another person) than if we take personal responsibility (such as when we regret a poor decision we just made). In addition, negative moods are less likely to increase helping if they cause us to become very self-focused (such as when we experience intense grief or depression or when we dwell on our own problems and concerns) than if they direct our focus outward (such as when we feel sad after watching a public service advertisement about child abuse) (Bagozzi & Moore, 1994; Gibbons & Wicklund, 1982; Tangney et al., 1996; Wood et al., 1990).

Role Models and Social Norms: A Helpful Standard

We mentioned earlier that children become more aware as they get older of the potential benefits of helping. How, in general, do children learn about helping? One way is through role models. Seeing important people in their lives behave prosocially, or antisocially, encourages children to follow suit. Role models can be real people in children's lives or characters they see on television (Moriarty & McCabe, 1977; Rushton, 1981a; Sprafkin et al., 1975). Indeed, although politicians, educators, researchers, and parents pay a great deal of attention to the negative effects of TV on children (discussed in Chapter 11 on Aggression), TV can also have positive effects on children through the modeling of prosocial behavior. After reviewing an extensive research literature, Susan Hearold (1986) concluded that the effect of prosocial TV on prosocial behavior was about twice as large as the effect of TV violence on aggressive behavior. She argued that rather than advocating primarily to "eliminate the negative" by removing shows with sex and violence, the public should focus more on "accentuating the positive" by encouraging the creation of more shows with prosocial themes and positive role models (p. 116).

Princess Diana talks to children who lost legs to landmines in Angola. Diana visited Angola in January, 1997, to rally support for a worldwide ban on the use of landmines. When high-profile people like Princess Diana volunteer their time for causes such as this, they can serve as role models, setting standards for others to follow.

Helpful models are important not only for children but for all of us. Imagine the following situations:

- You see someone at the side of the highway struggling to change a flat tire.
- You approach a table where volunteers are collecting money for famine-relief efforts.
- You hear the announcement of a blood-donation drive.

Now, think about your own behavior. Would you be more likely to help—change the tire, contribute money, donate blood—if you saw someone else helping first? Probably. Observing helpful models usually increases helping in these and other situations (Bryan & Test, 1967; Macaulay, 1970; Sarason et al., 1991).

Why do models of other people helping inspire us to help? Three reasons stand out. First, they provide an example of behavior for us to imitate directly. Second, when they are rewarded for their helpful behavior, models teach us that helping is valuable, which strengthens our own inclination to be helpful. Third, the behavior of models makes us think about and become more aware of the standards of conduct in our society.

General rules of conduct established by society are called **social norms.** These norms embody standards of socially approved and disapproved behavior. They are learned from what people say and from what they do (Rice & Grusec, 1975). Today, the mass media convey a great deal of information about normative expectations, and TV is an especially powerful influence (Hearold, 1986; Oskamp, 1988). Two sets of social norms bear directly on when people are likely to help. The first consists of norms based on fairness. As we mentioned in Chapter 7, the *norm of reciprocity* establishes quid-pro-quo transactions as a socially approved standard: People who give to you should be paid back (Schopler, 1970). Accordingly, people usually help those who have helped them, especially when the initial assistance was given voluntarily (Gross & Latané, 1974). Equity is the basis of another

"Those of us who have been blessed by this nation, those of us who enjoy success, if we are to be good citizens, it's incumbent upon all of us to reach back, down and across to a young person who wonders, 'Is there an American dream for me?'... If we don't reach them now, we might as well go back home and spend more money to build more jails."

—Retired General Colin Powell

social norm A general rule of conduct reflecting standards of social approval and disapproval.

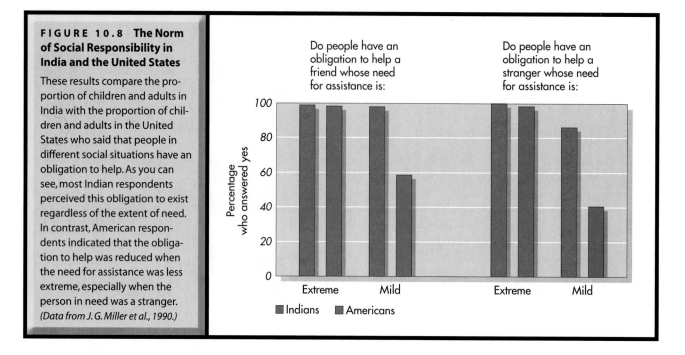

FIGURE 10.8 The Norm of Social Responsibility in India and the United States

These results compare the proportion of children and adults in India with the proportion of children and adults in the United States who said that people in different social situations have an obligation to help. As you can see, most Indian respondents perceived this obligation to exist regardless of the extent of need. In contrast, American respondents indicated that the obligation to help was reduced when the need for assistance was less extreme, especially when the person in need was a stranger. *(Data from J. G. Miller et al., 1990.)*

norm calling for fairness in our treatment of others. The *norm of equity* prescribes that when people are in a situation in which they feel overbenefited (receiving more benefits than earned), they should help those who are underbenefited (receiving fewer benefits than earned). Such help restores an equitable balance (Walster, Walster, & Berscheid, 1978).

Other help-relevant social norms go beyond an immediate sense of fairness to a larger sense of what is right. The **norm of social responsibility** dictates that people should help those who need assistance (Berkowitz, 1972). This norm creates a sense of duty and obligation, to which people respond by giving more help to those in greater need of it (Bornstein, 1994). The **norm of justice,** however, requires people to help when others *deserve* their assistance (Lerner & Meindl, 1981). This norm creates a standard of what is morally correct. Although the norm of social responsibility and the norm of justice often coincide and can be hard to tell apart, they differ in terms of the principles they express. The norm of social responsibility is person-based, calling on us to be responsive to people's needs regardless of how these needs came about. In contrast, the norm of justice is rule-based, calling on us to meet the needs of those who merit our assistance.

The social norms of reciprocity, equity, social responsibility, and justice can have powerful effects. Yet sometimes they fail to produce the helpful behavior they prescribe. Why? One problem with social norms is their generality. They are so general, so abstract, that it is not clear when they apply. When you encounter two people fighting, should you follow the norm prescribing "Help those in need" or the one instructing you to "Mind your own business" (Darley & Latané, 1970)?

Individuals differ considerably in what they regard as unfair or immoral and in the remedies they propose in different situations. Cultures also differ from each other in their perceptions and norms. For instance, Joan Miller and her colleagues have examined differences in how Hindu Indians and Americans view social norms. Most of the Hindu Indian college students who participated in one study viewed reciprocity as a moral obligation, while most of the American college students regarded it as a personal choice (Miller & Bersoff, 1994). Compared with someone who helped spontaneously, an individual who engaged in reciprocal helping was perceived as equally helpful by Indian students but as a less helpful person by American students. As illustrated in Figure 10.8, another study found that children and adults in

"From this day forward, when someone asks you to help a child, just say yes."

—Nancy Reagan (former U.S. First Lady known for her "Just say no" anti-drug campaign)

norm of social responsibility A moral standard emphasizing that people should help those who need assistance.

norm of justice A moral standard emphasizing that people should help those who deserve assistance.

the United States are less likely than children and adults in India to believe that people have an obligation to provide assistance to friends or strangers whose need for help is not extreme (J. G. Miller et al., 1990). It appears that the Hindu Indians who participated in this study regard social responsibilities as an absolute moral obligation, while Americans apply the norm of social responsibility more selectively.

Personal Influences: Who Is Likely to Help?

As we have just seen, social psychological research addressing the question "When do people help?" has been quite productive. What about the question "Who is likely to help?" When we think about extreme acts of helping, or of failing to help, or when we think about long-term, well-planned acts of helping such as volunteering at a clinic or shelter or serving as a Big Brother or Big Sister, we tend to wonder not about the situational influences but about the nature of the people involved. In this section, we consider some of the individual differences between people that address the question "Who is likely to help?"

The Altruistic Personality

Researchers interested in the question "Who is likely to help?" have tried to identify an *altruistic personality* that distinguishes people who help from those who don't. Some of their research has focused on whether certain people tend to be more helpful across situations than others and whether and to what extent these differences might be genetically based. Other research has sought to identify what general personality characteristics and traits comprise the altruistic personality. In this section, we review both of these lines of research.

Are Some People More Helpful Than Others?
When Daniel Santos's friends and co-workers learned of his heroics in jumping 150 feet off the Tappan Zee Bridge to save a stranger, they were not surprised. "That's just how he is," said a fellow volunteer firefighter. "If he sees something, he's going to go and try to help out that person." A receptionist at the company where he worked as a mechanic added, "He will help anyone at any place and any time." His sister noted that he leaped into the water even though he's not a strong swimmer. "He has a good heart," she said (Fitz-Gibbon & Siemaszko, 1996, p. 7).

Are there many people who are generally helpful across all situations? Are there others who are generally unhelpful? Although situational factors clearly can overwhelm individual differences in influencing helping behaviors in many contexts (Darley & Batson, 1973; Latané & Darley, 1970), researchers have demonstrated some evidence of individual differences in helping tendencies that endure over time and and across at least some situations. People who are more helpful than others in one situation are likely to be more helpful in other situations as well (Hampson, 1984; Rushton, 1981b).

According to J. Philippe Rushton and his colleagues (1984), this individual difference in helpfulness is in part genetically based. Studies of twins offer some support for Rushton's argument. Genetically identical (monozygotic) twins are more similar to each other in their helpful behavioral tendencies and their helping-related emotions and reactions, such as empathy, than are fraternal (dizygotic) twins, who share only a portion of their genetic make-up (Davis et al., 1994; Rushton et al., 1986; Zahn-Wexler et al., 1992). These findings suggest that there may be a heritable component to helpfulness.

"The purpose of human life is to serve and to show compassion and the will to help others."

—Albert Schweitzer

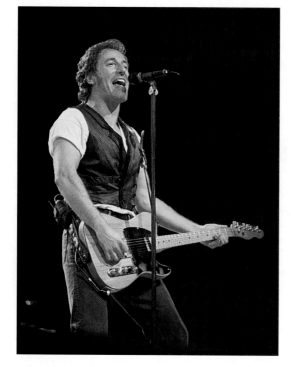

Rock star Bruce Springsteen may not seem to have a lot in common with Ted Turner and Mother Teresa and other people mentioned on this page as models of altruism, but like them, he has donated a tremendous amount of time and money to helping others. At every stop on his concert tours in recent years, Springsteen raises money for local causes, such as food banks, youth centers, and shelters.

What Is the Altruistic Personality? Even if we identify some people who help others a lot and other people who don't, we have not addressed the question of what distinguishes people who help from those who don't—other than their helpfulness, of course. What are the various components of the altruistic personality? Can we predict who is likely to be altruistic by looking at people's overall personalities?

Consider some examples of people who have acted very altruistically. Do they seem to have very similar personality traits and characteristics? Think, for example, about Oskar Schindler and how he cheated in business and in his marriage. Could anyone have predicted his altruistic actions from his overall personality? It is doubtful. What about more contemporary models of altruism? In 1997, Ted Turner, founder of cable stations CNN, TBS, and TNT and owner of sports teams (baseball's Atlanta Braves and basketball's Atlanta Hawks), pledged a personal donation of one *billion* dollars to the United Nations. Actor Paul Newman has donated all of the millions of dollars in profits that have been produced by his brands of salad dressing, spaghetti sauce, popcorn, and the like to charities, such as his camp for children who are living with a fatal disease. Until her death in 1997, Mother Teresa devoted her life to the poor in India. These three well-known figures seem quite different from each other in overall personality—except for their concern with helping others.

The quest to discover the altruistic personality has not been an easy one. Much of the research conducted over the years has failed to find consistent, reliable personality characteristics that predict helping behavior across situations. The situational variables that we've already discussed in this chapter have predicted people's behaviors much better than personality variables (Latané & Darley, 1970; Piliavin et al., 1981). Some more recent research has changed the nature of the quest, however, focusing on personality variables that predict helping in some specific situations rather than across all situations; and this research has been more successful in identifying traits that predict such behavior (Carlo et al., 1991; Penner et al., 1995). George Knight and his colleagues (1994) have suggested that an interacting "conglomerate" of numerous dispositional traits influences prosocial behavior and that the traits differ depending on the situation. For example, in dangerous emergencies, people who are high in self-confidence and independence are more likely to help than other people, but they are no more likely to help in response to a request to donate money to a charity (Wilson, 1976).

Personality variables that have been associated with greater helpfulness in some contexts include the following: being relatively high in empathy toward others; having a tendency to attribute the causes of events to individual control rather than external circumstances; tending toward a collectivist rather than an individualist orientation; and being more extroverted, more open to experience, and more agreeable (Bierhoff et al., 1991; Kosek, 1995; Moorman & Blakely, 1995). And whether or not people have the traits associated with prosocial behavior, if they can be convinced or motivated to believe that they *are* altruistic, their behavior may follow. For example, labeling someone as a helpful person increases that individual's helpful behavior (Kraut, 1973; Strenta & DeJong, 1981).

In sum, research provides some insight into the traits and characteristics that may be associated with helpful behavioral tendencies, but more research is needed before a conclusion can be

Fortune *Magazine's Five Most Generous Americans—1997*

Name	1997 Donation
1. Ted Turner	$1 billion
2. Kathryn Albertson	$660 million
3. George Soros	$540 million
4. Bill Gates	$210 million
5. Leonard Abramson	$100 million

reached about the makeup of the altruistic personality. The research thus far does point to two qualities that seem essential for such a personality: empathy and advanced moral reasoning. We focus on these qualities in the following section.

Empathy and Moral Reasoning

We have already discussed empathy in the context of Batson's empathy-altruism hypothesis, which emphasizes the role of empathy in triggering altruistic, as opposed to egoistic, motivations. Regardless of the true nature of the *motivation* to help, however, it is clear that empathy is an important predictor of helping behavior. Empathy involves taking the perspective of others. Empathic individuals witnessing someone suffering are likely to suffer along with that person and to feel sympathy and compassion for him or her. Being able to take the perspective of others and experience empathy are associated positively with helping and other prosocial behaviors in children and adults (Batson, 1991; Eisenberg et al., 1996; Hoffman, 1982; Litvack et al., 1997; Morgan et al., 1997; Roberts & Strayer, 1996).

In addition to empathy, a second characteristic associated with helping is moral reasoning. Children and adults who exhibit internalized and advanced levels of moral reasoning behave more altruistically than others (Carlo et al., 1996; Krebs & Rosenwald, 1994). Such moral reasoning involves adhering to moral standards independent of external social controls, and taking into account the needs of others when making decisions about courses of action. In contrast, people whose reasoning is focused on their own needs or on the concrete personal consequences that their actions are likely to have tend not to engage in many helping behaviors.

The combination of empathy and advanced moral reasoning may be an especially strong predictor of helping tendencies. Paul Miller and his colleagues (1996) propose that "cold" cognitive moral principles may not be enough to trigger self-sacrificing pro-social action; when these principles are activated together with the experience of "hot" empathic or sympathetic emotional responses to another's suffering, however, helping is much more likely. In one study, preschool children (four- to five-year-olds) watched a film in which a boy and girl got hurt from a fall.

"True kindness presupposes the faculty of imagining as one's own the suffering and joy of others."

—André Gide

Someone relatively low in empathic concern for another.

"It's always poor you, isn't it, Albert?"

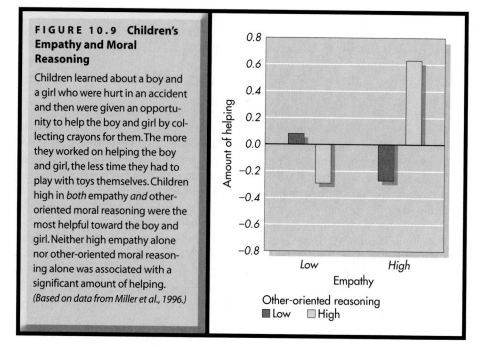

FIGURE 10.9 Children's Empathy and Moral Reasoning

Children learned about a boy and a girl who were hurt in an accident and then were given an opportunity to help the boy and girl by collecting crayons for them. The more they worked on helping the boy and girl, the less time they had to play with toys themselves. Children high in *both* empathy *and* other-oriented moral reasoning were the most helpful toward the boy and girl. Neither high empathy alone nor other-oriented moral reasoning alone was associated with a significant amount of helping. *(Based on data from Miller et al., 1996.)*

The children's empathic responses were measured through their facial reactions while they watched the film and their verbal and nonverbal self-reports of their feelings. The children's prosocial moral reasoning was assessed by their responses to a series of moral reasoning dilemmas in which the needs of the self are in conflict with those of another.

To measure the children's helping behavior, the experimenter told them that the boy and the girl from the film were in the hospital recovering from their fall, feeling fine but bored because there was nothing for them to do. The experimenter gave the children the option of either playing with very attractive toys or helping the boy and girl in the hospital by putting loose crayons into crayon boxes to send to them. Figure 10.9 illustrates the results. The children who were high in *both* moral reasoning and empathic emotions were especially likely to help the injured children by forgoing their own playing time to provide them with crayons.

Parental and Family Influences

Where do the abilities to empathize and reason morally come from? Parental behavior may make an important contribution to personal differences in these abilities (Koestner et al., 1990). A study by researchers in the Netherlands, for example, found that children raised in supportive, authoritative, and less restrictive environments behaved more prosocially and reasoned at a higher level about prosocial moral issues than did other children (Janssens & Dekovic, 1997). A study by researchers in Hong Kong found that altruistic children tended to come from family environments that were cohesive and harmonious and in which there was little open expression of anger, aggression, and conflict among family members. Altruistic orientation was also high in families that emphasized intellectual and cultural activities (Ma & Leung, 1995).

Parents often try to teach their children about prosocial behavior and moral reasoning. They can encourage children to share their toys with other children, for example, by saying, "I'll be unhappy with you if you don't share your toys with the other children." Alternatively, they can say, "The other children will be unhappy if you don't share your toys with them." The former approach puts the child's focus on the adult and the child's own desire not to be punished. The latter approach puts the child's focus on the potential recipients of his or her helpful behavior, encouraging perspective taking and empathy (McGath et al., 1995). Children of parents who use this latter approach, emphasizing empathy rather than direct rewards and punishments, tend to be more empathic and more likely to behave in helpful, prosocial ways than other children (Hoffman, 1994; Krevans & Gibbs, 1996; Zahn-Wexler et al., 1992).

Heroic helpers often acknowledge parental influence. Oskar Schindler had a troubled relationship with his father, but he respected the opinions of his father, who regarded Hitler with contempt. Other individuals who helped Jews escape from the Nazis describe an intense identification with at least one parent who was a model of high moral standards (London, 1970; Oliner & Oliner, 1988). Committed civil rights activists, interviewed in the mid-1960s, reported a similar pattern of strong parental identification (Rosenhan, 1970). The good that parents do can live after them.

Interpersonal Influences: Whom Do People Help?

However influential they might be, personal factors alone do not a helper make. The characteristics of the person in need are important as well. Are some people more likely than others to receive help? Are some helpers particularly responsive to certain kinds of individuals who need assistance? Here, we explore some of the interpersonal aspects of helping.

Perceived Characteristics of the Person in Need

Although many characteristics of a person in need might affect whether that individual is helped, researchers have paid special attention to two: the personal attractiveness of the person in need and whether or not the person seems responsible for being in the position of needing assistance.

Attractiveness In Chapter 9, we described the social advantages enjoyed by physically attractive individuals. The bias for beauty also affects helping, as Peter Benson and his colleagues (1976) observed in a large metropolitan airport. Darting into a phone booth to make a call, each of 604 travelers discovered some materials supposedly left behind accidentally by the previous caller (but actually planted by the experimenters): a completed graduate school application form, a photograph of the applicant, and a stamped, addressed envelope. In some packets, the photo depicted a physically attractive individual; in others, the person was relatively unattractive. What was a busy traveler to do? When the researchers checked their mail, they found that people were more likely to send in the materials of the good-looking applicants than those of the less attractive applicants.

Physical appearance, of course, is only one aspect of attractiveness. Friendly individuals also receive a more generous response (Lynn & Mynier, 1993). And sometimes, the charisma of one person can determine how much help other people receive. On November 7, 1991, Earvin "Magic" Johnson, Jr., announced to a stunned public that he had contracted HIV, the virus that causes AIDS. By coincidence, Louis Penner and Barbara Fritzsche (1993) had just completed a study in

Attractive people have a better chance than unattractive people of getting help when they need it. **True.**

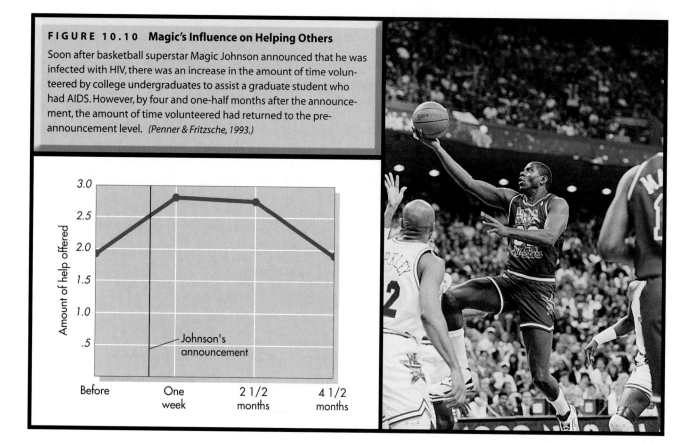

FIGURE 10.10   Magic's Influence on Helping Others
Soon after basketball superstar Magic Johnson announced that he was infected with HIV, there was an increase in the amount of time volunteered by college undergraduates to assist a graduate student who had AIDS. However, by four and one-half months after the announcement, the amount of time volunteered had returned to the pre-announcement level. *(Penner & Fritzsche, 1993.)*

which college undergraduates were given the opportunity to assist a graduate student who was described as having AIDS. These investigators decided to repeat their study three more times after Magic's announcement. As you can see in Figure 10.10, the amount of time participants were willing to volunteer increased after the announcement but then declined back to the pre-announcement baseline. It appears that for a while, the immense attractiveness of Magic Johnson spread like a protective cloak over others who were HIV-positive and increased the help they received. Unfortunately, once the shock wore off, so did the help.

Attributions of Responsibility   At some time or another, most students have had the experience of being asked to lend their class notes to a classmate. Has this ever happened to you? If so, you can compare your reactions with those of the students in a study conducted by Richard Barnes and his colleagues (1979). In this research, students received a call from an experimental confederate posing as another student, who asked to borrow their class notes to prepare for an upcoming exam. The reason for this request varied. To some students, the caller said, "I just don't seem to have the ability to take good notes. I really try to take good notes, but sometimes I just can't do it." Other students were told that "I just don't seem to have the motivation to take good notes. I really can take good notes, but sometimes I just don't try." You probably won't be surprised to learn that the caller received much more help from those who were informed he had tried yet failed than from those who were told he hadn't tried at all.

Bluntly stating that you didn't even try to help yourself may seem like an obvious way to ensure that others won't help you out. But even when the circumstances are more complex and the causes more subtle, people's beliefs about the needy individual's responsibility influence helping. The *attribution-affect-action theory* (or triple A, for short) describes the process (Schmidt & Weiner, 1988; Weiner, 1996).

When people attribute a person's need for assistance to factors beyond the individual's control, they do not hold that person responsible (attribution), they feel sympathy and pity for the person's plight (affect), and they are likely to help (action). However, when people perceive a person's difficulties as caused by controllable factors, they hold the person responsible, they feel angry or irritated, and they are less likely to help. For example, participants in an experiment by Pamela Dooley (1995) read scenarios about someone who had just been diagnosed with AIDS. If the participants read that the person had contracted the disease through a blood transfusion rather than through sexual activity or drug use, they considered the situation less controllable, and they felt more pity for the person. In addition, those who felt pity indicated a greater desire to engage in helping behaviors.

Ultimately, attributions of responsibility reside in the mind of the perceiver. And perceivers differ in the attributions they make for the same need for assistance. Political conservatives, for instance, are more likely to attribute personal responsibility than are political liberals (Zucker & Weiner, 1993). Are, then, conservatives less helpful? Not necessarily. When asked to allocate educational resources to an alcoholic, conservatives were less generous than liberals. But when the person in need was described as having successfully quit drinking and regularly attending Alcoholics Anonymous meetings, conservatives allocated more resources than did liberals (Skitka & Tetlock, 1993).

The Fit Between Giver and Receiver

The impact of political ideology on helping illustrates a general point. Some potential helpers are particularly responsive to some kinds of potential recipients. In this section, we look at a variety of ways in which helping depends on the fit between a giver and a receiver.

We are more likely to help similar, rather than dissimilar, others. Donald Reilly © 1996 from The New Yorker Collection. All Rights Reserved.

Similarity: Helping Those Just Like Us Similarity may be the closest fit of all. All kinds of similarity—from dress to attitudes to nationality—increase our willingness to help, and signs of dissimilarity decrease it (Dovidio, 1984). Indeed, similarity seems to be the common denominator for a number of psychological processes that affect helping. Similarity increases attraction, and dissimilarity decreases attraction (Byrne et al., 1986; Rosenbaum, 1986); and as we have seen, perceived attractiveness increases helping. Likewise, similarity increases empathy (Houston, 1990); and as we have seen, empathic concern increases helping.

The influence of similarity could even be a form of kinship selection. If similarity in appearance reflects the degree of genetic overlap (or, at least, if people think it does), then evolutionary psychologists and biologists would expect people to help similar-looking relatives more than dissimilar ones (Segal, 1993). We might also help similar, though biologically unrelated, individuals because we overgeneralize the assumption that what looks alike must genetically be alike (Krebs, 1987).

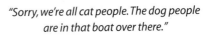

"Sorry, we're all cat people. The dog people are in that boat over there."

The strong, multiply determined effect of similarity on helping suggests that members of the same race should help each other more than members of different races. However, research on black-white helping in the United States indicates that the effects of racial similarity are highly variable. For instance, Faye Crosby and her colleagues (1980) found a same-race helping bias in 44 percent of the studies they reviewed. Sometimes, Whites were more biased; sometimes, Blacks. In the remaining studies, there was either no discrimination or reverse discrimination, in which people helped those of a different race more than they helped members of their own race.

There's no simple way to iron out all these inconsistencies, but we should examine some of the issues they raise. First, although helping can be a compassionate response to another, it can also be seen as a sign of superiority over the person who needs help (Rosen et al., 1986). Thus, cross-racial helping isn't always a sign of egalitarian attitudes. Second, public displays of racial prejudice risk social disapproval, and prejudiced individuals may bend over backward, in public at least, to avoid revealing their attitudes. As discussed in Chapter 5, however, modern racism relies on more subtle forms of discrimination. For example, if people are provided with an excuse not to help, racial discrimination in helping is more likely (Frey & Gaertner, 1986).

Intergroup biases in helping can be reduced significantly, however, if the members of the different groups can perceive themselves as members of a common group. Through fostering perceptions of shared identities, encouraging meaningful contact that defies group boundaries, and highlighting similarities on other dimensions unrelated to group distinctions, an ingroup and an outgroup can begin to see each other as more similar than different, thereby promoting helping and other positive behaviors (Dovidio, Gaertner, et al., 1997).

Closeness: A Little Help for Our Friends   As we would expect, people are usually more helpful toward those they know and care about than toward strangers or superficial acquaintances (Bell et al., 1995; Clark & Mills, 1993). People in a *communal* relationship, such as close friends or romantic partners, feel mutual responsibility for each other's needs. People in an *exchange* relationship, such as acquaintances or business associates, give help with the expectation of receiving comparable benefits in return—"If I help you move your furniture, you'd better give me a ride to the airport." When people are, or desire to be, in a communal relationship with each other, they attend more to each other's needs, are more likely to help, and are less likely to be concerned with keeping track of rewards and costs. People in a communal relationship also feel better about having helped the other, and they feel worse if they were unable to help (Williamson et al., 1996).

So, common sense seems correct here: People help their friends more than strangers or acquaintances. But there may be an exception to this general rule: What if a person's ego is threatened? According to the *self-evaluation maintenance model* (Erber & Tesser, 1994), we can respond in two very different ways to superior performance by a significant other. If the achievement occurs in an area not relevant to our own ego, we can indulge in the delight of BIRGing—basking in reflected glory, as described in Chapter 3. If the area is relevant to our own ego, however, we may experience envy and resentment.

To apply this perspective to helping behavior, suppose you have just finished working on a task and are told that you performed "a little below average." Then two other people take their turns at the same task; one of them is a stranger, and the other a close friend. You are asked to give some clues to each individual. The available clues differ in their level of difficulty. Some are easy and will boost the person's performance; others are so difficult that they will interfere with a good performance. Will you give your friend easier, more helpful clues than you give to the stranger?

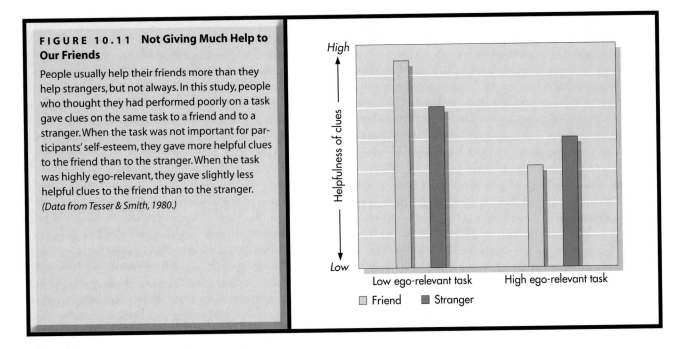

FIGURE 10.11 Not Giving Much Help to Our Friends

People usually help their friends more than they help strangers, but not always. In this study, people who thought they had performed poorly on a task gave clues on the same task to a friend and to a stranger. When the task was not important for participants' self-esteem, they gave more helpful clues to the friend than to the stranger. When the task was highly ego-relevant, they gave slightly less helpful clues to the friend than to the stranger. *(Data from Tesser & Smith, 1980.)*

As the self-evaluation maintenance model would predict, it depends on the task. When participants found themselves in the situation we've just described, those who believed that the task was a trivial game helped their friend more than they helped the stranger (Tesser & Smith, 1980). But when the task was important and relevant to their own self-esteem, participants were slightly less helpful to their friend than to the stranger (see Figure 10.11). In a conflict between our own egos and the welfare of a friend, the need to protect our self-esteem can sometimes overcome our helpful inclinations. The self-evaluation maintenance model applies even to very close relationships, such as married couples (Beach et al., 1996).

In any situation, people are more likely to help a friend succeed than a stranger. **False.**

Gender and Helping   Here's a quick, one-question quiz: Who helps more, men or women? Before you answer, consider the following situations:

A. Two strangers pass on the street. Suddenly, one of them needs help that might be dangerous to give. Other people are watching. The person in need is female.

B. Two individuals have a close relationship. Every so often, one of them needs assistance that takes time and energy to provide but is not physically dangerous. No one else is around to notice whether help is given. The person who needs help is either male or female.

Is your answer the same for both situations? It shouldn't be. Situation A is a classic male-helper scenario. Here, the helper is a "knight in shining armor"—physically brave and chivalrous, rescuing a lady in distress. Because social psychologists have tended to focus on these kinds of emergency situations, their research has found that, on the average, men are more helpful than women and women receive more help than do men (Eagly & Crowley, 1986).

Situation B is the classic female-helper scenario. Every day, millions of women—mothers, sisters, wives, and female friends—provide TLC for their loved ones (Kessler et al., 1985). Though it lacks the high drama of an emergency intervention, this type of helping, called "social support," plays a crucial role in the quality of our lives. Chapter 14 reports evidence indicating that social support is associated with better physical and psychological health.

Women seek help more often than men do. **True.**

Reactions to Receiving Help

Thus far, we've described factors that influence whether helping will occur. Now, we turn to what happens after it takes place. The last time someone helped you, how did you feel? Grateful, relieved, comforted—anything else? Embarrassed, obligated, inferior? Receiving help is often a positive experience, but sometimes it has drawbacks for the recipient. There are costs in providing help, and there can be costs in receiving it.

Help That Supports Versus Help That Threatens

Jeffrey Fisher and Arie Nadler have extensively examined people's reactions to receiving help (Fisher et al., 1982; Nadler & Fisher, 1986). According to their **threat-to-self-esteem model,** receiving help is experienced as *self-supportive* when the recipient feels appreciated and cared for, but as *self-threatening* when the recipient feels inferior and overly dependent. If recipients feel supported by the help they receive, they respond positively: feeling good, accepting the help, and being grateful to the donor. If, however, recipients feel threatened, they have a negative emotional reaction and evaluate both the help and the helper unfavorably.

There are three conditions under which receiving help is most likely to be perceived as threatening. First, individuals with high self-esteem tend to react more negatively to receiving help than do those with low self-esteem. Presumably, people who regard themselves as highly competent are especially sensitive to the implication that they are unable to take care of themselves. Second, being helped by a similar other highlights the contrast between the recipient's need for assistance and the generosity of the provider. This one difference between people alike in other ways may imply that the recipient is inferior. The third condition under which receiving help can be threatening involves the type of relationship the recipient has with the provider and the area in which help has been received. As would be expected from Tesser's self-evaluation maintenance model, receiving help from a significant other on an ego-relevant task can be threatening to an individual's self-esteem.

Usually, however, help from those who are close to us will be seen as supportive. High self-esteem does not appear to prompt negative reactions to assistance by a sibling (Searcy & Eisenberg, 1992). And the negative effects of similarity probably do not apply to close relationships, in which similarity is expected and desired (Wills, 1992). Even ego-relevant help may elicit positive, rather than negative, reactions from partners in an interdependent relationship (Clark, 1983; Cook & Pelfrey, 1985). In such relationships, feelings of inferiority are less likely to arise, as each person sometimes helps, sometimes receives help. Mutuality makes receiving help less threatening. So does a very young age. Because dependency is more acceptable for children than for adolescents and adults, children less often react negatively to being helped (Shell & Eisenberg, 1992).

People who are stigmatized by being the targets of negative stereotypes and feeling devalued in the larger society often face a difficult attributional dilemma when they receive help from members of nonstigmatized groups: Is the helping sincere and unassuming, is it well intentioned but patronizing, or is it controlling and designed to keep the recipient dependent? These are questions that members of nonstigmatized groups aren't as likely to consider when they receive help from another. Brenda Major and Jennifer Crocker and their colleagues have examined

threat-to-self-esteem model The theory that reactions to receiving assistance depend on whether help is perceived as supportive or threatening.

this issue in a number of experiments. For example, in one study, participants imagined themselves as stigmatized individuals who received a job either because of their qualifications or because of a stigmatizing condition that elicited sympathy from others. Participants reported lower self-esteem, more negative affect, and lowered work motivation when the job was offered out of sympathy (Blaine et al., 1995).

In another study (Schneider et al., 1996), black and white college students received *assumptive help*—help that they neither asked for nor gave any evidence of needing—from a same-sex white peer. The participants completed what they thought was the first of two parts of a "verbal-spatial aptitude task" that was allegedly an important predictor of future success. They believed that another participant had been working on the same task, and that they would be working together with this "partner" on the second part of the task. After completing the first part of the task, the participants were asked to exchange some personal information about themselves with the partner, including their sex and race. The participants believed that the partner had no knowledge of their performance on the first part of the test. When they received their partner's personal information as part of the exchange of information, half of the participants saw that the partner had written a special note on the form giving them a tip about how they "might do better next time" on the task if they realized there was a pattern to the answers, which the partner had apparently figured out. The other half of the participants did not receive a special note from the partner.

How would the participants react to the unsolicited advice about how they could do better? Keep in mind that the participants believed that this white partner was aware of their race but was unaware of how they had performed on the task. Apparently, this partner assumed that the participants had not figured out an important clue about the task. Although this assumption was indeed correct (the clue was designed to be so subtle that none of the participants would discover it on their own, and none of them did), participants might wonder why the partner made this assumption. White participants might simply assume that the partner was just being helpful and would have given this clue to anyone. Black participants might wonder, however, if the partner made this assumption because of their race. Consistent with this reasoning, the results revealed that black participants felt more depressed after the information exchange if the partner had offered unsolicited advice than if the partner had not; the partner's helping behavior had no such effect on the white participants. As can be seen in Figure 10.12, the black participants who received the assumptive help also had lower self-esteem about their competence than did other participants.

Results like these highlight a dilemma that a potential helper may face when interacting with a member of a stereotyped or stigmatized group. On the one hand, if help will be seen as threatening or controlling, it might be better not to offer any. On the other hand, not offering assistance can hurt a would-be recipient who truly needs it. Either way, the potential helper has reason to worry that his or her motives will be questioned (Crocker et al., 1998; Glick & Fiske, 1996; Kidda & Rosen, 1994). Furthermore, if the offer of help is rejected, the *helper's* self-esteem may be threatened (Cheuk & Rosen, 1996).

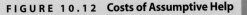

FIGURE 10.12   Costs of Assumptive Help

White and black students worked on the first part of a test. They then anticipated working on the second part of the test with a same-sex, white partner who allegedly had also just worked on the first part of the test. Some students then received unsolicited help from their partner in preparation for the next part of the test. Other participants received no such help. The white students' self-esteem concerning their own competence was unaffected by the unsolicited help. Black students, however, felt less competent if they were offered the help. *(Data from Schneider et al., 1996.)*

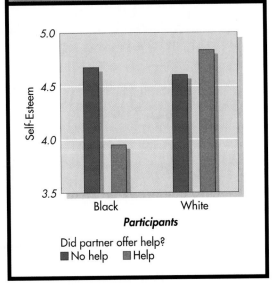

Seeking Help from Others

This chapter has focused on situations in which people are the passive recipients of help. However, people also seek help from others. Help-seeking can be a very constructive behavior, enabling lost drivers to finally get to their destinations, students to learn material better, and couples to survive problems in their relationships.

People's help-seeking behavior is influenced by how they have reacted to past experiences of being helped. If the reaction was positive, future help-seeking is encouraged. If the reaction was negative, however, subsequent efforts to obtain assistance will depend on the individual's *perceived control* over future events. An individual who has experienced threatening help and is pessimistic about the likelihood of future control feels helplessly dependent on the kindness of others (Coates et al., 1983). Help will again be sought, but at a high price to self-esteem. In general, highly dependent individuals seek help more than do those who are not as dependent (Bornstein et al., 1993). An individual who has experienced threatening help but is optimistic about the likelihood of future control reacts differently. This person avoids seeking help from others and relies instead on self-help efforts.

Gender also influences the willingness to seek help. Remember the time you and a member of the opposite sex got lost while driving in unfamiliar territory? Who wanted to stop early on and ask for directions? Who kept insisting that help wasn't necessary? For relatively minor problems, at least, men ask for help less frequently than do women (McMullen & Gross, 1983). Less socially acceptable for men, help-seeking is more threatening to their self-esteem (Wills & DePaulo, 1991).

There is a great irony in refusing to seek help in order to protect self-esteem. If your own success depends on obtaining information and assistance from others, then not seeking help increases the likelihood of failure and damage to self-esteem. The cure for this self-destructive paradox is to recognize "the utility of humility" (Weiss & Knight, 1980). Research on city-dwelling and kibbutz-residing Israelis indicates that such recognition is most likely when success is most important (Nadler, 1986). City residents valued individual achievement more than group accomplishment. Kibbutz residents, however, valued group accomplishment more than individual achievement. So when did people ask for help? When task performance was to be judged on the basis of individual scores, city dwellers sought more

"I would share my cookies, but I'm afraid I'll set up a cycle of dependency."

One of the potential costs of helping?

help than did those who lived on kibbutzim. But when task performance was to be judged on the basis of the average score of all group members, kibbutz residents sought more help than did city dwellers. If success really matters, people can swallow their pride and ask others to help them out.

The Helping Connection

A lthough whether or not people help others can be quite variable, there is a consistent theme that appears repeatedly in this chapter: a sense of connection.

The importance of a sense of connection is vividly demonstrated by a cross-cultural comparison. First, consider one of the great social tragedies of our time: homelessness. In the United States, one of the richest countries on earth, thousands of men, women, and children are without a home. Many sleep on the street, carry their belongings in grocery carts, and rummage through piles of garbage to find food.

Now, compare American homelessness with an anthropologist's account of life among the Moose (pronounced "MOH-say") in West Africa:

> *Moose welcome anyone who wishes to join the community and move into the village. New arrivals have only to say where they wish to build their homes, and the user of the land in question gives it up for the newcomer's residence. . . . Each of the two years that I lived there, the well ran dry and villagers had to walk miles to get water for themselves and their stock from other villages, carrying it home on their heads. Each of these other villages shared their water until their wells were nearly dry, without expecting any reciprocation for the water. Even in these circumstances, any stranger who comes into the village may ask for a drink, and any visitor is offered water.*
> *(Fiske, 1991, pp. 190–191)*

Among some of the poorest people on earth, no one goes without shelter or remains thirsty as long as anyone has water to drink.

How can we account for the extraordinary difference between American homelessness and Moose hospitality? Homelessness is, of course, a complex phenomenon affected by many specific economic and political factors. But it may also be a symptom of a profound loss of social connection in American society (Wuthnow, 1991). Among the Moose, no such loss has occurred. Their sense of being intimately connected to others binds them to those who live in their village and to strangers who arrive in their midst.

The relationship between helping and interpersonal connection runs like a bright red thread through much of the research on helping. For example:

- Evolutionary perspectives emphasize the genetic connection of reciprocal, kinship, and within-group helping.
- Two kinds of connections lie at the heart of the empathy-altruism hypothesis: the cognitive connection of perspective taking and the emotional connection of empathic concern.
- In an emergency, bystanders who know the victim or know each other are more likely to intervene.
- People who respond empathically to another's suffering and consider the plight of others in their own moral reasoning are more likely to help than are others.
- Perceived similarity increases helping.
- In a close relationship, it's easier to give and more comfortable to receive.

Taken as a whole, these theories and research findings suggest that helping requires the recognition of individual human beings with whom we can have a meaningful connection. Which brings us back to Oskar Schindler. He didn't know most of the people he rescued. He didn't share their religion or their nationality. But he felt a deep, personal sense of connection with them as individuals. Each of their lives mattered to him. And so, on their behalf, he wheeled and dealt, charmed and conned, spent his money and devised his schemes. There was nothing remarkable about Oskar before the war or afterward. For six long years, though, during some of the most horrible events in human history, he fulfilled his responsibility to help. Oskar Schindler may never have read the words that English poet John Donne wrote almost four hundred years ago. But he would have understood them:

No man is an island, entire of itself. Every man is a piece of the continent, a part of the main. If a clod be washed away by the sea, Europe is the less, as well as if a promontory were, as well as if a manor of thy friends or of thine own were. Any man's death diminishes me, because I am involved in mankind. And therefore never send to know for whom the bell tolls; it tolls for thee.

Review

Motivational Factors: Why Do People Help?

Evolutionary Factors in Helping

- Evolutionary perspectives emphasize three ways in which helping could become an innate, universal behavioral tendency: kinship selection, in which people protect their own genes by helping close relatives; reciprocal altruism, in which those who give also receive; and group selection, in which members of a social group help each other survive.

Rewards of Helping: Helping Others to Help Oneself

- People are much more likely to help when the potential rewards of helping seem high relative to the potential costs.

Overhelping: Being Cruel by Being Kind

- People sometimes appear to help others in order to hurt them. By providing public displays of help to someone who does not need help, individuals can sabotage the credit that the person would otherwise get for his or her successful performance.

Altruism or Egoism: The Great Debate

- According to the empathy-altruism hypothesis, taking the perspective of a person perceived to be in need creates the other-oriented emotion of empathic concern, which in turn produces the altruistic motive to reduce the other's distress.

- Not taking the other's perspective creates the self-oriented emotion of personal distress, which produces the egoistic motive to reduce one's own distress.

- When people are altruistically motivated, they will help even when escaping from the helping situation is easy.

- Alternatives to the empathy-altruism hypothesis include empathy-specific punishments for not helping and empathy-specific rewards for helping, such as negative state relief and empathic joy.

Distinguishing Among the Motivations to Help: Why Does It Matter?

- People's motivations influence whether or not they are likely to help someone in a particular situation.

- People who help someone for egoistic reasons will feel good or bad about their actions to the extent that they are rewarded for the actions, whereas people who help someone for altruistic reasons will feel good or bad as a function of the other person's fate.

- Helpers are more likely than observers to believe that their helpful behavior was motivated by altruism rather than egoism, and helpers may be offended when observers suggest egoistic motives.

- External rewards for helping diminish self-perceptions of being a helpful individual and decrease helpful behavior when rewards are no longer available.

- Awareness of internal rewards also diminishes self-perceptions of being a helpful individual, but this awareness can have various effects on actual helping.

Situational Influences: When Do People Help?

The Unhelpful Crowd

- Research on the bystander effect, in which the presence of others inhibits helping in an emergency, indicates why the five steps necessary for helping—noticing, interpreting, taking responsibility, deciding how to help, and providing help—may not be taken.

- The distractions of others and our own self-concerns may impair our ability to notice that someone needs help.

- Under ambiguous circumstances, some interpretations—such as the belief that an attacker and a victim have a close relationship or the mistaken inferences drawn from pluralistic ignorance—reduce bystander intervention.

- People may fail to take responsibility because they assume that others will—a phenomenon called diffusion of responsibility.

- Bystanders are less likely to offer direct aid when they do not feel competent to do so. They can, however, call for assistance from others.

- Even if people want to help, they tend not to do so if they fear that behaving in a helpful fashion will make them look foolish or if they conclude that there are other, less costly ways to reduce their shock and alarm.

The Place We Live

- Residents of densely populated urban areas are less likely to provide spontaneous, informal help to strangers than are residents of smaller or less densely populated communities.

Time Pressure

- When people are in a hurry, they are less likely to notice or choose to help others in need.

Emotional Factors in Helping

- A good mood increases helpfulness.

- People in a good mood may help in order to maintain their positive mood or because they have more positive thoughts and expectations about helpful behavior, the person in need, or social activities in general.

- A bad mood can often increase helpfulness, such as when people feel guilty about something.

- People in a bad mood may be motivated to help others in order to improve their mood.

- A bad mood is less likely to increase helpfulness if the bad mood is attributed to the fault of others, or if it causes the person to become very self-focused.

Role Models and Social Norms: A Helpful Standard

- Observing a helpful model increases helping.

- Social norms that promote helping are based on a sense of fairness or on standards about what is right.

- Cultural differences exist in how people interpret and apply social norms.

Personal Influences: Who Is Likely to Help?

The Altruistic Personality

- There is some evidence of relatively stable individual differences in helping tendencies.

- Some personality traits are associated with helpful behavioral tendencies, but no one set of traits appears to define the altruistic personality.

Empathy and Moral Reasoning

- Two qualities that do predict helping behaviors are empathy and advanced moral reasoning.

Parental and Family Influences

- Parental and family influences can promote empathy and advanced moral reasoning.

Interpersonal Influences: Whom Do People Help?

Perceived Characteristics of the Person in Need

- Attractive individuals are more likely to receive help than are those who are less attractive.

■ People are more willing to help when they attribute a person's need for assistance to uncontrollable causes rather than to events under the person's control. Some individuals are more likely than others to make attributions of personal responsibility.

The Fit Between Giver and Receiver

■ In general, perceived similarity to a person in need increases willingness to help. But research on racial similarity has yielded inconsistent results.

■ People usually help significant others more than strangers, except when helping threatens their own egos.

■ Men help female strangers in potentially dangerous situations more than women do; women help friends and relations in everyday situations more than men do.

Reactions to Receiving Help

Help That Supports Versus Help That Threatens

■ The threat-to-self-esteem model distinguishes between help perceived as supportive, which produces positive reactions, and help perceived as threatening, which creates negative reactions.

■ Help is most likely to be perceived as threatening by a recipient with high self-esteem who receives help from a similar provider or from a significant other on an ego-relevant task.

■ In close, interdependent relationships, receiving help is usually a positive experience.

■ Members of stigmatized groups sometimes feel threatened and depressed after receiving unsolicited help from members of nonstigmatized groups.

Seeking Help from Others

■ Receiving supportive help encourages the recipient to seek assistance again when needed.

■ Individuals who receive threatening help will seek further help if they are pessimistic about their ability to control future events but not if they anticipate being in control.

■ People are usually more willing to seek help from a person they are close to than from a stranger.

■ Women seek help more often than do men.

■ A greater desire for success increases willingness to seek the help necessary to succeed.

The Helping Connection

■ Theory and research seem to indicate that helping requires the recognition of meaningful connections among individuals.

Key Terms

PUTTING COMMON SENSE TO THE TEST

People are more likely to help someone in an emergency if the potential rewards seem high and the potential costs seem low.

True. *For both emergency situations and more long-term, well-planned helping, people's helping behaviors are determined in part by a cost-benefit analysis.*

In an emergency, a person who needs help has a much better chance of getting it if three other people are present than if only one other person is present.

False. *In several ways, the presence of others inhibits helping.*

People are much more likely to help someone when they're in a good mood.

True. *Compared to neutral moods, good moods tend to elicit more helping and other prosocial behaviors.*

People are much less likely to help someone when they're in a bad mood.

False. *Compared to neutral moods, negative moods often elicit more helping and prosocial behaviors. This effect depends on a number of factors, including whether people take responsibility for their bad mood or blame it on others; but in many circumstances, feeling bad leads to doing good.*

Attractive people have a better chance than unattractive people of getting help when they need it.

True. *People are more likely to help those who are attractive. This attractiveness can be based on physical appearance or friendliness.*

In any situation, people are more likely to help a friend succeed than a stranger.

False. *Although we tend to help those closest to us more than we help others, this tendency is often eliminated or even reversed if the task is very important to our own self-esteem and if our friend's success is threatening to our ego.*

Women seek help more often than men do.

True. *At least for relatively minor problems, men ask for help less frequently than women do.*

11 | Aggression

PREVIEW

In this chapter, we examine a disturbing aspect of human behavior: aggression. First, we ask, *"What is aggression?"* and consider its definition. After describing *cultural and gender differences*, we examine various theories concerning the *origins of aggression*. We next explore a variety of *situational factors* that influence when people are likely to behave aggressively. Finally, we focus on two critically important issues in our society: the *effects of media violence and pornography* on aggression and the *intimate violence* that can occur in close relationships. Throughout the chapter, we emphasize ways to prevent or reduce aggressive actions.

OUTLINE

As election day approached in November 1997, Rudy Giuliani, the incumbent mayor of New York City, and Ruth Messenger, his challenger, knew that the FBI's fall press releases about violent crime rates in cities throughout the United States would be big news among the city's voters. And they were right. Hungry for news during a relatively uneventful campaign, the New York media splashed the statistics across their front pages: During the first six months of 1997, there were 372 murders in New York City—an average of more than two murders every day.

More than two murders a day? One might suspect that numbers like that would have been ammunition to use against the mayor. But it wasn't the *challenger* who publicized the murder rate; it was the mayor himself—celebrating how *low* the numbers were—lower than they'd been in thirty years. Indeed, in contrast to the ultra-violent image suggested by TV shows such as *NYPD Blue*, New York City now had a murder rate per person that was far from the nation's highest; among 195 cities with a population of at least 100,000, New York City ranked only 71st. On New Year's Day of 1998, Mayor Giuliani began his second term as mayor, already one of the most popular mayors in the city's history, in large part because of numbers like *only* two murders per day.

T / F

_____ In virtually every culture, males are more violent than females.

_____ For virtually any category of aggression, males are more aggressive than females.

_____ Children who are spanked or otherwise physically disciplined (but not abused) for behaving aggressively tend to become less aggressive.

_____ Blowing off steam by engaging in safe but aggressive activities (such as sports) makes people less likely to aggress later.

_____ Exposure to TV violence in childhood is related to aggression later in life.

_____ Men are much more likely than women to aggress against their spouses or partners.

_____ Adults who as children were abused by their parents are less likely to inflict abuse on their own children than are other adults.

Rudolph Giuliani celebrates his re-election to his second term as mayor of New York City on November 4, 1997. Giuliani's tremendous popularity in the city was due in large part to the dramatic reduction in violent crime in New York during his first term.

According to the National Crime Victimization Survey, an estimated 2,700,000 violent crimes were committed in the United States in 1996.

If it weren't so serious, this might seem like an old joke: Do you want the good news or the bad news first? First, the good news: There were about 20,000 murders, 96,000 forcible rapes, and 1 million aggravated assaults reported in the United States in 1996, and each statistic represents a dramatic decrease from the previous few years. Now, the bad news: There were about 20,000 murders, 96,000 forcible rapes, and 1 million aggravated assaults reported in the United States in 1996.

Behind these statistics (see Table 11.1) are tragic stories. Think of someone you care deeply about—a parent, a brother or sister, a special teacher or coach, your best friend. Imagine that this person was taken away from you forever because of violence. Now imagine how many other people would suffer, too, because of the loss of this person. Then, multiply that suffering by almost 20,000 murders to get a sense of the toll taken by homicide in the United States in any given year.

And it is not only murder and other violent crimes that take their toll. For instance, look at schools in many countries around the world, and you're likely to see numerous acts of aggressive bullying. Debra Pepler and Wendy Craig (1995) set up hidden video cameras and microphones to get an unfiltered peek into aggression in schoolyards in Canada, and they saw bullying in midsized schools at a rate of once every seven minutes. These seemingly ordinary rites of childhood can lead to extraordinary suffering. Sonia Sharp (1995) found that approximately one-third of the secondary school students she studied in England reported incidents of being bullied that left them with feelings of panic or nervousness in school, recurring memories of the incidents, and impaired concentration in school. The injurious psychological effects of bullying are felt especially intensely by children

---

TABLE 11.1   The Violent Crime Clock

Although the rates of violent crime in the United States have declined in recent years, they are still distressingly high, as these statistics illustrate. The overall violent crime rate in the United States in the mid-1990s was almost twice as high as it was in the mid-1970s, almost four times as high as in the mid-1960s, and more than six times as high as in the mid-1950s. *(Based on Federal Bureau of Investigation statistics.)*

In the United States in 1996, there was, on average:

- One murder   every 27 minutes
- One forcible rape   every $5\frac{1}{2}$ minutes
- One hate crime*   every 49 minutes
- One aggravated assault   every 30 seconds

* Hate crimes are criminal offenses based on the offender's bias against a race, religion, ethnic/national-origin group, or sexual-orientation group.

with low self-esteem (Sharp, 1996). And all too often, some community is rocked when a student commits suicide after suffering from such acts of aggression, as students did in Burlington, Iowa; Cherokee County, Georgia; and small towns in northern Norway and Sweden (Marano, 1995).

There are few safe havens from aggression. Take a drive, and you might be another victim of "road rage," as aggressive drivers cut each other off and exchange heated words, gestures, and even gunshots. Read a college newspaper and learn about the violent hazing endured by fraternity pledges or military academy students. Watch sports on TV and see clips of the latest fight between a player and another player, coach, or fan—or perhaps between a coach and an umpire at a Little League game. Even mascots are getting into the act: Barney the purple dinosaur sued the "San Diego chicken" in late 1997 for pummeling a Barney look-alike at hockey and baseball games.

As historians review the twentieth century, they will note the stunning developments in technology that improved the quality of many aspects of people's lives, including developments in travel, communication, and health. But despite all this progress, the century will also be remembered for its violence: two world wars, the creation and use of weapons of mass destruction, biological warfare. As the twenty-first century begins, the human animal is as aggressive as ever. What can account for this aggression? Although it is often unsettling to think about aggression, the better we can understand this aspect of human behavior, the better equipped we will be to protect ourselves, our loved ones, and our society from its consequences. This chapter examines the origins and immediate triggers of aggression, as well as factors that reduce aggression. It focuses primarily on aggression by individuals; aggression by groups, such as rampaging mobs and warring nations, was discussed in Chapter 8.

"The most persistent sound which reverberates through men's history is the beating of war drums."

—Arthur Koestler

What Is Aggression?

The word is a familiar one, part of our everyday vocabulary, but the concept of "aggression" can be surprisingly hard to pin down. Consider, for example, the following actions. Which ones do you think are aggressive?

- Accidentally injuring someone
- Working tenaciously to try to sell a product to a customer
- Biting someone on the neck
- Spanking a child
- Swinging a stick at someone but missing
- Hurling insults at someone
- Deliberately failing to prevent harm
- Murdering for money
- Hiring someone to break a competitor's kneecaps
- Hitting others while in a rage

Researchers, too, have engaged in classification exercises like this in order to determine the meaning of aggression. Not everyone agrees on every point; by 1983, there were more than 250 different definitions of aggression in the psychological literature (Harré & Lamb, 1983). Most definitions used today share a number of common features, however. Putting them together, we can define **aggression** as behavior that is intended to injure another person who does not want to be injured.

aggression Behavior intended to injure another person who does not want to be injured.

This definition rules out the first example in our list. Accidentally injuring someone is not an aggressive act, because there is no intent to harm. People commonly refer to the second example as aggressive behavior ("She is a very aggressive salesperson"), but social psychologists classify this behavior as *assertive* rather than aggressive because there is no intent to injure. Biting someone on the neck is an act of aggression unless the person being bitten clearly wanted to be bitten in that way. A parent who spanks a child is not necessarily being aggressive, if the spanking is done in moderation with no intent to injure. Actions that produce harm as an unintended by-product are not aggressive; a physician who administers a painful treatment does not act aggressively. In contrast, actions that do not cause harm but were intended to do so are aggressive. Swinging a stick to injure someone is an aggressive act, even if there is no contact.

Of course, any definition that relies on an individual's intentions has a serious drawback. We can't see another person's intentions, so how do we know what they are? And whose view do we accept if people disagree about someone's intentions? When defined in terms of intent, aggression lies ultimately in the eye of the beholder. The consequences of a harmful act may be obvious to everyone, but its characterization as aggressive is a matter of subjective judgment.

Aggressive behaviors come in many forms. Words as well as deeds can be aggressive. Quarreling couples who intend their spiteful remarks to hurt are behaving aggressively. Even failure to act can be aggressive. If you know your boss is in a lousy mood and doesn't want to see anyone, but you deliberately decide not to warn a bouncy co-worker preparing to barge right in because you'd like to see this person lose some of that bounce, your inaction could be considered aggression.

To distinguish them from less harmful behaviors, extreme acts of aggression are called *violence*. Some other terms in the language of aggression refer to emotions and attitudes. *Anger* consists of strong feelings of displeasure in response to a perceived injury; the exact nature of these feelings (for example, outrage, hate, or irritation) depends on the specific situation. *Hostility* is a negative, antagonistic attitude toward another person or group. Anger and hostility are often closely connected to aggression, but not always. People can be angry at others and regard them with great hostility without ever trying to harm them. And aggression can occur without a trace of anger or hostility, as when a contract killer murders a perfect stranger in order to "make a killing" financially.

The aggression of a hired gun is an example of **instrumental aggression,** in which harm is inflicted as a means to a desired end. Aggression aimed at harming someone for personal gain, attention, or even self-defense fits this definition. If the aggressor believes that there is an easier way to obtain the goal, aggression would not occur.

In **emotional aggression,** the means and the end coincide. Harm is inflicted for its own sake. Emotional aggression is often impulsive, carried out in the heat of the moment. The jealous lover strikes out in rage; fans of rival soccer teams go at each other with fists and clubs. Emotional aggression, however, can also be calm, cool, and calculating. Revenge, so the saying goes, is a dish best served cold.

Of course, sometimes it is hard to distinguish between instrumental and emotional aggression. Why did Mike Tyson viciously bite Evander Holyfield's ear during their 1997 championship boxing match? Was it a deliberate attempt to escape the embarrassment of being beaten by his opponent for the second time, or did he simply lose control and lash out against him in frustration? Perhaps no one other than Tyson himself can answer this question.

The definitions we have discussed are crucial first steps in the study of aggression. They provide the framework for the theories and research described in the following pages. But aggression raises moral questions that go beyond scientific

instrumental aggression
Inflicting harm in order to obtain something of value.

emotional aggression
Inflicting harm for its own sake.

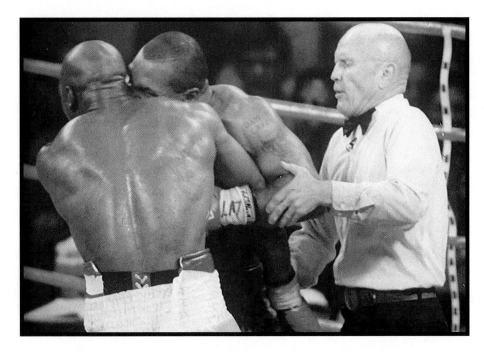

During their heavyweight boxing championship fight in June, 1997, former champion Mike Tyson viciously bites champion Evander Holyfield's ear. After chewing off pieces of both of Holyfield's ears, Tyson was disqualified, and a near-riot ensued in the ring. Was Tyson's attack an instance of instrumental aggression, in which he bit Holyfield's ears in order to stop a fight he felt he could not win, or emotional aggression, in which he lost his composure and snapped due to the frustration and pain he was experiencing?

findings. Is all aggression morally wrong? If not, when is aggression justifiable? Under what conditions is aggression preferable to other actions or responses? To answer such questions, each of us needs to carefully consider our own principles and values. Where do you draw the line?

Cultural and Gender Differences

J ust as not all types of aggression are alike, not all groups of people are alike in their attitudes and propensities toward aggression. Before we discuss the sources of aggression and what can be done about it, we need to consider how aggression is similar and how it differs across cultures and gender.

Cultural Variation

Cultures vary dramatically in how, and how much, their members aggress against each other. We can see this variation across societies and across specific groups, or subcultures, within a society.

Comparisons Across Societies   Like New York City, cities throughout the United States have enjoyed recent decreases in their rates of violent crimes; but the United States continues to be an exceptionally violent country. Its murder rate is one of the highest among industrialized nations, far worse than those in Canada, Australia, New Zealand, and much of Western Europe. However, several countries in Eastern Europe, Africa, Asia, and the Americas have much worse rates than the United States. Figure 11.1 illustrates some of the variation in homicide rates around the world.

The forms violence typically takes, and people's attitudes toward various kinds of aggression, also differ internationally. Relative to most of the world, the United

FIGURE 11.1   Violence Around the World

These figures indicate the number of murders per 100,000 people in each of several countries in 1994, according to United Nations statistics. As you can see, the frequency of murders varies widely around the world.

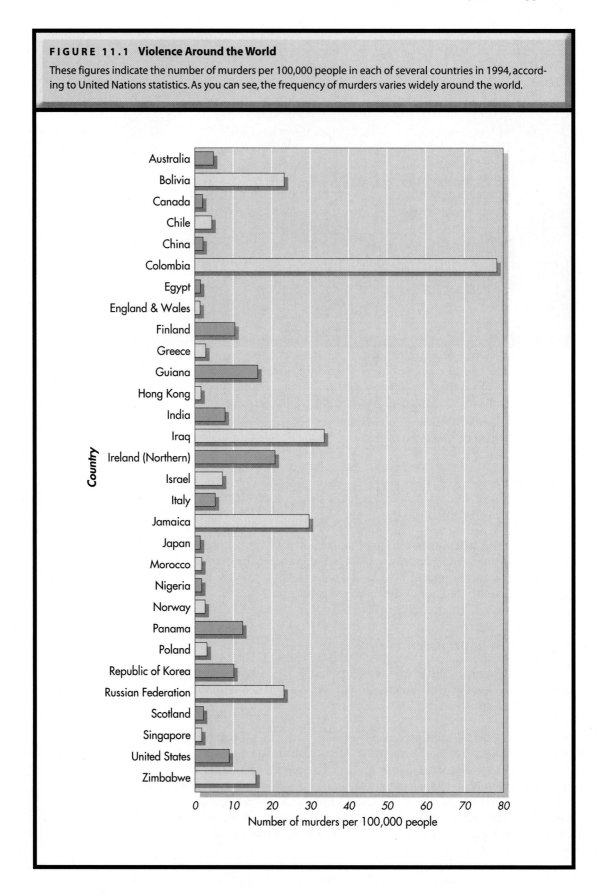

States has a tremendous amount of gun-related violence, and this violence tends to involve individuals rather than groups of people. Groups attacking other groups in political, ethnic, or tribal conflict are seen throughout the world but are particularly associated with the Middle East, Africa, and Eastern Europe. Until recently, violent mobs of European football (what Americans call "soccer") fans were common in England and Germany—behavior rarely seen at American sports events. Although this "hooliganism" has been less frequent recently in Western Europe, it seems to have been exported to Eastern Europe, as is evident in violence at games in Bucharest, Budapest, and Warsaw.

Cultures also differ in aggression involving children. For example, in Japan, it has been relatively common for Japanese adult businessmen to grope schoolgirls on public transportation—a practice that would be considered aggressive and unacceptable in many other cultures, including the far more violent United States (Kristof, 1997). Another example concerns female genital mutilation—any of several procedures in which, according to some estimates, approximately 6,000 girls a day have their genitals cut in many countries of Africa and Asia, as well as in New Zealand. The cultures that practice this consider it an important, sacred ritual; but the cultures that condemn it consider it an inhumane act of violence and have vigorously called for a world-wide ban (Swain, 1997).

Although violence seems to be just about everywhere, a handful of societies stand out as nonviolent exceptions. Bruce Bonta (1997) describes twenty-five societies around the world that are almost completely without violence. For example, the Chewong, who live in the mountains of the Malay Peninsula, do not even have words in their language for quarreling, fighting, aggression, or warfare. The most serious act of aggression noted during a year among the Ifaluk, who live on a small atoll in the Federated States of Micronesia, involved a man who "touched another on the shoulder in anger, an offense which resulted in a stiff fine." The Amish, the Hutterites, and the Mennonites are all societies that reside in the relatively violent United States (as well as in Canada) but remain remarkably nonviolent. Table 11.2 lists some of the other societies that Bonta identified as nonviolent. What makes all of these societies so peaceful? According to Bonta, all but two of these twenty-five societies strongly oppose competition and endorse cooperation in all aspects of their lives. This raises the possibility that cooperation and lack of competition may promote nonviolence.

Subcultures Within a Country

There are important variations in aggression within particular societies as a function of age,

TABLE 11.2 Nonviolent Societies

In addition to those discussed in the text, this table lists a few of the other societies that Bruce Bonta (1997) identified as nonviolent.

Society	Comments
Balinese (Indonesian island of Bali)	A researcher who was there for four years never even witnessed two boys fighting.
G/wi (Central Kalahari Desert of southern Africa)	They abhor violence and only take pleasure from fortunate events if they are in the company of group members.
Inuit (Arctic regions, including those in Siberia, Alaska, Canada, and Greenland)	They use strategies to control anger and prevent violence; they have a strong fear of aggression.
Ladakhis (Tibetan Buddhist society in northern India)	Villagers indicate that they have no memory of any fighting in the village.
Zapotec (Native American society in southern Mexico)	"Several researchers have been fascinated that one community is particularly peaceful, with very strong values that oppose violence, in contrast to other communities nearby where fighting and machismo are comparable with the rest of Mexico" (p. 320).

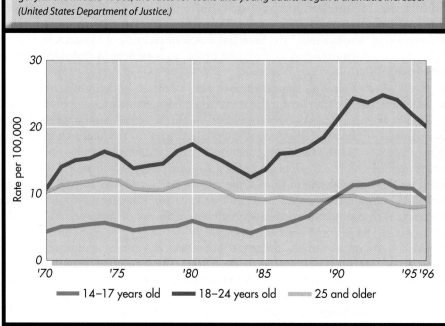

FIGURE 11.2   Murder Victims in the United States by Age, 1970–1996
These figures represent the number of murder victims per 100,000 people in each age category. In the middle 1980s, the rates for teens and young adults began a dramatic increase. *(United States Department of Justice.)*

class, race, and region. Identifying these differences can be critically important in understanding why, for example, violent crime rates in the United States have been decreasing, why these rates may increase in coming years, and why overall crime rates do not tell the complete story about the degree of violence that different groups of people are experiencing.

Teenagers and young adults, aged fourteen through twenty-four, have a much greater rate of involvement in violent crime—as both offenders and victims—than any other age group (see Figure 11.2). The fact that the American population has been aging in recent years is one of the reasons cited for the drop in violent crime rates. (Other factors that are noted frequently include longer jail sentences for criminals, more visible and community-oriented policing, a decline in the market for crack cocaine, tougher gun-control laws, and a booming economy.) As the post–World War II baby boomers began entering their forties and fifties in the mid–1990s, this large group of Americans became much less likely to commit acts of aggression and violence. Behind this calm may lurk a storm, however. There currently are more children under ten in the United States than at any time since the 1950s, and the number of teenagers is expected to start growing by about 1 percent a year through the year 2015, causing some criminologists to predict that the rates of violence will begin to rise again.

What about race? Despite the stories that get the most attention on the news, the large majority of murders are intra-racial rather than inter-racial. Among incidents involving one victim and one offender in the United States in 1995, 94 percent of black murder victims were killed by black offenders, and 84 percent of white murder victims were slain by white offenders. Nevertheless, African Americans live in a much more violent America than do Whites. Although there are far fewer black than white Americans, FBI statistics indicate that there were approximately the same number of black and white murder victims in 1996. For murders in which the offender was known, 52 percent of offenders were black and 45 percent white.

Regional differences are also striking. In the United States, the murder rate is consistently highest in the South, followed by the West. Many scholars have attributed the greater violence in the South and West to a "culture of honor" that is prevalent among white males in these regions. The culture of honor encourages violent responses to perceived threats against one's status as an honorable, powerful man (Cohen et al., 1998). We will focus more on the culture of honor later in the chapter (pp. 399–401).

Gender Differences

Despite all the variation across cultures, one thing is nearly universal: Men are more violent than women. This has been found in virtually all cultures studied around the world. According to U.S. Department of Justice data, 90 percent of murderers in 1996 were male, and 77 percent of murder victims were male. World Health Organization data indicate that for every 100,000 people in the country, 15.9 males and 4.2 females are murdered per year in the United States; 4.6 males and 2.4 females in Finland; 24.9 males and 6.7 females in the Russian Federation; and 31.5 males and 3.5 females in Mexico (Bulatao & VandenBos, 1996). Despite the significant variation in total violence from one country to another, the gender difference remains remarkably stable over time and place: Men commit the very large majority of homicides, and men comprise the very large majority of murder victims (Daly & Wilson, 1989; Kenrick, 1987).

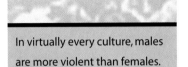

In virtually every culture, males are more violent than females. **True.**

Donald Reilly © 1995 from The New Yorker Collection. All Rights Reserved.

What about aggression in general, as opposed to violence? Even among children between three and six years old, boys show higher rates of physical aggression than girls (Loeber & Hay, 1997). Young boys play more aggressive games (mock fighting, cops and robbers) than girls, who tend to prefer more nurturant play (Jukes & Goldstein, 1993; Singer, 1994). Two-year-olds show different preferences for books: Boys like stories of violence and horror, and girls like more romantic tales (Collins-Standley et al., 1996). Indeed, even infants differ, with infant boys showing more anger and poorer regulation of their emotional states than infant girls (Weinberg & Tronick, 1997).

So, does all this mean that the stereotype that males are more aggressive than females is correct? Not necessarily. Most of the research has focused on the aggression typical of males: physical aggression. But think back to our definition of aggression: It concerns intent to injure. There are many ways to injure someone other than through physical means. Recent research has recognized this, and the results challenge the notion that males are more aggressive than females. The findings emerging can be summarized by a remark noted by Britt Galen and Marion Underwood (1997) in their research on aggression among adolescent girls and boys: "Boys may use their fists to fight, but at least it's over with quickly; girls use their tongues, and it goes on forever" (p. 589).

"It's a guy thing."

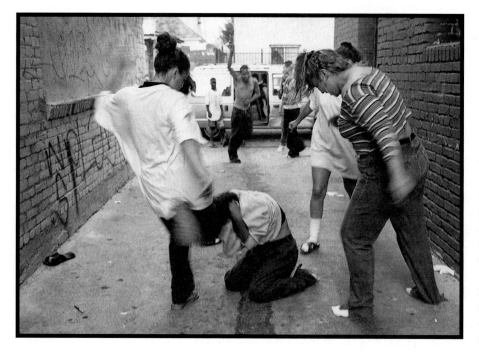

Men are more physically aggressive than women in most societies, but women, too, commit acts of physical violence. Here, a young woman is being brutally initiated into a gang by other female gang members.

Although boys tend to be more *overtly* aggressive than girls (Coie & Dodge, 1997), girls are often more *indirectly*, or *relationally*, aggressive than boys. These indirect, or relational, forms of aggression involve socially manipulating others in order to harm the target person, such as by spreading false stories, engaging in gossip and backbiting, and trying to get others to dislike the target. Nikki Crick and her colleagues (Crick et al., 1996; Crick & Grotpeter, 1995) believe that girls are more likely to use relational aggression because they typically care more about relationships and intimacy than boys do and so may see injuring someone socially as particularly effective. In studies conducted in several countries, including Finland, Argentina, Australia, and the United States, females were found to engage in indirect aggression more often than males (Björkqvist et al., 1992; Crick et al., 1997; Galen & Underwood, 1997; Hines & Fry, 1994; Owens & MacMullin, 1995).

Girls as young as preschool age tend to be more relationally aggressive than their male peers (Crick et al., 1997). The gender difference is clear through the school years, particularly from about age eleven. The difference begins to decline as the girls and boys become young adults, primarily because boys show a marked decrease in physical aggression from the age of fifteen to eighteen and a corresponding increase in their use of verbal and indirect aggression (Geen, 1998; Lagerspetz & Björkvist, 1994; Loeber & Hay, 1997).

Even the well-established gender difference in overt aggression appears to be an oversimplification. In a meta-analysis of sixty-four experiments, Ann Bettencourt and Norman Miller (1996) found that men consistently were more aggressive than women under neutral conditions but that this difference diminished significantly under conditions in which there was some clear provocation for the aggression, such as if the participants had been frustrated, insulted, or threatened. In many everyday life situations, however, men are quicker to aggress than women because they are more likely than women to interpret ambiguous situations as provoking (Bettencourt & Miller, 1996; Harris, 1995).

When girls or women can "hide" their overt aggression—from others or from themselves—their rates of aggression are more comparable with those of their male counterparts. When Debra Pepler and Wendy Craig (1995) videotaped children in schoolyards in Canada with hidden cameras, they found that bullying occurred at similar rates for girls and boys; but in interviews, girls were much less likely than boys to admit to bullying. In an experiment with female and male college students, Jennifer Lightdale and Deborah Prentice (1994) found that when experimental conditions were designed to make participants feel anonymous, men and women were equally aggressive. When the identities of the individuals were emphasized, however, women were less aggressive than men.

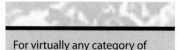

For virtually any category of aggression, males are more aggressive than females. **False.**

Origins of Aggression

Regardless of these various cultural and gender differences, aggression has been a prevalent part of human interaction throughout human history and around the world. It is not surprising that many have speculated about the origins of aggression. Where does it come from? Are we *born* aggressive, or are we *taught* to be aggressive? Many have argued for one side or the other of the "nature-nurture" debate—the "nature" side holding that aggression is an innate characteristic of human beings and the "nurture" side holding that aggression is learned through experience. In this section, we look at the theory and research most relevant to tracing the origins of human aggression. In reviewing each perspective, we examine how well it can account for the overall prevalence of aggression, as well as for the cultural and gender differences that we have discussed.

Is Aggression Innate?

Innate characteristics are not contingent on learning for their development, although they can be influenced by learning, culture, and other factors. Here, we examine three approaches to the issue of whether aggression is innate: instinct theories; evolutionary psychology accounts; and biological factors, including genes, hormones, and neurotransmitters.

Instinct Theories   On November 11, 1918, a human catastrophe finally ended. Covered in mud, lungs blasted by gas, millions of soldiers had died to gain bits and pieces of contested territory. For an Austrian physician named Sigmund Freud, the slaughter on the battlefields of Europe during World War I marked a turning point. Rejecting his prewar version of psychoanalysis, Freud (1920) proposed a grim new concept: the *death instinct*—a profound, unconscious desire to escape the tensions of living by becoming still, inanimate, dead. This impulse toward self-destruction does not, according to Freud, exist unchallenged. There is also a life instinct, which motivates human beings to preserve and reproduce themselves. Paradoxically, Freud considered aggression toward others to be a momentary victory for the life instinct. In aggression, the force of the death instinct is deflected outward at others rather than aimed inward toward the original target, the self.

Like Freud, Konrad Lorenz (1966) regarded aggression as an innate, instinctual motivation. Unlike Freud, who believed that the life and death instincts are antagonistic, Lorenz saw the will to live and the will to aggress as entirely compatible. Based on his observations of animals in their natural habitat, Lorenz argued that aggression secures an advantage in the struggle to survive. The individual who successfully aggresses against others gains access to valuable resources such as food, territory, and desirable mates. Because only those who survive are able to reproduce, natural selection would produce an aggressive instinct in humans as well as in other animals.

Despite the widespread attention that these theories received at the time they were formulated, they no longer have much influence on scientific research. The primary reason for their fall from favor is their reliance on circular reasoning. Why do people aggress? Because they have an aggressive instinct. How do we know that aggression is instinctive? Because people aggress. Case closed. But shut off from the exploration of testable alternatives, circular reasoning is a logical and scientific dead end. In addition, instinct theories cannot account adequately for the cultural and gender differences in aggression—except through more circular reasoning.

Evolutionary Psychology   There are clear similarities between Lorenz's instinct theory and evolutionary psychology, which uses principles of evolution to understand human social behavior. For example, Leda Cosmides and John Tooby share Lorenz's belief that human warfare originated in attempts to obtain valuable resources (Gibbons, 1993). These investigators, however, maintain that the earliest battles between men were fought over women rather than over food or land. To be well fed and have a safe territory can prolong life and indirectly enhance reproductive success—but having a mate is essential.

In contrast to Lorenz, evolutionary accounts emphasize genetic survival rather than survival of the individual. Because at least some of a person's genes can be transmitted through the reproductive success of genetic relatives, evolution should have favored the inhibition of aggression against those who are genetically related to us. For example, according to Martin Daly and Margo Wilson (1988, 1994, 1996), birth parents are much less likely to abuse or murder their own offspring than stepparents are to harm stepchildren. In two samples studied, preschool children living with a stepparent or foster parent were seventy to one hundred times more likely to be fatally abused than were children living with both biological parents.

What can account for the gender differences in aggression? From a strictly evolutionary perspective, for males to best ensure the survival of their genes, they should mate with attractive, healthy females and invest their time and resources only in offspring who are genetically related to them. Males are competitive with each other because females select high-status males for mating, and aggression is a means by which males traditionally have been able to achieve and maintain status. In addition, because human men, unlike women, cannot be sure that they are the true genetic parents of their children, men are predisposed to sexual jealousy. Behaviors triggered by sexual jealousy, including aggression and the threat of aggression, may be designed to enhance the male's confidence in his paternity of offspring. Consistent with evolutionary reasoning, crime statistics indicate that male-to-male violence is most likely to occur when one is perceived as challenging the other's status or social power, such as by attempting to humiliate him or to challenge his sexual relationships. Male-to-female violence is predominantly triggered by sexual jealousy (Buss & Kenrick, 1998; Buss & Shackelford, 1997; Wilson & Daly, 1996).

Evolutionary accounts have been challenged for a variety of reasons, including the historical and cultural diversity of human aggression (Ruback & Weiner, 1995). Within any society, the amount of aggression varies across time; and between societies, as illustrated in Figure 11.2, there are large differences in rates of violence. If aggression is innate and universal, how could people differ so much in when and where they display it? Faced with such variation, even some researchers who believe that aggression is an evolved characteristic have concluded that its occurrence is primarily determined by social factors (Lore & Schultz, 1993).

Responding to these challenges, evolutionary psychologists argue that the presence of cultural and historical variation is not inconsistent with evolution-based theories. Rather, evolutionary and social factors should be seen as compatible and complementary. Evolved psychological mechanisms develop in response to specific environmental contexts. David Buss (1995) points out, for example, that few doubt that our ability to develop calluses on our skin is an evolved physical reaction to environmental influences. Just because some people have lots of calluses and others don't does not invalidate the argument that evolutionary factors played a role in causing humans to evolve mechanisms that produce calluses to protect their skin. Similarly, the argument goes, one should not deny the role of evolution in human aggression just because some cultures are more violent than others. In addition, cultural differences themselves may be products of evolution, traced to different environmental pressures that required dissimilar adaptive responses (Buss & Malamuth, 1996).

Behavior Genetics   Evolutionary psychology involves tying together evolution, genetic transmission, and behavior. Behavior genetics settles for the complexities of connecting the latter two. Early in life, aggressiveness becomes a relatively stable personality characteristic—relative to other children, those who are high in aggressiveness when they are about eight years old are more likely to be aggressive later in life (Huesmann & Guerra, 1997). Can this aggressive personality type be due to genes?

To trace a line of genetic transmission (heritability), scientists examine differences between individuals or groups. Two types of studies are typically employed in research on humans. In twin studies, monozygotic twins (who are identical in their genetic make-up) are compared with dizygotic twins (who share only part of their genes). On any heritable trait, monozygotic twins will be more similar than dizygotic twins. Adoptee studies are also used in behavior genetics research. On any inherited trait, adopted children will resemble their biological parents more than they resemble their adoptive parents. Although twin and adoptee studies have produced some evidence supporting the heritability of human aggressive behavior (Carey, 1994; Gottesman & Goldsmith, 1994), the results overall have been somewhat mixed (Miles & Carey, 1997). More research, and particularly more research that uses diverse methods, needs to be done before a clearer picture of the heritability of aggression can be drawn.

The Role of Testosterone   In addition to the question of heritability, researchers have long been interested in determining what specific biological factors influence aggression (Renfrew, 1997). Because of the persistent sex differences in physical aggression found among humans and other animals, many researchers have wondered if testosterone plays a role. Although men and women both have this "male sex hormone," men usually have higher levels than do women. If testosterone affects aggressive behavior, then it could serve as the connection between biological gender and human aggression. A number of studies have documented an association between testosterone and aggression. These studies have used diverse samples of people, from prison inmates to college students to elderly men with dementias such as Alzheimer's disease. These studies tend to show a strong positive correlation between testosterone levels and physical aggression or violence (Berman et al., 1993; Dabbs et al., 1995; Orengo et al., 1997). One study found that college fraternities whose members tended to have higher testosterone levels were more rambunctious and exhibited more crude behavior than other fraternities; fraternities with lower testosterone levels tended to be more academically successful and socially responsible, and their members smiled more (Dabbs et al., 1996).

Intriguing as they are, such correlational findings cannot prove that testosterone causes aggression. There are other alternatives. For example, aggression can cause temporary increases in testosterone, if the aggression is successful. Even a game, such as tennis, chess, or a laboratory task, can temporarily increase the testosterone levels of winners and decrease the levels of losers (Gladue et al., 1989; Mazur & Lamb, 1980; Mazur et al., 1992). Stress may also be involved: Higher levels of stress are associated with higher levels of testosterone (Thompson et al., 1990). Testosterone levels are better predictors of antisocial behavior for individuals low in socioeconomic status than for those with greater income and education (Dabbs & Morris, 1990; Dabbs et al., 1990). Perhaps people who are poor and badly educated are more vulnerable to the kinds of stressors that simultaneously elevate both testosterone and aggression.

For ethical reasons, researchers do not manipulate people's levels of testosterone to measure its effects on aggression and other behaviors. But Stephanie Van Goozen and her colleagues (1995; Cohen-Ketteinis & Van Goozen, 1997) have studied individuals who were voluntarily manipulating their sex hormones—transsexuals undergoing sex reassignment treatments. The researchers administered tests of aggression to thirty-five female-to-male transsexuals and fifteen male-to-female transsexuals shortly before and three months after the start of cross-sex hormone treatment in a Dutch hospital. With their increase in male hormones, the female-to-male transsexuals exhibited increased aggression-proneness. In contrast, the deprivation of these hormones in the male-to-female group was associated with a decrease in aggression-proneness.

The Role of Serotonin Testosterone is not the only biological factor linked to human aggression. There has been an explosion of interest recently in the role of the neurotransmitter serotonin (Cleare & Bond, 1997; Cowley & Underwood, 1997/1998; Ferris et al., 1997; Pine et al., 1997; Siever & Frucht, 1997). Neurotransmitters such as serotonin act as chemical messengers in the nervous system, transmitting information. Serotonin appears to work like a braking mechanism to restrain impulsive acts of aggression. Low levels of serotonin in the nervous systems of humans and many animals are associated with high levels of aggression. Drugs that boost serotonin's activity can dampen aggressiveness, along with a range of other impulsive and socially deviant behaviors. Such drugs have even been used to treat "road rage"—people's impulsive acts of aggression and violence while driving (*St. Louis Post-Dispatch*, 1997). Is the lack of serotonin an innate cause of aggression?

Like testosterone, serotonin appears to be both a cause and a consequence of behaviors relevant to social status and dominance. In their work with vervet monkeys, for example, Gary Brammer and his colleagues (1994) found that individuals' social status influenced their levels of serotonin at least as much as their serotonin levels influenced their social status. Here again, biological and social factors interact with each other.

Is Aggression Learned?

Regardless of the precise contribution of genetic and biological factors, the importance of experience is clear: Aggressive behavior is strongly affected by learning (Bandura, 1973). Rewards obtained by aggression today increase its use tomorrow. Such rewards come in two flavors: *positive reinforcement*, when aggression produces desired outcomes, and *negative reinforcement*, when aggression prevents or stops undesirable outcomes. The child who gets a toy by hitting the toy's owner is likely to hit again. So, too, the child who can stop other children from teasing by shoving them away has learned the fateful lesson that aggression pays. Children who see aggression producing more good outcomes, and fewer bad ones, are more aggressive than other children (Boldizar et al., 1989).

Rewards are one part of the learning equation, but what about punishment? Punishment is often promoted as a way to reduce aggressive behavior. Can people learn not to act aggressively through punishment? New York City's Mayor Giuliani believes that the dramatic reduction in crime in the city in recent years is due in large part to swift, more effective punishment of all kinds of crimes, even relatively minor crimes such as vandalism, which sends the message that crime will lead to punishment. In fact, punishment can decrease aggression when it (a) immediately follows the aggressive behavior, (b) is strong enough to deter the

According to a 1997 Time/CNN poll, 67 percent of police chiefs said they don't think the death penalty deters homicides. In addition, 52 percent of Americans don't think the death penalty deters people from committing crime, and 60 percent don't think vengeance is a legitimate reason to execute a murderer, but 74 percent favor the death penalty.

—E. Pooley (Time, June 16, 1997)

aggressor, and (c) is consistently applied and perceived as fair and legitimate by the aggressor. However, such stringent conditions are seldom met. When courts are overburdened and prisons are overcrowded, as they are in the United States, the relationship between crime and punishment can seem more like a lottery than a rational system in which the punishment fits the crime (Berkowitz, 1993a; Smolowe, 1994).

There are some other problems with punishment as well. Punishment perceived as unfair or arbitrary can provoke retaliation, creating an escalating cycle of aggression. Perhaps most troubling is that punishment, especially when delivered in an angry or hostile manner, offers a model to imitate. Murray Straus and his colleagues (1997) have been outspoken critics of the use of *corporal punishment*—physical force (such as spanking, hitting, and pinching) intended to cause a child pain, but not injury, for the purpose of controlling or correcting the child's behavior. The large majority of children in the United States experience spanking and other forms of corporal punishment. Numerous studies, however, report a *positive* relationship between corporal punishment and the likelihood of aggression.

Correlational findings do not prove causality, however, and experiments using random assignment cannot be conducted to investigate spanking children. It is very possible that the aggressiveness of the children leads to more spanking, rather than the other way around. Some studies that have looked at this relationship longitudinally—measuring the use of corporal punishment and aggression at one time and measuring aggression at some later point—suggest that corporal punishment may indeed increase subsequent aggression. One study (Eron et al., 1991) reported that boys who received harsh punishment when they were eight years old were more aggressive than other males twenty-two years later on several measures of aggression, such as number of arrests, tendency to hit their spouses, and self-reported serious aggression. Another study (Straus et al., 1997) found that the more times a child was spanked during one week (as reported by the child's mother), the more likely the child was to display antisocial behavior, including aggression, two years later—even with the effects of the child's earlier antisocial behavior, gender, and ethnic background and the family's socioeconomic status ruled out. With these other factors controlled for, the researchers found that children who were spanked even once during that first week showed an increase in antisocial behavior two years later (Figure 11.3).

> Children who are spanked or otherwise physically disciplined (but not abused) for behaving aggressively tend to become less aggressive. **False.**

The relationship between parental corporal punishment and children's subsequent aggression is influenced by a number of factors, including the overall family environment, the emotions displayed by the parents during the punishment, and cultural and ethnic differences. For example, corporal punishment is less likely to increase aggressiveness when it is administered in the context of an overall warm and supportive parent-child relationship (Baumrind, 1996, 1997; Deater-Deckard & Dodge, 1997; Deater-Deckard et al., 1998).

Social Learning Theory The power of models to modify behavior is a crucial tenet of Albert

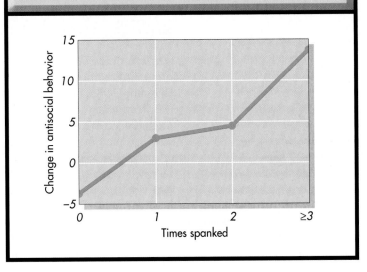

FIGURE 11.3 Spanking by Parents and Subsequent Antisocial Behavior by Children

In this study, researchers recorded the number of times in a week that children were spanked by parents and then measured the change after two years in the children's antisocial behavior. As you can see, the more the children were spanked, the more antisocial their behavior was two years later. *(Straus et al., 1997.)*

Young Palestinians imitate adult behavior by playing the "Intifada game."

Bandura's (1977b) **social learning theory.** Social learning theory emphasizes that we learn from the example of others as well as from direct experience with rewards and punishments. Models influence the prosocial, helpful behavior described in Chapter 10. They also affect antisocial, aggressive behavior. In an early study, Bandura and his associates (1961) observed the behavior of mildly frustrated children. Those who had previously watched an adult throw around, punch, and kick an inflatable doll were more aggressive when they later played with the doll than were those who had watched a quiet, subdued adult. These children followed the adult model's lead not only in degree of aggression but also in the kinds of aggression they exhibited. Subsequent research has amply demonstrated that a wide range of aggressive models can elicit a wide range of aggressive imitations. Furthermore, these models do not have to be present; people on TV—and even cartoon characters—can serve as powerful models of aggression (Bandura, 1983; Baron & Richardson, 1994; Berkowitz, 1993a).

Models who obtain desired goals through the use of aggression and are not punished for their behavior are the most likely to increase aggression among observers. But even those who are punished can have an effect. Postwar increases in homicide rates have been documented not only in rewarded, victorious countries that watched their soldiers prevail, but also in punished, defeated nations that saw their soldiers overwhelmed (Archer & Gartner, 1984). And for some, punishment seems to increase the influence of a model. Paul Hill, sentenced to death for murdering a physician and his bodyguard outside a Florida abortion clinic, said he didn't think of killing anyone himself until he saw Rachelle Shannon convicted for wounding a physician in Kansas: "I was encouraged and emboldened by her example."

We learn more than specific aggressive behaviors from aggressive models. We also develop more positive attitudes and beliefs about aggression in general, and we construct aggressive "scripts" to guide social behavior and social problem solving. These scripts can be activated automatically in various situations, leading to quick, often unthinking aggressive responses that follow the scripts we have been taught (Bandura, 1989; Huesmann, 1988).

Fortunately, changing the model can change the consequences: Nonaggressive models decrease aggressive behavior. Observing a nonaggressive response to a provoking situation teaches a peaceful alternative and strengthens existing restraints against aggression. In addition, observing someone who is calm and reasonable may help an angry person settle down rather than strike out. Aggression can spread like wildfire. But nonviolence, too, can be contagious (Baron & Kepner, 1970; Donnerstein & Donnerstein, 1976).

Socialization and Gender Differences: "Boys Will Be Boys"   To account for gender differences in aggression, learning approaches emphasize that males and

social learning theory The proposition that behavior is learned through the observation of others as well as through the direct experience of rewards and punishments.

females are taught different lessons about aggression—they are rewarded and punished differently for aggression and are presented with different models. Whether or not gender differences in aggressive behavior originated from innate biological factors, today they are maintained and perpetuated through lessons that are passed on from one generation to the next about the acceptability of various kinds and degrees of aggression.

Most researchers agree that social roles have a strong influence on gender differences in physical aggression (Eagly & Steffen, 1986; Eagly & Wood, 1991). As described in Chapter 5, males and females are socialized to fill different roles in society. Aggression tends to be more socially acceptable in stereotypically male roles than female roles.

When social norms constraining women from behaving aggressively are relaxed or are made less applicable to a particular situation, gender differences in aggression are reduced. This could account for the exceptions to the gender differences in aggression that we described earlier. When aggressive responses are justifiable because of a provocation, or when individuals are made to feel more anonymous and deindividuated and thus less connected to their norms and values, women exhibit as much aggression as men (Bettencourt & Miller, 1996; Lightdale & Prentice, 1994). In addition, although girls and boys often are taught (either explicitly or implicitly through rewards, punishments, and role models) that physical aggression is more acceptable for boys than girls, the same is not true for more indirect, relational kinds of aggression—the kinds that girls exhibit more than boys do.

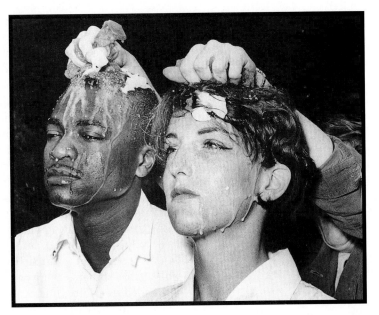

This photo, taken during the 1960's, shows civil rights demonstrators being trained to remain nonviolent despite the abusive and aggressive behavior they would encounter.

Socialization and Cultural Differences: Cultures of Honor   Socialization of aggression also varies from culture to culture. For example, Giovanna Tomada and Barry Schneider (1997) report that "Italians in traditional villages have been found to condone and encourage aggression among adolescent boys as an indication of their sexual prowess and as preparation for their dominant household role" (p. 601). Tomada and Schneider cite this as a reason why schoolyard bullying among elementary school boys is significantly higher in Central and Southern Italy than it is in Norway, England, Spain, or Japan (Genta et al., 1996). Similarly, some researchers believe that *machismo*—which in its most stereotyped characterization prescribes that challenges, abuse, and even differences of opinion "must be met with fists or other weapons" (Ingoldsby, 1991, p. 57) contributes to the fact that rates of violence are higher among Latin-American men than European-American men (Harris, 1995).

Machismo may represent one form of what anthropologists call a *culture of honor*, which emphasizes honor and social status, particularly for males, and the role of aggression in protecting that honor. Even minor conflicts or disputes are often seen as challenges to social status and reputation and can therefore trigger aggressive responses. Several such subcultures exist in the United States (and *Star Trek* fans might recognize the Klingon empire as an intergalactic example of a culture of honor). In an extensive series of studies, Dov Cohen and Richard Nisbett have focused on the culture of honor among white men in the American South. Nisbett and Cohen (1996) report that rates of violence are consistently higher in the South than in all other regions. For example, the South has led the rest of the country in

According to FBI statistics, the South consistently has the highest murder rate among regions in the United States, and the West consistently has the second highest rate. For 1996, the rates of murder per 100,000 residents in each region were as follows: Northeast 8.2; Midwest 7.6; South 11.3; West 9.9.

homicides ever since records have been kept. How did this culture originate? Nisbett and Cohen note that while northern towns were being settled mostly by farmers, the South was being settled by herders, whose "manly honor" was necessary to protect their flocks. The settlers of the South tended to come from herding cultures with inadequate law enforcement, and the herdsmen of the South had to protect their own herds from being stolen by others. As one North Carolina proverb observed, "Every man should be sheriff on his own hearth" (Fischer, 1989, p. 765).

Are southerners today more prone to honor-related aggression than people from other parts of the United States? Nisbett and Cohen believe so. They have collected data from surveys, field experiments, and laboratory experiments suggesting that the culture of honor persists today, and that this culture promotes violent behavior. Southerners are more likely than northerners to agree that "a man has the right to kill" in order to defend his family and house; and they are more accepting of using violence to protect one's honor (but not violence unrelated to the protection of honor) than are people from other parts of the country. In one series of experiments (Cohen et al., 1996), researchers investigated how white male students who had grown up either in the North or in the South responded to insults. The experiments, conducted on a large midwestern campus, involved an encounter that took place as the participant and the confederate were passing each other in a narrow hallway. The confederate did not give way to the participant, bumped into him, and hurled the insult. Compared with northerners, southerners were more likely to think that their masculine reputations had been threatened; exhibited greater physiological signs of being upset; appeared more physiologically primed for aggression (their testosterone levels rose); and engaged in more aggressive and dominant subsequent behavior (gave firmer handshakes) and were more unwilling to yield to a subsequent confederate as they walked toward each other in a very narrow hallway (see Figure 11.4).

Institutions support norms about the acceptability of honor-based violence. Cohen and Nisbett (1997) sent letters to employers all over the United States from a fictitious job applicant who admitted having been convicted of a felony. To

U.S. Marine paratroopers earn a pair of gold pins upon completion of ten training jumps. In February 1997, it was revealed, as captured on videotape, that this achievement is marked by "blood pinning"—a brutal hazing in which veteran Marines punch, pound, and grind the pins into the chests of the new initiates, who scream and writhe in pain. As military leaders try to crack down on this violent "rite of passage," others defend it as an important part of the "macho," honor-bound culture of the Marines.

FIGURE 11.4   Insult, Aggression, and the Southern Culture of Honor

White male participants from either North or South regions of the United States either were bumped and insulted by a male confederate, or they passed the confederate without incident (control condition). As you can see, the incident had a greater effect on southern participants. Specifically, they thought that they would be seen as less masculine (left); their testosterone levels increased more (center); and they were slower to yield to a confederate who later approached them in a narrow corridor (right). *(Cohen et al., 1996.)*

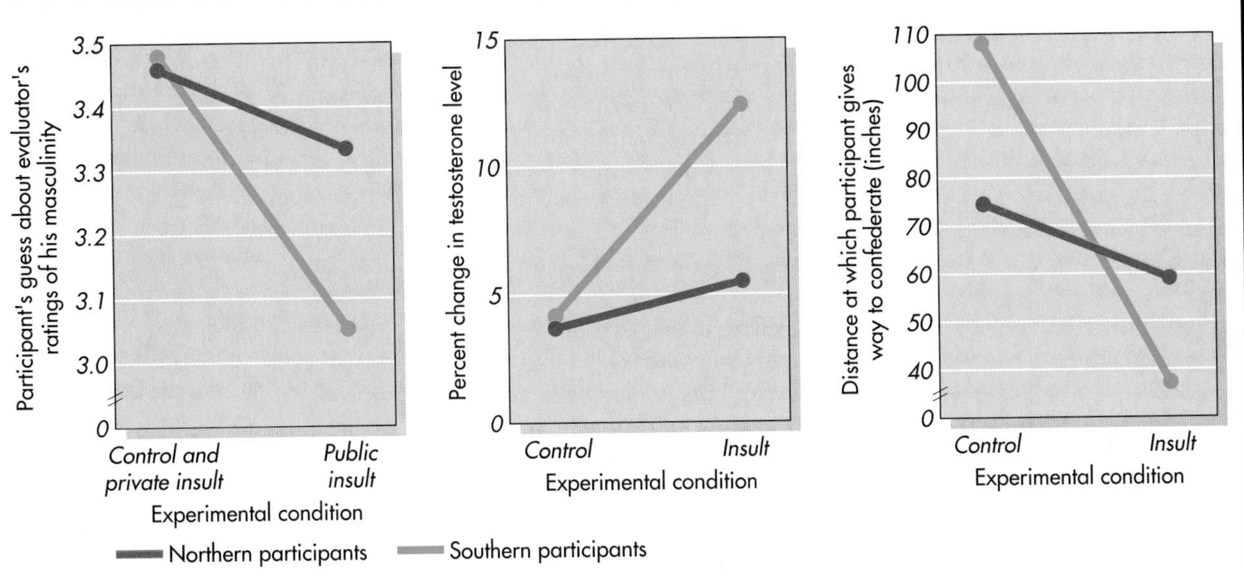

half the employers, the applicant reported that he had impulsively killed a man who had been having an affair with his fiancée and who tried to humiliate him verbally and then physically at a crowded bar. To the other half, the applicant reported that he had stolen a car because he needed the money to pay off debts. Employers from the South and the West (which has a culture of honor similar to the South's) were more likely than their northern counterparts to respond in an understanding and cooperative way to the letter from the convicted killer—but not from the auto thief.

Nature Versus Nurture: A False Debate?

The origins of aggression are a source not only of scientific disagreement but also of political controversy. Heated debates about funding research and treatment programs frequently occur among politicians who disagree strongly on whether aggression is, to any significant extent, attributable to genetic inheritance or stable biological characteristics present at birth. However important it may be, this contentious issue should not obscure the considerable agreement that exists on other points. The effects of learning are not disputed; aggression is, at least to some extent, "made" by experience. Nor is there any doubt that in aggression, as in all human behavior, biology and environment interact. Evolutionary accounts emphasize genetic predispositions as well as adaptations to immediate environmental contexts. Biological factors affect, and are affected by, social interactions. Social and cultural norms may have their roots in evolutionary and biological phenomena, but they exert direct influences on individuals today largely independent of their contemporary adaptive or biological significance. The debate between nature and nurture may rage on politically, but scientifically it is clear that the origins of human aggression represent a profound interaction of innate predispositions and environmental and social factors.

Situational Influences on Aggression

Whatever the ultimate causes of aggression, it is clear that specific, immediate situational factors can promote or inhibit aggressive thoughts and actions. In this section, we take a close look at several of these factors: frustration, negative affect, arousal, and factors that influence people's thoughts and information processing.

Frustration: Aggression as a Drive

In 1939, the year that World War II began, John Dollard and his colleagues published *Frustration and Aggression*, one of the most influential books on aggression ever written. This book sets forth two major propositions, which taken together are called the **frustration-aggression hypothesis:** (1) Frustration produced by interrupting a person's progress toward an expected goal will always elicit the motive to aggress. (2) All aggression is caused by frustration.

Dollard and his colleagues claimed that the motive to aggress is a psychological drive that resembles physiological drives like hunger. According to this theory, just as food deprivation elicits a hunger drive, so does frustration elicit an aggressive drive. Just as the hunger drive prompts the search for food, so does the aggressive drive prompt the attempt to inflict injury. But hunger does not always result in eating. Sometimes there's no food to be found or there's a fear that if one grabs a piece of another's feast, punishment will result. Similarly, the drive to aggress can be blocked if the source of the frustration is not present or the potential aggressor fears punishment for attacking.

Such obstacles, however, were not viewed by Dollard and his colleagues as permanent barriers against aggression. Instead, they believed that the aggressive drive seeps out in the form of **displacement.** Here, the inclination to aggress is deflected from the real target only to land on a substitute. After a bad day at work or at school, do you sometimes come home and yell at the first available target—be it man, woman, or beast? If so, what is the effect on you? Does yelling at an innocent bystander reduce your inclination to take revenge on the person who gave you a hard time?

The efficacy of such substitute actions was warmly endorsed by Dollard and his colleagues in their notion of **catharsis.** Just as hunger can be satisfied by hamburgers as well as by caviar, so any aggressive act should reduce the motive to engage in any other aggressive behavior. Since the Dollard group defined aggression quite broadly—to include making hostile jokes, telling violent stories, cursing, and observing the aggression of others, real or fictional—they held out the hope that engaging in some relatively harmless pursuit could drain away energy from more violent tendencies.

Problems and Limitations   Obviously, there is a connection between frustration and aggression. Break into a line of shoppers at the supermarket or interrupt a student cramming for an exam, and you can see it for yourself. But does frustration always produce the desire to aggress? And is all aggression the product of frustration?

frustration-aggression hypothesis The idea that (1) frustration always elicits the motive to aggress and (2) all aggression is caused by frustration.

displacement Aggressing against a substitute target because aggressive acts against the source of the frustration are inhibited by fear or lack of access.

catharsis A reduction of the motive to aggress that is said to result from any imagined, observed, or actual act of aggression.

Critics were quick to point out that the Dollard group had overstated their case. Early on, Neal Miller (1941), one of the originators of the hypothesis, acknowledged that frustration does not always produce aggressive inclinations. Subsequent research indicated that frustration is most likely to produce an aggressive response when people are kept from reaching an important goal to which they feel entitled (Blanchard & Blanchard, 1984; Worchel, 1974). The other absolute, that all aggression is caused by frustration, was soon overturned as well. In the following pages, we will consider many other causes of aggression.

The concept of displacement was also subjected to close scrutiny. In 1940, Carl Hovland and Robert Sears proposed that aggression by Whites against Blacks reflected the displacement of aggressive tendencies actually caused by economic frustration. Reviewing information on fourteen southern states from 1882 to 1930, these investigators found a strong negative correlation between economic indicators and the number of lynchings of African American men. When the southern economy declined, more lynchings occurred. Subsequent studies have confirmed this correlation between economic distress and racial violence (Beck & Tolnay, 1990; Hepworth & West, 1988).

Ervin Staub (1996) proposed recently that genocide and mass killing, such as during the Holocaust and the "ethnic cleansing" in the former Yugoslavia, may typically have their roots in societal frustrations arising from economic and social difficulties. These frustrations give rise to *scapegoating*—or blaming a particular minority group or groups for the problems the overall society is facing. In contrast, when the economy and social conditions are improving, aggression may decrease. Many believe that recent reductions in violent crimes in New York City and other cities across the United States are due to improvements in the U.S. economy.

However, these correlational findings do not prove the validity of the concept of displacement. Overall, evidence for the role of displacement in channeling aggressive behavior is inconclusive (Zillmann, 1979). As we will see later in this chapter, other processes can explain why it's possible to be provoked by one person but aggress against someone else.

Perhaps because it seemed to offer a way to control aggression, the concept of catharsis received particular attention. Dollard and his colleagues described catharsis as a two-step sequence. First, aggression reduces the level of physiological arousal. Second, because arousal is reduced, people are less angry and less likely to aggress further. It sounds logical, and many people believe it. For example, Gordon Russell and his colleagues (1995) reported that more than two-thirds of Canadian respondents in their research agreed with statements reflecting a belief in the effectiveness of catharsis (such as the statement that participating in aggressive sports is a good way to get rid of aggressive urges). Catharsis has been used by school administrators and others to justify violent sports (Bennett, 1991).

Exclusive: **The Most Daring Computer Cracker** ◆ **New Care for Alzheimer's Patients**

U.S.News & WORLD REPORT

JUNE 2, 1997 / $2.95

Road Rage

Why American drivers are ruder, meaner, and more dangerous than ever

As this cover story from an issue of U.S. News and World Report indicates, aggressive behavior on the road—what has been labelled "Road Rage"—is now a major problem in the United States, as well as in many parts of the world. A large majority of these acts of aggression stem from frustration—such as frustration about being stuck in traffic or cut off by another driver.

Since 1970, the mileage driven on U.S. roads has grown four times as fast as the population and eighteen times as fast as new roads (USA Today, January 16, 1998). Could this be a major source of frustration, which can cause "road rage"?

But, put to the test, catharsis has not lived up to its advertisement. Most researchers doubt that catharsis is the panacea that the Dollard group hoped it would be (Geen & Quanty, 1977). Here's why:

- Imagined aggression or the observation of aggressive models is more likely to increase arousal and aggression than to reduce them. Indeed, this is a central point of social learning theory.
- Actual aggression can lower arousal levels. However, if aggressive intent remains, "cold-blooded" aggression can still occur. Furthermore, if aggression-produced reduction of arousal feels good to the aggressor, this reward makes it more likely that aggression will occur again—another important point from social learning theory.
- Even relatively low levels of aggression can chip away at restraints against more violent behavior.

Aggressive behavior may well reduce the likelihood of further immediate aggression. In the long run, however, successful aggression sets the stage for more aggression later. In sum, relying on catharsis is dangerous medicine—more likely to inflame aggression than to put it out.

Frustration-Aggression Theory Revised   After bearing so much criticism, the frustration-aggression hypothesis seemed torn and tattered. But Leonard Berkowitz's (1989) reformulation put the hypothesis in a new perspective. According to Berkowitz, frustration is but one of many unpleasant experiences that can lead to aggression by creating negative, uncomfortable feelings. It is these negative feelings, not the frustration itself, that can trigger aggression. And as we'll see, negative feelings play a major role in influencing aggression.

Negative Affect

The key concept of negative affect opens all sorts of aggressive doors. In addition to frustrating experiences, a wide variety of noxious stimuli can create negative feelings and increase aggression: noise (Geen & McCown, 1984), crowding (Fisher et al., 1984), physical pain (Berkowitz, 1993b; Berkowitz & Heimer, 1989), threatened self-esteem (Baumeister et al., 1996), bad odors (Rotton & Frey, 1985), cigarette smoke (Zillmann et al., 1981), and having your home team lose a professional football playoff game (White, 1989). Reactions to a very common unpleasant condition, hot weather, are especially intriguing. Many people assume that temperature and tempers rise together, while others think it's just a myth. Who is right?

Heat and Aggression: Losing Your Cool   Craig Anderson and his colleagues have conducted extensive research on the question of whether heat leads to aggression; and data across time, cultures, and methodologies strongly support the notion that people lose their cool in hot temperatures and behave more aggressively (Anderson, 1989; Anderson & Anderson, 1998). More violent crimes occur in the summer than in the winter, during hot years than in cooler years, and in hot cities than in cooler cities at any given time of year. The numbers of political uprisings, riots, homicides, assaults, rapes, and reports of violence all peak in the summer months (see Figure 11.5). Indirect acts of aggression also increase in excessive heat. As temperatures rise to uncomfortable levels, laboratory participants become more likely to interpret ambiguous events in hostile terms (Rule et al., 1987), and drivers in cars without air-conditioning become more likely to honk their horns at motorists whose cars are stalled in front of them (Kenrick & MacFarlane, 1986). Alan Reifman and his colleagues (1991) found that as the temperature rises, major-league

---

Blowing off steam by engaging in safe but aggressive activities (such as sports) makes people less likely to aggress later.
False.

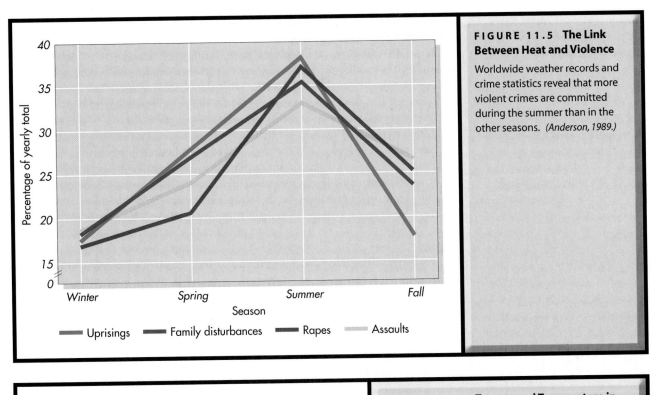

FIGURE 11.5 The Link Between Heat and Violence

Worldwide weather records and crime statistics reveal that more violent crimes are committed during the summer than in the other seasons. *(Anderson, 1989.)*

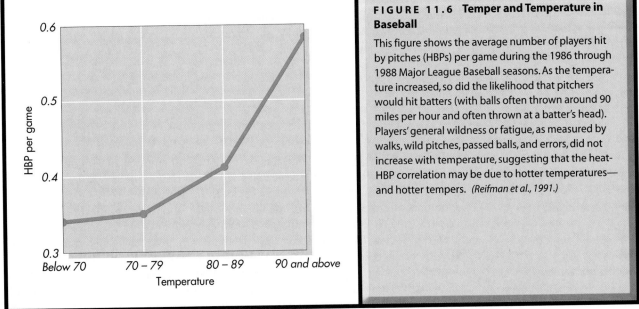

FIGURE 11.6 Temper and Temperature in Baseball

This figure shows the average number of players hit by pitches (HBPs) per game during the 1986 through 1988 Major League Baseball seasons. As the temperature increased, so did the likelihood that pitchers would hit batters (with balls often thrown around 90 miles per hour and often thrown at a batter's head). Players' general wildness or fatigue, as measured by walks, wild pitches, passed balls, and errors, did not increase with temperature, suggesting that the heat-HBP correlation may be due to hotter temperatures—and hotter tempers. *(Reifman et al., 1991.)*

baseball pitchers are more likely to hit batters with a pitch; the pitchers aren't wilder in general (such as in their number of walks or wild pitches)—just more likely to hit batters (see Figure 11.6).

Of course, the increase in aggressive behavior as the temperature rises can't continue indefinitely. At some point, aggression must decline, because people sicken and even die during extreme heat. According to the *negative affect escape model* (Baron, 1977; Baron & Richardson, 1994), as the intensity of noxious stimuli increases, so do negative affect and aggression—up to the point where nonaggressive responses such as escape or fatigue become dominant and aggression declines.

"By far, the worst thing about the firehouse was the heat. It got really, really hot inside there the last few weeks of shooting. We had no air conditioning and the hotter it got, the angrier we got."

—Jason, discussing his experiences on MTV's The Real World: Boston

However, evidence concerning where that turning point is—and whether it even exists within the range of temperatures that most people normally experience—has been mixed (Anderson & Anderson, 1998; Cohn & Rotton, 1997). In addition, uncomfortably cold temperatures may also increase aggressiveness, although people typically are better able to find relief from the cold than from the heat. In laboratory settings in which such escape is not available, aversively cold conditions do increase aggression (Anderson & Anderson, 1998).

Given the earlier discussion of the culture of honor and the high incidence of violence in the American South, you may wonder whether it is culture or heat that contributes to the violence. At this point, evidence points to both influences as important. Each probably has independent effects on aggression. In addition, they may interact with each other—for example, the relatively high temperatures of the region may support aggressive norms (Anderson & Anderson, 1996; Nisbett & Cohen, 1996).

Positive Affect: Reducing Retaliation   Like frustration and noxious stimuli, the unpleasant experience of provocation also increases aggression. Most aggressive incidents can be directly linked to some type of provocation (Anderson, 1998). But why does provocation trigger retaliatory aggression? The answer would seem to be a familiar one: negative affect. If so, then creating positive emotional reactions should cancel out negative feelings and thereby reduce retaliatory aggression. It does. In one study, participants were first provoked and angered by an experimental confederate (Baron & Ball, 1974). They were then shown funny cartoons or neutral pictures. Presented with an opportunity to retaliate by delivering electric shocks as part of a supposed learning experiment, those who had seen the cartoons delivered fewer shocks. Feeling good appears to be incompatible with anger and aggression. Feeling concerned about others has similar effects. An empathic response to another person reduces aggression against that individual (Miller & Eisenberg, 1988).

Approximately one-third of all murders in the United States stem from arguments, far more than from felonious activities such as robbery and arson.

Arousal: "Wired" for Action

Research on affect clearly indicates that the type of emotion (positive or negative) influences aggression. The intensity of arousal is important as well. In Chapter 9, we described the process of *excitation transfer*, in which the arousal created by one stimulus can intensify an individual's emotional response to another stimulus (Zillmann, 1984, 1996). For example, men who engaged in vigorous exercise were later more attracted to an attractive female than were those who had barely moved (White et al., 1981). Physical exercise is a highly arousing but emotionally neutral experience. Can it increase aggression as well as attraction?

For an answer, consider a study conducted by Dolf Zillmann and his colleagues (1972). Male participants were either angered or not angered by an experimental confederate and then either did or did not engage in strenuous physical exercise. Next, all participants were given the opportunity to shock the confederate in the context of a supposed learning experiment. As the researchers had predicted, angered participants who had exercised delivered shocks of greater intensity than did participants who had not been angered or who had not exercised. The scope of excitation transfer is not limited to physical exercise. Noise, violent motion pictures, arousing music—all have been shown to increase aggression (Zillmann, 1983). Heat has an interesting effect on arousal: Although people believe that heat lowers arousal, it actually increases it. This misperception makes heat a prime candidate for excitation transfer, as people are likely to misattribute arousal caused by heat to something else, such as anger, which can then lead to aggression (Anderson

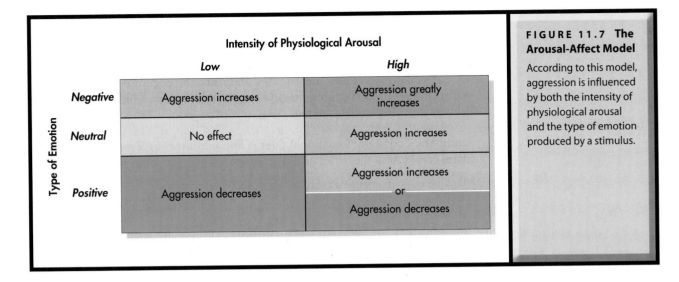

FIGURE 11.7 The Arousal-Affect Model

According to this model, aggression is influenced by both the intensity of physiological arousal and the type of emotion produced by a stimulus.

et al., 1996). Later in this chapter, we describe the effects of another arousing stimulus—pornography—on the inclination to aggress.

Thus far, we have treated the type of emotion and the intensity of physiological arousal as separate territories. But they can be unified. Focusing primarily on retaliatory aggression, the **arousal-affect model** (Sapolsky, 1984; Zillmann & Bryant, 1984) provides a systematic integration that summarizes a number of the findings we've discussed. As you can see in Figure 11.7, experiences that create negative emotions increase aggression; add high arousal, and the combination could be lethal. Experiences that are emotionally neutral have little impact on aggression, *unless* they are highly arousing. Experiences that create positive emotions and low arousal decrease aggression. Now comes the hard part: experiences that produce positive emotions and high arousal. Will aggression decrease because a positive emotional experience is incompatible with unpleasant angry feelings? Or will aggression increase because there's a lot of arousal available for transfer? It's a tough call and could go either way—depending on the individual, the situation, and the thoughts that come to mind.

Thought: Automatic and Deliberate

Step by step, we have been making our way toward a comprehensive theory of social and situational influences on aggression, particularly emotional aggression. We've examined several kinds of unpleasant experiences (frustration, noxious stimuli, and provocation) that create negative affect. We've considered how changes in negative affect (decreasing it by positive emotions, intensifying it by high arousal) produce corresponding changes in aggression. The next step is to add cognition. People don't just feel; they also think. What is the role of thought in aggressive behavior?

According to Leonard Berkowitz's **cognitive neoassociation analysis,** it has a star part. This theory proposes that feelings and thoughts interact. Negative affect automatically stimulates various thoughts, memories, and other reactions that are relevant to two basic tendencies: fight and flight. These automatic thoughts and reactions give rise to basic emotional experiences of anger and fear. How individuals ultimately respond to these automatic thoughts and emotions is influenced by subsequent higher-order cognitive processing. People interpret the situation they are in (Was that an insult or a joke?), think about how they feel (How angry am I?),

arousal-affect model The proposal that aggression is influenced by both the intensity of arousal and the type of emotion produced by a stimulus.

cognitive neoassociation analysis The view that unpleasant experiences create negative affect, which in turn stimulates associations connected with anger and fear. Emotional and behavioral outcomes then depend, at least in part, on higher-order cognitive processing.

make causal attributions for what led them to feel this way (I'm angry because of that remark), and weigh the consequences of acting on their feelings (What would be the risk of retaliation?). These thoughts produce more clearly differentiated feelings of anger or fear, as well as intentions to act (Berkowitz, 1993).

Let's take a closer look at two major influences on cognition: situational cues, which trigger automatic thoughts, and cognitive mediators, which influence more deliberate, higher-order thinking.

Automatic Cognition: Situational Cues   The deadliest aggression in the United States comes from the barrel of a gun.

- The large majority of murders are committed with guns.
- In several states, more people die from gunshots than from traffic accidents.
- Nearly half of all Americans have firearms in the home; those who keep guns are almost three times more likely to be killed at home as those who don't.
- In a national survey of students in the sixth through twelfth grades, 59 percent said they knew where to get a gun if they needed one, 15 percent said they'd carried a handgun in the past thirty days, and 11 percent said they'd been shot at.
- The number of gun-related murders committed by juvenile offenders aged ten to seventeen more than doubled from 1976 to 1992.

Faced with such gruesome statistics (*Newsweek*, 1995), the National Rifle Association (NRA) responds that guns should not be blamed. People, the NRA says, pull the trigger. Guns are the instrument, not the cause.

But are guns entirely neutral? Or does the presence of a weapon act as a situational cue that automatically triggers aggressive thoughts and feelings, thereby increasing the likelihood of aggression? In a classic study designed to address these questions, male participants who had been provoked by an experimental confederate delivered more shocks to him when a revolver and rifle were present (allegedly for use in a different study) than when badminton racquets and shuttlecocks were scattered about (Berkowitz & LePage, 1967). This tendency for the presence of guns to increase aggression is called the **weapons effect.** As Berkowitz put it: "The finger pulls the trigger, but the trigger may also be pulling the finger" (1968, p. 22).

Recent research by Craig Anderson and his colleagues (1996) gives further support to the idea that guns can have this effect. Participants exposed to pictures of guns automatically activated aggression-related thoughts. Hostile words like *assault, butcher, punch,* and *torture* were more accessible to these participants than to participants exposed to neutral pictures.

In general, any object or external characteristic that is associated with (1) successful aggression or (2) the negative affect of pain or unpleasantness can serve as an aggression-enhancing situational cue (Berkowitz, 1993a, 1993b). Such cues can have very strong effects, increasing people's hostility and likelihood of aggressing. In addition, stimuli that would not serve as aggression-enhancing cues for some people can be aggression-enhancing cues for others. People who tend to be aggressive associate significantly more cues with aggression and hostility than do people who are not as chronically aggressive; thus, they are particularly prone to automatically activating aggression-related thoughts (Bushman, 1996).

Higher-Order Cognition: Cognitive Control   Situational cues affect a network of automatic associations. More complex information about one's situation, however, influences the deliberate, thoughtful consideration that we call higher-order cognitive processing. For example, an angry person might refrain from acting aggressively if the potential costs of fighting seem too high. In this case, the person might choose to flee rather than fight. In addition, people whose cognitive beliefs about the acceptability of aggression imply that aggression is inappropriate in a particular

weapons effect The tendency of weapons to increase the likelihood of aggression by their mere presence.

situation, or whose moral values and principles mandate nonviolent behavior, may realize that better alternatives to aggression exist (Bandura et al., 1996; Huesmann & Guerra, 1997). The behavior of other people in the immediate situation can also influence an individual's considerations. If one or more others in a group are reacting aggressively to the situation, aggression can be contagious (Levy & Nail, 1993).

People's thoughts about the intentions of other people can determine whether they are likely to respond aggressively. For example, what if a person who has injured you claims that the action was unintentional? You have to think it over and decide whether you're convinced. If you are, the person may get a pass, and you are less likely to be angry or aggressive in response (Betancourt & Blair, 1992). Perhaps because it reduces the perception of intent, apologizing for having hurt someone reduces the victim's tendency to retaliate (Ohbuchi et al., 1989). **Mitigating information** indicating that an individual should not be held responsible for aggressive acts should also diminish perceived intent to harm. In criminal law, defendants are excused for aggression that is thought to result from insanity, coercion, ignorance, or self-defense. In our personal lives, too, we find room for forgiveness (Hodgins et al., 1996; McCullough et al., 1997). The friend whose love affair just broke up, the co-worker whose job is in danger—we don't hold them fully responsible for their actions. Whether we refrain from retaliating against them, however, may depend on when we learn about their stressful situation. In one study, participants who were aware of mitigating information before being attacked by another person stayed calm and were unaggressive. Those who learned about the other person's stressful situation only after being provoked experienced decreased physiological arousal but still retaliated (Zillmann & Cantor, 1976). Learning mitigating information can reduce our negative thoughts; but the negative affect that had been created may linger, leaving an increased likelihood of aggression (Dill & Anderson, 1995, Zillmann, 1996). Sometimes mitigating information is "too little, too late."

Whether or not perceivers interpret someone's actions as intentional or react to their apologies with understanding can vary as a function of individual differences. Socially maladjusted children, who are chronically aggressive and rejected by their peers, see hostile intent where others don't (Crick & Dodge, 1994). Such perceptions then increase their aggression, and their peers respond by rejecting them further, locking these children into an ever-escalating vicious cycle. Chronically aggressive adults similarly expect and perceive hostility in others' motives and behaviors (Dill et al., 1997). Individuals also differ in how they manage and express their anger. Some people tend to react to anger in constructive ways, such as by initiating communication designed to resolve conflict. Others react more destructively, lashing out at those around them. People who tend to manage their anger in destructive, maladaptive ways are prone to feelings of hostility directed at others as well as at themselves, leaving them more vulnerable to self-perpetuating cycles of negative affect, hostile cognitions, and aggression (Eisenberg et al., 1992; Tangney et al., 1996).

Some conditions make it more difficult to engage in higher-order processing. High arousal, for example, impairs the cognitive control of aggression (Zillmann et al., 1975). So does alcohol. Alcohol is implicated in the majority of violent crimes, suicides, and automobile fatalities. The evidence is quite clear about this point: Alcohol consumption often increases aggressive behavior (Bushman & Cooper, 1990). Even among individuals who are usually not aggressive and who are not provoked, those who drink more, aggress more (Bailey & Taylor, 1991). Moreover, clean living in the past will not protect you. People who usually drink very little are more responsive to the aggression-enhancing effects of alcohol than are those who have more experience with alcohol (Laplace et al., 1994).

But how does alcohol increase aggression? According to most investigators, drinking disrupts the way we process information (Leonard, 1989). Claude Steele

"Since war begins in the minds of men, it is in the minds of men that the defenses of peace must be constructed."

—Constitution of UNESCO

mitigating information Information about a person's situation indicating that he or she should not be held fully responsible for aggressive actions.

and Robert Josephs (1990) propose that intoxication causes what they call *alcohol myopia*—where there are multiple things to pay attention to, as is the case in most interpersonal situations, intoxicated people respond to initial, salient information about the situation but often miss later, more subtle indicators. They may focus on the perceived provocation but not on mitigating information or the potential costs of retaliating. A meta-analysis of forty-nine studies concerning alcohol and aggression found support for the idea that alcohol diminishes people's capacity to attend to multiple cues. The meta-analysis also indicated that another reason why alcohol increases aggression is because alcohol reduces anxiety, which in turn lowers people's inhibitions against aggressing (Ito et al., 1996).

Situational Influences: Multiple Causes, Multiple Cures

We have seen that negative affect, arousal, and aggression-related thoughts can lead to aggression. And a number of factors influence whether one is likely to experience negative affect, arousal, and aggressive thoughts, such as aversive experiences (frustration, crowding, heat, provocation), situational cues (guns, violent movies), and individual and cultural differences (chronic hostility, cultures of honor). Figure 11.8 diagrams how these various factors interact to lead to emotional aggression.

As can be seen from this figure, many events and conditions influence aggression. Moreover, the impact of any given situation often involves a variety of psychological factors. Hot temperatures, for instance, influence arousal and cognitions as well as affect (Anderson et al., 1995). Thus, we cannot hope for a single, simple cure. But multiple causes create the potential for multiple ways to reduce aggression. Indeed, one of the most successful types of treatment program for violent juvenile delinquents is called *multisystematic therapy*. This approach addresses individuals' problems at multiple levels, including the needs of the adolescents and the many contexts in which they are embedded, such as family, peers, school, and neighborhood (Tate et al., 1995). What about steps to reduce aggression more generally? Table 11.3 lists some of the possible steps suggested by the research we've reviewed. Personally, you may not agree that all of these actions are desirable—and you may prefer others that are not mentioned. What's important is to realize that each of us can do something to reduce aggression. There are many paths to take toward this common goal.

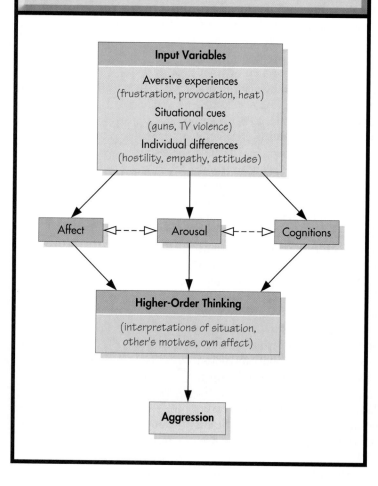

FIGURE 11.8   A Model of Situational Influences on Emotional Aggression

Unpleasant experiences and situational cues can trigger negative affect, high arousal, and aggression-related thoughts. Due to individual differences, some people are more likely than others to experience these feelings and thoughts. Higher-order thinking then shapes these feelings and thoughts into more well-defined emotions and behavioral intentions. Depending on the outcome of this thinking (which can occur beneath the individual's conscious awareness and can be affected by factors such as alcohol or stress), the individual may choose to aggress. *(Based on Anderson et al., 1996.)*

Input Variables

Aversive experiences
(frustration, provocation, heat)

Situational cues
(guns, TV violence)

Individual differences
(hostility, empathy, attitudes)

Affect ◁- - -▷ Arousal ◁- - -▷ Cognitions

Higher-Order Thinking

(interpretations of situation,
other's motives, own affect)

Aggression

> **TABLE 11.3 Some Steps to Reduce Aggression**
> Although there may be other reasons to endorse or reject these ideas, social psychological research on aggression suggests that each has the potential to reduce aggression.

Some Steps to Reduce Aggression

- Enlarge opportunities to achieve the goals valued by society (such as social approval, status, financial success) through nonviolent means.
- Reward nonaggressive behavior.
- Provide attractive models of peaceful behavior.
- Reduce all forms of aggression in our society, including physical punishment of children, capital punishment of criminals, and war.
- Reduce frustration by improving the quality of life in housing, health care, employment, and child care.
- Provide fans and air-conditioned shelters when it's hot.
- Reduce access to and display of weapons.
- Apologize when you've angered someone, and regard apologies as a sign of strength—not weakness. Encourage others to do likewise.
- Stop and think when you feel your temper rising. Control it instead of letting it control you.
- Discourage drinking and support efforts to provide treatment for alcohol abuse.

Media Effects: Scenes of Violence

Having looked at origins and specific factors that contribute to aggression, we now focus on a special topic that has been a major concern of politicians, families, and social scientists alike for many years: violence in television, film, and other media. We explore two types of mass media presentations—nonsexual violence and pornography—in which the display of aggression may elicit more of it.

Depictions of Nonsexual Violence

Testifying before a U.S. Senate subcommittee, social psychologist Leonard Eron reported some startling figures. Assuming that a child watches two to four hours of TV a day, Eron estimated that by the end of elementary school "he or she would have seen 8,000 murders and more than 100,000 other acts of violence" (DeAngelis, 1993). Might all this murder and mayhem on the screen spill over into real life? The senators thought so; and faced with mounting political pressure, the major TV networks agreed to insert a warning label before high-violence prime-time shows. In 1997, some of the networks adopted additional warning labels, such as warnings about sexual content and "mature" language. Posted at the beginning of many prime-time shows is a list of enough warning letters (V for violence, S for sex, etc.) to fill up a bowl of alphabet soup. It remains to be seen, however, whether these labels are effective in minimizing children's exposure to violent models.

Although most of the research on displays of nonsexual violence has focused on TV and movies, there are many other sources of violent presentations, such as this violent video game, Mortal Kombat.

Researchers have found that warning labels before TV shows can actually heighten viewer interest and attraction to the "forbidden fruit" (Bushman & Stack, 1996).

Violence on TV is not limited to the major networks or to prime time. There is violence on cable, on news shows, in commercials, and especially—and perhaps most troubling of all—on children's cartoons (*National Television Violence Study*, 1998). And then there are all those other sources of violent portrayals: movies, newspapers, newsmagazines, video games, virtual reality games, music videos, and song lyrics. Although most of the research on scenes of nonsexual violence has concentrated on TV and films, the findings point to some basic ways in which various kinds of violent depictions can increase the likelihood of aggressive behavior.

Immediate Effects   Does life imitate art? Sometimes it seems that way. Brad Bushman, whose work is cited in several places in this chapter, first became interested in research on media violence when a store owner he knew was the victim of a heinous crime: Two armed men came into the store and forced the owner and customers into the basement, forced them to drink Drano (a highly corrosive, toxic fluid used to clean plumbing pipes) and put duct tape over their mouths—the day after these men had allegedly watched (three times) the Clint Eastwood movie *Magnum Force*,

A Heath High School student screams at seeing the scene of the shooting in her school lobby, in Paducah, Kentucky, on December 1, 1997. A fourteen-year old student, Michael Carneal shot eight classmates—killing three of them—as they were finishing an informal prayer session. Investigators reported that Carneal may have been influenced by seeing the movie, The Basketball Diaries, which depicts a student who had been taunted by classmates dreaming that he returns to the classroom and shoots his tormentors. Carneal's rampage, in turn, may have influenced subsequent high-school shootings, as a series of such incidents occurred throughout the United States during the months that followed.

which features a scene depicting this very act of brutality (Leland, 1995). About a quarter century later, in December 1997, fourteen-year-old Michael Carneal shot to death three classmates and wounded five others as they gathered for a morning prayer in a high school in Kentucky. After seeing the 1995 film *The Basketball Diaries*—which opens with a character played by Leonardo DiCaprio shooting down classmates while others cheer him on—Carneal reportedly told friends that he might do something similar (Williams, 1997). Table 11.4 lists a few of the many violent incidents that may have been inspired by scenes in popular movies.

No one can ever prove that a specific fictional depiction was the primary cause of a specific act of violence. There are always other possibilities. But, as indicated earlier, research under controlled conditions in the laboratory has amply documented that aggressive models, live or on film, increase aggressive behavior among children and adults (Geen, 1998; Liebert & Sprafkin, 1988).

When exposure to violent images is manipulated in an experiment, the causal effect is clear. With control, however, comes artificiality, and doubts have been expressed about whether what is found in the lab will also occur in the real world (Freedman, 1988).

TABLE 11.4 Violent Fiction and Facts Although it's impossible to prove that any specific media depiction caused a specific violent action, there have been some close connections.	
Violent Fiction	**Subsequent Violent Fact**
The Basketball Diaries (movie starring Leonardo DiCaprio)	A 14-year old, allegedly inspired by the movie, shot to death three classmates and wounded five others as they gathered for a morning prayer in a high school in Kentucky.
Menace II Society (movie starring Tyrin Turner, Larenz Tate, and Jada Pinkett)	Four teens allegedly inspired by the movie killed one person and wounded another in a highway shooting.
Money Train (movie starring Wesley Snipes and Woody Harrelson)	In several incidents in New York City, people doused subway token collectors with flammable liquids and burned them, just as had been depicted in the movie.
Natural Born Killers (movie starring Woody Harrelson and Juliette Lewis)	Utah police claimed that a teenager obsessed with the movie murdered his stepmother and half-sister.
**** the Police* (song by gangsta rap group, N.W.A.)	Rifles used in the shooting of a police officer in North Carolina were emblazoned with the letters N.W.A.
The Program (movie starring James Caan, Halle Berry, and Omar Epps)	A young man died in Pennsylvania imitating a stunt in which college football players attempted to prove their manhood by lying on the white line in the middle of the highway (after a few incidents, the producers cut this scene from the movie).
Scream (movie starring Neve Campbell, Courtney Cox, and Drew Barrymore)	Three gunmen, wearing ghost masks and using scare tactics reminiscent of the movie, held up two Omaha restaurants.

Field experiments in a real-world setting such as a school offer one way to address this issue. When Wendy Wood and her colleagues (1991) examined both laboratory and field experiments conducted with children and adolescents, they found that exposure to aggressive films increased aggressive behavior in the laboratory, the classroom, the lunchroom, the playground, and the athletic field. Although laboratory experiments produced somewhat stronger results than those conducted in natural environments, the aggression-inducing effects of filmed models occurred in both types of settings. But what about the "real" real world—where no experiment is being conducted? Here, we must rely on correlational research, which cannot prove causation. Nevertheless, the positive correlation between amount of violent TV watched and aggressive behavior is quite robust (Huesmann & Miller, 1994).

Researchers have also looked at effects of violent imagery in the music industry as well. Many music videos and song lyrics depict violence and sexual aggression or

The British techno band Prodigy, *pictured here backstage after winning an award at the MTV Europe Music Awards in 1996, released a hit song called "Smack My Bitch Up" in 1997. Numerous groups, such as the National Organization of Women, protested the violent, anti-woman imagery in the song's lyrics, as well as in the video of the song, which showed women being hit and injected with drugs.*

Exposure to TV violence in childhood is related to aggression later in life. **True.**

habituation Adaptation to something familiar, so that both physiological and psychological responses are reduced.

cultivation The process by which the mass media (particularly television) construct a version of social reality for the public.

promote negative, hostile attitudes toward women (and, to a lesser extent, toward men). Rap (especially gangsta rap) and heavy metal music have received particular attention in this regard. James Johnson and his colleagues (1995) found that young African American males expressed greater acceptance of violence in general and violence toward women in particular—and a higher probability that they would engage in violence—if they had recently been exposed to violent rap music videos than if they had not. Several other studies have illustrated similar effects of gangsta rap and rock music videos (Hansen, 1995).

Long-Term Effects One question that has received a tremendous amount of attention is whether viewing violence at an early age is associated with more aggressive behavior at a later age. Most of the relevant research aimed at answering this question has concentrated on TV. The results of a twenty-two-year study, known as the Rip Van Winkle project, indicated that exposure to TV violence among eight-year-old boys was related to their aggression later in life, including self-reported aggression and the seriousness of criminal arrests at age thirty. This effect was independent of social class, intelligence, or parenting variables (Eron & Huesmann, 1984; Huesman & Miller, 1994). The effect was not observed, however, among females.

In an extensive cross-cultural study, Rowell Huesmann and Leonard Eron (1986) collaborated with researchers around the world to examine the relationship between TV violence and aggression among children in five different countries: Australia, Finland, Israel, Poland, and the United States. Researchers found evidence of a connection between early viewing of TV violence and later aggression for children in Finland, Poland, the United States, and urban areas in Israel. No such connection was established for Australian children or for those living on kibbutzim in Israel. The researchers believe that the correlation found among the children living on kibbutzim was weak because in this setting children watch very little violent TV. When they do, it is likely followed by a discussion of the implications of the violence—which may offer a lesson for all of us.

Beyond Imitation How can exposure to violent images as a child have long-term effects on adult aggression? One way is by influencing our values and attitudes toward aggression, making it seem more legitimate and even necessary for social interaction and resolution of social conflicts. Attitudes can also be affected through the process of **habituation.** A novel stimulus gets our attention and, if it's sufficiently interesting or exciting, elicits physiological arousal. But when we get used to something, our reactions diminish. Familiarity with violence reduces physiological arousal to new incidents of violence (Geen, 1981; Thomas, 1982). Desensitized to violence, we may become more accepting of it. For example, in one study, fourth- and fifth-grade girls and boys watched either a condensed version of the movie *The Karate Kid*, which depicts several brutal fights, or nonviolent scenes of Olympic competition. The students then saw two children on a TV monitor (the children supposedly were in an adjacent room) become violent toward each other. The students who had watched *The Karate Kid* were slower to seek out help, tolerating the violence more than the other children did (Molitor & Hirsch, 1994).

Another way that depictions of violence could change values and attitudes is through what George Gerbner and his colleagues (1986) call **cultivation.** Cultivation refers to the capacity of the mass media to construct a social reality that people perceive as true, even if it isn't. The media tend to depict the world as much more violent than it actually is. This can make people become more fearful, more distrustful, more likely to arm themselves, and more likely to behave aggressively in what they perceive as a threatening situation. Mass media cultivation may also affect the acceptability of aggressive behavior. Because the ultimate winners in the violent fights that are depicted in film and TV are the "good guys," aggression is justified, even if the initial aggressors (the "bad guys") suffer for their actions. Research on this issue reveals that viewers, especially angry ones, are usually more aggressive after watching justified aggression (Berkowitz, 1965). Seeing acceptable violence can make violence more acceptable.

Gallup polls have asked Americans about a dozen times since 1972, "Is there more crime in your area than there was a year ago, or less?" Each year, more respondents answered "More" than either "Less" or "Same." In 1997, despite the reduction in overall crime statistics in the United States, 46 percent said that there was more crime in their area than the year before, 32 percent said that there was less, and 20 percent said the incidence was the same.

What Can We Do About It?   Based on their review of the relevant research, a task force on television and society appointed by the American Psychological Association (APA) concluded that, "There is clear evidence that television violence can cause aggressive behavior and can cultivate values favoring the use of aggression to resolve conflicts" (Huston et al., 1992, p. 136). The Commission on Violence and Youth (1993), also appointed by APA, agreed and stated that "children's exposure to violence in the mass media, particularly at young ages, can have harmful lifelong consequences" (p. 33). However, both the task force and the commission recognized that the media do not operate in a vacuum. People are influenced by their families, peers, social values, and opportunities for education and employment. Nor are all individuals the same; individual differences in personality heat up or tone down the impact of exposure to aggres-

sive displays. The effects tend to be strong primarily for people who are high in trait aggressiveness, irritability, or hostility and for people who lack empathy (Anderson, 1997; Bushman, 1995; Zillmann & Weaver, 1997). Nevertheless, what we see in media presentations of violence is not a pretty picture.

What, then, can we do about it? Government censorship is one answer; but it is not a very popular one, for a number of reasons. In 1996, President Bill Clinton signed a bill that sets into motion the use of the "V chip" in television sets. This device will allow parents to block out programs that have been labeled as high in

Prospective studies examine the same individuals over a period of time so that changes in behavior can be observed. A number of such studies have investigated whether viewing TV violence at an early age is associated with aggressive behavior at a later age.

violence, sex, or other material deemed objectionable. Who does this labeling, and what criteria will be used, remain unclear. Furthermore, it is doubtful that children's cartoons will be blocked, although these are in many ways the most violent programs on television. Another alternative is to use public pressure to increase media self-censorship. Of course, the most powerful kind of public pressure would be a commercial boycott. If violence did not sell, the media would not produce it. Unfortunately, however, violence continues to be a money-maker.

At this point, education may well be the most effective approach. For example, treatment programs have been developed to curb children's undesirable reactions to TV (Eron, 1986; Singer & Singer, 1983). These programs recommend that parents select shows that provide compelling, vivid prosocial models for their children. An extensive review by Susan Hearold (1986) is encouraging in this regard. As discussed in Chapter 10, her analysis indicated that prosocial TV programs produce stronger effects on behavior than do antisocial TV programs. Parents have also been advised to watch television with their children and to teach them how TV differs from real life, how imitating TV characters can produce undesirable outcomes, and how children might be harmed by watching TV (Huesmann et al., 1983). This kind of ongoing parental tutorial takes significant time and effort. But given the extent of media depictions of violence in our society, strengthening children's critical viewing skills is a wise investment.

"What happened to 'Erotica'?"

One person's "art" can be another's "filth," highlighting the difficulties of trying to regulate the availability of pornography.   Sam Gross © 1997 from The New Yorker Collection. All Rights Reserved.

pornography   Explicit sexual material.

Pornographic Materials

Just as citizens, scientists, and politicians have been concerned about the consequences of mass media presentations of nonsexual violence, they have also been troubled by mass media displays of sexual material. Such displays are highly visible and widely available. Books, magazines, videos, and Internet sites cater to a wide range of sexual interests. Heavy metal, electronica, and rap groups often rely on obscenities to get their fans' attention. Dial-a-porn lines rake in millions of dollars. Opposition to pornography is equally prominent. Parents, religious leaders, consumer groups, and feminist activists lobby legislators and go to court to obtain greater restraints on the availability of sexually explicit materials.

Attempts to ban specific works, such as James Joyce's novel *Ulysses* and Robert Mapplethorpe's photos, indicate that the definitions of such terms as *obscenity*, *erotica*, and *pornography* are often a matter of personal opinion. One person's smut is another person's masterpiece. Because of the weight of subjective judgment in such definitions, the term **pornography** is used here to refer to explicit sexual material, regardless of its moral or aesthetic qualities. It is crucial, however, to distinguish between nonviolent and violent pornography in discussing the relationship between pornographic displays and aggression.

Nonviolent Pornography   Earlier in this chapter, we described the arousal-affect model, which proposes that both the type of emotion and the intensity of arousal produced by a stimulus influence aggression. The results of research on nonviolent pornography confirm the importance of these factors (Donnerstein et al., 1987). For many people, viewing attractive nudes elicits a pleasant emotional response and low levels of sexual arousal. Such materials usually reduce retaliatory aggression against a same-sex confederate. However, most people are more disturbed by crude displays of sexual activities. Their emotional response is negative, and their arousal is heightened by alarm, sexual feelings, or both. These kinds of pornographic materials usually increase aggression toward a same-sex confederate.

But what about aggression toward the opposite sex? Since the vast majority of pornography is designed to appeal to heterosexual males, investigators have been especially interested in whether pornographic materials have a specific effect on men's aggression against women. It does, but only when restraints that ordinarily inhibit male-to-female aggression are reduced such as when there are repeated opportunities to aggress (Donnerstein & Hallam, 1978).

Much of the research on pornography exposes participants to only one "dose" of pornography. What about viewing many pornographic images over an extended period of time? To investigate this issue, Dolf Zillmann and Jennings Bryant (1984) showed either eighteen or thirty-six pornographic films to male and female college students over the course of six weeks. These films were X-rated but nonviolent. Control participants saw neutral films or no films at all. After the exposure period, all participants returned to the laboratory for two follow-up sessions, which assessed (1) physiological arousal in response to new, unfamiliar pornography, (2) aggressiveness toward a same-sex confederate, and (3) attitudes.

This research revealed a clear habituation effect: Repeated prior exposure to pornography diminished physiological arousal in response to new pornography, especially among those who had previously been exposed to the greater number of pornographic films. As arousal subsided, so did the power of pornography to intensify aroused behaviors. After seeing new pornography, participants who had been exposed to a large number of pornographic films were less aggressive than control participants in response to provocation by a same-sex confederate. That's the good news.

But now here's the bad news. In the second follow-up session, participants read about a rape trial; they also expressed their opinion of the women's liberation movement. Those who had previously been exposed to a large number of pornographic films recommended a lighter sentence for the rapist and indicated less support for the women's liberation movement than did control participants. These results were obtained for both male and female participants. In addition, men who had been exposed to the larger amount of pornography reported more negative attitudes toward women than did the other participants. Once again, we see that habituation affects both arousal and attitudes. Prior exposure to large amounts of pornography can reduce arousal-based aggression but increase the kind of insensitive attitudes that could promote acceptance of future aggression.

Some nonviolent pornographic materials seem to specialize in trivializing rape and depersonalizing women as objects for sexual gratification, "with no human qualities other than [their] physical attributes" (Check & Guloien, 1989, p. 163). When James Check and Ted Guloien compared male participants who did not see any pornography with those who viewed dehumanizing pornography, they found that exposure to pornography increased participants' reports that they would force a woman to do something sexual against her will and would commit rape if they were assured of not getting caught.

Violent Pornography Adding violence to pornography greatly increases the possibility of harmful effects. Violent pornography is a triple threat: It brings together high arousal; negative emotional reactions such as shock, alarm, and disgust; and aggressive thoughts. According to a meta-analysis of 217 studies on the relation-

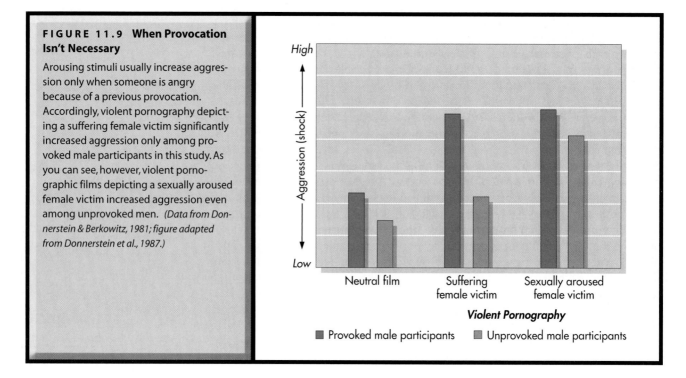

FIGURE 11.9 When Provocation Isn't Necessary

Arousing stimuli usually increase aggression only when someone is angry because of a previous provocation. Accordingly, violent pornography depicting a suffering female victim significantly increased aggression only among provoked male participants in this study. As you can see, however, violent pornographic films depicting a sexually aroused female victim increased aggression even among unprovoked men. *(Data from Donnerstein & Berkowitz, 1981; figure adapted from Donnerstein et al., 1987.)*

ship between TV violence and aggression, violent pornography had a stronger effect than any other type of program (Paik & Comstock, 1994). And there is substantial evidence that this effect is gender-specific. Male-to-male aggression is no greater after exposure to violent pornography than after exposure to highly arousing but nonviolent pornography. Male-to-female aggression, however, is markedly increased (Donnerstein & Malamuth, 1997; Linz et al., 1987; Malamuth & Donnerstein, 1982).

Like most experiences that intensify arousal (such as physical exercise), nonviolent pornography increases aggression only among individuals who have been provoked. But, like guns and alcohol, some violent pornography can increase aggression even in the absence of provocation. The prime ingredient in such materials is the portrayal of women as willing participants who "enjoy" their own victimization. In one study (Donnerstein & Berkowitz, 1981), violent pornography that emphasized the victim's suffering increased aggression only among men who had been provoked. But films that depicted female sexual response to acts of sexual violence increased aggression among both provoked and unprovoked male participants (see Figure 11.9).

We might like to believe that violent pornographic images are rare, found only in the most extreme varieties of hard-core porn. Not true. For example, in one survey of male college students, 36 percent reported having viewed materials during the preceding year that featured forced sexual acts against women; 25 percent said they had looked at materials depicting rape (Demaré et al., 1993). It is not uncommon for R-rated, "mainstream" movies to include sexually violent material, and this material can affect viewers' sexually related attitudes and beliefs. This was demonstrated in a field study that arranged for 115 college students to attend movies at campus theaters (Malamuth & Check, 1981). Half of these students saw the commercially successful movies *Swept Away* and *The Getaway*, both of which depict women who become sexually aroused by a sexual assault and romantically attracted to their assailant. The other half watched feature-length movies without sexually aggressive content. Several days later, all participants filled out a questionnaire in class along with the rest of their classmates. This questionnaire measured attitudes toward violence directed at women and beliefs about rape (see Table 11.5).

Compared with those who had not seen the movies depicting sexual assault, male students who had viewed these films reported greater acceptance of interpersonal violence against women and somewhat greater acceptance of rape myths. In contrast, women's acceptance of interpersonal violence against women and of rape myths tended to decline after viewing depictions of male-to-female sexual aggression. Figure 11.10 displays the findings for both men and women.

Some research examines the effects of combining exposure to violent pornography with individuals' negative attitudes toward women. Neil Malamuth has developed what he calls the "rapist's profile." Men fit the profile if they have relatively high levels of sexual arousal in response to violent pornography and also express attitudes and

TABLE 11.5 Attitudes About Sex and Aggression

Widely used in research on pornography, these two scales assess attitudes about violence toward women and beliefs about the nature of rape. A few items from each scale are shown here. *(Based on Burt, 1980.)*

Acceptance of Interpersonal Violence (Toward Women): AIV Scale

1. Being roughed up is sexually stimulating to many women.
2. Many times a woman will pretend she doesn't want to have intercourse because she doesn't want to seem loose, but she's really hoping the man will force her.
3. A man is never justified in hitting his wife.

Scoring: Persons scoring high in acceptance of violence toward women agree with items 1 and 2 but disagree with item 3.

Rape Myth Acceptance: RMA Scale

1. If a woman engages in necking or petting and she lets things get out of hand, it is her own fault if her partner forces sex on her.
2. Any female can get raped.
3. Many women have an unconscious wish to be raped, and may then unconsciously set up a situation in which they are likely to be attacked.
4. In the majority of rapes, the victim is promiscuous or has a bad reputation.

Scoring: Persons scoring high in acceptance of rape myths agree with items 1, 3, and 4 but disagree with item 2.

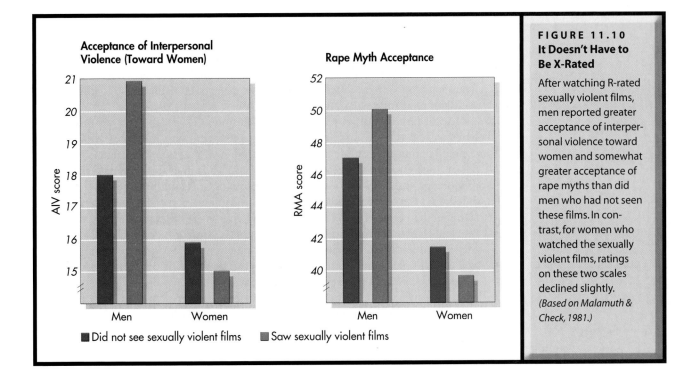

FIGURE 11.10 It Doesn't Have to Be X-Rated

After watching R-rated sexually violent films, men reported greater acceptance of interpersonal violence toward women and somewhat greater acceptance of rape myths than did men who had not seen these films. In contrast, for women who watched the sexually violent films, ratings on these two scales declined slightly. *(Based on Malamuth & Check, 1981.)*

opinions indicating acceptance of violence toward women. These individuals report more sexually coercive behavior in the past and more sexually aggressive intentions for the future. Among male college students given an opportunity to retaliate against a female confederate who had angered them, those who fit the rapist's profile were more aggressive (Malamuth, 1983, 1986). In another study illustrating the volatile mix of negative attitudes and violent pornography, Dano Demaré and his colleagues (1993) found that male college students' negative attitudes toward women and their frequent consumption of violent pornography each predicted the students' self-reported sexually aggressive intentions; the best prediction, however, was obtained when both pornography *and* attitudes were included in the equation.

Assessing the Possible Danger   Does the availability of pornography, then, increase the possibility of sexual assault? The correlational evidence bearing on the relationship between pornography and sex crimes is difficult to interpret (Marshall, 1989). Studies of retrospective reports by rapists about their experiences with pornography have yielded conflicting results (Malamuth & Billings, 1986). Nor do cross-cultural comparisons point to any clear relationship. Extremely violent pornography is widely available in Japan, but the incidence of rape is very low. India, in contrast, bans explicit sex (and even kissing) from commercial films but has a high incidence of rape (Pratap, 1990).

In the laboratory, the developing chain of evidence has a number of missing links. Because of ethical constraints, only relatively low levels of actual aggression have been studied, and this aggression has been nonsexual. Although pornography, especially violent pornography, does increase nonsexual aggression in the laboratory, it is not certain that these findings generalize to actual behavior. Studies of sexual aggression measure attitudes and self-reports, which can reflect or influence actual behavior but are not identical to it. Despite these limitations, however, existing research does indicate the clear possibility that pornography could contribute to sexual aggression against women.

What Can We Do About It?   The question of what to do about the potentially harmful effects of pornography leads to the same options described for depictions of nonsexual violence. Should pornography be banned? Should consumers be educated? Banning pornography raises a number of philosophical, political, and practical concerns. In addition, banning explicit sexual material would not prevent dehumanizing portrayals of women as sex objects or titillating but fully clothed scenes of rape and sexual assault.

According to Daniel Linz and his colleagues (1992), the real villains are violence, sexual or not, and the demeaning and degrading messages about women contained in pornographic depictions, violent or not. These researchers encourage educational efforts to increase viewers' critical skills in evaluating media depictions of violence and sex. A model for such efforts can be found in the debriefing provided to research participants exposed to violent pornography in experiments (Donnerstein et al., 1987). This debriefing emphasizes that rape myths are inaccurate and that violent pornography is unrealistic. Among individuals presented with this information, there are long-term reductions in acceptance of rape myths. Sex-education programs that emphasize the desirability of being respectful and considerate toward one's sexual partner may also be beneficial. In one study, a sex-education program conducted before participants were exposed to pornography reduced acceptance of rape myths and increased sympathy for rape victims (Intons-Peterson et al., 1989). Education and the public commitment required to implement it are important means of defense against sexual violence.

Intimate Violence: Trust Betrayed

ll violence is shocking, but aggression between intimates is especially disturbing. We want to feel safe with those we know and love; and yet far too often, that sense of security is destroyed by violence. Among the homicides committed in 1995, about half of the victims knew their murderer (see Figure 11.11). According to a three-year national survey, at least 75 percent of rapes are committed by a person the victim knows (Kilpatrick et al., 1992). The victims of intimate violence are children as well as adults, and the assault that takes place is often sexual as well as physical. In this section, we examine three major types of intimate violence: sexual aggression among college students, physical aggression between partners, and child abuse.

Sexual Aggression Among College Students

Acquaintance rape (often called "date rape") is a serious problem among college students. In the United States, over 25 percent of 3,187 female students surveyed on thirty-two college campuses reported having experienced either an attempted or a completed rape since age fourteen; over 50 percent of these assaults occurred during a date (Koss et al., 1987; Warshaw, 1988). When all types of unwanted sexual interactions are included, a majority of college women and about a third of college men say they have experienced coercive sexual contact (Cate & Lloyd, 1992; Struckman-Johnson & Struckman-Johnson, 1994). Rates of sexual coercion among Canadian college students appear to be similar (DeKeseredy et al., 1993).

A number of factors are associated with sexual aggression among college students. Two of the most important are gender and alcohol. First, both men and women report that men are more likely to engage in coercive behavior—psychological as well as physical—in order to obtain sex (Poppen & Segal, 1988). Second, alcohol consumption is involved in a majority of sexually aggressive incidents between college students (Cate & Lloyd, 1992). Not only does actual consumption increase aggressive behavior, but the mere *belief* that one has consumed alcohol (even if one hasn't) heightens sexual arousal and sexual interest (Baron & Richardson, 1994). The cognitive effects of intoxication, in which salient cues are noticed but subtle ones are missed, may disrupt interpersonal communication (Richardson & Hammock, 1991); and the anxiety-reducing effects of intoxication may

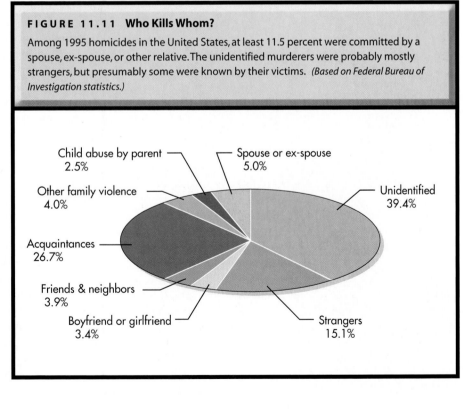

FIGURE 11.11 Who Kills Whom?
Among 1995 homicides in the United States, at least 11.5 percent were committed by a spouse, ex-spouse, or other relative. The unidentified murderers were probably mostly strangers, but presumably some were known by their victims. *(Based on Federal Bureau of Investigation statistics.)*

Child abuse by parent
2.5%

Spouse or ex-spouse
5.0%

Other family violence
4.0%

Unidentified
39.4%

Acquaintances
26.7%

Friends & neighbors
3.9%

Boyfriend or girlfriend
3.4%

Strangers
15.1%

weaken inhibitions against aggressive behavior (Ito et al., 1996; Seto & Barbaree, 1995).

A third important factor concerns attitudes toward rape and toward women. As we indicated earlier, men who fit Malamuth's concept of the rapist's profile—relatively high sexual arousal in response to violent pornography and attitudes indicating acceptance of violence toward women—report using more sexually coercive behavior. Both men and women who express greater acceptance of rape myths (see Table 11.5) also report greater use of coercive and aggressive tactics of sexual influence. Men's rape myth attitudes are also associated with hostility toward women, which itself promotes the use of these aggressive tactics (Christopher et al., 1993; Malamuth, 1996). Men who are self-centered rather than sensitive to others' needs and who have very impersonal, noncommittal, game-playing orientations in sexual relations are also more likely to engage in sexually aggressive behavior (Dean & Malamuth, 1997; Malamuth, 1996). In light of these findings, it is encouraging that rape-awareness workshops appear to reduce acceptance of rape myths and increase sympathy for a female rape victim (Szymanski et al., 1993). Again, education has a crucial role to play in reducing sexual aggression.

Physical Aggression Between Partners

In the United States, about one-third of female homicide victims are murdered by a husband or a boyfriend. In 1996, more than a thousand such murders were committed, and almost four hundred men were murdered by a wife or girlfriend. Of course, partner abuse is not limited to the United States; it is a worldwide phenomenon (Hoffman et al., 1994; Holloway, 1994). Neither is it a new development; it has occurred throughout history. Only in recent years, however, has a concerted effort been made to document the extent of this often very private form of violence—for example, through national surveys.

One of the most surprising results of national surveys in 1975 and 1985 was the high level of wife-to-husband abuse, which in terms of severe violence (such as kicking, hitting, beating, threatening with a weapon, and using a weapon) was consistently higher than the level of husband-to-wife abuse. Prospective research on aggression during the first years of marriage also found higher rates of wife-to-husband abuse (O'Leary et al., 1989). What these results don't reveal, however, is that women often use violence in self-defense rather than for intimidation. Nor do they reveal the consequences of spouse abuse. Usually these outcomes are more damaging to women, who are more often killed, seriously injured, or sexually assaulted during domestic disputes than are men (Browne, 1993; Stets & Straus, 1990). As Barbara Morse (1995) put it, "Women were more often the victims of severe partner assault and injury not because men strike more often, but because men strike harder" (p. 251).

The public image of rock star Tommy Lee and actress Pamela Anderson was glamorous and harmonious in the early days of their marriage. In this picture, Tommy rubs the belly of his pregnant wife in 1996. The private reality was quite different. In May, 1998, Tommy was sentenced to six months in prison for felony spousal abuse. After Tommy assaulted her while she was holding their infant son and their other young son looked on, Pamela said that she feared for the children's safety and filed for divorce.

Similar findings have been obtained in studies of violence among unmarried couples (Sugarman & Hotaling, 1989). Different types of intimate relationships, however, have different levels of violence. The average level of physical violence is lowest among dating couples, intermediate among married couples, and highest among unmarried couples who live together. The exact causes for the association between living together without marriage and physical abuse are not known, but it may result from the stresses and strains of living together without a strong commitment to the relationship (Stets, 1991; Stets & Straus, 1989).

Like most aggressive actions, violence between partners is multiply determined. Among the factors associated with increased partner aggression are personal characteristics (such as age, attitudes toward violence, drug and alcohol abuse, and personality), socioeconomic status (which includes income and education), interpersonal conflict, stress, social isolation, and the experience of growing up in a violent family (Gelles & Straus, 1988; Herzberger, 1996; Williams, 1992; Yoshikawa, 1994).

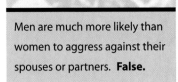

Men are much more likely than women to aggress against their spouses or partners. **False.**

Child Abuse

Children who grow up in a violent family not only witness aggression; they often bear the brunt of it. Tragically, child abuse is not a rare occurrence. It is estimated that each year in the United States over a million children are physically abused and over 150,000 are sexually abused. National survey data indicate that over 60 percent of rape victims are under eighteen. At least 2,000 children a year—five each day—die at the hands of their parents or caretakers (Cavaliere, 1995; Gelles & Cornell, 1990; National Center on Child Abuse and Neglect, 1988). David Finkelhor and Jennifer Dziuba-Leatherman (1994) conclude that the available evidence "strongly suggests that children are more victimized than adults are" (p. 173).

Children are abused by strangers as well as by family members, but severe abuse, particularly of young children, is more often inflicted by parents and caretakers. Boys suffer more physical abuse than do girls, and mothers are more likely than fathers to physically abuse their children (Straus et al., 1980). In contrast, girls suffer more sexual abuse than do boys, and fathers are more likely than mothers to sexually abuse their children (Russell, 1984).

Like partner aggression, child abuse is multiply determined. Among the factors associated with increased child abuse are personal characteristics of the abusing parent (such as personality and substance abuse) and of the child (younger children are more often abused by family members); the family's socioeconomic status; stressful experiences; social isolation; marital conflict; and the abusing parent's having been abused as a child (Belsky, 1993; Davies & Cummings, 1994; Herzberger, 1996).

The Cycle of Family Violence   At this point, you should begin to see a pattern emerging: the connection between violence in childhood and violence as an adult. This connection is called the **cycle of family violence.** Children who witness parental violence or who are themselves abused are more likely as adults to inflict abuse on intimate partners or, perhaps, to be victims of intimate violence (Malinosky-Rummell & Hansen, 1993; Simons et al., 1993). They are also more likely to abuse their own children. In turn, their children are more likely to interact violently with each other and to aggress against their parents (Patterson, 1984; Peek et al., 1985). This intergenerational transmission of domestic violence is by no means inevitable, however. Most people who witness or experience abuse in their families of origin are not abusive or abused in their families of procreation. The cycle of family violence refers to a greater tendency, not an absolute certainty.

Adults who as children were abused by their parents are less likely to inflict abuse on their own children than are other adults. **False.**

cycle of family violence
The transmission of domestic violence across generations.

Reducing Family Violence   Family violence is a matter of grave societal concern and, since it is caused by multiple factors, must be addressed by a variety of approaches. For example, reporting laws require certain individuals, such as physicians, to report suspected cases of child abuse. Since 1990, many states have enacted "stalking laws" making it illegal to harass, threaten, or follow individuals; these sorts of behaviors are often the prelude to violence inflicted on a former spouse. Though controversial, mandatory arrest policies for domestic assault have been enacted in several states as well. Shelters for battered women and their children provide protection and, often, various social services, such as legal referrals, psychological counseling, and employment assistance. Families in which a child has been abused may be required by court order to participate in family therapy; if necessary, an abused child can be removed from the home. Either by court order or voluntarily, many abusing men and women participate in group therapy sessions. Some cities and states require that police, prosecutors, and judges receive special training to help them better understand the causes and consequences of domestic violence.

Specific programs that protect victims of abuse and reduce the likelihood of continued violence by abusers are vitally important. But family violence takes place in a larger context. According to Jay Belsky (1993), poverty is "undoubtedly the major risk for child abuse and neglect" (p. 428). Thus, protecting families from violence also requires providing family members with educational and employment opportunities. Furthermore, as noted throughout this chapter, attitudes have a strong influence on aggressive behavior. If society legitimizes and glorifies violence, all of us are at risk.

Review

What Is Aggression?

- Aggression is behavior intended to injure another person who does not want to be injured.
- Anger is an emotional response to perceived injury; hostility is an antagonistic attitude.
- Instrumental aggression is a means to obtain a desired outcome.
- In emotional aggression, harm is inflicted for its own sake.

Cultural and Gender Differences

Cultural Variation

- The rates of violence and the forms violence takes vary dramatically from one society to another.
- Within a society, different subcultures exhibit different norms concerning aggression.
- Teenagers and young adults, African Americans, and people in the South are the groups most prone to violence in the United States.

Gender Differences

- Men are more violent than women in virtually every culture and time period that have been studied.
- Males tend to be more overtly, physically aggressive than females.
- Females are often more indirectly, or relationally, aggressive than males.
- When ordinary restraints against aggression are reduced, women are often as overtly aggressive as men.

Origins of Aggression

Is Aggression Innate?

- Both Freud and Lorenz regarded aggression as an innate instinct, but the circular reasoning of such instinct theories is unscientific.
- Evolutionary psychology views aggression as a universal, innate characteristic that has evolved from natural and sexual selection pressures.
- Evolutionary accounts propose that gender differences in aggression can be traced to competition for status (and the most desirable mates) and sexual jealousy.
- Some research suggests that individual differences in aggression are produced by genetic inheritance, but the overall evidence is somewhat mixed.

- The sex hormone testosterone and the neurotransmitter serotonin appear to play roles in human aggression.

Is Aggression Learned?

- Aggression is increased by rewards.
- Aggression is decreased by punishment only under specific conditions that are often not met in the real world.
- Physical punishment of children is associated with increases in their subsequent aggressive behavior.
- Social learning theory emphasizes the influence of models on the behavior of observers.
- Models who obtain desired goals through the use of aggression and are not punished for their behavior are the most likely to be imitated. But even punished models may encourage aggression by observers.
- Aggressive models teach not only specific behaviors but also more general attitudes and ideas about aggression.
- Peaceful models can decrease aggressive responses by observers.
- Gender and cultural differences in human aggression may be due in part to differences in socialization practices—lessons taught, reinforcements and punishments given, models offered, and roles and norms emphasized.
- A culture of honor promotes status-protecting aggression among white males in the American South and West.

Nature Versus Nurture: A False Debate?

- Human aggression clearly is affected by learning and experience.
- In aggression, as in all human behavior, biological and environmental influences interact.

Situational Influences on Aggression

Frustration: Aggression as a Drive

- The frustration-aggression hypothesis proposes that frustration always produces the motive to aggress and that all aggression is caused by frustration.
- But in fact, frustration produces many motives, and aggression is caused by many factors.
- According to the frustration-aggression hypothesis, displacement occurs if aggression against the source of frustration is inhibited. Research has yet to offer convincing support for this notion.
- The frustration-aggression hypothesis holds that engaging in any aggressive action reduces the motive to engage in further aggression, a process called catharsis. In the long run, however, aggression now is likely to increase aggression later.

- Frustration is only one of a number of unpleasant experiences that produce negative affect and increase aggression.

Negative Affect

- A wide variety of noxious stimuli can create negative feelings and increase aggression.
- Hot temperatures are associated with increased aggression and violence.
- Being attacked or insulted by someone is another experience that produces negative affect, and retaliation to provocation is a major source of aggressive behavior.
- Positive emotional responses are incompatible with negative affect and reduce retaliatory aggression.

Arousal: "Wired" for Action

- Highly arousing stimuli, neutral as well as negative, increase retaliatory aggression.
- The arousal-affect model proposes that both the type of emotion and the intensity of arousal influence aggression, which is greatest in response to experiences that combine negative affect and high arousal.

Thought: Automatic and Deliberate

- Berkowitz's cognitive-neoassociation analysis of aggression proposes that unpleasant experiences create negative affect, which in turn stimulates automatic associations connected with anger and fear. Behavioral and emotional outcomes then depend, at least in part, on higher-order cognitive processing.
- Situational cues associated with aggression, such as the presence of a gun, can automatically activate aggression-related thoughts and increase aggressive behavior.
- More deliberate thoughts that affect aggression include the perception of intent, which is reduced by mitigating information indicating that a person was not fully responsible for harmful acts.
- Individual differences, such as in chronic aggressiveness, influence how individuals interpret the aggression-related motives of others and how they react to mitigating information.
- High arousal impairs the cognitive control of aggression, as does alcohol.

Situational Influences: Multiple Causes, Multiple Cures

- Aggression is influenced by separate and interactive influences of affect, arousal, and cognitions.
- Because aggression is determined by many factors, there is no *one* way to end it, but there are many ways to reduce it.

Media Effects: Scenes of Violence

Depictions of Nonsexual Violence

■ In laboratory and field experiments, exposure to aggressive models increases aggressive behavior among adults and children.

■ Exposure to TV violence in childhood often is related to aggression later in life, although this relationship can vary by culture and gender.

■ Since we habituate to familiar stimuli, repeated observations of violence reduce physiological arousal to new incidents but may make aggression more acceptable.

■ Through cultivation of a social reality, the mass media can intensify fear of aggression and encourage aggressive behavior.

■ Educational efforts may be more successful than censorship in reducing media-induced aggression.

Pornographic Materials

■ Nonviolent pornography that is only mildly arousing reduces retaliatory aggression against someone of the same sex.

■ When normative restraints against male-to-female aggression are reduced, nonviolent but highly arousing pornography increases male-to-female aggression more than male-to-male aggression.

■ Extensive exposure to nonviolent pornography produces habituation, which reduces arousal-based aggression but increases callous attitudes that may lower restraints against future aggression.

■ Exposure to dehumanizing nonviolent pornography increases sexually aggressive intentions.

■ Violent pornography increases male-to-female aggression more than male-to-male aggression.

■ When a female is portrayed as enjoying violent sex, even unprovoked men become more aggressive and more accepting of violence against women.

■ The combination of interest in violent pornography and negative attitudes toward women is a strong predictor of self-reported sexual aggression in the past and sexually aggressive intentions for the future.

■ Education may be more effective than censorship in reducing sexual aggression.

Intimate Violence: Trust Betrayed

Sexual Aggression Among College Students

■ Men are more likely than women to engage in sexually coercive behavior.

■ Alcohol consumption is involved in a majority of sexually aggressive incidents.

■ Attitudes toward rape and toward women are associated with coercive sexual behavior.

Physical Aggression Between Partners

■ National surveys reveal that women engage in more aggressive behavior against a partner than do men; but women are more likely to be killed, seriously injured, or sexually abused by a partner.

■ The level of physical violence is higher among unmarried couples living together than among married or dating couples.

Child Abuse

■ Children are more likely to be victimized than adults.

■ Mothers are more likely than fathers to physically abuse their children; fathers are more likely than mothers to sexually abuse their children.

■ Children who witness parental violence or are themselves abused are more likely as adults to abuse their partners and their own children. But most people escape from this cycle of family violence.

■ Protecting the victims of family violence and preventing its recurrence require a wide range of interventions.

Key Terms

aggression *385*

arousal-affect model *407*

catharsis *402*

cognitive neoassociation analysis *407*

cultivation *415*

cycle of family violence *423*

displacement *402*

emotional aggression *386*

frustration-aggression hypothesis *402*

habituation *414*

instrumental aggression *386*

mitigating information *409*

pornography *416*

social learning theory *398*

weapons effect *408*

PUTTING COMMON SENSE TO THE TEST

In virtually every culture, males are more violent than females.

True. *In almost every culture and time period that have been studied, men commit the large majority of violent crimes.*

For virtually any category of aggression, males are more aggressive than females.

False. *Girls are often more indirectly, or relationally, aggressive than boys; and women often exhibit levels of aggression similar to men's when they have been provoked or when they feel relatively anonymous and deindividuated.*

Children who are spanked or otherwise physically disciplined (but not abused) for behaving aggressively tend to become less aggressive.

False. *Evidence indicates that the use of even a little physical punishment to discipline children is associated with increases in subsequent aggressive and antisocial behavior by the children, even years later, although this relationship may depend on a variety of other factors.*

Blowing off steam by engaging in safe but aggressive activities (such as sports) makes people less likely to aggress later.

False. *Although people may be less likely to aggress immediately after such activities, initial aggression makes future aggression more, not less, likely.*

Exposure to TV violence in childhood is related to aggression later in life.

True. *Laboratory experiments, field experiments, and correlational research all suggest a link between exposure to violence on TV and subsequent aggressive behavior.*

Men are much more likely than women to aggress against their spouses or partners.

False. *Some evidence suggests that women engage in more acts of serious aggression against their partners than men do; but men are much more likely to injure, sexually abuse, or kill their partners.*

Adults who as children were abused by their parents are less likely to inflict abuse on their own children than are other adults.

False. *Although most people who haved experienced such abuse do break the cycle of family violence, on average they are more likely to abuse their own children than are people who never experienced parental abuse.*

12 | Law

PREVIEW

This chapter examines applications of social psychology to the law. First, we consider three stages in the life of a jury trial: *jury selection,* an often controversial process; *the courtroom drama* in which confessions, eyewitnesses, and other types of evidence are presented; and *jury deliberation,* where the jury reaches a group decision. Next, we consider various *posttrial factors* such as sentencing and prison, the possible result of a guilty verdict. Finally, we discuss *perceptions of justice* both inside and outside the courtroom.

OUTLINE

It was called "the trial of the century." From the moment O. J. Simpson was named a suspect in the murders of his ex-wife Nicole Brown and her friend Ronald Goldman, it was apparent that this case would attract worldwide attention. Simpson was, after all, a Hall of Fame football hero, sportscaster, and actor. Now everyone would watch as police cars and a helicopter trailed him in his white Ford Bronco on a Los Angeles freeway. Celebrity, sports, sex, money, racial tension, and violence. This trial would have it all, and the stage was set.

As in live theater, the trial was packed with drama. Outside the courthouse, hundreds of TV cameras and microphones lined the parking lot. In an area that became known as "Camp O. J.," street musicians performed, bystanders held up signs, and vendors sold T-shirts, buttons, and other souvenirs. The courtroom itself was filled with journalists from all over the world, cameras, easels, a computer, and a wall-mounted projection screen. Yet it was so quiet you could hear a pin drop. At center stage were Simpson and his "dream team" lawyers, a team of prosecutors led by Marcia Clark, and Judge Lance Ito. Also in attendance were the jury, court personnel, photographers, reporters, families of the victims, and a select group of spectators. It was the toughest ticket in town.

PUTTING COMMON SENSE TO THE TEST

T / F

_____ Contrary to popular opinion, women are harsher as criminal trial jurors than men are.

_____ Without being beaten or threatened, innocent people sometimes confess to crimes they did not commit.

_____ Lie-detector tests can be beaten by suppressing arousal when questions about the crime are asked.

_____ Eyewitnesses find it relatively difficult to recognize members of a race other than their own.

_____ The more confident an eyewitness is about an identification, the more accurate it is likely to be.

_____ One can usually predict a jury's final verdict by knowing where the individual jurors stand the first time they vote.

In the so-called trial of the century, the most prominent actors were O.J. Simpson and his "dream team" defense lawyers Johnnie Cochran and Robert Shapiro (left), prosecutor Marcia Clark (right), and Judge Lance Ito (center).

The question for the jury was simple and to the point: Did Simpson stab his wife and her friend to death, and if so, was the act premeditated? To prove its case, the prosecution presented pictures, witnesses, blood-soaked socks and a glove, shoeprints, DNA tests, and the tape of a 911 phone call providing evidence that Simpson had been physically abusive of his wife. In turn, the defense argued that Simpson was at home at the time, that he would have been physically unable to overpower the two victims, and that the physical evidence could not be trusted. The trial, which lasted a full year and cost $9 million, included testimony from 126 witnesses and 857 exhibits. When it was over, the jury announced its controversial verdict: not guilty. For those who disagreed, Simpson was retried in a civil suit filed by the families of the victims. In February 1997, this second jury found Simpson liable for the murders and ordered him to pay the families over $30 million.

Regardless of how one felt about the O. J. Simpson trials, they served to illustrate the profound importance of social psychology at work in the legal system. The questions raised in this case, as in others: What kinds of people do lawyers select as jurors, and why? How reliable are confessions, eyewitnesses, and other types of evidence presented in court? How do juries reach their decisions, often after days or weeks of exhausting deliberation? And what factors influence the sentences imposed by judges? In this chapter, we take social psychology into the courtroom to answer these questions. But first, let's place the trial in a broader context.

In the American criminal justice system, trials are just the tip of an iceberg. Once a crime takes place, it must be detected and reported if it is to receive further attention. Through investigation, the police must then find a suspect and decide whether to make an arrest. If they do, the suspect is jailed or bail is set, and either a judge or a grand jury decides if there is sufficient evidence for a formal accusation. If there is, the prosecuting and defense lawyers begin a lengthy process known as "discovery," during which they gather evidence. At this point, many defendants plead guilty as part of a deal negotiated by the lawyers. In cases that do go to trial, the ordeal does not then end with a verdict. After conviction, the judge imposes a sentence, and the defendant decides whether to appeal to a higher court. For those in prison, decisions concerning their release are made by parole boards.

As Figure 12.1 illustrates, the criminal justice apparatus is complicated, and the actors behind the scenes are numerous. Yet through it all, the trial—a relatively infrequent event—is the heart and soul of the system. The threat of trial motivates parties to gather evidence and, later, to negotiate a deal. And when it's over, the trial forms the basis for sentencing and appeals decisions. Social psychologists have a lot to say about trials—and about other aspects of the legal system as well (Horowitz et al., 1998; Wrightsman et al., 1998). In the coming pages, we divide this event into three stages: jury selection, the presentation of evidence, and the jury's deliberations.

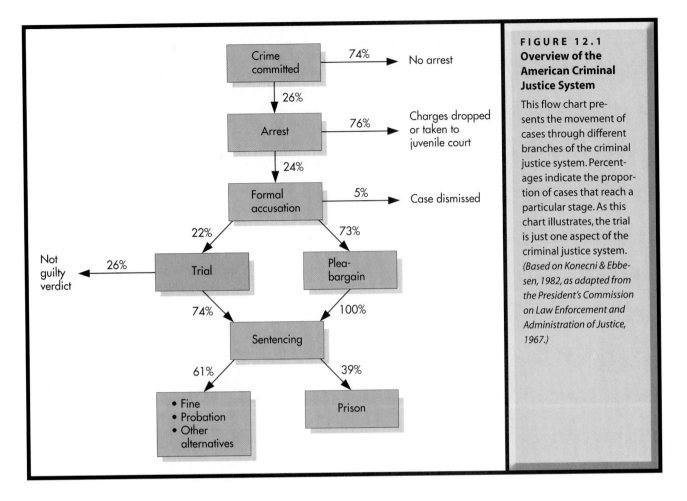

FIGURE 12.1
Overview of the American Criminal Justice System
This flow chart presents the movement of cases through different branches of the criminal justice system. Percentages indicate the proportion of cases that reach a particular stage. As this chart illustrates, the trial is just one aspect of the criminal justice system. *(Based on Konecni & Ebbesen, 1982, as adapted from the President's Commission on Law Enforcement and Administration of Justice, 1967.)*

Jury Selection

The first jury that tried O. J. Simpson consisted of four men and eight women. Two jurors were white, eight were black, one was Hispanic, and one was American Indian. Yet in the second trial, the civil jury had no black jurors on it. With millions of Los Angeles area residents to choose from in these cases, how were these particular groups selected, and why?

Jury selection is a three-stage process. First, the court uses voter registration lists, telephone directories, and other sources to compile a master list of eligible citizens who live in the community. Second, so that a representative sample from this community can be obtained, a certain number of people from the list are randomly drawn and summoned for duty. If you've ever been called, you know what happens next. Before people who appear in court are selected for a jury, they are subject to what is known as the **voir dire,** a pretrial interview in which the judge or the opposing lawyers question prospective jurors for signs of bias. If someone knows one of the parties, has an interest in the outcome of the case, or has already formed an opinion, the judge will excuse that person "for cause." In fact, if it can be proven that an entire community is biased, perhaps because of pretrial publicity, then the trial might be postponed or moved to another location.

Although the procedure seems straightforward, there is more to the story. In addition to de-selecting individuals who are clearly biased, lawyers are permitted to exercise **peremptory challenges.** That is, they can reject a certain limited number

voir dire The pretrial examination of prospective jurors by the judge or opposing lawyers to uncover signs of bias.

peremptory challenge A means by which lawyers can exclude a limited number of prospective jurors without the judge's approval.

of prospective jurors even if they seem fair and open-minded, and they can do so without having to state reasons or win the judge's approval. Why would a lawyer challenge someone who, at least on the surface, appears to be impartial? What guides the decision to accept some jurors and reject others? These questions make the voir dire particularly interesting to social psychologists (Hans & Vidmar, 1986; Kassin & Wrightsman, 1988).

Trial Lawyers as Intuitive Psychologists

Before the O. J. Simpson trial began, lawyers speculated that the ideal defense juror would be someone who is older, black, male, and a football fan. Indeed, trial lawyers have been known to use such strategies to select juries. Under pressure to make choices quickly and without much information, lawyers rely on implicit personality theories and stereotypes. As described in Chapter 4, an implicit personality theory is a set of assumptions that people make about how certain attributes are related to each other and to behavior. When people believe that all members of a group share the same attributes, these implicit theories are called stereotypes.

As far as trial practice is concerned, numerous how-to books claim that the astute lawyer can predict a juror's verdict by his or her gender, occupation, ethnic background, and other simple demographics (Fulero & Penrod, 1990). It has been suggested, for example, that athletes lack sympathy for fragile and injured victims, that engineers are unemotional, and that cabinetmakers are so meticulous in their work that they are never completely satisfied with the evidence. Rumor has it that some prosecutors exclude butchers from juries on the assumption that anyone who cuts up dead animals for a living will not easily be shocked by the details of a violent crime. Clarence Darrow, one of the most prominent trial attorneys of the twentieth century, advised that jurors of southern European descent favored the defense whereas those from Scandinavia favored the prosecution. Other lawyers have theorized that women are more skeptical as jurors than men—particularly in response to highly attractive female witnesses (Adler, 1994). Still others offer advice based on clothing, handwriting samples, body language, and astrology. Perhaps the most interesting rule of thumb is also the simplest: "If you don't like a juror's face, chances are he doesn't like yours either!" (Wishman, 1986, pp. 72–73).

If assumptions based on surface appearances were correct, it would be easy to predict how jurors would vote. But the folk wisdom of trial lawyers is not supported by research, as demographic factors such as gender, age, race, income, education, marital status, and occupation do not consistently predict juror verdicts (Hastie et al., 1983). To be sure, individuals may generally be prone to favor the prosecution or the defense—dispositions that can be measured using the Juror Bias Scale presented in Table 12.1 (Kassin & Wrightsman, 1983). Thus, when Andrea Chapdelaine and Sean Griffin

---

TABLE 12.1   Some Items Used to Measure Juror Bias

Taken from the Juror Bias Scale, these statements can be used to measure the extent to which people are predisposed to favor the criminal prosecution or the defense. Agreement with items 1, 2, and 5 indicate a bias for the prosecution, while agreement with items 3, 4, and 6 indicate a bias for the defense. *(Kassin & Wrightsman, 1983.)*

1. Too often jurors hesitate to convict someone who is guilty out of pure sympathy.
2. In most cases where the accused presents a strong defense, it is only because of a good lawyer.
3. The death penalty is cruel and inhumane.
4. Too many innocent people are wrongfully imprisoned.
5. Generally, the police make an arrest only when they are sure who committed the crime.
6. Circumstantial evidence is too weak to use in court.

(1997) administered this scale along with an attitude survey about the O. J. Simpson case, they found that respondents with higher prosecution-bias scores were more likely to judge Simpson as guilty. Research has also shown that jurors who have an authoritarian personality—which leads them to identify with figures of authority, while being punitive and intolerant of others who are nonconventional—are also generally prone to convict (Narby et al., 1993).

Clearly, there are individual differences among jurors. But just as clearly, simple and general cookbook recipes—such as "women are tougher than men in rape cases"—can prove hopelessly misleading. To illustrate the point, Norbert Kerr and others (1995) tested the most intuitive hypothesis of all: that jurors favor defendants who are similar to themselves in important ways. In one study, they presented mixed-race groups of participants with either a strong or weak case involving a black or white defendant. They found that when the evidence was weak, participants were more lenient in their verdicts toward the defendant of the same race. When the evidence was strong, however, participants were harsher against the defendant of the same race. Jurors may show the expected leniency bias toward similar defendants who may be innocent, but they are quick to distance themselves from similar others who seem guilty.

The intuitive approach to jury selection is flawed. Thus, although many experienced trial attorneys take pride in their jury-selection skills, researchers have found that lawyers cannot effectively predict how jurors will vote—either on the basis of their intuitive rules of thumb (Olczak et al., 1991) or by how prospective jurors answer questions during the voir dire (Kerr et al., 1991; Zeisel & Diamond, 1978). Apparently, whether a juror characteristic predicts verdicts depends on the specifics of each and every case. Hence the birth of a new, controversial service industry: scientific jury selection.

> Contrary to popular opinion, women are harsher as criminal trial jurors than men are. **False.**

Scientific Jury Selection

Rather than rely on their hunches, successful stock market investors, baseball managers, and gamblers play the odds whenever they can. Now, many trial lawyers do too. In recent years, the "art" of jury selection has been transformed into a "science."

It all began during the Vietnam War era, when the federal government prosecuted a group of antiwar activists known as the Harrisburg Seven. The case against the defendants was strong, and the trial was to be held in the conservative city of Harrisburg, Pennsylvania. To help the defense select a jury, sociologist Jay Schulman and his colleagues (1973) surveyed the local community by interviewing 840 residents. Two kinds of information were taken from each resident: demographics (for example, sex, race, age, and education) and attitudes relevant to the trial (for example, attitudes toward the government, the war, and political dissent). By correlating these variables, Schulman's team came up with a profile of the ideal defense juror: "a female Democrat with no religious preference and a white-collar job or a skilled blue-collar job" (p. 40). Guided by this result, the defense went on to select its jury. The rest is history. Against all odds, the trial ended in a hung jury, split 10 to 2 in favor of acquittal.

Twenty-five years later, in the criminal trial against O. J. Simpson, the defense team hired a jury consultant to help in the selection process. Based on pretrial surveys, this consultant predicted that black women would prove to be Simpson's strongest defenders. Indeed, public opinion polls and other research later confirmed the more general point that race may have played a role in this case (Murray et al., 1997). Prosecutor Marcia Clark also had the help of a jury consultant, and he found exactly the same result. However, Clark rejected his advice in favor of her intuitive belief that black women would be enraged by Simpson's history of domestic violence. Again, the rest is history. After four hours of deliberation, the criminal jury acquitted Simpson of all charges (Toobin, 1996).

Today, the technique known as **scientific jury selection** is used often, especially in civil trials in which large sums of money are at stake. The procedure is simple. Because lawyers are often not allowed to ask jurors intrusive and personal questions, they try to determine jurors' attitudes from known information about their backgrounds. This information can be obtained through a communitywide survey, in which statistical relationships are sought between general demographic factors and attitudes relevant to a particular case. Then, during the voir dire, lawyers ask prospective jurors about their backgrounds and use peremptory challenges to exclude those whose profiles are associated with unfavorable attitudes.

As you might expect, scientific jury selection is a controversial enterprise. Consultants are not legally permitted to communicate with or approach prospective jurors themselves—despite the tactics portrayed in John Grisham's (1996) novel *The Runaway Jury*. But are the techniques that are used effective? It's hard to say. On the one hand, trial lawyers who have used scientific jury selection boast an impressive winning percentage. On the other hand, it is impossible to know the extent to which these victories are attributable to the jury-selection surveys. Social psychologists assume that attitudes can influence verdicts and that scientific jury selection can help lawyers identify these attitudes. As we'll see, this linkage is found most clearly in cases involving capital punishment.

Before concluding our review of scientific jury selection, let's stop to consider an ethical question: Is justice enhanced or impaired by the intervention of professional jury consultants? Is the real goal for lawyers to eliminate jurors who are biased or to create juries slanted in their favor? Those who practice scientific jury selection argue that picking juries according to survey results is simply a more refined version of what lawyers are permitted to do by intuition. If there's a problem, they say, it is not in the *science* but in the *law* that permits attorneys to use peremptory challenges to exclude jurors who are not obviously biased. In response, critics argue that scientific jury selection tips the scales of justice in favor of wealthy clients who can afford the service—an outcome that widens even further the socioeconomic gap that exists within the courts.

Death Qualification

It was February 3, 1998, when thirty-eight-year-old ax murderer Karla Faye Tucker died by lethal injection in Huntsville, Texas. At 6:45 P.M., eight minutes after fatal chemicals were pumped into her arms, Tucker moaned, then moved her lips as in prayer, gasped twice, and died with her eyes open. Outside the prison walls, one group of protesters lit candles and sang songs, while another crowd cheered and waved signs that read "God bless the death penalty." Because Tucker was a woman and a born-again Christian, her execution drew worldwide attention. Pope John Paul II wrote a letter on her behalf, as did the European Parliament and the United Nations. On the question of her punishment, people were divided.

If you had to sentence someone to die, could you do it? Not everyone answers this question in the same way. Yet your answer could mean the difference between life and death for a defendant convicted of murder. Today, thirty-nine out of fifty states permit capital punishment. Among those that do, it is typically the jury that decides not only the verdict but the sentence as well. In cases involving crimes punishable by death, and in which the jury makes both decisions, a special jury-selection practice known as **death qualification** is used. In death qualification, judges may exclude all prospective jurors who say that they would refuse to vote for

Do you favor or oppose the death penalty for persons convicted of murder? In response to this question, 74 percent of Americans say they favor capital punishment.

scientific jury selection A method of selecting juries through surveys that yield correlations between demographics and trial-relevant attitudes.

death qualification A jury-selection procedure used in capital cases that permits judges to exclude prospective jurors who say they would not vote for the death penalty.

On the night of February 3, 1998, crowds gathered outside the Texas Department of Criminal Justice in Huntsville, where Karla Faye Tucker was put to death. As you can see, this particular group was morally opposed to her execution.

Worldwide, the most common methods of execution are by hanging, shooting, and beheading. In the United States, the most common methods are electrocution, poisonous gas, and lethal injection.

the death penalty. These jurors are excluded for the entire trial. To ensure that *sentencing* decisions are unbiased, it makes sense to exclude those who admit they are closed-minded. But does this same selection practice tip the balance toward the prosecution when it comes to the *verdict?* In other words, are death-qualified juries prone to convict?

Juries must often decide whether to sentence a convicted murderer to death—in this case, in a gas chamber.

Through a series of studies, Phoebe Ellsworth, Craig Haney, and their colleagues have examined this question. Their results showed that when compared with people who oppose the death penalty, those who support it are more prosecution-minded on a host of issues. For example, they are more concerned about crime, more trustful of police, more cynical about defense lawyers, and less tolerant of procedures that are designed to protect the accused (Fitzgerald & Ellsworth, 1984; Haney et al., 1994).

When it comes to verdicts, the difference between jurors who are death-qualified and those who are excluded on this ground can be substantial. In one study, 288 people watched a videotaped murder trial and then participated in mock juries. The results showed that jurors who said they were willing to impose the death penalty were more likely to vote guilty—both before and after deliberating—than were those who would have been excluded for their refusal to impose a death sentence (Cowan et al., 1984). Similar results have also been found in studies of real jurors (Moran & Comfort, 1986). In fact, Haney (1984) has found death qualification voir-dire questions themselves are biasing because they presume the defendant's guilt and communicate to prospective jurors that the courts consider death a desirable form of punishment. In his studies, even randomly selected mock jurors were more likely to vote for conviction—and for the death penalty—when they were exposed to such questions during the voir dire than when they were not.

"Are we to understand, then, that you would have no scruples about imposing the death penalty?"

No doubt this prospective juror would survive the death qualification test.

As the research evidence mounted, American courts had to face a sobering prospect. Had the hundreds of prisoners on death row been tried by juries that were biased against them? In the case of *Lockhart* v. *McCree* (1986), the United States Supreme Court considered the issue. To inform the Court of recent research, the American Psychological Association submitted an exhaustive review of the literature (Bersoff & Ogden, 1987)—but to no avail. In an opinion that disappointed many social psychologists, the Court rejected the research claims and ruled that death qualification does not violate a defendant's right to a fair trial.

Should the Supreme Court have been persuaded more by the evidence? Some say yes (Ellsworth, 1991); others say no (Elliott, 1991). Either way, it may now be important to devise alternative, nonprejudicial methods that can be used to select future capital juries. For example, research shows that many people who are excluded because of a *general* opposition to capital punishment admit that they would consider the death penalty for *specific* defendants found guilty of committing atrocious acts of violence—suggesting that perhaps these individuals should not be removed from the jury (Cox & Tanford, 1989). Clearly, and for many reasons, this issue is one that continues to spark interest among social psychologists (Costanzo, 1997).

The Courtroom Drama

Once a jury is selected, the trial officially begins, and much of the evidence previously gathered comes to life. The evidence produced in the courtroom can range far and wide, from confessions to autopsy results, medical tests, blood stains, hair samples, handwriting samples, fingerprints, photographs, diaries, and business documents. The trial itself is a well-orchestrated event. Lawyers for both sides make opening statements. Witnesses then answer questions under oath. Lawyers make closing arguments. The judge instructs the jury. Yet there are many problems in this all-too-human enterprise: The evidence may not be accurate or reliable, jurors may be biased by extraneous factors, and judges' instructions may fall on deaf ears. In this section, we identify some of the problems and possible solutions.

Confession Evidence

Beginning with the news that he was a suspect, climaxing the night that his white Bronco was followed by the Los Angeles police, and continuing with his physical presence inside the courtroom, all eyes were focused on O. J. Simpson. Few defendants command this extraordinary degree of attention. But when the defendant speaks, everyone listens. Sometimes, what they hear are pleas of innocence; at other times, they hear confessions.

Police Interrogations: Social Influence Under Pressure   Many years ago, police detectives would use bright lights, brute force, the rubber hose, and physical intimidation to get confessions. Today, however, "third degree" tactics are more psychological in nature. In *Criminal Interrogation and Confessions*, the most popular how-to manual written for the police, Fred Inbau, John Reid, and Joseph Buckley (1986) first advise interrogators to put suspects into a small, bare, soundproof room—a physical environment designed to arouse feelings of social isolation, helplessness, and discomfort. Next, they present a vivid nine-step procedure designed to get suspects to confess (see Table 12.2).

In general, there are two approaches contained within this method of interrogation. One approach is to befriend the suspect, offer sympathy and friendly advice, and "minimize" the offense by offering face-saving excuses or blaming the victim. Lulled into a false sense of security, and led to expect leniency, the suspect caves in. A second general approach is to frighten the suspect into submission by exaggerating the charges or pretending to have damaging evidence such as fingerprints or an eyewitness. In this scenario, the suspect is led to believe that it is futile to mount a defense. These techniques may sound as if they come from a television script, but in real life they are frequently used (Gudjonsson, 1992; Kassin, 1997). In an observational study of 182 live and videotaped interrogations, for example, Richard Leo (1996) found that police detectives used an average of five to six tactics per suspect.

The Risk of False Confessions   It could be argued that the use of trickery and deception do not pose a serious problem because innocent people never confess to crimes they did not commit. This assumption, however, is not always correct. As hard as it is to believe, there are a number of chilling cases on record.

> **TABLE 12.2   The Nine Steps of Interrogation**
> *(Inbau et al., 1986.)*
>
> 1. Confront the suspect with assertions of his or her guilt.
> 2. Develop "themes" that appear to justify or excuse the crime.
> 3. Interrupt all statements of innocence and denial.
> 4. Overcome all of the suspect's objections to the charges.
> 5. Keep the increasingly passive suspect from tuning out.
> 6. Show sympathy and understanding, and urge the suspect to tell all.
> 7. Offer the suspect a face-saving explanation for his or her guilty action.
> 8. Get the suspect to recount the details of the crime.
> 9. Convert that statement into a full written confession.

Sometimes innocent suspects confess under pressure as an act of *compliance*, merely to escape a bad situation. In one astonishing case, for example; four young men confessed independently to the shooting massacre of six Thai Buddhist monks in a Phoenix temple. Separately, each man was subject to late-night interrogations. One was questioned non-stop for twenty-one hours; another was told that his brothers would be arrested if he did not cooperate. All the men eventually confessed and spent seventy days in jail—until the real murderers were apprehended on the basis of ballistics evidence (Parloff, 1993).

There are other instances in which interrogation causes innocent suspects to believe that they might be guilty of the crime, illustrating an even stronger form of social influence known as *internalization*. This process was evident in the story of Paul Ingram, a man charged with rape and a host of satanic ritual cult crimes. For a period of six months, Ingram was hypnotized, informed of graphic crime details, told by a police psychologist that sex offenders typically repress their offenses, and urged by the minister of his church to confess. Eventually he "recalled" crime scenes to specification, pleaded guilty, and was sentenced to prison. In fact, there was no physical evidence that many of the alleged events had even occurred, and an expert who reviewed the case concluded that Ingram had been "brainwashed." At one point, this expert accused Ingram of a phoney crime. Ingram denied the charge at first, but eventually he confessed—and embellished the story in the process (Ofshe & Watters, 1994).

Is it really possible to convince people that they are guilty of an act they did not commit? Based on an analysis of actual cases, Kassin and Kiechel (1996) theorized that two factors can increase this risk: (1) a suspect who lacks a clear memory of the event in question and (2) the presentation of false evidence. To test this hypothesis, they recruited pairs of college students to work on a fast- or slow-paced computer task. At one point, the computer crashed, and students were accused of having caused the damage by pressing a key they had been specifically instructed to avoid. All students were truly innocent and denied the charge. In half the sessions, however, the second student (who was really a confederate) said that she had seen the student hit the forbidden key. Demonstrating the process of compliance, many students confronted by this false witness agreed to sign a confession handwritten by the experimenter. Next, demonstrating the process of internalization, some students later "admitted" their guilt to a stranger (also a confederate) after the experiment was supposedly over and the two were alone. In short, innocent people who are vulnerable to suggestion can be induced to confess and to internalize guilt by the presentation of false evidence—an interrogation tactic commonly used by the police (see Table 12.3).

TABLE 12.3   Factors That Promote False Confessions

As participants worked on a fast- or slow-paced task, the computer crashed, and they were accused of causing the damage by pressing a key they had been told to avoid. A confederate then said that she had or had not seen the participants hit the forbidden key. As shown, many participants signed a confession (compliance), and some even "admitted" their guilt in private to another confederate (internalization). Despite their innocence, many participants in the fast-false witness condition confessed on both measures. *(Kassin & Kiechel, 1996.)*

	Control		False Witness	
	Slow	Fast	Slow	Fast
Compliance	35%	65%	89%	100%
Internalization	0%	12%	44%	65%

Without being beaten or threatened, innocent people sometimes confess to crimes they did not commit. **True.**

Confessions and the Jury: An Attributional Dilemma   How does the legal system treat confessions brought out by various methods of interrogation? The procedure is straightforward. Whenever a suspect confesses but then withdraws the statement and goes to trial, the judge must determine whether the statement was voluntary or coerced. If the confession was clearly coerced—as when a suspect is isolated for a long period of time, deprived of food or sleep, threatened, or abused—it is excluded. If not, it is admitted into evidence for the jury to evaluate. Juries are thus confronted with a classic attributional dilemma: A suspect's statement may indicate guilt (personal attribution), or it may simply be a way to avoid the aversive consequences of silence (situational attribution). According to attribution theory, jurors should reject all confessions made in response to external pressure. But wait. Remember the fundamental attribution error? In Chapter 4, we saw that people tend to overattribute behavior to persons and overlook the influence of situational forces. Is it similarly possible that jurors view suspects who confess as guilty even if they were highly pressured to confess during interrogation?

To examine this question, Kassin and Sukel (1997) had mock jurors read one of three versions of a murder trial. In a control version that did not contain a confession, only 19 percent voted guilty. In a low-pressure version in which the defendant was said to have confessed immediately upon questioning, the conviction rate rose considerably, to 62 percent. But there was a third, high-pressure condition in which participants were told that the defendant had confessed out of fear and with his hands cuffed painfully behind his back. How did participants in this situation react? Reasonably, they judged the confession to be coerced, and they said it did not influence their verdicts. Yet the conviction rate in this situation significantly increased, this time to 50 percent. Apparently, people are powerfully influenced by evidence of a confession—even, sometimes, when they concede that this confession was coerced.

The jury's reaction to confession evidence may also depend on how that evidence is presented. Today, many police departments videotape confessions for presentation in court (Geller, 1993). But how are these events staged for the camera? As described in Chapter 4, research has shown that observers who watch two people engage in a conversation overemphasize the impact on that interaction of the person who is visually salient. On the basis of this finding, Daniel Lassiter and his colleagues (1992) taped a mock confession from three different camera angles so that either the suspect or the interrogator or both were visible. All participants heard the same exchange of words, but those who watched the suspect considered the situation to be less coercive than did those who focused on the interrogator. The practical implications are striking. When the camera directs all eyes at the accused, jurors are likely to underestimate the amount of pressure exerted by the "hidden" interrogator. Yet that is precisely the way that confessions are normally taped.

The Lie-Detector Test

Often, people confess after being told that they have failed the **polygraph,** or lie-detector, test. A polygraph is an electronic instrument that simultaneously records multiple channels of physiological arousal. The signals are picked up by sensors attached to different parts of the body. For example, rubber tubes are strapped around a suspect's torso to measure breathing; blood pressure cuffs are wrapped around the upper arm to measure pulse rate; and electrodes are placed on the fingertips to record sweat-gland activity, or perspiration. These signals are then boosted by amplifiers and converted into a visual display.

The polygraph is used to detect deception on the assumption that when people lie, they become anxious in ways that can be measured. Here's how the test is conducted. After convincing a suspect that the polygraph works and establishing his or her baseline level of arousal, the examiner asks a series of yes-no questions and compares how the suspect reacts to emotionally arousing *crime-relevant questions* ("Did you steal the money?") and *control questions* that are arousing but not relevant to the crime ("Did you take anything that did not belong to you when you were young?"). In theory, suspects who are innocent—whose denials are truthful—should be more aroused by the control questions, while guilty suspects—whose denials are false—should be more aroused by the crime-relevant questions.

Does the lie-detector test really work? Many people think it is foolproof, but scientific opinion is split (Iacono & Lykken, 1997). Some researchers report accuracy rates of about 90 percent (Honts, 1996; Raskin, 1986). Others say that such claims are exaggerated and misleading (Lykken, 1981). One well-documented problem is that truthful persons too often fail the test. For example, a study of polygraph records obtained from police files revealed that although 98 percent of suspects later known to be guilty were correctly identified as such, 45 percent of those who were eventually found innocent were judged deceptive (Patrick & Iacono, 1991). A second problem is that the test can be faked. Studies show that you can beat the polygraph by tensing your muscles, squeezing your toes, or using other countermeasures while answering the *control* questions. By artificially

polygraph A mechanical instrument that records physiological arousal from multiple channels; it is often used as a lie-detector test.

Lie-detector tests can be beaten by suppressing arousal when questions about the crime are asked. **False.**

inflating the responses to "innocent" questions, one can mask the stress that is aroused by lying on the crime-relevant questions (Honts et al., 1994).

What, then, are we to conclude? After carefully reviewing the research, Leonard Saxe and his colleagues (1985) determined that there is no simple answer. Under certain conditions—for example, when the suspect is naive and the examiner is competent—it is possible for the polygraph to detect truth and deception at fairly high levels of accuracy. Still, the problems are hard to overcome—which is why many states refuse to allow polygraph test results into evidence. As an alternative, some researchers are now trying to develop tests that distinguish between truth and deception through the measurement of involuntary electrical activity in the brain (Bashore & Rapp, 1993) and pupil dilation when the person being tested is visually re-exposed to an object related to the crime (Lubow & Fein, 1996). At this point, it is too early to tell whether these alternative methods will prove to be any more accurate (Rosenfeld, 1995).

Eyewitness Testimony

"I'll never forget that face!" When these words are uttered, police officers, judges, and juries all take notice. Sometimes, however, eyewitnesses make mistakes. Consider the sad story of William Jackson, identified by two crime victims, convicted, and sent to prison. Five years later, Jackson was proved innocent and released. But the damage had been done. "They took away part of my life, part of my youth," he said ("We're Sorry," 1982).

An estimated 77,000 people a year are charged with crimes solely on the basis of eyewitness evidence (Goldstein et al., 1989). Many of these eyewitness accounts are accurate, but many are not. In fact, U.S. Department of Justice researchers recently studied twenty-eight miscarriages of justice in which defendants who had been convicted by juries and imprisoned were later proved innocent by DNA evidence. All the defendants had been positively identified by one or more eyewitnesses (Connors et al., 1996).

After the tragic assassination of President John F. Kennedy, dozens of eyewitnesses came forward to describe what they saw. Some reported one gunman in the sixth-floor window of a nearby building; others reported two or three gunmen in the building; and still others thought the shots were fired from the ground. Such are the pitfalls of eyewitness testimony.

As eyewitnesses, people can be called on to remember just about anything, including a face, an accident, or a conversation. Over the years, hundreds of tightly controlled studies have been conducted. From this research, three conclusions can be drawn: (1) eyewitnesses are imperfect, (2) certain personal and situational factors systematically influence their performance, and (3) judges, juries, and lawyers are not well informed about these factors (Cutler & Penrod, 1995; Ross, Read, & Toglia, 1994; Sporer et al., 1996; Wells, 1993).

People tend to think that human memory is like a videotape camera: If you turn on the power and focus the lens, all events will be recorded for subsequent playback. Unfortunately, it's not that simple. Over the years, researchers have found it useful to view memory as a three-stage process involving the *acquisition*, *storage*, and *retrieval* of information. The first of these stages, acquisition, refers to a witness's perceptions at the time of the event in question. Second, the witness stores that information in memory to avoid forgetting. Third, the witness retrieves the information from storage when needed. This model suggests that errors can occur at three different points.

Acquisition   Some kinds of persons and events are more difficult to perceive than others. Common sense tells us that brief exposure time, poor lighting, distance, physical disguise, and distraction are all factors that can severely limit a witness's perceptions. Research has uncovered other, less obvious factors as well.

Consider the effects of a witness's emotional state. Often people are asked to recall a bloody shooting, or a car wreck, or an assault—emotional events that trigger high levels of stress. Arousal has a complex effect on memory. Realizing the importance of what they are seeing, highly aroused witnesses zoom in on the central features of an event—perhaps the culprit, the victim, or a weapon. As a direct result of this narrowed field of attention, however, arousal impairs a witness's memory for other less central details (Burke et al., 1992; Christianson, 1992). Alcohol, a drug often involved in crime, also causes problems. When participants in one study witnessed a live staged crime, those who had earlier consumed fruit juice were more accurate in their recollections than were those who had been served an alcoholic beverage (Yuille & Tollestrup, 1990).

The **weapon-focus effect** can also be an important factor. Research shows that when a criminal pulls out a gun, a razor blade, or a knife, witnesses are less able to identify that culprit than if no weapon is present (Steblay, 1992). There are two reasons for this effect. First, people are agitated by the sight of a menacing stimulus—as when participants in one study were approached by an experimenter holding a syringe or threatening to administer an injection (Maass & Kohnken, 1989). Second, even in a harmless situation, a witness's eyes lock in on a weapon like magnets—drawing attention away from the features of the face. To demonstrate, Elizabeth Loftus and her colleagues (1987) showed people slides of a customer who walked up to a bank teller and pulled out either a gun or a checkbook. By recording eye movements, these researchers found that people spent more time looking at the gun than at the checkbook. The net result was an impairment in their ability to identify the criminal in a lineup.

There is still another important consideration. By varying the racial make-up of participants and target persons in laboratory and real-life interactions, researchers discovered that people find it relatively difficult to recognize members of a race other than their own—an effect known as the **cross-race identification bias** (Bothwell et al., 1989; Brigham & Malpass, 1985; Malpass & Kravitz, 1969). To demonstrate, eighty-six convenience store clerks in El Paso, Texas, were asked to identify three customers—one white, one black, and one Mexican American— all experimental confederates who had stopped in and made a purchase earlier that

weapon-focus effect The tendency for the presence of a weapon to draw attention and impair a witness's ability to identify the culprit.

cross-race identification bias The tendency for people to have difficulty identifying members of a race other than their own.

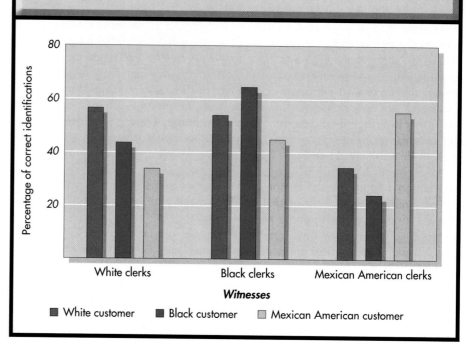

FIGURE 12.2   The Cross-Race Identification Bias

In this study, convenience store clerks tried to identify three customers—one white, one black, and one Mexican American—all of whom had stopped in during the day. As you can see, the clerks were more likely to correctly identify customers of their own racial or ethnic group. *(Platz & Hosch, 1988.)*

Eyewitnesses find it relatively difficult to recognize members of a race other than their own.
True.

day. Figure 12.2 shows that white, black, and Mexican American clerks were all most likely to make accurate identifications of customers belonging to their own racial or ethnic group (Platz & Hosch, 1988). To some extent, the problem that "they all look alike" stems from a lack of interracial contact. Thus, David Dunning and his colleagues (1998) found that the cross-race identification bias is *not* exhibited by white persons who are avid and knowledgeable fans of NBA basketball—a sport in which the majority of the players they watch are black.

Storage   In the fall of 1991, law professor Anita Hill accused Clarence Thomas, a nominee to the U.S. Supreme Court, of sexual harassment. She asserted that he had made certain statements ten years earlier—statements she said she could repeat word for word. A few years later, Whitewater prosecutor Kenneth Starr questioned several Arkansas associates of Bill and Hillary Clinton about financial transactions that had taken place years earlier. These stories have little in common, but both raise the same question: Can remembrances of the past be trusted?

As you might expect, memory for faces and events tends to decline with the passage of time. Longer intervals between an event and its retrieval are generally associated with increased forgetting (Shapiro & Penrod, 1986). But not all recollections fade, and time alone does not cause memory slippage. Consider the plight of those in Atlanta who witnessed firsthand the bombing at the 1996 Olympics. Afterward, they talked about the tragedy, read about it, heard what other bystanders had to say, and answered questions from investigators and reporters. By the time these witnesses were officially questioned, they had been exposed to so much post-event information that one wonders if their original memory was still "pure."

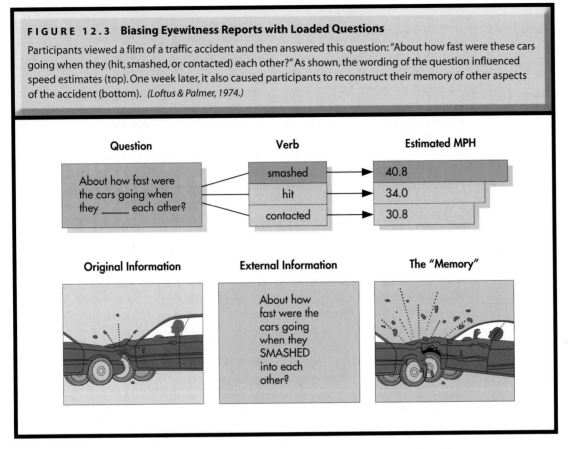

FIGURE 12.3 Biasing Eyewitness Reports with Loaded Questions
Participants viewed a film of a traffic accident and then answered this question: "About how fast were these cars going when they (hit, smashed, or contacted) each other?" As shown, the wording of the question influenced speed estimates (top). One week later, it also caused participants to reconstruct their memory of other aspects of the accident (bottom). *(Loftus & Palmer, 1974.)*

According to Elizabeth Loftus (1979), it probably was not. Based on her studies of eyewitness testimony, Loftus proposed a theory of reconstructive memory. After people observe an event, she said, later information about that event—whether it's true or not—becomes integrated into the fabric of their memory. A classic experiment by Loftus and John Palmer (1974) illustrates the point. Participants viewed a film of a traffic accident and then answered questions, including: "About how fast were the cars going when they *hit* each other?" Other participants answered the same question, except that the verb *hit* was replaced by *smashed, collided, bumped,* or *contacted.* All participants saw the same accident, yet the wording of the question affected their reports. Figure 12.3 shows that participants given the "smashed" question estimated the highest average speed and those responding to the "contacted" question estimated the lowest. But there's more. One week later, participants were called back for additional probing. Had the wording of the questions caused them to reconstruct their memories of the accident? Yes. When asked whether they had seen broken glass at the accident site (none was actually present), 32 percent of the "smashed" participants said they had. As Loftus had predicted, what these participants remembered of the accident was based on two sources: the event itself and postevent information.

This **misinformation effect** has aroused much controversy. It's clear that eyewitnesses can be compromised when they receive postevent information—as when they are told, for example, what other witnesses had reported (Shaw et al., 1997). But does postevent information actually alter or impair a witness's real memory, so that it can never be retrieved again (Belli et al., 1994; Weingardt et al., 1995)? Or do participants merely follow the experimenter's suggestion, leaving their true memory intact for retrieval under other conditions (Dodson & Reisberg, 1991;

misinformation effect The tendency for false postevent information to become integrated into people's memory of an event.

McCloskey & Zaragoza, 1985)? Although the debate rages on, an all-important practical lesson remains: Whether memory is truly altered or not, eyewitness *reports* are hopelessly biased by postevent information.

This phenomenon raises an additional question. If adults can be misled by postevent information, what about children? On August 2, 1988, Margaret Kelly Michaels, a twenty-six-year-old preschool teacher, was found guilty of 115 counts of sex abuse committed at the Wee Care Nursery School in New Jersey. The charges against her were shocking. For a period of over seven months, the jury was told, she danced nude in the classroom, stripped the children, licked peanut butter off their genitals, and raped them with knives, forks, spoons, and lego blocks.

Were the children's stories accurate? On the one hand, there were striking consistencies in the testimonies of nineteen child witnesses. On the other hand, social workers and investigators who conducted the interviews often prompted the children with suggestive leading questions, told them that Michaels was a bad person, urged them to describe acts they had initially denied, offered bribes for disclosures, and pressured those who claimed ignorance. Except for this testimony, there was no physical evidence of abuse and no other witnesses—even though the acts were supposed to have occurred during school hours in an open classroom. Michaels was found guilty and sentenced to forty-seven years in prison. After serving five of those years, she was released when the state appeals court overturned the conviction on the ground that the children's testimony could not be trusted. "One day you're getting ready for work and making coffee, minding your business," said Michaels, "and the next minute you are an accused child molester."

Can suggestive interview procedures cause young children to confuse appearance and reality? In recent years, thousands of sex abuse charges have been filed against babysitters, preschool teachers, family members, and strangers. In some of these cases, the suspects were falsely accused of performing ritual abuse as part of satanic cults (Bottoms & Davis, 1997). In light of these events, judges must struggle to decide: Are preschoolers competent to take the witness stand, or are they too suggestible, too prone to confuse reality and fantasy? To provide guidance to the courts, researchers have been studying children's eyewitness memory (Ceci & Bruck, 1995).

This research has evolved over the years. At first, simple laboratory experiments showed that preschoolers were more likely than older children and adults to incorporate misleading "trick" questions into their memories for simple stories (Ceci et al., 1987). Other studies showed that interviewers could get young children to change their memories, or at least their answers, simply by repeating a question over and over—a situation that implies that the answer given is not good enough (Poole & White, 1991). But are young children similarly suggestible about real-life, sometimes stressful, experiences?

In one study, nursery school children were told about a man named Sam Stone who was clumsy and always broke things. A month later, a man visited the school, spent time in the classroom, and left. The next day, the children were shown a ripped book and a soiled teddy bear and asked what happened. Reasonably, no one said that they saw Stone cause the damage. Over the next ten weeks, however, they were asked suggestive questions ("I wonder if Sam Stone was wearing long pants or short pants when he ripped the book?"). The result: When a new interviewer asked children to tell what happened, 72 percent of the three- and four-year-olds blamed Stone for the damage; 45 percent said they saw him do it. One child "recalled" that Stone took a paintbrush and painted melted chocolate on the bear. Others "saw" him spill coffee, throw toys in the air, rip the book in anger, and soak the book in warm water until it fell apart (Leichtman & Ceci, 1993). In a similar second study, children were manipulated into recalling one year later that an immunization shot they had received at the doctor's office either hurt, causing them to cry, or did not hurt (Bruck et al., 1995).

To summarize, misinformation and suggestive questions can bias a child's memory report—and preschoolers are particularly vulnerable in this regard. As such, the courts must distinguish between true and false claims—and do so on a case-by-case basis. In addition, clear research-based guidelines should be set for interviewing child witnesses in an objective, nonbiasing manner.

Retrieval For eyewitnesses, testifying is only the last in a series of efforts to retrieve what they saw from memory. Before witnesses reach the courtroom, they are questioned by police and lawyers, view a lineup or mug shots, and even assist in the construction of a facial composite or an artist's sketch of the perpetrator. Yet each of these experiences increases the risk of error and distortion.

Nothing an eyewitness does has greater impact than a lineup identification. When the police make an arrest, they often call on witnesses to view a lineup that includes the suspect and other individuals. This procedure may take place within days of a crime or months later. Either way, the lineup often results in tragic cases of mistaken identity. Through the application of eyewitness research findings, as we'll see, this risk can be reduced (Wells et al., 1998).

"Do you swear to tell your version of the truth as you perceive it, clouded perhaps by the passage of time and preconceived notions?"

© 1989 Sidney Harris.

Basically, four factors affect identification performance. The first is the lineup *construction*. A few years ago, comedian Richard Pryor performed in a skit on the TV show *Saturday Night Live* in which he appeared in a lineup next to a nun, a refrigerator, and a duck. Lo and behold, the eyewitness—having described a male criminal—picked Pryor. It obviously doesn't take a social psychologist to see the problem with this particular situation. To be fair, a lineup should contain four to eight innocent persons, or "foils," who match the witness's general description of the culprit (Lüüs & Wells, 1991) or resemble the suspect in general appearance (Nosworthy & Lindsay, 1990). Anything that makes the suspect distinctive, compared with the others, increases his or her chance of being selected (Buckhout, 1974). This is what happened to Steve Titus, a man mistakenly accused of rape when the police showed the victim his photograph along with photographs of five other men. Although the foils resembled Titus in appearance, his picture stood out like a sore thumb. It was smaller than all the others and was the only one without a border. Titus was also the only man in the group with a smile on his face (Loftus & Ketcham, 1991).

Second, lineup *instructions* to the witness are important. In a study by Roy Malpass and Patricia Devine (1981), students saw a staged act of vandalism, after which they attended a lineup. Half of the students received "biased" instructions: They were led to believe that the culprit was in the lineup. The others were told that he might or might not be present. Lineups were then presented either with or without the culprit. When the students received biased instructions, they felt compelled to

TABLE 12.4   Effects of Lineup and Instructions on False Identifications

After witnessing a crime, participants were told either that the culprit was in the lineup (biased instruction) or that he might or might not be present (unbiased instruction). Participants then viewed a lineup in which the real culprit was present or absent. Notice the percentage of participants in each group who identified an innocent person. Those who received the biased instruction were far more likely to make a false identification, picking an innocent person rather than no one at all—especially when the real culprit was not in the lineup. *(Malpass & Devine, 1981.)*

	Percentage of False Identifications	
	Unbiased Instructions	Biased Instructions
Culprit Present	0	25
Culprit Absent	33	78

When eyewitnesses look at a spread of photographs all at once, they tend to make relative judgments by picking the face that comes closest to the criminal. But when witnesses look through pictures one at a time, as shown here, they tend to make absolute judgments by comparing each face to their memory of the criminal. This latter procedure reduces the risk of a false identification.

identify *someone*—and often picked an innocent person (see Table 12.4). Additional studies have consistently confirmed this basic result (Steblay, 1997). Again, the story of Steve Titus is a case in point. The police told the victim to pick her assailant from a group of six photographs. After studying the pictures for several minutes and shaking her head in confusion, she was urged to concentrate and make a choice. "This one is the closest," she said. "It has to be this one" (Loftus & Ketcham, 1991, p. 38).

Third, the *format* of a lineup also influences whether a witness feels compelled to make a selection. When witnesses are shown a spread of photographs, they tend to make relative, multiple-choice-like judgments by picking the target who looks most like the suspect—a strategy that increases the risk of making a false identification. The solution? When the same photos are shown sequentially, one at a time, witnesses tend to make absolute judgments by comparing each target person with their memory of the criminal. This situation diminishes the risk of making a false identification (Lindsay et al., 1991; Lindsay & Wells, 1985). Indeed, Richard Gonzalez and others (1993) have found that in a procedure known as a *showup*—in which the police bring the suspect in alone, without foils—witnesses become cautious and make judgments that are more absolute than relative.

The fourth factor is perhaps the most subtle, as it pertains to *familiarity-induced biases*. Research shows that people often remember a face but forget the circumstances in which they saw it. In one study, for example, participants witnessed a staged crime and then looked through mugshots. A few days later, they were asked to view a lineup. The result was startling: Participants were just as likely to identify an innocent person whose photograph was in the mugshots as they were to pick the actual criminal! (Brown et al., 1977). This familiarity effect has been observed in many different studies (Brigham & Cairns, 1988; Gorenstein & Ellsworth, 1980). In fact, people are also likely to misidentify as the criminal an innocent bystander who happened to be at the crime scene (Ross, Ceci, Dunning, & Toglia, 1994). Apparently, witnesses often recognize a face but forget the circumstances in which they saw it.

Courtroom Testimony   Eyewitnesses can be inaccurate, but that's only part of the problem. The other part is that their testimony in the courtroom is persuasive and not easy to evaluate. To understand how juries view eyewitness testimony, Gary Wells, Rod Lindsay, and others conducted a series of experiments in which they staged the theft of a calculator in front of unsuspecting research participants, who were later cross-examined after trying to pick the culprit from a photo spread. Other participants, who served as mock jurors, observed the questioning and judged the witnesses. The results were sobering: Jurors overestimated how accurate the eyewitnesses were and could not distinguish between witnesses whose identifications were correct and those whose identifications were incorrect (Lindsay et al., 1981; Wells et al., 1979).

There appear to be two problems. First, the subject of human memory is not something people know about through common sense. Brian Cutler and his colleagues (1988), for example, found that mock jurors were simply not sensitive enough to the effects of lineup instructions, weapon focus, and other aspects of an eyewitnessing situation. Yet a witness's behavior may provide clues as to his or her accuracy. One possible way to distinguish between accurate and inaccurate identifications is by asking witnesses to describe the decision-making process. David Dunning and Lisa Beth Stern (1994) staged a crime and found that witnesses who made a correct identification from photographs described the judgment as quick, effortless, and automatic ("His face just popped out at me"). Those who were inaccurate described a more careful and deliberate process-of-elimination strategy ("I compared the photos with each other to narrow the choices"). The witness who recognizes the culprit's face is most likely to do so instantly, without much thought (Sporer, 1993).

The second problem is that participants in this study—and in others as well—based their judgments largely on how *confident* the witness was, a factor that does not reliably predict accuracy (Bothwell et al., 1987; Penrod & Cutler, 1995; Sporer et al., 1995; Wells & Murray, 1984). Why are eyewitness confidence and accuracy often not related? The reason is that confidence levels can be raised and lowered by factors that do not have an impact on identification accuracy.

To demonstrate, Elizabeth Lüüs and Wells (1994) staged a theft in front of pairs of participants and then had each participant separately identify the culprit from a photographic lineup. After the participants made an identification, the experimenter led them to believe that their partner, a co-witness, either had picked the same person, a similar-looking different person, or a dissimilar-looking different person or had said that the thief was not in the lineup. Participants were then questioned by a police officer about what they had seen and were asked, "On a scale from 1 to 10, how confident are you in your identification?" As shown in Figure 12.4, participants became more confident when told that a co-witness had picked the same person or a dissimilar alternative and less confident when told that the co-witness had selected a

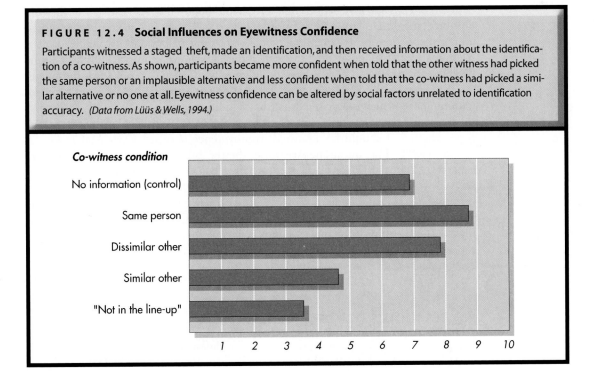

FIGURE 12.4 Social Influences on Eyewitness Confidence

Participants witnessed a staged theft, made an identification, and then received information about the identification of a co-witness. As shown, participants became more confident when told that the other witness had picked the same person or an implausible alternative and less confident when told that the co-witness had picked a similar alternative or no one at all. Eyewitness confidence can be altered by social factors unrelated to identification accuracy. *(Data from Lüüs & Wells, 1994.)*

The more confident an eyewitness is about an identification, the more accurate it is likely to be. **False.**

similar alternative or none at all. Other research confirms how important post-identification feedback can be. In a series of studies, John Shaw (1996) found that witnesses who are repeatedly questioned about their observations become increasingly confident over time—but not more accurate. Gary Wells and Amy Bradfield (1998) then found that witnesses given positive feedback about their false identifications also went on to reconstruct other aspects of the eyewitnessing experience. They reported, for example, that they had paid more attention to the event, had a better view of the culprit, and found it easier to make the identification. Clearly, eyewitnesses can become more or less confident about the entire experience as a result of social factors that are unrelated to identification accuracy.

The Eyewitness Expert   Having identified some of the problems with information obtained from eyewitnesses, social psychologists are in a position to put their knowledge to use by educating juries so they can better evaluate the evidence. But is this a goal that can and should be achieved? More and more, psychologists are being asked to testify as expert witnesses on coerced confessions, lie-detector tests, the suggestibility of children in abuse cases, and the coping behavior of rape victims and battered wives (Frazier & Borgida, 1992; Schuller & Vidmar, 1992).

One controversial form of expert testimony concerns the subject of eyewitness evidence. Like physicians who testify about a patient's medical condition, and like economists who testify on antitrust matters, eyewitness experts are often called by one party or the other to inform the jury about relevant theory and research (Kassin et al., 1989; Leippe, 1995). Does the jury need to be informed? In some cases, yes. Over the years, researchers have found that there's a great deal about eyewitness perception, memory, and communication that the average person does not know as a matter of common sense (Devenport et al., 1997). In fact, judges and lawyers themselves are not aware of many of the factors that influence eyewitness performance. To demonstrate, Veronica Stinson and her colleagues (1996, 1997) presented large groups of Florida judges and criminal defense lawyers with hypothetical cases, all of which included a lineup identification that varied in important ways. In general, these researchers found that the judges and lawyers could reasonably distinguish between lineups and instructions that were fair as opposed to suggestive. But they did not understand that witnesses are more likely to pick someone from photographs—even someone innocent—when the pictures are shown all at once (which leads people to make relative judgments) than when they are shown sequentially, one at a time (which leads people to make absolute judgments). Getting it backward, the judges and lawyers criticized the sequential format for not allowing witnesses to compare photographs—which is precisely what they should not do.

Psychologists disagree about whether advice from experts helps the jury—and, thus, whether it should be admitted into evidence (Loftus, 1983; McCloskey & Egeth, 1983). The question: Are juries better off with or without help from experts? Although it's too early to draw firm conclusions, research suggests two ways in which experts help jurors to be more competent. First, it's clear that eyewitness experts lead people to scrutinize the evidence more carefully. Since people in general place too much faith in eyewitness testimony, a dose of skepticism in this regard is a healthy outcome. Second, it is possible—but not yet certain—that expert testimony can help jurors to distinguish between accurate and inaccurate eyewitnesses (Cutler et al., 1989; Wells, 1986).

Nonevidentiary Influences

Early in the O. J. Simpson criminal trial, the defendant approached the jury box, lifted his pants, and displayed scars on his knees. A few days later, Denise Brown,

Nicole's sister, broke down and cried on the witness stand as gruesome pictures of her slain sister prompted a gasp in the courtroom. Also during the trial, Simpson's story was released in a book, prosecutor Marcia Clark became embroiled in a child custody suit with her ex-husband, and defense lawyers were caught withholding key evidence. In this case, however, as in others, the jury was shielded from some of these events and told to disregard the rest. The question is: To what extent are jurors influenced by information that is not in evidence?

Pretrial Publicity   Many cases find their way into the mass media long before they appear in court. Recent examples include the Oklahoma City bombing trials of Timothy McVeigh and Terry Nichols, the sexual assault case against sportscaster Marv Albert, the murder trial of the young British nanny, the "prom mom" trial involving the New Jersey teenager who gave birth at a prom and suffocated the newborn to death, the Texas cattlemen's lawsuit against entertainer Oprah Winfrey for critical statements she made about beef, and the many lawsuits filed against the tobacco industry. In each instance, the system struggles with this dilemma: Does exposure to pretrial news stories corrupt prospective jurors?

Public opinion surveys consistently show that the more people know about a case, the more likely they are to presume the defendant guilty, even when they claim to be impartial (Moran & Cutler, 1991). There is nothing particularly mysterious about this result. The information in news reports usually comes from the police or the district attorney's office, so it often reveals facts unfavorable to the defense. The real question is whether these reports have an impact on juries that go on to receive hard evidence in court and deliberate to a verdict.

To examine the effects of pretrial publicity, Geoffrey Kramer and his colleagues (1990) played a videotaped re-enactment of an armed robbery trial to hundreds of people participating in 108 mock juries. Before watching the tape, participants were exposed to news clippings about the case. Some read material that was neutral. Others received information that was incriminating—revealing, for example, that the defendant had a prior record or implicating him in a hit-and-run accident in which a small child was killed. Even though participants were instructed to base their decisions solely on the evidence, pretrial publicity had a marked effect. Among those exposed to neutral material, 33 percent voted guilty after deliberating in a jury. Among those exposed to the prejudicial material, that figure increased to 48 percent. What's worse, judges and defense lawyers could not identify in a simulated voir dire which jurors were biased by the publicity. As

"It is a capital mistake to theorize before you have all the evidence. It biases the judgment."

—Sir Arthur Conan Doyle

In 1997, Timothy McVeigh was convicted and sentenced to life for the Oklahoma City bombing murders. Based on the reasonable argument that McVeigh could not receive a fair trial in Oklahoma due to pretrial publicity, the trial had been moved to Denver, Colorado.

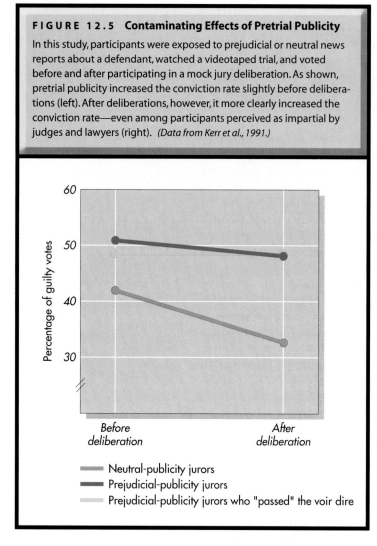

FIGURE 12.5 Contaminating Effects of Pretrial Publicity

In this study, participants were exposed to prejudicial or neutral news reports about a defendant, watched a videotaped trial, and voted before and after participating in a mock jury deliberation. As shown, pretrial publicity increased the conviction rate slightly before deliberations (left). After deliberations, however, it more clearly increased the conviction rate—even among participants perceived as impartial by judges and lawyers (right). *(Data from Kerr et al., 1991.)*

shown in Figure 12.5, 48 percent of those who were questioned and not challenged—jurors who said they were unaffected—went on to vote guilty (Kerr et al., 1991). The impact of pretrial publicity is even more powerful when the news is seen on television rather than in print (Ogloff & Vidmar, 1994).

Pretrial publicity is potentially dangerous in two respects. First, it often divulges information that is not later allowed into the trial record. Second is the matter of timing. Because many news stories precede the actual trial, jurors learn about certain facts even before they enter the courtroom. From what is known about the power of first impressions, the implications are clear. If jurors receive prejudicial news information about a defendant *before* trial, that information will distort the way they interpret the facts of the case. So, is there a solution? Since the biasing effects persist despite the practices of jury selection, the presentation of hard evidence, cautionary words from the judge, and jury deliberations, justice may demand that highly publicized cases be postponed or moved to other, less informed communities (Studebaker & Penrod, 1997).

Inadmissible Testimony Just as jurors are biased by news stories, they occasionally receive extralegal information within the trial itself. In his opening statement, for example, Simpson's lawyer—Johnnie Cochran—repeatedly referred to witnesses who would not later testify. With each passing reference, prosecutor Marcia Clark objected. Eventually, the judge issued a warning to Simpson's lawyer and ordered the jury to disregard the information. Then, just a few weeks later, the judge had to warn the prosecutors—and again instruct the jury to disregard that information.

If something seems wrong with this series of events, you should know that it is a scene often replayed in the courtroom. But can people really strike information from their minds the way court reporters can strike it from the record? Can people resist the forbidden fruit of inadmissible testimony? Although common sense suggests they cannot, the research is mixed. In one study, a group of mock jurors read about a murder case based on evidence so weak that not a single juror voted guilty. A second group read the same case, except that the prosecution introduced an illegally obtained tape recording of a phone call made by the defendant: "I finally got the money to pay you off…. When you read the papers tomorrow, you'll know what I mean." The defense argued that the illegal tape should not be admissible, but the judge disagreed. As a result, the conviction rate increased to 26 percent. In a third group, as in the second, the tape was brought in and the defense objected. Yet this time, the judge sustained the objection and told jurors to disregard the tape. The result: 35 percent voted for conviction (Sue et al., 1973). Other studies as well have revealed that "limiting instructions" do not deter jurors (Greene & Dodge, 1995; Pickel, 1995). In fact, when the disclosures to be disregarded are highly emotional in nature, such instructions may well increase their impact (Edwards & Bryan, 1997).

Why do people not follow a judge's instruction to disregard inadmissible evidence? Imagine yourself in the jury box, and three reasons will become apparent. First, the added instruction draws attention to the information in controversy. It's like being told *not* to think about white bears. As we saw in Chapter 3, trying to suppress a specific thought increases its tendency to intrude upon our consciousness (Wegner, 1994). A second reason is that a judge's instruction to disregard, like censorship, restricts a juror's decision-making freedom. Accordingly, it can backfire by arousing reactance. Thus, when a judge emphasizes the ruling by forbidding jurors from considering the information ("You have no choice but to disregard it"), they become even *more* likely to use it (Wolf & Montgomery, 1977). The third reason is the easiest to understand. Jurors want to reach the right decision. If they stumble onto relevant information, they want to use it—whether it satisfies the law's technical rules or not. In other words, jurors find it hard to ignore information that seems relevant to a case (Wissler & Saks, 1985).

To test this third hypothesis, Kassin and Sommers (1997) had mock jurors read a transcript of a double-murder trial that was based on relatively weak evidence, leading only 24 percent to vote guilty. Three other groups read the same case except that the state's evidence included a wiretapped phone conversation in which the defendant had confessed to a friend. In all cases, the defense lawyer objected to the disclosure. When the judge ruled to admit the tape into evidence, the conviction rate increased considerably, to 79 percent. But when the judge excluded the tape and instructed jurors to disregard it, their reaction depended on the reason for the tape's being excluded. When told to disregard the tape because it was barely audible and could not be trusted, participants mentally erased the information, as

"The proof was in the pudding, but the pudding was ruled inadmissible as evidence."

FIGURE 12.6   The Selective Impact of Inadmissible Testimony

In this experiment, mock jurors given admissible wiretap evidence against the defendant were more likely to vote guilty than control participants. When the judge ruled the tape inadmissible because it was unreliable, participants disregarded the information, as they should. When the tape was ruled inadmissible because it had been illegally obtained, however, participants used the information to vote guilty. It appears that jurors are unwilling to disregard testimony they see as relevant—even if instructed to do so by the judge. *(Kassin & Sommers, 1997, p. 1049.)*

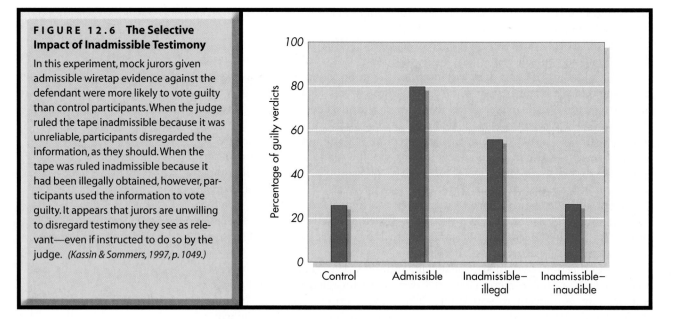

they should, and delivered the same 24 percent conviction rate as in the no-tape control group. But when told to disregard the item because it had been illegally obtained, 55 percent voted guilty. Despite the judge's warning, these latter participants were unwilling to ignore testimony they saw as highly relevant merely because of a legal "technicality" (see Figure 12.6).

The Judge's Instructions

One of the most important rituals in any trial is the judge's instruction to the jury. It is through these instructions that juries are educated about relevant legal concepts, informed of the verdict options, admonished to disregard extralegal factors, and advised on how to conduct their deliberations. To make verdicts adhere to the law, juries are supposed to comply with these instructions. The task seems simple enough, but there are problems.

To begin with, the jury's intellectual competence has been called into question. For years, the courts have doubted whether jurors understood their instructions. One skeptical judge put it bluntly when he said that "these words may as well be spoken in a foreign language" (Frank, 1949, p. 181). To some extent, he was right. When actual instructions are tested with mock jurors, the results reveal high levels of misunderstanding—a serious problem in light of the fact that jurors seem to have many preconceptions about crimes and the requirements of the law (Robinson & Darley, 1995; Smith, 1991). There is, however, reason for hope. Research has shown that when conventional instructions (which are poorly structured, esoteric, and filled with complex legal terms) are rewritten in plain English, comprehension rates increase markedly (Elwork et al., 1982; English & Sales, 1997).

Comprehension is a necessary first step, but presentation factors are also important. Consider the following study (Kassin & Wrightsman, 1979). Participants watched an auto-theft trial that included, for the defense, an all-important instruction stating that the defendant is presumed innocent and that the prosecutor must prove guilt beyond a reasonable doubt. The statement itself was easy to understand. The key, however, was its *timing*. Among mock jurors who never received the instruction, 63 percent voted guilty. When the instruction followed the evidence, as is the custom in most courts, the conviction rate remained high at 59 percent. Only when the instruction preceded the evidence did the rate drop, to

37 percent. Why did the postevidence instructions have so little impact? The researchers asked half of the participants for their opinions at various points during the trial and found that these mid-trial opinions were predictive of final verdicts. In other words, it was simply too late for a presumption-of-innocence instruction because many participants had already made up their minds. Indeed, Lynne FosterLee and her colleagues (1993) found that pre-evidence instructions generally increased the decision-making competence of mock jurors in a complex civil case.

In this Detroit courtroom, Dr. Jack Kevorkian was tried for an assisted suicide. Although physician-assisted suicide is illegal in Michigan, the jury in this case "nullified" the law in favor of their own conceptions of justice—and voted not guilty.

A lack of comprehension and poor timing are two reasons that a judge's instruction may have little impact. But there's a third reason: Juries sometimes disagree with the law—thus raising the controversial issue of **jury nullification.** You may not realize it, but juries, because they deliberate in private, can choose to disregard, or "nullify," the judge's instructions. The pages of history are filled with poignant examples. Consider the case of someone tried for euthanasia, or "mercy killing." By law, it is murder. But to the defendant, it might be a noble act performed on behalf of a loved one. Faced with this kind of conflict—an explosive moral issue on which public opinion is sharply divided (Brigham & Pfeifer, 1996; Sugarman, 1986)—juries often evaluate the issue in human terms, use their own notions of common-sense justice, and vote despite the law for acquittal (Finkel, 1995; Horowitz & Willging, 1991). This is what has happened in cases involving physician-assisted suicide, as often practiced by Jack Kevorkian, a retired pathologist. Kevorkian has presided over more than fifty deaths. For three of these incidents, he was tried for murder—and in all three he was acquitted by a jury.

Jury Deliberation

Anyone who has seen *Twelve Angry Men* can appreciate how colorful and passionate a jury's deliberation can be. This film classic opens with a jury eager to convict a young man of murder—no ifs, ands, or buts. The group selects a foreman and takes a show-of-hands vote. The result is an 11-to-1 majority, with actor Henry Fonda the lone dissenter. After many tense moments, Fonda manages to convert his peers, and the jury votes unanimously for acquittal.

It is often said that the unique power of the jury stems from the fact that individuals come together privately as one *group*. Is this assumption justified? *Twelve Angry Men* is a work of fiction, but does it realistically portray what transpires in the jury room? And in what ways does the legal system influence the group dynamics? By interviewing jurors after trials, and by recruiting people to participate on mock juries and then recording their deliberations, researchers have learned a great deal about the ways in which juries make their decisions.

jury nullification The jury's power to disregard, or "nullify," the law when it conflicts with personal conceptions of justice.

Leadership in the Jury Room

In theory, all jurors are created equal. In practice, however, dominance hierarchies develop. As in other decision-making groups, a handful of individuals lead the discussion, while others participate at a lower rate or watch from the sidelines, speaking only to cast their votes (Hastie et al., 1983). It's almost as if there is a jury within the jury. The question is, what kinds of people emerge as leaders?

It is often assumed that the foreperson is the leader. The foreperson, after all, calls for votes, acts as a liaison between the judge and jury, and announces the verdict in court. It seems like a position of importance, yet the selection process is very quick and casual. It's interesting that the foreperson selection outcomes do follow a predictable pattern (Stasser et al., 1982). People of higher occupational status or with prior experience on a jury are frequently chosen. Sex differences are also common. Norbert Kerr and his colleagues (1982) examined the records of 179 trials held in San Diego and found that 50 percent of the jurors were female but 90 percent of the forepersons were male. Other patterns, too, are evident. The first person who speaks is often chosen as foreperson (Strodtbeck et al., 1957). And when jurors deliberate around a rectangular table, those who sit at the heads of the table are more likely to be chosen than are those seated in the middle (Bray et al., 1978; Strodtbeck & Hook, 1961). Adding to the complete picture is the fact that men are more likely than women to speak first and take the prominent seats (Nemeth et al., 1976).

If you find such inequalities bothersome, fear not: Forepersons may act as nominal leaders, but they do *not* exert more than their fair share of influence over the group. In fact, although they spend more time than other jurors talking about procedural matters, they spend less time expressing opinions on the verdict (Hastie et al., 1983). Thus, it may be most accurate to think of the foreperson not as the jury's leader but as its moderator. In *Twelve Angry Men*, actor Martin Balsam—not Henry Fonda—was the foreperson. He was also among the least influential members of the jury.

The Dynamics of Deliberation

If the walls of the jury room could talk, they would tell us that the decision-making process typically passes through three stages (Hastie et al., 1983; Stasser et al., 1982). Like other problem-solving groups, juries begin in a relaxed *orientation* period during which they set an agenda, talk in open-ended terms, raise questions, and explore the facts. Then, once differences of opinion are revealed—usually after the first vote is taken—factions develop, and the

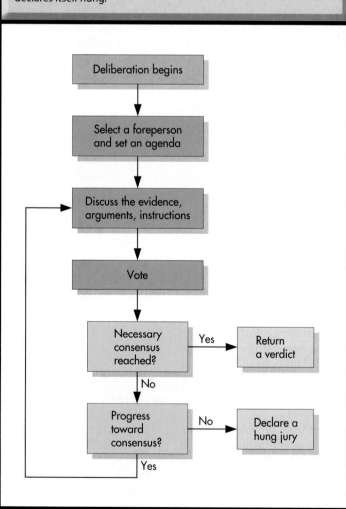

FIGURE 12.7   Jury Deliberations: The Process

Juries move through various tasks en route to a verdict. They begin by setting and reviewing the case. If all jurors agree, they return a verdict. If not, they continue to discuss the case until they reach a consensus. If the holdouts refuse to vote with the majority, the jury declares itself hung.

group shifts abruptly into a period of *open conflict*. With the battle lines sharply drawn, discussion takes on a more focused, argumentative tone. Together, jurors scrutinize the evidence, construct stories to account for that evidence, and discuss the judge's instructions (Pennington & Hastie, 1992). If all jurors agree, they return a verdict. If not, the majority tries to achieve a consensus by converting the holdouts through information and social pressure. If unanimity is achieved, the group enters a period of *reconciliation*, during which it smooths over the conflicts and affirms its satisfaction with the outcome. If the holdouts continue to disagree, the jury declares itself hung. This process is diagrammed in Figure 12.7.

When it comes to decision-making *outcomes*, deliberations tend to follow a predictable course first discovered by Harry Kalven and Hans Zeisel (1966). By interviewing the members of 225 criminal juries, they were able to reconstruct how these juries split on their very first vote. Out of 215 juries that opened with an initial majority, 209 reached a final verdict consistent with that first vote. This finding—later bolstered by the results of mock jury studies (Kerr, 1981; Sandys & Dillehay, 1995; Stasser & Davis, 1981; see Table 12.5)—led Kalven and Zeisel to conclude that "the deliberation process might well be likened to what the developer does for an exposed film; it brings out the picture, but the outcome is predetermined" (1966, p. 489). Henry Fonda's *Twelve Angry Men* heroics notwithstanding, one can usually predict the final verdict by knowing where the individual jurors stand the first time they vote.

There is one reliable exception to this majority-wins rule. It is that in criminal trials, deliberation tends to produce a **leniency bias** favoring the defendant. All other factors being equal, individual jurors are more likely to vote guilty on their own than in a group; they are also more prone to convict before deliberations than after (MacCoun & Kerr, 1988). Look again at Table 12.5, and you'll see that juries that are equally divided in their initial vote are ultimately likely to return not-guilty verdicts. Perhaps it is easier to raise a "reasonable doubt" in other people's minds than to erase all doubt. In this regard, it is interesting to note that in their classic study entitled *The American Jury* (1966), Kalven and Zeisel surveyed 555 judges who reported how they would have voted in some 3,500 jury trials. Judges agreed with their juries 78 percent of the time. When they disagreed, it was usually because the jury acquitted a defendant thought to be guilty by the judge. Perhaps these disagreements are due, in part, to the fact that juries decide as groups, and judges as individuals.

Knowing that the majority tends to prevail doesn't tell us *how* juries manage to resolve disagreements en route to a verdict. From the conformity studies discussed in Chapter 7, we know that there are two possibilities. Sometimes, people conform because, through a process of *informational influence*, they are genuinely persuaded by what others say. At other times, people yield to the pressures of *normative influence* by changing their overt behavior in the majority's direction even though they disagree in private. When it comes to the decision making of juries, justice demands that they reach a consensus through a vigorous exchange of views and information, not by heavy-handed social pressure. But is that how it works?

TABLE 12.5 The Road to Agreement: From Individual Votes to a Group Verdict

Research has shown that these verdicts are reached by mock juries that begin with different combinations of initial votes. You can see that the results support the majority-wins rule. But also note the evidence for a leniency bias: When the initial vote is split, juries gravitate toward acquittal. *(Kerr, 1981, as cited in Stasser et al., 1982.)*

Initial Votes (Guilty–Not Guilty)	Final Jury Verdicts (percent)		
	Conviction	Acquittal	Hung
6–0	100	0	0
5–1	78	7	16
4–2	44	26	30
3–3	9	51	40
2–4	4	79	17
1–5	0	93	7
0–6	0	100	0

leniency bias The tendency for jury deliberation to produce a tilt toward acquittal.

Research shows that juries achieve unanimity not by one process or the other but by a combination of both (Kaplan & Schersching, 1981). Research also shows that certain factors can upset the delicate balance between informational and normative influence. Social pressure is increased, for example, in juries that vote by a public roll call or show of hands (Davis et al., 1989) and in deadlocked juries that are called into the courtroom and urged by the judge to resolve their differences (Smith & Kassin, 1993).

Over the past thirty years, the U.S. Supreme Court has in two ways altered the decision-making dynamics of the jury. In the following pages, we look at these important changes and what they mean.

Jury Size: How Small Is Too Small?

How many people does it take to form a jury? In keeping with the British tradition, twelve has long been the magic number. Then, in the case of *Williams* v. *Florida* (1970), the defendant was convicted of armed robbery by a six-person jury. He appealed the verdict to the U.S. Supreme Court but lost. As a result of this precedent, American courts are today permitted to cut trial costs by using six-person juries in cases that do not involve the death penalty. Juries consisting of fewer than six are not permitted (*Ballew* v. *Georgia*, 1978).

What is the impact of a six-person jury? The Supreme Court approached the question as a social psychologist would. It sought to determine whether the change would affect the decision-making process. Unfortunately, the Court misinterpreted the available research so badly that Michael Saks concluded it "would not win a passing grade in a high school psychology class" (1974, p. 18). Consider whether a reduction in size affects the ability of those in the voting minority to resist normative pressures. The Supreme Court did not think it would. Citing Asch's (1956) conformity studies, the Court argued that an individual juror's resistance depends on the *proportional* size of the majority. But is that true? Is the lone dissenter caught in a 5-to-1 bind as well insulated from the group norm as the minority in a 10-to-2 split? The Court argued that these 83-to-17 percent divisions are psychologically identical. But wait. Asch's research showed exactly the opposite—that the mere presence of a single ally enables dissenters to maintain their independence better than anything else. Research has shown that the size of a jury has other effects too. Michael Saks and Molli Marti (1997) recently conducted a meta-analysis of studies involving fifteen thousand mock jurors who participated in over two thousand six-person or twelve-person juries. Overall, they found that the smaller juries were less likely to represent minority segments of the population. They were also more likely to reach a unanimous verdict—and to do so despite deliberating for shorter periods of time. Even in civil trials—in which juries have to make complex decisions on how much money to award the plaintiff—six-person groups spend less time discussing the case (Davis et al., 1997).

Less-Than-Unanimous Verdicts

The jury's size is not all that has changed. In 1972, the Supreme Court considered whether states may accept jury verdicts that are not unanimous. In one opinion, two defendants had been convicted by non-unanimous juries—one by a vote of 11 to 1, the other by 10 to 2 (*Apodaca* v. *Oregon*, 1972). In a second opinion, a guilty verdict was determined by a 9-to-3 margin (*Johnson* v. *Louisiana*, 1972). In both decisions, the Supreme Court upheld the convictions.

TABLE 12.6 *Johnson v. Louisiana* (1972): Contrasting Views

Notice the contrasting views in the U.S. Supreme Court's decision to permit non-unanimous jury verdicts. Justice White wrote the majority opinion, and Justice Douglas wrote the dissent. The decision was reached by a vote of 5 to 4.

Mr. Justice White, for the Majority:

We have no grounds for believing that majority jurors, aware of their responsibility and power over the liberty of the defendant, would simply refuse to listen to arguments presented to them in favor of acquittal, terminate discussion, and render a verdict. On the contrary, it is far more likely that a juror presenting reasoned argument in favor of acquittal could either have his arguments answered or would carry enough other jurors with him to prevent conviction. A majority will cease discussion and outvote a minority only after reasoned discussion has ceased to have persuasive effect or to serve any other purpose—when a minority, that is, continues to insist upon acquittal without having persuasive reasons in support of its position.

Mr. Justice Douglas, for the Minority:

Non-unanimous juries need not debate and deliberate as fully as most unanimous juries. As soon as the requisite majority is attained, further consideration is not required either by Oregon or by Louisiana even though the dissident jurors might, if given the chance, be able to convince the majority. . . . The collective effort to piece together the puzzle of historical truth . . . is cut short as soon as the requisite majority is reached in Oregon and Louisiana. . . . It is said that there is no evidence that majority jurors will refuse to listen to dissenters whose votes are unneeded for conviction. Yet human experience teaches us that polite and academic conversation is no substitute for the earnest and robust argument necessary to reach unanimity.

The Court was divided in its view of these cases. Five justices argued that a non-unanimous decision rule would not adversely affect the jury; four justices believed that it would reduce the intensity of deliberations and undermine the potential for minority influence. Table 12.6 presents these dueling points of view. Which do you find more convincing? Imagine yourself on a jury that needs only a 9-to-3 majority to return a verdict. You begin by polling the group and find that you already have the nine votes needed. What next? According to one script, the group continues to argue vigorously and with open minds. According to the alternative scenario, the group begins to deliberate, but the dissenters are quickly cast aside because their votes are not needed. Again, which scenario seems more realistic?

To answer that question, Reid Hastie and his colleagues (1983) recruited more than eight hundred people from the Boston area to take part in sixty-nine mock juries. After watching a reenactment of a murder trial, the groups were instructed to reach a verdict by a 12-to-0, a 10-to-2, or an 8-to-4 margin. The differences were striking. Compared with juries needing unanimous decisions, the others spent less time discussing the case and more time voting. After reaching the required number of votes, they often rejected the holdouts, terminated discussion, and returned a verdict. Afterward, participants in the non-unanimous juries rated their peers as more closed-minded and themselves as less informed and less confident about the verdict. What's worse, Hastie's team saw in tapes of the deliberations that majority-rule juries often adopted "a more forceful, bullying, persuasive style" (1983, p. 112).

If you're interested in a current jury trial and want to register your opinion in an online poll, visit this site: www.computek. net/jurytalk/

Today, a few states permit less-than-unanimous verdicts in criminal trials. A substantial number do so for civil cases. Yet research has shown that this procedure weakens jurors who are in the voting minority, breeds closed-mindedness, short-circuits the discussion, and leaves many jurors uncertain about the decision. Henry Fonda, step aside. The jury has reached its verdict.

Posttrial: To Prison and Beyond

Before taking O. J. Simpson to trial, the Los Angeles district attorney had to make a decision: If Simpson were to be convicted of first-degree murder, would the state seek the death penalty or life imprisonment? Fearful that jurors would hesitate to vote guilty, the district attorney's office chose not to seek the death penalty.

The Sentencing Process

For defendants convicted of crimes, the jury's verdict is followed by a sentence. Sentencing decisions—usually made by judges, not juries—are often controversial. One reason for the controversy is that many people see judges as being too lenient (Stalans & Diamond, 1990). Another reason is that people disagree on the goals served by imprisonment. For example, those who think that the purpose is to

In 1997, a Massachusetts jury convicted British au pair Louise Woodward of murder in the death of the infant for whom she cared. In a decision that reignited the concern about judicial disparity in sentencing, Judge Hiller Zobel overturned the verdict, reduced Woodward's sentence from life in prison to time served, and set her free.

punish, incapacitate, or deter offenders from committing future crimes prefer longer sentences than those who believe that prison should reform and rehabilitate convicted felons (McFatter, 1978).

Judges also disagree about sentencing-related issues. Thus, a common public complaint is that there is too much **sentencing disparity**—that punishments are inconsistent from one judge to the next. To document the problem, Anthony Partridge and William Eldridge (1974) compiled identical sets of files from twenty actual cases, sent them to fifty federal judges, and found major disparities in the sentences they said they would impose. In one case, for example, judges had read about a man who was convicted of extortion and tax evasion. One judge recommended a three-year prison sentence, while another recommended twenty years in prison and a fine of $65,000. It's hard to believe these two judges read the same case. But other studies uncovered similar differences. Recently, some judges have become particularly "creative" in the sentencing of convicted felons. For example, a judge in Houston ordered a piano teacher who molested two students to donate his piano to a local school, a South Dakota judge sentenced cattle rustlers to shovel manure for a week, and a Florida judge ordered drunk drivers to display a bumper sticker on their cars that said "Convicted DUI" (Wrightsman et al., 1998).

What seems to be the basis for disparity? Ebbe Ebbesen and Vladimir Konecni (1981) analyzed sentencing records in San Diego. As in previous research, they found a good deal of inconsistency, but not because the judges used idiosyncratic strategies or based decisions on extralegal factors. Rather, these judges tended to use the same strategy. They made decisions quickly and closely followed the pre-sentencing advice of probation officers. Sentencing disparity is a problem, in part, because judges get conflicting recommendations from those who advise them. And those who advise them differ in their beliefs about the purposes of imprisonment (Carroll et al., 1987). To reduce the disparities in the system, the U.S. Congress recently established a complicated but uniform set of sentencing guidelines. For better and for worse, these guidelines have made certain sentences mandatory—based on the severity of the crime and other factors that are seen as indicative of the defendant's responsibility.

The Prison Experience

It is no secret that many prisons are overcrowded—and that the situation has worsened as a result of the recently toughened sentencing guidelines. The federal prison system is now operating at close to 200 percent capacity (Mydans, 1996). It is also no secret that prison life can be cruel, violent, and degrading. The setting is highly oppressive and regimented, many prison guards are abusive, and many inmates fall into a state of despair (Paulus, 1988). Thus, it is natural for social psychologists to wonder: Is there something in the situation that leads guards and prisoners to behave as they do? Would the rest of us react in the same way?

For ethical reasons, one obviously cannot place research participants inside a real prison. So a team of researchers from Stanford University did the next best thing. They constructed their own prison in the basement of their psychology department building (Haney et al., 1973; Zimbardo et al., 1973). Complete with iron-barred cells, a solitary-confinement closet, and a recreation area for guards, the facility housed twenty-one participants—all healthy and stable men between the ages of seventeen and thirty who had answered a newspaper ad promising fifteen dollars a day for a two-week study of prison life. By the flip of a coin, half the participants were designated as guards; the other half became prisoners. Neither group was told specifically how to fulfill its role.

sentencing disparity Inconsistency of sentences for the same offense from one judge to another.

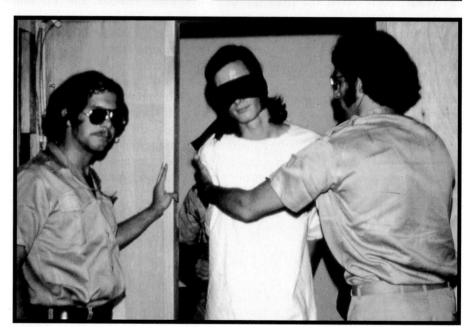

In this simulation study of prison behavior, subjects were arbitrarily assigned to be prisoners or guards. Local police officers arrested the prisoners, who were brought to a jail constructed at Stanford University. After several days, the guards took on cruel, authoritarian roles that demoralized the prisoners to such an extent that the experiment was terminated.

Based on current rates, an estimated 5 percent of all Americans (9 percent of men, 1 percent of women) will serve prison time during the course of their lives.

On the first day, each of the participant prisoners was unexpectedly "arrested" at his home, booked, fingerprinted, and driven to the simulated prison by officers of the local police department. These prisoners were then stripped, searched, and dressed in loose-fitting smocks with an identification number, a nylon stocking to cover their hair, rubber sandals, and a chain bolted to the ankle. The guards were dressed in khaki uniforms and supplied with nightsticks, handcuffs, reflector sunglasses, keys, and whistles. The rules specified that prisoners were to be called by number, routinely lined up to be counted, fed three bland meals, and permitted three supervised toilet visits per day. The stage was set. Participants were on their own. It remained to be seen just how seriously they would take their roles and react to one another in this novel setting.

The events of the next few days were startling. Filled with a sense of power and authority, a few guards became progressively more abusive. They harassed the inmates, forced them into crowded cells, woke them during the night, and subjected them to hard labor and solitary confinement. These guards were particularly cruel when they thought they were alone with a prisoner. The prisoners themselves were rebellious at first, but their efforts were met with retaliation. Soon they all became passive and demoralized. After thirty-six hours, the experimenters had to release their first prisoner, who was suffering from acute depression. On subsequent days, other prisoners had to be released. By the sixth day, those who remained were so shaken by the experience that the study was terminated. It is reassuring, if not remarkable, that after a series of debriefing sessions, participants seemed to show no signs of lasting distress.

This study has been criticized, for good reasons, on both methodological and ethical grounds (Banuazizi & Movahedi, 1975; Savin, 1973). In some ways, however, the results are impressive. Within a brief period of time, under relatively mild conditions, and with a group of men not prone to violence, the Stanford study recreated the prisoner and guard behaviors actually found behind prison walls. Apparently, even "normal" people can be dehumanized by their institutional roles. At this point, research with real inmates in real prisons is needed for a more thorough examination of the effects of overcrowding and other aspects of prison life (Ruback & Innes, 1988).

"It only makes a man worse to go to prison and be corrupted."

—E. M. Forster

Justice: A Matter of Procedure?

People tend to measure the success of a legal system by its ability to produce fair and accurate results. But is that all there is to justice? Let's step back for a moment from the specifics and ask if it is possible to define justice in a way that is unrelated to outcomes.

In a book entitled *Procedural Justice* (1975), John Thibaut and Laurens Walker proposed that our satisfaction with the way disputes are resolved—legal or otherwise—depends not only on outcomes but also on the procedures used to achieve those outcomes. Two aspects of procedure are important in this regard: One is *decision control*—whether a procedure affords the involved parties the power to accept, reject, or otherwise influence the final decision. The other is *process control*—whether it offers the parties an opportunity to present their case to a third-party decision maker. In the courtroom, of course, the disputants are limited in their decision control. Thus, their satisfaction must depend on whether they feel that they had a chance to express their views.

There are two ways to look at the effects of process control on perceptions of justice. Originally, it was thought that people want an opportunity to express their opinions only because having a *voice* in the process improves the odds of achieving a favorable ruling. In this view, process control is satisfying only because it increases decision control (Thibaut & Walker, 1978). Recent research, however, suggests that people value the chance to present their side of a story even when doing so does not influence the ultimate outcome. In other words, process control is more than just an instrumental means to an end. By making people feel that their voice is worth hearing, process control can be an end in itself (Lind et al., 1990; Lind & Tyler, 1988).

This aspect of the legal system is very important. It means, for example, that whether people agree or disagree with how a case turns out, they can at least find solace in the fact that both sides had their "day in court." Yet certain members of the legal community are openly critical of that so-called day in court. As law professor Alan Dershowitz put it, "Nobody really wants justice. Winning is the only thing to most participants in the criminal justice system, just as it is to professional athletes" (1982, p. xvi). Dershowitz's skepticism is centered on something that many of us take for granted: the **adversarial model** of justice. In the adversarial system—as practiced in North America, Great Britain, and a handful of other countries—the prosecution and defense oppose each other, each presenting one side of the story in an effort to win a favorable verdict. In contrast, most other countries use an **inquisitorial model,** in which a neutral investigator gathers the evidence from both sides and then presents the findings in court. With two such different methods of doing justice, social psychologists could not resist the temptation to make comparisons. Which system, they ask, do people prefer?

To make the comparison, Laurens Walker and his colleagues (1974) constructed a business simulation in which two companies competed for a cash prize. Assigned to the role of president of a company, participants learned that someone on their staff was accused of spying on the competition. To resolve the dispute, a "trial" was held. In some cases, the trial followed an adversarial procedure in which the two sides were presented by law students who were chosen by participants and whose payment was contingent on winning. Other cases followed an inquisitorial model in which a single law student—appointed by the experimenter and paid regardless of the outcome—presented both sides. Regardless of whether they had won or lost the verdict, participants who took part in an adversarial trial were more satisfied than those involved in an inquisitorial trial. Even impartial observers preferred the adversarial proceedings.

Other researchers have reported similar results, not only in the United States and Britain, whose citizens are used to the adversarial system, but in France and West Germany as well (Lind et al., 1978). It seems that any method that offers participants a voice in the proceedings—including methods that are nonadversarial—is seen as fair and just (Folger & Greenberg, 1985; Sheppard, 1985). Process control is desirable even among Chinese people, whose culture emphasizes social harmony and the resolution of disputes in ways that minimize conflict (Leung, 1987). In matters of justice, people are motivated not only by a desire for personal gain but by the need to be recognized, respected, and treated fairly by others (Tyler, 1994).

Closing Statement

adversarial model A dispute-resolution system in which the prosecution and defense present opposing sides of the story.

inquisitorial model A dispute-resolution system in which a neutral investigator gathers evidence from both sides and presents the findings in court.

This chapter focuses on the trial process, the events that precede it, and the events that follow from it. Yet we've only scratched the surface. In recent years, more and more judges, lawyers, and policy makers have come to recognize that social psychology can make important contributions to the legal system. Thus, with increasing frequency, social psychologists are called on for expert advice in and out of court and are cited in the opinions written by judges. Clearly, the gathering, presentation, and evaluation of evidence are imperfect human enterprises and subject to bias. Through an understanding of social psychology, however, we can now identify some of the problems—and perhaps even the solutions.

Review

- Embedded in a large criminal justice system, relatively few cases come to trial.
- Yet the trial is the heart and soul of the system.

Jury Selection

- Once called for service, prospective jurors are questioned by the judge or lawyers in a process known as voir dire.
- Those who exhibit a clear bias are excluded. Lawyers may also strike a limited number of others through the use of peremptory challenges.

Trial Lawyers as Intuitive Psychologists

- Pressured to make juror selections quickly, lawyers rely on implicit personality theories and stereotypes.
- But general demographic factors do not reliably predict how jurors will vote.

Scientific Jury Selection

- Lawyers sometimes hire psychologists to conduct surveys that identify correlations between demographics and trial-relevant attitudes.
- Scientific jury-selection raises ethical issues concerning its effects on justice.

Death Qualification

- In capital cases, prospective jurors who say they would not vote for the death penalty are excluded in a process known as death qualification.
- Jurors who favor the death penalty are more likely to find defendants guilty than are jurors who oppose the death penalty.

The Courtroom Drama

- Once the jury is selected, evidence previously gathered is presented in court.

Confession Evidence

- The police employ various methods of interrogation.
- One method is to befriend the suspect and "minimize" the offense; a second is to scare the suspect into believing that it is futile to deny the charges.
- Under pressure, people sometimes confess to crimes they did not commit.

- Although juries are supposed to reject coerced confessions, their verdicts are still influenced by such evidence.

The Lie-Detector Test

- By recording physiological arousal, the polygraph can be used as a lie-detector.
- Polygraphers report high rates of accuracy; but truthful persons are too often judged guilty, and the test can be faked.

Eyewitness Testimony

- Eyewitness memory is a three-stage process involving acquisition, storage, and retrieval.
- During acquisition, witnesses who are highly aroused zoom in on the central features of an event but lose their memory for peripheral details.
- The presence of a weapon hinders a witness's ability to identify the perpetrator.
- Witnesses have trouble recognizing members of a race other than their own.
- During storage, misleading postevent information influences eyewitness testimony.
- Research shows that young children are particularly suggestible in this regard.
- Lineups are biased when a suspect is distinctive, when the police imply that the criminal is in the lineup, when witnesses make relative judgments, and when the suspect is familiar for other reasons.
- In court, jurors overestimate eyewitnesses' accuracy and cannot distinguish between accurate and inaccurate witnesses.
- People are too readily persuaded by a witness's confdence—a factor that does not reliably predict identification accuracy.
- Psychologists are sometimes called to testify as experts on eyewitness evidence.

Nonevidentiary Influences

- The more pretrial knowledge people have about a case, the more likely they are to presume the defendant guilty.
- Research shows that pretrial publicity can bias jury verdicts.
- Once inadmissible testimony leaks out in court, the jury is contaminated by it.
- A judge's cautionary instruction may worsen the situation by drawing attention to the forbidden testimony, arousing reactance, or leading jurors to see the information as relevant.

The Judge's Instructions

- The judge's instructions often have little impact, in part because they are often incomprehensible.
- The instructions are usually delivered after the evidence—after many jurors have formed an opinion.
- Jurors may not follow instructions that conflict with their own conceptions of justice, a phenomenon known as jury nullification.

Jury Deliberation

Leadership in the Jury Room

- Dominance hierarchies develop in the jury room.
- Certain people are more likely than others to be elected foreperson, but the foreperson tends to play the role of moderator rather than that of group leader.

The Dynamics of Deliberation

- Jury deliberations pass through three stages: orientation, open conflict, and reconciliation.
- The period of open conflict is filled with informational and normative pressures.
- When it comes to outcomes, the initial majority typically wins, although deliberation tends to produce a leniency bias.

Jury Size: How Small Is Too Small?

- The U.S. Supreme Court has ruled that the use of six-person juries is acceptable.
- But these smaller groups do not deliberate for as long as twelve-person juries and contain less minority representation.

Less-Than-Unanimous Verdicts

- In some states, juries are permitted to reach verdicts by a less-than-unanimous majority.
- But research shows that once a required majority is reached, these juries reject the holdouts, terminate discussion, and return a verdict.

Posttrial: To Prison and Beyond

The Sentencing Process

- Many people believe that judges are too lenient and that punishments for the same offense are often inconsistent from one case to another.
- Part of the problem is that people have different views of the goals of sentencing.
- To minimize sentencing disparity, the U.S. government has legislated mandatory sentencing guidelines.

The Prison Experience

- Stanford researchers built a simulated prison and recruited male adults to act as guards and prisoners.
- Some guards were abusive, prisoners became passive, and the study had to be terminated.

Justice: A Matter of Procedure?

- Satisfaction with justice depends not only on winning and losing but also on the procedures used to achieve the outcome.
- People of all cultures prefer models of justice that offer participants a voice in the proceedings.

Closing Statement

- Increasingly, social psychologists have become involved in studying the legal system—identifying the problems and seeking solutions.

Key Terms

adversarial model *462*

cross-race identification bias *441*

death qualification *434*

inquisitorial model *462*

jury nullification *453*

leniency bias *455*

misinformation effect *443*

peremptory challenge *431*

polygraph *439*

scientific jury selection *434*

sentencing disparity *459*

voir dire *431*

weapon-focus effect *441*

PUTTING COMMON SENSE TO THE TEST

Contrary to popular opinion, women are harsher as criminal trial jurors than men are.

False. *Demographic factors such as gender do not consistently predict juror verdicts; men may be harsher in some cases, women in others.*

Without being beaten or threatened, innocent people sometimes confess to crimes they did not commit.

True. *Innocent suspects sometimes confess—either to escape an unpleasant situation or because they are led to believe they committed a crime they cannot recall.*

Lie-detector tests can be beaten by suppressing arousal when questions about the crime are asked.

False. *It is possible to beat a lie-detector test—but by elevating arousal when "innocent" questions are asked, not by trying to suppress arousal in response to "guilty" questions.*

Eyewitnesses find it relatively difficult to recognize members of a race other than their own.

True. *Researchers have observed this cross-race identification bias in both laboratory and field settings.*

The more confident an eyewitness is about an identification, the more accurate it is likely to be.

False. *Studies have shown that eyewitness confidence does not reliably predict accuracy, in part because confidence is influenced by post-identification factors.*

One can usually predict a jury's final verdict by knowing where the individual jurors stand the first time they vote.

True. *As a result of both informational and normative group influences, the preference of the initial voting majority usually prevails.*

Business

_____ Although flawed, job interviews consistently make for better hiring decisions.

_____ A problem with having workers evaluate their own job performance is that self-ratings are overly positive.

_____ The most effective type of leader is one who knows how to win support through the use of reward.

_____ People who feel "overpaid" work harder on the job than those who see their pay as appropriate.

_____ People losing money on an investment tend to cut their losses rather than hang tough.

Whenever two adults meet for the first time, the opening line of their conversation is predictable: "So, what do you do?" "Oh, I'm a (social psychologist). And you?" For many people, work is an integral part of their personal identity. Sure, most of us would rather spend next Monday morning lying on a warm and breezy beach, reading a novel, and sipping a tropical fruit drink, but most people spend more time working than playing. In large part, we work to make money. Yet jobs also provide us with activity, a sense of purpose, and a social community. Thus, people who lose their jobs are psychologically devastated—even when they are not to blame and even when they have enough money to see them through the period of unemployment (Price, 1992). Think about it. If you won $10 million in the lottery, would you continue to work? In a 1997 Gallup poll of over six hundred Americans, 40 percent said they would stop working, but 60 percent said they would continue—either at their current jobs or elsewhere. Thus, it is important to identify the social factors that influence this significant human experience.

This chapter considers applications of social psychology to business. First, we'll look at **industrial/organizational (I/O) psychology**—the study of human behavior in the workplace. This subdiscipline of psychology is broad and includes in its ranks both social and nonsocial psychologists who conduct research, teach in business schools or universities, and work in private industry. Whatever the setting, I/O psychology raises important practical questions about job interviewing, evaluations and promotions, leadership, motivation, and other aspects of life on the job. Next, we'll examine some social influences on economic decision making—in the stock market and elsewhere in the business world.

Ever since the classic Hawthorne study, I/O psychologists have examined various aspects of life in the workplace—even the motivational benefits of having a window office.

The impact of social psychological factors in the workplace was first recognized many years ago—thanks, oddly enough, to a study of industrial lighting. The year was 1927. Calvin Coolidge was president, Babe Ruth hit sixty home runs, Charles Lindbergh flew across the Atlantic for the first time, and the U.S. economy seemed sound, though it would soon become depressed. Just outside Chicago, the Hawthorne plant of the Western Electric Company employed thirty thousand men and women in the manufacture of telephones and central office equipment. As in other companies, management wanted to boost productivity. The bottom line was important.

At first, managers thought that they could make workers at the plant more productive by altering the illumination levels in the factory. Proceeding logically, they increased the lighting for one group of workers in a special test room, kept the same lighting in a control room, and compared the effects. Much to their surprise, productivity rates increased in both rooms. At that point, a team of psychologists was brought in to vary other conditions in the factory. Over the next five years, groups of employees from various departments were selected to do their work in a test room where, at different times, they were given more rest periods, coffee breaks, a free mid-morning lunch, shorter work days, shorter weeks, a new location, overtime, financial incentives, dimmer lights, or just a different method of payment. At one point, the researchers even went back and reinstated the original pre-study conditions inside the test room. Yet no matter what changes were made, productivity levels always increased.

The Hawthorne project, described in a classic book entitled *Management and the Worker* (Roethlisberger & Dickson, 1939), has had a great impact on the study of behavior in the workplace. At first, the researchers were both puzzled and discouraged. With positive effects observed among all test-room workers (even when the original pre-test conditions were in place), it seemed that the project had failed. Think about the results, however, and you'll see why these studies are important. With striking consistency, workers became more productive—not because of the specific changes made but because they had been singled out for special assignment. Many researchers have criticized the methods used in this study and the interpretation of the results (Adair, 1984; Parsons, 1974). Still, the phenomenon that has come to be known as the **Hawthorne effect** laid a foundation for I/O psychology.

The Hawthorne plant no longer exists, but the study conducted there has helped researchers to understand the profound impact of social influences in the workplace. Interested in the conditions that affect satisfaction, motivation, and performance, today's researchers study all aspects of life in the workplace—including vacation days off (Westman & Eden, 1997), background music and the use of stereo headsets (Oldham et al., 1995), sexual harassment (Pryor & McKinney,

industrial organizational (I/O) psychology The study of human behavior in business and other organizational settings.

Hawthorne effect The finding that workers who were observed increased their productivity regardless of what actual changes were made in the work setting.

1995; Stockdale, 1996), and the practice of observing workers by monitoring their activity on the computer (Aiello & Kolb, 1995; Stanton & Barnes-Farrell, 1996).

The three of us who wrote this textbook all work on college campuses, surrounded by students, professors, and administrators. We spend our time in classrooms, offices, laboratories, and libraries. For women and men in other occupations—store clerks, taxicab drivers, carpenters, doctors, corporate executives, farmers, teachers, accountants, musicians, firefighters, and airline pilots—the workplace is very different. Yet despite the diversity of roles and settings, certain common concerns arise: How are applicants selected for jobs? How is performance then evaluated? What makes for an effective leader who can influence others and mobilize their support? What motivates people to work hard and feel satisfied with this aspect of their lives? And what factors influence the kinds of economic decisions that people make? Let's enter the workplace and address these important questions.

What's important in a job? As reported in USA Today *(1996), the factors most often cited were: money (40%), likeable co-workers (30%), independence (26%), gratifying work (26%), and a nice setting (23%).*

Personnel Selection

For all kinds of organizations, the secret to success begins with the recruitment and development of a competent work staff. For that reason, personnel selection is the first important step (Borman et al., 1997; Landy et al., 1994).

Traditional Employment Interviews

Anyone who has ever applied for a desirable job knows that sometimes you have to climb hurdles and jump through hoops to get hired. The routine is a familiar one: You submit a résumé, fill out an application, and perhaps bring in samples of your work or take a standardized test of your abilities, personality traits, or honesty. You may even be put on the "hot seat" in a live face-to-face interview. In a traditional interview, a representative of the organization and an applicant meet in person to discuss the job. Interviews thus provide a two-way opportunity for the applicant and the employer to evaluate each other. What a social perception dilemma these opportunities present! As an applicant, you have only a half-hour or so to make a favorable impression. As an interviewer, you have the same brief period of time to penetrate the applicant's self-presentation and learn enough about that person to make a sound hiring decision.

Very few employers would consider hiring a complete stranger for a responsible position without an interview. Think about it. Would you? Like most of us, you probably trust your ability to size people up. In the words of one professional headhunter (a consultant who helps companies find qualified executives), "A good interviewer can probe the candidate's basic mental and emotional patterns and determine whether he will fit not only the job but also the company" (Bauman, 1982). But the question remains: Do interviews promote sound hiring or decisions that are biased by various personal characteristics? Civil rights laws explicitly forbid employers to discriminate on the basis of sex, race, age, religion, national origin, or disability. Does the interview process itself intensify or diminish these possible sources of bias? And are interviews valid and predictive of performance?

Research suggests that interviewing has mixed effects. On the positive side, live interviews may actually diminish the tendency to make simple stereotyped judgments. Studies on the effects of gender have shown that when prospective employers rate applicants from résumés and other written material, they tend to evaluate

Today, according to Fortune *magazine, more and more job seekers and companies first "meet" online. Jobs are posted on sites such as Online Career Center (www.occ.com)—and most large corporations have their own Web sites. Some companies even have "cyber-recruiters" who scan the Internet for people who have posted their résumés.*

—Martin, 1998

FIGURE 13.1 The Bias for Beauty in Hiring

In this study, managers rank-ordered four job applicants: two men and two women—one of each attractive, the other plain. As shown, a majority selected an attractive male or female applicant as their top choice. *(Marlowe et al., 1996.)*

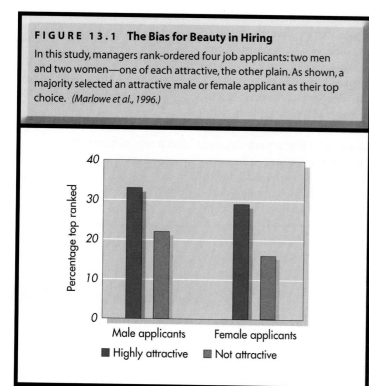

men more highly than they do comparable women (Marlowe et al., 1996; Powell, 1987)—at least for occupations that are not stereotypically feminine (Glick et al., 1988). As employers receive more information about an applicant's credentials, however, this bias is reduced (Tosi & Einbender, 1985). What happens in a live interview? Does gender become more salient, or do job-relevant attributes take over? To answer this question, Laura Graves and Gary Powell (1988) studied 483 interviewers who visited college campuses to recruit prospective graduates for entry-level corporate jobs. While on campus, each interviewer rated one student and answered this question: "What are the chances that this applicant will receive a job offer from your company?" Of the applicants sampled, 53 percent were male, 47 percent female. More to the point, there was no evidence of sex discrimination, as men and women were equally likely to get hired. Perhaps the face-to-face interaction brings to life an applicant's speaking ability, social skills, interest in the company, and other relevant attributes that do not show up on paper.

Although employers have become increasingly sensitive about discriminatory hiring practices, there is one possible source of bias that is more difficult to regulate: physical attractiveness. Except for certain types of work (such as modeling), beauty is not relevant to performance on the job. Yet as we saw in Chapter 9, people favor others who are good-looking. Does this bias operate in hiring situations? To answer this question, Cynthia Marlowe and others (1996) presented a set of job application folders—including résumés, data sheets, and photographs—to 112 male and female managers of a financial institution. Believing they were evaluating actual prospective employees, each manager rank-ordered four equivalent and qualified applicants: two men and two women—one of each of whom was highly attractive. So who was selected? Look at Figure 13.1, and you'll see that there was a slight tendency to favor male applicants, but that physical appearance had an even greater impact; as 62 percent of all managers selected an attractive applicant as their top choice. On a positive note, the results showed that managers who had the most experience did not exhibit the bias for beauty. It remains to be seen, however, whether physical attractiveness would play a greater or lesser role in face-to-face hiring situations.

Although interviews sometimes result in the right selection of employees, they often lack predictive validity (Harris, 1989). Part of the problem may be that job applicants present themselves in a positive light, as you'd expect, and that those who engage in the most self-promotion (not necessarily those who are best qualified) are most likely to get hired (Stevens & Kristof, 1995). Another problem is that an employer's preconceptions about an applicant can distort the whole interview process. For example, when white participants in one study questioned an applicant who was black rather than white, they sat farther away and held shorter interviews—a "distant" interpersonal style that causes interviewees to behave in a more nervous and awkward manner (Word et al., 1974). And when participants in another experiment were led to believe that an applicant was not suitable for a particular job, they prepared interview questions that sought negative rather than positive information (Binning et al., 1988).

In a field study illustrating the problem, Amanda Phillips and Robert Dipboye (1989) surveyed 34 managers from different branch offices of a large corporation and 164 job applicants whom these managers had interviewed. They found that the managers' pre-interview expectations, which were based on written application materials, influenced the kinds of interviews they conducted as well as the outcomes: The higher their expectations, the more time they spent "recruiting" rather than evaluating and the more likely they were to make a favorable hiring decision. Similarly, Thomas Dougherty and his colleagues (1994) found that interviewers with positive rather than negative expectations sounded warmer, more outgoing, and more cheerful. They also gave more information and spent more time promoting the company. It seems that job interviews can become part of a vicious cycle, or self-fulfilling prophecy. Without realizing it, employers use the opportunity to create realities that bolster their preexisting beliefs (see Figure 13.2).

> Although flawed, job interviews consistently make for better hiring decisions. **False.**

"Scientific" Alternatives to Traditional Interviews

Face-to-face interviews bring to life both job-relevant and irrelevant personal characteristics. Given that the process is so variable, should interviews be eliminated? Should they, perhaps, be computerized—leaving applicants to interact with companies via a programmed sequence of questions and answers administered on a microcomputer? Cyberspace interviews may offer a forum for an initial screening of applicants. Chances are, however, not too many people would feel comfortable making important life decisions in such an impersonal manner. Is it possible, then, to preserve the human touch of an interview while eliminating bias and error?

To improve the prediction of job performance, organizations have sought more "scientific" methods of selection. Some firms in the United States and in Europe use *graphology*, or handwriting analysis, to predict job-relevant traits such as honesty, sales ability, and leadership potential (Rafaeli & Klimoski, 1983). Controlled research, however, does not support the claim that handwriting can be used in this way. In one study, for example, professional graphologists tried to predict various aspects of job performance by analyzing the handwriting contained in the autobiographical sketches of bank employees. From the information in those same materials, the researchers also made predictions about these employees. A comparison of predicted and actual performance revealed that the graphologists were no better than the researchers. In fact, they were no more accurate than they would have been if they had made their predictions by flipping a coin (Ben-Shakhar et al., 1986).

Some organizations use the *polygraph*, or lie-detector test, as a screening device. As described in Chapter 12, the polygraph is an instrument that records physiological arousal in different parts of the body. Based on the assumption that lying creates stress, a polygraph examiner conducts an interview and compares the interviewee's level of arousal in response to various questions. Those who administer lie-detector

If you are on the job market and have access to the Internet, you can practice by taking part in a "virtual interview": www. aboutwork.com/ace/virtual. html

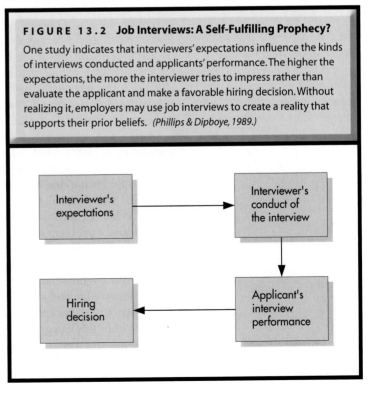

FIGURE 13.2 Job Interviews: A Self-Fulfilling Prophecy?
One study indicates that interviewers' expectations influence the kinds of interviews conducted and applicants' performance. The higher the expectations, the more the interviewer tries to impress rather than evaluate the applicant and make a favorable hiring decision. Without realizing it, employers may use job interviews to create a reality that supports their prior beliefs. *(Phillips & Dipboye, 1989.)*

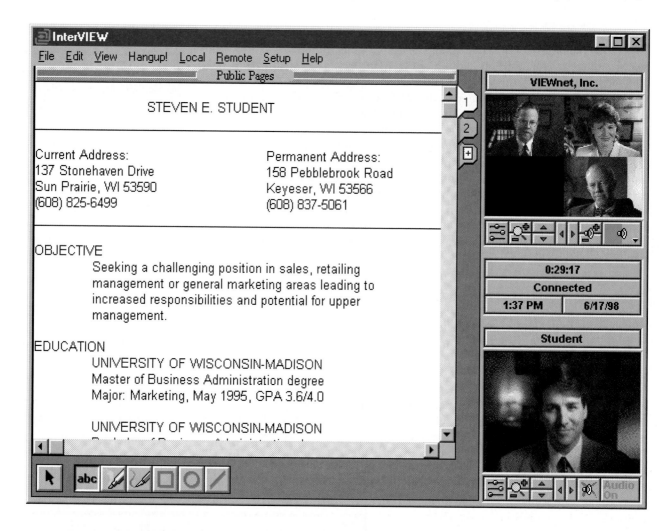

InterVIEW is a computerized interviewing system. Many organizations are beginning to use this and other commercial software as a low-cost first step in the recruitment of college seniors.

tests argue that it enhances their ability to identify prospective employees who are honest. But opponents argue that the test invades an individual's privacy, that it is too easily misused, and that its results are not sufficiently accurate (Saxe et al., 1985). For these reasons, the U.S. government in 1988 passed the Employee Polygraph Protection Act, a bill limiting the use of lie-detector tests to jobs in law enforcement, national security, and public safety.

Standardized Tests   On Christmas Eve, 1996, Dan Reeves resigned as head coach of the New York Giants football team. At his press conference, Reeves criticized the team for basing decisions on which college players to draft too heavily on psychological tests that all rookies must take. "So how valid is a two-hour test?" he asked. "When a psychologist has more to do with the draft than you do as a head coach, I have a problem with that" (Rhoden, 1996).

Today, many companies use standardized written tests in the selection process. Three general types of tests are used for this purpose. Some are designed to measure various cognitive abilities, such as general intelligence or achievement, job-specific knowledge and skills, or "street smarts" and common sense—all of which may contribute to success on the job (Hunter & Hunter, 1984; Sternberg et al., 1995). Within this category are "situational judgment tests" containing hypothetical scenarios that describe relevant work situations in which a problem has arisen. In a multiple-choice format, applicants must choose the most effective course of action (Motowidlo et al., 1990).

Other tests are designed to measure personality traits of possible relevance to work-related outcomes, such as leadership potential, helpfulness, lateness, absenteeism, and theft. For example, research shows that people who score high rather than low in the trait of conscientiousness are more likely in general to perform well on the job—and, more specifically, that people who score as extroverted rather than introverted are more likely to succeed as business managers and salespersons. Increasingly, it is evident that certain personality traits are useful for predicting success and failure in the workplace (Goffin et al., 1996; Hogan et al., 1996; Salgado, 1997).

Third, many companies have recently begun to administer **integrity tests**— questionnaires designed specifically to assess an applicant's honesty and character through questions concerning drug abuse, shoplifting, petty theft, and other transgressions. The responses are scored by computer. Narrative profiles are provided, and arbitrary cutoff scores are often used to determine if an applicant has passed or failed (Camara & Schneider, 1994).

A major concern about integrity tests is that applicants might be able to fake them— either on their own or with the help of coaching. But is this the case? Let's consider the two different types of tests currently in use: (1) *overt* integrity tests, in which the purpose is obvious to the test-taker, and (2) *covert* tests, in which items measure broad personality characteristics that are not clearly related to the workplace. To examine the susceptibility of these tests to faking, George Alliger and his colleagues (1996) gave both overt and covert tests to college students. Some were told to just take the tests, others were instructed to "fake good," and still others were coached and

Comment to avoid on a résumé: "Am a perfectionist and rarely if if ever forget details."

—Fortune, 1997

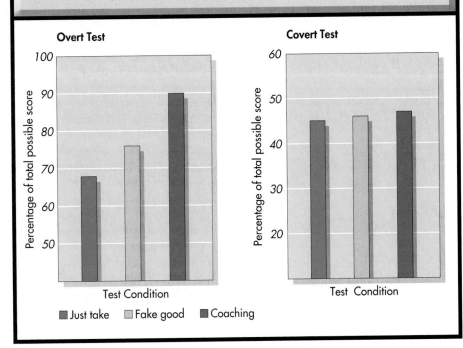

FIGURE 13.3 Can Integrity Tests Be Faked?
Alliger and others (1996) gave college students overt and covert integrity tests. Some just took the test; others were told to "fake good"; others were coached. On the overt test, scores increased for subjects who faked good or were coached (left). On the covert test, scores were unaffected by these interventions (right).

given specific strategies for how to beat the tests. Look at Figure 13.3, and you'll see how well the students did. On the overt test, scores increased for those instructed to fake good and then increased again among those who were specifically coached. On the covert personality test, however, scores were unaffected by these interventions. When it comes to faking, the covert tests, quite literally, passed the test.

But are such instruments sufficiently valid for use in personnel selection? Although there is reason for skepticism, the research thus far suggests that both types of tests do predict various work-related behaviors (Goldberg et al., 1991; Sackett et al., 1989). In an experiment using overt integrity tests, Michael Cunningham and others (1994) found that actual job applicants scored higher on the tests than did nonmotivated research participants—and that their scores match

integrity test Paper-and-pencil questionnaire designed to test a job applicant's honesty and character.

those obtained from participants specifically instructed to fake good. Does this self-presentation bias compromise a test's validity? Not necessarily. In a second experiment, these same investigators overpaid participants by $5 and found that those with high rather than low test scores were more likely to return the extra cash. Other researchers, too, have found this result (Barrick & Mount, 1996). Thus, when Deniz Ones and others (1993) conducted a meta-analysis of tests administered to thousands of workers, they found that test scores were highly predictive of job performance and of counterproductive behaviors such as theft, absenteeism, lateness, and disciplinary problems.

Structured Interviews   Another way to improve selection judgments is through the use of **structured interviews.** A structured interview is like a standardized test in that the same information is obtained in the same situation from all applicants, who are then compared on a common, relevant set of dimensions (Campion et al., 1988). By asking the same set of questions or using the same set of tasks, employers can prevent themselves from unwittingly conducting biased interviews that merely confirm their preconceptions. Over the years, research has shown that structured interviews are better than conventional interviews in the selection of insurance agents, sales clerks, and other workers (Wiesner & Cronshaw, 1988). In this context, Michael Campion and others (1994) have found that past-oriented questions ("How did you react when…?") elicit more predictive information from job applicants than do future-oriented questions ("What would you do if…?").

To create a structured setting for selection and evaluation purposes, many organizations now use **assessment centers,** in which several applicants take part in a group of activities—written tests, role-playing exercises, and so on—that are monitored by a group of evaluators. Instead of one method (an interview) and one evaluator (an interviewer), multiple methods and evaluators are used. Assessment centers are widely assumed to be more effective than traditional interviews at identifying applicants who will succeed in a particular position (Gaugler et al., 1987; Thornton & Byham, 1982). As companies struggle to cut their hiring costs, however, these assessments are often streamlined—involving fewer evaluators, fewer exercises, briefer exercises, and other types of shortcuts (Borman et al., 1997).

For many years, researchers focused on the ways in which different personnel selection procedures serve employers. As we noted earlier, however, the hiring process is an interpersonal two-way street in which organizations and applicants both form impressions of each other. So how do job seekers feel about the methods just described? What is *your* reaction to these methods? Research shows that people generally see concrete, job-specific tests and interview situations as most fair— and dislike being evaluated by more general, standardized tests of intelligence, personality, and honesty (Rosse et al., 1994; Rynes & Connerly, 1993). For employers on the lookout for strong recruits, the perceived fairness of the selection process that is used may well influence whether top applicants accept the offers that are made.

structured interview Interview in which each job applicant is asked a standard set of questions and evaluated on the same criteria.

assessment center Structured setting in which job applicants are exhaustively tested and judged by multiple evaluators.

Affirmative Action

Affirmative action—the policy whereby preferences in hiring, admissions, and promotion are given to women and underrepresented minority groups—is among the most emotional and explosive social issues of our time. On one side of the debate, many liberals argue that preferential treatment is necessary as a way to overcome past inequities. On the other side, many conservatives claim that the policy results in unfair reverse discrimination. Surveys show that Americans are sharply divided on the issue—with women more supportive than men, and blacks more supportive than whites (Kravitz & Platania, 1993). It comes as no surprise, then, that in a large-scale study of federal government workers, female and minority employees saw their organizations as less supportive of affirmative action than did their white male co-workers (Parker et al., 1997).

As the political debate rages, numerous questions are being raised. According to Rupert Nacoste (1996), affirmative action affects those whom the policy is designed to help, those who feel excluded by it, the organizations that implement it, and the interactions among these three interested groups. In addition, Nacoste argues that people react not to the abstract concept of affirmative action but to the procedures that are used to implement the concept—and these reactions can set off "procedural reverberations" within the system. For example, people will be dissatisfied and the system will reverberate to the extent that the policy is set secretly rather than in the open, to the extent that interested parties have no opportunity to express their views, and to the extent that group membership considerations are seen as more important than the individual contributions of each applicant. Nacoste's notion of procedural interdependence is diagrammed in Figure 13.4.

As you might expect, people who do not personally benefit from affirmative action react negatively to the policy—and to those targeted to benefit from it (Clayton, 1996; Heilman et al., 1996; Maio & Esses, 1998). But what about the recipients of this policy? Does affirmative action psychologically undermine those whom it is intended to help? In an interesting series of studies, Madeline Heilman and her colleagues selected male and female college students to serve as leaders of a two-person task. The students were then led to believe that they had been chosen

FIGURE 13.4 Affirmative Action: Effects on Individuals, Groups, and Organizations

Affirmative action affects target group members whom the policy is designed to help, nontarget group members who feel excluded by it, organizations that implement it, and the interactions among these groups. According to Nacoste, people's reactions to affirmative action procedures can set off "procedural reverberations" (P) within the system. *(Nacoste, 1996.)*

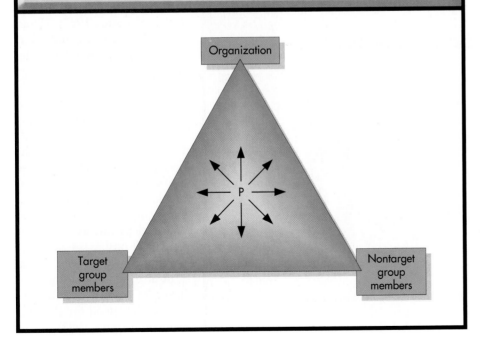

for the leadership role either by a preferential selection process based on gender or by a merit-selection process based on their credentials and qualifications. As depicted in Figure 13.5, the women (but not the men) who thought they had been chosen because of their gender later devalued their own task performance—even after receiving positive feedback (Heilman et al., 1987). They were also less likely afterward to recommend female job applicants for an entry-level position (Heilman et al., 1993). This research may help to explain why female business managers who think they were hired through affirmative action are often unhappy with their work (Chacko, 1982). It may also explain an observation made by black law professor Stephen Carter, in his book *Reflections of an Affirmative Action Baby*, that minorities "resist being thought of as beneficiaries" (1991, p. 21).

There are three explanations as to why preferential selection practices might have a range of negative effects. First, people perceive a procedure as unjust to the extent that it excludes those who are qualified simply because of their non-membership in a group (Barnes Nacoste, 1994; Heilman et al., 1996). Second, recipients become less able to attribute success on the job to their own abilities and efforts, leading them and co-workers to harbor doubts about their competence (Heilman et al., 1992; Major et al., 1994). Third, preferential selection is seen as a form of assistance—a situation that can trigger a defensive reaction among recipients for whom receiving help threatens their self-esteem (Pratkanis & Turner, 1996).

Are the recipients of affirmative action doomed to feel stigmatized, like second-class citizens in the workplace? Not necessarily. The way people react to a preferential selection procedure depends on how that procedure is structured and implemented. A good deal of research now shows that people draw negative inferences about themselves and others when employment selections are made *solely* on the basis of sex, skin color, or ethnic background. But everyone's reactions to a preferential selection process are more favorable when it's clear that merit-based factors also play a role and that the person chosen is competent and qualified for the position (Arthur et al., 1992; Heilman et al., 1993; Major et al., 1994; Nacoste, 1987). Thus, Anthony Pratkanis and Marlene Turner (1996) offer guidelines on how to manage affirmative action programs in order to make them seem supportive rather than threatening to all concerned (see Table 13.1). In the meantime, the fiery political debate may have overshadowed a key point: that in our multicultural society, many organizations (such as police departments, universities, small businesses, and corporations) benefit from having a diverse staff—and that the hiring of women and minorities can be "good for the bottom line" (Annin, 1995).

FIGURE 13.5　Paradoxical Effects of Affirmative Action on Women

College students assigned to act as task leaders were led to believe that they had been selected on the basis of merit or gender. The selection method had no effect on the self and other evaluations made by male leaders. However, women who thought they had been selected because of gender later devalued their own job performance (left) and were less favorable toward a female job applicant (right). *(Data from Heilman et al., 1987; Heilman et al., 1993.)*

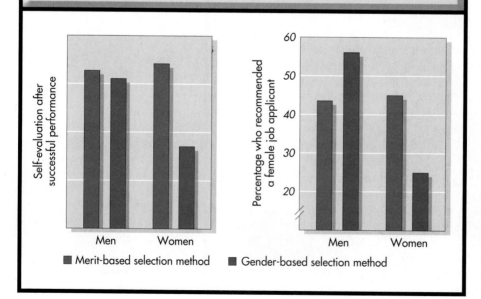

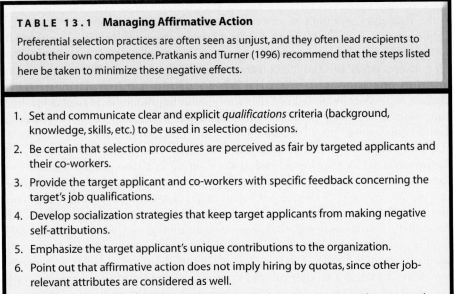

TABLE 13.1 Managing Affirmative Action

Preferential selection practices are often seen as unjust, and they often lead recipients to doubt their own competence. Pratkanis and Turner (1996) recommend that the steps listed here be taken to minimize these negative effects.

1. Set and communicate clear and explicit *qualifications* criteria (background, knowledge, skills, etc.) to be used in selection decisions.

2. Be certain that selection procedures are perceived as fair by targeted applicants and their co-workers.

3. Provide the target applicant and co-workers with specific feedback concerning the target's job qualifications.

4. Develop socialization strategies that keep target applicants from making negative self-attributions.

5. Emphasize the target applicant's unique contributions to the organization.

6. Point out that affirmative action does not imply hiring by quotas, since other job-relevant attributes are considered as well.

7. Recognize that affirmative action is not a panacea and that it cannot be expected to solve all the problems faced by the targeted groups.

Performance Appraisals

E ven after a person is hired for a job, the evaluation process continues. Nobody enjoys being scrutinized by a boss—or by anyone else, for that matter. Still, **performance appraisal**—the process of evaluating an employee's work and communicating the results to that person—is an inevitable fact of life in the workplace. Performance appraisals provide a basis for placement decisions, transfers, promotions, changes in salary, bonuses, and layoffs. They also give feedback to employees about their status within the organization. It's no wonder that I/O psychologists have studied this process in great detail.

It would be easy if a worker's performance could be measured by *objective*, quantifiable criteria—as when typists are judged by the number of words they type in a minute, automobile dealers by the number of cars they sell, and doctors by the number of patients they treat. Quantitative measures like these are often not available, however, nor do they take into account the quality of work. By necessity, then, performance appraisals are usually based on *subjective* measures—perceptions of employees by their supervisors, co-workers, customers, clients, and sometimes even themselves (Landy & Farr, 1983).

Supervisor Ratings

Based on the assumption that supervisors are informed about the performance of their subordinates, they are most often called on to make evaluations. But are these ratings accurate? And is the process fair? The process has both benefits and drawbacks. On the one hand, research shows that supervisors are influenced more by a worker's job knowledge, ability, technical proficiency, and dependability than by less relevant factors such as friendliness (Borman et al., 1995). On the other hand, as we'll see, evaluators predictably fall prey to many of the social perception biases described elsewhere in this book.

performance appraisal
The process of evaluating an employee's work within the organization.

Over the years, several appraisal-related problems have been identified. One is the *halo effect*, a failure to discriminate among distinct aspects of a worker's performance (Cooper, 1981). In Chapter 4, we saw that people's impressions of one another are guided by various implicit personality theories—that is, by the preconceptions we have about the relationships among different traits. Believing someone is warm, we assume that he or she is also generous and good-natured. In a similar manner, supervisors who believe that a worker is unproductive may also rate that same worker negatively on teamwork, loyalty, independence, creativity, and other distinct dimensions. Halo effects are most pronounced when evaluators rate someone they don't know well or when a time delay has caused their memory of performance to fade (Kozlowski et al., 1986; Murphy & Balzer, 1986). Without having concrete information, people fall back on past impressions and implicit theories and assume that one aspect of performance implies other aspects as well. Note, however, that although this effect often leads people to make judgments that are in error, there are times when the halo we see over others is real (Murphy et al., 1993).

Second, it may be difficult for supervisors to make repeated evaluations of the same worker, each time through fresh eyes. In a series of experiments, participants were asked to watch a teacher present three videotaped lectures and then to evaluate his or her speaking ability, clarity, preparation, rapport, and so on (Murphy et al., 1985; Smither et al., 1988). For some, the first two lectures were low in quality; for others, they were high in quality. On the third tape, all participants watched the same average performance. The result? Even though participants rated each lecture independently, their final evaluations showed signs of a *contrast effect:* Those who had first observed negative performances judged the average lecture more favorably than did those who had watched the positive performances. Practically speaking, this finding suggests that supervisors who conduct multiple performance appraisals may judge an employee's work in light of previous observations. One performance sets a standard for another. It's no wonder that entertainers worry about taking the stage right after a "tough act to follow."

A third problem is that evaluators are often indiscriminate in their numerical ratings of others. Because of what is known as the *restriction of range problem*, some people provide uniformly high, lenient ratings; others are inclined to give negative, low ratings; and still others gravitate toward the center of the numerical scale. In all cases, people who use a restricted range of ratings fail to make adequate distinctions. Sometimes, the differences between raters are considerable. In a meta-analysis of twenty-five studies—some conducted in the workplace, others in the laboratory—John Georgesen and Monica Harris (1998) found that people who are in power, compared to those who are not, consistently give lower performance ratings to others who are in subordinate positions.

Self-Evaluations

Although performance appraisals are most typically made by supervisors, input is often sought from co-workers, clients, customers, and others whose opinions are relevant. You may not realize it, but by filling out course-evaluation surveys in college, you may have had an influence on tenure and promotion decisions involving your own professors.

One particularly interesting source of information comes from self-evaluations. If you've ever had to describe yourself in a job application, you know that a self-evaluation is not exactly a lesson in modesty. As discussed in Chapter 3, people generally perceive themselves in overly flattering terms, taking credit for success, denying the blame for failure, having an inflated sense of control, and exhibiting unrealistic optimism about the future. Add the fact that people like to present themselves favorably to others, and it comes as no surprise that self-evaluations in the workplace are consistently more positive than the ratings made by supervisors (Campbell & Lee, 1988)—and are less predictive of job success (Shore et al., 1992). For example, recent studies have shown that workers underestimate the number of times they have been absent compared with their co-workers (Harrison & Shaffer, 1994; Johns, 1994).

Another reason why self-evaluations should be taken with a grain of salt is that individuals differ in the extent to which they tend to present themselves in a positive light. Research shows that the more power people have in an organization, the higher are their self-evaluations (Georgesen & Harris, 1998). Similarly, studies have shown that men are more boastful in general than women—and more likely to overestimate their own performance (Beyer, 1990). Insofar as work appraisals are based on self-evaluations, then, these differences put both subordinates and female employees at a disadvantage.

A problem with having workers evaluate their own job performance is that self-ratings are overly positive. **True.**

New and Improved Methods of Appraisal

Performance appraisals cannot always be trusted. When more objective measures of work output are not available, however, organizations have no choice but to rely on the imperfect human judge. For researchers, the challenge is to find ways to boost the accuracy of the evaluations that are made.

One solution concerns the timing of evaluations in relation to the observation of performance. Evaluations are less prone to error when made right after performance than when there's a delay of days, weeks, or months. Alternatively, evaluators should take notes and keep clear records of their observations—perhaps using behavioral checklists. Part of the problem is that once memory for details begins to fade, evaluators fall back on stereotypes and other biases (Murphy & Balzer, 1986; Sanchez & De La Torre, 1996). A second solution is to increase the number of evaluators used. As in assessment centers, a multiple-rater system—in which a final evaluation represents the average of ratings made by independent sources with different perspectives—is better than a single rater (Conway & Huffcut, 1997; Sackett & Wilson, 1982). Whatever bias a single individual brings to bear on his or her performance ratings can thus be offset, to some extent, by the ratings of others. Third, it is possible to teach some of the skills necessary for making accurate appraisals. Various training programs have been developed; and research suggests that accuracy can be boosted by alerting evaluators to the biases of social perception, focusing their attention on job-relevant behaviors, sharpening their memory skills, informing them of performance norms that serve as a frame of reference within the organization, and providing them with practice and feedback in the use of rating scales (Bernardin & Beatty, 1984; Day & Sulsky, 1995; Hedge & Kavanagh, 1988). No system will ever be perfect, but much improvement is possible—particularly when people are motivated to be accurate (Salvemini et al., 1993).

Due Process Considerations

Part of the problem with performance appraisals is that people exhibit social perception biases that often result in a loss of accuracy. In this all-too-human enterprise, however, there's also another problem: fairness. Appraisals of job performance—because they influence personnel decisions—are often biased, sometimes even deliberately distorted, by those motivated by political and self-serving agendas within the workplace. Particularly at the executive level, office politics is an organizational fact of life (Gioia & Longnecker, 1994).

To enhance fairness, Robert Folger and his colleagues (1992) have proposed a "due process" model of performance appraisal. In general, this model is designed to guard the rights of employees in the same way that the criminal justice system seeks to protect the accused. The model consists of three principles. The first is that there should be *adequate notice*—that is, clear performance standards that employees can understand and ask questions about. The second is that employees should receive a *fair hearing* in which they are evaluated by a supervisor who knows their work, and in which they receive timely feedback as well as an opportunity to present their own case. The third principle is that appraisals should be based on *evidence* of job performance—not on prejudice, corruption, or other external considerations. As indicated by research on how people react to pay raises (Folger & Konovsky, 1989) and the implementation of affirmative action policies (Nacoste, 1996), procedural fairness (*how* decisions are made) can be just as important as a favorable outcome (*what* decisions are made). Thus, workers who are dissatisfied with their pay are more likely to retaliate (for example, by calling in sick, stealing or wasting the company's supplies, or damaging equipment) when they see the procedures used to determine pay as unfair and when they were not consulted about the decision (Skarlicki & Folger, 1997).

Leadership

If you could fire your current boss, would you? In a Gallup poll of American workers, 24% said yes.

What personal and situational factors make for effective leaders? At the Center for Creative Leadership, located in Greensboro, North Carolina, consultants try to evaluate managers by observing work team interactions through a one-way mirror.

Regardless of where you're employed, the work experience depends in large part on the quality of the leadership in the organization. A leader is someone who can move a group of people toward a common goal. What personal and situational factors make for effective leaders? There is no single formula. Some leaders succeed by winning supporters, others by mending fences, uniting rivals, negotiating deals, building coalitions, solving problems, or stirring emotions. Whatever the strategy, there is one common denominator: Good leadership requires social influence (Bass, 1990; Hollander & Offermann, 1990; House & Podsakoff, 1994).

The Classic Trait Approach

One approach to the study of leadership is to identify the traits that characterize "natural-born" leaders who have the "right stuff." According to the Great Person Theory of history, exceptional individuals rise up to determine the course of human events. This approach has had some support over the years, as certain traits—such as ambition, intelligence, a need for power, self-confidence, a high energy level, and an ability to be flexible and adapt to change—are characteristic of people who go on to become leaders (Hogan et al., 1994; Kenny & Zaccaro, 1983). Even physical height may play a role—a possibility suggested by research showing that male and female managers in a corporation were, on average, more than an inch taller than nonmanagement employees (Egolf & Corder, 1991). In this regard, it's striking that between the years 1900 and 1996, the tallest candidate for U.S. president won an astonishing twenty-two out of twenty-four elections (1972 and 1976 being the only exceptions).

On the basis of past research, Shelley Kirkpatrick and Edwin Locke (1991) argue that certain personality characteristics are predictably associated with successful leadership among business executives. In particular, they point to the central importance of *cognitive ability* (intelligence, an ability to quickly process large amounts of information), *drive* (a need for achievement, ambition, and a high energy level), *leadership motivation* (a desire to influence others for the purpose of reaching a common goal), *expertise* (specific knowledge of technical issues relevant to the organization), *creativity* (an ability to generate original ideas), *self-confidence* (faith in one's own abilities and ideas), *integrity* (openness of communication, reliability, and honesty), and *flexibility* (a willingness to adapt to the needs of followers and changes in the situation). As Kirkpatrick and Locke (1991) put it, "Regardless of whether leaders are born or made, it is unequivocally clear that leaders are not like other people" (p. 58).

In contrast to this approach, more situationally oriented theories were introduced based on the notion that the emergence of a given leader depends on time, place, and circumstances—that different situations call for different types of leaders. Thus, as the needs, expectations, and resources of a group change, so will the person best suited to lead it. Studies of presidential leadership illustrate the point. David Winter (1987) found that presidential candidates are more likely to be elected and then reelected when their primary motive in life—whether it is for achievement, power, or affiliation—matches what Americans want most at that time. An alternative to the trait perspective, then, is a view that leadership is the product of a unique interaction between personal and situational factors.

Contingency Models of Leadership

Illustrative of this interactional perspective is Fred Fiedler's (1967) **contingency model of leadership.** Fiedler argues that a key difference among leaders is whether they are primarily *task oriented* (single-mindedly focused on the job) or *relations oriented* (concerned about the feelings of employees). The amount of control that a leader has determines which type of leadership is more effective. Leaders enjoy *high situational control* when they have good relations with their staff, a position of power, and a clearly structured task. In contrast, leaders exhibit *low situational control* when they have poor relations with their staff, limited power, and a task that is not clearly defined.

Combining these personal and situational components, studies of various work groups suggest that task-oriented leaders are the most effective in clear-cut

contingency model of leadership The theory that leadership effectiveness is determined both by the personal characteristics of leaders and by the control afforded by the situation.

situations that are either low or high in control and that relations-oriented leaders perform better in situations that afford a moderate degree of control. In low-control situations, groups need guidance, which task-oriented leaders provide by staying focused on the job. In high-control situations, where conditions are already favorable, these same leaders maintain a relaxed, low profile. Relations-oriented leaders are different. They offer too little guidance in low-control situations, and they meddle too much in high-control situations. In ambiguous situations, however, relations-oriented leaders—precisely because of their open, participative, social style—motivate workers to solve problems in creative ways.

Many—but not all—studies of military units, sports teams, schools, hospitals, and other organizations support Fiedler's contingency model (Peters et al., 1985; Schriesheim et al., 1994; Strube & Garcia, 1981; Vecchio, 1983). Even though support for the model is not unanimous, however, the main point is well taken: Good leadership requires a match between personal style and the demands of a specific situation (Fiedler & Chemers, 1984). A mismatch—that is, the wrong type of person for the situation—can have negative consequences for both the leader and the organization. For example, Martin Chemers and his colleagues (1985) surveyed college administrators to determine both their leadership style and their situational control. They found that mismatches were associated with increased job stress, stress-related illness, and absence from work—symptoms that diminish a leader's productivity and competence (Fiedler & Garcia, 1987; Fiedler et al., 1992).

One of the most important tasks for any leader is to make decisions. In the two-way street between leaders and followers, however, it is often important to solicit the opinions of others. How much participation should leaders invite? According to the **normative model of leadership** proposed by Victor Vroom and Philip Yetton (1973), leaders vary widely in this regard. Some are highly autocratic and directive (they invite no feedback from workers), while others are highly participative (they frequently seek and use suggestions from workers). For effective long-term leadership, the key is to invite just the right amount of worker participation—not too much (which is often not efficient), and not too little (which can lower morale). As to what constitutes the right amount, Vroom and Yetton argued that it depends on various factors—such as the clarity of the problem, the informa-

Shown at his famous "I have a dream" speech in Washington D.C., in August 1963. Martin Luther King, Jr. was a transformational leader who inspired massive change by making supporters believe that anything was possible.

normative model of leadership The theory that leadership effectiveness is determined by the amount of feedback and participation that leaders invite from workers.

tion available to the leader and followers, and whether it's more important that the decision be right or have support.

Although the ideal leader is one who adjusts his or her style to meet the situation, people in general prefer leaders who involve them in important decisions. Research thus shows that participative decision making boosts worker morale, motivation, and productivity—and reduces turnover and absenteeism rates. Benefits such as these have been found especially in situations where employees want to have input (Vroom & Jago, 1988) and when they are involved in decision making directly rather than through elected representatives (Rubenowitz et al., 1983).

Transactional Leadership

Although contingency models take both persons and situations into account, Edwin Hollander (1985) criticizes these "top-down" views of leadership in which the workers are portrayed as inert, passive, and faceless creatures to be soothed or aroused at the management's discretion. Instead, leadership is seen as a two-way social exchange in which there is mutual and reciprocal influence between a leader and his or her followers. According to Hollander, a good **transactional leader** is one who gains compliance and support from followers by setting clear goals for them, by offering tangible rewards, by providing assistance, and by fulfilling psychological needs in exchange for an expected level of job performance. Thus, transactional leadership rests on the leader's willingness and ability to reward subordinates who keep up their end of the bargain—and to correct those who do not.

Transformational Leadership

Think about some of the greatest leaders of the twentieth century, those who were able to transform the status quo by making supporters believe that anything is possible. Martin Luther King, Jr., was that kind of leader. So were Franklin D. Roosevelt, Mahatma Gandhi, John F. Kennedy, and Nelson Mandela. In the book *In Search of Excellence*, Thomas Peters and Robert Waterman (1982) studied sixty-two of America's best businesses and found that their success was due largely to the ability of leaders to elicit extraordinary efforts from ordinary human beings.

Perhaps the most prominent current model of such leadership is Bill Gates—chairman and CEO of Microsoft, the world's leading provider of software for the personal computer. In 1975, Gates dropped out of Harvard and founded Microsoft. Long before it seemed possible to most people, he envisioned a day when there would be a PC in every home and office. Then in 1996, as it became clear that the future promise of computers resides in cyberspace, he shocked the business community by completely refocusing Microsoft around the Internet. In an industry that demands the ability to anticipate the future, adapt quickly to change, take great risks, and enlist support from others, Gates is a leader. Today, he is also the richest person in the world.

"Most people think of a great leader as someone who can give rousing speeches that fire up the troops.... But, to be successful in the long term, a leader must be frank with employees about the challenges as well as the opportunities they face." (Bill Gates)

transactional leader A leader who gains compliance and support from followers primarily through goal setting and the use of rewards.

"The transactional leader works within the constraints of the organization; the transformational leader changes the organization."

—Bernard Bass

The most effective type of leader is one who knows how to win support through the use of reward. **False.**

If you can access the Internet and want to learn more about the Multifactor Leadership Questionnaire, you can visit this site: www.leadership. mindgarden.com/demo/ intro/mlq.html

transformational leader A leader who inspires followers to transcend their own needs in the interest of a common cause.

What's so special about Bill Gates and other great leaders? Based on the work of political scientist James MacGregor Burns (1978), Bernard Bass (1998) calls them **transformational leaders.** Transformational leaders motivate followers to transcend their personal needs in the interest of a common cause—particularly in times of growth, change, and crisis. Through consciousness raising and raw emotional inspiration, they articulate a clear vision for the future and then mobilize others to join in that vision. Over the years, Bass and his colleagues have asked people who work for business managers and executives, military officers, school principals, government bureaucrats, fire chiefs, and store owners to describe the most outstanding leaders they know (Bass & Avolio, 1990; Hater & Bass, 1988). As shown in Table 13.2, the descriptions revealed four attributes: charisma, inspirational motivation, intellectual stimulation, and an individualized consideration of others.

To measure the extent to which individuals possess the attributes of transactional and transformational leadership styles, Bass (1985) devised the Multifactor Leader Questionnaire. Using this instrument, many researchers have studied leadership in different cultures and in different types of organizations—including automakers, express-mail companies, multinational corporations, banks, government agencies, and military groups. Others have varied the use of the different leadership styles in controlled laboratory settings. Indicating that inspiration is universally a more powerful motivator than reward, the results consistently have shown that transformational leaders are more effective than transactional leaders (Bass, 1998; Lowe et al., 1996).

TABLE 13.2   Characteristics of Transformational Leaders

When people are asked to describe the best leaders they know, four characteristics are most often cited: charisma, an ability to inspire others, intellectual stimulation, and individualized consideration. These attributes are evident in the self-descriptions given here. *(Based on Bass & Avolio, 1990.)*

Characteristic	Description	Sample Items
Charisma	Has a vision; gains respect, trust, and confidence; promotes a strong identification of followers.	I have a sense of mission which I communicate to them. They are proud to be associated with me.
Inspiration	Gives pep talks, increases optimism and enthusiasm, and arouses emotion in communications.	I present a vision to spur them on. I use symbols and images to focus their efforts.
Intellectual Stimulation	Actively encourages a re-examination of existing values and assumptions; fosters creativity and the use of intelligence.	I enable them to think about old problems in new ways. I place strong emphasis on careful problem solving before taking action.
Individualized Consideration	Gives personal attention to all members, acts as advisor and gives feedback in ways that are easy to accept, understand, and use for personal development.	I coach individuals who need it. I express my appreciation when they do a good job.

Leadership Among Women and Minorities

Look at the leaders of America's Fortune 500 companies, and you'll find that less than 5 percent of all board-of-directors members are women—a percentage that is not much higher in the health-care industry, government, or educational institutions. Now look at the percentage of African Americans, Hispanics, and Asians in the top ranks of the same organizations, and you'll find that they fare even worse. Even today, you can count on one hand the number of U.S. senators who are female or the number of major-league baseball managers who are black. Despite progress that has been made in entry- and middle-level positions, working women and minorities who seek positions of leadership still seem blocked by a "glass ceiling"—a barrier so subtle that it is transparent yet so strong that it keeps them from reaching the top of the hierarchy (Morrison & Von Glinow, 1990). Women may also encounter "glass walls" that keep them from moving laterally within an organization—for example, from positions in public relations to those in core areas such as production, marketing, and sales (Lopez, 1992).

Many women are highly qualified for positions of power. Research shows that male and female managers have very similar aspirations, abilities, values, and job-related skills. Indeed, Alice Eagly and Blair Johnson (1990) meta-analyzed the results of 150 studies of sex differences in leadership and found that female leaders in the workplace are as task oriented as their male counterparts. Similarly, Eagly and her colleagues (1995) found that male and female leaders are equally effective. The only difference seems to be that men are more controlling and women more democratic in their approaches. As a result, men may be more effective as leaders in positions that require a more directive style (for example, in the military), whereas women may be more effective in managerial settings that require openness and cooperation.

In 1997, Madeleine Albright broke through the proverbial glass ceiling and became the first woman ever to serve as the U.S. Secretary of State.

This portrayal of women leaders is consistent with Judy Rosener's (1990) impression, as reported in the *Harvard Business Review*, that although female executives used to feel a need to prove they were tough, today's generation of leading women are drawing successfully on qualities that are traditionally viewed as feminine. It's also consistent with Sally Helgesen's (1990) observation that female managers interact more with subordinates, invite them to participate in the decision-making process, share information and power, and spin more extensive networks, or "webs of inclusion"—a leadership style she calls the "feminine advantage."

So what's wrong? If women are competent at leadership, why have so few managed to reach the top? For women, the path to power—from their entry into the labor market, to recruitment in an organization, and up the promotion ladder—is something of an "obstacle course" (Ragins & Sundstrom, 1989). One problem is that many women are deeply conflicted about having to juggle a career and family responsibilities (Crosby, 1991). As a result, women—even in the executive ranks—take more leaves of absence and are somewhat less mobile (Lyness & Thompson, 1997). Another problem is societal. Lingering stereotypes portray women as followers rather than as leaders, and many people are uneasy about women who assume leadership roles. In one study, men and women who were seated at the head of the table in all-male or all-female groups were automatically tagged as leaders. Yet in mixed-sex groups, this head-of-the-table bias applied only to men who sat in that position (Porter et al., 1985). In another study, participants were observed from behind a one-way mirror as they took part in a discussion group with male and female confederates who were trained to behave similarly. Regardless of their sex, all confederates who played an assertive role were quite reasonably perceived as leaders. Yet participants smiled and nodded less often, and frowned more often, in response to female leaders—a subtle but sure sign of disapproval (Butler & Geis, 1990). Combining the results of sixty-one studies, Eagly and others (1992) concluded that female leaders are devalued in comparison to equivalent men when they adopt a "masculine" style of leadership (directive and task focused) or occupy "masculine" positions (for example, as business manager or athletic coach).

Statistics show that minorities also fight an uphill battle for leadership positions in the workplace. In interviews, 84 percent of black MBA graduates from five prestigious business schools said they believed that race had a negative impact on their salaries, performance appraisals, and promotions (Jones, 1986). Research does not clearly show that employee evaluations are biased by race (Sackett & DuBois, 1991; Waldman & Avolio, 1991). Still, in light of what social psychologists know about the subtleties of modern racism, as described in Chapter 5, business leaders should beware of the indirect ways in which minorities are handicapped in the pursuit of leadership. For example, a study of African Americans in the banking industry revealed that they often feel excluded socially from informal work groups, are not "networked," and lack the sponsors, role models, and mentors that are so helpful for upward mobility within an organization (Irons & Moore, 1985). Similarly, a study of business school graduates revealed that African American and Hispanic men were less likely than others to establish mentoring relationships with the influential white men in their respective companies (Dreher & Cox, 1996).

Motivation

What motivates individuals to work hard, and to work well? What determines *your* on-the-job performance? Are you driven by strictly economic concerns, or do you have other personal needs to fulfill? There is no single answer. At work, as in the rest of life, our behavior often stems from the convergence of many different motives.

Economic Reward Models

Out of necessity, people work to make a living. In strictly economic terms, however, payment is more complicated than it may appear. To begin with, an employee's overall satisfaction with his or her compensation depends not only on salary (gross income, take-home pay) but also on raises (upward or downward changes in pay, how these changes are determined), method of distribution (number of checks received, salary differences within the company), and benefits (vacation time, sick leave, insurance, pensions, and other services). Each of these factors is part of the formula for satisfaction (Heneman & Schwab, 1985; Judge & Welbourne, 1994). In fact, many rewards are not monetary but symbolic—such as titles, office size, location, carpeting, furnishings, windows, and the ability to regulate access by others (Becker, 1981; Sundstrom, 1986).

Perhaps the most popular theory of worker motivation is Victor Vroom's (1964) **expectancy theory.** According to Vroom, people are rational decision makers who analyze the benefits and costs of the possible courses of action. Accordingly, he says, workers become motivated and exert effort when they believe that: (1) their effort will result in improved performance, (2) their performance will be recognized and rewarded, and (3) the rewards offered—both monetary and symbolic—are valuable and desirable. Over the years, expectancy theory has been used with some success to predict worker attendance, productivity, and other job-related behaviors (Mitchell, 1974; Van Eerde & Thierry, 1996). Research has also shown that people perform better at work and are more productive when they are given specific goals and clear standards for success and failure than when they're simply told to "do your best" (Locke & Latham, 1990).

What are the practical implications of expectancy theory? In recent years, organizations have devised some new and innovative motivational programs. A survey of 1,600 companies revealed that many of them use (1) individual incentive programs that provide an opportunity to earn time off or extra pay; (2) small-group incentive plans, in which members of a work unit can win bonuses for reaching specified goals; (3) profit-sharing plans, in which workers earn money from company profits; (4) recognition programs that single out "employees of the month" for gifts or trophies; and (5) pay-for-knowledge plans that raise salaries for workers who are flexible and can perform different jobs within a work unit (Horn, 1987).

"We reward top executives at the agency with a unique incentive program. Money."

Bonuses, Bribes, and Intrinsic Motivation

People may strive for reward, but there's more to money than just economics and more to motivation than just the size of a paycheck. Social psychological factors must also be considered. Under certain conditions, reward systems that increase *extrinsic motivation* may undermine *intrinsic motivation*. As we saw in Chapter 3, people are said to be extrinsically motivated when they engage in an activity for money, recognition, or other tangible rewards. In contrast, people are said to be intrinsically motivated when they perform for the sake of interest, challenge, or sheer enjoyment. Business leaders want employees to feel intrinsically motivated and committed to their work. So where do expectancy theory and incentive programs fit in? Is tangible reward the bottom line or not?

expectancy theory The theory that workers become motivated when they believe that their efforts will produce valued outcomes.

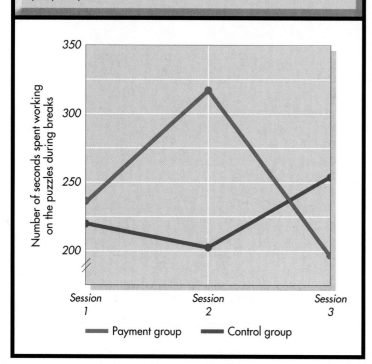

Research shows that when people start getting paid for a task they already enjoy, they sometimes lose interest in it. In the first demonstration of this effect, Edward Deci (1971) recruited college students to work for three one-hour sessions on block-building puzzles they found interesting. During the first and third sessions, all participants were treated in the same manner. In the second session, however, half were paid one dollar for each puzzle they completed. To measure intrinsic motivation, Deci left participants alone during a break in the first and third sessions and recorded the amount of time they spent on the puzzles rather than on other available activities. Compared with participants in the unrewarded group, those who had been paid in the second session later showed less interest in the puzzles when the money was no longer available (see Figure 13.6).

This paradoxical finding—that rewards undermine intrinsic motivation—has been observed in numerous studies (Deci & Ryan, 1985; Lepper & Greene, 1978; Tang & Hall, 1995). By making people feel controlled rather than autonomous, various extrinsic factors commonly found in the workplace—punishment, close supervision, evaluation, deadlines, and competition—also have adverse effects on motivation and performance. Thus, Teresa Amabile (1996) found that people who were paid for artistic activities, compared with others who were not paid, produced less creative work—a finding that applies to creative problem-solving situations as well (McGraw & McCullers, 1979). To be maximally productive, people must feel internally driven, not compelled by outside forces.

But wait. If money undermines intrinsic motivation, should employers *not* use monetary incentives? Are the pay-for-performance programs often used in the workplace doomed to fail, as some have suggested (Kohn, 1993)? Not necessarily. To answer this question, it's important to realize that a reward can be interpreted in two ways, depending on how it is presented. On the one hand, being offered payment can make a person feel bribed, bought off, and controlled, which can result in the detrimental effects just described. On the other hand, rewards often provide people with positive information about the quality of their performance—as when people earn bonuses, scholarships, and verbal praise from others they respect. Research now shows that just as controlling rewards can lower intrinsic motivation, informational rewards can have the opposite positive effect (Cameron & Pierce, 1994; Eisenberger, 1992; Eisenberger & Cameron, 1996). Studying an office machine company, Deci and his colleagues (1989) found that the less controlling the managers were, the more satisfied workers were with the company as a whole. Indeed, when Studs Terkel (1974) interviewed secretaries, stockbrokers, baseball players, garbage collectors, and other workers, over and over again he heard two complaints: The employees were being too closely watched, or "spied on," and they were getting too little positive feedback—in other words, too much control and not enough strokes.

Equity Considerations

A second aspect of payment that influences motivation is the perception that it is fair. According to *equity theory*, presented in Chapter 9, people want rewards to be equitable. In other words, the ratio between inputs and outcomes should be the same for the self as it is for others. Relative to co-workers, then, the more effort you exert and the more you contribute, the more money you should earn. If you feel overpaid or underpaid, however, you will experience distress—and try to relieve it by (1) restoring actual equity, say, by working less or getting a raise, or (2) convincing yourself that equity already exists (Cropanzano, 1993; Greenberg, 1982).

Equity theory has some fascinating implications for behavior in the workplace. Consider Jerald Greenberg's (1988) study of employees in a large insurance firm. To allow for refurbishing, nearly two hundred workers had to be moved temporarily from one office to another. Randomly, the workers were assigned to offices that usually belonged to others who were higher, lower, or equal in rank. Predictably, the higher the rank, the more spacious the office, the fewer the occupants, and the larger the desk. Would the random assignments influence job performance? By keeping track of the number of insurance cases processed, and by rating the complexity of the cases and the quality of the decisions made, Greenberg was able to derive a measure of job performance for each worker before, during, and after the office switch. To restore equity, he reasoned, workers assigned to higher-status offices would feel overcompensated and improve their job performance, and those sent to lower-status offices would feel undercompensated and lower their performance. That is exactly what happened. Figure 13.7 shows that the results offered sound support for equity theory.

Satisfaction depends not only on equity outcomes but also on the belief that the used to determine those outcomes were fair and clearly communicated (Brockner & Wiesenfeld, 1996; Folger, 1986; Moorman, 1991). For example, Greenberg (1990) studied workers in three manufacturing plants owned by the same parent company. Business was slow, so the company reduced its payroll through temporary pay cuts. Would the cuts make workers feel underpaid? If so, how would the workers restore equity? Concerned that the policy might trigger employee theft, Greenberg randomly varied the conditions in the three plants. In

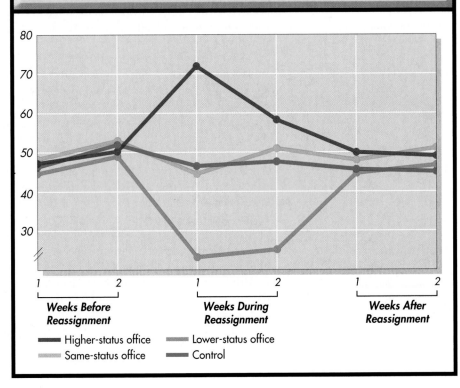

FIGURE 13.7 Equity in the Workplace

Insurance company workers were moved temporarily to offices that were higher, lower, or equal in status to their own rank. Supporting equity theory, those assigned to higher-status offices increased their job performance, and those sent to lower-status offices showed a decrease. When workers were reassigned to original offices, productivity levels returned to normal. *(Greenberg, 1988.)*

"Productivity is up nine percent since I made everyone a vice-president."

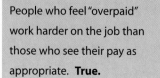

People who feel "overpaid" work harder on the job than those who see their pay as appropriate. **True.**

one, the employees were told, without an explanation, that they would receive a 15 percent pay cut for ten weeks. In the second, the same pay cut was accompanied by an explanation and expressions of regret. In the third plant, salaries were not cut. By keeping track of inventories for the ten weeks before, during, and after the pay cuts, Greenberg was able to estimate the employee theft rate. The result: Workers whose pay had been cut stole more from the company, presumably to restore equity—but only when not provided with an adequate explanation for their loss. In the laboratory too, research participants who were underpaid for their time often restored equity by stealing—particularly when they were not given a valid explanation (Greenberg, 1993).

Equity in the workplace is important, perhaps more for men than for women. In studies of reward allocation, people are led to believe that they and a partner are working at a task for which they will be paid. They work separately, receive false feedback on their performance, and then are told that they must decide how to divide a joint reward. In this situation, women typically pay themselves less than men do and react less strongly when they are underpaid by others (Major & Deaux, 1982). The sex difference in self-payment is found even among male and female college students who had similar pay experiences in their summer jobs (Desmarais & Curtis, 1997). A study of male and female graduates of an Ivy League business school showed that the men were more likely to negotiate starting salaries that were higher than those initially offered (Gerhart & Rynes, 1991).

The gender wage gap has been narrowing in recent years, but at a snail's pace. In 1980, American women earned only 60 cents for every dollar that men were paid. By 1990, the figure was up slightly, to 68 cents. By 1996, it had climbed to 75 cents. This disparity may explain why, in a survey of career expectations among male and female college seniors, the women expected to earn $1,238 less than the men upon entering the job market and $18,659 less at the peak of their careers (Jackson et al., 1992).

There are several possible explanations for this gender wage gap. The first is that women expect lower pay than men do, even when they are just as qualified—an expectation that stems, perhaps, from a history of discrimination (Major & Konar, 1984). Second, women tend to care less about money and more about interpersonal relationships (Crosby, 1982). Third, women may be satisfied with less money because they compare themselves with other women—not with their more highly paid male colleagues (Bylsma et al., 1995; Chesler & Goodman, 1976). Fourth, women tend to rate themselves less favorably than do men; so even when they work harder and perform better, they still feel less entitled (Major, McFarlin, & Gagnon, 1984). Whatever the explanation, these findings have to make you wonder. Will working women of the future be content to remain underpaid relative to men? Is the gender wage gap here to stay? Not necessarily. If the difference in reward expectations is rooted in experience, it should diminish as successive generations of women become more established in high-paying careers.

Economic Decision Making

O ctober 19, 1987, was called Black Monday. On that day, the stock market dived even more deeply than it had during the famous crash of 1929, resulting in an estimated loss of $500 billion. Worst of all, no one really knew why. Was the economy on the verge of collapse, or were psychological factors to blame? Some analysts sought rational economic reasons, citing a rise in the American trade deficit, an increase in the prime lending rate, and political events at home and abroad. Others said the crash was triggered by false beliefs, fear-arousing rumors, conformity pressures, and other social influences—all compounded by the speed with which brokers could buy and sell stocks via computers. Forget interest rates, trade deficits, and the gross national product, they said; if you want to predict the market, talk to investors.

Social Influences in the Stock Market

The odds of making money are far better in the stock market than in gambling casinos—the majority of investors come out ahead. In many ways, however, choosing stocks is like gambling. In *A Random Walk Down Wall Street*, economist Burton Malkiel (1981) reported that over the long haul, mutual fund portfolios compiled by experts perform no better than groups of randomly selected stocks. Thus, when *Consumer Reports* evaluated the advice given by professional brokers, it concluded that "a monkey throwing darts at the stock pages . . . could probably do as well in overall investment performance, perhaps even better" (Shefrin & Statman, 1986, p. 52).

But don't some professionals turn a greater profit than others? And if stock prices rise and fall in reaction to economic conditions, can't the astute investor take advantage of these relationships? The answer to both questions is "not necessarily." It's true that some brokers perform better than others for a period of time, perhaps even four or five years. But investors are no more likely to succeed after a string of wins than after a string of losses. Since many traders have access to the same information, and since prices can change at a moment's notice, movements in the market cannot be predicted with reliability. The only way to guarantee profit is to use confidential information—an illegal activity.

If stock market decisions are not made on strictly economic grounds, then what are they based on? Recent research suggests that predictions of the future on Wall Street are influenced by social psychological factors. Shortly after the October 1987 crash, economist Robert Shiller sent questionnaires to a group of active traders to try to determine what caused the crisis. For the approximately one thousand investors who responded, the key event was news concerning the market itself—including a sharp decline that occurred on the morning of the crash. In other words, price movements in the stock market were triggered not by objective economic information but by other price movements in the market. Does this phenomenon ring a bell? Research on the processes of social comparison (Chapter 3) and conformity (Chapter 7) has shown that when people feel they cannot clearly and concretely measure their own opinion, they turn to others for guidance. Perhaps that is why investors are more influenced by news and stock market tips during periods of rising or falling prices than during periods of relative stability (Schachter et al., 1985).

With respect to coin flips and other chance events, gamblers often assume that hot streaks are due to turn cold, and vice versa. Yet when it comes to games of skill, such as basketball, people often make the opposite assumption—that a hot streak

On October 27, 1997, the U.S. stock market plummeted from 7714 to 7164. In absolute terms, the 550 point drop was the largest ever. But because the market was at an all-time high, the 7.2% decline was far less damaging than the crashes of 1929 and 1987.

forecasts continued success, while a cold spell predicts failure. Both assumptions are incorrect. One event does not imply another. But what about the ups and downs of the stock market? Do either of these beliefs influence the decisions made by investors?

To explore this question, Stanley Schachter and his colleagues (1987) presented college students with recent price histories of stocks that had increased, decreased, or remained stable over a three-week period. The conventional wisdom of Wall Street is that investors should "buy low and sell high." Yet most participants decided to buy stocks that were on the rise and sell those that were on the decline. In a follow-up study, similar decisions were made by a more sophisticated group of students attending the business school at Columbia University.

Do people always go with the flow of the marketplace, or do they sometimes follow the smart "buy low and sell high" rule? Paul Andreasson (1987) argued that the answer depends on attributions. According to Andreasson, investors may well follow conventional wisdom. But what about price changes for which they have a ready explanation? What if a rise in stock prices is attributed to certain world events? As far as the stock market is concerned, attributions such as these can produce a self-fulfilling prophecy by leading investors to believe that the changes will persist—that rising prices will continue to climb and declining prices will continue to fall.

To test his hypothesis, Andreasson simulated a stock market on the computer and found that without news stories to explain the fluctuations, research participants assumed that prices would return to previous levels. The result: They bought stocks when the price was low and sold when the price was high. However, those who also received *Wall Street Journal* explanations for the changes pursued the less

In the cover story of a March 1998 issue, Business Week *predicted that the world economy will suffer in the year 2000 if drastic measures are not taken to correct all the computers that are programmed for the twentieth century. Could this fear trigger a self-fulfilling prophecy—and actually* cause *the economy to weaken?*

"Jitters on Wall Street today over rumors that Alan Greenspan said, 'A rich man can as soon enter Heaven as a camel fit through the eye of a needle.'"

profitable strategy, buying stocks that were climbing (based on the assumption that they would continue to do so) and selling those that were on the decline (based on the same assumption of continuity). Even unpublished rumors can have this effect. Nicholas DiFonzo and Prashant Bordia (1997) conducted a stock market simulation in which unconfirmed rumors were presented to some participants but not others. Interestingly, the participants said that the rumors were not credible and did not sway their decisions. Yet they traded on rumors as if they were hard facts. It doesn't stretch the imagination to see how all these findings might relate to Black Monday. Faced with changes in the market, the financial news media often seize upon current events for a quick explanation. In some cases, rumors spread like fire through the business community. Whether the news is true or false is irrelevant. Either way, it can turn an initial dip in the market into a steep dive.

Commitment, Entrapment, and Escalation

Stock market behavior, like all business decisions made by individuals and organizations, is complicated by another social factor. Hersh Shefrin and Meir Statman (1985) believe that some investors lack the self-control necessary for sound investment decisions. When people own shares of a stock that is climbing, they often sell too early so they can enjoy the quick pleasure of making a profit. This tendency is easy to understand. But when people own stock that is falling, they often wait too long before selling in the hope that they might avoid a financial loss. Why do people—and organizations—often continue to hang on in a failing situation? When the handwriting is on the wall, why compound the problem by throwing good money after bad?

In *Too Much Invested to Quit*, Alan Teger (1980) described a dollar-auction game that illustrates part of the dilemma. Imagine yourself in the following situation. The auctioneer tells you and other participants that a one-dollar bill is about to be sold. As in a typical auction, the highest bidder will receive the dollar in exchange for the amount bid. Yet contrary to convention, the second highest bidder must also pay the amount bid—and will receive nothing in return. You and the other participants are asked not to communicate, and the minimum opening bid is set at five cents. Then before you know it, the bidding begins. In laboratory experiments, two participants compete in the auction. They are supplied with a small amount of money that is theirs to keep, and they are free to quit the experiment at any time. What happens next can be startling. Some pairs reasonably choose to take the money and run without making a single bid. Other pairs, however, get involved in escalating bidding wars. According to Teger, bidding for the dollar frequently climbs into the five-dollar range—more than the amount allocated for play by the experimenter. On one occasion, the auctioneer had to terminate the game after the two participants had bid $24.95 and $25.00.

The dollar auction helps us understand how people can become financially overcommitted in real life. In Chapter 8, we saw that individuals and groups can become *entrapped* by their own initial commitments as they try to justify or salvage investments already made. In business, the economic conditions in which an investment is made sometimes justify continued commitment. When there is a reasonable likelihood of success, and when potential earnings are high relative to the additional necessary costs, it may pay to persist. With certain long-term investments, sizable up-front costs simply have to be endured before the delayed benefits are likely to materialize. As in the dollar auction, however, entrapment may also occur when economic conditions do not provide a basis for optimism.

Why do investors, business executives, and others who are losing money on a failing investment so often "hang tough," only to sink deeper and deeper? Why do supervisors who recommend that a worker be hired later overrate that worker's job performance compared with others in the company who were not involved in the hiring (Schoorman, 1988)? And why do NBA basketball teams continue to start players who were selected as top draft picks but have not performed well (Staw & Hoang, 1995)? One explanation for this **escalation effect** is that while people ordinarily avoid taking large financial risks to gain money, they are often willing to take risks to keep from losing money. When offered a hypothetical choice between a certain gain of $1,000 and a fifty-fifty shot at a gain of $2,500, most people choose the smaller guaranteed alternative. Yet when offered a choice between a certain loss of $1,000 and a fifty-fifty shot at a loss of $2,500, most people roll the dice (Kahneman & Tversky, 1979).

Our aversion to loss may account for part of the problem, but it's clear that social psychological factors also contribute heavily to the escalation effect. Research has shown that those individuals who make the decisions that lead to loss are more likely than others to persist, or even to invest further—when they feel personally responsible (Bazerman et al., 1982; Whyte, 1991). Why? According to Barry Staw, Joel Brockner, and others, people often remain committed to a failing course of action to justify their prior decisions, protect their self-esteem, or save face in front of others (Bobocel & Meyer, 1994; Brockner & Rubin, 1985; Staw & Ross, 1987). Thus, Staw and his colleagues (1997) found that banks were less likely to cut their losses on bad business and real estate loans when the executives who had funded those loans were still with the bank than when they were not.

In organizations, escalation can be minimized by removing those who made the initial losing investment from the decision making later on. Thankfully, individual investors can also learn to use various de-escalation strategies designed to make them more responsive to available evidence and keep them from throwing good money after bad (Simonson & Staw, 1992). In their research, for example, Richard Larrick and his colleagues (1990) found that people often violate the **sunk cost principle** of economics, which states that only future costs and benefits, not past commitments, or "sunk costs," should be considered in making a decision. To appreciate the practical implications, imagine that you've bought a fifteen-dollar ticket to a basketball game weeks in advance. Now, on the day of the game, you don't feel well, it's snowing, and your favorite player is injured. Do you still go to the game to make sure you use the ticket? Not wanting to "waste" the money, many of us would go—even though the money is already sunk, and even though we would have to bear the added costs of getting sick, driving in bad weather, and sitting through a boring game. To see if there is a more "rational" economic choice, ask yourself this question: Would you go to the game if someone called on game day and offered you a free ticket? If you said that you would go if you'd paid for the ticket but not if it were free, then—like investors who don't know when to cut their losses—you fell into the sunk cost trap and should have stayed home.

In a study of University of Michigan professors, Larrick and his colleagues (1990) found that the economists were more likely than their counterparts in other disciplines to use the sunk cost principle—not only in hypothetical problems but also in personal decisions. More important, they found that other people can be taught to apply the rule as well. Indeed, a full month after one brief training session, college students were more likely to report using the rule in their own private lives. Sometimes a little knowledge can go a long way.

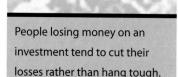

People losing money on an investment tend to cut their losses rather than hang tough. **False.**

escalation effect The tendency for investors to remain committed to a losing course of action.

sunk cost principle The economic rule of thumb that only future costs and benefits, not past commitments, should be considered in making a decision.

Review

- The classic Hawthorne studies showed that worker productivity was increased by the attention paid to the workers.
- In the workplace and other business settings, behavior is heavily influenced by social psychological factors.

Personnel Selection

- Recruiting a competent staff is the first important step in the development of a successful organization.

Traditional Employment Interviews

- Employment interviews may actually diminish the tendency to make simple stereotyped judgments.
- But interviews often give rise to poor selection decisions, in part because of applicant self-presentations and in part because of interviewer expectations that bias the interview.

"Scientific" Alternatives to Traditional Interviews

- Many companies use standardized tests of cognitive ability, personality, and integrity as part of the selection process.
- Although overt integrity tests are easy to fake, the results are predictive of performance on the job.
- A more effective selection method is the structured interview, in which all applicants are evaluated in a standardized manner.
- Many organizations use assessment centers, in which multiple applicants take part in multiple activities that are monitored by a group of evaluators.

Affirmative Action

- Affirmative action affects those whom it is designed to help, those who feel excluded by it, the organizations that implement it, and the interactions among these three groups.
- Research shows that women devalue their own performance when they think they were preferentially selected.
- But reactions are more favorable when procedures are seen as fair, when merit-based factors are thought to play a role, and when the person chosen is seen as qualified for the position.

Performance Appraisals

- Performance appraisals involve the evaluation of an employee and communication of the results to that person.

- Sometimes objective measures of performance are available, but usually evaluations are based on subjective judgments.

Supervisor Ratings

- Research shows that supervisor ratings are based largely on job-relevant characteristics.
- These ratings may be biased by the halo effect, contrast effects, and a tendency to use a restricted range on an evaluation rating scale.

Self-Evaluations

- Self-evaluations also figure into performance appraisals, but these evaluations tend to be self-serving and inflated.
- Self-evaluations are higher among those who have power in an organization; in addition, they are higher among men than women.

New and Improved Methods of Appraisal

- Performance appraisals can be improved by making ratings shortly after observation or taking careful notes, using multiple raters, and training raters in the necessary skills.

Due Process Considerations

- Procedural fairness (not just outcomes) is an important factor in the way people react to evaluations of their performance.

Leadership

- Everyone agrees that leadership requires social influence.

The Classic Trait Approach

- One approach is to identify the traits that characterize people who naturally appear to have leadership qualities.
- In contrast, situational theories are based on the notion that different situations call for different types of leaders.

Contingency Models of Leadership

- In Fiedler's contingency model, task-oriented leaders excel in high- and low-control situations, whereas relations-oriented leaders are effective in moderate-control situations.
- According to the normative model, leaders range from autocratic to participative, and the key to good leadership is to invite just the right amount of worker participation.

Transactional Leadership

■ Transactional leaders reward followers who keep up their end of the bargain and correct those who do not.

Transformational Leadership

■ Transformational leaders motivate followers through their charisma, inspiration, intellectual stimulation, and personal concern for others.
■ Studies show that transformational leaders are more effective than transactional leaders.

Leadership Among Women and Minorities

■ Despite recent gains, working women and minorities are still underrepresented in positions of leadership.
■ Many women are qualified, but they encounter obstacles at home and at work, where people hold lingering stereotypes about women in leadership roles.
■ Part of the problem for minorities is that they are excluded from social networks and influential mentors in the workplace.

Motivation

■ Both economic and social factors influence motivation in the workplace.

Economic Reward Models

■ On the economic side, Vroom's expectancy theory states that workers behave in ways designed to produce the most desirable outcome.
■ Various incentive programs are thus used to motivate by reward.

Bonuses, Bribes, and Intrinsic Motivation

■ When people perceive a reward as a bribe and a means of controlling their behavior, they lose interest in the work itself.
■ But when a reward is presented as a bonus, which provides positive information about the quality of performance, it can enhance intrinsic motivation.

Equity Considerations

■ Equity theory says that the ratio between inputs and outcomes should be the same for all workers.
■ Consistent with the theory, research shows that workers do adjust their productivity levels upward when they feel overpaid and downward when they feel underpaid.
■ For various reasons, women accept as equitable a lower level of pay than men do.

Economic Decision Making

■ Economic decisions are often heavily influenced by social psychological factors.

Social Influences in the Stock Market

■ Sharp changes in the stock market can be triggered by news of what other investors are doing.
■ The goal in the stock market is to buy low and sell high, yet studies show that various factors can lead investors to follow less profitable strategies.
■ Stock market simulations have shown that investors can be influenced by news stories and unconfirmed rumors, both of which can set in motion a self-fulfilling prophecy.

Commitment, Entrapment, and Escalation

■ People often become entrapped by their initial commitments, leading them to stick to failing courses of action and throw good money after bad.
■ At an organizational level, escalation can be minimized by removing those who made the initial losing investment from later decision making.
■ Individually, people can be taught de-escalation strategies, such as the rule that only future costs and benefits, not past commitments, are relevant to economic decisions.

Key Terms

assessment center *474*

contingency model of leadership *481*

escalation effect *494*

expectancy theory *487*

Hawthorne effect *468*

industrial organizational (I/O) psychology *468*

integrity test *473*

normative model of leadership *482*

performance appraisal *477*

structured interview *474*

sunk cost principle *494*

transactional leader *483*

transformational leader *484*

PUTTING COMMON SENSE TO THE TEST

Although flawed, job interviews consistently make for better hiring decisions.

False. *Although interviews may lessen the tendency among employers to make simple stereotyped judgments, they often lack predictive validity.*

A problem with having workers evaluate their own job performance is that self-ratings are overly positive.

True. *Self-evaluations of job performance are not only more positive than ratings made by others but also less predictive of success.*

The most effective type of leader is one who knows how to win support through the use of reward.

False. *Great leaders articulate a vision and then inspire others to join in that vision and work for a common cause.*

People who feel "overpaid" work harder on the job than those who see their pay as appropriate.

True. *People who feel overpaid work harder to restore their sense of equity.*

People losing money on an investment tend to cut their losses rather than hang tough.

False. *People often remain committed to a failing course of action in order to justify the initial decision to themselves and others.*

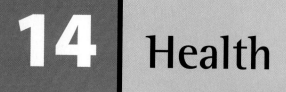

Health

PREVIEW

This chapter explores the social psychology of physical and mental health. We focus first on the links between *stress and health*. Two questions are then asked in this regard: *What causes stress,* and *how does stress affect the body?* Next we examine *processes of appraisal* as well as various *ways of coping with stress.* Finally, we discuss some of the social influences on *treatment and prevention*.

T / F

_____ The accumulation of daily hassles does more to make people sick than catastrophes or major life changes.

_____ Like humans, zebras get ulcers.

_____ Stress can weaken the heart, but it cannot affect the immune system.

_____ When it comes to physical health, research does not support popular beliefs about the power of positive thinking.

_____ People who have lots of friends are healthier and live longer than those who live more isolated lives.

_____ As role models, celebrities have great influence over public health-care decisions.

When Laurence Sterne, an eighteenth-century English novelist, weighed the value of good health, he concluded that it was "above all gold and treasure." Most would agree. Because health matters so much, health care is always near the top of the list of priorities in every country. The long and complex debate about health care in the United States, likely to continue in one form or another into the next century, clearly illustrates the intensity of feelings about this issue. Everyone cares about health and its care—including social psychologists.

The reasons that social psychologists study *mental health*—and such disorders as anxiety and depression—are obvious. We humans are inherently social creatures, and our psychological well-being can be both damaged and repaired by our relationships with other people. But social psychologists are also intensely interested in *physical health*, a domain normally associated with medicine. Working in universities, medical schools, hospitals, and government agencies, many social psychologists are deeply involved in an emerging area of **health psychology**—the application of psychology to the promotion of physical health and the prevention and treatment of illness (Salovey et al., 1998; Taylor et al., 1997). You may wonder, What does social psychology have to do with catching a cold, having a heart attack, or being afflicted by cancer? If you could turn the clock back a few years and ask your family doctor, his or her reply would be "nothing." In the past, physical illness was considered a purely biological event. But this strict medical perspective has now given way to a broader model, which holds that health is a joint product of biological, psychological, and social factors.

health psychology
The study of physical health and illness by psychologists from various areas of specialization.

According to the World Health Organization (1997), average life expectancy ranges from a low of forty in Sierra Leone up to eighty in Japan. In the United States, the average life expectancy is seventy-six.

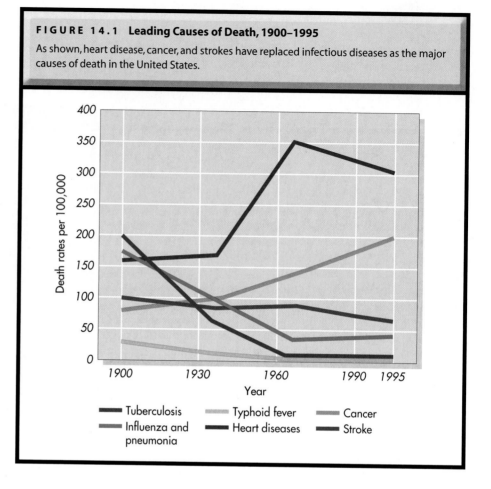

FIGURE 14.1   Leading Causes of Death, 1900–1995

As shown, heart disease, cancer, and strokes have replaced infectious diseases as the major causes of death in the United States.

For up-to-date health statistics, you can visit the World Health Organization and the National Center for Health Statistics online at www.who.org/ and at www.cdc.gov/nchshome.html

Part of the reason for this expanded view is that illness patterns over the years have changed in significant ways. Before the twentieth century, the principal causes of death in the United States were contagious diseases such as polio, smallpox, tuberculosis, typhoid fever, malaria, influenza, and pneumonia. Today, none of these infectious illnesses is a leading killer. Instead, Americans are most likely to die, in order of risk, from heart disease, cancer, strokes, and accidents (AIDS is eighth on the list)—problems that are sometimes preventable through changes in our lifestyles, outlooks, and behavior (see Figure 14.1). In light of the very useful social psychology research that has been conducted in recent years, this chapter focuses first on stress—what causes it, what it does to the body, and how we appraise stressful situations in an effort to cope. Then we look at social influences on the treatment and prevention of illness.

Stress and Health

stress An unpleasant state of arousal in which people perceive the demands of an event as taxing or exceeding their ability to satisfy or alter those demands.

Stress is an unpleasant state of arousal that arises when we perceive that the demands of a situation threaten our ability to cope effectively. Nobody knows the precise extent of the problem, but stress is a potent killer. Regardless of who you are, when you were born, or where you live, you have no doubt experienced stress. Sitting in rush-hour traffic, packing your belongings to move, getting married or divorced, losing hours of work to a computer crash, getting into an argument with a close friend, worrying about an unwanted pregnancy or the health of your child, living in a high-crime neighborhood, struggling to make financial ends meet, and caring for a loved one who is sick—these are the kinds of stresses and strains we all must live with. Whether the stress is short-term or long-term, serious or mild, no one is immune, and there is no escape. But there are ways to cope.

According to Richard Lazarus and Susan Folkman (1984), the stress-and-coping process can be seen as an ongoing transaction between a person and his or her environment. Faced with an event that may prove threatening, our subjective **appraisal** of the situation determines how we will experience the stress and what **coping** strategies we will use—that is, what thoughts, feelings, and behaviors we will employ to try to reduce the stress. At times, people also take proactive steps to keep a potentially stressful event from occurring in the first place (Aspinwall & Taylor, 1997). As we'll see, effective coping helps to maintain good health; ineffective coping can cause harm.

In the next two sections, we examine two questions of relevance to health and well-being: (1) What causes stress? (2) How does stress "get into" the body? Then we look at appraisal and coping—processes that account for why an event that flattens one person can prove harmless to another. As all the pieces come together, we'll see that the answers to these questions provide a broad and useful model of the stress-and-coping process (see Figure 14.2).

At every age, from birth to retirement, more males than females die each year. Note the effect on the U.S. population.

	Male	Female
At conception	56%	44%
Under 5	51%	49%
Under 30	51%	49%
50–54	49%	51%
Over 65	41%	59%
Over 85	29%	71%
Over 100	18%	82%
All ages	49%	51%

What Causes Stress?

There are many different sources of stress, or **stressors,** and these can be defined and measured in different ways (Cohen et al., 1995). What events do *you* find stressful? Try jotting down some of the stressors in your own life, and you'll probably find that the items on your list can be sorted into three major categories: crises and catastrophes, major life events, and daily hassles.

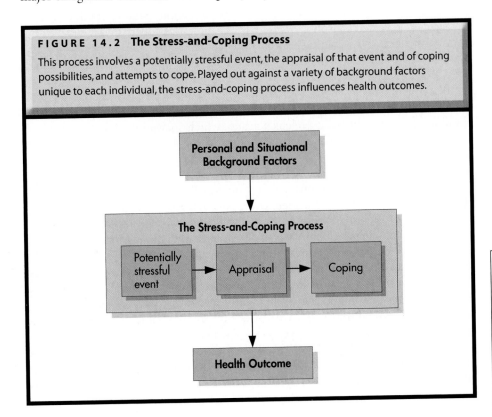

FIGURE 14.2 The Stress-and-Coping Process
This process involves a potentially stressful event, the appraisal of that event and of coping possibilities, and attempts to cope. Played out against a variety of background factors unique to each individual, the stress-and-coping process influences health outcomes.

appraisal The process by which people make judgments about the demands of potentially stressful events and their ability to meet those demands.

coping Efforts to reduce stress.

stressor Anything that causes stress.

Crises and Catastrophes

It was the winter of 1998 when El Niño wreaked havoc on many parts of the United States. In Florida, tornados packing winds of up to 210 miles per hour whipped through the state, threw cars into houses, wrapped trailers around trees, and killed dozens of residents. One twister snatched an eight-month-old baby from his father's arms, killing the child. At about the same time, torrential rainfalls in California caused flooding, loosened the ground, collapsed hillsides, and set off avalanches of mud along parts of the coast, buckling walls and burying cars. The storms of El Niño dealt a devastating blow to many people. Other events that have similarly traumatic effects include plane crashes, car accidents, wars, sexual and violent crimes, divorce, and the death of a parent, spouse, or child.

The harmful effects of catastrophic stressors on health are well documented. The 1979 accident at the Three Mile Island nuclear plant in Pennsylvania illustrates the point. Near-meltdown in the core of a nuclear reactor exposed residents of surrounding communities to radioactive gases and required the evacuation of over 100,000 people. Studies conducted after the accident revealed sharply increased stress among residents living close to the plant, with mothers of young children suffering the most (Hartsough & Savitsky, 1984). At least some residents still exhibited symptoms up to six years later, though stress reactions had dissipated by the end of a decade (Baum & Fleming, 1993).

On February 23, 1998, severe storms in Oscelona County, Florida wrecked havoc on many lives. As captured in this aerial photograph, trucks and cars were thrown into homes and roofs were completely blown off. The stress aroused by such natural disasters can have negative long-term effects on health and well-being.

Natural disasters can be just as upsetting. Paul and Gerald Adams (1984) examined the public records in Othello, Washington, before and after the 1980 eruption of the Mount Saint Helens volcano, which spewed thick layers of ash all over the area. They discovered post-eruption increases in calls made to a mental health crisis line, police reports of domestic violence, referrals to a local alcohol treatment center, and visits to the hospital emergency room.

Then there was the earthquake that shook the San Francisco Bay area in 1989. Houses collapsed, highways buckled, overpasses fell apart, water mains burst, and fires raged out of control. The death toll was sixty-two and thousands were left homeless. By coincidence, Susan Nolen-Hoeksema and Jannay Morrow (1991) had administered some trauma-relevant measures to a group of Stanford University students two weeks before the earthquake. Follow-up assessments ten days later, and again after six weeks, provided these investigators with that rarest of studies: a before-and-after examination of coping. They found that people who had initially been more distressed and those who had encountered more danger during the quake experienced the greatest psychological distress afterward.

The scarring effects of large-scale natural disasters are without dispute. Based on their review of fifty-two studies, Anthony Rubonis and Leonard Bickman (1991) found that high rates of psychological disorders—such as anxiety, phobias, depression, alcohol abuse, and somatic complaints—are common among residents of areas that were hit by these catastrophic events. In a recent study of disasters involving 377 counties, a team of researchers found that, compared with the years preceding each disaster, the suicide rate increased—by 14 percent after floods, by 31 percent after hurricanes, and by 63 percent after earthquakes (Krug et al., 1998).

War in particular leaves deep and permanent psychological scars. Soldiers in combat believe they have to kill or be killed. They suffer intense anxiety and see horrifying injuries, death, and destruction—which leaves them with images and emotions that do not fade. Given this level of stress, it's not surprising that when the war is over, some veterans suffer greatly. In World War I, the problem was called "shell shock." In World War II, it was called "combat fatigue." It is now referred to as **posttraumatic stress disorder (PTSD)** and can be identified

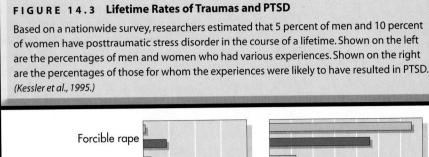

FIGURE 14.3   Lifetime Rates of Traumas and PTSD

Based on a nationwide survey, researchers estimated that 5 percent of men and 10 percent of women have posttraumatic stress disorder in the course of a lifetime. Shown on the left are the percentages of men and women who had various experiences. Shown on the right are the percentages of those for whom the experiences were likely to have resulted in PTSD. *(Kessler et al., 1995.)*

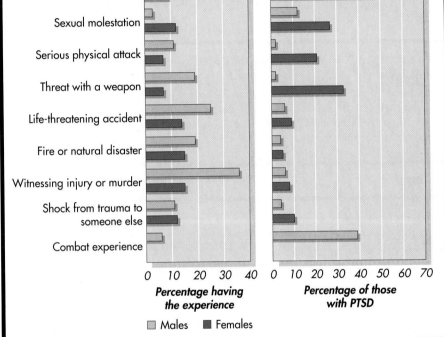

by the presence of such enduring symptoms as recurring anxiety, sleeplessness, nightmares, flashbacks, intrusive thoughts, attentional problems, and social withdrawal. A survey of veterans who served during Operation Desert Storm revealed that 16 to 19 percent reported various PTSD symptoms four to ten months after coming home (Sutker et al., 1993).

For some individuals, PTSD can last much longer. To evaluate the extent of the problem, researchers at the Centers for Disease Control (1988) compared seven thousand Vietnam combat veterans with seven thousand noncombat veterans who had served in the military at the same time, more than twenty years earlier. They found that although the Vietnam War was a distant memory to most Americans, 15 percent of those who had seen combat—twice as many as in the comparison group—reported lingering symptoms of posttraumatic stress disorder. Those who had experienced the most traumatic experiences (crossing enemy lines, being ambushed or shot at, handling dead bodies) were five times more likely to suffer from nightmares, flashbacks, startle reactions, and other problems (Goldberg et al., 1990). Similar results have been found among older veterans of World War II and the Korean War (Fontana & Rosenheck, 1994). When a Vietnam vet, who in 1968 had lost both legs and part of his hands to a booby trap in Danang Province, committed suicide in 1994, his widow suggested a fitting memorial: "To the list of names of victims of the Vietnam War, add the name of Lewis Puller. He suffered terrible wounds that never really healed."

posttraumatic stress disorder (PTSD) A condition in which a person experiences enduring physical and psychological symptoms after an extremely stressful event.

Over the years, clinical psychologists have observed that PTSD can be caused by traumas off the battlefield as well. Based on a nationwide survey of six thousand Americans, from fifteen to fifty-four years old, Ronald Kessler and others (1995) estimated that 8 percent of the population (5 percent of men, 10 percent of women) have posttraumatic stress disorder in the course of a lifetime—and that the symptoms often persist for many years. Figure 14.3 (page 503) indicates that various types of experiences can produce these traumas. In a study of Miami residents caught in a major hurricane, Gail Ironson and others (1997) found that after a few months, one-third exhibited symptoms of PTSD—and that the more injury, property damage, and loss they had suffered from the storm, the more severe their symptoms were. Situations over which we have no control may be particularly traumatic. For example, people involved in serious automobile accidents exhibited more PTSD symptoms and suffered for a longer period of time when the other driver was responsible for what happened than when they were to blame (Delahanty et al., 1997).

Major Life Events

Some people are lucky enough to avoid major catastrophes. But nobody can avoid stress. Indeed, perhaps, change itself causes stress by forcing us to adapt to new circumstances. This hypothesis was first proposed by Thomas Holmes and Richard Rahe (1967), who interviewed hospital patients and found that their illnesses had often been preceded by major changes in some aspect of their lives. Some of the changes were negative (getting hurt, divorced, or fired), but others were positive (getting married or promoted or having a baby). To measure life stress, Holmes and Rahe thus devised the Social Readjustment Rating Scale (SRRS)—a checklist of forty-three major life events, each assigned a numerical value based on the amount of readjustment it requires (see Table 14.1).

The simple notion that change is inherently stressful has an intuitive ring about it. But are positive and negative events really equivalent in their effects simply because they introduce change? Probably not. It now appears that positive and negative events have different implications for stress and coping. One reason for this difference lies in the nature of the emotional experience. Most researchers today believe that positive and negative emotions are distinct and relatively independent (Goldstein & Strube, 1994; Watson, 1988). Happiness is not the absence of distress, nor is distress the absence of happiness—and a person can experience both feelings simultaneously (Carver & Scheier, 1990). The emotional consequences of positive and negative life events thus run on separate

TABLE 14.1 Sample Items from the Social Readjustment Rating Scale

The events listed, in order of stressfulness, can be used to estimate the amount of recent stress in your life (you'll notice that this scale omits many events common among college students—such as graduation and relationships with friends and lovers). *(Holmes & Rahe, 1967.)*

Life Event	Value
1. Death of spouse	100
2. Divorce	73
3. Jail term or imprisonment	63
4. Death of a close family member	63
5. Major personal injury or illness	53
6. Marriage	50
7. Losing one's job	47
8. Pregnancy	40
9. Sexual difficulties	39
10. Addition of a new family member	39
11. Change in financial state	37
12. Death of a close friend	36
13. Change to a different line of work	36
14. Taking out a large mortgage	31
15. Change in status at work	29
16. Son or daughter leaving home	29
17. Outstanding personal achievement	28
18. Major change in work hours or conditions	20
19. Move to a new residence	20
20. Transfer to a new school	20
21. Taking out a loan (e.g., for a new car)	17
22. Change in sleeping habits	16
23. Change in eating habits	15
24. Vacation	13
25. Minor law violations (traffic tickets, etc.)	11

tracks. So, it seems, do the health consequences (Taylor, 1991). Although negative life events are frequently associated with distress and physical illness (Sarason & Sarason, 1984), positive events do not appear to have negative long-term effects on health (Stewart et al., 1986; Thoits, 1983).

Microstressors: The Hassles of Everyday Life

Think again about the sources of stress in your life, and catastrophes or exceptional events spring to mind. Yet the most common source of stress arises from the hassles that irritate us every day. Environmental factors such as population density, loud noise, extreme heat or cold, and cigarette smoke are all sources of stress. Car problems, waiting in lines, losing keys, bad work days, money troubles, and other "microstressors" also place a constant strain on us. Unfortunately, there is nothing "micro" about the impact of these stressors on our health and well-being. Studies show that the accumulation of daily hassles contributes more to illness than do major life events (Kohn et al., 1991), with interpersonal conflicts being the most upsetting of our daily stressors and having a longer-lasting impact than most others (Bolger et al., 1989).

Some daily aggravations are architecturally induced. Take, for example, two common types of college dormitories: those with long corridors (as shown in Figure 14.4A) and those divided into suites (Figure 14.4B). When Andrew Baum and Stuart Valins (1979) compared first-year college students living in these two types of dorms, they found that corridor residents experienced more stress than those in suites. But why? The answer lies in the way these spatial arrangements affect social

Major life events can be stressful—particularly when they are negative. After being forced to testify to a Washington D.C. grand jury about her daughter, Monica Lewinsky, Marcia Lewis was visibly shaken. According to her attorney, Ms. Lewis was too distraught at the time to complete her testimony.

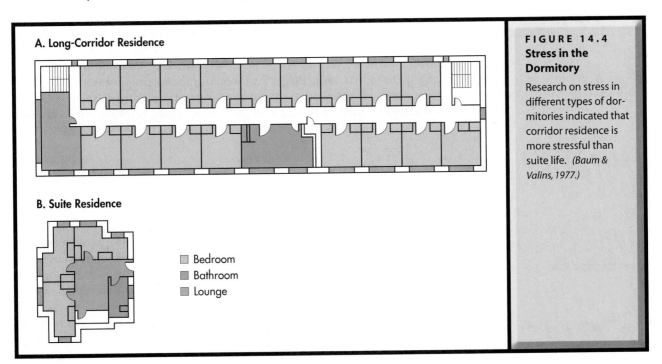

A. Long-Corridor Residence

B. Suite Residence

■ Bedroom
■ Bathroom
■ Lounge

FIGURE 14.4
Stress in the Dormitory

Research on stress in different types of dormitories indicated that corridor residence is more stressful than suite life. *(Baum & Valins, 1977.)*

Heavy rush-hour traffic on Storrow Drive, in Boston, is the kind of microstressor that plagues urban commuters on a daily basis.

control. Because corridor residents have to share more space with more people (such as in the bathroom and lounge areas), it is more difficult for them to avoid unwanted social contacts. Research on prison overcrowding reveals a similar pattern, as the number of inmates sharing a space has a greater effect on stress than does the total amount of space available (Paulus, 1988).

Living in a noisy place—downtown in a busy city, amidst construction, close to a highway, or near an airport—can also be stressful. In a naturalistic test of this hypothesis, Gary Evans and others (1998) studied two groups of German children who were comparable except in one way: A new international airport was opening near where some of them lived. The investigators measured blood pressure both before and after the airport opened and found that in the communities affected by aircraft noise, children exhibited a rise in blood pressure relative to those living in the quiet comparison groups. Up to eighteen months after the airport had opened, these children also gave lower ratings of the quality of life.

There is another source of stress that plagues some people five or six days a week. At work, relentless job pressures can grind away at a person over time and cause *burnout*—a state of emotional exhaustion characterized by a feeling of distance from others and a diminished sense of personal accomplishment. School teachers, doctors, nurses, police officers, social workers, and others in human-service professions are particularly at risk for burnout. Research shows that people who are burned out describe themselves as used up, drained, frustrated, callous, hardened, apathetic, lacking in energy, and without motivation (Cordes & Dougherty, 1993; Maslach, 1982). Research also shows people are most likely to experience burnout when there are not enough resources at work (such as support from supervisors, friendly relationships with co-workers, autonomy, and opportunities for advancement) to meet the demands of the job (Lee & Ashforth, 1996).

The accumulation of daily hassles does more to make people sick than catastrophes or major life changes. **True.**

How Does Stress Affect the Body?

The term *stress* was first popularized by Hans Selye (1936), an endocrinologist. As a young medical student, Selye noticed that patients who were hospitalized for different illnesses often had similar symptoms, such as muscle weakness, a loss of weight and appetite, and a lack of ambition. Maybe these symptoms were part of a generalized response to an attack on the body, he thought. In the 1930s, Selye tested this hypothesis by exposing laboratory rats to various stressors, including heat, cold, heavy exercise, toxic substances, food deprivation, and electric shock. As anticipated, the different stressors all produced a similar physiological response: enlarged adrenal glands, shrunken lymph nodes, and bleeding stomach ulcers. Selye borrowed a term from engineering and called the reaction *stress*, a word that quickly became part of everyday language.

The General Adaptation Syndrome

According to Selye, the body naturally responds to stress in a three-staged process he called the **general adaptation syndrome** (see Figure 14.5). Sparked by the recognition of a threat—such as a predator, enemy soldier, speeding car, or virus—the body has an initial *alarm* reaction. To meet the challenge, adrenaline and other hormones are poured into the bloodstream, creating physiological arousal.

Heart rate, blood pressure, and breathing rates increase, while slower, long-term functions such as growth, digestion, and the operation of the immune system are inhibited. At this stage, the body mobilizes all of its resources to ward off the threat. Next comes a *resistance* stage, during which the body remains aroused and on the alert. There is continued release of stress hormones, and local defenses are activated. But if the stress persists for a prolonged period of time, the body will fall into an *exhaustion* stage. According to Selye, our anti-stress resources are limited. In fact, however, research has shown that exhaustion occurs not because our stress-fighting resources are limited but because their overuse causes other systems in the body to break down, which puts us at risk for illness and even death.

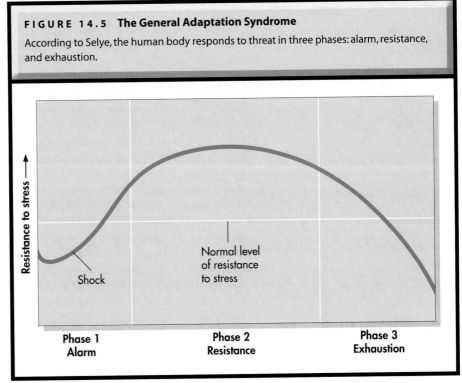

FIGURE 14.5 The General Adaptation Syndrome
According to Selye, the human body responds to threat in three phases: alarm, resistance, and exhaustion.

Selye's basic model thus makes an important point: Stress may be an adaptive short-term reaction to threat, but over time it compromises our health and well-being.

This stress response is found in all mammals. So why, asks neuroscientist Robert Sapolsky (1994), don't zebras get ulcers? Sapolsky notes that the physiological stress response is superbly designed through evolution to help animals mobilize to fight or escape in acute emergencies. For the zebra, this occurs when a hungry lion leaps out from a bush and sprints at top speed across the savanna. For humans, it occurs in combat or in competitive sports and perhaps even on first dates and in job interviews. But think about the list of situations you find stressful, and you'll see that people become anxious over things that would make no sense to a zebra. "We humans live well enough and long enough, and are smart enough, to generate all sorts of stressful events purely in our heads," notes Sapolsky. "From the perspective of the evolution of the animal kingdom, psychological stress is a recent invention" (p. 5). The reason that stress causes ulcers and other illnesses, then, is that the response is designed for acute physical emergencies, yet we turn it

Anthony Robbins proposes a two step formula for handling stress: (1) Don't sweat the small stuff, and (2) Remember that it's all small stuff.

general adaptation syndrome A three-stage process (alarm, resistance, and exhaustion) by which the body responds to stress.

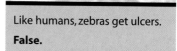

Like humans, zebras get ulcers.
False.

For more information about heart disease, you can visit the American Heart Association's Web site: www.amhrt.org/

on often and for prolonged periods of time as we worry about taxes, mortgages, marital problems, career goals, and the inevitability of death.

What Stress Does to the Heart

Coronary heart disease (CHD) is a narrowing of the blood vessels that carry oxygen and nutrients to the heart muscle. It is currently the leading cause of death in the United States. An estimated 69 million Americans suffer from CHD. For many, the result is a heart attack, which occurs when the blood supply to the heart is blocked. This causes an uncomfortable feeling of pressure, fullness, squeezing, or pain in the center of the chest—and sometimes also sweating, dizziness, nausea, fainting, and shortness of breath. Every year, 1.5 million Americans have heart attacks. One-third do not survive.

Several factors are known to increase the risk of CHD. The three most important are hypertension, or high blood pressure; cigarette smoking; and high cholesterol (others include a family history of CHD, obesity, and lack of exercise). People with one of these three major risk factors are twice as likely to develop CHD, those with two risk factors are three and a half times as likely, and those with all three are six times as likely. These statistics are compelling and should not be taken lightly. Combined, however, these variables account for fewer than half the known cases of CHD. What's missing from the equation is the fourth major risk factor: stress.

In 1956, cardiologists Meyer Friedman and Ray Rosenman were studying the relationship between cholesterol and coronary heart disease. After noticing that husbands were more likely than their wives to have CHD, they speculated that work-related stress might be the reason (at the time, most women did not work outside the home). To test this hypothesis, Friedman and Rosenman interviewed three thousand healthy middle-aged men. Those who seemed to be the most hard-driving, competitive, impatient, time-conscious, and quick to anger were classified as having a **Type A behavior pattern**. Roughly an equal number of men who were easygoing, relaxed, and laid back were classified as having a Type B pattern of behavior. Interestingly, out of 258 men who went on to have heart attacks over the following nine years, 69 percent had been classified as Type A's and only 31 percent as Type B's (Rosenman et al., 1975).

The Type A behavior pattern is made up of a cluster of traits—including competitive drive, a sense of time urgency, and a dangerous mix of anger, cynicism, and hostility (Friedman & Booth-Kewley, 1987; Matthews, 1988). In interviews and written questionnaires, Type A's report that they walk fast, talk fast, work late, interrupt speakers in midsentence, detest waiting in lines, race through yellow lights when they drive, lash out at others in frustration, strive to win at all costs, and save time by doing many things at once. In contrast, "there are those who breeze through the day as pleased as park rangers—despite having deadlines and kids and a broken down car and charity work and scowling Aunt Agnes living in the spare bedroom" (Carey, 1997, p. 75).

By the early 1980s, the influence of the Type A behavior pattern on CHD was widely accepted. A panel of distinguished scientists convened by the National Heart, Lung and Blood Institute concluded that the Type A pattern was a risk factor for CHD, comparable to more traditional risks such as high blood pressure, smoking, high blood cholesterol, and obesity (Review Panel, 1981). But science, like time, moves on. Later studies of the link between Type A and CHD obtained weaker results (Matthews & Haynes, 1986). In fact, the results varied depending on how Type A was measured and the kind of population being studied (Matthews, 1988; Miller et al., 1991). Certainty about the bad effects of "hurry sickness" and "workaholism" began to crumble.

Type A behavior pattern
A pattern of behavior characterized by extremes of competitive striving for achievement, a sense of time urgency, hostility, and aggression.

One issue that arose concerned measurement. Specifically, it turns out that the strength of the link between Type A behavior and coronary heart disease depends on how people are diagnosed. In their original study, Friedman and Rosenman classified men by means of a structured interview in which they could observe their verbal and nonverbal behavior. Afterward, however, many psychologists—in their haste to pursue this vital line of research—tried to identify Type A people using quick, easy-to-administer questionnaires instead of time-consuming interviews. The questionnaires, however, were not as predictive. Apparently, the Type A pattern is more evident from a person's interview *behavior* (whether he or she constantly checks the time, speaks quickly, interrupts the interviewer, and makes restless fidgety movements) than from his or her *self-reports*. When interviews are used to make the diagnosis, 70 percent of men who have CHD also have a Type A behavior pattern—compared with only 46 percent of those who are healthy (Miller et al., 1991).

"I hope you don't mind. We're workaholics."

The Type A behavior pattern was also refined conceptually, and a new line of inquiry sprang up. Perhaps the Type A behavior pattern is too broad, too all-encompassing. If so, could there be a specific component that is most damaging to health? Yes. It now appears that the main toxic ingredient in CHD is *hostility*—as seen in people who are constantly angry, resentful, cynical, suspicious, and mistrustful of others. People who are always in a negative emotional state, and are quick to blow up, are besieged by stress. Because the heart is a dumb pump and the blood vessels mere hoses, the health result is predictable: "The cardiovascular stress-response basically consists of making them work harder for a while, and if you do that on a regular basis, they will wear out, just like any pump or hoses you could buy at Sears" (Sapolsky, 1994, p. 42). It's no wonder that in the long run, the trait of hostility is significantly associated with CHD (T. Q. Miller et al., 1996; Siegman & Smith, 1994). In this regard, Table 14.2 presents some questions that Redford Williams (1993) uses to help people assess their own level of hostility.

TABLE 14.2 How "Hostile" Is Your Pattern of Behavior?
(Williams, 1993.)

- When in the express checkout line at the supermarket, do you often count the items in the baskets of the people ahead of you to be sure they aren't over the limit?
- When an elevator doesn't come as quickly as it should, do your thoughts quickly focus on the inconsiderate behavior of the person on another floor who's holding it up?
- When someone criticizes you, do you quickly begin to feel annoyed?
- Do you frequently find yourself muttering at the television during a news broadcast?
- When you are held up in a slow line in traffic, do you quickly sense your heart pounding and your breath quickening?

What else explains the connection between hostility and coronary heart disease? One possibility is that hostile people are less health-conscious—that they tend to smoke more, consume more caffeine and alcohol, exercise less, sleep less, and eat less healthy foods and are also less likely to comply with health advice from their doctors (Leiker & Hailey, 1988; Siegler, 1994). A second explanation is that hostile people are physiologically reactive. In tense social situations, they react with greater increases in blood pressure, pulse rate, and adrenaline—a hormone that accelerates the build-up of fatty plaques on the artery walls, causing hardening of the arteries (Blascovich & Katkin, 1993; Harbin, 1989; Krantz & Manuck, 1984; Suls & Wan, 1993).

What Stress Does to the Immune System

Increasingly, it has become clear that psychological stress produces a wide range of effects on the body—including increases in the risk of chronic back pain, diabetes, appendicitis, upper respiratory infections, arthritis, herpes, gum disease, common colds, and some forms of cancer. How can stress have so wide a range of disabling effects? Answer: by compromising the body's immune system—the first line of defense against illness (Glaser & Kiecolt-Glaser, 1994).

This color-enhanced microscopic image shows two "natural killer" immune cells (in yellow) engulfing and destroying a leukemia cell (in red). The human immune system contains more than a trillion specialized white blood cells.

The **immune system** is a complex surveillance system that fights bacteria, viruses, parasites, fungi, and other "nonself" substances that invade the body. The system contains more than a trillion specialized white blood cells called *lymphocytes* that circulate throughout the bloodstream and secrete chemical antibodies. These sharklike search-and-destroy cells patrol the body twenty-four hours a day and attack trespassers. The immune system is also equipped with large scavenger cells that zero in on viruses and cancerous tumors. Serving as a "sixth sense" for foreign invaders, the immune system continually renews itself. During the few seconds it takes to read this sentence, your body will have produced 10 million new lymphocytes.

Today, many health psychologists specialize in the subfield of **psychoneuroimmunology,** or **PNI** (*psycho* for mind, *neuro* for the nervous system, and *immunology* for the immune system). These researchers have found that stress can affect the immune system, at least temporarily. The medical community used to reject the idea, but no longer. What changed? First, animal experiments showed that rats exposed to noise, overcrowding, or inescapable shocks, as well as primates separated from their social companions, exhibit a drop in immune cell activity compared with non-exposed animals (Coe, 1993; Moynihan & Ader, 1996). A link was also observed in humans. Intrigued by the fact that people often become sick and die shortly after they are widowed, R. W. Barthrop and others (1977) took

immune system A biological surveillance system that detects and destroys "nonself" substances that invade the body.

psychoneuroimmunology (PNI) A subfield of psychology that examines the links among psychological factors, the brain and nervous system, and the immune system.

blood samples from twenty-six men and women whose spouses had recently died. Compared with nonwidowed controls, these grief-stricken spouses exhibited a weakened immune response. This demonstration was the first of its kind.

Additional studies soon revealed weakened immune responses in NASA astronauts after their reentry into the atmosphere and splashdown, in people deprived of sleep for a prolonged period of time, in students in the midst of final exams, in men and women recently divorced or separated, in people caring for a family member with Alzheimer's disease, in snake phobics exposed to a live snake, and in workers who have just lost their jobs (O'Leary, 1990). Even in the laboratory, people who are given complex arithmetic problems to solve or painful stimuli to tolerate exhibit changes in immune cell activity—changes that last for one or more hours after the stress has subsided (Cohen & Herbert, 1996).

In a particularly intriguing study, Arthur Stone and others (1994) paid forty-eight adult volunteers to take a harmless but novel protein pill every day for twelve weeks—a substance that would lead the immune system to respond by producing an antibody. Every day, the participants completed a diary in which they reported on their moods and on experiences at work, at home, in financial matters, in leisure activities, and in relationships with their friends, spouses, and children. The participants also gave daily saliva samples that were later used to measure the amount of antibody produced. The results were striking, as are their implications: The more positive events participants experienced in a given day, the more antibody was produced. The more negative events they experienced, the less antibody was produced. In a direct way, then, daily experiences can strengthen or weaken our immune system's ability to protect us from illness.

It appears that psychological states "get into" the immune system. But how? As illustrated in Figure 14.6, there are two possible ways this can happen. First, people who are under great stress tend to smoke more, use more alcohol and drugs, sleep less, exercise less, and have poorer diets—behaviors that tend to compromise the immune system. For example, one study showed that when healthy male adults were kept awake between 3:00 and

At the Johnson Space Center, in Houston, former astronaut and U.S. Senator John Glenn prepares for his recent shuttle mission. Research shows that the stress of space travel—particularly reentry into the earth's atmosphere—temporarily weakens an astronaut's immune responses.

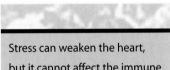

Stress can weaken the heart, but it cannot affect the immune system. **False.**

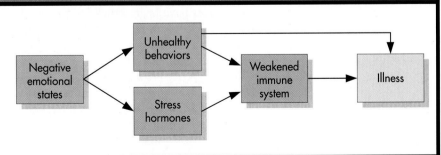

FIGURE 14.6 Pathways from Stress to Illness

Hostility, stress, and other negative emotional states may cause illness in two ways: (1) by promoting unhealthful behaviors (more alcohol, less sleep, and so on) and (2) by triggering the release of hormones that weaken the immune system.

7:00 A.M., immune cell activity diminished—and returned to normal only after a full night of uninterrupted sleep (Irwin et al., 1994). Second, stress triggers the release of adrenaline and other stress hormones into the bloodstream—and these hormones tend to suppress immune cell activity (Dhabhar & McEwen, 1995). The result is a temporary lowering of the body's resistance (Cohen & Williamson, 1991).

The Links Between Stress and Illness

If stress weakens the immune system, are people who are stressed more likely to become sick? Sheldon Cohen and others (1993) conducted a fascinating, elaborate study to help answer this question. They paid 420 volunteers to spend nine days in a medical experiment—and risk exposure to a common cold virus. In the first two days, participants filled out several questionnaires, including one that measured recent stressful experiences in their lives. They were also given a physical examination, including a blood test. Then, to simulate the person-to-person transmission of a virus, the researchers dropped a clear liquid solution into each participant's nose. Those randomly assigned to the control group received only a saline solution. Others, less fortunate, received a cold virus in doses that tend to produce illness rates of 20 to 60 percent.

For the next week, participants were quarantined in large apartments, where they were examined daily by a nurse who took their temperatures, extracted mucus samples, and looked for signs of colds, such as sneezing, watery eyes, stuffy nose, and sore throat (participants did not realize it, but the nurse also kept track of the number of tissues they used). All participants were healthy at the start of the project—and not a single one in the saline control group developed a cold. Yet among those exposed to a virus, 82 percent became infected, and 46 percent of those who were infected caught a cold, symptoms and all. A virus is a virus, and there is no escape. Most interesting, however, is that life stress made a difference. Among those who became infected, high-stress participants were more likely to catch a cold than were low-stress participants—53 percent compared with 40 percent. In short, people whose lives are filled with stress are particularly vulnerable to illness.

Does stress have similar effects on more serious illnesses? Can it, for example, hasten the spread of cancer? In an early test of this hypothesis, Madeline Visintainer and others (1982) implanted tumorous cancer cells into laboratory rats, some of which were then exposed repeatedly to shocks they could not escape. After one month, 50 percent of the animals not shocked died of cancer. Yet relative to that baseline, the death rate climbed to 73 percent among those subjected to the inescapable shock. This study was among the first to show that psychological states—such as a feeling of helplessness—can influence the spread of cancer.

The growth of tumors in helpless white laboratory rats is interesting, but does the same principle apply to people? For obvious ethical reasons, researchers cannot fill humans with despair or inject lethal tumors into their bodies to test the cause-and-effect chain directly. But they can examine the medical records of people whose lives have been struck by tragedy. Investigations of this sort have revealed that cancer appears more often than normal in people prone to being in a negative emotional state (Sklar & Anisman, 1981). In one large-scale study, investigators looked up two thousand male employees of the Western Electric Company in Chicago whose personalities had been assessed in 1958. At the time, test scores had indicated that some of the men were low in self-esteem, unhappy, and depressed. The result? Some twenty years later, these men were more likely than their co-workers to have died of cancer (Persky et al., 1987). Let's be clear about what these results mean. Nobody disputes the notion that cancer is caused by exposure to toxic substances and other biological factors. But individuals who are clinically depressed or under great stress have weakened immune systems—which, in some cases, may result in a higher death rate from cancer and other diseases (Andersen et al., 1994; Herbert & Cohen, 1993).

Processes of Appraisal

Some 2,500 years ago, an anonymous author wrote an extraordinary poem about human suffering: the Book of Job. A pious and prosperous man as the poem begins, Job is soon beset by great calamities. He loses his property, his children, and his health. Job and his friends try to understand how these terrible things could happen. His friends argue that Job's plight must be a punishment sent by God and tell Job to repent. Because he believes that his sufferings far exceed any wrongdoing on his part, Job cannot accept this explanation. In despair, he doubts his capacity to withstand continued hardship and longs for death. But eventually Job finds strength and peace through trusting in God's will.

From the perspective of the stress-and-coping model shown in Figure 14.2, Job and his friends were engaged in the process of appraisal. They thought about possible explanations for Job's suffering and formed expectations about his ability to cope with his situation. These same themes are found in research on stress and coping.

Attributional and Explanatory Styles

Depression is a mood disorder characterized by feelings of sadness, low self-esteem, pessimism, apathy, and slowed thought processes. Other symptoms include disturbances in sleeping and eating patterns, and reduced sexual interest. Per year, 3 percent of the U.S. population experiences a major depression. Many more suffer from brief, mild bouts with the blues. The problem is so widespread that it has been called the "common cold" of psychological disorders.

About twice as many women as men seek treatment for being depressed. During the course of a lifetime, an estimated 12 percent of American men and 21 percent of women will suffer from a major depression (Kessler et al., 1994; Nolen-Hoeksema & Girgus, 1994), though the gender disparity is somewhat smaller in less developed nations (Culbertson, 1997). Although there are many possible causes of depression, many social psychologists have focused on the attributions that people make for the positive and negative events of their lives.

In 1975, Martin Seligman argued that depression results from **learned helplessness,** the acquired expectation that one cannot control important outcomes. In a classic series of experiments, Seligman had found that dogs strapped into a harness and exposed to painful electric shocks soon became passive and gave up trying to escape—even in new situations where escape was possible. In contrast, dogs that had not received uncontrollable shocks quickly learned the escape routine. As applied to humans, this finding suggested that prolonged exposure to uncontrollable events may similarly cause apathy, inactivity, a loss of motivation, and pessimism. Among human research participants, those exposed to inescapable bursts of noise thus failed to protect themselves in a later situation where the noise could be easily avoided. Seligman was quick to note that people who are exposed to uncontrollable events become, in many ways, like depressed individuals: discouraged, pessimistic about the future, and lacking in initiative. Thus, he saw depression as a form of learned helplessness.

learned helplessness A phenomenon in which experience with an uncontrollable event creates passive behavior toward a subsequent threat to well-being.

FIGURE 14.7   The Reformulated Model of Learned Helplessness

According to this model, stable and global attributions for an uncontrollable event create the expectation of a lack of control over future events. This expectation then produces depressed behavior and feelings. An internal attribution is said to lead to low self-esteem, which characterizes many depressed individuals.

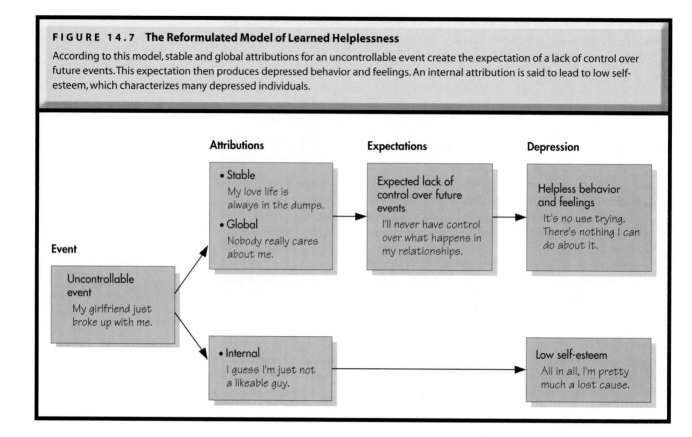

Lynn Abramson and others (1978) soon proposed a reformulated model of learned helplessness. This model holds that lacking any control in one situation is not by itself sufficient to produce helplessness and inactivity in a completely different situation. What matters is the person's *attributions* for that initial lack of control. Specifically, the attributions can vary along three dimensions:

- *Internal versus external.* Does the person attribute the initial lack of control to personal characteristics (internal) or to outside forces in the environment (external)?
- *Stable versus unstable.* Is the lack of control attributed to factors that are seen as relatively permanent (stable) or as temporary (unstable)?
- *Global versus specific.* Is the cause seen as extending to other situations in the person's life (global) or as limited to a particular situation (specific)?

According to the reformulated model, individuals who make *stable* and *global* attributions for an uncontrollable event are more likely to expect more of the same from future events—which means passive and helpless behavior in new situations. Those who make *internal* attributions by blaming themselves are said to be more likely to develop low self-esteem. Taken together, this attributional "triple whammy" locks the person into the worst possible box: a bleak future caused by his or her own unchangeable characteristics (see Figure 14.7).

Abramson, along with Gerald Metalsky and Lauren Alloy (1989) more recently proposed that depression springs from *hopelessness*, a state of mind brought on by the negative self-attributions that people make for failure. In this regard, they note that some individuals possess a **depressive explanatory style**—a tendency to attribute bad events to factors that are internal rather than external ("It's my fault"), stable rather than unstable ("It will not change"), and global rather than specific ("It affects other parts of my life"). Many studies now support this

depressive explanatory style
A habitual tendency to attribute negative events to causes that are stable, global, and internal.

proposition. Whether people are trying to explain social rejection, a sports defeat, low grades, or their inability to solve an experimenter's puzzle, those who are depressed are more likely than others to blame factors that are within the self, unlikely to change, and broad enough to impair other aspects of their lives. The result: a sense of hopelessness and despair (Metalsky et al., 1993).

Everyone suffers occasional setbacks. But people who have a depressive explanatory style find it more difficult to weather the storms. Based on their review of over a hundred studies, Paul Sweeney and others (1986) thus found a clear association between a depressive explanatory style and being depressed. There may even be long-term health implications. Christopher Peterson and others (1988) collected personal essays written in the 1940s by ninety-nine men who had just graduated from Harvard, and analyzed these materials to determine what each man's explanatory style had been in his youth. Thirty-five years later, those who had initially had a depressive, pessimistic explanatory style had more health problems than did their more optimistic peers. Why? A later study by Leslie Kamen-Siegel and colleagues (1991) provides a clue. By taking blood samples, these researchers found that people with a depressive explanatory style also exhibited a weaker immune response. Keep in mind that links between explanatory style and health are only correlational—and subject to interpretation with regard to cause and effect.

Perceptions of Control

Stress affects people differently, an observation that led Suzanne Kobasa and her colleagues (1982) to wonder why some of us are more resilient than others. Kobasa studied some two hundred business executives who were under stress. Many said they were frequently sick, affirming the link between stress and illness; others had managed to stay healthy. The two groups were similar in terms of age, education, job status, income, and ethnic and religious background. But from various tests, it was clear that they differed in their attitudes toward themselves, their jobs, and the people in their lives. Based on these differences, Kobasa identified a personality style she called *hardiness* and concluded that hardy people have three characteristics: (1) commitment, a sense of purpose with regard to work, family, and other domains; (2) challenge, an openness to new experiences and a desire to embrace change; and (3) control, the belief that one has the power to influence important future outcomes.

Research supports the general point that hardiness serves as a buffer against stress (Funk, 1992)—and that the perception of control is the most important ingredient (Florian et al., 1995). Studies have shown that the harmful effects of crowding, noise, heat, and other stressors are reduced when people think they can exert control over these aspects of their environment (Glass & Singer, 1972). The perception of control is especially meaningful for people whose lives are regulated to a large extent by others. For example, elderly residents of nursing homes who were given more control over daily routines became happier and more active (Langer & Rodin, 1976; Schulz, 1976). In addition, continuing expectations of control had positive effects on future health and longevity (Rodin & Langer, 1977; Schulz & Hanusa, 1978). Other studies have also illustrated the point: Patients with coronary heart disease, cancer, and AIDS are better adjusted, emotionally, when they think they can influence the course of their illness (Helgeson, 1992; Reed et al., 1993; Rodin, 1986; Thompson et al., 1993).

The perception of control refers to the expectation that our behaviors can produce satisfying outcomes. But people also differ in the extent to which they believe that they can perform these behaviors in the first place. These concepts seem

"Amazing, three failed marriages, scores of disastrous relationships, many financial reversals, and countless physical ailments, but through it all I've always had good luck parking."

related; but in fact they refer to different beliefs, both of which are necessary for us to feel that we control the important outcomes in our lives (Skinner, 1996). According to Albert Bandura (1997), the latter expectations are based on feelings of competence, or **self-efficacy.** Some individuals may be generally more confident than others, says Bandura, but self-efficacy is a state of mind that varies from one specific task and situation to another. In other words, you may have high self-efficacy about meeting new people, but not about raising your grades. Or you may have high self-efficacy about solving a math problem but not about writing a paper.

Research on self-efficacy has shown that the more of it you have at a particular task, the more likely you are to take on that task, try hard, persist in the face of failure, and succeed. As Bandura (1997) notes, the implications for mental and physical health are particularly striking. For example, individuals with high self-efficacy on health-related matters are more likely, if they want, to stop smoking, abstain from alcohol, stay physically fit, and tolerate the pains of arthritis, childbirth, and migraine headaches (Maddux, 1991; O'Leary, 1985). People who have a high level of self-efficacy about their ability to cope with stress also exhibit an enhanced functioning of the immune system (Wiedenfeld et al., 1990).

Optimism and Hope

The reason it's so important to understand the attributions we make about past outcomes and our perceptions of control in present situations is that both have implications for our outlook on the future. In his book *Learned Optimism*, Seligman (1991) argues that optimism, a generalized tendency to expect positive outcomes, is characterized by a nondepressive explanatory style. According to Seligman, an optimist tends to blame failure on factors that are external, temporary, and specific—and credit success to factors that are internal, permanent, and global. Think about your own view of the future. Are you the eternal optimist who looks on the bright side and expects good things to happen? Or do you tend to believe in

self-efficacy A person's belief that he or she is capable of the specific behavior required to produce a desired outcome in a given situation.

Murphy's Law, that if something can go wrong, it will? By asking questions such as these, Michael Scheier and Charles Carver (1985) categorized college students along this dimension and found that dispositional optimists reported fewer illness symptoms during the semester than did pessimists. Correlations between optimism and health are common. Studies have shown that optimists are more likely to take a problem-focused approach in coping with stress; complete a rehabilitation program for alcoholics; make a quicker, fuller recovery from coronary artery bypass surgery; and, among gay men concerned about AIDS, take a more active approach to the threat (Scheier & Carver, 1992). Optimism is also associated with better adjustment among patients with arthritis (Long & Sangster, 1993) and breast cancer (Carver et al., 1993).

The notion that health springs from optimism is profoundly well documented in the **placebo effect**—the tendency for an inactive drug or treatment to improve a patient's condition because he or she believes in its effectiveness. In past years, sick people were forced to consume potions made of frog sperm, lizard tongues, crocodile dung, fly specks, unicorn horns, and ground snake. They were also subjected to shock treatments, forced vomiting, bloodletting, freezing, and blistering. It seems a miracle anyone survived. Yet accounts of early medical practices indicate that many were "cured" by these peculiar remedies. Why? The placebo effect gives patients faith and hope—an important part of the healing process. Today this psychological aspect of treatment is taken for granted in medical circles (Brown, 1998; Harrington, 1997).

In an early demonstration of the placebo effect, Robert Sternbach (1964) gave volunteer participants a white sugar pill that contained no active ingredients. At first, these participants were told that the pill contained a drug that would stimulate a strong churning sensation in the stomach. The next time, they were told that it would reduce their stomach activity and make them feel full. On a third occasion, they were informed that the pill was only a placebo. The result: Participants always swallowed the same tablet, yet they exhibited measurable changes in stomach activity consistent with expectations. More recently, Montgomery and Kirsch (1996) recruited volunteers for an experiment on pain. These volunteers placed the index finger from each hand in a device onto which a metal bar was lowered, putting pressure on the fingers. On one finger, but not the other, the experimenter applied a brownish, medicinal-smelling "local anesthetic" to reduce pain. The solution was only a mixture of iodine, oil of thyme, and water and had no anesthetic properties, but participants rated the pain to the placebo-treated finger as less intense and less unpleasant.

Over the years, placebos have been used to treat allergies, headaches, insomnia, skin rashes, upset stomachs, chronic pain, and other ailments. Thus, to evaluate the effectiveness of any new drug, or other form of treatment, researchers must show that people who received that drug improved more than others who *believed* they received it but did not. Only then can the true effect of the treatment be separated from the powerful placebo effect. Somehow, beliefs transform reality.

There's an old saying, "Where there's life, there's hope." Perhaps the opposite is also true: "Where there's hope, there's life." In a remarkable illustration of this possibility, Susan Everson and others (1996) studied 2,428 middle-aged men in Finland. Based on the extent to which they agreed with two simple statements ("I feel that it is impossible to reach the goals I would like to strive for" and "The future seems hopeless, and I can't believe that things are changing for the better"), the men were initially classified as having a high, medium, or low sense of hopelessness. When the investigators checked the death records roughly six years later, they found that the more hopeless the men were at the start, the more likely they were to have died of various causes—even when the men were otherwise equated for their age and prior health status. Compared with those who were low in hopelessness, the

"The optimist proclaims we live in the best of all possible worlds; and the pessimist fears this is true."

—James Cabell

"For a wide range of afflictions, 30 to 40 percent of patients experience relief after taking a placebo."

—Walter A. Brown

When it comes to physical health, research does not support popular beliefs about the power of positive thinking. **False.**

placebo effect The tendency for an ineffectual drug or treatment to improve a patient's condition because he or she believes in its effectiveness.

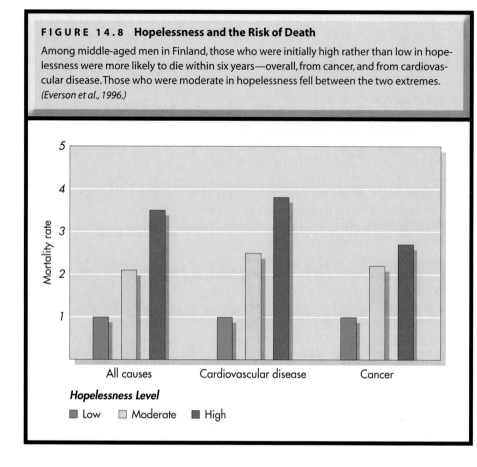

FIGURE 14.8   Hopelessness and the Risk of Death

Among middle-aged men in Finland, those who were initially high rather than low in hope-lessness were more likely to die within six years—overall, from cancer, and from cardiovas-cular disease. Those who were moderate in hopelessness fell between the two extremes. *(Everson et al., 1996.)*

highs were more than twice as likely to die from cancer and four times more likely to die of cardiovascular disease (see Figure 14.8). These results thus bring to life what Norman Cousins (1989) described as "the biology of hope."

Pollyanna's Health

Pollyanna is the name of the upbeat heroine created by American writer Eleanor Porter. Although Pollyanna used to get bad press for her boundless belief that even the most ominous cloud has a bright silver lining, the research in this section suggests that Pollyanna should be an extraor-dinarily healthy person.

Let's be clear about what the research means. No credi-ble scientist believes that our explanatory styles, perceptions of control, or outlook on the future are the *sole* determinants of our health and well-being. Positive thinking cannot guarantee good health. So although we should appreciate the powers of the mind to influence the body, it would be a cruel mistake to blame victims of illness for having a "bad attitude" (Krantz & Hedges, 1987). As Howard Friedman (1991) put it, in *The Self-Healing Personality*, "We must walk a fine line between blaming patients on the one hand and absolving them of any role in their health on the other" (p. 96).

It's also important to recognize that there may be limits to positive thinking, especially if it leads us to see ourselves and the events around us in ways that are not realistic. As we saw in Chapter 3, people who have overly positive rather than realis-tic views of themselves are sometimes disliked by their own friends. In a series of studies, Colvin and others (1995) found that self-enhancing men were seen as rela-tively boastful and inconsiderate of others, while self-enhancing women were seen as defensive, sensitive to criticism, and overreactive to minor setbacks. It may also be detrimental for people to believe that they have control over events when, in fact, they do not. Thus, in a study of patients suffering from a loss of kidney function, those who felt they had control over their health became more depressed, not less, after having a transplant that failed (Christensen et al., 1991). Faced with some set-backs, a sense of control can help us bounce back. But setting control expectations too high can do more harm than good in the wake of negative outcomes.

Which brings us back to Job. At the end of this Biblical account, Job recovers his health, his property, and his family prosperity. He does not, however, regain the sense of personal control and optimism that he enjoyed prior to being struck by calamity. Instead, Job's hard-won serenity is based on his belief that life has mean-ing and purpose. Such beliefs may be especially important for those confronted with highly stressful experiences, such as the loss of a child (McIntosh et al., 1993). Pollyanna has her charm, but Job is a hero of the human condition.

"The most important thing in illness is never to lose heart."

—Nikolai Lenin

TABLE 14.3 Ways of Coping with Stress

These statements describe some coping strategies that people say they use. The strategies are listed in order from those that are relatively common to those that are less common *(Carver et al., 1989).*

Planning/Active Coping

- I try to come up with a strategy about what to do.
- I take additional action to try to get rid of the problem.

Positive Reinterpretation

- I look for something good in what is happening.
- I try to make it seem more positive.

Acceptance

- I learn to live with it.
- I accept that this has happened and can't be changed.

Seeking Social Support

- I talk to someone about how I feel.
- I ask people who had similar experiences what they did.

Restraint Coping

- I force myself to wait for the right time to do something.
- I make sure not to make matters worse by acting too soon.

Focusing on/Venting Emotions

- I get upset and let my emotions out.
- I let my feelings out.

Suppression of Competing Activities

- I put aside other activities to concentrate on this.
- … if necessary let other things slide a little

Mental Disengagement

- I turn to work … to take my mind off things.
- I go to the movies or watch TV, to think about it less.

Turning to Religion

- I seek God's help.
- I try to find comfort in my religion.

Behavioral Disengagement

- I give up the attempt to get what I want.
- I admit to myself that I can't deal with it.

Denial

- I refuse to believe that it has happened.
- I pretend that it hasn't really happened.

Alcohol and Drugs

- I drink alcohol or take drugs to think about it less.

Ways of Coping with Stress

Stress is inevitable. No one can prevent it. But people can try to minimize its harmful effects on health. To understand how some people keep their composure while others crumble under the pressure, it is useful to examine the *coping* process and ask, What are some adaptive ways to cope with stress? Like Job, many people react to misfortune and tragedy by actively searching for meaning in their lives (Terry, 1994). But there are numerous other ways to cope. Based on the self-reports of many people, Charles Carver and others (1989) constructed a multidimensional questionnaire called COPE that measures twelve distinct methods of coping (see Table 14.3).

While acknowledging that people can use many different coping strategies, Richard Lazarus and Susan Folkman (1984) distinguished two general types. The first is **problem-focused coping,** cognitive and behavioral efforts to reduce stress by overcoming the source of the problem. Difficulties in school? Study harder, hire a tutor, or reduce your workload. Marriage on the rocks? Talk it out or see a counselor. Problems at work? Consult with your boss or look for another job. As indicated in several of the items in Table 14.3, the goal is to attack the source of stress. A second approach is **emotion-focused coping,** which consists of various efforts to manage our emotional reactions to a stressful situation rather than trying to change it. If you're struggling at school, at work, or in a romantic relationship, you can keep a stiff upper lip, accept what is happening, tune out, or vent your emotions. According to Lazarus and Folkman, and as supported by research (Reese et

problem-focused coping
Cognitive and behavioral efforts to alter a stressful situation.

emotion-focused coping
Cognitive and behavioral efforts to reduce the distress produced by a stressful situation.

al., 1997), we tend to take an active, problem-focused approach when we think we can overcome a stressor but fall back on an emotion-focused approach when we perceive the problem to be out of our control.

Problem-Focused Coping

Problem-focused coping seems like the prime candidate for a starring role in the war against stress. Surely our most active, direct, and assertive efforts are associated with better health (Aspinwall & Taylor, 1992). And clearly we often do benefit from confronting a stressor head-on rather than avoiding it. Consider something we are all guilty of on occasion: procrastination, a purposive delay in the beginning or completing of a task, which is often accompanied by feelings of discomfort (Ferrari et al., 1995). In a longitudinal study of college students enrolled in a health psychology class, Dianne Tice and Roy Baumeister (1997) administered at the start of the semester a questionnaire that assesses the extent to which people generally tend to procrastinate. True to their word, those students who were classified as procrastinators on the basis of their test scores turned in their term papers later than did their classmates—and also received lower grades. Even more interesting was the relationship to daily reports of stress and physical health. Early on, while procrastinators were in the "putting it off" stage of their projects, they were relatively stress-free compared with others. Later in the semester, however, as the deadline neared and passed, procrastinators were under greater stress and reported having more symptoms of illness. In the end, the short-term benefits of avoidance were outweighed by the long-term costs.

In dealing with essential tasks, it is better to confront and control than to avoid. But is this always the more beneficial approach? There are three reasons why sometimes it is not. First, to exert control a person must stay vigilant, alert, and actively engaged—which is physiologically taxing (Light & Obrist, 1980). Second, control also brings with it the burden of responsibility—and the fear that these efforts will fail (Burger et al., 1983; Rodin et al., 1980). Third, a controlling orientation can cause problems if it leads us to develop an over-controlling, stress-inducing, Type A pattern of behavior—whether that means always having the last word in an argument, "driving" from the back seat of a car, or planning every last detail of a leisurely vacation. Not all events are within our control or important enough to worry about. Thus, there are times when it is better to just let go (Friedland et al., 1992; Wright et al., 1990).

When we use the word *control*, we usually have in mind active efforts to manage something: win an argument, work out a marital problem, change a job requirement. But control

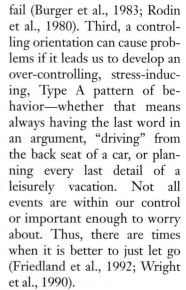

After falling from a horse, which left him paralyzed, actor Christopher Reeve has raised millions of dollars for spinal injury research. "You have only two choices," he said. "Either you vegetate and look out the window or activate and try to effect change." (Carey, 1997, p. 78.)

comes in many guises. Knowledge, for instance, is a form of control. Knowing why something is happening increases your chance of making sure it goes your way—if not now, then the next time. Sometimes, we can cope effectively with tragedies— such as technological disasters (Solomon et al., 1989) and spousal abuse (Andrews, 1992)—by blaming the perpetrators for their actions. In these situations, holding others responsible can force a helpful response, such as financial compensation or police protection.

But what about self-blame? Is it adaptive to cope with a bad situation by blaming oneself? According to Ronnie Janoff-Bulman (1979), it depends on whether you blame your behavior or yourself as a person. People can change their own behavior, she notes, so behavioral self-blame paves the way for control in an effort to reduce current stresses or avoid future ones. In contrast, it is not adaptive to blame your own enduring personal characteristics, which are hard to change. As with the depressive explanatory style described earlier, characterological self-blame may well breed resignation and pessimism about the future. In short, behavioral self-blame should be adaptive; characterological self-blame should be maladaptive.

The most extensive test of these predictions has come in a set of studies examining women's adjustment after having been raped. As would be expected, characterological self-blame is sometimes a stronger predictor of psychological distress than is behavioral self-blame (Hill & Zautra, 1989). But both types of self-blame seem to be associated with increased distress (Frazier & Schauben, 1994; Meyer & Taylor, 1986). Contrary to prediction, then, rape victims who blame their own behavior for what happened do *not* cope better than those who blame their character—though behavioral self-blame may have some advantages for coping with less traumatic experiences (Anderson et al., 1994).

Emotion-Focused Coping

Look back at Table 14.3, and you'll see many instances of emotion-focused coping, such as acceptance, denial, a focusing on or venting of emotions, mental and behavioral disengagement, or a turning to religion. By and large, there are two general ways to cope with the emotional aspects of stress: shutting down and opening up. This section examines the health effects of each of these strategies.

Shutting Down: Suppressing Unwanted Thoughts Often, we react to stress by shutting down and trying to deny or suppress the unpleasant thoughts and feelings. A severe trauma with long-lasting consequences—such as the death of a loved one, life-threatening illness, job loss, or divorce—can cause us to question some of our most basic and cherished assumptions about personal invulnerability, the meaningfulness of life, and self-worth (Janoff-Bulman & Timko, 1987). People who are confronted with serious threats to their worldviews often need psychological breathing space—and time to incorporate the trauma without demolishing their psychological integrity. If unable to avoid or deny these threats early in the coping process, they may become overwhelmed.

One specific and, at times, adaptive form of avoidance coping is distraction. Consider what happens when terrorists or street criminals take innocent victims hostage. Police surround the airplane or building, and negotiations begin. We all hold our breath, concerned about getting the hostages out alive and in good health. Are certain ways of coping with this frightening situation particularly effective? To help answer this question, fifty-seven airline employees voluntarily participated in a remarkable training exercise conducted by the Special Operations and Research Staff of the FBI Academy (Auerbach et al., 1994; Strentz & Auerbach, 1988). Some of the volunteers were trained in problem-focused coping techniques such as

In a daring rescue, French commandos stormed an Air France jetliner, killed four Algerian terrorists who had hijacked the plane and murdered two passengers, and freed 173 passengers and crew. Simulation research conducted by the FBI examined what techniques would help people cope effectively when they were held hostage.

helping each other, interacting with their captors, and gathering intelligence. Others were trained in emotion-focused techniques designed to decrease anxiety—such as distraction, deep breathing, and muscle relaxation. Volunteers in a control condition did not receive any specific instruction.

After the training session, the volunteers were "abducted" by FBI agents acting as terrorists. Automatic weapons were fired (with blanks), and bloody injuries were simulated. The volunteers were then "held captive" in one room and isolated by having pillow cases placed over their heads. A few cooperative "hostages" were released. Four days later, other FBI agents "stormed" the building and "rescued" the remaining hostages. The exercise was conducted in a very realistic manner, and the volunteers reported that it had been exceedingly stressful. Their self-reports of the experience as well as observations of their behavior revealed that those who had been instructed in anxiety-management techniques coped better than those given problem-solving training or no training at all. In this kind of situation, where individuals have little actual control over events, distraction and other emotion-focused techniques were more effective in reducing distress than were problem-focused efforts to exert control.

Although potentially effective, the suppression of unwanted thoughts from awareness can also have a peculiar, paradoxical effect. As described in Chapter 3, Daniel Wegner (1994) conducted a series of experiments in which he told people not to think of a white bear and found that they could not then keep the image from popping to mind. What's more, he found that among participants who were permitted later to think about the bear, those who had earlier tried to suppress the image were unusually preoccupied with it, providing evidence of a rebound effect. Sometimes, the harder you try not to think about something, the less likely you are to succeed. The solution: focused distraction. When Wegner told participants to imagine a tiny red Volkswagen every time the forbidden white bear intruded into consciousness, the rebound effect vanished.

What do white bears and red cars have to do with coping? Lots. When people try to block stressful thoughts from awareness, the problem may worsen. That's where focused distraction comes in. In a study of pain tolerance, Delia Cioffi and James Holloway (1993) had people put a hand into a bucket of ice-cold water and keep it there until they could no longer bear the pain. One group was instructed to avoid thinking about the sensation. A second group was told to form a mental picture of their room at home. Afterward, those who had coped through suppression were slower to recover from the pain than were those who had used focused self-distraction. To manage stress—whether it's caused by physical pain, a strained romance, final exams, or problems at work—distraction ("think about lying on the beach") is a better coping strategy than mere suppression ("don't think about the pain").

Keeping secrets and holding in strong emotions may also be physically taxing. In the laboratory, James Gross and Robert Levenson (1997) showed female students funny, sad, and neutral films. Half the time, they instructed the students to not let their feelings show. From a hidden camera, videotapes confirmed that when asked to conceal their feelings, the students were less expressive. But physiological recordings revealed that as they watched the funny and sad films, the students exhibited a greater cardiovascular response when they tried to inhibit their feelings than when they did not. Physiologically, the effort to suppress the display of emotion backfired.

A recent study by Steve Cole and others (1996) pushes this point a suggestive but profound step further. These investigators identified eighty gay men in the Los Angeles area who were newly infected with the HIV virus but had no symptoms, administered various psychological tests, and monitored their progress every six months for nine years. They found that in men who were partly "in the closet"— compared with those who were completely open about their homosexuality—the infection spread more rapidly, causing them to die sooner. This correlation does not *prove* that "coming out" is healthier than "staying in," but it is consistent with the increasingly popular notion that concealing one's innermost thoughts and feelings can prove harmful in the long run.

Opening Up: Confronting One's Demons   The research just described suggests that just as shutting down, at times, can have benefits, so too can the opposite form of coping: opening up. According to James Pennebaker (1990), psychotherapy, self-help groups, and various religious rituals all have something in common: They offer a chance for people to confide in someone, spill their guts, confess, and talk freely about their troubles—maybe for the first time.

To test for the healing power of opening up, Pennebaker went on to conduct a series of controlled studies in which he brought college students into a laboratory and asked them to talk into a tape recorder or write for twenty minutes either about past traumas or about trivial daily events. While speaking or writing, the students were physiologically aroused and upset. Many tearfully recounted accidents, failures, instances of sex abuse, loneliness, rape, the divorce of their parents, shattered relationships, death, and their fears about the future. Soon, however, these students felt better than ever. Pennebaker found that when they opened up, their systolic blood pressure levels rose during the disclosures but then later dipped below their pre-experiment levels. The students even exhibited a decline in their number of visits to the campus health center over the next six months. Other studies, too, have shown that keeping personal secrets can be stressful and that "letting it out" and "getting it off your chest" can have true therapeutic effects on mental and physical health—effects that are especially strong when the events being described are highly traumatic (Pennebaker, 1997; Smyth, 1998). It appears that confession may be good for the body as well as the soul.

Why does it help to open up? Why do *you* sometimes feel the need to talk out your problems? One possibility, recognized many years ago by Sigmund Freud, is that the experience

Ten days after his only son, Ennis, was murdered on a California highway, comedian Bill Cosby candidly discussed the tragedy in an interview with CBS news anchor Dan Rather. Deeply wounded, Cosby (who has a doctoral degree in education) may well have appreciated the coping benefits of opening up.

provides a much-needed *catharsis*, a discharge of tension—like taking the lid off a boiling pot of water to slow the boiling. Another interpretation, favored by Pennebaker, is that talking about a problem can help you to sort out your thoughts, understand the problem better, and gain *insight*, in cognitive terms. Whatever the reason, it's clear that opening up, perhaps to someone else, can be therapeutic—provided that the listener can be trusted. This last point is critical: Despite the potential for gain, opening up can also cause great distress when the people we choose to confide in react with rejection or unwanted advice, or, worse, disclose what was said to others (Kelly & McKillop, 1996).

Self-Focus: Getting Trapped Versus Getting Out   In Chapter 3, we saw that people spend relatively little time actually thinking about themselves—and when they do, they often wish they were doing something else (Csikszentmihalyi & Figurski, 1982). According to self-awareness theory, self-focus brings out our personal shortcomings the way staring in a mirror draws our attention to every blemish on the face. It comes as no surprise, then, that self-focus seems to intensify some of the most undesirable consequences of emotion-focused coping. Here's the script.

The state of self-awareness can be induced in us by external stimuli such as mirrors, cameras, and audiences. Mood, too, plays a role. Peter Salovey (1992) found that, compared with a neutral mood state, both positive and negative moods increase awareness of the self. Thus, when a stressful event occurs, the negative feelings that arise magnify self-focus. What happens next depends on a person's self-esteem, as people with a negative self-concept experience more negative moods when self-focused than do those with a positive self-concept (Sedikides, 1992). The end result is a self-perpetuating feedback loop: Being in a bad mood triggers self-focus, which in people with a negative self-concept makes the mood even worse. This vicious circle forms the basis for a self-focus model of depression (Pyszczynski & Greenberg, 1992). Round and round it goes, digging the pit of depression deeper and deeper. In this case, coping with stress by focusing on your own feelings only makes things worse.

Caught in this self-awareness trap, why don't people break out? One reason may be that depressed, self-focused individuals don't feel capable of escape through distraction (Lyubomirsky & Nolen-Hoeksema, 1993). In fact, those who do manage to escape often jump from the frying pan straight into the fire. According to Roy Baumeister (1991), people engage in smoking, drinking, overeating, drug use, promiscuous sexual behavior, masochistic sexual behavior, self-mutilation, and ultimately suicide as ways to "escape the self" in times of stress. To be sure, these kinds of distraction have nothing to recommend them.

Women and men differ in the likelihood of getting trapped in a self-focused state in response to negative emotions. Over the years, research has shown that women are

Healthy distractions like exercise are a good way to break out of the trap of self-focused depression. Unhealthy distractions, like an alcohol binge, reduce self-focus at a self-destructive cost.

more likely to ruminate and confront their negative feelings, while men tend to resort to using alcohol, physical activity, and other means of distraction (Nolen-Hoeksema & Girgus, 1994). Across a variety of ethnic groups, women are more likely to report being depressed, and men are more likely to engage in antisocial behaviors and substance abuse (Dohrenwend et al., 1992). Women brood; men act out. Both suffer.

Thankfully, there are healthier alternatives. For example, to redirect attention away from the self, it helps to become absorbed in an activity such as aerobic exercise, gardening, or reading a book. Whatever the activity, it should be difficult, demanding, and fully engaging. Ralph Erber and Abraham Tesser (1992) found that people who were in a bad mood felt better after performing a difficult task than did those who performed a simple task or none at all. Difficult tasks, it appears, can "absorb" a bad mood. Meditation can have beneficial effects for the same reason. Referring to his own techniques of focused relaxation, cardiologist

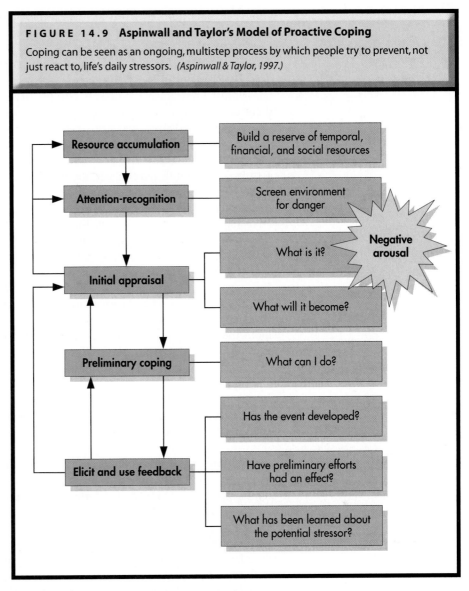

FIGURE 14.9 Aspinwall and Taylor's Model of Proactive Coping

Coping can be seen as an ongoing, multistep process by which people try to prevent, not just react to, life's daily stressors. *(Aspinwall & Taylor, 1997.)*

Herbert Benson recommends that people sit comfortably, close their eyes, relax the muscles, breathe deeply, and silently utter some word over and over again. Says Benson (1993), "By practicing two basic steps—the repetition of a sound, word, phrase, prayer, or muscular activity; and a passive return to the repetition whenever distracting thoughts recur—you can trigger a series of physiological changes that offer protection against stress" (p. 256).

Proactive Coping

According to Lisa Aspinwall and Shelley Taylor (1997), people often benefit from **proactive coping,** which consists of up-front efforts to ward off or modify the onset of a stressful event. As illustrated in Figure 14.9, coping can thus be seen as an ongoing process by which we try to prevent as well as react to the bumps and bruises of daily life. Also as shown, the first line of defense in this regard consists of the accumulation of resources—personal, financial, social, and otherwise—that can later, if needed, serve as a buffer against stress. In this section, we look at two such

proactive coping Up-front efforts to ward off or modify the onset of a stressful event.

"resources": becoming involved in multiple self-relevant activities and having a network of friendships to draw on for social support.

Self-Complexity   People can occupy many different roles in life—friend, lover, psychology major, tennis player, employee, party animal, family member, and so on—or just a few. Research on **self-complexity** indicates that individuals who view themselves as having many distinct roles or identities are less prone to feel the sting of psychological distress and stress-related illness than are those with fewer roles to play (Linville, 1987). There are exceptions to this rule, of course, as when people have many *negative* identities (Woolfolk et al., 1995). But having multiple *positive* identities is helpful, particularly for individuals who have experienced traumatic events (Morgan & Janoff-Bulman, 1994).

It makes sense that people who enact multiple roles benefit from not having all their identity eggs in one basket. But wait. Don't they suffer from overload? Concern about having to juggle multiple roles has recently increased in the United States as large numbers of married women with children have entered the work force, while maintaining primary responsibility for child care and housework (Blair & Johnson, 1992; Peterson & Gerson, 1992). Nevertheless, it appears that having multiple roles is associated with an increase in well-being. There are two strands of evidence for this proposition. First, employed women who have positive attitudes about their jobs experience less distress and better physical health than do unemployed women (Repetti et al., 1989). Second, among married men, those who find their family relationships rewarding suffer less distress from problems at work (Barnett et al., 1992). Based on their research on dual-earner couples, Rosalind Barnett and her colleagues (1993) see an emerging similarity in role patterns. For many men and women, their well-being depends on the quality of their experiences both at work and at home.

Social Support   If the world is crashing down around you, what do you do? Do you try to stop it? Do you try to manage your emotions? Or do you try to get some help from others? Throughout this textbook, we have seen that no man (or woman) is an island, that human beings are social animals, that people need people, and that to get by you need a little help from your friends. But does our social nature, and do our connections to others, have anything to do with health? Do close family ties, lovers, buddies, community support groups, and relationships at work serve as a buffer against stress? The answer is yes. An overwhelming amount of evidence now shows that **social support** has therapeutic effects on both our psychological and physical health (Uchino et al., 1996; Wills, 1990).

David Spiegel, of Stanford University's School of Medicine, came to appreciate the value of social connections several years ago when he organized support groups for women with advanced breast cancer. The groups met weekly in ninety minute sessions to laugh, cry, share stories, and discuss ways of coping. Spiegel had fully expected the women to benefit, emotionally, from the experience. But he found something else he did not expect: These women lived an average of eighteen months longer than did similar others who did not attend the groups. According to Spiegel (1993), "The added survival time was longer than any medication or other known medical treatment could be expected to provide for women with breast cancer so far advanced" (pp. 331–332).

Similar discoveries have been made by other researchers. In one study, Lisa Berkman and Leonard Syme (1979) surveyed seven thousand residents of Alameda County, California; conducted a nine-year follow-up of mortality rates; and found that the more social contacts people had, the longer they lived. In fact, those who lived alone, had very few close friends or relatives, and did not participate in community groups died at a rate two to five times greater than those with more

self-complexity The number of distinct roles or identities people believe they have.

social support The helpful coping resources provided by friends and other people.

extensive social networks. This was true of men and women, young and old, rich and poor, and people from all racial and ethnic backgrounds. James House and others (1988) studied 2,754 adults interviewed during visits to their doctors. He found that the most socially active men were two to three times less likely to die within nine to twelve years than those of similar age who were more isolated. Socially active women were almost two times less likely to die. According to House, social isolation is, statistically, just as predictive of an early death as smoking or high cholesterol—especially among men (Pilisuk et al., 1993; Rogers, 1995).

Research findings like these are now common. Married people are more likely than those who are unmarried to survive cancer for five years (Taylor, 1990), gay men infected with HIV are less likely to contemplate suicide if they have close ties than if they do not (Schneider et al., 1991), and people who have a heart attack are less likely to have a second one if they live with someone than if they live alone (Case et al., 1992). Among students buried in schoolwork, and among the spouses of cancer patients, more social support is also associated with a stronger immune response (Baron et al., 1990; Jemmott & Magloire, 1988). Based on their review of eighty-one studies, Bert Uchino, John Cacioppo, and Janice Kiecolt-Glaser (1996) concluded that in times of stress, having social support lowers blood pressure, lessens the secretion of stress hormones, and strengthens immune responses. There's no doubt about it: Being isolated from other people is hazardous to your health.

Our social connections can be therapeutic for many reasons. Friends may encourage us to get out, exercise, eat regularly, stop smoking or drinking, or seek professional help. Emotionally, friends give sympathy and reassurance in difficult times. Perhaps having a good friend around boosts our confidence, self-esteem, and sense of security. On an intellectual level, having someone to talk to provides a sounding board, new perspectives, advice, and information as we struggle for solutions to our problems. Communicating helps us sort things out in our own minds (Clark, 1993).

The value of social support is so basic that *any* bond formed with another living being—even the companionship of a pet— may promote health and survival. For example, Judith Siegel (1990) found that stress-buffering effects are not confined to social support from humans. In her study, over a thousand individuals sixty-five years of age or older were asked whether they owned a pet. The number of negative events experienced in the previous six months was also assessed. Participants then reported every two months for a year on how many times they had contacted a physician. The result: Among people with many negative life events, those with pet dogs had fewer contacts with physicians. Perhaps animals have a calming and comforting influence on us. Karen Allen and her colleagues (1991) found that when women—all of whom owned pet dogs—worked on a stressful laboratory task, those who had their pets with them became less physiologically aroused (as measured by changes in blood pressure, perspiration, and pulse rate) than those who were either alone or had a human friend present. As companions, dogs—like close friends not looking to evaluate us (Kors et al., 1997)—are wonderfully nonjudgmental.

The benefits of social support can occur across a range of domains. Think for a moment about your entire social network. What happens when one part of it goes sour? Does it help to have support elsewhere? It seems so. In a study of college students, perceived support from a friend reduced distress when there was conflict with a roommate. Similarly, perceived support from a

People who have lots of friends are healthier and live longer than those who live more isolated lives. **True.**

Research shows that pets as well as people provide us with companionship and social support—and can serve as a buffer against stress.

A street scene in India illustrates the density of its population in some urban areas. Faced with a lack of control over social contracts in over-crowded situations, individuals withdraw from others, lose social support, and experience greater psychological distress.

roommate reduced psychological distress when there was conflict with a friend (Lepore, 1992). Like multiple positive identities and satisfying social roles, multiple sources of support promote well-being.

Although researchers agree that social support is vital to health, they do not agree about how to measure it. In a large number of studies, social support was defined by the *number of social contacts* a person has. This measure is predictive, but a simple social contact model has some limitations. One is that it glosses over the fact that people who are stuck in bad social relationships are more distressed, not less (Rook, 1984). Even good social relationships can heighten stress—particularly in women, who tend to do more of the "caring." According to Vicki Helgeson (1994), excessive attention to either one's own well-being or that of others increases health risks. For men and women alike, a more balanced perspective is healthier (Saragovi et al., 1997). A second reason why a simple count of social contacts does not adequately measure social support is that having too many contacts can actually reduce levels of support. Consider the plight of the urban poor in India, packed into over-crowded residences of up to eleven people per room. They are more stressed than those living in less crowded conditions—and have *less* social support (Evans et al., 1989). Why? Despite living among others, people who feel crowded tend to withdraw, resulting over time in a loss of social support (Evans & Lepore, 1993).

A second model of social support emphasizes the quality of a person's relationships rather than their quantity. The *intimacy model* predicts that the key is to have a close relationship with a significant other—someone who's emotionally on call for late night conversations. Often, this prediction proves true. Women who enjoy an intimate relationship with a spouse or boyfriend are less likely to become depressed than are those who lack such a relationship (Brown & Harris, 1978; Costello, 1982). Similarly, among gay and bisexual men infected with HIV, those with a history of close, confiding relationships have lower levels of suicidal intent (Schneider et al., 1991).

A third approach defines social support in terms of its *perceived availability* (Sarason et al., 1983). Compared with those who doubt the adequacy of their social resources, individuals who think that ample support is available cope more effectively—for example, in school (Cutrona et al., 1994) and after an abortion (Major & Cozzarelli, 1992). In almost any demanding situation that you can imagine, perceived support is associated with better adjustment—even though these perceptions are not always accurate (Lakey & Cassady, 1990). Why is the perception of support so important? According to Irwin Sarason and his colleagues (1994), people who perceive that they have others to turn to are "social optimists" who have a strong sense of self-efficacy, high self-esteem, good social skills, and a positive outlook about future interactions. They also tend to interpret the behaviors of others as being helpful (Lakey et al., 1992).

Understanding what social support is and how it operates is important in the study of health because many of life's problems and prospects occur in a social context—and because so much of how we cope with stress involves other people. As we will see in the next section, treatment and prevention are also influenced by our relations with others.

Treatment and Prevention

Social psychologists contribute in different ways to the development of treatment and prevention programs. Here, we focus first on social influences on treatment effectiveness and then on ways to increase people's healthy behaviors.

Treatment: The "Social" Ingredients

Often, what ails us can be treated through medical intervention. The treatments vary widely—from a simple change in diet to vitamin supplements, aspirins, antibiotics and other drugs, surgery, and the like. There's no doubt about it. Medicine is often vital to health. In addition, however, treatment has an important social component—what the family doctor used to call "bedside manner." What are the active social ingredients? To begin to answer this question, let's consider research on the benefits of psychotherapy. Over the years, studies have shown that although there are vastly different schools of thought and techniques for doing psychotherapy, all approaches are effective and, surprisingly, all are generally equivalent (Seligman, 1995; Smith et al., 1980). Apparently, despite the surface differences, all psychotherapies have a great deal in common at a deeper level—and these common factors, more than the specific techniques used, provide the active ingredients necessary for change. What are some of these factors?

First, all healers—regardless of whether they are doctors, psychologists, or others—provide *social support*, a close human relationship characterized by warmth, expressions of concern, a shoulder to cry on, and someone to talk to. Earlier, we discussed the benefits to health and longevity of having social contacts. In psychological therapy, studies have shown that the better the "working alliance" is between a therapist and client, the more favorable the outcome is likely to be (Horvath & Luborsky, 1993). As psychotherapist Hans Strupp (1996) put it, "The simple and incontrovertible truth is that if you are anxious or depressed, or if you are experiencing difficulties with significant people in your life, chances are that you feel better if you talk to someone you can trust" (p. 1017).

Second, all therapies offer a ray of *hope* to people who are sick, demoralized, unhappy, or in pain. In all aspects of life, people are motivated by positive expectations. Although some of us are generally more optimistic than others, optimism is a specific expectation that can be increased or decreased in certain situations (Armor & Taylor, 1998). Indeed, a common aspect of all treatments is that they communicate positive expectations. It has been suggested that high expectations alone can spark change even when they are not justified (Prioleau et al., 1983). This suggestion is consistent with the placebo effect described earlier, whereby patients improve after being given an inactive drug or treatment. Believing can help make it so—which is how faith healers, shamans, and witch doctors all over the world have managed to perform "miracle cures" with empty rituals. Even modern medicine capitalizes on the power of hope. As Walter Brown (1998) puts it, "The symbols and rituals of healing—the doctor's office, the stethoscope, the physical examination—offer reassurance" (p. 91).

A third important ingredient is *choice*. Allowing patients to make meaningful choices, such as deciding on a type of treatment, increases the effectiveness of treatments for alcoholism (Miller, 1985) and obesity (Mendonca & Brehm, 1983). Even relatively minor choices—such as being able to decide the order in which various procedures will be performed—can reduce psychological distress (Miller & Mangan, 1983). The choice to undergo an effortful or costly treatment is particularly beneficial in this regard. The person who voluntarily pays in time, money, or discomfort needs to self-justify that investment—a predicament sure to arouse cognitive dissonance (see Chapter 6). One way to reduce dissonance is to become super-motivated to succeed: "Why have I chosen to do this? Because I really want to get better." Since highly motivated individuals should be more careful and conscientious about carrying out the prescribed treatment, they should improve more.

Danny Axsom (1989) tested this proposition in a study of snake phobias. Participants, all highly snake-phobic, either were or were not given an explicit choice about undertaking a treatment that was described as either requiring "extreme exertion" or being "so easy." Among the four experimental conditions, participants given an explicit choice about continuing an effortful treatment reported the greatest motivation to change their phobic behavior and came closest to the five-foot-long New Jersey corn snake used to measure approach behavior.

Prevention: Getting the Message Across

We live in what could aptly be described as the era of prevention in that many serious health threats are preventable. Just watch TV, read a newspaper, or leaf through any magazine: There are programs for AIDS prevention, campaigns to persuade smokers to break the habit, sunscreens that protect the skin from harmful rays, and laws that mandate the use of seat belts. To a large extent, we know what to do and what not to do to promote good health and to avoid disease and injury. But just how do we convince ourselves and others to translate that knowledge into action?

Nowhere is this problem more acute than among people who suffer from AIDS. Earlier in this chapter, we noted that heart attacks, cancer, strokes, and accidents are now more common causes of death than infectious diseases. But AIDS, the first truly global epidemic, continues to spread at an alarming rate. It has been called a recently exploded microbiological time bomb (Mann, 1992). In 1981, five homosexual men in North America were diagnosed with AIDS and were among only 189 cases reported that year. By 1996, the number of cases in North America had skyrocketed to three-quarters of a million—and included heterosexual men, women, and children. Worldwide, an estimated 22 million people are currently infected with HIV. The World Health Organization projects that by the year 2000, these numbers will climb even higher. From 1992 to 1996, the numbers stabilized in North America, Australia, and Western Europe; but there was an increase in live cases of 43 percent in Latin America, 37 percent in sub-Saharan Africa, 46 percent in North Africa and the Middle East, 238 percent in Eastern Europe and Central Asia, 261 percent in South and Southeast Asia, and 658 percent in East Asia and the Pacific (Purvis, 1997).

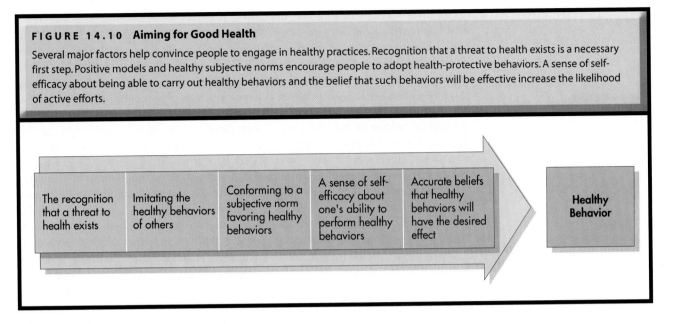

FIGURE 14.10   Aiming for Good Health
Several major factors help convince people to engage in healthy practices. Recognition that a threat to health exists is a necessary first step. Positive models and healthy subjective norms encourage people to adopt health-protective behaviors. A sense of self-efficacy about being able to carry out healthy behaviors and the belief that such behaviors will be effective increase the likelihood of active efforts.

The AIDS virus is transmitted from one person to another in infected blood, semen, and vaginal secretions. People who are HIV-positive may have no symptoms for several years and may not even realize they are infected. Eventually, however, the virus will ravage the immune system by destroying lymphocytes that help ward off disease. What's so scary about AIDS is that it appears fatal, that it is increasing at a rate of one new case every few seconds, and that there is no vaccine that can prevent it (Greene, 1993). At present, the most effective way to control the spread of AIDS is to alter people's beliefs, motivations, and risk-taking behavior (Fisher et al., 1994; Gerrard et al., 1996)—and that's where social psychology comes in. Across a range of perspectives, several basic factors emerge (see Figure 14.10).

The first step toward good health depends on the relative pleasure to be derived from healthy versus unhealthy behaviors. If a healthy behavior is more enjoyable than an unhealthy one, then presumably all we need to do is try it out and we'll be convinced. Usually, however, it's not this easy. Many unhealthy habits are sinfully enjoyable, and many healthy behaviors (at least initially) may require extra effort. To be convinced to switch, then, people have to recognize that their health is at risk. Perhaps because this is such an obvious first step, too much emphasis may sometimes be placed on it. As described in Chapter 6, graphic fear appeals are a popular method of persuasion in public service advertisements: the gory lung-cancer operation to scare smokers into quitting, the bloody accident victim to get people to use seat belts. Fear appeals can increase the incentive to change, but their ultimate impact depends on the strength of the arguments—and whether the message also contains reassuring advice on how to avoid the threatened danger (Leventhal, 1970; Rogers, 1983; Witte, 1992).

The role of risk perceptions may have been overestimated. Most models of prevention assume that perceived risk increases the likelihood of adopting healthy behaviors and avoiding risky ones. But *higher* perceived risk is often associated with *more* risky behaviors (Goldman & Harlow, 1993). The explanation of this apparent contradiction is timing. Since most research examines perceived risk and behavior simultaneously, what we're getting is an accurate read-out of current conditions (Weinstein & Nicolich, 1993). If you are engaging in more risky behaviors, you are, in fact, running a higher risk.

An adequate test of the effects of perceived risk requires prospective research, in which perceptions are measured first and then behavior is assessed at a later

For more information concerning AIDS, the Centers for Disease Control provides a toll-free number: 1-800-342-2437.

In 1998, the Centers for Disease Control announced that the incidence of new AIDS cases had declined 12 percent in 1997—the first reduction ever.

time. Investigations of this sort indicate that perceived vulnerability is associated with preventive behaviors in some health areas but not in others. For example, an individual's perception of the risk of getting AIDS appears to have little if any relationship to whether that person will adopt safe-sex practices (Gerrard et al., 1993). When it comes to sex, people need to know the risks involved—but such knowledge is seldom sufficient to change behavior (van der Pligt et al., 1993).

The next two steps toward good health involve other people. When those around us behave in healthful ways, they provide role models that help establish healthy norms. Direct modeling can be useful. For example, we are more likely to wear seat belts if we see others wearing theirs (Howell et al., 1990). Celebrities in particular have a great deal of influence over public health issues. In the most poignant moment of the 1996 Olympics, former heavyweight boxing champion Muhammad Ali—who now suffers from Parkinson's disease, a motor disorder—stood upright with his arm trembling and his face frozen and lit the ceremonial flame. The National Parkinson's Foundation, which went on to adopt a torch as its symbol, was flooded with donations. In another instance, several years ago, former first lady Nancy Reagan decided to undergo a mastectomy rather than breast-conserving surgery. Over the next six months, there was a 25 percent decline in the number of women choosing the breast-conserving surgery that she had rejected (Nattinger et al., 1998). In light of these influences, it is troubling to see role models of unhealthy behavior among professional athletes, entertainers, politicians, and others who occupy center stage. An analysis of the most popular movies from 1977 to 1988, for example, revealed that after a decline in the mid-1980s, depictions of smoking, drinking, illegal drug use, and other risky habits rose toward the end of the decade (Terre et al., 1991).

Besides eliciting direct imitation, models also contribute to the development of subjective norms, our beliefs about how others expect us to behave. According to the theories of reasoned action (Fishbein, 1980) and planned behavior (Ajzen, 1991) presented in Chapter 6, both attitudes and subjective norms should affect our intentions to take action. And they do. Both positive attitudes toward safe sex and perceived pressure from significant others increase intentions to practice safe sex (Chan & Fishbein, 1993; Cochran et al., 1992). In fact, a whole range of health-related behavioral intentions—such as flossing teeth, driving carefully, eating low-fat foods, washing hands after using the bathroom, and getting enough sleep—are triggered by a combination of attitudes and subjective norms (Finlay et al., 1997).

Intervention strategies that use social pressure can be very effective. In a series of studies, Jeffrey Kelly and others (1991, 1992) found that self-reports by gay men of high-risk sexual behavior diminished after opinion leaders in the gay community had been trained to advocate safe-sex practices to their peers. Unfortunately, subjective norms often sustain unhealthy behaviors. There are two reasons why this occurs. First, as an instance of the false-consensus effect described in Chapter 4, people who smoke or drink excessively overestimate the prevalence of such practices among their peers (Chassin et al., 1990; Suls et al., 1988). Second, these inflated estimates serve to support and increase the unhealthy practices at a later time (Marks et al., 1992). For example, Deborah Prentice and Dale Miller (1996) have found that college students who overestimate the level of alcohol use on campus at the start of a school year are eventually more likely to conform to this misperception in their own attitudes and behavior. Confronted by this closed circle, the best way to cut through it is to provide accurate information about who does what. Prentice and Miller found that students who took part in a program designed to correct their misperceptions of campus norms actually drank less alcohol six months later.

The fourth step to health emphasizes a person's confidence in his or ability to succeed. Self-efficacy—the belief that we can do what needs to be done—enhances both the adoption and the maintenance of various healthy behaviors, including safe-sex practices, nonsmoking, and abstinence from alcohol (Goldman & Harlow,

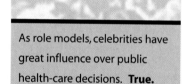

As role models, celebrities have great influence over public health-care decisions. **True.**

1993; Maddux, 1991). If people don't know how to perform the necessary corrective behaviors, then they should be taught. For example, smoking-prevention programs often teach children techniques for resisting peer pressures and refusing the offer of a cigarette (Baum, 1984; Evans et al., 1984).

Finally, people need solid, accurate information about the effectiveness of the healthy behaviors they are urged to adopt (Weinstein, 1989). If people believe that something works, they will be more likely to develop positive attitudes and try it out. Beware, however, of someone who is too easily convinced. In one study, participants who had been reassured that a proposed prevention program was highly likely to be successful were quite positive in their evaluation of the program—regardless of the quality of the arguments that supported its probable success (Gleicher & Petty, 1992). Participants provided with a lower expectation of success were more discerning: They based their evaluations on the quality of the arguments presented. In the short run, people can be tricked by false promises. But in the long run, accurate information will usually prevail.

By now, the social nature of prevention should be abundantly clear. Information about health risks and the benefits of preventive measures comes from other people. What people do and what they say provide models and establish norms. Even our own sense of self-efficacy is influenced by others who teach us what we need to know. It also goes the other way around: Just as other people influence us, so too do we influence others. Prevention is very much a social phenomenon in which we all participate.

Review

Stress and Health

- Stress is an unpleasant state that arises when we perceive that the demands of an event strain our ability to cope effectively.
- A person's appraisal of a situation determines how stress is experienced and how he or she copes.
- Coping responses consist of the thoughts, feelings, and behaviors by which people attempt to reduce stress.

What Causes Stress?

- There are many different causes of stress, or stressors.

Crises and Catastrophes

- Natural disasters and other catastrophic events can have harmful, long-term effects on mental and physical health.
- People with posttraumatic stress disorder suffer from specific psychological and physical symptoms long after the event is over.
- Soldiers exposed to heavy combat are especially likely to suffer from posttraumatic stress disorder.

Major Life Events

- Early research suggested that all change is stressful.
- However, more recent studies suggest that only negative events are harmful.

Microstressors: The Hassles of Everyday Life

- The most common source of stress arises from what seem like minor everyday hassles.
- Living in shared space that does not afford control over one's social contacts, constant noise, and relentless job pressures are all stressful in this regard.

How Does Stress Affect the Body?

- Selye coined the term *stress* upon observing that different stressors produce similar physiological effects on the body.

The General Adaptation Syndrome

- The body responds to stress in three stages: alarm, resistance, and exhaustion.
- The stress response is designed for acute emergencies—not for the constant long-term stress that humans often experience.

What Stress Does to the Heart

- Stress is a major risk factor in coronary heart disease (CHD).
- Early research suggested that the hard-driving Type A behavior pattern is strongly predictive of CHD.

- This link was found when the Type A pattern was assessed in structured interviews but not when it was measured by questionnaire.
- More recent research suggests that hostility is the "toxic" element in the Type A behavior pattern.

What Stress Does to the Immune System

- The immune system contains specialized white blood cells called lymphocytes that detect and destroy "nonself" substances in the body.
- Laboratory and field research shows that stress affects the activity of these cells, sometimes resulting in a weakened immune response.
- Stress can "get into" the immune system by causing people to behave in unhealthy ways or by triggering the release of stress hormones that suppress immune cell activity.

The Links Between Stress and Illness

- Because stress weakens the immune system, people who are under stress are more likely to catch a cold when exposed to a virus.
- There may also be a link between negative emotional states and serious diseases such as cancer, but the evidence is less strong.

Processes of Appraisal

Attributional and Explanatory Styles

- In the learned helplessness model of depression, exposure to an uncontrollable event was said to spark passive, apathetic, depression-like symptoms.
- In contrast, the reformulated model highlights the importance of the attributions people make for their lack of control.
- The depressive explanatory style is a tendency to make stable, global, internal attributions for negative events; it is associated with depression and perhaps physical illness.

Perceptions of Control

- Some individuals are more resilient than others in the face of stress, a trait called hardiness.
- The key ingredient of hardiness is the belief that one has the power to control future outcomes through one's own behavior.
- Depending on the situation, people may feel high or low in self-efficacy, the belief that they can perform the behaviors needed to produce positive outcomes.

Optimism and Hope

- Some individuals are characteristically more optimistic than others.

- Optimism and hope at one point in time are associated with a range of positive health outcomes later.
- The notion that hope is important to health is evident in the well-documented placebo effect.

Pollyanna's Health

- Positive thinking is associated with good health, but the causal relationship is unclear.
- Unrealistic positive illusions may have undesirable interpersonal and health consequences.

Ways of Coping with Stress

Problem-Focused Coping

- In problem-focused coping, people try to reduce stress by overcoming the source of the problem.
- Problem-focused coping is often effective, but at times there are drawbacks.
- For example, exerting control is physiologically taxing and can increase stress rather than reduce it.
- Also, both behavioral and characterological self-blame are associated with increased distress.

Emotion-Focused Coping

- In emotion-focused coping, people try to manage the emotional turmoil produced by a stressful situation.
- In situations that one cannot control, mental distraction and avoidance can reduce stress.
- But the suppression from awareness of unwanted thoughts and feelings can backfire, causing us to become preoccupied with them.
- Research shows that opening up and confronting one's feelings about upsetting events improves mental and physical health.
- Among people with low self-esteem, self-focus worsens their mood and heightens their distress.
- In contrast, it is helpful to become absorbed in demanding external activities such as reading, exercise, and gardening.

Proactive Coping

- As a first line of defense, people can ward off stress through proactive coping efforts such as the accumulation of resources.
- Having many different roles and identities serves as a buffer against stressors in any one domain of life.
- Friendships and other sources of social support have strong beneficial effects on physical health and psychological well-being.
- Even the companionship of a pet dog is beneficial to health.
- All researchers agree that social support is healthy, but they measure it in different ways.

- Measures of social support include: the sheer number of social contacts a person has, the presence of at least one close relationship, and the perceived availability of social support.

Treatment and Prevention

Treatment: The "Social" Ingredients

- Medical treatment includes an important social component.
- Doctors, therapists, and other health-care workers provide patients with social support and a ray of hope.
- Choice of treatment is also an important factor—particularly when patients choose an effortful treatment, which increases their sense of commitment.

Prevention: Getting the Message Across

- Many causes of death are preventable through changes in lifestyle and behavior—which is where social psychology comes in.
- First, people have to recognize that a threat to their health exists.
- The behaviors of others serve as important role models for healthy or unhealthy imitation.
- Subjective norms (beliefs about what others expect us to do) can also encourage healthy or unhealthy behaviors.
- A sense of self-efficacy enhances the adoption and maintenance of healthy behaviors.
- Accurate information is needed to sustain people's commitment to healthy behaviors.

Key Terms

PUTTING COMMON SENSE TO THE TEST

The accumulation of daily hassles does more to make people sick than catastrophes or major life changes.

True. *Car problems, arguments with friends, and other "microstressors" contribute more to our levels of stress than larger but less frequent stressors.*

Like humans, zebras get ulcers.

False. *Stress causes ulcers in humans, not zebras. That's because the stress response is designed for acute emergencies; but in people, it is activated often and for long periods of time.*

Stress can weaken the heart, but it cannot affect the immune system.

False. *Recent research has shown that stress and other psychological states can alter the activity of white blood cells in the immune system—and affect our resistance to illness.*

When it comes to physical health, research does not support popular beliefs about the power of positive thinking.

False. *Consistently, people who are optimistic—and situations that promote optimism—are associated with better health outcomes.*

People who have lots of friends are healthier and live longer than those who live more isolated lives.

True. *Across a range of studies, researchers have found that social support is strongly associated with positive health outcomes.*

As role models, celebrities have great influence over public health-care decisions.

True. *As a result of all the media attention given to celebrities, the health-care decisions they make exert a great deal of influence on others.*

Glossary

actor-observer effect   The tendency to attribute our own behavior to situational causes and the behavior of others to personal factors. (*p. 109*)

adversarial model   A dispute-resolution system in which the prosecution and defense present opposing sides of the story. (*p. 462*)

aggression   Behavior intended to injure another person who does not want to be injured. (*p. 385*)

altruistic   Motivated by the desire to increase another's welfare. (*p. 345*)

applied research   Research whose goals are to enlarge the understanding of naturally occurring events and to find solutions to practical problems. (*p. 27*)

appraisal   The process by which people make judgments about the demands of potentially stressful events and their ability to meet those demands. (*p. 501*)

arousal-affect model   The proposal that aggression is influenced by both the intensity of arousal and the type of emotion produced by a stimulus. (*p. 407*)

arousal:cost-reward model   The proposition that people react to emergency situations by acting in the most cost-effective way to reduce the arousal of shock and alarm. (*p. 357*)

assessment center   Structured setting in which job applicants are exhaustively tested and judged by multiple evaluators. (*p. 474*)

attachment style   The way a person typically interacts with significant others. (*p. 318*)

attitude   A positive, negative, or mixed reaction to a person, object, or idea. (*p. 173*)

attitude scale   A multiple-item questionnaire designed to measure a person's attitude toward some object. (*p. 175*)

attribution theory   A group of theories that describe how people explain the causes of behavior. (*p. 101*)

audience inhibition   Reluctance to help for fear of making a bad impression on observers. (*p. 357*)

availability heuristic   The tendency to estimate the likelihood that an event will occur by how easily instances of it come to mind. (*p. 104*)

base-rate fallacy   The finding that people are relatively insensitive to consensus information presented in the form of numerical base rates. (*p. 104*)

basic research   Research whose goal is to increase the understanding of human behavior, often by testing hypotheses based on a theory. (*p. 27*)

bask in reflected glory (BIRG)   Increasing self-esteem by associating with others who are successful. (*p. 79*)

behavioral genetics   A subfield of psychology that examines the role of genetic factors in behavior. (*p. 18*)

belief in a just world   The belief that individuals get what they deserve in life, an orientation that leads people to disparage victims. (*p. 110*)

belief perseverance   The tendency to maintain beliefs even after they have been discredited. (*p. 117*)

bogus pipeline   A phony lie-detector device that is sometimes used to get respondents to give truthful answers to sensitive questions. (*p. 175*)

brainstorming   A technique that attempts to increase the production of creative ideas by encouraging group members to speak freely without criticizing their own or others' contributions. (*p. 271*)

bystander effect   The effect whereby the presence of others inhibits helping. (*p. 352*)

catharsis   A reduction of the motive to aggress that is said to result from any imagined, observed, or actual act of aggression. (*p. 402*)

central route to persuasion   The process by which a person thinks carefully about a communication and is influenced by the strength of its arguments. (*p. 181*)

central traits   Traits that exert a powerful influence on overall impressions. (*p. 114*)

cognitive dissonance theory   The theory that holding inconsistent cognitions arouses psychological tension that people become motivated to reduce. (*p. 199*)

cognitive neoassociation analysis   The view that unpleasant experiences create negative affect, which in turn stimulates associations connected with anger and fear. Emotional and behavioral outcomes then depend, at least in part, on higher-order cognitive processing. (*p. 407*)

collective   People engaged in common activities but having minimal direct interaction. (*p. 249*)

collective effort model   The theory that individuals will exert effort on a collective task to the degree that they think their individual efforts will be important, relevant, and meaningful for achieving outcomes that they value. (*p. 254*)

collectivism   A cultural orientation in which interdependence, cooperation, and social harmony take priority over personal goals. (*p. 221*)

communal relationship   A relationship in which the participants expect and desire mutual responsiveness to each other's needs. (*p. 318*)

companionate love   A secure, trusting, stable partnership. (*p. 321*)

compliance   Changes in behavior that are elicited by direct requests. (*p. 224*)

confederate   Accomplice of an experimenter who, in dealing with the real participants in an experiment, acts as if he or she is also a participant. (*p. 47*)

confirmation bias   The tendency to seek, interpret, and create information that verifies existing beliefs. (*p. 116*)

conformity   The tendency to change our perceptions, opinions, or behavior in ways that are consistent with group norms. (*p. 213*)

construct validity   The extent to which the measures used in a study measure the variables they were designed to measure and the manipulations in an experiment manipulate the variables they were designed to manipulate. *(p. 28)*

contact hypothesis   The theory that direct contact between hostile groups will reduce prejudice under certain conditions. *(p. 161)*

contingency model of leadership   The theory that leadership effectiveness is determined both by the personal characteristics of leaders and by the control afforded by the situation. *(p. 481)*

contrast effect   A tendency to perceive stimuli that differ from expectations as being even more different than they really are. *(p. 134)*

coping   Efforts to reduce stress. *(p. 501)*

correlational research   Research designed to measure the association between variables that are not manipulated by the researcher. *(p. 36)*

correlation coefficient   A statistical measure of the strength and direction of the association between two variables. *(p. 36)*

correspondent inference theory   A theory holding that we make inferences about a person when his or her actions are freely chosen, are unexpected, and result in a small number of desirable effects. *(p. 101)*

counterfactual thinking   A tendency to imagine alternative events or outcomes that might have occurred but did not. *(p. 105)*

covariation principle   A principle of attribution theory holding that people attribute behavior to factors that are present when a behavior occurs and absent when it does not. *(p. 102)*

cross-cultural research   Research designed to compare and contrast people of different cultures. *(p. 19)*

cross-race identification bias   The tendency for people to have difficulty identifying members of a race other than their own. *(p. 441)*

cultivation   The process by which the mass media (particularly television) construct a version of social reality for the public. *(p. 415)*

cycle of family violence   The transmission of domestic violence across generations. *(p. 423)*

death qualification   A jury-selection procedure used in capital cases that permits judges to exclude prospective jurors who say they would not vote for the death penalty. *(p. 434)*

debriefing   A disclosure, made to participants after research procedures are completed, in which the researcher explains the purpose of the research, attempts to resolve any negative feelings, and emphasizes the scientific contribution made by the participants' involvement. *(p. 49)*

deception   In the context of research, a method that provides false information to participants. *(p. 47)*

deindividuation   The loss of a person's sense of individuality and the reduction of normal constraints against deviant behavior. *(p. 256)*

dependent variable   In an experiment, a factor experimenters measure to see if it is affected by the independent variable. *(p. 41)*

depressive explanatory style   A habitual tendency to attribute negative events to causes that are stable, global, and internal. *(p. 514)*

diffusion of responsibility   The belief that others will or should take the responsibility for providing assistance to a person in need. *(p. 355)*

discrimination   Any behavior directed against persons because of their membership in a particular group. *(p. 129)*

displacement   Aggressing against a substitute target because aggressive acts against the source of the frustration are inhibited by fear or lack of access. *(p. 402)*

distraction-conflict theory   A theory holding that the presence of others will produce social facilitation effects only when those others distract from the task and create attentional conflict. *(p. 251)*

door-in-the-face technique   A two-step compliance technique in which an influencer prefaces the real request with one that is so large that it is rejected. *(p. 229)*

downward social comparisons   Defensive tendency to compare ourselves with others who are worse off than we are. *(p. 80)*

egocentric bias   Bias toward perceiving and recalling oneself as a central actor in past events. *(p. 66)*

egoistic   Motivated by the desire to increase one's own welfare. *(p. 345)*

elaboration   The process of thinking about and scrutinizing the arguments contained in a persuasive communication. *(p. 182)*

emotional aggression   Inflicting harm for its own sake. *(p. 386)*

emotion-focused coping   Cognitive and behavioral efforts to reduce the distress produced by a stressful situation. *(p. 519)*

empathy-altruism hypothesis   The proposition that empathic concern for a person in need produces an altruistic motive for helping. *(p. 346)*

entrapment   The condition in which commitments to a failing course of action are increased to justify investments already made. *(p. 274)*

equity theory   The theory that people are most satisfied with a relationship when the ratio between benefits and contributions is similar for both partners. *(p. 316)*

escalation effect   The tendency for investors to remain committed to a losing course of action. *(p. 494)*

evaluation apprehension theory   A theory holding that the presence of others will produce social facilitation effects only when those others are seen as potential evaluators. *(p. 251)*

evolutionary psychology   A subfield of psychology that uses the principles of evolution to understand human social behavior. *(p. 18)*

exchange relationship   A relationship in which the participants expect and desire strict reciprocity in their interactions. *(p. 318)*

excitation transfer   The process whereby arousal caused by one stimulus is added to arousal from a second stimulus and the combined arousal is attributed to the second stimulus. *(p. 322)*

expectancy theory   The theory that workers become motivated when they believe that their efforts will produce valued outcomes. *(p. 487)*

experiment   A form of research that can demonstrate causal relationships because (1) the experimenter has control over the events that occur and (2) participants are randomly assigned to conditions. *(p. 39)*

experimental realism   The degree to which experimental procedures are involving to participants and lead them to behave naturally and spontaneously. *(p. 47)*

experimenter expectancy effects   The effects produced when an experimenter's expectations about the results of an experiment affect his or her behavior toward a participant and thereby influence the participant's responses. *(p. 45)*

external validity   The degree to which there can be reasonable confidence that the results of a study would be obtained for other people and in other situations. *(p. 45)*

facial electromyograph (EMG)   An electronic instrument that records facial muscle activity associated with emotions and attitudes. *(p. 176)*

facial feedback hypothesis   The hypothesis that changes in facial expression can lead to corresponding changes in emotion. *(p. 59)*

false-consensus effect   The tendency for people to overestimate the extent to which others share their opinions, attributes, and behaviors. *(p. 104)*

foot-in-the-door technique   A two-step compliance technique in which an influencer sets the stage for the real request by first getting a person to comply with a much smaller request. *(p. 227)*

frustration-aggression hypothesis   The idea that (1) frustration always elicits the motive to aggress and (2) all aggression is caused by frustration. *(p. 402)*

fundamental attribution error   The tendency to focus on the role of personal causes and underestimate the impact of situations on other people's behavior. *(p. 106)*

general adaptation syndrome   A three-stage process (alarm, resistance, and exhaustion) by which the body responds to stress. *(p. 507)*

good mood effect   The effect whereby a good mood increases helping behavior. *(p. 360)*

graduated and reciprocated initiatives in tension-reduction (GRIT)   A strategy for unilateral, persistent efforts to establish trust and cooperation between opposing parties. *(p. 283)*

group   Two or more persons perceived as related because of their interactions, membership in the same social category, or common fate. *(p. 129)*

group polarization   The exaggeration through group discussion of initial tendencies in the thinking of group members. *(p. 263)*

groupthink   A group decision-making style characterized by an excessive tendency among group members to seek concurrence. *(p. 266)*

guilt   Feelings of discomfort or distress produced by people's belief that they have violated their own personal standards or their fear that others will perceive such violations. *(p. 361)*

habituation   Adaptation to something familiar, so that both physiological and psychological responses are reduced. *(p. 414)*

hard-to-get effect   The tendency to prefer people who are highly selective in their social choices over those who are more readily available. *(p. 310)*

Hawthorne effect   The finding that workers who were observed increased their productivity regardless of what actual changes were made in the work setting. *(p. 468)*

health psychology   The study of physical health and illness by psychologists from various areas of specialization. *(p. 499)*

hindsight bias   The tendency, once an event has occurred, to overestimate one's ability to have foreseen the outcome. *(p. 66)*

hypothesis   A testable prediction about the conditions under which an event will occur. *(p. 27)*

idiosyncrasy credits   Interpersonal "credits" that a person earns by following group norms. *(p. 223)*

illusory correlation   An overestimate of the association between variables that are only slightly or not at all correlated. *(p. 135)*

immune system   A biological surveillance system that detects and destroys "nonself" substances that invade the body. *(p. 510)*

implicit personality theory   A network of assumptions people make about the relationships among traits and behaviors. *(p. 114)*

impression formation   The process of integrating information about a person to form a coherent impression *(p. 111)*

independent variable   In an experiment, a factor experimenters manipulate to see if it affects the dependent variable. *(p. 41)*

individualism   A cultural orientation in which independence, autonomy, and self-reliance take priority over group allegiances. *(p. 221)*

industrial organizational (I/O) psychology   The study of human behavior in business and other organizational settings. *(p. 468)*

informational influence   Influence that produces conformity when a person believes others are correct in their judgments. *(p. 216)*

information integration theory   The theory that impressions are based on (1) perceiver dispositions and (2) a weighted average of a target person's traits. *(p. 112)*

informed consent   An individual's deliberate, voluntary decision to participate in research, based on the researcher's description of what will be required during such participation. *(p. 49)*

ingroup favoritism   The tendency to discriminate in favor of ingroups over outgroups. *(p. 146)*

inoculation hypothesis   The idea that exposure to weak versions of a persuasive argument increases later resistance to that argument. *(p. 197)*

inquisitorial model   A dispute-resolution system in which a neutral investigator gathers evidence from both sides and presents the findings in court. *(p. 462)*

instrumental aggression   Inflicting harm in order to obtain something of value. *(p. 386)*

insufficient deterrence   A condition in which people refrain from engaging in a desirable activity, even when only mild punishment is threatened. *(p. 202)*

insufficient justification   A condition in which people freely perform an attitude-discrepant behavior without receiving a large reward. *(p. 201)*

integrative agreement   A negotiated resolution to a conflict in which all parties obtain outcomes that are superior to what they would have obtained from an equal division of the contested resources. *(p. 286)*

integrity test   Paper-and-pencil questionnaire designed to test a job applicant's honesty and character *(p. 473)*

interactionist perspective   An emphasis on how both an individual's personality and environmental characteristics influence behavior. *(p. 14)*

internal validity   The degree to which there can be reasonable certainty that the independent variables in an experiment caused the effects obtained on the dependent variables. *(p. 44)*

interrater reliability   The degree to which different observers agree on their observations. *(p. 31)*

intimate relationship   A close relationship between two adults involving at least one of the following: emotional attachment, fulfillment of psychological needs, and interdependence. *(p. 314)*

jealousy   The reaction to a perceived threat to a relationship. *(p. 328)*

jigsaw classroom   A cooperative learning method used to reduce racial prejudice through interaction in group efforts. *(p. 164)*

jury nullification   The jury's power to disregard, or "nullify," the law when it conflicts with personal conceptions of justice. *(p. 453)*

kinship selection   Preferential helping of genetic relatives, so that genes held in common will survive. *(p. 339)*

learned helplessness   A phenomenon in which experience with an uncontrollable event creates passive behavior toward a subsequent threat to well-being. *(p. 513)*

leniency bias   The tendency for jury deliberation to produce a tilt toward acquittal. *(p. 455)*

loneliness   A feeling of deprivation about existing social relations. *(p. 297)*

low-balling   A two-step compliance technique in which the influencer secures agreement with a request but then increases the size of that request by revealing hidden costs. *(p. 228)*

matching hypothesis   The proposition that people are attracted to and form relationships with those who are similar to them in particular characteristics, such as physical attractiveness. *(p. 309)*

mere exposure effect   The phenomenon whereby the more often people are exposed to a stimulus, the more positively they evaluate that stimulus. *(p. 299)*

mere presence theory   A theory holding that the mere presence of others is sufficient to produce social facilitation effects. *(p. 251)*

meta-analysis   A set of statistical procedures used to review a body of evidence by combining the results of individual studies to measure the overall reliability and strength of particular effects. *(p. 47)*

minority influence   The process by which dissenters produce change within a group. *(p. 223)*

misinformation effect   The tendency for false postevent misinformation to become integrated into people's memory of an event. *(p. 443)*

mitigating information   Information about a person's situation indicating that he or she should not be held fully responsible for aggressive actions. *(p. 409)*

modern racism   A form of prejudice that surfaces in subtle ways when it is safe, socially acceptable, and easy to rationalize. *(p. 158)*

multicultural research   Research designed to examine racial and ethnic groups within cultures. *(p. 19)*

mundane realism   The degree to which the experimental situation resembles places and events in the real world. *(p. 47)*

need for affiliation   The desire to establish and maintain many rewarding interpersonal relationships. *(p. 295)*

need for closure   A desire to reduce cognitive uncertainty, which heightens the importance of first impressions. *(p. 115)*

need for cognition (NC)   A personality variable that distinguishes people on the basis of how much they enjoy effortful cognitive activities. *(p. 194)*

need for evaluation   A tendency to form positive and negative attitudes toward the people, objects, and issues we encounter. *(p. 174)*

negative state relief model   The proposition that people help others in order to counteract their own feelings of sadness. *(p. 348)*

nonverbal behavior   Behavior that reveals a person's feelings without words—through facial expressions, body language, and vocal cues. *(p. 95)*

normative influence   Influence that produces conformity when a person fears the negative social consequences of appearing deviant. *(p. 216)*

normative model of leadership   The theory that leadership effectiveness is determined by the amount of feedback and participation that leaders invite from workers. *(p. 482)*

norm of justice   A moral standard emphasizing that people should help those who deserve assistance. *(p. 364)*

norm of social responsibility   A moral standard emphasizing that people should help those who need assistance. *(p. 364)*

obedience   Behavior change produced by the commands of authority. *(p. 232)*

outgroup homogeneity effect   The tendency to assume that there is greater similarity among members of outgroups than among members of ingroups. *(p. 131)*

overjustification effect   The tendency for intrinsic motivation to diminish for activities that have become associated with reward or other extrinsic factors. *(p. 61)*

passionate love   Romantic love characterized by high arousal, intense attraction, and fear of rejection. *(p. 321)*

peremptory challenge   A means by which lawyers can exclude a limited number of prospective jurors without the judge's approval. *(p. 431)*

performance appraisal   The process of evaluating an employee's work within the organization. *(p. 477)*

peripheral route to persuasion   The process by which a person does not think carefully about a communication and is influenced instead by superficial cues. *(p. 181)*

personal attribution   Attribution to internal characteristics of an actor, such as ability, personality, mood, or effort. *(p. 101)*

persuasion   The process by which attitudes are changed. *(p. 180)*

placebo effect   The tendency for an ineffectual drug or treatment to improve a patient's condition because he or she believes in its effectiveness. *(p. 517)*

pluralistic ignorance   The state in which people mistakenly believe that their own thoughts and feelings are different from those of others, even though everyone's behavior is the same. *(p. 355)*

polygraph   A mechanical instrument that records physiological arousal from multiple channels; it is often used as a lie-detector test. (p. 439)

pornography   Explicit sexual material. (p. 416)

posttraumatic stress disorder (PTSD)   A condition in which a person experiences enduring physical and psychological symptoms after an extremely stressful event. (p. 503)

prejudice   Negative feelings toward persons based on their membership in certain groups. (p. 143)

primacy effect   The tendency for information presented early in a sequence to have more impact on impressions than information presented later. (p. 115)

priming   The tendency for recently used words or ideas to come to mind easily and influence the interpretation of new information. (p. 113)

private conformity   The change of beliefs that occurs when a person privately accepts the position taken by others. (p. 216)

private self-consciousness   A personality characteristic of individuals who are introspective, often attending to their own inner states. (p. 74)

proactive coping   Up-front efforts to ward off or modify the onset of a stressful event. (p. 525)

problem-focused coping   Cognitive and behavioral efforts to alter a stressful situation. (p. 519)

psychological reactance   The theory that people react against threats to their freedom by asserting themselves and perceiving the threatened freedom as more attractive. (p. 198)

psychoneuroimmunology (PNI)   A subfield of psychology that examines the links among psychological factors, the brain and nervous system, and the immune system. (p. 510)

public conformity   A superficial change in overt behavior, without a corresponding change of opinion, produced by real or imagined group pressure. (p. 216)

public self-consciousness   A personality characteristic of individuals who focus on themselves as social objects, as seen by others. (p. 74)

racism   Prejudice and discrimination based on a person's racial background. (p. 157)

random assignment   A method of assigning participants to the various conditions of an experiment so that each participant in the experiment has an equal chance of being in any of the conditions. (p. 39)

random sampling   A method of selecting participants for a study so that everyone in a population has an equal chance of being in the study. (p. 34)

realistic conflict theory   The theory that hostility between groups is caused by direct competition for limited resources. (p. 145)

reciprocity   A mutual exchange between what we give and receive—for example, liking those who like us. (p. 309)

relative deprivation   Feelings of discontent aroused by the belief that one fares poorly compared with others. (p. 145)

scientific jury selection   A method of selecting juries through surveys that yield correlations between demographics and trial-relevant attitudes. (p. 434)

self-awareness theory   The theory that self-focused attention leads people to notice self-discrepancies, thereby motivating either an escape from self-awareness or a change in behavior. (p. 73)

self-complexity   The number of distinct roles or identities people believe they have. (p. 526)

self-concept   The sum total of an individual's beliefs about his or her own personal attributes. (p. 57)

self-disclosure   Revelations about the self that a person makes to others. (p. 325)

self-efficacy   A person's belief that he or she is capable of the specific behavior required to produce a desired outcome in a given situation. (p. 516)

self-esteem   An affective component of the self, consisting of a person's positive and negative self-evaluations. (p. 70)

self-fulfilling prophecy   The process by which one's expectations about a person eventually lead that person to behave in ways that confirm those expectations. (p. 118)

self-handicapping   Behaviors designed to sabotage one's own performance in order to provide a subsequent excuse for failure. (p. 78)

self-monitoring   The tendency to change behavior in response to the self-presentation concerns of the situation. (p. 85)

self-perception theory   The theory that when internal cues are difficult to interpret, people gain self-insight by observing their own behavior. (p. 59)

self-presentation   Strategies people use to shape what others think of them. (p. 82)

self-schema   A belief people hold about themselves that guides the processing of self-relevant information. (p. 69)

sentencing disparity   Inconsistency of sentences for the same offense from one judge to another. (p. 459)

sexism   Prejudice and discrimination based on a person's gender (p. 150)

situational attribution   Attribution to factors external to an actor, such as the task, other people, or luck. (p. 101)

sleeper effect   A delayed increase in the persuasive impact of a noncredible source. (p. 188)

social categorization   The classification of persons into groups on the basis of common attributes. (p. 131)

social cognition   The study of how people perceive, remember, and interpret information about themselves and others. (p. 16)

social comparison theory   The theory that people evaluate their own abilities and opinions by comparing themselves to others. (p. 63)

social dilemma   A situation in which a self-interested choice by everyone creates the worst outcome for everyone. (p. 276)

social exchange theory   A perspective that views people as motivated to maximize benefits and minimize costs in their relationships with others. (p. 315)

social facilitation   A process whereby the presence of others enhances performance on easy tasks but impairs performance on difficult tasks. (p. 250)

social identity theory   The theory that people favor ingroups over outgroups in order to enhance their self-esteem. (p. 146)

social impact theory   The theory that social influence depends on the strength, immediacy, and number of source persons relative to target persons. (p. 240)

social learning theory   The proposition that behavior is learned through the observation of others as well as through the direct experience of rewards and punishments. (p. 398)

social loafing   A group-produced reduction in individual output on easy tasks where contributions are pooled. *(p. 252)*

social norm   A general rule of conduct reflecting standards of social approval and disapproval. *(p. 363)*

social perception   A general term for the processes by which people come to understand one another. *(p. 91)*

social psychology   The scientific study of how individuals think, feel, and behave in regard to other people and how individuals' thoughts, feelings, and behaviors are affected by other people. *(p. 5)*

social role theory   The theory that small gender differences are magnified in perception by the contrasting social roles occupied by men and women. *(p. 154)*

social support   The helpful coping resources provided by friends and other people. *(p. 526)*

stereotype   A belief that associates a group of people with certain traits. *(p. 130)*

stress   An unpleasant state of arousal in which people perceive the demands of an event as taxing or exceeding their ability to satisfy or alter those demands. *(p. 500)*

stressor   Anything that causes stress. *(p. 501)*

structured interview   Interview in which each job applicant is asked a standard set of questions and evaluated on the same criteria. *(p. 474)*

subject variable   Variable that characterizes pre-existing differences among the participants in a study. *(p. 43)*

subliminal presentation   A method of presenting stimuli so faintly or rapidly that people do not have any conscious awareness of having been exposed to them. *(p. 131)*

sunk cost principle   The economic rule of thumb that only future costs and benefits, not past commitments, should be considered in making a decision. *(p. 494)*

superordinate goal   Shared goal that can be achieved only through cooperation among individuals or groups. *(p. 144)*

superordinate identity   The perception by members of different groups that they all belong to a larger whole. *(p. 287)*

that's-not-all technique   A two-step compliance technique in which the influencer begins with an inflated request, then

decreases its apparent size by offering a discount or bonus. *(p. 230)*

theory   An organized set of principles used to explain observed phenomena. *(p. 27)*

theory of planned behavior   The theory that attitudes toward a specific behavior combine with subjective norms and perceived control to influence a person's actions. *(p. 177)*

threat-to-self-esteem model   The theory that reactions to receiving assistance depend on whether help is perceived as supportive or threatening. *(p. 374)*

transactional leader   A leader who gains compliance and support from followers primarily through goal setting and the use of rewards. *(p. 483)*

transformational leader   A leader who inspires followers to transcend their own needs in the interest of a common cause. *(p. 484)*

triangular theory of love   A theory proposing that love has three basic components—intimacy, passion, and commitment—which can be combined to produce eight subtypes. *(p. 320)*

two-factor theory of emotion   The theory that the experience of emotion is based on two factors: physiological arousal and a cognitive interpretation of that arousal. *(p. 64)*

Type A behavior pattern   A pattern of behavior characterized by extremes of competitive striving for achievement, a sense of time urgency, hostility, and aggression. *(p. 508)*

voir dire   The pretrial examination of prospective jurors by the judge or opposing lawyers to uncover signs of bias. *(p. 431)*

weapon-focus effect   The tendency for the presence of a weapon to draw attention and impair a witness's ability to identify the culprit. *(p. 441)*

weapons effect   The tendency of weapons to increase the likelihood of aggression by their mere presence. *(p. 408)*

what-is-beautiful-is-good stereotype   The belief that physically attractive individuals also possess desirable personality characteristics. *(p. 304)*

References

Abbey, A. (1982). Sex differences in attributions for friendly behavior: Do males misperceive females' friendliness? *Journal of Personality and Social Psychology, 42,* 830–838.

Abbey, A. (1987). Misperceptions of friendly behavior as sexual interest: A survey of naturally occurring incidents. *Psychology of Women Quarterly, 11,* 173–194.

Abeles, R. P. (1976). Relative deprivation, rising expectations and black militancy. *Journal of Social Issues, 32,* 119–137.

Abelson, R. P. (1981). Psychological status of the script concept. *American Psychologist, 36,* 715–729.

Abelson, R. P., Aronson, E., McGuire, W. J., Newcomb, T. M., Rosenberg, M. J., & Tannenbaum, P. H. (1968). *Theories of cognitive consistency: A sourcebook.* Chicago: Rand McNally.

Abramis, D. J. (1994). Work role ambiguity, job satisfaction, and job performance: Meta-analyses and review. *Psychological Reports, 75,* 1411–1433.

Abramson, L. Y., Metalsky, G. I., & Alloy, L. B. (1989). Hopelessness depression: A theory-based subtype of depression. *Psychological Review, 96,* 358–372.

Abramson, L. Y., Seligman, M. E. P., & Teasdale, J. (1978). Learned helplessness in humans: Critique and reformulation. *Journal of Abnormal Psychology, 87,* 49–74.

Acker, M., & Davis, M. H. (1992). Intimacy, passion, and commitment in adult romantic relationships: A test of the triangular theory of love. *Journal of Social and Personal Relationships, 9,* 21–50.

Adair, J. G. (1984). The Hawthorne effect: A reconsideration of the methodological artifact. *Journal of Applied Psychology, 69,* 334–345.

Adams, P. R., & Adams, G. R. (1984). Mount Saint Helens's ashfall: Evidence for a disaster stress reaction. *American Psychologist, 39,* 252–260.

Aderman, D. (1972). Elation, depression, and helping behavior. *Journal of Personality and Social Psychology, 24,* 91–101.

Aderman, D., Brehm, S. S., & Katz, B. (1974). Empathic observation of an innocent victim: The just world revisited. *Journal of Personality and Social Psychology, 29,* 342–347.

Adler, S. J. (1994). *The jury: Trial and error in the American courtroom.* New York: Times Books.

Adorno, T., Frenkel-Brunswik, E., Levinson, D., & Sanford, R. N. (1950). *The authoritarian personality.* New York: Harper.

Aguinis, H., Pierce, C. A., & Quigley, B. M. (1993). Conditions under which a bogus pipeline procedure enhances the validity of self-reported cigarette smoking: A meta-analytic review. *Journal of Applied Social Psychology, 23,* 352–373.

Aiello, J. R., & Kolb, K. J. (1995). Electronic performance monitoring and social context: Impact on productivity and stress. *Journal of Applied Psychology, 80,* 339–353.

Ainsworth, M., Blehar, M. C., Waters, E., & Wall, S. (1978). *Patterns of attachment: A psychological study of the strange situation.* Hillsdale, NJ: Erlbaum.

Ajzen, I. (1991). The theory of planned behavior. *Organizational Behavior and Human Decision Processes, 50,* 179–211.

Ajzen, I., & Fishbein, M. (1977). Attitude-behavior relations: A theoretical analysis and review of empirical research. *Psychological Bulletin, 84,* 888–918.

Ajzen, I., & Madden, T. J. (1986). Prediction of goal-directed behavior: Attitudes, intentions, and perceived behavioral control. *Journal of Experimental Social Psychology, 22,* 453–474.

Aldag, R. J., & Fuller, S. R. (1993). Beyond fiasco: A reappraisal of the groupthink phenomenon and a new model of group decision processes. *Psychological Bulletin, 113,* 533–552.

Alicke, M. D., & Largo, E. (1995). The role of the self in the false consensus effect. *Journal of Experimental Social Psychology, 31,* 28–47.

Alicke, M. D., LoSchiavo, F. M., Zerbst, J., & Zhang, S. (1997). The person who outperforms me is a genius: Maintaining perceived competence in upward social comparison. *Journal of Personality and Social Psychology, 73,* 781–789.

Allen, B. (1995). Gender stereotypes are not accurate: A replication of Martin (1987) using diagnostic vs. self-report and behavioral criteria. *Sex Roles, 32,* 583–600.

Allen, J. B., Kenrick, D. T., Linder, D. E., & McCall, M. A. (1989). Arousal and attribution: A response-facilitation alternative to misattribution and negative-reinforcement models. *Journal of Personality and Social Psychology, 57,* 261–270.

Allen, K. M., Blascovich, J., Tomaka, J., & Kelsey, R. M. (1991). Presence of human friends and pet dogs as moderators of autonomic responses to stress in women. *Journal of Personality and Social Psychology, 61,* 582–589.

Allen, V. L. (1965). Situational factors in conformity. In L. Berkowitz (Ed.), *Advances in Experimental Social Psychology, 2,* 133–175.

Allen, V. L., & Levine, J. M. (1969). Consensus and conformity. *Journal of Experimental Social Psychology, 5,* 389–399.

Allen, V. L., & Levine, J. M. (1971). Social support and conformity: The role of independent assessment of reality. *Journal of Experimental Social Psychology, 7,* 48–58.

Alley, T. R. (1988). *Social and applied aspects of perceiving faces.* Hillsdale, NJ: Erlbaum.

Alliger, G. M., Lilienfeld, S. O., & Mitchell, K. E. (1996). The susceptibility of overt and covert integrity tests to coaching and faking. *Psychological Science, 7,* 32–39.

Allison, S. T., & Kerr, N. L. (1994). Group correspondent biases and the provision of public goods. *Journal of Personality and Social Psychology, 66,* 688–698.

Allison, S. T., McQueen, L. R., & Schaerfl, L. M. (1992). Social decision making processes and the equal partitionment of shared resources. *Journal of Experimental Social Psychology, 28,* 23–42.

Allison, S. T., & Messick, D. M. (1985). Effects of experience on performance in a replenishable resource trap. *Journal of Personality and Social Psychology, 49,* 943–948.

Allport, F. H. (1924). *Social psychology.* Boston: Houghton Mifflin.

Allport, F. H., et al. (1953). The effects of segregation and the consequences of desegregation: A social science statement. *Minneapolis Law Review, 37,* 429–440.

Allport, G. W. (1954). *The nature of prejudice.* Reading, MA: Addison-Wesley.

Allport, G. W. (1985). The historical background of social psychology. In G. Lindzey & E. Aronson (Eds.), *Handbook of social psychology* (3rd ed., Vol. I, pp. 1–46). New York: Random House.

Allport, G. W., & Postman, L. J. (1947). *The psychology of rumor.* New York: Holt.

Aloise-Young, P. A. (1993). The development of self-presentation: Self-promotion in 6- to 10-year-old children. *Social Cognition, 11,* 201–222.

Altman, I. (1973). Reciprocity of interpersonal exchange. *Journal for Theory of Social Behavior, 3,* 249–261.

Altman, I., & Taylor, D. A. (1973). *Social penetration: The development of interpersonal relationships.* New York: Holt, Rinehart and Winston.

Amabile, T. M. (1996). *Creativity in context.* New York: Westview.

Amabile, T. M., Hill, K. G., Hennessey, B. A., & Tighe, E. M. (1994). The work preference inventory: Assessing intrinsic and extrinsic motivation orientations. *Journal of Personality and Social Psychology, 66,* 950–967.

Amato, P. R. (1983). Helping behavior in urban and rural environments: Field studies based on a taxonomic organization of helping episodes. *Journal of Personality and Social Psychology, 45,* 571–586.

Ambady, N., & Rosenthal, R. (1993). Half a minute: Predicting teacher evaluations from thin slices of nonverbal behavior and physical attractiveness. *Journal of Personality and Social Psychology, 64,* 431–441.

American Psychological Association (1992). Ethical principles of psychologists and code of conduct. *American Psychologist, 47,* 1597–1611.

Amir, Y. (1969). Contact hypothesis in ethnic relations. *Psychological Bulletin, 71,* 319–342.

Andersen, B. L., Kiecolt-Glaser, J. K., & Glaser, R. (1994). A biobehavioral model of cancer stress and disease course. *American Psychologist, 49,* 389–404.

Andersen, S. M., & Ross, L. (1984). Self-knowledge and social inference: I. The impact of cognitive/affective and behavioral data. *Journal of Personality and Social Psychology, 46,* 280–293.

Anderson, C. A. (1989). Temperature and aggression: Ubiquitous effects of heat on occurrence of human violence. *Psychological Bulletin, 106,* 74–96.

Anderson, C. A. (1997). Effects of violent movies and trait irritability on hostile feelings and aggressive thoughts. *Aggressive Behavior, 23,* 161–178.

Anderson, C. A. (1998). Aggression and violence. In *The Encyclopedia of Psychology.* Washington, DC: American Psychological Association.

Anderson, C. A., & Anderson, K. B. (1996). Violent crime rate studies in philosophical context: A destructive testing approach to heat and southern culture of violence effects. *Journal of Personality and Social Psychology, 70,* 740–756.

Anderson, C. A., & Anderson, K. B. (1998). Temperature and aggression: Paradox, controversy, and a (fairly) clear picture. In R. Geen & E. Donnerstein (Eds.), *Human aggression: Theories, research, and implications for policy.* New York: Academic Press.

Anderson, C. A., Anderson, K. B., & Deuser, W. E. (1996). Examining an affective framework: Weapon and temperature effects on aggressive thoughts, affect, and attitudes. *Personality and Social Psychology Bulletin, 22,* 366–376.

Anderson, C. A., & Bushman, B. J. (1997). External validity of trivial experiments: The case of laboratory aggression. *Review of General Psychology, 1,* 19–41.

Anderson, C. A., Deuser, S. E., & DeNeve, K. M. (1995). Hot temperatures, hostile affect, hostile cognition, and arousal: Tests of a general model of affective aggression. *Personality and Social Psychology Bulletin, 21,* 434–448.

Anderson, C. A., Lepper, M. R., & Ross, L. (1980). Perseverance of social theories: The role of explanation in the persistence of discredited information. *Journal of Personality and Social Psychology, 39,* 1037–1049.

Anderson, C. A., Miller, R. S., Riger, A. L., Dill, J. C., & Sedikides, C. (1994). Behavioral and characterological attributional styles as predictors of depression and loneliness: Review, refinement, and test. *Journal of Personality and Social Psychology, 66,* 549–558.

Anderson, C. A., & Sechler, E. S. (1986). Effects of explanation and counterexplanation on the development and use of social theories. *Journal of Personality and Social Psychology, 50,* 24–34.

Anderson, J. L., Crawford, C. B., Nadeau, J., & Lindberg, T. (1992). Was the Duchess of Windsor right? A cross-cultural review of the socioecology of ideals of female body shape. *Ethology and Sociobiology, 13,* 197–227.

Anderson, N. H. (1965). Averaging versus adding as a stimulus combination rule in impression formation. *Journal of Experimental Social Psychology, 70,* 394–400.

Anderson, N. H. (1981). *Foundations of information integration theory.* New York: Academic Press.

Anderson, N. H., & Hubert, S. (1963). Effects of concomitant verbal recall on order effects in personality impression formation. *Journal of Verbal Learning and Verbal Behavior, 2,* 379–391.

Andreasson, P. B. (1987). On the social psychology of the stock market: Aggregate attributional effects and the regressiveness of prediction. *Journal of Personality and Social Psychology, 53,* 490–496.

Andrews, B. (1992). Attribution processes in victims of marital violence: Who do women blame and why? In J. H. Harvey, T. L. Orbuch, & A. L. Weber (Eds.), *Attributions, accounts, and close relationships* (pp. 176–193). New York: Springer-Verlag.

Annin, P. (1995, April 3). Battleground Chicago: Report from the front: How racial preferences really work—or don't. *Newsweek,* pp. 26–33.

Antonioni, D. (1996). Two strategies for responding to stressors: Managing conflict and clarifying work expectations. *Journal of Business and Psychology, 11,* 287–295.

Apodaca v. *Oregon,* 406 U.S. 404 (1972).

Apple, W., Streeter, L. A., & Krauss, R. M. (1979). Effects of pitch and speech rate on personal attributions. *Journal of Personality and Social Psychology, 37,* 715–727.

Archer, D., & Gartner, R. (1984). *Violence and crime in cross-national perspective.* New Haven, CT: Yale University Press.

Archer, D., Iritani, B., Kimes, D. D., & Barrios, M. (1983). Five studies of sex differences in facial prominence. *Journal of Personality and Social Psychology, 45,* 725–735.

Archibald, F. S., Bartholomew, K., & Marx, R. (1995). Loneliness in early adolescence: A test of the cognitive discrepancy model of loneliness. *Personality and Social Psychology Bulletin, 21,* 296–301.

Arendt, H. (1963). *Eichmann in Jerusalem: A report on the banality of evil.* New York: Viking.

Argote, L., Devadas, R., & Melone, N. (1990). The base-rate fallacy: Contrasting processes and outcomes of group and individual judgment. *Organizational Behavior and Human Decision Processes, 46,* 296–310.

Argote, L., Insko, C. A., Yovetich, N., & Romero, A. A. (1995). Group learning curves: The effects of turnover and task complexity on group performance. *Journal of Applied Social Psychology, 25,* 512–529.

Arkin, R. M. (1981). Self-presentation styles. In J. T. Tedeschi (Ed.), *Impression management theory and social psychological research* (pp. 311–333). New York: Academic Press.

Armor, D. A., & Taylor, S. E. (1998). Situated optimism: Specific outcome expectancies and self-regulation. *Advances in Experimental Social Psychology, 30,* 309–379.

Armour, S. (1998, February 17). Office ethics: Teams make it hard to tattle. *USA Today,* p. 6B.

Aron, A., Aron, E. N., & Smollan, D. (1992). Inclusion of Other in the Self Scale and the structure of interpersonal closeness. *Journal of Personality and Social Psychology, 63,* 596–612.

Aron, A., Aron, E. N., Tudor, M., & Nelson, G. (1991). Close relationships as including other in the self. *Journal of Personality and Social Psychology, 60,* 241–253.

Aron, A., Dutton, D. G., Aron, E. N., & Iverson, A. (1989). Experiences of falling in love. *Journal of Social and Personal Relationships, 6,* 243–257.

Aron, A., & Westbay, L. (1996). Dimensions of the prototype of love. *Journal of Personality and Social Psychology, 70,* 535–551.

Aronoff, J., Barclay, A. M., & Stevenson, L. A. (1988). The recognition of threatening facial stimuli. *Journal of Personality and Social Psychology, 54,* 647–655.

Aronoff, J., Woike, B. A., & Hyman, L. M. (1992). Which are the stimuli in facial displays of anger and happiness? *Journal of Personality and Social Psychology, 62,* 1050–1066.

Aronson, E. (1969). The theory of cognitive dissonance: A current perspective. In L. Berkowitz (Ed.), *Advances in experimental social psychology* (Vol. 4, pp. 1–34). New York: Academic Press.

Aronson, E. (1988). *The social animal.* San Francisco, CA: Freeman.

Aronson, E., Blaney, N., Stephan, C., Sikes, J., & Snapp, M. (1978). *The jigsaw classroom.* Beverly Hills, CA: Sage.

Aronson, E., Brewer, M., & Carlsmith, J. M. (1985). Experimentation in social psychology. In G. Lindzey & E. Aronson (Eds.), *Handbook of social psychology* (Vol. 1, 3rd ed., pp. 441–486). New York: Random House.

Aronson, E., & Carlsmith, J. M. (1963). Effect of severity of threat on the devaluation of forbidden behavior. *Journal of Abnormal and Social Psychology, 66,* 584–588.

Aronson, E., & Carlsmith, J. M. (1968). Experimentation in social psychology. In G. Lindzey & E. Aronson (Eds.), *Handbook of social psychology* (Vol. 2, 2nd ed., pp. 1–79). Reading, MA: Addison-Wesley.

Aronson, E., & Cope, V. (1968). My enemy's enemy is my friend. *Journal of Personality and Social Psychology, 8,* 8–12.

Aronson, E., & Linder, D. (1965). Gain and loss of esteem as determinants of interpersonal attractiveness. *Journal of Experimental Social Psychology, 1,* 156–172.

Aronson, E., & Mills, J. (1959). The effect of severity of initiation on liking for a group. *Journal of Abnormal and Social Psychology, 59,* 177–181.

Arthur, W., Jr., Doverspike, D., & Fuentes, R. (1992). Recipients' affective responses to affirmative action interventions: A cross-cultural perspective. *Behavioral Sciences and the Law, 10,* 229–243.

Asch, S. E. (1946). Forming impressions of personality. *Journal of Abnormal and Social Psychology, 41,* 258–290.

Asch, S. E. (1951). Effects of group pressure upon the modification and distortion of judgments. In H. Guetzkow (Ed.), *Groups, leadership, and men.* Pittsburgh, PA: Carnegie Press.

Asch, S. E. (1955, November). Opinions and social pressure. *Scientific American,* pp. 31–35.

Asch, S. E. (1956). Studies of independence and conformity: A minority of one against a unanimous majority. *Psychological Monographs, 70,* 416.

Asch, S. E., & Zukier, H. (1984). Thinking about persons. *Journal of Personality and Social Psychology, 46,* 1230–1240.

Asendorpf, J. B., Warkentin, V., & Baudonniere, P. M. (1996). Self-awareness and other-awareness II: Mirror self-recognition, social contingency awareness, and synchronic imitation. *Developmental Psychology, 32,* 313–321.

Askenasy, H. (1978). *Are we all Nazis?* Secaucus, NJ: Lyle Stuart.

Aspinwall, L. G., & Taylor, S. E. (1992). Modeling cognitive adaptation: A longitudinal investigation of the impact of individual differences and coping on college adjustment and performance. *Journal of Personality and Social Psychology, 63,* 989–1003.

Aspinwall, L. G., & Taylor, S. E. (1993). The effects of social comparison direction, threat, and self-esteem on affect, self-evaluation, and expected success. *Journal of Personality and Social Psychology, 64,* 708–722.

Aspinwall, L. G., & Taylor, S. E. (1997). A stitch in time: Self-regulation and proactive coping. *Psychological Bulletin, 121,* 417–436.

Associated Press. (1988, October 10). Skirting the issue? *The National Law Journal,* p. 43.

Auerbach, S. M., Kiesler, D. J., Strentz, T., Schmidt, J. A., & Serio, C. D. (1994). Interpersonal impacts and adjunction to the stress of simulated captivity: An empirical test of the Stockholm Syndrome. *Journal of Social and Clinical Psychology, 13,* 207–221.

Aukett, R., Richie, J., & Mill, K. (1988). Gender differences in friendship patterns. *Sex Roles, 19,* 57–66.

Axelrod, R. (1984). *The evolution of cooperation.* New York: Basic Books.

Axsom, D. (1989). Cognitive dissonance and behavior change in psychotherapy. *Journal of Experimental Social Psychology, 25,* 234–252.

Axsom, D., & Cooper, J. (1985). Cognitive dissonance and psychotherapy: The role of effort justification in inducing weight loss. *Journal of Experimental Social Psychology, 21,* 149–160.

Axtell, R. E. (1993). *Do's and taboos around the world* (3rd ed.). New York: John Wiley.

Babad, E., & Katz, Y. (1991). Wishful thinking—against all odds. *Journal of Applied Social Psychology, 21,* 1921–1938.

Bagley, C., Bolitho, F., & Bertrand, L. (1997). Norms and construct validity of the Rosenberg self-esteem scale in Canadian high school populations: Implications for counselling. *Canadian Journal of Counselling, 31,* 82–92.

Bagozzi, R. P., & Moore, D. J. (1994). Public service advertisements: Emotions and empathy guide prosocial behavior. *Journal of Marketing, 58,* 56–70.

Bailey, D. S., & Taylor, S. P. (1991). Effects of alcohol and aggressive disposition on human physical aggression. *Journal of Research in Personality, 25,* 334–342.

Baldwin, M., & Fehr, B. (1995). On the instability of attachment style ratings. *Personal Relationships, 2,* 247–261.

Bales, R. F. (1958). Task roles and social roles in problem-solving groups. In E. E. Maccoby, T. M. Newcomb, & E. L. Hartley (Eds.), *Readings in social psychology* (3rd ed., pp. 437–447). New York: Holt.

Ballew v. *Georgia,* 435 U.S. 223 (1978).

Banaji, M. R., & Hardin, C. D. (1996). Automatic gender stereotyping. *Psychological Science, 7,* 136–141.

Banaji, M. R., Hardin, C., & Rothman, A. J. (1993). Implicit stereotyping in person judgment. *Journal of Personality and Social Psychology, 65,* 272–281.

Banaji, M. R., & Steele, C. M. (1989). Alcohol and self-evaluation: Is a social cognition approach beneficial? *Social Cognition, 7,* 137–151.

Bancroft, J. (Ed.) (1997). *Researching sexual behavior: Methodological issues.* Bloomington: Indiana University Press.

Bandura, A. (1973). *Aggression: A social learning analysis.* Englewood Cliffs, NJ: Prentice-Hall.

Bandura, A. (1977). *Social learning theory.* Englewood Cliffs, NJ: Prentice-Hall.

Bandura, A. (1983). Psychological mechanisms of aggression. In R. G. Geen & E. I. Donnerstein (Eds.), *Aggression: Theoretical and empirical reviews: Vol. l. Theoretical and methodological issues* (pp. 1–40). New York: Academic Press.

Bandura, A. (1989). *Social cognitive theory.* Englewood Cliffs, NJ: Erlbaum.

Bandura, A. (1990). Selective activation and disengagement of moral control. *Journal of Social Issues, 46,* 27–46.

Bandura, A. (1997). *Self-efficacy: The exercise of control.* New York: W. H. Freeman.

Bandura, A., Barbaranelli, C., Caprara, G. V., & Pastorelli, C. (1996). Mechanisms of moral disengagement in the exercise of moral agency. *Journal of Personality and Social Psychology, 71,* 364–374.

Bandura, A., Ross, R., & Ross, S. (1961). Transmission of aggression through imitation of aggressive models. *Journal of Abnormal and Social Psychology, 63,* 575–582.

Banuazizi, A., & Movahedi, S. (1975). Interpersonal dynamics in a simulated prison: A methodological analysis. *American Psychologist, 30,* 152–160.

Bar-Tal, D. (1990). Causes and consequences of delegitimization: Models of conflict and ethnocentrism. *Journal of Social Issues, 46,* 65–81.

Bar-Tal, D. (1996). Development of social categories and stereotypes in early childhood: The case of "the Arab" concept formation, stereotype and attitudes by Jewish children in Israel. *International Journal of Intercultural Relations, 20,* 341–370.

Bargh, J. A. (1997). The automaticity of everyday life. In R. S. Wyer (Ed.), *The automaticity of everyday life: Advances in social cognition* (Vol. 10, pp. 1–61). Mahwah, NJ: Erlbaum.

Bargh, J. A., Chaiken, S., Govender, R., & Pratto, F. (1992). The generality of the automatic attitude activation effect. *Journal of Personality and Social Psychology, 62,* 893–912.

Bargh, J. A., Chaiken, S., Raymond, P., & Hymes, C. (1996). The automatic evaluation effect: Unconditional automatic attitude activation with a pronunciation task. *Journal of Experimental Social Psychology, 31,* 104–128.

Bargh, J. A., Chen, M., & Burrows, L. (1996). Automaticity of social behavior: Direct effects of trait construct and stereotype activation on action. *Journal of Personality and Social Psychology, 71,* 230–244.

Bargh, J. A., Lombardi, W. J., & Higgins, E. T. (1988). Automaticity of chronically accessible constructs in person x situation effects on person perception: It's just a matter of time. *Journal of Personality and Social Psychology, 55,* 599–605.

Bargh, J. A., & Pietromonaco, P. (1982). Automatic information processing and social perception: The influence of trait information presented outside of conscious awareness on impression formation. *Journal of Personality and Social Psychology, 43,* 437–449.

Barley, S. R., & Bechky, B. A. (1994). In the backrooms of science: The work of technicians in science labs. *Work and Occupations, 21,* 85–126.

Barnes Nacoste, R. (1994). If empowerment is the goal . . .: Affirmative action and social interaction. *Basic and Applied Social Psychology, 15,* 87–112.

Barnes, R. D., Ickes, W., & Kidd, R. F. (1979). Effects of the perceived intentionality and stability of another's dependency on helping behavior. *Personality and Social Psychology Bulletin, 5,* 367–372.

Barnett, R. C., Marshall, N. L., & Pleck, J. H. (1992). Men's multiple roles and their relationship to men's psychological distress. *Journal of Marriage and the Family, 54,* 358–367.

Barnett, R. C., Marshall, N. L., Raudenbush, S. W., & Brennan, R. T. (1993). Gender and the relationship between job experience and psychological distress: A study of dual-earner couples. *Journal of Personality and Social Psychology, 64,* 794–806.

Baron, R. A. (1977). *Human aggression.* New York: Plenum.

Baron, R. A. (1997). The sweet smell of . . . helping: Effects of pleasant ambient fragrance on prosocial behavior in shopping malls. *Personality and Social Psychology Bulletin, 23,* 498–503.

Baron, R. A., & Ball, R. L. (1974). The aggression-inhibiting influence of nonhostile behavior. *Journal of Experimental Social Psychology, 10,* 23–33.

Baron, R. A., & Kepner, C. R. (1970). Model's behavior and attraction toward the model as determinants of adult aggressive behavior. *Journal of Personality and Social Psychology, 14,* 335–344.

Baron, R. A., & Richardson, D. R. (1994). *Human aggression* (2nd ed.). New York: Plenum.

Baron, R. M. (1988). An ecological framework for establishing a dual-mode theory of social knowing. In D. Bar-Tal & A. W. Kruglanski (Eds.), *The social psychology of knowledge* (pp. 48–82). New York: Cambridge University Press.

Baron, R. S. (1986). Distraction-conflict theory: Progress and problems. In L. Berkowitz (Ed.), *Advances in experimental social psychology* (Vol. 19, pp. 1–40). Orlando, FL: Academic Press.

Baron, R. S., Cutrona, C. E., Hicklin, D., Russell, D. W., & Lubaroff, D. M. (1990). Social support and immune function among spouses of cancer patients. *Journal of Personality and Social Psychology, 59,* 344–352.

Baron, R. S., Hoppe, S. I., Kao, C. F., Brunsman, B., Linneweh, B., & Rogers, D. (1996). Social corroboration and opinion extremity. *Journal of Experimental Social Psychology, 32,* 537–560.

Baron, R. S., Vandello, J. A., & Brunsman, B. (1996). The forgotten variable in conformity research: Impact of task importance on social influence. *Journal of Personality and Social Psychology, 71,* 915–927.

Baron, R., Logan, H., Lilly, J., Inman, M., & Brennan, M. (1994). Negative emotion and message processing. *Journal of Experimental Social Psychology, 30,* 181–201.

Barrick, M. R., & Mount, M. K. (1996). Effects of impression management and self-deception on the predictive validity of personality constructs. *Journal of Applied Psychology, 81,* 261–272.

Barthrop, R. W., Lazarus, L., Luckhurst, E., Kiloh, L. G., & Penny, R. (1977). Depressed lymphocyte function after bereavement. *Lancet, 1,* 834–839.

Basden, B. H., Basden, D. R., Bryner, S., & Thomas, R. L. III. (1997). A comparison of group and individual remembering: Does collaboration disrupt retrieval strategies? *Journal of Experimental Psychology: Learning, Memory, and Cognition, 23,* 1176–1191.

Bashore, T. R., & Rapp, P. E. (1993). Are there alternatives to traditional polygraph procedures? *Psychological Bulletin, 113,* 3–22.

Bass, B. M. (1985). *Leadership and performance beyond expectations.* New York: Free Press.

Bass, B. M. (1990). *Bass & Stogdill's handbook of leadership: Theory, research, & managerial applications* (3rd ed.). New York: Free Press.

Bass, B. M. (1997). Does the transactional-transformational leadership paradigm transcend organizational and national boundaries? *American Psychologist, 52,* 130–139.

Bass, B. M. (1998). *Transformational leadership: Industry, military, and educational impact.* Mahwah, NJ: Erlbaum.

Bass, B. M., & Avolio, B. J. (1990). *Manual: The multifactor leadership questionnaire.* Palo Alto, CA: Consulting Psychologists Press.

Bassili, J. N., & Provencal, A. (1988). Perceiving minorities: A factor-analytic approach. *Personality and Social Psychology Bulletin, 14,* 5–15.

Batson, C. D. (1991). *The altruism question.* Hillsdale, NJ: Erlbaum.

Batson, C. D. (1997). Self-other merging and the empathy-altruism hypothesis: Reply to Neuberg et al. (1997). *Journal of Personality and Social Psychology, 73*(3), 517–522.

Batson, C. D. (1998). Altruism and prosocial behavior. In D. T. Gilbert, S. T. Fiske, & G. Lindzey (Eds.), *The handbook of social psychology* (4th ed., Vol. 2, pp. 282–316). New York: McGraw-Hill.

Batson, C. D., Batson, J. G., Griffitt, C. A., Barrientos, S., Brandt, J. R., Sprengelmeyer, P., & Bayly, M. J. (1989). Negative-state relief and the empathy-altruism hypothesis. *Journal of Personality and Social Psychology, 56,* 922–933.

Batson, C. D., Batson, J. G., Slingsby, J. K., Harrell, K. L., Peekna, H. M., & Todd, R. M. (1991). Empathic joy and the empathy-altruism hypothesis. *Journal of Personality and Social Psychology, 61,* 413–426.

Batson, C. D., Batson, J. G., Todd, R. M., Brummett, B. H., Shaw, L. L., & Aldeguer, C. M. R. (1995). Empathy and the collective good: Caring for one of the others in a social dilemma. *Journal of Personality and Social Psychology, 68,* 619–631.

Batson, C. D., Cochran, P. J., Biederman, M. F., Blosser, J. L., Ryan, M. J., & Vogt, B. (1978). Failure to help when in a hurry: Callousness or conflict? *Personality and Social Psychology Bulletin, 4,* 97–101.

Batson, C. D., Coke, J. S., Jasnoski, M. L., & Hanson, M. (1978). Buying kindness: Effect of an extrinsic incentive for helping on perceived altruism. *Personality and Social Psychology Bulletin, 4,* 86–91.

Batson, C. D., Duncan, B. D., Ackerman, P., Buckley, T., & Birch, K. (1981). Is empathic emotion a source of altruistic motivation? *Journal of Personality and Social Psychology, 40,* 290–302.

Batson, C. D., Dyck, J. L., Brandt, J. R., Batson, J. G., Powell, A. L., McMaster, M. R., & Griffitt, C. (1988). Five studies testing two new egoistic alternatives to the empathy-altruism hypothesis. *Journal of Personality and Social Psychology, 55,* 52–77.

Batson, C. D., Early, S., & Salvarani, G. (1997). Perspective taking: Imagining how another feels versus imagining how you would feel. *Personality and Social Psychology Bulletin, 23,* 751–758.

Batson, C. D., O'Quin, K., Fultz, J., Vanderplas, M., & Isen, A. M. (1983). Influence of self-reported distress and empathy on egoistic versus altruistic motivation to help. *Journal of Personality and Social Psychology, 45,* 706–718.

Batson, C. D., Sager, K., Garst, E., Kang, M., Rubchinsky, K., & Dawson, K. (1997). Is empathy-induced helping due to self-other merging? *Journal of Personality and Social Psychology, 73,* 495–509.

Batson, C. D., & Weeks, J. L. (1996). Mood effects of unsuccessful helping: Another test of the empathy-altruism hypothesis. *Personality and Social Psychology Bulletin, 22,* 148–157.

Baugh, S. G., & Graen, G. B. (1997). Effects of team gender and racial composition on perceptions of team performance in cross-functional teams. *Group and Organization Management, 22,* 366–383.

Baum, A. (Ed.). (1984). Social psychology and cigarette smoking [Special issue]. *Journal of Applied Social Psychology, 14*(3).

Baum, A., & Fleming, I. (1993). Implications of psychological research on stress and technological accidents. *American Psychologist, 48,* 665–672.

Baum, A., & Valins, S. (1977). *Architecture and social behavior: Psychological studies of social density.* Hillsdale, NJ: Erlbaum.

Baum, A., & Valins, S. (1979). Architectural mediation of residential density and control: Crowding and the regulation of social contact. In L. Berkowitz (Ed.), *Advances in experimental social psychology* (Vol. 12, pp. 131–175). New York: Academic Press.

Bauman, M. H. (1982, August 16). What you can and can't learn from interviews. *The Wall Street Journal.*

Baumeister, R. F. (1982). A self-presentational view of social phenomena. *Psychological Bulletin, 91,* 3–26.

Baumeister, R. F. (1984). Choking under pressure: Self-consciousness and paradoxical effects of incentives on skillful performance. *Journal of Personality and Social Psychology, 46,* 610–620.

Baumeister, R. F. (1991). *Escaping the self.* New York: Basic Books.

Baumeister, R. F. (1998). The self. In G. Lindzey, S. T. Fiske, & D. Gilbert (Eds.), *The handbook of social psychology* (4th ed.). New York: Oxford University Press.

Baumeister, R. F., & Leary, M. R. (1995). The need to belong: Desire for interpersonal attachments as a fundamental human motivation. *Psychological Bulletin, 117,* 497–529.

Baumeister, R. F., & Scher, S. J. (1988). Self-defeating behavior patterns among normal individuals: Review and analysis of common self-destructive tendencies. *Psychological Bulletin, 104,* 3–22.

Baumeister, R. F., & Tice, D. M. (1984). Role of self-presentation and choice in cognitive dissonance under forced compliance: Necessary or sufficient causes? *Journal of Personality and Social Psychology, 46,* 5–13.

Baumeister, R. F., Chesner, S. P., Sanders, P. S., & Tice, D. M. (1988). Who's in charge here? Group leaders do lend help in emergencies. *Personality and Social Psychology Bulletin, 14,* 17–22.

Baumeister, R. F., Smart, L., & Boden, J. M. (1996). Relation of threatened egotism to violence and aggression: The dark side of high self-esteem. *Psychological Review, 103,* 5–33.

Baumeister, R., Stillwell, A. M., & Hetherington, T. F. (1994). Guilt: An interpersonal approach. *Psychological Bulletin, 115,* 243–267.

Baumrind, D. (1996). A blanket injunction against disciplinary use of spanking is not warranted by the data. *Pediatrics, 98,* 828–831.

Baumrind, D. (1997). Necessary distinctions. *Psychological Inquiry, 8,* 176–229.

Baxter, L. A. (1987). Self-disclosure and disengagement. In V. J. Derleg & J. H. Berg (Eds.), *Self-disclosure: Theory, research, and therapy* (pp. 155–174). New York: Plenum.

Bazerman, M. H., Beekun, R. I., & Schoorman, F. D. (1982). Performance evaluation in dynamic context: The impact of a prior commitment to the ratee. *Journal of Applied Psychology, 67,* 873–876.

Bazerman, M. H., Messick, D. M., Tenbrunsel, A. E., Wade-Benzoni, K. A. (Eds.) (1997). *Environment, ethics, and behavior: The psychology of environmental valuation and degradation.* San Francisco, CA: Jossey-Bass.

Bazerman, M. H., & Neale, M. A. (1992). *Negotiating rationally.* New York: Free Press.

Beach, S. R. H., Tesser, A., Mendolia, M., Anderson, P., et al. (1996). Self-evaluation maintenance in marriage: Toward a performance ecology of the marital relationship. *Journal of Family Psychology, 10,* 379–396.

Beaman, A. L., Cole, C. M., Preston, M., Klentz, B., & Steblay, N. M. (1983). Fifteen years of foot-in-the-door research: A meta-analysis. *Personality and Social Psychology Bulletin, 9,* 181–196.

Beaman, A. L., Klentz, B., Diener, E., & Svanum, S. (1979). Objective self-awareness and transgression in children: A field study. *Journal of Personality and Social Psychology, 37,* 1835–1846.

Beck, E. M., & Tolnay, S. E. (1990). The killing fields of the deep south: The market for cotton and the lynching of blacks, 1882–1930. *American Sociological Review, 55,* 526–539.

Becker, F. D. (1981). *Workspace.* New York: Praeger.

Beggan, J. K. (1992). On the social nature of nonsocial perception: The mere ownership effect. *Journal of Personality and Social Psychology, 62,* 229–237.

Bell, J., Grekul, J., Lamba, N., Minas, C., & Harrell, W. A. (1995). The impact of cost on student helping behavior. *Journal of Social Psychology, 135,* 49–56.

Belli, R. F., Lindsay, D. S., Gales, M. S., & McCarthy, T. T. (1994). Memory impairment and source misattribution in postevent misinformation experiments with short retention intervals. *Memory and Cognition, 22,* 40–54.

Belmore, S. M. (1987). Determinants of attention during impression formation. *Journal of Experimental Psychology: Learning, Memory, and Cognition, 13,* 480–489.

Belsky, J. (1993). Etiology of child maltreatment: A developmental-ecological analysis. *Psychological Bulletin, 114,* 413–434.

Bem, D. J. (1965). An experimental analysis of self-persuasion. *Journal of Experimental Social Psychology, 1,* 199–218.

Bem, D. J. (1967). Self-perception: An alternative interpretation of cognitive dissonance phenomena. *Psychological Review, 74,* 183–200.

Bem, D. J. (1972). Self-perception theory. In L. Berkowitz (Ed.), *Advances in experimental social psychology* (Vol. 6, pp. 1–62). New York: Academic Press.

Bem, S. L. (1981). Gender schema theory: A cognitive account of sex typing. *Psychological Review, 88,* 354–364.

Ben-Shakhar, G., Bar-Hillel, M., Bilu, Y., Ben-Abba, E., & Flug, A. (1986). Can graphology predict occupational success? Two empirical studies and some methodological ruminations. *Journal of Applied Psychology, 71,* 645–653.

Benbow, C. P., Lubinski, D., & Hyde, J. S. (1997). Mathematics: Is biology the cause of gender differences in performance? In M. R. Walsh (Ed.), *Women, men, and gender: Ongoing debates* (pp. 271–287). New Haven, CT: Yale University Press.

Bennett, J. C. (1991). The irrationality of the catharsis theory of aggression as justification for educators' support of interscholastic football. *Perceptual and Motor Skills, 72,* 415–418.

Benson, H. (1993). The relaxation response. In D. Goleman & J. Gurin (Eds.), *Mind body medicine: How to use your mind for better health* (pp. 233–257). Yonkers, NY: Consumer Reports Books.

Benson, P. L., Karabenick, S. A., & Lerner, R. M. (1976). Pretty pleases: The effects of physical attractiveness, race, and sex on receiving help. *Journal of Experimental Social Psychology, 12,* 409–415.

Berg, J. H., & McQuinn, R. D. (1986). Attraction and exchange in continuing and noncontinuing dating relationships. *Journal of Personality and Social Psychology, 50,* 942–952.

Berglas, S., & Jones, E. E. (1978). Drug choice as a self-handicapping strategy in response to noncontingent success. *Journal of Personality and Social Psychology, 36,* 405–417.

Berkman, L., & Syme, S. L. (1979). Social networks, host resistance, and mortality: A nine-year follow-up study of Alameda County residents. *American Journal of Epidemiology, 109,* 186–204.

Berkowitz, L. (1965). Some aspects of observed aggression. *Journal of Personality and Social Psychology, 2,* 359–369.

Berkowitz, L. (1968). Impulse, aggression, and the gun. *Psychology Today, 2*(4), pp. 18–22.

Berkowitz, L. (1972). Social norms, feelings, and other factors affecting helping and altruism. In L. Berkowitz (Ed.), *Advances in experimental social psychology.* (Vol. 6, pp. 63–108). New York: Academic Press.

Berkowitz, L. (1989). Frustration-aggression hypothesis: Examination and reformulation. *Psychological Bulletin, 106,* 59–73.

Berkowitz, L. (1993a). *Aggression: Its causes, consequences, and control.* New York: McGraw-Hill.

Berkowitz, L. (1993b). Pain and aggression: Some findings and implications. *Motivation and Emotion, 17,* 277–293.

Berkowitz, L., & Donnerstein, E. (1982). External validity is more than skin deep: Some answers to criticisms of laboratory experiments. *American Psychologist, 37,* 245–257.

Berkowitz, L., & Heimer, K. (1989). On the construction of the anger experience: Aversive events and negative priming in the frustration of feelings. In L. Berkowitz (Ed.), *Advances in experimental social psychology* (Vol. 22, pp. 1–37). San Diego: Academic Press.

Berkowitz, L., & LePage, A. (1967). Weapons as aggression-eliciting stimuli. *Journal of Personality and Social Psychology, 7,* 202–207.

Berman, M., Gladue, B., & Taylor, S. (1993). The effects of hormones, Type A behavior pattern, and provocation on aggression in men. *Motivation and Emotion, 17,* 125–138.

Bernardin, H. J., & Beatty, R. W. (1984). *Performance appraisal: Assessing human behavior at work.* Boston: Kent.

Berndt, T. J. (1979). Developmental changes in conformity to peers and parents. *Developmental Psychology, 15,* 606–616.

Berry, D. S., & Finch Wero, J. L. (1993). Accuracy in face perception: A view from ecological psychology. *Journal of Personality, 61,* 497–520.

Berry, D. S., & Zebrowitz-McArthur, L. (1986). Perceiving character in faces: The impact of age-related craniofacial changes in social perception. *Psychological Bulletin, 100,* 3–18.

Berry, J. W. (1979). A cultural ecology of social behavior. *Advances in Experimental Social Psychology, 12,* 177–206.

Berry, J. W., Poortinga, Y. H., Segall, M. H., & Dasen, P. R. (1992). *Cross-cultural psychology: Research and application.* Cambridge, UK: Cambridge University Press.

Berscheid, E. (1966). Opinion change and communicator-communicatee similarity and dissimilarity. *Journal of Personality and Social Psychology, 4,* 670–680.

Berscheid, E., Dion, K., Walster, E., & Walster, G. W. (1971). Physical attractiveness and dating choice: A test of the matching hypothesis. *Journal of Experimental Social Psychology, 7,* 173–189.

Berscheid, E., & Meyers, S. A. (1996). A social categorical approach to a question about love. *Personal Relationships, 3,* 19–43.

Berscheid, E., & Peplau, L. A. (1983). The emerging science of relationships. In H. H. Kelley, E. Berscheid, A. Christenson, J. H. Harvey, T. L. Huston, G. Levinger, E. McClintock, L. A. Peplan, & D. R. Peterson, *Close relationships* (pp. 1–19). New York: Freeman.

Berscheid, E., & Reis, H. T. (1998). Attraction and close relationships. In D. Gilbert, S. Fiske, & G. Lindzey (Eds.), *Handbook of social psychology* (4th ed.). New York: McGraw-Hill.

Berscheid, E., Snyder, M., & Omoto, A. M. (1989). The relationship closeness inventory: Assessing the closeness of interpersonal relationships. *Journal of Personality and Social Psychology, 57,* 792–807.

Berscheid, E., & Walster, E. (1974a). A little bit about love. In T. Huston (Ed.), *Foundations of interpersonal attraction* (pp. 355–381). New York: Academic Press.

Berscheid, E., & Walster, E. (1974b). Physical attractiveness. In L. Berkowitz (Ed.), *Advances in experimental social psychology* (Vol. 7, pp. 157–215). New York: Academic Press.

Berscheid, E., Walster, E., & Campbell, R. (1972). *Grow old along with me.* Unpublished manuscript, Department of Psychology, University of Minnesota.

Bersoff, D. N., & Ogden, D. W. (1987). In the Supreme Court of the United States: *Lockhart v. McCree. American Psychologist, 42,* 59–68.

Betancourt, H., & Blair, I. (1992). A cognition (attribution)-emotion model of violence in conflict situations. *Personality and Social Psychology Bulletin, 18,* 343–350.

Bettencourt, B. A., Brewer, M. B., Croak, M. R., & Miller, N. (1992). Cooperation and the reduction of intergroup bias: The role of reward structure and social orientation. *Journal of Experimental Social Psychology, 28,* 301–319.

Bettencourt, B. A., & Miller, N. (1996). Gender differences in aggression as a function of provocation: A meta-analysis. *Psychological Bulletin, 119,* 422–447.

Betzig, L. (1989). Causes of conjugal dissolution: A cross-cultural study. *Current Anthropology, 30,* 654–676.

Beyer, S. (1990). Gender differences in the accuracy of self-evaluations of performance. *Journal of Personality and Social Psychology, 59,* 960–970.

Bickman, L. (1974). The social power of a uniform. *Journal of Applied Social Psychology, 4,* 47–61.

Bierbrauer, G. (1979). Why did he do it? Attributions of obedience and the phenomenon of dispositional bias. *European Journal of Social Psychology, 9,* 67–84.

Bierhoff, H. W., Klein, R., & Kramp, P. (1991). Evidence for the altruistic personality from data on accident research. *Journal of Personality, 59,* 263–280.

Biernat, M., Vescio, T. K., & Manis, M. (1998). Judging and behaving toward members of stereotyped groups. A shifting standards perspective. In C. Sedikides, J. Schopler, & C. A. Insko (Eds.), *Intergroup cognition and intergroup behavior* (pp. 151–175). Mahwah, NJ: Erlbaum.

Binning, J. F., Goldstein, M. A., Garcia, M. F., & Scatteregia, J. H. (1988). Effects of preinterview impressions on questioning strategies in same- and opposite-sex employment interviews. *Journal of Applied Psychology, 73,* 30–37.

Bisanz, G. L., & Rule, B. G. (1989). Gender and the persuasion schema: A search for cognitive invariants. *Personality and Social Psychology Bulletin, 15,* 4–18.

Björkqvist, K., Österman, K., & Kaukiainen, A. (1992). The development of direct and indirect aggressive strategies in males and females. In K. Björkqvist & P. Niemelä (Eds.), *Of mice and women: Aspects of female aggression* (pp. 51–64). San Diego: Academic Press.

Blaine, B., Crocker, J., & Major, B. (1995). The unintended negative consequences of sympathy for the stigmatized. *Journal of Applied Social Psychology, 25,* 889–905.

Blair, S. L., & Johnson, M. P. (1992). Wives' perceptions of the fairness of the division of household labor: The intersection of housework and ideology. *Journal of Marriage and the Family, 54,* 570–581.

Blake, R. R., & Mouton, J. S. (1984). *Solving costly organizational conflicts.* San Francisco: Jossey-Bass.

Blanchard, D. C., & Blanchard, R. J. (1984). Affect and aggression: An animal model applied to human behavior. In R. J. Blanchard & D. C. Blanchard (Eds.), *Advances in the study of aggression* (Vol. 1, pp. 1–62). New York: Academic Press.

Blascovich, J., & Katkin, E. S. (Eds.). (1993). *Cardiovascular reactivity to psychological stress and disease.* Washington, DC: American Psychological Association.

Blascovich, J., Wyer, N. A., Swart, L. A., & Kibler, J. L. (1997). Racism and racial categorization. *Journal of Personality and Social Psychology, 72,* 1364–1372.

Blass, T. (1984). Social psychology and personality: Toward a convergence. *Journal of Personality and Social Psychology, 47,* 1013–1027.

Blass, T. (1991). Understanding behavior in the Milgram obedience experiment: The role of personality, situations, and their interactions. *Journal of Personality and Social Psychology, 60,* 398–413.

Blass, T. (1992). The social psychology of Stanley Milgram. *Advances in Experimental Social Psychology, 25,* 227–329.

Blass, T., & Krackow, A. (1991, June). *The Milgram obedience experiments: Students' views vs. scholarly perspectives and actual findings.* Paper presented at the annual meeting of the American Psychological Society, Washington, DC.

Bless, H., Schwarz, N., & Wieland, R. (1996). Mood and the impact of category membership and individuating information. *European Journal of Social Psychology, 26,* 935–959.

Bobo, L. (1988). Attitudes toward the black political movement: Trends, meaning, and effects of racial policy preferences. *Social Psychology Quarterly, 51,* 287–302.

Bobocel, D. R., & Meyer, J. P. (1994). Escalating commitment to a failing course of action: Separating the roles of choice and justification. *Journal of Applied Psychology, 79,* 360–363.

Bochner, S. (1994). Cross-cultural differences in the self-concept: A test of Hofstede's individualism/collectivism distinction. *Journal of Cross Cultural Psychology, 25,* 273–283.

Bochner, S., & Insko, C. A. (1966). Communicator discrepancy, source credibility, and opinion change. *Journal of Personality and Social Psychology, 4,* 614–621.

Bodenhausen, G. V. (1990). Stereotypes as judgmental heuristics: Evidence of circadian variations in discrimination. *Psychological Science, 1,* 319–322.

Bodenhausen, G. V., & Macrae, C. N. (1998). Stereotype activation and inhibition. In R. S. Wyer, Jr. (Ed.), *Stereotype activation and inhibition: Advances in Social Cognition* (Vol. 11). Mahwah, NJ: Erlbaum.

Boldizar, J. P., Perry, D. G., & Perry, L. (1989). Outcome values and aggression. *Child Development, 60,* 571–579.

Bolger, N., DeLongis, A., Kessler, R. C., & Schilling, E. A. (1989). Effects of daily stress and negative mood. *Journal of Personality and Social Psychology, 57,* 808–818.

Bond, C. F., Jr., & Titus, L. T. (1983). Social facilitation: A meta-analysis of 241 studies. *Psychological Bulletin, 94,* 265–292.

Bond, R., & Smith, P. B. (1996). Culture and conformity: A meta-analysis of studies using Asch's (1952b, 1956) line judgment task. *Psychological Bulletin, 119,* 111–137.

Boninger, D. S., Brock, T. C., Cook, T. D., Gruder, C. L., & Romer, D. (1990). Discovery of reliable attitude change persistence resulting from a transmitter tuning set. *Psychological Science, 1,* 268–271.

Boninger, D. S., Krosnick, J. A., & Berent, M. K. (1995). Origins of attitude importance: Self-interest, social identification, and value relevance. *Journal of Personality and Social Psychology, 68,* 61–80.

Bonta, B. D. (1997). Cooperation and competition in peaceful societies. *Psychological Bulletin, 121,* 299–320.

Borgida, E., & Campbell, B. (1982). Belief relevance and attitude-behavior consistency: The moderating role of personal experience. *Journal of Personality and Social Psychology, 42,* 239–247.

Borman, W. C., Hanson, M. A., & Hedge, J. W. (1997). Personnel selection. *Annual Review of Psychology, 48,* 299–337.

Borman, W. C., White, L. A., & Dorsey, D. W. (1995). Effects of ratee task performance and interpersonal factors on supervisor and peer performance ratings. *Journal of Applied Psychology, 80,* 168–177.

Bornstein, R. F. (1989). Exposure and affect: Overview and meta-analysis of research, 1968–1987. *Psychological Bulletin, 106,* 265–289.

Bornstein, R. F. (1994). Dependency as a social cue: A meta-analytic review of research on the dependency-helping relationship. *Journal of Research in Personality, 28,* 182–213.

Bornstein, R. F., & D'Agostino, P. R. (1992). Stimulus recognition and the mere exposure effect. *Journal of Personality and Social Psychology, 63,* 545–552.

Bornstein, R. F., Krukonis, A. B., Manning, K. A., Mastrosimone, C. C., & Rossner, S. C. (1993). Interpersonal dependency and health service utilization in a college student sample. *Journal of Social and Clinical Psychology, 12,* 262–279.

Bothwell, R. K., Brigham, J. C., & Malpass, R. S. (1989). Cross-racial identification. *Personality and Social Psychology Bulletin, 15,* 19–25.

Bothwell, R. K., Deffenbacher, K. A., & Brigham, J. C. (1987). Correlation of eyewitness accuracy and confidence: Optimality hypothesis revisited. *Journal of Applied Psychology, 72,* 691–695.

Bottoms, B. L., & Davis, S. L. (1997). The creation of satanic ritual abuse. *Journal of Social and Clinical Psychology, 16,* 112–132.

Bouas, K. S., & Komorita, S. S. (1996). Group discussion and cooperation in social dilemmas. *Personality and Social Psychology Bulletin, 22,* 1144–1150.

Bradbury, T. N. (Ed.) (1998). *The developmental course of marital dysfunction.* New York: Cambridge University Press.

Bradbury, T. N., & Fincham, F. D. (1992). Attributions and behavior in marital interaction. *Journal of Personality and Social Psychology, 63,* 613–628.

Brammer, G. L., Raleigh, M. J., & McGuire, M. T. (1994). Neurotransmitters and social status. In L. Ellis (Ed.), *Social stratification and socioeconomic inequality, Vol. 2: Reproductive and interpersonal aspects of dominance and status* (pp. 75–91). Westport, CT: Praeger/Greenwood.

Branscombe, N. R., & Wann, D. L. (1994). Collective self-esteem consequences of outgroup derogation when a valued social identity is on trial. *European Journal of Social Psychology, 24,* 641–657.

Branscombe, N. R., Wann, D. L., Noel, J. G., & Coleman, J. (1993). In-group or out-group extremity: Importance of the threatened social identity. *Personality and Social Psychology Bulletin, 19,* 381–388.

Brauer, M., Judd, C. M., & Gliner, M. D. (1995). The effects of repeated expressions on attitude polarization during group discussions. *Journal of Personality and Social Psychology, 68,* 1014–1029.

Bray, R. M., Johnson, D., & Chilstrom, J. T., Jr. (1982). Social influence by group members with minority opinions: A comparison of Hollander & Moscovici. *Journal of Personality and Social Psychology, 43,* 78–88.

Bray, R. M., Struckman-Johnson, C., Osborne, M., McFarlane, J., & Scott, J. (1978). The effects of defendant status on decisions of student and community juries. *Social Psychology, 41,* 256–260.

Brean, H. (1958, March 31). What hidden sell is all about. *Life,* pp. 104–114.

Breckler, S. J. (1984). Empirical validation of affect, behavior, and cognition as distinct components of attitude. *Journal of Personality and Social Psychology, 47,* 1191–1205.

Brehm, J. W. (1956). Post-decision changes in desirability of alternatives. *Journal of Abnormal and Social Psychology, 52,* 384–389.

Brehm, S. S. (1992). *Intimate relationships* (2nd ed.). New York: McGraw-Hill.

Brehm, S. S., & Brehm, J. W. (1981). *Psychological reactance: A theory of freedom and control.* New York: Academic Press.

Brewer, M. B. (1988). A dual process model of impression formation. In T. K. Srull & R. S. Wyer, Jr. (Eds.), *Advances in social cognition* (Vol. 1, pp. 1–36). Hillsdale, NJ: Erlbaum.

Brewer, M. B. (1991). The social self: On being the same and different at the same time. *Personality and Social Psychology Bulletin, 17,* 475–482.

Brewer, M. B. (1993). Social identity, distinctiveness, and in-group homogeneity. *Social Cognition, 11,* 150–164.

Brewer, M. B. (1995). Managing diversity: The role of social identities. In S. E. Jackson & M. N. Ruderman (Eds.), *Diversity in work teams: Research paradigms for a changing workplace* (pp. 47–68). Washington, DC: American Psychological Association.

Brewer, M. B., & Brown, R. J. (1998). Intergroup relations. In D. T. Gilbert, S. T. Fiske, & G. Lindzey (Eds.), *The handbook of social psychology* (4th ed., Vol. 2, pp. 554–594). New York: McGraw-Hill.

Brewer, M. B., & Miller, N. (1984). Beyond the contact hypothesis: Theoretical perspectives on desegregation. In N. Miller & M. B. Brewer (Eds.), *Groups in contact: The psychology of desegregation* (pp. 281–302). New York: Academic Press.

Briggs, S. R., & Cheek, J. M. (1988). On the nature of self-monitoring: Problems with assessment, problems with validity. *Journal of Personality and Social Psychology, 54,* 663–678.

Brigham, J. C., & Cairns, D. L. (1988). The effect of mugshot inspections on eyewitness identification accuracy. *Journal of Applied Social Psychology, 18,* 1394–1410.

Brigham, J. C., & Malpass, R. S. (1985). The role of experience and contact in the recognition of faces of own- and other-race persons. *Journal of Social Issues, 41,* 139–155.

Brigham, J. C., & Pfeifer, J. E. (1996). Euthanasia: An introduction. *Journal of Social Issues, 52,* 1–11.

Brinthaupt, R. M., Moreland, R. L., & Levine, J. M. (1991). Sources of optimism among prospective group members. *Personality and Social Psychology Bulletin, 17,* 36–43.

Brockner, J. (1983). Low self-esteem and behavioral plasticity: Some implications. In L. Wheeler & P. Shaver (Eds.), *Review of personality and social psychology* (Vol. 4, pp. 237–271). Beverly Hills, CA: Sage.

Brockner, J., & Rubin, J. Z. (1985). *Entrapment in escalating conflicts: A social psychological analysis.* New York: Springer-Verlag.

Brockner, J., & Wiesenfeld, B. M. (1996). An integrative framework for explaining reactions to decisions: Interactive effects of outcomes and procedures. *Psychological Bulletin, 120,* 189–208.

Brodkey, H. (1993, July 5). The central face. *The New Yorker,* p. 31.

Bronfenbrenner, U. (1961). The mirror-image in Soviet-American relations. *Journal of Social Issues, 17,* 45–56.

Brown, B. B., Clasen, D. R., & Eicher, S. A. (1986). Perceptions of peer pressure, peer conformity dispositions, and self-reported behavior among adolescents. *Developmental Psychology, 22,* 521–530.

Brown, E., Deffenbacher, K., & Sturgill, W. (1977). Memory for faces and the circumstances of encounter. *Journal of Applied Psychology, 62,* 311–318.

Brown, G. W., & Harris, T. (1978). *Social origins of depression: A study of psychiatric disorder in women.* New York: Free Press.

Brown, J. D. (1991). Staying fit and staying well: Physical fitness as a moderator of life stress. *Journal of Personality and Social Psychology, 60,* 555–561.

Brown, J. D., & Dutton, K. A. (1995). The thrill of victory, the complexity of defeat: Self-esteem and people's emotional reactions to success and failure. *Journal of Personality and Social Psychology, 68,* 712–722.

Brown, J. D., Novick, N. J., Lord, K. A., & Richards, J. M. (1992). When Gulliver travels: Social context, psychological closeness, and self-appraisals. *Journal of Personality and Social Psychology, 62,* 717–727.

Brown, J. D., & Smart, S. A. (1991). The self and social conduct: Linking self-representations to prosocial behavior. *Journal of Personality and Social Psychology, 60,* 368–375.

Brown, R. (1965). *Social psychology.* New York: Free Press.

Brown, R. (1986). *Social psychology* (2nd ed.). New York: Free Press.

Brown, R., & Kulik, J. (1977). Flashbulb memories. *Cognition, 5,* 73–99.

Brown, V., & Paulus, P. B. (1996). A simple dynamic model of social factors in group brainstorming. *Small Group Research, 27,* 91–114.

Brown, W. A. (1998, January). The placebo effect. *Scientific American,* pp. 90–95.

Browne, A. (1993). Violence against women by male partners: prevalence, outcomes, and policy implications. *American Psychologist, 48,* 1077–1087.

Brownell, K. D., & Fairburn, C. G. (Eds.) (1995). *Eating disorders and obesity: A comprehensive handbook.* New York: Guilford Press.

Bruch, M. A., Gorsky, J. M., Collins, T. M., & Berger, P. A. (1989). Shyness and sociability examined: A multicomponent analysis. *Journal of Personality and Social Psychology, 57,* 904–915.

Bruck, M., Ceci, S. J., Francoeur, E., & Barr, R. (1995). "I hardly cried when I got my shot!" Influencing children's reports about a visit to their pediatrician. *Child Development, 66,* 193–208.

Bruner, J. S., & Potter, M. C. (1964). Interference in visual recognition. *Science, 144,* 424–425.

Bruner, J. S., & Tagiuri, R. (1954). Person perception. In G. Lindzey (Ed.), *Handbook of social psychology* (Vol. 2, pp. 634–654). Reading, MA: Addison-Wesley.

Bryan, J. H., & Test, M. A. (1967). Models and helping: Naturalistic studies in aiding behavior. *Journal of Personality and Social Psychology, 6,* 400–407.

Bryson, J. B. (1991). Modes of response to jealousy-evoking situations. In P. Salovey (Ed.), *The psychology of jealousy and envy* (pp. 178–207). New York: Guilford.

Buckhout, R. (1974, December). Eyewitness testimony. *Scientific American,* pp. 23–31.

Buehler, R., & Griffin, D. (1994). Change-of-meaning effects in conformity and dissent: Observing construal processes over time. *Journal of Personality and Social Psychology, 67,* 984–996.

Bulatao, E. Q., & VandenBos, G. R. (1996). Workplace violence: Its scope and the issues. In G. R. VandenBos & E. Q. Bulatao (Eds.), *Violence on the job: Identifying risks and developing solutions* (pp. 1–23). Washington, DC: American Psychological Association.

Bull, R., & Rumsey, N. (1988). *The social psychology of facial appearance.* New York: Springer-Verlag.

Burger, J. M. (1986). Increasing compliance by improving the deal: The that's-not-all technique. *Journal of Personality and Social Psychology, 51,* 277–283.

Burger, J. M. (1991). Changes in attributions over time: The ephemeral fundamental attribution error. *Social Cognition, 9,* 182–193.

Burger, J. M., Brown, R., & Allen, C. K. (1983). Negative reactions to personal control. *Journal of Social and Clinical Psychology, 1,* 322–342.

Burger, J. M., Horita, M., Kinoshita, L., Roberts, K., & Vera, C. (1997). Effects of time on the norm of reciprocity. *Basic and Applied Social Psychology, 19,* 91–100.

Burger, J. M., & Petty, R. E. (1981). The low-ball compliance technique: Task or person commitment? *Journal of Personality and Social Psychology, 40,* 492–500.

Burke, A., Heuer, F., & Reisberg, D. (1992). Remembering emotional events. *Memory and Cognition, 20,* 277–290.

Burman, B., & Margolin, G. (1992). An analysis of the association between marital relationships and health problems: An interactional perspective. *Psychological Bulletin, 112,* 39–63.

Burnkrant, R. E., & Howard, D. J. (1984). Effects of the use of introductory rhetorical questions versus statements on information processing. *Journal of Personality and Social Psychology, 47,* 1218–1230.

Burns, J. M. (1978). *Leadership.* New York: Harper & Row.

Burnstein, E., Crandall, C., & Kitayama, S. (1994). Some neo-Darwinian decision rules for altruism: Weighing cues for inclusive fitness as a function of the biological importance of the decision. *Journal of Personality and Social Psychology, 67,* 773–789.

Burnstein, E., & Schul, Y. (1982). The informational basis of social judgments: The operations in forming an impression of another person. *Journal of Experimental Social Psychology, 18,* 217–234.

Burt, M. C. (1980). Cultural myths and supports for rape. *Journal of Personality and Social Psychology, 38,* 217–230.

Bushman, B. J. (1984). Perceived symbols of authority and their influence on compliance. *Journal of Applied Social Psychology, 14,* 501–508.

Bushman, B. J. (1988). The effects of apparel on compliance: A field experiment with a female authority figure. *Personality and Social Psychology Bulletin, 14,* 459–467.

Bushman, B. J. (1995). Moderating role of trait aggressiveness in the effects of violent media on aggression. *Journal of Personality and Social Psychology, 69,* 950–960.

Bushman, B. J. (1996). Individual differences in the extent and development of aggressive cognitive-associative networks. *Personality and Social Psychology Bulletin, 22,* 811–819.

Bushman, B. J., & Cooper, H. M. (1990). Effects of alcohol on human aggression: An integrative research review. *Psychological Bulletin, 107,* 341–354.

Bushman, B. J., & Stack, A. D. (1996). Forbidden fruit versus tainted fruit: Effects of warning labels on attraction to television violence. *Journal of Experimental Psychology: Applied, 2,* 207–226.

Buss, A. H. (1980). *Self-consciousness and social anxiety.* San Francisco: Freeman.

Buss, D. M. (1989). Sex differences in human mate preferences: Evolutionary hypotheses tested in 37 cultures. *Behavioral and Brain Sciences, 12,* 1–14.

Buss, D. M. (1994). *The evolution of desire: Strategies of human mating.* New York: Basic Books.

Buss, D. M. (1995). Evolutionary psychology: A new paradigm for psychological science. *Psychological Inquiry, 6,* 1–30.

Buss, D. M., Gomes, M., Higgins, D. S., & Lauterbach, K. (1987). Tactics of manipulation. *Journal of Personality and Social Psychology, 52,* 1219–1229.

Buss, D. M., & Kenrick, D. T. (1998). Evolutionary social psychology. In D. T. Gilbert, S. T. Fiske, & G. Lindzey (Eds.), *The handbook of social psychology* (4th ed., Vol. 2, pp. 982–1026). New York: McGraw-Hill.

Buss, D. M., Larsen, R. J., Westen, D., & Semmelroth, J. (1992). Sex differences in jealousy: Evolution, physiology, and psychology. *Psychological Science, 3,* 251–255.

Buss, D. M., & Malamuth, N. M. (Eds.) (1996). *Sex, power, conflict: Evolutionary and feminist perspectives.* New York: Oxford University.

Buss, D. M., & Schmitt, D. P. (1993). Sexual strategies theory: An evolutionary perspective on human mating. *Psychological Review, 100,* 204–232.

Buss, D. M., & Shackelford, T. K. (1997). From vigilance to violence: Mate retention tactics in married couples. *Journal of Personality and Social Psychology, 72,* 346–361.

Butler, D., & Geis, F. L. (1990). Nonverbal affect responses to male and female leaders: Implications for leadership evaluations. *Journal of Personality and Social Psychology, 58,* 48–59.

Buunk, B. P. (1991). Jealousy in close relationships: An exchange-theoretical perspective. In P. Salovey (Ed.), *The psychology of jealousy and envy* (pp. 148–177). New York: Guilford.

Buunk, B. P., Angleitner, A., Oubaid, V., & Buss, D. M. (1996). Sex differences in jealousy in evolutionary and cultural perspective: Tests from the Netherlands, Germany, and the United States. *Psychological Science, 7,* 359–363.

Buunk, B., & Hupka, R. B. (1987). Cross-cultural differences in the elicitation of sexual jealousy. *Journal of Sex Research, 23,* 12–22.

Bylsma, W. H., Major, B., & Cozzarelli, C. (1995). The influence of legitimacy appraisals on the determinants of entitlement beliefs. *Basic and Applied Social Psychology, 17,* 223–237.

Byrne, D. (1971). *The attraction paradigm.* New York: Academic Press.

Byrne, D. (1997). An overview (and underview) of research and theory within the attraction paradigm. *Journal of Social and Personal Relationships, 14,* 417–431.

Byrne, D., & Clore, G. L. (1970). A reinforcement model of evaluative processes. *Personality: An International Journal, 1,* 103–128.

Byrne, D., Clore, G. L., & Smeaton, G. (1986). The attraction hypothesis: Do similar attitudes affect anything? *Journal of Personality and Social Psychology, 51,* 1167–1170.

Cacioppo, J. T., Crites, S. L., Berntson, G. G., & Coles, M. G. H. (1993). If attitudes affect how stimuli are processed, should they not affect the event-related brain potential? *Psychological Science, 4,* 108–112.

Cacioppo, J. T., Gardner, W. L., & Bernston, G. G. (1997). Beyond bipolar conceptualizations and measures: The case of attitudes and evaluative space. *Personality and Social Psychology Review, 1,* 3–25.

Cacioppo, J. T., & Petty, R. E. (1981). Electromyograms as measures of extent and affectivity of information processing. *American Psychologist, 36,* 441–456.

Cacioppo, J. T., & Petty, R. E. (1982). The need for cognition. *Journal of Personality and Social Psychology, 42,* 116–131.

Cacioppo, J. T., Petty, R. E., Feinstein, J. A., & Jarvis, W. B. G. (1996). Dispositional differences in cognitive motivation: The life and times of individuals varying in need for cognition. *Psychological Bulletin, 119,* 197–253.

Cacioppo, J. T., Petty, R. E., Losch, M. E., & Kim, H. S. (1986). Electromyographic activity over facial muscle regions can differentiate the valence and intensity of affective reactions. *Journal of Personality and Social Psychology, 50,* 260–268.

Cacioppo, J. T., Petty, R. E., & Morris, K. (1983). Effects of need for cognition on message evaluation, recall, and persuasion. *Journal of Personality and Social Psychology, 45,* 805–818.

Cacioppo, J. T., Priester, J. R., & Bernston, G. G. (1993). Rudimentary determinants of attitudes. II. Arm flexion and extension have differential effects on attitudes. *Journal of Personality and Social Psychology, 65,* 5–17.

Cadenhead, A. C., & Richman, C. L. (1996). The effects of interpersonal trust and group status on prosocial and aggressive behaviors. *Social Behavior and Personality, 24,* 169–184.

Cahn, D. D. (1992). *Conflict in intimate relationships.* New York: Guilford.

Callaway, M. R., Marriott, R. G., & Esser, J. K. (1985). Effects of dominance on group decision making: Toward a stress-reduction explanation of groupthink. *Journal of Personality and Social Psychology, 49,* 949–952.

Camacho, L. M., & Paulus, P. B. (1995). The role of social anxiousness in group brainstorming. *Journal of Personality and Social Psychology, 68,* 1071–1080.

Camara, W. J., & Schneider, D. L. (1994). Integrity tests: Facts and unresolved issues. *American Psychologist, 49,* 112–119.

Cameron, J., & Pierce, W. D. (1994). Reinforcement, reward, and intrinsic motivation: A meta-analysis. *Review of Educational Research, 64,* 363–423.

Campbell, D. J., & Lee, C. (1988). Self-appraisal in performance evaluation: Development versus evaluation. *Academy Management Review, 13,* 302–313.

Campbell, J. D., & Fairey, P. J. (1989). Informational and normative routes to conformity. *Journal of Personality and Social Psychology, 57,* 457–468.

Campion, M. A., Campion, J. E., & Hudson, J. P. (1994). Structured interviewing: A note on incremental validity and alternative question types. *Journal of Applied Psychology, 79,* 998–1002.

Campion, M. A., Pursell, E. D., & Brown, B. K. (1988). Structured interviewing: Raising the psychometric properties of the employment interview. *Personnel Psychology, 41,* 25–42.

Carey, B. (1997, April). Don't face stress alone. *Health,* pp. 74–76, 78.

Carey, G. (1994). Genetics and violence. In A. J. Reiss, K. A. Miczek, & J. A. Roth (Eds.), *Understanding and preventing violence: Vol. 2. Biobehavioral influences* (pp. 21–57). Washington, DC: National Academy Press.

Carlo, G., Eisenberg, N., Troyer, D., Switzer, G., & Speer, A. L. (1991). The altruistic personality: In what contexts is it apparent? *Journal of Personality and Social Psychology, 61,* 450–458.

Carlo, G., Koller, S. H., Eisenberg, N., Da Silva, M. S., & Frohlich, C. B. (1996). A cross-national study on the relations among prosocial moral reasoning, gender role orientations, and prosocial behaviors. *Developmental Psychology, 32,* 231–240.

Carlson, M., Charlin, V., & Miller, N. (1988). Positive mood and helping behavior: A test of six hypotheses. *Journal of Personality and Social Psychology, 55,* 211–229.

Carlson, M., & Miller, N. (1987). Explanation of the relation between negative mood and helping. *Psychological Bulletin, 102,* 91–108.

Carnegie, D. (1936). *How to win friends and influence people.* New York: Pocket Books. (Reprinted in 1972)

Carnevale, P. J. (1985). Mediation of international conflict. *Applied Social Psychology Annual, 6,* 87–105.

Carroll, J. M., & Russell, J. A. (1996). Do facial expressions signal specific emotions? Judging emotion from the face in context. *Journal of Personality and Social Psychology, 70,* 205–218.

Carroll, J. S., Perkowitz, W. T., Lurigio, A. J., & Weaver, F. M. (1987). Sentencing goals, causal attributions, ideology, and personality. *Journal of Personality and Social Psychology, 52,* 107–118.

Carter, S. L. (1991). *Reflections of an affirmative action baby.* New York: Basic Books.

Cartwright, D. (1971). Risk taking by individuals and groups: An assessment of research employing choice dilemmas. *Journal of Personality and Social Psychology, 20,* 245–261.

Cartwright, D. (1979). Contemporary social psychology in historical perspective. *Social Psychology Quarterly, 42,* 82–93.

Cartwright, D., & Zander, A. (1960). Group cohesiveness: Introduction. In D. Cartwright & A. Zander (Eds.), *Group dynamics: Research and theory* (2nd ed., pp. 69–94). Evanston, IL: Row, Peterson.

Carver, C. S., Pozo, C., Harris, S. D., Noriega, V., Scheier, M. F., Robinson, D. S., Ketcham, A. S., Moffet, Jr., F. L., & Clark, K. C. (1993). How coping mediates the effect of optimism on distress: A study of women with early stage breast cancer. *Journal of Personality and Social Psychology, 65,* 375–390.

Carver, C. S., & Scheier, M. F. (1981). *Attention and self-regulation: A control-theory approach to human behavior.* New York: Springer-Verlag.

Carver, C. S., & Scheier, M. F. (1990). Origins and functions of positive and negative affect: A control-process view. *Psychological Review, 97,* 19–35.

Carver, C. S., Scheier, M. F., & Weintraub, J. K. (1989). Assessing coping strategies: A theoretically based approach. *Journal of Personality and Social Psychology, 56,* 267–283.

Case, R. B., Moss, A. J., Case, N., McDermott, M., & Eberly, S. (1992). Living alone after myocardial infarction: Impact on prognosis. *Journal of the American Medical Association, 267,* 515–519.

Cassidy, J., Kirsh, S. J., Scolton, K. L., & Parke, R. D. (1996). Attachment and representations of peer relationships. *Developmental Psychology, 32,* 892–904.

Cate, R. M., & Lloyd, S. A. (1988). Courtship. In S. Duck (Ed.), *Handbook of personal relationships: Theory, research, and interventions* (pp. 409–427). New York: Wiley.

Cate, R. M., & Lloyd, S. A. (1992). *Courtship.* Newbury Park, CA: Sage.

Cavaliere, F. (1995, August). Parents killing kids: A nation's shame. *American Psychological Association Monitor,* p. 34.

Ceci, S. J., Peters, D., & Plotkin, J. (1985). Human subjects review, personal values, and the regulation of social science research. *American Psychologist, 40,* 994–1002.

Ceci, S. J., Ross, D. F., & Toglia, M. P. (1987). Suggestibility of children's memory: Psycholegal implications. *Journal of Experimental Psychology, 116,* 38–49.

Centers for Disease Control Vietnam Experience Study. (1988). Health status of Vietnam veterans: I. Psychosocial characteristics. *Journal of the American Medical Association, 259,* 2701–2707.

Chacko, T. I. (1982). Women and equal employment opportunity: Some unintended effects. *Journal of Applied Psychology, 67,* 119–123.

Chaiken, S. (1979). Communicator physical attractiveness and persuasion. *Journal of Personality and Social Psychology, 37,* 1387–1397.

Chaiken, S. (1980). Heuristic versus systematic information processing and the use of source versus message cues in persuasion. *Journal of Personality and Social Psychology, 39,* 752–766.

Chaiken, S. (1987). The heuristic model of persuasion. In M. P. Zanna, J. M. Olson, & C. P. Herman (Eds.), *Social influence: The Ontario symposium* (Vol. 5, pp. 3–39). Hillsdale, NJ: Erlbaum.

Chaiken, S., & Baldwin, M. W. (1981). Affective-cognitive consistency and the effect of salient behavioral information on the self-perception of attitudes. *Journal of Personality and Social Psychology, 41,* 1–12.

Chaiken, S., & Maheswaran, D. (1994). Heuristic processing can bias systematic processing: Effects of source credibility, argument ambiguity, and task importance on attitude judgment. *Journal of Personality and Social Psychology, 66,* 460–473.

Chaiken, S., Liberman, A., & Eagly, A. (1989). Heuristic and systematic information processing within and beyond the persuasion context. In J. Uleman and J. A. Bargh (Eds.), *Unintended thought* (pp. 212–252). New York: Guilford.

Chan, D. K., & Fishbein, M. (1993) Determinants of college women's intentions to tell their partners to use condoms. *Journal of Applied Social Psychology, 23,* 1455–1470.

Chandrashekaran, M., Walker, B. A., Ward, J. C., & Reingen, P. H. (1996). Modeling individual preference evolution and choice in a dynamic group setting. *Journal of Marketing Research, 33,* 211–223.

Chapdelaine, A., & Griffin, S. F. (1997). Beliefs of guilt and recommended sentence as a function of juror bias in the O. J. Simpson trial. *Journal of Social Issues, 53,* 477–485.

Chapdelaine, A., Kenny, D. A., & LaFontana, K. M. (1994). Matchmaker, matchmaker, can you make me a match? Predicting liking between two unacquainted persons. *Journal of Personality and Social Psychology, 67,* 83–91.

Chapman, L. J. (1967). Illusory correlation in observational report. *Journal of Verbal Learning and Verbal Behavior, 6,* 151–155.

Chassin, L., Presson, C. C., & Sherman, S. J. (1990). Social psychological contributions to the understanding and prevention of adolescent cigarette smoking. *Personality and Social Psychology Bulletin, 16,* 133–151.

Check, J. V. P., & Guloien, T. H. (1989). Reported proclivity for coercive sex following repeated exposure to sexually violent pornography, nonviolent dehumanizing pornography, and erotica. In D. Zillmann & J. Bryant (Eds.), *Pornography: Research advances and policy considerations* (pp. 159–184). Hillsdale, NJ: Erlbaum.

Cheek, J. M., & Melchior, L. A. (1990). Shyness, self-esteem, and self-consciousness. In H. Leitenberg (Ed.), *Handbook of social and evaluation anxiety.* New York: Plenum.

Chemers, M. M., Hays, R. B., Rhodewalt, F., & Wysocki, J. (1985). A person-environment analysis of job stress: A contingency model explanation. *Journal of Personality and Social Psychology, 49,* 628–635.

Chemers, M. M., Oskamp, S., & Costanzo, M. A. (Eds.) (1995). *Diversity in organizations: New perspectives for a changing workplace.* Thousand Oaks, CA: Sage.

Chen, M., & Bargh, J. A. (1997). Nonconscious behavioral confirmation processes: The self-fulfilling consequences of automatic stereotype activation. *Journal of Experimental Social Psychology, 33,* 541–560.

Chen, Z., Lawson, R. B., Gordon, L. R., & McIntosh, B. (1996). Groupthink: Deciding with the leader and the devil. *Psychological Record, 46,* 581–590.

Cheng, P. W., & Novick, L. R. (1990). A probabilistic contrast model of causal induction. *Journal of Personality and Social Psychology, 58,* 545–567.

Cherlin, A. J. (1992). *Marriage, divorce, remarriage* (2nd ed.). Cambridge, MA: Harvard University Press.

Chesler, P., & Goodman, E. J. (1976). *Women, money, and power.* New York: Morrow.

Cheuk, W. H., & Rosen, S. (1996). The moderating influence of perceived importance on rejected helpers' reactions. *Basic and Applied Social Psychology, 18,* 195–210.

Christensen, A., & Heavey, C. L. (1993). Gender differences in marital conflict: The demand/withdraw interaction pattern. In S. Oskamp & M. Costanzo (Eds.), *Gender issues in contemporary society* (pp. 113–141). Newbury Park, CA: Sage.

Christensen, A. J., Turner, C. W., Smith, T. W., Holman, J. M., Jr., & Gregory, M. C. (1991). Health locus of control and depression in end-stage renal disease. *Journal of Counseling and Clinical Psychology, 59,* 419–424.

Christensen, L. (1988). Deception in psychological research: When is its use justified? *Personality and Social Psychology Bulletin, 14,* 664–675.

Christianson, S. (1992). Emotional stress and eyewitness memory: A critical review. *Psychological Bulletin, 112,* 284–309.

Christopher, F. S., Owens, L. A., & Stecker, H. L. (1993). Exploring the dark side of courtship: A test of a model of male premarital sexual aggressiveness. *Journal of Marriage and the Family, 55,* 469–479.

Cialdini, R. B. (1993). *Influence: Science and practice* (3rd ed.). Glenview, IL: Scott, Foresman.

Cialdini, R. B., & Ascani, K. (1976). Test of a concession procedure for inducing verbal, behavioral, and further compliance with a request to give blood. *Journal of Applied Psychology, 61,* 295–300.

Cialdini, R. B., Baumann, D. J., & Kenrick, D. T. (1981). Insights from sadness: A three-step model of the development of altruism as hedonism. *Developmental Review, 1,* 207–223.

Cialdini, R. B., Borden, R. J., Thorne, A., Walker, M. R., Freeman, S., & Sloan, L. R. (1976). Basking in reflected glory: Three (football) field studies. *Journal of Personality and Social Psychology, 34,* 366–375.

Cialdini, R. B., Brown, S. L., Lewis, B. P., Luce, C., & Neuberg, S. L. (1997). Reinterpreting the empathy-altruism relationship: When one into one equals oneness. *Journal of Personality and Social Psychology, 73,* 481–494.

Cialdini, R. B., Cacioppo, J. T., Bassett, R., & Miller, J. A. (1978). Low-ball procedure for producing compliance: Commitment then cost. *Journal of Personality and Social Psychology, 36,* 463–476.

Cialdini, R. B., & De Nicholas, M. E. (1989). Self-presentation by association. *Journal of Personality and Social Psychology, 57,* 626–631.

Cialdini, R. B., & Fultz, J. (1990). Interpreting the negative mood-helping literature via "mega" analysis: A contrary view. *Psychological Bulletin, 107,* 210–214.

Cialdini, R. B., Kallgren, C. A., & Reno, R. R. (1991). A focus theory of normative conduct: A theoretical refinement and reevaluation of the role of norms in human behavior. *Advances in Experimental Social Psychology, 24,* 201–234.

Cialdini, R. B., Reno, R. R., & Kallgren, C. A. (1990). A focus theory of normative conduct: Recycling the concept of norms to reduce littering in public places. *Journal of Personality and Social Psychology, 58,* 1015–1026.

Cialdini, R. B., Schaller, M., Houlihan, D., Arps, K., Fultz, J., & Beaman, A. L. (1987). Empathy-based helping: Is it selflessly or selfishly motivated? *Journal of Personality and Social Psychology, 52,* 749–758.

Cialdini, R. B., & Trost, M. R. (1998). Influence, social norms, conformity, and compliance. In D. T. Gilbert, S. T. Fiske, & G. Lindzey (Eds.), *The handbook of social psychology* (4th ed.). New York: Oxford University Press.

Cialdini, R. B., Trost, M. R., & Newsom, J. T. (1995). Preference for consistency: The development of a valid measure and the discovery of surprising behavioral implications. *Journal of Personality and Social Psychology, 69,* 318–328.

Cialdini, R. B., Vincent, J. E., Lewis, S. K., Catalan, J., Wheeler, D., & Darby, B. L. (1975). Reciprocal concessions procedure for inducing compliance: The door-in-the-face technique. *Journal of Personality and Social Psychology, 31,* 206–215.

Cini, M. A., Moreland, R. L., & Levine, J. M. (1993). Group staffing levels and responses to prospective and new group members. *Journal of Personality and Social Psychology, 65,* 723–734.

Cioffi, D., & Holloway, J. (1993). Delayed costs of suppressed pain. *Journal of Personality and Social Psychology, 64,* 274–282.

Clark, L. F. (1993). Stress and the cognitive-conversational benefits of social interaction. *Journal of Social and Clinical Psychology, 12,* 25–55.

Clark, M. S. (1983). Reactions to aid in communal and exchange relationships. In J. D. Fisher, A. Nadler, & B. DePaulo (Eds.), *New directions in helping: Vol. 1. Recipient reactions to aid* (pp. 281–304). New York: Academic Press.

Clark, M. S. (1984). Record keeping in two types of relationships. *Journal of Personality and Social Psychology, 47,* 549–557.

Clark, M. S., & Mills, J. (1979). Interpersonal attraction in exchange and communal relationships. *Journal of Personality and Social Psychology, 37,* 12–24.

Clark, M. S., & Mills, J. (1993). The difference between communal and exchange relationships: What it is and is not. *Personality and Social Psychology Bulletin, 19,* 684–691.

Clark, R. D., III, & Maass, A. (1990). The effects of majority size on minority influence: *European Journal of Psychology, 20,* 99–117.

Clark, R. D., III, & Word, L. E. (1972). Why don't bystanders help? Because of ambiguity? *Journal of Personality and Social Psychology, 24,* 392–400.

Clary, E. G., & Orenstein, L. (1991). The amount and effectiveness of help: The relationship of motives and abilities to helping behavior. *Personality and Social Psychology Bulletin, 17,* 58–64.

Clayton, S. (1996). Reactions to social categorization: Evaluating one argument against affirmative action. *Journal of Applied Social Psychology, 26,* 1472–1493.

Cleare, A. J., & Bond, A. J. (1997). Does central serotonergic function correlate inversely with aggression? A study using d-fenfluramine in healthy subjects. *Psychiatry Research, 69,* 89–95.

Clifford, M. M., & Walster, E. H. (1973). The effect of physical attractiveness on teacher expectations. *Sociology of Education, 46,* 248–258.

Coates, D., Renzaglia, G. J., & Embree, M. C. (1983). When helping backfires: Help and helplessness. In J. D. Fisher, A. Nadler, & B. DePaulo (Eds.), *New directions in helping: Vol. 1. Recipient reactions to aid* (pp. 251–279). New York: Academic Press.

Cochran, S. D., Mays, V. M., Ciarletta, J., Caruso, C., & Mallon, D. (1992). Efficacy of the theory of reasoned action in predicting AIDS-related sexual risk reduction among gay men. *Journal of Applied Social Psychology, 22,* 1481–1501.

Coe, C. L. (1993). Psychosocial factors and immunity in nonhuman primates: A review. *Psychosomatic Medicine, 55,* 298–308.

Cohen, D., & Nisbett, R. E. (1997). Field experiments examining the culture of honor: The role of institutions in perpetuating norms about violence. *Personality and Social Psychology Bulletin, 23,* 1188–1199.

Cohen, D., Nisbett, R. E., Bowdle, B. F., & Schwarz, N. (1996). Insult, aggression, and the southern culture of honor: An "experimental ethnography." *Journal of Personality and Social Psychology, 70,* 945–960.

Cohen, D., Vandello, J., & Rantilla, A. K. (1998). The sacred and the social: Honor and violence in cultural context. In P. Gilbert & B. Andrews (Eds.), *Shame: Interpersonal behavior, psychopathology, and culture.* Cambridge: Oxford University Press.

Cohen, E. G. (1984). The desegregated school: Problems in status power and interethnic climate. In N. Miller, & M. B. Brewer (Eds.), *Groups in contact: The psychology of desegregation* (pp. 77–96). New York: Academic Press.

Cohen, S., & Herbert, T. (1996). Health psychology: Psychological factors and physical disease from the perspective of human psychoneuroimmunology. *Annual Review of Psychology, 47,* 113–142.

Cohen, S., Kessler, R. C., & Gordon, L. U. (1995). *Measuring stress: A guide for health and social scientists.* New York: Oxford University Press.

Cohen, S., Tyrrell, D. A. J., & Smith, A. P. (1993). Negative life events, perceived stress, negative affect, and susceptibility to the common cold. *Journal of Personality and Social Psychology, 64,* 131–140.

Cohen, S., & Williamson, G. (1991). Stress and infectious disease in humans. *Psychological Bulletin, 109,* 5–24.

Cohen-Ketteinis, P. T., & van Goozen, S. H. M. (1997). Sex reassignment of adolescent transsexuals: A follow-up study. *Journal of the American Academy of Child and Adolescent Psychiatry, 36,* 263–271.

Cohn, E. G., & Rotton, J. (1997). Assault as a function of time and temperature: A moderator-variable time-series analysis. *Journal of Personality and Social Psychology, 72,* 1322–1334.

Coie, J. D., & Dodge, K. A. (1997). Aggression and antisocial behavior. In W. Damon & N. Eisenberg (Eds.), *Handbook of child psychology* (Vol. 3). New York: Wiley.

Cole, S. W., Kemeny, M. E., Taylor, S. E., Visscher, B. R., & Fahey, J. L. (1996). Accelerated course of human immunodeficiency virus infection in gay men who conceal their homosexual identity. *Psychosomatic Medicine, 58,* 219–231.

Collins, N. L., & Miller, L. C. (1994). Self-disclosure and liking: a meta-analytic review. *Psychological Bulletin, 116,* 457–475.

Collins, R. L. (1996). For better or worse: The impact of upward social comparison on self-evaluations. *Psychological Bulletin, 119,* 51–69.

Collins-Standley, T., Gan, S., Yu, H., & Zillmann, D. (1996). Choice of romantic, violent, and scary fairy-tale books by preschool girls and boys. *Child Study Journal, 26,* 279–302.

Colvin, C. R., & Block, J. (1994). Do positive illusions foster mental health? An examination of the Taylor and Brown formulation. *Psychological Bulletin, 116,* 3–20.

Colvin, C. R., Block, J., & Funder, D. C. (1995). Overly positive self-evaluations and personality: Negative implications for mental health. *Journal of Personality and Social Psychology, 68,* 1152–1162.

Commission on Violence and Youth. (1993). *Violence and youth: Psychology's response* (Vol. I). Washington, DC: American Psychological Association.

Condry, J., & Condry, S. (1976). Sex differences: A study of the eye of the beholder. *Child Development, 47,* 812–819.

Connors, E., Lundregan, T., Miller, N., & McEwen, T. (1996). *Convicted by juries, exonerated by science: Case studies in the use of DNA evidence to establish innocence after trial.* Washington, DC: U.S. Department of Justice.

Conway, J. M., & Huffcut, A. I. (1997). Psychometric properties of multisource performance ratings: A meta-analysis of subordinate, supervisor, peer, and self-ratings. *Human Performance, 10,* 331–360.

Conway, M. (1995). *Flashbulb memories.* Mahwah, NJ: Erlbaum.

Cook, S. W. (1984). The 1954 social science statement and school desegregation: A reply to Gerard. *American Psychologist, 39,* 819–832.

Cook, S. W. (1985). Experimenting on social issues: The case of school desegregation. *American Psychologist, 40,* 452–460.

Cook, S. W., & Pelfrey, M. (1985). Reactions to being helped in cooperating interracial groups: A context effect. *Journal of Personality and Social Psychology, 49,* 1231–1245.

Cook, T. D., & Campbell, D. T. (1979). *Quasi-experimentation: Design and analysis issues for field settings.* Chicago: Rand McNally.

Cooley, C. H. (1902). *Human nature and the social order.* New York: Schocken Books. (Reprinted in 1964)

Coombs, C. H. (1987). The structure of conflict. *American Psychologist, 42,* 355–363.

Cooper, H., & Good, T. (1983). *Pygmalion grows up: Studies in the expectation communication process.* New York: Longman.

Cooper, J., & Fazio, R. H. (1984). A new look at dissonance theory. In L. Berkowitz (Ed.), *Advances in experimental social psychology* (Vol. 17, pp. 229–267). New York: Academic Press.

Cooper, J., Zanna, M. P., & Goethals, G. R. (1974). Mistreatment of an esteemed other as a consequence affecting dissonance reduction. *Journal of Experimental Social Psychology, 10,* 224–233.

Cooper, M. L., Frone, M. R., Russell, M., & Mudar, P. (1995). Drinking to regulate positive and negative emotions: A motivational model of alcohol use. *Journal of Personality and Social Psychology, 69,* 990–1005.

Cooper, W. H. (1981). Ubiquitous halo. *Psychological Bulletin, 90,* 218–224.

Coopersmith, S. (1967). *The antecedents of self-esteem.* San Francisco: Freeman.

Coovert, M. D., & Reeder, G. D. (1990). Negativity effects in impression formation: The role of unit formation and schematic expectations. *Journal of Experimental Social Psychology, 26,* 49–62.

Copeland, J. T. (1994). Prophecies of power: Motivational implications of social power for behavioral confirmation. *Journal of Personality and Social Psychology, 67,* 264–277.

Cordes, C. L., & Dougherty, T. W. (1993). A review and integration of research on job burnout. *Academy of Management Review, 18,* 621–656.

Cose, E. (1997). *Color-blind: Seeing beyond race in a race-obsessed world.* New York: HarperCollins.

Costa, R. M. (1982, March 6). Latin and Greek are good for you. *New York Times,* p. 23.

Costanzo, M. (1997). *Just revenge: Costs and consequences of the death penalty.* New York: St. Martin's Press.

Costello, C. G. (1982). Social factors associated with depression: A retrospective community study. *Psychological Medicine, 12,* 329–339.

Cota, A. A., Evans, C. R., Dion, K. L., Kilik, L., & Longman, R. S. (1995). The structure of group cohesion. *Personality and Social Psychology Bulletin, 21,* 572–580.

Cottrell, N. B. (1968). Performance in the presence of other human beings: Mere presence, audience, and affiliation effects. In E. C. Simmel, R. A. Hoppe, & G. A. Milton (Eds.), *Social facilitation and imitative behavior* (pp. 91–110). Boston: Allyn & Bacon.

Cottrell, N. B., Wack, D. L., Sekerak, G. J., & Rittle, R. H. (1968). Social facilitation of dominant responses by the presence of an audience and the mere presence of others. *Journal of Personality and Social Psychology, 9,* 245–250.

Cousins, N. (1989). *Head first: The biology of hope.* New York: Dutton.

Cowan, C. L., Thompson, W. C., & Ellsworth, P. C. (1984). The effects of death qualification on jurors' predisposition to convict and on the quality of deliberation. *Law and Human Behavior, 8,* 53–80.

Cowley, G. (1996, June 3). The biology of beauty. *Newsweek,* pp. 61–69.

Cowley, G., & Underwood, A. (1997/1998, December/January). A little help from serotonin. *Newsweek,* p. 78.

Cox, M., & Tanford, S. (1989). An alternative method of capital jury selection. *Law and Human Behavior, 13,* 167–183.

Cox, T. H., Lobel, S. A., & McLeod, P. L. (1991). Effects of ethnic group cultural differences on cooperative and competitive behavior on a group task. *Academy of Management Journal, 34,* 827–847.

Coyne, J. C. (1994). Self-reported distress: Analog or ersatz depression? *Psychological Bulletin, 116,* 29–45.

Cramer, R. E., McMaster, M. R., Bartell, P. A., & Dragna, M. (1988). Subject competence and the minimization of the bystander effect. *Journal of Applied Social Psychology, 18,* 1133–1148.

Crick, N. R., Bigbee, M. A., & Howes, C. (1996). Gender differences in children's normative beliefs about aggression: How do I hurt thee? Let me count the ways. *Child Development, 67,* 1003–1014.

Crick, N. R., Casas, J. F., & Mosher, M. (1997). Relational and overt aggression in preschool. *Developmental Psychology, 33,* 579–588.

Crick, N. R., & Dodge, K. A. (1994). A review and reformulation of social information-processing mechanisms in children's social adjustment. *Psychological Bulletin, 115,* 74–101.

Crick, N. R., & Grotpeter, J. K. (1995). Relational aggression, gender, and social-psychological adjustment. *Child Development, 66,* 710–722.

Crocker, J., & Luhtanen, R. (1990). Collective self-esteem and ingroup bias. *Journal of Personality and Social Psychology, 58,* 60–67.

Crocker, J., Major, B., & Steele, C. M. (1998). Social stigma. In D. T. Gilbert, S. T. Fiske, & G. Lindzey (Eds.), *The handbook of social psychology* (4th ed., Vol. 2, pp. 504–553). New York: McGraw-Hill.

Crocker, J., Voelkl, K., Testa, M., & Major, B. (1991). Social stigma: The affective consequences of attributional ambiguity. *Journal of Personality and Social Psychology, 60,* 218–228.

Cronbach, L. J. (1955). Processes affecting scores on "understanding of others" and "assumed similarity." *Psychological Bulletin, 52,* 177–193.

Cropanzano, R. (Ed.) (1993). *Justice in the workplace: Approaching fairness in human resource management.* Hillsdale, NJ: Erlbaum.

Crosby, F. (1976). A model of egoistical relative deprivation. *Psychological Review, 83,* 85–113.

Crosby, F. (1982). *Relative deprivation and working women.* New York: Oxford University Press.

Crosby, F. (1984). The denial of personal discrimination. *American Behavioral Scientist, 27,* 371–386.

Crosby, F. J. (1991). *Juggling.* New York: Free Press.

Crosby, F., Bromley, S., & Saxe, L. (1980). Recent unobtrusive studies of black and white discrimination and prejudice: A literature review. *Psychological Bulletin, 87,* 546–563.

Cross, S. E., & Madson, L. (1997). Models of the self: Self-construals and gender. *Psychological Bulletin, 122,* 5–37.

Crowley, A. E., & Hoyer, W. D. (1994). An integrative framework for understanding two-sided persuasion. *Journal of Consumer Research, 20,* 561–574.

Croyle, R., & Cooper, J. (1983). Dissonance arousal: Physiological evidence. *Journal of Personality and Social Psychology, 45,* 782–791.

Crutchfield, R. S. (1955). Conformity and character. *American Psychologist, 10,* 195–198.

Csikszentmihalyi, M., & Figurski, T. J. (1982). Self-awareness and aversive experience in everyday life. *Journal of Personality, 50,* 15–28.

Culbertson, F. M. (1997). Depression and gender: An international review. *American Psychologist, 52,* 25–31.

Cunningham, M. R. (1979). Weather, mood, and helping behavior: Quasi experiments with the sunshine Samaritan. *Journal of Personality and Social Psychology, 37,* 1947–1956.

Cunningham, M. R. (1986). Measuring the physical in physical attractiveness: Quasi-experiments on the sociobiology of female facial beauty. *Journal of Personality and Social Psychology, 50,* 925–935.

Cunningham, M. R., Barbee, A. P., & Pike, C. L. (1990). What do women want? Facialmetric assessment of multiple motives in the perception of male facial physical attractiveness. *Journal of Personality and Social Psychology, 59,* 61–72.

Cunningham, M. R., Roberts, A. R., Wu, C., Barbee, A. P., & Druen, P. B. (1995). "Their ideas of beauty are, on the whole, the same as ours": Consistency and variability in the cross-cultural perception of female physical attractiveness. *Journal of Personality and Social Psychology, 68,* 261–279.

Cunningham, M. R., Shaffer, D. R., Barbee, A. P., Wolff, P. L., & Kelley, D. J. (1990). Separate processes in the relation of elation and depression to helping: Social versus personal concerns. *Journal of Experimental Social Psychology, 26,* 13–33.

Cunningham, M. R., Steinberg, J., & Grev, R. (1980). Wanting to and having to help: Separate motivations for positive mood and guilt-induced helping. *Journal of Personality and Social Psychology, 38,* 181–192.

Cunningham, M. R., Wong, D. T., & Barbee, A. P. (1994). Self-presentation dynamics on overt integrity tests: Experimental studies of the Reid Report. *Journal of Applied Psychology, 79,* 643–658.

Curtis, R. C., & Miller, K. (1986). Believing another likes or dislikes you: Behaviors making the beliefs come true. *Journal of Personality and Social Psychology, 51,* 284–290.

Cutler, B. L., & Penrod, S. D. (1995). *Mistaken identification: The eyewitness, psychology, and the law.* New York: Cambridge University Press.

Cutler, B. L., Penrod, S. D., & Dexter, H. R. (1989). The eyewitness, the expert, and the jury. *Law and Human Behavior, 13,* 311–332.

Cutler, B. L., Penrod, S. D., & Stuve, T. E. (1988). Juror decision making in eyewitness identification cases. *Law and Human Behavior, 12,* 41–55.

Cutrona, E. C., Cole, V., Colangelo, N., Assouline, S. G., & Russell, D. W. (1994). Perceived parental social support and academic achievement: An attachment theory perspective. *Journal of Personality and Social Psychology, 66,* 369–378.

Dabbs, J. M., Jr., Carr, T. S., Frady, R. L., & Riad, J. K. (1995). Testosterone, crime, and misbehavior among 692 male prison inmates. *Personality and Individual Differences, 18,* 627–633.

Dabbs, J. M., Jr., Hargrove, M. F., & Heusel, C. (1996). Testosterone differences among college fraternities: Well-behaved vs. rambunctious. *Personality and Individual Differences, 20,* 157–161.

Dabbs, J. M., Jr., Hopper, C. H., & Jurkovic, G. J. (1990). Testosterone and personality among college students and military veterans. *Personality and Individual Differences, 11,* 1263–1269.

Dabbs, J. M., Jr., & Morris, R. (1990). Testosterone, social class, and antisocial behavior in a sample of 4,462 men. *Psychological Science, 1,* 209–211.

Daily Telegraph (1997, September 6). Three more photographers placed under investigation, p. A8.

Daly, M., & Wilson, M. (1988). *Homicide.* New York: Aldine de Gruyter.

Daly, M., & Wilson, M. (1989). Homicide and cultural evolution. *Ethology and Sociobiology, 10,* 99–110.

Daly, M., & Wilson, M. (1994). Some differential attributes of lethal assaults on small children by stepfathers versus genetic fathers. *Ethology and Sociobiology, 15,* 207–217.

Daly, M., & Wilson, M. (1996). Violence against stepchildren. *Current Directions in Psychological Science, 5,* 77–81.

Danheiser, P. R., & Graziano, W. G. (1982). Self-monitoring and cooperation as a self-presentational strategy. *Journal of Personality and Social Psychology, 42,* 497–505.

Darby, B. L. (1975). Reciprocal concessions procedure for inducing compliance: The door-in-the-face technique. *Journal of Personality and Social Psychology, 31,* 206–215.

Darley, J. M., & Batson, C. D. (1973). From Jerusalem to Jericho: A study of situational and dispositional variables in helping behavior. *Journal of Personality and Social Psychology, 27,* 100–108.

Darley, J. M., & Fazio, R. (1980). Expectancy confirmation processes arising in the social interaction sequence. *American Psychologist, 35,* 867–881.

Darley, J. M., & Gross, P. H. (1983). A hypothesis-confirming bias in labeling effects. *Journal of Personality and Social Psychology, 44,* 20–33.

Darley, J. M., & Latané, B. (1970). Norms and normative behavior: Field studies of social interdependence. In J. Macauley & L. Berkowitz (Eds.), *Altruism and helping behavior* (pp. 83–101). New York: Academic Press.

Darwin, C. (1872). *The expression of the emotions in man and animals.* London: John Murray.

Davidson, A. R., & Jaccard, J. J. (1979). Variables that moderate the attitude-behavior relation: Results of a longitudinal survey. *Journal of Personality and Social Psychology, 37,* 1364–1376.

Davidson, A. R., Yantis, S., Norwood, M., & Montano, D. E. (1985). Amount of information about the attitude object and attitude-behavior consistency. *Journal of Personality and Social Psychology, 49,* 1184–1198.

Davies, P. T., & Cummings, E. M. (1994). Marital conflict and child adjustment: An emotional security hypothesis. *Psychological Bulletin, 116,* 387–411.

Davis, J. H., Au, W. T., Hulbert, L., Chen, X., & Zarnoth, P. (1997). Effects of group size and procedural influence on consensual judgments of quantity: The example of damage awards and mock civil juries. *Journal of Personality and Social Psychology, 73,* 703–718.

Davis, J. H., Kameda, T., Parks, C., Stasson, M., & Zimmerman, S. (1989). Some social mechanics of group decision-making: The distribution of opinion, polling sequence, and implications for consensus. *Journal of Personality and Social Psychology, 57,* 1000–1012.

Davis, M. H. (1994). *Empathy: A social psychological approach.* Madison, WI: Browon & Benchmark.

Davis, M. H., Luce, C., & Kraus, S. J. (1994). The heritability of characteristics associated with dispositional empathy. *Journal of Personality, 62,* 369–391.

Davis, S. (1990). Men as success objects and women as sex objects: A study of personal advertisements. *Sex Roles, 23,* 43–50.

Dawkins, R. (1989). *The selfish gene* (2nd ed.). Oxford: Oxford University Press.

Day, D. D., & Sulsky, L. M. (1995). Effects of frame-of-reference training and information configuration on memory organization and rating accuracy. *Journal of Applied Psychology, 80,* 158–167.

Dean, K. E., & Malamuth, N. M. (1997). Characteristics of men who aggress sexually and of men who imagine aggressing: Risk and moderating variables. *Journal of Personality and Social Psychology, 72,* 449–455.

DeAngelis, T. (1993, August). *APA Monitor,* p. 16.

Deater-Deckard, K., & Dodge, K. A. (1997). Externalizing behavior problems and discipline revisited: Nonlinear effects and variation by culture, context, and gender. *Psychological Inquiry, 8,* 161–175.

Deater-Deckard, K., Dodge, K. A., Bates, J. E., & Pettit, G. S. (1998). Multiple-risk factors in the development of externalizing behavior problems: Group and individual differences. *Development and Psychopathology.*

Deaux, K., & Emswiller, T. (1974). Explanations for successful performance on sex-linked tasks: What is skill for the male is luck for the female. *Journal of Personality and Social Psychology, 29,* 80–85.

Deaux, K., & Lewis, L. L. (1984). The structure of gender stereotypes: Interrelationships among components and gender label. *Journal of Personality and Social Psychology, 46,* 991–1004.

Deaux, K., & Major, B. (1987). Putting gender into context: An interactive model of gender-related behavior. *Psychological Review, 94,* 369–389.

DeBono, K. G. (1987). Investigating the social-adjustive and value-expressive functions of attitudes: Implications for persuasion processes. *Journal of Personality and Social Psychology, 52,* 279–287.

Deci, E. L. (1971). Effects of externally mediated rewards on intrinsic motivation. *Journal of Personality and Social Psychology, 18,* 105–115.

Deci, E. L., Connell, J. P., & Ryan, R. M. (1989). Self-determination in a work organization. *Journal of Applied Psychology, 74,* 580–590.

Deci, E. L., & Ryan, R. M. (1985). *Intrinsic motivation and self-determination in human behavior.* New York: Plenum.

De Dreu, C. K. W., Yzerbyt, V. Y., & Leyens, J.-Ph. (1995). Dilution of stereotype-based cooperation in mixed-motive interdependence. *Journal of Experimental Social Psychology, 31,* 575–593.

DeJong, W. (1979). An examination of self-perception mediation of the foot-in-the-door effect. *Journal of Personality and Social Psychology, 37,* 2221–2239.

DeKeseredy, W. S., Schwartz, M. D., & Tait, K. (1993). Sexual assault and stranger aggression on a Canadian university campus. *Sex Roles, 28,* 263–277.

Delahanty, D. L., Herberman, H. B., Fullerton, C. S., Ursano, R. J., Craig, K. J., Hayward, M. C., & Baum, A. (1997). Acute and chronic distress and posttraumatic stress disorder as a function of responsibility for serious motor vehicle accidents. *Journal of Consulting and Clinical Psychology, 65,* 560–567.

Demaré, D., Lips, H. M., & Briere, J. (1993). Sexually violent pornography, anti-women attitudes, and sexual aggression: A structural equation model. *Journal of Research in Personality, 27,* 285–300.

DePaulo, B. M. (1992). Nonverbal behavior and self-representation. *Psychological Bulletin, 111,* 203–243.

DePaulo, B. M., Charlton, K., Cooper, H., Lindsay, J. J., & Muhlenbruck, L. (1997). The accuracy-confidence correlation in the detection of deception. *Personality and Social Psychology Review, 1,* 346–357.

DePaulo, B. M., Epstein, J. A., & LeMay, C. S. (1990). Responses of the socially anxious to the prospect of interpersonal evaluation. *Journal of Personality, 58,* 623–640.

DePaulo, B. M., & Kashy, D. A. (1998). Everyday lies in close and casual relationships. *Journal of Personality and Social Psychology, 74,* 63–79.

DePaulo, B. M., Lassiter, G. D., & Stone, J. I. (1982). Attentional determinants of success at detecting deception and truth. *Personality and Social Psychology Bulletin, 8,* 273–279.

DePaulo, B. M., & Tang, J. (1994). Social anxiety and social judgment: The example of detecting deception. *Journal of Research in Personality, 28,* 142–153.

Deppe, R. K., & Harackiewicz, J. M. (1996). Self-handicapping and intrinsic motivation: Buffering intrinsic motivation from the threat of failure. *Journal of Personality and Social Psychology, 70,* 868–876.

Derlega, V. J., Metts, S., Petronio, S., & Margulis, S. T. (1993). *Self-disclosure.* Newbury Park, CA: Sage.

Derlega, V. J., Wilson, M., & Chaikin, A. L. (1976). Friendship and disclosure reciprocity. *Journal of Personality and Social Psychology, 34,* 578–587.

Dershowitz, A. M. (1982). *The best defense.* New York: Vintage Books.

Desforges, D. M., Lord, C. G., Pugh, M. A., Sia, T. L., et al. (1997). Role of group representativeness in the generalization part of the contact hypothesis. *Basic and Applied Social Psychology, 19,* 183–204.

Desmarais, S., & Curtis, J. (1997). Gender and perceived pay entitlement: Testing for effects of experience with income. *Journal of Personality and Social Psychology, 72,* 141–150.

DeSteno, D. A., & Salovey, P. (1996). Evolutionary origins of sex differences in jealousy? Questioning the "fitness" model. *Psychological Science, 7,* 367–372.

Detroit News (1997, November 25). Belle Isle bridge murder verdict upheld, p. C3.

Deutsch, F. M. (1989). The false consensus effect: Is the self-justification hypothesis justified? *Basic and Applied Social Psychology, 10,* 83–99.

Deutsch, M., & Gerard, H. B. (1955). A study of normative and informational social influences upon individual judgment. *Journal of Abnormal and Social Psychology, 51,* 629–636.

Deutsch, M., & Krauss, R. M. (1960). The effect of threat upon interpersonal bargaining. *Journal of Abnormal and Social Psychology, 61,* 181–189.

Devenport, J. L., Penrod, S. D., & Cutler, B. L. (1997). Eyewitness identification evidence: Evaluating commonsense evaluations. *Psychology, Public Policy, and Law, 3,* 338–361.

Devine, P. G. (1989). Stereotypes and prejudice: Their automatic and controlled components. *Journal of Personality and Social Psychology, 56,* 5–18.

de Waal, F. B. M. (1996) *Good natured: The origins of right and wrong in humans and other animals.* Cambridge, MA: Harvard University Press.

Dhabhar, F., & McEwen, B. (1995). *Journal of Immunology, 154,* 5511–5527.

Diener, E. (1979). Deindividuation, self-awareness, and disinhibition. *Journal of Personality and Social Psychology, 37,* 1160–1171.

Diener, E. (1980). Deindividuation: The absence of self-awareness and self-regulation in group members. In P. B. Paulus (Ed.), *Psychology of group influence* (pp. 209–242). Hillsdale, NJ: Erlbaum.

Diener, E., Fraser, S. C., Beaman, A. L., & Kelem, R. T. (1976). Effects of deindividuation variables on stealing among Halloween trick-or-treaters. *Journal of Personality and Social Psychology, 33,* 178–183.

Diener, E., Wolsic, B., & Fujita, F. (1995). Physical attractiveness and subjective well-being. *Journal of Personality and Social Psychology, 69,* 120–129.

Dietz-Uhler, B. (1996). The escalation of commitment in political decision-making groups: A social identity approach. *European Journal of Social Psychology, 26,* 611–629.

DiFonzo, N., & Bordia, P. (1997). Rumor and prediction: Making sense (but losing dollars) in the stock market. *Organizational Behavior and Human Decision Processes, 71,* 329–353.

Dijksterhuis, A., & van Knippenberg, A. (1996). The knife that cuts both ways: Facilitated and inhibited access to traits as a result of stereotype activation. *Journal of Experimental and Social Psychology, 32,* 271–288.

Dill, J. C., & Anderson, C. A. (1995). Effects of frustration justification on hostile aggression. *Aggressive Behavior, 21,* 359–369.

Dill, K. E., Anderson, C. A., Anderson, K. B., & Deuser, W. E. (1997). Effects of aggressive personality on social expectations and social perceptions. *Journal of Research in Personality, 31,* 272–292.

Dillard, J. P. (1991). The current status of research on sequential-request compliance techniques. *Personality and Social Psychology Bulletin, 17,* 283–288.

Dimberg, U., & Ohman, A. (1996). Behold the wrath: Psychophysiological responses to facial stimuli. *Motivation and Emotion, 20,* 149–181.

Dindia, K., & Allen, M. (1992). Sex differences in self-disclosure: A meta-analysis. *Psychological Bulletin, 112,* 106–124.

Dion, K. K., Berscheid, E., & Walster, E. (1972). What is beautiful is good. *Journal of Personality and Social Psychology, 24,* 285–290.

Dion, K. K., & Dion, K. L. (1996). Cultural perspectives on romantic love. *Personal Relationships, 3,* 5–17.

Dion, K. L. (1979). Intergroup conflict and intragroup cohesiveness. In W. G. Austin & S. Worchel (Eds.), *The social psychology of intergroup relations* (pp. 211–224). Pacific Grove, CA: Brooks/Cole.

Dion, K. L., & Cota, A. A. (1991). The Ms. stereotype: Its domain and the role of explicitness in title preference. *Psychology of Women Quarterly, 15,* 403–410.

Dion, K. L., & Dion, K. K. (1976). Love, liking and trust in heterosexual relationships. *Personality and Social Psychology Bulletin, 2,* 187–190.

Dodd, D. K. (1985). Robbers in the classroom: A deindividuation exercise. *Teaching in Psychology, 12,* 89–91.

Dodson, C., & Reisberg, D. (1991). Indirect testing of eyewitness memory: The (non)effect of misinformation. *Bulletin of the Psychonomic Society, 29,* 333–336.

Doherty, K., Weigold, M. F., & Schlenker, B. R. (1990). Self-serving interpretations of motives. *Personality and Social Psychology Bulletin, 16,* 485–495.

Dohrenwend, B. P., Levav, I., Shrout, P. E., Schwartz, S., Naveh, G., Link, B. G., Skodol, A. E., & Stueve, A. (1992). Socioeconomic status and psychiatric disorders: The causation-selection issue. *Science, 255,* 946–952.

Dollard, J., Doob, L. W., Miller, N. E., Mowrer, O. H., & Sears, R. R. (1939). *Frustration and aggression.* New Haven, CT: Yale University Press.

Donne, J. (1975). Meditation, 17. In A. Raspa (Ed.), *Devotions upon emergent occasions* (p. 87). Montreal: McGill-Queen's University Press. (Original work published 1624)

Donnerstein, E., & Berkowitz, L. (1981). Victim reactions in aggressive erotic films as a factor in violence against women. *Journal of Personality and Social Psychology, 41,* 710–724.

Donnerstein, E., & Donnerstein, M. (1976). Research in the control of interracial aggression. In R. G. Geen and E. C. O'Neal (Eds.), *Perspectives on aggression* (pp. 133–168). New York: Academic Press.

Donnerstein, E., & Hallam, J. (1978). Facilitating effects of erotica on aggression against women. *Journal of Personality and Social Psychology, 36,* 1270–1277.

Donnerstein, E., Linz, D., & Penrod, S. (1987). *The question of pornography.* New York: Free Press.

Donnerstein, E., & Malamuth, N. (1997). Pornography: Its consequences on the observer. In L. B. Schlesinger & E. Revitch (Eds.), *Sexual dynamics of anti-social behavior* (2nd ed., pp. 30–49). Springfield, IL: Charles C Thomas.

Dooley, P. A. (1995). Perceptions of the onset controllability of AIDS and helping judgments: An attributional analysis. *Journal of Applied Social Psychology, 25,* 858–869.

Dornbusch, S. M., Hastorf, A. H., Richardson, S. A., Muzzy, R. E., & Vreeland, R. S. (1965). The perceiver and the perceived: Their relative influence on categories of interpersonal perception. *Journal of Personality and Social Psychology, 1,* 434–440.

Dougherty, T. W., Turban, D. B., & Callender, J. C. (1994). Confirming first impressions in the employment interview: A field study of interviewer behavior. *Journal of Applied Psychology, 79,* 659–665.

Dovidio, J. F. (1984). Helping behavior and altruism: An empirical and conceptual overview. In L. Berkowitz (Ed.), *Advances in experimental social psychology* (Vol. 17, pp. 361–427). New York: Academic Press.

Dovidio, J. F., Brigham, J. C., Johnson, B. T., & Gaertner, S. L. (1996). Stereotyping, prejudice, and discrimination: Another look. In C. N. Macrae, C. Stangor, & M. Hewstone (Eds.), *Stereotypes and stereotyping* (pp. 276–319). New York: Guilford.

Dovidio, J. F., Ellyson, S. L., Keating, C. F., Heltman, K., & Brown, C. E. (1988). The relationship of social power to visual displays of dominance between men and women. *Journal of Personality and Social Psychology, 54,* 233–242.

Dovidio, J. F., Evans, N., & Tyler, R. (1986). Racial stereotypes: The contents of their cognitive representations. *Journal of Experimental Social Psychology, 22,* 22–37.

Dovidio, J. F., & Gaertner, S. L. (1997). On the nature of contemporary prejudice: The causes, consequences, and challenges of aversive racism. In J. L. Eberhardt & S. T. Fiske (Eds.), *Racism: The problem and the response.* Thousand Oaks, CA: Sage.

Dovidio, J. F., Gaertner, S. L., Validzic, A., Matoka, K., Johnson, B., & Frazier, S. (1997). Extending the benefits of recategorization: Evaluations, self-disclosure, and helping. *Journal of Experimental Social Psychology, 33,* 401–420.

Dovidio, J. F., Kawakami, K., Johnson, C., Johnson, B., & Howard, A. (1997). On the nature of prejudice: Automatic and controlled processes. *Journal of Experimental Social Psychology, 33,* 510–540.

Dovidio, J. F., Piliavin, J. A., Gaertner, S. L., Schroeder, D. A., & Clark, R. D., II. (1991). The arousal: cost-reward model and the process of intervention: A review of the evidence. In M. S. Clark (Ed.), *Review of personality and social psychology 12: Prosocial behavior* (pp. 86–118). Newbury Park, CA: Sage.

Downs, A. C., & Lyons, P. M. (1995). Natural observations of the links between attractiveness and initial legal judgments. *Personality and Social Psychology Bulletin, 17,* 541–547.

Dreher, G. F., & Cox, T. H., Jr. (1996). Race, gender, and opportunity: A study of compensation attainment and the establishment of mentoring relationships. *Journal of Applied Psychology, 81,* 297–308.

Drigotas, S. M., & Rusbult, C. E. (1992). Shall I stay or should I go? A dependence model of breakups. *Journal of Personality and Social Psychology, 62,* 62–87.

Duck, S., & Wright, P. H. (1993). Reexamining gender differences in same-gender friendships: A close look at two kinds of data. *Sex Roles, 28,* 709–727.

Duclos, S. E., Laird, J. D., Schneider, E., Sexter, M., Stern, L., & Van Lighten, O. (1989). Emotion-specific effects of facial expressions and postures on emotional experience. *Journal of Personality and Social Psychology, 57,* 100–108.

Dudley, B. S., Johnson, D. W., & Johnson, R. T. (1996). Conflict-resolution training and middle school students' integrative negotiation behavior. *Journal of Applied Social Psychology, 26,* 2038–2052.

Duff, K. J., & Newman, L. S. (1997). Individual differences in the spontaneous construal of behavior: Idiocentrism and the automatization of the trait inference process. *Social Cognition, 15,* 217–241.

Dunning, D., Griffin, D. W., Milojkovic, J. D., & Ross, L. (1990). The overconfidence effect in social prediction. *Journal of Personality and Social Psychology, 58,* 568–581.

Dunning, D., & Hayes, A. F. (1996). Evidence for egocentric comparison in social judgment. *Journal of Personality and Social Psychology, 71,* 213–229.

Dunning, D., Li, J., & Malpass, R. S. (1998, March). Basketball fandom and cross-race identification among European-Americans: Another look at the contact hypothesis. Paper presented at the American Psychology-Law Society, Redondo Beach, CA.

Dunning, D., Perie, M., & Story, A. L. (1991). Self-serving prototypes of social categories. *Journal of Personality and Social Psychology, 61,* 957–968.

Dunning, D., & Sherman, D. A. (1997). Stereotypes and tacit inference. *Journal of Personality and Social Psychology, 73,* 459–471.

Dunning, D., & Stern, L. B. (1994). Distinguishing accurate from inaccurate eyewitness identifications via inquiries about decision processes. *Journal of Personality and Social Psychology, 67,* 818–835.

Dunton, B. C., & Fazio, R. H. (1997). An individual difference measure of motivation to control prejudiced reactions. *Personality and Social Psychology Bulletin, 23,* 316–326.

Dutton, D. G., & Aron, A. P. (1974). Some evidence for heightened sexual attraction under conditions of high anxiety. *Journal of Personality and Social Psychology, 30,* 510–517.

Duval, S., & Wicklund, R. A. (1972). *A theory of objective self-awareness.* New York: Academic Press.

Duval, T. S., Duval, V. H., & Mulilis, J. P. (1992). Effects of self-focus, discrepancy between self and standard, and outcome expectancy favorability on the tendency to match self to standard or to withdraw. *Journal of Personality and Social Psychology, 62,* 340–348.

Eagly, A. H. (1987). *Sex differences in social behavior: A social-role interpretation.* Hillsdale, NJ: Erlbaum.

Eagly, A. H., Ashmore, R. D., Makhijani, M. G., & Longo, L. C. (1991). What is beautiful is good, but . . . : A meta-analytic review of research on the physical attractiveness stereotype. *Psychology Bulletin, 110,* 107–128.

Eagly, A. H., & Carli, L. L. (1981). Sex of researchers and sex-typed communications as determinants of sex differences in influenceability: A meta-analysis of social influence studies. *Psychological Bulletin, 90,* 1–20.

Eagly, A. H., & Chaiken, S. (1998). Attitude structure and function. In D. Gilbert, S. Fiske, & G. Lindzey (Eds.), *Handbook of social psychology* (4th ed.). New York: McGraw-Hill.

Eagly, A. H., Chen, S., Chaiken, S., & Shaw-Barnes, K. (1998). The impact of attitudes on memory: An affair to remember. *Psychological Bulletin,* in press.

Eagly, A. H., & Chravala, C. (1986). Sex differences in conformity: Status and gender-role interpretations. *Psychology of Women Quarterly, 10,* 203–220.

Eagly, A. H., & Crowley, M. (1986). Gender and helping behavior: A meta-analytic review of the social psychological literature. *Psychological Bulletin, 100,* 283–308.

Eagly, A. H., & Johnson, B. T. (1990). Gender and leadership style: A meta-analysis. *Psychological Bulletin, 108,* 233–256.

Eagly, A. H., Karau, S. J., & Makhijani, M. G. (1995). Gender and effectiveness of leaders: A meta-analysis. *Psychological Bulletin, 117,* 125–145.

Eagly, A. H., Makhijani, M. G., & Klonsky, B. G. (1992). Gender and evaluation of leaders: A meta-analysis. *Psychological Bulletin, 111,* 3–22.

Eagly, A. H., & Steffen, V. J. (1986). Gender and aggressive behavior: A meta-analytic review of the social psychology literature. *Psychological Bulletin, 100,* 309–330.

Eagly, A. H., & Wood, W. (1982). Inferred sex differences in status as a determinant of gender stereotypes about social influence. *Journal of Personality and Social Psychology, 43,* 915–928.

Eagly, A. H., & Wood, W. (1991). Explaining sex differences in social behavior: A meta-analytic perspective. *Personality and Social Psychology Bulletin, 17,* 306–315.

Eagly, A. H., Wood, W., & Chaiken, S. (1978). Causal inferences about communicators and their effect on opinion change. *Journal of Personality and Social Psychology, 36,* 424–435.

Eagly, A. H., Wood, W., & Fishbaugh, L. (1981). Sex differences in conformity: Surveillance by the group as a determinant of male nonconformity. *Journal of Personality and Social Psychology, 40,* 384–394.

Ebbesen, E. B., & Konecni, V. J. (1981). The process of sentencing adult felons: A causal analysis of judicial decisions. In B. D. Sales (Ed.), *The trial process* (pp. 413–458). New York: Plenum.

Eden, D. (1990). Pygmalion without interpersonal contrast effects: Whole groups gain from raising manager expectations. *Journal of Applied Psychology, 75,* 394–398.

Edney, J. J. (1979). The nuts game: A concise commons dilemma analog. *Environmental Psychology and Nonverbal Behavior, 3,* 252–254.

Edwards, K. (1990). The interplay of affect and cognition in attitude formation and change. *Journal of Personality and Social Psychology, 59,* 202–216.

Edwards, K., & Bryan, T. S. (1997). Judgmental biases produced by instructions to disregard: The (paradoxical) case of emotional information. *Personality and Social Psychology Bulletin, 23,* 849–864.

Edwards, K., & Smith, E. E. (1996). A disconfirmation bias in the evaluation of arguments. *Journal of Personality and Social Psychology, 71,* 5–24.

Egolf, D. B., & Corder, L. E. (1991). Height differences between low and high job status female and male corporate employees. *Sex Roles, 24,* 365–373.

Ehrlichman, H., & Eichenstein, R. (1992). Private wishes: Gender similarities and differences. *Sex Roles, 26,* 399–422.

Eisenberg, N., Cialdini, R. B., McCreath, H., & Shell, R. (1987). Consistency-based compliance: When and why do children become vulnerable? *Journal of Personality and Social Psychology, 52,* 1174–1181.

Eisenberg, N., Fabes, R. A., Carlo, G., & Karbon, M. (1992). Emotional responsivity to others: Behavioral correlates and socialization antecedents. In N. Eisenberg & R. A. Fabes (Eds.), *Emotion and its regulation in early development* (pp. 57–73). San Francisco: Jossey-Bass.

Eisenberg, N., Fabes, R. A., Murphy, B., Karbon, M., Smith, M., & Maszk, P. (1996). The relations of children's dispositional empathy-related responding to their emotionality, regulation, and social functioning. *Developmental Psychology, 32,* 195–209.

Eisenberger, R. (1992). Learned industriousness. *Psychological Review, 99,* 248–267.

Eisenberger, R., & Cameron, J. (1996). Detrimental effects of reward: Reality or myth? *American Psychologist, 51,* 1153–1166.

Eisenberger, R., Cotterell, N., & Marvel, J. (1987). Reciprocation ideology. *Journal of Personality and Social Psychology, 53,* 743–750.

Ekman, P., & Davidson, R. J. (1993). Voluntary smiling changes regional brain activity. *Psychological Science, 4,* 342–345.

Ekman, P., Davidson, R. J., & Friesen, W. V. (1990). The Duchenne smile: Emotional expression and brain physiology II. *Journal of Personality and Social Psychology, 58,* 342–353.

Ekman, P., & Friesen, W. V. (1974). Detecting deception from the body or face. *Journal of Personality and Social Psychology, 29,* 288–298.

Ekman, P., Friesen, W. V., O'Sullivan, M., Chan, A., Diacoyanni-Tarlatzis, I., Heider, K., Krause, R., LeCompte, W. A., Pitcairn, T., Ricci-Bitti, P., Scherer, K., Tomita, M., & Tzavaras, A. (1987). Universals and cultural differences in the judgments of facial expressions of emotion. *Journal of Personality and Social Psychology, 53,* 712–717.

Ekman, P., & O'Sullivan, M. (1991). Who can catch a liar? *American Psychologist, 46,* 913–920.

Elkin, R. A., & Leippe, M. R. (1986). Physiological arousal, dissonance, and attitude change: Evidence for a dissonance-arousal link and a "don't remind me" effect. *Journal of Personality and Social Psychology, 51,* 55–65.

Elliot, A. J., & Devine, P. G. (1994). On the motivational nature of cognitive dissonance: Dissonance as psychological discomfort. *Journal of Personality and Social Psychology, 67,* 382–394.

Elliot, A. J., & Harackiewicz, J. M. (1994). Goal setting, achievement orientation, and intrinsic motivation: A mediational analysis. *Journal of Personality and Social Psychology, 66,* 968–980.

Elliott, R. (1991). Social science data and the APA: The *Lockhart* brief as a case in point. *Law and Human Behavior, 15,* 59–76.

Ellsworth, P. C. (1991). To tell what we know or wait for Godot? *Law and Human Behavior, 15,* 77–90.

Elms, A., & Milgram, S. (1966). Personality characteristics associated with obedience and defiance toward authoritative command. *Journal of Experimental Research in Personality, 1,* 282–289.

Elwork, A., Sales, B. D., & Alfini, J. J. (1982). *Making jury instructions understandable.* Charlottesville, VA: Miche.

English, P. W., & Sales, B. D. (1997). A ceiling or consistency effect for the comprehension of jury instructions. *Psychology, Public Policy, and Law, 3,* 381–401.

Enrico, D. (1998, January 5). Experts doubt effectiveness of Apple's star-studded ads. *USA Today*, p. 12B.

Enzle, M. E., & Anderson, S. C. (1993). Surveillant intentions and intrinsic motivation. *Journal of Personality and Social Psychology, 64*, 257–266.

Enzle, M. E., Hansen, R. D., & Lowe, C. A. (1975). Causal attribution in the mixed-motive game: Effects of facilitory and inhibitory environmental forces. *Journal of Personality and Social Psychology, 31*, 50–54.

Epstein, J. L. (1985). After the bus arrives: Resegregation in desegregated schools. *Journal of Social Issues, 41*, 23–43.

Erber, R., & Tesser, A. (1992). Task effort and the regulation of mood: The absorption hypothesis. *Journal of Experimental Social Psychology, 28*, 339–359.

Erber, R., & Tessser, A. (1994). Self-evaluation maintenance: A social psychological approach to interpersonal relationships. In R. Erber & R. Gilmour (Eds.), *Theoretical frameworks for personal relationships* (pp. 211–233). Hillsdale, NJ: Erlbaum.

Eron, L. D. (1986). Interventions to mitigate the psychological effects of media violence on aggressive behavior. In L. R. Huesmann & N. M. Malamuth (Eds.), *Journal of Social Issues: Media Violence and Antisocial Behavior, 42*(3), 155–169.

Eron, L. D., & Huesmann, L. R. (1984). The control of aggressive behavior by changes in attitudes, values, and the conditions of learning. In R. J. Blanchard & D. C. Blanchard (Eds.), *Advances in the study of aggression* (Vol. 1, pp. 139–171). New York: Academic Press.

Eron, L. D., Huesmann, L. R., & Zelli, A. (1991). The role of parental variables in the learning of aggression. In. D. J. Pepler & K. H. Rubin (Eds.), *The development and treatment of childhood aggression* (pp. 169–188). Hillsdale, NJ: Erlbaum.

Evans, G. W., Bullinger, M., & Hygge, S. (1998). Chronic noise exposure and physiological response: A prospective study of children living under environmental stress. *Psychological Science, 9*, 75–77.

Evans, G. W., & Lepore, S. J. (1993). Household crowding and social support: A quasiexperimental analysis. *Journal of Personality and Social Psychology, 65*, 308–316.

Evans, G. W., Palsane, M. N., Lepore, S. J., & Martin, J. (1989). Residential density and psychological health: The mediating effects of social support. *Journal of Personality and Social Psychology, 57*, 994–999.

Evans, R. I., Smith, C. K., & Raines, B. E. (1984). Deterring cigarette smoking in adolescents: A psychosocial-behavioral analysis of an intervention strategy. In A. Baum, S. E. Taylor, & J. E. Singer (Eds.), *Handbook of psychology and health: Vol. 4. Social psychological aspects of health* (pp. 301–318). Hillsdale, NJ: Erlbaum.

Everson, S. A., et al. (1996). Hopelessness and risk of mortality and incidence of myorcardial infarction and cancer. *Psychosomatic Medicine, 58*, 133–121.

Fabes, R. A., Fultz, J., Eisenberg, N., May-Plumlee, T., & Christopher, F. S. (1989). Effects of rewards on children's prosocial motivation: A socialization study. *Developmental Psychology, 25*, 509–515.

Fazio, R. H. (1987). Self-perception theory: A current perspective. In M. P. Zanna, J. M. Olson, & C. P. Herman (Eds.), *Social influence: The Ontario Symposium* (Vol. 5, pp. 129–150). Hillsdale, NJ: Erlbaum.

Fazio, R. H. (1990). Multiple processes by which attitudes guide behavior: The MODE model as an integrative framework. In M. P. Zanna (Ed.), *Advances in experimental social psychology* (Vol. 23, pp. 75–109). New York: Academic Press.

Fazio, R. H., Effrein, E. A., & Falender, V. J. (1981). Self-perceptions following social interactions. *Journal of Personality and Social Psychology, 41*, 232–242.

Fazio, R. H., Jackson, J. R., Dunton, B. C., & Williams, C. J. (1995). Variability in automatic activation as an unobtrusive measure of racial attitudes. A bona fide pipeline? *Journal of Personality and Social Psychology, 69*, 1013–1027.

Fazio, R. H., & Zanna, M. P. (1981). Direct experience and attitude-behavior consistency. In L. Berkowitz (Ed.), *Advances in experimental social psychology* (Vol. 14, pp. 162–202). New York: Academic Press.

Fazio, R. H., Zanna, M. P., & Cooper, J. (1977). Dissonance and self perception: An integrative view of each theory's proper domain of application. *Journal of Experimental Social Psychology, 13*, 464–479.

Feeney, J. A., & Noller, P. (1990). Attachment style as a predictor of adult romantic relationships. *Journal of Personality and Social Psychology, 58*, 281–291.

Fehr, B. (1996). *Friendship processes.* Thousand Oaks, CA: Sage Publications.

Fehr, B., & Russell, J. A. (1991). The concept of love viewed from a prototype perspective. *Journal of Personality and Social Psychology, 60*, 425–438.

Fein, E., & Schneider, S. (1996). *The rules: Time-tested secrets for capturing the heart of Mr. Right.* New York: Warner Books.

Fein, S. (1996). Effects of suspicion on attributional thinking and the correspondence bias. *Journal of Personality and Social Psychology, 70*, 1164–1184.

Fein, S., & Spencer, S. J. (1997). Prejudice as self-image maintenance: Affirming the self through derogating others. *Journal of Personality and Social Psychology, 73*, 31–44.

Fein, S., Goethals, G. R., & Kassin, S. M. (1998). *Social influence and presidential debates.* Manuscript under review, Williams College.

Fein, S., Morgan, S. J., Norton, M. I., & Sommers, S. R. (1997). Hype and suspicion: The effects of pretrial publicity, race, and suspicion on jurors' verdicts. *Journal of Social Issues, 53*, 487–502.

Feingold, A. (1988). Matching for attractiveness in romantic partners and same-sex friends: A meta-analysis and theoretical critique. *Psychological Bulletin, 104*, 226–235.

Feingold, A. (1992a). Gender differences in mate selection preferences: A test of the parental investment model. *Psychological Bulletin, 112*, 125–139.

Feingold, A. (1992b). Good-looking people are not what we think. *Psychological Bulletin, 111*, 304–341.

Feingold, A. (1994). Gender differences in personality: a meta-analysis. *Psychological Bulletin, 116*, 429–456.

Felson, R. B. (1989). Parents and the reflected appraisal process: A longitudinal analysis. *Journal of Personality and Social Psychology, 56*, 965–971.

Fenigstein, A., & Abrams, D. (1993). Self-attention and the egocentric assumption of shared perspectives. *Journal of Experimental Social Psychology, 29*, 287–303.

Fenigstein, A., Scheier, M. F., & Buss, A. H. (1975). Public and private self-consciousness: Assessment and theory. *Journal of Consulting and Clinical Psychology, 43*, 522–527.

Ferrari, J. R., Johnson, J. L., & McCown, W. G. (Eds.) (1995). *Procrastination and task avoidance: Theory, research, and treatment.* New York: Plenum.

Ferris, C. F., Melloni, R. H. Jr., Koppel, G., & Perry, K. W. et. al. (1997). Vasopressin/serotonin interactions in the anterior hypothalamus control aggressive behavior in golden hamsters. *Journal of Neuroscience, 17*, 4331–4340.

Fershtman, M. (1997). Cohesive group detection in a social network by the segregation matrix index. *Social Networks, 19*, 193–208.

Festinger, L. (1950). Informal social communication. *Psychological Review, 57*, 271–282.

Festinger, L. (1954). A theory of social comparison processes. *Human Relations, 7,* 117–140.

Festinger, L. (1957). *A theory of cognitive dissonance.* Stanford, CA: Stanford University Press.

Festinger, L., & Carlsmith, J. M. (1959). Cognitive consequences of forced compliance. *Journal of Abnormal and Social Psychology, 58,* 203–210.

Festinger, L., Pepitone, A., & Newcomb, T. (1952). Some consequences of de-individuation in a group. *Journal of Abnormal and Social Psychology, 47,* 382–389.

Festinger, L., Schachter, S., & Back, K. W. (1950). *Social pressures in informal groups: A study of human factors in housing.* New York: Harper.

Fiedler, F. E. (1967). *A theory of leadership effectiveness.* New York: McGraw-Hill.

Fiedler, F. E., & Chemers, M. M. (1984). *Improving leadership effectiveness: The leader match concept* (2nd ed.). New York: Wiley.

Fiedler, F. E., & Garcia, J. E. (1987). *Leadership: Cognitive resources and performance.* New York: Wiley.

Fiedler, F. E., Murphy, S. E., & Gibson, F. W. (1992). Inaccurate reporting and inappropriate variables: A reply to Vecchio's (1990) examination of cognitive resource theory. *Journal of Applied Psychology, 77,* 372–374.

Fields-Meyer, T., Weinstein, F., Wilson, M., & Sandler, B. (September 11, 1995). Death in a crowded place. *People,* pp. 99–100.

Fincham, F. D., & Bradbury, T. N. (1993). Marital satisfaction, depression, and attributions: A longitudinal analysis. *Journal of Personality and Social Psychology, 64,* 442–452.

Fine, M. A., & Sacher, J. A. (1997). Predictors of distress following relationship termination among dating couples. *Journal of Social and Clinical Psychology, 16,* 381–388.

Finkel, N. J. (1995). *Commonsense justice: Jurors' notions of the law.* Cambridge, MA: Harvard University Press.

Finkelhor, D., & Dziuba-Leatherman, J. (1994). Victimization of children. *American Psychologist, 49,* 173–183.

Finlay, K. A., Trafimow, D., & Jones, D. (1997). Predicting health behaviors from attitudes and subjective norms: Between-subjects and within-subjects analyses. *Journal of Applied Social Psychology, 27,* 2015–2031.

Fischer, C. S. (1976). *The urban experience.* New York: Harcourt Brace Jovanovich.

Fischer, D. H. (1989). *Albion's seed: Four British folkways in America.* New York: Oxford University Press.

Fischhoff, B. (1975). Hindsight ≠ foresight: The effect of outcome knowledge on judgment under uncertainty. *Journal of Experimental Psychology: Human Perception and Performance, 1,* 288–299.

Fishbein, M. (1980). A theory of reasoned action: Some applications and implications. In H. E. Howe & M. M. Page (Eds.), *Nebraska Symposium on Motivation* (Vol. 27, pp. 65–116). Lincoln: University of Nebraska Press.

Fishbein, M., & Ajzen, I. (1972). Attitudes and opinions. In P. H. Mussen & M. R. Rosenzweig (Eds.), *Annual Review of Psychology, 23,* 487–544.

Fishbein, M., & Ajzen, I. (1975). *Beliefs, attitudes, intention, and behavior: An introduction to theory and research.* Reading, MA: Addison-Wesley.

Fishbein, M., & Stasson, M. (1990). The role of desires, self-predictions, and perceived control in the prediction of training session attendance. *Journal of Applied Social Psychology, 20,* 173–198.

Fisher, J. D., Bell, P. A., & Baum, A. (1984). *Environmental psychology* (2nd ed.). New York: Holt, Rinehart and Winston.

Fisher, J. D., Fisher, W. A., Williams, S. S., & Malloy, T. E. (1994). Empirical tests of an information-motivation-behavioral skills model of AIDS-preventive behavior with gay men and heterosexual university students. *Health Psychology, 13,* 238–250.

Fisher, J. D., Nadler, A., & Whitcher-Alagna, S. (1982). Recipient reactions to aid. *Psychological Bulletin, 91,* 27–54.

Fisher, R. J., & Keashly, L. (1990). A contingency approach to third party intervention. In R. J. Fisher (Ed.), *The social psychology of intergroup and international conflict resolution* (pp. 234–238). New York: Springer.

Fiske, A. P. (1991). The cultural relativity of selfish individualism: Anthropological evidence that humans are inherently sociable. In M. S. Clark (Ed.), *Review of personality and social psychology: Vol. 12. Prosocial behavior* (pp. 176–214). Newbury Park, CA: Sage.

Fiske, A. P. (1992). The four elementary forms of sociality: Framework for a unified theory of social relations. *Psychological Review, 99,* 689–723.

Fiske, A. P., Kitayama, S., Markus, H. R., & Nisbett, R. E. (1998). The cultural matrix of social psychology. In D. T. Gilbert, S. T. Fiske, & G. Lindzey (Eds.), *The handbook of social psychology* (4th ed., Vol. 2, pp. 915–981). New York: McGraw-Hill.

Fiske, S. T., Bersoff, D. N., Borgida, E., Deaux, K., & Heilman, M. E. (1991). Social science research on trial: Use of sex stereotyping research in *Price Waterhouse v. Hopkins. American Psychologist, 46,* 1049–1060.

Fiske, S. T., Bersoff, D. N., Borgida, E., Deaux, K., & Heilman, M. E. (1997). What constitutes a scientific review? A majority reply to Barrett and Morris. In M. R. Walsh (Ed.), *Women, men, and gender: Ongoing debates.* New Haven, CT: Yale University Press.

Fiske, S. T., & Neuberg, S. L. (1990). A continuum of impression formation from category-based to individuating processes: Influences of information and motivation on attention and interpretation. In M. P. Zanna (Ed.), *Advances in experimental social psychology* (Vol. 23, pp. 1–74). New York: Academic Press.

Fitz-Gibbon, J., & Siemaszko, C. (September 11, 1996). Hero's pals not surprised. *New York Daily News,* p. 3.

Fitzgerald, J. M. (1988). Vivid memories and the reminiscence phenomenon: The role of self-narrative. *Human Development, 31,* 261–273.

Fitzgerald, R., & Ellsworth, P. C. (1984). Due process vs. crime control: Death qualification and jury attitudes. *Law and Human Behavior, 8,* 31–52.

Fleming, J. S., & Courtney, B. E. (1984). The dimensionality of self-esteem: II. Hierarchical facet model for revised measurement scales. *Journal of Personality and Social Psychology, 46,* 404–421.

Fletcher, G. J. O., Danilovics, P., Fernandez, G., Peterson, D., & Reeder, G. D. (1986). Attributional complexity: An individual differences measure. *Journal of Personality and Social Psychology, 51,* 875–884.

Florian, V., Mikulincer, M., & Taubman, O. (1995). Does hardiness contribute to mental health during a stressful real-life situation? The roles of appraisal and coping. *Journal of Personality and Social Psychology, 68,* 687–695.

Folger, R. (1986). Rethinking equity theory: A referent cognitions model. In H. W. Bierhoff, R. L. Cohen, & J. Greenberg (Eds.), *Justice in social relations* (pp. 145–162). New York: Plenum.

Folger, R., & Greenberg, J. (1985). Procedural justice: An interpretive analysis of personnel systems. In K. Rowland & G. Ferris (Eds.), *Research in personnel and human resource management* (Vol. 3, pp. 141–183). Greenwich, CT: JAI Press.

Folger, R., & Konovsky, M. A. (1989). Effects of procedural and distributive justice on reactions to pay raise decisions. *Academy of Management Journal, 32,* 115–130.

Folger, R., Konovsky, M. A., & Cropanzano, R. (1992). A due process metaphor for performance appraisal. *Research in Organizational Behavior, 14,* 129–177.

Folkes, V. S. (1982). Forming relationships and the matching hypothesis. *Personality and Social Psychology Bulletin, 8,* 631–636.

Follett, M. P. (1942). Constructive conflict. In H. C. Metcalf & L. Urwick (Eds.), *Dynamic administration: The collected papers of Mary Parker Follett* (pp. 30–49). New York: Harper.

Fontana, A., & Rosenheck, R. (1994). Traumatic war stressors and psychiatric symptoms among World War II, Korean, and Vietnam war veterans. *Psychology and Aging, 9,* 27–33.

Forgas, J. P. (1992). Mood and the perception of atypical people: Affect and prototypicality in person memory and impressions. *Journal of Personality and Social Psychology, 62,* 863–875.

Forgas, J. P. (1995). Mood and judgment: The Affect Infusion Model (AIM). *Psychological Bulletin, 117,* 39–66.

Forgas, J. P., & Bower, G. H. (1987). Mood effects on person-perception judgments. *Journal of Personality and Social Psychology, 53,* 53–60.

Foroughi, A., Perkins, W. C., & Jelassi, M. T. (1995). An empirical study of an interactive, session-oriented computerized negotiation support system (NSS). *Group Decision and Negotiation, 4,* 485–512.

Forsyth, D. R. (1990). *Group dynamics* (2nd ed.). Pacific Grove, CA: Brooks/Cole.

Forsythe, S. M. (1990). Effects of applicant's clothing on interviewer's decision to hire. *Journal of Applied Social Psychology, 20,* 1579–1595.

Foster, C. A., Witcher, B. S., Campbell, W. K., & Green, J. D. (1998). Arousal and attraction: Evidence for automatic and controlled processes. *Journal of Personality and Social Psychology, 74,* 86–101.

FosterLee, L., Horowitz, I. A., & Bourgeois, M.J. (1993). Juror competence in civil trials: Effects of preinstruction and evidence technicality. *Journal of Applied Psychology, 78,* 14–21.

Fosterling, F. (1992). The Kelley model as an analysis of variance analogy: How far can it be taken? *Journal of Experimental Social Psychology, 28,* 475–490.

Frable, D. E. S. (1989). Sex typing and gender ideology: Two facets of the individual's gender psychology that go together. *Journal of Personality and Social Psychology, 56,* 95–108.

Franck, K. A. (1980). Friends and strangers: The social experience of living in urban and non-urban settings. *Journal of Social Issues, 36*(3), 52–71.

Frank, J. (1949). *Courts on trial.* Princeton, NJ: Princeton University Press.

Frank, M. G., & Ekman, P. (1997). The ability to detect deceit generalizes across different types of high-stake lies. *Journal of Personality and Social Psychology, 72,* 1429–1439.

Frank, M. G., Ekman, P., & Friesen, W. V. (1993). Behavioral markers and recognizability of the smile of enjoyment. *Journal of Personality and Social Psychology, 64,* 83–93.

Frazier, P. A., & Borgida, E. (1992). Rape trauma syndrome: A review of case law and psychological research. *Law and Human Behavior, 16,* 293–311.

Frazier, P., & Schauben, L. (1994). Causal attributions and recovery from rape and other stressful events. *Journal of Social and Clinical Psychology, 13,* 1–14.

Fredrickson, B. L., Roberts, T. A., Noll, S. M., Quinn, D. M., & Twenge, J. M. (1998). The swimsuit becomes you: Sex differences in self-objectification, restrained eating, and math performance. *Journal of Personality and Social Psychology.*

Freedman, J. L. (1988). Television violence and aggression: What the evidence shows. *Applied Social Psychology Annual, 8,* 144–162.

Freedman, J. L., & Fraser, S. C. (1966). Compliance without pressure: The foot-in-the-door technique. *Journal of Personality and Social Psychology, 4,* 195–202.

Freedman, J. L., & Sears, D. O. (1965). Warning, distraction, and resistance to influence. *Journal of Personality and Social Psychology, 1,* 262–266.

Freud, S. (1905). Fragments of an analysis of a case of hysteria. *Collected papers* (Vol. 3). New York: Basic Books. (Reprinted in 1959)

Freud, S. (1920). *Beyond the pleasure principle: A study of the death instinct in human aggression* (J. Strachey, Trans.). New York: Bantam Books. (Reprinted in 1959)

Frey, D. L., & Gaertner, S. L. (1986). Helping and the avoidance of inappropriate interracial behavior: A strategy that perpetuates a nonprejudiced self-image. *Journal of Personality and Social Psychology, 50,* 1083–1090.

Friedland, N. (1990). Attribution of control as a determinant of cooperation in exchange interactions. *Journal of Applied Social Psychology, 20,* 303–320.

Friedland, N., Keinan, G., & Regev, Y. (1992). Controlling the uncontrollable: Effects of stress on illusory perceptions of controllability. *Journal of Personality and Social Psychology, 63,* 923–931.

Friedman, H. S. (1991). *The self-healing personality.* New York: Henry Holt.

Friedman, H. S., & Booth-Kewley, S. (1987). The "disease-prone personality": A meta-analytic view of the construct. *American Psychologist, 42,* 539–555.

Friedrich, J., Fethersonhaugh, D., Casey, S., & Gallagher, D. (1996). Argument integration and attitude change: Suppression effects in the integration of one-sided arguments that vary in persuasiveness. *Personality and Social Psychology Bulletin, 22,* 179–191.

Friend, R., Rafferty, Y., & Bramel, D. (1990). A puzzling misinterpretation of the Asch "conformity" study. *European Journal of Social Psychology, 20,* 29–44.

Friman, P. C., Allen, K. D., Kerwin, M. L. E., & Larzelere, R. (1993). Changes in modern psychology: A citation analysis of the Kuhnian displacement thesis. *American Psychologist, 48,* 658–664.

Fulero, S., & Penrod, S. D. (1990). Attorney jury selection folklore: What do they think and how can psychology help? *Forensic Reports, 3,* 223–259.

Fultz, J., & Nielsen, M. E. (1993). Anticipated vicarious affect and willingness to be exposed to another's suffering. *Basic and Applied Social Psychology, 14,* 273–283.

Funder, D. C. (1982). On the accuracy of dispositional vs. situational attributions. *Social Cognition, 1,* 205–222.

Funder, D. C. (1987). Errors and mistakes: Evaluating the accuracy of social judgment. *Psychological Bulletin, 101,* 75–90.

Funk, S. C. (1992). Hardiness: A review of theory and research. *Health Psychology, 11,* 335–345.

Furnham, A. (1993). Just world beliefs in twelve societies. *Journal of Social Psychology, 133,* 317–329.

Furnham, A., & Skae, E. (1997). Changes in the stereotypical portrayal of men and women in British television advertisements. *European Psychologist, 2,* 44–51.

Gaertner, S. L., Mann, J. A., Dovidio, J. F., Murrell, A. J., & Pomare, M. (1990). How does cooperation reduce intergroup bias? *Journal of Personality and Social Psychology, 59,* 692–704.

Gaertner, S. L., Mann, J. A., Murrell, A. J., & Dovidio, J. F. (1989). Reducing intergroup bias: The benefits of recategorization. *Journal of Personality and Social Psychology, 57,* 239–249.

Gagnon, A., & Bourhis, R. Y. (1996). Discrimination in the minimal group paradigm: Social identity or self-interest? *Personality and Social Psychology Bulletin, 22,* 1289–1301.

Galen, B. R., & Underwood, M. K. (1997). *Developmental Psychology, 33,* 589–600.

Gallup, G. G., Jr. (1977). Self-recognition in primates: A comparative approach to the bidirectional properties of consciousness. *American Psychologist, 32,* 329–337.

Gallupe, R. B., Bastianutti, L. M., & Cooper, W. H. (1991). Unblocking brainstorms. *Journal of Applied Psychology, 76,* 137–142.

Gamson, W. A., Fireman, B., & Rytina, S. (1982). *Encounters with unjust authority.* Homewood, IL: Dorsey.

Gan, S., Zillmann, D., & Mitrook, M. (1997). Stereotyping effect of Black women's sexual rap on White audiences. *Basic and Applied Social Psychology, 19,* 381–399.

Gangestad, S. W. (1993). Sexual selection and physical attractiveness: Implications for mating dynamics. *Human Nature, 4,* 205–235.

Gangestad, S., & Snyder, M. (1991). Taxonomic analysis redux: Some statistical considerations for testing a latent class model. *Journal of Personality and Social Psychology, 61,* 141–146.

Gaugler, B. B., Rosenthal, D. B., Thornton, G. C., III, & Bentson, C. (1987). Meta-analysis of assessment center validity. *Journal of Applied Psychology, 72,* 493–511.

Gavin, L., & Furman, W. (1989). Age difference in adolescents' perceptions of their peer groups. *Developmental Psychology, 25,* 827–834.

Geen, R. G. (1981). Behavioral and physiological reactions to observed violence: Effects of prior exposure to aggressive stimuli. *Journal of Personality and Social Psychology, 40,* 868–875.

Geen, R. G. (1998). Aggression and antisocial behavior. In D. T. Gilbert, S. T. Fiske, & G. Lindzey (Eds.), *The handbook of social psychology* (4th ed., Vol. 2, pp. 317–356). New York: McGraw-Hill.

Geen, R. G., & McCown, E. J. (1984). Effects of noise and attack on aggression and physiological arousal. *Motivation and Emotion, 8,* 231–241.

Geen, R. G., & Quanty, M. B. (1977). The catharsis of aggression: An evaluation of a hypothesis. In L. Berkowitz (Ed.), *Advances in experimental social psychology* (Vol. 10, pp. 1–37). New York: Academic Press.

Geis, F. L., Brown, V., Jennings (Walstedt), J., & Porter, N. (1984). TV commercials as achievement scripts for women. *Sex Roles, 10,* 513–525.

Geiselman, R. E., Haight, N. A., & Kimata, L. G. (1984). Context effects in the perceived physical attractiveness of faces. *Journal of Experimental Social Psychology, 20,* 409–424.

Geller, W. A. (1993). *Videotaping interrogations and confessions.* Washington, DC: National Institute of Justice.

Gelles, R. J., & Cornell, C. P. (1990). *Intimate violence in families* (2nd ed.). Newbury Park, CA: Sage.

Gelles, R. J., & Straus, M. A. (1988). *Intimate violence.* New York: Simon & Schuster.

Genta, M. L., Menesini, E., Fonzi, A., Costabile, A., & Smith, P. K. (1996). Bullies and victims in schools in Central and South Italy. *European Journal of Psychology of Education, 11,* 97–110.

George, J. M., & Brief, A. P. (1992). Feeling good–doing good: A conceptual analysis of the mood at work—organizational spontaneity relationship. *Psychological Bulletin, 112,* 310–329.

Georgesen, J. C., & Harris, M. J. (1998). Why's my boss always holding me down? A meta-analysis of power effects on performance evaluations. *Personality and Social Psychology Review,* in press.

Gerard, H. B., Whilhelmy, R. A., & Connolley, R. S. (1968). Conformity and group size. *Journal of Personality and Social Psychology, 8,* 79–82.

Gerbner, G., Gross, L., Morgan, M., & Signorielli, N. (1986). Living with television: The dynamics of the cultivation process. In J. Bryant & D. Zillmann (Eds.), *Perspectives on media effects* (pp. 17–40). Hillsdale, NJ: Erlbaum.

Gergen, K. J. (1973). Social psychology as history. *Journal of Personality and Social Psychology, 26,* 309–320.

Gergen, K. J. (1994). Exploring the postmodern: Perils or potentials? *American Psychologist, 49,* 412–416.

Gerhart, B., & Rynes, S. (1991). Determinants and consequences of salary negotiations by male and female MBA graduates. *Journal of Applied Psychology, 76,* 256–262.

Gerrard, M., Gibbons, F. X., & Bushman, B. J. (1996). Relation between perceived vulnerability to HIV and precautionary sexual behavior. *Psychological Bulletin, 119,* 390–409.

Gerrard, M., Gibbons, F. X., Warner, T. D., & Smith, G. E. (1993). Perceived vulnerability to HIV infection and AIDS-preventive behavior: A critical review of the evidence. In J. B. Pryor & G. D. Reeder (Eds.), *The social psychology of HIV infection* (pp. 59–84). Hillsdale, NJ: Erlbaum.

Gersick, C. J. G. (1988). Time and transition in work teams: Toward a new model of group development. *Academy of Management Journal, 21,* 9–41.

Gersick, C. J. G. (1994). Pacing strategic change: The case of a new venture. *Academy of Management Journal, 37,* 9–45.

Gibbons, A. (1993). Evolutionists take the long view on sex and violence. *Science, 261,* 987–988.

Gibbons, F. X. (1978). Sexual standards and reactions to pornography: Enhancing behavioral consistency through self-focused attention. *Journal of Personality and Social Psychology, 36,* 976–987.

Gibbons, F. X. (1990). Self-attention and behavior: A review and theoretical update. In M. P. Zanna (Ed.), *Advances in experimental social psychology* (Vol. 23, pp. 249–303). New York: Academic Press.

Gibbons, F. X., & McCoy, S. B. (1991). Self-esteem, similarity, and reactions to active versus passive downward comparison. *Journal of Personality and Social Psychology, 60,* 414–424.

Gibbons, F. X., & Wicklund, R. A. (1982). Self-focused attention and helping behavior. *Journal of Personality and Social Psychology, 43,* 462–474.

Giesler, R. B., Josephs, R. A., & Swann, W. B., Jr. (1996). Self-verification in clinical depression: The desire for negative evaluation. *Journal of Abnormal Psychology, 105,* 358–368.

Giesler, R. B., & Swann, W. B., Jr. (1998). Self-verification and depression. In T. Joiner & J. C. Coyne (Eds.), *Recent advances in interpersonal approaches to depression.* Washington, D.C.: American Psychological Association.

Gigone, D., & Hastie, R. (1993). The common knowledge effect: Information sharing and group judgment. *Journal of Personality and Social Psychology, 65,* 959–974.

Gigone, D., & Hastie, R. (1997). Proper analysis of the accuracy of group judgments. *Psychological Bulletin, 121,* 149–167.

Gilbert, D. T., Giesler, R. B., & Morris, K. A. (1995). When comparisons arise. *Journal of Personality and Social Psychology, 69,* 227–236.

Gilbert, D. T., & Hixon, J. G. (1991). The trouble of thinking: Activation and application of stereotypic beliefs. *Journal of Personality and Social Psychology, 60,* 509–517.

Gilbert, D. T., & Jones, E. E. (1986). Perceiver-induced constraint: Interpretations of self-generated reality. *Journal of Personality and Social Psychology, 50,* 269–280.

Gilbert, D. T., & Krull, D. S. (1988). Seeing less and knowing more: The benefits of perceptual ignorance. *Journal of Personality and Social Psychology, 54,* 193–202.

Gilbert, D. T., & Malone, P. S. (1995). The correspondence bias. *Psychological Bulletin, 117,* 21–38.

Gilbert, D. T., McNulty, S. E., Giuliano, T. A., & Benson, J. E. (1992). Blurry words and fuzzy deeds: The attribution of obscure behavior. *Journal of Personality and Social Psychology, 62,* 18–25.

Gilbert, D. T., Pelham, B. W., & Krull, D. S. (1988). On cognitive busyness: When person perceivers meet persons perceived. *Journal of Personality and Social Psychology, 54,* 733–740.

Gilbert, D. T., & Silvera, D. H. (1996). Overhelping. *Journal of Personality and Social Psychology, 70,* 678–690.

Gilbert, S. J. (1981). Another look at the Milgram obedience studies: The role of the gradated series of shocks. *Personality and Social Psychology Bulletin, 7,* 690–695.

Gillig, P. M., & Greenwald, A. G. (1974). Is it time to lay the sleeper effect to rest? *Journal of Personality and Social Psychology, 29,* 132–139.

Gilovich, T. (1991). *How we know what isn't so: The fallibility of human reason in everyday life.* New York: Free Press.

Giner-Sorolla, R., & Chaiken, S. (1997). Selective use of heuristic and systematic processing under defensive motivation. *Personality and Social Psychology Bulletin, 23,* 84–97.

Gioia, D. A., & Longnecker, C. O. (1994). Delving into the dark side: The politics of executive appraisal. *Organizational Dynamics, 22,* 47–58.

Gladue, B. A., Boechler, M., & McCaul, K. D. (1989). Hormonal response to competition in human males. *Aggressive Behavior, 15,* 409–422.

Glaser, R., & Kiecolt-Glaser, J. K. (Eds.) (1994). *Handbook of stress and immunity.* San Diego: Academic Press.

Glass, D. C., & Singer, J. E. (1972). *Urban stress.* New York: Academic Press.

Gleicher, F., & Petty, R. E. (1992). Expectations of reassurance influence the nature of fear-stimulated attitude change. *Journal of Experimental Social Psychology, 28,* 86–100.

Gleick, E. (1997). The marker we've been waiting for. *Time,* April 7, 1997, pp. 31–36.

Glick, P., & Fiske, S. T. (1996). The Ambivalent Sexism Inventory: Differentiating hostile and benevolent sexism. *Journal of Personality and Social Psychology, 70,* 491–512.

Glick, P., Zion, C., & Nelson, C. (1988). What mediates sex discrimination in hiring decisions? *Journal of Personality and Social Psychology, 55,* 178–186.

Godfrey, D. K., Jones, E. E., & Lord, C. G. (1986). Self-promotion is not ingratiating. *Journal of Personality and Social Psychology, 50,* 106–115.

Goethals, G. R., Cooper, J., & Naficy, A. (1979). Role of foreseen, foreseeable, and unforeseeable behavioral consequences in the arousal of cognitive dissonance. *Journal of Personality and Social Psychology, 37,* 1179–1185.

Goethals, G. R., & Darley, J. (1977). Social comparison theory: An attributional approach. In J. M. Suls & R. L. Miller (Eds.), *Social comparison processes: Theoretical and empirical perspectives* (pp. 259–278). Washington, DC: Hemisphere.

Goethals, G. R., & Reckman, R. (1973). The perception of consistency in attitudes. *Journal of Experimental Social Psychology, 9,* 491–501.

Goffin, R. D., Rothstein, M. G., & Johnston, N. G. (1996). Personality testing and the assessment center: Incremental validity for managerial selection. *Journal of Applied Psychology, 81,* 746–756.

Goffman, E. (1955). On face-work: An analysis of ritual elements in social interaction. *Psychiatry, 18,* 213–231.

Goffman, E. (1959). *The presentation of self in everyday life.* Garden City: Doubleday.

Goldberg, J., True, W. R., Eisen, S. A., & Henderson, W. G. (1990). A twin study of the effects of the Vietnam War on posttraumatic stress disorder. *Journal of the American Medical Association, 263,* 1227–1232.

Goldberg, L. R. (1978). Differential attribution of trait-descriptive terms to oneself as compared to well-liked, neutral, and disliked others: A psychometric analysis. *Journal of Personality and Social Psychology, 36,* 1012–1028.

Goldberg, L. R. (1993). The structure of phenotypic personality. *American Psychologist, 48,* 26–34.

Goldberg, L. R., Grenier, J. R., Guion, R., Sechrest, L. B., & Wing, H. (1991). *Questionnaires used in the prediction of trustworthiness in pre-employment selection decisions: An A.P.A. task force report.* Washington, DC: American Psychological Association.

Goldberg, P. (1968). Are women prejudiced against women? *Transaction, 5,* 28–30.

Goldhagen, D. J. (1996). *Hitler's willing executioners: Ordinary Germans and the Holocaust.* New York: Knopf.

Goldman, J. A., & Harlow, L. L. (1993). Self-perception variables that mediate AIDS-preventive behavior in college students. *Health Psychology, 12,* 489–498.

Goldman, M. (1986). Compliance employing a combined foot-in-the-door and door-in-the-face procedure. *Journal of Social Psychology, 126,* 111–116.

Goldstein, A. G., Chance, J. E., & Schneller, G. R. (1989). Frequency of eyewitness identification in criminal cases: A survey of prosecutors. *Bulletin of the Psychonomic Society, 27,* 71–74.

Goldstein, M. D., & Strube, M. J. (1994). Independence revisited: The relation between positive and negative affect in a naturalistic setting. *Personality and Social Psychology Bulletin, 20,* 57–64.

Gonzalez, R., Ellsworth, P. C., & Pembroke, M. (1993). Response biases in lineups and showups. *Journal of Personality and Social Psychology, 64,* 525–537.

Gorassini, D. R., & Olson, J. M. (1995). Does self-perception change explain the foot-in-the-door effect? *Journal of Personality and Social Psychology, 69,* 91–105.

Gorenstein, G. W., & Ellsworth, P. C. (1980). Effect of choosing an incorrect photograph on a later identification by an eyewitness. *Journal of Applied Psychology, 65,* 616–622.

Gorman, C. (1994, September 19). Let's not be too hasty. *Time,* p. 71.

Gosselin, P., Kirouac, G., & Dore, F. Y. (1995). Components and recognition of facial expression in the communication of emotion by actors. *Journal of Personality and Social Psychology, 68,* 83–96.

Gottesman, I. I., & Goldsmith, H. H. (1994). Developmental psychopathology of antisocial behavior: Inserting genes into its ontogenesis and epigenesis. In C. A. Nelson (Ed.), *Threats to optimal development: Integrating biological, psychological, and social risk factors. The Minnesota symposia on child psychology* (Vol. 27, pp. 69–104). Hillsdale, NJ: Erlbaum.

Gottlieb, J., & Carver, C. S. (1980). Anticipation of future interaction and the bystander effect. *Journal of Experimental Social Psychology, 16,* 253–260.

Gottman, J. M. (1994). *What predicts divorce?* Hillsdale, NJ: Erlbaum.

Gottman, J. M., & Levenson, R. L. (1988). The social psychophysiology of marriage. In P. Noller & M. A. Fitzpatrick (Eds.), *Perspectives on marital interaction* (pp. 182–200). Clevedon, England: Multilingual Matters.

Gottman, J. M., & Levenson, R. W. (1992). Marital processes predictive of later dissolution: Behavior, physiology, and health. *Journal of Personality and Social Psychology, 63,* 221–233.

Gould, S. J. (1992, November 19). The confusion over evolution. *New York Review of Books,* pp. 47–54.

Gouldner, A. W. (1960). The norm of reciprocity: A preliminary statement. *American Sociological Review, 25,* 161–178.

Graham, S. (1992). "Most of the subjects were white and middle class": Trends in published research on African Americans in selected APA journals, 1970–1989. *American Psychologist, 47,* 629–639.

Grammer, K., & Thornhill, R. (1994). Human facial attractiveness and sexual selection: The role of averageness and symmetry. *Journal of Comparative Psychology, 108,* 233–242.

Granberg, D., & Brent, E. (1983). When prophecy bends: The preference-expectation link in U.S. presidential elections. *Journal of Personality and Social Psychology, 45,* 477–491.

Graves, L. M., & Powell, G. N. (1988). An investigation of sex discrimination in recruiters' evaluations of actual applicants. *Journal of Applied Psychology, 73,* 20–29.

Gray, J. (1997). *Men are from Mars, women are from Venus.* New York: HarperCollins.

Greenberg, J. (1982). Approaching equity and avoiding inequity in groups and organizations. In J. Greenberg & R. L. Cohen (Eds.), *Equity and justice in social behavior* (pp. 389–435). New York: Academic Press.

Greenberg, J. (1988). Equity and workplace status: A field experiment. *Journal of Applied Psychology, 73,* 606–613.

Greenberg, J. (1990). Employee theft as a reaction to under-payment inequity: The hidden costs of pay cuts. *Journal of Applied Psychology, 75,* 561–568.

Greenberg, J. (1993). Stealing in the name of justice: Informational and interpersonal moderators of theft reactions to underpayment equity. *Organizational Behavior and Human Decision Processes, 54,* 81–103.

Greenberg, J., & Pyszczynski, T. (1985). The effects of an overheard ethnic slur on evaluations of the target: How to spread a social disease. *Journal of Experimental Social Psychology, 21,* 61–72.

Greenberg, J., Pyszczynski, T., Solomon, S., Rosenblatt, A., et al. (1990). *Journal of Personality and Social Psychology, 58,* 308–318.

Greenberg, J., Solomon, S., & Pyszczynski, T. (1997). Terror management theory of self-esteem and cultural worldviews: Empirical assessments and conceptual refinements. *Advances in Experimental Social Psychology, 29,* 61–139.

Greenberg, L. (1979). Genetic component of bee odor in kin recognition. *Science, 206,* 1095–1097.

Greenberg, M. S., & Westcott, D. R. (1983). Indebtedness as a mediator of reactions to aid. In J. D. Fisher, A. Nadler, & B. M. DePaulo (Eds.), *New directions in helping: Vol. 1. Recipient reactions to aid* (pp. 85–112). New York: Academic Press.

Greene, C. N. (1989). Cohesion and productivity in work groups. *Small Group Behavior, 20,* 70–86.

Greene, E., & Dodge, M. (1995). The influence of prior record evidence on juror decision-making. *Law and Human Behavior, 19,* 67–78.

Greene, W. C. (1993, September). AIDS and the immune system. *Scientific American,* pp. 99–105.

Greenwald, A. G. (1968). Cognitive learning, cognitive responses to persuasion, and attitude change. In A. Greenwald, T. Brock, & T. Ostrom (Eds.), *Psychological foundations of attitudes* (pp. 147–170). New York: Academic Press.

Greenwald, A. G. (1980). The totalitarian ego: Fabrication and revision of personal history. *American Psychologist, 35,* 603–618.

Greenwald, A. G., & Banaji, M. R. (1995). Implicit social cognition: Attitudes, self-esteem, and stereotypes. *Psychological Review, 102,* 4–27.

Greenwald, A. G., McGhee, D. E., & Schwartz, J. L. K. (1998). Measuring individual differences in implicit cognition: The implicit association test. *Journal of Personality and Social Psychology.*

Greenwald, A. G., Pratkanis, A. R., Leippe, M. R., & Baumgardner, M. H. (1986). Under what conditions does theory obstruct research progress? *Psychological Review, 93,* 216–229.

Greenwald, A. G., Spangenberg, E. R., Pratkanis, A. R., & Eskenazi, J. (1991). Double-blind tests of subliminal self-help audiotapes. *Psychological Science, 2,* 119–122.

Grisham, J. (1996). *The runaway jury.* New York: Bantam Books.

Gross, A. E., & Crofton, C. (1977). What is good is beautiful. *Sociometry, 40,* 85–90.

Gross, A. E., & Latané, J. G. (1974). Receiving help, reciprocation, and interpersonal attraction. *Journal of Applied Social Psychology, 4,* 210–223.

Gross, J. J., & Levenson, R. W. (1997). Hiding feelings: The acute effects of inhibiting negative and positive emotion. *Journal of Abnormal Psychology, 106,* 95–103.

Gross, S. R., & Miller, N. (1997). The "golden section" and bias in perceptions of social consensus. *Personality and Social Psychology Review, 1,* 241–271.

Grossman, M., & Wood, W. (1993). Sex differences in intensity of emotional experience: A social role interpretation. *Journal of Personality and Social Psychology, 65,* 1010–1020.

Gruder, C. L., Cook, T. D., Hennigan, K. M., Flay, B. R., Alessis, C., & Halamaj, J. (1978). Empirical tests of the absolute sleeper effect predicted from the discounting cue hypothesis. *Journal of Personality and Social Psychology, 36,* 1061–1074.

Grusec, J. E. (1991). The socialization of altruism. In M. S. Clark (Ed.), *Prosocial behavior. Review of personality and social psychology* (Vol. 12, pp. 9–33). Newbury Park, CA: Sage.

Gudjonsson, G. (1992). *The psychology of interrogations, confessions, and testimony.* Chichester: John Wiley.

Gudykunst, W., & Bond, M. H. (1997). Intergroup relations across cultures. In J. W. Berry, M. H. Segall, & C. Kagitçibasi (Eds.), *Handbook of cross-cultural psychology: Social behavior and applications* (2nd ed., Vol. 3, pp. 119–161). Needham Heights, MA: Allyn & Bacon.

Guerin, B. (1986). Mere presence effects in humans: A review. *Journal of Experimental Social Psychology, 22,* 38–77.

Guimond, S., & Dubé-Simard, L. (1983). Relative deprivation theory and the Quebec nationalist movement: The cognition-emotion distinction and the personal-group deprivation issue. *Journal of Personality and Social Psychology, 44,* 526–535.

Gully, S. M., Devine, D. J., & Whitney, D. J. (1995). A meta-analysis of cohesion and performance: Effects of level of analysis and task interdependence. *Small Group Research, 26,* 497–520.

Gump, B. B., & Kulik, J. A. (1997). Stress, affiliation, and emotional contagion. *Journal of Personality and Social Psychology, 72,* 305–319.

Gwaltney, L. (1986). *The dissenters.* New York: Random House.

Hakmiller, K. L. (1966). Threat as a determinant of downward comparison. *Journal of Experimental Social Psychology* (Suppl. 1), 32–39.

Halberstam, D. (1972). *The best and the brightest.* New York: Random House.

Halford, W. K., Hahlweg, K., & Dunne, M. (1990). The cross-cultural consistency of marital communication associated with marital distress. *Journal of Marriage and the Family, 52,* 487–500.

Hamermesh, D. S., & Biddle, J. E. (1994). Beauty and the labor market. *American Economic Review, 84,* 1174–1195.

Hamilton, D. L., & Gifford, R. K. (1976). Illusory correlation in interpersonal perception: A cognitive basis of stereotypic judgments. *Journal of Experimental Social Psychology, 12,* 392–407.

Hamilton, D. L., & Rose, T. L. (1980). Illusory correlation and the maintenance of stereotypic beliefs. *Journal of Personality and Social Psychology, 39,* 832–845.

Hamilton, W. D. (1964). The genetical evolution of social behavior: I and II. *Journal of Theoretical Biology, 7,* 1–52.

Hammersla, J. F., & Frease-McMahan, L. (1990). University students' priorities: Life goals vs. relationships. *Sex Roles, 23,* 1–14.

Hampson, R. B. (1984). Adolescent prosocial behavior: Peer-group and situational factors associated with helping. *Journal of Personality and Social Psychology, 46,* 153–162.

Han, G., & Park, B. (1995). Children's choice in conflict: Application of the theory of individualism-collectivism. *Journal of Cross-Cultural Psychology, 26,* 298–313.

Han, S., & Shavitt, S. (1994). Persuasion and culture: Advertising appeals in individualistic and collectivistic societies. *Journal of Experimental Social Psychology, 30,* 326–350.

Haney, C. (1984). On the selection of capital juries: The biasing effects of the death-qualification process. *Law and Human Behavior, 8,* 121–132.

Haney, C., Banks, C., & Zimbardo, P. (1973). Interpersonal dynamics in a simulated prison. *International Journal of Criminology and Penology, 1,* 69–97.

Haney, C., Hurtado, A., & Vega, L. (1994). "Modern" death qualification: New data on its biasing effects. *Law and Human Behavior, 18,* 619–633.

Hans, V. P., & Vidmar, N. (1986). *Judging the jury.* New York: Plenum.

Hansen, C. H. (1995). Predicting cognitive and behavioral effects of gangsta rap. *Basic and Applied Social Psychology, 16,* 43–52.

Hansen, C. H., & Hansen, R. D. (1988). Finding the face in the crowd: An anger superiority effect. *Journal of Personality and Social Psychology, 54,* 917–924.

Hansen, J. E., & Schuldt, W. J. (1984). Marital self-disclosure and marital satisfaction. *Journal of Marriage and the Family, 46,* 923–926.

Harackiewicz, J. M., & Elliot, A. J. (1993). Achievement goals and intrinsic motivation. *Journal of Personality and Social Psychology, 65,* 904–915.

Harbin, T. J. (1989). The relationship between the Type A behavior pattern and physiological responsivity: Quantitative review. *Psychophysiology, 26,* 110–119.

Hardin, G. (1968). The tragedy of the commons. *Science, 162,* 1243–1248.

Haritos-Fatouros, M. (1988). The official torturer: A learning model for obedience to the authority of violence. *Journal of Applied Social Psychology, 18,* 1107–1120.

Harkins, S. G., & Petty, R. E. (1981). Effects of source magnification of cognitive effort on attitudes: An information

processing view. *Journal of Personality and Social Psychology, 40,* 401–413.

Harkins, S. G., & Petty, R. E. (1982). Effects of task difficulty and task uniqueness on social loafing. *Journal of Personality and Social Psychology, 43,* 1214–1229.

Harkins, S. G., & Petty, R. E. (1987). Information utility and the multiple source effect. *Journal of Personality and Social Psychology, 52,* 260–268.

Harkins, S. G., & Szymanski, K. (1987). Social loafing and social facilitation: New wine in old bottles. In C. Hendrick (Ed.), *Review of personality and social psychology: Group processes and intergroup relations* (Vol. 9, pp. 167–188). Beverly Hills, CA: Sage.

Harmon-Jones, E., Brehm, J. W., Greenberg, J., Simon, L., & Nelson, D. E. (1996). Evidence that the production of aversive consequences is not necessary to create cognitive dissonance. *Journal of Personality and Social Psychology, 70,* 5–16.

Harré, R., & Lamb, R. (1983). *The encyclopedic dictionary of psychology.* Oxford, England: Basil Blackwell.

Harrington, A. (Ed.) (1997). *The placebo effect: An inter-disciplinary exploration.* Cambridge, MA: Harvard University Press.

Harris, C. R., & Christenfeld, N. (1996). Gender, jealousy, and reason. *Psychological Science, 7,* 364–366.

Harris, M. B. (1995). Ethnicity, gender, and evaluations of aggression. *Aggressive Behavior, 21,* 343–357.

Harris, M. J., Moniz, A. J., Sowards, B. A., & Krane, K. (1994). Mediation of interpersonal expectancy effects: Expectancies about the elderly. *Social Psychology Quarterly, 57,* 36–48.

Harris, M. J., & Perkins, R. (1995). Effects of distraction on interpersonal expectancy effects: A social interaction test of the cognitive busyness hypothesis. *Social Cognition, 13,* 163–182.

Harris, M. J., & Rosenthal, R. (1985). Mediation of interpersonal expectancy effects. *Psychological Bulletin, 97,* 363–386.

Harris, M. M. (1989). Reconsidering the employment interview: A review of recent literature and suggestions for future research. *Personnel Psychology, 42,* 691–726.

Harrison, A. A., & Connors, M. M. (1984). Groups in exotic environments. In L. Berkowitz (Ed.), *Advances in experimental social psychology* (Vol. 8, pp. 49–87). Orlando, FL: Academic Press.

Harrison, D. A., & Shaffer, M. A. (1994). Comparative examinations of self-reports and perceived absenteeism norms: Wading through Lake Wobegon. *Journal of Applied Psychology, 79,* 240–251.

Hartsough, D. M., & Savitsky, J. C. (1984). Three Mile Island: Psychology and environmental policy at a crossroads. *American Psychologist, 39,* 1113–1122.

Harvey, J. H. (1995). *Odyssey of the heart: The search for closeness, intimacy, and love.* New York: Freeman.

Harvey, J. H., & Omarzu, J. (1997). Minding the close relationship. *Personality and Social Psychology Review, 1,* 224–240.

Harvey, J. H., Town, J. P., & Yarkin, K. L. (1981). How fundamental is the "fundamental attribution error"? *Journal of Personality and Social Psychology, 43,* 345–346.

Hass, R. G. (1981). Effects of source characteristics on the cognitive processing of persuasive messages and attitude change. In R. Petty, T. Ostrom, & T. Brock (Eds.), *Cognitive responses in persuasion* (pp. 141–172). Hillsdale, NJ: Erlbaum.

Hass, R. G. (1984). Perspective taking and self-awareness: Drawing an E on your forehead. *Journal of Personality and Social Psychology, 46,* 788–798.

Hass, R. G., & Eisenstadt, D. (1990). The effects of self-focused attention on perspective-taking and anxiety. *Anxiety Research, 2,* 165–176.

Hass, R. G., & Grady, K. (1975). Temporal delay, type of forewarning, and resistance to influence. *Journal of Experimental Social Psychology, 11,* 459–469.

Hass, R. G., Katz, I., Rizzo, N., Bailey, J., & Moore, L. (1992). When racial ambivalence evokes negative affect, using a disguised measure of mood. *Personality and Social Psychology Bulletin, 18,* 786–797.

Hastie, R. (1984). Causes and effects of causal attribution. *Journal of Personality and Social Psychology, 46,* 44–56.

Hastie, R., Penrod, S. D., & Pennington, N. (1983). *Inside the jury.* Cambridge, MA: Harvard University Press.

Hatch, O. G. (1982). Psychology, society, and politics. *American Psychologist, 37,* 1031–1037.

Hater, J. J., & Bass, B. M. (1988). Superiors' evaluations and subordinates' perceptions of transformational and transactional leadership. *Journal of Applied Psychology, 73,* 695–702.

Hatfield, E. (1988). Passionate and companionate love. In R. J. Sternberg & M. L. Barnes (Ed.), *The psychology of love* (pp. 191–217). New Haven, CT: Yale University Press.

Hatfield, E., Greenberger, E., Traupmann, J., & Lambert, P. (1982). Equity and sexual satisfaction in recently married couples. *Journal of Sex Research, 18,* 18–32.

Hatfield, E., & Rapson, R. L. (1987). Passionate love: New directions in research. In W. H. Jones & D. Perlman (Eds.), *Advances in personal relationships* (Vol. 1, pp. 109–139). Greenwich, CT: JAI Press.

Hatfield, E., & Rapson, R. L. (1993). *Love, sex, and intimacy: Their psychology, biology, and history.* New York: HarperCollins.

Hatfield, E., & Sprecher, S. (1986). *Mirror, mirror. . . . The importance of looks in everyday life.* Albany, NY: State University of New York Press.

Haupt, A. L., & Leary, M. R. (1997). The appeal of worthless groups: Moderating effects of trait self-esteem. *Group Dynamics, 1,* 124–132.

Haverkamp, B. E. (1993). Confirmatory bias in hypothesis testing for client-identified and counselor self-generated hypotheses. *Journal of Counseling Psychology, 40,* 303–315.

Hawkins, S. A., & Hastie, R. (1990). Hindsight: Biased judgments of past events after the outcomes are known. *Psychological Bulletin, 107,* 311–327.

Hays, R. B. (1985). A longitudinal study of friendship development. *Journal of Personality and Social Psychology, 48,* 909–924.

Hazan, C., & Shaver, P. (1987). Romantic love conceptualized as an attachment process. *Journal of Personality and Social Psychology, 52,* 511–524.

Hearold, S. (1986). A synthesis of 1043 effects of television on social behavior. In G. Comstock (Ed.), *Public communication and behavior* (Vol. 1, pp. 65–133). Orlando, FL: Academic Press.

Heatherton, T. F., & Polivy, J. (1991). Development and validation of a scale for measuring state self-esteem. *Journal of Personality and Social Psychology, 60,* 895–910.

Heaton, T. B. (1991). Time related determinants of marital dissolution. *Journal of Marriage and the Family, 53,* 285–295.

Hedge, A., & Yousif, Y. H. (1992). Effects of urban size, urgency, and cost on helpfulness: A cross-cultural comparison between the United Kingdom and the Sudan. *Journal of Cross Cultural Psychology, 23,* 107–115.

Hedge, J. W., & Kavanagh, M. J. (1988). Improving the accuracy of performance evaluations: Comparison of three methods of performance appraiser training. *Journal of Applied Psychology, 73,* 68–73.

Heider, F. (1958). *The psychology of interpersonal relations.* New York: Wiley.

Heilman, M. E., Block, C. J., & Lucas, J. A. (1992). Presumed incompetent? Stigmatization and affirmative action efforts. *Journal of Applied Psychology, 77,* 536–544.

Heilman, M. E., Kaplow, S. R., Amato, M. A., & Stathatos, P. (1993). When similarity is a liability: Effects of sex-based preferential selection on reactions to like-sex and different-sex others. *Journal of Applied Psychology, 78,* 917–927.

Heilman, M. E., McCullough, W. F., & Gilbert, D. (1996). The other side of affirmative action: Reactions of nonbeneficiaries to sex-based preferential selection. *Journal of Applied Psychology, 81,* 346–357.

Heilman, M. E., Rivero, J. C., & Brett, J. F. (1991). Skirting the competence issue: Effects of sex-based preferential selection on task choices of women and men. *Journal of Applied Psychology, 76,* 99–105.

Heilman, M. E., Simon, M. C., & Repper, D. P. (1987). Intentionally favored, unintentionally harmed? Impact of sex-based preferential selection on self-perceptions and self-evaluations. *Journal of Applied Psychology, 72,* 62–68.

Heinberg, L. J., & Thompson, J. K. (1995). Body image and televised images of thinness and attractiveness: A controlled laboratory investigation. *Journal of Social and Clinical Psychology, 14,* 325–338.

Heine, S. J., & Lehman, D. R. (1995). Cultural variation in unrealistic optimism: Does the West feel more invulnerable than the East? *Journal of Personality and Social Psychology, 68,* 595–607.

Helgesen, S. (1990). *The female advantage: Women's ways of leadership.* New York: Doubleday Currency.

Helgeson, V. S. (1992). Moderators of the relation between perceived control and adjustment to chronic illness. *Journal of Personality and Social Psychology, 63,* 652–666.

Helgeson, V. S. (1994). Relation of agency and communion to well-being: Evidence and potential explanations. *Psychological Bulletin, 116,* 412–428.

Heller, J. F., Pallak, M. S., & Picek, J. M. (1973). The interactive effects of intent and threat on boomerang attitude change. *Journal of Personality and Social Psychology, 26,* 273–279.

Henchy, T., & Glass, D. C. (1968). Evaluation apprehension and the social facilitation of dominant and subordinate responses. *Journal of Personality and Social Psychology, 10,* 446–454.

Hendrick, S. S., & Hendrick, C. (1992). *Romantic love.* Newbury Park, CA: Sage.

Hendrick, S. S., & Hendrick, C. (1993). Lovers as friends. *Journal of Social and Personal Relationships, 10,* 459–466.

Hendrick, S. S., & Hendrick, C. (1995). Gender differences and similarities in sex and love. *Personal Relationships, 2,* 55–65.

Heneman, H. G., & Schwab, D. P. (1985). Pay satisfaction: Its multidimensional nature and measurement. *International Journal of Psychology, 20,* 129–141.

Henley, N. M. (1977). *Body politics: Power, sex, and nonverbal communication.* Englewood Cliffs, NJ: Prentice-Hall.

Henry, R. A. (1995). Improving group judgment accuracy: Information sharing and determining the best member. *Organizational Behavior and Human Decision Processes, 62,* 190–197.

Hense, R. L., Penner, L. A., & Nelson, D. L. (1995). Implicit memory for age stereotypes. *Social Cognition, 13,* 399–415.

Hensley, T. R., & Griffin, G. W. (1986). Victims of groupthink. *Journal of Conflict Resolution, 30,* 497–531.

Hepworth, J. T., & West, S. G. (1988). Lynchings and the economy: A time-series reanalysis of Hovland and Sears (1940). *Journal of Personality and Social Psychology, 55,* 239–247.

Herbert, T. B., & Cohen, S. (1993). Stress and immunity in humans: A meta-analytic review. *Psychosomatic Medicine, 55,* 364–379.

Herman, C. P., Zanna, M. P., & Higgins, E. T. (1986). *Physical appearance, stigma, and social behavior: The Ontario Symposium* (Vol. 3). Hillsdale, NJ: Erlbaum.

Hertel, G., & Fiedler, K. (1994). Affective and cognitive influences in a social dilemma game. *European Journal of Social Psychology, 24*, 131–145.

Hertz-Lazarowitz, R., & Miller, N. (Eds.) (1992). *Interaction in cooperative groups: The theoretical anatomy of group learning.* Cambridge, England: Cambridge University Press.

Herzberger, S. D. (1996). *Violence within the family: Social psychological perspectives.* Madison, WI: Brown & Benchmark.

Hewstone, M., & Lord, C. G. (1998). Changing intergroup cognitions and intergroup behavior: The role of typicality. In C. Sedikides, J. Schopler, & C. A. Insko (Eds.), *Intergroup cognition and intergroup behavior* (pp. 367–392). Mahwah, NJ: Erlbaum.

Hewstone, M., Macrae, C. N., Griffiths, R., Milne, A. B., & Brown, R. (1994). Cognitive models of stereotype change: (5). Measurement, development, and consequences of subtyping. *Journal of Experimental Social Psychology, 30*, 505–526.

Higgins, E. T. (1989). Self-discrepancy theory: What patterns of self-beliefs cause people to suffer? In L. Berkowitz (Ed.), *Advances in experimental social psychology* (Vol. 22, pp. 93–136). New York: Academic Press.

Higgins, E. T., King, G. A., & Mavin, G. H. (1982). Individual construct accessibility and subjective impressions and recall. *Journal of Personality and Social Psychology, 43*, 35–47.

Higgins, E. T., & Rholes, W. S. (1978). "Saying is believing": Effects of message modification on memory and liking for the person described. *Journal of Experimental Social Psychology, 14*, 363–378.

Higgins, E. T., Rholes, C. R., & Jones, C. R. (1977). Category accessibility and impression formation. *Journal of Experimental Social Psychology, 13*, 141–154.

Higgins, R. L., & Harris, R. N. (1988). Strategic "alcohol" use: Drinking to self-handicap. *Journal of Social and Clinical Psychology, 6*, 191–202.

Higgins, R. L., Synder, C. R., & Berglas, S. (1990). *Self-handicapping: The paradox that isn't.* New York: Plenum.

Hill, C. A. (1987). Affiliation motivation: People who need people . . . but in different ways. *Journal of Personality and Social Psychology, 52*, 1008–1018.

Hill, J. L., & Zautra, A. J. (1989). Self-blame attributions and unique vulnerability as predictors of post-rape demoralization. *Journal of Social and Clinical Psychology, 8*, 368–375.

Hilton, J. L., & Darley, J. M. (1985). Constructing other persons: A limit on the effect. *Journal of Experimental Social Psychology, 21*, 1–18.

Hilton, J. L., & Darley, J. M. (1991). The effects of interaction goals on person perception. *Advances in Experimental Social Psychology, 24*, 235–267.

Hilton, J. L., & Darley, J. M. (1991). The effects of interaction goals on person perception. In M. P. Zanna (Ed.), *Advances in experimental social psychology* (Vol. 24, pp. 235–267). San Diego: Academic Press.

Hilton, J. L., & Fein, S. (1989). The role of typical diagnosticity in stereotype-based judgments. *Journal of Personality and Social Psychology, 57*, 201–211.

Hilton, J. L., Fein, S., & Miller, D. T. (1993). Suspicion and dispositional inference. *Personality and Social Psychology Bulletin, 19*, 501–512.

Hilton, J. L., & von Hippel, W. (1990). The role of consistency in the judgment of stereotype-relevant behaviors. *Personality and Social Psychology Bulletin, 16*, 430–448.

Hilton, J. L., & von Hippel, W. (1996). Stereotypes. In J. T. Spence, J. M. Darley, & D. J. Foss (Eds.), *Annual review of psychology* (Vol. 47, pp. 237–271). Palo Alto, CA: Annual Reviews.

Hines, N. J., & Fry, D. P. (1994). Indirect modes of aggression among women of Buenos Aires, Argentina. *Sex Roles, 30*, 213–236.

Hinsz, V. B. (1995). Group and individual decision making for task performance goals: Processes in the establishment of goals in groups. *Journal of Applied Social Psychology, 25*, 353–370.

Hinsz, V. B., Tindale, R. S., Nagao, D. H., Davis, J. H., & Robertson, B. A. (1988). The influence of the accuracy of individuating information on the use of base rate information in probability judgment. *Journal of Experimental Social Psychology, 24*, 127–145.

Hinsz, V. B., Tindale, R. S., & Vollrath, D. A. (1997). The emerging conceptualization of groups as information processors. *Psychological Bulletin, 121*, 43–64.

Hirt, E. R., Deppe, R. K., & Gordon, L. J. (1991). Self-reported versus behavioral self-handicapping: Empirical evidence for a theoretical distinction. *Journal of Personality and Social Psychology, 61*, 981–991.

Hirt, E. R., Zillman, D., Erickson, G. A., & Kennedy, C. (1992). Costs and benefits of allegiance: Changes in fans' self-ascribed competencies after team victory versus defeat. *Journal of Personality and Social Psychology, 63*, 724–738.

Hitler, A. (1933). *Mein Kampf* (E. T. S. Dugdale, Trans.). Cambridge, MA: Riverside.

Hixon, J. G., & Swann, W. B., Jr. (1993). When does introspection bear fruit? Self-reflection, self-insight, and interpersonal choices. *Journal of Personality and Social Psychology, 64*, 35–43.

Hodgins, H. S., Liebeskind, E., & Schwartz, W. (1996). Getting out of hot water: Facework in social predicaments. *Journal of Personality and Social Psychology, 71*, 300–314.

Hodson, G., & Sorrentino, R. M. (1997). Groupthink and uncertainty orientation: Personality differences in reactivity to the group situation. *Group Dynamics, 1*, 144–155.

Hoffman, K. L., Demo, D. H., & Edwards, J. N. (1994). Physical wife abuse in a non-Western society: An integrated theoretical approach. *Journal of Marriage and the Family, 56*, 131–146.

Hoffman, M. L. (1982). Development of prosocial motivation: Empathy and guilt. In N. Eisenberg (Ed.), *The development of prosocial behavior* (pp. 281–313). New York: Academic Press.

Hoffman, M. L. (1994). Discipline and internalization. *Developmental Psychology, 30*, 26–28.

Hofling, C. K., Brotzman, E., Dalrymple, S., Graves, N., & Pierce, C. (1966). An experimental study of nurse-physician relations. *Journal of Nervous and Mental Disease, 143*, 171–180.

Hofstede, G. (1980). *Culture's consequences.* Beverly Hills, CA: Sage.

Hogan, R., Curphy, G. J., & Hogan, J. (1994). What we know about leadership: Effectiveness and personality. *American Psychologist, 49*, 493–504.

Hogan, R., Hogan, J., & Roberts, B. W. (1996). Personality measurement and employment decisions: Questions and answers. *American Psychologist, 51*, 469–477.

Hogg, M. A., & Abrams, D. (1990). Social motivation, self-esteem and social identity. In D. Abrams & M. Hogg (Eds.), *Social identity theory: Constructive and critical advances* (pp. 28–47). New York: Springer-Verlag.

Hogg, M. A., Cooper-Shaw, L., & Holzworth, D. W. (1993). Group prototypicality and depersonalized attraction in small interactive groups. *Personality and Social Psychology Bulletin, 19*, 452–465.

Hogg, M. A., Turner, J. C., & Davidson, B. (1990). Polarized norms and social frames of reference: A test of the self-categorization theory of group polarization. *Basic and Applied Social Psychology, 11,* 77–100.

Hollander, E. P. (1958). Conformity, status, and idiosyncrasy credit. *Psychological Review, 65,* 117–127.

Hollander, E. P. (1985). Leadership and power. In G. Lindzey & E. Aronson (Eds.), *Handbook of social psychology* (3rd ed., Vol. 2, pp. 485–537). New York: Random House.

Hollander, E. P., & Offermann, L. R. (1990). Power and leadership in organizations. *American Psychologist, 45,* 179–189.

Holloway, M. (1994). Trends in women's health: A global view. *Scientific American, 271* (2), 76–83.

Holmes, J. G., & Murray, S. L. (1996). Conflict in close relationships. In E. T. Higgins & A. W. Kruglanski (Eds.), *Social psychology: Handbook of basic principles* (pp. 622–654). New York: Guilford.

Holmes, T. H., & Rahe, R. H. (1967). The Social Readjustment Rating Scale. *Journal of Psychosomatic Research, 11,* 213–218.

Holsti, O. R. (1962). The belief system and national images: A case study. *Journal of Conflict Resolution, 6,* 244–252.

Holtgraves, T., & Yang, J. N. (1992). Interpersonal underpinnings of request strategies: General principles and differences due to culture and gender. *Journal of Personality and Social Psychology, 62,* 246–256.

Holtzworth-Munroe, A., & Jacobson, N. S. (1987). An attributional approach to marital dysfunction and therapy. In J. E. Maddux, C. D. Stoltenberg, & R. Rosenwein (Eds.), *Social processes in clinical and counseling psychology* (pp. 153–170). New York: Springer-Verlag.

Homans, G. C. (1961). *Social behavior.* New York: Harcourt, Brace & World.

Honeycutt, J. M., Woods, B. L., & Fontenot, K. (1993). The endorsement of communication conflict rules as a function of engagement, marriage and marital ideology. *Journal of Social and Personal Relationships, 10,* 285–304.

Honts, C. R. (1996). Criterion development and validity of the CQT in field application. *Journal of General Psychology, 123,* 309–324.

Honts, C. R., Raskin, D. C., & Kircher, J. C. (1994). Mental and physical countermeasures reduce the accuracy of polygraph tests. *Journal of Applied Psychology, 79,* 252–259.

Hoorens, V., & Nuttin, J. M. (1993). Overvaluation of own attributes: Mere ownership or subjective frequency? *Social Cognition, 11,* 177–200.

Horn, J. C. (1987, July). Bigger pay for better work. *Psychology Today,* pp. 54–57.

Horowitz, I. A., & Willging, T. E. (1991). Changing views of jury power: The nullification debate, 1787–1988. *Law and Human Behavior, 15,* 165–182.

Horowitz, I. A., Willging, T. E., & Bordens, K. S. (1998). *The psychology of law: Integrations and applications* (2nd ed.). New York: Longman.

Horvath, A. O., & Luborsky, L. (1993). The role of the therapeutic alliance in psychotherapy. *Journal of Consulting and Clinical Psychology, 61,* 561–573.

House, J. S., Landis, K. R., & Umberson, D. (1988). Social relationships and health. *Science, 241,* 540–545.

House, R. J., & Podsakoff, P. M. (1994). Leadership effectiveness: Past perspectives and future directions for research. In J. Greenberg (Ed.), *Organizational behavior: The state of the science* (pp. 45–82). Hillsdale, NJ: Erlbaum.

Houston, D. A. (1990). Empathy and the self: Cognitive and emotional influences on the evaluation of negative affect in others. *Journal of Personality and Social Psychology, 59,* 859–868.

Houts, A. C., Cook, T. D., & Shadish, W. R., Jr. (1986). The person-situation debate: A critical multiplist perspective. *Journal of Personality, 54,* 52–105.

Houts, R. M., Robins, E., & Huston, T. L. (1996). Compatibility and the development of premarital relationships. *Journal of Marriage and the Family, 58,* 7–20.

Hovland, C. I., Janis, I. L., & Kelley, H. H. (1953). *Communication and persuasion: Psychological studies of opinion change.* New Haven, CT: Yale University Press.

Hovland, C. I., Lumsdaine, A. A., & Sheffield, F. D. (1949). *Experiments on mass communication.* Princeton, NJ: Princeton University Press.

Hovland, C. I., & Sears, R. R. (1940). Minor studies in aggression: VI. Correlation of lynchings with economic indices. *Journal of Psychology, 9,* 301–310.

Hovland, C. I., & Weiss, W. (1951). The influence of source credibility on communication effectiveness. *Public Opinion Quarterly, 15,* 635–650.

Howard, D. J. (1990a). The influence of verbal responses to common greetings on compliance behavior: The foot-in-the-mouth effect. *Journal of Applied Social Psychology, 20,* 1185–1196.

Howard, D. J. (1990b). Rhetorical question effects on message processing and persuasion: The role of information availability and the elicitation of judgment. *Journal of Experimental Social Psychology, 26,* 217–239.

Howell, R. H., Owen, P. D., & Nocks, E. C. (1990). Increasing safety belt use: Effects of modeling and trip length. *Journal of Applied Social Psychology, 20,* 254–263.

Huesmann, L. R. (1988). An information processing model for the development of aggression. *Aggressive Behavior, 14,* 13–24.

Huesmann, L. R., & Eron, L. D. (Eds.). (1986). *Television and the aggressive child: A cross-national comparison.* Hillsdale, NJ: Erlbaum.

Huesmann, L. R., Eron, L. D., Klein, R., Brice, P., & Fischer, P. (1983). Mitigating the imitation of aggressive behaviors by changing children's attitudes about media violence. *Journal of Personality and Social Psychology, 44,* 899–910.

Huesmann, L. R., & Guerra, N. G. (1997). Children's normative beliefs about aggression and aggressive behavior. *Journal of Personality and Social Psychology, 72,* 408–419.

Huesmann, L. R., & Miller, L. S. (1994). Long-term effects of repeated exposure to media violence in childhood. In L. R. Huesmann (Ed.), *Aggressive Behavior: Current Perspectives* (pp. 153–186). New York: Plenum.

Hull, J. G., & Young, R. D. (1983). Self-consciousness, self-esteem, and success-failure as determinants of alcohol consumption in male social drinkers. *Journal of Personality and Social Psychology, 44,* 1097–1109.

Hull, J. G., Young, R. D., & Jouriles, E. (1986). Applications of the self-awareness model of alcohol consumption: Predicting patterns of use and abuse. *Journal of Personality and Social Psychology, 51,* 790–796.

Humphreys, K., & Rappaport, J. (1993). From the community mental health movement to the war on drugs: A study in the definition of social problems. *American Psychologist, 48,* 892–901.

Hunter, J. D., & Hunter, R. F. (1984). Validity and utility of alternative predictors of job performance. *Psychological Bulletin, 96,* 72–98.

Huston, A., Donnerstein, E., Fairchild, H., Feshbach, N. D., Katz, P. A., Murray, J. P., Rubinstein, E. A., Wilcox, B. L., & Zuckerman, D. (1992). *Big world, small screen: The role of television in American society.* Lincoln: University of Nebraska Press.

Huston, T. L., & Vangelisti, A. L. (1991). Socioemotional behavior and satisfaction in marital relationships: A longitudinal study. *Journal of Personality and Social Psychology, 61,* 721–733.

Iacono, W. G., & Lykken, D. T. (1997). The validity of the lie-detector test: Two surveys of scientific opinion. *Journal of Applied Psychology, 82,* 426–433.

Ickes, W., Bissonnette, V., Garcia, S., & Stinson, L. L. (1990). Implementing and using the Dyadic Interaction Paradigm. In C. Hendrick & M. S. Clark (Eds.), *Review of personality and social psychology: Vol. 11. Research methods in personality and social psychology* (pp. 16–44). Newbury Park, CA: Sage.

Imai, Y. (1991). Effects of influence strategies, perceived social power and cost on compliance with requests. *Japanese Psychological Research, 33,* 134–144.

Inbau, F. E., Reid, J. E., & Buckley, J. P. (1986). *Criminal interrogation and confessions* (3rd ed.). Baltimore: Williams & Wilkins.

Ingham, A. G., Levinger, G., Graves, J., & Peckham, V. (1974). The Ringelmann effect: Studies of group size and group performance. *Journal of Experimental Social Psychology, 10,* 371–384.

Ingoldsby, B. B. (1991). The Latin American family: Familism vs. machismo. *Journal of Comparative Family Studies, 23,* 47–62.

Ingram, R. E. (1990). Self-focused attention in clinical disorders: Review and a conceptual model. *Psychological Bulletin, 107,* 156–176.

Insko, C. A., Drenan, S., Solomon, M. R., Smith, R., & Wade, T. J. (1983). Conformity as a function of the consistency of positive self-evaluation with being liked and being right. *Journal of Experimental Social Psychology, 19,* 341–358.

Insko, C. A., & Schopler, J. (1998) Differential distrust of groups and individuals. In C. Sedikides, J. Schopler, & C. A. Insko (Eds.), *Intergroup cognition and intergroup behavior* (pp. 75–107). Mahwah, NJ: Erlbaum.

Insko, C. A., Schopler, J., Graetz, K. A., & Drigotas, S. M. (1994). Interindividual-intergroup discontinuity in the prisoner's dilemma game. *Journal of Conflict Resolution, 38,* 87–116.

Insko, C. A., Sedlak, A. J., & Lipsitz, A. (1982). A two-valued logic or two-valued balance resolution of the challenge of agreement and attraction effects in p-o-x triads, and a theoretical perspective on conformity and hedonism. *European Journal of Social Psychology, 12,* 143–167.

Intons-Peterson, M. J., Roskos-Ewoldsen, B., Thomas, L., Shirley, M., & Blut, D. (1989). Will educational materials reduce negative effects of exposure to sexual violence? *Journal of Social and Clinical Psychology, 8,* 256–275.

Irons, E. D., & Moore, G. W. (1985). *Black managers: The case of the banking industry.* New York: Praeger.

Ironson, G., et al. (1997). Posttraumatic stress symptoms, intrusive thoughts, loss, and immune function after Hurricane Andrew. *Psychosomatic Medicine, 59,* 128–141.

Irwin, M., Mascovich, S., Gillin, J. C., Willoughby, R., Pike, J., & Smith, T. L. (1994). Partial sleep deprivation reduces natural killer cell activity in humans. *Psychosomatic Medicine, 56,* 493–498.

Isen, A. M. (1970). Success, failure, attention, and reaction to others: The warm glow of success. *Journal of Personality and Social Psychology, 15,* 294–301.

Isen, A. M. (1984). Toward understanding the role of affect in cognition. In R. S. Wyer & T. K. Srull (Eds.), *Handbook of social cognition* (Vol. 3, pp. 179–236). Hillsdale, NJ: Erlbaum.

Isen, A. M., Clark, M., & Schwartz, M. H. (1976). Duration of the effect of good mood on helping: "Footprints in the sands of time." *Journal of Personality and Social Psychology, 34,* 385–393.

Isen, A. M., & Levin, P. A. (1972). Effect of feeling good on helping: Cookies and kindness. *Journal of Personality and Social Psychology, 21,* 384–388.

Isen, A. M., Shalker, T. E., Clark, M., & Karp, L. (1978). Affect, accessibility of material in memory, and behavior: A cognitive loop? *Journal of Personality and Social Psychology, 36,* 1–12.

Ito, T. A., Miller, N., & Pollock, V. E. (1996). Alcohol and aggression: A meta-analysis on the moderating effects of inhibitory cues, triggering events, and self-focused attention. *Psychological Bulletin, 120,* 60–82.

Izard, C. E. (1990). Facial expressions and the regulation of emotions. *Journal of Personality and Social Psychology, 58,* 487–498.

Jackson , S. E., May, K. E., & Whiteney, K. (1995). Understanding the dynamics of diversity in decision making teams. In R. A. Guzzo & E. Salas (Eds.), *Team effectiveness and decision making in organizations* (pp. 204–261). San Francisco: Jossey-Bass.

Jackson, J. M. (1986). In defense of social impact theory: Comment on Mullin. *Journal of Personality and Social Psychology, 50,* 511–513.

Jackson, J. M., & Williams, K. D. (1985). Social loafing on difficult tasks: Working collectively can improve performance. *Journal of Personality and Social Psychology, 49,* 937–942.

Jackson, L. A., Gardner, P. D., & Sullivan, L. A. (1992). Explaining gender differences in self-pay expectations: Social comparison standards and perceptions of fair pay. *Journal of Applied Psychology, 77,* 651–663.

Jackson, S. E., & Schuler, R. S. (1985). A meta-analysis and conceptual critique of research on role ambiguity and role conflict in work settings. *Organizational Behavior, 36,* 16–78.

Janis, I. L. (1968). Attitude change via role playing. In R. Abelson, E. Aronson, W. McGuire, T. Newcomb, M. Rosenberg, & P. Tennenbaum (Eds.), *Theories of cognitive consistency: A sourcebook* (pp. 810–818). Chicago: Rand McNally.

Janis, I. L. (1982). *Groupthink* (2nd ed.). Boston: Houghton Mifflin.

Janis, I. L., & Feshbach, S. (1953). Effects of fear arousing communications. *Journal of Abnormal and Social Psychology, 48,* 78–92.

Janis, I. L., Kaye, D., & Kirschner, P. (1965). Facilitating effects of "eating while reading" on responsiveness to persuasive communications. *Journal of Personality and Social Psychology, 1,* 181–186.

Janis, I. L., & King, B. T. (1954). The influence of role playing on opinion change. *Journal of Abnormal and Social Psychology, 49,* 211–218.

Jankowiak, W. R., & Fischer, E. F. (1992). A cross-cultural perspective on romantic love. *Ethnology, 31,* 149–155.

Janoff-Bulman, R. (1979). Characterological versus behavioral self-blame: Inquiries into depression and rape. *Journal of Personality and Social Psychology, 37,* 1798–1809.

Janoff-Bulman, R., & Timko, C. (1987). Coping with traumatic life events: The role of denial in light of people's assumptive worlds. In C. R. Snyder & C. E. Ford (Eds.), *Coping with negative life events: Clinical and social psychological perspectives* (pp. 135–159). New York: Plenum.

Jansari, A., & Parkin, A. J. (1996). Things that go bump in your life: Explaining the reminiscence bump in autobiographical memory. *Psychology and Aging, 11,* 85–91.

Janssens, J. M. A. M., & Dekovic, M. (1997). Child rearing, prosocial moral reasoning, and prosocial behaviour. *International Journal of Behavioral Development, 20,* 509–527.

Jarvis, W. B. G., & Petty, R. E. (1996). The need to evaluate. *Journal of Personality and Social Psychology, 70,* 172–194.

Jemmott, J. B., III, & Magloire, K. (1988). Academic stress, social support, and secretory immunoglobulin A. *Journal of Personality and Social Psychology, 55,* 803–810.

Jennings (Walstedt), J., Geis, F. L., & Brown, V. (1980). Influence of television commercials on women's self-confidence and independent judgment. *Journal of Personality and Social Psychology, 38,* 203–210.

Jepson, C., & Chaiken, S. (1990). Chronic issue-specific fear inhibits systematic processing of persuasive communications. *Journal of Social Behavior and Personality, 5,* 61–84.

Johansson, G., von Hofsten, C., & Jansson, G. (1980). Event perception. *Annual Review of Psychology, 31,* 27–53.

John, O. P., Cheek, J. M., & Klohnen, E. C. (1996). On the nature of self-monitoring: Construct explication with Q-sort ratings. *Journal of Personality and Social Psychology, 71,* 763–776.

Johns, G. (1994). Absenteeism estimates by employees and managers: Divergent perspectives and self-serving perceptions. *Journal of Applied Psychology, 79,* 229–239.

Johnson v. Louisiana, 406 U.S. 356 (1972).

Johnson, B. T., & Eagly, A. H. (1989). Effects of involvement on persuasion: A meta-analysis. *Psychological Bulletin, 106,* 290–314.

Johnson, D. J., & Rusbult, C. E. (1989). Resisting temptation: Devaluation of alternative partners as a means of maintaining commitment in close relationships. *Journal of Personality and Social Psychology, 57,* 967–980.

Johnson, J. D., Jackson, L. A., & Gatto, L. (1995). Violent attitudes and deferred academic aspirations: Deleterious effects of exposure to rap music. *Basic and Applied Social Psychology, 16,* 27–41.

Johnson, R. D., & Downing, L. L. (1979). Deindividuation and valance of cues: Effects on prosocial and antisocial behavior. *Journal of Personality and Social Psychology, 37,* 1532–1538.

Johnson, R. W., Kelly, R. J., & LeBlane, B. A. (1995). Motivational basis of dissonance: Aversive consequences or inconsistency. *Personality and Social Psychology Bulletin, 21,* 850–855.

Johnston, L. C., & Macrae, C. N. (1994). Changing social stereotypes: The case of the information seeker. *European Journal of Social Psychology, 24,* 581–592.

Jones, E. E. (1964). *Ingratiation: A social psychological analysis.* New York: Appleton-Century-Crofts.

Jones, E. E. (1990). *Interpersonal perception.* New York: Freeman.

Jones, E. E., & Davis, K. E. (1965). A theory of correspondent inferences: From acts to dispositions. In L. Berkowitz (Ed.), *Advances in experimental social psychology* (Vol. 2, pp. 219–266). New York: Academic Press.

Jones, E. E., Davis, K. E., & Gergen, K. (1961). Role playing variations and their informational value for person perception. *Journal of Abnormal and Social Psychology, 63,* 302–310.

Jones, E. E., & Harris, V. A. (1967). The attribution of attitudes. *Journal of Experimental Social Psychology, 3,* 1–24.

Jones, E. E., & Nisbett, R. E. (1972). The actor and the observer: Divergent perceptions of causality. In E. E. Jones, D. E. Kanouse, H. H. Kelley, R. E. Nisbett, S. Valins, & B. Weiner (Eds.), *Attribution: Perceiving the causes of behavior* (pp. 79–94). Morristown, NJ: General Learning Press.

Jones, E. E., & Pittman, T. S. (1982). Toward a general theory of strategic self presentation. In J. Suls (Ed.), *Psychological perspectives on the self.* Hillsdale, NJ: Erlbaum.

Jones, E. E., Rhodewalt, F., Berglas, S., & Skelton, J. A. (1981). Effects of strategic self-presentation on subsequent self-esteem. *Journal of Personality and Social Psychology, 41,* 407–421.

Jones, E. E., Rock, L., Shaver, K. G., Goethals, G. R., & Ward, L. M. (1968). Pattern of performance and ability attribution: An unexpected primary effect. *Journal of Personality and Social Psychology, 10,* 317–340.

Jones, E. E., & Sigall, H. (1971). The bogus pipeline: A new paradigm for measuring affect and attitude. *Psychological Bulletin, 76,* 349–364.

Jones, E. W. (1986). Black managers: The dream deferred. *Harvard Business Review, 64,* 84–93.

Josephs, R. A., Markus, H. R., & Tafarodi, R. W. (1992). Gender and self-esteem. *Journal of Personality and Social Psychology, 63,* 391–402.

Jost, J. T., & Banaji, M. R. (1994). The role of stereotyping in system justification and the production of false consciousness. *British Journal of Social Psychology, 33,* 1–27.

Judge, T. A., & Welbourne, T. M. (1994). A confirmatory investigation of the dimensionality of the Pay Satisfaction Questionnaire. *Journal of Applied Psychology, 79,* 461–466.

Jukes, J. A., & Goldstein, J. H. (1993). Preference for aggressive toys. *International Play Journal, 1,* 81–91.

Jussim, L., Coleman, L. M., & Lerch, L. (1987). The nature of stereotypes: A comparison and integration of three theories. *Journal of Personality and Social Psychology, 52,* 536–546.

Jussim, L., Eccles, J., & Madon, S. (1996). Social perception, social stereotypes, and teacher expectations: The quest for the powerful self-fulfilling prophecy. *Advances in Experimental Social Psychology, 28,* 281–387.

Kagan, J. (1994). *Galen's prophecy: Temperament in human nature.* New York: Basic Books.

Kahle, L. R., & Homer, P. M. (1985). Physical attractiveness of the celebrity endorser: A social adaptation perspective. *Journal of Consumer Research, 11,* 954–961.

Kahneman, D., & Miller, D. T. (1986). Norm theory: Comparing reality to its alternatives. *Psychological Review, 93,* 136–153.

Kahneman, D., Slovic, P., & Tversky, A. (Eds.). (1982). *Judgment under uncertainty: Heuristics and biases.* New York: Cambridge University Press.

Kahneman, D., & Tversky, A. (1979). Prospect theory: An analysis of decisions under risk. *Econometrika, 47,* 263–291.

Kalick, S. M., & Hamilton, T. E., III. (1986). The matching hypothesis revisited. *Journal of Personality and Social Psychology, 51,* 673–682.

Kalick, S. M., Zebrowitz, L. A., Langlois, J. H., & Johnson, R. M. (1998). Does human facial attractiveness honestly advertise health? Longitudinal data on an evolutionary question. *Psychological Science, 9,* 8–13.

Kallgren, C. A., & Wood, W. (1986). Access to attitude-relevant information in memory as a determinant of attitude-behavior consistency. *Journal of Experimental Social Psychology, 22,* 328–338.

Kalven, H., & Zeisel, H. (1966). *The American jury.* Boston: Little, Brown.

Kameda, T., & Sugimori, S. (1993). Psychological entrapment in group decision making: An assigned decision rule and a groupthink phenomenon. *Journal of Personality and Social Psychology, 65,* 282–292.

Kamen-Siegel, L., Rodin, J., Seligman, M. E. P., & Dwyer, J. (1991). Explanatory style and cell-mediated immunity in elderly men and women. *Health Psychology, 10,* 229–235.

Kang, M.-E. (1997). The portrayal of women's images in magazine advertisements: Goffman's gender analysis revisited. *Sex Roles, 37,* 979–996.

Kaplan, D. E., Tharp. M., Madden, M., & Witkin, G. (1997/1998, December 29/January 5). *U.S. News and World Report.*

Kaplan, M. F., & Schersching, C. (1981). Juror deliberation: An information integration analysis. In B. Sales (Ed.), *The trial process* (pp. 235–262). New York: Plenum.

Karau, S. J., & Williams, K. D. (1993). Social loafing: A meta-analytic review and theoretical integration. *Journal of Personality and Social Psychology, 65,* 681–706.

Karau, S. J., & Williams, K. D. (1997). The effects of group cohesiveness on social loafing and social compensation. *Group Dynamics, 1,* 156–168.

Karney, B. R., & Bradbury, T. N. (1995). The longitudinal course of marital quality and stability: A review of theory, method, and research. *Psychological Bulletin, 118,* 3–34.

Karney, B. R., & Bradbury, T. N. (1997). Neuroticism, marital interaction, and the trajectory of marital satisfaction. *Journal of Personality and Social Psychology, 72,* 1075–1092.

Karpinski, A. T., & von Hippel, W. (1996). The role of the linguistic intergroup bias in expectancy maintenance. *Social Cognition, 14,* 141–163.

Kashima, Y., & Kerekes, A. R. Z. (1994). A distributed memory model of averaging phenomena in person impression formation. *Journal of Experimental Social Psychology, 30,* 407–455.

Kassin, S. M. (1997). The psychology of confession evidence. *American Psychologist, 52,* 221–233.

Kassin, S. M., Ellsworth, P. C., & Smith, V. L. (1989). The "general acceptance" of psychological research on eyewitness testimony: A survey of the experts. *American Psychologist, 44,* 1089–1098.

Kassin, S. M., & Kiechel, K. L. (1996). The social psychology of false confessions: Compliance, internalization, and confabulation. *Psychological Science, 7,* 125–128.

Kassin, S. M., & Sommers, S. R. (1997). Inadmissible testimony, instructions to disregard, and the jury: Substantive versus procedural considerations. *Personality and Social Psychology Bulletin, 23,* 1046–1054.

Kassin, S. M., & Sukel, H. (1997). Coerced confessions and the jury: An experimental test of the "harmless error" rule. *Law and Human Behavior, 21,* 27–46.

Kassin, S. M., & Wrightsman, L. S. (1979). On the requirements of proof: The timing of judicial instruction and mock juror verdicts. *Journal of Personality and Social Psychology, 37,* 1877–1887.

Kassin, S. M., & Wrightsman, L. S. (1983). The construction and validation of a Juror Bias Scale. *Journal of Research in Personality, 17,* 423–442.

Kassin, S. M., & Wrightsman, L. S. (1988). *The American jury on trial: Psychological perspectives.* Washington, DC: Hemisphere.

Katz, D., & Braly, K. W. (1933). Racial stereotypes of 100 college students. *Journal of Abnormal and Social Psychology, 28,* 280–290.

Katz, I., Wackenhut, J., & Hass, G. (1986). Racial ambivalence, value duality, and behavior. In J. F. Dovidio & S. L. Gaertner, (Eds.), *Prejudice, discrimination, and racism: Theory and research* (pp. 35–60). Orlando, FL: Academic Press.

Katzev, A. R., Warner, R. L., & Acock, A. C. (1994). Girls or boys? Relationship of child gender to marital instability. *Journal of Marriage and the Family, 56,* 89–100.

Keelan, J. P. R., Dion, K. L., & Dion, K. K. (1994). Attachment style and heterosexual relationships among young adults: A short-term panel study. *Journal of Social and Personal Relationships, 11,* 201–214.

Kelley, H. H. (1950). The warm-cold variable in first impressions of persons. *Journal of Personality, 18,* 431–439.

Kelley, H. H. (1967). Attribution theory in social psychology. In D. Levine (Ed.), *Nebraska Symposium on Motivation* (Vol. 15, pp. 192–241). Lincoln: University of Nebraska Press.

Kelley, H. H. (1983). Love and commitment. In H. H. Kelley, E. Berscheid, A. Christenson, J. H. Harvey, T. L. Huston, G. Levinger, E. McClintock, L. A. Peplau, & D. R. Peterson, *Close relationships* (pp. 265–314). New York: Freeman.

Kelley, H. H., & Stahelski, A. J. (1970). Social interaction basis of cooperators' and competitors' beliefs about others. *Journal of Personality and Social Psychology, 16,* 66–91.

Kelly, A. E., & McKillop, K. J. (1996). Consequences of revealing personal secrets. *Psychological Bulletin, 120,* 450–465.

Kelly, J. A., St. Lawrence, J. S., Diaz, Y. E., Stevenson, L. Y., Hauth, A. C., Brasfield, T. L., Kalichman, S. C., Smith, J. E., & Andrew, M. E. (1991). HIV risk behavior reduction following intervention with key opinion leaders of a population: An experimental community-level analysis. *American Journal of Public Health, 81,* 168–171.

Kelly, J. A., St. Lawrence, J. S., Stevenson, L. Y., Hauth, A. C., Kalichman, S. C., Diaz, Y. E., Brasfield, T. L., Koob, J. J., & Morgan, M. G. (1992). Community AIDS/HIV risk reduction: The effects of endorsements by popular people in three cities. *American Journal of Public Health, 82,* 1483–1489.

Kelman, H. C. (1961). Processes of opinion change. *Public Opinion Quarterly, 25,* 57–78.

Kelman, H. C. (1967). Human use of human subjects: The problem of deception in social psychology experiments. *Psychological Bulletin, 67,* 1–11.

Kelman, H. C., & Hamilton, V. L. (1989). *Crimes of obedience: Toward a social psychology of authority and responsibility.* New Haven, CT: Yale University Press.

Kelman, H. C., & Hovland, C. I. (1953). "Reinstatement" of the communicator in delayed measurement of opinion change. *Journal of Abnormal and Social Psychology, 48,* 327–335.

Kenny, D. A. (1994). *Interpersonal perception: A social relations analysis.* New York: Guilford.

Kenny, D. A., Albright, L., Malloy, T. E., & Kashy, D. A. (1994). Consensus in interpersonal perception: Acquaintance and the Big Five. *Psychological Bulletin, 116,* 245–258.

Kenny, D. A., & DePaulo, B. M. (1993). Do people know how others view them? An empirical and theoretical account. *Psychological Bulletin, 114,* 145–161.

Kenny, D. A., Horner, C., Kashy, D. A., & Chu, L. (1992). Consensus at zero acquaintance: Replication, behavioral cues, and stability. *Journal of Personality and Social Psychology, 62,* 88–97.

Kenny, D. A., & Zaccaro, S. J. (1983). An estimate of variance due to traits in leadership. *Journal of Applied Psychology, 68,* 678–685.

Kenrick, D. T. (1987). Gender, genes, and the social environment: A biosocial interactionist perspective. In P. Shaver & C. Hendrick (Eds.), *Sex and gender. Review of personality and social psychology* (Vol. 7, pp. 14–43). Newbury Park, CA: Sage.

Kenrick, D. T., Gabrielidis, C., Keefe, R. C., & Cornelius, J. S. (1996). Adolescents' age preferences for dating partners: Support for an evolutionary model of life-history strategies. *Child Development, 67,* 1499–1511.

Kenrick, D. T., Gutierres, S. E., & Goldberg, L. L. (1989). Influence of popular erotica on judgments of strangers and mates. *Journal of Experimental Social Psychology, 25,* 159–167.

Kenrick, D. T., & Keefe, R. C. (1992). Age preferences in mates reflect sex differences in human reproductive strategies. *Behavioral and Brain Sciences, 15,* 75–133.

Kenrick, D. T., & MacFarlane, S. W. (1986). Ambient temperature and horn honking: A field study of the heat/aggression relationship. *Environment and Behavior, 18,* 179–191.

Kenrick, D. T., Montello, D. R., Gutierres, S. E., & Trost, M. R. (1993). Effects of physical attractiveness on affect and perceptual judgments: When social comparison overrides social reinforcement. *Personality and Social Psychology Bulletin, 19,* 195–199.

Kernis, M. H., & Waschull, S. B. (1995). The interactive roles of stability and level of self-esteem: Research and theory. *Advances in Experimental Social Psychology, 27,* 93–141.

Kerr, N. L. (1981). Social transition schemes: Charting the group's road to agreement. *Journal of Personality and Social Psychology, 41,* 684–702.

Kerr, N. L. (1992a). Efficacy as a causal and moderating variable in social dilemmas. In W. B. G. Liebrand, D. M. Messick, & H. A. M. Wilke (Eds.), *Social dilemmas: Theoretical issues and research findings* (pp. 59–80). Oxford: Pergamon Press.

Kerr, N. L. (1992b). Issue importance and group decision making. In S. Worchel, W. Wood, & J. A. Simpson (Eds.), *Group process and productivity* (pp. 68–88). Newbury Park, CA: Sage.

Kerr, N. L., & Bruun, S. E. (1983). Dispensibility of member effort and group motivation losses: Free-rider effects. *Journal of Personality and Social Psychology, 44,* 78–94.

Kerr, N. L., Harmon, D. L., & Graves, J. K. (1982). Independence of multiple verdicts by jurors and juries. *Journal of Applied Social Psychology, 12,* 12–29.

Kerr, N. L., Hymes, R. W., Anderson, A. B., & Weathers, J. E. (1995). Defendant-juror similarity in mock juror judgments. *Law and Human Behavior, 19,* 545–567.

Kerr, N. L., & Kaufman-Gilliland, C. M. (1994). Communication, commitment, and cooperation in social dilemmas. *Journal of Personality and Social Psychology, 66,* 513–529.

Kerr, N. L., Kramer, G. P., Carroll, J. S., & Alfini, J. J. (1991). On the effectiveness of voir dire in criminal cases with prejudicial pretrial publicity: An empirical study. *American University Law Review, 40,* 665–701.

Kessler, R. C., et al. (1994). Lifetime and 12-month prevalence of DSM-III-R psychiatric disorders in the United States. *Archives of General Psychiatry, 51,* 8–19.

Kessler, R. C., McLeod, J. D., & Wethington, E. (1985). The costs of caring: A perspective on the relationship between sex and psychological distress. In I. G. Sarason & B. R. Sarason (Eds.), *Social support: Theory, research and applications* (pp. 491–506). Dordrecht, The Netherlands: Martinus Nijhoff.

Kessler, R. C., Sonnega, A., Bromet, E., Hughes, M., & Nelson, C. B. (1995). Posttraumatic stress disorder in the National Comorbidity Survey. *Archives of General Psychiatry, 52,* 1048–1060.

Key, W. B. (1973). *Subliminal seduction.* Englewood Cliffs, NJ: Signet.

Key, W. B. (1989). *The age of manipulation.* New York: Holt.

Kidda, M., & Rosen, S. (1994). Helping as controlling: Normative and dispositional control perspectives affect aid-giving. *Journal of Social Behavior and Personality, 9,* 335–348.

Kiesler, C. A. (1971). *The psychology of commitment.* New York: Academic Press.

Kiesler, C. A., & Kiesler, S. B. (1969). *Conformity.* Reading, MA: Addison-Wesley.

Kihlstrom, J. F., & Cantor, N. (1984). Mental representations of the self. In L. Berkowitz (Ed.), *Advances in experimental social psychology* (Vol. 17, pp. 1–47). New York: Academic Press.

Kilham, W., & Mann, L. (1974). Level of destructive obedience as a function of transmitter and executant roles in the Milgram obedience paradigm. *Journal of Personality and Social Psychology, 29,* 696–702.

Kilpatrick, D. G., Edmunds, C. N., & Seymour, A. (1992). *Rape in America.* Arlington, VA: National Victim Center.

Kim, P. H. (1997). When what you know can hurt you: A study of experiential effects on group discussion and performance. *Organizational Behavior and Human Decision Processes, 69,* 165–177.

Kimmel, P. R. (1994). Cultural perspectives on international negotiations. *Journal of Social Issues, 50,* 179–196.

Kinsey, A. C., Pomeroy, W. B., & Martin, C. E. (1948). *Sexual behavior in the human male.* Philadelphia: Saunders.

Kinsey, A. C., Pomeroy, W. B., Martin, C. E., & Gebhard, P. H. (1953). *Sexual behavior in the human female.* Philadelphia: Saunders.

Kirkpatrick, L. A., & Hazan, C. (1994). Attachment styles and close relationships: A four-year prospective study. *Personal Relationships, 1,* 123–142.

Kirkpatrick, S. A., & Locke, E. A. (1991). Leadership: Do traits matter? *Academy of Management Executive, 5,* 48–60.

Kitayama, S., Markus, H. R., Matsumoto, H., & Norasakkunkit, V. (1997). Individual and collective processes in the construction of the self: Self-enhancement in the United States and self-criticism in Japan. *Journal of Personality and Social Psychology, 72,* 1245–1267.

Kite, M. E. (1992). Age and the spontaneous self-concept. *Journal of Applied Social Psychology, 22,* 1828–1837.

Kitson, G. C., & Morgan, L. A. (1990). The multiple consequences of divorce: A decade review. *Journal of Marriage and the Family, 52,* 913–924.

Klein, J. G. (1991). Negativity effects in impression formation: A test in the political arena. *Personality and Social Psychology Bulletin, 17,* 412–418.

Klein, W. M. (1997). Objective standards are not enough: Affective, self-evaluative, and behavioral responses to social comparison information. *Journal of Personality and Social Psychology, 72,* 763–774.

Klein, W. M., & Kunda, Z. (1992). Motivated person perception: Constructing justifications for desired beliefs. *Journal of Experimental Social Psychology, 28,* 145–168.

Kleinke, C. L. (1986). Gaze and eye contact: A research review. *Psychological Bulletin, 100,* 78–100.

Kleinke, C. L., Paterson, T. R., & Rutledge, T. R. (1998) Effects of self-generated facial expressions of mood. *Journal of Personality and Social Psychology, 74,* 272–279.

Knapp, A., & Clark, M. S. (1991). Some detrimental effects of negative mood on individuals' ability to solve resource dilemmas. *Personality and Social Psychology Bulletin, 17,* 678–688.

Knight, G. P., Johnson, L. G., Carlo, G., & Eisenberg, N. (1994). A multiplicative model of the dispositional antecedents of a prosocial behavior: Predicting more of the people more of the time. *Journal of Personality and Social Psychology, 66,* 178–183.

Knowles, E. S. (1983). Social physics and the effects of others: Tests of the effects of audience size and distance on social judgments and behavior. *Journal of Personality and Social Psychology, 45,* 1263–1279.

Knox, R. E., & Inskter, J. A. (1968). Postdecision dissonance at post-time. *Journal of Personality and Social Psychology, 8,* 319–323.

Knox, R. E., & Safford, R. K. (1976). Group caution at the race track. *Journal of Experimental Social Psychology, 12,* 317–324.

Kobasa, S. C., Maddi, S. R., & Kahn, S. (1982). Hardiness and health: A prospective study. *Journal of Personality and Social Psychology, 42,* 168–177.

Kobrynowicz, D., & Branscombe, N. R. (1997). Who considers themselves victims of discrimination? Individual difference predictors of perceived gender discrimination in women and men. *Psychology of Women Quarterly, 21,* 347–363.

Koestner, R., Franz, C., & Weinberger, J. (1990). The family origins of empathic concern: A 26-year longitudinal study. *Journal of Personality and Social Psychology, 58,* 709–717.

Kohn, A. (1993). *Punished by rewards.* Boston: Houghton Mifflin.

Kohn, P. M., Lafreniere, K., & Gurevich, M. (1991). Hassles, health, and personality. *Journal of Personality and Social Psychology, 61,* 478–482.

Kolditz, T. A., & Arkin, R. M. (1982). An impression management interpretation of the self-handicapping strategy. *Journal of Personality and Social Psychology, 43,* 492–502.

Komorita, S. S., Chan, D. K-S., & Parks, C. (1993). The effects of reward structure and reciprocity in social dilemmas. *Journal of Experimental Social Psychology, 29,* 252–267.

Komorita, S. S., & Parks, C. D. (1994). *Social dilemmas.* Madison, WI: Brown & Benchmark.

Konecni, V. J., & Ebbesen, E. B. (1982). *The criminal justice system: A social-psychological analysis.* San Francisco: Freeman.

Kors, D. J., Linden, W., & Gerin, W. (1997). Evaluation interferes with social support: Effects on cardiovascular stress reactivity in women. *Journal of Social and Clinical Psychology, 16,* 1–23.

Korte, C. (1980). Urban-nonurban differences in social behavior and social psychological models of urban impact. *Journal of Social Issues, 36* (3), 29–51.

Kosek, R. B. (1995). Measuring prosocial behavior of college students. *Psychological Reports, 77,* 739–742.

Koss, M. P., Gidycz, C. A., & Wisniewski, N. (1987). The scope of rape: Incidence and prevalence of sexual aggression and victimization in a national sample of higher education students. *Journal of Consulting and Clinical Psychology, 55,* 162–170.

Kowalski, R. M. (1993). Inferring sexual interest from behavioral cues: Effects of gender and sexually relevant attitudes. *Sex Roles, 29,* 13–36.

Kowalski, R. M. (1996). Complaints and complaining: Functions, antecedents, and consequences. *Psychological Bulletin, 119,* 179–196.

Kowalski, R. M., & Wolfe, R. (1994). Collective identity orientation, patriotism, and reactions to national outcomes. *Personality and Social Psychology Bulletin, 20,* 533–540.

Kozlowski, S. W., Kirsch, M. P., & Chao, G. T. (1986). Job knowledge, ratee familiarity, conceptual similarity, and halo error: An exploration. *Journal of Applied Psychology, 71,* 45–49.

Kraines, D., & Kraines, V. (1995). Evolution of learning among Pavlov strategies in a competitive environment with noise. *Journal of Conflict Resolution, 39,* 439–466.

Kramer, G. P., Kerr, N. L., & Carroll, J. S. (1990). Pretrial publicity, judicial remedies, and jury bias. *Law and Human Behavior, 14,* 409–438.

Kramer, R. M., & Brewer, M. B. (1984). Effects of group identity on resource use in a simulated commons dilemma. *Journal of Personality and Social Psychology, 46,* 1044–1057.

Krantz, D. S., & Hedges, S. M. (1987). Some cautions for research on personality and health. *Journal of Personality, 55,* 351–357.

Krantz, D. S., & Manuck, S. B. (1984). Acute psychophysiologic reactivity and risk of cardiovascular disease: A review and methodological critique. *Psychological Bulletin, 96,* 435–464.

Kraus, S. J. (1995). Attitudes and the prediction of behavior: A meta-analysis of the empirical literature. *Personality and Social Psychology Bulletin, 21,* 58–75.

Krauss, R. M., Chen, Y., & Chawla, P. (1996). Nonverbal behavior and nonverbal communication: What do conversational hand gestures tell us? *Advances in Experimental Social Psychology, 28,* 389–450.

Kraut, R. E. (1973). Effects of social labeling on giving to charity. *Journal of Experimental Social Psychology, 9,* 551–562.

Kravitz, D. A., & Martin, B. (1986). Ringelmann rediscovered: The original article. *Journal of Personality and Social Psychology, 50,* 936–941.

Kravitz, D. A., & Platania, J. (1993). Attitudes and beliefs about affirmative action: Effects of target and of respondent sex and ethnicity. *Journal of Applied Psychology, 78,* 928–938.

Krebs, D. (1987). The challenge of altruism in biology and psychology. In C. Crawford, M. Smith, & D. Krebs (Eds.), *Sociobiology and psychology: Ideas, issues, and applications* (pp. 81–118). Hillsdale, NJ: Erlbaum.

Krebs, D., & Rosenwald, A. (1994). Moral reasoning and moral behavior in conventional adults. In B. Puka (Ed.), *Fundamental research in moral development* (pp. 111–121). New York: Garland.

Krevans, J., & Gibbs, J. C. (1996). Parents' use of inductive discipline: Relations to children's empathy and prosocial behavior. *Child Development, 67,* 3263–3277.

Kristof, N. D. (1997, April 2). Tokyo journal: A plain school uniform as the latest aphrodisiac. *New York Times,* p. A4.

Kroon, M. B. R., 't Hart, P., & van Kreveld, D. (1991). Managing group decision making processes: Individual versus collective accountability and groupthink. *International Journal of Conflict Management, 2,* 91–115.

Krueger, J. (1998). On the perception of social consensus. *Advances in Experimental Social Psychology, 30,* 163–240.

Krueger, J., & Clement, R. W. (1994). The truly false consensus effect: An ineradicable and egocentric bias in social perception. *Journal of Personality and Social Psychology, 67,* 596–610.

Krug, E. G., Kresnow, M., Peddicord, J. P., Dahlberg, L. L., Powell, K. E., Crosby, A. E., & Annest, J. L. (1998). Suicide after natural disasters. *New England Journal of Medicine, 338,* 373–378.

Kruglanski, A. W. (1986). Freeze-think and the Challenger. *Psychology Today, 20,* 48–49.

Kruglanski, A. W., & Freund, T. (1983). The freezing and unfreezing of lay-inferences: Effects of impressional primacy, ethnic stereotyping, and numerical anchoring. *Journal of Experimental Social Psychology, 19,* 448–468.

Kruglanski, A. W., & Mayseless, O. (1988). Contextual effects in hypothesis testing: The role of competing alternatives and epistemic motivations. *Social Cognition, 6,* 1–20.

Kruglanski, A. W., & Webster, D. M. (1991). Group members' reactions to opinion deviates and conformists at varying degrees of proximity to decision deadline and of environmental noise. *Journal of Personality and Social Psychology, 61,* 212–225.

Kruglanski, A. W., & Webster, D. M. (1996). Motivated closing of the mind: "Seizing" and "freezing." *Psychological Review, 103,* 263–283.

Kulik, J. A., & Mahler, H. I. M. (1989). Stress and affiliation in a hospital setting: Preoperative roommate preferences. *Personality and Social Psychology Bulletin, 15,* 183–193.

Kulik, J. A., Mahler, H. I. M., & Earnest, A. (1994). Social comparison and affiliation under threat: Going beyond the affiliate-choice paradigm. *Journal of Personality and Social Psychology, 66,* 301–309.

Kulik, J. A., Mahler, H. I. M., & Moore, P. J. (1996). Social comparison and affiliation under threat: Effects of recovery from major surgery. *Journal of Personality and Social Psychology, 71,* 967–979.

Kunda, Z. (1987). Motivated inference: Self-serving generation and evaluation of causal theories. *Journal of Personality and Social Psychology, 53,* 636–647.

Kunda, Z. (1990). The case of motivated reasoning. *Psychological Bulletin, 108,* 480–498.

Kunda, Z., & Oleson, K. C. (1997). When exceptions prove the rule: How extremity of deviance determines the impact of deviant examples on stereotypes. *Journal of Personality and Social Psychology, 72,* 965–979.

Kunda, Z., Sinclair, L., & Griffin, D. (1997). Equal ratings but separate meanings: Stereotypes and the construal of traits. *Journal of Personality and Social Psychology, 72,* 720–734.

Kuntz-Wilson, W., & Zajonc, R. B. (1980). Affective discrimination of stimuli that cannot be recognized. *Science, 207,* 557–558.

Kurdek, L. A. (1991a). Correlates of relationship satisfaction in cohabiting gay and lesbian couples: Interpretation of contextual, investment, and problem-solving models. *Journal of Personality and Social Psychology, 61,* 910–922.

Kurdek, L. A. (1991b). The dissolution of gay and lesbian couples. *Journal of Social and Personal Relationships, 8,* 265–278.

Kurdek, L. A. (1992). Relationship stability and relationship satisfaction in cohabiting gay and lesbian couples: A prospective longitudinal test of the contextual and interdependence models. *Journal of Social and Personal Relationships, 9,* 125–142.

Kurdek, L. A. (1994). Areas of conflict for gay, lesbian, and heterosexual couples: What couples agree about influences relationship satisfaction. *Journal of Marriage and the Family, 56,* 923–934.

Kurland, N. B. (1995). Ethical intentions and theories of reasoned action and planned behavior. *Journal of Applied Social Psychology, 25,* 297–313.

Lagerspetz, K. M. J., & Björkvist, K. (1994). Indirect aggression in boys and girls. In L. R. Huesman (Eds.), *Aggressive behavior: Current perspectives* (pp. 131–150). New York: Plenum.

Laird, J. D. (1974). Self-attribution of emotion: The effects of expressive behavior on the quality of emotional experience. *Journal of Personality and Social Psychology, 29,* 475–486.

Lakey, B., & Cassady, P. B. (1990). Cognitive processes in perceived social support. *Journal of Personality and Social Psychology, 59,* 337–343.

Lakey, B., Moineau, S., & Drew, J. B. (1992). Perceived social support and individual differences in the interpretation and recall of supportive behaviors. *Journal of Social and Clinical Psychology, 11,* 336–348.

Lamb, C. S., Jackson, L. A., Cassiday, P. B., & Priest, D. J. (1993). Body figure preferences of men and women: A comparison of two generations. *Sex Roles, 28,* 345–358.

Lambert, A. J., Khan, S. R., Lickel, B. A., & Fricke, K. (1997). Mood and the correction of positive versus negative stereotypes. *Journal of Personality and Social Psychology, 72,* 1002–1016.

Lamm, H., & Myers, D. G. (1978). Group-induced polarization of attitudes and behavior. In L. Berkowitz (Ed.), *Advances in experimental social psychology* (Vol. 11, pp. 145–195). New York: Academic Press.

Landau, T. (1989). *About faces: The evolution of the human face.* New York: Anchor Books.

Landy, F. J., & Farr, J. L. (1983). *The measurement of work performance: Methods, theory, and applications.* New York: Academic Press.

Landy, F. J., Shankster, L. J., & Kohler, S. S. (1994). Personnel selection and placement. *Annual Review of Psychology, 45,* 261–296.

Langer, E. J. (1989). *Mindfulness.* Reading, MA: Addison-Wesley.

Langer, E. J., Blank, A., & Chanowitz, B. (1978). The mindlessness of ostensibly thoughtful action. *Journal of Personality and Social Psychology, 36,* 635–642.

Langer, E. J., & Rodin, J. (1976). The effects of choice and enhanced personal responsibility for the aged: A field experiment in an institutional setting. *Journal of Personality and Social Psychology, 34,* 191–198.

Langlois, J. H., Ritter, J. M., Casey, R. J., & Sawin, D. B. (1995). Infant attractiveness predicts maternal behaviors and attitudes. *Developmental Psychology, 31,* 464–472.

Langlois, J. H., Ritter, J. M., Roggman, L. A., & Vaughn, L. S. (1991). Facial diversity and infant preferences for attractive faces. *Developmental Psychology, 27,* 79–84.

Langlois, J. H., & Roggman, L. A. (1990). Attractive faces are only average. *Psychological Science, 1,* 115–121.

Langlois, J. H., Roggman, L. A., & Musselman, L. (1994). What is average and what is not average about attractive faces? *Psychological Science, 5,* 214–220.

Lanzetta, J. T. (1955). Group behavior under stress. *Human Relations, 8,* 29–52.

Lanzetta, J. T., & Englis, B. G. (1989). Expectations of cooperation and competition and their effects on observers' vicarious emotional responses. *Journal of Personality and Social Psychology, 56,* 543–554.

LaPiere, R. T. (1934). Attitudes vs. action. *Social Forces, 13,* 230–237.

Laplace, A. C., Chermack, S. T., & Taylor, S. P. (1994). Effects of alcohol and drinking experience on human physical aggression. *Personality and Social Psychology Bulletin, 20,* 439–444.

Larrick, R. P., Morgan, J. N., & Nisbett, R. E. (1990). Teaching the use of cost-benefit reasoning in everyday life. *Psychological Science, 1,* 362–370.

Larsen, K. S. (1990). The Asch conformity experiment: Replication and transhistorical comparisons. *Journal of Social Behavior and Personality, 5,* 163–168.

Lassiter, G. D. (1988). Behavior perception, affect, and memory. *Social Cognition, 6,* 150–176.

Lassiter, G. D., Slaw, R. D., Briggs, M. A., & Scanlan, C. R. (1992). The potential for bias in videotaped confessions. *Journal of Applied Social Psychology, 22,* 1838–1851.

Lassiter, G. D., Stone, J. I., & Rogers, S. L. (1988). Memorial consequences of variation in behavior perception. *Journal of Experimental Social Psychology, 24,* 222–239.

Latané, B. (1981). The psychology of social impact. *American Psychologist, 36,* 343–356.

Latané, B., & Darley, J. M. (1968). Group inhibition of bystander intervention. *Journal of Personality and Social Psychology, 10,* 215–221.

Latané, B., & Darley, J. M. (1970). *The unresponsive bystander: Why doesn't he help?* New York: Appleton-Century-Crofts.

Latané, B., & L'Herrou, T. (1996). Spatial clustering in the conformity game: Dynamic social impact in electronic groups. *Journal of Personality and Social Psychology, 70,* 1218–1230.

Latané, B., Liu, J. H., Nowak, A., Bonevento, M., & Zheng, L. (1995). Distance matters: Physical space and social impact. *Personality and Social Psychology Bulletin, 21,* 795–805.

Latané, B., & Werner, C. (1978). Regulation of social contact in laboratory rats: Time, not distance. *Journal of Personality and Social Psychology, 36,* 1128–1137.

Latané, B., Williams, K., & Harkins, S. (1979). Many hands make light the work: The causes and consequences of social loafing. *Journal of Personality and Social Psychology, 37,* 822–832.

Latané, B., & Wolf, S. (1981). The social impact of majorities and minorities. *Psychological Review, 88,* 438–453.

Lau, R. R. (1985). Two explanations for negativity effects in political behavior. *American Journal of Political Science, 29,* 119–138.

Laughlin, P. R., & Ellis, A. L. (1986). Demonstrability and social combination processes on mathematical intellective tasks. *Journal of Experimental Social Psychology, 22,* 177–189.

Laumann, E. O., Gagnon, J. H., Michael, R. T., & Michaels, S. (1994). *The social organization of sexuality.* Chicago: University of Chicago Press.

Laupa, M., & Turiel, E. (1993). Children's concepts of authority and social contexts. *Journal of Educational Psychology, 85*, 191–197.

Lavallee, L. F., & Campbell, J. D. (1995). Impact of personal goals on self-regulation processes elicited by daily negative events. *Journal of Personality and Social Psychology, 69*, 341–352.

Lavine, H., & Snyder, M. (1996). Cognitive processing and the functional matching effect in persuasion: The mediating role of subjective perceptions of message quality. *Journal of Experimental Social Psychology, 32*, 580–604.

Lazarus, R. S. (1984). On the primacy of cognition. *American Psychologist, 39*, 124–129.

Lazarus, R. S., & Folkman, S. (1984). *Stress, appraisal, and coping.* New York: Springer.

Leana, C. R. (1985). A partial test of Janis' groupthink model: Effects of group cohesiveness and leader behavior on defective decision making. *Journal of Management, 11*, 5–17.

Leary, M. R., & Kowalski, R. M. (1990). Impression management: A literature review and two-component model. *Psychological Bulletin, 107*, 34–47.

Leary, M. R., & Kowalski, R. M. (1995). *Social anxiety.* New York: Guilford Press.

Leary, M. R., Haupt, A. L., Strausser, K. S., & Chokel, J. T. (1998). Calibrating the sociometer: The relationship between interpersonal appraisals and state self-esteem. *Journal of Personality and Social Psychology.*

Leary, M. R., Springer, C., Negel, L., Ansell, E., & Evans, K. (1998). The causes, phenomenology, and consequences of hurt feelings. *Journal of Personality and Social Psychology.*

Leary, M. R., Tambor, E. S., Terdal, S. T., & Downs, D. L. (1995). Self-esteem as an interpersonal monitor: The sociometer hypothesis. *Journal of Personality and Social Psychology, 68*, 518–530.

Leary, M. R., Tchividjian, L. R., & Kraxberger, B. E. (1994). Self-presentation can be hazardous to your health: Impression management and health risk. *Health Psychology, 13*, 461–470.

Le Bon, G. (1895). *Psychologie des foules.* Paris: Félix Alcan.

Lee, J. A. (1977). A typology of styles of loving. *Personality and Social Psychology Bulletin, 3*, 173–182.

Lee, J. A. (1988). Love-styles. In R. J. Sternberg & M. L. Barnes (Ed.), *The psychology of love* (pp. 38–67). New Haven, CT: Yale University Press.

Lee, R. T., & Ashforth, B. E. (1996). A meta-analytic examination of the correlates of the three dimensions of job burnout. *Journal of Applied Psychology, 81*, 123–133.

Lee, Y. T., & Ottati, V. (1995). Perceived in-group homogeneity as a function of group membership salience and stereotype threat. *Personality and Social Psychology Bulletin, 21*, 610–619.

Lehman, D. R., Lempert, R. O., & Nisbett, R. E. (1988). The effects of graduate training on reasoning: Formal discipline and thinking about everyday-life events. *American Psychologist, 43*, 431–442.

Leichtman, M. D., & Ceci, S. J. (1995). The effects of stereotypes and suggestions on preschoolers' reports. *Developmental Psychology, 31*, 568–578.

Leigh, B. C., & Stacy, A. W. (1993). Alcohol outcome expectancies: Scale construction and predictive utility in higher-order confirmatory models. *Psychological Assessment, 5*, 216–229.

Leiker, M., & Hailey, B. J. (1988). A link between hostility and disease: Poor health habits? *Behavioral Medicine, 14*, 129–133.

Leinbach, M. D., & Fagot, B. I. (1993). Categorical habituation to male and female faces: Gender schematic processing in infancy. *Infant Behavior and Development, 16*, 317–332.

Leippe, M. (1995). The case for expert testimony about eyewitness memory. *Psychology, Public Policy, and Law, 1*, 909–959.

Leippe, M. R., & Eisenstadt, D. (1994). Generalization of dissonance reduction: Decreasing prejudice through induced compliance. *Journal of Personality and Social Psychology, 67*, 395–413.

Leitenberg, H., & Henning, K. (1995). Sexual fantasy. *Psychological Bulletin, 117*, 469–496.

Leland, J. (1995, December 11). "Copycat" crimes in New York's subways reignite the debate: Do TV and movies cause actual mayhem? *Newsweek*, p. 46.

Leo, J. (1996, June 17). Let's lower our self-esteem. *U.S. News & World Report*, p. 25.

Leo, R. A. (1996). Inside the interrogation room. *The Journal of Criminal Law and Criminology, 86*, 266–303.

Leonard, K. E. (1989). The impact of explicit aggressive and implicit nonaggressive cues on aggression in intoxicated and sober roles. *Personality and Social Psychology Bulletin, 15*, 390–400.

Lepore, L., & Brown, R. (1997). Category and stereotype activation: Is prejudice inevitable? *Journal of Personality and Social Psychology, 72*, 275–287.

Lepore, S. J. (1992). Social conflict, social support, and psychological distress: Evidence of cross-domain buffering effects. *Journal of Personality and Social Psychology, 63*, 857–867.

Lepper, M. R., & Greene, D. (Eds.). (1978). *The hidden costs of reward.* Hillsdale, NJ: Erlbaum.

Lepper, M. R., Greene, D., & Nisbett, R. E. (1973). Undermining children's intrinsic interest with extrinsic reward: A test of the "overjustification" hypothesis. *Journal of Personality and Social Psychology, 28*, 129–137.

Lerner, M. J. (1980). *The belief in a just world: A fundamental delusion.* New York: Plenum.

Lerner, M. J., & Meindl, J. R. (1981). Justice and altruism. In J. P. Rushton & R. M. Sorrentino (Eds.), *Altruism and helping behavior: Social, personality, and developmental perspectives* (pp. 213–232). Hillsdale, NJ: Erlbaum.

Lerner, M. J., & Simmons, C. H. (1966). Observers' reaction to the "innocent victim": Compassion or rejection? *Journal of Personality and Social Psychology, 4*, 203–210.

Leung, K. (1987). Some determinants of reactions to procedural models for conflict resolution: A cross-national study. *Journal of Personality and Social Psychology, 53*, 898–908.

Leventhal, H. (1970). Findings and theory in the study of fear communications. In L. Berkowitz (Ed.), *Advances in experimental social psychology* (Vol. 5, pp. 119–186). New York: Academic Press.

Leventhal, H., Watts, J. C., & Pagano, F. (1967). Effects of fear and instructions on how to cope with danger. *Journal of Personality and Social Psychology, 6*, 313–321.

Levesque, M. J. (1997). Meta-accuracy among acquainted individuals: A social relations analysis of interpersonal perception and metaperception. *Journal of Personality and Social Psychology, 72*, 66–74.

Levine, J. M. (1989). Reaction to opinion deviance in small groups. In P. B. Paulus (Ed.), *Psychology of group influence* (2nd ed., pp. 187–231). Hillsdale, NJ: Erlbaum.

Levine, J. M., & Moreland, R. L. (1990). Progress in small group research. *Annual Review of Psychology, 41*, 585–634.

Levine, J. M., & Moreland, R. L. (1994). Group socialization: Theory and research. In W. Stroebe & M. Hewstone (Eds.), *European Review of Social Psychology* (Vol. 5, pp. 305–336). Chichester, England: Wiley.

Levine, J. M., & Moreland, R. L. (1998). Small groups. In D. T. Gilbert, S. T. Fiske, & G. Lindzey (Eds.), *The handbook of social psychology* (4th ed., Vol. 2, pp. 415–469). New York: McGraw-Hill.

Levine, J. M., Moreland, R. L., & Ryan, C. S. (1998). Group socialization and intergroup relations. In C. Sedikides, J. Schopler, & C. A. Insko (Eds.), *Intergroup Cognition and Intergroup Behavior.* Mahwah, NJ: Erlbaum.

Levine, J. M., & Thompson, L. (1996). Intragroup conflict. In E. T. Higgins & A. W. Kruglanski (Eds.), *Social psychology: Handbook of basic principles* (pp. 745–776). New York: Guilford.

Levine, R. A., & Campbell, D. T. (1972). *Ethnocentrism: Theories of conflict, ethnic attitudes, and group behavior.* New York: Wiley.

Levine, R. B. (1993). Is love a luxury? *American Demographics, 15* (2), 27–28.

Levine, R. V., Martinez, T. S., Brase, G., & Sorenson, K. (1994). Helping in 36 U.S. cities. *Journal of Personality and Social Psychology, 67* (1), 69–82.

Levy, D. A., & Nail, P. R. (1993). Contagion: A theoretical and empirical review and reconceptualization. *Genetic, Social, and General Psychology Monographs, 119,* 233–284.

Levy, G. D., & Haaf, R. A. (1994). Detection of gender-related categories by 10-month-old infants. *Infant Behavior and Development, 17,* 457–459.

Lewin, K. (1935). *A dynamic theory of personality.* New York: McGraw-Hill.

Lewin, K. (1947). Group decision and social change. In T. M. Newcomb & E. L. Hartley (Eds.), *Readings in social psychology* (pp. 330–344). New York: Holt.

Lewin, K. (1951). Problems of research in social psychology. In D. Cartwright (Ed.), *Field theory in social science* (pp. 155–169). New York: Harper & Row.

Lewis, B. P., & Linder, D. E. (1997). Thinking about choking? Attentional processes and paradoxical performance. *Personality and Social Psychology Bulletin, 23,* 937–944.

Lewis, M., & Brooks-Gunn, J. (1979). *Social cognition and the acquisition of self.* New York: Plenum.

Liebert, R. M., & Sprafkin, J. (1988). *The early window* (3rd ed.). New York: Pergamon Press.

Liebowitz, M. R. (1983). *The chemistry of love.* Boston: Little, Brown.

Lifton, R. J. (1986). *The Nazi doctors: Medical killing and the psychology of genocide.* New York: Basic Books.

Light, K. C., & Obrist, P. A. (1980). Cardiovascular response to stress: Effects of opportunity to avoid shock experience, and performance feedback. *Psychophysiology, 17,* 243–252.

Lightdale, J. R., & Prentice, D. A. (1994). Rethinking sex differences in aggression: Aggressive behavior in the absence of social roles. *Personality and Social Psychology Bulletin, 20,* 34–44.

Likert, R. (1932). A technique for the measurement of attitudes. *Archives of Psychology, 140,* 1–55.

Lind, E. A., Erickson, B. E., Friedland, N., & Dickenberger, M. (1978). Reactions to procedural models for adjudicative conflict resolution: A cross national study. *Journal of Conflict Resolution, 22,* 318–341.

Lind, E. A., Kanfer, R., & Farley, P. C. (1990). Voice, control, and procedural justice: Instrumental and noninstrumental concerns in fairness judgments. *Journal of Personality and Social Psychology, 59,* 952–959.

Lind, E. A., & Tyler, T. R. (1988). *The social psychology of procedural justice.* New York: Plenum.

Linder, D. E., Cooper, J., & Jones, E. E. (1967). Decision freedom as a determinant of the role of incentive magnitude in attitude change. *Journal of Personality and Social Psychology, 6,* 245–254.

Lindsay, R. C. L., Lea, J. A., & Fulford, J. A. (1991). Sequential lineup presentation: Technique matters. *Journal of Applied Psychology, 76,* 741–745.

Lindsay, R. C. L., & Wells, G. L. (1985). Improving eyewitness identifications from lineups: Simultaneous versus sequential lineup presentations. *Journal of Applied Psychology, 70,* 556–564.

Lindsay, R. C. L., Wells, G. L., & Rumpel, C. M. (1981). Can people detect eyewitness-identification accuracy within and across situations? *Journal of Applied Psychology, 66,* 79–89.

Lindskold, S., & Han, G. (1988). GRIT as a foundation for integrative bargaining. *Personality and Social Psychology Bulletin, 14,* 335–345.

Lindskold, S., Han, G., & Betz, B. (1986). The essential elements of communication in the GRIT strategy. *Personality and Social Psychology Bulletin, 12,* 179–186.

Linville, P. (1998). The heterogeneity of homogeneity. In J. Cooper & J. Darley (Eds.), *Attribution processes, person perception, and social interaction: The legacy of Ned Jones.* Washington, DC: American Psychological Association.

Linville, P. W. (1987). Self-complexity as a cognitive buffer against stress-related illness and depression. *Journal of Personality and Social Psychology, 52,* 663–676.

Linville, P. W., Fischer, G. W., & Fischoff, B. (1992). Perceived risk and decision making involving AIDS. In J. B. Pryor & G. D. Reeder (Eds.), *The social psychology of HIV infection.* Hillsdale, NJ: Erlbaum.

Linville, P. W., Fischer, G. W., & Salovey, P. (1989). Perceived distributions of the characteristics of in-group and out-group members: Empirical evidence and a computer simulation. *Journal of Personality and Social Psychology, 57,* 165–188.

Linville, P. W., Fischer, G. W., & Yoon, C. (1996). Perceived covariation among the features of ingroup and outgroup members: The outgroup covariation effect. *Journal of Personality and Social Psychology, 70,* 421–436.

Linville, P. W., & Jones, E. E. (1980). Polarized appraisals of out-group members. *Journal of Personality and Social Psychology, 38,* 689–703.

Linz, D., Donnerstein, E., & Penrod, S. (1987). The findings and recommendations of the Attorney General's Commission on Pornography: Do the psychological "facts" fit the political fury? *American Psychologist, 42,* 946–953.

Linz, D., Wilson, B. J., & Donnerstein, E. (1992). Sexual violence in the mass media: Legal solutions, warnings, and mitigation through education. *Journal of Social Issues, 48,* 145–171.

Littlepage, G., Robison, W., & Reddington, K. (1997). Effects of task experience and group experience on group performance, member ability, and recognition of expertise. *Organizational Behavior and Human Decision Processes, 69,* 133–147.

Litvack, M. W., McDougall, D., & Romney, D. M. (1997). The structure of empathy during middle childhood and its relationship to prosocial behavior. *Genetic, Social and General Psychology Monographs, 123,* 303–324.

Lloyd, J. W., Eberhardt, M. J., & Drake, G. P., Jr. (1996). Group versus individual reinforcement contingencies within the context of group study conditions. *Journal of Applied Behavior Analysis, 29,* 189–200.

Lloyd, S. A., Cate, R. M., & Henton, J. M. (1984). Predicting premarital relationship stability: A methodological refinement. *Journal of Marriage and the Family, 46,* 71–76.

Locher, P., Unger, R., Sociedade, P., & Wahl, J. (1993). At first glance: Accessibility of the physical attractiveness stereotype. *Sex Roles, 28,* 729–743.

Locke, E. A., & Latham, G. P. (1990). *A theory of goal setting and task performance.* Englewood Cliffs, NJ: Prentice Hall.

Lockhart v. *McCree,* 54 U.S.L.W. 4449 (1986).

Locksley, A., Borgida, E., Brekke, N., & Hepburn, C. (1980). Sex stereotypes and social judgment. *Journal of Personality and Social Psychology, 39,* 821–831.

Loeber, R., & Hay, D. (1997). Key issues in the development of aggression and violence from childhood to early adulthood. *Annual Review of Psychology, 48,* 371–410.

Loftus, E. F. (1979). *Eyewitness testimony.* Cambridge, MA: Harvard University Press.

Loftus, E. F. (1983). Silence is not golden. *American Psychologist, 38,* 564–572.

Loftus, E. F., & Ketcham, K. (1991). *Witness for the defense: The accused, the eyewitness, and the expert who puts memory on trial.* New York: St. Martin's Press.

Loftus, E. F., & Palmer, J. C. (1974). Reconstruction of automobile destruction: An example of the interaction between language and memory. *Journal of Verbal Learning and Verbal Behavior, 13,* 585–589.

Loftus, E. F., Loftus, G. R., & Messo, J. (1987). Some facts about "weapon focus." *Law and Human Behavior, 11,* 55–62.

London, P. (1970). The rescuers: Motivational hypotheses about Christians who saved Jews from the Nazis. In J. R. Macaulay & L. Berkowitz (Eds.), *Altruism and helping behavior* (pp. 241–250). New York: Academic Press.

Long, B. C., & Sangster, J. I. (1993). Dispositional optimism/pessimism and coping strategies: Predictors of psychosocial adjustment of rheumatoid and osteoarthritis patients. *Journal of Applied Social Psychology, 23,* 1069–1091.

Long, E. C. J., & Andrews, D. W. (1990). Perspective taking as a predictor of marital adjustment. *Journal of Personality and Social Psychology, 59,* 126–131.

Longley, J., & Pruitt, D. G. (1980). Groupthink: A critique of Janis's theory. In L. Wheeler (Ed.), *Review of personality and social psychology* (Vol. 1, pp. 74–93). Beverly Hills, CA: Sage.

Lopez, J. A. (1992, March 3). Study says women face glass walls as well as ceilings. *Wall Street Journal,* pp. B1, B8.

Lord, C. G., Desforges, D. M., Fein, S., Pugh, M., & Lepper, M. R. (1994). Typicality effects in attitudes toward social policies: A concept-mapping approach. *Journal of Personality and Social Psychology, 66,* 658–673.

Lore, R. K., & Schultz, L. A. (1993). Control of human aggression: A comparative perspective. *American Psychologist, 48,* 16–25.

Lorenz, K. (1966). *On aggression.* New York: Harcourt, Brace & World.

Lortie-Lussier, M. (1987). Minority influence and idiosyncrasy credit: A new comparison of the Moscovici and Hollander theories of innovation. *European Journal of Social Psychology, 17,* 431–446.

Losch, M. E., & Cacioppo, J. T. (1990). Cognitive dissonance may enhance sympathetic tonus, but attitudes are changed to reduce negative affect rather than arousal. *Journal of Experimental Social Psychology, 26,* 289–304.

Lott, A. J., & Lott, B. E. (1974). The role of reward in the formation of positive interpersonal attitudes. In T. L. Huston (Ed.), *Foundations of interpersonal attraction* (pp. 171–189). New York: Academic Press.

Lott, B. (1985). The devaluation of women's competence. *Journal of Social Issues, 41,* 43–60.

Lovdal, L. T. (1989). Sex role messages in television commercials: An update. *Sex Roles, 21,* 715–724.

Lowe, K., Kroeck, K., & Sivasubramaniam, N. (1996). Effectiveness correlates of transformational and transactional leadership: A meta-analytic review of the MLQ literature. *Leadership Quarterly, 7,* 385–425.

Lubow, R. E., & Fein, O. (1996). Pupillary size in response to a visual guilty knowledge test: A new technique for the detection of deception. *Journal of Experimental Psychology: Applied, 2,* 164–177.

Luks, A. (1988, October). Helper's high. *Psychology Today,* pp. 39–40.

Lupfer, M. B., Clark, L. F., Hutcherson, H. W. (1990). Impact of context on spontaneous trait and situational attributions. *Journal of Personality and Social Psychology, 58,* 239–249.

Lüüs, C. A. E., & Wells, G. L. (1991). Eyewitness identification and the selection of distractors for lineups. *Law and Human Behavior, 15,* 43–58.

Lüüs, C. A. E., & Wells, G. L. (1994). The malleability of eyewitness confidence: Co-witness and perseverance effects. *Journal of Applied Psychology, 79,* 714–723.

Lykken, D. T. (1981). *A tremor in the blood: Uses and abuses of the lie detector.* New York: McGraw-Hill.

Lykken, D. T., & Tellegen, A. (1993). Is human mating adventitious or the result of lawful choice? A twin study of mate selection. *Journal of Personality and Social Psychology, 65,* 56–68.

Lyness, K. S., & Thompson, D. E. (1997). Above the glass ceiling? A comparison of matched samples of female and male executives. *Journal of Applied Psychology, 82,* 359–375.

Lynn, M., & Mynier, K. (1993). Effect of server posture on restaurant tipping. *Journal of Applied Social Psychology, 23,* 678–685.

Lyubomirsky, S., & Nolen-Hoeksema, S. (1993). Self-perpetuating properties of dysphoric rumination. *Journal of Personality and Social Psychology, 65,* 339–349.

Ma, H. K., & Leung, M. C. (1995). The relation of altruistic orientation to family social environment in Chinese children. *Psychologia, 38,* 109–115.

Maass, A., Ceccarelli, R., & Rudin, S. (1996). Linguistic intergroup bias: Evidence for in-group-protective motivation. *Journal of Personality and Social Psychology, 71,* 512–526.

Maass, A., & Clark, R. D., III. (1984). Hidden impact of minorities: Fifteen years of minority influence research. *Psychological Bulletin, 95,* 428–450.

Maass, A., & Kohnken, G. (1989). Eyewitness identification: Simulating the "weapon effect." *Law and Human Behavior, 13,* 397–408.

Maass, A., Milesi, A., Zabbini, S., & Stahlberg, D. (1995). Linguistic intergroup bias: Differential expectancies or in-group protection? *Journal of Personality and Social Psychology, 68,* 116–126.

Maass, A., Volpato, C., & Mucchi-Faina, A. (1996). Social influence and the verifiability of the issue under discussion: Attitudinal versus objective items. *British Journal of Social Psychology, 35,* 15–26.

Macaulay, J. R. (1970). A shill for charity. In J. Macaulay & L. Berkowitz (Eds.), *Altruism and helping behavior* (pp. 43–59). New York: Academic Press.

Maccoby, E. E., & Jacklin, C. N. (1974). *The psychology of sex differences.* Stanford, CA: Stanford University Press.

MacCoun, R. J., & Kerr, N. L. (1988). Asymmetric influence in mock jury deliberation: Jurors' bias for leniency. *Journal of Personality and Social Psychology, 54,* 21–33.

Macionis, J. J. (1997). *Sociology* (6th ed.). Upper Saddle River, NJ: Prentice Hall.

Mackie, D. M., Asuncion, A. G., & Rosselli, F. (1992). Impact of positive affect on persuasion processes. *Review of Personality and Social Psychology, 14,* 247–270.

Mackie, D. M., & Cooper, J. (1984). Attitude polarization: Effects of group membership. *Journal of Personality and Social Psychology, 46,* 575–585.

Mackie, D. M., & Worth, L. T. (1989). Processing deficits and the mediation of positive affect in persuasion. *Journal of Personality and Social Psychology, 57,* 27–40.

Mackie, D. M., Worth, L. T., & Asuncion, A.G. (1990). Processing of persuasive in-group messages. *Journal of Personality and Social Psychology, 58,* 812–822.

MacLeod, C., & Campbell, L. (1992). Memory accessibility and probability judgments: An experimental evaluation of the availability heuristic. *Journal of Personality and Social Psychology, 63,* 890–902.

Macrae, C. N., Bodenhausen, G. V., & Milne, A. B. (1995). The dissection of selection in person perception: Inhibitory processes in social stereotyping. *Journal of Personality and Social Psychology, 69,* 397–407.

Macrae, C. N., Bodenhausen, G. V., & Milne, A. B. (1998). Saying no to unwanted thoughts: Self-focus and the regulation of mental life. *Journal of Personality and Social Psychology, 74,* 578–589.

Macrae, C. N., Bodenhausen, G. V., Milne, A. B., & Jetten, J. (1994). Out of mind but back in sight: Stereotypes on the rebound. *Journal of Personality and Social Psychology, 67,* 808–817.

Macrae, C. N., Milne, A. B., & Bodenhausen, G. V. (1994). Stereotypes as energy-saving devices: A peek inside the cognitive toolbox. *Journal of Personality and Social Psychology, 66,* 37–47.

Madden, T. J., Ellen, P. S., & Ajzen, I. (1992). A comparison of the theory of planned behavior and the theory of reasoned action. *Personality and Social Psychology Bulletin, 18,* 3–9.

Maddux, J. E. (1991). Self-efficacy. In C. R. Snyder & D. R. Forsyth (Eds.), *Handbook of social and clinical psychology: The health perspective* (pp. 57–78). New York: Pergamon Press.

Maddux, J. E., & Rogers, R. W. (1980). Effects of source expertness, physical attractiveness, and supporting arguments on persuasion: A case of brains over beauty. *Journal of Personality and Social Psychology, 39,* 235–244.

Madey, S. F., Simo, M., Dillworth, D., Kemper, D., Toczynski, A., & Perella, A. (1996). They do get more attractive at closing time, but only when you are not in a relationship. *Basic and Applied Social Psychology, 18,* 387–393.

Maio, G. R., & Esses, V. M. (1998). The social consequences of affirmative action: Deleterious effects on perceptions of groups. *Personality and Social Psychology Bulletin, 24,* 65–74.

Major, B., Carrington, P. I., & Carnevale, P. J. D. (1984). Physical attractiveness and self-esteem: Attributions for praise from an other-sex evaluator. *Personality and Social Psychology Bulletin, 10,* 43–50.

Major, B., & Cozzarelli, C. (1992). Psychosocial predictors of adjustment to abortion. *Journal of Social Issues, 48,* 121–142.

Major, B., & Crocker, J. (1993). Social stigma: The affective consequences of attributional ambiguity. In D. M. Mackie & D. L. Hamilton (Eds.), *Affect, cognition, and stereotyping: Interactive processes in intergroup perception* (pp. 345–370). New York: Academic Press.

Major, B., & Deaux, K. (1982). Individual differences in justice behavior. In J. Greenberg & R. L. Cohen (Eds.), *Equity and justice in social behavior* (pp. 13–76). New York: Academic Press.

Major, B., Feinstein, J., & Crocker, J. (1994). Attributional ambiguity of affirmative action. *Basic and Applied Social Psychology, 15,* 113–142.

Major, B., & Konar, E. (1984). An investigation of sex differences in pay expectations and their possible causes. *Academy of Management Journal, 27,* 777–792.

Major, B., McFarlin, D. B., & Gagnon, D. (1984). Overworked and underpaid: On the nature of gender differences in personal entitlement. *Journal of Personality and Social Psychology, 47,* 1399–1412.

Malamuth, N. M. (1983). Factors associated with rape as predictors of laboratory aggression against women. *Journal of Personality and Social Psychology, 45,* 432–442.

Malamuth, N. M. (1986). Predictors of naturalistic sexual aggression. *Journal of Personality and Social Psychology, 50,* 953–962.

Malamuth, N. M. (1996). The confluence model of sexual aggression: Feminist and evolutionary perspectives. In D. M. Buss & N. M. Malamuth (Eds.), *Sex, power, conflict: Evolutionary and feminist perspectives* (pp. 269–295). New York: Oxford University Press.

Malamuth, N. M., & Billings, V. (1986). The function and effects of pornography: Sexual communications versus the feminist model in light of research findings. In J. Bryant & D. Zillmann (Eds.), *Perspectives on media effects* (pp. 83–108). Hillsdale, NJ: Erlbaum.

Malamuth, N. M., & Check, J. V. P. (1981). The effects of mass media exposure on acceptance of violence against women: A field experiment. *Journal of Research in Personality, 15,* 436–446.

Malamuth, N. M., & Donnerstein, E. I. (1982). The effects of aggressive-pornographic mass media stimuli. In L. Berkowitz (Ed.), *Advances in experimental social psychology* (Vol. 15, pp. 103–136). New York: Academic Press.

Malinosky-Rummell, R., & Hansen, D. J. (1993). Long-term consequences of childhood physical abuse. *Psychological Bulletin, 114,* 68–79.

Malkiel, B. (1981). *A random walk down Wall Street* (2nd ed.). New York: Norton.

Malle, B. F., & Knobe, J. (1997). Which behaviors do people explain? A basic actor-observer asymmetry. *Journal of Personality and Social Psychology, 72,* 288–304.

Malloy, T. E., & Albright, L. (1990). Interpersonal perception in a social context. *Journal of Personality and Social Psychology, 58,* 419–428.

Malpass, R. S., & Devine, P. G. (1981). Eyewitness identification: Lineup instructions and the absence of the offender. *Journal of Applied Psychology, 66,* 482–489.

Malpass, R. S., & Kravitz, J. (1969). Recognition for faces of own and other race. *Journal of Personality and Social Psychology, 13,* 330–334.

Manis, M., Nelson, T. E., & Shedler, J. (1988). Stereotypes and social judgment: Extremity, assimilation, and contrast. *Journal of Personality and Social Psychology, 55,* 28–36.

Mann, J. M. (1992). AIDS—The second decade: A global perspective. *Journal of Infectious Diseases, 165,* 245–250.

Mann, L. (1981). The baiting crowd in episodes of threatened suicide. *Journal of Personality and Social Psychology, 41,* 703–709.

Mann, T. (1994). Informed consent for psychological research: Do subjects comprehend consent forms and understand their legal rights? *Psychological Science, 5,* 140–143.

Manz, C. C., & Sims, H. P., Jr. (1982). The potential for "groupthink" in autonomous work groups. *Human Relations, 35,* 773–784.

Marano, H. E. (1995). Big. Bad. Bully. *Psychology Today, 28,* 51–56, 62–82.

Margolin, G., & Wampold, B. E. (1981). A sequential analysis of conflict and accord in distressed and nondistressed marital partners. *Journal of Consulting and Clinical Psychology, 49,* 554–567.

Markman, K. D., & Weary, G. (1996). The influence of chronic control concerns on counterfactual thought. *Social Cognition, 14,* 292–316.

Marks, G., Graham, J. W., & Hansen, W. B. (1992). Social projection and social conformity in adolescent alcohol use: A longitudinal analysis. *Personality and Social Psychology Bulletin, 18,* 96–101.

Marks, G., & Miller, N. (1982). Target attractiveness as a mediator of assumed attitude similarity. *Personality and Social Psychology Bulletin, 8,* 728–735.

Markus, H. (1977). Self-schemata and processing information about the self. *Journal of Personality and Social Psychology, 35,* 63–78.

Markus, H., Hamill, R., & Sentis, K. P. (1987). Thinking fat: Self-schemas for body weight and the processing of weight-relevant information. *Journal of Applied Social Psychology, 17,* 50–71.

Markus, H. R., & Kitayama, S. (1991). Culture and the self: Implications for cognition, emotion, and motivation. *Psychological Review, 98,* 224–253.

Markus, H., & Nurius, P. (1986). Possible selves. *American Psychologist, 41,* 954–969.

Marlowe, C. M., Schneider, S. L., & Nelson, C. E. (1996). Gender and attractiveness biases in hiring decisions: Are more experienced managers less biased? *Journal of Applied Psychology, 81,* 11–21.

Marlowe, D., & Gergen, K. (1969). Personality and social interaction. In G. Lindzey & E. Aronson (Eds.), *The handbook of social psychology* (2nd ed., pp. 590–665). Reading, MA: Addison-Wesley.

Marques, J. M. (1990). The black sheep effect: Outgroup homogeneity in social comparison settings. In D. Abrams & M. Hogg (Eds.), *Social identity theory: Constructive and critical advances* (pp. 131–151). New York: Springer-Verlag.

Marsh, H. W., & Parker, J. W. (1984). Determinants of student self-concept: Is it better to be a relatively large fish in a small pond even if you don't learn to swim as well? *Journal of Personality and Social Psychology, 47,* 213–231.

Marshall, L. (1979). Sharing, talking, and giving: Relief of social tensions among !Kung Bushmen. In R. B. Lee & I. DeVore (Eds.), *Kalahari hunter-gatherers: Studies of the !Kung San and their neighbors* (pp. 349–372). Cambridge, England: Cambridge University Press.

Marshall, W. L. (1989). Pornography and sex offenders. In D. Zillmann & J. Bryant (Eds.), *Pornography: Research advances and policy considerations* (pp. 185–214). Hillsdale, NJ: Erlbaum.

Martin, C. L. (1987). A ratio measure of sex stereotyping. *Journal of Personality and Social Psychology, 52,* 489–499.

Martin, C. L., Eisenbud, L., & Rose, H. (1995). Children's gender-based reasoning about toys. *Child Development, 66,* 1453–1471.

Martin, C. L., & Parker, S. (1995). Folk theories about sex and race differences. *Personality and Social Psychology Bulletin, 21,* 45–57.

Martin, C. L., Wood, C. H., & Little, J. K. (1990). The development of gender stereotype components. *Child Development, 61,* 1891–1904.

Martin, J. (1998, March 2). Changing jobs? Try the net. *Fortune.*

Martz, L. (1987, May 25). "It Was My Idea." *Newsweek,* 16–19.

Maslach, C. (1979). Negative emotional biasing of unexplained arousal. *Journal of Personality and Social Psychology, 37,* 953–969.

Maslach, C. (1982). *Burnout: The cost of caring.* Englewood Cliffs, NJ: Prentice Hall.

Mathes, E. W. (1992). *Jealousy: The psychological data.* Lanhan, MD: University Press of America.

Mathur, M., & Chattopadhyay, A. (1991). The impact of moods generated by TV programs on responses to advertising. *Psychology and Marketing, 8,* 59–77.

Matthews, K. A. (1988). Coronary heart disease and Type A behaviors: Update on and alternative to the Booth-Kewley and Friedman (1987) quantitative review. *Psychological Bulletin, 104,* 373–380.

Matthews, K. A., & Haynes, S. G. (1986). Type A behavior pattern and coronary disease risk: Update and critical evaluation. *American Journal of Epidemiology, 123,* 923–958.

Maznevski, M. L. (1994). Understanding our differences: Performance in decision-making groups with diverse members. *Human Relations, 47,* 531–552.

Mazur, A., Booth, A., & Dabbs, J. M. (1992). Testosterone and chess competition. *Social Psychology Quarterly, 55,* 70–77.

Mazur, A., & Lamb, T. A. (1980). Testosterone, status, and mood in human males. *Hormones and Behavior, 14,* 236–246.

McAdams, D. P. (1989). *Intimacy: The need to be close.* New York: Doubleday.

McArthur, L. A. (1972). The how and what of why: Some determinants and consequences of causal attribution. *Journal of Personality and Social Psychology, 22,* 171–193.

McCauley, C. (1989). The nature of social influence in groupthink: Compliance and internalization. *Journal of Personality and Social Psychology, 57,* 250–260.

McCloskey, M., & Egeth, H. (1983). Eyewitness identification: What can a psychologist tell a jury? *American Psychologist, 38,* 550–563.

McCloskey, M., & Zaragoza, M. (1985). Misleading postevent information and memory for events: Arguments and evidence against memory impairment hypotheses. *Journal of Experimental Psychology, 114,* 3–18.

McConahay, J. B. (1983). Modern racism and modern discrimination: The effects of race, racial attitudes, and context on simulated hiring decisions. *Personality and Social Psychology Bulletin, 9,* 551–558.

McConahay, J. B. (1986). Modern racism, ambivalence, and the modern racism scale. In J. F. Dovidio & S. L. Gaertner (Eds.), *Prejudice, discrimination, and racism: Theory and research* (pp. 91–125). Orlando, FL: Academic Press.

McCrae, R. R., & Costa, P. T., Jr. (1997). Personality trait structure as a human universal. *American Psychologist, 52,* 509–516.

McCullough, M. E., Worthington, E. L., Jr., & Rachal, K. C. (1997). Interpersonal forgiving in close relationships. *Journal of Personality and Social Psychology, 73,* 321–336.

McCusker, C., & Carnevale, P. J. (1995). Framing in resource dilemmas: Loss aversion and the moderating effects of sanctions. *Organizational Behavior and Human Decision Processes, 61,* 190–201.

McDougall, W. (1908). *An introduction to social psychology.* London: Methuen.

McFarland, C., & Buehler, R. (1995). Collective self-esteem as a moderator of the frog-pond effect in reactions to performance feedback. *Journal of Personality and Social Psychology, 68,* 1055–1070.

McFatter, R. M. (1978). Sentencing strategies and justice: Effects of punishment philosophy on sentencing decisions. *Journal of Personality and Social Psychology, 36,* 1490–1500.

McGarty, C., Turner, J. C., Hogg, M. A., David, B., et al. (1992). Group polarization as conformity to the prototypical group member. *British Journal of Social Psychology, 31,* 1–19.

McGath, M. P., Wilson, S. R., & Frassetto, S. J. (1995). Why some forms of induction are better than others at encouraging prosocial behavior. *Merrill Palmer Quarterly, 41,* 347–360.

McGillicuddy, N. B., Pruitt, D. G., & Syna, H. (1984). Perceptions of fairness and strength of negotiation. *Personality and Social Psychology Bulletin, 10,* 402–409.

McGraw, K. O., & McCullers, J. C. (1979). Evidence of a detrimental effect of extrinsic incentives on breaking a mental set. *Journal of Experimental Social Psychology, 15,* 285–294.

McGuire, W. J. (1964). Inducing resistance to persuasion. In L. Berkowitz (Ed.), *Advances in experimental social psychology* (Vol. 1, pp. 192–229). New York: Academic Press.

McGuire, W. J. (1967). Some impending reorientations in social psychology: Some thoughts provoked by Kenneth Ring. *Journal of Experimental Social Psychology, 3,* 124–139.

McGuire, W. J. (1968). Personality and susceptibility to social influence. In E. F. Borgatta & W. W. Lambert (Eds.), *Handbook of personality theory and research* (pp. 1130–1187). Chicago: Rand McNally.

McGuire, W. J. (1969). The nature of attitudes and attitude change. In G. Lindzey & E. Aronson (Eds.), *Handbook of social psychology* (2nd ed., Vol. 3, pp. 136–314). Reading, MA: Addison-Wesley.

McGuire, W. J., & McGuire, C. V. (1988). Content and process in the experience of self. In L. Berkowitz (Ed.), *Advances in experimental social psychology* (Vol. 20, pp. 97–144). New York: Academic Press.

McGuire, W. J., McGuire, C. V., & Winton, W. (1979). Effects of household sex composition on the salience of one's gender in the spontaneous self-concept. *Journal of Experimental Social Psychology, 15,* 77–90.

McIntosh, D. N. (1996). Facial feedback hypothesis: Evidence, implications, and directions. *Motivation and Emotion, 20,* 121–147.

McIntosh, D. N., Silver, R. C., & Wortman, C. B. (1993). Religion's role in adjustment to a negative life event: Coping with the loss of a child. *Journal of Personality and Social Psychology, 65,* 812–821.

McLeod, P. L., Lobel, S. A., & Cox, Jr., T. H. (1996). Ethnic diversity and creativity in small groups. *Small Group Research, 27,* 248–264.

McMullen, P. A., & Gross, A. E. (1983). Sex differences, sex roles, and health-related help-seeking. In B. M. DePaulo, A. Nadler, & J. D. Fisher (Eds.), *New directions in helping: Vol. 2. Help-Seeking* (pp. 233–263). New York: Academic Press.

Mead, G. H. (1934). *Mind, self, and society.* Chicago: University of Chicago Press.

Medvec, V. H., Madey, S. F., & Gilovich, T. (1995). When less is more: Counterfactual thinking and satisfaction among olympic medalists. *Journal of Personality and Social Psychology, 69,* 603–610.

Medvec, V. H., & Savitsky, K. (1997). When doing better means feeling worse: The effects of categorical cutoff points on counterfactual thinking and satisfaction. *Journal of Personality and Social Psychology, 72,* 1284–1296.

Medved, M. (1996, September 21). *Daily Telegraph,* p. 5.

Meeus, W. H. J., & Raaijmakers, Q. A. W. (1995). Obedience in modern society: The Utrecht studies. *Journal of Social Issues, 51,* 155–175.

Melamed, T. (1991). Individual differences in romantic jealousy: The moderating effect of relationship characteristics. *European Journal of Social Psychology, 21,* 455–461.

Meleshko, K. G. A., & Alden, L. E. (1993). Anxiety and self-disclosure: Toward a motivational model. *Journal of Personality and Social Psychology, 64,* 1000–1009.

Mendonca, P. J., & Brehm, S. S. (1983). Effects of choice on behavioral treatment of overweight children. *Journal of Social and Clinical Psychology, 1,* 343–358.

Merikle, P., & Skanes, H. E. (1992). Subliminal self-help audiotapes: A search for placebo effects. *Journal of Applied Psychology, 77,* 772–776.

Merton, R. (1948). The self-fulfilling prophecy. *Antioch Review, 8,* 193–210.

Messick, D. M., & Cook, K. S. (Eds.). (1983). *Equity theory: Psychological and sociological perspectives.* New York: Praeger.

Messick, D. M., & Mackie, D. M. (1989). Intergroup relations. *Annual Review of Psychology, 40,* 51–81.

Messick, D. M., Wilke, H., Brewer, M. B., Kramer, R. M., Zemke, P. E., & Lui, L. (1983). Individual adaptation and structural change as solutions to social dilemmas. *Journal of Personality and Social Psychology, 44,* 294–309.

Metalsky, G. I., Joiner, T. E., Hardin, T. S., & Abramson, L. Y. (1993). Depressive reactions to failure in a naturalistic setting: A test of the hopelessness and self-esteem theories of depression. *Journal of Abnormal Psychology, 102,* 101–109.

Meyer, C. B., & Taylor, S. E. (1986). Adjustment to rape. *Journal of Personality and Social Psychology, 50,* 1226–1234.

Michaels, J. W., Edwards, J. N., & Acock, A. C. (1984). Satisfaction in intimate relationships as a function of inequality, inequity, and outcomes. *Social Psychology Quarterly, 47,* 347–357.

Mickelson, K. D., Kessler, R. C., & Shaver, P. R. (1997). Adult attachment in a nationally representative sample. *Journal of Personality and Social Psychology, 73,* 1092–1106.

Miles, D. R., & Carey, G. (1997). Genetic and environmental architecture on human aggression. *Journal of Personality and Social Psychology, 72,* 207–217.

Miles, J. A., & Greenberg, J. (1993). Using punishment threats to attenuate social loafing effects among swimmers. *Organizational Behavior and Human Decision Processes, 56,* 246–265.

Milgram, S. (1963). Behavioral study of obedience. *Journal of Abnormal and Social Psychology, 67,* 371–378.

Milgram, S. (1970). The experience of living in cities. *Science, 167,* 1461–1468.

Milgram, S. (1974). *Obedience to authority: An experimental view.* New York: Harper & Row.

Milgram, S., Bickman, L., & Berkowitz, L. (1969). Note on the drawing power of crowds of different size. *Journal of Personality and Social Psychology, 13,* 79–82.

Milgram, S., & Sabini, J. (1978). On maintaining urban norms: A field experiment in the subway. In A. Baum, J. E. Singer, & S. Valins (Eds.), *Advances in environmental psychology* (Vol. 1). Hillsdale, NJ: Erlbaum.

Milgram, S., & Toch, H. (1969). Collective behavior: Crowds and social movements. In G. Lindzey & E. Aronson (Eds.), *The handbook of social psychology* (2nd ed., Vol. 4, pp. 507–610). Reading, MA: Addison-Wesley.

Millar, M. G., & Millar, K. U. (1990). Attitude change as a function of attitude type and argument type. *Journal of Personality and Social Psychology, 59,* 217–228.

Millar, M. G., & Millar, K. U. (1996). The effects of direct and indirect experience on affective and cognitive responses and the attitude-behavior relation. *Journal of Experimental Social Psychology, 32,* 561–579.

Millar, M. G., & Tesser, A. (1989). The effects of affective-cognitive consistency and thought on the attitude-behavior relation. *Journal of Experimental Social Psychology, 25,* 189–202.

Miller, A. G. (1986). *The obedience experiments: A case study of controversy in social science.* New York: Praeger.

Miller, A. G., Jones, E. E., & Hinkle, S. (1981). A robust attribution error in the personality domain. *Journal of Experimental Social Psychology, 17,* 587–600.

Miller, B. C. (1993). Families, science, and values: Alternative view of parenting effects and adolescent pregnancy. *Journal of Marriage and the Family, 55,* 7–21.

Miller, C. T. (1984). Self-schemas, gender, and social comparison: A clarification of the related attributes hypothesis. *Journal of Personality and Social Psychology, 46,* 1222–1229.

Miller, D. T., & McFarland, C. (1987). Pluralistic ignorance: When similarity is interpreted as dissimilarity. *Journal of Personality and Social Psychology, 53,* 298–305.

Miller, J. G. (1984). Culture and the development of everyday social explanation. *Journal of Personality and Social Psychology, 46,* 961–978.

Miller, J. G., & Bersoff, D. M. (1994). Cultural influences on the moral status of reciprocity and the discounting of endogenous motivation. *Personality and Social Psychology Bulletin, 20,* 592–602.

Miller, J. G., Bersoff, D. M., & Harwood, R. L. (1990). Perceptions of social responsibility in India and in the United States: Moral imperatives or personal decisions? *Journal of Personality and Social Psychology, 58,* 33–47.

Miller, M. L., & Thayer, J. F. (1989). On the existence of discrete classes in personality: Is self-monitoring the correct joint to carve? *Journal of Personality and Social Psychology, 57,* 143–155.

Miller, N. E. (1941). The frustration-aggression hypothesis. *Psychological Review, 48,* 337–342.

Miller, N., & Brewer, M. B. (Eds.) (1984). *Groups in contact: The psychology of desegregation.* New York: Academic Press.

Miller, N., & Campbell, D. T. (1959). Recency and primacy in persuasion as a function of the timing of speeches and measurements. *Journal of Abnormal and Social Psychology, 59,* 1–9.

Miller, N., & Carlson, M. (1990). Valid theory-testing meta-analyses further question the negative state relief model of helping. *Psychological Bulletin, 107,* 215–225.

Miller, P. A., & Eisenberg, N. (1988). The relation of empathy to aggressive and externalizing/antisocial behavior. *Psychological Bulletin, 103,* 324–344.

Miller, P. A., Eisenberg, N., Fabes, R. A., & Shell, R. (1996). Relations of moral reasoning and vicarious emotion to young children's prosocial behavior toward peers and adults. *Developmental Psychology, 32,* 210–219.

Miller, S. M., & Mangan, C. E. (1983). Interacting effects of information and coping style in adapting to gynecologic stress: Should the doctor tell all? *Journal of Personality and Social Psychology, 45,* 223–236.

Miller, T. Q., Smith, T. W., Turner, C. W., Guijarro, M. L., & Hallet, A. J. (1996). A meta-analytic review of research on hostility and physical health. *Psychological Bulletin, 119,* 322–348.

Miller, T. Q., Turner, C. W., Tindale, R. S., Posavac, E. J., & Dugon, B. L. (1991). Reasons for the trend toward null findings in research on Type A behavior. *Psychological Bulletin, 110,* 469–485.

Miller, W. R. (1985). Motivation for treatment: A review with special emphasis on alcoholism. *Psychological Bulletin, 98,* 84–107.

Milliken, F. J., & Martins, L. L. (1996). Searching for common threads: Understanding the multiple effects of diversity in organizational groups. *Academy of Management Review, 21,* 402–433.

Miranda, S. M. (1994). Avoidance of groupthink: Meeting management using group support systems. *Small Group Research, 25,* 105–136.

Mita, T. H., Dermer, M., & Knight, J. (1977). Reversed facial images and the mere exposure hypothesis. *Journal of Personality and Social Psychology, 35,* 597–601.

Mitchell, T. R. (1974). Expectancy models of job satisfaction, occupational preference, and effort: A theoretical, methodological, and empirical appraisal. *Psychological Bulletin, 81,* 1096–1112.

Moghaddam, F. M., Taylor, D. M., & Wright, S. C. (1993). *Social psychology in cross-cultural perspective,* New York: W. H. Freeman and Co.

Mohamed, A. A., & Wiebe, F. A. (1996). Toward a process theory of groupthink. *Small Group Research, 27,* 416–430.

Molitor, F., & Hirsch, K. W. (1994). Children's toleration of real-life aggression after exposure to media violence: A replication of the Drabman and Thomas studies. *Child Study Journal, 24,* 191–207.

Monteith, M. J., Devine, P. G., & Zuwerink, J. R. (1993). Self-directed versus other-directed affect as a consequence of prejudice-related discrepancies. *Journal of Personality and Social Psychology, 64,* 198–210.

Monteith. M. J., Sherman, J. W., & Devine, P. G. (1998). *Personality and Social Psychology Review, 2,* 63–82.

Montepare, J. M., & McArthur, L. Z. (1988). Impressions of people created by age-related qualities of their gaits. *Journal of Personality and Social Psychology, 55,* 547–556.

Montgomery, G., & Kirsch, I. (1996). Mechanisms of placebo pain reduction: An empirical investigation. *Psychological Science, 7,* 174–176.

Moore, B. S., Underwood, B., & Rosenhan, D. L. (1973). Affect and altruism. *Developmental Psychology, 8,* 99–104.

Moore, T. E. (1982). Subliminal advertising: What you see is what you get. *Journal of Marketing, 46,* 38–47.

Moorhead, G., & Montanari, J. R. (1986). An empirical investigation of the groupthink phenomenon. *Human Relations, 39,* 399–410.

Moorman, R. H. (1991). Relationship between organizational justice and organizational citizenship behaviors: Do fairness perceptions influence employee citizenship? *Journal of Applied Psychology, 76,* 845–855.

Moorman, R. H., & Blakely, G. L. (1995). Individualism-collectivism as an individual difference predictor of organizational citizenship behavior. *Journal of Organizational Behavior, 16,* 127–142.

Moran, G., & Comfort, C. (1986). Neither "tentative" nor "fragmentary": Verdict preference of impaneled felony jurors as a function of attitude toward capital punishment. *Journal of Applied Psychology, 71,* 146–155.

Moran, G., & Cutler, B. L. (1991). The prejudicial impact of pretrial publicity. *Journal of Applied Social Psychology, 21,* 345–367.

Moray, N. (1959). Attention in dichotic listening: Affective cues and the influence of instructions. *Quarterly Journal of Experimental Psychology, 11,* 56–60.

Moreland, R. L., & Beach, S. R. (1992). Exposure effects in the classroom: The development of affinity among students. *Journal of Experimental Social Psychology, 28,* 255–276.

Moreland, R. L., Hogg, M. A., & Hains, S. C. (1994). Back to the future: Social psychological research on groups. *Journal of Experimental Social Psychology 30,* 527–555.

Morgan, H. J., & Janoff-Bulman, R. (1994). Positive and negative self-complexity: Patterns of adjustment following traumatic versus non-traumatic life experiences. *Journal of Social and Clinical Psychology, 13,* 63–85.

Morgan, M. M., Goddard, H. W., & Givens, S. N. (1997). Factors that influence willingness to help the homeless. *Journal of Social Distress and the Homeless, 6,* 45–56.

Mori, D., Chaiken, S., & Pliner, P. (1987). Eating lightly and the self-presentation of femininity. *Journal of Personality and Social Psychology, 53,* 693–702.

Moriarty, D., & McCabe, A. E. (1977). Studies of television and youth sport. In *Ontario Royal Commission on Violence in the*

Communications Industry report (Vol. 5). Toronto: Queen's Printer for Ontario.

Moriarty, T. (1975). Crime, commitment, and the responsive bystander: Two field experiments. *Journal of Personality and Social Psychology, 31,* 370–376.

Morris, M. W., & Peng, K. (1994). Culture and cause: American and Chinese attributions for social and physical events. *Journal of Personality and Social Psychology, 67,* 949–971.

Morrison, A. M., & Von Glinow, M. A. (1990). Women and minorities in management. *American Psychologist, 45,* 200–208.

Morse, B. J. (1995). Beyond the Conflict Tactics Scale: Assessing gender differences in partner violence. *Violence and Victims, 10,* 251–272.

Moscovici, S. (1980). Toward a theory of conversion behavior. In L. Berkowitz (Ed.), *Advances in Experimental Social Psychology, 6,* 149–202.

Moscovici, S. (1985). Social influence and conformity. In G. Lindzey & E. Aronson (Eds.), *The handbook of social psychology* (3rd ed., pp. 347–412). New York: Random House.

Moscovici, S., Lage, E., & Naffrechoux, M. (1969). Influence of a consistent minority on the responses of a majority in a color perception task. *Sociometry, 32,* 365–380.

Moscovici, S., & Personnaz, B. (1991). Studies in social influence VI: Is Lenin orange or red? Imagery and social influence. *European Journal of Social Psychology, 21,* 101–118.

Moscovici, S., & Zavalloni, M. (1969). The group as a polarizer of attitudes. *Journal of Personality and Social Psychology, 12,* 125–135.

Moskowitz, G. B. (1993). Individual differences in social categorization: The influence of personal need for structure on spontaneous trait inferences. *Journal of Personality and Social Psychology, 65,* 132–142.

Moskowitz, G. B. (1996). The mediational effects of attributions and information processing in minority social influence. *British Journal of Social Psychology, 35,* 47–66.

Motowidlo, S. J., Dunnette, M. D., & Carter, G. W. (1990). An alternative selection procedure: The low-fidelity simulation. *Journal of Applied Psychology, 75,* 640–647.

Mouton, J., Blake, R., & Olmstead, J. (1956). The relationship between frequency of yielding and the disclosure of personal identity. *Journal of Personality, 24,* 339–347.

Moynihan J. A., & Ader, R. (1996). Psychoneuroimmunology: Animal models of disease. *Psychosomatic Medicine, 58,* 546–558.

Muehlenhard, C. L. (1988). Misinterpreted dating behaviors and the risk of date rape. *Journal of Social and Clinical Psychology, 6,* 20–37.

Mueller, J. H. (1982). Self-awareness and access to material rated as self-descriptive and nondescriptive. *Bulletin of the Psychonomic Society, 19,* 323–326.

Mugny, G. (1982). *The power of minorities.* London: Academic Press.

Mugny, G., & Perez, J. A. (1991). *Social psychology of minority influence.* Cambridge: Cambridge University Press.

Mullen, B. (1983). Operationalizing the effect of the group on the individual: A self-attention perspective. *Journal of Experimental Social Psychology, 19,* 295–322.

Mullen, B. (1985). Strength and immediacy of sources: A meta-analytic evaluation of the forgotten elements of social impact theory. *Journal of Personality and Social Psychology, 48,* 1458–1466.

Mullen, B. (1986). Atrocity as a function of lynch mob composition: A self-attention perspective. *Personality and Social Psychology Bulletin, 12,* 187–197.

Mullen, B., Anthony, T., Salas, E., & Driskell, J. E. (1994). Group cohesiveness and quality of decision making: An integration of tests of the groupthink hypothesis. *Small Group Research, 25,* 189–204.

Mullen, B., & Copper, C. (1994). The relation between group cohesiveness and performance: An integration. *Psychological Bulletin, 115,* 210–227.

Mullen, B., Dovidio, J. F., Johnson, C., & Copper, C. (1992). In-group and out-group differences in social projection. *Journal of Experimental Social Psychology, 28,* 422–440.

Mullen, B., Johnson, C., & Salas, E. (1991). Productivity loss in brainstorming groups: A meta-analytic integration. *Basic and Applied Social Psychology, 12,* 3–23.

Murphy, K. R., & Balzer, W. K. (1986). Systematic distortions in memory-based behavior ratings and performance evaluation: Consequences for rating accuracy. *Journal of Applied Psychology, 71,* 39–44.

Murphy, K. R., Balzer, W. K., Lockhart, M. C., & Eisenman, E. J. (1985). Effects of previous performance on evaluations of present performance. *Journal of Applied Psychology, 70,* 72–84.

Murphy, K. R., Jako, R. A., & Anhalt, R. L. (1993). Nature and consequences of halo error: A critical analysis. *Journal of Applied Psychology, 78,* 218–225.

Murray, C. B., Kaiser, R., & Taylor, S. (1997). The O. J. Simpson verdict: Predictors of beliefs about innocence or guilt. *Journal of Social Issues, 53,* 455–475.

Murray, S. L., Holmes, J. G., & Griffin, D. W. (1996). The benefits of positive illusions: Idealization and the construction of satisfaction in close relationships. *Journal of Personality and Social Psychology, 70,* 79–98.

Murstein, B. I. (1972). Physical attractiveness and marital choice. *Journal of Personality and Social Psychology, 22,* 8–12.

Murstein, B. I. (1986). *Paths to marriage.* Beverly Hills, CA: Sage.

Murstein, B. I. (1987). A clarification and extension of the SVR theory of dyadic pairing. *Journal of Marriage and the Family, 49,* 929–933.

Mwangi, M. W. (1996). Gender roles portrayed in Kenyan television commercials. *Sex Roles, 34,* 205–214.

Mydans, S. (1996, August 12). Federal prison system close to capacity. *New York Times,* pp. A12, C18.

Myers, D. G., & Bishop, G. D. (1970). Discussion effects on racial attitudes. *Science, 169,* 778–779.

Myers, D. G., & Diener, E. (1995). Who is happy? *Psychological Science, 6,* 10–19.

Myers, D. G., & Lamm, H. (1976). The group polarization phenomenon. *Psychological Bulletin, 83,* 602–627.

Nacoste, R. W. (1987). But do they care about fairness? The dynamics of preferential treatment and minority interest. *Basic and Applied Social Psychology, 8,* 177–191.

Nacoste, R. W. (1996). Social psychology and the affirmative action debate. *Journal of Social and Clinical Psychology, 15,* 261–282.

Nadler, A. (1986). Helpseeking as a cultural phenomenon: Differences between city and kibbutz dwellers. *Journal of Personality and Social Psychology, 51,* 976–982.

Nadler, A., & Fisher, J. D. (1986). The role of threat to self-esteem and perceived control in recipient reactions to help: Theory development and empirical validation. In L. Berkowitz (Ed.), *Advances in experimental social psychology* (Vol. 19, pp. 81–122). New York: Academic Press.

Nagao, D. H., Tindale, R., Hinsz, V., & Davis, J. H. (1985). *Individual and group biases in information processing.* Paper presented at the annual meeting of the American Psychological Association, Los Angeles.

Nando Times, (1997, September 5). Good Samaritan Laws, pp. 1–2.

Narby, D. J., Cutler, B. L., & Moran, G. (1993). A meta-analysis of the association between authoritarianism and jurors' perceptions of defendant culpability. *Journal of Applied Psychology, 78*, 34–42.

Nardi, P. M., & Sherrod, D. (1994). Friendship in the lives of gay men and lesbians. *Journal of Social and Personal Relationships, 11*, 185–199.

National Center on Child Abuse and Neglect. (1988). *Study findings: Study of national incidence and prevalence of child abuse and neglect: 1988*. Washington, DC: U.S. Department of Health and Human Services.

National Law Journal (1990). Rock group not liable for deaths (September 10), p. 33.

National Television Violence Study, Vol. 2 (1998). Thousand Oaks, CA: Sage.

Nattinger, A. B., et al. (1998). Celebrity medical care decisions can influence others. *Journal of the American Medical Association, 279*, 788–789.

Neck, C. P., & Moorhead, G. (1995). Groupthink remodeled: The importance of leadership, time pressure, and methodical decision-making procedures. *Human Relations, 48*, 537–557.

Neisser, U. (1981). John Dean's memory: A case study. *Cognition, 9*, 1–22.

Nemeth, C. (1986). Differential contributions of majority and minority influence. *Psychological Review, 93*, 23–32.

Nemeth, C., & Brilmayer, A. G. (1987). Negotiation versus influence. *European Journal of Social Psychology, 17*, 45–56.

Nemeth, C., Endicott, J., & Wachtler, J. (1976). From the '50s to the '70s: Women in jury deliberations. *Sociometry, 39*, 38–56.

Nemeth, C., & Kwan, J. (1987). Minority influence, divergent thinking, and detection of correct solutions. *Journal of Applied Social Psychology, 17*, 788–799.

Nemeth, C., Mayseless, O., Sherman, J., & Brown, Y. (1990). Exposure to dissent and recall of information. *Journal of Personality and Social Psychology, 58*, 429–437.

Neuberg, S. L. (1989). The goal of forming accurate impressions during social interactions: Attenuating the impact of negative expectancies. *Journal of Personality and Social Psychology, 56*, 374–386.

Neuberg, S. L., Cialdini, R. B., Brown, S. L., & Luce, C., Sagarin, B. J., & Lewis, B. P. (1997). Does empathy lead to anything more than superficial helping? Comment on Batson et al. (1997). *Journal of Personality and Social Psychology, 73*, 510–516.

Neuberg, S. L., & Fiske, S. T. (1987). Motivational influences on impression formation: Outcome dependency, accuracy-driven attention, and individuating processes. *Journal of Personality and Social Psychology, 53*, 431–444.

Neuberg, S. L., Judice, T. N., Virdin, L. M., & Carrillo, M. A. (1993). Perceiver self-presentational goals as moderators of expectancy influences: Ingratiation and the disconfirmation of negative expectancies. *Journal of Personality and Social Psychology, 64*, 409–420.

Neuberg, S. L., & Newsom, J. T. (1993). Personal need for structure: Individual differences in the desire for simple structure. *Journal of Personality and Social Psychology, 65*, 113–131.

Newcomb, T. M. (1961). *The acquaintance process*. New York: Holt, Rinehart and Winston.

Newman, L. S. (1993). How individualists interpret behavior: Idiocentrism and spontaneous trait inference. *Social Cognition, 11*, 243–269.

Newman, L. S., & Uleman, J. S. (1989). Spontaneous trait inference. In J. S. Uleman & J. A. Bargh (Eds.), *Unintended thought* (pp. 155–188). New York: Guilford.

Newtson, D. (1974). Dispositional inference from effects of actions: Effects chosen and effects foregone. *Journal of Experimental Social Psychology, 10*, 487–496.

Newtson, D., Hairfield, J., Bloomingdale, J., & Cutino, S. (1987). The structure of action and interaction. *Social Cognition, 5*, 191–237.

Nezlek, J. B., & Pilkington, C. J. (1994). Perception of risk in intimacy and social participation. *Personal Relationships, 1*, 45–62.

Nezlek, J. B., Imbrie, M., & Shean, G. D. (1994). Depression and everyday social interaction. *Journal of Personality and Social Psychology, 67*, 1101–1111.

Nieva, V. F., & Gutek, B. A. (1981). *Women and work: A psychological perspective*. New York: Praeger.

Nisbett, R. E., & Cohen, D. (1996). *Culture of honor: The psychology of violence in the South*. Boulder, CO: Westview.

Nisbett, R. E., Fong, G. T., Lehman, D. R., & Cheng, P. W. (1987). Teaching reasoning. *Science, 238*, 625–631.

Nisbett, R. E., & Ross, L. (1980). *Human inference: Strategies and shortcomings of social judgment*. Englewood Cliffs, NJ: Prentice-Hall.

Nisbett, R. E., & Wilson, T. D. (1977). Telling more than we can know: Verbal reports on mental processes. *Psychological Review, 84*, 231–259.

Noel, J. G., Wann, D. L., & Branscombe, N. R. (1995). Peripheral ingroup membership status and public negativity toward outgroups. *Journal of Personality and Social Psychology, 68*, 127–137.

Nolen-Hoeksema, S., & Girgus, J. S. (1994). The emergence of gender differences in depression during adolescence. *Psychological Bulletin, 115*, 424–443.

Nolen-Hoeksema, S., & Morrow, J. (1991). A prospective study of depression and posttraumatic stress symptoms after a natural disaster: The 1989 Loma Prieta earthquake. *Journal of Personality and Social Psychology, 61*, 115–121.

Noller, P., & Fitzpatrick, M. A. (1990). Marital communication in the eighties. *Journal of Marriage and the Family, 52*, 832–843.

Noller, P., Feeney, J. A., Bonnell, D., & Callan, V. J. (1994). A longitudinal study of conflict in early marriage. *Journal of Social and Personal Relationships, 11*, 233–252.

Northcraft, G. B., Polzer, J. T., Neale, M. A., & Kramer, R. M. (1995). Diversity, social identity, and performance: Emergent social dynamics in cross-functional teams. In S. E. Jackson & M. N. Ruderman (Eds.), *Diversity in work teams: Research paradigms for a changing workplace* (pp. 69–96). Washington, DC: American Psychological Association.

Norton, K. I., Olds, T. S., Olive, S., & Dank, S. (1996). Ken and Barbie at life size. *Sex Roles, 34*, 287–294.

Nosworthy, G. J., & Lindsay, R. C. L. (1990). Does nominal lineup size matter? *Journal of Applied Psychology, 75*, 358–361.

Nowak, M., & Sigmund, K. (1993). A strategy of win-stay, lose-shift that outperforms tit-for-tat in the Prisoner's Dilemma game. *Nature, 364*, 56–58.

O'Connor, K. M., & Carnevale, P. J. (1997). A nasty but effective negotiation strategy: Misrepresentation of a common-value issue. *Personality and Social Psychology Bulletin, 23*, 504–515.

O'Connor, S. C., & Rosenblood, L. K. (1996). Affiliation motivation in everyday experience: A theoretical comparison. *Journal of Personality and Social Psychology, 70*, 513–522.

Offner, A. K., Kramer, T. J., & Winter, J. P. (1996). The effects of facilitation, recording, and pauses on group brainstorming. *Small Group Research, 27*, 283–298.

Ofshe, R., & Watters, E. (1994). *Making monsters: False memories, psychotherapy, and sexual hysteria*. New York: Charles Scribner's Sons.

Ogilvy, D. (1985). *Ogilvy on advertising*. New York: Vintage Books.

Ogloff, J. R. P., & Vidmar, N. (1994). The impact of pretrial publicity on jurors: A study to compare the relative effects of television and print media in a child sex abuse case. *Law and Human Behavior, 18,* 507–525.

Ohbuchi, K., Kameda, M., & Agarie, N. (1989). Apology as aggression control: Its role in mediating appraisal of and response to harm. *Journal of Personality and Social Psychology, 56,* 219–227.

O'Keefe, D. J., & Figge, M. (1997). A guilt-based explanation of the door-in-the-face influence strategy. *Human Communication Research, 42,* 64–81.

Olczak, P. V., Kaplan, M. F., & Penrod, S. (1991). Attorneys' lay psychology and its effectiveness in selecting jurors: Three empirical studies. *Journal of Social Behavior and Personality, 6,* 431–452.

Oldham, G. R., Cummings, A., Mischel, L. J., Schmidtke, J. M., & Zhou, J. (1995). Listen while you work? Quasi-experimental relations between personal-stereo headset use and employee work response. *Journal of Applied Psychology, 80,* 547–564.

O'Leary, A. (1985). Self-efficacy and health. *Behaviour Research and Therapy, 23,* 437–451.

O'Leary, A. (1990). Stress, emotion, and human immune function. *Psychological Bulletin, 108,* 363–382.

O'Leary, K. D., & Smith, D. A. (1991). Marital interaction. *Annual Review of Psychology, 42,* 191–212.

O'Leary, K. D., Barling, J., Arias, I., Rosenbaum, A., Malone, J., & Tyree, A. (1989). Prevalence and stability of physical aggression between spouses: A longitudinal analysis. *Journal of Consulting and Clinical Psychology, 57,* 263–268.

O'Leary-Kelly, A. M., Martocchio, J. J., & Frink, D. D. (1994). A review of the influence of group goals on group performance. *Academy of Management Journal, 37,* 1285–1301.

Oliner, S. P., & Oliner, P. M. (1988). *The altruistic personality: Rescuers of Jews in Nazi Europe.* New York: Free Press.

Oliver, M. G., & Hyde, J. S. (1993). Gender differences in sexuality: A meta-analysis. *Psychological Bulletin, 114,* 29–51.

Olmeda, R. A., & Gentile, D. (1996, September 14). Hero prayed and plunged. *New York Daily News,* p. 4.

Olson, J. M., Herman, C. P., & Zanna, M. P. (Eds.). (1986). *Relative deprivation and social comparison: The Ontario Symposium* (Vol. 4). Hillsdale, NJ: Erlbaum.

Olson, M. (1965). *The logic of collective action.* Cambridge, MA: Harvard University Press.

Olzak, S., & Nagel, J. (1986). *Competitive ethnic relations.* New York: Academic Press.

Omoto, A. M., & Snyder, M. (1995). Sustained helping without obligation: Motivation, longevity of service, and perceived attitude change among AIDS volunteers. *Journal of Personality and Social Psychology, 68,* 671–686.

O'Neill, A. M., Green, M., & Cuadros, P. (1996, September 2). *People,* p. 72.

Ones, D. S., Viswesvaran, C., & Schmidt, F. L. (1993). Comprehensive meta-analysis of integrity test validities: Findings and implications for personnel selection and theories of job performance. *Journal of Applied Psychology, 78,* 679–703.

Operario, D., & Fiske, S. (1998). Power plus prejudice: Socio-cultural and psychological foundations of racial oppression. In J. L. Eberhardt & S. T. Fiske (Eds.), *Racism: The problem and the response.* Thousand Oaks, CA: Sage.

Orbell, J. M., Dragt, van de A. J. C., & Dawes, R. M. (1988). Explaining discussion-induced cooperation. *Journal of Personality and Social Psychology, 54,* 811–819.

Orbell, J., Dawes, R., & Schwartz-Shea, P. (1994). Trust, social categories, and individuals: The case of gender. *Motivation and Emotion, 18,* 109–128.

Orengo, C. A., Kunik, M. E., Ghusn, H., & Yudofsky, S. C. (1997). Correlation of testosterone with aggression in demented elderly men. *Journal of Nervous and Mental Disease, 185,* 349–351.

Orne, M. T. (1962). On the social psychology of the psychological experiment: With particular reference to demand characteristics and their implications. *American Psychologist, 17,* 776–783.

Ortmann, A., & Hertwig, R. (1997). Is deception acceptable? *American Psychologist, 52,* 746–747.

Orwell, G. (1942). Looking back on the Spanish War. In S. Orwell & I. Angus (Eds.), *The collected essays, journalism and letters of George Orwell: Vol. 2. My country right or left, 1940–1943* (pp. 249–267). New York: Harcourt, Brace & World. (Reprinted in 1968)

Osborn, A. F. (1953). *Applied imagination.* New York: Scribner.

Osgood, C. E. (1962). *An alternative to war or surrender.* Urbana: University of Illinois Press.

Oskamp, S. (1965). Attitudes toward U.S. and Russian actions: A double standard. *Psychological Reports, 16,* 43–46.

Oskamp, S. (Ed.). (1988). *Television as a social issue: Applied social psychology annual* (Vol. 8). Newbury Park, CA: Sage.

Ostrom, T. M., & Sedikides, C. (1992). Out-group homogeneity effects in natural and minimal groups. *Psychological Bulletin, 112,* 536–552.

Ottati, V. C., Riggle, E. J., Wyer, R. S., Schwarz, N., & Kuklinski, J. (1989). Cognitive and affective bases of opinion survey responses. *Journal of Personality and Social Psychology, 57,* 404–415.

Otto, A. L., Penrod, S. D., & Dexter, H. R. (1994). The biasing impact of pretrial publicity on juror judgments. *Law and Human Behavior, 18,* 453–469.

Owens, L. D., & MacMullin, C. E. (1995). Gender differences in aggression in children and adolescents in South Australian schools. *International Journal of Adolescence and Youth, 6,* 21–35.

Oxley, N. L., Dzindolet, M. T., & Paulus, P. B. (1996). The effects of facilitators on the performance of brainstorming groups. *Journal of Social Behavior and Personality, 11,* 633–646.

Packard, V. (1957). *The hidden persuaders.* New York: Pocket Books.

Paik, H., & Comstock, G. (1994). The effects of television violence on antisocial behavior: A meta-analysis. *Communication Research, 21,* 516–546.

Pallak, S. R. (1983). Salience of a communicator's physical attractiveness and persuasion: A heuristic versus systematic processing interpretation. *Social Cognition, 2,* 158–170.

Park, B. (1986). A method for studying the development of impressions of real people. *Journal of Personality and Social Psychology, 51,* 907–917.

Parker, C. P., Baltes, B. B., & Christiansen, N. D. (1997). Support for affirmative action, justice perceptions, and work attitudes: A study of gender and racial-ethnic group differences. *Journal of Applied Psychology, 82,* 376–389.

Parkinson, S. (1994). Scientific or ethical quality? *Psychological Science, 5,* 137–138.

Parks, C. D. (1994). The predictive ability of social values in resource dilemmas and public goods games. *Personality and Social Psychology Bulletin, 20,* 431–438.

Parks, C. D., Henager, R. F., & Scamahorn, S. D. (1996). Trust and reactions to messages of intent in social dilemmas. *Journal of Conflict Resolution, 40,* 134–151.

Parks, C. D., & Vu, A. D. (1994). Social dilemma behavior of individuals from highly individualist and collectivist cultures. *Journal of Conflict Resolution, 38,* 708–718.

Parloff, R. (1993, May). False confessions: Standard interrogations by Arizona law enforcement officials led to four matching confessions to the murders of nine people at a Buddhist temple. *American Lawyer,* pp. 58–62.

Parrott, W. G., & Smith, R. H. (1993). Distinguishing the experiences of envy and jealousy. *Journal of Personality and Social Psychology, 64,* 906–920.

Parsons, H. M. (1974). What happened at Hawthorne? *Science, 183,* 922–932.

Partridge, A., & Eldridge, W. B. (1974). *The second circuit sentencing study: A report to the judges of the second circuit.* Washington, DC: Federal Judicial Center.

Patrick, C. J., & Iacono, W. G. (1991). Validity of the control question polygraph test: The problem of sampling bias. *Journal of Applied Psychology, 76,* 229–238.

Patterson, G. R. (1984). Siblings: Fellow travelers in coercive family processes. In R. J. Blanchard & D. C. Blanchard (Eds.), *Advances in the study of aggression* (Vol. 1, pp. 173–215). New York: Academic Press.

Patterson, M. L. (1983). *Nonverbal behavior: A functional perspective.* New York: Springer-Verlag.

Paulhus, D., Graf, P., & Van Selst, M. (1989). Attentional load increases the positivity of self-presentation. *Social Cognition, 7,* 389–400.

Paulus, P. B. (1988). *Prison crowding: A psychological perspective.* New York: Springer-Verlag.

Paulus, P. B., & Dzindolet, M. T. (1993). Social influence processes in group brainstorming. *Journal of Personality and Social Psychology, 64,* 575–586.

Paulus, P. B., Dzindolet, M. T., Poletes, G., & Camacho, L. M. (1993). Perception of performance in group brainstorming: The illusion of group productivity. *Personality and Social Psychology Bulletin, 19,* 78–89.

Paulus, P. B., Larey, T. S., Putman, V. L., & Leggett, K. L. (1996). Social influence processes in computer brainstorming. *Basic and Applied Social Psychology, 18,* 3–14.

Paulus, P. B., & Paulus, L. E. (1997). Implications of research on group brainstorming for gifted education. *Roeper Review, 19,* 225–229.

Paunonen, S. V. (1989). Consensus in personality judgments: Moderating effects of target-rater acquaintanceship and behavior observability. *Journal of Personality and Social Psychology, 56,* 823–833.

Pavitt, C. (1994). Another view of group polarizing: The "reasons for" one-sided oral argumentation. *Communication Research, 21,* 625–642.

Peek, C. W., Fischer, J. L., & Kidwell, J. S. (1985). Teenage violence toward parents: A neglected dimension of family violence. *Journal of Marriage and the Family, 47,* 1051–1058.

Pelham, B. W. (1995). Self-investment and self-esteem: Evidence for a Jamesian model of self-worth. *Journal of Personality and Social Psychology, 69,* 1141–1150.

Pelham, B. W., & Swann, W. B., Jr. (1989). From self-conceptions to self-worth: The sources and structure of self-esteem. *Journal of Personality and Social Psychology, 57,* 672–680.

Pendry, L. F., & Macrae, C. N. (1994). Stereotypes and mental life: The case of the motivated but thwarted tactician. *Journal of Experimental Social Psychology, 30,* 303–325.

Pendry, L. F., & Macrae, C. N. (1996). What the disinterested perceiver overlooks: Goal-directed social categorization. *Personality and Social Psychology Bulletin, 22,* 249–256.

Pennebaker, J. W. (1990). *Opening up.* New York: Morrow.

Pennebaker, J. W. (1997). Writing about emotional experiences as a therapeutic process. *Psychological Science, 8,* 162–166.

Pennebaker, J. W., Colder, M., & Sharp, L. K. (1990). Accelerating the coping process. *Journal of Personality and Social Psychology, 58,* 528–537.

Pennebaker, J. W., Dyer, M. A., Caulkins, R. J., Litowitz, D. L., Ackreman, P. L., Anderson, D. B., & McGraw, K. M. (1979). Don't the girls get prettier at closing time: A country and western application to psychology. *Personality and Social Psychology Bulletin, 5,* 122–125.

Penner, L. A., & Fritzsche, B. A. (1993). Magic Johnson and reactions to people with AIDS: A natural experiment. *Journal of Applied Social Psychology, 23,* 1035–1050.

Penner, L. A., Fritzsche, B. A., Craiger, J. P., & Freifeld, T. S. (1995). Measuring the prosocial personality. In J. Butcher & C. Spielberger (Eds.), *Advances in personality assessment* (Vol. 10, pp. 147–163). Hillsdale, NJ: Erlbaum.

Pennington, N., & Hastie, R. (1992). Explaining the evidence: Tests of the story model for juror decision making. *Journal of Personality and Social Psychology, 62,* 189–206.

Penrod, S. D., & Cutler, B. (1995). Witness confidence and witness accuracy: Assessing their forensic relation. *Psychology, Public Policy, and Law, 1,* 817–845.

People (1996, December 30). She gave a helping hand to a distant—very distant—relation. P. 66.

Peplau, L. A., & Perlman, D. (Eds.) (1982). *Loneliness: A sourcebook of current theory, research, and therapy.* New York: Wiley.

Pepler, D. J., & Craig, W. M. (1995). A peek behind the fence: Naturalistic observations of aggressive children with remote audiovisual recording. *Developmental Psychology, 31,* 548–553.

Perdue, C. W., Dovidio, J. F., Gurtman, M. B., & Tyler, R. B. (1990). Us and them: Social categorization and the process of intergroup bias. *Journal of Personality and Social Psychology, 59,* 475–486.

Perlman, D., & Oskamp, S. (1971). The effects of picture context and exposure frequency on evaluations of negroes and whites. *Journal of Experimental and Social Psychology, 7,* 503–514.

Perrett, D. I., May, K. A., & Yoshikawa, S. (1994). Facial shape and judgments of female attractiveness. *Nature, 368,* 239–242.

Persky, V. W., Kempthorne-Rawson, J., & Shekelle, R. B. (1987). Personality and risk of cancer: 20-year follow-up of the Western Electric Study. *Psychosomatic Medicine, 49,* 435–449.

Peters, L. H., Hartke, D. D., & Pohlmann, J. T. (1985). Fiedler's contingency theory of leadership: An application of the meta-analytic procedures of Schmidt and Hunter. *Psychological Bulletin, 97,* 274–285.

Peters, T. J., & Waterman, R. H. (1982). *In search of excellence: Lessons from America's best-run companies.* New York: Warner.

Peterson, C., Seligman, M. E. P., & Vaillant, G. E. (1988). Pessimistic explanatory style is a risk factor for physical illness: A thirty-five-year longitudinal study. *Journal of Personality and Social Psychology, 55,* 23–27.

Peterson, R. R., & Gerson, K. (1992). Determinants of responsibility for child care arrangements among dual-earner couples. *Journal of Marriage and the Family, 54,* 527–536.

Pettigrew, T. F. (1969). Racially separate or together? *Journal of Social Issues, 25,* 43–69.

Pettigrew, T. F. (1991). Normative theory in intergroup relations: Explaining bad harmony and conflict. *Psychology and Developing Societies, 3,* 3–16.

Pettigrew, T. F., & Martin, J. (1987). Shaping the organizational context for black American inclusion. *Journal of Social Issues, 43,* 41–78.

Pettigrew, T. F., & Meertens, R. W. (1995). Subtle and blatant prejudice in western Europe. *European Journal of Social Psychology, 25,* 57–75.

Petty, R. E., & Cacioppo, J. T. (1983). The role of bodily responses in attitude measurement and change. In J. Cacioppo & R. Petty (Eds.), *Social psychophysiology: A sourcebook* (pp. 51–101). New York: Guilford.

Petty, R. E., & Cacioppo, J. T. (1984). The effects of involvement on response to argument quantity and quality: Central and peripheral routes to persuasion. *Journal of Personality and Social Psychology, 46,* 69–81.

Petty, R. E., & Cacioppo, J. T. (1986). *Communication and persuasion: Central and peripheral routes to attitude change.* New York: Springer-Verlag.

Petty, R. E., & Cacioppo, J. T. (1990). Involvement and persuasion: Tradition versus integration. *Psychological Bulletin, 107,* 367–374.

Petty, R. E., Cacioppo, J. T., & Goldman, R. (1981). Personal involvement as a determinant of argument-based persuasion. *Journal of Personality and Social Psychology, 41,* 847–855.

Petty, R. E., Cacioppo, J. T., & Heesacker, M. (1981). Effects of rhetorical questions on persuasion: A cognitive response analysis. *Journal of Personality and Social Psychology, 40,* 432–440.

Petty, R. E., Harkins, S. G., Williams, K. D., & Latané, B. (1977). The effects of group size on cognitive effort and evaluation. *Personality and Social Psychology Bulletin, 3,* 579–582.

Petty, R. E., & Krosnick, J. A. (Eds.) (1993). *Attitude strength: Antecedents and consequences.* Hillsdale, NJ: Erlbaum.

Petty, R. E., & Krosnick, J. A. (Eds.) (1995). *Attitude strength: Antecedents and consequences.* Mahwah, NJ: Erlbaum.

Petty, R. E., Schumann, D. W., Richman, S. A., & Strathman, A. J. (1993). Positive mood and persuasion: Different roles for affect under high- and low-elaboration conditions. *Journal of Personality and Social Psychology, 64,* 5–20.

Petty, R. E., & Wegener, D. T. (1998). Attitude change: Multiple roles for persuasion variables. In D. Gilbert, S. Fiske, & G. Lindzey (Eds.), *Handbook of social psychology* (4th ed.). New York: McGraw-Hill.

Petty, R. E., Wegener, D. T., & Fabrigar, L. R. (1997). Attitudes and attitude change. *Annual Review of Psychology, 48,* 609–647.

Pfau, M., Kenski, H. C., Nitz, M., & Sorenson, J. (1990). Efficacy of inoculation strategies in promoting resistance to political attack messages: Application to direct mail. *Communication Monographs, 57,* 25–43.

Phillips, A. P., & Dipboye, R. L. (1989). Correlational tests of predictions from a process model of the interview. *Journal of Applied Psychology, 74,* 41–52.

Pickel, K. L. (1995). Inducing jurors to disregard inadmissible evidence: A legal explanation does not help. *Law and Human Behavior, 19,* 407–424.

Piliavin, I. M., Piliavin, J. A., & Rodin, J. (1975). Costs, diffusion, and the stigmatized victim. *Journal of Personality and Social Psychology, 32,* 429–438.

Piliavin, J. A., & Callero, P. L. (1991). *Giving blood: The development of an altruistic identity.* Baltimore: Johns Hopkins.

Piliavin, J. A., Dovidio, J. F., Gaertner, S. L., & Clark, R. D., III. (1981). *Emergency intervention.* New York: Academic Press.

Pilisuk, M., Montgomery, M. B., Parks, S. H., & Acredolo, C. (1993). Loss of control, life stress, and social networks: Gender differences in health status of the elderly. *Sex Roles, 28,* 147–166.

Pillemer, D. B., Picariello, M. L., Law, A. B., & Reichman, J. S. (1996). Memories of college: The importance of educational episodes. In D. C. Rubin (Ed.), *Remembering our past: Studies in autobiographical memory* (pp. 318–337). New York: Cambridge University Press.

Pine, D. S., Coplan, J. D., Wasserman, G. A., Miller, L. S., Fried, J. E., Davies, M., Cooper, T. B., Greenhill, L., Shaffer, D., & Parsons, B. (1997). Neuroendocrine response to fenfluramine challenge in boys: Associations with aggressive behavior and adverse rearing. *Archives of General Psychiatry, 54,* 839–846.

Pittman, T. S. (1975). Attribution of arousal as a mediator of dissonance reduction. *Journal of Experimental Social Psychology, 11,* 53–63.

Pittman, T. S., & Heller, J. F. (1987). Social motivation. *Annual Review of Psychology, 38,* 461–489.

Platz, S. J., & Hosch, H. M. (1988). Cross-racial/ethnic eyewitness identification: A field study. *Journal of Applied Social Psychology, 18,* 972–984.

Pliner, P., & Chaiken, S. (1990). Eating, social motives, and self-presentation in women and men. *Journal of Experimental Social Psychology, 26,* 240–254.

Polivy, J., Garner, D. M., & Garfinkel, P. E. (1986). Causes and consequences of the current preference for thin female physiques. In C. P. Herman, M. P. Zanna, & E. T. Higgins (Eds.), *The Ontario Symposium: Vol. 3. Physical appearance, stigma, and social behavior* (pp. 89–112). Hillsdale, NJ: Erlbaum.

Polzer, J. T. (1996). Intergroup negotiations: The effects of negotiating teams. *Journal of Conflict Resolution, 40,* 678–698.

Poole, D. A., & White, L. T. (1991). Effects of question repetition on the eyewitness testimony of children and adults. *Developmental Psychology, 27,* 975–986.

Pooley, E. (1997, June 16). Death or life? *Time,* pp. 30–36.

Poppen, P. J., & Segal, N. J. (1988). The influence of sex and sex role orientation on sexual coercion. *Sex Roles, 19,* 689–701.

Porter, N., Geis, F. L., Cooper, E., & Newman, E. (1985). Androgyny and leadership in mixed-sex groups. *Journal of Personality and Social Psychology, 49,* 808–823.

Postmes, T., & Spears, R. (1998). Deindividuation and antinormative behavior: A meta-analysis. *Psychololgical Bulletin, 123,* 238–259.

Povinelli, D. J., Rulf, A. B., & Bierschwale, D. T. (1994). Absence of knowledge attribution and self-recognition in young chimpanzees. *Journal of Comparative Psychology, 108,* 74–80.

Powell, G. N. (1987). The effects of sex and gender on recruitment. *Academy of Management Review, 12,* 731–743.

Powell, M. C., & Fazio, R. M. (1984). Attitude accessibility as a function of repeated attitudinal expression. *Personality and Social Psychology Bulletin, 10,* 139–148.

Powlishta, K. K. (1995). Intergroup processes in childhood: Social categorization and sex role development. *Developmental Psychology, 31,* 781–788.

Prapavessis, H., & Carron, A. V. (1997). Sacrifice, cohesion, and conformity to norms in sport teams. *Group Dynamics, 1,* 231–240.

Pratap, A. (1990, August 13). "Romance and a little rape." *Time,* p. 69.

Pratkanis, A. R. (1992). The cargo-cult science of subliminal persuasion. *Skeptical Inquirer, 16,* 260–272.

Pratkanis, A., & Aronson, E. (1992). *Age of propaganda: The everyday use and abuse of persuasion.* San Francisco: Freeman.

Pratkanis, A. R., Eskenazi, J., & Greenwald, A. G. (1994). What you expect is what you believe (but not necessarily what you get): A test of the effectiveness of subliminal self-help audiotapes. *Basic and Applied Social Psychology, 15,* 251–276.

Pratkanis, A. R., Greenwald, A. G., Leippe, M. R., & Baumgardner, M. H. (1988). In search of reliable persuasion effects: III. The sleeper effect is dead. Long live the sleeper effect. *Journal of Personality and Social Psychology, 54,* 203–218.

Pratkanis, A. R., & Turner, M. E. (1994). Nine principles of successful affirmative action: Mr. Branch Rickey, Mr. Jackie Robinson, and the integration of baseball. *Nine: A Journal of Baseball History and Social Policy Perspectives, 3,* 36–65.

Pratkanis, A. R., & Turner, M. E. (1996). The proactive removal of discriminatory barriers: Affirmative action as effective help. *Journal of Social Issues, 52,* 111–132.

Pratto, F., & Bargh, J. A. (1991). Stereotyping based on apparently individuating information: Trait and global components of sex stereotypes under attention overload. *Journal of Experimental Social Psychology, 27,* 26–47.

Pratto, F., & John, O. P. (1991). Automatic vigilance: The attention-grabbing power of negative social information. *Journal of Personality and Social Psychology, 61,* 380–391.

Pratto, F., Stallworth, L. M., Sidanius, J., & Siers, B. (1997). The gender gap in occupational attainment: A social dominance approach. *Journal of Personality and Social Psychology, 72,* 37–53.

Prentice, D. A. (1990). Familiarity and differences in self- and other-representations. *Journal of Personality and Social Psychology, 59,* 369–383.

Prentice, D. A., & Miller, D. T. (1993). Pluralistic ignorance and alcohol use on campus: Some consequences of misperceiving the social norm. *Journal of Personality and Social Psychology, 64,* 243–256.

Prentice, D. A., & Miller, D. T. (1996). Pluralistic ignorance and the perpetuation of social norms by unwitting actors. *Advances in Experimental Social Psychology, 28,* 161–209.

Prentice, D. A., Miller, D. T., & Lightdale, J. R. (1994). Asymmetries in attachments to groups and to their members: Distinguishing between common-identity and common-bond groups. *Personality and Social Psychology Bulletin, 20,* 484–493.

Prentice-Dunn, S., & Rogers, R. W. (1980). Effects of deindividuating situational cues and aggressive models on subjective deindividuation and aggression. *Journal of Personality and Social Psychology, 39,* 104–113.

Prentice-Dunn, S., & Rogers, R. W. (1982). Effects of public and private self-awareness on deindividuation and aggression. *Journal of Personality and Social Psychology, 43,* 503–513.

Prentice-Dunn, S., & Rogers, R. W. (1983). Deindividuation in aggression. In R. G. Geen & E. I. Donnerstein (Eds.), *Aggression: Theoretical and empirical reviews: Vol. 2. Issues in research* (pp. 155–171). New York: Academic Press.

President's Commission on Law Enforcement and Administration of Justice (1967). *The challenge of crime in a free society.* Washington, DC: U.S. Government Printing Office.

Price, R. H. (1992). Psychosocial impact of job loss on individuals and families. *Current Directions in Psychological Science, 1,* 9–11.

Price, S. L. (1997, December 8). What ever happened to the White athlete? *Sports Illustrated,* pp. 30–55.

Priester, J. R., Cacioppo, J. T., & Petty, R. E. (1996). The influence of motor processes on attitudes toward novel versus familiar semantic stimuli. *Personality and Social Psychology Bulletin, 22,* 442–447.

Priester, J. R., & Petty, R. E. (1995). Source attributions and persuasion: Perceived honesty as a determinant of message scrutiny. *Personality and Social Psychology Bulletin, 21,* 637–654.

Prioleau, L., Murdock, M., & Brody, N. (1983). An analysis of psychotherapy versus placebo studies. *Behavioral and Brain Sciences, 6,* 275–310.

Propp, K. M. (1995). An experimental examination of biological sex as a status cue in decision-making groups and its influence on information use. *Small Group Research, 26,* 451–474.

Pruitt, D. G. (1998). Social conflict. In D. T. Gilbert, S. T. Fiske, & G. Lindzey (Eds.), *The handbook of social psychology* (4th ed., Vol. 2, pp. 410–503). New York: McGraw-Hill.

Pruitt, D. G., & Carnevale, P. J. (1993). *Negotiation in social conflict.* Pacific Grove, CA: Brooks/Cole.

Pruitt, D. G., & Kressel, K. (1985). The mediation of social conflict: An introduction. *Journal of Social Issues, 41*(2), 1–10.

Pryor, J. B., & Merluzzi, T. V. (1985). The role of expertise in processing social interaction scripts. *Journal of Experimental Social Psychology, 21,* 362–379.

Purvis, A. (1997, January 6). The global epidemic. *Time,* pp. 76–78.

Pyszczynski, T., & Greenberg, J. (1992). *Hanging on and letting go.* New York: Springer-Verlag.

Qualter, T. H. (1962). *Propaganda and psychological warfare.* New York: Random House.

Quattrone, G. A. (1986). On the perception of a group's variability. In S. Worchel & W. G. Austin (Eds.), *Psychology of intergroup relations* (2nd ed.). Chicago: Nelson Hall.

Quattrone, G. A., & Jones, E. E. (1980). The perception of variability within ingroups and outgroups: Implications for the law of small numbers. *Journal of Personality and Social Psychology, 38,* 141–152.

Radecki-Bush, C., Farrell, A. D., & Bush, J. P. (1993). Predicting jealous responses: The influence of adult attachment and depression on threat appraisal. *Journal of Social and Personal Relationships, 10,* 569–588.

Rafaeli, A., & Klimoski, R. J. (1983). Predicting sales success through handwriting analysis: An evaluation of the effects of training and handwriting sample context. *Journal of Applied Psychology, 68,* 212–217.

Ragins, B. R., & Sundstrom, E. (1989). Gender and power in organizations: A longitudinal perspective. *Psychological Bulletin, 105,* 51–88.

Rajecki, D. W. (1982). *Attitudes.* Sunderland, MA: Sinauer.

Rajecki, D. W., Bledsoe, S. B., & Rasmussen, J. L. (1991). Successful personal ads: Gender differences and similarities in offers, stipulations, and outcomes. *Basic and Applied Social Psychology, 12,* 457–469.

Raskin, D. C. (1986). The polygraph in 1986: Scientific, professional, and legal issues surrounding application and acceptance of polygraph evidence. *Utah Law Review,* 29–74.

Read, S. J. (1987). Constructing causal scenarios: A knowledge structure approach to causal reasoning. *Journal of Personality and Social Psychology, 52,* 288–302.

Reed, G. M., Taylor, S. E., & Kemeny, M. E. (1993). Perceived control and psychological adjustment in gay men with AIDS. *Journal of Applied Social Psychology, 23,* 791–824.

Reeder, G. D. (1993). Trait-behavior relations and dispositional inference. *Personality and Social Psychology Bulletin, 19,* 586–593.

Reeder, G. D., & Brewer, M. B. (1979). A schematic model of dispositional attribution in interpersonal perception. *Psychological Review, 86,* 61–79.

Reese, F. L., Kliewer, W., & Suarez, T. (1997). Control appraisals as moderators of the relationship between intrusive thoughts and coping. *Journal of Applied Social Psychology, 27,* 1131–1145.

Reeve, J., & Deci, E. L. (1996). Elements of the competitive situation that affect intrinsic motivation. *Personality and Social Psychology Bulletin, 22,* 24–33.

Regan, D. T. (1971). Effects of a favor and liking on compliance. *Journal of Experimental Social Psychology, 7,* 627–639.

Regan, D. T., & Kilduff, M. (1988). Optimism about elections: Dissonance reduction at the ballot box. *Political Psychology, 9*, 101–107.

Regan, P. C., & Berscheid, E. (1997). Gender differences in characteristics desired in a potential sexual and marriage partner. *Journal of Psychology and Human Sexuality, 9*, 25–37.

Regan, P. C., & Berscheid, E. (1999). *Lust: What we know about human sexual desire.* Thousand Oaks, CA: Sage.

Regan, P. C., Kocan, E. R., & Whitlock, T. (1998). Ain't love grand! A prototype analysis of the concept of romantic love. *Journal of Social and Personal Relationships, 15*, 411–420.

Reicher, S., & Levine, M. (1994). On the consequences of deindividuation manipulations for the strategic communication of self: Identifiability and the presentation of social identity. *European Journal of Social Psychology, 24*, 511–524.

Reifman, A., Klein, J. G., & Murphy, S. T. (1989). Self-monitoring and age. *Psychology and Aging, 4*, 245–246.

Reifman, A. S., Larrick, R. P., & Fein, S. (1991). Temper and temperature on the diamond: The heat-aggression relationship in major-league baseball. *Personality and Social Psychology Bulletin, 17*, 580–585.

Reisenzein, R. (1983). The Schachter theory of emotion: Two decades later. *Psychological Bulletin, 94*, 239–264.

Remley, A. (1988, October). The great parental value shift: From obedience to independence. *Psychology Today*, 56–59.

Renfrew, J. W. (1997). *Aggression and its causes: A biopsychosocial approach.* New York: Oxford University Press.

Reno, R. R., Cialdini, R. B., & Kallgren, C. A. (1993). The trans-situational influence of norms. *Journal of Personality and Social Psychology, 64*, 104–112.

Repetti, R. L., Matthews, K. A., & Waldron, I. (1989). Employment and women's health: Effects of paid employment on women's mental and physical health. *American Psychologist, 44*, 1394–1401.

Report of the Presidential Commission on the Space Shuttle Challenger Accident. (1986, June 6). Washington, D.C., U.S. Government Printing Office.

Review Panel on Coronary-Prone Behavior and Coronary Heart Disease (1981). Coronary-prone behavior and coronary heart disease: A critical review. *Circulation, 63*, 1199–1215.

Rhee, E., Uleman, J. S., Lee, H. K., & Roman, R. J. (1995). Spontaneous self-descriptions and ethnic identities in individualistic and collectivistic cultures. *Journal of Personality and Social Psychology, 69*, 142–152.

Rhoden, W. C. (1996, December 24). A two-hour psychological test turns into Giants' lightning rod. *New York Times*, pp. B1, B10.

Rhodes, G., & Tremewan, T. (1996). Averageness, exaggeration, and facial attractiveness. *Psychological Science, 7*, 105–110.

Rhodes, N., & Wood, W. (1992). Self-esteem and intelligence affect influenceability: The mediating role of message reception. *Psychological Bulletin, 111*, 156–171.

Rhodewalt, F. (1990). Self-handicappers: Individual differences in the preference for anticipatory, self-protective acts. In R. L. Higgins, C. R. Synder, & S. Berglas (Eds.), *Self-handicapping: The paradox that isn't*, pp. 69–106. New York: Plenum.

Rhodewalt, F., & Agustsdottir, S. (1986). Effects of self-presentation on the phenomenal self. *Journal of Personality and Social Psychology, 50*, 47–55.

Rhodewalt, F., Morf, C., Hazlett, S., & Fairfield, M. (1991). Self-handicapping: The role of discounting and augmentation in the preservation of self-esteem. *Journal of Personality and Social Psychology, 61*, 122–131.

Rhodewalt, F., Sandonmatsu, D. M., Tschanz, B., Feick, D. L., & Waller, A. (1995). Self-handicapping and interpersonal trade-offs: The effects of claimed self-handicaps on observers' performance evaluations and feedback. *Personality and Social Psychology Bulletin, 21*, 1042–1050.

Rice, M. E., & Grusec, J. E. (1975). Saying and doing: Effects on observer performance. *Journal of Personality and Social Psychology, 32*, 584–593.

Richardson, D. R., & Hammock, G. S. (1991). Alcohol and acquaintance rape. In A. Parrot & L. Bechofer (Eds.), *Acquaintance rape: The hidden crime* (pp. 83–95). New York: Wiley.

Ringelmann, M. (1913). Recherches sur les moteurs animés: Travail de l'homme. *Annales de l'Institut National Agronomique, 2e série, tom XII*, 1–40.

Roberts, W., & Strayer, J. (1996). Empathy, emotional expressiveness, and prosocial behavior. *Child Development, 67*, 449–470.

Robins, R. R., Spranca, M. D., & Mendelsohn, G. A. (1996). The actor-observer effect revisited: Effects of individual differences and repeated social interactions on actor and observer attributions. *Journal of Personality and Social Psychology, 71*, 375–389.

Robinson, I., Ziss, K., Ganza, B., Katz, S, & Robinson, E. (1991). Twenty years of the sexual revolution, 1965–1985: An update. *Journal of Marriage and the Family, 53*, 216–220.

Robinson, P. H., & Darley, J. M. (1995). *Justice, liability, and blame.* San Francisco: Westview Press.

Rodin, J. (1986). Aging and health: Effects of the sense of control. *Science, 233*, 1271–1276.

Rodin, J., & Langer, E. J. (1977). Long-term effects of a control-relevant intervention with the institutionalized aged. *Journal of Personality and Social Psychology, 35*, 897–902.

Rodin, J., Rennert, K., & Solomon, S. L. (1980). Intrinsic motivation for control: Fact or fiction. In A. Baum & J. E. Singer (Eds.), *Advances in environmental psychology: Vol. 2. Applications of personal control* (pp. 131–148). Hillsdale, NJ: Erlbaum.

Roesch, S. C., & Amirkhan, J. H. (1997). Boundary conditions for self-serving attributions: Another look at the sports pages. *Journal of Applied Social Psychology, 27*, 245–261.

Roese, N. J. (1997). Counterfactual thinking. *Psychological Bulletin, 121*, 133–148.

Roese, N. J., & Jamieson, D. W. (1993). Twenty years of bogus pipeline research: A critical review and meta-analysis. *Psychological Bulletin, 114*, 363–375.

Roese, N. J., & Olson, J. M. (1994). Attitude importance as a function of repeated attitude expression. *Journal of Experimental Social Psychology, 30*, 39–51.

Roese, N. J., & Olson, J. M. (Eds.) (1995). *What might have been: The social psychology of counterfactual thinking.* Hillsdale, NJ: Erlbaum.

Roethlisberger, F. J., & Dickson, W. J. (1939). *Management and the worker.* Cambridge, MA: Harvard University Press.

Rofé, Y. (1984). Stress and affiliation: A utility theory. *Psychological Review, 91*, 235–250.

Rogers, M., Miller, N., Mayer, F. S., & Duval, S. (1982). Personal responsibility and salience of the request for help: Determinants of the relation between negative affect and helping behavior. *Journal of Personality and Social Psychology, 43*, 956–970.

Rogers, R. G. (1995). Marriage, sex, and mortality. *Journal of Marriage and the Family, 57*, 515–526.

Rogers, R. W. (1983). Cognitive and psychological processes in fear appeals and attitude change: A revised theory of protection motivation. In J. Cacioppo & R. Petty (Eds.), *Social psychophysiology: A sourcebook* (pp. 153–176). New York: Guilford.

Rogers, R. W., & Mewborn, R. C. (1976). Fear appeals and attitude change: Effects of a threat's noxiousness, probability of occurrence, and the efficacy of coping responses. *Journal of Personality and Social Psychology, 34,* 54–61.

Rohrer, J. H., Baron, S. H., Hoffman, E. L., & Swander, D. V. (1954). The stability of autokinetic judgments. *Journal of Abnormal and Social Psychology, 49,* 595–597.

Romzek, B. S., & Dubnick, M. J. (1987). Accountability in the public sector: Lessons from the Challenger tragedy. *Public Administration Review, 47,* 227–238.

Rook, K. S. (1984). The negative side of social interaction: Impact on psychological well-being. *Journal of Personality and Social Psychology, 46,* 1097–1108.

Rook, K. S. (1987). Reciprocity of social exchange and social satisfaction among older women. *Journal of Personality and Social Psychology, 52,* 145–154.

Rook, K. S., & Peplau, L. A. (1982). Perspectives on helping the lonely. In L. A. Peplau & D. Perlman (Eds.), *Loneliness: A sourcebook of current theory, research and therapy* (pp. 351–378). New York: Wiley.

Rose, S., & Frieze, I. H. (1993). Young singles' contemporary dating scripts. *Sex Roles, 28,* 499–509.

Rosen, S., Tomarelli, M. M., Kidda, M. L., Jr., & Medvin, N. (1986). Effects of motive for helping, recipient's inability to reciprocate, and sex on devaluation of the recipient's competence. *Journal of Personality and Social Psychology, 50,* 729–736.

Rosenbaum, M. E. (1986). The repulsion hypothesis: On the nondevelopment of relationships. *Journal of Personality and Social Psychology, 51,* 1156–1166.

Rosenberg, M. (1965). *Society and the adolescent self-image.* Princeton, NJ: Princeton University Press.

Rosener, J. B. (1990). Ways women lead. *Harvard Business Review, 68,* 119–125.

Rosenfeld, J. P. (1995). Alternative views of Bashore and Rapp's (1993) alternatives to traditional polygraphy: A critique. *Psychological Bulletin, 117,* 159–166.

Rosenhan, D. L. (1970). The natural socialization of altruistic autonomy. In J. R. Macaulay & L. Berkowitz (Eds.), *Altruism and helping behavior* (pp. 251–268). New York: Academic Press.

Rosenhan, D. L., Salovey, P., & Hargis, K. (1981). The joys of helping: Focus of attention mediates the impact of positive affect on altruism. *Journal of Personality and Social Psychology, 40,* 899–905.

Rosenman, R. H., Brand, R. J., Jenkins, C. D., Friedman, M., Strau, R., & Wurm, M. (1975). Coronary heart disease in the Western Collaborative Group Study: Final follow-up experience of 8 1/2 years. *Journal of the American Medical Association, 233,* 872–877.

Rosenthal, R. (1966). *Experimenter effects in behavioral research.* New York: Appleton-Century-Crofts.

Rosenthal, R. (1976). *Experimenter effects in behavioral research.* New York: Irvington.

Rosenthal, R. (1985). From unconscious experimenter bias to teacher expectancy effects. In J. B. Dusek, V. C. Hall, & W. J. Meyer (Eds.), *Teacher expectancies* (pp. 37–65). Hillsdale, NJ: Erlbaum.

Rosenthal, R. (1991). *Meta-analytic procedures for social research* (2nd ed.). Newbury Park, CA: Sage.

Rosenthal, R., & Jacobson, L. (1968). *Pygmalion in the classroom: Teacher expectation and pupils' intellectual development.* New York: Holt, Rinehart and Winston.

Rosnow, R. L., & Rosenthal, R. (1993). *Beginning behavioral research: A conceptual primer.* New York: Macmillan.

Ross, D. F., Ceci, S. J., Dunning, D., & Toglia, M. P. (1994). Unconscious transference and mistaken identity: When a witness misidentifies a familiar but innocent person. *Journal of Applied Psychology, 79,* 918–930.

Ross, D. F., Read, J. D., & Toglia, M. P. (Eds.) (1994). *Adult eyewitness testimony: Current trends and developments.* New York: Cambridge University Press.

Ross, E. A. (1908). *Social psychology: An outline and source book.* New York: Macmillan.

Ross, J., & Staw, B. M. (1986). Expo 86: An escalation prototype. *Administrative Science Quarterly, 31,* 274–297.

Ross, L. (1977). The intuitive psychologist and his shortcomings: Distortions in the attribution process. In L. Berkowitz (Ed.), *Advances in experimental social psychology* (Vol. 10, pp. 174–221). New York: Academic Press.

Ross, L., Amabile, T. M., & Steinmetz, J. L. (1977). Social roles, social control, and biases in social-perception processes. *Journal of Personality and Social Psychology, 35,* 485–494.

Ross, L., Bierbrauer, G., & Hoffman, S. (1976). The role of attribution processes in conformity and dissent. *American Psychologist, 31,* 148–157.

Ross, L., Greene, D., & House, P. (1977). The false consensus phenomenon: An attributional bias in self-perception and social-perception processes. *Journal of Experimental Social Psychology, 13,* 279–301.

Ross, M. (1989). The relation of implicit theories to the construction of personal histories. *Psychological Review, 96,* 341–357.

Ross, M., & Sicoly, F. (1979). Egocentric biases in availability and attribution. *Journal of Personality and Social Psychology, 37,* 322–336.

Rosse, J. G., Miller, J. L., & Stecher, M. D. (1994). A field study of job applicants' reactions to personality and cognitive ability testing. *Journal of Applied Psychology, 79,* 987–992.

Rothbaum, F., & Tsang, B. Y. (1998). Lovesongs in the United States and China: On the nature of romantic love. *Journal of Cross-Cultural Psychology, 29,* 306–319.

Rotton, J., & Frey, J. (1985). Air pollution, weather, and violent crimes: Concomitant time-series analysis of archival data. *Journal of Personality and Social Psychology, 49,* 1207–1220.

Roy, M. C., Gauvin, S., & Limayem, M. (1996). Electronic group brainstorming: The role of feedback on productivity. *Small Group Research, 27,* 215–247.

Ruback, R. B., & Innes, C. A. (1988). The relevance and irrelevance of psychological research: The example of prison crowding. *American Psychologist, 43,* 683–693.

Ruback, R. B., & Weiner, N. A. (Eds.). (1995). *Interpersonal violent behaviors: Social and cultural aspects.* New York: Springer Publishing.

Rubenowitz, S., Norrgren, F., & Tannenbaum, A. S. (1983). Some social psychological effects of direct and indirect participation in ten Swedish companies. *Organization Studies, 4,* 243–259.

Rubenstein, C. M., & Shaver, P. (1982). *In search of intimacy.* New York: Delacorte.

Rubenstein, S. (1996, August 29). Letting Binti just be herself. *San Francisco Chronicle,* p. A17.

Rubin, D. C. (Ed.) (1996). *Remembering our past: Studies in autobiographical memory.* New York: Cambridge University Press.

Rubin, J. Z. (1994). Models of conflict management. *Journal of Social Issues, 50,* 33–45.

Rubin, J. Z., Provenzano, F. J., & Luria, Z. (1974). The eye of the beholder: Parents' views on sex of newborns. *American Journal of Orthopsychiatry, 44,* 512–519.

Rubin, J. Z., Pruitt, D. G., & Kim, S. H. (1994). *Social conflict: Escalation, stalemate, and settlement.* New York: McGraw-Hill.

Rubin, M., & Hewstone, M. (1998). Social identity theory's self-esteem hypothesis: A review and some suggestions for clarification. *Personality and Social Psychology Review, 2,* 40–62.

Rubin, Z. (1973). *Liking and loving.* New York: Holt, Rinehart and Winston.

Rubin, Z., Hill, C. T., Peplau, L. A., & Dunkel-Schetter, C. (1980). Self-disclosure in dating couples: Sex roles and the ethic of openness. *Journal of Marriage and the Family, 42,* 305–317.

Rubonis, A. V., & Bickman, L. (1991). Psychological impairment in the wake of disaster: The disaster-psychopathology relationship. *Psychological Bulletin, 109,* 384–399.

Rudman, L. A., & Borgida, E. (1995). The afterglow of construct accessibility: The behavioral consequences of priming men to view women as sexual objects. *Journal of Experimental Social Psychology, 31,* 493–517.

Ruggiero, K. M., & Major, B. N. (1998). Group status and attributions to discrimination: Are low or high status group members more likely to blame their failure on discrimination? *Personality and Social Psychology Bulletin.*

Ruggiero, K. M., & Taylor, D. M. (1997). Why minority group members perceive or do not perceive the discrimination that surrounds them: The role of self-esteem and perceived control. *Journal of Personality and Social Psychology, 72,* 373–389.

Rule, B. G., Taylor, B. R., & Dobbs, A. R. (1987). Priming effects of heat on aggressive thoughts. *Social Cognition, 5,* 131–143.

Runciman, W. C. (1966). *Relative deprivation and social justice: A study of attitudes to social inequality in twentieth century England.* Berkeley: University of California Press.

Rusbult, C. E. (1983). A longitudinal test of the investment model: The development (and deterioration) of satisfaction and commitment in heterosexual involvement. *Journal of Personality and Social Psychology, 45,* 101–117.

Rusbult, C. E., & Buunk, B. P. (1993). Commitment processes in close relationships: An interdependence analysis. *Journal of Social and Personal Relationships, 10,* 175–204.

Rusbult, C. E., & Martz, J. M. (1995). Remaining in an abusive relationship: An investment model analysis of nonvoluntary dependence. *Personality and Social Psychology Bulletin, 21,* 558–571.

Ruscher, J. B. (1998). Prejudice and stereotyping in everyday communication. In M. P. Zanna (Ed.), *Advances in experimental social psychology* (Vol. 30, pp. 241–307). San Diego: Academic Press.

Rushton, J. P. (1981a). Television as a socializer. In J. P. Rushton & R. M. Sorrentino (Eds.), *Altruism and helping behavior: Social, personality, and developmental perspectives.* Hillsdale, NJ: Erlbaum.

Rushton, J. P. (1981b). The altruistic personality. In J. P. Rushton & R. M. Sorrentino (Eds.), *Altruism and helping behavior: Social, personality, and developmental perspectives* (pp. 251–266). Hillsdale, NJ: Erlbaum.

Rushton, J. P., Fulker, D. W., Neale, M. C., Nias, D. K. B., & Eysenck, H. J. (1986). Altruism and aggression: The heritability of individual differences. *Journal of Personality and Social Psychology, 50,* 1192–1198.

Rushton, J. P., Russell, R. J. H., & Wells, P. A. (1984). Genetic similarity theory: Beyond kin selection. *Behavior Genetics, 14,* 179–193.

Russell, D. E. H. (1984). *Sexual exploitation.* Beverly Hills, CA: Sage.

Russell, D., Peplau, L. A., & Cutrona, C. E. (1980). The revised UCLA Loneliness Scale: Concurrent and discriminant validity evidence. *Journal of Personality and Social Psychology, 39,* 472–480.

Russell, G. W., Arms, R. L., & Bibby, R. W. (1995). Canadians' belief in catharsis. *Social Behavior and Personality, 23,* 223–228.

Russell, J. A. (1994). Is there universal recognition of emotion from facial expression? A review of cross-cultural studies. *Psychological Bulletin, 115,* 102–141.

Rutkowski, G. K., Gruder, C. L., & Romer, D. (1983). Group cohesiveness, social norms, and bystander intervention. *Journal of Personality and Social Psychology, 44,* 545–552.

Ruvolo, A., & Markus, H. (1992). Possible selves and performance: The power of self-relevant imagery. *Social Cognition, 9,* 95–124.

Ryan, C. S., Judd, C. M., & Park, B. (1996). Effects of racial stereotypes on judgments of individuals: The moderating role of perceived group variability. *Journal of Experimental Social Psychology, 32,* 71–103.

Rynes, S. L., & Connerly, M. L. (1993). Applicant reactions to alternative selection procedures. *Journal of Business and Psychology, 4,* 261–277.

Saal, F. E., Johnson, C. B., & Weber, N. (1989). Friendly or sexy? It may depend on whom you ask. *Psychology of Women Quarterly, 13,* 263–276.

Sackett, P. R., Burris, L. R., & Callahan, C. (1989). Integrity testing for personnel selection: An update. *Personnel Psychology, 42,* 491–525.

Sackett, P. R., & DuBois, C. L. Z. (1991). Rater-ratee race effects on performance evaluation: Challenging meta-analytic conclusions. *Journal of Applied Psychology, 76,* 873–877.

Sackett, P. R., & Wilson, M. A. (1982). Factors affecting the consensus judgment process in managerial assessment centers. *Journal of Applied Psychology, 67,* 10–17.

Sacks, O. (1985). *The man who mistook his wife for a hat.* New York: Summit.

Saenz, D. S. (1994). Token status and problem-solving deficits: Detrimental effects of distinctiveness and performance monitoring. *Social Cognition, 12,* 61–74.

Safer, M. (1980). Attributing evil to the subject, not the situation: Student reactions to Milgram's film on obedience. *Personality and Social Psychology Bulletin, 6,* 205–209.

Sagar, H. A., & Schofield, J. W. (1980). Racial and behavioral cues in black and white children's perceptions of ambiguously aggressive acts. *Journal of Personality and Social Psychology, 39,* 590–598.

Saks, M. J. (1974). Ignorance of science is no excuse. *Trial, 10,* 18–20.

Saks, M. J., & Marti, M. W. (1997). A meta-analysis of the effects of jury size. *Law and Human Behavior, 21,* 451–468.

Salgado, J. F. (1997). The five factor model of personality and job performance in the European community. *Journal of Applied Psychology, 82,* 30–43.

Salovey, P. (Ed.) (1991). *The psychology of jealousy and envy.* New York: Guilford Press.

Salovey, P. (1992). Mood-induced focus of attention. *Journal of Personality and Social Psychology, 62,* 699–707.

Salovey, P., Mayer, J. D., & Rosenhan, D. L. (1991). Mood and helping: Mood as a motivator of helping and helping as a regulator of mood. In M. S. Clark (Ed.), *Prosocial behavior* (Vol. 12, pp. 215–237). Newbury Park, CA: Sage.

Salovey, P., & Rodin, J. (1984). Some antecedents and consequences of social-comparison jealousy. *Journal of Personality and Social Psychology, 47,* 780–792.

Salovey, P., Rothman, A. J., & Rodin, J. (1998). Health behavior. In D. Gilbert, S. Fiske, & G. Lindzey (Eds.), *Handbook of social psychology* (4th ed.). New York: McGraw-Hill.

Salvemini, N. J., Reilly, R. R., & Smither, J. W. (1993). The influence of rater motivation on assimilation effects and accuracy in performance ratings. *Organizational Behavior and Human Decision Processes, 55*, 41–60.

Sanchez, J. I., & De La Torre, P. (1996). A second look at the relationship between rating and behavioral accuracy in performance appraisal. *Journal of Applied Psychology, 81*, 3–10.

Sanders, G. S. (1981). Driven by distraction: An integrative review of social facilitation theory and research. *Journal of Experimental Social Psychology, 17*, 227–251.

Sanders, G. S., & Baron, R. S. (1977). Is social comparison irrelevant for producing choice shifts? *Journal of Experimental Social Psychology, 13*, 303–314.

Sanderson, D. W. (1993). *Smileys.* Sebastopol, CA: O'Reilly.

Sandys, M., & Dillehay, R. C. (1995). First-ballot votes, pre-deliberation dispositions, and final verdicts in jury trials. *Law and Human Behavior, 19*, 175–195.

Sanna, L. J. (1992). Self-efficacy theory: Implications for social facilitation and social loafing. *Journal of Personality and Social Psychology, 62*, 774–786.

Sanoff, A. P., & Leight, K. (1994). Altruism is in style. *U.S. News and World Report* (*America's Best Colleges: 1994 College Guide*), pp. 25–28.

Santee, R. T., & Maslach, C. (1982). To agree or not to agree: Personal dissent amid social pressure to conform. *Journal of Personality and Social Psychology, 42*, 690–700.

Santos, M. D., Leve, C., & Pratkanis, A. R. (1994). Hey buddy, can you spare seventeen cents? Mindful persuasion and the pique technique. *Journal of Applied Social Psychology, 24*, 755–764.

Sapolsky, B. S. (1984). Arousal, affect, and the aggression-moderating effect of erotica. In N. M. Malamuth & E. I. Donnerstein (Eds.), *Pornography and sexual aggression* (pp. 85–113). New York: Academic Press.

Sapolsky, R. M. (1994). *Why zebras don't get ulcers: A guide to stress, diseases, and coping.* New York: Freeman.

Saragovi, C., Koestner, R., Aube, J., & Di Dio, L. (1997). Agency, communion, and well-being: Extending Helgeson's (1994) model. *Journal of Personality and Social Psychology, 73*, 593–609.

Sarason, I. G., Levine, H. M., Basham, R. B., & Sarason, B. R. (1983). Assessing social support: The social support questionnaire. *Journal of Personality and Social Psychology, 44*, 127–139.

Sarason, I. G., & Sarason, B. R. (1984). Life changes, moderators of stress, and health. In A. Baum, S. E. Taylor, & J. E. Singer (Eds.), *Handbook of psychology and health: Vol. 4. Social psychological aspects of health* (pp. 279–299). Hillsdale, NJ: Erlbaum.

Sarason, I. G., Sarason, B. R., & Pierce, G. R. (1994). Social support: Global and relationship-based levels of analysis. *Journal of Social and Personal Relationships, 11*, 295–312.

Sarason, I. G., Sarason, B. R., Pierce, G. R., Shearin, E. N., & Sayers, M. H. (1991). A social learning approach to increasing blood donations. *Journal of Applied Social Psychology, 21*, 896–918.

Sarnoff, I., & Zimbardo, P. (1961). Anxiety, fear, and social affiliation. *Journal of Abnormal and Social Psychology, 62*, 356–363.

Sato, K. (1987). Distribution of the cost of maintaining common resources. *Journal of Experimental Social Psychology, 23*, 19–31.

Saulnier, K., & Perlman, D. (1981). The actor-observer bias is alive and well in prison: A sequel to Wells. *Personality and Social Psychology Bulletin, 7*, 559–564.

Savin, H. B. (1973). Professors and psychological researchers: Conflicting values in conflicting roles. *Cognition, 2*, 147–149.

Saxe, L., Dougherty, D., & Cross, T. (1985). The validity of polygraph testing: Scientific analysis and public controversy. *American Psychologist, 38*, 355–366.

Schachter, S. (1951). Deviation, rejection, and communication. *Journal of Abnormal and Social Psychology, 46*, 190–207.

Schachter, S. (1959). *The psychology of affiliation: Experimental studies of the sources of gregariousness.* Stanford, CA: Stanford University Press.

Schachter, S. (1964). The interaction of cognitive and physiological determinants of emotional state. In L. Berkowitz (Ed.), *Advances in experimental social psychology* (Vol. 1, pp. 49–80). New York: Academic Press.

Schachter, S., Hood, D., Gerin, W., Andreasson, P. B., & Rennert, M. (1985). Some causes and consequences of dependence and independence in the stock market. *Journal of Economic Behavior and Organization, 6*, 339–357.

Schachter, S., Ouellette, R., Whittle, B., & Gerin, W. (1987). Effects of trends and of profit or loss on the tendency to sell stock. *Basic and Applied Social Psychology, 8*, 259–271.

Schachter, S., & Singer, J. (1962). Cognitive, social, and physiological determinants of the emotional state. *Psychological Review, 69*, 379–399.

Schachter, S., & Singer, J. (1979). Comments on the Maslach and Marshall-Zimbardo experiments. *Journal of Personality and Social Psychology, 37*, 989–995.

Schafer, R. B., & Keith, P. M. (1980). Equity and depression among married couples. *Social Psychology Quarterly, 43*, 430–435.

Schaller, M. (1991). Social categorization and the formation of social stereotypes: Further evidence for biased information processing in the perception of group-behavior correlations. *European Journal of Social Psychology, 21*, 25–35.

Schaller, M., & Cialdini, R. B. (1988). The economics of empathic helping: Support for a mood management motive. *Journal of Experimental Social Psychology, 24*, 163–181.

Schaller, M., & Conway, L. G., III (1998). *From cognition to culture: The origins of stereotypes that really matter.* Unpublished manuscript, University of British Columbia.

Scharfe, E., & Bartholomew, K. (1994). Reliability and stability of adult attachment patterns. *Personal Relationships, 1*, 23–43.

Scheier, M. F., & Carver, C. S. (1983). Two sides of the self: One for you and one for me. In J. Suls and A. G. Greenwald (Eds.), *Psychological perspectives on the self* (Vol. 2, pp. 123–157). Hillsdale, NJ: Erlbaum.

Scheier, M. F., & Carver, C. S. (1985). Optimism, coping, and health: Assessment and implications of generalized outcome expectancies. *Health Psychology, 4*, 219–247.

Scheier, M. F., & Carver, C. S. (1992). Effects of optimism on psychological and physical well-being: Theoretical overview and empirical update. *Cognitive Therapy and Research, 16*, 201–228.

Scheier, M. F., Carver, C. S., & Gibbons, F. X. (1979). Self-directed attention, awareness of bodily states, and suggestibility. *Journal of Personality and Social Psychology, 37*, 1576–1588.

Scher, S. J., & Cooper, J. (1989). Motivational basis of dissonance: The singular role of behavioral consequences. *Journal of Personality and Social Psychology, 56*, 899–906.

Schittekatte, M., & van Hiel, A. (1996). Effects of partially shared information and awareness of unshared information on information sampling. *Small Group Research, 27*, 431–448.

Schlenker, B. R. (1982). Translating actions into attitudes: An identity-analytic approach to the explanation of social conduct. In L. Berkowitz (Ed.), *Advances in experimental social psychology* (Vol. 15, pp. 193–247). New York: Academic Press.

Schlenker, B. R., & Trudeau, J. V. (1990). The impact of self-presentations on private self-beliefs: Effects of prior self-beliefs and misattribution. *Journal of Personality and Social Psychology, 58,* 22–32.

Schlenker, B. R., & Weigold, M. F. (1992) Interpersonal processes involving impression regulation and management. *Annual Review of Psychology, 43,* 133–168.

Schlenker, B. R., Weigold, M. F., & Hallam, J. R. (1990). Self-serving attributions in social context: Effects of self-esteem and social pressure. *Journal of Personality and Social Psychology, 58,* 855–863.

Schmidt, F. L. (1992). What do data really mean? Research findings, meta-analysis, and cumulative knowledge in psychology. *American Psychologist, 47,* 1173–1181.

Schmidt, G., & Weiner, B. (1988). An attribution-affect-action theory of behavior: Replications of judgments of help-giving. *Personality and Social Psychology Bulletin, 14,* 610–621.

Schneider, D. J. (1973). Implicit personality theory: A review. *Psychological Bulletin, 79,* 294–309.

Schneider, D. M., & Watkins, M. J. (1996). Response conformity in recognition testing. *Psychonomic Bulletin & Review, 3,* 481–485.

Schneider, M. E., Major, B., Luhtanen, R., & Crocker, J. (1996). Social stigma and the potential costs of assumptive help. *Personality and Social Psychology Bulletin, 22,* 201–209.

Schneider, S. G., Taylor, S. E., Hammen, C., Kemeny, M. E., & Dudley, J. (1991). Factors influencing suicide intent in gay and bisexual suicide ideators: Differing models for men with and without human immunodeficiency virus. *Journal of Personality and Social Psychology, 61,* 776–778.

Schoeneman, T. J., & Rubanowitz, D. E. (1985). Attributions in the advice columns: Actors and observers, causes and reasons. *Personality and Social Psychology Bulletin, 11,* 315–325.

Schofield, J. W. (1982). *Black and white in school: Trust, tension, or tolerance?* New York: Praeger.

Schoorman, F. D. (1988). Escalation bias in performance appraisals: An unintended consequence of supervisor participation in hiring decisions. *Journal of Applied Psychology, 73,* 58–62.

Schopler, J. (1970). An attribution analysis of some determinants of reciprocating a benefit. In J. R. Macaulay & L. Berkowitz (Eds.), *Altruism and helping behavior* (pp. 231–238). New York: Academic Press.

Schopler, J., Insko, C. A., Drigotas, S. M., Wieselquist, J., Pemberton, M. B., & Cox, C. (1995). The role of identifiability in the reduction of interindividual-intergroup discontinuity. *Journal of Experimental Social Psychology, 31,* 553–574.

Schopler, J., Insko, C. A., Graetz, K. A., Drigotas, S., Smith, V. A., & Dahl, K. (1993). Individual-group discontinuity: Further evidence for mediation by fear and greed. *Personality and Social Psychology Bulletin, 19,* 419–431.

Schriesheim, C. A., Tepper, B. J., & Tetrault, L. A. (1994). Least preferred co-worker score, situational control, and leadership effectiveness: A meta-analysis of contingency model performance predictions. *Journal of Applied Psychology, 79,* 561–573.

Schroeder, D. A., Dovidio, J. F., Sibicky, M. E., Matthews, L. L., & Allen, J. L. (1988). Empathy concern and helping behavior: Egoism or altruism? *Journal of Experimental Social Psychology, 24,* 333–353.

Schroeder, D. A., Penner, L. A., Davidio, J. F., & Piliavin, J. A. (1995). *The psychology of helping and altruism: Problems and puzzles.* New York: McGraw-Hill.

Schuller, R. A., & Vidmar, N. (1992). Battered woman syndrome evidence in the courtroom: A review of the literature. *Law and Human Behavior, 16,* 273–291.

Schulman, J., Shaver, P., Colman, R., Emrick, B., & Christie, R. (1973, May). Recipe for a jury. *Psychology Today,* pp. 37–44, 77, 79–84.

Schultz, B., Ketrow, S. M., & Urban, D. M. (1995). Improving decision quality in the small group: The role of the reminder. *Small Group Research, 26,* 521–541.

Schultz, N. R., Jr., & Moore, D. (1984). Loneliness: Correlates, attributions, and coping among older adults. *Personality and Social Psychology Bulletin, 10,* 67–77.

Schulz, R. (1976). Effects of control and predictability on the physical and psychological well-being of the institutionalized aged. *Journal of Personality and Social Psychology, 33,* 563–573.

Schulz, R., & Hanusa, B. H. (1978). Long-term effects of control and predictability-enhancing interventions: Findings and ethical issues. *Journal of Personality and Social Psychology, 36,* 1194–1201.

Schwartz, S. H., & Gottlieb, A. (1980). Bystander anonymity and reaction to emergencies. *Journal of Personality and Social Psychology, 39,* 418–430.

Schwarz, N. (1990). Feelings as information: Information and motivational functions as affective states. In E. T. Higgins et al. (Eds.), *Handbook of motivation and cognition: Foundations of social behavior* (Vol. 2, pp. 527–561). New York: Guilford.

Schwarz, N., Bless, H., & Bohner, G. (1991). Mood and persuasion: Affective states influence the processing of persuasive communications. In M. P. Zanna (Ed.), *Advances in experimental social psychology* (Vol. 24, pp. 161–199). New York: Academic Press.

Schwarz, N., Groves, R. M., & Schuman, H. (1998). Survey methods. In D. Gilbert, S. Fiske, & G. Lindzey (Eds.), *Handbook of social psychology* (4th ed.). New York: McGraw-Hill.

Schwarz, N., Hippler, H. J., Deutsch, B., & Strack, F. (1985). Response scales: Effects of category range on reported behavior and comparative judgments. *Public Opinion Quarterly, 49,* 388–395.

Schwarz, N., & Kurz, E. (1989). What's in a picture? The impact of face-ism on trait attribution. *European Journal of Social Psychology, 19,* 311–316.

Schwarz, N., Strack, F., Hilton, D., & Naderer, G. (1991). Base rates, representativeness, and the logic of conversation: The contextual relevance of "irrelevant" information. *Social Cognition, 9,* 67–84.

Schwarz, N., & Sudman, S. (Eds.) (1996). *Answering questions: Methodology for determining cognitive and communicative processes in survey research.* San Francisco: Jossey-Bass.

Schwarzwald, J., Raz, M., & Zvibel, M. (1979). The applicability of the door-in-the-face technique when established behavioral customs exist. *Journal of Applied Social Psychology, 9,* 576–586.

Scott, L., & O'Hara, M. W. (1993). Self-discrepancies in clinically anxious and depressed university students. *Journal of Abnormal Psychology, 102,* 282–287.

Searcy, E., & Eisenberg, N. (1992). Defensiveness in response to aid from a sibling. *Journal of Personality and Social Psychology, 62,* 422–433.

Sears, D. O. (1986). College sophomores in the laboratory: Influences of a narrow data base on social psychology's view of human nature. *Journal of Personality and Social Psychology, 51,* 515–530.

Sears, D. O., & Allen, H. M., Jr. (1984). The trajectory of local desegregation controversies and whites' opposition to busing. In N. Miller & M. B. Brewer (Eds.), *Groups in contact: The psychology of desegregation* (pp. 123–151). New York: Academic Press.

Sears, D. O., & Kinder, D. R. (1985). Whites' opposition to busing: On conceptualizing and operationalizing group conflict. *Journal of Personality and Social Psychology, 48,* 1141–1147.

Sedikides, C. (1992). Attentional effects on mood are moderated by chronic self-conception valence. *Personality and Social Psychology Bulletin, 18,* 580–584.

Sedikides, C. (1993). Assessment, enhancement, and verification determinants of the self-evaluation process. *Journal of Personality and Social Psychology, 65,* 317–338.

Sedikides, C., & Anderson, C. A. (1994). Causal perceptions of intertrait relations: The glue that holds person types together. *Personality and Social Psychology Bulletin, 20,* 294–302.

Sedikides, C., & Jackson, J. M. (1990). Social impact theory: A field test of source strength, source immediacy and number of targets. *Basic and Applied Social Psychology, 11,* 273–281.

Sedikides, C., & Skowronski, J. J. (1995). On the sources of self-knowledge: The perceived primacy of self-reflection. *Journal of Social and Clinical Psychology, 14,* 244–270.

Sedikides, C., & Skowronski, J. J. (1997). The symbolic self in evolutionary context. *Personality and Social Psychology Review, 1,* 80–102.

Seeger, J. A. (1983). No innate phases in group problem solving. *Academy of Management Review, 8,* 683–689.

Segal, N. L. (1993). Twin, sibling, and adoption methods: Tests of evolutionary hypotheses. *American Psychologist, 48,* 943–956.

Seligman, C., Bush, M., & Kirsch, K. (1976). Relationship between compliance in the foot-in-the-door paradigm and size of first request. *Journal of Personality and Social Psychology, 33,* 517–520.

Seligman, M. E. P. (1975). *On depression, development, and death.* San Francisco: Freeman.

Seligman, M. E. P. (1991). *Learned optimism.* New York: Knopf.

Seligman, M. E. P. (1995). The effectiveness of psychotherapy: The *Consumer Reports* Study. *American Psychologist, 50,* 965–974.

Selye, H. (1936). A syndrome produced by diverse nocuous agents. *Nature, 138,* 32.

Seto, M. C., & Barbaree, H. E. (1995). The role of alcohol in sexual aggression. *Clinical Psychology Review, 15,* 545–566.

Shackelford, T. K., & Larsen, R. J. (1997). Facial asymmetry as an indicator of psychological, emotional, and physiological distress. *Journal of Personality and Social Psychology, 72,* 456–466.

Shaffer, D. R., Smith, J. E., & Tomarelli, M. (1982). Self-monitoring as a determinant of self-disclosure reciprocity during the acquaintance process. *Journal of Personality and Social Psychology, 43,* 163–175.

Shanab, M. E., & Yahya, K. A. (1977). A behavioral study of obedience in children. *Journal of Personality and Social Psychology, 35,* 530–536.

Shanab, M. E., & Yahya, K. A. (1978). A cross cultural study of obedience. *Bulletin of the Psychonomic Society, 11,* 267–269.

Shapiro, P. N., & Penrod, S. (1986). Meta-analysis of facial identification studies. *Psychological Bulletin, 100,* 139–156.

Sharp, S. (1995). How much does bullying hurt? The effects of bullying on the personal well-being and educational progress of secondary aged students. *Educational and Child Psychology, 12* (2), 81–88.

Sharp, S. (1996). Self-esteem, response style and victimization: Possible ways of preventing victimization through parenting and school based training programmes. *School Psychology International, 17,* 347–357.

Sharpsteen, D. J., & Kirkpatrick, L. A. (1997). Romantic jealousy and adult romantic attachment. *Journal of Personality and Social Psychology, 72,* 627–640.

Shaver, K. G. (1970). Defensive attribution: Effects of severity and relevance on the responsibility assigned for an accident. *Journal of Personality and Social Psychology, 14,* 101–113.

Shaver, P., Hazan, C., & Bradshaw, D. (1998). Love as attachment: The integration of three behavioral systems. In R. J. Sternberg & M. L. Barnes (Eds.), *The psychology of love* (pp. 68–99). New Haven, CT: Yale University Press.

Shaver, P., & Rubenstein, E. (1980). Childhood attachment experience and adult loneliness. In L. Wheeler (Ed.), *Review of personality and social psychology* (Vol. 1, pp. 42–73). Beverly Hills, CA: Sage.

Shavitt, S., Swan, S., Lowery, T. M., & Wanke, M. (1994). The interaction of endorser attractiveness and involvement in persuasion depends on the goal that guides message processing. *Journal of Consumer Psychology, 3,* 137–162.

Shaw, J. S., III (1996). Increases in eyewitness confidence resulting from postevent questioning. *Journal of Experimental Psychology: Applied, 2,* 126–146.

Shaw, J. S., III., Garven, S., & Wood, J. M. (1997). Co-witness information can have immediate effects on eyewitness memory reports. *Law and Human Behavior, 21,* 503–523.

Shaw, L. L., Batson, C. D., & Todd, R. M. (1994). Empathy avoidance: Forestalling feeling for another in order to escape the motivational consequences. *Journal of Personality and Social Psychology, 67,* 879–887.

Shea, C. (1996, January 12). New students uncertain about racial preferences. *Chronicle of Higher Education,* p. A33.

Shefrin, H. M., & Statman, M. (1985). The disposition to sell winners too early and ride losers too long: Theory and evidence. *Journal of Finance, 40,* 777–790.

Shefrin, H. M., & Statman, M. (1986, February). How not to make money in the stock market. *Psychology Today,* pp. 52–57.

Shell, R. M., & Eisenberg, N. (1992). A developmental model of recipients' reactions to aid. *Psychological Bulletin, 111,* 413–433.

Sheppard, B. H. (1985). Justice is no simple matter: Case for elaborating our model of procedural fairness. *Journal of Personality and Social Psychology, 49,* 953–962.

Sheppard, B. H., Hartwick, J., & Warshaw, P. R. (1988). The theory of reasoned action: A meta-analysis of past research with recommendations for modifications and future research. *Journal of Consumer Research, 15,* 325–343.

Shepperd, J. A. (1993a). Productivity loss in performance groups: A motivation analysis. *Psychological Bulletin, 113,* 67–81.

Shepperd, J. A. (1993b). Student derogation of the Scholastic Aptitude Test: Biases in perceptions and presentations of college board scores. *Basic and Applied Social Psychology, 14,* 455–473.

Shepperd, J. A., & Arkin, R. M. (1991). Behavioral other-enhancement: Strategically obscuring the link between performance and evaluation. *Journal of Personality and Social Psychology, 60,* 79–88.

Sherif, M. (1936). *The psychology of social norms.* New York: Harper.

Sherif, M. (1966). *In common predicament: Social psychology of intergroup conflict and cooperation.* Boston: Houghton Mifflin.

Sherif, M., Harvey, L. J., White, B. J., Hood, W. R., & Sherif, C. W. (1961). *The Robbers Cave experiment: Intergroup conflict and cooperation.* Middletown, CT: Wesleyan University Press. (Reprinted in 1988)

Sherman, S. J., Presson, C., & Chassin, L. (1984). Mechanisms underlying the false consensus effect: The special role of threats to the self. *Personality and Social Psychology Bulletin, 10,* 127–138.

Shore, T. H., Shore, L. M., & Thornton, G. C., III. (1992). Construct validity of self- and peer evaluations of performance dimensions in an assessment center. *Journal of Applied Psychology,* 77, 42–54.

Shotland, R. L., & Heinold, W. D. (1985). Bystander response to arterial bleeding: Helping skills, the decision-making process, and differentiating the helping response. *Journal of Personality and Social Psychology,* 49, 347–356.

Shotland, R. L., & Stebbins, C. A. (1980). Bystander response to rape: Can a victim attract help? *Journal of Applied Social Psychology,* 10, 510–527.

Shotland, R. L., & Stebbins, C. A. (1983). Emergency and cost as determinants of helping behavior and the slow accumulation of social psychological knowledge. *Social Psychology Quarterly,* 46, 36–46.

Shotland, R. L., & Straw, M. K. (1976). Bystander response to an assault: When a man attacks a woman. *Journal of Personality and Social Psychology,* 34, 990–999.

Shrauger, J. S., & Schoeneman, T. (1979). Symbolic interactionist view of the self-concept: Through the looking-glass darkly. *Psychological Bulletin,* 86, 549–573.

Sibicky, M. E., Schroeder, D. A., & Dovidio, J. F. (1995). Empathy and helping: Considering the consequences of intervention. *Basic and Applied Social Psychology,* 16, 435–453.

Sieber, J. E., & Stanley, B. (1988). Ethical and professional dimensions of socially sensitive research. *American Psychologist,* 43, 49–55.

Siegel, J. M. (1990). Stressful life events and use of physician services among the elderly: The moderating role of pet ownership. *Journal of Personality and Social Psychology,* 58, 1081–1086.

Siegler, I. C. (1994). Hostility and risk: Demographic and lifestyle variables. In A. W. Siegman & T. W. Smith (Eds.), *Anger, hostility, and the heart* (pp. 199–214). Hillsdale, NJ: Erlbaum.

Siegman, A. W., & Boyle, S. (1993). Voices of fear and anxiety and sadness and depression: The effects of speech rate and loudness on fear and anxiety and sadness and depression. *Journal of Abnormal Psychology,* 102, 430–437.

Siegman, A. W., & Smith, T. W. (1994). *Anger, hostility, and the heart.* Hillsdale, NJ: Erlbaum.

Siever, L. J., & Frucht, W. (1997). *The new view of self: How genes and neurotransmitters shape your mind, your personality, and your mental health.* New York: Macmillan.

Sigall, H., & Page, R. (1971). Current stereotypes: A little fading, a little faking. *Journal of Personality and Social Psychology,* 18, 247–255.

Sigelman, L., & Welch, S. (1991). *Black Americans' views of racial inequality: The dream deferred.* New York: Cambridge University Press.

Signorielli, N., McLeod, D., & Healy, E. (1994). Gender stereotypes in MTV commercials: The beat goes on. *Journal of Broadcasting and Electronic Media,* 38, 91–101.

Silka, L. (1989). *Intuitive judgments of change.* New York: Springer-Verlag.

Silver, W. M., & Bufanio, K. M. (1996). The impact of group efficacy and group goals on group task performance. *Small Group Research,* 27, 347–359.

Silverstein, B., Perdue, L., Peterson, B., & Kelly, E. (1986). The role of the mass media in promoting a thin standard of bodily attractiveness for women. *Sex Roles,* 14, 519–532.

Sime, J. D. (1983). Affiliative behavior during escape to building exits. *Journal of Environmental Psychology,* 3, 21–41.

Simons, R. L., Johnson, C., Beaman, J., & Conger, R. D. (1993). Explaining women's double jeopardy: Factors that mediate the association between harsh treatment as a child and violence by a husband. *Journal of Marriage and the Family,* 55, 713–723.

Simonson, I., & Staw, B. W. (1992). Deescalation strategies: A comparison of techniques for reducing commitment to losing courses of action. *Journal of Applied Psychology,* 77, 419–426.

Simpson, J. A. (1987). The dissolution of romantic relationships: Factors involved in relationship stability and emotional distress. *Journal of Personality and Social Psychology,* 53, 683–692.

Simpson, J. A., Campbell, B., & Berscheid, E. (1986). The association between romantic love and marriage: Kephart (1967) twice revisited. *Personality and Social Psychology Bulletin,* 12, 363–372.

Simpson, J. A., & Gangestad, S. W. (1992). Sociosexuality and romantic partner choice. *Journal of Personality,* 60, pp. 31–51.

Simpson, J. A., Gangestad, S. W., & Lerma, M. (1990). Perception of physical attractiveness: Mechanisms involved in the maintenance of romantic relationships. *Journal of Personality and Social Psychology,* 59, 1192–1201.

Simpson, J. A., & Kenrick, D. T. (Eds.) (1997). *Evolutionary social psychology.* Mahwah, NJ: Erlbaum.

Simpson, J. A., Rholes, W. S., & Phillips, D. (1996). Conflicts in close relationships: An attachment perspective. *Journal of Personality and Social Psychology,* 71, 899–914.

Sinclair, R. C., Hoffman, C., Mark, M. M., Martin, L. M., & Pickering, T. L. (1994). Construct accessibility and the misattribution of arousal: Schachter and Singer revisited. *Psychological Science,* 5, 15–19.

Singelis, T. M. (1994). The measurement of independent and interdependent self-construals. *Personality and Social Psychology Bulletin,* 20, 580–591.

Singer, J. L. (1994). Imaginative play and adaptive development. In J. H. Goldstein (Ed.), *Toys, play, and child development* (pp. 6–26). New York: Cambridge University Press.

Singer, J. L., & Singer, D. G. (1983). Psychologists look at television: Cognitive, developmental, personality, and social policy implications. *American Psychologist,* 38, 826–834.

Singh, D. (1993). Adaptive significance of female physical attractiveness: Role of waist-to-hip ratio. *Journal of Personality and Social Psychology,* 65, 293–307.

Singh, D. (1995). Female judgment of male attractiveness and desirability for relationships: Role of waist-to-hip ratio and financial status. *Journal of Personality and Social Psychology,* 69, 1089–1101.

Sistrunk, F., & McDavid, J. W. (1971). Sex variable in conforming behavior. *Journal of Personality and Social Psychology,* 17, 200–207.

Skarlicki, D. P., & Folger, R. (1997). Retaliation in the workplace: The roles of distributive, procedural, and interactional justice. *Journal of Applied Psychology,* 82, 434–443.

Skinner, E. A. (1996). A guide to constructs of control. *Journal of Personality and Social Psychology,* 71, 549–570.

Skitka, L. J., & Tetlock, P. E. (1993). Providing public assistance: Cognitive and motivational processes underlying liberal and conservative policy preferences. *Journal of Personality and Social Psychology,* 65, 1205–1223.

Sklar, L. S., & Anisman, H. (1981). Stress and cancer. *Psychological Bulletin,* 89, 369–406.

Skov, R. B., & Sherman, S. J. (1986). Information-gathering processes: Diagnosticity, hypothesis confirmatory strategies, and perceived hypothesis confirmation. *Journal of Experimental Social Psychology,* 22, 93–121.

Skowronski, J. J., & Carlston, D. E. (1989). Negativity and extremity biases in impression formation: A review of explanations. *Psychology Bulletin,* 105, 131–142.

Slamecka, N. J., & Graff, P. (1978). The generation effect: Delineation of a phenomenon. *Journal of Experimental Psychology: Human Learning and Memory,* 4, 592–604.

Slovic, P., Fischhoff, B., & Lichtenstein, S. (1982). Facts versus fears: Understanding perceived risk. In D. Kahneman, P. Slovic, & A. Tversky (Eds.), *Judgment under uncertainty: Heuristics and biases* (pp. 463–489). New York: Cambridge University Press.

Smeaton, G., Byrne, D., & Murnen, S. K. (1989). The repulsion hypothesis revisited: Similarity irrelevance or dissimilarity bias? *Journal of Personality and Social Psychology, 56,* 54–59.

Smith, H. J., & Tyler, T. R. (1997). Choosing the right pond: The impact of group membership on self-esteem and group-oriented behavior. *Journal of Experimental Social Psychology, 33,* 146–170.

Smith, H. S., & Cohen, L. H. (1993). Self-complexity and reactions to a relationship breakup. *Journal of Social and Clinical Psychology, 12,* 367–384.

Smith, K. D., Keating, J. P., & Stotland, E. (1989). Altruism reconsidered: The effect of denying feedback on a victim's status to empathic witnesses. *Journal of Personality and Social Psychology, 57,* 641–650.

Smith, M. L., Glass, G. V., & Miller, T. I. (1980). *The benefits of psychotherapy.* Baltimore: Johns Hopkins University Press.

Smith, P. B., & Bond, M. H. (1993). *Social psychology across cultures: Analysis and perspective.* New York: Harvester/Wheatsheaf.

Smith, S. S., & Richardson, D. (1983). Amelioration of deception and harm in psychological research: The important role of debriefing. *Journal of Personality and Social Psychology, 44,* 1075–1082.

Smith, T. W., Snyder, C. R., & Perkins, S. C. (1983). The self-serving function of hypochondriacal complaints: Physical symptoms as self-handicapping strategies. *Journal of Personality and Social Psychology, 44,* 787–797.

Smith, V. L. (1991). Prototypes in the courtroom: Lay representations of legal concepts. *Journal of Personality and Social Psychology, 61,* 857–872.

Smith, V. L., & Kassin, S. M. (1993). Effects of the dynamite charge on the deliberations of deadlocked mock juries. *Law and Human Behavior, 17,* 625–643.

Smither, J. W., Reilly, R. R., & Buda, R. (1988). Effect of prior performance information on ratings of present performance: Contrast versus assimilation revisited. *Journal of Applied Psychology, 73,* 487–496.

Smitherman, H. O. (1992). Helping: The importance of cost/reward considerations on likelihood to help. *Psychological Reports, 71,* 305–306.

Smolowe, J. (1993, Fall Special Issue). "Intermarried . . . with children." *Time,* pp. 64–65.

Smolowe, J. (1994, February 7). ". . . And throw away the key." *Time.* pp. 54–59.

Smyth, J. M. (1998). Written emotional expression: Effect sizes, outcome types, and moderating variables. *Journal of Consulting and Clinical Psychology, 66,* 174–184.

Snyder, C. R., & Higgins, R. L. (1988). Excuses: Their effective role in the negotiation of reality. *Psychological Bulletin, 104,* 23–35.

Snyder, C. R., Higgins, R. L., & Stucky, R. J. (1983). *Excuses: Masquerades in search of grace.* New York: Wiley.

Snyder, C. R., Lassegard, M. A., & Ford, C. E. (1986). Distancing after group success and failure: Basking in reflected glory and cutting off reflected failure. *Journal of Personality and Social Psychology, 51,* 382–388.

Snyder, M. (1974). The self-monitoring of expressive behavior. *Journal of Personality and Social Psychology, 30,* 526–537.

Snyder, M. (1987). *Public appearances private/realities: The psychology of self-monitoring.* New York: Freeman.

Snyder, M. (1992). Motivational foundations of behavioral confirmation. In M. P. Zanna (Ed.), *Advances in experimental social psychology* (Vol. 25, pp. 67–114). San Diego: Academic Press.

Snyder, M. (1993). Basic research and practical problems: The promise of a "functional" personality and social psychology. *Personality and Social Psychology Bulletin, 19,* 251–264.

Snyder, M., & DeBono, K. (1985). Appeals to image and claims about quality: Understanding the psychology of advertising. *Journal of Personality and Social Psychology, 49,* 586–597.

Snyder, M., & Gangestad, S. (1986). On the nature of self-monitoring: Matters of assessment, matters of validity. *Journal of Personality and Social Psychology, 51,* 125–139.

Snyder, M., & Haugen, J. A. (1994). Why does behavioral confirmation occur? A functional perspective on the role of the perceiver. *Journal of Experimental Social Psychology, 30,* 218–246.

Snyder, M., & Monson, T. C. (1975). Persons, situations, and the control of social behavior. *Journal of Personality and Social Psychology, 32,* 637–644.

Snyder, M., & Swann, W. B., Jr. (1978). Behavioral confirmation in social interaction: From social perception to social reality. *Journal of Personality and Social Psychology, 36,* 1202–1212.

Snyder, M., Tanke, E. D., & Berscheid, E. (1977). Social perception and interpersonal behavior: On the self-fulfilling nature of social stereotypes. *Journal of Personality and Social Psychology, 35,* 656–666.

Solomon, S. D., Regier, D. A., & Burke, J. D. (1989). Role of perceived control in coping with disaster. *Journal of Social and Clinical Psychology, 8,* 376–392.

Spanier, G. B. (1992). Divorce: A comment about the future. In T. L. Orbuch (Ed.), *Close relationship loss: Theoretical approaches* (pp. 207–212). New York: Springer-Verlag.

Special report: A crime as American as a Colt .45. (1995, August 15). *Newsweek,* 22–23, 45.

Spence, J. T., Deaux, K., & Helmreich, R. L. (1985). Sex roles in contemporary American society. In G. Lindzey & E. Aronson (Eds.), *Handbook of social psychology* (Vol. 2, 3rd ed., pp. 149–178). New York: Random House.

Spencer, S. J., Steele, C. M., & Quinn, D. (1999). Stereotype threat and women's math performance. *Journal of Experimental Social Psychology.*

Spiegel, D. (1993). Social support: How friends, family, and groups can help. In D. Goleman & J. Gurin (Eds.), *Mind body medicine: How to use your mind for better health* (pp. 331–350). Yonkers, NY: Consumer Reports Books.

Spivey, C. B., & Prentice-Dunn, S. (1990). Assessing the directionality of deindividuated behavior: Effects of deindividuation, modeling, and private self-consciousness on aggressive and prosocial responses. *Basic and Applied Social Psychology, 11,* 387–403.

Sporer, S. L. (1993). Eyewitness identification accuracy, confidence, and decision times in simultaneous and sequential lineups. *Journal of Applied Psychology, 78,* 22–33.

Sporer, S. L., Malpass, R. S., & Koehnken, G. (Eds.) (1996). *Psychological issues in eyewitness identification.* Mahwah, NJ: Erlbaum.

Sporer, S. L., Penrod, S. D., Read, J. D., & Cutler, B. L. (1995). Choosing, confidence, and accuracy: A meta-analysis of the confidence-accuracy relation in eyewitness identification studies. *Psychological Bulletin, 118,* 315–327.

Sprafkin, J. N., Liebert, R. M., & Poulos, R. W. (1975). Effects of a prosocial televised example on children's helping. *Journal of Experimental Child Psychology, 20,* 119–126.

Sprecher, S. (1994). Two sides to the breakup of dating relationships. *Personal Relationships, 1,* 199–222.

Sprecher, S., & Regan, P. C. (1998). Passionate and companionate love in courting and young married couples. *Sociological Inquiry.*

Sprecher, S., Sullivan, Q., & Hatfield, E. (1994). Mate selection preferences: Gender differences examined in a national sample. *Journal of Personality and Social Psychology, 66,* 1074–1080.

Sproull, L., Subramani, M., Kiesler, S., Walker, J. H., & Waters, K. (1996). When the interface is a face. *Human Computer Interaction, 11,* 97–124.

St. Louis Post-Dispatch (1997, December 15). Health update: Prozac. P. A4.

Stalans, L. J., & Diamond, S. S. (1990). Formation and change in lay evaluations of criminal sentencing: Misperception and discontent. *Law and Human Behavior, 14,* 199–214.

Stangor, C., & Lange, J. E. (1994). Mental representations of social groups: Advances in understanding stereotypes and stereotyping. *Advances in Experimental Social Psychology, 26,* 357–416.

Stangor, C., Lynch, L., Changming, D., & Glass, B. (1992). Categorization of individuals on the basis of multiple social features. *Journal of Personality and Social Psychology, 62,* 207–218.

Stanley, S. M., & Markman, H. J. (1992). Assessing commitment in personal relationships. *Journal of Marriage and the Family, 54,* 595–608.

Stanton, J. M., & Barnes-Farrell, J. L. (1996). Effects of electronic performance monitoring on personal control, task satisfaction, and task performance. *Journal of Applied Psychology, 81,* 738–745.

Stapel, D. A., & Koomen, W. (1998). When stereotype activation results in (counter)stereotypical judgments: Priming stereotype-relevant traits and exemplars. *Journal of Experimental Social Psychology, 34,* 136–163.

Stasser, G. (1992). Pooling of unshared information during group discussions. In S. Worchel, W. Wood, & J. A. Simpson (Eds.), *Group process and productivity* (pp. 48–67). Newbury Park, CA: Sage.

Stasser, G., & Davis, J. H. (1981). Group decision making and social influence: A social interaction sequence model. *Psychological Review, 88,* 523–551.

Stasser, G., Kerr, N. L., & Bray, R. M. (1982). The social psychology of jury deliberations: Structure, process, and product. In N. Kerr & R. Bray (Eds.), *The psychology of the courtroom* (pp. 221–256). New York: Academic Press.

Stasser, G., Stewart, D. D., & Wittenbaum, G. M. (1995). Expert roles and information exchange during discussion: The importance of knowing who knows what. *Journal of Experimental Social Psychology, 31,* 244–265.

Stasser, G., & Titus, W. (1985). Pooling of unshared information in group decision making: Biased information sampling during discussion. *Journal of Personality and Social Psychology, 48,* 1467–1478.

Stasson, M. F., & Bradshaw, S. D. (1995). Explanations of individual-group performance differences: What sort of "bonus" can be gained through group interaction? *Small Group Research, 26,* 296–308.

Staub, E. (1996). Cultural-societal roots of violence: The examples of genocidal violence and of contemporary youth violence in the United States. *American Psychologist, 51,* 117–132.

Staw, B. M., Barsade, S. G., & Koput, K. W. (1997). Escalation at the credit window: A longitudinal study of bank executives' recognition and write-off of problem loans. *Journal of Applied Psychology, 82,* 130–142.

Staw, B. M., & Hoang, H. (1995). Sunk costs in the NBA: Why draft order affects playing time and survival in professional basketball: *Administrative Science Quarterly, 40,* 474–493.

Staw, B. M., & Ross, J. (1987). Behavior in escalation situations: Antecedents, prototypes, and solutions. In L. L. Cummings and B. M. Staw (Eds.), *Research in organizational behavior* (Vol. 9). Greenwich, CT: JAI Press.

Steblay, N. M. (1987). Helping behavior in rural and urban environments: A meta-analysis. *Psychological Bulletin, 102,* 346–356.

Steblay, N. M. (1992). A meta-analytic review of the weapon-focus effect. *Law and Human Behavior, 16,* 413–424.

Steblay, N. M. (1997). Social influence in eyewitness recall: A meta-analytic review of lineup instruction effects. *Law and Human Behavior, 21,* 283–297.

Steele, C. M. (1988). The psychology of self-affirmation: Sustaining the integrity of the self. In L. Berkowitz (Ed.), *Advances in experimental social psychology* (Vol. 21, pp. 261–302). New York: Academic Press.

Steele, C. M. (1997). A threat in the air: How stereotypes shape intellectual identity and performance. *American Psychologist, 52,* 613–629.

Steele, C. M., & Aronson, J. (1995). Stereotype vulnerability and the intellectual test performance of African Americans. *Journal of Personality and Social Psychology, 69,* 797–811.

Steele, C. M., & Josephs, R. A. (1990). Alcohol myopia: Its prized and dangerous effects. *American Psychologist, 45,* 921–933.

Steele, C. M., Spencer, S. J., & Lynch, M. (1993). Self-image resilience and dissonance: The role of affirmational resources. *Journal of Personality and Social Psychology, 64,* 885–896.

Stein, M. B., Walker, J. R., & Forde, D. R. (1996). Public-speaking fears in a community sample. *Archives of General Psychiatry, 53,* 169–174.

Steiner, I. D. (1972). *Group process and productivity.* New York: Academic Press.

Stephan, W. G. (1985). Intergroup relations. In G. Lindzey & E. Aronson (Eds.), *Handbook of social psychology* (Vol. 2, pp. 599–658). New York: Random House.

Stephan, W. G. (1986). The effects of school desegregation: An evaluation 30 years after Brown. In M. J. Saks & L. Saxe (Eds.), *Advances in applied social psychology* (Vol. 3, pp. 181–206). Hillsdale, NJ: Erlbaum.

Stepper, S., & Strack, F. (1993). Proprioceptive determinants of emotional and nonemotional feelings. *Journal of Personality and Social Psychology, 64,* 211–220.

Sternbach, R. A. (1964). The effects of instructional sets on autonomic responsivity. *Psychophysiology, 1,* 67–72.

Sternberg, R. J. (1986). A triangular theory of love. *Psychological Review, 93,* 119–135.

Sternberg, R. J. (1997). Construct validation of the triangular love scale. *European Journal of Social Psychology, 27,* 313–335.

Sternberg, R. J., & Barnes, M. L. (Eds.) (1998). *The psychology of love.* New Haven, CT: Yale University Press.

Sternberg, R. J., Wagner, R. K., Williams, W. M., & Horvath, J. A. (1995). Testing common sense. *American Psychologist, 50,* 912–927.

Stets, J. E. (1991). Cohabiting and marital aggression: The role of social isolation. *Journal of Marriage and the Family, 53,* 669–680.

Stets, J. E., & Straus, M. A. (1989). The marriage license as a hitting license: A comparison of assaults in dating, cohabiting, and married couples. *Journal of Family Violence, 41,* 33–52.

Stets, J. E., & Straus, M. A. (1990). Gender differences in reporting marital violence and its medical and psychological consequences. In M. A. Straus & R. J. Gelles (Eds.), *Physical violence in American families: Risk factors and adaptations to violence in 8,145 families* (pp. 151–165). New Brunswick, NJ: Transaction Publishers.

Stevens, C. K., & Kristof, A. L. (1995). Making the right impression: A field study of applicant impression management during job interviews. *Journal of Applied Psychology, 80,* 587–606.

Stewart, A. J., Sokol, M., Healy, J. M., Jr., & Chester, N. L. (1986). Longitudinal studies of psychological consequences of life changes in children and adults. *Journal of Personality and Social Psychology, 50,* 143–151.

Stice, E., & Shaw, H. E. (1994). Adverse effects of the media-portrayed thin-ideal on women and linkages to bulimic symptomatology. *Journal of Social and Clinical Psychology, 13,* 288–308.

Stinson, V., Devenport, J. L., Cutler, B. L., & Kravitz, D. A. (1996). How effective is the presence-of-counsel safeguard? Attorney perceptions of suggestiveness, fairness, and correctability of biased lineup procedures. *Journal of Applied Psychology, 81,* 64–75.

Stinson, V., Devenport, J. L., Cutler, B. L., & Kravitz, D. A. (1997). How effective is the motion-to-suppress safeguard? Judges perceptions of the suggestiveness and fairness of biased lineup procedures. *Journal of Applied Psychology, 82,* 211–220.

Stockdale, M. S. (1996). *Sexual harassment in the workplace: Perspectives, frontiers, and response strategies.* Thousand Oaks, CA: Sage.

Stogdill, R. (1972). Group productivity, drive, and cohesiveness. *Organizational Behavior and Human Performance, 8,* 26–43.

Stoltzfus, N. (1996). *Resistance of the heart: Intermarriage and the Rosenstrasse protest in Nazi Germany.* New York: Norton.

Stone, A. A., Neale, J. M., Cox, D. S., Napoli, A., Valdimarsdottir, H., & Kennedy-Moore, E. (1994). Daily events are associated with a secretory immune response to an oral antigen in men. *Health Psychology, 13,* 440–446.

Stone, B., Jones, C., & Betz, B. (1996). Response of cooperators and competitors in a simulated arms race. *Psychological Reports, 79,* 1101–1102.

Stone, J., Wiegand, A. W., Cooper, J., & Aronson, E. (1997). When exemplification fails: Hypocrisy and the motive for self-integrity. *Journal of Personality and Social Psychology, 72,* 54–65.

Stone, W. F., Lederer, G., & Christie, R. (Eds.) (1993). *Strength and weakness: The authoritarian personality today.* New York: Springer-Verlag.

Stoner, J. A. F. (1961). *A comparison of individual and group decisions involving risk.* Unpublished manuscript, Massachusetts Institute of Technology, Cambridge, MA.

Storms, M. D. (1973). Videotape and the attribution process: Reversing actors' and observers' points of view. *Journal of Personality and Social Psychology, 27,* 165–175.

Stotland, E. (1969). Exploratory investigations of empathy. In L. Berkowitz (Ed.), *Advances in experimental social psychology* (Vol. 4, pp. 271–313). New York: Academic Press.

Strauman, T. J. (1992). Self-guides, autobiographical memory, and anxiety and dysphoria: Toward a cognitive model of vulnerability to emotional distress. *Journal of Abnormal Psychology, 101,* 87–95.

Strauman, T. J., Lemieux, A. M., & Coe, C. L. (1993). Self-discrepancy and natural killer cell activity: Immunological consequences of negative self-evaluation. *Journal of Personality and Social Psychology, 64,* 1042–1052.

Straus, M. A. (1994). *Beating the devil out of them: Corporal punishment in American families.* San Francisco: Jossey-Bass.

Straus, M. A., Gelles, R. J., & Steinmetz, S. K. (1980). *Behind closed doors.* Garden City, NY: Anchor Books.

Straus, M. A., Sugarman, D. B., & Giles-Sims, J. (1997). Spanking by parents and subsequent antisocial behavior of children. *Archives of Pediatrics and Adolescent Medicine, 151,* 761–767.

Street, M. D. (1997). Groupthink: An examination of theoretical issues, implications, and future research suggestions. *Small Group Research, 28,* 72–93.

Strenta, A., & DeJong, W. (1981). The effect of a prosocial label on helping behavior. *Social Psychology Quarterly, 44,* 142–147.

Strentz, T., & Auerbach, S. M. (1988). Adjustment to the stress of simulated captivity: Effects of emotion-focused versus problem-focused preparation on hostages differing in locus of control. *Journal of Personality and Social Psychology, 55,* 652–660.

Strodtbeck, F. L., & Hook, L. (1961). The social dimensions of a twelve-man jury table. *Sociometry, 24,* 397–415.

Strodtbeck, F. L., James, R., & Hawkins, C. (1957). Social status in jury deliberations. *American Sociological Review, 22,* 713–719.

Stroebe, W., & Diehl, M. (1991). You can't beat good experiments with correlational evidence: Mullen, Johnson, and Sala's meta-analytic misinterpretations. *Journal of Basic and Applied Social Psychology, 12,* 25–32.

Stroebe, W., & Diehl, M. (1994). Why groups are less effective than their members: On productivity losses in idea generating groups. In W. Stroebe & M. Hewstone (Eds.), *European Review of Social Psychology* (Vol. 5, pp. 272–303). Chichester, England: Wiley.

Strube, M. J., & Garcia, J. E. (1981). A meta-analytical investigation of Fiedler's contingency model of leadership effectiveness. *Psychological Bulletin, 90,* 307–321.

Struch, N., & Schwartz, S. H. (1989). Intergroup aggression: Its predictors and distinctness from in-group bias. *Journal of Personality and Social Psychology, 56,* 364–373.

Struckman-Johnson, C. J., Gilliland, R. G., Struckman-Johnson, D. L., & North, T. C. (1990). The effects of fear of AIDS and gender on responses to fear-arousing condom advertisements. *Journal of Applied Social Psychology, 20,* 1396–1410.

Struckman-Johnson, C., & Struckman-Johnson, D. (1994). Men pressured and forced into sexual experience. *Archives of Sexual Behavior, 23,* 93–114.

Strupp, V. H. (1996). The tripartite model and the *Consumer Reports* study. *American Psychologist, 51,* 1017–1024.

Studebaker, C. A., & Penrod, S. D. (1997). Pretrial publicity: The media, the law, and common sense. *Psychology, Public Policy, and Law, 3,* 428–460.

Sue, S., Smith, R. E., & Caldwell, C. (1973). Effects of inadmissible evidence on the decisions of simulated jurors: A moral dilemma. *Journal of Applied Social Psychology, 3,* 345–353.

Suedfeld, P., Wallace, M. D., & Thachuk, K. L. (1993). Changes in integrative complexity among Middle East leaders during the Persian Gulf crisis. *Journal of Social Issues, 49,* 183–199.

Sugarman, D. B. (1986). Active versus passive euthanasia: An attributional analysis. *Journal of Applied Social Psychology, 16,* 60–76.

Sugarman, D. B., & Hotaling, G. T. (1989). Dating violence: Prevalence, context, and risk markers. In M. A. Pirog-Good & J. E. Stets (Eds.), *Violence in dating relationships: Emerging social issues* (pp. 3–32). New York: Praeger.

Suls, J., & Wan, C. K. (1993). The relationship between trait hostility and cardiovascular reactivity: A quantitative review and analysis. *Psychophysiology, 30,* 615–636.

Suls, J., Wan, C. K., & Sanders, G. S. (1988). False consensus and false uniqueness in estimating the prevalence of health-protective behaviors. *Journal of Applied Social Psychology, 18,* 66–79.

Suls, J., & Wills, T. A. (Eds.). (1991). *Social comparison: Contemporary theory and research.* Hillsdale, NJ: Erlbaum.

Sundstrom, E. (1986). *Work places.* New York: Cambridge University Press.

Sundstrom, E., Busby, P. L., & Bobrow, W. S. (1997). Group process and performance: Interpersonal behaviors and decision quality in group problem solving by consensus. *Group Dynamics, 1,* 241–253.

Surra, C. A., & Huston, T. L. (1987). Mate selection as a social transition. In D. Perlman & S. Duck (eds.), *Intimate relationships: Development, dynamics, and deterioration* (pp. 88–120). Newbury Park, CA: Sage.

Sutker, P. B., Uddo, M., Brailey, K., & Allain, A. N., Jr., (1993). War-zone trauma and stress-related symptoms in Operation Desert Shield/Storm (ODS) returnees. *Journal of Social Issues, 49,* 33–49.

Swain, P. (1997, October 25). Culture battle over a cruel mutilation. *The Dominion* (Wellington), p. 25.

Swallow, S. R., & Kuiper, N. A. (1993). Social comparison in dysphoria and nondysphoria: Differences in target similarity and specificity. *Cognitive Therapy and Research, 17,* 103–122.

Swann, W. B., Jr. (1984). Quest for accuracy in person perception: A matter of pragmatics. *Psychological Review, 91,* 457–477.

Swann, W. B., Jr. (1987). Identity negotiation: Where two roads meet. *Journal of Personality and Social Psychology, 53,* 1038–1051.

Swann, W. B., Jr. (1997). The trouble with change: Self-verification and allegiance to the self. *Psychological Science, 8,* 177–180.

Swann, W. B., Jr., & Ely, R. J. (1984). A battle of wills: Self-verification versus behavioral confirmation. *Journal of Personality and Social Psychology, 46,* 1287–1302.

Swann, W. B., Jr., & Hill, C. A. (1982). When our identities are mistaken: Reaffirming self-conceptions through social interaction. *Journal of Personality and Social Psychology, 43,* 59–66.

Swann, W. B., Jr., Hixon, J. G., & De La Ronde, C. (1992). Embracing the bitter "truth": Negative self-concepts and marital commitment. *Psychological Science, 3,* 118–121.

Swann, W. B., Jr., Stein-Seroussi, A., & Giesler, B. J. (1992). Why people self-verify. *Journal of Personality and Social Psychology, 62,* 392–401.

Sweeney, P. D., Anderson, K., & Bailey, S. (1986). Attributional style in depression: A meta-analytic review. *Journal of Personality and Social Psychology, 50,* 974–991.

Swim, J. K. (1994). Perceived versus meta-analytic effect sizes: An assessment of the accuracy of gender stereotypes. *Journal of Personality and Social Psychology, 66,* 21–36.

Swim, J. K., Aikin, K. J., Hall, W. S., & Hunter, B. A. (1995). Sexism and racism: Old-fashioned and modern prejudices. *Journal of Personality and Social Psychology, 68,* 199–214.

Swim, J., Borgida, E., Maruyama, G., & Myers, D. G. (1989). Joan McKay versus John McKay: Do gender stereotypes bias evaluations? *Psychological Bulletin, 105,* 409–429.

Szymanski, L. A., Devlin, A. S., Chrisler, J. C., & Vyse, S. A. (1993). Gender role and attitudes toward rape in male and female college students. *Sex Roles, 29,* 37–57.

Tajfel, H. (Ed.). (1982). *Social identity and intergroup relations.* London: Cambridge University Press.

Tajfel, H., Billig, M. G., Bundy, R. P., & Flament, C. (1971). Social categorization and intergroup behavior. *European Journal of Social Psychology, 1,* 149–178.

Tanford, S., & Penrod, S. (1984). Social influence model: A formal integration of research on majority and minority influence processes. *Psychological Bulletin, 95,* 189–225.

Tang, S., & Hall, V. C. (1995). The overjustification effect: A meta-analysis. *Applied Cognitive Psychology, 9,* 365–404.

Tangney, J. P., Wagner, P. E., Hill-Barlow, D., Marschall, D. E., & Gramzow, R. (1996). Relation of shame and guilt to constructive versus destructive responses to anger across the lifespan. *Journal of Personality and Social Psychology, 70,* 797–809.

Tannen, D. (1990). *You just don't understand: Women and men in conversation.* New York: Morrow.

Tarde, G. (1890). *Les lois de l'imitation. Étude sociologique.* Paris: Félix Alcan.

Tassinary, L. G., & Cacioppo, J. T. (1992). Unobservable facial actions and emotion. *Psychological Science, 3,* 28–33.

Tate, D. C., Reppucci, N. D., & Mulvey, E. P. (1995). Violent juvenile delinquents: Treatment effectiveness and implications for future action. *American Psychologist, 50,* 777–781.

Tavris, C. (1992). *The mismeasure of woman.* New York: Simon & Schuster.

Taylor, D. M., & Moghaddam, F. M. (1994). *Theories of intergroup relations* (2nd ed.). Westport, CT: Praeger.

Taylor, S. E. (1989). *Positive illusions: Creative self-deceptions and the healthy mind.* New York: Basic Books.

Taylor, S. E. (1990). Health psychology: The science and the field. *American Psychologist, 45,* 40–50.

Taylor, S. E. (1991). Asymmetrical effects of positive and negative events: The mobilization-minimization hypothesis. *Psychological Bulletin, 110,* 67–85.

Taylor, S. E., & Brown, J. D. (1988). Illusion and well-being: A social psychological perspective on mental health. *Psychological Bulletin, 103,* 193–210.

Taylor, S. E., & Brown, J. D. (1994). Positive illusions and well-being revisited: Separating fact from fiction. *Psychological Bulletin, 116,* 21–27.

Taylor, S. E., Falke, R. L., Shoptaw, S. J., & Lichtman, R. R. (1986). Social support, support groups, and the cancer patient. *Journal of Consulting and Clinical Psychology, 54,* 608–615.

Taylor, S. E., & Fiske, S. T. (1975). Point of view and perceptions of causality. *Journal of Personality and Social Psychology, 32,* 439–445.

Taylor, S. E., & Lobel, M. (1989). Social comparison activity under threat: Downward evaluation and upward contacts. *Psychological Review, 96,* 569–575.

Taylor, S. E., Repetti, R. L., & Seeman, T. (1997). Health psychology: What is an unhealthy environment and how does it get under the skin? *Annual Review of Psychology, 48,* 411–447.

Taylor, S. L., O'Neal, E. C., Langley, T., & Butcher, A. H. (1991). Anger arousal, deindividuation, and aggression. *Aggressive Behavior, 17,* 193–206.

Tedeschi, J. T. (Ed.). (1981). *Impression management theory and social psychological research.* New York: Academic Press.

Tedeschi, J. T. (1997, October). *Lab experiments under-represent the construct of aggression.* Paper presented to the New England Social Psychological Association, Williamstown, MA.

Tedeschi, J. T., Schlenker, B. R., & Bonoma, T. V. (1971). Cognitive dissonance: Private ratiocination or public spectacle? *American Psychologist, 26,* 685–695.

Teger, A. (1980). *Too much invested to quit.* New York: Pergamon Press.

Teitelbaum, S., & Geiselman, R. E. (1997). Observer mood and cross-racial cognition of faces. *Journal of Cross Cultural Psychology, 28,* 93–106.

Terkel, S. (1974). *Working.* New York: Pantheon Books.

Terkel, S. (1992). *Race: How blacks and whites think and feel about the American obsession.* New York: New Press.

Terre, L., Drabman, R. S., & Speer, P. (1991). Health-relevant behaviors in media. *Journal of Applied Social Psychology, 21,* 1303–1319.

Terry, D. J. (1994). Determinants of coping: The role of stable and situational factors. *Journal of Personality and Social Psychology, 66,* 895–910.

Tesser, A. (1978). Self-generated attitude change. In L. Berkowitz (Ed.), *Advances in experimental social psychology* (Vol. 11, pp. 288–338). New York: Academic Press.

Tesser, A. (1980). Self-esteem maintenance in family dynamics. *Journal of Personality and Social Psychology, 39,* 77–91.

Tesser, A. (1988). Toward a self-evaluation maintenance model of social behavior. In L. Berkowitz (Ed.), *Advances in experimental social psychology* (Vol. 21, pp. 181–227). New York: Academic Press.

Tesser, A. (1993). The importance of heritability in psychological research: The case of attitudes. *Psychological Review, 100,* 129–142.

Tesser, A., & Collins, J. E. (1988). Emotion in social reflection and comparison situations: Intuitive, systematic, and exploratory approaches. *Journal of Personality and Social Psychology, 55,* 695–709.

Tesser, A., & Smith, J. (1980). Some effects of task relevance and friendship on helping: You don't always help the one you like. *Journal of Experimental Social Psychology, 16,* 582–590.

Tesser, A., Pilkington, C. J., & McIntosh, W. D. (1989). Self-evaluation maintenance and the mediational role of emotion: The perception of friends and strangers. *Journal of Personality and Social Psychology, 57,* 442–456.

Tetlock, P. E. (1988). Monitoring the integrative complexity of American and Soviet foreign policy rhetoric: What can be learned? *Journal of Social Issues, 44,* 101–131.

Tetlock, P. E. (1998). Social psychology and world politics. In D. T. Gilbert, S. T. Fiske, & G. Lindzey (Eds.), *The handbook of social psychology* (4th ed., Vol. 2, pp. 868–912). New York: McGraw-Hill.

Tetlock, P. E., Peterson, R. S., McQuire, C., Chang, S., & Feld, P. (1992). Assessing political group dynamics: A test of the groupthink model. *Journal of Personality and Social Psychology, 63,* 403–425.

t'Hart, P., Stern, E., & Sundelius, B. (1995). *Beyond groupthink.* Stockholm: Stockholm Center for Organizational Research.

Thibaut, J. W., & Kelley, H. H. (1959). *The social psychology of groups.* New York: Wiley.

Thibaut, J., & Walker, L. (1975). *Procedural justice: A psychological analysis.* Hillsdale, NJ: Erlbaum.

Thibaut, J., & Walker, L. (1978). A theory of procedure. *California Law Review, 66,* 541–566.

Thibodeau, R. (1989). From racism to tokenism: The changing face of blacks in *New Yorker* cartoons. *Public Opinion Quarterly, 53,* 482–494.

Thibodeau, R., & Aronson, E. (1992). Taking a closer look: Reasserting the role of the self-concept in dissonance theory. *Personality and Social Psychology Bulletin, 18,* 591–602.

Thoits, P. A. (1983). Dimensions of life events that influence psychological distress: An evaluation and synthesis of the literature. In H. B. Kaplan (Ed.), *Psychosocial stress: Trends in theory and research* (pp. 33–103). New York: Academic Press.

Thomas, M. H. (1982). Physiological arousal, exposure to a relatively lengthy aggressive film, and aggressive behavior. *Journal of Research in Personality, 16,* 72–81.

Thompson, L. (1990). Negotiation behavior and outcomes: Empirical evidence and theoretical issues. *Psychological Bulletin, 108,* 515–532.

Thompson, L. (1991). Information exchange in negotiation. *Journal of Experimental Social Psychology, 27,* 161–179.

Thompson, L. (1995). "They saw a negotiation": Partisanship and involvement. *Journal of Personality and Social Psychology, 68,* 839–853.

Thompson, L., & Hrebec, D. (1996). Lose-lose agreements in interdependent decision making. *Psychological Bulletin, 120,* 396–409.

Thompson, L., Peterson, E., & Brodt, S. E. (1996). Team negotiation: An examination of integrative and distributive bargaining. *Journal of Personality and Social Psychology, 70,* 66–78.

Thompson, L., Valley, K. L., & Kramer, R. M. (1995). The bittersweet feeling of success: An examination of social perception in negotiation. *Journal of Experimental Social Psychology, 31,* 467–492.

Thompson, S. C., Kohles, J. C., Otsuki, T. A., & Kent, D. R. (1997). Perceptions of attitudinal similarity in ethnic groups in the US: Ingroup and outgroup homogeneity effects. *European Journal of Social Psychology, 27,* 209–220.

Thompson, S. C., Sobolew-Shubin, A., Galbraith, M. E., Schwankovsky, L., & Cruzen, D. (1993). Maintaining perceptions of control: Finding perceived control in low-control circumstances. *Journal of Personality and Social Psychology, 64,* 293–304.

Thompson, W. M., Dabbs, J. M., Jr., & Frady, R. L. (1990). Changes in saliva testosterone levels during a 90-day shock incarceration program. *Criminal Justice and Behavior, 17,* 246–252.

Thornton, B. (1992). Repression and its mediating influence on the defensive attribution of responsibility. *Journal of Research in Personality, 26,* 44–57.

Thornton, B., & Moore, S. (1993). Physical attractiveness contrast effect: Implications for self-esteem and evaluation of the social self. *Personality and Social Psychology Bulletin, 19,* 474–480.

Thornton, B., Hogate, L., Moirs, K., Pinette, M., & Presby, W. (1986). Physiological evidence for an arousal-based motivational bias in the defensive attribution of responsibility. *Journal of Experimental Social Psychology, 22,* 148–162.

Thornton, G. C., III, & Byham, W. C. (1982). *Assessment centers and managerial performance.* New York: Academic Press.

Thurstone, L. L. (1928). Attitudes can be measured. *American Journal of Sociology, 33,* 529–544.

Tice, D. M. (1991). Esteem protection or enhancement? Self-handicapping motives and attributions differ by trait self-esteem. *Journal of Personality and Social Psychology, 60,* 711–725.

Tice, D. M., & Baumeister, R. F. (1997). Longitudinal study of procrastination, performance, stress, and health: The costs and benefits of dawdling. *Psychological Science, 8,* 454–458.

Tidwell, M. C. O., Reis, H. T., & Shaver, P. R. (1996). Attachment, attractiveness, and social interaction: A diary study. *Journal of Personality and Social Psychology, 71,* 729–745.

Tilker, H. A. (1970). Socially responsible behavior as a function of observer responsibility and victim feedback. *Journal of Personality and Social Psychology, 14,* 95–100.

Time, (1994, June 27). p. 26.

Tisak, M. S., & Tisak, J. (1996). My sibling's but not my friend's keeper: Reasoning about responses to aggressive acts. *Journal of Early Adolescence, 16,* 324–339.

Tobin, R. J., & Eagles, M. (1992). U.S. and Canadian attitudes toward international interactions: A cross-national test of the double-standard hypothesis. *Basic and Applied Social Psychology, 13,* 447–459.

Tolstedt, B. E., & Stokes, J. P. (1984). Self-disclosure, intimacy, and the depenetration process. *Journal of Personality and Social Psychology, 46,* 84–90.

Tomada, G., & Schneider, B. H. (1997). Relational aggression, gender, and peer acceptance: Invariance across culture, stability over time, and concordance among informants. *Developmental Psychology, 33,* 601–609.

Toobin, J. (1996, September 9). The Marcia Clark verdict. *New Yorker,* pp. 58–71.

Top, T. J. (1991). Sex bias in the evaluation of performance in the scientific, artistic, and literary professions: A review. *Sex Roles, 24,* 73–106.

Tosi, H. L., & Einbender, S. W. (1985). The effects of the type and amount of information in sex discrimination research: A meta-analysis. *Academy of Management Journal, 28,* 712–723.

Tougas, F., Brown, R., Beaton, A. M., & Joly, S. (1995). Neosexism: Plus ça change, plus c'est pareil. *Personality and Social Psychology Bulletin, 21,* 842–849.

Tourangeau, R., Rasinksi, K. A., & D'Andrade, R. (1991). Attitude structure and belief accessibility. *Journal of Experimental Social Psychology, 27,* 48–75.

Tourangeau, R., Smith, T. W., & Rasinski, K. A. (1997). Motivation to report sensitive behaviors on surveys: Evidence from a bogus pipeline experiment. *Journal of Applied Social Psychology, 27,* 209–222.

Trafimow, D., Silverman, E. S., Fan, R. M. T., & Law, J. S. F. (1997). The effects of language and priming on the relative accessibility of the private self and collective self. *Journal of Cross-Cultural Psychology, 28,* 107–123.

Trafimow, D., Triandis, H. C., & Goto, S. G. (1991). Some tests of the distinction between the private and collective self. *Journal of Personality and Social Psychology, 60,* 649–655.

Triandis, H. C. (1994). *Culture and social behavior.* New York: McGraw-Hill.

Triandis, H. C. (1995). *Individualism and collectivism.* Boulder, CO: Westview.

Tripathi, R. C., & Srivastava, R. (1981). Relative deprivation and intergroup attitudes. *European Journal of Social Psychology, 11,* 313–318.

Triplett, N. (1897-1898). The dynamogenic factors in pacemaking and competition. *American Journal of Psychology, 9,* 507–533.

Tripp, C., Jensen, T. D., & Carlson, L. (1994). The effects of multiple product endorsements by celebrities on consumers' attitudes and intentions. *Journal of Consumer Research, 20,* 535–547.

Trivers, R. L. (1971). The evolution of reciprocal altruism. *Quarterly Review of Biology, 46,* 35–57.

Trivers, R. L. (1972). Parental investment and sexual selection. In B. Campbell (Ed.), *Sexual selection and the descent of man* (pp. 136–179). Chicago: Aldine-Atherton.

Trivers, R. L. (1985). *Social evolution.* Menlo Park, CA: Benjamin/ Cummings.

Troll, L. E., & Skaff, M. M. (1997). Perceived continuity of self in very old age. *Psychology and Aging, 12,* 162–169.

Trope, Y. (1986). Identification and inferential processes in dispositional attribution. *Psychological Review, 93,* 239-257.

Trope, Y., & Alfieri, T. (1997). Effortfulness and flexibility of dispositional judgment processes. *Journal of Personality and Social Psychology, 73,* 662–674.

Trope, Y., Bassock, M., & Alon, E. (1984). The questions lay interviewers ask. *Journal of Personality, 52,* 90-106.

Tucker, P., & Aron, A. (1993). Passionate love and marital satisfaction at key transition points in the family life cycle. *Journal of Social and Clinical Psychology, 12,* 135-147.

Tuckman, B. W. (1965). Developmental sequence in small groups. *Psychological Bulletin, 63,* 384–399.

Tuckman, B. W., & Jensen, M. A. (1977). Stages of small-group development revisited. *Group and Organization Studies, 2,* 419–427.

Turner, J. C. (1987). *Rediscovering the social group: A self-categorization theory.* Oxford, England: Basil Blackwell.

Turner, J. C. (1991). *Social influence.* Pacific Grove, CA: Brooks/Cole.

Turner, J. C., & Oakes, P. J. (1989). Self-categorization theory and social influence. In P. B. Paulus (Ed.), *Psychology of group influence* (2nd ed., pp. 233-275). Hillsdale, NJ: Erlbaum.

Turner, J. C., Oakes, P. J., Haslam, S. A., & McGarty, C. (1994). Self and collective: Cognition and social context. *Personality and Social Psychology Bulletin, 20,* 454-463.

Turner, M. E., & Pratkanis, A. R. (1994). Affirmative action as help: A review of recipient reactions to preferential selection and affirmative action. *Basic and Applied Social Psychology, 15,* 43–70.

Turner, M. E., Pratkanis, A. R., Probasco, P., & Leve, C. (1992). Threat, cohesion, and group effectiveness: Testing a social identity maintenance perspective on groupthink. *Journal of Personality and Social Psychology, 63,* 781-796.

Turner, S. M., & Beidel, D. C. (1989). Social phobia: Clinical syndrome, diagnosis, and comorbidity. *Clinical Psychology Review, 9,* 3–18.

Turner-Bowker, D. M. (1996). Gender stereotyped descriptors in children's picture books: Does "curious Jane" exist in the literature? *Sex Roles, 35,* 461–488.

Tversky, A., & Kahneman, D. (1973). Availability: A heuristic for judging frequency and probability. *Cognitive Psychology, 5,* 207–232.

Tyler, T. R. (1994). Psychological models of the justice motive: Antecedents of distributive and procedural justice. *Journal of Personality and Social Psychology, 67,* 850–863.

Tyler, T. R., & Smith, H. J. (1998). Social justice and social movements. In D. T. Gilbert, S. T. Fiske, & G. Lindzey (Eds.), *The handbook of social psychology* (4th ed., Vol. 2, pp. 595–629). New York: McGraw-Hill.

Tyler, T., Lind, E. A., Ohbuchi, K., Sugawara, I., & Huo, Y. J. (1998). Conflict with outsiders: Disputing within and across cultural boundaries. *Personality and Social Psychology Bulletin, 24,* 137–146.

Uchino, B. N., Cacioppo, J. T., & Kiecolt-Glaser, J. K. (1996). The relationship between social support and physiological processes: A review with emphasis on underlying mechanisms and implications for health. *Psychological Bulletin, 119,* 488–531.

U.S. Bureau of the Census (1994). *Statistical Abstract of the United States: 1994.* Washington, DC: The Reference Press.

U.S. Department of Health, Education, and Welfare. (1974, May 30). Protection of human subjects. *Federal Register, 39*(105): 18914–20 (45CFR, part 46).

USA Today (1998, January 16). P. 1A.

Vaillant, G. E. (1977). *Adaptation to life.* Boston: Little, Brown.

Valacich, J. S., Dennis, A. R., & Connolly, T. (1994). Idea generation in computer-based groups: A new ending to an old story. *Organizational Behavior and Human Decision Processes, 57,* 448–467.

Vallone, R. P., Griffin, D. W., Lin, S., & Ross, L. (1990). Overconfident prediction of future actions and outcomes by self and others. *Journal of Personality and Social Psychology, 58,* 582–592.

van der Pligt, J., Otten, W., Richard, R., & van der Velde, F. (1993). Perceived risk of AIDS: Unrealistic optimism and self-protective action. In J. B. Pryor & G. D. Reeder (Eds.), *The social psychology of HIV infection* (pp. 39–58). Hillsdale, NJ: Erlbaum.

VanderStoep, S. W., & Shaughnessy, J. J. (1997). Taking a course in research methods improves reasoning about real-life events. *Teaching of Psychology, 24,* 122–124.

VanderZee, K. I., Buunk, B. P., DeRuiter, J. H., Tempelaar, R., VanSonderen, E., & Sanderman, R. (1996). Social comparison and the subjective well-being of cancer patients. *Basic and Applied Social Psychology, 18,* 453–468.

Van Dyne, L., & Saavedra, R. (1996). A naturalistic minority influence experiment: Effects on divergent thinking, conflict, and originality in work-groups. *British Journal of Social Psychology, 35,* 151–167.

Van Eerde, W., & Thierry, H. (1996). Vroom's expectancy models and work-related criteria: A meta-analysis. *Journal of Applied Psychology, 81,* 575–586.

Van Goozen, S. H. M., Cohen-Kettenis, P. T., Gooren, L. J. G., & Frijda, N. H., et al. (1995). Gender differences in behaviour: Activating effects of cross-sex hormones. *Psychoneuroendocrinology, 20,* 343–363.

Van Lange, P. A. M. (1992). Rationality and morality in social dilemmas: The influence of social value orientations. In W. B. G. Liebrand, D. M. Messick, & H. A. M. Wilke (Eds.), *Social dilemmas: Theoretical issues and research findings* (pp. 133–146). Oxford: Pergamon Press.

Van Lange, P. A., & Liebrand, W. B. (1991). The influence of other's morality and own social value orientation on cooperation in the Netherlands and the U. S. A. *International Journal of Psychology, 26,* 429–449.

Van Vugt, M., Van Lange, P. A. M., & Meertens, R. E. (1996). Commuting by car or public transportation? A social dilemma analysis of travel mode judgments. *European Journal of Social Psychology, 26,* 373–395.

Vaughan, K. (1997, November 22). Racist describes killing black man. *Rocky Mountain News,* p. 5A.

Vecchio, R. P. (1983). Assessing the validity of Fiedler's contingency model of leadership effectiveness: A closer look at Strube and Garcia. *Psychological Bulletin, 93,* 404–408.

Vinokur, A., & Burnstein, E. (1974). Effects of partially shared persuasive arguments on group-induced shifts: A group-problem-solving approach. *Journal of Personality and Social Psychology, 29,* 305–315.

Visintainer, M., Volpicelli, J., & Seligman, M. (1982). Tumor rejection in rats after inescapable or escapable shock. *Science, 216,* 437–439.

von Hippel, W., Sekaquaptewa, D., & Vargas, P. (1995). On the role of encoding processes in stereotype maintenance. *Advances in Experimental Social Psychology, 27,* 177–254.

Vonk, R., & van-Knippenberg, A. (1995). Processing attitude statements from in-group and out-group members: Effects of within-group and within-person inconsistencies on reading times. *Journal of Personality and Social Psychology, 68,* 215–227.

Von Lang, J., & Sibyll, C. (Eds.). (1983). *Eichmann interrogated* (R. Manheim, Trans.). New York: Farrar, Straus & Giroux.

Vrij, A. (1997). Wearing black clothes: The impact of offenders' and suspects' clothing on impression formation. *Applied Cognitive Psychology, 11,* 47–53.

Vroom, V. H. (1964). *Work and motivation.* New York: Wiley.

Vroom, V. H., & Jago, A. G. (1988). *Managing participation in organizations.* Englewood Cliffs, NJ: Prentice-Hall.

Vroom, V. H., & Yetton, P. W. (1973). *Leadership and decision-making.* Pittsburgh: University of Pittsburgh Press.

Waldman, D. A., & Avolio, B. J. (1991). Race effects in performance evaluations: Controlling for ability, education, and experience. *Journal of Applied Psychology, 76,* 897–901.

Walker, L., LaTour, S., Lind, E. A., & Thibaut, J. (1974). Reactions of participants and observers to modes of adjudication. *Journal of Applied Social Psychology, 4,* 295–310.

Walster, E. (1966). Assignment of responsibility for important events. *Journal of Personality and Social Psychology, 3,* 73–79.

Walster, E., Aronson, V., Abrahams, D., & Rottman, L. (1966). The importance of physical attractiveness in dating behavior. *Journal of Personality and Social Psychology, 4,* 508–516.

Walster, E., & Festinger, L. (1962). The effectiveness of "overheard" persuasive communications. *Journal of Abnormal and Social Psychology, 65,* 395–402.

Walster, E., Walster, G. W., & Berscheid, E. (1978). *Equity: Theory and research.* Boston: Allyn & Bacon.

Walster, E., Walster, G. W., Piliavin, J., & Schmidt, L. (1973). "Playing hard-to-get": Understanding an elusive phenomenon. *Journal of Personality and Social Psychology, 26,* 113–121.

Walster, E., Walster, G. W., & Traupmann, J. (1978). Equity and premarital sex. *Journal of Personality, 36,* 82–92.

Warren, B. L. (1966). A multiple variable approach to the assortive mating phenomenon. *Eugenics Quarterly, 13,* 285–298.

Warshaw, R. (1988). *I never called it rape.* New York: Harper & Row.

Watson, D. (1982). The actor and the observer: How are their perceptions of causality divergent? *Psychological Bulletin, 92,* 682–700.

Watson, D. (1988). The vicissitudes of mood measurement: Effects of varying descriptors, time frames, and response formats on measures of positive and negative affect. *Journal of Personality and Social Psychology, 55,* 128–141.

Watson, D., Clark, L. A., McIntyre, C., & Hamaker, S. (1992). Affect, personality, and social activity. *Journal of Personality and Social Psychology, 63,* 1011–1025.

We're sorry: A case of mistaken identity. (1982, October 4). *Time,* p. 45.

Weary, G., & Edwards, J. A. (1994). Individual differences in causal uncertainty. *Journal of Personality and Social Psychology, 67,* 308–318.

Weber, J. G. (1994). The nature of ethnocentric attribution bias: Ingroup protection or enhancement? *Journal of Experimental Social Psychology, 30,* 482–504.

Weber, R., & Crocker, J. C. (1983). Cognitive processes in the revision of stereotypic beliefs. *Journal of Personality and Social Psychology, 45,* 961–967.

Webster, D. M. (1993). Motivated augmentation and reduction of the overattribution bias. *Journal of Personality and Social Psychology, 65,* 261–271.

Webster, D. M., Kruglanski, A. W., & Pattison, D. A. (1997). Motivated language use in intergroup contexts: Need-for-closure effects on the linguistic intergroup bias. *Journal of Personality and Social Psychology, 72,* 1122–1131.

Webster, D. M., Richter, L., & Kruglanski, A. W. (1996). On leaping to conclusions when feeling tired: Mental fatigue effects on impressional primacy. *Journal of Experimental Social Psychology, 32,* 181–195.

Wegener, D. T., & Petty, R. E. (1994). Mood management across affective states: The hedonic contingency hypothesis. *Journal of Personality and Social Psychology, 66,* 1034–1048.

Wegener, D. T., Petty, R. E., & Smith, S. M. (1995). Positive mood can increase or decrease message scrutiny: The hedonic contingency view of mood and message processing. *Journal of Personality and Social Psychology, 69,* 5–15.

Wegner, D. M. (1980). The self in prosocial action. In D. M. Wegner & R. R. Vallacher (Eds.), *The self in social psychology* (pp. 131–157). New York: Oxford University Press.

Wegner, D. M. (1994). Ironic processes of mental control. *Psychological Review, 101,* 34–52.

Wegner, D. M. (1997). When the antidote is the poison: Ironic mental control processes. *Psychological Science, 8,* 148–153.

Wegner, D. M., Ansfield, M., & Pilloff, D. (1998). The putt and the pendulum: Ironic effects of the mental control of action. *Psychological Science, 9,* 196–199.

Wegner, D. M., Lane, J. D., & Dimitri, S. (1994). The allure of secret relationships. *Journal of Personality and Social Psychology, 66,* 287–300.

Weinberg, K. M., & Tronick, E. Z. (1997). Maternal depression and infant maladjustment: A failure of mutual regulation. In

J. Noshpitz (Ed.), *The handbook of child and adolescent psychiatry*. New York: Wiley.

Weiner, B. (1985). "Spontaneous" causal thinking. *Psychological Bulletin, 97,* 74–84.

Weiner, B. (1996). Searching for order in social motivation. *Psychological Inquiry, 7,* 199–216.

Weingardt, K. R., Loftus, E. F., & Lindsay, D. S. (1995). Misinformation revisited: New evidence on the suggestibility of memory. *Memory and Cognition, 23,* 72–82.

Weinstein, N. D. (1980). Unrealistic optimism about future life events. *Journal of Personality and Social Psychology, 39,* 806–820.

Weinstein, N. D. (1989). Effects of personal experience on self-protective behavior. *Psychological Bulletin, 105,* 31–50.

Weinstein, N. D., & Nicolich, M. (1993). Correct and incorrect interpretations of correlations between risk perceptions and risk behaviors. *Health Psychology, 12,* 235–245.

Weiss, D. E. (1991). *The great divide.* New York: Simon & Schuster.

Weiss, H. M., & Knight, P. A. (1980). The utility of humility: Self-esteem, information search, and problem-solving efficiency. *Organizational Behavior and Human Performance, 25,* 216–223.

Weldon, E., & Gargano, G. M. (1988). Cognitive loading: The effects of accountability and shared responsibility on cognitive effort. *Personality and Social Psychology Bulletin, 14,* 159–171.

Weldon, M. S., & Bellinger, K. D. (1997). Collective memory: Collaborative and individual processes in remembering. *Journal of Experimental Psychology: Learning, Memory, and Cognition, 23,* 1160–1175.

Wells, G. L. (1986). Expert psychological testimony: Empirical and conceptual analyses of effects. *Law and Human Behavior, 10,* 83–95.

Wells, G. L., Small, M., Penrod, S., Malpass, R. S., Fulero, S. M., & Brimacombe, C. A. E. (1998). Eyewitness Identification Procedures: Recommendations for Lineups and Photospreads. *Law and Human Behavior.*

Wells, G. L., & Bradfield, A. L. (1998). "Good, you identified the suspect": Feedback to eyewitnesses distorts their reports of the witnessing experience. *Journal of Applied Psychology, 83,* 360–376.

Wells, G. L., Lindsay, R. C. L., & Ferguson, T. J. (1979). Accuracy, confidence, and juror perceptions in eyewitness identification. *Journal of Applied Psychology, 64,* 440–448.

Wells, G. L., & Murray, D. M. (1984). Eyewitness confidence. In G. Wells & E. Loftus (Eds.), *Eyewitness testimony: Psychological perspectives* (pp. 155–170). New York: Cambridge University Press.

Wells, G. L., & Petty, R. E. (1980). The effects of overt head-movements on persuasion: Compatibility and incompatibility of responses. *Basic and Applied Social Psychology, 1,* 219–230.

Westman, M., & Eden, D. (1997). Effects of a respite from work on burnout: Vacation relief and fade-out. *Journal of Applied Psychology, 82,* 516–527.

Wheeler, L., & Kim, Y. (1997). What is beautiful is culturally good: The physical attractiveness stereotype has different content in collectivist cultures. *Personality and Social Psychology Bulletin, 23,* 795–800.

Wheeler, L., Koestner, R., & Driver, R. E. (1982). Related attributes in the choice of comparison others. *Journal of Experimental Social Psychology, 18,* 489–500.

Wheeler, L., & Miyake, K. (1992). Social comparison in everyday life. *Journal of Personality and Social Psychology, 62,* 760–773.

Wheeler, L., Reis, H. T., & Bond, M. H. (1989). Collectivism-individualism in everyday social life: The middle kingdom and the melting pot. *Journal of Personality and Social Psychology, 57,* 79–86.

Whitbeck, L. B., & Hoyt, D. R. (1994). Social prestige and assortive mating: A comparison of students from 1956 and 1988. *Journal of Social and Personal Relationships, 11,* 137–145.

White, G. F. (1989). Media and violence: The case of professional football championship games. *Aggressive Behavior, 15,* 423–433.

White, G. L. (1981). A model of romantic jealousy. *Motivation and Emotion, 5,* 295–310.

White, G. L., Fishbein, S., & Rutstein, J. (1981). Passionate love: The misattribution of arousal. *Journal of Personality and Social Psychology, 41,* 56–62.

White, G. L., & Mullen, P. E. (1989). *Jealousy: Theory, research, and clinical strategies.* New York: Guilford.

White, J. E. (1997, May 5). "I'm just who I am." *Time,* pp. 32–36.

White, P. A., & Younger, D. P. (1988). Differences in the ascription of transient internal states to self and other. *Journal of Experimental Social Psychology, 24,* 292–309.

Whittaker, J. O., & Meade, R. D. (1967). Social pressure in the modification and distortion of judgment: A cross-cultural study. *International Journal of Psychology, 2,* 109–113.

Whyte, G. (1991). Diffusion of responsibility: Effects on the escalation tendency. *Journal of Applied Psychology, 76,* 408–415.

Whyte, G. (1993). Escalating commitment in individual and group decision making: A prospect theory approach. *Organizational Behavior and Human Decision Processes, 54,* 430–455.

Wicker, A. W. (1969). Attitudes versus actions: The relationship between verbal and overt behavioral responses to attitude objects. *Journal of Social Issues, 25*(4), 41–78.

Wicklund, R. A. (1975). Objective self-awareness. In L. Berkowitz (Ed.), *Advances in experimental social psychology* (Vol. 8, pp. 233–275). New York: Academic Press.

Wicklund, R. A., & Frey, D. (1980). Self-awareness theory: When the self makes a difference. In D. M. Wegner & R. R. Vallacher (Eds.), *The self in social psychology* (pp. 31–54). New York: Oxford University Press.

Widmeyer, W. N., & Ducharme, K. (1997). Team building through team goal setting. *Journal of Applied Sport Psychology, 9,* 97–113.

Widmeyer, W. N., & Loy, J. W. (1988). When you're hot, you're hot! Warm-cold effects in first impressions of persons and teaching effectiveness. *Journal of Educational Psychology, 80,* 118–121.

Wiedenfeld, S. A., O'Leary, A., Bandura, A., Brown, S., Levine, S., & Raska, K. (1990). Impact of perceived self-efficacy in coping with stressors on components of the immune system. *Journal of Personality and Social Psychology, 59,* 1082–1094.

Wiederman, M. W., & Allgeier, E. R. (1992). Gender differences in mate selection criteria: Sociobiological or socioeconomic explanation? *Ethology and Sociobiology, 13,* 115–124.

Wiesner, W. H., & Cronshaw, S. F. (1988). A meta-analytic investigation of the impact of interview format and degree of structure on the validity of the employment interview. *Journal of Occupational Psychology, 61,* 275–290.

Wiggins, J. S. (Ed.) (1996). *The five-factor model of personality: Theoretical perspectives.* New York: Guilford.

Wilder, D. A. (1977). Perception of groups, size of opposition, and social influence. *Journal of Experimental Social Psychology, 13,* 253–268.

Wilder, D. A. (1986). Social categorization: Implications for creation and reduction of intergroup bias. In L. Berkowitz (Ed.), *Advances in experimental social psychology* (Vol. 19, pp. 291–355). New York: Academic Press.

Wilder, D. A. (1993). The role of anxiety in facilitating stereotypic judgment of outgroup behavior. In D. M. Mackie & D. L. Hamilton (Eds.), *Affect, cognition, and stereotyping: Interactive processes in group perception* (pp. 87–109). San Diego: Academic Press.

Wilder, D. A., Simon, A. F., & Myles, F. (1996). Enhancing the impact of counterstereotypic information: Dispositional attributions for deviance. *Journal of Personality and Social Psychology, 71*, 276–287.

Williams v. *Florida*, 399 U.S. 78 (1970).

Williams, J. E., & Best, D. L. (1982). *Measuring sex stereotypes: A thirty nation study.* Beverly Hills, CA: Sage.

Williams, K. D. (1998). Social ostracism. In R. Kowalski (Ed.), *Aversive interpersonal behavior.* New York: Plenum.

Williams, K. D., Nida, S. A., Baca, L. D., & Latané, B. (1989). Social loafing and swimming: Effects of identifiability on individual and relay performance of intercollegiate swimmers. *Basic and Applied Social Psychology, 10*, 73–81.

Williams, K. R. (1992). Social sources of marital violence and deterrence: Testing an integrated theory of assaults between partners. *Journal of Marriage and the Family, 54*, 620–629.

Williams, M. (1997, December 5). Movie "factor" in school shootings. *Atlanta Constitution*, p. 3A.

Williams, R. (1993). *Anger kills.* New York: Times Books.

Williamson, G. M., & Clark, M. S. (1989). Providing help and desired relationship type as determinants of changes in moods and self-evaluations. *Journal of Personality and Social Psychology, 56*, 722–734.

Williamson, G. M., & Clark, M. S. (1992). Impact of desired relationship type on affective reactions to choosing and being required to help. *Personality and Social Psychology Bulletin, 18*, 10–18.

Williamson, G. M., Clark, M. S., Pegalis, L. J., & Behan, A. (1996). Affective consequences of refusing to help in communal and exchange relationships. *Personality and Social Psychology Bulletin, 22*, 34–47.

Wills, T. A. (1981). Downward comparison principles in social psychology. *Psychological Bulletin, 90*, 245–271.

Wills, T. A. (Ed.) (1990). Social support in social and clinical psychology [Special issue]. *Journal of Social and Clinical Psychology, 9*

Wills, T. A. (1992). The helping process in the context of personal relationships. In S. Spacapan & S. Oskamp (Eds.), *Helping and being helped: Naturalistic studies* (pp. 17–48). Newbury Park, CA: Sage.

Wills, T. A., & DePaulo, B. M. (1991). Interpersonal analysis of the help-seeking process. In C. R. Snyder & D. R. Forsyth (Eds.), *Handbook of social and clinical psychology: The health perspective* (pp. 350–375). New York: Pergamon Press.

Wilson, D. S., & Sober, E. (1994). Reintroducing group selection to the human behavioral sciences. *Behavioral and Brain Sciences, 17*, 585–654.

Wilson, D. W. (1981). Is helping a laughing matter? *Psychology, 18*, 6–9.

Wilson, J. P. (1976). Motivation, modeling, and altruism: A Person X Situation analysis. *Journal of Personality and Social Psychology, 34*, 1078–1086.

Wilson, M. I., & Daly, M. (1996). Male sexual proprietariness and violence against wives. *Current Directions in Psychological Science, 5*, 2–7.

Wilson, T. D. (1985). Strangers to ourselves: The origins and accuracy of beliefs about one's own mental states. In J. H. Harvey & G. Weary (Eds.), *Attribution: Basic issues and applications* (pp. 9–36). New York: Academic Press.

Wilson, T. D., & LaFleur, S. J. (1995). Knowing what you'll do: Effects of analyzing reasons on self-prediction. *Journal of Personality and Social Psychology, 68*, 21–35.

Wilson, T. D., & Schooler, J. W. (1991). Thinking too much: Introspection can reduce the quality of preferences and decisions. *Journal of Personality and Social Psychology, 60*, 181–192.

Winch, R. F., Ktsanes, I., & Ktsanes, V. (1954). The theory of complementary needs in mate selection: An analytic and descriptive study. *American Sociological Review, 19*, 241–249.

Winter, D. G. (1987). Leader appeal, leader performance, and the motive profiles of leaders and followers: A study of American presidents and elections. *Journal of Personality and Social Psychology, 52*, 41–46.

Wishman, S. (1986). *Anatomy of a jury: The system on trial.* New York: Times Books.

Wissler, R. L., & Saks, M. J. (1985). On the inefficacy of limiting instructions: When jurors use prior conviction evidence to decide on guilt. *Law and Human Behavior, 9*, 37–48.

Witte, K. (1992). Putting the fear back into fear appeals: The extended parallel process model. *Communication Monographs, 59*, 329–349.

Witteman, P. A. (1990, April 30). Vietnam: 15 years later. *Time*, pp. 19–21.

Wittenbrink, B., Judd. C. M., & Park, B. (1997). Evidence for racial prejudice at the implicit level and its relationship with questionnaire measures. *Journal of Personality and Social Psychology, 72*, 262–274.

Wolf, S., & Montgomery, D. A. (1977). Effects of inadmissible evidence and level of judicial admonishment to disregard on the judgments of mock jurors. *Journal of Applied Social Psychology, 7*, 205–219.

Wood, G. (1978). The knew-it-all-along effect. *Journal of Experimental Psychology: Human Perception and Performance, 4*, 345–353.

Wood, J. (1989). Theory and research concerning social comparisons of personal attributes. *Psychological Bulletin, 106*, 231–248.

Wood, J. V., Giordano-Beech, M., Taylor, K. L., Michela, J. L., & Gaus, V. (1994). Strategies of social comparison among people with low self-esteem: Self-protection and self-enhancement. *Journal of Personality and Social Psychology, 67*, 713–731.

Wood, J. V., Saltzberg, J. A., & Goldsamt, L. A. (1990). Does affect induce self-focused attention? *Journal of Personality and Social Psychology, 58*, 899–908.

Wood, J. V., Taylor, S. E., & Lichtman, R. R. (1985). Social comparison in adjustment to breast cancer. *Journal of Personality and Social Psychology, 49*, 1169–1183.

Wood, N., & Cowan, N. (1995). The cocktail party phenomenon revisited: How frequent are attention shifts to one's name in an irrelevant auditory channel? *Journal of Experimental Psychology: Learning, Memory, and Cognition, 21*, 255–260.

Wood, W. (1987). Meta-analytic review of sex differences in group performance. *Psychological Bulletin, 102*, 53–71.

Wood, W., Kallgren, C. A., & Preisler, R. M. (1985). Access to attitude-relevant information in memory as a determinant of persuasion: The role of message attributes. *Journal of Experimental Social Psychology, 21*, 73–85.

Wood, W., & Karten, S. J. (1986). Sex differences in interaction style as product of perceived sex differences in competence. *Journal of Personality and Social Psychology, 50*, 341–347.

Wood, W., Lundgren, S., Ouellette, J. A., Busceme, S., & Blackstone, T. (1994). Minority influence: A meta-analytic review of social influence processes. *Psychological Bulletin, 115*, 323–345.

Wood, W., Polek, D., & Aiken, C. (1985). Sex differences in group task performance. *Journal of Personality and Social Psychology, 48*, 63–71.

Wood, W., Pool, G. J., Leck, K., & Purvis, D. (1996). Self-definition, defensive processing, and influence: The normative impact of majority and minority groups. *Journal of Personality and Social Psychology, 71*, 1181–1193.

Wood, W., Wong, F. Y., & Chachere, J. G. (1991). Effects of media violence on viewers' aggression in unconstrained social interaction. *Psychological Bulletin, 109,* 371–383.

Woolfolk, R. L., Novalany, J., Gara, M. A., Allen, L. A., & Polino, M. (1995). Self-complexity, self-evaluation, and depression: An examination of form and content within the self-schema. *Journal of Personality and Social Psychology, 68,* 1108–1120.

Worchel, S. (1974). The effect of three types of arbitrary thwarting on the instigation to aggression. *Journal of Personality, 42,* 300–318.

Word, C. O., Zanna, M. P., & Cooper, J. (1974). The nonverbal mediation of self-fulfilling prophecies in interracial interaction. *Journal of Experimental Social Psychology, 10,* 109–120.

Worth, L. T., & Mackie, D. M. (1987). Cognitive mediation of positive affect in persuasion. *Social Cognition, 5,* 76–94.

Wright, L., von Bussman, K., Friedman, A., Khoury, M., & Owens, F. (1990). Exaggerated social control and its relationship to the Type A behavior pattern. *Journal of Research in Personality, 24,* 258–269.

Wright, P. H. (1982). Men's friendships, women's friendships and the alleged inferiority of the latter. *Sex Roles, 8,* 1–20.

Wright, P. H., & Keple, T. W. (1981). Friends and parents of a sample of high school juniors: An exploratory study of relationship intensity and interpersonal rewards. *Journal of Marriage and the Family, 43,* 559–570.

Wright, R. A., & Contrada, R. J. (1986). Dating selectivity and interpersonal attraction: Toward a better understanding of the "elusive phenomenon." *Journal of Social and Personal Relationships, 3,* 131–148.

Wright, R. A., Wadley, V. G., Danner, M., & Phillips, P. N. (1992). Persuasion, reactance, and judgments of interpersonal appeal. *European Journal of Social Psychology, 22,* 85–91.

Wrightsman, L. S., & Kassin, S. M. (1993). *Confessions in the courtroom.* Newbury Park, CA: Sage.

Wrightsman, L. S., Nietzel, M. T., & Fortune, W. H. (1998). *Psychology and the Legal System* (4th ed.). Pacific Grove, CA: Brooks/Cole.

Wuthnow, R. (1991). *Acts of compassion.* Princeton, NJ: Princeton University Press.

Yoshikawa, H. (1994). Prevention as cumulative protection: Effects of early family support and education on chronic delinquency and its risks. *Psychological Bulletin, 115,* 28–54.

Young, R. K., Kennedy, A. H., Newhouse, A., Browne, P., & Thiessen, D. (1993). The effects of names on perceptions of intelligence, popularity, and competence. *Journal of Applied Social Psychology, 23,* 1770–1788.

Youngs, G. A. (1986). Patterns of threat and punishment reciprocity in a conflict setting. *Journal of Personality and Social Psychology, 51* (3), 541–546.

Yuille, J. C., & Tollestrup, P. A. (1990). Some effects of alcohol on eyewitness memory. *Journal of Applied Psychology, 75,* 268–273.

Yzerbyt, V. Y., Leyens, J. P., & Bellour, F. (1995). The ingroup overexclusion effect: Identity concerns in decisions about group membership. *European Journal of Social Psychology, 25,* 1–16.

Zaccaro, S. J., & McCoy, M. C. (1988). The effects of task and interpersonal cohesiveness on performance of a disjunctive group task. *Journal of Applied Social Psychology, 18,* 837–851.

Zahn-Wexler, C., Robinson, J. L., & Emde, R. N. (1992). The development of empathy in twins. *Developmental Psychology, 28,* 1038–1047.

Zajonc, R. B. (1965). Social facilitation. *Science, 149,* 269–274.

Zajonc, R. B. (1968). Attitudinal effects of mere exposure. *Journal of Personality and Social Psychology Monograph Supplement, 9*(2), 1–27.

Zajonc, R. B. (1980). Compresence. In P. B. Paulus (Ed.), *Psychology of group influence* (pp. 35–60). Hillsdale, NJ: Erlbaum.

Zajonc, R. B. (1984). On the primacy of affect. *American Psychologist, 39,* 117–123.

Zajonc, R. B. (1993). Brain temperature and subjective emotional experience. In M. Lewis & J. M. Haviland (Eds.), *Handbook of emotions* (pp. 209–220). New York: Guilford.

Zajonc, R. B., Heingartner, A., & Herman, E. M. (1969). Social enhancement and impairment of performance in the cockroach. *Journal of Personality and Social Psychology, 13,* 82–92.

Zajonc, R. B., Murphy, S. T., & Inglehart, M. (1989). Feeling and facial efference: Implications of the vascular theory of emotion. *Psychological Review, 96,* 395–416.

Zanna, M. P., & Cooper, J. (1974). Dissonance and the pill: An attribution approach to studying the arousal properties of dissonance. *Journal of Personality and Social Psychology, 29,* 703–709.

Zanna, M. P., & Rempel, J. K. (1988). Attitudes: A new look at an old concept. In D. Bar-Tal & A. Kruglanski (Eds.), *The social psychology of knowledge* (pp. 315–334). New York: Cambridge University Press.

Zaraté, M., & Sandoval, P. (1995). The effects of contextual cues on making occupational and gender categorizations. *British Journal of Social Psychology, 34,* 353–362.

Zebrowitz-McArthur, L. A. (1996). *Reading faces.* Boulder, CO: Westview.

Zebrowitz-McArthur, L. A., & McDonald, S. M. (1991). The impact of litigants' babyfacedness and attractiveness on adjudications in small claims courts. *Law and Human Behavior, 15,* 603–624.

Zebrowitz-McArthur, L. A., Tenenbaum, D. R., & Goldstein, L. H. (1991). The impact of job applicants' facial maturity, gender, and academic achievement on hiring recommendations. *Journal of Applied Social Psychology, 21,* 525–548.

Zeisel, H., & Diamond, S. (1978). The effect of peremptory challenges on jury and verdict: An experiment in a federal district court. *Stanford Law Review, 30,* 491–531.

Zillmann, D. (1979). *Hostility and aggression.* Hillsdale, NJ: Erlbaum.

Zillmann, D. (1983). Arousal and aggression. In R. G. Geen & E. I. Donnerstein (Eds.), *Aggression: Theoretical and empirical reviews: Vol. l. Theoretical and methodological issues* (pp. 75–101). New York: Academic Press.

Zillmann, D. (1984). *Connections between sex and aggression.* Hillsdale, NJ: Erlbaum.

Zillmann, D. (1996). Sequential dependencies in emotional experience and behavior. In R. D. Kavanaugh, B. Zimmerberg, & S. Fein (Eds.), *Emotion: Interdisciplinary perspectives.* Mahwah, NJ: Erlbaum.

Zillmann, D., Baron, R., & Tamborini, R. (1981). Social costs of smoking: Effects of tobacco smoke on hostile behavior. *Journal of Applied Social Psychology, 11,* 548–561.

Zillmann, D., & Bryant, J. (1984). Effects of massive exposure to pornography. In N. M. Malamuth & E. I. Donnerstein (Eds.), *Pornography and sexual aggression* (pp. 115–138). New York: Academic Press.

Zillmann, D., Bryant, J., Cantor, J. R., & Day, K. D. (1975). Irrelevance of mitigating circumstances in retaliatory behavior at high levels of excitation. *Journal of Research in Personality, 9,* 282–293.

Zillmann, D., & Cantor, J. R. (1976). Effect of timing of information about mitigating circumstances on emotional responses to provocation and retaliatory behavior. *Journal of Experimental Social Psychology, 12,* 38–55.

Zillmann, D., Katcher, A. H., & Milavsky, B. (1972). Excitation transfer from physical exercise to subsequent aggressive behavior. *Journal of Experimental Social Psychology, 8,* 247–259.

Zillmann, D., & Weaver, J. B. (1989). Pornography and men's sexual callousness toward women. In D. Zillmann & J. Bryant (Eds.), *Pornography: Research advances and policy considerations* (pp. 95–125). Hillsdale: Erlbaum.

Zillmann, D., & Weaver, J. B., III. (1997). Psychoticism in the effect of prolonged exposure to gratuitous media violence on the acceptance of violence as a preferred means of conflict resolution. *Personality and Individual Differences, 22,* 613–627.

Zimbardo, P. G. (1969). The human choice: Individuation, reason, and order versus deindividuation, impulse, and chaos. *Nebraska Symposium on Motivation, 17,* 237–307.

Zimbardo, P. G. (1970). The human choice: Individuation, reason, and order versus deindividuation, impulse, and chaos. In W. J. Arnold & D. Levine (Eds.), *Nebraska Symposium on Motivation: 1969* (Vol. 17, pp. 237–307). Lincoln: University of Nebraska Press.

Zimbardo, P. G. (1977). *Shyness.* New York: Jove.

Zimbardo, P. G. (1985, June). Laugh where we must, be candid where we can. *Psychology Today,* pp. 43–47.

Zimbardo, P. G., Banks, W. C., Haney, C., & Jaffe, D. (1973, April 8). The mind is a formidable jailer: A Pirandellian prison. *New York Times Magazine,* pp. 38–60.

Zimbardo, P. G., LaBerge, S., & Butler, L. D. (1993). Psychophysiological consequences of unexplained arousal: A posthypnotic suggestion paradigm. *Journal of Abnormal Psychology, 102,* 466–473.

Zucker, G. S., & Weiner, B. (1993). Conservatism and perceptions of poverty: An attributional analysis. *Journal of Applied Social Psychology, 23,* 925–943.

Zuckerman, M., DePaulo, B. M., & Rosenthal, R. (1981). Verbal and nonverbal communication of deception. In L. Berkowitz (Ed.), *Advances in experimental social psychology* (Vol. 14, pp. 1–59). New York: Academic Press.

Zuckerman, M., & Kieffer, S. C. (1994). Race differences in faceism: Does facial prominence imply dominance? *Journal of Personality and Social Psychology, 66,* 86–92.

Zuckerman, M., Knee, C. R., Hodgins, H. S., & Miyake, K. (1995). Hypothesis confirmation: The joint effect of positive test strategy and acquiescence response set. *Journal of Personality and Social Psychology, 68,* 52–60.

Zuckerman, M., Lazzaro, M. M., & Waldgeir, D. (1979). Undermining effects of the foot-in-the-door technique with extrinsic rewards. *Journal of Applied Social Psychology, 9,* 292–296.

Zuwerink, J. R., & Devine, P. G. (1996). Attitude importance and resistance to persuasion: It's not just the thought that counts. *Journal of Personality and Social Psychology, 70,* 931–944.

Credits

Chapter 1: **p. 2** *(Opener):* Richard Pasley/Stock Boston. **p. 5:** © Stewart Cohen/Tony Stone Images. **p. 6:** © AP/Wide World Photos. **p. 9:** © Michael Newman/PhotoEdit. **p. 12:** © Gray Mortimore/Tony Stone Images. **p. 13** *(left):* © Rick Friedman/ Black Star. **p. 13** *(right):* © Alan L. Detrick/Photo Researchers. **p. 14:** © National Archives and Records Administration. **p. 17:** © Lorne Resnick/Tony Stone Images.

Chapter 2: **p. 22** *(Opener):* Comstock. **p. 25:** © Lisa Quinones/Black Star. **p. 26:** © AP/Wide World Photos. **p. 28:** © Kate Connell/Tony Stone Images. **p. 29:** *Table 2.1* M. Rosenberg, *Society and the Adolescent Self-Image.* Copyright © 1965. Reprinted by permission. **p. 30:** *Table 2.2* "How Many Hours of TV Did They Watch?" from N. Schwarz, H. J. Hippler, B. Deutsch, and F. Strack, "Response scales: effects of category range on reported behavior and comparative judgements," *Public Opinion Quarterly, 49* (1985): 388–395, published by The University of Chicago Press. Reprinted by permission of the publisher. **p. 31:** © Brian Smith/Stock Boston. **p. 32:** © Dan McCoy/Rainbow. **p. 34:** © Richard B. Levine. **p. 35** *(top):* © Robert Brenner/PhotoEdit. **p. 35** *(bottom):* © UPI/Corbis-Bettmann. **p. 36:** © Anthony Edgeworth/The Stock Market. **p. 41:** © L. Migdale/Photo Researchers. **p. 43:** *Figure 2.3* "Alcohol and Aggression: The Results" from K.E. Leonard, "The impact of explicit aggressive and implicit nonaggressive cues on aggression in intoxicated and sober roles," *Personality and Social Psychology Bulletin, 15* (1989): 390–400. Reprinted by permission of Sage Publications, Inc. **p. 45:** © Will & Deni McIntyre/Photo Researchers.

Chapter 3: **p. 54** *(Opener):* Marie Brimberg/Woodfin Camp. **p. 56:** © Ursula Markus/Photo Researchers. **p. 61:** © Jonathan Alcorn/ZUMA Press. **p. 62:** *Figure 3.1* From M.R. Lepper, D. Greene, and K.E. Nisbett, "Undermining, children's intrinsic interest with extrinsic reward: A test of the 'overjustification' hypothesis," *Journal of Personality and Social Psychology, 28* (1973): 129–137. Copyright © 1973 by the American Psychological Association. Reprinted by permission of the American Psychological Association and the author. **p. 65** *(left):* © Visual/ Gamma-Liaison. **p. 65** *(right):* © Visual/Gamma-Liaison. **p. 66:** *Figure 3.2* Bahrick, H.P., Hall, L.K., and Berger, S.A., "Accuracy and distortion in memory for high school grades." From *Psychological Science, 7* (1996): 265–271, Blackwell Publishers. Reprinted by permission of the publisher. **p. 67** *(left):* © J.P. Laffont/Sygma. **p. 67** *(right):* © Jeffrey Cadge/The Image Bank. **p. 68:** *Figure 3.3* From H.R. Markus and S. Kitayama, "Culture and the self: Implications for cognition, emotion, and motivation", *Psychological Review,* 98 (1991): 226. Copyright © 1991 by the American Psychological Association. Reprinted by permission. **p. 69:** *Figure 3.4* D. Trafimow, E.S. Silverman, R. Fan, and J.S.F. Law, "The effects of language and primitive in the relative accessibility of the private self and collective self," *Journal of Cross-Cultural Psychology 28* (1997). Copyright © 1997. Reprinted by permission of Sage Publications, Inc. **p. 74:** *Table*

3.1 From A. Fenigstein, M.F. Scheier, and A.H. Buss, "Public and private self-consciousness: Assessment and theory," *Journal of Consulting and Clinical Psychology 43* (1975): 522–527. Copyright © 1975 by the American Psychological Association. Reprinted by permission. **p. 75** *(top):* Figure 3.7 C.R. Snyder, R.L. Higgins, and R.J. Stucky, *Excuses: Masquerades in Search of Grace.* Copyright 1983. Reprinted by permission. **p. 75** *(bottom):* © Pierre-Paul Poulin/Sygma. **p. 77:** © Bachmann/Photo Researchers. **p. 78:** *Figure 3.9* From M.R. Lepper, D. Greene, and K.E. Nisbett, "Undermining children's intrinsic interest with extrinsic reward: A test of 'overjustification' hypothesis," *Journal of Personality and Social Psychology, 28* (1973): 129–137. Copyright © 1973 by the American Psychological Association. Reprinted by permission. **p. 79:** © J.L. Atlan/Sygma. **p. 81:** © Phyllis L. Méras. **p. 83:** © Brooks Kraft/Sygma. **p. 85:** *Figure 3.10* From W.B. Swann, Jr., A. Stein-Sercussi, and B.J. Giesler, *Journal of Personality and Social Psychology, 62* (1992): 392–401. Copyright © 1992 by the American Psychological Association. Reprinted by permission. **p. 86:** *Table 3.2* "Self-Monitoring Scale," from M. Snyder and S. Gangestad "On the nature of self monitoring: Matters of assessment, matters of validity," *Journal of Personality and Social Psychology 51,* (1986): 125–139. Copyright © 1986 by the American Psychological Association. Reprinted by permission.

Chapter 4: **p. 90** *(Opener):* David Hamilton/The Image Bank. **p. 92** *(left):* © AP/Wide World Photos. **p. 92** *(right):* © Reuters/Charles Platiau/Archive Photos. **p. 93:** © Corbis-Bettmann. **p. 94:** © AP/Wide World Photos. **p. 95:** © American Psychological Association. **p. 96** *(bottom right):* © Harry Scull/Allsport. **p. 97** *(top):* *Figure 4.2* "Some common e-mail 'emotions'," Reprinted with permission from *Smileys,* copyright © 1993, O'Reilly and Associates, Inc. For orders and information call 800-998-9938. **p. 97** *(bottom):* © Reuters/ Ahmed Jadallah/Archive Photos. **p. 98:** © AP/Wide World Photos. **p. 99** *(left):* © Agence France Press/Corbis-Bettmann. **p. 99** *(right):* © CNP/Archive Photos. **p. 100:** *Table 4.1* From P. Ekman and M. O'Sullivan, "Who can catch a liar?," *American Psychologist, 46* (1991): 913–920. Copyright © 1991 by the American Psychological Association. Reprinted by permission. **p. 102:** *Figure 4.3* "What Does This Speechwriter Really Believe?" from, "The attribution of attitudes," E.G. Jones and K.E. Harris, *Journal of Experimental and Social Psychology, 3* (1967): 1–24. Reprinted by permission of the Academic Press. **p. 105:** *Table 4.2* From J. Krueger and R.W. Clement, "The truly false consensus effect: An ineradicable and egocentric bias in social perception," *Journal of Personality and Social Psychology 64* (1994): 600. Copyright © 1994 by the American Psychological Association. Reprinted by permission. **p. 106:** © Photofest. **p. 107** *(top):* *Figure 4.5* L. Ross, T.M. Amabile, and J.L. Steinmetz, "Social roles, social control, and biases in social perception processes," *Journal of Personality and Social Psychology 35* (1977): 485–494. Copyright © 1977 by the American Psychological Association. Reprinted by permission. **p. 108:**

T., and Birch, K. "Is empathetic emotion a source of altruistic motivation?" *Journal of Personality and Social Psychology*, 40 (1981): 290–302. Copyright © 1981 by the American Psychological Association. Reprinted by permission. **p. 350:** *Figure 10.5* Fabes, R.A., Fultz, J., Eisenberg, N., May-Plumlee, T., and Christopher, F.S. "Effects of rewards on children's prosocial motivation: A socialization study," *Developmental Psychology*, 25 (1989): 509–515. Copyright © 1989 by the American Psychological Association. Reprinted by permission. **p. 351:** *Table 10.1* Omoto, A.M. and Snyder, M. "Sustained helping without obligation: Motivation, longevity of service, and perceived attitude change among AIDS volunteers," *Journal of Personality and Social Psychology*, 68 (1995): 671–686. Copyright © 1995 by the American Psychological Association. Reprinted with permission. **p. 352:** © New York Times Pictures. **p. 354:** © Bob Strong/The Image Works. **p. 356:** © Charles H. Porter IV/Sygma. **p. 358:** *Table 10.2* "Helping in the USA," from "Helpfulness Index: How U.S. Cities Rank," *The Boston Globe*, July 7, 1994, copyright © 1994, The Boston Globe. Reprinted by courtesy of The Boston Globe. **p. 360:** *Figure 10.7* Baron, R.A. "The sweet smell of . . . helping: Effects of pleasant ambient fragrance on prosocial behavior in shopping malls," *Personality and Social Psychology Bulletin*, 23 (1997): 498–503. Copyright 1997. Reprinted by permission. **p. 363:** © AP/Wide World Photos. **p. 364:** *Figure 10.8* Miller, J.G., Bersoff, D.M., and Harwood, R.L. "Perceptions of social responsibility in India and in the United States: Moral imperatives or personal decisions?" *Journal of Personality and Social Psychology*, 58 (1990): 33–47. Copyright © 1990 by the American Psychological Association. Reprinted with permission. **p. 366:** © Michael J. Okoniewski/Gamma-Liaison. **p. 368:** *Figure 10.9* Miller, P.A., Eisenberg, N., Fabes, R.A., and Shell, R. "Relations of moral reasoning and vicarious emotion to young children's prosocial behavior toward peers and adults," *Developmental Psychology*, 32 (1996): 210–219. Copyright © 1996 by the American Psychological Association. Reprinted with permission. **p. 370** © *(left):* *Figure 10.10* From L.A. Penner and B.A. Fritzsche. "Magic Johnson and reactions to people with AIDS," *Journal of Applied Social Psychology*, 23 (1993): 1035–1050. Copyright © 1993 by V.H. Winston & Son, Inc. Reprinted by permission. **p. 370** *(right):* © AP/Wide World Photos. **p. 375:** *Figure 10.12* Schneider, M.E., Major, B., Luhtanen, R., and Crocker, J. "Social stigma and the potential costs of assumptive help," *Personality and Social Psychology Bulletin*, 22 (1996): 201–209. Reprinted by permission.

Chapter 11: **p. 382:** © *(Opener):* Tom Walker/Stock Boston. **p. 384:** © Les Stone/Sygma. **p. 387:** © C. Karlson/LVJ/ Gamma-Liaison. **p. 389:** *Table 11.2* Bonta, Bruce "Cooperation and competition in non-violent societies," *Psychological Bulletin*, 121 (1997): 299–320. Copyright © 1997 by the American Psychological Association. Reprinted with permission. **p. 392:** © Robert Yager/Tony Stone Images. **p. 397:** *Figure 11.3* From: M.A. Straus, D.B. Sugarman, J.Giles-Sims. "Spanking by Parents and Subsequent Antisocial Behavior by Children," *Archives of Pediatrics and Adolescent Medicine*, 151 (1997): 761–767. Reprinted by permission. **p. 398:** © Esaias Baitel/ Gamma-Liaison. **p. 399:** © UPI/Corbis-Bettmann. **p. 400:** © Reuters/TV-NBC/Archive Photos. **p. 401:** *Figure 11.4* Cohen, D., Nisbett, R.E., Bowdle, B.F., and Schwart, N. "Insult, aggression, and the southern culture of honor: An experimental ethnography," *Journal of Personality and Social Psychology*, 70 (1996): 945–960. Copyright © 1996 by the American Psychological Association. Reprinted by permission of the American Psychological Association and the author. **p. 403:**

Photo illustration by William Duke. © 1998. **p. 405** *(top): Figure 11.5* Anderson, C.A. "Temperature and Aggression: Ubiquitous effects of heat on occurrence of human violence," *Psychological Bulletin*, 106 (1989): 74–96. Copyright © 1989 by the American Psychological Association. Reprinted by permission of the American Psychological Association and the author. **p. 405** *(bottom): Figure 11.6* Reifman, A.S., Larrick, R.P., Fein, S. "Temper and temperature on the diamond: The heat-aggression relationship in major-league baseball," *Personality and Social Psychology Bulletin*, 17 (1991): 580–585. Copyright 1991. Reprinted by permission. **p. 410:** *Figure 11.8* Anderson, C.A., Anderson, K.B., and Deuser, W.E. "Examining an affective framework: Weapon and temperature effects on aggressive thoughts, affect, and attitudes," *Personality and Social Psychology Bulletin*, 22 (1996): 366–376. Copyright 1996. Reprinted by permission. **p. 412** *(top):* Yvonne Hemsey/Gamma-Liaison. **p. 412** *(bottom):* © AP/Wide World Photos. **p. 414:** © Andrew Murray/Sygma. **p. 415:** © Comstock, Inc. **p. 418:** *Figure 11.9* Donnerstein, E., Linz, D., and Penrod, S. "The Question of Pornography: Research Findings and Policy Implications," *Journal of Personality and Social Psychology*, 41 (1981): 710–724. Copyright © 1981 by the American Psychological Association. Adapted with permission. **p. 419:** *Table 11.5* From M.C. Burt, "Cultural myths and supports for rape," *Journal of Social Psychology*, 38 (1980): 217–230. Copyright © 1980 by the American Psychological Association. Reprinted by permission. **p. 419:** *Figure 11.10* From: N.M. Malamuth and J.V.P. Check, "The effects of mass media exposure on acceptance of violence against women. A field experiment," *Journal of Research in Personality*, 15 (1981): 436–446. Copyright © 1981 by Academic Press. Reprinted by permission of Academic Press and the authors. **p. 422:** Reuters/Kim Kulish/Archive Photos.

Chapter 12: **p. 428** © *(Opener):* Superstock. **p. 430** *(left):* © AP/Wide World Photos. **p. 430** *(middle):* © David Butow/Black Star. **p. 430** *(right):* © AP/Wide World Photos. **p. 432:** *Table 12.1* Kassin, S.M. & Wrightsman, L.S. "The Construction and Validation of a Juror Bias Scale," from *Journal of Research in Personality*, 17 (1983): 423–442. Reprinted by permission of Academic Press. **p. 435** *(top)* © AP/Wide World Photos. **p. 435** *(bottom):* © Taylor /Fabricuius/Gamma-Liaison. **p. 436:** © *(Cartoon)* The cartoon by Lee Lorenz is reproduced from *Disorderly Conduct, Verbatim Excerpts from Actual Court Cases*, selected by Rodney R. Jones, Charles M. Sevilla, and Gerald F. Uelman, by permission of W.W. Norton and Company, Inc. Illustrations copyright © Lee Lorenz. **p. 438:** *Table 12.3* "Factors That Promote False Confessions," from S. M. Kassin and K. L. Kiechel, "The Social Psychology of False Confessions: Compliance, Internalization, and Confabulation," *Psychological Science*, (1996). Copyright © 1996. Reprinted with permission. **p. 440:** Zapruder Film: Copyright 1967 (Renewed 1995) LMH Co. c/o James Lorin Silverberg, Esq. Washington, D.C. 202-466-2787. All Rights Reserved. For Zapruder Film documentary contact: "Zapruder Film," MPI Media Group, 1-800-323-0442. **p. 442:** *Figure 12.2* From: S.J. Platz and H.M. Hosch, "Cross-racial ethnic eyewitness justification: A field study," *Journal of Applied Social Psychology*, 18 (1988): 972–984. Copyright 1988. Reprinted by permission of V.H. Winston & Sons, Inc. **p. 443:** *Figure 12.3:* From E. F. Loftus and J. C. Palmer, "Reconstruction of automobile destruction: An example of the interaction between language and memory," *Journal of Verbal Learning and Verbal Behavior*, 13 (1974): 585–589. **p. 446:** © David E. Dempster. **p. 446:** *Table 12.4* Malpass, R., and Devine, P. "Eyewitness identification: Lineup instructions and the absence of the offender," *Journal of Applied Psychology*, 66

(1981): 482–489. Copyright © 1981 by the American Psychological Association. Reprinted with permission. **p. 447:** *Figure 12.4* Lüüs, C.A.E., and Wells, G.L. "The malleability of eyewitness confidence: Co-witness and perseverance effects," *Journal of Applied Psychology*, 79 (1994): 713–714. Copyright © 1994 by the American Psychological Association. Reprinted with permission. **p. 449:** © AP/Wide World Photos. **p. 450:** *Figure 12.5* "Contaminating Effects of Pretrial Publicity," from Kerr, N.I., Kramer, G.P., Carroll, J.S., & Alfinin, J.J. "On the effectiveness of voir dire in criminal cases with prejudicial pretrial publicity: An empirical study," *American University Law Review*, 40 (1981): pp. 665–701. Reprinted with permission. **p. 452:** *Figure 12.6* From: Kassin and Sommers, *Law and Human Behavior*, 21, (1997): 27–46. Copyright © 1997. Reprinted with permission. **p. 453:** © Brian Bohannon-Booth News Service/Sygma. **p. 455:** *Table 12.5* From G. Strasser, N. Kerr, and R. Bray © (eds.), "The social psychology of jury deliberations: Structure, process, and product," *The Psychology of the Courtroom*. Copyright © 1982 by the Academic Press. Reprinted by permission of the Academic Press and the authors. **p. 458** *(left):* © Jim Bourg/Gamma-Liaison. **p. 458** *(right):* © Jim Bourg/Gamma-Liaison. **p. 460** *(top left):* © P.G. Zimbardo, Inc., Stanford, CA. **p. 460** *(top right):* © P.G. Zimbardo, Inc., Stanford, CA. **p. 460** *(top middle):* © P.G. Zimbardo, Inc., Stanford, CA.

Chapter 13: **p. 466** © *(Opener):* David Graham/Black Star. **p. 468:** © Robert C. Shafer/Folio. **p. 470:** *Figure 13.1* Marlowe, C.M., Schenider, S.L., and Nelson, C.E. "Gender and attractiveness biases in hiring decisions: Are more experienced managers less biased?" *Journal of Applied Psychology*, 81 (1996): 11–21. Copyright © 1996 by the American Psychological Association. Reprinted with permission. **p. 471:** *Figure 13.2* From R.L. Dipboye and T.M. Macan, "A process view of the selection-recruitment interview" appearing in *Readings in Personnel in Human Resource Management*. Copyright 1989. Reprinted by permission of West Publishing. **p. 472:** © VIEWnet, Inc. **p. 473:** *Figure 13.3* From Alliger, G. M. Lillienfeld, S.O., & Mitchell, K.E. "The susceptibility of overt and convert integrity tests to coaching and faking," from *Psychological Science*, 7 (1996): 32–39. Reprinted by permission. **p. 475:** *Figure 13.4* "Affirmative Action: Effects on Individuals, Groups, and Organizations," from Nacoste, R.W. Social psychology and the affirmative action debate. *Journal of Social and Clinical Psychology*, 15 (1996): 261–282. Copyright © 1996. Reprinted with permission. **p. 480:** © Jay Dickman. **p. 483:** © Porter Gifford/Gamma-Liaison. **p. 482:** © Topham/ The Image Works. **p. 484:** *Table 13.2* Reproduced by special permission of the Publisher, MIND GARDEN, Inc., 1690 Woodside Road #202, Redwood City, CA 94061 (650) 261-3500 from the **Multifactor Leadership Questionnaire** by Bernard M. Bass and Bruce J. Avolio. Copyright © 1990 by Bernard M. Bass and Bruce J. Avolio. All rights reserved. Further reproduction is prohibited without the Distributor's written consent. **p. 485:** © Dirck Halstead/Gamma-Liaison. **p. 488:** *Figure 13.6* Deci, E.L. "Effects of externally mediated rewards on intrinsic motivation," *Journal of Psychology and Social Psychology*, 18 (1971): 105–115. Copyright © 1971 by the American Psychological Association. Reprinted with permission. **p. 489:** *Figure 13.7* Greenberg, J. "Equity and workplace status: A field experiment," *Journal of Applied Psychology*, 73 (1988): 606–613. Copyright © 1988 by the American Psychological Association. Reprinted with permission. **p. 492** *(top):* Reprinted from the March, 2, 1998, issue of *Business Week* by special permission © 1998 by McGraw Hill Companies.

Chapter 14: **p. 498** © *(Opener):* A. Ramey/Woodfin Camp. **p. 502:** © Red Huber/Orlando Sentinel/Sygma. **p. 503:** *Figure 14.3* From: R.C. Kessler, A. Sonnega, E. Bromet, M. Hughes, and C.B. Nelson,"Posttraumatic stress disorder in the National Comorbidity Survey," *Archives of General Psychiatry*, 52 (1995): 1048–1060. Reprinted by permission. **p. 504:** *Table 14.1* From T.H. Holmes and R.H. Rahe. "The social readjustment rating scale," *Journal of Psychosomatic Research*, 11 (1967): 213–218. Reprinted by permission. **p. 505** *(top):* © AP/Wide World Photos. **p. 505** *(bottom):* *Figure 14.4* A. Baum and S. Valins, *Architecture and Social Behavior: Psychological Studies of Social Density*. Copyright © 1977 by Lawrence Erlbaum Associates, Inc. Reprinted by permission. **p. 506:** © Bill Horsman/ Stock Boston. **p. 509:** *Table 14.2* "How Hostile Is Your Pattern of Behavior?," from *Anger Kills* by Redford B. Williams, M.D. and Virginia Williams, Ph.D. Copyright © 1993 by Redford B. Williams, M.D. and Virginia Williams, Ph.D. Reprinted by permission of Times Books, a division of Random House, Inc. **p. 510:** © Meckes/Ottawa/Photo Researchers. **p. 511** *(top):* © Paul S. Howell/Gamma-Liaison. **p. 518:** *Figure 14.8* "Hopelessness and the Risk of Death," from Everson, S.A. et al. "Hopelessness and risk morality and incidence of myorcardial infarction and cancer," *Psychosomatic Medicine*, 58 (1996): 121–133. Reprinted by permission. **p. 519:** *Table 14.3* Carver, C.S., Scheier, M.F., and Weintraub, J.K. "Assessing coping strategies: A theoretically based approach," *Journal of Personality and Social Psychology*, 56 (1989): 267–283. Copyright © 1989 by the American Psychological Association. Reprinted with permission. **p. 520:** © AP/Wide World Photos. **p. 522:** © Serge Pagano/Sipa. **p. 523:** © AP/Wide World Photos. **p. 524** *(left):* © Jon Feingersh/ The Stock Market. **p. 524** *(right):* © Bob Daemmrich/Stock Boston. **p. 525:** *Figure 14.9* Aspinwall and Taylor. "A stitch in time: self-regulation and proactive coping," *Psychological Bulletin*, 121 (1997): 417–436. Copyright © 1997 by the American Psychological Association. Reprinted with permission. **p. 527:** © Myrleen Ferguson Cate/PhotoEdit. **p. 528:** © Porterfield/Chickering/Photo Researchers.

Name Index

Page numbers followed by *c* indicate captions; page numbers followed by *f* indicate figures; page numbers followed by *t* indicate tables.

Subject Index

Page numbers followed by *c* indicate captions; page numbers followed by *f* indicate figures; page numbers followed by *t* indicate tables.